KIPLING: THE CRITICAL HERITAGE

THE CRITICAL HERITAGE SERIES

GENERAL EDITOR: B. C. SOUTHAM, M.A., B.LITT. (OXON.)

Formerly Department of English, Westfield College, University of London

---

Volumes in the series include

KIPLING

THE CRITICAL HERITAGE

Edited by
ROGER LANCELYN GREEN
B.Litt., M.A. (Oxon.)

NEW YORK
BARNES & NOBLE, INC.

First Published
in Great Britain 1971

Published in the United States of America 1971
by Barnes & Noble Inc, New York, N.Y.
© *Roger Lancelyn Green 1971*

ISBN 0 389 04081 9

Printed in Great Britain

General Editor's Preface

The reception given to a writer by his contemporaries and near-contemporaries is evidence of considerable value to the student of literature. On one side we learn a great deal about the state of criticism at large and in particular about the development of critical attitudes towards a single writer; at the same time, through private comments in letters, journals or marginalia, we gain an insight upon the tastes and literary thought of individual readers of the period. Evidence of this kind helps us to understand the writer's historical situation, the nature of his immediate reading-public, and his response to these pressures.

The separate volumes in the *Critical Heritage Series* present a record of this early criticism. Clearly, for many of the highly productive and lengthily reviewed nineteenth- and twentieth-century writers, there exists an enormous body of material; and in these cases the volume editors have made a selection of the most important views, significant for their intrinsic critical worth or for their representative quality—perhaps even registering incomprehension!

For earlier writers, notably pre-eighteenth century, the materials are much scarcer and the historical period has been extended, sometimes far beyond the writer's lifetime, in order to show the inception and growth of critical views which were initially slow to appear.

In each volume the documents are headed by an Introduction, discussing the material assembled and relating the early stages of the author's reception to what we have come to identify as the critical tradition. The volumes will make available much material which would otherwise be difficult of access and it is hoped that the modern reader will be thereby helped towards an informed understanding of the ways in which literature has been read and judged.

B.C.S.

To

EDMUND BLUNDEN

with gratitude and affection

Contents

CONTENTS

CONTENTS

Acknowledgments

I should like to thank the following for their kind permission to reprint and quote copyright material: Mrs. George Bambridge for the various quotations from Kipling's works in prose and verse; John Murray Ltd. for the parody by Barry Pain from the *Cornhill Magazine*; the *Contemporary Review* and his literary executors for the article by J. M. Barrie; William Heinemann Ltd. for the article by Edmund Gosse published by them in his *Questions at Issue* (1893); Methuen & Co. Ltd. for the article on Kipling in *Reading for Pleasure* by R. Ellis Roberts and for the 1893 review by George Saintsbury, collected by J. W. Oliver, A. M. Clarke and A. Muir in *A Last Vintage* (1950); William Blackwood and Sons Ltd. for the article and review by J. H. Millar and for the review by Mrs. Oliphant, which all appeared in *Blackwood's Magazine*; Miss D. E. Collins for the review of *Just So Stories* by G. K. Chesterton, and to her and The Bodley Head Ltd. for extracts from his volume *Heretics*; The Estate of Sir Arthur Conan Doyle and John Murray Ltd. for the extract from *Through the Magic Door*; the Executors of Ford Madox Ford for the extracts from *The Critical Attitude*; the Estates of H. G. Wells and the publishers for extracts from *The New Machiavelli* (now published by Penguin Books) and *The Outline of History* (subsequently revised by G. P. Wells and Raymond Postgate and published by Cassell & Co. Ltd., and Doubleday & Co. Inc.); Mrs. T. S. Eliot and Faber & Faber Ltd. for the review by T. S. Eliot; Mr. Edmund Blunden for the extract from his review of *The Irish Guards*, in the *Nation and Athenaeum*; the *Saturday Review of Literature* (New York) for the review, 'Horace, Book Five', by Christopher Morley; Professor Bonamy Dobrée for his article from the *Monthly Criterion* and the extract from his *Rudyard Kipling: Realist and Fabulist*; the Literary Executors of Gilbert Frankau for the extract from his article in the *London Magazine*; the Cambridge University Press for extracts from F. J. Harvey Darton's *Children's Books in England*; the Kipling Society for papers by L. C. Dunsterville and André Maurois from the *Kipling Journal*; Mr. Dennis Gwynn and Mrs. T. G. Moorhead for the article by their father Stephen Gwynn; The Editor of the *Times Literary Supplement* for the review by T. Humphrey Ward (1890) in *The Times*, and the anonymous obituary

ACKNOWLEDGMENTS

Article from the *T.L.S.* of 25th January 1936; the Literary Executors of George Moore for the extracts from his article on 'Kipling and Loti' reprinted in *Avowals*, published by William Heinemann Ltd.; Mr. Hugh Noyes for the article from the *Bookman* by his father, Alfred Noyes; the Executors of the late Dr. Neil Munro for his article from *Good Words*; the Society of Authors as the literary representative of the Estate of Richard Le Gallienne for his article in *Munsey's Magazine*; J. M. Dent & Sons Ltd. for the extract from *On Some Living Poets* by Sir Arthur Quiller-Couch.

Note on the text

The text of reviews and articles in this volume is taken whenever possible from the original periodical in which each first appeared, and not from subsequent reprints in book form. Where such were made, the original article was usually revised—in some cases many years later, often after Kipling's death. Minor mistakes and misprints (e.g. slips of a word in titles of stories or poems) have been corrected. Longer passages in prose, and more than a few consecutive lines of verse (except when detailed reference is made to them) have been omitted, and references given to the standard editions. In the case of Kipling's prose works, page and line references are to Macmillan's Uniform and Pocket Editions; in the case of the verse to Hodder and Stoughton's *Rudyard Kipling's Verse: Definitive Edition* (1940, frequently reprinted) herein referred to as DV.

Preface

Except in the case of extracts from letters by Robert Louis Stevenson (No. 10), Henry James (No. 11), and Lafcadio Hearn (No. 23), the three reviews by Lionel Johnson (No. 15) (which appeared within about the space of a year) and the two extracts from books by H. G. Wells (No. 46), all the items are arranged in the chronological order of their first appearance. This is of particular interest and importance in the case of Kipling whose critical adventures have been perhaps the strangest experienced by any great writer. And the end is not yet. As explained in the Introduction, the present selection does not carry these adventures further than 1936, the year of Kipling's death. Most of the more outstanding critical essays published since 1940 have already been collected in the volumes edited by Andrew Rutherford and Elliot L. Gilbert described in the Book List at the end of the present volume—where the chief critical and biographical studies of Kipling published in the same period are also listed.

Kipling has taken longer than most writers to pass through the valley of the shadow of criticism: his recent emergence on the further shore has been startling—and is likely to be even more so as his works receive deeper and more dispassionate study in academic and other circles. 'But that is another story.'

ROGER LANCELYN GREEN

Introduction

'It is time that the line should be firmly drawn between criticism and reviewing,' wrote Andrew Lang in 1890; 'the brief contemporary notice is not criticism . . . to me criticism seems more valuable and other . . . [By criticism] I mean reasoned and considered writing on the tried masterpieces of the world, or even ingenious and entertaining writing about new books. To have a clever and accomplished man telling you, in his best manner, what thoughts come into his mind after reading even a new novel, is no trifling pleasure among the pale and shadowy pleasures of the mind.'

Even at its very best criticism is no more than a handmaid to the Muses. The few really great practitioners may produce brief works of literature, but in relation to the works which inspired them, no results can be more than the *hors-d'œuvre* or the dessert to the main meal—however great a relish is added to the banquet by the best additions of even Lamb or Hazlitt, F. R. Leavis or C. S. Lewis.

The best criticism is a stimulant to make the lazy or unobservant reader look for more in the author than he notices at a casual reading. Much of the interest of the sort of early criticism that is half-reviewing is to see the dawning and unfolding of appreciation and realization of a new author with no place then in literature, who is now regarded as a classic. Another interest is of an historical kind: to follow an author's course through the tastes and prejudices and predictions—literary, ethical, social or political—of his period.

Rudyard Kipling is the most controversial author in English Literature. Even today his place on Parnassus remains undecided—though a place there he is generally agreed to have, even if some critics would seek it near the summit while others relegate him to the foothills.

This volume shows the remarkable nature of Kipling's reception by the critics. His sudden leap to the forefront of contemporary authors during the first few months after his return to England at just under twenty-four—hailed as a successor to Dickens by the leading reviewers, and with enthusiasm but a little more discrimination by his contemporaries among novelists; the serious studies as of a major writer by leading critics such as Lang (No. 12) and Gosse (No. 17) in this country, by Howells (No. 28) and Charles Eliot Norton (No. 27) in America during the next ten years; and then the sudden descent into obliquity due almost entirely to political reasons beneath the pens of the Liberal critics of the turn of the century—with no falling off at all among the reading public. And finally the beginnings of his slow climb back towards consideration as a great writer—most of which has come since his death and, as easily available in other volumes, is outside the scope of this book.

As early as 1923, Edward Shanks wrote in the *London Mercury* [Vol. VII, pp. 274-5, 284, January 1923] of Kipling's

leap into a position in English political thought and feeling which, it is safe to say, no other English imaginative writer (even Milton not excepted) has ever occupied. Hence, too, comes the difficulty of looking at him dispassionately as an imaginative writer. We do not often mix together our enjoyment of litera-ture and our partisan interest in politics, but when we do it we do it thoroughly.

So it comes about that we find even critics who maintain that Mr. Kipling does not write well . . . Time, and severe impartial standards, winnowing his work, will winnow much of it away; but they will certainly leave something that is unique.

I

KIPLING IN ENGLISH LITERATURE

The interesting moment of Kipling's eruption into English literature is well described by R. G. Collingwood in *The Principles of Art* (1938). After writing of what he calls 'Magical Art' as 'an art which is rep-resentative and therefore evocative of emotion, and evokes of set purpose some emotions rather than others in order to discharge them into the affairs of practical life', he goes on [p. 70]:

The change of spirit which divides Renaissance and modern art from that of the Middle Ages consists in the fact that medieval art was frankly and definitely magical, while Renaissance and modern art was not. I say 'was' not, because the climax of this non-magical or anti-magical period in the history of art was reached in the late nineteenth century, and the tide is now visibly turning. But there were always eddies in the tide-stream. There were cross-currents even in the nineties, when English literary circles were dominated by a school of so-called aesthetes professing the doctrine that art must not subserve any utilitarian end but must be practised for its own sake alone. This cry of art for art's sake was in some ways ambiguous; it did not, for example, distinguish art proper from amusement, and the art which its partisans admired and practised was in fact a shameless amusement art, amusing a select and self-appointed clique; but in one way it was perfectly definite: it ruled out magical art altogether. Into the perfumed and stuffy atmosphere of this china-shop burst Rudyard Kipling, young, nervous, short-sighted, and all on fire with the notion of using his very able pen to evoke and canalize the emotions which in his Indian life he had found to be associated with the governing of the British Empire. The aesthetes were horrified, not because they disapproved of imperialism, but because they disapproved of magical art; Kipling had blundered right up against their most cherished taboo. What was worse, he made a huge success of it. Thousands of people who knew those emotions as the steam in the engine of their daily work took him to their hearts. But Kipling was a morbidly sensitive little man, and the rebuff he had met with from the aesthetes blasted the early summer of his life. Henceforth he was torn between two ideals, and could pursue neither with undivided allegiance.

When Kipling arrived in London in the autumn of 1889 'Art for Art's Sake' was still being preached by Oscar Wilde (No. 16) and practised to a greater or lesser extent by writers such as Robert Louis Stevenson and Henry James (see their correspondence about 'the infant monster of a Kipling', Nos. 10 and 11).

A few years earlier Rider Haggard had set the critical bee-hive humming like Mowgli's hornets' nest with several 'big stones' such as *She* and *Allan Quartermain*. Kipling did not raise a like storm, though Henry James and 'J. K. S.' (No. 13) were anxious to bracket them together.

But the more orthodox view was still given by George Meredith when the American editor S. S. McClure visited him, after hearing of Kipling from Sidney Colvin as 'a new writer who seemed to have red blood in him', and asked: 'Mr. Meredith, Mr. Colvin thinks very highly of a new writer named Rudyard Kipling. He believes he is the coming man. Do you know anything about him?'

'The coming man,' said Meredith emphatically, 'is James Barrie.' [*McClure's Magazine*, Vol. XLII, p. 108, March 1914.]

Stevenson also set Barrie above Kipling, but second to Henry James (No. 10). For, as J. A. Hammerton wrote [in *Barrie: The Story of Genius*, 1929, pp. 140–1]:

The reader whose memory goes back to the year 1889 may recall the thrilling interest which the world of book-lovers was then taking in the performances of two young competitors for literary fame. Kipling, with his sudden spate of shilling story books that had first been 'tried' out on his Anglo-Indian audience and his virile *Barrack-Room Ballads* . . . seemed to shoot ahead of Barrie for the moment . . .

Kipling and Barrie were admittedly the two foremost names among the bright band of new writers who seemed to arrive at the critical moment to breathe a hopeful and purposeful spirit into a literature which, with the decadent trend of the waning century, was threatening to become morbid and joyless. It is true that Stevenson had already brought into contemporary fiction a new sensitiveness to form, and that Meredith, Hardy, and many another good, if lesser, Victorian was still in his vigour . . .

And Barrie himself, who had already achieved his own burst into early fame, greeted his new rival with true generosity: 'The great question is, can he write?' he asked in a short article called 'The Man from Nowhere' [*British Weekly*, 2 May 1890]. 'To which my own answer is that no young man of such capacity has appeared in our literature for years . . . few, if any, novelists who have become great did such promising work at his age.'

The popularity of Kipling's work in the nineties owed a great deal to its novelty. As C. S. Lewis wrote many years later ['Kipling's World' in *Literature and Life*, 1948, pp. 59-60]:

To put the thing in its shortest possible way, Kipling is first and foremost the poet of work. It is really remarkable how poetry and fiction before his time had avoided this subject. They had dealt almost exclusively with men in their 'private hours'—with love-affairs, crimes, sport, illness and changes of fortune . . . With a few exceptions imaginative literature in the eighteenth and nineteenth centuries had quietly omitted, or at least thrust into the background, the sort of thing which in fact occupies most of the waking hours of most men. And this did not merely mean that certain technical aspects of life were unrepresented. A whole range of strong sentiments and emotions—for many men, the strongest of all—went with them. For, as Pepys once noted with surprise, there is a great pleasure in talking of business. It was Kipling who first reclaimed for literature this enormous territory.

With this new literary dimension went also the new use of language —a frankness and a largeness in the use of the 'language of common men' that shocked many, delighted many more, and brought for all a refreshing blast of genuine fresh air into the hot-house atmosphere of the *fin-de-siècle*. 'Here's Literature! Here's Literature at last!' David Masson, elderly Professor of Literature and Rhetoric at Edinburgh is said to have declared to his astonished students, waving over his head a copy of the *Scots Observer* containing 'Danny Deever', in February 1890.

Seventy-five years later Mr Jack Dunman was writing of Kipling in *Marxism Today* (August 1965):

There is in fact no other considerable writer, except Hugh McDiarmid, who has written, or attempted to write, poetry in working-class language; it is a pity that the left-wing poets of the thirties, including Spender and Auden, made no attempt to study his methods . . . There is one other point about the poetry which workers should consider—his deep interest in machinery. No other poet in this country thus far has written so effectively about it. Working-class language is used extensively in the short stories, many of which are about working-class characters and no others . . . He had a profound sense of history, and therefore of change and development; but his history was always human, and human of the common people; never of kings and aristocrats.

And the other great novelty of Kipling's literary achievement was virtually to introduce the short story into English literature—and write perhaps the greatest examples of this genre that we can boast even now.

Curiously enough, only a few months before his discovery of Kipling's short stories, Andrew Lang was writing in the Introduction to a collection of tales from the French, *The Dead Leman, and other Stories* (published in June 1889):

In England, short stories—tales which may be read in half an hour—are not so popular as they are in France. This may perhaps be explained, and certainly it must be regretted. In a brief narrative, or romance, nothing should be wasted, nothing should be superfluous, all should converge rapidly so as to produce the desired effect, or to enhance the interest of the given situation. Hence it is a misfortune that English taste is intolerant of short stories. They are welcomed in a magazine or journal; when collected they are looked on with suspicion. Not long ago a critic in *Blackwood's Magazine* rebuked Mr. Stevenson for publishing a set of *contes* in a volume, as if the performance were almost dishonourable. Some strange prejudice whispers, apparently, that a short story must be a 'pot boiler', or at best a rough sketch. Almost the reverse of this theory is often true.

A writer has an idea, say, a set of characters, or a given situation, which ought to be given in some twenty pages. But he is made to understand that he cannot afford thus to waste his idea. If he treats it as it should be treated, he produces a magazine tale which is not very remunerative; and if he were to write a dozen small masterpieces, and reprint them in a volume, he would have, at best, a little praise as the reward of his toil . . .

In France the *conte*, or short story has always been more fortunate . . . Many circumstances made the short story popular in France. Perhaps the more quick and eager intellect of the people does not dread, as we dread, the effort of awakening the attention afresh a dozen times in one volume. In England, we seem to dislike this effort. We prefer to make it only once, to get interested in the characters once for all, and then to loiter with them through, perhaps, 400,000 words of more or less consecutive narrative. If this theory be correct, short stories will never have much success in England, and, consequently, will not often be well written, because there is no prize in praise or money offered to him who writes them well. It would be hard to mention a single collection of *contes* which has really prospered among English-speaking people, except the stories of Poe. Experience proves that the least excellent of Hawthorne's romances is better liked than his volumes of little masterpieces. We seem to hate literary kickshaws, and to clamour for a round of literary beef. Older authors, Fielding and Dickens, at first mixed up brief tales in their long stories, but such tales were felt to be superfluous. Only one of them is immortal, 'Wandering Willie's Tale' in *Redgauntlet*, that perfect model of a *conte* in whose narrow range, humour, poetry, the grotesque, the terrible are combined as in no other work of man.

Within a year of this, Kipling had entirely altered the literary scene in England with regard to short stories. He arrived with one big volume and six small ones of short stories already written and collected —*Plain Tales from the Hills*, *Soldiers Three*, *The Story of the Gadsbys*, *In Black and White*, *Under the Deodars*, *The Phantom Rickshaw* and *Wee Willie Winkie*—and soon had a host of readers waiting for him to collect the stories which were appearing in magazines in 1890 into *Life's Handicap* in 1891.

But it will be noticed how at first most of his critics were suspending judgment until he had written the novel which they assumed he would attempt as the real test of his potentialities as a great writer. *The Light that Failed* at the end of 1890 was written partly as a bid for these laurels—and proved that Kipling had been right in choosing the short story as the literary type most fitted to his genius. *The Naulahka* (1892) proved that he was not to excel in the romance of adventure either; only in 1901 the 'nakedly picaresque' (*Something of Myself*, p. 228) *Kim* showed the one form of longer narrative in which he could write a masterpiece—and *Kim* stands alone, though for convenience sake it is classed as a novel.

This is not the place to enter into the circumstances which made Kipling a writer of short stories but not a novelist in the ordinary sense. Much lay, doubtless, in the whole cast of his mind; something perhaps in the brute fact that for two years he was allowed just the space for a 2,400 word 'Plain Tale' each week in the *Civil and Military Gazette*. But the fact remains that he conquered his reading public in England mainly with collections of short stories in volume form— and from 1890 the short story boomed in England, whether written by Kipling or Stevenson or Maugham, by Conan Doyle or G. K. Chesterton or Saki.

As several critics have pointed out right from the beginning of his career, Kipling learnt to write as a journalist and turned his experiences of daily reporting on Indian papers to good use when he 'graduated into literature'. As Frank Swinnerton put it in his Foreword to Hilton Brown's *Rudyard Kipling* (1945) Kipling was 'the first journalist, since Defoe, to bring a sense of news to the service of fiction, he excelled in the yarn'.

The result of this journalistic background and its unexpected development was well described by Desmond MacCarthy in his obituary article on Kipling in the *Sunday Times* of 19 January 1936:

His style, while loved by the unliterary, often irritated the literary because the aim of his virtuosity was always a *violent precision*. His adjectives and phrases start from the page. He forced you first and foremost to see, to hear, to touch, to smell—above all to see and smell—as vividly as words can make you do those things. When the greatest vividness was inconsistent with an aesthetic impression—well, in his work aesthetic sensitiveness went by the board . . .

Although his style possessed one of the most important qualifications for immense popularity, namely, unflagging vigour, it displayed at the same time an unpopular quality—extreme virtuosity. In his later work, especially, his prose was marked by an acrobatic verbal ingenuity hardly equalled by Meredith. It seems on the face of it strange that an author who is sometimes difficult, an author who must be read slowly, who is so tremendously concentrated and was latterly elliptical, should have continued to appeal to non-literary readers. Kipling is a writer whose phrases must be allowed to soak a moment in the mind before they expand, as those little Japanese pellets do which blossom into flower only when they have lain awhile on the surface of a cup of water.

Yet with all his extravagant and undisguised word-craft, he remained a favourite author of thousands upon thousands of readers who are ordinarily impatient of that kind of writing. No author, too, had a more various audience of admirers, while, oddly enough, it was among literary people, among artists and critics, that this master-craftsman was apt to meet with grudging appreciation. They admitted his genius, his power, but they often wrote and talked as though they were sorry that they had to. What were the qualities which made him admired by millions and yet often crabbed by those who loved, as he did, the painful art of writing?

II

KIPLING AND HIS CRITICS

'The qualities which made him admired by millions' are there for us all to enjoy and discover according to our own individual powers of appreciation and understanding; our own good fortune if we find ourselves naturally in tune with even some of what Kipling wrote in prose or verse, and our ability (and humility) in recognizing his achievements even if we do not admire them.

'Kipling is intensely loved and hated,' said C. S. Lewis. 'Hardly any reader likes him a little.' This should be less true now than when he said it twenty-one years ago since the winnowing process may have made it easier for the uncommitted reader to begin with the best of Kipling, and the passage of time should have brought nearer the happy day when his political opinions will matter no more than those of Milton or Swift or William Morris.

But there is danger here too. Any serious student or reader must read and study all Kipling's stories and all his poems and verses to choose the best—and should do so before reading any criticism or listening to any one else's views on which these are. Even anthologies (several have been issued by Macmillan, one in Dent's Everyman Library, and a number in the United States) should be used only with reserve and read only as introductions—if introduction is deemed necessary.

From time to time during more than forty years since its foundation the Kipling Society (which averages a thousand members) has tried, as a matter of interest, to decide by a majority vote which are Kipling's twelve best (or most popular) stories—but without any very satisfactory results. Even the process of counting votes has only really succeeded in singling out the twelve stories which members feel they should include. But most lists run on the lines: 'Such and such stories obviously ought to be included, but my own favourites are this and that.' One member submitted his twelve favourite stories and the three he disliked most—and those three were included among another member's twelve favourites. On another occasion, at a meeting about fifty strong, a leading Kipling scholar remarked: 'There is probably somewhere in the world a Kipling reader who would include every single one of the stories among his twelve favourites—except, of course, that utterly abominable " —— ".' Whereupon another member immediately exclaimed: 'Oh, that's always been one of my favourites!'

Even among contemporary critics of a single new volume this extraordinary variety of choice is apparent. Thus George Saintsbury (No. 25), when reviewing *Many Inventions*, singled out 'Brugglesmith' and 'Judson and the Empire' as among those he liked best, while Percy Addleshaw in the *Academy* (1 July 1893) included these two with

'The Children of the Zodiac' as 'quite the worst things Mr. Kipling ever wrote—and they are very bad'. Saintsbury liked 'Children of the Zodiac' least, but does not even mention the two, 'In the Rukh' and 'A Matter of Fact', which Addleshaw considered the best. However, Saintsbury's absolute favourites, 'My Lord the Elephant' and 'His Private Honour' were at least admitted to the second class by Addleshaw.

And of the same collection Andrew Lang noted in the *Cosmopolitan* [Vol. XV, p. 616, September 1893]:

Among books of fiction, Mr. Kipling's *Many Inventions* is far the most popular, and deserves its popularity. There are great varieties of excellence in the tales. The fun of 'The Children of the Zodiac' I fail to see, but 'In the Rukh' is a surprising piece of modified were-wolfism; 'The Finest Story in the World' is one of the five or six best stories in the world. 'The Lost Legion' shows a new kind of skill in the supernatural, and the three soldiers are as good as ever, except in 'Love o' Women', which seems to my taste, rather dully disagreeable than really 'powerful'. But it *is* all a matter of taste.

Looking back over the critical reception of his works only a month or two before his death, Kipling wrote in *Something of Myself* [pp. 210-11]:

I am afraid that I was not much impressed by reviews. But my early days in London were unfortunate. As I got to know literary circles and their critical output, I was struck by the slenderness of some of the writers' equipment. I could not see how they got along with so casual a knowledge of French work and, apparently, of much English grounding that I had supposed indispensable. Their stuff seemed to be a day-to-day traffic in generalities, hedged by trade considerations. Here I expect I was wrong but making my own tests (the man who had asked me out to dinner to discover what I had read gave me the notion), I would ask simple questions, misquote or misattribute my quotations; or (once or twice) invent an author. The result did not increase my reverence. Had they been newspaper men in a hurry, I should have understood; but the gentlemen were presented to me as Priests and Pontiffs . . .

With this should be compared Kipling's poem 'In Partibus' and story 'The Three Young Men', written in December 1889 for the *Civil and Military Gazette* and rescued from intended oblivion by the American pirate publication of *Abaft and Funnel* (1909). Otherwise he was absolutely true in saying [*Something of Myself*, pp. 84-5] 'I have never directly or indirectly criticized any fellow-craftsman's output, or encouraged any man or woman to do so; nor have I approached any persons that they might be led to comment on my output.'

There were, of course, obvious exceptions to Kipling's sweeping condemnation of the literary knowledge and basic scholarship of his critics and reviewers. Even in the earlier period he was reviewed and his work studied seriously by men as widely read in European and Classical literature as Lang and Whibley and Henley and Gosse, as well as those who then or later held Chairs in English Literature such as J. H. Millar, Saintsbury, Quiller-Couch and Norton, while Sir William Hunter (No. 3) brought unrivalled knowledge of the Oriental setting of the earlier stories; and his critics also included novelists from Henry James and J. M. Barrie to Ford Madox Ford and Ian Hay, and later on Somerset Maugham and J. B. Priestley, besides poets from Alfred Noyes and Richard Le Gallienne to T. S. Eliot and Edmund Blunden.

But the majority of reviews and much of the criticism that was intended to be more serious were indeed such as Kipling describes, and he rightly ignored them—and understandably paid little attention even to the more worthwhile studies by those better qualified to make them.

For, contrary to much that has been said, Kipling was a truly modest man, and very humble in the conviction that a man's best work came from without—at the promptings of his 'daemon', as he himself would have put it.

Two extracts from the private diary of his closest friend, Rider Haggard, are of interest in this context. [They have been published by Morton N. Cohen in his *Rudyard Kipling to Rider Haggard: The Record of a Friendship* (1965), pp. 84, 100]:

23 March 1915 . . . I asked him what he was doing to occupy his mind amidst all these troubles. He answered, like myself, writing stories, adding, 'I don't know what they are worth, I only know they ain't literature.' Like all big men Kipling is very modest as to his own productions. Only little people are vain . . .
22 May 1918 . . . I commented on the fact that he had wide fame and was known as 'the great Mr. Kipling', which should be a consolation to him. He thrust the idea away with a gesture of disgust. 'What is it worth—what *is* it all worth?' he answered. Moreover he went on to show that anything any of us did *well* was no credit to us: that it came from somewhere else: 'We are only telephone wires.' As example he instanced (I think) 'Recessional' in his own case and *She* in mine. 'You didn't write *She* you know,' he said, 'something wrote it through you!' or some such words.

It should be added that Kipling himself was not only very well read indeed in English and French literature [see *Kipling's Reading* by Ann M. Weygandt (1939) for the majority of references and quotations in his published works], but took a keen interest in most of his contemporaries, and wrote enthusiastically to those whom he knew even slightly. Except in the case of Rider Haggard, whose imaginative achievement he understood and appreciated as few have done, most of these letters remain unpublished. Besides more obvious authors, he wrote letters of praise and criticism to such writers as Barrie and Henley, Conan Doyle, Stanley Weyman and A. E. W. Mason, Mrs Molesworth and E. Nesbit—to name only a few. And contemporary reminiscences and letters bear testimony to his friendly interest and wide appreciation. For example:

Anthony Hope wrote to a friend after meeting Kipling at lunch in November 1900: 'He was kind and interesting about *Quisanté* . . . He is a singularly attractive fellow, genuine and brimming with life.' [Sir Charles Mallet: *Anthony Hope and his Books* (1935), p. 155.]

Baroness Orczy, staying in the same hotel in Bath in 1915, wrote in her auto-biography: 'I had many a talk with that very dear and very great man. It would be impossible to imagine anyone distinguished as he was, more simple and unaffected, so full of charm and understanding. He made me very happy with his generous praise of my work, telling me just what he admired in it, and why in his opinion it had been so successful and popular.' [*Links in the Chain of Life* (1947), pp. 147–8.]

A. E. W. Mason wrote in a letter to a friend from Cairo, 29 February 1929: 'Kipling and his wife are out here at this hotel. I never knew him really well before but he is quite charming. He was wildly enthusiastic about [*The Prisoner in the Opal*] which is always pleasant.' [Roger Lancelyn Green: *A. E. W. Mason* (1952), p. 192.]

'F. Anstey' [T. Anstey Guthrie] wrote in his autobiography: 'In 1900 he wrote me an extraordinary kind and generous letter about *The Brass Bottle*, then running as a serial in the pages of the *Strand Magazine*.' [*A Long Retrospect* (1936), p. 147.]

Doubtless Kipling too received many letters of appreciation and criticism from his literary contemporaries, but these have not survived. Like Lang, he destroyed all incoming correspondence, hoping—vainly—that those to whom he wrote would do likewise, objecting to the publication of letters, reminiscences and all forms of 'the higher cannibalism' [*Something of Myself*, p. 191]. 'Seek not to question other than the works I leave behind' (Epilogue to his poetical works), he begged: but it was too much to expect.

As for published criticism, he wrote: 'attacking or attacked, so long as you have breath on no provocation explain'—and held to this rule throughout his career.

'Years ago he gave us fair warning he would not work with an eye to his public, and he never has,' complained a critic in the New York *Bookman* in March 1902. 'There is no sign in Kipling's writings that he has ever learnt anything from his critics or made any concessions to his public's demands. Take it or leave it has been his attitude from the first. In his own good time, after people had despaired of him, he wrote *Kim*. We told him distinctly that was the kind of thing we wanted of him, and asked him to do it again; whereupon he undertook the conduct of the British Government through the agency of bad verse . . . As mere literary pleasure-lovers his readers have a right to complain . . . Other writers have at one time or another paid some attention to criticism. There was George Meredith, for instance, whom no one would accuse of pliancy. He was swerved entirely from his early course by criticism. And Thomas Hardy, the only other living novelist of Kipling's rank, was influenced by it to his own and our advantage. But from Kipling, as from a Tammany watermain, we must take things as they come, knowing that protests are in vain.'

III

CRITICAL RECEPTION

Whether he paid any attention to it or not, Kipling received an immense amount of criticism, from short reviews to full-scale articles by leading critics, followed within ten years of his first appearance in literary London by a flow of book-length studies that by now far exceeds his own original output; if books containing essays and chapters on him are included, the library of the Kipling Society can boast well over two hundred volumes of biography and criticism—and even so cannot claim absolute completeness.

His earliest volumes were reviewed fairly extensively by Indian papers in the English language—but with little realization that here was anything out of the ordinary. Nor did any reviewer do much more than make conventional critical noises.

Departmental Ditties (1886), for example, was greeted by the *Times of India* as 'a very pleasant companion for a lonely half-hour, or to while away the tedium of a railway journey'. The *Indian Daily News* went a little further, declaring that 'the pieces are bright and clever, with occasional touches which indicate that the author may some day reach to higher flights than the lampooning of weak or corrupt officialism'. The *Sind Gazette* went further still, averring that 'they are full of humour and spirit, and, brief as they are, have the genuine ring, and display a poetical faculty of a high order'.

Little more than this was said, except that the *Advocate of India* felt that 'he had attacked the public departments of this country, dealing with them in a spirit of genial fun which reminds one of Bon Gaultier and Aliph Cheem', the *Bombay Gazette* compared 'The Story of Uriah' to *The Biglow Papers*, and *The Englishman* felt that 'they will suffer little by comparison with the best work of Praed or Locker'.

But such fame was purely local. E. Kay Robinson who became editor of the *Civil and Military Gazette* towards the end of 1886, wrote later ['Kipling in India', *McClure's Magazine*, Vol. VII, July 1896]:

Having to my great delight 'discovered' Kipling (though his name was already a household word throughout India) in 1886, I thought that the literary world at home should share my pleasure. He was just then publishing his first little book in India; but the *Departmental Ditties* were good enough, as I thought at the time, and as afterwards turned out, to give him a place among English writers of the day. So I obtained eight copies, and distributed them, with recommendatory letters, among editors of English journals . . . So far as I could ascertain, not a single one of those papers condescended to say a word about the unpretentious little volume.

One copy, however—whether from among Robinson's eight or another source—came into the hands of Andrew Lang, who reviewed it in his monthly causerie, the famous 'At the Sign of the Ship', in *Longman's Magazine* [Vol. VIII, pp. 675-6, October 1886]—the first item (No. 1) in the present volume.

Lang failed to spot the author's name (reproduced in facsimile at the foot of the front wrapper)—or to realize what the signature over 'Assistant—Department of Public Journalism, Lahore District' was: for he notes 'the modest author does not give his name'.

The next step is odd, and has never been fully explained. In October 1887 Kipling wrote to his friend Mrs F. C. Burton (the 'original' of Mrs Hauksbee, to whom *Plain Tales* was dedicated as 'The Wittiest Woman in India'): 'With moderate good luck and the recommendation of a man in London, I get a rather nasty story into *Longman's Magazine* about Christmas time.'

The 'man in London' was Vereker Hamilton; the recommendation came from Ian Hamilton (afterwards General Sir Ian Hamilton), and the story was 'The Mark of the Beast' [later published in the *United Service Magazine* June, and the *Pioneer* 12–14 July 1890, before being collected in *Life's Handicap*, 1891]—possibly in an even 'nastier' version.

The story (apparently with the author unnamed) was shown to Lang by Vereker Hamilton. Lang (who was literary adviser to Charles Longman, editor of *Longman's Magazine*) returned it to Vereker with a letter (no longer extant) containing the sentence: 'I would gladly give Ian a fiver if he had never been the means of my reading this poisonous stuff, which has left an extremely disagreeable impression on my mind.' Surprised by this, but doubtless recollecting Lang's supersensitiveness to any descriptions of cruelty or torture, Vereker took it to William Sharp, 'a man of quite different tastes from Lang'. But Sharp was even more decisive, writing: 'I would like to hazard a guess that the writer is very young and that he will die mad before he has reached the age of thirty.'[1]

(At variance with the usual account, H. B. Marriott-Watson (1863–1921), the novelist, wrote in 1904 that 'The Mark of the Beast', sent by Ian Hamilton, 'reached Mr. Andrew Lang, who read it with interest, and advised the author to get it translated into French, as it would never pass in this country'. Marriott-Watson knew Lang well, and may have had this version of the events from him. [Cutting from unidentified periodical dated 18 July 1904 in the Library of the Kipling Society.])

Lang apparently did not know who had written the story which he found so upsetting (and did not recommend for *Longman's Magazine*). For in 1888 C. F. Hooper, who was learning the publishing business with Thacker and Spink of Calcutta, publishers in that year of Kipling's second book, *Plain Tales from the Hills*, was told 'to try to sell it in London'. Hooper had little success, only sixteen copies being subscribed; but he persuaded the editor of the *Saturday Review* to review it [9 June 1888] (No. 2). [See C. F. Hooper's article 'Kipling's Younger Days', *Saturday Review*, Vol. CLXI, pp. 308–9, 7 March 1936.]

The editor who reviewed *Plain Tales* was Walter Herries Pollock [1850–1926]. Lang was a close friend of his, and wrote each week for the *Saturday Review* at the time—so he cannot have missed seeing the review, and probably reading the book. Certainly it was recorded by Mrs Hill, wife of the Professor with whom Kipling was lodging at Allahabad at the time, in her diary for April 1888: 'I shall never forget the glee with which RK came in one afternoon saying, "What do you suppose I just came across in reading the proof of this week's English letter?" Andrew Lang says: "Who is Mr. Rudyard Kipling?" He was so pleased that they really had heard of him in England, for in all modesty he intends to make his mark in the world.' [Edmonia Hill: 'The Young Kipling', *Atlantic Monthly*, Vol. CLVII, pp. 406–15, April 1936.]

Meanwhile a family friend got a review of *Departmental Ditties* into the *Academy* of 1 September 1888 (No. 3): 'The first analytical essay

by a writer who knew Kipling's background, and knew India', Charles
Carrington calls it in the authorized biography. [Charles Carrington:
Rudyard Kipling—His Life and Work (1955), p. 131.]

Hunter had been on Lord Dufferin's staff, but returned to England to
take up a career in journalism, and Kipling had already addressed a
long (uncollected) ode to him in the *Pioneer* of 1 June 1888, to the effect:

> You're far too good! Ask L[a]ng, ask Ar[no]ld, ask
> The S[avi]le and the S[ava]ge where men call
> Who nightly gibber 'neath the penny mask,
> And scribble crudities on Time's blank wall,
> How golden is the guerdon of their task,
> Hark! From the weltering Strand the newsboys bawl:
> 'Murder in Paddin'ton! Revoltin' Story!!'
> "Untin' in Injia!' Hunter, is *this* glory?

Somehow, early in 1889, a copy of *Soldiers Three* got to England
and was reviewed anonymously in the *Spectator* of 23 March (No. 4).
But the next definite step was chronicled by Mrs Hill in her diary for
9 March 1889 when she and her husband were already at Calcutta with
Kipling at the beginning of their trip to England via Japan and America,
described in *From Sea to Sea*: 'The covers were torn off from the whole
six of the Wheeler edition on account of some postal law, and the
letterpress sent on to England to Andrew Lang, so that Ruddy may
be already introduced when he arrives in London.' (This may have
been done earlier than the date of the entry, and the books arrived in
time for the *Spectator* review of *Soldiers Three*.)

The six Wheeler paperbound volumes, later collected into two in
England as *Soldiers Three* and *Wee Willie Winkie*, had received only
superficial reviews in India. 'His knowledge of Anglo-Indian human
nature, which is ordinary human nature under great provocation, is
profound—we were going to say awful—and he can go from grave
to gay with the facility of a true artist,' was the most interesting comment the *Home and Colonial Mail* could make; and the *Civil and Military Gazette* followed the same line: 'His pictures of Anglo-Indian life
are finished works of art, full of go and brightness, true to nature in
its many aspects, and enlivened with a quaint fancy, a ready wit, and a
faculty of phrase and expression seldom met with.'

Looking back in 1890, and forgetting that he had not then known
who wrote *Departmental Ditties*, Lang commented on the fact that he
had been the first to review it in England, and went on:

Mr. Kipling's name was new to me, and, much as I admired his verses, I heard no more of him till I received *The Story of the Gadsb's*, *In Black and White*, and *Under the Deodars*. They were all unpretending little tomes, clad in grey paper, and published in India. Then, on reading them, one saw that a new star in literature had swum into one's ken. [*Harper's Weekly*, 30 August 1890.]

Lang advised Sampson Low, Marston and Co., to publish the Wheeler booklets in England (he is supposed to have exclaimed: 'Eureka! A genius has come to light!' [Edward E. Long: 'The Discovery of Rudyard Kipling', the *London Magazine*, 1926]), and proceeded to review *In Black and White* and *Under the Deodars* in the *Saturday Review* of 10 August 1889 (No. 5). Lang had met Kipling (who arrived in London about 5 October) and introduced him to Haggard [see letter of 26 October to Lang in Morton N. Cohen's *Rudyard Kipling to Rider Haggard* (1965), pp. 25–7] before writing his next review, of *Plain Tales from the Hills* (also anonymous) in the *Daily News* of 2 November.

Lang and others may have prepared the way for Kipling by making his name known to a small public that appreciated good literature and suggesting that critics should look out for him. But on his arrival in London he made his own way into popular fame by the arresting excellence of his stories and poems.

That the word had got about, and his books were being read when he arrived is shown by the recollections of Sidney Low, at that time editor of the *St. James's Gazette:*

I spent an afternoon reading *Soldiers Three* and when I went out to a dinner-party that evening I could talk of nothing but this marvellous youth who had dawned upon the eastern horizon. My host, a well-known journalist and critic of those days, laughed at my enthusiasm which he said would hardly be justified by the appearance of another Dickens. 'It may be,' I answered hotly, 'that a greater than Dickens is here.'

I got Wheeler [Stephen Wheeler, who had been Kipling's first editor on the *Civil and Military Gazette* at Lahore] to put me in touch with Kipling on his arrival in London, and one morning there walked into my office a short, dark, young man with a bowler hat, a rather shabby tweed overcoat, an emphatic voice, a charming smile, and behind his spectacles a pair of the brightest eyes I had ever seen. He told me that he had his way to make in English literature, and intended to do it, though at the time he was young, very poor, and (in this country) quite unknown. I suggested that he might help to keep his pot boiling by writing sketches and short stories for the *St. James's*, which suggestion he willingly accepted . . .

A day or two later he sent me a contribution, which I received with delight and promptly printed. This, so far as I know, was the first piece from Kipling's pen published in England. [D. Chapman-Huston: *The Lost Historian—Sidney Low* (1936), pp. 78–9.]

These stories, which appeared weekly from 21 November ('The Comet of a Season') to 28 December ('The Battle of Rupert Square') were all unsigned (Kipling continued to contribute in prose and verse until the end of March 1890, but some later items were signed and others may not be his), and cannot have helped him to make his name known.

This he did, however, with the aid of the one important introduction which he brought with him, to Mowbray Morris (1847–1911), editor of *Macmillan's Magazine*, who had once been art editor of the *Pioneer* of Allahabad. Even so Kipling began with a pseudonym for his first two poems 'The Ballad of the King's Mercy' and 'The Ballad of East and West', which appeared as by 'Yussuf' in November and December 1889. But the December issue also contained the first signed story, 'The Incarnation of Krishna Mulvaney', and thereafter followed almost monthly such famous stories as 'The Head of the District', 'The Courting of Dinah Shadd', 'The Man Who Was', 'Without Benefit of Clergy', 'On Greenhow Hill', and several poems —all by September 1890, and all signed.

The *Barrack-Room Ballads* began in the *Scots Observer* (edited by W. E. Henley) with 'Danny Deever' on 22 February 1890, and were received with enthusiasm; while stories and poems appeared also in other periodicals such as the *Fortnightly*, *Longman's*, *Lippincott's*, *Harper's* and even the *Fishing Gazette* during that first year with its amazing productivity.

Kipling's meteoric rise to fame is well sketched by J. M. Barrie in his article 'The Man from Nowhere', published over the pseudonym Gavin Ogilvy in the *British Weekly* on 2 May 1890:

. . . Two society papers made themselves at one time a debating society for discussing Mr. Rudyard Kipling, 'The Man from Nowhere', as he then called himself. That 'everybody knows Mr. Kipling's books', was *The World's* argument, and that 'nobody ever heard of Mr. Kipling', was *Truth's*. As a result, while *The World* and other papers thought Mr. Kipling such a celebrity that they vied with each other in describing the tags of his bootlaces, *Truth* and other papers talked contemptuously of log-rolling.

At the time of the *World–Truth* debate Mr. Kipling was a novelist who, six months previous, was almost quite unknown in this country. Therefore, his detractors seemed to urge, it is absurd that he can be a great man already. No, said his admirers, it is only remarkable, and therefore worth making a greater shout over. They certainly shouted so loudly as to justify the other side in calling him, not the Man from Nowhere, but the Man with many Friends. But to his friends let this folly be charged, not to him. Even if he did take their indiscriminate eulogies a little complacently, can we, with any generosity, blame a young man for liking to hear his work extolled? Whether Mr. Kipling has influential friends is a small matter. The great question is, can he write? To which my own answer is that no young man of such capacity has appeared in our literature for years.

The very next day in the *Scots Observer* (see No. 7 below) W. E. Henley was almost echoing Barrie's words—and Sidney Low's enthusiasm of six months earlier:

When Kipling is writing at his best, of Mulvaney or the Man who would be King, . . . you are made to feel with all your strength that here is such a promise as has not been perceived in English letters since young Mr. Dickens broke in suddenly upon the precincts of immortality as the creator of Pickwick and the Wellers.

And both these echoed an anonymous review of reprints of *Departmental Ditties* and *Soldiers Three* less than a week earlier in the *Athenaeum* [No. 3261, p. 528, 26 April 1890], which might be by Theodore Watts-Dunton:

What position Mr. Kipling may ultimately attain to it is impossible upon his present performances to predict with any certainty; yet if he should prove capable of filling a larger canvas than he has yet essayed, he might conceivably become a second Dickens. His sparkling and cynical trifles are comparable to those *Sketches by Boz* which first brought the great English novelist to the notice of the public; but it remains to be seen whether he can give the public what will answer to a *David Copperfield* or *A Tale of Two Cities*. He has shown himself extraordinarily prolific since his arrival in this country, and some of his later work seems to be of a higher imaginative quality than his earlier studies. What we look for now is that he shall begin 'majora canere,' and, avoiding the nemesis that waits upon over-productiveness, concentrate his undoubted gifts upon the treatment of more important themes than even the amusing vagaries of Tommy Atkins and the risky situations of Simla society.

All this is confirmed shortly by Kipling in *Something of Myself* [pp. 78-9, 88]:

My small stock-in-trade of books had become known in certain quarters; and there was an evident demand for my stuff. I do not recall that I stirred a hand to help myself. Things happened to me. I went by invitation to Mowbray

Morris, the editor of *Macmillan's Magazine* . . . He took from me an Indian tale and some verses . . .

Then more tales were asked for, and the editor of the *St. James's Gazette* wanted stray articles, signed and unsigned . . .

About this time was an interview in a weekly paper, where I felt myself on the wrong side of the counter and that I ought to be questioning my questioner. Shortly after, that same weekly made me a proposition which I could not see my way to accept, and then announced that I was 'feeling my oats', of which, it was careful to point out, it had given me my first sieveful. Since, at that time, I was overwhelmed, not to say scared, by the amazing luck that had come to me, the pronouncement gave me confidence. If that was how I struck the external world—good! For naturally I considered the whole universe was acutely interested in me only—just as a man who strays into a skirmish is persuaded he is the pivot of the action . . .

I was plentifully assured, *viva voce* and in the Press cuttings—which is a drug that I do not recommend to the young—that 'nothing since Dickens' compared with my 'meteoric rise to fame', etc. (But I was more or less inoculated, if not immune, to the coarser sorts of print.)

'People talked, quite reasonably, of rockets and sticks,' added Kipling, and went on to quote the immortal lines by 'that genius J. K. S.'—'which I would have given much to have written myself' (No. 13).

Besides reproof in verse, parody also could contain genuine—and sometimes devastating—criticism. Barry Pain seems to have been about the first in the field with his parody of a *Plain Tale* in the *Cornhill Magazine* in October 1890 (No. 9)—which shows up some of Kipling's early weaknesses with kindly mockery.

E. V. Lucas (1868–1938) late in 1892 in the *Privateer* (an ephemeral magazine issued at University College, London, which survived only for eleven numbers) included in a series of amusing 'Literary Recipes' one for 'Kipling Chutnee':

This pickle has a peculiar mordant quality which distinguishes it from all others. The chief ingredient is unwashed English, chopped, broken, and bruised with a brazen instrument. Then work in chips and fragments of cynicism, 'B.V.' [James Thomson, author of *The City of Dreadful Night*]'s poems, the seven cardinal sins, the *Soldier's Pocket Book*, the *Civil Service Regulations*, Simla manners, profanity, an Ekka pony, the Southern Cross, and genius. Spice with a Tipperary brogue.

Again, Owen Seaman in 'The Ballad of the Kipperling' in *Punch* (13 January 1894), hits off very neatly the facility of some of Kipling's verse, and his inordinate delight in 'jargon'. But later examples tend to be vindictive without conveying any real criticism, as in the case of Max Beerbohm's 'P.C., X, 36' in *A Christmas Garland* (1912), pp. 11–20. At least nine caricatures and two critical articles emanated from the pen of the unconscionable Max, as well as this parody: 'This incomparable master of the smirk and titter,' wrote Charles Carrington, 'was, as a rule, gentle, except when he touched upon one topic. He hated Rudyard Kipling. He set himself to destroy Kipling's reputation and, later, to assure the world that it had been destroyed, with no small degree of success among the literary coteries, but with no visible effect upon Kipling's ever-growing fame and influence in wider circles.' [*Rudyard Kipling*, p. 341.]

Such parodies as R. C. Lehmann's 'Burra Murra Boko', Number Two of the second series of Mr Punch's Prize Novels [*Punch*, Vol. XCIX, p. 173, 11 October 1890]; Anthony C. Deane's 'A Very Nearly Story' [*Punch*, Vol. CXXIII, p. 248, 8 October 1902] and the Kipling item in St John Hankin's *Lost Masterpieces* [*Punch*, Vol. CXXV, p. 254, 14 October 1903] are little more than mildly amusing and do not have much to say as criticism. Lehmann also wrote an attack on 'The Islanders' [*Punch*, Vol. CXXII, p. 52, 15 January 1902], from a political rather than a literary angle which, Kipling declared, nearly made him break his rule of never answering criticism:

I had written during the Boer War a set of verses based on unofficial criticisms of many serious junior officers . . . Nobody loved them, and indeed they were not conciliatory; but *Punch* took them rather hard. This was a pity because *Punch* would have been useful at that juncture. I knew none of its staff, but I asked questions and learned that *Punch* on this particular issue was—non-Aryan 'and German at that' . . . I swallowed my spittle at once. Israel is a race to leave alone. It abets disorder. [*Something of Myself*, pp. 223–4.]

But indeed from the end of the century onwards most parody of Kipling was from a political angle, as most criticism soon tended to become. His role as prophet was neatly summed up, and without animus, in an anonymous Alphabet of Authors contributed to the *London Magazine* about 1902:

> K is for Kipling
> A builder of rhymes,
> Who 'lest we forget'
> All our national crimes
> Sets them forth at great length
> In large type in *The Times*.

A little earlier, in their *Lives of the 'Lustrious* (1901) C. L. Graves and E. V. Lucas had also made gently satiric protest against Kipling's new role:

KIPLING, RUDYARD, Poet Laureate and Recruiting Sergeant, was born all over the world, some eighteen years ago. After a lurid infancy at Westward Ho! in the company of Stalky & Co., he emigrated to India at the age of six and swallowed it whole. In the following year the British Empire was placed in his charge, and it is still there. A misgiving that England may have gone too far in the matter of self-esteem having struck him in 1897, he wrote 'The Recessional', but there are signs that he has since forgotten it . . . He lives in Cape Colony, which is a suburb of Rottingdean, and at intervals puts forth a fascinating book, or a moral essay in *The Times* . . . [Quoted in full in E. V. Lucas: *Reading, Writing and Remembering* (1932), pp. 212–13.]

Whether or not Kipling was 'The Man with Many Friends', even those most interested in his success mingled blame with their praise, and by no means practised the gentle art of log-rolling. To take one example, Andrew Lang who had done more to help Kipling to make his way in the literary world than any other of his earlier critics shows by a selection of his more casual utterances that he did not necessarily admire all that Kipling wrote:

What *does* Kipling mean by that story in *Longman's*? I admire him awfully, but one or two such performances as that would make me set about a volume of selections. [Unpublished letter to Rider Haggard: April 1890.] [The story was the uncollected 'For One Night Only'.]

I don't care for *The Light that Failed*! [Unpublished letter to Walter Herries Pollock: 3 April 1891.]

'Love-o'-Women' seems to my taste, rather dully disagreeable than really 'powerful'. [*Cosmopolitan* (N.Y.), Vol. XV, p. 616, September 1893.]

Of new books here, Mr. Rudyard Kipling's *Jungle Book* is perhaps the most interesting, certainly the most original. One likes to hear dull owls hoot that Mr. Kipling will 'write himself out'. Nobody is less likely to exhaust his stores of reflection, humour and observation . . . [Mowgli and the wolves] are delightful to read about, for 'grown-ups', and the pretty volume is a paradise for children . . . Oh, blessed province of fancy, and dear jungle of the imagination, whither we can flee and be at peace, if he who guides us, like Mr. Kipling, has the secret of the branch of gold. [*Cosmopolitan*, Vol. XVII, p. 503, August 1894.]

As my sympathies are not wholly engaged with *Stalky and Co.* in their long and successful combat with their masters, I prefer to say very little about these heroes. Whatever they may be they are not normal schoolboys. Their eternal use of the word 'giddy' is teasing; their slang is not 'of the centre' . . . More agreeable fellows are Mr. Eden Phillpots's heroes in that delightful book *The Human Boy* . . . Then I am wholly captivated by those perfect little trumps, Mrs. Nesbit's characters in *The Treasure Seekers* . . . [*Longman's Magazine*, Vol. XXXV, p. 184, December 1899.]

Mr. Kipling in *Kim* in *Cassell's Magazine* is once more the Mr. Kipling who first won our hearts. His theme is India, where he is always at his best; and we learn more of the populace, the sects, the races, the lamas, the air, the sounds, scents and smells from a few pages than from libraries of learned authors. [*Longman's Magazine*, Vol. XXXVII, p. 570, April 1901.]

Before political bias took the place of literary criticism, beginning with Robert Buchanan's 'The Voice of the Hooligan' (No. 33) in 1899, the more scholarly critics had attempted to treat fully and dispassionately of such work as was before them from the simple standpoint of literature. Lang at the beginning of 1891 (No. 12) was followed by Barrie (No. 14) and Gosse (No. 17) and Henry James (No. 21), with a more grudging acceptance from Francis Adams (No. 20) and the fuller studies by Charles Eliot Norton (No. 27) and J. H. Millar (No. 29).

Millar's lengthy and leisurely pontification in *Blackwood's Magazine* in 1898 is typical—and the best—of a number of anonymous studies of great length in the 'Reviews'; Rowland Prothero, Baron Ernle (1851–1937) wrote twenty pages on 'The Tales of Mr. Kipling' in the *Edinburgh Review* [Vol. CLXXIV, pp. 132–51] in July 1891; the Rev. William Barry, Catholic apologist, (1849–1930) thirty pages on 'Mr. Rudyard Kipling's Tales' in the *Quarterly Review* [Vol. CLXXV, pp. 132–61] in July 1892, and Henry Heathcote Statham, authority on art and music, (1839–1924) preceded Millar with an article of twenty-two pages on 'The Works of Mr. Rudyard Kipling' in the *Edinburgh Review* [Vol. CLXXXVII, pp. 203–26] in January 1898.

After them Kipling became the butt of political prejudice, and his literary attainments were more and more ignored by critics, or assumed not to exist outside the popular fancy. An occasional reviewer broke away from what was fast becoming a stereotyped ready-made label; but on the whole no serious criticism of Kipling was written during the first two decades of the present century.

An honourable exception was Holbrook Jackson (1874–1948) in his excellent study *The Eighteen Nineties* (1913), where he gave Kipling a whole chapter of sensible and well-balanced description, setting him reasonably in his period, and attempting no overall judgments.

The first award of the Nobel Prize for Literature to Kipling in 1907 did little to reinstate him as a great writer in his own country. Books of the stature of *Puck of Pook's Hill* (1906) and *Rewards and Fairies* (1910) were dismissed on the back pages of periodicals as scarcely worthy of notice: the *Athenaeum's* note on the former is typical:

In his new part—the missionary of empire—Mr. Kipling is living the strenuous life. He has frankly abandoned story telling, and is using his complete and powerful armoury in the interest of patriotic zeal. [No. 4119, p. 404, 6 October 1906.]

It was, of course, understandable when Kipling was appealing for conscription and warning the country of its unreadiness for the European war which he foresaw as imminent, in public speeches, in impassioned verses set up 'in large type in *The Times*', and even in such stories as 'The Army of a Dream' [*Morning Post*, 15–18 June 1904; collected in *Traffics and Discoveries* the same year] and 'The Edge of the Evening' [*Pall Mall Magazine*, December 1913; collected in *A Diversity of Creatures*, 1917] and the allegory of 'The Mother Hive' [*Windsor Magazine*, December 1908; collected in *Actions and Reactions*, 1909], that those who disagreed with him should look with suspicion on all else that he wrote.

Naturally an author's deeply-held convictions may find some reflection in most of what he writes, and Kipling did see parallels between past and present in his historical stories (which is only to repeat the cliché that history repeats itself); but though the Puck stories became immediately popular—among his most popular works, in fact—it took a generation before they were considered seriously as important historical fiction. Then the historian G. M. Trevelyan set them at the top of Kipling's achievement, declaring in 1953 that:

He tells us tale after tale of the ancient history of England, as he imagines it, with a marvellous historical sense, I think . . . As a piece of historical imagination I know of nothing in the world better than the third story in *Puck* called 'The Joyous Venture', in which the Viking ship coasts Africa to find gold, and fight gorillas in the tropical forest. I can see no fault in it, and many a merit. [See further in his *A Layman's Love of Letters* (1954), pp. 27–35. Also on Kipling's historical stories see J. I. M. Stewart in the *Kipling Journal*, No. 153, p. 9, March 1965, and his other writings on Kipling.]

The First World War proved Kipling right in many respects—as he said in his poetic tribute to Lord Roberts, it was 'the War that he had descried'. But prophets of woe are usually execrated before the event and seldom praised for their prescience after it.

Perhaps Kipling was considered harmless, a toothless tiger, by early postwar writers—even as approaching the image of a 'grand old man of letters'—and he was often described (with an implied shrug) as 'an institution'.

Overseas Maurice Hutton, lecturing in Montreal in 1918, felt able to take Kipling as a serious craftsman [the *University Magazine*, Montreal, Vol. XVII, No. 4, pp. 589–618, December 1918]; but in England the first attempt came, surprisingly, from the greatest poet of the new literary movement, T. S. Eliot, in a review of Kipling's verse in the *Athenaeum* of 9 May 1919 (No. 50).

The real beginning of modern Kipling criticism, however, came from Professor Bonamy Dobrée in a long article in the *Monthly Criterion* for December 1927 (No. 55)—later enlarged and reprinted in his *The Lamp and the Lute* (1929, revised 1964)—a prelude to his full-scale study *Rudyard Kipling: Realist and Fabulist* (1967).

But in 1919 E. T. Raymond [Edward Raymond Thompson] was writing in his *All and Sundry* [pp. 177–85], with much second-hand and facile generalizations, the startling conviction that 'Mr. Rudyard Kipling is not perhaps a spent force. But it seems safe to say that he will never again be more than a minor one.'

Though there were dissenting murmurs in America (see Nos. 53 and 54 below), this remained the general critical opinion until well after Kipling's death on 18 January 1936. That event brought forth the usual chorus of polite tributes—of little critical value and remarkable in this case for their extreme caution. The best of the obituary studies seem to have been the article by Desmond MacCarthy quoted earlier in this Introduction, and the anonymous essay in the *Times Literary Supplement* which concludes the present volume (No. 61). A good study of the reaction—or lack of it—after Kipling's death is given by Hilton Brown in the first chapter of his *Rudyard Kipling: A New Appreciation* (1943).

IV

SALES, HOME AND OVERSEAS

The critical reaction against Kipling seems to have made little difference to his popularity. Sales figures are not available, as one would expect with an author who valued his privacy as highly as Kipling did, but it can be stated from reliable evidence that the only sharp falling-off in sales, and that only a temporary one, came in 1919 after a 'boom' period during the War.

Charles Carrington who, though even he did not have full access to the sales figures, was able to make some kind of estimate of the overall picture, wrote in 1955 [*Rudyard Kipling*, p. xxi]:

According to the verdict of the critics, Kipling's literary credit reached its zenith in the early eighteen-nineties, declined and was almost extinguished before his death, to be revived by some connoisseurs in the nineteen-forties. By another criterion, his reputation moved through quite different phases. Not only his most approved writings but all his authorized work, year after year, and decade after decade, remained in the class that the book trade calls 'best-sellers', and were still in that class twenty years after his death, although these books were never issued in cheap editions . . . Kipling, like Dickens and Defoe, was a popular writer whose work had a 'sensational' success that did not die with the season, that did not need puffing by the reviewers. From 1890 to 1932, and even to 1955, there was no lack of buyers for this line of goods even though the publicists no longer urged the public to acquire it. When his politics were most out of fashion, he still had no lack of readers . . .

And Charles Morgan, writing the history of Kipling's publishers in 1943 [*The House of Macmillan*, pp. 151-2] had already described how, during Kipling's lifetime—

It became, as the years passed, almost a game to invent new dresses for his work —uniform editions, pocket editions, the Edition de Luxe in red and gold, the Bombay Edition, the Service Edition intended for the pack or pocket of soldiers in the 1914 War. There were, also, school editions, and gigantic volumes in which all the dog stories or all the Mowgli stories or all the humorous stories were assembled, and year by year the wise men held their breath and wondered whether by now the public demand for old wine in new bottles was exhausted. The cautious feared it might be, but they were always wrong.[2]

Only the magnificent Sussex Editions, prepared by Kipling during the last year of his life though not published until 1937-8, failed to sell as quickly as was anticipated, and some of the 525 sets (35 volumes at £87 10s. od. per set) were unsold in 1940 and perished in the Blitz. Very few, however, seem to have been destroyed, and the remaining majority of sets average £500 to £600 when they come up for sale two or three times a year.

In the United States the Kipling sales seem to have been less steady, but at least as great on aggregate—beginning with a host of pirate editions before the 1891 Copyright Act, and once more proliferating in paperbacks as the earlier volumes go out of copyright under the different system, which dates from first publication and not, as here, from author's death.

The critical reception seems to have been much the same as in England, but a little slower in recognizing a major author.

Speaking a bit sarcastically of American popular taste, Andrew Lang wrote [*Harper's Weekly*, 30 August] in 1890:

I do not anticipate for Mr. Kipling a very popular popularity. He does not compete with Miss Braddon or Mr. E. P. Roe. His favourite subjects are too remote and unfamiliar for a world that likes to be amused with matters near home and passions that do not stray far from the drawing-room or the parlor.

And he was shown to have hit off the American reaction pretty fairly by an anonymous writer a month later in *Harper's Magazine* [October 1890, Vol. LXXXI, pp. 801–2]:

It is pathetic that people read Haggard and Rudyard Kipling when such artistic and important books as Harold Frederic's are available.

And the author (possibly the Editor, H. M. Alden, 1869–1919) goes on to speak contemptuously of 'the Rudyard Kipling fad'.

But the 'fad' grew by leaps and bounds, and Roger Burlingame records [*Of Many Books*, 1946, p. 249] the extraordinary success of *Departmental Ditties* and *Barrack-Room Ballads:*

These verses were, of course, novel in subject and rhythm; they caught on surprisingly in America—being so British in substance—until Kipling's public here equalled or exceeded that in the homeland.

He records, however, that by the end of the century 'Kipling and Barrie were no longer among the ten at the top: Gilbert Parker, William J. Locke and Mrs. Humphrey Ward took their places.'

The reaction at the beginning of the twentieth century seems to have been almost as strong in America as in England, and may be typified by quotation from Arthur Bartlett Maurice's review of *Kim* in the New York *Bookman* [Vol. XIV, pp. 146–9] in October 1901:

There was, once upon a time—somehow it seems very many years ago—a young man who left his home in English India and came to Europe and America, bringing with him a dressing case filled with the manuscripts of marvellous tales about soldiers and civilians . . . That, in a word, was the Mr. Kipling of other days whom men deservedly called great. Unfortunately, it is not the Mr. Kipling of today.

It should be understood that mediocre and meaningless though *Kim* is, it is not to be classed with some of Mr. Kipling's other recent literary efforts—especially with some attempts at verse of which he has of late been guilty. For instance, there was 'The Lesson', an alleged poem, which treated of England's political and military mistakes in the war in the Transvaal. Now, 'The Lesson' was absolutely and flatly unspeakable bosh . . .

[After an inaccurate synopsis] And there you have *Kim*, a jumble of native phrases, of extraneous conversations, of Eastern mysticism, redeemed and brought into a certain concrete form by that craft which Mr. Kipling could not fail to acquire in the years of his apprenticeship and of his genius. It is all so cold, so dead, so lifeless. Mr. Kipling seems to have gone raking through the cinders of his youth in search of the bits of half-burned coals with which to make a little flame and warmth. The old spontaneous fire seems to have irrevocably gone.

On the continent of Europe Kipling took and still holds a high place which seems to have suffered little from adverse political climates— even, strangely enough, in Germany and Russia. His books have been continuously translated into most languages, French taking precedence over a close tie between German, Italian and Swedish.

When he was at his lowest ebb with English critics, one finds no change on the continent. In 1902 Guido Milanesi [in *Rivista d'Italia: Lettere Scienze ed Arte*, Rome, May 1902] is prophesying immortality for *The Seven Seas* and *The Jungle Books*, describing Kipling as a poet—'the poet of the practical spirit'—and accusing English critics of underestimating the greatness of *Plain Tales from the Hills* because they cannot accept its extreme realism.

André Chrevillon [*Revue de Paris*, 15 February 1908] was hailing Kipling six years later as a literary genius—even if some of his political ideas were out of fashion. And J. Castellanos was translating his poems into Spanish and lecturing on them as the work of a great contemporary writer in 1914 [published in *Los Optimistas: Ensayos Literarios*, Madrid, c. 1918]. 'Public taste has shifted to Meredith, Wells, Shaw and Joyce,' wrote André Chaumeix in 1933 [*Le Mois*, April]. 'But Rudyard Kipling can wait serenely for the judgement of the future.' And in his obituary article ['La Grandeur de Kipling', *Revue de France*, 15 February 1936] Claude Farrere ended a glowing tribute with the assertion that 'Rudyard Kipling is better understood by certain French readers than by the immense majority of the British public.'

Kipling himself, always a Francophil, and one who had read French as easily as English since his schooldays, claimed [*Something of Myself*, pp. 227–8] that Prévost was the subconscious inspiration of *The Light that Failed*, and goes on: 'I was confirmed in my belief when the French took to that *conte* with relish, and I always fancied that it walked better in translation than in the original.'

By the time of his death Kipling's works could be found in translation (other than European) ranging from Bengali, Hindustani and Urdu to Chinese, Japanese, Korean, Brazilian and Yiddish. [See Flora V. Livingston: *Supplement to Bibliography of the Works of Rudyard Kipling,* Cambridge, Mass., 1938, pp. 201–31 for a good representative list.]

As far as post-revolutionary Russia is concerned an interesting note appeared in the *Author*, winter number, in 1958, drawn from the findings of the Director of the All Union Chamber of Publications in Moscow:

According to statistics he has produced for the years 1918 to July 1st 1958, more than 77 million copies of works by British authors (including works appearing in anthologies) have been published in the USSR. The number of British authors represented is 236, and the number of languages in which their works have been published is 54. Dickens comes top of the list with nearly ten million copies to his credit (18 languages). He is followed by Wells with nearly seven million copies (16 languages). Conan Doyle, Kipling and Swift are in the next group—between four and five million each, Kipling being published in 34 languages, Swift in 42 and Conan Doyle in 9. In the three-to-four-million group come Defoe, Galsworthy, Shakespeare and Scott; Defoe being the most translated of the three (36 languages). Between two and three million are Robert Louis Stevenson and A. J. Cronin (15 and 6 languages respectively), and in the one-to-two-million group comes James Aldridge, with Jerome K. Jerome. A large group in the half-million area includes Byron, Burns, Charlotte Brontë, Hardy, Walter Greenwood, Conrad, Thackeray, Fielding and Shaw.

During a visit paid to Oxford by a group of Russian professors of English literature the same year, the *Guardian* (21 July 1958) noted that: 'They are surprised by the different value given to certain English writers by Russian and English critical opinion—notably the importance attached to Lawrence and Joyce here and our neglect of Kipling and Galsworthy.' And 'Atticus' in the *Sunday Times* of 6 May 1962 recorded a conversation between the English poet Edwin Brock and the young Russian poet Evgeni Evtushenko:

'For my last book,' said the Russian modestly, 'there were orders for 200,000 copies.' He seemed amazed when Brock murmured that a young British poet was lucky to sell a thousand copies . . .

'I shouldn't think anyone here has made a living out of poetry since Tennyson,' ventured Brock.

'Kipling must have made money out of poetry,' said Evtushenko. 'You know, the most popular poet in Moscow is Kipling.'

'But Kipling was an imperialist.'

The Russian smiled and quoted Kipling in Russian with evident approval.

Kipling's popularity throughout the British Empire seems to have been at least as great as in the mother country—and it does not seem to have suffered for long as former dominions and colonies achieved their varying forms of independence.

Thus, in the early years of Kipling's fame we find the Australian novelist 'Rolf Boldrewood' [Thomas Alexander Browne, 1826–1915, quoted in Simon Nowell-Smith's *Letters to Macmillan*, 1967, p. 213] writing to his publisher on 20 July 1891:

I have just been reading your edition of *The Light that Failed*. In my humble opinion Mr. Rudyard Kipling is the strongest and most original writer in his own department since Dickens.

From the middle of his career a Canadian writer, Edgar Pelham [*University Magazine* (Montreal), Vol. VII, pp. 261–5, April 1908, in an article on 'English Poetry since Tennyson'] contrasted Kipling's 'kettledrums in the street' with Yeats's 'flute in the hushed forest', and compared the realism of the one with the idealism of the other. Kipling, he maintained, was inferior to Yeats in harmony and imagination, but Kipling was original in 'introducing into poetry the primitive nature sentiment', though he did not lean on traditional, literary primitivism. Kipling, 'rather than conveying the beauty of ocean, best conveys its mystery and strength'.

In the same year, an Indian writer, Kiran Nath Dhar ['Some Indian Novels' in the *Calcutta Review*, Vol. CXXVII, pp. 561–83, October 1908] declared that Kipling 'was more truly Anglo-Indian than any other writer. His short stories are vivid, and a genuine sympathy for all things Indian pervades his works.'

Between then and independence Indian writers naturally tended to denigrate Kipling and credit him less and less with any understanding of the native Indian outlook and point of view. But with independence an accomplished fact, political axes ceased to be ground far more quickly than they have here, and in 1957 as eminent a writer and critic as Nirad C. Chaudhuri was writing [in *Encounter*, Vol. VIII, pp. 47–53, April 1957]:

'In *Kim* its author wrote not only the finest novel in the English language with an Indian theme, but also one of the greatest of English novels in spite of the theme. This rider is necessary, because the association of anything in English literature with India suggests a qualified excellence, an achievement which is to be judged by its special standards, or even a work which in form and content has in it more than a shade of the second-rate. But *Kim* is great by any standards that ever obtained in any age of English literature.

V

KIPLING CRITICISM TO-DAY

But it is not proposed to deal in the present volume with the Kipling criticism of the last thirty years. The most important critical essays have been collected by Andrew Rutherford in *Kipling's Mind and Art* (1964) and by Elliot L. Gilbert in *Kipling and the Critics* (1965); and there have been several individual studies. The official biography, *Rudyard Kipling: His Life and Work* (1955) by Charles Carrington contains many quotations from earlier criticism, besides its author's own expert and judicious comments. In 1959 J. M. S. Tompkins produced her full-scale study *The Art of Rudyard Kipling*, the best and fullest critical assessment so far made, and other writers since then have written on various sides of his literary achievement. (See Select Bibliography on pp. 396–7 of the present volume.)

In his Preface to Hilton Brown's book quoted above, Frank Swinnerton wrote: 'Until Mr. T. S. Eliot caused consternation among the genteel by analysing his virtues as a poet he was safely dismissed by them as a sort of literary bounder who was somehow responsible for the Boer War.'

Eliot's essay, a study in thirty-two pages, introduced *A Choice of Kipling's Verse* in 1941, and is also too well known and easily accessible to quote here. He was not quite the first to treat Kipling seriously, if we include a rather cautious and non-committal lecture by W. L. Renwick published in the *Durham University Journal* [Vol. XXXII, pp. 3–16] in January 1940, and collected by Rutherford. Edmund Wilson had also just preceded Eliot with his notorious article 'The Kipling that Nobody Read' in the *Atlantic Monthly* [Vol. CLXVII] of February and March 1941 and reprinted at the end of the year in his *The Wound and the Bow* (also included by Rutherford in his collection). And both of these had been forestalled by Edward Shanks in his book *Rudyard Kipling: A Study in Literature and Political Ideas* published in 1940—a volume still not altogether superseded.

But Eliot's determination to treat Kipling as a major writer provoked a good deal of strenuous confutations and expressions of opinion, notably from Boris Ford in *Scrutiny* (11 January 1942), George Orwell in *Horizon* [Vol. V, pp. 111–25, February 1942] and Lionel Trilling in *Nation* [New York: Vol. CLVII, pp. 436 etc., 16 October 1943] —all collected in Elliot L. Gilbert's volume and the second two by Rutherford.

The best re-assessment preceding the volumes by Carrington and Tompkins was, however, the lecture on 'Kipling's World' delivered by C. S. Lewis before the English Association and first published in their *Literature and Life* (1948), since when it has been reprinted in several places, and is included in Gilbert's volume.

Lewis insisted that Kipling 'was a very great writer', even if there were certain things about him which you did not like or even considered a serious blot. To Lewis the blot on Kipling was that 'he is the slave of the Inner Ring'; to other critics it can be his supposed streak of cruelty, his insistence on the Law, or his conviction (for a time at least) that the British Empire offered the best hope of world peace and prosperity.

Critics are apt to be led into over-emphasizing their personal views or special pre-occupation—and others seem unable or unwilling to make the necessary historical metempsychosis to understand the outlook of Kipling's contemporaries—forgetting that the greatest social and intellectual change in recorded history has taken place since Kipling was a young man in India nearly a century ago.

Some critics seem to be 'too clever by half', looking for double-meanings and hidden allegories and allusions. They may add to a reader's enjoyment, even if they cannot prove their points. A good example of this is in the excellent study *Aspects of Kipling's Art* (1964) by Professor C. A. Bodelsen which treats several of the stories, notably the final one, 'Teem: A Treasure-Hunter', as if they were literary Chinese-puzzles, carved ivory ring within ring. There is much amusement in it for the reader, and he often underlines meanings that we may have missed. But we are too often left at the end with the uneasy feeling that we have been sharing in an amusing game, like that played by the Sherlock Holmes Society, rather than arriving at a truer understanding of Kipling's stories.

More dangerous is the psychological approach initiated by Edmund Wilson, who found distrust, hate and cruelty as dominant traits of Kipling's work, and then set to work conscientiously to prove his thesis by exaggerating the unhappy period at Southsea, the harshness of the 'twelve bleak houses by the shore' at Westward Ho! and the 'seven years hard' in India. Most of this has been either disproved, or shown to be in need of drastic toning-down and re-statement by the biographical works published since Wilson's essay; but the attitude still persists as more than a mere echo of Robert Buchanan and H. G. Wells.

31

Another approach is the frankly clinical psychoanalysis. But so far this seems to have been inept, and based on such shaky foundations of pre-conception and sheer ignorance as to be hardly worth considering.

As an example of this so-called criticism may be taken the article by Thomas N. Cross, M.D., 'Rudyard Kipling's Sense of Identity', published in the *Michigan Quarterly Review* [Vol. IV, No. 4, pp. 245–53] in October 1965. This also bases Kipling's literary and political outlook on his sufferings as a child at Southsea. But it can easily be disproved. The 'Devil Boy' whose cruelties were described by Kipling in the story 'Baa, Baa, Black Sheep' and forty years later in his autobiographical fragment *Something of Myself,* is called 'Harry' in the story, and his parents are 'Uncle Harry' and 'Auntie Rosa' (Dr Cross adds a note that Kipling and his sister called Mrs Holloway 'Auntie Rosa', though 'she was not a relative as various biographers have assumed' —I have not so far discovered any of those 'biographers'). And he goes on:

In all that he wrote—more than thirty-six volumes—Kipling used thousands of names; but never once did he use the name Harry. He did, however, use the expression 'By the Lord Harry!'—reflecting, I think, at least something of Harry's power over him.

Mr R. E. Harbord, the President of The Kipling Society, who has been preparing a Reader's Guide to Kipling's works for the last twenty years, writes: 'There are 4 Harrys and 11 Henrys in the Verse; 14 Harrys and 20 Henrys in the Prose—total 49.'

The names given to the couple and their son in the story should surely have been considered by any serious scholar as fictional, unless he could prove that they were the actual names. Dr Cross could have discovered from the *Kipling Journal*, No. 139 (September 1961) that the names of the parents were Captain Pryse Agar Holloway and Sarah Holloway. Their son's name eluded research until about the time the article was written, but was only published after it: he was, in fact, Henry Thomas Holloway [see my *Kipling and the Children* (1965), pp. 29–30].

As for the expression 'By the Lord Harry!' it was a common ejaculation much used in the nineties, and may be found easily in the works of Rider Haggard, Conan Doyle and any other writer of the period.

Conclusions based on such flimsy evidence and ignorance of the very rudiments of research can surely be dismissed as worthless.

Before turning from the end to the beginning of Kipling criticism, as exhibited in the following pages, we can do no better than read and take to heart the opening paragraph of Professor Dobrée's *Rudyard Kipling: Realist and Fabulist*:

Rudyard Kipling, it is now coming generally to be acknowledged, has been more grotesquely misunderstood, misrepresented, and in consequence denigrated, than any other known writer. I have attempted here to present him as outside any of the camps into which careless readers have wished to, indeed have, put him, either in praise or in blame. I say 'careless readers' because I have found that most of those who so readily label him have not really read him, or have done so with preconceived notions of what he wished to impart. Not long ago a distinguished man of letters and lecturer wrote to me: 'People are not only blinded, but *deafened* by prejudice. If you talk (as I sometimes do . . .) about him, *nobody hears what you say*. They simply switch off their aids, or have an automatic cut-out.' Thus I have not attempted, except by occasional incidental remarks, to refute the ill-based accusations made against him. An unbiased view of the totality of his work makes such labour unnecessary.

NOTES

1 Vereker Hamilton: *Things That Happened* (1925), pp. 186–9; Ian Hamilton: *Listening for the Drums* (1944), p. 203; Coulson Kernahan: *Nothing Quite Like Kipling Had Happened Before* (1944), p. 47; Ian B. W. Hamilton: *The Happy Warrior: A Life of General Sir Ian Hamilton* (1966), p. 77.

2 There seem to have been twenty-one Collected Editions of Kipling's works between 1890 and 1965, nine of these limited sets at high prices: eleven (three of them early and not completed) in America, ten in England and one (Tauchnitz, 19 volumes) on the Continent. This does not include school editions, translations into foreign languages, nor such selections— each of more than a thousand pages—as *The One Volume Kipling* (1928) and *A Kipling Pageant* (1935), both published in America; nor the various editions of his Collected Verse of which there seem to have been nine before the *Definitive Edition* of 1940.

1. Andrew Lang introduces Kipling's First Book

1886

The earliest review in Great Britain so far discovered was contained in Andrew Lang's monthly *causerie* 'At the Sign of the Ship' in *Longman's Magazine*, Vol. VIII, pp. 675–6, October 1886. (Lang did not realize that the name in facsimile handwriting on the 'envelope' was that of the author. See pages 13–14 of Introduction.)

Andrew Lang (1844–1912), poet, scholar, folklorist and essayist, was the leading literary critic and reviewer of the last two decades of the century. He was among the first to recognize and encourage many writers of the period, notably Stevenson, Bridges, Kipling and De la Mare, besides the romance-writers from Haggard, Doyle and Weyman to A. E. W. Mason and John Buchan.

There is a special variety of English *Vers de Société*, namely the Anglo-Indian species. A quaint and amusing example of this literature has reached me, named *Departmental Ditties*. The modest author does not give his name. The little book is published in the shape of an official paper, 'No. 1. of 1886'. The envelope is the cover. No poem, and this is an excellent arrangement, occupies more than one of the long narrow pages. Would that all poems were as brief. The Radical should read *Departmental Ditties* and learn how gaily *Jobus et Cie* govern India:

> 'Who shall doubt' the secret hid
> Under Cheops' pyramid,
> Was that the contractor 'did'
>   Cheops out of several millions?
>
> Or that Joseph's sudden rise
> To Comptroller of Supplies,
> Was a fraud of monstrous size
>   On King Pharaoh's swart civilians?

Here we learn how Ahasuerus Jenkins, merely because he 'had a tenor voice of super Santley tone', became a power in the state.

Very curious is the tale of Jones, who left his newly-wedded bride, and went to the Hurrom Hills above the Afghan border, and whose heliographic messages home were intercepted and interpreted by General Bangs.

> With damnatory dash and dot he'd heliographed his wife
> Some interesting details of the General's private life.

On the whole, these are melancholy ditties. Jobs, and posts, and pensions, and the wives of their neighbours appear (if we trust the satirist) to be much coveted by her Majesty's Oriental civil servants. The story of Giffen, who was broken and disgraced, and saved a whole countryside at the expense of his own life, and who is now worshipped (by the natives) in Bengal, is worthy of Bret Harte.

The Indian poet has kept the best wine to the last, and I like his poem 'In Spring-time' so much that (supreme compliment!) I have copied it out here . . . [the poem is quoted in full: see DV, p. 78].

2. *Plain Tales from the Hills* Reaches England

1888

Anonymous review of *Plain Tales from the Hills* (Thacker and Spink, London and Calcutta, 1888) in the *Saturday Review*, No. 1702, Vol. LXV, pp. 697–8 (9 June 1888) under the heading 'Novels and Stories', with seven other novels by various authors —none now remembered.

Probably by Walter Herries Pollock (1850–1926), the editor— author of minor verse, fiction, criticism, etc. C. F. Hooper (then a member of the firm of Thacker and Spink) recorded in an article 'Kipling's Younger Days'—*Saturday Review*, 7 March 1936, that he was trying to sell *Plain Tales* in London, but had no success until he persuaded the Editor of the *Saturday Review* to review it.

There is a good deal in a title. Could there be a much less attractive title than *Plain Tales from the Hills*? Residents in British India and subscribers to the *Civil and Military Gazette* may know what it means, and hasten to get hold of the book accordingly; but to the untravelled inhabitants of London and the United Kingdom generally it would seem almost as hopeful to undertake the perusal of a volume entitled *Straight Talks from Beulah*. We should suggest to Mr. Kipling to change the name of his book to *The Other Man; and Other Stories*, not because 'The Other Man' is his best plain tale, which it is not, but because it would look well on the bookstalls. There are forty plain tales, of which twenty-eight have appeared separately in a newspaper, and the other twelve are, in the modest words of the author, 'more or less new'. Each tale is extremely short, the average length being just under seven pages. Nevertheless, for the profitable disposal of odds and ends of time or for a cross-country journey in stopping trains on Sunday it would be hard to find better reading. Mr. Kipling knows and appreciates the English in India, and is a born story-teller and a man of humour into the bargain. He is also singularly versatile, and equally at home in humour and pathos. 'Thrown Away', a story of a commonplace youth who killed himself in despair merely for want of proper training, is little short of genuine tragedy, and is full of a grim humour which is decidedly telling. 'The Three Musketeers' and 'A Friend's Friend' are farce of a high order. Four of the stories—and four of the best—concern the British private in regiments stationed in India. An inimitable Irishman appears in each of them, and relates his experiences with a delightful freshness and good humour. The following extract occurs in an astonishing story of the taking of a town by Burmese Dacoits. The British detachment could not discover where the Dacoits abode; but

evenshually we *puckarowed* wan man. 'Trate him tinderly,' sez the Lift'nint. So I tuk him away into the jungle, wid the Burmese Interprut'r an' my clanin'-rod. Sez I to the man: 'My paceful squireen,' sez I, 'you shquot on your hunkers an' dimonstrate to *my* frind here, where *your* frinds are whan they're at home.' Wid that I introjuced him to the clanin'-rod, an' he comminst to jabber; the Interprut'r inturprutin' in betweens, an' me helpin' the Intelligince Departmint wid my clanin'-rod whan the man misremimbered.

It has been explained just before that: 'Tis only a *dah* and a Snider that makes a dacoit. Widout thim he's a paceful cultivator, an' felony for to shoot.'

Another remarkable military story is 'The Madness of Private Ortheris'. Ortheris goes out shooting with his friend Mulvaney and the author . . . [26 lines, mainly quotations from the story, with synopsis] . . . The military stories happen to have been dwelt on here, but there are many tales of civilians, and indeed of natives, that are really quite as good. The reader should not omit to peruse the headnotes of the stories, especially when they are in verse. It seems probable that a considerable proportion are Mr. Kipling's own. One advantage in the extreme shortness of the stories is that, as they are read in a few minutes, their incidents are easily forgotten, and they may be read again with fresh pleasure after a short interval. For this reason, and because it is small, the book is one to buy, and not merely to get from the library.

3. Sir William Hunter on Departmental Ditties

1888

Signed review in the *Academy*, No. 852, pp. 128–9 (1 September 1888).

Sir William Wilson Hunter (1840–1900) was a well-known Indian civilian, historian and publicist, author of several learned works on India, notably *The Indian Empire: its Peoples, History and Products* (1895), and a member of the Governor-General's Council 1881–7.

Charles Carrington calls this review 'the first analytical essay by a writer who knew Kipling's background, and knew India'.

Mr. Kipling's ditties have well earned the honours of a third edition. They possess the one quality which entitles *vers de société* to live. For they reflect with light gaiety the thoughts and feelings of actual men and women, and are true as well as clever. Neither wit nor sparkling epigram, nor the laboriously laughable rhyme, but this element of truth alone can save the poet of a set from oblivion.

As Pope admits us to a real belle's toilette in the reign of Queen Anne and allows us to look over her hand at ombre; or as Praed preserves alive the political coterie-life of half-a-century ago; or as Bret Harte, in his sadder way, places us down among the saloon-gamblers of the West with their stray gleams of compunction and tenderness— so Mr. Kipling achieves the feat of making Anglo-Indian society flirt and intrigue visibly before our eyes. It is not, as he discloses it, a very attractive society. Its flirtations will seem rather childish to a London coquette, its intrigues very small to a parliamentary wire-puller. But, if Mr. Kipling makes his little Simla folk rather silly, he also makes them very real. The Mayfair matron, accustomed to calmly play her musical pawns at her matinées, will indeed marvel that any woman should take the trouble which the Simla lady took to capture one singing subaltern. The 'Legend of the Indian Foreign Office' may seem to the diplomatic youth whose windows look out on Downing Street to be better suited to the civic parlour of some small pushing mayor. Although, however, Mr. Kipling's stage is a narrow one, his players are very much alive, and they go through their pranks in quite fresh dresses, and with all the accessories of true tears and ogles, audible sighs and laughter.

It is a curious little world to which he introduces us. The few English men of letters who have passed a portion of their lives in India, from Philip Francis to Macaulay, and the still rarer stray scholar from foreign parts, like Csoma de Koros, who has sojourned there, seem to have found Anglo-Indian society sometimes bizarre, and more often intolerably dull. It is this weariness of uncongenial social surroundings which gives to Sir Alfred Lyall's poems their note of peculiar pathos. In spite of the brilliance of his own career, India is ever to him the Land of Regrets. The merry little people who flirt through Mr. Kipling's ditties look out on the scene with altogether different eyes. They may detest the country and dislike the natives, but they find their own small lives vastly amusing. Their personal tastes and their code of public morals are equally simple. Their highest ideal of enjoyment would seem, according to Mr. Kipling, to be a stringed band and a smooth floor. Their most serious aim in life, we learn from the same observer, is 'an appointment'—signifying thereby not an opportunity for doing work, but a device for drawing pay. This great object of existence in the ditties is apparently best to be achieved by flirting, fibbing, and conjugal collusion. Thus Mr. Potiphar Gubbins, the hero of one poem, gets hoisted over the heads of his brother engineers by the fascinations of his wife—an attractive and a complaisant young person who, for reasons of her own, has married Potiphar, although 'coarse as a chimpanzee'. Another piece relates how Mr. Sleary, an impecunious subaltern secretly engaged to a lady in England, obtains an appointment by proposing to the daughter of an Indian official. Having secured the post, he frightens his fiancée Number Two out of the engagement by pretending to have epileptic fits, then nobly marries fiancée Number One, and lives with her happily ever after on the produce of his fraud. In the ditty of Delilah, a veteran Simla charmer wheedles a State secret out of an aged Councillor and betrays it to a younger admirer, who, in turn, promptly betrays it to the press. In the story of Uriah, an officer is despatched to Quetta and dies there, in order that his wife may more freely amuse herself at Simla with the senior who got him sent out of the way. A private secretary-ship is the well-earned reward of a young gentleman who receives a kiss by mistake at a masked ball, and who has the extraordinary chivalry or prudence not to publish the lady's name. These little *contes*, with various duller, if more decorous, jobs like that of the Chatham colonel, may seem poor stuff for verse. But Mr. Kipling handles each situation with a light touch and a gay malice, which make it difficult to be quite sure whether he sincerely admires his pretty marionettes, or whether he is not inwardly chafing and raging at the people among whom he is condemned to live. He very calmly expounds the scheme of creation in his curious Anglo-India world:

[quotes first four stanzas of 'A General Summary': DV p. 4]

If this were Mr. Kipling's highest flight his poems would scarcely have reached a third edition. But in the midst of much flippancy and cynicism come notes of a pathetic loneliness and a not ignoble dis-content with himself, which have something very like the ring of genius. Making verses, however clever, for the mess-room and the lawn tennis-club cannot be an altogether satisfying lifework. To Mr. Kipling, as to Sir Alfred Lyall in our own time, or to poor Leyden in the past, and, indeed, to every man of the true literary temperament who has had to spend his years in India, that country is still the 'sultry and sombre Noverca—the Land of Regrets'. There are many stanzas and not a few poems in this little volume which go straight to the heart of all who have suffered or are now suffering, the long pain of tropical exile. For besides the silly little world which disports itself throughout most of the ditties, there is another Anglo-Indian world which for high aims, and a certain steadfastness in effort after the personal in-terest in effort is well nigh dead, has never had an equal in history. Some day a writer will arise—perhaps this young poet is the destined man—who will make that nobler Anglo-Indian world known as it really is. It will then be seen by what a hard discipline of endurance our countrymen and countrywomen in India are trained to do England's greatest work on the earth. Heat, solitude, anxiety, ill-health, the never-ending pain of separation from wife and child, these are not the experiences which make men amusing in after-life. But these are the stern teachers who have schooled one generation of Anglo-Indian administrators after another to go on quietly and resolutely, if not hopefully, with their appointed task. Of this realistic side of Anglo-

Indian life Mr. Kipling also gives glimpses. His serious poems seem to me the ones most full of promise. Taken as a whole, his book gives hope of a new literary star of no mean magnitude rising in the east. An almost virgin field of literary labour there awaits some man of genius. The hand which wrote 'The Last Department' in this little volume is surely reserved for higher work than breaking those poor pretty Simla butterflies on the wheel.

4. An Early Review of *Soldiers Three*

1889

Anonymous review from the *Spectator*, Vol. LXII, pp. 403–4, 23 March 1889; reprinted in the *Kipling Journal*, Vol. VII, No. 52, pp. 27–30, December 1939.

There is no evidence as to who wrote this review, but it may well have been by John St. Loe Strachey (1860–1927), at that time on the staff of the *Spectator* (of which he was editor and proprietor from 1898 to 1925), who was a family friend of the Lockwood Kiplings.

As a wholesome corrective to what may be called the oleographic style of depicting military life, now so much in vogue, Mr. Kipling's brilliant sketches of the barrack-room, realistic in the best sense of the word, deserve a hearty welcome. Here be no inanities of the officers' mess, no apotheosis of the gilded and tawny-moustachioed dragoon, no languid and lisping lancer, no child-sweethearts—none, in fact, of the sentimental paraphernalia familiar to readers of modern military fiction. Here, instead, we have Tommy Atkins as the central figure: and not Tommy on parade, but in those moods when the natural man finds freest expression—amorous, pugnacious, and thievish—a somewhat earthy personage on the whole, but with occasional gleams of chivalry and devotion lighting up his cloudy humanity. Too many so-called realists seem to aim at representing man as continuously animal, without any intervals in which his higher nature emerges at all. But Mr. Kipling happily does not belong to this school. The actualities of barrack-room life are not extenuated, but the tone of the whole is sound and manly. The author does not gloss over the animal tendencies of the British private, but he shows how in the grossest natures sparks of nobility may lie hid.

He has taken three widely different types of British soldier, a Yorkshireman, a Cockney, and a 'Paddy from Cork', and in spite of the savagery of the first, the cynicism of the second, and the thrasonical complacency of the third, we can fully comprehend the attractions which their company is supposed to have offered to the narrator. Of a truth it must indeed have been 'better to sit out with Mulvaney than to dance many dances', if Mulvaney in the flesh was at all like his literary representation. 'Hit a man an' help a woman, and ye can't be far wrong, anyways'—one of his own maxims—sums up very adequately the philosophy of this combative but chivalrous warrior, whose voluble tongue and droll humour render him the most conspicuous figure of this quaintly assorted but most attacked trio. Private Mulvaney—he was 'a Corp'ril wanst', but he was 'rejuced afterwards'—he is really a humorist of a very high order, witness the following passage:

[quotes 'Black Jack', *Soldiers Three*, p. 100, lines 11–20]

Mr. Kipling has a genius for reproducing quaint and characteristic Hibernicisms. How expressive for example are the words in which Mulvaney describes the court paid by an unscrupulous officer to a girl whom he wished to elope with him: 'So he went menowderin', and minanderin', and blandandherin' round an' about the Colonel's daughter.' In another place he speaks of some men who 'can swear so as to make green turf crack'. Who but an Irishman again would think of addressing a ghost as 'ye frozen thief of Genesis', or who would speak of a 'little squidgereen' of an officer?

Some of the stories in this collection introduce us to the realities of warfare in a surprisingly vivid fashion, and here also Mulvaney's sayings are full of life and originality. For example, he tells how in a peculiarly bloody engagement with some hill tribes, an Irish soldier was anxious to avenge a comrade: "Tim Coulan'll slape aisy to-night", sez he wid a grin (after bayoneting a Pathan): and the next minute his head was in two halves, an' he went down grinnin' by sections.'

There is a strange power in the following grim picture of another episode of the same fight:

[quotes 'With the Main Guard', *Soldiers Three*, p. 70, line 20, to p. 71, line 10]

Mr. Kipling is equally at home in the Yorkshire and Whitechapel dialects; and perhaps the most purely humorous narrative in the book is 'Private Learoyd's Story', a tale of successful imposture, in which the dog-fancying instinct of the Yorkshireman has full scope. The victim is thus described by the narrator; the last sentence speaks volumes:

[quotes 'Private Learoyd's Story', *Soldiers Three*, p, 17, lines 10 to 19]

Another very happy touch is Private Learoyd's contemptuous dismissal of the caressing nonsense which womenkind lavish upon dogs, as 'thot sort o' talk, at a dog o' sense mebbe thinks nowt on, tho' he bides it by reason o' his breedin' '.

The point of this story consists in the successful substitution of a very vicious cur for a fox-terrier, for the theft of which the Eurasian lady described above had offered a very heavy bribe to the narrator. How this was done is best described in the words of two of the conspirators. Mulvaney was the first to conceive the idea of palming off another dog on their covetous friend:

[quotes 'Private Learoyd's Story', *Soldiers Three*, p. 24, line 10, to p. 25, line 11]

The perusal of these stories cannot fail to inspire the reader with the desire to make further acquaintance with the other writings of the author. They are brimfull of humanity and a drollery that never degenerates into burlesque. In many places a note of genuine pathos is heard. Mr. Kipling is so gifted and versatile, that one would gladly see him at work on a larger canvas. But to be so brilliant a teller of short stories is in itself no small distinction.

5a. Andrew Lang on 'Mr. Kipling's Stories'

1889

Unsigned review of *In Black and White* and *Under the Deodars* from the *Saturday Review*, Vol. LXVIII, pp. 165–6, 10 August 1889. Lang had recently received the six Wheeler's Railway Library booklets, and was recommending their publication in England to Sampson Low, Marston & Co. (See Introduction, pp. 15–16.)

The worst of recommending Mr. Wheeler's publications, which we do very heartily, is that apparently they are difficult to procure. They appear in paper-covered little volumes; but these volumes are not found on English railway bookstalls. Very little that is so new and so good can be discovered in those shrines of fugitive literature. Mr. Kipling is a new writer, or a writer new to the English as distinct from the Anglo-Indian public. He is so clever, so fresh, and so cynical that he must be young; like other people, he will be kinder to life when he has seen more of it. Clever people usually begin with a little aversion, which is toned down, in life as in love, to a friendly resignation, if it is not toned up to something warmer by longer experience. Mr. Kipling's least cynical stories are those in *In Black and White*, studies of native life and character. He is far happier with Afghan homicides and old ford-watchers, and even with fair Lalun, 'whose profession was the most ancient in the world', and whose house was built upon the city wall, than with the flirts and fribbles of the hills. His 'black men' (as Macaulay would have called them) are excellent men, full of courage, cunning, revenge, and with points of honour of their own. We are more in sympathy with their ancient semi-barbarism than with the inexpensive rank and second-hand fashion of Simla.

An invidious critic might say, and not untruly, that Mr. Kipling has, consciously or unconsciously, formed himself on the model of Mr. Bret Harte. He has something of Mr. Harte's elliptic and allusive manner, though his grammar is very much better. He has Mr. Harte's liking for good qualities where they have the charm of the unexpected. Perhaps the similarity is increased by the choice of topics and events on the fringes of alien civilizations. It may also be conjectured that Mr. Kipling is not ignorant of 'Gyp's' works. In any case he has wit, humour, observation; he can tell a story, and he does not always disdain pathos, even when the pathetic is a little too obvious. People will probably expect Mr. Kipling, with all these graces of his, to try his hand at a long novel. We are a nation that likes quantity. But it may very probably turn out that Mr. Kipling is best at short stories and sketches.

Perhaps the most excellent of his tales is 'Dray Wara Yow Dee', the confession to an Englishman of a horse-dealer from the Northern frontier. This character, in his cunning and his honesty, his madness of revenge, his love, his misery, his honour, is to our mind a little masterpiece. There is a poetry and a melancholy about the picture which it would be hard, perhaps impossible, to find in more than one or two barbaric or savage portraits from a European hand. His confession must be read; we shall not spoil it by analysis. The 'Judgment of Dungara' is as good, in a comic and cynical manner; so is the tale of a 'sahib, called Yankum Sahib'. Missionaries ought to get the former by heart, and magistrates the latter. 'Gemini', the story of Ram Dass and Durga Dass, might make a Radical Indophile laugh, and might teach him a good deal about his clients. 'In Flood Time' is a little prose idyl of epical strength; there is something primitive in the adventure and something very sympathetic in the old warder of the ford who tells the tale. The 'Sending of Dana Da' is an Icelandic kind of miracle worked on esoteric Buddhists to their confusion and sorrow. The sending wherewith Dana Da vexed Lone Sahib was a sending of kittens, not nice young vivacious kittens, but kittens in their babyhood, and they vexed Lone Sahib sore. 'On the City Wall' is the last, and certainly one of the very best, of the stories; the tale of conspiracy, riot, prison-breaking, organized by Lalun the Fair and Wali Dad, 'a young Mahommedan who was suffering acutely from Education of the English variety, and knew it'. This Wali Dad is as clever a study as that of the Pathan horse thief; his modern melancholy, infidelity, *Weltschmerz*, and all the rest of it, leave him at bottom as thorough a Moslem fanatic as ever yelled 'Ya Hasan! Ya Hussain!' How the British soldiers quell a multitude of yelling fanatics, without drawing a bayonet or firing a shot, is pleasant to read. And, at the end of the riot, there we find Agnostic Wali Dad, 'shoeless, turbanless, and frothing at the mouth; the flesh on his chest bruised and bleeding from the vehemence with which he had smitten himself'. Wherefore we part from Wali Dad respecting him rather more than in his character of educated Unbeliever; for the attitude and actions of the fanatic were more sincere than the sighs and sneers of 'the product'.

On the whole, Mr. Kipling's *Under the Deodars* is more conventional and less interesting than his studies of native life. There is comparatively little variety in 'playing lawn-tennis with the Seventh Commandment'. Mr. Kipling, in his preface, intimates that Anglo-Indian society has other and more seemly diversions. Any persons who wish to see the misery, the seamy, sorry side of irregular love affairs, may turn to 'The Hill of Illusion'. It is enough to convert a man or woman on the verge of guilt by reminding them that, after all, they will be no happier than they have been, and much less respectable. 'A Wayside Comedy' contains a tragedy almost impossible in its absurd and miserable complexity of relations. Only a very small and very remote Anglo-Indian station could have produced this comedy, or tolerated it; and yet what were the wretched men and women to do on this side of suicide? The freaks of Mrs. Hauksbee and Mrs. Mallowe are more commonplace and rather strained in their cleverness. But, on the whole, the two little volumes, with Mr. Kipling's *Departmental Ditties*, give the impression that there is a new and enjoyable talent at work in Anglo-Indian literature.

5b. Andrew Lang welcomes 'An Indian Story-teller'

1889

Unsigned review of *Plain Tales from the Hills* in the *Daily News* (2 November 1889).

'Who will show us some new thing?' is the constant demand of criticism. As Jeames grew tired of beef and mutton, and wished that some new animal was invented, so the professional student of contemporary fiction wearies, ungratefully, of the regular wholesome old joints—of the worthy veteran novelists. This fastidiousness has its good side, it gives every beginner a chance of pleasing; but, on the other hand, it tempts people to overestimate an author merely because he is not yet stale and hackneyed, or at least familiar. We know pretty well what the eminent old hands can do, they seldom surprise us agreeably. What the new hand does is likely to have the merit of a surprise. Thus Mr. Rudyard Kipling's *Plain Tales from the Hills* (Thacker and Co.) take us captive, pretty much as his friend, Private Mulvaney, with twenty-five naked recruits, took the Burmese town of Lungtungpen. It was the dash, the strangeness, and the unexpectedness of Private Mulvaney's expedition that did the business; the fort was not captured according to the theories of war. Thus we must be more on the watch than the Burmese garrison, and must not surrender at discretion to a literary recruit. This warning is needful because Mr. Kipling's tales really are of an extraordinary charm and fascination, not to all readers no doubt, but certainly to many men. His is more a man's book than a woman's book. The 'average' novel reader, who likes her three stout volumes full of the love affairs of an ordinary young lady in ordinary circumstances, will not care for Mr. Kipling's brief and lively stories. There is nothing ordinary about them. The very scenes are strange, scenes of Anglo-Indian life, military and official; of native life; of the life of half-castes and Eurasians. The subjects in themselves would be a hindrance and a handicap to most authors, because the general reader is much averse to the study of Indian matters, and is baffled by *jhairuns*, and *khitmatgars*, and the rest of it. Nothing but the writer's unusual vivacity, freshness, wit, and knowledge of things little known—the dreams of opium smokers, the ideas of private soldiers, the passions of Pathans and wild Border tribes, the magic which is yet a living force in India, the loves of secluded native widows, the habits of damsels whose house, like Rahab's, is on the city wall— nothing but these qualities keeps the English reader awake and excited. It may safely be said that *Plain Tales from the Hills* will teach more of India, of our task there, of the various peoples whom we try to rule, than many Blue Books. Here is an unbroken field of actual romance, here are incidents as strange as befall in any city of dream, any Kôr or Zu-Vendis, and the incidents are true.

Mr. Kipling's romances are not all of equal value; far from it. Several of them might indeed be left out with no great loss. But the best are very good indeed. For example, to read 'The False Dawn' is to receive quite a new idea of the possibilities of life, and of what some people call 'the potentialities of passion'. Cut down to the quick, it only tells how a civil servant, in love with one sister, proposed to another in the darkness of a dust storm. But the brief, vivid narrative; the ride to the old tomb in the sultry tropical midnight, 'the horizon to the north, carrying a faint, dun-coloured feather, the hot wind lashing the orange trees; the wandering, blind night of dust; the lightning spurting like water from a sluice; the human passions breaking forth as wildly as the fire from Heaven; the headlong race in the whirlwind and the gloom; the dust-white, ghostly men and women'— all these make pictures as real as they are strange. 'I never knew anything so un-English in my life,' says Mr. Kipling; and well he may. It is more like a story from another world than merely from another continent. A window is opened on the future, and we have a glimpse of what our race may become when our descendants have lived long in alien lands, in changed conditions—for example, in the electric air of South Africa. There will be new and passionate types of character in 'the lands not yet meted out'.

The natives of India have been dwelling for countless centuries in the region which can make even Englishmen 'un-English'. Mr. Kipling's tales of native life are particularly moving and unwonted. Perhaps the very best, the account of a Hindoo and Moslem riot, called 'On the City Wall' is not in this volume, and we miss here the Pathan story of love and revenge. But, if anyone wishes to 'grue', as the Ettrick Shepherd has it, to shudder, he may try 'In the House of Suddhoo'. He will not only be taught to shiver, though the magic employed was a mere imposture, but he will learn more of what un-educated natives believe, than official records and superficial books of travel can tell him. There is nothing approaching it in modern litera-ture, except the Pakeha Maori's account of a native séance in a Tohun-ga's hut in New Zealand. The Voice, the twittering, spiritual Voice that flew about the darkness, talking now from the roof, now from the floor, now without, now within, impressed the Pakeha Maori till it said, 'Give the priest my gun'. Then the English observer began to doubt the genuine nature of the ghost. In the same way when the dead head of the native child spoke as it floated on the brass basin in the haunted house of Suddhoo, the English spectator can hardly help being moved, till the dry lips declare that the fee of the sorcerer must be doubled. 'Here the mistake from the artistic point of view came in.' But the tragic consequences came in too, inevitably. Mr. Kipling acts Asmodeus here, and, as it were, lifts the roof from the native house. The roof is only half lifted, with a terrible effect, in the roman-tic story 'Beyond the Pale', the half-told and never-to-be-finished record of an Englishman's *amour* with a young native widow. On the other hand, in 'The Gate of a Hundred Sorrows', the whole life of a half-caste opium smoker, all the spectacle of will and nerve hopelessly relaxed and ruined, is transparent and masterly. At first three pipes enabled him to see the red and yellow dragons fight on his neighbour's cap. Now it needs a dozen pipes, and soon he will see their last battle, and slip into another sleep, in 'The Gate of a Hundred Sorrows'. The tales of English existence, official and military, are often diverting and witty; occasionally flippant and too rich in slang. Mr. Kipling may have the vivacity of Guy De Maupassant, but he has neither his pessim-ism, nor, unluckily, the simplicity of his style. There is yet a good deal to be learned by this born storyteller, and there is always the danger that, with experience and self-restraint, may come timidity and lack of force. The last story of the volume promises, or seems to promise, a novel on a theme quite untouched, the existence of a broken-down Englishman, a white pariah fallen among the dark places of 'the Serzi where the horse-traders live'. These stories, whatever their merits, are an addition to the new exotic literature, of which M. Pierre Loti is the leader in France. They have not M. Loti's style, nor his romantic gloom and desolation; their defects are a certain knowingness and familiarity, as of one telling a story in a smoking-room rather late in the evening. But that is a very curable fault, and it is natural to expect much from a talent so fresh, facile, and spontaneous, working in a field of such unusual experiences.

6. 'Mr. Kipling's Writings'

1890

Anonymous article in *The Times*, 25 March 1890. The Editor of the *Times Literary Supplement* kindly informs me that it was by Humphrey Ward.

Thomas Humphrey Ward (1845–1926)—husband of the novelist 'Mrs. Humphrey Ward'—was a Fellow and Tutor of Brasenose College, Oxford, and joined the staff of *The Times* in 1881. He is best remembered for his edition of *The English Poets*, 1881. There is no evidence that he had ever met Kipling when he wrote this article.

India has given us an abundance of soldiers and administrators but she has seldom given us a writer. There is no question, however, that she has done this in the person of the author of the numerous short stories and verses of which we give the titles below. Mr. Rudyard Kipling has the merit of having tapped a new vein, and of having worked it out with real originality. He is even now a very young man, in spite of his seven or eight small volumes; in fact, we believe he is not yet twenty-five. The son of an Englishman who has long been head of the Government School of Art at Lahore, Mr. Kipling was, in the usual way, sent home in early childhood to be educated, and at sixteen or so returned to India to earn his bread. He soon showed that his faculties of keen observation and incisive writing were already developed to an extent far beyond his years. Circumstances appear to have thrown him into journalism, and his talent soon found its proper scope in the stories that he wrote for different Indian papers, especially for the *Week's News*. They made an impression, and when they came to be reprinted Mr. Kipling found himself famous in Indian society as the writer of sketches which were generally accepted as representing, with a fair amount of truth and a great amount of pungency, scenes of a very diverse kind. For he does not confine himself to one class of subjects. He is at home at Simla, and in the life of 'the station', but he is very far from considering that the English ladies and gentlemen there assembled either constitute the whole of India, or, indeed, are the personages best worth studying there. He deals also with that unfortunate result of our settlement in India, the Eurasian, and some of the most brilliant of his tales have this seldom successful growth for their topic. Again, one of his favourite studies lies in the lower ranks of the British Army, and he may, indeed, be almost called the discoverer, as far as India is concerned, of 'Tommy Atkins' as a hero of realistic romance. But if English ladies and gentlemen are, numerically speaking, almost as nothing in comparison with the millions of natives, the private soldiers are not much more numerous, and it was not to be expected that a writer so open-eyed as Mr. Kipling should represent these as including all that was worth description in the life of that vast continent. Accordingly some of the best and most penetrating of the *Plain Tales from the Hills* and the whole of the little collection called *In Black and White* deal with various aspects of native life, and in this department Mr. Kipling's serious and seemingly almost instinctive knowledge is not less evident than in his stories of European life. In fact, from the artistic point of view we should be inclined to place these stories at the top of all his compositions. That very grim story 'In the House of Suddhoo', the tragedy called 'Beyond the Pale', and one or two of the 'Black and White' series seem to be almost the best of Mr. Kipling's writings, perhaps because they appear to lift the veil from a state of society so immeasurably distant from our own and to offer us glimpses of unknown depths and gulfs of human existence.

Nothing is more difficult to review than a collection of short stories. Three-fourths of the charm must lie in the stories themselves, in the plot, and in the characters whom the author can at most indicate by a few strong touches. The reviewer, however, cannot follow him, and cannot tell the stories again one after another; and the only alternative left to him, that of generalizing as to the writer's method and the world in which he moves, is at best unsatisfactory. But Mr. Kipling provides a certain connection between the stories that make up his different books; he does not leave his labyrinth entirely without a thread. There is, for example, a strong family likeness among the tales which he tells of his 'Three Musketeers'—three private soldiers of the Indian army, linked together by a close and romantic friendship, different as are their races and characters. The Irishman, Mulvaney, the cockney, Ortheris, and the big Yorkshireman, Learoyd, are comrades in weal or woe, proud of the regiment, devoted to each other, given to a certain amount of quarrelling over their cups, and of horseplay at any time, but at bottom admirable specimens of their class and profession, and interesting by the tenacity of their affection for one another. Whether they have their exact personal counterparts in real life, we cannot say; probably Mr. Kipling, like a true novelist, has taken but the germs of these characters from fact and developed them by his imagination alone. But they are singularly consistent, and poor Mulvaney especially, the strongest and the best of the three, who was a corporal once but had to be 'rejuced' for drunkenness, is a truly attaching creature from his strength and his little weaknesses. The comedy, the dull hard work, and the not unfrequent tragedy of life in the ranks are admirably given in the stories which concern these three soldiers. In some of them we see hard fighting, as in that called 'With the Main Guard', which contains a truly brilliant account, put in the mouth of the Irishman, of a struggle between the 'Tyrone' regiment and the Afghans. In 'Black Jack' a section of the same imaginary regiment is set upon murdering its sergeant, and Mulvaney tells how he was able to upset the little conspiracy. 'In the Matter of a Private' is a gruesome tale of a soldier who literally runs amuck with his Martini-Henry in a fit of heat hysteria; and we may here remark that in nothing is Mr. Kipling more successful than in his truly lurid descriptions and indications of what Indian heat can be, and what its effect on the minds and bodies of the Europeans who have to suffer it. We in England seem to take for granted that India is hot, but scarcely one of us makes any attempt to realize what that heat really means, especially to the men on whom our power there really reacts, our private soldiers, with their few comforts, their dreary, enforced leisure, and their almost irresistible temptations for getting into mischief. Mr. Kipling has used to the full the novelist's right and the novelist's power of bringing home a practical fact like this to his readers, and although his aim is artistic in the first place and practical only in the second, he will certainly not be unwilling that the British Government as well as the British people should come nearer to realizing what these terrible conditions of life actually imply. It is not, however, all tragedy and all horror with Private Mulvaney and his friends. Persons with so keen a sense of humour as these three are likely to find plenty of occupation for it even in India, and this we are happy to say Mr. Kipling's heroes do.

Plain Tales from the Hills is the longest of the volumes, and, as its title implies, it deals mostly with Simla life. The picture that Mr. Kipling gives is not altogether a pleasant one; but then he does not profess to be an optimist or to represent society as all varnish and veneer. And probably he himself would be the last to maintain that his Mrs. Reiver and Mrs. Mallowe, and even the great Mrs. Hauksbee, 'the most wonderful woman in India', represent Anglo-Indian society as a whole, or that even at Simla men and women have nothing to do but to make love where they ought not. Still, those who have had the most experience in India—by which we do not mean those who have moved longest and most smoothly along the official groove—will recognize that in many respects these stories give a true picture of what is at all events not an inconsiderable section of Indian society. If it fails of being quite a first-rate picture, it is because Mr. Kipling, though an admirably direct writer, is comparatively wanting in style. People have compared him with Guy de Maupassant, not, let it be observed, that he shows any disposition to emulate the French writer in his choice of subjects, (which would be, indeed, even now, an impossibility for an Englishman), but because of his incisive power of drawing vignette portraits and of representing in half-a-dozen pages a complete action. There is, however, an important difference. Guy de Maupassant is a stylist of the first order, and this Mr. Kipling is not yet, whatever he may come to be. His admirers, however, may fairly hope that, in this respect as in others, he may go very much further than he has yet gone. Many of the stories which he has lately published in the English magazines—for he has returned to England, probably for good—show a distinct advance in artistic power on any of those he published in India, and the volume called *Departmental Ditties*, clever and bright as it is, is in no respect on the same level as certain verses which have appeared with and without his name during the present year in British periodicals. Even so, we are far from asserting that Mr. Kipling has yet made any claim to a place in the first rank of contemporary writers. He has given evidence of a knowledge of Indian life which would be extraordinary in any writer and is phenomenal in one so young. He has shown a truly remarkable power of telling a story dramatically and vividly. He has written a number of amusing occasional verses, not without point and sting. But, as yet, he has not attempted 'the long distance race', and the question in which the rapidly-growing number of his readers are now most interested is the question whether he possesses staying power. We sincerely hope that he does, and that he will show it in good time; but, meanwhile, it is to be hoped he will not write himself out. Modern magazines and their eager editors are a dangerous snare in the way of a bright, clever, and versatile writer, who knows that he has caught the public taste.

7. W. E. Henley on 'The New Writer'

1890

Anonymous review of *Soldiers Three*, *Plain Tales from the Hills* and *Departmental Ditties* in the *Scots Observer* (3 May 1890). Besides evidence of style, a reference in a letter quoted by John Connell in his *W. E. Henley* (1949, p. 194) makes the ascription to Henley virtually certain.

William Ernest Henley (1849–1903) is best known as a minor poet. But 'as a critic', wrote Meredith, 'he was one of the main supports of good literature in our time', and Kipling called him 'a jewel of an editor'. Besides other noteworthy ventures he edited the *Scots* (later *National*) *Observer* from 1889 to 1894 and published in it most of Kipling's *Barrack-Room Ballads*, beginning with 'Danny Deever' on 22 February 1890. His other contributors ranged from R. L. Stevenson, Thomas Hardy, J. M. Barrie and Andrew Lang to W. B. Yeats, H. G. Wells, Alice Meynell and Kenneth Grahame.

Mr. Kipling is so fervently engaged just now in cutting his old records and making himself new records to cut that perhaps it is hardly fair to discuss him in respect of the works of his youth. But himself has challenged criticism; and as the aforesaid works of youth are marked by most of the qualities that distinguish those of his riper years—(he is, we believe, a man of five- or six-and-twenty)—it may be well to take him pretty much as he is revealed in them, and see what are his faults, his virtues what, and what his chances in the future.

To begin with the spots upon the sun: Mr. Kipling is not nearly so complete a master of the tongue that Shakespeare spake as he is of the atrocious lingo—a mixture of all the slangs in the world with a rank, peculiar flavour of its own—of Thomas Atkins. In writing English he is often inadequate, he is often pert, and he is sometimes even common; but in dialect he is nearly always an artist. That is, he has so steeped himself in Atkinsese, he is so thoroughly conscious of its capacities and so quick with the essentials of its genius, that he can and does use it not only to state facts and express ideas withal but also as a means of producing those effects in the arrangement of words that belong to pure art. This, of course, is less true of *Soldiers Three* than of certain *Barrack-Room Ballads* known to readers of this journal; but it is true in a sense of much of the speech of Mulvaney and Learoyd, while in the later work the medium is handled to a purpose that could not, it seems, have been achieved in any other. The material is of the vilest—is the very dregs of language, in fact; but the artist has come that way, and has produced an effect—by the orchestration as it were of such low-lived and degraded vocables as (say) the equivalents of 'bloomin'' and 'beggar'—that in its way and degree is comparable to that of those great Miltonic polysyllables which seem to have been dictated by Apollo himself. Once, and only once, has Mr. Kipling done anything of the sort in plain English; and even then—it was in that noble 'Ballad of East and West' which remains thus far his master-piece, alike in inspiration and in execution—the quality of the result was by no means extraordinary. And this is really the principal count in our indictment. What he has to tell is now and then of such un-common excellence that one resents the faults of his method with a sense of peculiar exasperation. The stuff is so good of the one part that it is a sin and a shame it is not better of the other. True it is in many of his stories in prose he abounds in worrying little tricks and mannerisms; that at times he is self-conscious to the point of being well-nigh unbearable; that he is capable of being so clever as to con-trive to miss his point and go out with the face of his intention veiled from the eyes of man; that he has sometimes no story to tell you, and that sometimes he does but spoil his story in the telling. But all these are maladies most incident to youth, and one regards them not: they are there, and they will pass, and no more need be said about them. What concerns one chiefly is the fact that the man's style has commonly so rich and curious a savour of newspaperese and is—unless he is pro-jecting himself into somebody else, and uttering that somebody else in dialect—unworthy of the matter it conveys.

For, the truth is, that matter is often of so extraordinary a quality that in these days one knows not where to look for its like. Mr. Kipling has been thrice fortunate in experience, and it is a thing to reflect upon with pride and a lively sense of favours to come that here at last is something that may well turn out to be a force in literature. His verse may be, and often is, pure doggerel; but it hits you. His prose may be, and often is, self-conscious, jerky, incapable of persuasiveness; but when he is putting it to the best use of which it is thus far capable—when, for instance, Mulvaney is delivering himself of that terrific experience of his at Silver's Theatre, or you are listening to the delirium of Mrs. Gadsby, or that crazy Sancho of the blackguard, red-haired Quixote that wanted to be king is telling what came of his chief's desire—then you have to attend with all your ears, and then you are made to feel with all your strength that here is such a promise as has not been perceived in English letters since young Mr. Dickens broke in suddenly upon the precincts of immortality as the creator of Pickwick and the Wellers. Mr. Kipling, indeed, has that rarest gift of all—the gift of not merely suggesting character and emotion but of so creating and so realising character that the emotion it expresses appears the living and unalterable truth. Sir Walter had it when he liked, Dickens had it often, Thackeray had it now and then, Mr. Meredith has it sometimes; Mr. Kipling has shown more than once that he, too, has it in him to be great as these were great, and that in the presentation of character and emotion he may hope, if he keep the right way, to vie with the heroes until himself attains to heroism. It is a far cry from now to then, of course; but to be five-and-twenty, and have put Kamal and the Colonel's Son on their feet, and set them face to face with each other, and made them swagger it out as they do—to have done that, we say, is to have given hostages to expectation, and placed oneself in the position of them of whom much is asked, and whose failure were a national misfortune, even as their triumph is a triumph for the race. Mr. Kipling has but to be patient, to forget that he is somebody before his time, to be prepared to meet failure half-way, to put off the vanity of superfluous industry, to avoid cleverness as he would avoid the devil, to write—(as Mozart wrote *Don Juan*) 'for himself and two or three friends'; and the issue is not doubtful.

It is late in the day to begin talking of Mulvaney and Ortheris and Learoyd; so we shall let them go on speaking for themselves—speaking as surely three of Her Imperial Majesty's army never spoke before. It is late, too, for anybody to discuss the merits and demerits of a book in everybody's hands, which appears to be what is the matter with *Plain Tales from the Hills*; so no more shall here be said of it than that 'The Taking of Lung-Tung-Pen' and 'The Madness of Private Ortheris' are good enough to be read at least three times apiece and then remembered with the good things of minor literature. And this fourth edition of *Departmental Ditties* is not particularly suggestive either.

There is a convention of Anglo-Indian verse, of course; and of course it is worth noting that the poet of Potiphar Gubbins and Pagett, M.P., is no prodigy but the result of a certain process of evolution. He is the best, perhaps; for he has sung the dirge of Jack Barrett, and is the maker of a certain 'Ballad of Burial' and 'Possibilities' and 'The Undertaker's Horse'—(all three of them clamouring for better technique)—and has told the strange and moving story of how Giffen—Giffen the drunkard and the renegade—became the local god. But there were Anglo-Indian poets before him as there were men of might before Agamemnon; and it may be that his supremacy is largely an effect of the effort that preceded his and the convention he found ready to his hand. Of the ten new numbers included in the present edition, the three best —'The Ballad of Fisher's Boarding-House' and 'The Grave of the Hundred Heads' and 'The Galley Slave'—are out of place in their environment. The themes of them are tragic, the manner befits the theme, the effect is spoiled by a certain sense of incongruity, and to get the full of it you have to go back on them and take them apart from their surroundings. They have so little in common, indeed, with Sleary and Delilah Aberystwith and the light loves and lighter chatter of Simla that their introduction is felt and resented as a mistake in art. It would not have mattered so much had they been bad; but all are good—'The Galley Slave', in especial, being almost good enough to vie with 'The Ballad of East and West' for the place of honour in Mr. Kipling's whole metrical achievement. In a sense too, it is typical of the writer. The rhythm is coarse, and the *facture* by no means irreproachable; but to read it without emotion is impossible. It is a man's work done for men; and it puts before you the feeling of the Anglo-Indian for the Indian Empire in terms so single-hearted and so strong as to make you glory in the name of Briton and exult in the work your race has done.

8. Charles Whibley on 'Good Stuff and Bad'

1890

Anonymous review of reprints of *In Black and White* and *The Story of the Gadsbys* in the *Scots Observer* (20 September 1890). Credited to Whibley by John Connell in his *W. E. Henley* (1949, p. 194).

Charles Whibley (1859–1930), scholar, critic and wit was a close friend of W. E. Henley with whom he worked in most of the latter's editorial ventures, and with whom he produced the Tudor Translations series. Later he contributed 'Musings Without Method' each month to *Blackwood's Magazine* for twenty-five years. Carrington describes him as 'a scholarly *bon-viveur* with a well-earned liver complaint'.

It was one of Matthew Arnold's justest canons that a man of letters must be appraised by his best work. If you wish to appreciate the poems of Wordsworth, he said in effect, or the collection of books known as the New Testament, you must first strip them of their absurdities and irrelevancies and there will then remain for your enjoyment a pearl of great price. The surest winnower, indeed, is Time, who suffers no chaff on his threshing-floor. But the man of genius never lived that did not give the hostile among his contemporaries reason to blaspheme. It would be an easy matter, by an unscrupulous choice of examples, to prove that Mr. Kipling was little better than a smart journalist; but if we boldly attempt to anticipate the work of Time and discard what is merely 'copy', there will be left a very great deal to which only a man of genius could set his name.

The misfortune is that good and bad are sent out into the world together. The alliance is not a permanent one, but though it endures but a brief while it is imprudent. *In Black and White* exhibits the same glaring inequalities to which Mr. Kipling has accustomed us. When the two stories are set side by side it is difficult to believe that the author of 'In Flood-Time' also wrote 'The Sending of Dana Da'. The latter is perhaps worthy to beguile a railway journey; the former is one of the finest examples of its genre in the language. He who can read it without a thrill is dead to words. Never has the relentless might of the flood found clearer expression. The rain-swollen river dashes and swirls through the whole story. The horror of the populous stream is set forth in the simplest terms, and yet it grips the reader as the Mariner's skinny hand gripped the Wedding Guest. 'There were dead beasts in the driftwood on the piers, and others caught by the neck in the lattice-work—buffaloes and kine, and wild pig, and deer one or two, and snakes and jackals past counting. Their bodies were black upon the left side of the bridge.' When the Strong One of Barhwi, rising above the 'wave of the wrath of the river', puts forth his hand to swim and it falls on the knotted hair of a dead man, it is impossible to repress a shudder. With such skill and restraint is the scene presented, its darkness and awe overwhelm you. And not only has Mr. Kipling arranged his material with the perception of the artist, but as a piece of English the description could not be bettered. The words fit the idea like a garment, and you are conscious all the while of receiving the precise impression which the writer intended to convey. To achieve which is a triumph of art.

No less masterly is 'Dray Wara Yow Dee'. Its theme is the fury and passion of jealousy. The local colour is luridly Eastern, and none but Mr. Kipling, who knows the native of India as he was never known before, could so rightly have felt, so rightly have expressed, the situation. The Oriental's ferocity is curiously tinctured with a heart-whole trustfulness in fate.

'Surely I shall overtake him,' says the seeker after vengeance, 'surely God hath him in the hollow of His hand against my claiming! There shall no harm befall Daoud Shah till I come; for I would fain kill him quick and whole with the life sticking firm in his body. A pomegranate is sweetest when the cloves break away unwilling from the rind. Let it be in the daytime, that I may see his face and my delight may be crowned.'

If it is by work such as this that Mr. Kipling is to be judged, it may be claimed for him that he is among the most distinguished of those who have enriched English literature with short stories. But no man may spend his life fashioning masterpieces, whether small or great: and were *In Black and White* robbed of the stories we have named little enough would be left. 'At Twenty-Two' has its moments, it is true, and 'On the City Wall' contains an admirable sketch of Lalun, 'a member of the most ancient profession in the world', as well as a street-fighter described with energy and gusto. But it does not hold together, and it emphatically fails to give the impression of completion and achievement which in 'Dray Wara Yow Dee' and 'In Flood-Time' is irresistible.

There have been men who learned Greek in their cradle, and Mr. Kipling was born with an insight into life. The knowledge of human feeling and human impulse he displays in *The Story of the Gadsbys* would be miraculous did we not reflect that it is intuitive: he probably knew as much at fifteen as he does at twenty-five. The book is intensely dramatic, and is packed with action and emotion. It has serious faults of diction which are all the more irritating to the reader because they might so easily have been avoided. In more than one scene Mr. Kipling crosses the line which divides art from reporting. He seems to forget that the written word does not produce the same effect as the spoken. A duologue conducted in the slang of the mess-room only becomes vulgar when it is crystallised into literary form. Words and phrases have one value in life, another in literature, and it is the artist's business to translate, not to transcribe. The reader wearies of such expressions as 'regimental shop o' sorts', and the jarring note lingers long in the brain. By a bolder generalisation Mr. Kipling might have given the impression that all his characters were talking slang, and refrained from using a single doubtful phrase. But his characters, though their accent is not always irreproachable, have the blood and bone of reality. There is not one but lives and convinces the reader of his life. Captain Gadsby's explanation with Mrs. Herriott is done with amazing dexterity and with that impartial recognition of the facts that holds the scales of sympathy even. There is a haunting pathos in 'The Valley of the Shadow', and the situation, almost new to literature, is handled with a fine discretion. When Gadsby, uncertain if his wife will live another hour, stumbles into the garden and merely says in answer to Mafflin's inquiry, 'Your curb's too loose,' the touch is so true that it is hard to believe that Mr. Kipling was not a witness of the scene. None, except Count Tolstoi, has introduced the unimportant in an emotional crisis with better tact. And with how sure a hand is drawn the picture of Gadsby 'funking a fall on parade!' The effect of marriage upon the Captain of the Pink Hussars is the result of inspiration rather than of observation. The man who 'led at Amdheran after Bogul-Deasin went under, and came out of the show dripping like a butcher,' is afraid to gallop in column of troop! Where in literature has the demoralisation of comfort found clearer and stronger expression?

9. 'The Sincerest Form of Flattery'

1890

Anonymous parody first published in the *Cornhill Magazine*, N.S. Vol. XV, pp. 367–9 (October 1890).

By Barry Pain (1864–1928), the 'inventor' of 'The New Humour' exemplified in his *In a Canadian Canoe* (1891) and in the writings of Jerome K. Jerome. He wrote excellent parodies in prose and verse, the earlier examples of which were collected in his *Playthings and Parodies* (1892)—in which the following parody of *Plain Tales* occupies pp. 3–8.

This is not a tale. It is a conversation which I had with a complete stranger. If you ask me why I talked to him, I have no very good reason to give. I would simply tell you to spend three hours of solitude in that same compartment on that same line. You may not know the line; which is neither your loss nor the company's gain. I do, and I had spent three hours alone on it; and at the end of three hours I longed for human converse. I was prepared to talk Persian poetry to an assistant commissioner; I was ready to talk to anyone about anything; I would have talked to a pariah dog; talked kindly, too.

So when the complete stranger got in I began at once. You see, I did not know then that he was an inaccurate young man. I thought he was a nicely-dressed average specimen. It never does to judge from appearances. I once knew a T.G., or rather, Tranter of the Bombay side knew him; but that is another story. First we talked weather, and then we talked horse. He smoked my cheroots, and I told him several things which were quite true. He began to look a little uneasy, as if he were not used to that kind of talk. Then he told me the story of the little mare which he bought in Calcutta. He gave RS.175 for her. It was thought by his friends at the time that he had been too generous; she had a very bad cough and a plaintive look in the eyes.

'I have now had her for two years,' he said, slowly removing my cheroot from his lips, 'and she has not got over that cough yet. She also continues to look plaintive. But she is fast. The other day I drove her sixty miles along the road in an *ekka*.'

I was given to understand that the time had been five hours, twenty minutes, and a decimal. Well, a country-bred mare will go almost any pace you like to ask. I should have thought about believing the man if he had not put in the decimal. As it was, I never really wanted to call him a liar until he picked up the book which I had been reading. It was a copy of *Plain Tales from the Hills*, and it lay on the seat by my side. I have a liking for that book, and I often read it. It is a good book.

'Can you understand,' he asked, 'why that book is so popular in England? Perhaps you will allow me to explain. I understand books as well as I understand horses and men. First, note this. Even in your schooldays you probably saw the difference between the prose of Cicero and the conversational Latin of Plautus.'

This last remark enabled me to place the man. He was, it seemed, a full-sized Oxford prig. They are fond of throwing their education about like that. Which is loathly in them. But they do it. I explained to him that I had never been to school.

'Well, then, to come down to your level,' he continued. 'You have read English books, and you must have seen that written English is not like spoken English. When we speak, for instance—to take quite a minor point—we often put a full stop before the relative clauses—add them as an afterthought.'

Which struck me as being true.

'But when we write we only put a comma. The author of *Plain Tales from the Hills* saw this, and acted on the principle. He punctuated his writing as he did his speaking; and used more full stops than any man before him. Which was genius.'

I think—I am not sure, but I think—that at this point I blushed.

Secondly, the public want to be mystified. They like references to things of which they have never heard. They read the sporting papers for that reason. So this man wrote of Anglo-Indian life, and put very little explanation into it. It was all local colour. Do you suppose the average cockney knows what 'P.W.D. accounts' are? Of course he doesn't. But he likes to be treated as if he did. The author noted this point. And that also shows genius. Thirdly, the public do *not* like the good man, nor do they like the bad man. They like the man-who-has-some-good-in-him-after-all. 'I am cynical,' says our author, 'and desperately worldly, and somewhat happy-go-lucky, yet I, the same man, am interested in children. Witness my story of Tods and my great goodness to Muhammed Din. With all my cynicism I have a kind heart. Was I not kind even unto Jellaludin? I am the man-who-has-some-good-in-him-after-all. Love me!' Genius again. Fourthly, take the subject-matter—soldiers, horses, and flirts. Of these three the public never weary. It may not have been genius to have seen that. And the public like catch-words. I knew a girl once who did the serio-comic business at the————; but that is another story. To recognise the beauty of catch-words may not be genius either. But it *is* genius to say more than you know, and to seem to know more than you say—to be young and to seem old. There are people who are connected with the Government of India who are so high that no one knows anything about them except themselves, and their own knowledge is very superficial. Is our author afraid? Not a bit. He speaks of them with freedom but with vagueness. He says Up Above. And the public admire the freedom, and never motice the vagueness. Bless the dear public!

The train and the complete stranger stopped simultaneously. I was not angry. 'How do you come to know the workings of the author's mind?' I asked.

I put the question calmly, and I waited to see him shrivel.

He never shrivelled. He was getting his gun-case out from under the seat. 'I am the author,' he said blandly. 'Good afternoon.' Then he got out.

He was so bland that I should have quite believed him if I had not written the book myself. As it is, I feel by no means sure about it.

Which is curious.

10. Extracts from Robert Louis Stevenson's Letters

1890-94

Extracts from letters by Robert Louis Stevenson (1850–1894), the most popular of the great writers of the Nineties—until the appearance of Kipling. These are taken from the Tusitala Edition of Stevenson's works, to which references are given below—except in the case of the letter to Richard Le Gallienne which was published in that writer's *The Romantic Nineties* (1926, p. 81). It should be remembered that R.L.S. set 'style' above all else in his literary judgments.

To Henry James. August 1890. Vol. XXXIII, p. 306:
'Kipling is too clever to live.'

To Henry James. 29 December 1890. Vol. XXXIV, p. 45:
'Kipling is by far the most promising young man who has appeared since—ahem—I appeared. He amazes me by his percocity and various endowment. But he alarms me by his copiousness and haste. He should shield his fire with both hands "and draw up all his strength and sweetness in one ball". ("Draw all his strength and all his sweetness up into one ball?" I cannot remember Marvell's words.) So the critics have been saying to me; but I was never capable of—and surely never guilty of—such a debauch of production. At this rate his works will soon fill the habitable globe; and surely he was armed for better conflicts than these succinct sketches and flying leaves of verse? I look on, I admire, I rejoice for myself; but in a kind of ambition we all have for our tongue and literature I am wounded. If I had this man's fertility and courage, it seems to me I could heave a pyramid.

Well, we begin to be old fogies now; and it was high time *something* rose to take our places. Certainly Kipling has the gifts; the fairy godmothers were all tipsy at his christening: what will he do with them?'

To Charles Baxter. 18 July 1892. Vol. XXXIV, pp. 208–9:
'Glad to hear Henley's prospects are fair: his new volume [*The Song of the Sword, and Other Verses*] is the work of a real poet. He is one of those who can make a noise of his own with words, and in whom experience strikes an individual note. There is perhaps no more genuine poet living, bar the Big Guns ... How poorly Kipling compares! He is all smart journalism and cleverness; it is all bright and shallow and limpid, like a business paper—a good one, *s'entend*; but there is no blot of heart's blood and the Old Night; there are no harmonics, there is scarce harmony to his music; and in Henley—all these; a touch, a sense within sense, a sound outside the sound, the shadow of the inscrutable, eloquent beyond all definition.'

To Henry James. 5 December 1892. Vol. XXXIV, p. 273:
'Hurry up with another book of stories. I am now reduced to two of my contemporaries, you and Barrie—O, and Kipling—you and Barrie and Kipling are now my Muses Three. And with Kipling, as you know, there are reservations to be made. And you and Barrie don't write enough. I should say I also read Anstey when he is serious ... But Barrie is a beauty, *The Little Minister* and *The Window in Thrums*, eh? Stuff in that young man; but he must see and not be too funny. Genius in him, but there's a journalist at his elbow—there's the risk.'

To Richard Le Gallienne. 28 December 1893. *The Romantic Nineties*, p. 81:
'You are still young, and you may live to do much. The little artificial popularity of style in England tends, I think, to die out; the British pig returns to his true love, the love of the style-less, of the shapeless, of the slapdash and the disorderly. Rudyard Kipling, with all his genius, his Morrowbie-Jukeses, and At-the-end-of-the-Passages, is a move in that direction, and it is the wrong one. There is trouble coming, I think; and you may have to hold the fort for us in evil days.'

To Will H. Low. 15 January 1894. Vol. XXXV, p. 111:
'Here is a long while I have been waiting for something *good* in art; and what have I seen? Zola's *Débâcle* and a few of Kipling's tales ...'

[Note by Sidney Colvin, editor of Stevenson's *Letters*, in the Tusitala Edition, Vol. XXXIV, pp. 45–46. 'In 1890, on first becoming acquainted with Mr. Kipling's *Soldiers Three*, Stevenson had written off his congratulations red-hot. "Well and indeed, Mr. Mulvaney," so ran the first sentences of his note, "but it's as good as meat to meet in with you sir. They tell me it was a man of the name of Kipling made ye; but indeed and they can't fool me; it was the Lord God Almighty that made you." Taking the cue thus offered, Mr. Kipling had written back in the character of his own Irishman, Terence Mulvaney, addressing Stevenson's Highlander, Alan Breck Stewart . . .'

Colvin includes Stevenson's answer to this, in the character of Alan —but it is of little interest and contains no criticism. The rest of Stevenson's original letter, and any others in the correspondence, have not so far been traced.]

11. Extracts from Letters of Henry James

1890–99

Henry James (1843–1916), American novelist resident in England, was an early acquaintance of Kipling's at the Savile Club, but got to know him well via their mutual friendship for Wolcott Balestier with whom Kipling was collaborating in *The Naulahka* by July 1890. He wrote an Introduction to the American collection of Kipling's stories, *Mine Own People*, in 1891 (see No. 21, below). For the other side of the correspondence with Stevenson see No. 10 above.

The extracts from his letters are quoted from *The Letters of Henry James* (2 vols.), edited by Percy Lubbock in 1920, except for two from Charles Carrington's *Rudyard Kipling*, 1955.

To Robert Louis Stevenson. 21 March 1890. *Letters*: Vol. I, p. 158: 'We'll tell you all about Rudyard Kipling—your nascent rival; he has killed one immortal—Rider Haggard; the star of the hour, aged 24 and author of remarkable Anglo-Indian and extraordinarily observed barrack life—Tommy Atkins—tales.'

To Robert Louis Stevenson. 12 January 1891. *Letters*: Vol. I, p. 182:
'The only news in literature here—such is the virtuous vacancy of our consciousness—continues to be the infant monster of a Kipling. I enclose, in this, for your entertainment a few pages I have lately written about him, to serve as the preface to an (of course authorized) American *recueil* of some of his tales. [*Mine Own People*. See No. 21.] I may add that he has just put forth his longest story yet—a thing in *Lippincott* ['The Light that Failed'—shorter version with happy ending—in January 1891 number of *Lippincott's Monthly Magazine*, Vol. XLVII, pp. 3–97] which I also send you herewith—which cuts the ground somewhat from under my feet, inasmuch as I find it the most youthfully infirm of his productions (in spite of great 'life'), much wanting in composition and in narrative and explicative, or even implicative, art.'

To Robert Louis Stevenson. 30 October 1891. Carrington, p. 188:
'That little black demon of a Kipling will perhaps have leaped upon your silver strand by the time this reaches you. He publicly left England to embrace you many weeks ago—carrying literary genius out of the country with him in his pocket.' [Kipling reached New Zealand on 18 October—but was not able to get to Samoa to see Stevenson.]

To William James. 6 February 1892. Carrington, p. 193:
'I saw the Rudyard Kiplings off by the *Teutonic* the other day . . . She was poor Wolcott Balestier's sister and is a hard devoted capable little person whom I don't in the least understand his marrying . . . Kipling strikes me personally as the most complete man of genius (as distinct from fine intelligence) that I have ever known.'

To Robert Louis Stevenson. 19 March 1892. *Letters*: Vol. I, p. 193:
'We lately clubbed together, all, to despatch to you an eye-witness in the person of the genius or the *genus*, in himself, Rudyard, for the concussion of whose extraordinary personality with your own we are beginning soon to strain the listening ear. We devoutly hope that this time he will really be washed upon your shore. With him goes a new little wife—whose brother—Wolcott Balestier, lately dead, in much youthful promise and performance (I don't allude, in saying that, especially to the literary part of it,) was a very valued young friend of mine.' [Again Kipling failed to reach Samoa, this time on account of

the failure of his bank which left him almost penniless in Yokohama on 9 June 1892 on his wedding trip round the world.]

To Jonathan Sturges. 5 November 1896. *Letters*: Vol. I, p. 256:
'. . . We will talk of many things—and among them of Rudyard Kipling's *Seven Seas*, which he has just sent me. I am laid low by the absolutely uncanny talent—the prodigious special faculty of it. It's all *violent*, without a dream of nuance or a hint of 'distinction'; all prose trumpets and castanets and such—with never a touch of the fiddle-string or a note of the nightingale. But it's magnificent and masterly in its way, and full of the most insidious art. He's a rum 'un—and one of the very few first *talents* of the time. There's a vilely idiotic reference to his 'coarseness' in this a.m.'s. *Chronicle*. The coarseness of 'The Mary Gloster' is absolutely one of the most triumphant 'values' of that triumphant thing.'

To Grace Norton. 25 December 1897. *Letters*: Vol. I, p. 278:
'His ballad future may still be big. But my view of his prose future has much shrunken in the light of one's increasingly observing how little life he can make use of. Almost nothing civilized save steam and patriotism—and the latter only in verse, where I *hate* it so, especially mixed up with God and goodness, that that half spoils my enjoyment of his great talent. Almost nothing of the complicated soul or of the female form or of any other question of *shades*—which latter constitutes, to my sense, the real formative literary discipline. In his earliest time I thought he perhaps contained the seeds of an English Balzac; but I have given that up in proportion as he has come down steadily from the simple in subject to the more simple—from the Anglo-Indians to the natives, from the natives to the Tommies, from the Tommies to the quadrupeds, from the quadrupeds to the fish, and from the fish to the engines and screws.'

To Charles Eliot Norton. 28 November 1899. Vol. I, p. 349:
'The great little Rudyard struck me as quite on his feet again, and very sane and sound and happy. Yet I am afraid you will think me a very disgusted person if I show my reserves again, over *his* recent incarnations. I can't swallow his loud, brazen patriotic verse—an exploitation of the patriotic idea, for that matter, which seems to me not really much other than the exploitation of the name of one's mother or one's wife. Two or three times a century—yes; but not every month. He is,

however, such an embodied little talent, so economically constructed for all use and no waste, that he will get again upon a good road—leading *not* into mere multitudinous noise. His talent I think quite diabolically great; and this in spite—here I am at it again!—of the misguided, the unfortunate Stalky. Stalky gives him away, aesthetically, as a man in his really now, as regards our roaring race, bardic condition, should not have allowed himself to be given. That is not a thing, however, that, in our paradise of criticism, appears to occur to so much as three persons, and meanwhile the sale, I believe, is tremendous.'

12. Andrew Lang on 'Mr. Kipling's Stories'

1891

Critical essay from Andrew Lang's *Essays in Little* (published January 1891), pp. 198–205.

For Lang's earlier writings on Kipling see above, pp. 44–50 etc.

The wind bloweth where it listeth. But the wind of literary inspiration has rarely shaken the bungalows of India, as, in the tales of the old Jesuit missionaries, the magical air shook the frail 'medicine tents', where Huron conjurors practised their mysteries. With a world of romance and of character at their doors, Englishmen in India have seen as if they saw it not. They have been busy in governing, in making war, making peace, building bridges, laying down roads, and writing official reports. Our literature from that continent of our conquest has been sparse indeed, except in the way of biographies, of histories, and of rather local and unintelligible *facetiæ*. Except the novels by the author of 'Tara', and Sir Henry Cunningham's brilliant sketches, such as 'Dustypore', and Sir Alfred Lyall's poems, we might almost say that India has contributed nothing to our finer literature. That old haunt of history, the wealth of character brought out in that confusion of races, of religions, and the old and new, has been wealth untouched, a treasure-house sealed: those pagoda trees have never been shaken. At last there comes an Englishman with eyes, with a pen extraordinarily deft, an observation marvellously rapid and keen; and, by good luck, this Englishman has no official duties: he is neither a soldier, nor a judge; he is merely a man of letters. He has leisure to look around him, he has the power of making us see what he sees; and, when we have lost India, when some new power is ruling where we ruled, when our empire has followed that of the Moguls, future generations will learn from Mr. Kipling's works what India was under English sway.

It is one of the surprises of literature that these tiny masterpieces in prose and verse were poured, 'as rich men give that care not for their gifts', into the columns of Anglo-Indian journals. There they were thought clever and ephemeral—part of the chatter of the week. The subjects, no doubt, seemed so familiar, that the strength of the handling, the brilliance of the colour, were scarcely recognised. But Mr. Kipling's volumes no sooner reached England than the people into whose hands they fell were certain that here were the beginnings of a new literary force. The books had the strangeness, the colour, the variety, the perfume of the East. Thus it is no wonder that Mr. Kipling's repute grew up as rapidly as the mysterious mango tree of the conjurors. There were critics, of course, ready to say that the thing was merely a trick, and had nothing of the supernatural. That opinion is not likely to hold its ground. Perhaps the most severe of the critics has been a young Scotch gentleman, writing French, and writing it wonderfully well, in a Parisian review. He chose to regard Mr. Kipling as little but an imitator of Bret Harte, deriving his popularity mainly from the novel and exotic character of his subjects. No doubt, if Mr. Kipling has a literary progenitor, it is Mr. Bret Harte. Among his earlier verses a few are what an imitator of the American might have written in India. But it is a wild judgment which traces Mr. Kipling's success to his use, for example, of Anglo-Indian phrases and scraps of native dialects. The presence of these elements is among the causes which have made Englishmen think Anglo-Indian literature tediously provincial, and India a bore. Mr. Kipling, on the other hand, makes us regard the continent which was a bore as an enchanted land, full of marvels and magic which are real. There has, indeed, arisen a taste for exotic literature: people have become alive to the strangeness and fascination of the world beyond the bounds of Europe and the United

States. But that is only because men of imagination and literary skill have been the new conquerors—the Corteses and Balboas of India, Africa, Australia, Japan, and the isles of the southern seas. All such conquerors, whether they write with the polish of M. Pierre Loti, or with the carelessness of Mr. Boldrewood, have, at least, seen new worlds for themselves; have gone out of the streets of the over-populated lands into the open air; have sailed and ridden, walked and hunted; have escaped from the fog and smoke of towns. New strength has come from fresher air into their brains and blood; hence the novelty and buoyancy of the stories which they tell. Hence, too, they are rather to be counted among romanticists than realists, however real is the essential truth of their books. They have found so much to see and to record, that they are not tempted to use the microscope, and pore for ever on the minute in character. A great deal of realism, especially in France, attracts because it is novel, because M. Zola and others have also found new worlds to conquer. Yet certain provinces in those worlds were not unknown to, but were voluntarily neglected by, earlier explorers. They were the 'Bad Lands' of life and character: surely it is wiser to seek quite new realms than to build mud huts and dunghills on the 'Bad Lands'.

Mr. Kipling's work, like all good work, is both real and romantic. It is real because he sees and feels very swiftly and keenly; it is romantic, again, because he has a sharp eye for the reality of romance, for the attraction and possibility of adventure, and because he is young. If a reader wants to see petty characters displayed in all their meannesses, if this be realism, surely certain of Mr. Kipling's painted and frisky matrons are realistic enough. The seamy side of Anglo-Indian life: the intrigues, amorous or semi-political—the slang of people who describe dining as 'mangling garbage'—the 'games of tennis with the seventh commandment'—he has not neglected any of these. Probably the sketches are true enough, and pity 'tis 'tis true: for example, the sketches in *Under the Deodars* and in *The Gadsbys*. That worthy pair, with their friends, are to myself as unsympathetic almost, as the characters in *La Conquête de Plassans*. But Mr. Kipling is too much a true realist to make their selfishness and pettiness unbroken, unceasing. We know that 'Gaddy' is a brave, modest, and hard-working soldier; and, when his silly little bride (who prefers being kissed by a man with waxed moustaches) lies near to death, certainly I am nearer to tears than when I am obliged to attend the bed of Little Dombey or of Little Nell. Probably there is a great deal of slangy and unrefined Anglo-Indian society; and, no doubt, to sketch it in its true colours is not beyond the province of art. At worst it is redeemed, in part, by its constancy in the presence of various perils—from disease, and from 'the bullet flying down the pass'. Mr. Kipling may not be, and very probably is not, a reader of 'Gyp'; but The Gadsbys, especially, reads like the work of an Anglo-Indian disciple, trammelled by certain English conventions. The more Pharisaic realists—those of the strictest sect—would probably welcome Mr. Kipling as a younger brother, so far as Under the Deodars and The Gadsbys are concerned, if he were not occasionally witty and even flippant, as well as realistic. But, very fortunately, he has not confined his observation to the leisures and pleasures of Simla; he has looked out also on war and on sport, on the life of all native tribes and castes; and has even glanced across the borders of 'The Undiscovered Country'.

Among Mr. Kipling's discoveries of new kinds of characters, probably the most popular is his invention of the British soldier in India. He avers that he 'loves that very strong man, Thomas Atkins'; but his affection has not blinded him to the faults of the beloved. Mr. Atkins drinks too much, is too careless a gallant in love, has been educated either too much or too little, and has other faults, partly due, apparently, to recent military organisation, partly to the feverish and unsettled state of the civilised world. But he is still brave, when he is well led; still loyal, above all, to his 'trusty chum'. Every Englishman must hope that, if Terence Mulvaney did not take the city of Lungtung Pen as described, yet he is ready and willing so to take it. Mr. Mulvaney is as humorous as Micky Free, but more melancholy and more truculent. He has, perhaps, 'won his way to the mythical' already, and is not so much a soldier, as an incarnation, not of Krishna, but of many soldierly qualities. On the other hand, Private Ortheris, especially in his frenzy, seems to shew all the truth, and much more than the life of, a photograph. Such, we presume, is the soldier, and such are his experiences and temptations and repentance. But nobody ever dreamed of telling us all this, till Mr. Kipling came. As for the soldier in action, the 'Taking of Lungtung Pen', and the 'Drums of the Fore and Aft', and that other tale of the battle with the Pathans in the gorge, are among the good fights of fiction. They stir the spirit, and they should be distributed (in addition, of course, to the Soldier's Pocket Book) in the ranks of the British army. Mr. Kipling is as well informed about the soldier's women-kind as about the soldier; about Dinah Shadd as about Terence Mulvaney. Lever never instructed us on these matters:

73

Micky Free, if he loves, rides away; but Terence Mulvaney is true to his old woman. Gallant, loyal, reckless, vain, swaggering, and tender-hearted, Terence Mulvaney, if there were enough of him, 'would take St. Petersburg in his drawers'. Can we be too grateful to an author who has extended, as Mr. Kipling in his military sketches has extended, the frontiers of our knowledge and sympathy?

It is a mere question of individual taste; but, for my own part, had I to make a small selection from Mr. Kipling's tales, I would include more of his studies in Black than in White, and many of his excursions beyond the probable and natural. It is difficult to have one special favourite in this kind; but perhaps the story of the two English adventurers among the freemasons of unknown Kafiristan (in the 'Phantom Rickshaw') would take a very high place. The gas-heated air of the Indian newspaper office is so real, and into it comes a wanderer who has seen new faces of death, and who carries with him a head that has worn a royal crown. The contrasts are of brutal force; the legend is among the best of such strange fancies. Then there is, in the same volume, 'The Strange Ride of Morrowbie Jukes', the most dreadful nightmare of the most awful Bunker in the realms of fancy. This is a very early work; if nothing else of Mr. Kipling's existed, his memory might live by it, as does the memory of the American Irishman by the 'Diamond Lens'. The sham magic of 'In the House of Suddhu' is as terrible as true necromancy could be, and I have a *faiblesse* for the 'Bisara of Pooree'. 'The Gate of the Hundred Sorrows', is a realistic version of 'The English Opium Eater', and more powerful by dint of less rhetoric. As for the sketches of native life—for example, 'On the City Wall'—to English readers they are no less than revelations. They testify, more even than the military stories, to the author's swift and certain vision, his certainty in his effects. In brief, Mr. Kipling has conquered worlds, of which, as it were, we knew not the existence.

His faults are so conspicuous, so much on the surface, that they hardly need to be named. They are curiously visible to some readers who are blind to his merits. There is a false air of hardness (quite in contradiction to the sentiment in his tales of childish life); there is a knowing air; there are mannerisms, such as 'But that is another story'; there is a display of slang; there is the too obtrusive knocking of the nail on the head. Everybody can mark these errors; a few cannot overcome their antipathy, and so lose a great deal of pleasure.

It is impossible to guess how Mr. Kipling will fare if he ventures on one of the usual novels, of the orthodox length. Few men have succeeded both in the *conte* and the novel. Mr. Bret Harte is limited to the *conte*; M. Guy de Maupassant is probably at his best in it. Scott wrote but three or four short tales, and only one of these is a masterpiece. Poe never attempted a novel. Hawthorne is almost alone in his command of both kinds. We can live only in the hope that Mr. Kipling, so skilled in so many species of the *conte*, so vigorous in so many kinds of verse, will also be triumphant in the novel; though it seems unlikely that its scene can be in England, and though it is certain that a writer who so cuts to the quick will not be happy with the novel's almost inevitable 'padding'. Mr. Kipling's longest effort, *The Light which Failed*, can, perhaps, hardly be considered a test or touchstone of his powers as a novelist. The central interest is not so powerful, the characters are not so sympathetic, as are the interest and the characters of his short pieces. Many of these persons we have met so often that they are not mere passing acquaintances, but already find in us the loyalty due to old friends.

13. J. K. Stephen: 'A Protest in Verse'

1891

First published in the *Cambridge Review* (February 1891) and collected the same year in '*Lapsus Calami*, by J.K.S.'.

James Kenneth Stephen (1859–1892), son of Sir James Fitzjames Stephen, was a barrister and Fellow of Trinity College, Cambridge. He produced two slim volumes of superb parodies and light verse, *Lapsus Calami* and *Quo, Musa, Tendis?*, both published in 1891 shortly before his tragically early death in February 1892.

Kipling wrote in *Something of Myself* (1937), pp. 92–3:
'People talked, quite reasonably, of rockets and sticks; and that genius, J.K.S., brother to Herbert Stephen, dealt with Haggard and me in some stanzas which I would have given much to have written myself ... It ran joyously through all the papers. It still hangs faintly in the air and, as I used to warn Haggard, may continue as an aroma when all but our two queer names are forgotten.'

To R.K.

As long I dwell on some stupendous
and tremendous (Heaven defend us!)
Monstr'-inform'-ingens-horrendous
Demoniaco-seraphic
Penman's latest piece of graphic
BROWNING

Will there never come a season
Which shall rid us from the curse
Of a prose which knows no reason
And an unmelodious verse:
When the world shall cease to wonder
At the genius of an Ass,
And a boy's eccentric blunder
Shall not bring success to pass:

When mankind shall be delivered
From the clash of magazines,
And the inkstand shall be shivered
Into countless smithereens:
When there stands a muzzled stripling,
Mute, beside a muzzled bore:
When the Rudyards cease from kipling
And the Haggards Ride no more.

14. J. M. Barrie on 'Mr. Kipling's Stories'

1891

Signed article from the *Contemporary Review*, Vol. LIX, pp. 364–372 (March 1891).

James Matthew Barrie (1860–1937), though now remembered for his plays, was at first considered to be the great coming novelist on the strength of his sketches of Scottish character in *Auld Licht Idylls* (1888) and *A Window in Thrums* (1889). Both Meredith and Stevenson set him above Kipling, and were not disappointed when he too essayed the full-length novel in 1891 with *The Little Minister*. Barrie had already welcomed his young rival with typical generosity a year earlier in an article 'The Man from Nowhere' in the *British Weekly* (2 May 1890): for quotations from this see Introduction pp. 17–18.

The best of our fiction is by novelists who allow that it is as good as they can give, and the worst by novelists who maintain that they could do much better if the public would let them. They want to be strong, but the public, they say, prohibits it. In the meantime, Mr. Kipling has done what we are to understand they could do if they dared. He has brought no mild wines from India, only liqueurs, and the public has drunk eagerly. His mission is to tell Mr. Grant Allen and the others that they may venture to bring their 'Scarlet Letter' out of their desks and print it. Mr. Kipling has done even more than that. He has given the reading public a right not to feel ashamed of itself on second thoughts, which is a privilege it seldom enjoys. Now that the Eurekas over his discovery are ended we have no reason to blush for them. Literary men of mark are seldom discovered; we begin to be proud of them when they are full-grown, or afterwards. True, every other season a new writer is the darling of London, but not by merit, and presently he is pilloried for standing on the pedestal where our whim placed him. Mankind has no mercy for the author about whom it has deceived itself. But here is a literary 'sensation' lifted on high because he is worth looking at. Doubtless the circumstances were favourable. Most writers begin with one book, but he came from India with half a dozen ready, and fired them at the town simultaneously. A six-shooter attracts more attention than a single barrel. Alarming stories of his youth went abroad at the same time, and did him no harm among a people who love to say 'Oh my! and 'Fancy!' over precocity. Many men have begun to write as early as Mr. Kipling, but seldom so boldly. His audacity alone might have carried him shoulder-high for a brief period. His knowledge of life, 'sufficient to turn your hair grey', would have sent ladies from the musical prodigies whom they fed on sweets, and the theatrical prodigies who (according to the interviews) play when at home with dolls, to the literary prodigy whose characters swear most awful. From the first only the risky subjects seem to have attracted Mr. Kipling. He began by dancing on ground that most novelists look long at before they adventure a foot. His game was leapfrog over all the passions. One felt that he must have been born *blasé*, that in his hurry to be a man he had jumped boyhood, which is perhaps why his boy and girl of *The Light that Failed* are a man and woman playing in vain at being children. The task he set himself was to peer into humanity with a very bright lantern, of which he holds the patent, and when he encountered virtue he passed it by respectfully as not what he was looking for. It is a jewel, no doubt, but one that will not gleam sufficiently in the light of that lantern. In short, he was in search of the devil (his only hero so far) that is in all of us, and he found him and brought him forth for inspection, exhibiting him from many points of view in a series of lightning flashes. Lightning, however, dazzles as well as reveals, and after recovering their breath, people began to wonder whether Mr. Kipling's favourite figure would look like this in daylight. He has been in no hurry to answer them, for it is in these flashes that the magic lies; they are his style.

'It would be a good thing,' Mr. Mark Twain says, 'to read Mr. Kipling's writings for their style alone, if there were no story back of it.' This might be a good thing if it were not impossible, the style being the story. As well might one say, 'It would be a good thing to admire a Rubens for the way it is painted alone, though there were no picture back of it;' or, 'It would be a good thing to admire correct spelling, though there were no word back of it.' Words are what we spell ideas with. Here, then, is the difference between style and matter. The ideas are the matter, and the spelling is the style. But style and

matter, we have been saying, are one. So they are, even as the letters
that make a word are the word. Unless we have the right letters
arranged in the one way we do not have the word, and, similarly,
without the right words arranged in the one way, we do not get the
idea. Were we as capable at spelling ideas as at spelling words, we could
estimate a writer as easily as a schoolmaster corrects a boy's exercise.
Unfortunately, when we sit down to criticise we must write at the top
of our paper, 'But we don't know the way ourselves'. The author
under our lens is at the same time our teacher, for we only know how
the idea he is putting together should be spelled after we have seen
him spell it. So difficult is his task that he has done a big thing if the
spelling is nearly right; if, that is to say, we can recognise the idea, as
we know a word though there may be a letter missing or upside down.
An idea correctly spelled is so beautiful that we read the truth in its
face. It carries conviction. How does Mr. Kipling spell his ideas?
therefore, is a way of asking what is his style, which sums up his worth.
Most will admit that of our living novelists Mr. Meredith and Mr.
Hardy spell the greatest ideas best. Doubtless Mr. Stevenson is correct
more often than any of his contemporaries, certainly a dozen times for
Mr. Kipling's once; but, on the other hand, it should be said that the
younger writer tries to spell the bigger ideas. While Mr. Stevenson
sets his horse at ideas of one syllable and goes over like a bird, Mr.
Kipling is facing Mesopotamia and reaching the other side, perhaps
on his head or muddy. Still he has got through it, if not over it. He
rides a plucky little donkey that shies at nothing and sticks in nothing.
We have his style in that sentence in which Mulvaney wakes from a
drunken bout and 'feels as tho' a she-cat had littered in my mouth'.
This is not an idea perfectly spelled. *She*-cat is unnecessary; Tom-
cats do not litter. But though it is by coarseness that Mr. Kipling gains
his end, which is to make us feel suddenly sick, he does gain it, and so
he is an artist. Some admit his humour, his pathos, his character-
drawing, his wonderful way of flashing a picture before our eyes till
it is as vivid as a landscape seen in lightning—in short, his dramatic
power—and yet add with a sigh, 'What a pity he has no style!' This
surely is saying in one breath that he is and he isn't. These qualities
they have allowed him are his style. They are his spelling of ideas.
Nevertheless, he is to Mr. Stevenson as phonetic spelling is to pure
English. He is not a Christian, but a Kristyān. His words are often
wrong, but he groups them so that they convey the idea he is in
pursuit of. We see at once that his pathos is potatoes. It is not legitimate,

but it produces the desired effects. There are sentences without verbs. He wants perpetually to take his readers by surprise, and has them, as it were, at the end of a string, which he is constantly jerking. With such a jerk he is usually off from one paragraph to the next. He writes Finis with it. His style is the perfection of what is called journalese, which is sometimes not on speaking terms with Lindley Murray.[1]

He owes nothing to any other writer. No one helped to form him. He never imitated, preparatory to making a style for himself. He began by being original, and probably when at school learned calligraphy from copy lines of his own invention. If his work suggests that of any other novelists, it is by accident; he would have written thus though they had never existed. By some he has been hailed as a Dickens, which seems mere cruelty to a young man. A Dickens should never be expected. He must always come as a surprise. He is too big to dream about. But there is a swing, an exuberance of life in some of Mr. Kipling's practical jokes that are worthy of the author of 'Charles O'Malley'. Rather let us say that certain of Lever's roaring boys are worthy of Mr. Kipling. 'The Taking of Lungtungpen' and 'The Man who would be King' are beyond Lever; indeed, for the second of these two stories, our author's masterpiece, there is no word but magnificent. It is about two scamps, stone-broke, who, as they can get no other employment, decide to be kings. They borrow a map of India, fix upon their territory, and become monarchs after a series of adventures that make the reader's head swim. Finally, their weakness for women and liquor dethrones them, and the one is sent back to civilised parts with the other's head in a bag. Positively it is the most audacious thing in fiction, and yet it reads as true as *Robinson Crusoe*. Daniel Dravot the First throws Mulvaney. I like to think that he was Mulvaney all the time. Thus should that warrior's career have closed. It is Mr. Bret Harte that Mr. Kipling most resembles. He, too, uses the lantern flash; Mulvaney would have been at home in Red Gulch and Mr. Oakhurst in Simla. Let us, in fanciful mood, suppose we presented a town to our novelists and asked each to write a book about the persons in it that interested him most. The majority would begin their novel as soon as they found a young man and woman who made forty years between them. Without mentioning names, we know who would wait for a murder as the beginning of all good things, and who would go to the East-end in search of a lady from the West, and who would

[1] [Author of the standard *English Grammar*, 1795]

81

stroll into the country and who would seek (and find) a Highlander, and who would inquire for a pirate with no female connections. But Mr. Harte and Mr. Kipling would discover their quarry in the ne'er-do-wells and treat them not dissimilarly. Mr. Kipling has one advantage. He is never theatrical as Mr. Harte sometimes is. Both are frequently pathetic, but the one ever draws back from bathos, while the other marches into it, and is fitly rewarded if we smile instead of weep. There is more restraint in Mr. Kipling's art. But Mr. Harte is easily first in his drawing of women. It is in their women that most of our leading novelists excel. No doubt (the sex tells us so) the women are all wrong, for no man really knows anything about women except that they are a riddle. It is enough, however, to put the riddle delightfully, as so many do, Mr. Harte among them. We are in love with his girls, and so all is well. Here, unfortunately, Mr. Kipling fails. Mr. Stevenson is in the same predicament, but that, one almost dares to conclude, is because he lacks interest in the subject; he cunningly contrives men who can get on without the other sex, and such is his fascination that we let this pass. The 'duel between the sexes', however, is Mr. Kipling's theme (which increases his chances of immortality), and there is a woman in most of his stories. Yet who remembers her? The three soldiers' tales are often about women, and these wonderful soldiers you could not forget if you would, but the women are as if they had never been. The author's own favourite is Mrs. Hauksbee, the grass widow, whom the 'boys' love, and she is an adept at drawing back from the brink, while they go over or are saved according to her whim. She is clever and good-natured, and has a sense of humour, and that she is a pernicious woman is no subject for complaint. She belongs to the dirty corner, of which we have to speak presently. But she is drawn with little subtlety. We only know her superficially. We should forget her like the rest did she not appear so frequently. The real Mrs. Hauksbee is to be found in the works of other novelists. Yet she is better than the usually vulgar girls of Simla, to whom she occasionally restores a lover. Girlhood is what is wanted, and so far it has proved beyond him. In *The Light that Failed*, Maisie, the heroine, is utterly uninteresting, which is the one thing a heroine may not be. We never know her, and this is not because she is an intricate study. She is merely offered as a nice girl, with an ambition to have her person and paint-brush described in the *Star's* fashionable column. But she is colourless, a nonentity. On the other hand, she has a friend called 'the red-haired girl', whom we do care for, but probably only because we see her in three brief flashes. If she came into the light of day she might prove as dull as Maisie.

Some have taken Mr. Kipling's aim to be the representation oι India as it is, and have refused to believe that Indian life—especially Anglo-Indian life—is as ugly as he paints it. Their premiss granted, few would object to their conclusion except such as judge England by the froth of society or by its dregs. But Mr. Kipling warns us against this assumption. In the preface to one of his books—a preface that might stand in front of all—he 'assures the ill-informed that India is not entirely inhabited by men and women playing tennis with the Seventh Commandment ... The drawback of collecting dirt in one corner is that it gives a false notion of the filth of the room.' The admission of his aim herein contained contracts his ambition into a comparatively little thing, but it should silence much of the hostile criticism. That he is entitled as an artist to dwell chiefly on the dirty corner of the room will surely be admitted. A distinguished American writer maintains that certain subjects taken up by daring novelists should be left to the doctors; but is not this a mistake? The novelist's subject is mankind, and there is no part of it of which he has not the right to treat. By his subject never, by his treatment of it always, should he be judged. If he does not go about the work honestly, so much the worse for him. If his motives are unworthy, nothing is surer in this world than that tomorrow, if not today, he will be found out. Many in England seem to have forgotten this, and Mr. Kipling has done noble work in reminding them of it by example. He refuses to be caged, and that is all a novelist need do to be free. The dirty corner is Mr. Kipling's, to write about if he chooses, and he may do it with the highest motives, that is to say, as an artist, and according as he does it well or ill shall we esteem him. From all points of view but one he does it amazingly well. Assuredly we are made to see that dirty corner. We get it from north, south, east and west. But we are never allowed to estimate its size; there is no perspective; the blaze of light is always on the one spot; we never see the rest of the room. It is not enough for Mr. Kipling to say that he is only concerned with the corner, and so can keep the room in darkness. By all means let the corner be his subject; but we shall never know all about it until we can fit it into that of which it is a part. In other words, we must be shown the room in order to know the corner. Suppose an artist, instead of choosing the human figure for his subject, were to limit himself to the human hand, his work might be as fine as Mr. Kipling's, and yet it would be incom-

plete. We should not know whether that hand needed sixes or nines in
gloves, unless we saw the person it belonged to, and the artist could not
satisfy us by merely intimating that the figure is not all hand, as Mr.
Kipling remarks that the room is not all dirty corner. We want to see
the whole room lighted up that we may judge the dirty corner by
comparison. No doubt it is this want of perspective that has made
many uneasy about Mr. Kipling's work. He has startled them, and
then left them doubtful whether it was done legitimately. There is
something wrong, they feel, and they have a notion that they could
put their finger on it if the stories were English instead of Indian, and
long instead of short. Hence, apparently, has arisen a noisy demand for
English novels from him. They are to be his test. In answer, one may
conclude, to this request, he has written several English stories recently,
one of them his 'first long story'. Mr. Kipling, having a respect for his
calling, always writes as well as he can, and these stories, we are told,
have been rewritten as many times as Mr. Ruskin would have lovers
serve years for their ladies. It is, however, by the result alone that he
is to be judged, and the result is not great. Those of the stories that
deal with 'Society', are more ambitious than the *feuilletons* of the Society
journals, but merit no longer life. *The Record of Badalia Herodsfoot* is
much better; but it is merely a very clever man's treatment of a land
he knows little of. We are only shown the conventional East-end, and
there is something grim in Mr. Kipling become conventional. The
only point the story has in common with the Indian sketches is that it
makes straight for the dirty corner. But it has one inspired moment,
when Badalia dances on the barrow. As for *The Light that Failed*, one
hasty critic finds not even cleverness in it; while another says it would
make ninety-seven ordinary novels, and proves his argument by
pointing out that Mr. Kipling knows there are three kinds of soap.
Mr. Kipling knows even more than this; but despite its vigour and
picturesqueness, the story would probably have attracted little notice
had it been an unknown man, and such as it might have got would
have been won by its almost brutal cynicism. High as the author
stands as a writer of short stories, *The Light that Failed* proves that the
moment he takes to writing novels he has many contemporaries to
make up upon, as also that, if he is to do it, he must abandon some of
his own methods in favour of some of theirs.

His chief defect is ignorance of life. This seems a startling charge to
bring against one whose so-called knowledge of life has frightened the
timid. But it is true. One may not often identify an author with any

of his characters, but if Dick Heldar had written instead of painted, or
Mr. Kipling had painted instead of written, it would have been difficult
to distinguish the one artist from the other. Dick gives us his views on
art and life in *The Light that Failed*, and his creator in that story and
others, and they correspond. They are very smart views, and gaudy.
Mr. Kipling is most tender in his treatment of Dick become blind.
Such a man would not, we think, have fallen in love with Maisie the
characterless, and instead of sitting in his blindness turning her letters
over in his hand, and purring placidly when she is willing, in pity, to
be his, he would probably have blown out his brains. But Dick and
the letters make an affecting picture. There is something else in the
story, however, far more touching; and the author is not aware of it,
which adds greatly to the pathos. It is the revolting cynicism of Dick,
who thinks he is at least a man, and is really anything but that. Though
Dick had kept his eyesight, he could not have become a great artist
without growing out of the ideas he was so proud of. He was always
half blind to the best in life, just as Mr. Kipling is. Yet he was so
brilliant, so honest, so streaked with good, that one does not sneer at
his boyish cynicism, but is sad because he became blind before he ever
saw properly. He is under the curse of thinking he knows everything.
He believes that because he has knocked about the world in shady
company he has no more to learn. It never dawns on him that he is but
a beginner in knowledge of life compared to many men who have
stayed at home with their mothers. He knows so little where is the fire
in which men and women are proved that he has crossed a globe for
it, which is like taking a journey to look for one's shadow. He is so
ignorant of art as to think it the greatest thing in the world. Poor Dick
comes to London, gloating over the stir he is to make, and thus
addresses a row of semi-detached villas: 'Oh, you rabbit-hutches! Do
you know what you have to do later on? You have to supply me with
men-servants and maid-servants'—here he smacked his lips—'and the
peculiar treasure of kings. Meantime I'll get clothes and boots, and
presently I will return and trample on you.' And why is Master Dick
to trample on these people? Because they have not the artistic instinct.
This is what it is to be a heaven-born artist according to Messrs.
Heldar and Kipling. We know it from scores of the stories. There is
no sympathy with humanity, without which there never was and
never will be a great novelist. Sympathy is the blood of the novel.
True, Mr. Kipling has an affection for the Mulvaney type, but it is
only because they too, are artists in their own way. When full of drink

and damns they are picturesque, they have a lordly swagger, they are saved by being devil-may-cares. But if they drank tea instead of whisky, if it was their own wives they walked out with, if they were not ashamed to live respectably in semi-detached villas, if they were grocers who thought almanacks art, or double-chinned professional men who only admired the right picture when they had an explanatory catalogue in their hand, if they were costermongers whose dissipation was the People's Palace, then would they be as cattle. Ninety-nine in every hundred of the population are for trampling on. With the mass of his fellow-creatures Mr. Kipling is out of touch, and thus they are an unknown tongue to him. He will not even look for the key. At present he is a rare workman with a contempt for the best material.

Should Mr. Kipling learn that he can be taught much by grocers, whose views of art are bounded by Adelphi dramas and Sunday-school literature, he may rise to be a great novelist, for the like of him at his age has seldom been known in fiction. His work of the past twelve months is a flat contradiction to the statement that he is written out. Some of the recent stories in *Macmillan's Magazine* rank among his best. It has been pointed out that 'he cannot go on writing these sketches for ever', that they must lose in freshness, that all his characters will soon be used up. But this only means that we could not write them for ever, which is quite true, as we could not have written them at all. We have no right to demand long novels from him, we should be content to revel in the sketches, but if, as we have been led to believe, his intentions run in that direction, we know enough of him to be convinced that he should lay his scene in India. The cry for an English novel has been curiously unreasonable. The example our great novelists have set him is not to write of England, but of what he knows best. If by an accident it has usually been England with them, it is India by accident with him.

The Light that Failed is not much, but, like *The Story of the Gadsbys*, it reveals the great gift of character-drawing by means of dialogue, and as a first attempt in a new method it is in one respect little short of a triumph. Hitherto he had always worked by means of the lantern flash. He took an hour of a man's life and condensed it into a moment. What we were shown was less a printed page that had to be read than a picture which we could take in at once. He had it thus before himself. He could grip it all in his hand. He never required to wonder how one part should play into another. Not in this way can the novel be written. It does not aim at immediate and incessant effects. The chapter, which could swallow half-a-dozen sketches, is not considered by itself, but as the small part of the whole, and it is as a whole that the novel is judged. To forget this is to lose thought of symmetry. No doubt Scott wrote too quickly, but his speed was a real advantage in one way, for it kept his mind on the story as a whole. Having mastered the flash, one might have feared that Mr. Kipling had also become its slave. In *The Story of the Gadsbys* he uses it as much as in the short sketches. That tale is in eight chapters, but each is complete in itself. We get eight events in the Gadsbys' life squeezed into eight minutes, and the result is not a novel. It is only a series of fine pictures. But when he began *The Light that Failed*, Mr. Kipling had realised that the novel in flashes will no more do than liqueurs in tumblers. He broke away from the old method, and he has produced a real novel, though not a great one. Here is proof that there are latent capabilities in him which may develop, and show him by-and-by grown out of knowledge. If he is as conscientious in the future as he has been in the past, and discovers that nothing lives in literature save what is ennobling, he may surprise us again.

15. Three Reviews by Lionel Johnson

1891-2

Three signed reviews which appeared in the *Academy*, Vol. XXXIX, pp. 319–20 (4 April 1891); Vol. XL, pp. 327–8 (17 October 1891) and Vol. XLI, pp. 509–10 (28 May 1892). Subsequently collected in *Reviews and Critical Papers* by Lionel Johnson, (1921) pp. 17–51.

Lionel Pigot Johnson (1867–1902) minor poet and critic. Besides volumes of poems, and a number of reviews such as those collected in the 1921 volume, Johnson wrote *The Art of Thomas Hardy* (1894) and on Irish poetry.

(1). *The Light that Failed* (1891)

'Good Lord! who can account for the fathomless folly of the public?' 'They're a remarkably sensible people.' 'They're subject to fits, if that's what you mean; and you happen to be the object of the latest fit among those who are interested in what they call art. Just now you're a fashion, a phenomenon, or whatever you please.'

This is part of a conversation between Dick Heldar, a young artist whose work has taken the public, and his best friend Torpenhow. Mr. Kipling will not think me discourteous, if I confess that these wise words bear for me a second application to himself. Thanks to the incessant criticism, panegyric, detraction and talk inflicted upon his work in the last year, one feels an unreasoning desire, either to defer the study of Mr. Kipling till the hubbub die down, or to assume an indifference towards him, in the name of sober sense. Either course would be foolish, and neither is possible. Whatever else be true of Mr. Kipling, it is the first truth about him that he has power: not a clever trick, nor a happy knack, nor a flashy style, but real intrinsic power. The reader of contemporary books, driven mad by the distracting affectations, the contemptible pettiness of so much modern work, feels his whole heart go out towards a writer with mind and muscle in him, not only nerves and sentiment. To get into the grip of a new writer; not to saunter arm in arm with him, listening to his tedious and familiar elegancies: that is what we want. Style, the perfection of workmanship, we cannot do without that; but still less can we endure the dexterous and polished imitation of that. It is easy enough to find fault with Mr. Kipling, to deplore certain technical failures, to cry out against his lack of grace; but perfect workmanship is the last good gift, and granted only to the faithful and the laborious in literature. A writer whose first books have flesh and blood, mind and meaning in them, has the right to hope for all things. But the public is less kind than uncritical, when it admires 'achieved perfection' in writings that have achieved much else that is good, but not yet that.

The present volume gives us the story 'as it was originally conceived by the writer', not as it appeared in *Lippincott's Magazine*. There, as most of us know, the story has a pleasant and conventional close, with a marriage of the consolatory sort, familiar to English readers. It is difficult to think well of Mr. Kipling in this matter; such a conclusion was impossible, upon the stated premises. But the book in its true form is finely and desperately logical. Briefly expressed, this is the idea: A boy and a girl, brought up together not too happily, part as chidlren, when the boy's sentiments of mere companionship begin to deepen into love, of a childish sort indeed, yet perfectly real. The boy leads a rough, adventurous life about the world, and after the most varied experiences, wins a sudden and perhaps precarious success in art. His life has been that of an Elizabethan adventurer, in the altered manner of this century: a life of the reckless sort, wild and free, with all the virtues of *camaraderie*, and with few of the more decorous moral excellences. Settled, more or less, in London, he meets the girl again, whom he has never forgotten; she, too, is an artist, full of ambition, eager for recognition, and singularly selfish. She refuses to think of love and marriage; and he devotes himself, half in hopes, half in despair, to her service in art. From the effect of an early wound he grows blind; and the culminating point of interest is reached when the question presents itself to the girl, whom he has loved and served, whether now, in mere compassion and self-respect, she will marry him, and so pay back his devotion by an act of willing self-denial. In sheer selfishness, perfectly natural and immensely strong, she prefers her freedom and her foolish dreams of fame. He cannot endure the idle agony of his life, cut off from all the best things in the world; and he makes his way out to the Soudan, the old scene of his early life, and is there killed, dying in his friend's arms.

The story has a double interest: the interest of character in Maisie the heroine, and the interest of dramatic life and action in Dick the hero and in his friends. Hero and heroine are not the right words, but let that pass. Now the first thought that occurs to one well acquainted with Mr. Kipling's work, upon reading this, his longest book, is of this sort: why is the interest of character so slight and the interest of action and of life so strong? Scenes of superb vigour and animation, passages of wonderful force and movement, these have struck us and taken hold upon us; but the characters, emotions, the mind and soul of Maisie and Dick have not been felt, and do not remain with us. We remember how they looked, talked, bore themselves in various situations; we still hear their characteristic phrases, we still see their attitudes and motions; but themselves, their inner reality, for all the power and mind of the book, are strange to us. Perhaps this may be the reason. Mr. Kipling, before all things, is an observer, not a thinker. Certainly no one can observe life without colouring or shaping his observations by his thoughts; each has his own way of observing life, according to his own habit and cast of mind. But it is not so much the reflections upon life, as the reflections of life, that Mr. Kipling values; and he leaves the bare facts, in all their intensity and vividness, to create the impression which he desires us to receive. There must be no waste of words, no flow of sentiment, no dwelling upon motives; take the facts, he seems to say, as lifelike as I can show them, and make what you can of them. This may be called cynicism, but it need not be that. Without question it is an effective literary method; but, and here is the difficulty, it is a method of very limited application. It will excellently serve for a brilliant sketch of certain scenes, where the men and women act and speak in character, with all the appropriate peculiarities of manner and speech. A third-class smoking-carriage full of soldiers, labourers and city clerks, each with his personal or professional dialect and style, and with that curious force and energy which belong to the less cultured—Mr. Kipling's manner serves perfectly to give us that. But a drawing-room full of more sophisticated and of less intelligible persons, all possessing the complicated emotions and using the subtle language of a life externally refined: what will his robust method make of that? Here we turn to Mr. Henry James. He will in twenty pages bring home to us the passion or the intellect at work in that room, perhaps during one hour only; yet each word will be essential and indispensable. If Mr. James try his hand upon coarser material, he fails at once: witness many pages of *The Princess Casamassima*. Hitherto Mr. Kipling has been successful when dealing with life of a certain vehement intensity, not only in the emotions of it, but in the outward manner: his soldiers, with their heartiness, or roughness, or swagger, or strength, men 'of strange oaths'—full of experience, yet children after all in many things—these are admirable. Or his natives of India, whose circumstances, sordid or picturesque, dignified or pathetic, are felt to be impressive—these he can present to us in perfection. But in whatever he handles well, there must be salient points rather than delicate shades. 'One crowded hour of glorious life', splendid and intoxicating, he can render into words of marvellous intensity; some scene of touching pitifulness, quite simple and human, he can draw with touches absolutely true and right. He is master of human nature in the rough, in its primitive or unconventional manifestations. His rapid sketches, carefully as they are designed, give an impression rather of an immense capacity of eye than of a fineness of sympathy and understanding. His work of this 'coloured and figured' sort is unrivalled, and stands alone; no one has done anything quite like it. But Mr. Kipling is, or seems to be, so fascinated by these lively effects that he wishes to treat everything in the same way, which is irritating. He appears almost to despise whatever is not vivid and impressive; to look at everything from the standpoint of a man who knows camps and barracks, wild countries and native quarters. He attempts to play Othello to his ignorant reader's Desdemona, in a manner almost ludicrous. A writer may be intimate with Valparaiso and Zanzibar without being superior to the reader, who knows only Bloomsbury and Kensington, or Oxford and Manchester. It is impossible to take English life of all kinds by storm, for literary purposes, with the methods applicable to military stations in India. And so, whilst in this book the scenes in the Soudan, and the riotous humours of special correspondents, are convincing and true to the inexperienced reader, there is a great deal which rings false. Torpenhow's warning comes into our mind, 'Take care, Dick: remember, this isn't the Soudan'. When Mr. Kipling is concerned with Maisie's character, and the less obvious emotions of life, we are constantly thinking, take care: remember, this isn't an Irish private. One striking fact illustrates this comparative incapacity for treating delicate or sophisticated sentiments: we cannot remember the phrases used.

Professional terms, technical slang, all varieties of masculine dialect and expression, are easily remembered by Mr. Kipling's readers; everything forcible and boisterous. But of Dick's conversation with Maisie, of the sentiment and psychological description, we can quote not one word. Take away from Mr. Kipling his salient points and lively effects, and then his style becomes merely commonplace. And even in his best passages, the strained expression, the unrelaxed determination to be vigorous, grows wearisome. Contrast with Mr. Kipling the enchanting style of Pierre Loti; that strangely ironical and gentle style, so caressing and unforgettable. For *Les trois Dames de la Kasbah*, we would give many a Plain Tale from the Hills. And, ultimately, Mr. Kipling's incessant vigilance, lest he fall into the hackneyed and the tame, produces an effect of brilliant vulgarity: an effect wholly unjust to Mr. Kipling, yet an inevitable result of his method, when carried to excess. Surely, one protests, we do not want special correspondence, even composed with genius.

Apart from this mannerism, Mr. Kipling's work has innumerable good qualities. Restraint, a dislike of the superfluous, how rare is that just now! To take one small instance: Mr. Kipling makes Dick quote Emerson and Marvell, but he does not mention them by name. In actual life, we do not mention the authors of our quotations; we quote what we suppose familiar to our companions. But in books there seems to come upon the writer a desire to exhibit his reading; he mentions Emerson and Marvell. It is an infinitely small matter, but it is precisely characteristic of Mr. Kipling. Directness, also; only Mr. Meredith, Mr. Hardy, and Mr. Stevenson, to name three very varied writers, can so give us the absolutely right and infallible phrase. Mr. Kipling, with 'his eye on the object', is astounding; with no accumulation of detail, no tiresome minuteness, he brings before us the very reality of life and of character, so far as character can be shown in sketches of talk and action. For there are these limitations to Mr. Kipling's art; within them I recognise with gratitude and admiration a fine writer. But, outside them, I seem to see, if I may make a vigorous quotation in Mr. Kipling's manner, 'another good man gone wrong'. Let us hope for the best, and enjoy what is already in so great a measure so excellent.

(2). *Life's Handicap: Being Stories of Mine Own People* (1891)

Mr. Kipling has gathered into a volume twenty-seven stories: the best of them have been already recognised by readers of the magazines as

Mr. Kipling's finest work. The book is so characteristic, for good and bad, of its author, that it may be interesting to attempt a classification of these twenty-seven stories. Eight of them, with certain limitations, are excellent: 'The Incarnation of Krishna Mulvaney', 'The Courting of Dinah Shadd', 'On Greenhow Hill', 'The Man Who Was', 'Without Benefit of Clergy', 'Through the Fire', 'The Finances of the Gods', and 'Little Tobrah'. To these may be added the Preface. They deal with the famous triumvirate of privates, with the British army, and with the comedy and tragedy of native life and character. Two stories, 'At the End of the Passage' and 'The Mark of the Beast', are concerned with the grim and terrible possibilities and impossibilities of sickness, weariness, fear, superstition, climate, work, and, to put it plainly, the devil, as shown by the experiences of Englishmen in India. Three more, 'The Return of Imray', 'Bubbling Well Road', and 'Bertran and Bimi', are powerful stories of the horrible, without any mixture of mystery and impossibility. Three, 'The Mutiny of the Mavericks', 'The Head of the District' and 'Namgay Doola', have, more or less directly, a political moral wrapped up in them. Five more, 'The Amir's Homily', 'Jews in Shushan', 'The Limitations of Pambe Serang', 'The City of Dreadful Night' and 'The Dream of Duncan Parrenness', are mediocre examples of Mr. Kipling's various manners; and of these the fourth is the most striking. The remaining six, in my sincere and humble opinion, do not deserve publication: 'The Lang Men o'Larut', 'Reingelder and the German Flag', 'The Wandering Jew', 'Moti Guj', 'Georgie Porgie' and 'Naboth'. The volume ends with some of Mr. Kipling's best verses.

This is, of course, merely a classification made according to the mind of one particular reader, with his own tastes and prejudices. Among the stories which I think the worst, is one which many readers have ranked among the best. But, upon the whole, I think that most readers would accept the classification in its spirit and intention.

The one great fault in Mr. Kipling's work is, not its 'brutality', nor its fondness for strong effects, but a certain taint of bad manners, from the literary point of view. He insists upon spicing his stories with an ill-flavoured kind of gossip, wholly irrelevant, and very offensive. For example: 'The Man Who Was', an admirable story, full of that indefinable spirit, military patriotism and regimental pride, is spoilt by this pointless passage:

And indeed they were a regiment to be admired. When Lady Durgan, widow of the late Sir John Durgan, arrived in their station, and after a short time had been proposed to by every single man at mess, she put the public sentiment very neatly when she explained that they were all so nice that unless she could marry them all, including the colonel and some majors already married, she was not going to content herself with one hussar. Wherefore she wedded a little man in a Rifle Regiment, being by nature contradictious: and the White Hussars were going to wear crape on their arms, but compromised by attending the wedding in full force, and lining the aisle with unutterable reproach. She had jilted them all—from Bassett-Holmer, the senior captain, to little Mildred, the junior subaltern, who could have given her four thousand a year and a title.

I hate to mutilate a book; but I hope to read this story often; and, rather than meet the offence and the annoyance of that silly stuff, in a story otherwise splendid, I have obliterated the passage. Too often, in reading Mr. Kipling, we are forced to say, 'That would make a good special report', or 'That's a telling bit of war correspondence': yet special reports and war correspondence are good things of their kind. But the passage just quoted shows merely the contemptible smartness of a society journal; and of a very inferior specimen. I do not say that the thing did not, could not, or should not, happen: I do say that Mr. Kipling, as an artist, one careful to preserve the tone and the proportion of his work, commits a grave offence against his art by such a fall from the fine to the trivial, without just cause. And from the frequency of his offence, in every book that he has written, it would seem that he does not feel the common sentiments of natural good breeding and of artistic reticence. Two expressions in a stirring passage of the same story jar upon us in the same way:

The talk rose higher and higher, and the regimental band played between the courses, as is the immemorial custom, till all tongues ceased for a moment with the removal of the dinner-slips, and the first toast of obligation, when an officer rising said, 'Mr. Vice, the Queen,' and little Mildred from the bottom of the table answered, 'The Queen, God bless her,' and the big spurs clanked as the big men heaved themselves up and drank the Queen, upon whose pay they were falsely supposed to settle their mess bills. That sacrament of the mess never grows old, and never ceases to bring a lump into the throat of the listener wherever he be by sea or by land.

What is the point here of dragging in the familiar fact that the Queen's pay is insufficient for a modern officer under modern circumstances? It sounds like the petty, ill-conditioned criticism of some Cockney money-lender: it is a crying false note, coming just in that place. Again, 'toast of obligation' and 'sacrament of the mess' are phrases in which it is difficult not to see a flippant reference to two ecclesiastical and sacred terms. These things are fatal to the perfection of a story: and Mr. Kipling's taste for them is his worst enemy. But it may be observed that they do not occur except when Mr. Kipling is dealing with English officers and civilians: his 'common' soldiers and his Indian natives, under all circumstances and conditions, talk, and are treated by Mr. Kipling, without these petty offences against good taste. Ortheris and Mulvaney, Ameera and Khoda Dad Khan, in every mood or situation, are allowed by Mr. Kipling to live without those peculiar tricks and tones, which in his stories are the essential notes of the English gentleman in India. His officers and his civil servants, Orde, Tallentire, Hummil, Spurstow, Lowndes, Mottram, Strickland, and 'I', one and all talk with a strained intensity, a bitter tone, a sharp conciseness, an abbreviation of epigram, a clever slang, which are meant to denote, partly their cultured intellects and partly that sentiment of fatality and dogged endurance which Mr. Kipling would have us believe to be the invariable result of official work in India. The Empire, the Administration, the Government, become in Mr. Kipling's hands necessary and yet amusing powers, in whose service Englishmen are willing to toil and sweat, knowing that *il n'y pas d'homme nécessaire*, but content to go on, relieved by making cynical epigrams about life and death, and everything before, between, or after them. The consciousness of duty becomes the consciousness of a mechanical necessity: the sentiment of loyalty is caricatured into a cynical perseverance. One thinks of Dalhousie and of the Lawrences. Mr. Kipling has had experience of English life and work in India: his readers, for the most part, have not. But I would ask any reader, who has known English officers and civilians, before, during, and after their Indian service, whether he has found them quite so brilliant or quite so ill-bred, quite so epigrammatic or quite so self-conscious, as these creatures of Mr. Kipling. Is it that before leaving home, or while home on leave, or when done with India, they are natural Englishmen; but that an Indian climate, and a share in Indian administration, turn them into machines: men who seem to talk like telegrams, and to think in shorthand, and to pose, each as a modern Atlas, helping to uphold the Indian Empire, and swearing pessimist oaths at its weight? Mr. Kipling presents English rule in India, for purposes of effective fiction, as a huge and ironical joke, or, to use one of his favourite words, as a 'grim' comedy. In fact, whenever he gives us the views of life held by men of education and official responsibility, they are the views expressed by his title, *Life's Handicap*. You start with your chances and make the best of the race, sure to be tripped up half-way by the irony of the fates and powers, or baulked at the very finish. In 'The Head of the District', a dying man sees his wife crossing the river to meet him, and knows that she will come too late; and his last words are: 'That's Polly,' he said simply, though his mouth was wried with agony. 'Polly and—the grimmest practical joke ever played on a man. Dick—you'll—have—to—explain.'

The one story in the book, admirable from first to last, is 'The Courting of Dinah Shadd': the tragedy of his life, told by Mulvaney. The Irishman's story is told with perfect truth and pity: Mr. Kipling makes not one mistake in sentiment. But had Mulvaney's colonel told the story of *his* life, Mr. Kipling would have filled it with cheap jests and cynicisms, gall and bitterness.

Years ago, *Werther* first, and *Childe Harold* afterwards, brought into fashion the philosophy of woe and want, and tragic heroics: a perverted sensibility, an affectation of misery and despair: its victims or devotees wept over their sorrows and shrieked at their gods. But the posture was tiring, and at last literature renounced it. Just now, a new philosophy is coming into fashion: it is required of a man that he be virile, robust and bitter. Laugh at life, and jest with the world: waste no words and spare no blushes: whatever you do, do it doggedly, and whatever you say, put a sting into it. In sentiment, let Voltaire talking Ibsen be your ideal: in life, rival the Flying Dutchman for recklessness, the Wandering Jew for restlessness, and the American rowdy for readiness to act. Life is short, so stuff it full: art is long, so cut it short. Various men have various methods: some writers cut art short by reducing it to impressions, some by reducing it to epigrams. Whichever you do, care nothing for beauty and truth, but everything for brevity and effect. You may lead your readers to believe that you have stayed at home and analysed yourself till you were sick of yourself; or that you have raged round the world and found all hollow, without you and within. You can make literature an affair of nerves or an affair of blood: you may paint life grey, or paint it red. But if you would be a modern man of letters, before all else, ignore the Ten Commandments and the Classics. Swear by the sciences, which you have not studied, and the foreign literature, which you read in translation: if you want to make a hit, bring the *Iliad* up to date: you need only double the bloodshed, and turn the long speeches into short, smart, snapping cynicisms.

Some of these follies, which many writers now take for virtues, are but the accidental vices of Mr. Kipling's work; and it is because he can write so well that I have ventured to suggest that he often writes far too badly. A writer suddenly and deservedly welcomed with great praise is at once imitated by all sorts of incapable persons; and for one story which has something of his real charm and power, there are twenty with nothing but his casual levities and unfortunate mannerisms. For example, 'The Mark of the Beast' is a story of an incident among the more unnecessary horrors of life in India, brought about by 'the power of the Gods and Devils of Asia'. An Englishman pays a drunken insult to Hanuman, the monkey-god, in his temple at night: a leper, a 'Silver Man', just drops his head upon the man's breast, and nothing more. And gradually, with dreadful warnings and signs, the man's nature is changed into a beast's, a wolf's. It is an uncanny, haunting story, told with a singular power: but Mr. Kipling does not seem to know wherein consist the real horror and fascination of his own work. A passage of pure and perfect excellence is often followed by one of simple bad taste and feebleness. For example: while Fleete, the were-wolf, is lying bound in the house, with his two friends watching, the cry of the Silver Man is heard outside. They determine to capture him, and go into the garden: and 'in the moonlight we could see the leper coming round the corner of the house. He was perfectly naked, and from time to time he mewed and stopped to dance with his shadow.' That sentence gave me a literal shudder of sudden fear, like the fear of a child in the dark: for complete effectiveness, in the narration of a fearful story, it could not be beaten. It is horrible, but the horror is not strained and emphasised; the simple words do their work naturally. The two men succeed in capturing the leper; they resolve to torture him into removing the spell from their friend. 'When we confronted him with the beast, the scene was beyond description. The beast doubled backwards into a bow as though he had been poisoned with strychnine, and moaned in the most pitiable fashion.' Well, that is right enough in its way; but Mr. Kipling adds, 'several other things happened also, but they cannot be put down here'. And 'Strickland shaded his eyes with his hands for a moment, and we set to work. This part is not to be printed.' A row of asterisks follows. Now this suggestion of un-mentionable horror is a piece of the very worst possible art: Mr. Kipling means to thrill us with absolute horror, to fill us with shudder-ing apprehensions of absolute fearfulness. He fails: we feel nothing but wonder and contempt, to find so able a writer fall into so pitiable a device. And he is constantly leading us up to the doors of a sealed chamber of horrors, and expecting us to be smitten with dread. The fearful and the terrible are not necessarily loathsome to the senses, matters of blood and noisome pestilence: they are produced by appeals to the imagination and to the intellect. Running through Mr. Kipling's work, and spoiling its value, is this strain of bad taste: irritated by silly sentiment, he takes up silly cynicism; angry with foolish shamefacedness, he adopts a foolish shamelessness. Rather than let his work win its way by the subtle powers of its ideas, he prefers to force our attention by the studied abruptness of his phrases. It is characteristic of the times: General Booth and Mr. Stanley, the German Emperor and General Boulanger, have done much the same thing in practical affairs. But Mr. Kipling, in his profession, is a greater man than they in theirs and we continue to hope against hope for his ultimate purification and perfection.

(3). *Barrack-Room Ballads and Other Verses* (1892)

The two divisions of this book disclose the strength and the weakness of Mr. Kipling: triumphant success and disastrous failure. Certainly, there are weak things among the strong, and strong things among the weak; but the good and the bad, for the most part, are separated, the wheat from the tares. The 'Barrack-Room Ballads' are fine and true; the 'Other Verses', too many of them, are rhetorical and only half true. It is more important, then, as it is more pleasant, to consider first, and at the greater length, the 'Barrack-Room Ballads'.

They are written in the dialect of 'the common soldier', of 'Tommy Atkins'; they are composed in his spirit also. It is a curious reflection that the British Army at large, and the British soldier in particular, have received so little attention in literature of any excellence. We have plenty of heroic poems, as Mr. Henley and many others know well; plenty of verse alive with the martial spirit, with the 'pomp and circumstance of glorious war'; plenty of things hardly less great than Wordsworth's 'Happy Warrior', or the Laureate's 'Ode on Wellington'. But of the British Army, as a way of daily life, as composed of individual men, as full of marked personal characteristics and peculiarities, our poets great and small have had little conception. What Smollett in prose, and Dibdin in verse, did for the Navy, no one has yet done for the Army. Famous achievements and signal successes of armies, or of regiments, or of individual men, have been sung. Agincourt, Flodden, Blenheim, Waterloo, the Crimea, the Mutiny, have inspired praises, not always stilted and official; but the personal sentiments of the British soldier have not been the theme of any British poet worth naming. Certain criticisms which I have read of these Ballads have dwelt upon the technical difficulty of their dialect. Such criticism is of a piece with the prevailing apathy and ignorance concerning the Army. Little wonder that Special Committees and Royal Commissions are required to look into its state, while so many critics of literature, whose pride and business it is to be omniscient, are baffled by the technical terms or the appropriate slang of these Ballads. Poems thick with archaeological terms, with foreign phrases, with recondite learning and allusions, are accepted without demur. Mr. Kipling's Indian stories have roused no protest; but when he sings the common soldier in a common way, these omnivorous critics are aghast at the uncouth and mysterious language.

There are twenty of these Ballads; and there can hardly be said to be one failure among them, although two or three are of marked inferiority to the rest, and although the greater number look poor by the side of the four or five masterpieces. The most noticeable thing about them, on a first reading, is their swinging, marching music. The accents and beat of the verse fall true and full, like the rhythmical tramp of men's feet. Take such rhythms and measures as

> For it was—'Belts, belts, belts, an' that's one for you!'
> An' it was—'Belts, belts, belts, an' that's done for you!'

Or as

> When first under fire, an' you're wishful to duck,
> Don't look nor take 'eed at the man that is struck,
> Be thankful you're livin', and trust to your luck,
>   And march to your front like a soldier.
>   Front, front, front, like a soldier,
>   Front, front, front, like a soldier,
>   Front, front, front, like a soldier,
>   So-oldier *of* the Queen!

Or, best of all, as

>   On the road to Mandalay,
>   Where the old Flotilla lay;
> Can't you 'ear their paddles chunkin' from Rangoon to Mandalay?
>   On the road to Mandalay,
>   Where the flyin' fishes play,
> An' the dawn comes up like thunder outer China 'crost the bay!

They go with a swing and a march, an emphasis and a roll, which may delude the inexperienced into thinking them easy to 'rattle off'. I should be greatly surprised to hear that Mr. Kipling thought the same.

The Ballads deal with a few marked incidents, experiences, and emotions from the private soldier's point of view; some general and unlocalised, but most peculiar to military life in the East. All Mr. Kipling's undiverted and undiluted strength has gone into these vivid Ballads; phrase follows phrase, instinct with life, quivering and vibrating with the writer's intensity. No superfluity, no misplaced condescension to sentiment, no disguising of things ludicrous or ugly or unpleasant; Tommy Atkins is presented to the ordinary reader, with no apologies and with no adornments.

> We aren't no thin red 'eroes, nor we aren't no blackguards too,
> But single men in barricks, most remarkable like you,

he sings: in a genial and, at the same time, an acute expostulation with the people, who exalt him in war but despise him in peace, in the amiable manner lately described by the Duke of Connaught. But no panegyrics could give the civilian a truer sense of the soldier's life, in its rough and ready hardships, than the experiences of camp and battle in these pages; their grim pleasantry in describing the little accidents of a battery charge, the perversities of the commissariat camel, the dangers that await the "arf made' recruits in the East, the humours of the 'time-expired', the fascinations of 'loot', the joys of the 'cells', the fatigue and the exhilaration of 'route marchin' '. Then we have the generous recognition of 'Fuzzy-Wuzzy', the Soudanese:

> So 'ere's to you, Fuzzy-Wuzzy, at your 'ome in the Soudan;
> You're a pore benighted 'eathen, but a first-class fightin' man;
> An' 'ere's to you, Fuzzy-Wuzzy, with your 'ayrick 'ead of 'air—
> You big black boundin' beggar—for you broke a British square!

And an eulogy no less generous is bestowed upon the native water-carrier, 'our regimental bhisti, Gunga Din'.

The most poetical, in the sense of being the most imaginative and heightened in expression, is 'Danny Deever', hanged for shooting a comrade.

> "Is cot was right-'and cot to mine,' said Files-on-Parade.
> "E's sleepin' out an' far to-night,' the Colour-Sergeant said.
> ' I've drunk 'is beer a score o' times,' said Files-on-Parade.
> "E's drinkin' bitter beer alone,' the Colour-Sergeant said.

And perhaps the most winning of them all is 'Mandalay': the Burmese girl and her lover, the British soldier, his sickness and disgust at London and England after those old times in the East.

> I'm learnin' 'ere in London what the ten-year soldier tells,
> 'If you've 'eard the East a-callin', you won't never 'eed naught else'

—which would seem to be the experience of Mr. Kipling also.

There is plenty of matter in these Ballads to which 'inquisiturient' critics, to use Milton's word, can take objection: the moral and dogmatic theology of the soldier, as indicated by Mr. Kipling, is somewhat unauthorised and lax. But Mr. Kipling has no ambition to paint him, except in his own colours; and, very seriously contemplated, these Ballads give a picture of life and character more estimable and praiseworthy for many rugged virtues of generosity, endurance, heartiness, and simplicity, than are the lives and characters of many 'gentlemen of England, who stay at home at ease'.

Mr. Kipling's 'Other Verses' are less pleasant reading. Their rhetorical energy is splendid. At times they ring true to nature; but for the most part they are spasmodic, ranting, overstrained. For example, the volume opens with a poem to the praise of one whose death Mr. Kipling has an especial right to lament, while all lovers of literature have also their regrets. It imagines the great dead in a Valhalla of the windiest sort. There, beyond the farthest ways of sun, or comet, or star, or 'star-dust', 'live such as fought, and sailed, and ruled, and loved, and made our world'. There 'they sit at wine with the Maidens Nine and the Gods of the Elder Days'; and

> 'Tis theirs to sweep through the ringing deep where Azrael's outposts are,
> Or buffet a path through the Pit's red wrath when God goes out to war
> Or hang with the reckless Seraphim on the rim of a red-maned star.

There 'they whistle the Devil to make them sport who know that Sin is vain;' but that is not all:

> And ofttimes cometh our wise Lord God, master of every trade,
> And tells them tales of His daily toil, of Edens newly made;
> And they rise to their feet as He passes by, gentlemen unafraid.

It is a Paradise, an Elysium, a Valhalla, of 'the Strong Men'.

The hollow insincerity of this rhetoric is little short of marvellous; not, I need hardly say, that I impute any insincerity to the writer's spirit and intention. I mean, that the imaginative design of the poem, aiming at the heroic and the sublime, falls into a bathos worthy of

Nat Lee. 'The reckless Seraphim', to put it quite frankly, are absurd; and so is the whole attempt, by a mystical use of vague astronomy, to represent in a new fashion the home and the life of the great dead. I can attach no meaning to the jumble of 'Maidens Nine' and 'Gods of the Elder Days' and 'Azrael' and 'the Pit' and 'the Devil' and 'our wise Lord God': if it be all metaphorical, a large and half-Oriental dream, it loses all semblance of reality; if it be more soberly meant, I prefer not to characterise it, but rather turn to Dante or to Virgil. Dante has no lack of strength and power; and I am more at home, with reverence be it said, in his *Paradiso*, with *il santo atleta*, than with the self-satisfied 'Strong Men' of Mr. Kipling. Yet, like all that he writes with any degree of excellence, these lines have fine things in them: witness the description of him who walked from his birth 'in simpleness and gentleness and honour and clean mirth': a just and noble praise.

Mr. Kipling has run riot in chaunting the glories of action; for still, as Mr. Stevenson has it,

> For still the Lord is Lord of might;
> In deeds, in deeds, he takes delight.

It is very true; but he takes delight in other things also; and this glorification of the Strong, the Virile, the Robust, the Vigorous is fast becoming as great a nuisance and an affectation as were the True and the Beautiful years ago. It is so easy to bluster and to brag; so hard to remember that 'they also serve who only stand and wait'. Indeed, there seems to be no virtue which Mr. Kipling would not put under the head of valour; virtue, to him, is *virtus*, and all the good qualities of man are valorous. From that point of view, saints and sinners, soldiers and poets, men of science and men of art, if they excel in their chosen works, are all Strong Men. That may be fair enough as a view of the matter to be sometimes emphasised; but we can have too much of it.

In some of the finest pieces Mr. Kipling is a prey to the grandiose aspect of things. 'The English Flag', for example, in which the Winds of the World witness to England's greatness, is grievously spoiled by exaggeration of tone. We know that England is great, that Englishmen have done great things, that the fame of her glory has filled the corners of the earth; but we have no occasion to shriek about it, to wax hysterically wroth with those who deny it. Shakespeare's great burst of loyal pride, Milton's solemn utterance, Wordsworth's noble verses, Browning's 'Home Thoughts from Abroad', the Laureate's stately lyrics, do not brag and bluster and protest. 'What should they know

of England, who only England know?' cries Mr. Kipling; as though
nothing short of ocular demonstration and a tourist's ticket could make
the 'poor little street-bred people' believe in the greatness of England
by North, South, East and West. The occasion upon which the verses
were written may justify some of this agitated declamation; but the
tone is habitual with Mr. Kipling. Again, the delightful satire of
'Tomlinson', the man with no soul of his own, whose God and whose
virtues and whose rites came all 'from a printed book', would be far
more telling if there were some recognition of the fact that a man may
be equally contemptible who 'posts o'er land and ocean without rest',
with no more soul than a thistledown. I am duly sorry to rely so much
upon 'printed books'; but I remember certain exhortations to the
theoretic life in Plato and Aristotle, certain passages in Dante about
l'antica Rachele, the Lady of Contemplation, and in Milton about 'the
cherub Contemplation', whom he wished for 'first and chiefest'.
Doubtless, this is to take Mr. Kipling's satire too seriously, and to have
no sense of humour; but I am in Mr. Kipling's debt for so great a
number of delights that I am the more moved to exclaim against his
defects. I want to enjoy all that he writes. All that he urges against the
effeminate, miserable people who take their whole standard of life and
conduct from the opinions that they meet, and the society that surrounds them, is admirable; but it is not the whole truth. Perhaps, as
Mr. Stevenson suggests, there is no such thing as the whole truth.

Of the remaining poems, far the best are the 'Ballad of East and
West', a thing to stir the blood like a trumpet; the 'Conundrum of the
Workshops', a charming satire upon critics and criticism; and the
ballads of the 'Clampherdown' and the 'Bolivar'. The fierce and
stinging verses against the Irish members concerned in the famous
Commission are too virulent in their partisanship to be quite successful,
even in the eyes of those who agree with them in the main. Of the
Indian legends and ballads, we may say nothing; most of them have
some force and spirit, but they do not equal the similar work of Sir
Alfred Lyall.

Let me conclude by expressing my thanks once more for the
'Barrack-Room Ballads'; in them, their unforced vigour and un-
exaggerated truth, I can forget all excesses of rhetoric, all extravagances
of tone.

16. Oscar Wilde: Two Extracts

1891

Extracts from 'The True Function and Value of Criticism' (The *Nineteenth Century*, Vol. XXVIII, July, September 1890; reprinted with additions, bracketed below, in *Intentions* 1891) and a letter about a criticism of the above published in *The Times* (25 September 1891), under the heading 'An Anglo-Indian's Complaint'.

Oscar Wilde (1854–1900) was a great dramatist and minor story-teller and versifier. His occasional criticism lacked depth but supplied a number of brilliant and sometimes telling epigrams. Kipling began by imitating him (e.g. in 'Ave Imperatrix' and in his early, and mainly uncollected, Indian sketches and stories), but ended by writing in *Something of Myself* of 'the suburban Toilet-Club school favoured by the late Mr. Oscar Wilde'.

(1) ... He who would stir us now by fiction must either give us an entirely new background or reveal to us the soul of man in its innermost workings. The first is for the moment being done for us by Mr. Rudyard Kipling. As one turns over the pages of his *Plain Tales from the Hills*, one feels as if one were seated under a palm-tree reading life by superb flashes of vulgarity. The jaded, second-rate Anglo-Indians are in exquisite incongruity with their surroundings. The mere lack of style in the story-teller gives an odd journalistic realism to what he tells us. From the point of view of literature Mr. Kipling is a genius who drops his aspirates. From the point of view of life, he is a reporter who knows vulgarity better than anyone has ever known it. Dickens knew its clothes [and its comedy]. Mr. Kipling knows its essence [and its seriousness]. He is our first authority on the second-rate [and has seen marvellous things through keyholes, and his backgrounds are real works of art].

(2) ... There is no reason why Mr. Rudyard Kipling should not select vulgarity as his subject-matter, or part of it. For a realistic artist,

certainly, vulgarity is a most admirable subject. How far Mr. Kipling's stories really mirror Anglo-Indian society I have no idea at all, nor, indeed, am I ever much interested in any correspondence between art and nature. It seems to me a matter of entirely secondary importance.

17. Edmund Gosse: 'Rudyard Kipling'

1891

Signed article in the *Century Magazine*, Vol. XLII, pp. 901–10 (October 1891). Much of this was reprinted in the author's *Questions at Issue* (1893).

Sir Edmund William Gosse (1849–1928) was a minor poet and a major critic and biographer throughout most of Kipling's working life. He is remembered for his 'grim memoir' *Father and Son* (1907), but in his day was an influential critic. He was one of the circle at the Savile Club who welcomed Kipling's advent to literary London at the end of 1889. He introduced him to Wolcott Balestier, and he, with his wife and son, made up half the congregation at Kipling's wedding to Balestier's sister in January 1892.

Two years ago there was suddenly revealed to us, no one seems to remember how, a new star out of the East. Not fewer distinguished men of letters profess to have 'discovered' Mr. Kipling than there were cities of old in which Homer was born. Yet, in fact, the discovery was not much more creditable to them than it would be, on a summer night, to contrive to notice a comet flaring across the sky. Not only was this new talent robust, brilliant, and self-asserting, but its reception was prepared for by a unique series of circumstances. The fiction of the Anglo-Saxon world, in its more intellectual provinces, had become curiously femininized. Those novel-writers who cared to produce subtle impressions upon their readers, in England and America, had become extremely refined in taste and discreet in judgment. People who were not content to pursue the soul of their next-door neighbor through all the burrows of self-consciousness had no choice but to take ship with Mr. Rider Haggard for the 'Mountains of the Moon'. Between excess of psychological analysis and excess of superhuman romance, there was a great void in the world of Anglo-Saxon fiction. It is this void which Mr. Kipling, with something less than one hundred short stories, one novel, and a few poems, has filled by his exotic realism and his vigorous rendering of unhackneyed experience. His temperament is eminently masculine, and yet his imagination is strictly bound by existing laws. The Evarras of the novel had said: 'Thus gods are made,/And whoso makes them otherwise shall die,' when, behold, a young man comes up out of India, and makes them quite otherwise, and lives.

The vulgar trick, however, of depreciating other writers in order to exalt the favorite of a moment was never less worthy of practice than it is in the case of the author of *Soldiers Three*. His relation to his contemporaries is curiously slight. One living writer there is, indeed, with whom it is not unnatural to compare him—Pierre Loti. Each of these men has attracted the attention, and then the almost exaggerated admiration, of a crowd of readers drawn from every class. Each has become popular without ceasing to be delightful to the fastidious. Each is independent of traditional literature, and affects a disdain for books. Each is a wanderer, a lover of prolonged exile, more at home among the ancient races of the East than among his own people. Each describes what he has seen, in short sentences, with highly colored phrases and local words, little troubled to obey the laws of style if he can but render an exact impression of what the movement of physical life has been to himself. Each produces on the reader a peculiar thrill, a voluptuous and agitating sentiment of intellectual uneasiness, with the spontaneous art of which he has the secret. Totally unlike in detail, Rudyard Kipling and Pierre Loti have these general qualities in common, and if we want a literary parallel to the former, the latter is certainly the only one that we can find. Nor is the attitude of the French novelist to his sailor friends at all unlike that of the Anglo-Indian civilian to his soldier chums. To distinguish we must note very carefully the difference between Mulvaney and *mon frère Yves*; it is not altogether to the advantage of the latter.

The old rhetorical manner of criticism was not meant for the discussion of such writers as these. The only way in which, as it seems to me, we can possibly approach them, is by a frank confession of their personal relation to the feelings of the critic. I will therefore admit that I cannot pretend to be indifferent to the charm of what Mr. Kipling writes. From the first moment of my acquaintance with it it has held me fast. It excites, disturbs, and attracts me; I cannot throw off its disquieting influence. I admit all that is to be said in its disfavor. I force myself to see that its occasional cynicism is irritating and strikes a false note. I acknowledge the broken and jagged style, the noisy newspaper bustle of the little peremptory sentences, the cheap irony of the satires on society. Often—but this is chiefly in the earlier stories—I am aware that there is a good deal too much of the rattle of the piano at some café concert. But when all this is said, what does it amount to? What but an acknowledgment of the crudity of a strong and rapidly developing young nature? You cannot expect a creamy smoothness while the act of vinous fermentation is proceeding.

> Wit will shine
> Through the harsh cadence of a ruggèd line;
> A noble error, and but seldom made,
> When poets are by too much force betray'd;
> Thy generous fruits, though gather'd ere their prime,
> Still show a quickness, and maturing time
> But mellows what we write to the dull sweets of rime.

In the following pages I shall try to explain why the sense of these shortcomings is altogether buried for me in delighted sympathy and breathless curiosity. Mr. Kipling does not provoke a critical suspension of judgment. He is vehement, and sweeps us away with him; he plays upon a strange and seductive pipe, and we follow him like children. As I write these sentences, I feel how futile is this attempt to analyse his gifts, and how greatly I should prefer to throw this paper to the winds, and listen to the magician himself. I want more and more, like Oliver Twist. I want all those 'other stories'; I wish to wander down all those by-paths that we have seen disappear in the brushwood. If one lay very still and low by the watch-fire, in the hollow of Ortheris's great-coat, one might learn more and more of the inextinguishable sorrows of Mulvaney. One might be told more of what happened, out of the moonlight, in the blackness of Amir Nath's Gully. I want to know how the palanquin came into Dearsley's possession, and what became of Kheni Singh, and whether the seal-cutter did really die in the House of Suddhoo. I want to know who it is who dances the *Halli Hukk*, and how, and why, and where. I want to know what happened at Jagadhri, when the Death Bull was painted. I want to know all the things that Mr. Kipling does not like to tell—to see the devils of the East 'rioting as the stallions riot in spring'. It is the strength of this new story-teller that he re-awakens in us the primitive emotions of curiosity, mystery, and romance in action. He is the master of a new kind of terrible and enchanting peepshow, and we crowd around him begging for 'just one more look'. When a writer excites and tantalizes us in this way, it seems a little idle to discuss his style. Let pedants, then, if they will, say that Mr. Kipling has no style; yet if so, how shall we designate such passages as this, frequent enough among his more exotic stories?

Come back with me to the north and be among men once more. Come back when this matter is accomplished and I call for thee. The bloom of the peach orchards is upon all the valley, and *here* is only dust and a great stink. There is a pleasant wind among the mulberry trees, and the streams are bright with snow-water, and the caravans go up and the caravans go down, and a hundred fires sparkle in the gut of the pass, and tent-peg answers hammer-nose, and pony squeals to pony across the drift-smoke of the evening. It is good in the north now. Come back with me. Let us return to our own people. Come!

The private life of Mr. Rudyard Kipling is not a matter of public interest, and I should be very unwilling to exploit it, even if I had the means of doing so. The youngest of living writers should really be protected for a few years longer against those who chirp and gabble about the unessential. All that needs to be known, in order to give him his due chronological place, is that he was born in Bombay in Christmas week, 1865, and that he is therefore only in his twenty-sixth year yet. The careful student of what he has published will collect from it the impression that Mr. Kipling was in India at an age when few European children remain there; that he returned to England for a brief period; that he began a career on his own account in India at an unusually early age; that he has led life of extraordinary vicissitude, as a journalist, as a war correspondent, as a civilian in the wake of the army; that an insatiable curiosity has led him to shrink from no experience that might help to solve the strange riddles of Oriental existence; and that he is distinguished from other active, adventurous, and inquisitive persons in that his capacious memory retains every impression that it captures. Beyond this, all that must here be said about the man is that his stories began to be published—I think about eight years ago—in local newspapers of India, that his first book of verse, *Departmental Ditties*, appeared in 1886, while his prose stories were not collected from a Lahore journal, of which he was the sub-editor, until 1888, when a volume of *Plain Tales from the Hills* appeared in Calcutta. In the same year six successive pamphlets or thin books appeared in an 'Indian Railway Library', published at Allahabad, under the titles of *Soldiers Three*, *The Gadsbys*, *In Black and White*, *Under the Deodars*, *The Phantom Rickshaw*, and *Wee Willie Winkie*. These formed the literary baggage of Mr. Rudyard Kipling when, in 1889, he came home to find himself suddenly famous at the age of twenty-three.

Since his arrival in England Mr. Kipling has not been idle. In 1890 he brought out a Christmas annual called *The Record of Badalia Herodsfoot*, and a short novel, *The Light that Failed*. Already in 1891 he has published a fresh collection of tales called (in America) *Mine Own People* [*Life's Handicap*] and a second miscellany of verses. This is by no means a complete record of his activity, but it includes the names of all his important writings. At an age when few future novelists have yet produced anything at all, Mr. Kipling is already voluminous. It would be absurd not to acknowledge that a danger lies in this precocious fecundity. It would probably be an excellent thing for every one concerned if this brilliant youth could be deprived of pens and ink for a few years and be buried again somewhere in the far East. There should be a 'close time' for authors no less than for seals, and the extraordinary fullness and richness of Mr. Kipling's work does not completely reassure us.

The publications which I have named above have not, as a rule, any structural cohesion. With the exception of *Badalia Herodsfoot* and *The Light that Failed* which deal with phases of London life, their contents might be thrown together without much loss of relation. The general mass so formed could then be re-divided into several coherent sections. It may be remarked that Mr. Kipling's short stories, of which, as I have said, we hold nearly a hundred, mainly deal with three or four distinct classes of Indian life. We may roughly distinguish these as the British soldier in India, the Anglo-Indian, the Native, and the British child in India. In the following pages I shall endeavor to characterize his treatment of these four classes, and finally to say a word about him as a poet.

There can be no question that the side upon which Mr. Kipling's talent has most delicately tickled British curiosity, and British patriotism too, is his revelation of the soldier in India. A great mass of our countrymen are constantly being drafted out to the East on Indian service. They serve their time, are recalled, and merge in the mass of our population; their strange temporary isolation between the civilian and the native and their practical inability to find public expression for their feelings make these men—to whom, though we so often forget it, we owe the maintenance of the English Empire in the East—an absolutely silent section of the community. Of their officers we may know something, although 'A Conference of the Powers' may perhaps have awakened us to the fact that we know very little. Still, people like Tick Boileau and Captain Mafflin of the Duke of Derry's Pink Hussars are of ourselves; we meet them before they go out and when they come back; they marry our sisters and our daughters; and they lay down the law about India after dinner. Of the private soldier, on the other hand, of his loves and hates, sorrows and pleasures, of the way in which the vast, hot, wearisome country and its mysterious inhabitants strike him, of his attitude towards India, and of the way in which India treats him, we know, or knew until Mr. Kipling enlightened us, absolutely nothing. It is not surprising, then, if the novelty of this portion of his writings has struck ordinary English readers more than that of any other.

This section of Mr. Kipling's work occupies the seven tales called *Soldiers Three* and a variety of stories scattered through his other books. In order to make his point of view that of the men themselves, not spoiled by the presence of superior officers or by social restraint of any sort, the author takes upon himself the character of an almost silent young civilian who has gained the warm friendship of three soldiers, whose intimate companion and chum he becomes. Most of the military stories, though not all, are told by one of these three, or else recount their adventures or caprices. Before opening the book called *Soldiers Three*, however, the reader will do well to make himself familiar with the opening pages of a comparatively late story, 'The Incarnation of Krishna Mulvaney', in which the characteristics of the famous three are more clearly defined than elsewhere. Mulvaney, the Irish giant, who has been the 'grizzled, tender, and very wise Ulysses' to successive generations of young and foolish recruits, is a great creation. He is the father of the craft of arms to his associates; he has served with various regiments from Bermuda to Halifax; he is 'old in war, scarred, reckless, resourceful, and in his pious hours an unequalled soldier'. Learoyd, the second of these friends, is 'six-and-a-half feet of slow-moving, heavy-footed Yorkshireman, born on the wolds, bred in the dales, and educated chiefly among the carriers' carts at the back of York railway-station'. The third is Ortheris, a little man as sharp as a needle, 'a fox-terrier of a cockney', an inveterate poacher and dog-stealer.

Of these three strongly contrasted types the first and the third live in Mr. Kipling's pages with absolute reality. I must confess that Learoyd is to me a little shadowy, and even in a late story, 'On Greenhow Hill', which has apparently been written in order to emphasize the outline of the Yorkshireman, I find myself chiefly interested in the incidental part, the sharp-shooting of Ortheris. It seems as though Mr. Kipling required, for the artistic balance of his cycle of stories, a third figure, and had evolved Learoyd while he observed and created Mulvaney and Ortheris, nor am I sure that places could not be pointed out where Learoyd, save for the dialect, melts undistinguishably into an incarnation of Mulvaney. The others are studied from the life, and by an observer who goes deep below the surface of conduct. How penetrating the study is, and how clear the diagnosis, may be seen in one or two stories which lie somewhat outside the popular group. It is no superficial idler among men who has taken down the strange notes on military hysteria which inspire 'The Madness of Ortheris' and 'In the Matter of a Private', while the skill with which the battered giant Mulvaney, who has been a corporal and then has been reduced for misconduct, who to the ordinary view and in the eyes of all but the wisest of his officers is a dissipated blackguard, is made to display the rapidity, wit, resource, and high moral feeling which he really possesses, is extraordinary.

We have hitherto had in English literature no portraits of private soldiers like these, and yet the soldier is an object of interest and of very real, if vague and inefficient, admiration to his fellow-citizens. Mr. Thomas Hardy has painted a few excellent soldiers, but in a more romantic light and a far more pastoral setting. Other studies of this kind in fiction have either been slight and unsubstantial, or else they have been, as in the baby-writings of a certain novelist who has enjoyed popularity for a moment, odious in their sentimental unreality. There seems to be something essentially volatile about the soldier's memory. His life is so monotonous, so hedged in by routine, that he forgets the details of it as soon as the restraint is removed, or else he looks back upon it to see it bathed in a fictitious haze of sentiment. The absence of sentimentality in Mr. Kipling's version of the soldier's life in India is one of its great merits. What romance it assumes under his treatment is due to the curious contrasts it encourages. We see the ignorant and raw English youth transplanted, at the very moment when his instincts begin to develop, into a country where he is divided from everything which can remind him of his home, where by noon and night, in the bazaar, in barracks, in the glowing scrub jungle, in the ferny defiles of the hills, everything he sees and hears and smells and feels produces on him an unfamiliar and an unwelcome impression. How he behaves himself under these new circumstances, what code of laws still binds his conscience, what are his relaxations, and what his observations, these are the questions which we ask and which Mr. Kipling essays for the first time to answer.

Among the short stories which Mr. Kipling has dedicated to the British soldier in India there are a few which excel all the rest as works of art. I do not think that any one will deny that of this inner selection none exceeds in skill or originality 'The Taking of Lungtungpen'. Those who have not read this little masterpiece have yet before them the pleasure of becoming acquainted with one of the best short stories not merely in English but in any language. I do not know how to praise adequately the technical merit of this little narrative. It possesses to the full that masculine buoyancy, that power of sustaining an extremely spirited narrative in a tone appropriate to the action, which is one of Mr. Kipling's rare gifts. Its concentration, which never descends into obscurity, its absolute novelty, its direct and irresistible appeal to what is young and daring and absurdly splendid, are unsurpassed. To read it, at all events to admire and enjoy it, is to recover for a moment a little of that dare-devil quality that lurks somewhere in the softest and the baldest of us. Only a very young man could have written it, perhaps, but still more certainly only a young man of genius.

A little less interesting, in a totally different way, is 'The Daughter of the Regiment', with its extraordinarily vivid account of the breaking-out of cholera in a troop-train. Of 'The Madness of Ortheris' I have already spoken; as a work of art this again seems to me somewhat less remarkable, because carried out with less completeness. But it would be hard to find a parallel, of its own class, to 'The Rout of the White Hussars', with its study of the effects of what is believed to be supernatural on a gathering of young fellows who are absolutely without fear of any phenomenon of which they comprehend the nature. In a very late story, 'The Courting of Dinah Shadd', Mr. Kipling has shown that he is able to deal with the humors and matrimonial amours of India barrack-life just as rapidly, fully, and spiritedly as with the more serious episodes of a soldier's career. The scene between Judy Sheehy and Dinah, as told by Mulvaney in that story, is pure comedy, without a touch of farce.

On the whole, however, the impression left by Mr. Kipling's military stories is one of melancholy. Tommy Atkins, whom the author knows so well and sympathizes with so truly, is a solitary being in India. In all these tales I am conscious of the barracks as of an island in a desolate ocean of sand. All around is the infinite waste of India, obscure, monotonous, immense, inhabited by black men and pariah dogs, Pathans and green parrots, kites and crocodiles, and long solitudes of high grass. The island in this sea is a little collection of young men, sent out from the remoteness of England to serve 'the Widder', and to help to preserve for her the rich and barbarous empire of the East. This microcosm of the barracks has its own laws, its own morals, its own range of emotional sentiment. What these are the new writer has (not told us, for that would be a long story) but shown us that he himself has divined. He has held the door open for a moment, and has revealed to us a set of very human creations. One thing, at least, the biographer of Mulvaney and Ortheris has no difficulty in persuading us, namely, that 'God in his wisdom has made the heart of the British soldier, who is very often an unlicked ruffian, as soft as the heart of a little child, in order that he may believe in and follow his officers into tight and nasty places.'

The Anglo-Indians with whom Mr. Kipling deals are of two kinds. I must confess that there is no section of his work which appears to me so insignificant as that which deals with Indian 'society'. The eight tales which are bound together as *The Story of the Gadsbys* are doubtless very early productions. I have been told, but I know not whether on good authority, that they were published before the author was twenty-one. Judged as the observation of Anglo-Indian life by so young a boy, they are, it is needless to say, astonishingly clever. Some pages in them can never, I suppose, come to seem unworthy of later fame. The conversation in 'The Tents of Kedar', where Captain Gadsby breaks to Mrs. Herriott that he is engaged to be married, and absolutely darkens her world to her during 'a Naini Tal dinner for thirty-five', is of consummate adroitness. What a 'Naini Tal[1] dinner' is I have not the slightest conception, but it is evidently something very sumptuous and public, and if any practised hand of the old social school could have contrived the thrust and parry under the fire of

[1][Naini Tal is a hill station near Lucknow.]

seventy critical eyes better than young Mr. Kipling has done, I know not who that writer is. In quite another way the pathos of the little bride's delirium in 'The Valley of the Shadow' is of a very high, almost of the highest, order.

But, as a rule, Mr. Kipling's 'society' Anglo-Indians are not drawn better than those which other Indian novelists have created for our diversion. There is a sameness in the type of devouring female, and though Mr. Kipling devises several names for it, and would fain persuade us that Mrs. Herriott, and Mrs. Reiver, and Mrs. Hauksbee possess subtle differences which distinguish them, yet I confess I am not persuaded. They all—and the Venus Annodomini as well—appear to me to be the same high-colored, rather ill-bred, not wholly spoiled professional coquette. Mr. Kipling seems to be too impatient of what he calls 'the shiny top-scum stuff people call civilization' to paint these ladies very carefully. 'The Phantom Rickshaw', in which a hideously selfish man is made to tell the story of his own cruelty and of his mechanical remorse, is indeed highly original, but here it is the man, not the woman, in whom we are interested. The proposal of marriage in the dust-storm in 'False Dawn', a theatrical, lurid scene, though scarcely natural, is highly effective. The archery contest in 'Cupid's Arrows' needs only to be compared with a similar scene in 'Daniel Deronda' to show how much more closely Mr. Kipling keeps his eye on detail than George Eliot did. But these things are rare in this class of his stories, and too often the Anglo-Indian social episodes are choppy, unconvincing, and not very refined.

All is changed when the central figure is a man. Mr. Kipling's officials and civilians are admirably vivid and of an amazing variety. If any one wishes to know why this new author has been received with joy and thankfulness by the Anglo-Saxon world, it is really not necessary for him to go further for a reason than to the moral tale of 'The Conversion of Aurelian McGoggin'. Let the author of that tract speak for himself.

Every man is entitled to his own religious opinions;

but no man—least of all a junior—has a right to thrust these down other men's throats. The government sends out weird civilians now and again; but McGoggin was the queerest exported for a long time. He was clever—brilliantly clever—but his cleverness worked the wrong way. Instead of keeping to the study of the vernaculars, he had read some books written by a man called Comte, I think, and a man called Spencer, and a Professor Clifford. [You will find these books in the Library.] They deal with people's insides from the point

of view of men who have no stomachs. There was no order against his reading
them, but his mama should have smacked him. . . . I do not say a word against
this creed. It was made up in town, where there is nothing but machinery and
asphalt and building—all shut in by the fog. . . . But in this country [India],
where you really see humanity—raw, brown, naked humanity—with nothing
between it and the blazing sky, and only the used-up, over-handled earth under-
foot, the notion somehow dies away, and most folk come back to simpler
theories.

Those who will not come back to simpler theories are prigs, for
whom the machine-made notion is higher than experience. Now Mr.
Kipling, in his warm way, hates many things, but he hates the prig for
preference. Aurelian McGoggin, better known as the Blastoderm, is a
prig of the over-educated type, and upon him falls the awful calamity
of sudden and complete nerve-collapse. Lieutenant Golightly, in the
story which bears his name, is a prig who values himself for spotless
attire and clockwork precision of manner; he therefore is mauled and
muddied up to his eyes, and then arrested under painfully derogatory
conditions. In 'Lispeth' we get the missionary prig, who thinks that
the Indian instincts can be effaced by a veneer of Christianity. Mr.
Kipling hates 'the sheltered life'. The men he likes are those who have
been thrown out of their depth at an early age, and taught to swim off
a boat. The very remarkable story of 'Thrown Away' shows the effect
of preparing for India by a life 'unspotted from the world' in England;
it is as hopelessly tragic as any in Mr. Kipling's somewhat grim
repertory.

Against the régime of the prig Mr. Kipling sets the régime of
Strickland. Over and over again he introduces this mysterious figure,
always with a phrase of extreme approval. Strickland is in the police,
and his power consists in his determination to know the East as the
natives know it. He can pass through the whole of Upper India,
dressed up as a fakir, without attracting the least attention. Sometimes,
as in 'Beyond the Pale', he may know too much. But this is an exception, and personal to himself. Mr. Kipling's conviction is that this is
the sort of man to pervade India for us, and that one Strickland is
worth a thousand self-conceited civilians. But even below the Indian
prig, because he has at least known India, is the final object of Mr.
Kipling's loathing, 'Pagett, M.P.', the radical English politician who
comes out for four months to set everybody right. His chastisement is
always severe and often comic. But in one very valuable paper, which
Mr. Kipling must not be permitted to leave unreprinted, 'The

Enlightenments of Pagett, M.P.', he has dealt elaborately and quite seriously with this noxious creature. Whether Mr. Kipling is right or wrong, far be it from me in my ignorance to pretend to know. But his way of putting these things is persuasive.

Since Mr. Kipling has come back from India he has written about society 'of sorts' in England. Is there not perhaps in him something of Pagett, M.P., turned inside out? As a delineator of English life, at all events, he is not yet thoroughly master of his craft. Everything he writes has vigor and picturesqueness. But 'The Lamentable Comedy of Willow Wood' is the sort of thing that any extremely brilliant Burman, whose English, if slightly odd, was nevertheless unimpeachable, might write of English ladies and gentlemen, having never been in England. *The Record of Badalia Herodsfoot* was in every way better, more truly observed, more credible, more artistic, but yet a little too cynical and brutal to come straight from life. And last of all there is the novel of *The Light that Failed*, with its much-discussed two endings, its oases of admirable detail in a desert of the undesirable, with its extremely disagreeable woman, and its far more brutal and detestable man, presented to us, the precious pair of them, as typical specimens of English society. I confess that it is *The Light that Failed* that has wakened me to the fact that there are limits to this dazzling new talent, the éclat of which had almost lifted us off our critical feet.

The conception of Strickland would be very tantalizing and incomplete if we were not permitted to profit from his wisdom and experience. But, happily, Mr. Kipling is perfectly willing to take us below the surface, and to show us glimpses of the secret life of India. In so doing he puts forth his powers to their fullest extent, and I think it cannot be doubted that the tales which deal with native manners are not merely the most curious and interesting which Mr. Kipling has written, but are also the most fortunately constructed. Every one who has thought over this writer's mode of execution will have been struck with the skill with which his best work is restrained within certain limits. When inspiration flags with him, indeed, his stories may grow too long, or fail, as if from languor, before they reach their culmination. But his best short stories—and among his best we include the majority of his native Indian tales—are cast at once, as if in a mould; nothing can be detached from them without injury. In this consists his great technical advantage over almost all his English rivals; we must look to France or to America for stories fashioned in this way. In several of his tales of Indian manners this skill reaches its highest because most complicated expression. It may be comparatively easy to hold within artistic bonds a gentle episode of European amorosity. To deal, in the same form, but with infinitely greater audacity, with the muffled passions and mysterious instincts of India, to slur over nothing, to emphasize nothing, to give in some twenty pages the very spicy odour of the East, this is marvelous.

Not less than this Mr. Kipling has done in a little group of stories which I cannot but hold to be the culminating point of his genius so far. If the remainder of his writings were swept away, posterity would be able to reconstruct its Rudyard Kipling from 'Without Benefit of Clergy', 'The Man who Would be King', 'The Strange Ride of Morrowbie Jukes', and 'Beyond the Pale'. More than that, if all record of Indian habits had been destroyed, much might be conjectured from them of the pathos, the splendor, the cruelty, and the mystery of India. From 'The Gate of the Hundred Sorrows' more is to be gleaned of the real action of opium-smoking, and the causes of that indulgence, than from many sapient debates in the British House of Commons. We come very close to the confines of the moonlight-colored world of magic in 'The Bisara of Pooree'. For pure horror and for the hopeless impenetrability of the native conscience there is 'The Recrudescence of Imray'. In a revel of color and shadow, at the close of the audacious and Lucianic story of 'The Incarnation of Krishna Mulvaney', we peep for a moment into the mystery of 'a big queen's praying at Benares'.

Admirable, too, are the stories which deal with the results of attempts made to melt the Asiatic and the European into one. The red-headed Irish-Thibetan who makes the king's life a burden to him in the fantastic story of 'Namgay Doola' represents one extremity of this chain of grotesque Eurasians: Michele D'Cruze, the wretched little black police inspector, with a drop of white blood in his body, who wakes up to energetic action at one supreme moment of his life, is at the other. The relapse of the converted Indian is a favorite theme with this cynical observer of human nature. It is depicted in 'The Judgment of Dungara', with a rattling humor worthy of Lever, where the whole mission, clad in white garments woven of the scorpion nettle, go mad with fire and plunge into the river, while the trumpet of the god bellows triumphantly from the hills. In 'Lispeth' we have a study—much less skilfully worked out, however—of the Indian woman carefully Christianized from childhood reverting at once to heathenism when her passions reach maturity.

The lover of good literature, however, is likely to come back to the four stories which we named first in this section. They are the very flower of Mr. Kipling's work up to the present moment, and on these we base our highest expectations for his future. 'Without Benefit of Clergy' is a study of the Indian woman as wife and mother, uncovenanted wife of the English civilian and mother of his son. The tremulous passion of Ameera, her hopes, her fears, and her agonies of disappointment, combine to form by far the most tender page which Mr. Kipling has written. For pure beauty the scene where Holden, Ameera, and the baby count the stars on the housetop for Tota's horoscope is so characteristic that, although it is too long to quote in full, its opening paragraph must here be given as a specimen of Mr. Kipling's style in this class of work.

Ameera climbed the narrow staircase that led to the flat roof. The child, placid and unwinking, lay in the hollow of her right arm, gorgeous in silver-fringed muslin, with a small skull-cap on his head. Ameera wore all that she valued most. The diamond nose-stud that takes the place of the Western patch in drawing attention to the curve of the nostril, the gold ornament in the center of the forehead studded with tallow-drop emeralds and flawed rubies, the heavy circlet of beaten gold that was fastened round her neck by the softness of the pure metal, and the clinking curb-patterned silver anklets hanging low over the rosy ankle-bones. She was dressed in jade-green muslin, as befitted a daughter of the Faith, and from shoulder to elbow and elbow to wrist ran bracelets of silver tied with floss silk; frail glass bangles slipped over the wrist in proof of the slenderness of the hand, and certain heavy gold bracelets that had no part in her country's ornaments, but, since they were Holden's gifts, and fastened with a cunning European snap, delighted her immensely.

They sat down by the low white parapet of the roof, overlooking the city and its light.

What tragedy was in store for the gentle astrologer, or in what darkness of waters the story ends, it is needless to repeat here.

In 'The Strange Ride of Morrowbie Jukes' a civil engineer stumbles by chance on a ghastly city of the dead who do not die, trapped into it, down walls of shifting sand, on the same principle as the ant-lion secures its prey, the parallel being so close that one half suspects Mr. Kipling of having invented a human analogy to the myrmeleon. The abominable settlement of living dead men is so vividly described, and the wonders of it are so calmly, and, as it were, so temperately discussed, that no one who possesses the happy gift of believing can fail to be persuaded of the truth of the tale. The character of Gunga Dass, a Deccanee Brahmin whom Jukes finds in this reeking village, and who, reduced to the bare elements of life, preserves a little, though exceedingly little, of his old traditional obsequiousness, is an admirable study. But all such considerations are lost, as we read the story first, in the overwhelming and Poe-like horror of the situation and the extreme novelty of the conception.

A still higher place, however, I am inclined to claim for the daring invention of 'The Man who Would be King'. This is a longer story than is usual with Mr. Kipling, and it depends for its effect, not upon any epigrammatic surprise or extravagant denouement of the intrigue, but on an imaginative effort brilliantly sustained through a detailed succession of events. Two ignorant and disreputable Englishmen, exiles from social life, determine to have done with the sordid struggle, and to close with a try for nothing less than empire. They are seen by the journalist who narrates the story to disappear northward from the Kumharsan Serai disguised as a mad priest and his servant starting to sell whirligigs to the Ameer of Kabul. Two years later there stumbles into the newspaper office a human creature bent into a circle, and moving his feet one over the other like a bear. This is the surviving adventurer, who, half dead and half dazed, is roused by doses of raw whisky into a condition which permits him to unravel the squalid and splendid chronicle of adventures beyond the utmost rim of mountains, adventures on the veritable throne of Kafiristan. The tale is recounted with great skill as from the lips of the dying king. At first, to give the needful impression of his faint, bewildered state, he mixes up his narrative, whimpers, forgets, and repeats his phrases; but by the time the curiosity of the reader is fully arrested, the tale has become limpid and straightforward enough. When it has to be drawn to a close, the symptoms of aphasia and brain-lesion are repeated. This story is conceived and conducted in the finest spirit of an artist. It is strange to the verge of being incredible, but it never outrages possibility, and the severe moderation of the author preserves our credence throughout.

It is in these Indian stories that Mr. Kipling displays more than anywhere else the accuracy of his eye and the retentiveness of his memory. No detail escapes him, and, without seeming to emphasize the fact, he is always giving an exact feature where those who are in possession of fewer facts or who see less vividly are satisfied with a shrewd generality.

In Mr. Kipling's first volume there was one story which struck quite a different note from all the others, and gave promise of a new delineator of children. 'Tods' Amendment', which is a curiously constructed piece of work, is in itself a political allegory. It is to be noticed that when he warms to his theme the author puts aside the trifling fact that Tods is an infant of six summers, and makes him give a clear statement of collated native opinion worthy of a barrister in ample practice. What led to the story, one sees without difficulty, was the wish to emphasize the fact that unless the Indian government humbles itself, and becomes like Tods, it can never legislate with efficiency, because it never can tell what all the *jhampanis* and *saises* in the bazaar really wish for. If this were all, Mr. Kipling in creating Tods would have shown no more real acquaintance with children than other political allegorists have shown with sylphs or Chinese philosophers. But Mr. Kipling is always an artist, and in order to make a setting for his child-professor of jurisprudence, he invented a really convincing and delightful world of conquering infancy. Tods, who lives up at Simla with Tods' mama, and knows everybody, is 'an utterly fearless young pagan', who pursues his favorite kid even into the sacred presence of the Supreme Legislative Council, and is on terms of equally well-bred familiarity with the Viceroy and with Futteh Khan, the villainous loafer *khit* from Mussoorie.

To prove that 'Tods' Amendment' was not an accident, and also, perhaps, to show that he could write about children purely and simply, without any afterthought of allegory, he brought out, as the sixth instalment of the 'Indian Railway Library', a little volume entirely devoted to child-life. Of the four stories contained in this book one is among the finest productions of its author, while two others are very good indeed. There are also, of course, the children in *The Light that Failed*, although they are too closely copied from the author's previous creations in 'Baa, Baa, Black Sheep'; and in other writings of his children take a position sufficiently prominent to justify us in considering this as one of the main divisions of his work.

In his preface to *Wee Willie Winkie* Mr. Kipling has sketched for us the attitude which he adopts towards babies. 'Only women,' he says, but we may doubt if he means it, 'understand children thoroughly; but if a mere man keeps very quiet, and humbles himself properly, and refrains from talking down to his superiors, the children will sometimes be good to him, and let him see what they think about the world.' This is a curious form of expression, and suggests the naturalist more than the lover of children. So might we conceive a successful zoologist describing the way to note the habits of wild animals and birds, by keeping very quiet, and lying low in the grass, and refraining from making sudden noises. This is, indeed, the note by which we may distinguish Mr. Kipling from such true lovers of childhood as Mrs. Ewing. He has no very strong emotion in the matter, but he patiently and carefully collects data, partly out of his own faithful and capacious personal memory, partly out of what he observes.

The Tods type he would probably insist that he has observed. A finer and more highly developed specimen of it is given in *Wee Willie Winkie*, the hero of which is a noble infant of overpowering vitality, who has to be put under military discipline to keep him in any sort of domestic order, and who, while suffering under two days' confinement to barracks (the house and veranda), saves the life of a headstrong girl. The way in which Wee Willie Winkie—who is of Mr. Kipling's favorite age, six—does this is at once wholly delightful and a terrible strain to credence. The baby sees Miss Allardyce cross the river, which he has always been forbidden to do, because the river is the frontier, and beyond it are bad men, goblins, Afghans, and the like. He feels that she is in danger, he breaks mutinously out of barracks on his pony and follows her, and when she has an accident, and is surrounded by twenty hill-men, he saves her by his spirit and by his complicated display of resource. To criticize this story, which is told with infinite zest and picturesqueness, seems merely priggish. Yet it is contrary to Mr. Kipling's whole intellectual attitude to suppose him capable of writing what he knows to be supernatural romance. We have therefore to suppose that in India infants 'of the dominant race' are so highly developed at six, physically and intellectually, as to be able to ride hard, alone, across a difficult river, and up pathless hilly country, to contrive a plan for succoring a hapless lady, and to hold a little regiment of savages at bay by mere force of eye. If Wee Willie Winkie had been twelve instead of six, the feat would have been just possible. But then the romantic contrast between the baby and his virile deeds would not have been nearly so piquant. In all this Mr. Kipling, led away by sentiment and a false ideal, is not quite the honest craftsman that he should be.

But when, instead of romancing and creating, he is content to observe children, he is excellent in this as in other branches of careful natural history. But the children he observes, are, or we much misjudge him, himself. 'Baa, Baa, Black Sheep' is a strange compound of work at first and second hand. Aunty Rosa (delightfully known, without a suspicion of supposed relationship, as 'Anti-rosa'), the Mrs. Squeers of the Rocklington lodgings, is a sub-Dickensian creature, tricked out with a few touches of reality, but mainly a survival of early literary hatreds. The boy Harry and the soft little sister of Punch are rather shadowy. But Punch lives with an intense vitality, and here, without any indiscretion, we may be sure that Mr. Kipling has looked inside his own heart and drawn from memory. Nothing in the autobiographies of their childhood by Tolstoi and Pierre Loti, nothing in Mr. R. L. Stevenson's 'Child's Garden of Verses', is more valuable as a record of the development of childhood than the account of how Punch learned to read, moved by curiosity to know what the 'falchion' was with which the German man split the Griffin open. Very nice, also, is the reference to the mysterious rune, called 'Sonny, my Soul',[1] with which mama used to sing Punch to sleep.

By far the most powerful and ingenious story, however, which Mr. Kipling has yet dedicated to a study of childhood is 'The Drums of The Fore and Aft'. 'The Fore and Aft' is a nickname given in derision to a crack regiment, whose real title is 'The Fore and Fit', in memory of a sudden calamity which befell them on a certain day in an Afghan pass, when if it had not been for two little blackguard drummer-boys, they would have been woefully and contemptibly cut to pieces, as they were routed, by a dashing troop of Ghazis. The two little heroes, who only conquer to die, are called Jakin and Lew, stunted children of fourteen, 'gutter-birds' who drink and smoke and 'do everything but lie', and are the disgrace of the regiment. In their little souls, however, there burns what Mr. Pater would call a 'hard, gem-like flame' of patriotism, and they are willing to undergo any privation, if only they may wipe away the stigma of being 'bloomin' non-combatants'. In the intervals of showing us how that stain was completely removed, Mr. Kipling gives us not merely one of the most thrilling and effective battles in fiction, but a singularly delicate portrait of two grubby little souls turned white and splendid by an element of native greatness. It would be difficult to point to a page of modern English more poignant than that which describes how 'the only acting-drummers who were took along',—and—left, behind, moved forward across the pass alone to the enemy's front, and sounded on drum and fife the return of the regiment to duty. But perhaps the most remarkable feature of the whole story is that a record of shocking British retreat

[1] [The hymn 'sun of my soul . . .']

and failure is so treated as to flatter in its tenderest susceptibilities the pride of British patriotism.

Mr. Kipling's début was made in a volume of verse, called *Departmental Ditties*, which has continued to enjoy considerable popularity and has frequently been reprinted. This collection of comical and satirical pieces representative of Indian official life has, however, very slight literary value. The verses in it are mostly imitations of popular English and American bards, with but here and there a trace of the true accent of the author in such strong though ill-executed strains as 'The Story of Uriah', and 'The Song of the Women'. In other cases they follow, but more faintly, the lines of the author's prose stories. It cannot be said that in this collection Mr. Kipling soars above the 'Ali Babas' and 'Aliph Cheems' who strike an agreeable lyre for the entertainment of their fellow Anglo-Indians. No claim for the title of poet could be founded on literary baggage so slight as *Departmental Ditties*.

Of late years, however, Mr. Kipling has put forward, in a great variety of directions, essays in verse which deserve much higher consideration. He has indulged the habit of prefixing to his prose stories fragments of poems which must be his own, for there is nobody else to claim them. Some of these are as vivid and tantalizing as the tiny bits we possess of lost Greek tragedians. Among them is to be found this extract from a 'barrack-room ballad' used to introduce the story of 'The Madness of Private Ortheris':

> Oh! where would I be when my froat was dry?
> Oh! where would I be when the bullets fly?
> Oh! where would I be when I come to die?
>   Why,
> Somewheres anigh my chum,
>   If 'e's liquor 'e'll give me some,
>   If I'm dying 'e'll 'old my 'ead,
> An' 'e'll write 'em 'ome when I'm dead.
>   God send us a trusty chum!

There must have been not a few readers who, like the present writer, on finding this nugget of ballad-doggerel, felt that here was a totally unworked field just touched by the spade, and left. Happily, Mr. Kipling has digged farther and deeper, and he has written a series of barrack-room ballads which are unique in their kind, and of which scarcely one but is of definite and permanent value. The only writer who has, to my mind, in any degree anticipated the mixture of vulgar and realistic phraseology with the various elements of pathos combined in the lives of rough young men exiled from home is the Australian poet Adam Lindsay Gordon, whom Mr. Kipling greatly excels in variety of metre and force of language. Except in its sardonic form, humor has never been a prominent feature of Mr. Kipling's prose. I hardly know an instance of it not disturbed by irony or savagery, except the story of 'Moti Guj', the mutineer elephant. But in some of the *Barrack-Room Ballads* there is found the light of a genuine humor. What can be more delightful, for instance, than this appreciative description of Fuzzy-Wuzzy, by one of the Soudan force who has had to deal with him in the bush?

[quotes last stanza of 'Fuzzy-Wuzzy': DV, pp. 400–1]

But more often, underneath the rollicking storm of the verses, there may be heard the melancholy which is characteristic of so much of the best modern writing, the murmur of that *Weltschmerz* which is never far off, at all events, from Mr. Kipling's verse. It sometimes seems as though it were the author himself who speaks to us in the soldier's impatience at the colorlessness and restraint of Western life. And it is with the exquisite melody of his own ballad of 'Mandalay' that we leave the author who has so strangely moved and fascinated us, who has enlarged our horizon on one wholly neglected side, and from whom, in the near future, we have a right to expect so much imaginative invigoration. But what is he saying?

Ship me somewhere east of Suez where the best is like the worst,
Where there are n't no Ten Commandments, an' a man can raise a thirst;
For the temple-bells are callin', an' it's there that I would be—
By the old Moulmein Pagoda, lookin' lazy at the sea—
        On the road to Mandalay,
        Where the old flotilla lay,
With our sick beneath the awnings when we went to Mandalay!
        Oh, the road to Mandalay,
        Where the flyin'-fishes play,
An' the dawn comes up like thunder out er China 'crost the bay!

Ah, yes! Mr. Kipling, go back to the far East! Yours is not the talent to bear with patience the dry-rot of London or of New York. Disappear, another Waring, and come back in ten years' time with a fresh and still more admirable budget of precious loot out of Wonderland!

18. The *Bookman* estimate; 'Kipling'

1891

Two articles from the *Bookman* (London), Vol. I, pp. 28–30 and 63–6 (October and November 1891), signed 'Y. Y.', and both headed 'The Work of Rudyard Kipling'.

The author has not so far been identified. Works of reference all give him as Robert Lynd (1879–1949) who used this pseudonym —but in 1891 Lynd was only twelve years old, and there were earlier essays and verses signed 'Y. Y.' even than this.

PART I

This attempt to estimate the work of Mr. Kipling shall be mainly illustrated from his last book, *Life's Handicap*, which is fairly representative, and will be freshest in the reader's memory. Is such an estimate premature? Is it unfair? I think not, and for this reason. If his career is not yet closed, at least one phase of it is. Nothing he may yet do is likely to alter, to enhance or impair, the rank he has already taken as an Observer and Recorder of what he has seen of Nature and Man. For such he is—nothing less, nor more.

On the very threshold lie three stumbling-blocks. First, the perplexing form in which his work has been presented to us. From time to time his stray stories have been hunted up and issued in small volumes, arranged on no apparent principle. Many were not worth re-printing—mere doting-Colonel-yarns of the nullah-in-the-foreground type, mess-room practical jokes, and dingy Simla scandals. These I shall simply ignore. All his best work might well have been wrought into his two books, *Black and White* and *Soldiers Three*. Secondly, he is furiously popular. His books sell like the *Sporting Life* or Dr. Farrar's Sermons—and to the same buyers. He has been cuddled by the lewd people of the baser sort, who fancy themselves Athenians because they rave over Τι καινότερον—Robert Elsmeres, Shes, Hes, Hermaphrodites, or what not. Lastly, he has been imported as an Infant Prodigy all the way from India, where he has performed with applause before all the crowned, uncrowned and discrowned heads. Here we at once get into the heart of the question.

Mr. Kipling is neither an Infant—if he ever was one—nor a Prodigy; but his training has been prodigious, if you like—at least in our sleek days. His writings as yet contain no avowedly autobiographical element. It would therefore be impertinent to repeat all that I have been privileged to learn about his early career, and I apologise for mentioning even so much as is directly to my purpose. His gifts of eye and mind are hereditary. Exiled to England like other Indian children he at last broke his chain, found his way back, and sacrificing the advantages of a finished education entered as a mere youth the hard school of journalism. Thus much, and no more.

'But oh, think how wonderfully young!' Granted. Young he was—young he still is—in savage energy, fearless dash, careless confidence; but in other respects old—wonderfully old. He had seen much, heard much, noted much—more perhaps than is well for a lad—while other youthful eyes were riveted mostly on lexicons and cricket-stumps. And that too in a land of varied races and rival civilisations and strange old obsolete, yet living religions, where even a boy who will see and think becomes perforce somewhat of a philosopher. True, he has not been ground small in our educational mill. But is that loss or gain? To us, I think, almost wholly gain. We have enough and to spare of prize graduates, quite as clever as he, who are going to turn out Bacons, Gibbons, and Matthew Arnolds. But somehow they are all so dreadfully alike. Send them to India—as we do in fact. Tell them to look at a jungle, or a Jain temple; they will see just what Ruskin taught them to look for and nothing beyond. Bid them discourse of sepoys, priests, zenanas, village life; they will give you only the same views that other cautious, well-expressed persons have cautiously expressed so well before them. Ask them to judge, to criticise; they will try to tell you not what they themselves think, but what they think the majority of their cultured tribe must be thinking. Among so many Levites surely we have room for one sturdy Ishmael. He has never been taught to see, hear, reflect and describe in the proper Levitical, academical, second-hand way. He just has to do the best he can. What is that best? How has it been developed by his exceptional training? Space only permits me to hastily touch a few points.

As an observer and recorder Mr. Kipling is not really an Impressionist, but rather a Selecter. He does not—even in his 'City of Dreadful

Night'—give us a mere sidelight on a passing mood; he seems to see the whole, and make us see it too, by selecting and dashing down a very few intensely significant points. I do not mean that he draws a skeleton of the man or the landscape for our fancy to clothe at will. He takes the skeleton for granted, and just accentuates those half-dozen features of physiognomy which give the keynote to our first view and our last lingering memory of a man or a picture. Those who have visited or read much about India have the background and general composition already in their mind's eye; Mr. Kipling adds the magic touches—and the picture lives. His method is the reverse of Balzac's, but to me at least, as satisfying.

This power of selection naturally involves dramatic art, the instinct of construction and the ineffable tact of omission. These gifts he sometimes misuses and abuses, and too often wholly neglects, as in the ill-judged introductions to some of his stories. But at its best his art is supreme. 'The Finances of the Gods' is a masterpiece—so tiny, so compact, so homogenous—prologue, legend and epilogue, so simply graceful, so paternally tender, such an interior—one almost fancies Metsu painting an Indian conversation-piece—such a seeming lightness, such a deep undercurrent of significance—nothing less than the infiltration, the saturation of a nation's whole life by a Faith to us impossibly grotesque! You think this exaggeration? then clearly you have only skimmed the story instead of studying, analysing, and dissecting it. Another short sketch, 'Little Tobrah', illustrates still more signally the instinctive knowledge of what to omit. Its intense directness is electric. But enough, for pages would not suffice for analysing the varied forms of Mr. Kipling's dramatic art, varied because unconventional.

Again, note his youthful confidence. Right or wrong he never hesitates, balances, shuffles, sees both ways at once—clearly he never practised writing essays for the headmaster.

Humour he possesses, but it is of the grim, broad, not wholly happy, Yorkshire type—the humour of experience. His wit is less striking, save in his felicitous and pregnant epigrams; for example take this—'the Russian is a delightful person till he tucks in his shirt', or this—'East of Suez, some hold, the direct control of Providence ceases'.

His narrative style may lack symmetry and taste, but now and then phrases flash out of native force and beauty. This of a caged wild beast asleep—'troubled by some dream of the forests of his freedom'—or this of the Amir—'His word is red law; by the gust of his passion falls the leaf of man's life, and his favour is terrible'—though here perhaps we may trace an Oriental model. Indeed, long passages might be selected of vivid, nay majestic force, or pathetic beauty marred only by a few blemishes. When he observes most keenly, he describes most eloquently, as you will own if you study the perfect sentence on page 37 about the Indian starlight. And above all he has never learnt the trick of reeling off neat pages of something or other about nothing.

One other feature in his rich variety—variety, look you, not versatility. His method never changes, but he applies it with equal force to such varied material, such diverse experiences—for experiences they must surely be. His German, his Fenian, his Rajah, his Yorkshire Methodist, his Malay murderer, his Burmese priest, his Moslem mullah, even Bimi the orang-outang, are as Shakspearian as his Soldiers Three—that is, each is a veritably individual specimen of a district generic type. Once rightly conceive the relations of individual, species and genus—that is, if you can—and you may conjure up a living man in ten lines, instead of manufacturing him in a whole chapter.

The final result of this peculiar self-training is an attitude, a manner, a style of presentation wholly personal and individual. There is something like it in much of the nervous, high-pressure work of the best American, and probably also Anglo-Indian, journalism. Yet not quite the same. Mr. Kipling will of course find imitators, but among his predecessors, can we point to a single page which could be mistaken for his best work? Whether it be good, whether it be bad, he has added yet another to the many forms of English literature.

Such are the more obvious merits of his books, viewed from the purely literary and artistic side. But he has also *les défauts de ses qualités*. These, and with them far deeper and more suggestive questions—the moral significance, the human interest, the philosophic bearing, the present achievement and the future promise of his work—remain yet untreated.

PART II

It has been already hinted that Mr. Kipling has the defects which spring from his merits. His quick, bold style of presentation often strains and fatigues the attention; his scenic construction, when extended to trifles, sometimes sinks to burlesque; his dogmatic assurance and daring satire is bound to stab many a respectable prejudice. Further, a self-formed style must always seem a tacit outrage upon the great accepted models unless itself rises to the rank of a model. Mr.

Kipling's style is no model, nor is it even quite original. Tainted with the flippancy of journalism and the distressing smartness of trans-Atlantic buffoonery, it is by no means that of the artless child of Nature who 'pipes but as the throstles sing'. Superfine vulgarians have called him vulgar. Vulgar he is not. His occasional untowardness or forwardness has no real affinity to the innately vulgar and subtly vulgarising tone of a Charles Reade or a Theodore Hook. To me, indeed, his errors of taste seem but the price we pay for the unconventional evolution of his genius. And so far we gain more than we lose.

Good print is well; good style is better; best of all is good matter. Such, at least, is the due order of excellence in the eyes of the sober Bookman, who would not love books so well, loved he not knowledge more. In Mr. Kipling's manner I have pointed to some admirable qualities marred by a few glaring yet pardonable blemishes. It remains to ask what is it that he has to say—wherein and how far are we the richer or the better for it?

One verdict has been given already. The big battalions of railway-readers on whose *popularis aura* our writers are now wafted to fame—that myriad-eyed Argus intent on Tit-bits, Scraps and Orts, has long since decided with the enviable promptitude to be expected of a critic who sees his way at a glance into the inmost Secret of Bradshaw. *Life's Handicap* has amused and excited him—what more would you have? Yet the oracles of the smoking carriage are truer than their echoes in the penny press. The morning paper which at present I take in, in a brief notice just admires and quotes the (really unsatisfactory) Preface, decides that the stories are 'very smart and imbued with a strong worldly philosophy', and closes by singling out three as 'especially striking', of which the first, I own, is excellent, the second peculiarly inartistic and repulsive, the third the one palpable failure in the series. Yet even such criticism serves its turn. Few care to dig deeper. The popular interest in Humanity is mainly centred on its choicest specimen—oneself. Millions ride in cabs; only hundreds criticise the horse; only tens study the cabman. Smart and worldly—such is the very last word of the railroad critics who only read as they run.

He who leisurely turns the pages will seek and will find more than amusement. Much that seems, much that is, wholly new will startle him; he will ask himself: are these things true? how did the author get hold of them? what does he really think about them? what would he have me think? what do I think? Of some such train of thought, limited to his best prose work, here are a few results.

His avowed purpose is described in the Preface thus—'Chiefly I write of Life and Death, and men and women and Love and Fate'. This is true enough, though the Preface is but a disingenuous mystification contradicted by its business-like last sentences—a mere clever *jeu d'esprit* composed to bind together a random collection of stories. Men, and in a less degree women and children—even brutes, as dogs, apes and elephants, in so far as they present inchoate human elements— are Mr. Kipling's absorbing theme.

His peculiar attitude towards Nature proves this. True, he has the artist-eye. His reading of Indian scenery is, I am assured, not less exactly truthful than it seems. But he has nothing of the Wordsworthian, vague, yearning sympathy with Nature. His marvellous, often terrible, pictures of elemental phenomena—seasons, heat, cold, rain and flood— are always drawn in the light of man's enjoyment or misery. If ever his landscape lacks some foreground figures their place is supplied by a human suggestion of loneliness. He is no pious Pantheist to whom the earth is but a great globular god, with Rydal Mount for its pole—an all-sufficing Paradise sadly marred by the intrusion of Adam's children with their odious railways and waterworks. True, in a splendid night description he says: 'the earth was a grey shadow more unreal than the sky. We could hear her breathing lightly in the pauses between the howling of the jackals and the movement of the wind in the tamarisks;' but then he adds his touches of human interest, the 'fitful mutter of musketry-fire leagues away', a 'native woman singing in some un-seen hut', and the 'mail-train thundering by'. For this 'even breathing of the crowded earth' is not the charming repose of flowers and trees and pretty birds; he is thinking of the mighty Indian soil strewn with myriad tired, stark men, as it were some vast beach at the tremulous pause of the low tide of humanity. To him the earth is the Lord's and the fulness thereof, but that lord is Mankind. No mystical hypostatic union of the human Soul with the divine Nature of sunsets, waterfalls, larks, and lesser celandines: Nature, the world, is simply the home, the environment of man, the mere scenery of the supreme drama of human struggle, failure, or success.

In what spirit, by what method, has he studied men? The answer is involved in the further question of his veracity. And here I find myself at fault. On the one hand a high—perhaps the very highest—authority on India tells me that Mr. Kipling's portraitures of native character and opinions are simply brilliant imaginative creations based only on limited and superficial observation. On the other hand, I confess that my own experience seldom clashes with his European characters, and that his Oriental element, which is infinitely the more interesting, seems to strengthen, but never conflict with the impressions left by such masters as Burton and Meadows Taylor, and by the only Hindu of first-rate intellect and real learning whose mind I ever studied at leisure. This presumption I do not justify, but may fairly palliate by large concessions. I grant that in his coarser work Mr. Kipling has contented himself with conventional types like his Simla flirts, and wooden officials; that he has never penetrated the inner working of the mighty machine of Government; that of the highest class, both native and English, he has little to say, and that mostly in a vein of comic exaggeration and contemptuous raillery, for all this is patent. For instance, he makes the 'Very Greatest of All the Viceroys' promote a native pet from Bengal to the North West Service. Surely this was beyond the power even of the Most Mischievous of All the Mediocrities, though the satire is fair enough in principle. Again, in his satirical and allegorical sketches he takes strange licences; for example, in 'Namgay Doolah' a savage family with three-fourths of Thibetan and only one-fourth of Irish blood, all have red hair, and by pure hereditary instinct cut off cows' tails, wear black masks, and take blood-money to betray their own kin. But this, like 'Naboth', is clearly allegory. Again, elephant yarns are probably the Indian equivalent for English dog-stories; hence the farcical exaggerations of 'Moti Guj'. Granted, too, that so young a man cannot possibly have studied profoundly and exhaustively every inch of the ground he covers, granted much more—for these concessions are but my own suggestions—the dilemma remains, either a creative genius well-nigh incredible, or a very considerable basis of experience. For my own part, inclining to the latter, I would fain combine both views, and in this way. Where Mr. Kipling is careless, or deficient, or wrong is precisely where we have no lack of trustworthy guides. Great men, great matters, great theories—not such are his true province, but the infinitely little, yet supremely significant trifles which cling closest round the core of humanity. Of these, the statesman, the statistician, the traveller is silent. They will tell you correctly all about the Native—his land-system, his creed, his literature, his social system, his customs, his manners, his general un-Englishism—and you wonder at the odd creature. The Storyteller takes up the lifeless image, adds a few bold touches, making it odder than ever, but you cease to wonder—it seems after all but a man of like passions with yourself, to be either familiarly kicked, or taken by the hand. It seems—nay, it is. For correctness is not truth. The practised eye may detect in these native portraits many discrepancies, errors, and omissions; the outsider, rightly or wrongly, will feel them to be true, and deny that even genius can make bricks without straw. He will even doubt whether the high official mind can fully gauge the opportunities for seeing and hearing which a varied, more or less Bohemian, unofficial life may have afforded. On these Mr. Kipling has built up a definite body of opinion. Little of personal reminiscence can be detected, save in his short novel; most of his stories have been picked up, some wholly invented, but into each he weaves the already arranged and labelled results of his observation—each at least reads like a first-hand experience. Whether an Observer or a Creator, he is equally original. It may be that, like Darwin with his Cirripedia, he at first concentrated himself on a few typical characters, and by this training matured his power of rapidly discriminating each new type he comes across. He does not present, of course, George Eliot's close analysis of complex and conflicting motive—his men are active animals, not ruminants—but in a masterly way he does single out what we may call the main efficient cause of conduct, whether it be a ruling passion or a momentary impulse. And to find it he goes down to the very depths.

Mark, too, his careful racial discrimination. He never confounds the turns and tricks of thought of his Irish, Yorkshire, and Cockney soldiers, or of his varied Orientals. How boldly in 'Pambe Serang' does he contrast the Malay and African traits! How grandly he brings out in the 'Amir's Homily' the secret of Eastern despotism! How exquisitely in the last pages of 'Without Benefit of Clergy' that loveliest of Oriental traits, the courteous, unobtrusive, reverent sympathy with one stricken of God. Vambéry, Burton, Morier, even Palgrave, no doubt bring us nearer to the secret of Moslem character; he alone is at home with all sorts and conditions of men. Take the rigmarole evidence of the coolies (p. 12); there you have the Bengali as ages of servitude have made him, a well-meaning, fawning, crafty, yet transparent liar— the liar of instinct of self-preservation. Or take 'Through the Fire', or 'Little Tobrah'; how utterly un-European is every feeling, every motive, every standard of conduct, yet how utterly human! Correct or not, it is—surely it must be—true.

And it would be truer still if he dared. We live a century too late and too soon for speaking out; but sometimes, as in 'On the Wall', he throws off the fetters. Bold or reticent by turns, he never discloses his ethical system. Probably it is yet incomplete. Like Zola, he never comments or moralises, but so artfully arranges the facts that the inferences become irresistible. In 'Without Benefit of Clergy'—the very title is polemical—those inferences amount to a homily.

If his ethics are obscure, they are always manly. Courage, endurance, fidelity, discipline, the joy of living, of working, of fighting—every spring of virile conduct he delights in. This naturally implies a certain tincture of brutal coarseness, already sufficiently bewailed by the critics. I will therefore only say—and say emphatically—that to this coarseness we owe the purity, the depth, and the intensity of his pathos. In that superb study, 'Greenhow Hill', are a few lines, the death of 'Liza' when for a brief moment the Woman survives the Saint, to which I know no parallel whatever in literature, so poignant its feeling, so profound its philosophy, so instinctive its truth. He only who has studied the coarse animalism of strong men can understand and portray their flashes of supreme tenderness and their numb, speechless grief. Herein we trace the only true affinity to the work of Mr. Bret Harte. Rugged yet affecting pathos is perhaps the highest attribute of Mr. Kipling's genius, and it comes of his penetrating insight into the hearts of men, not indeed the whole heart—a Tito Melema is beyond his grasp—but its inmost part, its most strenuous pulsation, the secret of its very self.

I pass lightly over his two most obvious errors of conception, both results of an imperfect training. Sometimes he stoops to the Supernatural, sinking as low as the prophecies in 'Dinah Shadd', the dog rubbish in 'Imray', the snake lies on page 232, and that vile tale, 'The Mark of the Beast'. Again, he has not yet shaken off his morbid love of journalistic 'horrors', 'shocking discoveries'—that is to say, putrid corpses, painful suffering, and spilled blood. Such 'horrors' do not shock—they only disgust.

Finally, his attitude towards the world of men is very much that of an eager, attentive, observant, sharp-eyed sight-seer. Much in him that looks like sympathy is really only strong interest. He always preserves a certain cynical aloofness; he never, like Dickens, fondles his puppets; none of them, not even Mulvaney, seems dearer to him than another. Hence his somewhat repellent, unfriendly personality as an author. Contrast him with Lamb or Montaigne or Rabelais; of them in no sense could Flaubert say: '*l'œuvre est tout, l'homme est rien.*' And why? Because no one doubts the rounded completeness of the philosophy which Rabelais chose to conceal, or disdained to explain. Mr. Kipling's reticence is less suggestive. I doubt whether he yet has, or ever will have, a philosophy—a broad universal scheme into which all his thoughts and experiences can be harmoniously fitted. But without it no great, creative work is possible. Fielding had his great, tender humanity, Dickens his sentimental optimism, Goethe his belief in Spirit, Scott his trust in providential justice—one has the Christian faith, another fatalism—but all have some sheet anchor. Mr. Kipling, like so many of us, has none. And mark this—it is just when genius after its first daring flights is settling down for maturer triumphs that the lack of early discipline is felt. As it is with the painter so is it with the author. For then the mind, grasping to attain some higher, firmer, wider standpoint, falls back upon the half-forgotten, long-despaired, but never wholly eradicated teaching of school and college; self-discipline reproduces an echo of the ferule; law, order, precept, method, system, resume their sway, and Genius, now heated to fluidity in the fires of life, at last pours smoothly into the matrix chiselled for it by the master-spirits of all the ages. The scholar has become a man, both are fused into the philosopher. I wish, but dare not hope, that Mr. Kipling may yet attain that rich, ripe, sober, benevolent spirit, that repose of the heart, that balance of the brain, which makes the great humanist. His fresh start, *The Light that Failed*, was a false one. He may go on multiplying for our delight his Indian experiences; he may study new types in the West; but can a man feel a youth's quick impressions, or describe them with a youth's audacious energy? He may strengthen, but cannot alter his place in literature. That place is not beside the great masters of imperishable fiction, but high among those vivid, veracious, but fragmentary painters of life and manners by whose inestimable aid, as de Caylus aptly says: '*on sait vivre sans avoir vécu.*'

19. Mrs. Oliphant reviews *Life's Handicap*

1891

From an anonymous review of new books under the general heading of 'The Old Saloon' in *Blackwood's Magazine*, Vol. CL, pp. 728–35 (November 1891), credited to Mrs. Oliphant by *The Wellesley Index*.

Margaret Oliphant (1828–1897), well-known Scottish novelist, historian and biographer, had a life-long connection with *Blackwood's Magazine* in which much of her fiction appeared, as well as reviews: she also wrote the history of the publishing firm of William Blackwood and Sons. Kipling quotes from her best-known novel, *A Beleagured City* (1880) in *Stalky and Co.* (p. 123).

We know of no recent success in the world of literature which is at all equal to that of the young man who came to us from India a few years ago with a name unknown, and in that very short period has made himself such a reputation that everything he writes is not only looked for with eagerness by readers, but is enough to make the temporary fortune of any newspaper or cheap print which is fortunate enough to secure the blazon of that name. When we say he came to us unknown, we do not mean to ignore the fact that he brought with him from that distant empire of which the mass of us, who are not connected with any of the Indian services (a large exception, by the way), are so little acquainted—a blast of reputation and the work upon which that reputation was founded, the *Plain Tales*, in which the great Mulvaney and his comrades were first made known to the world: along with some other views of Indian soldiers and Indian civilians equally novel and wonderful. These revelations of a new world, pure gold of genius and poetic insight, were alloyed by many conventional and quite distasteful visions of something odious beyond the other developments of that generally odious thing 'society'—in the East: which no doubt had appeared, in various mess-rooms, club-rooms, and drawing-rooms, acquainted with Mrs. Hauksbee in her various incarnations, to be 'the

real thing', more thrilling and full of interest than mere stories about
natives and private soldiers. Mrs. Hauksbee was much in the front of
our young man's productions when he came to us with those early
works, not perhaps quite sure of his own genius nor of what was its
strength, and disposed to think (as we have been credibly informed)
in his youthful over-acquaintance and inacquaintance with life, that
his own precocious success was merely a 'boom', and would not last.
His last volume has completely proved, if proof had been necessary,
the inappropriateness of this conclusion. Mr. Rudyard Kipling, we
imagine, must now have discovered himself, his wonderful powers,
and the just direction of them, as he has discovered so many other
things. Not that it is easy to limit the application of these powers. He
came from India, the country of his education, and, we understand,
predilection, which he understands as few do, and cast his eyes by some
chance upon the slums of London—of which he forthwith produced a
tremendous picture, such as made into instant and vivid life the scenes
which a hundred ineffectual pens and voices have endeavoured to lay
before us. We saw the paper in which this extraordinary *aperçu* of a
situation and characters [*sic*] which must have been entirely new to the
writer only long enough for a single hurried reading; but it was enough
to make the London of those awful streets, and their strange but entirely true heroine, as real to us as any of the masterpieces of fiction.
The name of the woman was absurd. She was called Badaliah Hinds-
foot[1]—a name impossible both for fact and fiction; but this was the
only thing unreal about her. The story was also, perhaps, too painful
for a trim and permanent new edition; yet we hope we may have it
so ere long.

Those, however, who wish to avoid pain must not go to Mr.
Rudyard Kipling for pleasure. The thrill of emotion which he has the
gift to send tingling through and through his reader is not of the easy
kind. It is far from being the best of all possible worlds which he reveals
to us; but it is something better. It is a world in which every cruel ill
is confronted by that struggling humanity which is continually over-
borne, yet always victorious—victorious in defeat, in downfall, and in
death: the spirit of man made, even when he knows it not, in the image
of God. His conception of the race is the same as that which Browning
died singing:

One who never turned his back, but marched breast forward.

[1] [Badalia Herodsfoot, reprinted in *Many Inventions*, 1893]

Yet his conception of life is not, as Browning's was, optimistic. Perhaps indeed he has no clearly developed conception of life: he knows that the strangest effort often ends in overthrow; perhaps he may believe that it can do no other. Yet while we stand by his Indian civilian, cut down unnoted in the vast world of darkness against which he is struggling in the name of law and mercy; his soldiers slaughtered in some battle the very name of which will never be known—our souls are penetrated not by the sense of failure, but of the terrible and splendid warfare of everlasting good against overwhelming yet temporary evil. It is something very different from the story of the Good Apprentice; living happy ever after is not the fate to which his heroes, or even his heroines, attain. His men are not always moral; they are distinguished by none of the niceties of the drawing-room (that is to say, those among them who are so, are odious, and surrounded by still more odious womankind); they are faulty, troublesome, impracticable. The soldiers get drunk as often as they can, and swear freely on all occasions; they are not too scrupulous about bloodshed. Yet what our young missionary makes us see with the clearness of light is, that these rough fellows are struggling too, in their way, on the side of righteousness, and that when all this hay, straw, and stubble of mortal error is swept away, the meaning and purpose and essence of the men will not be lost.

Along with this, and perhaps the highest result of Mr. Rudyard Kipling's work is to roll away for us the veil which covers that vast and teeming world, the responsibility of which, for good or evil, before God, the British nation has taken upon its shoulders—India, in so many of its differing nations and phases, and what is going on within it. How he has acquired his marvellous acquaintance, so impartial and so complete, we have no means of knowing; each scene bears so strong a stamp of reality that, as with a portrait painted by one of the masters of human physiognomy and expression, we say instinctively: 'This must be a perfect likeness': the men prove themselves, from the Head of the District to the drummers of the Fore and Aft, from the little naked brown child in the bazaar to the old devotee who has retired to await his death in the temple. The landscape, the atmosphere, even the temperature—that stifling of awful heat, those breakings of great storms, the dust, the blaze, the air that burns, all rise before us; but chiefly, and above all, the servants of that majesty of England, of whom, when they are not our sons and brothers, we know so little. The reader may study a hundred authentic and instructive works upon India without coming to a knowledge of the way in which that Government is carried on, which a glimpse at this record will give him. The civilians out in obscure districts, with neither hopes of fame nor wealth, who live there knowing that far the likeliest thing is that they will die there, and never be heard of more, one man following another with a grim heroism, knowledge of all the risks, and determined indifference to them—is of itself a revelation which sweeps away in a moment all the modern cant of a weakened race and unheroic age. Unheroic! With the commonplace Competition Wallah marching up into the dust and glare to relieve a comrade who is dying or succeed one who is dead, at a moment's notice, knowing that he will probably be relieved himself after a horrible year or two, or month or two, in the same grim way—Smith dead, Brown to take his place— a mere item in a list, nothing more. The breast tightens, the eyes fill, as we read. They lie in the desert where they fell, scores, nay, hundreds of them, the British supremacy built up upon their tombstones—if they have so much as that to show where they lie to form its foundations; and what they suffer in the meantime only themselves and Mr. Rudyard Kipling knows. Here is the *mise-en-scène*—the place and the men:

[quotes 'At the End of the Passage', *Life's Handicap*, pp. 182, line 1, to 185, line 5]

We may add the account these same men give of the various occupations from which they have come to the spare entertainment of the engineer's hut. The explanation is made apropos of a speech read to them out of an English paper in which appointments in India were described as retained for 'scions of the aristocracy who took care to maintain their lavish scale of incomes, to avoid or stifle any enquiries into the nature and conduct of their administration, while they themselves force the unhappy peasant to pay with the sweat of his brow', etc. The civil servant describes his position with various amusing and instructive details:

[quotes 'At the End of the Passage', *Life's Handicap*, pp. 188, line 21, to 189, line 27]

The engineer who is the host is worst off of all. His English subcontractor has died 'accidentally' by the going off of his gun, and he himself is half mad with sleeplessness, but will not ask for leave because the man who would relieve him has a delicate wife at Simla, whom he can visit weekly where he is, and who would insist on following were he sent to Hummil's desert post. 'It's murder to bring a woman here just now. Burkett hasn't the physique of a rat. If he came here he'd go out: and I know she hasn't any money, and I'm pretty sure she'd go out too. I'm salted in a sort of way, and I'm not married. Wait till the rains, and then Burkett can get thin down here.' The story of this hero, and how he perishes at the post he will not let another man encounter the dangers of, is told in the terrible story called the 'End of the Passage'. So much for the servants of the English Government in the burning plains. We ourselves think this story one of the most sad and terrible in the book, though perhaps the 'Man who Was' is still more piteously tragic. The great horror of the volume, the 'Mark of the Beast', affects our particular imagination less, insomuch as it has, as the children say, a happy ending, the man being set free from the horrible enchantment. But it is idle to call these marvellous glimpses into a strange life stories, in the ordinary sense of the word—they are revelations, of what men can do, of what perhaps devils may.

The soldiers, again, are portrayed with more love and sympathy than the civilians, and with not less vivid touches. The 'Drummers of the Fore and Aft' (not in this book) is an epic which has seized upon every man from the age of ten upwards—and we say not man invidiously, as shutting out woman, but collectively as including her. These have entered into the English language, and are, though so young, mere babies of tales, rooted like Shakespeare. The soldiers, even in their most tragic moments, are gayer than the civil servants. The battle in the 'Main Guard' (also not in this volume) is like Homer or Sir Walter. The Pathans and the Englishmen, drunk with fighting, love and applaud each other as each cuts down his man, and the sergeant, withdrawn for a moment from the deadly struggle, who sits on the 'little orficer bhoy' to keep his immature strength out of it, while the youngster struggles and roars threats of punishment, is an immortal group. We will not attempt to quote anything from stories so well known, except in the little unconsidered details which a hasty reader full of excitement for the narrative might slip over in his haste. Here is an indication of the ways of the bivouac and the relations between officers and men, accustomed to lead and follow in the real and awful game of war, though for the moment only playing at it in the manœuvres of a sham campaign.

[quotes 'The Courting of Dinah Shadd', *Life's Handicap*, pp. 42, line 33, to 43, line 25; and p. 47, lines 6 to 16]

This is a very pretty picture of one of the armies in the world in which there is the greatest distance between officers and men—'the men moaning melodiously' after the lieutenant is one of the happiest touches.

This, however, is not all that we owe to Mr. Rudyard Kipling. Behind those bands of Englishmen, Scotsmen (he gives our countrymen but little attention, yet introduces one here and there for a moment, just to show that he can give the speech and accent of a Scot without ridicule or mistake, the all-comprehending boy), and Irishmen, whom he loves, and to whom he does full justice, lies the vast world of India, which also, in the great and unfathomable experience of his less than thirty years, this wonderful youth has penetrated and made his own. The niggers whom foolish young officers scorn—the wily and flattering races that bow down before the Sahibs; the fierce Borderers, who own their master when they see him, but are ready, like children, to take immediate advantage of a priest's murmur that the British Raj is over; the pathetic feminine creatures, half children, half women, whom the white men love and ride away; the old sages squatted in the cool recesses of the temples; the noble chief, who, having been poor himself and worked for his living, has no mercy on the vagabond who steals to live. These are stories, no doubt, and most entertaining stories, full of human nature, piquant in its difference, overwhelming in its resemblances to our own— with all the strange circumstances of ignorance and wisdom, unlike ours, that make it a revelation to us. There has been a question lately in the papers, of a decoration for literature, a share in the honours so freely going about the world, for literary men. Some of the debaters— indeed most of them—have taken a high tone, and attributed to writers the ineffable pretension of being above everything of the kind. Why? We do not pretend to know, the writers of books being but men, not contemptuous of any good thing that their trade may bring them, were it no more (but what is more?—the Garter itself is only that) than a piece of ribbon. If her Majesty's Ministers will be guided by us (which perhaps is not extremely probable; yet we confess we should like the command of a Minister's ear for several shrewd suggestions), they will bestow a Star of India without more ado upon this young man of genius, who has shown us all what the India empire means. Perhaps Lord Salisbury has not time, poor gentleman! with all the weight of State upon him, to refresh his soul with stories; but we dare be bound Mr. Balfour has, who, to speak as do the children of today, is up to everything. Sir Edwin Arnold had a good right to that star, probably suggested by his own poem, which showed us Buddha in his more-than-half Christianity—wonderful shadow of the Christ that was to be, not to be lightly touched by the ignorant missionary; and we would award it to a few others we know of—the author, for instance, of the 'City of Sunshine',[1] and perhaps he of Mr. Isaacs'.[2] But there is no Indian potentate, no general, no political agent, no member of council, who has a better right to the Indian decoration than this errant storyteller. We have all read a great deal about that vast continent, and the extraordinary British rule which is over it, without in most cases understanding very much. But here it lies, a hundred nationalities, a world unknown, under the blazing sky— innumerable crowds of human creatures, like the plains they inhabit, stretching into distance further than any eye can see. Never was there more astonishing picture than that, all done in black and white, which is called the 'City of Dreadful Night'. We pant in the air which is no air, we sicken for the evanescent breath of dawn, we walk between the white bodies asleep, not dead, that lie in every corner, we hear the *muezzin* climb the stairs to give forth his cry upon the stillness, as if we were there in bodily sight and hearing. It is a magic, it is an enchantment. If her Majesty herself, who knows so much, desires a fuller knowledge of her Indian empire, and how it is ruled and defended and fought for every day against all the Powers of Darkness, we desire respectfully to recommend to the Secretary for India that he should place no sheaves of despatches in the royal hands, but Mr. Rudyard Kipling's books. There are only two volumes of them, besides sundry small *brochures*. A good bulky conscientious three-volume novel holds many words. But there lies India, the most wonderful conquest and possession that any victorious kingdom ever made, the greatest fief, perhaps, that ever was held for God. These are great words: and the young magician upon whose lips we hang does not hesitate to show us what imperfect instruments the Raj of the white empire is upheld, men themselves stumbling and labouring upon the path of life, taking that great name as often in vain as speaking it in reverence— storming, fighting, sinning, forgetting themselves often, yet never forgetting the strong rule and curb with which, a handful themselves

[1] [*City of Sunshine* (1877) by Alexander Allardyce]
[2] [*Mr. Isaacs* (1882) by F. Marion Crawford]

they hold millions, always with an obdurate and steadfast direction towards Justice and Truth.

No patriot leader could do a better work. We dwell upon none of the literary qualities of this achievement. These are for lesser efforts. What Mr. Rudyard Kipling has done is an imperial work, and worthy of an imperial reward. The Star of India! a small thing the critic might say; but in this modern condition of affairs, when it is no longer the fashion to give a man as much land as he can ride round in a summer day—as much as there is to give. It would be a good beginning of a new system in respect to that unacknowledged craft which is bid to content itself with what little good it can do in its generation and the fickle applauses of popular fame. It is well to consider, however, another good thing that Mr. Kipling has done. He has proved that the public, though apt to be beguiled by Mr. Jerome K. Jerome and the 'Mystery of a Hansom Cab',[1] has yet sense enough to recognise something better when it sees it—for which also we are much beholden to him: it restores our faith in human nature: though how Mulvaney and his friends can share the quarters, even on a railway bookstall, of the sentimental Bootles[2] and his men and babies, we confess we are at a loss to conceive.

It was said, we believe, of our young man, that though superlative in the art (which he has brought so strongly into fashion) of the short story, he was incapable of writing a long one. In answer to which, his daemon produced at a sitting *The Light that Failed*. We remember sitting up to read that story through the moonlight hours of an Italian midnight, until the blueness of the morning began to lighten over the sea, and the grey olives twinkled silvery in that first dawn which comes before the sun. Much experience hath made us calm, and might, as one would think, take the edge off any interest or excitement of a tale. But it is not so; and like a youth with the spell of strong feelings upon us, we seized the pen to write to the author. But paused, as Gobind in Dhunni Bhagat's Chubara might have done; for youth in these days is apt to contemn experience, and better loves the praises of his kind. Here, however, by the dignified hand of Maga, the ever young, is that letter which was never written, bidding the young genius All-hail! and more power to his elbow, to relapse into vernacular speech, which is always more convincing than the high-flown.

[1] [1886. By 'Fergus Hume']
[2] [*Bootles' Baby*, by John Strange Winter]

20. Francis Adams on 'Rudyard Kipling'

1891

Signed article from the *Fortnightly Review*, Vol. LVI, pp. 686–700 (November 1891).

Francis William Lauderdale Adams (1862–1893), minor poet and essayist of promise who died young, also wrote a long article on 'Mr. Kipling's Verse' in the *Fortnightly Review*, Vol. LX, pp. 185–216 (November 1893)—but in it politics triumph over literary criticism even more than here. With Kipling, Adams tells us, 'the drop is always straight from the stars into the puddles'—but he equates stars with sentimental Liberal views and puddles with Tory imperialism.

It was inevitable that sooner or later someone should make a systematic effort, in the interests (say) of literature and art, to exploit India and the Anglo-Indian life. England has awakened at last to the astonishing fact of her world-wide Empire, and has now an ever-growing curiosity concerning her great possessions *outre mer*. The writer who can 'explain', in a vivid and plausible manner, the social conditions of India, Australia, Canada, and South Africa—who can show, even approximately, how people there live, move, and have their being, is assured of at least a remarkable vogue. Several vogues of this sort have already been won on more or less inadequate grounds: have been won, and lost and the cry is still: 'They come!' From among them all, so far, one writer alone, led on to fortune on this flood-tide in the affairs of men, has consciously and deliberately aimed high; taken his work seriously, and attempted to add something to the vast store of our English literature. The spectacle of a writer of fiction who is also a man of letters, and not merely a helpless caterer for the circulating libraries and the railway bookstalls, is unfortunately as rare among us as it is frequent among our French friends. Literature and Art are organized in France, and have prestige and power. In England they are impotent and utterly at the mercy of Philistine and imperfectly-educated newspaper men, who, professed caterers for the ignorant and stupid cravings of the average English person, male and female (and especially female), foist upon us painters, poets, novelists, and musicians of the most hopeless mediocrity. In France this sort of thing is impossible. Such efforts would only provoke a smile. People would say to you when you were taking seriously a poet (for instance) like Mr. Lewis Morris, or Sir Edwin Arnold, or a novelist like Mr. Besant or Mr. Haggard: 'Why, you must be joking! These gentlemen are not writers—are not artists at all. Surely you know that what they concern themselves with is the nourishment of the babes and sucklings who have to be provided with pap somehow; but serious workers, contributors to critical and creative thought—*allez!*' It seems something to be at last able to go to our French friends, and say: 'Well, here at any rate we have a young Englishman who has won a remarkable vogue, and for all that *is* a serious worker, *is* a contributor to critical and creative thought, *is* an artist, *is* a writer'—to be able to go and say this, and to advance reasons for our belief in it of sufficient cogency to extort, perhaps, from our friends a genuine assent. If for this alone, we ought to be grateful to Mr. Rudyard Kipling, our Anglo-Indian story-teller.

From the very beginning Mr. Kipling struck a strong and solemn personal note. To his first booklet, *Soldiers Three*, a collection of seven 'stories of barrack-room life', and designed to 'illustrate' one of 'the four main features of Anglo-Indian life', viz., the military, he attached the following sombre, proud, and yet pitiful *envoi*:

[quotes 'A Dedication' (DV. pp. 637–8) in full]

Certainly three of these tales constituted something very like a revelation not only of one of 'the four main features of Anglo-Indian life', but also of a new writer of considerable force and originality. Nothing like either 'The Big Drunk Draf', or 'With the Main Guard', had been presented to the reading public before, and the praise of the long *bazaar* was justifiable enough. But as a gallery of characters, as manifest fictional creations, the success of the book is not great. Indeed, one of the weakest sides of all Mr. Kipling's work is just the want of this very gift, on the assured possession of which he seems to pique himself. His characterization is never excellent; often it is mediocre; sometimes it is abominable. He cannot escape from his own subjectivity. Never was work more acutely personal than his. Never did a writer consciously or unconsciously insist with such passionate persistence on the special form of milieu which has given him what he feels to be (so far at least) the dominant factor in his view of things. And this is why, in nine cases out of ten, his dramatis personae melt away so rapidly in the memory, leaving us with nothing but the impression of an admirably piquant and clever delineation. He has probably spent more time and trouble over his 'Soldiers Three', Mulvaney, Ortheris, and Learoyd, than over any other of the characters of his tales; yet Mulvaney alone is recognizable as anything approaching an organic creation. Mr. Kipling sacrifices everything to his mordant individuality. Mulvaney, the drunken, pugnacious, loquacious, kindly Irish ruffian of the old school, will tell you how, 'Brazenose walked into the gang wid his sword, like Diarmid av the Gowlden Collar,' and will not mention the name of the Queen in ordinary conversation without devoutly invoking upon her the blessing of the Creator! Ortheris, the little vulgar rascal of a cockney, urges his comrade on to an adventure with the quotation:

> Go forth, return in glory,
>   To Clusium's royal 'ome:
> And round these bloomin' temples 'ang
>   The bloomin' shields o' Rome.

And, when he is rebuked for loquacity under trial, inquires: 'D'you stop your parrit screamin' of a 'ot day when the cage is a-cookin' 'is pore little pink toes orf?' Similarly a regimental carpenter likens the splitting open of a boat to 'a cock-eyed Chinese lotus', or a London street-girl entreats: 'But cou-couldn't you take and live with me till Miss Right comes along? I'm only Miss Wrong, I know, but I'd,' etc., etc. I respectfully submit that the speaker here is Mr. Rudyard Kipling, not Mulvaney, nor Ortheris, nor another. Instances of this sort of utterly inartistic insertion of little bits of Mr. Rudyard Kipling into Mr. Rudyard Kipling's 'rude figures of a rough-hewn race', are very plentiful, and are certainly not edifying samples of the way he shows his god-like 'power over these'. But how, when taken from the larger point of view, this defect limits the value of his criticism of the main features of Anglo-Indian life, which he designs to 'illustrate'! Today we are all full of eagerness and curiosity to know of what sort our short-service soldiers are. Mr. Kipling dedicates his booklet to 'that very strong man, T. Atkins', who is surely the very person in question. But what does he tell us about him? Little or nothing. It is the old long-service man who is his game. Into the mouth of Mulvaney, who gives us most of the military criticism, is put the ancient and stock abuse of the short-service system, backed up with the stock and ancient chauvinism about the glory and gain of the good old gentleman officer, all of the olden time, the individual with the courage of a mastiff and the brains of a rabbit. The poor old Irishman in his degradation is even made consolingly to kick himself with the reflection that, if he could have kept out of one big drink a month, he would have been an honorary lieutenant by this time, 'a nuisance to my betthers, a laughin' stock to my equils, an' a curse to meself'. And thus we settle the modern military question, incidentally throwing in a few jeers at Lord Wolseley as a drawing-room man, who doesn't know his business. With what heartfelt rapture, on the other hand, do we approach the sacred exhibitions of the Old Style! Take the first toast at the mess, which is the same as Mulvaney's loyal conversational prayer. 'That Sacrament of the Mess', says Mr. Kipling solemnly and deliberately in his own person, 'never grows old and never ceases to bring a lump into the throat of the listener, be he by sea or by land.' Dirkovitch [a mere unregenerate Cossack] 'rose with his "brothers glorious", but he did not understand. No one but an officer [the italics are mine] can tell what that means; and the bulk', etc., etc. And this in the year of grace 1891! Now what I want to know is this. Does Mr. Rudyard Kipling, in his most calm and disillusionized hours, in the dead unhappy night, and when the rain is on the roof, seriously believe in this sort of thing? If so, then he is indeed in a condition past even that in which the Lord might be asked to have mercy on his soul. For 'with stupidity the gods themselves contend in vain'. There are other excesses to which the sightless tradition of the old hide-bound, Jingoistic, Anglo-Indian officialism leads Mr. Kipling, but they are excusable and even defensible. It is only abject silliness which can be neither defended nor excused. None the less, he carries some of these excesses to considerable length. Dickie, the most gentle and lovable of his male characters, blind, and going to his death, 'stretches himself on the floor' [of a carriage in an armed train at Suakim] 'wild with delight at the sounds and the smells' of the machine-gun, pouring out lead through its five noses upon hapless Arabs, fighting for their freedom in their native land. ' "God is very good—never thought I'd hear this again. Give 'em hell, men! oh, give 'em hell!" he cried.'

The exceeding goodness of God in relation to Englishmen and 'niggers' seems always to consist in the opportunity and ability of the former to give the latter 'hell'. Never once in his tales does Mr. Kipling appear to be aware that these same miserable aliens may have a point of view of their own—they also. There is always the tacit assumption of the fact that they are made merely to be fought with, conquered, and ruled, which is simply the sentiment of the Exeter Hall of the Jingoes, who should surely look with greater favour than they do on their Christian brethren. For are they not both after the same thing? The missionary going even one better in his desire for the servitude not only of the body but of the spirit, which of course is *his* special way of 'giving 'em hell'. I am not quarrelling with this genial and enlightened manner of treating the 'inferior races'. I am only saying that in the case of Mr. Rudyard Kipling it makes one feel how much less interesting and valuable his criticism on the Indian people is than it might be. Ah, if only kindly nature had given him as much brain-power as she has given him pictorial talent, what a rendering of the Anglo-Indian life we might have had! It would have been final. There would have been no need for anyone even to try to do this contemporary phase of it over again.

Pieces of his description of fighting have been spoken of as unparalleled. Wonderful as was his first effort in this direction, the 'jam' in 'the gut betune two hills, as black as a bucket an' as thin as a gurl's waist', where the Pathans waited 'like rats in a pit', for the onslaught of the two regiments, one of which (the Black Tyrone) 'had seen their dead'—wonderfully as this was presented in the Mulvaneyan brogue, when Mr. Kipling trusted to himself alone he did better and achieved a masterpiece. 'The Drums of the Fore and Aft' is one of those performances which are apt to reduce criticism to the mere tribute of a respectful admiration. It is absolutely and thoroughly well done. It 'explains' everybody and everything. We follow the raw-recruited regiment step by step in the process of its demoralization. We feel the approach of the inevitable catastrophe. Equally clear is the demonstration of the personal incident of the two little drummer-boys, who are to be on this occasion the chance gods from the machine. It all passes before us like a piece of illuminated life. And with what dramatic power is it all gathered together and swept forward to the culminating scene, where the two lads step out from the rocks with drum and fife, 'and the old tune of the old Line shrills and rattles'. Then from the purely descriptive writing which follows, take a specimen like this:

'The English were not running. They were hacking and hewing and stabbing . . . The Fore and Aft held their fire till one bullet could drive through five or six men, and the front of the Afghan force gave on the volley. They then selected their men, and slew them with deep gasps and short hacking coughs, and groanings of leather belts against strained bodies.'

Scarcely less fine is the charge of the Lancers, which

'detached the enemy from his base as a sponge is torn from a rock, and left him ringed about with fire in that pitiless plain. And as a sponge is chased round the bath-tub by the hand of the bather, so were the Afghans chased.'

Whenever Mr. Kipling touches on a battle-scene, especially a mêlée, he writes with this absolute mastery of it all. It is real pictorial magic. The charge of Arabs on the square on the Nile bank (*The Light that Failed*, chap. ii.) is too long for full quotation here, and too perfect to be mutilated; the following may be taken as a sample of the way in which he can render a personal incident in such surroundings. It is from a tale in his last book, *Life's Handicap*, 'The Mutiny of the Mavericks', which is for the most part a worthless piece of special pleading, but which ends with this admirable portrayal of the madness of a coward:

Dan and Horse Egan kept themselves in the neighbourhood of Mulcahy. Twice the man would have bolted back in the confusion. Twice he was heaved, kicked, and shouldered back again into the unpaintable *inferno* of a hotly contested charge. At the end, the panic excess of his fear drove him into madness beyond all human courage. His eyes staring at nothing, his mouth open and frothing, and breathing as one in a cold bath, he went forward demented, while Dan toiled after him. The charge checked at a high mud wall. It was Mulcahy who scrambled up tooth and nail and hurled down among the bayonets the amazed Afghan who barred his way. It was Mulcahy, keeping to the straight line of the rabid dog, who led a collection of ardent souls at a newly unmasked battery and flung himself on the muzzle of a gun, as his companions danced among the gunners. It was Mulcahy who ran wildly on from that battery into the open plain, where the enemy were retiring in sullen groups. His hands were empty, he had lost helmet and belt, and he was bleeding from a wound in the neck . . . Dan and Horse Egan, panting and distressed, had thrown themselves down upon the ground by the captured guns, when they noticed Mulcahy's charge. . . . The last of a hurrying crowd of Afghans turned at the noise of shod feet behind him, and shifted his knife ready to hand. This, he saw, was no time to take prisoners. Mulcahy tore on, sobbing; the straight-held blade went home through the defenceless breast, and the body pitched forward almost before a shot from Dan's rifle brought down the slayer. The two Irishmen went out to bring in their dead.

'Description,' said Byron, in his riper time, when he had begun to understand himself a little, 'description is my *forte*'. It is also Mr. Rudyard Kipling's.

The second of the four main features of the Anglo-Indian life is the domestic, and Mr. Kipling chooses *The Story of the Gadsbys* as his typical illustration of it. The difference, however, between the 'domestic' feature and the last of the four, which he denominates the 'social' feature, is slight, and the latter term is quite comprehensive enough for the two. Here, indeed, he is on his special ground. Here his critical limitations do not come into play; his pet prejudices and theories are unaffected, and he sets himself to render Anglo-Indian 'society' as seen and felt from within as well as from without, with an unimpeachable disinterestedness. *The Story of the Gadsbys* showed, in at least one scene of that dramatized 'tale without a plot' ('The Tents of Kedar'), a really remarkable gift of dialogue. It was true drawing-room comedy of a high order, and indeed throughout the whole of the piece the talking and gesturing of the puppets were undeniably actual. In the *Soldiers Three* there was a piece of first-rate dialogue ('The Solid Muldoon', pp. 45, 46, the talk between Mulvaney and Annie Bragin), but it is obviously one thing to write two pages of conversation and quite another to write eighty. The characters chosen for analysis, however, are on a rather low plane and prove tedious when treated at such length. Seven pages of the silly delirium of a silly girl are rather too large an instalment of predetermined pathos on one note, coming on the top of two even larger and more monotonous instalments of honeymooning and conjugal 'tiffing'. An obviously much-experienced I.C.S. man has a felicitous phrase for the Anglo-Indian 'society' ladies, married or single. He calls them 'fire-balloons', and every type of 'fire-balloon', from the empty-headed little girl aforesaid (whose maiden experience so soon corroborates the touching aphorism of her maiden friend that 'being kissed by a man who *didn't* wax his moustache was like eating an egg without salt') through the savage man-exploiting Mrs. Reiver up to Mrs. Hauksbee, 'the most wonderful woman in India',—everyone of them he treats with a loving, patient, and elaborate detail. Some of them are not worth it, 'the most wonderful woman in India' among them (he dedicates *Plain Tales from the Hills*, with a mild fatuity, 'to the wittiest woman in India', who must run that terrible Mrs. Hauksbee close);[1] but others

---

[1] [They were, in fact, the same: Mrs. F. C. Burton]

are drawn with the hand of a master, and are among his most living creations. The same is to be said of most of the men.

Here, then, we have at last the Anglo-Indian 'society' life of today, and we see it from every side. Duty and red tape tempered by picnics and adultery—it is a singular spectacle. But we are to ascribe much, very much, to the climate. Simla holds 'the only existence in this desolate land worth the living'. For the rest, it is six months purgatory and six months hell. 'One of the many curses of our life in India is the want of atmosphere in the painter's sense. There are no half-tints worth noticing. Men stand out all crude and raw, with nothing to tone them down, and nothing to scale them against.' For instance, we speak of 'all the pleasures of a quiet English wooing, quite different from the brazen businesses of the East, when half the community stand back and bet on the result, and the other half wonder what Mrs. So-and-so will say to it'. Thus Minnie Threegan competes successfully with her 'poor, dear mamma' (who is not precisely a widow) for Mr. Gadsby, who, in his turn, throws over Mrs. Herriott (also apparently not a widow to any alarming extent) in order to enter into the matrimonial 'garden of Eden'. Out of the six tales specially designed to 'illustrate' the 'social' life of the Anglo-Indians, five are based, some more, some less, on adultery. In the way of short stories Mr. Kipling has done nothing better than the three central ones—'At the Pit's Mouth', 'A Wayside Comedy', and 'The Hill of Illusion'; the last containing the most admirably sustained piece of dialogue he has yet written. The other side to the picture of the reckless, light-hearted revelry of the Hills is to be found in the doggedly heroic work of, at any rate, the male portion of these people down in the Plains. Picnics, rides and drives, with garden-parties and promenades, are suddenly forgotten in a scene like this:

The atmosphere within was only 104°, as the thermometer bore witness, and heavy with the foul smell of badly-trimmed kerosene lamps; and this stench, combined with that of native tobacco, baked brick and dried earth, sends the heart of many a strong man down to his boots, for it is the smell of the Great Indian Empire when she turns herself for six months into a house of torment.

The temper induced by this sort of thing, when mixed up well with fever and finally flavoured with cholera *ad libitum*, is scarcely likely to be lamb-like. 'It's an insult to the intelligence of the Deity,' observes one of the sufferers, 'to pretend we're anything but tortured rebels.' Who shall be surprised, then, that when the tortured rebels go away for a holiday to 'the only existence in this desolate land worth the living', they are devotees of the gospel of eating, drinking, and being merry, for only too obvious reasons? At the bad times this same gospel leads to astonishing effects in the way of kindliness and self-sacrifice. A savage Stoicism holds all things cheap, even death. 'Bah! how these Christians funk death!' It is the grim and contemptuous jeer of the eternal heathen, whose heart says to him with a fraternal candour, 'Dust thou art, and to dust thou shalt return, and what on earth does it matter?' Yet what a depth of passion and emotion lies in these Stoics, and how paltry and factitious all other men seem beside them— children babbling of the moon or cowards sucking at their spiritual opium pipes to drug their 'funk' into 'faith'. Mr. Kipling loves his heathens with all his heart, and even the silliest of his 'fire-balloons' seeks not succour 'from on high' in the troubles and agonies of 'life's handicap'. As for his men, they have all more or less of the nature of the eternal barbarian, the atavistic impulse of ruthless action which lies so deeply and so ineradicably in almost all of us, under the thin veneer of our civilized refinement and 'good manners'. Speaking of his Dickie, he calls it the

go-fever, which is more real than many doctor's diseases, waking and raging, urging him, who loved Maisie beyond anything in the world, to go away and taste the old, hot, unregenerate life again—to scuffle, swear, gamble, and live light lives with his fellows; to take ship and know the sea once more, and by her beget pictures; to talk to Binat among the sands of Port Said, while Yellow Tina mixed the drinks. . . .

and so on. Very little respect or care has he, therefore, for those who shout to us perpetually: 'Great is the Respectability of the English people!' 'Oh, you rabbit hutches!' cries out Dickie, in the black hour of his poverty in London, 'do you know what you've got to do later on? You have to supply me with men-servants and maid-servants'— here he smacked his lips—'and the peculiar treasure of kings. Meantime I'll get clothes and boots, and presently I will return and trample on you.' Strange, passing strange, that in the throat of men who talk like this a lump should rise, 'be they by sea or by land', at the mystic formula which sums up the cult of the Sovereign who doesn't rule. Yet such, it appears, are we English, a 'peculiar people' in all conscience. Nor is even the saving grace of humour denied to our Anglo-Indian storyteller, to temper the foolisher aspects of that bilious and fiery jingoism of the devastated and terrible clime. The preface to *Life's*

Handicap is a delicious proof of this, and paragraphs, sentences and phrases, that have the true piquant flavour, are rarely to seek. Yet his touch is not by any means always certain. His false characterization has its parallel in false criticism, sometimes merely the smart superficialities of the imperfectly-educated journalist (to whom culture stands for nothing more than 'culchaw), at other times quite shocking tributes of respect and admiration to tenth-rate personages. Mr. Kipling knows little beyond modern English prose. The secret of the art and literature of the great Continental peoples is hid from him. He is too young, and he has lived too hard, not to be considerably in the dark about himself. The pose he prefers to take is that of the utmost smartness and cocksureness available. How else is one to explain the insertion of work absolutely vile and detestable in his latest book? The *sacra fames auri* might explain such composition; but it is another thing in the full flood-tide of your vogue, with name, and fame, and fortune all at your hand, to write in this way of your work:

> The depth and dream of my desire,
> The bitter paths wherein I stray,
> Thou knowest Who hast made the fire,
> Thou knowest Who hast made the clay.
>
> One stone the more swings to her place
> In that dread Temple of Thy worth—
> It is enough that thro' Thy grace
> I saw nought common on Thy earth.
>
> Take not that vision from my ken;
> Oh, whatso'er may spoil or speed,
> Help me to need no aid from men
> That I may help such men as need!

to write like this, and then to present to us such unspeakably mediocre and wretched stuff as 'The Lang Men o' Larut' or 'Namgay Doola!' 'Under any circumstances, remember,' says the sagacious Dickie, in the character of the pictorial journalist in the heyday of his London vogue, 'four-fifths of everybody's work must be bad. But the remnant is worth the trouble for its own sake.' Very true: but is this any reason that a man who can give us such a splendid sample of storytelling as 'The Courting of Dinah Shadd', or touch the very spring of the *lacrimae rerum* in the piteous narrative of 'The Man who was', should proceed to inflict on us work which even the most sympathetic criti-

cism can only designate as beneath contempt? Mr. Kipling asks too
much of his most devoted admirers when he leaves them to try and
justify the existence of 'Namgay Doola' and 'The Lang Men o' Larut',
and even 'The Incarnation of Krishna Mulvaney'. Balzac could not
afford to sign his name to such rubbish. For Mr. Rudyard Kipling to
do so, is to send snakes to strangle his reputation in its cradle.

'In India,' he says, speaking in his proper person, 'you really see
humanity—raw, brown, naked humanity—with nothing between it
and the blazing sky, and only the used-up, over-handled earth under
foot.' One of the results of the overwhelming nature of this fact is that,
at any rate in any close consideration of the 'native feature' you are
soon driven to take refuge in 'simpler theories' than those current
among the benighted English home officials. Herein, of course, is the
great difference between these and the Anglo-Indian officials. The
latter have ever treated the native feature from the simpler theory
point of view. Hence the stupendous success of our Indian administration as an administration from the days of Clive to those of Lord
Lytton and onwards. Our sympathetic comprehension of the races we
have ruled, our intimate knowledge and appreciation of their religious
and social feelings; all this is due to the simpler theories of our Anglo-
Indian officials, civil and military. The events of the year 1857 were
the crowning proof of this. In that year we simplified even these
simpler theories into the one simplest theory of all. 'We gave 'em
hell' to an extent that they have never forgotten, and Mr. Kipling
smiles cunningly over the still active native prejudice against being
blown away from the mouths of cannons. The foolish person in search
of a little disinterested information about things may find the so-called
Indian Mutiny an unexplained historical phenomenon and eagerly
hope for some enlightenment on the subject from a writer who is
'illustrating' the native feature. He will get little or none from Mr.
Kipling. Firstly, he will find the scantiest mention or even allusion to
the social movements of the natives. They are viewed merely as a
huge mass of raw, brown, naked humanity to be manipulated by the
civil and military officials for the arcane purposes of the Great Indian
Empire, or by the inspired amateur detective (Strickland is Mr. Kipling's name for him) as material for his dexterous energy and sagacity,
or by the male portion of the Anglo-Indians as a happy hunting-ground
for more or less animating, if monotonous, sexual experiences 'without benefit of clergy'. We see the officials perpetually hustling the

child-like natives about all over the country. We see Strickland or somebody else, not quite so clever perhaps, but still far too clever for child-like natives, perpetually exposing their villainies. We see rows of Anglo-Indian bachelors of all sorts (some the most commonplace sorts) inspiring dark-eyed little native girls with dog-like adorations.

There is in these narratives all the ability of the thoroughly good storyteller we know, here and there bits of excellent dialogue (the final scene in 'The Sending of Dana Da', for example), the same exquisite little descriptive cameos, the same rapid and piquant dogmatism—one has nothing less to praise here than in the tales of the 'military' feature, but unhappily also nothing more. Now and then vivid touches seem to bring us into contact with the peculiar and essential nature of the more active members of the alien races, and we realize for a moment something of the qualities in them which have made history; but how rare and partial such glimpses are! Thus Mr. Kipling shows us the Afghan Amir in his Court, and 'the long tail of feudal chiefs, men of blood, fed and cowed with blood'. But such things are not his game. It is the little personal experiences and the 'begetting of pictures' from the same that he is keen for. This is what interests and absorbs him. 'If I were Job ten times over,' says one of his characters in the most unnatural manner for the character, and in the most natural manner for Mr. Rudyard Kipling, 'I should be so interested in what was going to happen next that I'd stay in and watch'. And he makes his Mrs. Hauksbee repeat the sentiment. 'Colour, light, and motion,' he says elsewhere with his own voice, 'without which no man has much pleasure in living'. He loves the demonstrative instinct of the Oriental. 'You cannot explain things to the Oriental. You must show.' He has in him, too, the Oriental love of storytelling for its own sake; and even their superstition strikes a responsive chord in him. 'I have lived long enough in this India,' he says, 'to know that it is best to know nothing'. And on the force of this he mars a little masterpiece like 'The Courting of Dinah Shadd' with a large allowance of second-rate second-sight prediction, which is fulfilled to the letter. I cannot tell whether it is simply due to the benumbing chill of incredulity, but his deliberately supernatural tales, from 'The Phantom Rickshaw' downwards, impress me as distinct failures. On the other hand, when he deals in natural horror (take 'At the Pit's Mouth' as a sample, or 'The Other Man') I often find him a master.

But do not let me seem to strike with too great insistence the note of depreciation and disappointment. That would be to be unjust as well as ungracious. The best Mr. Kipling has to give, he gives, and the best of that best is veritably good, and what more should we ask of him? Nowhere in his more elaborate efforts to delineate child-life (and some of them are something rather like successes) does he give us so perfect a piece of work as the little child-idyll called 'The Story of Muhammad Din': nowhere does this gift of natural horror find more artistically harrowing expression than in 'The Gate of the Hundred Sorrows', or in 'Bubbling Well Road': nowhere does he paint the *ewig Weibliche* with a more liquid depth of simple love than in 'Lispeth' or 'Beyond the Pale'. And all of these are stories that illustrate the native feature.

There is one obvious quality in all literary work without which the name or fame of a writer has no possible chance of survival, and that is the literary quality. Its manifestations are many, far more diverse, indeed, than jejune critics like Matthew Arnold will admit. Arnold loved to quote a line of Sophocles above a line of Homer, a line of Dante below a line of Shakspeare, and to assure us that these were all perfect samples of 'style'. The fact is, that of style in the sense known to Sophocles or Milton, Shakspeare and Homer had little, and Dante had less. Shakspeare achieves his immortality through a verbal magic unequalled in the world's literature. No man ever created such lines and phrases. Dante (to take his case alone) achieves his immortality by something quite different—by a sheer and simple sincerity of outlook. He watches, and watches, and watches, till he sees things before him with an actuality that burns achingly into his sight, and what he sees he puts down simply—as he sees it; but style in the sense of Sophocles, verbal magic in the sense of Shakspeare, he has little or none of either.

Our business here is obviously with things on a smaller scale, but the same line of judgment must be held as with those of the largest. No one can claim for Mr. Kipling the possession of a real prose style, or, indeed, of anything approaching it. He cannot even, at least in this respect, for a moment be placed beside his French contemporaries and fellow storytellers—Maupassant and Bourget, let alone the great names of French and English prose. Such style, *qua* style, as he has is mere ephemeral and journalistic smartness, and he never begins to do good work till he has consciously forgotten all about it, and has set himself down to paint his 'pictures' or express his emotions as he best may. Neither has he that sheer and simple sincerity of outlook, that patient and relentless realism which (for example) lifts the best work of Zola so high. His youth and ardour, worked to white-heat by the Indian climate and his hard life, have intensified his individualism to such a pitch that he cannot get out of himself—cannot render anyone or anything objectively. The types he hates he caricatures, and mingles up men, and women, and children with puppets tricked out in semblance of the same, with a splendid want of discrimination. What side, then, of this precious, this indispensable quality does he possess as the 'Open, Sesame', of the years to come, where newspaper 'boomers' cease from troubling and serious workers are at rest? The reply can happily be given without much hesitation. Beyond all question (to put it in the particular form) he has the gift, both of the happy simile and of the happy phrase. 'You pass through big still deodar forests, and under big still cliffs, and over big still grass-downs swelling like a woman's breasts; and the wind across the grass, and the rain among the deodars says: "Hush—hush—hush."' A touch of verbal trickery here, and Nature is rendered purely in the focus of the spectator's subjectivity, but how well she is rendered! Or, again:

A large, low moon turned the tops of the spear-grass to silver, and the stunted camelthorn-bushes and sour tamarisks into the likeness of trooping devils. The smell of the sun had not left the earth, and little aimless winds, blowing across the rose-gardens to the southward, brought the scent of dried roses and water.

He is almost as keen a connoisseur of scents and smells as M. Guy de Maupassant. He realizes their powers. Several such samples have been given already. Here are the Himalayas from the nasal point of view.

The monkeys sang sorrowfully to each other as they hunted for dry roots in the fern-wreathed trees, and the last puff of the day-wind brought from the unseen villages the scent of damp wood-smoke, hot cakes, dripping under-growth, and rotting pine-cones. That is the true smell of the Himalayas, and if once it creeps into the blood of a man, that man will, at the last, forgetting all else, return to the hills to die.

Admirable, indeed, are these little descriptive cameos, which he strews broadcast. Sometimes they are enclosed in two or three lines. 'The witchery of the dawn turned the grey river-reaches to purple, gold, and opal: and it was as though the lumbering barge crept across the splendour of a new Heaven.' Again he achieves the same result in one single perfect epithet. 'The drinking earth'—three words to describe the drought-laden Indian land under the heavy, unceasing downpour of the longed-for, welcome rains. 'Nothing save the spikes of the rain without and the smell of the drinking earth in my nostrils.' Verbal magic of this sort is of the poet: it is thrown out whole, so to say, not constructed. Or take this: 'There was nothing but grass everywhere, and it was impossible to see two yards in any direction. *The grass-stems held the heat exactly as boiler tubes do.*' No more: not another word. Oh, veritably in Art the part is ever greater than the whole. Naturally enough, when he deliberately sets himself down to exploit this supreme gift of his, he succeeds but moderately. 'The City of Dreadful Night' may be taken as a good example. It is excellent better-class journalism, and all the third-rate 'word-painters' are in raptures over it, but (alas!) it is not the third-rate, or the second-rate, or even the first-rate word painters who precisely know what they are talking about. Yet (alas! once more) for how much do they and their wrong-headed praise and undiscriminating enthusiasm count in the creation of vogues! Must a man ever owe three-fourths of his temporary success to his defects and limitations? Smartness and superficiality, Jingoism and aggressive cock-sureness, *rococo* fictional types and overloaded pseudo-prose, how much too much have these helped to make the name of our young Anglo-Indian storyteller familiar to the readers of the English-speaking race all over the earth!

Grant to him, however, as we surely must, the possession of verbal magic, of this striking aspect of our precious and indispensable literary quality, and add to it such gifts as have been enumerated in our short review of his work, and surely the case for taking it and its creator seriously has been clearly made out. On the other hand, we must not for a moment lose sight of the fact with which we started in our consideration of his claims to a permanent literary position. We are dealing with things on a scale which can only be called small, and his limitations, his aberrations are very real and very grave. The time is past when a writer of talent could win such a position, even for a generation, by the most nimble and vivid variations of a 'criticism of life' adapted to the use of the nursery or the schoolroom. Loud-tongued, fractious and numerous though it still is, the Noble Army of Blockheads no longer exercises that perfect tyranny it did fifteen or twenty years ago. It is yet able to dispense the loaves and fishes, but its judgments, overwhelming though they be for a short time, are being perpetually upset by the small, but ever-growing section of the public that begins in Art and Literature to know its right hand from its left. It will not be long before people come to tell Mr. Kipling that they are sick to death of his continual efforts to galvanize his most puppet-like puppets into the dreary semblance of life. 'No more

Mulvaney, Ortheris, and Learoyd, an you love us! No more Mrs. Hauksbee, and Strickland, and Mrs. What's-her-name. They are only visible and palpable object-lessons of your inability to create characters!' Such an inability at this present time, when characterization is being more and more recognized as the supreme gift of the writer and artist, is a vital matter. Then, again, although Mr. Kipling is young and full of vigour, what are we left to infer from the undeniable fact that the ascending force in his work is very slight? Nay, we might question its existence. His work has not gone on improving in his successive efforts. He has never excelled 'The Big Drunk Draf', or 'The Drums of the Fore and Aft', or 'At the Pit's Mouth', or 'Gemini', each in their special style, and these (if I do not mistake) are all from his earlier period. There is nothing in any degree better—shall I say there is nothing in any degree so good?—in the whole collection of stories gathered up in *Plain Tales from the Hills* and *Life's Handicap*. Any attempt to classify Mr. Kipling, to give him a place, and his true place, in our modern fiction would be premature. Hope (which, according to the Latin phrase, is 'the expectation of good') clings to this saving clause. But after his next book will this still be so? What should we make of another huge slice of the 'Incarnation of Krishna Mulvaney' style of thing, and 'Namgay Doola', and 'The Lang Men of Larut'?

But, once more, let me not seem to strike the unjust and ungracious note of depreciation and disappointment, especially at the close of my review. We should be thankful for what we have got; but, if we chiefly show our thankfulness by energetically asking for more, let us not fall under the suspicion of want of generosity. The case, we say, for taking Mr. Kipling seriously has surely been made out beyond cavil. His vogue may pass—it seems passing somewhat already—as all vogues pass; but, at least, we shall not be able to declare of it, as of so many of its fellows—and, indeed, of some which seem at this hour to stand above all such changes and chances—that it was won on such inadequate grounds that a total extinction and oblivion were, in mercy to the vileness of the English artistic taste, its most expedient as well as its worthiest fate. That can never be said of the man who could describe Anglo-Indian society as in 'At the Pit's Mouth', who could tell a story like 'The Courtship of Dinah Shadd', who could do a piece of such splendid analytical and dramatic work as 'The Drums of the Fore and Aft'.

21. Henry James's Introduction to *Mine Own People*

1891

Introduction to authorized collection of stories, five of which had been 'pirated' in *The Courting of Dinah Shadd* (1890) with 'A Biographical and Critical Sketch' by Andrew Lang (also 'pirated'). Issued in March 1891 by John W. Lovell Company of New York. James's 'Introduction' occupies pages [vii]–xxvi.

James wrote to his brother a few days later (6 February 1892) that 'Kipling strikes me personally as the most complete man of genius (as distinct from fine intelligence) that I have ever known'. But after 1900 he lost touch both with him and his work. (See above, No. 11.)

It would be difficult to answer the general question whether the books of the world grow, as they multiply, as much better as one might suppose they ought, with such a lesson on wasteful experiment spread perpetually behind them. There is no doubt, however, that in one direction we profit largely by this education: whether or no we have become wiser to fashion, we have certainly become keener to enjoy. We have acquired the sense of a particular quality which is precious beyond all others—so precious as to make us wonder where, at such a rate, our posterity will look for it, and how they will pay for it. After tasting many essences we find freshness the sweetest of all. We yearn for it, we watch for it and lie in wait for it, and when we catch it on the wing (it flits by so fast), we celebrate our capture with extravagance. We feel that after so much has come and gone it is more and more of a feat and a *tour de force* to be fresh. The tormenting part of the phenomenon is that, in any particular key, it can happen but once—by a sad failure of the law that inculcates the repetition of goodness. It is terribly a matter of accident; emulation and imitation have a fatal effect upon it. It is easy to see, therefore, what importance the epicure may attach to the brief moment of its bloom. While that lasts we all are epicures.

This helps to explain, I think, the unmistakable intensity of the general relish for Mr. Rudyard Kipling. His bloom lasts, from month to month, almost surprisingly—by which I mean that he has not worn out even by active exercise the particular property that made us all, more than a year ago, so precipitately drop everything else to attend to him. He has many others which he will doubtless always keep; but a part of the potency attaching to his freshness, what makes it as exciting as a drawing of lots, is our instinctive conviction that he cannot, in the nature of things, keep that; so that our enjoyment of him, so long as the miracle is still wrought, has both the charm of confidence and the charm of suspense. And then there is the further charm, with Mr. Kipling, that this same freshness is such a very strange affair of its kind—so mixed and various and cynical, and, in certain lights, so contradictory of itself. The extreme recentness of his inspiration is as enviable as the tale is startling that his productions tell of his being at home, domesticated and initiated, in this wicked and weary world. At times he strikes us as shockingly precocious, at others as serenely wise. On the whole, he presents himself as a strangely clever youth who has stolen the formidable mask of maturity and rushes about making people jump with the deep sounds, the sportive exaggerations of tone, that issue from its painted lips. He has this mark of a real vocation, that different spectators may like him—must like him, I should almost say—for different things: and this refinement of attraction, that to those who reflect even upon their pleasures he has as much to say as to those who never reflect upon anything. Indeed there is a certain amount of room for surprise in the fact that, being so much the sort of figure that the hardened critic likes to meet, he should also be the sort of figure that inspires the multitude with confidence—for a complicated air is, in general, the last thing that does this.

By the critic who likes to meet such a bristling adventurer as Mr. Kipling I mean of course the critic for whom the happy accident of character, whatever form it may take, is more of a bribe to interest than the promise of some character cherished in theory—the appearance of justifying some foregone conclusion as to what a writer or a book 'ought', in the Ruskinian sense, to be: the critic in a word, who has, *a priori*, no rule for a literary production but that it shall have genuine life. Such a critic (he gets much more out of his opportunities, I think, than the other sort) likes a writer exactly in proportion as he is a challenge, an appeal to interpretation, intelligence, ingenuity, to what is elastic in the critical mind—in proportion indeed as he may be a negation of things familiar and taken for granted. He feels in this case how much more play and sensation there is for himself.

Mr. Kipling, then, has the character that furnishes plenty of play and of vicarious experience—that makes any perceptive reader foresee a rare luxury. He has the great merit of being a compact and convenient illustration of the surest source of interest in any painter of life—that of having an identity as marked as a window-frame. He is one of the illustrations, taken near at hand, that help to clear up the vexed question, in the novel or the tale, of kinds, camps, schools, distinctions, the right way and the wrong way; so very positively does he contribute to the showing that there are just as many kinds, as many ways, as many forms and degrees of the 'right', as there are personal points of view. It is the blessing of the art he practises that it is made up of experience conditioned, infinitely, in this personal way—the sum of the feeling of life as reproduced by innumerable natures; natures that feel through all their differences, testify through their diversities. These differences, which make the identity, are of the individual; they form the channel by which life flows through him, and how much he is able to give us of life—in other words, how much he appeals to us—depends on whether they form it solidly.

This hardness of the conduit, cemented with a rare assurance, is perhaps the most striking idiosyncrasy of Mr. Kipling; and what makes it more remarkable is that accident of his extreme youth which, if we talk about him at all, we cannot affect to ignore. I cannot pretend to give a biography or a chronology of the author of *Soldiers Three*, but I cannot overlook the general, the importunate fact that, confidently as he has caught the trick and habit of this sophisticated world, he has not been long of it. His extreme youth is indeed what I may call his window-bar—the support on which he somewhat rowdily leans while he looks down at the human scene with his pipe in his teeth; just as his other conditions (to mention only some of them), are his prodigious facility, which is only less remarkable than his stiff selection; his unabashed temperament, his flexible talent, his smoking-room manner, his familiar friendship with India—established so rapidly, and so completely under his control; his delight in battle, his 'cheek' about women—and indeed about men and about everything; his determination not to be duped, his 'imperial' fibre, his love of the inside view, the private soldier and the primitive man. I must add further to this list of attractions the remarkable way in which he makes us aware that he has been put up to the whole thing directly by life (miraculously, in his teens), and not by the communications of others. These elements, and many more, constitute a singularly robust little literary character (our use of the diminutive is altogether a note of endearment and enjoyment), which, if it has the rattle of high spirits and is in no degree apologetic or shrinking, yet offers a very liberal pledge in the way of good faith and immediate performance. Mr. Kipling's performance comes off before the more circumspect have time to decide whether they like him or not, and if you have seen it once you will be sure to return to the show. He makes us prick up our ears to the good news that in the smoking-room too there may be artists; and indeed to an intimation still more refined—that the latest development of the modern also may be, most successfully, for the canny artist to put his victim off the guard by imitating the amateur (superficially, of course) to the life.

These, then, are some of the reasons why Mr. Kipling may be dear to the analyst as well as, M. Renan says, to the simple. The simple may like him because he is wonderful about India, and India has not been 'done'; while there is plenty left for the morbid reader in the surprise of his skill and the *fioriture* of his form, which are so oddly independent of any distinctively literary note in him, any bookish association. It is as one of the morbid that the writer of these remarks (which doubtless only too shamefully betray his character) exposes himself as most consentingly under the spell. The freshness arising from a subject that—by a good fortune I do not mean to underestimate—has never been 'done', is after all less of an affair to build upon than the freshness residing in the temper of the artist. Happy indeed is Mr. Kipling, who can command so much of both kinds. It is still as one of the morbid, no doubt—that is, as one of those who are capable of sitting up all night for a new impression of talent, of scouring the trodden field for one little spot of green—that I find our young author quite most curious in his air, and not only in his air but in his evidently very real sense, of knowing his way about life. Curious in the highest degree and well worth attention is such an idiosyncrasy as this in a young Anglo-Saxon. We meet it with familiar frequency in the budding talents of France, and it startles and haunts us for an hour. After an hour, however, the mystery is apt to fade, for we find that the wondrous initiation is not in the least general, is only exceedingly special, and is, even with this limitation, very often rather conventional. In a word, it is with the ladies that the young Frenchman takes his ease, and more particularly with ladies selected expressly to make this attitude convincing. When *they* have let him off, the dimnesses too often encompass him. But for Mr. Kipling there are no dimnesses anywhere, and if the ladies are indeed violently distinct they are only strong notes in a universal loudness. This loudness fills the ears of Mr. Kipling's admirers (it lacks sweetness, no doubt, for those who are not of the number), and there is really only one strain that is absent from it—the voice, as it were, of the civilised man; in whom I of course also include the civilised woman. But this is an element that for the present one does not miss—every other note is so articulate and direct.

It is a part of the satisfaction the author gives us that he can make us speculate as to whether he will be able to complete his picture altogether (this is as far as we presume to go in meddling with the question of his future) without bringing in the complicated soul. On the day he does so, if he handles it with anything like the cleverness he has already shown, the expectation of his friends will take a great bound. Meanwhile, at any rate, we have Mulvaney, and Mulvaney is after all tolerably complicated. He is only a six-foot saturated Irish private, but he is a considerable pledge of more to come. Hasn't he, for that matter, the tongue of a hoarse syren, and hasn't he also mysteries and infinitudes almost Carlylese? Since I am speaking of him I may as well say that, as an evocation, he has probably led captive those of Mr. Kipling's readers who have most given up resistance. He is a piece of portraiture of the largest, vividest kind, growing and growing on the painter's hands without ever outgrowing them. I can't help regarding him, in a certain sense, as Mr. Kipling's tutelary deity—a landmark in the direction in which it is open to him to look furthest. If the author will only go as far in this direction as Mulvaney is capable of taking him (and the inimitable Irishman is, like Voltaire's Habakkuk, *capable de tout*), he may still discover a treasure and find a reward for the services he has rendered the winner of Dinah Shadd. I hasten to add that the truly appreciative reader should surely have no quarrel with the primitive element in Mr. Kipling's subject-matter, or with what, for want of a better name, I may call his love of low life. What is that but essentially a part of his freshness? And for what part of his freshness are we exactly more thankful than for just this smart jostle that he gives the old stupid superstition that the amiability of a storyteller is the amiability of the people he represents—that their vulgarity, or depravity, or gentility, or fatuity are tantamount to the same qualities in the painter himself? A blow from which, apparently, it will not easily recover is dealt this infantine philosophy by Mr. Howells when, with the most distinguished dexterity and all the detachment of a master, he handles some of the clumsiest, crudest, most human things in life—answering surely thereby the playgoers in the sixpenny gallery who howl at the representative of the villain when he comes before the curtain.

Nothing is more refreshing than this active, disinterested sense of the real; it is doubtless the quality for the want of more of which our English and American fiction has turned so woefully stale. We are ridden by the old conventionalities of type and small proprieties of observance—by the foolish baby-formula (to put it sketchily) of the picture and the subject. Mr. Kipling has all the air of being disposed to lift the whole business off the nursery carpet, and of being perhaps even more affable than he is disposed. One must hasten of course to parenthesise that there is not, intrinsically, a bit more luminosity in treating of low life and of primitive man than of those whom civilisation has kneaded to a finer paste: the only luminosity in either case is in the intelligence with which the thing is done. But it so happens that, among ourselves, the frank, capable outlook, when turned upon the vulgar majority, the coarse, receding edges of the social perspective, borrows a charm from being new; such a charm as, for instance, repetition has already despoiled it of among the French—the hapless French who pay the penalty as well as enjoy the glow of living intellectually so much faster than we. It is the most inexorable part of our fate that we grow tired of everything, and of course in due time we may grow tired even of what explorers shall come back to tell us about the great grimy condition, or with unprecedented items and details, about the grey middle state which darkens into it. But the explorers, bless them! may have a long day before that; it is early to trouble about reactions, so that we must give them the benefit of every presumption. We are thankful for any boldness and any sharp curiosity, and that is why we are thankful for Mr. Kipling's general spirit and for most of his excursions.

Many of these, certainly, are into a region not to be designated as superficially dim, though indeed the author always reminds us that India is above all the land of mystery. A large part of his high spirits, and of ours, comes doubtless from the amusement of such vivid, heterogeneous material, from the irresistible magic of scorching suns, subject empires, uncanny religions, uneasy garrisons and smothered-up women—from heat and colour and danger and dust. India is a portentous image, and we are duly awed by the familiarities it undergoes at Mr. Kipling's hands and by the fine impunity, the sort of fortune that favours the brave, of *his* want of awe. An abject humility is not his strong point, but he gives us something instead of it—vividness and drollery, the vision and the thrill of many things, the misery and strangeness of most, the personal sense of a hundred queer contacts and risks. And then in the absence of respect he has plenty of knowledge, and if knowledge should fail him he would have plenty of invention. Moreover, if invention should ever fail him, he would still have the lyric string and the patriotic chord, on which he plays admirably; so that it may be said he is a man of resources. What he gives us, above all, is the feeling of the English manner and the English blood in conditions they have made at once so much and so little their own; with manifestations grotesque enough in some of his satiric sketches and deeply impressive in some of his anecdotes of individual responsibility.

His Indian impressions divide themselves into three groups, one of which, I think, very much outshines the others. First to be mentioned are the tales of native life, curious glimpses of custom and superstition, dusky matters not beholden of the many, for which the author has a remarkable flair. Then comes the social, the Anglo-Indian episode, the study of administration and military types and of the wonderful rattling, riding ladies who, at Simla and more desperate stations, look out for husbands and lovers; often, it would seem, the husbands and lovers of others. The most brilliant group is devoted wholly to the common soldier, and of this series it appears to me that too much good is hardly to be said. Here Mr. Kipling, with all his offhandness, is a master; for we are held not so much by the greater or less oddity of the particular yarn—sometimes it is scarcely a yarn at all, but something much less artificial—as by the robust attitude of the narrator, who never arranges or glosses or falsifies, but makes straight for the common and the characteristic. I have mentioned the great esteem in which I hold Mulvaney—surely a charming man and one qualified to adorn a higher sphere. Mulvaney is a creation to be proud of, and his two comrades stand as firm on their legs. In spite of Mulvaney's social possibilities they are all three finished brutes; but it is precisely in the finish that we delight. Whatever Mr. Kipling may relate about them for ever will encounter readers equally fascinated and unable fully to justify their faith.

Are not those literary pleasures after all the most intense which are the most perverse and whimsical, and even indefensible? There is a logic in them somewhere, but it often lies below the plummet of criticism. The spell may be weak in a writer who has every reasonable and regular claim, and it may be irresistible in one who presents himself with a style corresponding to a bad hat. A good hat is better than a bad one, but a conjurer may wear either. Many a reader will never be able to say what secret human force lays its hand upon him when Private Ortheris, having sworn 'quietly into the blue sky', goes mad with home-sickness by the yellow river and raves for the basest sights and sounds of London. I can scarcely tell why I think 'The Courting of Dinah Shadd' a masterpiece (though, indeed, I can make a shrewd guess at one of the reasons), nor would it be worth while perhaps to attempt to defend the same pretension in regard to 'On Greenhow Hill'—much less to trouble the tolerant reader of these remarks with a statement of how many more performances in the nature of 'The End of the Passage' (quite admitting even that they might not represent Mr. Kipling at his best), I am conscious of a latent relish for. One might as well admit while one is about it that one has wept profusely over 'The Drums of the Fore and Aft', the history of the 'Dutch courage' of two dreadful dirty little boys, who, in the face of Afghans scarcely more dreadful, saved the reputation of their regiment and perished, the least mawkishly in the world, in a squalor of battle incomparably expressed. People who know how peaceful they are themselves and have no bloodshed to reproach themselves with needn't scruple to mention the glamour that Mr. Kipling's intense militarism has for them and how astonishingly contagious they find it, in spite of the unromantic complexion of it—the way it bristles with all sorts of uglinesses and technicalities. Perhaps that is why I go all the way even with *The Gadsbys*—the Gadsbys were so connected (uncomfortably it is true) with the Army. There is fearful fighting—or a fearful danger of it—in 'The Man who would be King': is that the reason we are deeply affected by this extraordinary tale? It is one of them, doubtless, for Mr. Kipling has many reasons, after all, on his side, though they don't equally call aloud to be uttered.

One more of them, at any rate, I must add to these unsystematised remarks—it is the one I spoke of a shrewd guess at in alluding to 'The Courting of Dinah Shadd'. The talent that produces such a tale is a talent eminently in harmony with the short story, and the short story is, on our side of the Channel and of the Atlantic, a mine which will take a great deal of working. Admirable is the clearness with which Mr. Kipling perceives this—perceives what innumerable chances it gives, chances of touching life in a thousand different places, taking it up in innumerable pieces, each a specimen and an illustration. In a word, he appreciates the episode, and there are signs to show that this shrewdness will, in general, have long innings. It will find the detachable, compressible 'case' an admirable, flexible form; the cultivation of which may well add to the mistrust already entertained by Mr. Kipling, if his manner does not betray him, for what is clumsy and tasteless in the time-honoured practice of the 'plot'. It will fortify him in the conviction that the vivid picture has a greater communicative value than the Chinese puzzle. There is little enough plot in such a perfect little piece of hard representation as 'The End of the Passage', to cite again only the most salient of twenty examples.

But I am speaking of our author's future, which is the luxury that I meant to forbid myself—precisely because the subject is so tempting. There is nothing in the world (for the prophet) so charming as to prophesy, and as there is nothing so inconclusive the tendency should be repressed in proportion as the opportunity is good. There is a certain want of courtesy to a peculiarly contemporaneous present even in speculating, with a dozen deferential precautions, on the question of what will become in the later hours of the day of a talent that has got up so early. Mr. Kipling's actual performance is like a tremendous walk before breakfast, making one welcome the idea of the meal, but consider with some alarm the hours still to be traversed. Yet if his breakfast is all to come the indications are that he will be more active than ever after he has had it. Among these indications are the unflagging character of his pace and the excellent form, as they say in athletic circles, in which he gets over the ground. We don't detect him stumbling; on the contrary, he steps out quite as briskly as at first and still more firmly. There is something zealous and craftsman-like in him which shows that he feels both joy and responsibility. A whimsical, wanton reader, haunted by a recollection of all the good things he has seen spoiled; by a sense of the miserable, or, at any rate, the inferior, in so many continuations and endings, is almost capable of perverting poetic justice to the idea that it would be even positively well for so surprising a producer to remain simply the fortunate, suggestive, unconfirmed and unqualified representative of what he has actually done. We can always refer to that.

22. An Open Letter to Rudyard Kipling

1892

From *Letters to Eminent Hands* (1892), pp. 56–61. The book (suggested by Andrew Lang's *Letters to Dead Authors*, 1886) was published over the pseudonym '*i*' [iota], but was later acknowledged by its author. Other living authors addressed included Hardy, George Moore, R. L. Stevenson, Lang, Anstey, Bret Harte, etc.

Gleeson White (1851–1898) was best known as an art critic, his publications including *English Illustration* (1897) and *Master Painters of Britain*, 4 vols. (1897–8). He also edited *Ballads and Rondeaux* (1887), *The Pageant* (1896–7) and other volumes notable in the nineties.

TO RUDYARD KIPLING, ESQ.

Sir,

What is to hinder your fame being 'dispershed most notoriously in sev'ril volumes'? Today under the novel spell of your genius we are all in the uncritical stage of hero-worship. First came the rumour of another new genius 'from the East', after the manner of creeds from time immemorial; next, during a period of ignorant but vicious antagonism, and an inward resolve to stand upon one's dignity, refusing to accept a new genius at any man's bidding, we read a chance thing of yours, and were still more decided to keep a firm attitude of neutrality. Then, alas for our consistency, came *Departmental Ditties*, *Plain Tales from the Hills*, and so on to *Life's Handicap*, compelling an abject down-climb and complete surrender; since when, we have delighted to pass on the badge of servitude to the unenlightened, and be your most obedient and humble servants.

Having thus become converts, it was curious to find 'Cheop's Pyramid' familiar; and it would be interesting to ask how many of its present admirers remember it quoted as from a pamphlet 'in the shape of an official paper, the envelope is the cover', in *The Sign of the Ship*, October 1886. The Indian *vers de société*, by the modest author who did not give his name, were then formally introduced to London, as any doubter may see by reference to his set of *Longman's Magazine*, if he be wise enough to bind those pleasant monthly gossips of men and books.

Now while a nation is grovelling at your feet, will you display an English contempt towards such servile adulation, or the kindly forbearance with a tinge of deeper brotherhood that, we fancy, underlies all your cynicism? For you write of 'niggers' and children with a loving pen—not sentimentally, nor patronisingly, but with the manlier tone of kinship with the least of these, that whined as it may be by specious hypocrites, is yet the noblest truth of our common life.

The gods be thanked that although you are popular you have humour. Can it be that the British public is awakening to that salt of life? After periods of theological meanderings and savage blood-letting, it is good to think that Bret Harte is yet a power and that you are becoming one. On every side, if you look hard for it—in spite of 'fads' and comic papers, in spite of burlesques at the theatres and comic songs—there appears to be a streak of humour lightening the dull grey sky. We have had a serious epoch—gloomy in literature, gloomy in art and in its professionally comic element gloomier than words may say. Is it passing away? Dickens roused the nation to its last hearty laugh. Du Maurier has made us smile; Gilbert has delighted a comparative few; but the whole mass of English people still affect to believe *Ally Sloper* a comic person, instead of a tragedian of some rude power. Ouïda is powerful; but Miss Rhoda Broughton's humour nearly lost her respectability. To be cynical, even though you have humour—as Mr. Lang for instance—is pardoned: to be humorous without much cynicism is not, or was not until lately, permissible. Heaps of people voted *Vice Versa* a dull book. There are those who fail to find the *Bab Ballads* funny, or Mr. Anstey's *Burglar Bill* an uproariously amusing collection. But from the cliques who believe in such things, and the crowd who are—so we hope—about to welcome you, it may be that the English lack of humour will be a reproach out of date soon, and that *Merry England* will no longer indicate an excellent but somewhat obscure magazine, but be a worthy term to apply to our great empire, which knows no sunset and has no name.

To have made India a real place to dwellers in Great Britain is in itself an imperial conquest. *Mr. Isaacs*,[1] *The Dilemma*,[2] and a few other novels awoke English stay-at-homes to the fact that there was an English society in India. Mr. Phil Robinson[3] added the beasts and birds; and now you have thrown in the rank and file of the British Army and a few million natives to complete our mental picture of the great empire that was not officially recognised in *Whitaker's Almanac* as a part of the British Crown until recent years, and is still to most people but an excuse for a party cry, or a useful place to acquire enlarged livers and reduced pensions.

From America comes news of a 'Rudyard Kipling' Society for the study of your works. Philadelphia claims the honour of this somewhat premature attempt to exploit you. Personal paragraphs full of charming detail are already showing the brilliant invention of the Western boys. Will you find them as charming as the dusky Eastern ones, or will you return to the Orient disgusted with our commonplace lot? Yet Anglo-Indian colonels, who proffer much detail of your early life unasked, spin a yarn as colourless and respectable as though you were a person of no genius whatever, and had never lived in a place 'where the best is like the worst—where there aren't no Ten Commandments, an' a man can raise a thirst'.

It is to be hoped that, cleverly as you depict society and its foibles and keenly conscious as you are that even its puppets are men and women with passions, it will not monopolise your pen. The hand that sketched *Soldiers Three* and *Black and White* can do greater work. The studies of native life collected under various titles have importance far beyond their relative size. 'Without Benefit of Clergy', 'The Man who Was', and a dozen others are each told in few pages, and yet fill a space on the shelves of the real library we carry with us wherever we go, entirely beyond the whole series of volumes by many quite respectable authors. 'Danny Deever' alone is a masterpiece hard to parallel. 'Rizpah' with all its grim horror affects us less strongly, for the humour of 'Danny Deever' adds awful force to the tragedy so wonderfully told. Like a clever impressionist your aim is for colour, air and light, with the supreme moment only. Your art is modern in its breadth and classical in its restraint. No words are too mean or common for you to use, but you employ them with the vivid, direct power that is itself proof of mastery. Only those who grope for *the* word, and,

---

[1] [1882. By F. Marion Crawford]
[2] [1876. By Sir George Chesney]
[3] [*In My Indian Garden*, 1878]

failing, have to make shift with a possible synonym, can realise the delight of finding a writer who knows his trade, can handle his tools deftly, and is aware of the enormous wealth of material at hand in the vernacular of the masses hitherto deemed undignified for literary uses.

You show that hybrid monstrosities, Latinised polysyllables or scientific terminology dragged from its lawful place are none of them required to make good honest English. The power of making colloquial prose telling and yet understanded of the people is an enviable gift, and you possess it; and for it we ought all—yourself as well as ourselves—to thank the gods and pray that the example may not be in vain.

You have the daring of youth with the knowledge that comes later. It has been said there was never a 'prodigy' in painting, and rarely in literature; but you are not far off becoming an example of the latter. You dare also to be frank and nearly raise the blush to Mrs. Grundy's cheek. 'The Taking of Lungtungpen', for instance, is a shock to her 'dasincy' as much as to 'Lift'nint Brazenose'. We recall Marryat's open-air humour, or the breezy animal spirits of Fielding and Smollett when such pages appear, and long more than ever for a unanimous and vigorous protest against the societies for the suggestion of pruriency that weigh us down.

The large virtue of Purity we all prize, but the small vice of Prudery should be shocked to death; and there are not wanting signs that you may help to do it. There are many pages of Indian life and manners, no doubt familiar to you, that would terrify a respectable Philistine to hear. Although we are so used to condoning English vices, we have still a shudder left for alien ones; and if it is not within your programme to revive our code of morality, a study of Eastern manners is a good tonic to spur our jaded sensibility to call right and wrong by their proper names, and not confound sins against society with sins against natural morality.

But here creeps in the cant of the day, and all unwittingly you are requested to be a moralist with a mission. For this—ten thousand pardons—the parochial influences will tell after years spent under their sway. The didactic moralising called art criticism, and the sermons in stones, parables in paint, and homilies in marble we have been taught to expect have naturally dulled our love of Art; and cause us even now to forget that in an artist we have no more right to look for a reformer of society than to expect a bishop, say, to know aught of art. If they both chance to stray into the domains of the other, it is, as a rule, the worse for their own kingdoms. So, forbearing all hope that you will do much to convert us, let us thank you for amusing us, for awakening our sense of humour to a new response and touching our hearts in a way not perilous to true manly dignity; and above all for the creation of the undying *Soldiers Three*, and the budget of songs worthy of such heroes. To have spurred the money-grubbing apathy of this prosaic generation to show new interest in its fighting-men is a supreme achievement; for if in the course of events we have suddenly to fight for the honour and existence of Old England as a nation, the spirit aroused in raw recruits by your rollicking songs might be worth more than the addition of a million mercenaries to our little army, and prove, even as the 'Marseillaise' or the 'Watch by the Rhine' has shown before, the overwhelming power of a war-cry that touches the hearts and nerves the sinews of those in battle. Such sentiments as those expressed in 'The Drums of the Fore and Aft', or 'the Young British Soldier'—

> When you're wounded and left on Afghanistan's plains,
> An' the women come out to cut up your remains,
> Just roll to your rifle, an' blow out your brains,
> And go to your Gawd like a soldier—

are worth all the excellent leaflets on temperance, all the plaintive stories of the Hedley Vicars type—nay, may even be more powerful than the graphic summary of the life of a Havelock, in evoking the simple obedience and pagan stoicism which are worth as much today as ever they were in the stern prose of warfare.

From Rudyard Kipling as a writer of short stories to the same author as the saviour of an empire is a far cry; yet precedents exist to show that such a forecast however improbable can hardly be deemed impossible. But whether you become a mythological entity or remain merely a first-rate storyteller, matters little; the love you have won from British hearts is hardly a passing fancy, but a good life-long devotion that will stick to you, and possibly bore you with its indiscriminating laudation for many a long year.

23. Letters from Lafcadio Hearn
1892–8

Extracts quoted from *The Life and Letters of Lafcadio Hearn* (1906) by Elizabeth Bisland.

Lafcadio Hearn (1850–1904), half English and half Greek, was the well-known writer on Japan who married a Japanese girl, took Japanese nationality, and became Professor of English Literature at Tokyo University.

---

1. From Lafcadio Hearn to Ellwood Hendrick: April 1892: '. . . I hate the Jesuit; but he has a particular cleverness of his own indeed. I hate him first because he is insincere, as you suggest; then I hate him because he is morbid, with a priestly morbidness—sickly, cynical, unhealthy. I like Kipling's morbidness, which is manly and full of enormous resolve and defiance in the teeth of God and hell and nature.'

2. From Lafcadio Hearn to Ellwood Hendrick: January 1895: '. . . Kipling is priceless—the single story of Puran Bhagat is worth a kingdom; and the suggestive moral of human life is such a miracle! I can't tell you what pleasure it gave me.'

3. From Lafcadio Hearn to Ellwood Hendrick: February 1897: '. . . Oh! have you ever read those two marvellous things of Kipling's last—"McAndrews' Hymn", and "The Mary Gloster"? Especially the "Mary Gloster"! I have no more qualified ideas about Kipling. He is to my fixed conviction the greatest of living English poets, and greater than all before him in the line he has taken. As for England, he is her modern Saga-man—skald, scôp, whatever you like; lineal descendants of those fellows to whom the Berserker used to say: "Now you just stand right here, and see us fight so that you can make a song about it." '

4. From Lafcadio Hearn to Mitchell McDonald: December 1898: '. . . Ah! I had almost forgotten. I *have* Kipling's "Day's Work" already. It is great—very great. Don't mistake him, even if he seems too colloquial at times. He is the greatest living English poet and English storyteller. Never in this world will I be able to write one page to compare with a page of his. He makes me feel so small, that after reading him I wonder why I am such an ass as to write at all.'

24. Quiller-Couch on Kipling's Verse

1893

From signed article 'Reviews and Reminders. II. On Some Living English Poets' (review of *Barrack-Room Ballads* and eight other volumes of contemporary verse) in the *English Illustrated Magazine*, Vol. X, No. 120, pp. 901–3 (September 1893).

Sir Arthur T. Quiller-Couch (1863–1944), scholar, novelist, appointed Professor of English Literature at Cambridge in 1912. 'Q' lived by his fiction and by journalism until he received the chair at Cambridge, but had already edited *The Oxford Book of English Verse* and contributed literary *causeries* and reviews to the *Pall Mall Magazine* ('From a Cornish Window') and *The Speaker* for periods of several years. He is best remembered for his Cambridge lectures of later years.

... 'Is English Poetry Dead?' Well here, in the first place comes Mr. William Ernest Henley, who has truculence enough at any rate to answer that question in Captain Timothy Edward's fashion; and here also comes Mr. Rudyard Kipling to supply plenty more in the very unlikely case of Mr. Henley's running short. I put these two writers together for the moment because their work (in verse) though very different in method and texture, has certain points of resemblance too salient to be ignored. The sudden growth of Mr. Henley's influence among young writers both of verse and prose strikes me as about the most remarkable phenomenon in the recent history of English letters. I believe (though I speak without precise knowledge) that it may be said to date from the summer of 1888, when his *A Book of Verse* was published by Mr. David Nutt. This little volume sounded a clear challenge. Its temper no less than its unusual handling of rhythm bespoke the innovator. And this challenge Mr. Henley repeated in 1890 with his *Views and Reviews*—and again last year with his *Song of the Sword and other Verses*. But the secret of Mr. Henley's influence has been his editorship of the *National* (late the *Scots'*) *Observer*. He stepped into this post at a time when many were disposed to shake their heads over his future and prophesy that his fine stream of originality, missing its proper channel, would waste itself in the sands. But in the nick of time —though he is perhaps too stout to admit this—came the right kind of opportunity; a captaincy for a born fighter and leader of men.

He can count many young men of talent within the circle of his influence, and one at least of genius. For good or ill that was an important day for Mr. Rudyard Kipling when he and Mr. Henley met; and as a poet one must allow that at present he seems immeasurably the better for it. Others may find more than facile vulgarity in *Departmental Ditties*. Having searched once and twice, I do not; save only in the penultimate poem 'The Galley-Slave', which really gave some promise of the splendid work to come. For the *Barrack Room* volume does indeed contain verse for which 'splendid' is the only term—so radiantly it glitters with incrustations of barbaric words. It has genius in it, of course, in the grim effectiveness (for instance) of 'Danny Deever':

[quotes DV. p. 398 (last stanza)]

and in the simple solemnity of the refrain

> Ford, ford, ford o'Kabul river.
> Ford o'Kabul river in the dark!

in every line of 'East and West'—in almost every line of 'The English Flag', and throughout in the stirring 'Envoi', a poem that takes you by the heart and shakes you. But the first reflection to which this volume gives rise is that which Mr. Henley once made upon Dickens. 'He developed into an artist in words . . . but his development was his own work, and it is a fact that should redound eternally to his honour that he began in newspaper English . . . and went on to become an exemplar.' Mr. Kipling suffers and must suffer, the penalty which awaits every writer who wins renown in youth and has henceforward to develop under the public's eye. Because he has originality he will be continually making experiments in his art; and whenever an experiment fails a dozen critics will arise in their seats and announce that this young author is deteriorating. 'Thus and thus,' they say, 'is poetry written'—

> Thus Gods are made
> And who so makes them otherwise shall die.

We may take comfort in the thought that Mr. Kipling is the last man in the world to listen to them.

To set forth, as only art can, the beauty and the joy of living, the beauty and the blessedness of death, the glory of battle and adventure, the nobility of devotion—to a cause, an ideal, a passion even—the dignity, of resistance, the sacred quality of patriotism.

This was Mr. Henley's ambition, as he declares, when he selected and arranged the other day that capital book of verse for boys *Lyra Heroica*; and this, too, would seem to be the aim of his own poetry. It may stand as his artistic creed—his and Mr. Kipling's. But while Mr. Kipling assails us with simple and even vulgar metres and dazzling crudities of speech, Mr. Henley's versification is learned and elaborate, and his language charged with literary feeling. The *Barrack Room Ballads* are just doggerel in apotheosis, doggerel lifted out of its sphere by a touch of genius. *The London Voluntaries* are ripe and well-considered achievements in rhythm. Each poet loves the highly coloured word; but the word which Mr. Henley selects has taken its colour from a score of literary reminiscences . . . Mr. Henley loves life for the romance in it, and has a beautiful word for its romantic associations. Mr. Kipling finds the East enchanting, for instance, by right of having been born there; Mr. Henley by right of having made acquaintance with it in the pages of the *Arabian Nights Entertainments* . . .

[After two more paragraphs on Henley, 'Q' goes on to review volumes by Norman Gale, George Meredith, Richard Le Gallienne, Arthur Symons, James Dryden Hosken, William Watson (three collections) and T. E. Brown.]

25. George Saintsbury on *Many Inventions*

1893

Review from unidentified periodical, reprinted in *A Last Vintage: Essays and Papers by George Saintsbury* (1950), pp. 178–9.

George Saintsbury (1845–1933), after twenty years of journalism, succeeded David Masson as Professor of Rhetoric and English Literature at Edinburgh University from 1895 to 1915. He is remembered for his many scholarly and critical works such as *A Short History of English Literature* (1898), *A History of English Prosody* (1906–21), *A History of English Criticism* (1911) and *The Peace of the Augustans* (1916). His only Dedication was of *Notes on a Cellar Book* (1920) to Kipling, in which he regretted that he had never had the chance of reviewing any of his books—obviously forgetting this short, early estimate.

Many Inventions is not only good, but very good. I am inclined to think it, using words carefully, the best volume that Mr. Kipling has done. It is, of course, unequal; nobody could write fourteen different tales of the widest range of subject and style and not be unequal. Of course one reader will like this better than that, and another that better than this. The stories draw nigh with fitful success to that 'True Romance' which Mr. Kipling has celebrated, in verse as heartfelt if not quite as finished as he has ever written, at the beginning of the book, and has not extolled too much. For what is romance but creation? and what is creation if not divine? As for the separate stories, I confess to being in something like the frame of mind of Miss Snevellicci's papa—'I love 'em every one,' but as a person of taste must speak with graduated affection, I think I like 'My Lord the Elephant' most as a whole, and 'The Children of the Zodiac' least. The 'Finest Story in the World' which is itself a legend of metempsychosis, has affected me in a very strange fashion, for it seems to me that (in another state of existence, of course) I heard Mr. Kipling tell it, and tell it better than here. 'His

Private Honour' is the noblest and most complete; the conclusion of 'Love o' Women' (which seems to me as a whole to suffer from ups and downs) is the most passionate and accomplished, I am too much of a Jingo to be quite a fair judge of 'Judson and the Empire' or 'A Conference of Powers', but it is to me a blessed thing to think that Mr. Kipling, like Kingsley before him, will breed up Jingos by the thousand. *Badalia Herodsfoot*, though excellent, has been done better before by Dickens and others, with a little less freedom of speech than Mr. Kipling is nowadays permitted to use. I would not wish for a better farce than 'Brugglesmith'; (did Mr. Kipling ever dree the more terrible weird not of being unable to get away from an adhesive drunken man, but of having to look after an evasive one?) And of the more imaginative and ghostly pieces 'The Lost Legion' seems to me to bear the bell. But what a jejune enumeration of personal inpressions is this! For the book is to be read and rejoiced over by the reader, not analysed or even pronounced on by the critic, 'which is 'is 'abit', as Mr. Kipling's friend the policeman says.

26. S. R. Crockett 'On Some Tales of Mr. Kipling's'

1895

Signed article from the *Bookman* (London), Vol. VII, pp. 139–40 (February 1895).

Samuel Rutherford Crockett (1860–1914), Scottish minister and novelist, began in the 'Kailyard School' and graduated as an historical romance writer of considerable power, *The Black Douglas* (1899) being his most outstanding work. He is also remembered for his children's story *Sir Toady Lion* (1897).

In a lonely Sussex house a number of men sat together. The cheerful dinner was done, the ingle flamed, and whenever one, rising, chanced to open the cottage door, the freshness of the still and breathing spring night stole in. There were among these men editors, critics, dons, and writers—modest men all, who yet had tried, each within his possible, to do something. There was talk and turmoil—the incidence of liking, the extreme dissidence of dissent. From argument they went to criticism, and in the forecasting of the future, reputations suffered. All the while the great editor sat above them (in a smoking-jacket), as the gods sit, dividing good and evil. Finally they fell upon a new play.

They resolved to write out, each for himself, a list of the best half-dozen of Mr. Kipling's short stories. The papers were folded. They were put into the hat, and the editor, well-accustomed, made out the final result. 'The Man who would be King' stood proudly at the head of every list, followed by 'At the End of the Passage', 'Without Benefit of Clergy', 'The Drums of the Fore-and-Aft', and I forget what other.

It is a game that anyone can try, and the results may be varied from theirs. But the fact stood clear that men of book and pen read Kipling for their own pleasure; and, what is more, remember him.

Afterward they fell a-talking of the author. They recalled how he flashed upon the world, various discoverers claiming him—like a new planet with an Adams and a Leverrier on the staff of every paper.

'In Vishnu-land what Avatar?' cried Browning long ago from among the tangled bowers of 'Bells and Pomegranates', when Waring took his wayward forth-going out of the ken of men—to return, not Waring, but merely Alfred Domett, a forgotten New Zealand statesman with an unmanageable epic. For Kipling, and not Domett, was to be the Avatar of Vishnu-land.

To myself the Revealer of the East was made plain one day when a curious-looking book came to me from India, bearing a strange imprint, as though Charles Dickens had been inventing names for the publishers of the Orient.[1]

On the sandhills of Colwyn the Elder I lay and read, while a wind from the sea whipped the leaves. I found a new language. I trod among unknown allusions. The East, the skirts of which I had trod, spoke to me for the first time with authentic voice.

For Fortune was good to me. She opened the book at a Jubilee Ode, which, had a careful eye noted the image and superscription thereof, would assuredly not have been read. For who in the later eighties would read Jubilee Odes, compound of the patriotism and the champagne of the day before yesterday?

But this ran on in other fashion. And small wonder it was that staid Anglo-Indians marvelled what snake had crept within the robustly military columns of their favourite journal, and was now hissing at them with erected crest.

> By the well where the bullocks go,
> Silent and blind and slow,
> By the field where the young corn dies,
> In the face of the sultry skies,
> They have heard as the dull earth hears,
> The sound of the wind of an hour,
> The sound of a great Queen's voice:
> 'My God hath granted me years.
> Hath granted dominion and power,
> And I bid you, O land, rejoice!'
>
> But the ploughman settled the share
> More deep in the grudging clod,
> For he saith, 'The wheat is my care,
> And the rest is the will of God!'

[1] [*Departmental Ditties* (3rd. Edn.), Thacker & Spink: Calcutta, 1888]

Thus the words came grimly, solemnly, laden with sympathy for India's inarticulate millions—hopeless, futureless, undesirous even of speech. It is possible that these words, and others in the same set of verses, are oftener remembered by one to whom they told of a new power beginning to be eloquent in the East, than even by the man who wrote them himself.

And there is something here which Mr. Kipling has never yet given rein to—perhaps the preaching strain in the background of his soul. He 'believes in God and the angels', like Colonel John Hay's prairie pioneer, and still more perhaps in the Law Inexorable which strikes once and no more, And, in that case, the preaching is sure to come.

Then the grey paper books began to pour, and we laughed and fought with the much-enduring Mulvaney, trained 'tarriers and poops' with Jock, longed for London 'and the stinks of her' with the Cockney Ortheris.

And we that were of the heather and the salt water were just as mad as the others. The style? queried the critic, whose duty it was to keep his head among the smother of our admiration. Bah! We did not care for the style. It was great story-telling—bold, free, effortless. And we found a sentence to fling at the critic too: 'And over the bastions of Fort Amara, broke the pitiless day. ' "Better that!" we cried at him.'

And then, as Mr. Kipling himself might say, 'there was a great silence between the howling of the jackals'.

As each succeeding book came to us, it grew clearer that the romance writer of the specialist had come to us. He grasped the mechanism of life—and that not only in the Orient. On the seas he 'knew the ropes'. Down in the engineer's grimy Inferno who but him had been keeping an eye upon the gauges. Doctors said; 'None but a doctor could have known that!' Military men claimed him as a comrade. Mr. Thomas Atkins, private in the line, declared him (with the Adjective) to be a time-expired gentleman-ranker. Newspaper men knew him for one who understood how 'to fake the paper' when moribund royalty will not die, the premier will not resign, or the wires are down in the North.

Clearer than the events of our last year's holiday lived the tale for us. We opened the pages at random, and so that Mr. Kipling told of India, in a trice we were transported. Wet, weariness, and day-worry were forgotten. In a moment there was blown across our nostrils the acrid whiff of wood smoke—the danker smell of rotting leaves, and of rushing hill torrents that flow from the caverns under—the true Himalaya smell—which, as Mr. Kipling says, when once a man smells, he will surely come back even from the ends of the earth to smell it again 'ere he die.

Or, as it may happen, we sweltered in the flaring daylong heats on some God-forsaken Indian embankment. We rode about the pine-woods of Simla and watched the star rise over the glacier.

The compact multifarious Indies pushed and shouldered through the tranced pages—Bengali, Sikh, Pathan, men meek of countenance, ghouls fiendish of eye, ill-favoured and treacherous men with long hair from the hills of the horse thieves on the North-Western frontier. We rode a-foraying with the Zukka Kehl, and knew all the while that the alert police officer on the other side of the frontier was going to catch us every time. In which case we should as surely be hanged for the greater glory of Law and Order. And so it ought to be. For when will ever Mr. Kipling give a chance to the horse that never knew a bridle, and the gipsying blood that will call no man master while the world lasts?

But what a new world it was, and what service and thank we owed to the caravels of the Columbus of the East, who pursued Mr. Bret Harte across the prairies and through the gulches, and bore eastward from the Farthest West the secret of its barbaric saga. The pre-Kipling generation had only to glimpse the word 'Indian' at the head of an article, or upon the title of a book, to retreat with a boredom that verged upon disgust. Just as the Indian Budget, or indeed Indian discussions generally, cleared the benches in the House of Commons, so the Indian tale, suggesting tiger-shooting and blue books with an occasional Mahatma, was left alone, untended, to die on the waste. It was once indeed permitted to Mr. Marion Crawford; but editors told him not to do it again, and he wisely obeyed them. Now Mr. Kipling changed all that, and the tribes of the East spoke to us authentic, every man in his own tongue. And more than all our hearts are stirred for Tommy Atkins, whether he might be hanged, like Danny Deever, high as Haman in the hollow square of the regiment, or whether he might finish his career in the worthiest way, as a commissaire outside the 'Grand Metropole'.

> Give him a letter,
> Can't do no better,
> Late Troop-Sergeant-Major, an'—runs with a letter!
> Think what he's been,
> Think what he's seen,
> Think of his pension an'
> GOD SAVE THE QUEEN.

And the faults? To another be the ungracious task for the drums have begun to roll, and the fever's in the blood.

Mr. Kipling may sometimes be inclined, as Mr. Stevenson says, to the heresy of Cain, in that he would let his brother go to the devil his own way. But I think that oftener he will be ready to square him up, and help him as the friendly private helped Mulvaney, 'to preserve his formation', till he lies down among the long grass for his longer rest. For we are inclined to think less of ourselves as it nears the sundown, and as our feet overpass more of 'The Long Trail—the Trail that is always new'.

If an apprentice at the writing trade may say the word, there are some verses of Mr. Kipling's which have often made him work the willinger and the worthier, so far as work he may.

> If there be good in that I wrought,
>   Thy hand compelled it, Master, Thine;
> Where I have failed to meet Thy thought,
>   I know, through thee, the blame is mine.
>
> One instant's toil to Thee denied,
>   Stands all eternity's offence,
> Of what I did with Thee to guide,
>   To Thee, through Thee, be excellence.
>
> Take not that vision from my ken,
>   O whatso'er may spoil or speed—
> Help me to need no aid from men,
>   That I may help such men as need.

27. Charles Eliot Norton on 'The Poetry of Rudyard Kipling'

1897

Signed article from the *Atlantic Monthly*, Vol. LXXIX, pp. 111–15 (January 1897).

Charles Eliot Norton (1827–1908) was Professor of the History of Art at Harvard 1875–98 and editor of Carlyle's letters and reminiscences (1883 and 1887). 'We are both of us awed, and if the truth be told a little scared at your article in the *Atlantic Monthly*,' wrote Kipling to Norton on 31 December 1896. 'You are the only man except my father and Uncle Ned [Burne-Jones] whose disapproval or advice slays me; and I will say just as one says to one's father when one is little, "I'll try to think and be better next time". But, even now, the notion that *you* should have reviewed me rather makes me gasp.'

During the last two or three years, we have often heard the lament that the Victorian era of poetry was closed: that with the death of Tennyson the last great voice had fallen silent; that only the small harpers with their glees were left, such as Chaucer saw sitting at the feet of the mighty masters of old; or that if one or two who might claim to belong to the band of fame lingered on, they were now old men, and their voices were no longer heard or were faint with age. But the lament was futile, however it might seem to be justified by the verse of the new Poet Laureate. Pye was Poet Laureate at the beginning of the century, as Austin is at its end. But before Pye died Scott and Wordsworth had already secured their seats among the immortals, and England, at the end of the century no less than at the beginning, is still the nursing mother of poets; and though Tennyson and his compeers be dead, her genius, with its eternal youth, is still finding fresh expression for itself, inspired with a novel poetic spirit as genuine as any that has moulded English verse.

This splendid continuous fertility of English genius, this unbroken poetic expression of English character and life from Chaucer to Rudyard Kipling, is unparalleled in the moral and intellectual history of any other race. For five full centuries England has had such a succession of poets as no other land can boast. There is no reason to fear that the succession will fail. One dynasty may follow another, but the throne will not lack a king. It is a change of dynasty which we are witnessing now, and it was the mistaking of this for a break in succession that has given occasion to the lament that the Victorian era of poetry had ended.

As we look back over the poetry of the century, two main inspiring motives, exhibiting a natural evolution of poetic doctrine and influence, are clearly distinguishable. The one, of which Wordsworth is the representative, proceeded direct from external nature in her relations to man; while the other, with many representatives from Keats to Tennyson, Arnold, Clough and Browning, was derived from human nature, from man himself in his various relations to the universe and to his kind. And all these latter poets, however they might differ in their look upon life, treated it either ideally and romantically, or else as matter mainly of introspective reflection and sentiment. Poetry with them was not so much an image of life as, on the one hand a scenic representation of it, and on the other a criticism of it. In their kind, the finer dramatic lyrics of Browning, scenic representations of life, may long stand unsurpassed, while for criticism and exposition of life of the intellectual order Clough and Arnold may have no rivals, as Tennyson may have none in the field of pure sentiment in exquisite lyrical form.

The poetry inspired by these motives was the adequate expression of the ideals of the age—of its shifting creeds, its doubts, its moral perplexities, its persistent introspection. The mood lasted for full fifty years, and never did the prevailing mood of the higher life of a people find nobler or more complete utterance. But meanwhile the process of mental and spiritual evolution was going on. The mood was gradually changing; the poets themselves, by uttering it, were exhibiting its limitations; it was a phase of the spiritual life of man, of which no age exhibits the full orb. A new generation had been growing up under these poets, with its own conceptions and aspirations and its new modes of confronting the conditions of existance. It found the poetic motives of the earlier part of the century insufficient; neither external nature nor human nature in any select aspect was what it cared most about. It had taken to heart the instructions of the poets; it aimed 'to see life steadily and see it *whole*', or, in Clough's words, 'to look straight out upon the big plain things that stare one in the face'. It took the whole world for its realm and was moved to depict it in its actual aspect and what was called its reality. The realists of yesterday or to-day are the legitimate offspring of the romanticists and idealists of the mid-century, following, as is often the habit of sons, a different course from that which their fathers pursued. The new spirit showed itself at first in prose fiction. It was weak and often misdirected. It waited for its poet. For realism—the aim to see the world and to depict it as it is—required for the fit performance of its work the highest exercise of the poetic imagination. The outward thing, the actual aspect, is in truth the real thing and the true aspect only when seen by the imaginative vision. To see a thing truly, a man must as Blake says, look *through*, not *with* the eye. The common reporter sees *with* his eye, and, meaning to tell the truth, tells a falsehood. But the imagination has insight, and what it sees is reality.

It is now some six or seven years since *Plain Tales from the Hills* gave proof that a man who saw through his eyes was studying life in India and was able to tell us what he saw. And those who read the scraps of verse prefixed to many of his stories, if they knew what poetry was, learned that their writer was at least potentially a poet, not by virtue of fantasy alone, but by his mastery of lyrical versification. The rhythm of these fragments had swing and ease and variety, and there was one complete little set of verses, at the head of the last story in the book, which made clear the writer's title to the name of poet. We had not then seen *Departmental Ditties and Other Verses*, or *Ballads and Barrack-Room Ballads*: they came to us before long, and showed that the qualities which distinguished Mr. Kipling's stories were not lacking in his poems. There was the same sure touch, the same insight, the same imaginative sympathy with all varieties of life, and the same sense of the moral significance of life even in its crudest, coarsest, and most vulgar aspects. Many of these verses were plainly the work of youth—of a boy full of talent, but not yet fully master of his own capacities, not yet wholly mastered by his own genius. They had a boyish audacity and extravagance; they were exuberant; there was too much talent in them, usurping the place and refusing the control of genius: but underneath their boyishness, and though their manner was not yet wholly subdued to art, there was a vital spirit of fresh and vigorous originality which, combined with extraordinary control of rhythmical expression, gave sure promise of higher manly achievement.

Mr. Kipling's progress as poet has been plain to those who have read the pieces from his hand which have appeared in magazine and newspaper in England and America, or have had their place in his volumes of stories during the last four or five years. A good part of this scattered verse is now gathered into *The Seven Seas*, but this volume is by no means a complete collection, and there are poems omitted from it which the lover of poetry can ill spare, and for which he would readily exchange some of those included in it.

But in spite of omissions and inclusions alike to be regretted, *The Seven Seas* contains a notable addition to the small treasury of enduring English verse, an addition sufficient to establish Mr. Kipling's right to take place in the honourable body of those English poets who have done England service in strengthening the foundations of her influence and of her fame. The dominant tone of his verse is indeed the patriotic; and it is the tone of the new patriotism, that of imperial England, which holds as one all parts of her wide-stretched empire, and binds them close in the indissoluble bond of common motherhood, and with the ties of common convictions, principles, and aims, derived from the teachings and traditions of the motherland, and expressed in the best verses of her poets. It is this passionate, moral, imperial patriotism that inspires the first poem in the book, 'The Song of the English', and which recurs again and again through its pages.

But if this be the dominant tone, easily recognized by every reader, the full scale which includes it and every other tone of Mr. Kipling's verse is that of actual life seen by the imagination intensely and comprehensively, and seen by it always, in all conditions and under all forms, as a moral experience, with the inevitable consequences resulting from the good or evil use of it.

The gift of imagination, with which as a quality Mr. Kipling is endowed as few men have ever been, has quickened and deepened his sympathies with men of every class and race, and given him free entrance to their hearts. He 'draws the thing as he sees it for the God of things as they are;' and the thing as he sees it is the relation of experience and conduct, while the rule of life which he deduces from it is that of 'Law, Duty, Order and Restraint, Obedience, Discipline'. He does not enforce this rule as a preacher from the pulpit, but, as Shakespeare teaches it, by the simple exhibition of life in its multiplicity and apparent confusion.

'What is a poet?' asks Wordsworth, and he answers his question: 'He is a man speaking to men . . . carrying everywhere with him relationship and love . . . He binds together by passion and knowledge the vast empire of human society.' And this vast empire of society includes the mean and the vulgar no less than the noble and the refined, Tommy Atkins and Bill 'Awkins as well as McAndrew and True Thomas. The recklessness, the coarseness, the brutality of Tommy Atkins, the spirit of the beast in man, all appear in the *Barrack-Room Ballads*, but not less his courage, his fidelity, his sense of duty, his obscure but deep-seated sentiment. The gist of all these Ballads is the display of the traits of human nature which makes this semi-savage 'most remarkable like you'. Yet it will not be only the fastidious and the super-refined reader who will find that some of the ballads might well be spared. There is more than one in this last volume which offends the taste by coarseness insufficiently redeemed by humour or by suggestion of virtue obscured by vulgarity, diminishes the charm of the book as a whole, and interferes with the commendation of it which might otherwise be hearty and unqualified. And yet, in condemning these few pieces, and in regretting their association with nobler work, I am reminded of a sentence in the *Apologie of Poetrie* of Sir John Harington, printed in the year 1591, which runs as follows:

But this I say, and I think I say truly: that there are many good lessons to be learned out of these poems, many good uses to be had of them, and that therefore they are not, nor ought not to be, despised by the wiser sort, but so to be studied and employed as was intended by the writer and deviser thereof, which is to soften and polish the hard and rough disposition of men, and make them capable of virtue and good discipline.

But enough of blame and of excuse. From the reek of the barrack-room we come out with delight to the open air and to the fresh breezes of the sea. For the sea has touched Mr. Kipling's imagination with its magic and its mystery, and never are his sympathies keener than with the men who go down upon it, and with the vast relations of human life to the waters that encircle the earth. Here too is manifest his love of England, the mistress of the sea. The ocean is the highway of her sons, and the paths of the ocean which they travel from one end of the earth to the other are paths from one region to another of her imperial dominion.

The passion for the sea, the mastery of its terrors, the confident but distrustful familiarity with it of the English seaman, have never had such expression as Mr. Kipling has given to them. From his splendid paean of 'The English Flag'—'What is the flag of England, winds of the world declare', to 'The Song of the English'—

We have fed our sea for a thousand years,
And she calls us, still unfed,
Though there's never a wave of all her waves
But marks our English dead

—his imagination dwells with vivifying emotion on the heroic combats—now victories, now defeats—of his race with the winds and the waves from which they draw their strength. All that belongs to the story of man upon the sea—the line-of-battle ship, the merchantman, the tramp steamer, the derelict, the little cargo-boats, the lighthouse, the bell-buoy—has its part in his verse of human experience. And so vivid are his appreciations of the poetic significance of even the most modern and practical of the conditions and aspects of sea life that in 'McAndrew's Hymn', a poem of surpassing excellence alike in conception and in execution, Mr. Kipling has sung the song of the marine steam-engine and all its machinery, from furnace-bars to screw, in such wise as to convert their clanging beats and throbs into a sublime symphony in accord with the singing of the morning stars. He has thus fulfilled a fine prophecy of Wordsworth's, that when the time should come, if it should ever come, when the discoveries and applications of science shall become

familiarized to men, and shall be ready to put on, as it were, a form of flesh and blood, the Poet will lend his divine spirit to aid the transfiguration, and will welcome the Being thus produced as a dear and genuine inmate of the household of man.

Such a poem as 'McAndrew's Hymn' is a masterpiece of realism in its clear insight into real significance of common things, and in its magnificent expression of it. Here Mr. Kipling is at his best, revealing the admirable quality of his imaginative vision and obeying the true command of his genius. It is not strange that the insistence of his varied and vigorous talents should often, during youth, when the exercise of talents is so delightful and so delusive, have interfered with his perfect obedience to the higher law of his inward being. And the less strange is it because of the ready acceptance of the work of talent by the world and by the critics, and their frequent lack of readiness of appreciation of the novel modes of genius. Moreover, this age of ours, like every other age, is full of false and misleading doctrines of art, of which the fallacies are often to be discovered by the artist only through his own hard experience. But the interested reader of Mr. Kipling's verse will not fail to note that almost from the beginning there were indications of his being possessed by the spirit which, whether it be called realist or idealist, sees things as they are; delights in their aspect; finds the shows of the earth good, yet recognizes that they all are but veils, concealments, and suggestions of the things better than themselves, of ideals always to be striven after, never to be attained. The dull-eyed man finds life dull and the earth unpoetic. He is McAndrew's 'damned ijjit' who asks: 'Mr. McAndrew, don't you think steam spoils romance at sea?' But the poet finds to-day as entertaining as any day that ever dawned, and man's life as interesting and as romantic as it ever was in old times. Yet he is not satisfied; he reveals this human life to himself as well as to his fellows; he gives to it its form of beauty; but for himself there is a something for which he longs, which he seeks for, and which always eludes him. It is his beloved, it is his ideal; it is what Mr. Kipling, in one of his most beautiful poems, and one in which he gives expression to his deepest self, calls the True Romance. This poem begins:

> Thy face is far from this our war,
>   Our call and counter-cry,
> I shall not find Thee quick and kind,
>   Nor know Thee till I die:
> Enough for me in dreams to see
>   And touch Thy garments' hem;
> Thy feet have trod so near to God
>   I may not follow them.

It is this poem which more than any other gives the key to the interpretation of Mr. Kipling's work in general, and displays its controlling aim. And more than this, it gives assurance of better work to come than any which Mr. Kipling has yet achieved. For as with every man who holds to a high ideal, pursuing it steadily, each step is a step in advance, so is it with the poet. The imagination, if it be a genuine faculty, and not a mere quality, is not to be worn out and exhausted by use. Nay, rather, it grows stronger with exercise; it is constantly quickened by each new experience; its insight becomes deeper and more keen. It is the poets in whom imagination is a secondary quality who, as they grow old, fail to equal their youthful selves. But the poets whose imagination is the essence of their being lose nothing, but gain always with advance of years. They are the real idealists.

I have said too little, in what precedes, concerning the gifts possessed by Mr. Kipling which would be matters of chief consideration with a minor poet—gifts subsidiary to his imagination, though dependent on it for their excellence—the frequent perfect mating of word with sentiment, the graphic epithet, the force, freedom, directness, and simplicity of diction, the exquisite movement and flow of rhythm, the felicity of rhyme. It would be easy to illustrate these qualities of his poetry by the selection of verses in which they are displayed; but there is little need to do so, for the poems are already familiar, not only to the readers of poetry, but to many who have hardly read any other verse. The *Barrack-Room Ballads*, set to old tunes, are already sung wherever the British soldier plants his camp. The correspondent of the London *Times*, who accompanied the recent expedition to Dongola, told in one of his letters how, while he was writing, he heard the soldiers outside his tent singing one of Kipling's songs.

The study of the forms of Mr. Kipling's verse must be left for some other occasion. It is enough now gratefully to recognize that he continues the great succession of royal English poets, and to pay to him the homage which is his due.

28. W. D. Howells on 'The Laureate of the Larger England'

1897

Signed review of *The Seven Seas* from *McClure's Magazine*, Vol. VIII, pp. 453–5 (March 1897).

William Dean Howells (1837–1920), famous American novelist and critic, was editor of *Atlantic Monthly* for ten years 'encouraging realism among the contributors' who included Mark Twain, Bret Harte and Henry James. Later he carried on the same policy as a member of the staff of *Harper's Magazine*.

If Mr. Rudyard Kipling should remain the chief poet of his race in his time, his primacy would be the most interesting witness of the imperial potentialities of that race in literature. He was not born English, if that means born in England, but the keynote of his latest volume is a patriotism intense beyond anything expressed by other English poets. He is so intense in the English loyalty which always mystifies us poor Americans, that one has a little difficulty in taking him at his word in it. But he is most serious, and in the presence of the fact one cannot help wondering how far the ties of affection, the sentiment of a merely inherited allegiance, can stretch. If we had not snapped them so summarily a century ago should we be glowing and thrilling at the name of England, which now awakens only a cold disgust in us, or at the notion of an anthropomorphic majesty, which only makes us smile? One cannot read 'A Song of the English' in Mr. Kipling's new book without thinking we might, though as it is we read it without a responsive heart-throb, or any feeling but wonder for its beauty and sincerity.

Its patriotism is not love of the little England, 'encompassed by the inviolate seas' on the west coast of Europe; but the great England whose far-strewn empire feels its mystical unity in every latitude and longitude of the globe. It has its sublimity, that emotion, and its reason, though we cannot share it; and it is only in asking ourselves why a man of any nation, any race, should so glory in its greatness or even its goodness when he has the greatness, the goodness of all humanity to glory in, that we are sensible of the limitations of this outborn Englishman. Possibly when we broke with England we broke more irreparably with tradition than we imagined, and liberated ourselves to a patriotism not less large than humanity. Possibly it has been for much more than we knew that we have made a home here for all mankind, and America is yet to make her own home in the heart of every man. At any rate, it seems certain that if we had not taught England that sharp lesson of a hundred years ago in colonial government, there would be no such imperial England as we see today, and no such poet of the imperial English race to sing her grandeur as he who holds the first place today among English poets.

Upon this hypothesis we may claim Mr. Kipling, whether he likes it or not, as in some sort American. He has, in fact, given us a kind of authority to do so by divining our actual average better than any American I can think of offhand, in this very extraordinary poem, where he supposes the spirit of America to speak at a well-known moment of civic trouble:

[quotes the whole of 'An American' (DV. pp. 184–5)]

The American spirit speaks here as if with the blended voices of Emerson and Ironquil; and it is from no one essentially alien to us that knowledge of us so subtle can come. I am tempted to call the piece the most important thing, intellectually, in Mr. Kipling's new volume of *The Seven Seas*. To me, it gives a sense of his penetration and his grasp that nothing else does, though there are many other things in the book which I like as well and which have the force and charm possible only from the habit of thinking in tones and colors. These things all bear witness to his uncommon quality as a poet, but if it is something more to be a humanist, then the piece I have quoted marks him as a poet with this distinction to his advantage.

Of course the last book of Mr. Kipling does not make the impression of novelty which his earlier verse made. A man can be novel but once, and for the artist in every kind all surprises after the first are to be in the way of greater strength and depth. These are what keep him new; and no mere variety without them can save his novelty from staling. Certain things this poet gave assurance of in the beginning almost in full measure: dramatic instinct, picturesque emotion, and a mighty music as of drums and trumpets. His verse always marched, with the bands playing, and the flags flying; and it marches so still, but not more bravely; that would be difficult. What it could do and does do is to impart the effect of a sort of veteran solidity in its splendors; everything is more perfect; without losing dash or dare, it is steadier and more equal. The years have not passed without enlarging the poet to vaster ranges of feeling, and giving him new light on his own thoughts and experiences. This is all they can do for any of us; when they do it for one of the best of us it is to the common good of all.

In the new *Barrack-Room Ballads* here, there is, to be sure, nothing with the peculiar thrill of 'Danny Deever', nothing with the peculiar homesick, heartsick touch of 'Mandalay', but there are other things as moving and as true, with a plunge of tragedy into depths which were not sounded before, however the surface was troubled. I could allege this or that in proof, but the temper of the whole book is the best proof, and I must let this witness also for something else that I feel strongly in it: the constant individuality, the constant impersonality. No poet has more distinctly made himself felt than this poet who has always merged and hidden himself in his types, his characters. The terms upon which he could do his kind of work at all were purely dramatic. He could never stand for himself alone; he must always stand for some one else too. He must not move us with his melancholy, his rapture, his passion, except as he makes it appear that of another. With all his love of the heroic, he is one of the least romantic of the poets because the least subjective. But when I have said that he is the least subjective, I am in instant doubt of my position, except as it concerns his expression. As concerns his impression, he is one of the most subjective. He has not so much gone out to that imperial England of his as received it into himself, and given it forth again with the color, the stamp of his mind upon it. For the first time in literature that empire is imagined.

It is imagined with pride in 'The Song of the English', and with a certain pain and futile appeal in this lovely poem, which I like much better, and find the tenderest and sweetest in the whole book.

[quotes the whole of 'The Flowers' (DV. pp. 190–1)]

I think the appeal, here, is futile, because it is from the ardor of the younger world to the indifference of the elder, which must grow more and more with age. It is in the nature of exile to turn with unforgetting fondness to home, but the home soon forgets the exile, or if it does not forget, cannot care for him. The inviolate seas that keep the insular England safe cannot keep her alive to the love that glows for her in the far-off lands they sever from her; and it appears to those who are politically of neither the larger nor the lesser England that if ever her mighty empire is to perish, it will die first at the heart. Canada will not grow cold first, nor Africa, nor Australasia, nor India, but England herself. It has happened so with all empires; and it is not material that empires should survive, the English more than the Roman. But it is very material that what is good in English feeling and English thinking should still inherit the earth; that is far better than English fighting or English ruling; and I do not know anything more significant of what may be hereafter than the fact that the English poet who continues the great tradition of English poetry most conspicuously should not be English born, should not have been reared under English skies, or islanded by English seas. I do not forget the beautiful, the exquisite verse of William Watson when I praise that of Rudyard Kipling; but it seems to me I am sensible of a vaster promise, a more assured future in his work; and there is no one else to name with him. He is, by virtue of his great gift, the laureate of that larger England whose wreath it is not for any prime minister to bestow; but wherever the English tongue is written or spoken, those who are native to it may claim a share in his recognition. He stands for the empire of that language which grows more and more the only English empire which has a common history and a common destiny.

29. J. H. Millar: 'The Works of Mr. Kipling'

1898

Anonymous article in *Blackwood's Magazine*, Vol. CLXIV, pp. 470–82 (October 1898), Authorship confirmed by *Blackwood's Contributors' Book* now in the National Library of Scotland. (See *Wellesley Index*, p. 10.)

John Hepburn Millar (1864–1929), son of Lord Craighill, became an Advocate in 1889, was lecturer in Scottish Literature at Glasgow 1911–12 and Professor of Constitutional Law and Constitutional History at Edinburgh 1909–25. Besides much criticism he wrote *A Literary History of Scotland* (1903) and several other volumes on literature and law.

Literary reputations have often been rapidly won. To wake one morning and find himself famous has been the lot of many a writer besides the poet, the England of whose time—the England, that is to say, of the Peninsula and Waterloo—the England of Wellington, Scott, and Castlereagh—is pronounced by Mr. Stephen Phillips to have been 'for the most part petty and hypocritical'! (See the *Cornhill Magazine* for January 1898, p. 21.) Our fathers were almost as much on the alert as ourselves for the appearance of a new genius; but never have men of letters succeeded in reaching the substantial honour of a 'collected edition' so early in life as at the present day. That distinction used to be jealously reserved for veterans. Now it is liberally bestowed upon authors who (one hopes) have at least as many years of at least as good work before as behind them. We do not grumble at the innovation. The old style of 'edition de luxe', whose inconveniences were so feelingly portrayed by the late Mr. du Maurier, has fortunately gone out of fashion; and the new style is sure to be convenient for reading as well as ornamental to the bookshelf. The resources of typography are freely drawn upon for its production, and the result is something eminently pleasant to the eye, whether the contents of the volumes are to be desired to make one wise or the reverse. From our lips, therefore, no word of disparagement shall fall with reference to the edition of Mr. Kipling's works, the publication of which has just been completed. The printing is all that could be desired, though no more than was to be expected from the celebrated house founded by the late Mr. Robert Clark, that 'warrior' and hero of a hundred well-fought golf-matches. Mr. Kipling, too, has done well in refraining from introducing prefaces—a sort of writing which calls for a touch of the Magician's own wand. But were the edition as mean and unworthy in externals as it is handsome and sumptuous, we should none the less welcome it as supplying a convenient pretext for attempting to weigh in the critical balance the productions of the most remarkable writer of his generation.

It is not much more than ten years since the attention of the English public was first attracted to an unknown author (with a name suspiciously like a *nom de guerre*) by the appearance of some spirited prose sketches and of one or two ballads, possessing the genuine ring of poetry, in the pages of a contemporary. The attention so drawn was riveted by certain poems from the same pen in which a new and original note was undoubtedly struck, and which Mr. Henley was the means of introducing to the world in a vivacious weekly periodical. Thenceforward, Mr. Kipling's literary career is matter of common knowledge. It has been his portion to gain the ear of the great non-literary reading public, and at the same time to win the enthusiastic applause of that limited body of men whose pleasure in a work of art is derived from a perception of the means as well as of the end. Such good fortune falls to few. There are writers whose work is keenly appreciated by their literary brethren, but who make little or no impression upon 'the great heart of the people'. Of such, Mr. Stevenson was a typical representative. There are others, again, who sell their tens of thousands, yet whose glaring faults of taste effectually repel the sympathies of the educated minority, the *cachet* of whose approbation, while they profess to despise, they secretly long for. But the critic to whose palate the works of Miss Corelli or Mr. Caine are as ungrateful as a meal of dust and ashes, is well aware that from the point of view of literature neither the lady nor the gentleman exists. Their performances will have as much significance for the competent critic of the future as the *Dagonet Ballads* or Captain Coe's finals. So, too, the reviewer to whose hardened sensibilities the pathos and the humour of the Kailyard alike appeal in vain, has more than a suspicion that Messrs. Crockett and

Maclaren will not enter into the reckoning of our sons' sons. But he knows that Mr. Barrie is certain to count. And even so it is with Mr. Kipling. You may lay your finger on faults real or imaginary; you may find his verse flashy and his prose irritating. But you cannot (being in full possession of your senses) pass him by; you cannot maintain that, in estimating the literary forces and tendencies of our age, it is possible to leave him out of account. As well ignore Dickens in a review of Victorian literature; as well ignore Keene in a review of Victorian art.

Perhaps the most striking feature of Mr. Kipling's work is the wide range over which it expatiates. Subjects the most diverse are handled with the same air of ease and intimacy; and no other writer is so well entitled to repeat with proper pride the most familiar and the most hackneyed of Terentian sentiments, 'For to admire and for to see, for to behold this world so wide'—that is his *métier*; and we may proceed with the quotation and add that 'he can't drop it if he tried'. How or where Mr. Kipling acquired his 'extensive and peculiar' knowledge of the physical world, of the human heart, and of animated nature, is no business of ours. As he himself sings—

'When 'Omer smote 'is blomin' lyre
'Ed 'eard men sing by land an' sea;
An' what 'e thought 'e might require
'E went an' took—the same as me!'

No doubt in 'The Three Musketeers' he allows the world a glimpse of one of his methods of collecting raw material. But there are matters innumerable in his writings for which there is no accounting unless we are prepared to concede to him a full measure of that faculty of divination which is heaven's best gift to a chosen few.

It is a commonplace that Shakespeare was accustomed to handle with astounding felicity and correctness the technical phraseology of the law, of the *manège*, of venery, and of many other departments of human activity. It being, of course, impossible that a Warwickshire yokel, whom we know to have been but imperfectly educated, could have acquired so minute a knowledge of so many complicated subjects, a sapient school of critics has not hesitated to assure us that the author of the Shakespearean plays was not one but many—was a lawyer, a Jehu, a Nimrod, a Papist, a Protestant, a Jesuit, a Puritan—was anything you please, in short, but a man with an unrivalled *flair* for the niceties of language, and an unequalled share of IMAGINATION— that quality of all others most abhorrent to the dunce. Let us adopt this singular fallacy for a moment, and see to what conclusion it leads us in Mr. Kipling's case.

It is plain, to begin with, that Mr. Kipling must have studied long and ardently at all the best schools and universities in the world. How else could he have acquired his thorough acquaintance with zoology (*vide* the *Jungle Books*), with geography, including the use of the globes (*vide* 'The Flag of England' and 'The Children of the Zodiac'), with archaeology (*vide* 'The Story of Ung'), and with botany (*vide* 'The Flowers')? It is equally beyond dispute that he served a long apprentice-ship on the sea; and it seems likely that he first gratified his passion for that element by taking service in a Greek galley and afterwards in that of a Viking. He must then have occupied a post on the following vessels in succession—a chinese pig-boat, a Bilbao-tramp, a New England fishing-smack, a British man-of-war, and an Atlantic liner. It was certainly in the engine-room of the last named vessel that he learned those details about machinery which he reproduces so faith-fully in 'M'Andrew's Hymn'.

We infer that Mr. Kipling next withdrew for a few years' complete rest to the solitude of the jungle. He there added materially to his knowledge of natural history, and familiarised himself thoroughly with the manners and customs of bird, beast, and reptile. (If he did not, how on earth *could* he have written the *Jungle Books*?) It is also quite obvious that he has held a large number of appointments in the Indian Civil Service; and that he served for a considerable period in the ranks of the army. No sane man can doubt that he took part in several hot engagements, and fought in at least one Soudan cam-paign. A good many years must also have been passed by Mr. Kipling in disguise among the natives. By no other means could he have be-come conversant with their habits of thought and ways of life. It is further beyond dispute that he must have slummed in London; that at one time he must have had a studio of his own; and that the inside of a newspaper office must have been during a certain period of his life a place of almost daily resort.

Our chain of reasoning is now almost complete, and we defy any one to snap it. No man can acquire a knowledge of the terminology of soldiering, or sailoring, or tinkering, or tailoring, unless he has been a soldier, or a sailor, or a tinker, or a tailor. But human life is too short for a man to be all four, and, *a fortiori*, for a man to follow fifty occu-pations. *Argal*, Kipling is but the name of an amanuensis or hack, through whose pen certain eminent soldiers, sailors, tinkers, tailors, etc., have chosen, for some undisclosed reason, to tell their story to the world. Such, without exaggeration, is the reasoning of the dullards who have presumed to tamper with the fame of England's greatest poet.

While Mr. Kipling surveys mankind from China to Peru, he does so not from the dubious point of view of the cosmopolitan but from the firm vantage-ground of a Briton. It is merely his due to attribute to him the chief share among men of letters in that revival of the Imperial sentiment, both in these islands and in our colonies, which has been so striking a phenomenon of recent years. To have reawakened a great people to a sense of its duties and responsibilities, to have fanned the drooping flame of an enlightened but fervent patriotism—these are achievements of which few indeed can boast. It is, we trust, unnecessary to disclaim all intention of disparaging the good work performed by great men in years when the country seemed plunged in a fatal lethargy, and men appeared to have grown indifferent or insensible to England's mission and destiny. Lord Tennyson, for example, has no stronger claim upon the reverence and affection of all generations of his countrymen than the fact that from time to time he set the trumpet to his lips and blew a strain whose echoes will never cease to encourage and to inspire. But old and neglected truths sometimes require to be presented in a new garb; and abstract principles constantly need to be driven home by concrete illustrations. It has been Mr. Kipling's enviable task to bring down patriotism from the closet to the street, and to diffuse its beneficent influence among millions who had hitherto remained untouched.

As so frequently happens, Mr. Kipling's teaching fell upon willing ears. The English nation is patient and long-suffering enough. It is also extraordinarily loyal in its allegiance to its chosen favourites. But the Government which mismanaged the affairs of this country from 1880 to 1885 was kind enough to supply at least two specimens of the application of Liberal principles to foreign politics which can never be forgotten. The shameful peace concluded after our defeat at Majuba Hill—a peace so pregnant with trouble and disaster—was not rendered more palatable to a people which loves honesty and plain-dealing by the sanctimonious cant characteristically employed to justify it. The projected relinquishment of a portion of Egypt might, indeed, have passed at the time without exciting the national resentment. But the cold-hearted abandonment of Gordon aroused a storm of indignation which in reality has been the motive-power of that series of laborious yet brilliant operations whose culmination was successfully attained a few weeks ago. The better-informed classes of Englishmen were at the same time aware that, in the East, Lord Ripon had embarked upon a course of policy, the ultimate result, if not the conscious design, of which must be the overthrow of British power in India. Worse, if worse were possible, remained behind. The most audacious and malignant of blows was presently struck at the integrity of the empire by hands the measure of whose evil-doing not even Majuba Hill and Khartoum had sufficed to fill up. The dismemberment of the United Kingdom was solemnly and seriously offered as the price of political support to a faction 'steeped to the lips in treason'. This master-stroke was attended by at least one happy consequence. The nobler elements in the Liberal party were for ever severed from the baser, and became practically fused with the Conservatives. No wonder that men's hearts were longing for an outspoken proclamation on the side of loyalty and empire! No wonder that the Jubilee celebrations of 1887 were hailed as an outward and visible sign of the reawakening of the national spirit! Yet they announced merely the inception of a great movement. It is surely no vain imagination to suppose that the Jubilee rejoicings of last year possessed a deeper significance and were informed with a more exalted spirit than those of ten years before. The soul of the nation seemed to be more profoundly stirred. Ideas and aspirations of a loftier order seemed to have taken root in the nation's heart. And if such indeed were the case, it was to Rudyard Kipling more than to any other writer that the change was due, just as it was he who seized upon the unspoken national thought and enshrined it in imperishable verse. On one Englishman of eminence, and one alone, it is to be feared, did the writings of Mr. Kipling during the last decade fail to produce a perceptible impression. From childhood to old age the more poignant emotions of patriotism and the fine sense of national honour were, unhappily, strangers to the bosom of William Ewart Gladstone.

We make no apology for this apparent digression; for Mr. Kipling's most characteristic work is really saturated with politics—not the politics of Taper or Tadpole, or even of Mr. Rigby, but the politics of true statesmanship. No patriot assuredly can forget the signal service which he rendered to his country, at a moment when the horizon was darker than one now cares to think of, by the publication of 'Cleared'. It is not only one of the most trenchant pieces of rhetoric in any language (Juvenal himself might be proud to claim it for his own), but it furnishes an absolute and conclusive answer to the contemptible sophistries by which men who had once had at least a bowing acquaintance with honesty were fain to palliate their connection and co-operation with ruffians and assassins. But the truth is, that no more formidable attack has been delivered upon Liberalism in the present generation than Mr. Kipling's work, taken as a whole. The shameless lies by which the friends of disaffection and the devotees of so-called philanthropy have never scrupled to fortify their cause, crumble to atoms at the touch of the artist whose highest aspiration it is 'to draw the Thing as he sees It for the God of Things as They are'. The precious time-dishonoured formulae become meaningless when confronted with the very essence of practical experience. Mr. Kipling has taken the pains (in 'The Enlightenments of Padgett, M.P.') to set forth his opinions in direct and almost didactic shape; but a story like 'The Head of the District' is more valuable than many such discourses, and illuminates the situation as with a flash. Here are facts, stubborn facts, which it is the very *raison d'être* of Liberalism to ignore, but the ignoring of which means the end of all government worthy of the name. It is of a piece with his sound and comprehensive view of politics that Mr. Kipling should strike the true note in comparing the relative value and importance of the man of action and the man of letters. He is guiltless of the affectation of depreciating his own calling. But his judgment coincides with that invariably pronounced by Sir Walter Scott. 'A Conference of the Powers' is in many ways by much the least felicitous of the numerous productions of his pen. Nowhere else is his touch so uncertain; nowhere else does the author strike one as being so much of a *poseur*; nowhere else does he come so near to trespassing upon the unconsciously ridiculous. But, despite its manifold imperfections, it teaches lessons which we fear that many journalists and many more pretentious writers have yet to learn.

The particular quarter of the globe in which Mr. Kipling reduces Liberal principles *ad absurdum* is of course India; and, though the universe is his by right of conquest, India is, no question, his particular domain. 'Twas there his earliest triumphs were achieved; and with it the most instructive portion of his work is concerned. Whatever his excellences or defects, it was he and no other who first brought home to the average Englishman something like an adequate conception of what our Indian Empire means. We all knew that there was a subtle and mysterious charm about the East. Those who had read the *Arabian Nights* and *Tancred* had a faint conception of its potency. Those who were fortunate enough to have relatives in the Company's or the Queen's service were, of course, in the enjoyment of a much ampler knowledge. The Mutiny taught us something, though that something was gradually being forgotten. But it was not until Mr. Kipling's arrival on the scene that 'the man on the knife-board' was dumped down, as it were, by the compelling force of an irresistible will among a mass of 'raw, brown, naked humanity'; that he realised the existence of a vast body of fellow subjects to whom his favourite catchwords (such as 'liberty' and 'progress') would have been absolutely unintelligible; and that he was enabled to apprehend, however imperfectly, the magnitude of the work which it has been the privilege of England to initiate and carry on in the East Indies through the instrumentality of a handful of her sons. One of the main secrets, we believe, of the extraordinary vividness with which Mr. Kipling represents scenes so wholly different from anything in the experience of the average Englishman is that he never pauses to make preliminary explanations. His early writings, by a fortunate accident, were addressed to an Anglo-Indian audience upon whom such explanations would have been thrown away. They knew Jakko and Peliti's, and Tara-Devi, and Benmore and Boileaugunge as well as a man-about-town knows Piccadilly or an East-ender Epping Forest. Tonga-bars and rikshaws, dâk-bungalows and saises, pipals and walers, had no mysteries for them. A glossary would have been more of an impertinence and a superfluity for them than a glossary of the dialect of the *Sporting Times* would be to the ordinary middle-aged and middle-class householder. Hence Mr. Kipling grew accustomed to waste no time in commentary, and the sudden plunge into a strange atmosphere and into unfamiliar 'shop' and slang which he compels the English reader to take is eminently bracing and delightful, though it takes away the breath to start with. In his hands we may truly say that new things become familiar and familiar things new. Which (to borrow a form of sentence much affected by himself) is half the battle.

A vivid impression, it is true, is not necessarily a correct one, and it is quite natural that there should be more than one opinion as to the truth of Mr. Kipling's sketches of Anglo-Indian society. Here his detractors (if he any have) will find the most promising material for animadversion. None of his stories, indeed, is wholly outside the region of possibility; while many of them doubtless had a more or less solid 'foundation in fact'. Some of the *Plain Tales* read like nothing so much as a reproduction of the current gossip of a day now dead and gone, with a proper alteration of names, dates, and immaterial surroundings. Human nature, after all, is not vastly different at Simla from human nature elsewhere. Why should jobbery and favouritism, which find a home in every clime, pass India by? In what country have men not been occasionally preferred to high office through the influence of pretty women? Doubtless merit swelters in the plains from time to time, while stupidity and incompetence are promoted to the honours and emoluments which they never earned. 'Tis a mere question of the thermometer. In more temperate zones, *'virtus laudater et—alget'*. Thus most of Mr. Kipling's anecdotes are probably, in one sense, well-authenticated. Chapter and verse could be cited for every one of them; and regarded as a collection of isolated and independent details they may be said to be literally true to life. But when these details come to be considered as parts of a greater whole, when the picture invites criticism as a complete work of art, the matter assumes an entirely different complexion. The Government of India is emphatically *not* conducted at headquarters in obedience to the dictates of intriguing hussies and their unscrupulous hangers-on. No more is the Government of Great Britain. Yet a satirist with the necessary adroitness could present the world with a description of the social and political life of London which would be absolutely horrifying and absolutely misleading, yet of which each individual stroke should have been painfully copied from the living model. He would be able to quote facts in proof of the existence among us of failings and of vices notoriously inconsistent with social or political wellbeing. But if he inferred, for example, universal corruption from the records of the divorce-court, he would be as wide of the mark as if, from a perusal of their light literature, he drew the conclusion that the French attach no sanctity to family life. The analogy we have suggested should put us on our guard against accepting as typical and representative personages or episodes with no claim to being anything of the kind. To hit off the exact proportion in which the component elements in the character of any community are blended is never an easy task, and its difficulty is not diminished for the storyteller by the fact that the baser ingredients lend themselves to his legitimate purposes in proportion as they are pungent and high-flavoured.

There are, to be quite frank, a few of Mr. Kipling's literary offspring which we would throw to the wolves without the least compunction. Mrs. Hauksbee 'won't do'; and no more will the 'boys' who make love to her. What in the rest of Mr. Kipling's work is knowledge degenerates too often into knowingness, a very different quality, when he begins to depict Indian Society. We become conscious of a certain aggressiveness in his touch—of the absence of the tone of true fashion—of more than a hint of that uneasy familiarity which may be frequently observed in the very young or the hopelessly shy. The ladies are not exactly patterns of good breeding, while the men who associate with them have a cheap swagger which Ouïda's guardsmen would despise. So at least some devil's advocate might argue with no little plausibility. There is unquestionably much better stuff in such slight sketches as 'Bubbling Well Road' or 'The Finances of the Gods' than in a thousand elaborate pieces of the type of 'Mrs. Hauksbee Sits Out', which leave behind the disagreeable suspicion that the author deliberately tried to scandalise. Sailing near the wind is a dangerous and undignified past-time for a writer of Mr. Kipling's calibre.

Nothing, indeed, is more extraordinary in this portion of Mr. Kipling's work than the interminglings of good and bad, worthy and base, essential and trifling. Cheek by jowl with smart snip-snap you find something that probes the inmost recesses of your soul. Only a few pages of print separate a specimen of flippant superficiality like 'The Education of Otis Yeere' from a masterpiece of analysis and penetration like 'The Hill of Illusion'. And *The Story of the Gadsbys*—at once the glory and the shame of Mr. Kipling's prose-muse—what is it but a field where wheat and tares grow together in careless and inextricable confusion? To read that singular drama for the seventh or eighth time is to pass once more from delight to disgust and again to delight—is to marvel that genius which can soar so high should ever be content to stoop so low. At one moment the author discloses some of the deepest secrets of the human heart—secrets which most men take half a lifetime to find out—with a frankness and a simplicity which attest his extreme youth; at another his facetiousness is such as a respectable pot-house would reprobate, and his view of life too raffish for even a military lady-novelist to adopt. The most moving pathos alternates with the most brazen-faced vulgarity, and the most vital facts of human existence are handled with the raw cocksureness of an inspired schoolboy. *The Gadsbys* is the most amazing monument of precocity in all literature. Yet who can doubt that its faults, palpable and serious though they be, are upon a general balance outweighed by its merits? Or who would not swallow the opening scene, albeit with a wry face, rather than give up that later episode, where the author's method is so simple yet so telling, and its outcome makes so irresistible an appeal to the primary emotions—we mean the scene of Mrs. Gadsby's illness and delirium? If in none other of his writings he has sinned so grievously, in none has he made so ample an atonement.

In estimating the accuracy of Mr. Kipling's picture of the English in India the critic is entitled to fall back upon his knowledge of the corresponding ranks of society at home; but no such assistance is available when he comes to consider Mr. Kipling's treatment of native life. Its fidelity to the original has never, so far as we are aware, been impugned, and there are few besides Mr. Kipling himself who possess the qualifications necessary for sitting in judgment on this department of his work. For him, as for Strickland, 'the streets and the bazaars and the sounds in them are full of meaning', though he would probably be the first to admit how superficial any European's knowledge of the inner life of the 'black man' must needs be. It is not safe, to be sure, to take Mr. Kipling seriously at all times. Extravaganza is a form of art to which he occasionally condescends with the happiest results. What else are 'The Germ Destroyer' and 'Pig' in the *Plain Tales*? And what is 'The Incarnation of Krishna Mulvaney' but rollicking, incomparable, irresistible farce? But nobody can suppose for a moment that 'In Flood Time' or 'On the City Wall' was written 'with intent to deceive'; and even if a hundred pedants were to suggest a hundred reasons for suspecting the fidelity of his portraiture, we should prefer to maintain the attitude of unshaken faith, and to enjoy what is so admirably calculated to produce enjoyment. For, to tell the truth, the native tales carry their credentials on their very face. Like holograph documents, they must be allowed the privilege of proving themselves; and if work at once so powerful and so exquisite as 'Without Benefit of Clergy' happens not to be true to nature, so much the worse for nature. The description of life at a Rajput King's Court in *The Naulahka* is worth countless blue-books and innumerable tracts as a revelation of the inveterate habits of thought and of the social customs which a beneficent Government must attempt by slow degrees to accommodate as far as possible to the ethical standards of the West.

Mr. Kipling's military stories have probably enjoyed the greatest vogue of all his writings in this country, and not without reason. The subject of everyday life in the British army, though a tempting one, had been practically left untouched, and clamoured for a man of genius to 'exploit' it. We know with what complete success he took it up. 'Who can withstand Mulvaney, Learoyd, and Ortheris? ' 'Tis immortial fame the gentleman's going to give us,' predicted the first-named, and the prophecy bids fair to come true. Since the deathless Pickwick and his faithful band desisted from their wanderings, no group of personages has gained so well-assured a footing in the affections of the public as these same 'soldiers three'. Men do not love them, perhaps, for their own sakes. As studies of character they count for comparatively little. They are not discriminated with any great nicety, and the marked difference in their speech dispenses with all necessity for the finer and more delicate strokes of the brush. We cannot pretend to look upon Mulvaney as a Milesian Prometheus, with the vultures of remorse preying upon his vitals; nor does Learoyd seem to be distinguishable in any particular from our old friend the Yorkshireman of the stage. The claim which the trio really have upon our undying gratitude and regard arises mainly from their being the mouthpiece of the author for a series of stories which hold their own with any in our language in point of variety, humour, spirit, and power. It is unnecessary to expatiate on their merits, though we may call attention to the extraordinary felicity and appropriateness of their respective settings, of which Mulvaney and his comrades are *pars magna*. Nor is it possible to arrange them in order of excellence. Each seems the best until the next is read. We should not quarrel seriously with any one who indicated a special preference for 'The Courting of Dinah Shadd' and 'With the Main Guard', the latter being Mr. Kipling's best war-piece, with the exception of 'The Lost Legion'. But we cannot pass from them without congratulating the British private upon having at last found his *vates sacer*, and the army generally upon having fallen in with a writer who has taught the least imaginative of nations what manful work its soldiers are doing for it. There is a fine healthy ring in all Mr. Kipling's utterances about her Majesty's forces. But his inspiration was curiously anticipated by a writer who in other respects is his very antithesis. Tom Robertson was timid, artificial, and conventional. Mr. Kipling is dashing, original, and bold. Tom Robertson seems hopelessly out of date. Mr. Kipling is essentially *dans le train*. But he must be a rare hand indeed at the splitting of a hair who can detect any appreciable distinction or difference between the tone and sentiment of 'Ours'[1] and those of 'The Big Drunk Draf''', or 'Only a Subaltern', or 'The Man Who Was', or 'His Private Honour'.

The rough classification which, for convenience sake, we have made of Mr. Kipling's short stories is not quite exhaustive. There remain a

---

[1] [A play (1866) by T. W. Robertson, author of *Caste*]

fair number which are not tales of Anglo-Indian society, nor tales of native life, nor yet tales of the British army. There are, for instance, what we may call the tales of physical horror. Among these are 'Bertran and Bimi', 'A Matter of Fact', and 'The Mark of the Beast'; and, without embarking upon the general question whether such topics as they deal with fall within the legitimate sphere of art, we confess that we could have willingly spared them. The stories of the supernatural, on the other hand, like 'At the End of the Passage', we could spare by no possibility whatever. Finally, there is a small class which stands by itself in virtue of possessing in an especial degree the characteristic excellence of its creator's genius. 'The Finest Story in the World' will always stand out as perhaps the most striking illustration of Mr. Kipling's versatility. The deeper problems it suggests may be put on one side; what is of real moment is the snatches from the galley-slave's experience. Here are the same matchless power of presenting a scene and suggesting an atmosphere, the same realistic commemoration of minute details, the same idealistic selection of the relevant and the essential, which distinguished the Indian narratives, and all applied to a state of facts long since passed away. Yet even this miracle of invention and artifice must give place to 'The Man who would be King', which we venture to consider Mr. Kipling's *chef-d'œuvre* in prose. The fable makes considerable drafts on one's credulity at the outset; but the drafts are instantly honoured, and the reader, falling more and more under the master's spell, is whirled along triumphantly to the close. No time to take breath or to reflect, so impetuous and irresistible is the torrent. Those to whom emotions are as daily bread will find there a truly bounteous repast.

Whether a writer of short stories can write long ones and vice versa has often been acrimoniously debated; but one thing is plain, that Mr. Kipling has not yet proved the affirmative. *The Light that Failed* and *The Naulahka* have their moments. They are much more readable than most contemporary novels, and the latter is as thrilling as *Treasure Island*. But to compare them with, say, 'The Drums of the Fore and Aft' would be ridiculous. Perhaps one reason of their failure is the thoroughly uninteresting character of the hero and heroine. Who cares much for Dick and Maisie? Who for Nicholas Tarvin and Kate Sheriff? Better by far the society of Mowgli and the wolves—than whom indeed more agreeable company is not to be found without much seeking. None of Mr. Kipling's works has the same graciousness and charm as the *Jungle Books*, none is so wise, so considerate, so kindly. If, before trying them yourself, you follow the old maxim and 'Try them on the dog', the result is certain to be satisfactory. Children adore them, and add the animals to that menagerie which Robin, Dickie, Flapey and Pecksey[1] used to adorn. And if, fortified by the success of your experiment, you try them on yourself, you will thenceforth use no others. The reader will perhaps forgive an uncontrollable lapse into the dignified phraseology of latter-day criticism.

The peculiar attraction of Mr. Kipling's prose work lies much less in any solicitude for style than in his unique fertility of imagination. He need never beat about the bush, for it disgorges a hare every two minutes; nor has he time to be fastidious in his choice of words. In some of his earlier pieces his manner is almost vicious. It is like 'the picture-writing of a half-civilised people', to borrow an apt metaphor of his own—crude, jerky, flippant. The straining after smartness and sensation is too evident, and the flash epigram is too frequent and favourite an ornament. That these faults have been to a great extent corrected by the maturer taste and sounder discretion of advancing years is perfectly true. But they are not wholly eradicated, and Mr. Kipling has still to vindicate his title to be considered as a model of English style. That he could make it good if he pleased, we have not the least doubt. A descriptive passage like the following proves that he has little to learn:

Over our heads burned the wonderful Indian stars, which are not all pricked in on one plane, but, preserving an orderly perspective, draw the eye through the velvet darkness of the void up to the barred doors of heaven itself. The earth was a grey shadow, more unreal than the sky. We could hear her breathing lightly in the pauses between the howling of the jackals, the movement of the wind in the tamarisks, and the fitful mutter of musketry-fire, leagues away to the left. A native woman from some unseen hut began to sing, the mail-train thundered past on its way to Delhi, and a roosting crow cawed drowsily. Then there was a belt-loosening silence about the fires, and the even breathing of the crowded earth took up the story.

There is no doubt about that as a piece of English; but the great bulk of Mr. Kipling's most vigorous and successful prose-work is not in ordinary English but in dialect. It is in the lingo of the Cockney, the Irishman, or the Yorkshireman; or it is in a tongue specially invented for the use of birds and beasts; or it is in a language designed to reproduce the characteristic nuances of oriental thought and feeling. It is through such a medium that Mr. Kipling's genius seems to find its

[1] [Bird characters in The Robins (1786) by Mrs. Trimmer]

most ample and fitting expression; and perhaps it is on that account that his long stories are disappointing. They are necessarily in more or less literary English, for dialect cannot be maintained beyond a certain length of time without fatiguing the reader.

That Mr. Kipling has performed prodigies of ingenuity, and of more than ingenuity, with dialect in verse as well as in prose, is no more than the truth. He has indeed accomplished what, perhaps, was never achieved before. He has selected a *patois* the associations of which were wholly mean, commonplace, ludicrous, and degrading, and has made it the vehicle of poetry characterised by qualities the very reverse of these. But his verse, whether in plain English or in dialect, is superior to his prose in plain English, because poetry is more exacting than prose. It is the paradox of poetry that it permits no synonyms. The poet is in perpetual quest of the one inevitable word, and only the true poet can find it. Now in Mr. Kipling's poetry the right word emerges at the right moment, and no one can doubt that it *is* the right word.

> So it's knock out your pipes an' follow me!
> An' it's finish off your swipes an' follow me!
> Oh, 'ark to the fifes *a-crawlin'*!
> Follow me—follow me 'ome!

Does not the word we have italicised almost make one catch one's breath by its startling appropriateness? But we must not begin to quote, or this article would never end.

The technical difficulties of poetry have no terrors for Mr. Kipling. His command of rhythm and metre is absolute. No measure is too intricate for him to master, and some of the pleasure with which his verse is read is due to the apparent facility with which he handles a complicated scheme of versification. We think we can detect that Mr. Swinburne engaged some portion of Mr. Kipling's youth; but the influence of that master is not obtrusive in his later productions. For pure poetical prestidigitation we never read anything to compare with the stanza prefixed to chapter vii, of *The Naulahka*. Even Mr. Gilbert, in the happiest hours of his plenary Aristophanic inspiration, never equalled that. But luckily there is infinitely more in Mr. Kipling's poetry than mere nimbleness of wit or mechanical dexterity. His highest flights are high indeed, and it is true of his best work, as of all the world's greatest poetry, that it can be read and re-read without losing its freshness. New beauties are ever to be discovered, and the old ones shine with brighter lustre. His record as a poet is one of steady and rapid progress. His very earliest efforts are perhaps scarcely superior to the best verse in *Punch*, when the letterpress of that journal was worth reading. Among all the *Departmental Ditties* there is but one—'Possibilities'—whose original flavour and half-pathetic, half-cynical humour indicate something transcending extreme cleverness. 'The Ballad of East and West' was the first plain manifestation of genius; while in his subsequent volumes—in the *Barrack-room Ballads* and in *The Seven Seas*—there are poems whose authorship not even the greatest of England's singers need be eager to disavow. 'The Flag of England', 'A Song of the English', 'The Last Chantey', 'M'Andrew's Hymn',—these are strains that dwell in the memory and stir the blood. They have a richness and fulness of note very different from the shrill and reedy utterance of many who have attempted to tune their pipe to the pitch of courage and of patriotism. Yet even they sink into comparative insignificance beside that 'Recessional' which fifteen months ago took England by storm, and which seemed to concentrate in itself the glowing patriotism of a Shakespeare, the solemn piety of a Milton, and the measured stateliness of a Dryden. For sheer ingenuity and lightness of touch, indeed, 'The Song of the Banjo' cannot be matched. (Why, by the by, has the fate of 'the younger son' such a fascination for Mr. Kipling's muse?) But we are not prepared to put it in the same rank as the best of the *Barrack-room Ballads*, though what the best are we shall not be rash enough to say. Let the reader make his own selection.

To frame a concise yet exhaustive judgment upon Mr. Kipling is impossible, so various are his gifts, so rich his endowment. A glowing imagination, an inexhaustible invention, a profound knowledge of the human heart—these are three of his choicest possessions. Yet how inadequately does so bald a statement sum up the rich profusion of his talents! How beggarly and feeble seem the resources of language to do justice to his great achievements! It is good to think that in all human probability he will be long with us to continue his work and to enhance his fame. There will never be wanting persons to dissuade from patriotism, and to point out how expensive the exercise of that virtue is apt to be. It is well for us that a great writer should be in our midst strengthening the weak hands and confirming the feeble knees. Much as he has accomplished in the past, there remains much for him to accomplish in the future, and if in the course of providence we should be spared to survey Mr. Kipling's work thirty years hence, we make no doubt that much of priceless value will have been added to its tale. For the constant burden of his song teaches the lesson which it most behoves the younger generation to learn. 'Law, Orrder, Duty, an' Restraint, Obedience, Discipline!'—these are the foundations of a prosperous State. The Laws of the Jungle are the Laws of the Universe, and we shall be fortunate indeed if, when times of stress and peril arrive, we have realised what our fathers learned in sorrow and tribulation and what their sons are too prone to forget—

> But the head and the hoof of the Law
> And the haunch and the hump is—Obey!

30. 'The Madness of Mr. Kipling'

1898

Article signed 'An Admirer' in *Macmillan's Magazine*, Vol. LXXIX, pp. 131-5 (December 1898): credited to Stephen Gwynn by *The Wellesley Index*.

Stephen Lucius Gwynn (1864-1950), Irish poet and critic, author of studies of Swift, Goldsmith, Scott, Tennyson, Thomas Moore, Stevenson and others.

There is no gratitude more sincere than that which is paid to the man who can amuse us; and few of us would be slow to admit that Mr. Kipling has made the world more amusing. He is one of the most agreeable luxuries that we possess, and for what should we be grateful if not for luxuries? But there are times when gratitude sees, like Desdemona, a divided duty. Should it blind us to the shortcomings of a favourite author? Or should it make us indignant when he produces work seriously below his best level? There is a case to be made out for either side, and of course no artist can reasonably be expected to produce nothing but masterpieces. But when one sees a writer wilfully making play in a definitely wrong direction, it is surely permissible to remonstrate. There are a dozen stories in Mr. Kipling's new book, *The Day's Work*; three of them are, as I think it will be generally allowed, in his best manner; half-a-dozen more are no worse than many good things in his earlier work; but the other three, though in their way clever enough, no doubt, like everything else of their author's, do, I must say, awaken a desire to protest. And some of the protests which must be made against them apply partially to the other stories. But let us analyse the volume.

Over 'The Tomb of his Ancestors', which relates the adventures of Lieutenant John Chinn among the Bhils and his hereditary domination, there will surely be no dispute; nor is there likely, I take it, to be much over 'William the Conqueror', a love-story set against a background of Indian famine. Here is a passage I should like to quote before turning Devil's Advocate. One Scott, of the Irrigation Department in the Punjab, has been ordered down to fight the famine in the Madras Presidency, and, since the rice-eating people will sooner starve than eat unfamiliar grains, he has been forced to give the grain to goats and feed perishing babies on their milk. After a month of milking and baby-feeding he returns to the central camp, where 'William', a hard-riding young lady with a preference for men of action, has been busy also.

He had no desire to make any dramatic entry, but an accident of the sunset ordered it that, when he had taken off his helmet to get the evening breeze, the low light should fall across his forehead and he could not see what was before him; while one waiting at the tent door beheld, with new eyes, a young man, beautiful as Paris, a god in a halo of golden dust, walking slowly at the head of his flock, while at his knee ran small naked Cupids.

That is a pretty picture, and tells all the more against the severe realism of its setting.

The other one of the first three is 'The Bridge Builders', which, for my own part, I should put in a class by itself, ranking it higher than anything of its author's except only 'The Man that would be King'. But it is open to certain objections, and not unreasonable ones. Mr. Kipling suffers from a mania, which is really only the perversion of his best quality. His passionate desire for concrete information makes his whole work a storehouse of curious and sometimes very interesting facts; but with the desire to know all about everything goes a desire to be able to call everything by its right name, and this has bred a kind of collector's mania, a craving for strange words. If Mr. Kipling discovers a new term—a technical term for choice, but any flower of American slang will do nearly as well—he is as happy as an entomologist with a new beetle, and as anxious to produce it. Now a story which turns upon a triumph of modern engineering gives great scope to this bent of mind, and the consequence is that the first three or four pages of 'The Bridge Builders' are sprinkled thick with words like 'spile-pier', 'borrow-pit', 'trusses' and 'revetments'. Tastes differ about the result. To myself it appears to convey the atmosphere which Mr. Kipling wants to attain, and certainly the picture of the bridge rises distinct enough; but to many other people it seems a disagreeable pedantry, and indisposes them to follow with proper attention what comes after. About that also there are two opinions; one fervent admirer said to me that the story broke off just at the interesting part, where the flood came down on the unfinished bridge, and went off into a silly dream. But the peculiar bent of the author's mind, while it gives him the keenest interest in the bridge as a bridge, makes him also see in it not merely a bridge but a symbol. The spanning of the Ganges is not merely an engineering achievement; it stands for a type of the losing battle which the old gods of the East fight against new and spiritual forces. Still, in the use of symbols there always lurks a snare, and though I should defend with enthusiasm the symbolism of this story, which lies a good deal nearer to poetry than to prose, I am constrained to admit that it sins by a trifle of obscurity; and in the other stories the use of a figurative method leads the author into errors much worse than obscurity. In short, as Devil's Advocate, I should sum up my indictment by accusing Mr. Kipling first of an abuse of technical jargon, secondly, and this is a more serious matter, of an abuse of symbolism.

The two faults are at their worst when they occur together, and indeed they are traceable back to one source. Everybody felt that there was symbolism, or allegory, involved in the two *Jungle Books*, but nobody resented it, for the stories were fundamentally interesting. The presence of Mowgli added the human link which is needed to bring us into sympathy, and the animals talked credibly. Animals must, and do, talk, and it seems natural that they should talk as Mr. Kipling makes them. But when it comes to engines discoursing on a railway-siding, or the different parts of a ship holding converse, credibility ceases, and, as Horace observes, *incredulus odi*—the incredible is a bore. But the reason why Mr. Kipling falls into this error is sufficiently simple. He has a passion for machinery, and very rightly, since the marine engine, even more than Finlayson's bridge, is to this age what the Parthenon was to Athens. Probably his sincerest aspiration expresses itself in McAndrew's phrase: 'Oh for another Robbie Burns to sing the song of steam.'

Mr. Kipling may live to sing the song of steam yet, but for the present he trails us somewhat heavily at the heels of his hobby. Machines may be alive to him, but they are not alive to us. Nobody would object to his technicalities when they are used so admirably as in the story 'Bread Upon the Waters', a capital yarn with that touch of something more in it that puts Mr. Kipling miles above so excellent a spinner of yarns as Mr. Jacobs. Mr. Jacobs would never have realised that McPhee had a Shekinah in 'the matter o' fair runnin' '. But in that other story of a steamer, 'The Devil and the Deep Sea', I confess that the technicalities overpower me. It was no doubt an admirable thing that Mr. Kipling should have plotted out exactly what would happen in the engine-room if a five-inch shell fractured the bolts that held the connecting-rod to the forward crank; but the description will be worse than Hebrew to the average reader, for it is not merely unintelligible but tantalising. This, however, Mr. Kipling knows well enough, and he takes his chance; for my own part I willingly accept the bewilderment for the subsequent picture of the repairing. I cannot understand what is being done, but I can feel the feverish activity and the sense of amazing resourcefulness. It enlarges one's view of the possibilities in human nature to read of man, stripped to the skin and reduced all but to a state of nature, at grapple desperately and successfully to improvise the most complicated weapons of civilisation.

But what I suspect Mr. Kipling of not knowing is that a symbol has only value when it translates into the concrete something less intelligible in the abstract; and that an allegory is only tolerable when its story is so interesting that one tacitly forgives it for being an allegory. Finlayson's bridge over the Ganges seems to me an excellent symbol, a material incident to show a spiritual conflict; the *Jungle-Book* stories are admirable allegories because there is very little allegory in them; we are haunted by a sense of some further meaning, not knocked over the head with a moral. But the sketch called 'A Walking Delegate' is an allegory naked and not ashamed. Mr. Kipling has a profound antipathy to Socialism, and a profound belief in 'the day's work'; that renders him a valuable prophet, and in one of his cleverest poems, 'An Imperial

Rescript', he put the case against an artificial limitation of man's energy more convincingly than could be done by a legion of blue-books. But he has now chosen to represent the contempt of real workers for the idle demagogue in terms of horseflesh, and the result is, to speak plainly, nonsense. These are not the ideas of horses, for the conception of combination for a common end is essentially foreign to them; and if Mr. Kipling wanted to write the dialogue it is hard to see why he should not have written it about men. Very probably he would say it amused him to write it in this way; and that is an unanswerable argument when what amuses the writer amuses the reader also. This Walking Delegate is a caricature of a man, but he is not in the least like a horse. The other horses are like horses, but the situation is not one that could conceivably arise among horses. Swift saw the possibilities long ago, and exhausted the dramatic contrast between a man's conventions and the rules of life among decent animals, in circumstances fabulous, of course, but not inconceivable. And I confess that even the better features of the story—for instance, the insight into the experiences of a New York tram-horse—are marred to me by the dialect. There may possibly be some fascination about a tongue in which people say 'nope' and 'yep' for 'no' and 'yes', but I do not feel it; and there are surely enough authors already engaged in garnering the rank crop of American vulgarisms. To a certain extent these have infected Mr. Kipling's own style already; we find him talking about 'slugging' a guard, 'cramping' a coupé, and so forth; and before the century is out, he may be writing 'vim' and 'brainy' with the best of them.

'The Ship that Found Herself' is another allegory, or symbol as you choose. If an organisation—a State, for instance—is to be worth its place in the world, all the bits in that organisation have to do their separate work in the best way they can and not mind if their toes are trodden on, because that is inevitable. That is the moral of innumerable tales in Mr. Kipling's work, and a very admirable moral it is. Servants of the State have to realise that they are parts of a machine, the whole of which depends on the loyalty of every part. That is all very well as a metaphor or illustration. But when you come to writing a story to show how all the parts of a ship, the rivets, stringers, garboard-strake, and heaven knows what else, have feelings to be considered and how each learns a common lesson—why then you are very apt to be a bore. And when you bring in the steam as a kind of guardian angel with a tendency to be facetious, you approach to being intolerable.

And yet I must admit that I have heard an intelligent man speaking of this book describe 'The Maltese Cat' as the best story in it, and next to that he placed 'The Ship that Found Herself' and '·007'. There are things to interest one, as well as many to annoy one in the story of the ship; it is doubtless a graphic account of the process of adjustment which actually takes place on a first voyage; but '·007' is beyond me. Here all Mr. Kipling's manias break loose at once—there is the madness of American slang, the madness of technical jargon, and the madness of believing that silly talk, chiefly consisting of moral truisms, is amusing because you put it into the mouths of machines, for machines in Mr. Kipling have mouths. Here is a sample:

'I've trouble enough in my own division,' said a lean, light suburban loco with very shiny brake-shoes. 'My commuters wouldn't rest till they got a parlour-car. They've hitched her back of all, and she hauls worse'n a snowplough. I'll snap her off some day sure, and then they'll blame anyone except their fool-selves. They'll be askin' me to haul a vestibuled next.'

Now in this I do not know what 'brake-shoes', 'commuters', or a 'vestibuled' may be, and as Mr. Kipling has already surfeited me with strange knowledge and unfamiliar terms, I would not thank him to tell me. It is enough that he should let loose upon us all the unknown possibilities of our own tongue without borrowing abominations from America. But the pith of my objection is to this silly perversion of symbolism. It is no doubt perfectly true that complicated machines have their idiosyncrasies, their personalities even, if you please; a bicycle can be nearly as annoying as a horse. For once in a way it may be good fun to push the fancy a little further and attribute to them sentient life, but Mr. Kipling has overdone the thing. If we take 'The Ship that Found Herself' seriously, as I believe he means it to be taken, it is an exaggeration—what Mr. Ruskin used to call a pathetic fallacy; and the thing is capable of indefinite and appalling extension. If Mr. Kipling fell ill (which heaven forbid) or had any reason to interest himself in the inside of a chemist's shop, we might have the different pills bragging to one another, and tincture of quinine comparing its function in the universe with that of a black draught. Why not? It is all in 'the day's work'.

In all seriousness, be his faults what they may, Mr. Kipling has something of nearly every virtue that an author can be credited with. His work is obviously wrought up to the last limit of care; he does not produce too much—indeed, we would welcome more; but he does not seem to have a sure critical instinct. This pedantry of technical terms seems to grow on him, and the craze for symbolism, with the accompanying belief that a thing gains by being said round a corner instead of straight out, might very conceivably mar the work of the one man among us from whom our prose literature has much to expect. And not our prose literature only. Years ago, Mr. Kipling spoilt a poem in which there were almost the best verses he ever wrote, 'L'Envoi', with unnecessary and crabbed nautical terms, all the more annoying because in the same poem he had two or three times over got the real poetry of the thing, whose accidental details he wearied us with cataloguing. Clever as it is, this is not poetry:

> See the shaking funnels roar, with the Peter at the fore,
> And the fenders grind and heave,
> And the derricks clack and grate, as the tackle hooks the crate,
> And the fall rope whines through the sheave.

But there can be no mistake about this:

> Then home, get her home, where the drunken rollers comb,
> And the shouting seas drive by,
> And the engines stamp and ring, and the wet bows reel and swing
> And the Southern Cross rides high!

'McAndrew's Hymn' makes interesting reading, no doubt, but it also misses being poetry, because Mr. Kipling is too much set on the detail and cannot hide his knowledge; what he wants to celebrate is the power, and he only shows us the machinery. And the other fault, excessive indulgence in symbolism, which, as I have said, makes even 'The Bridge-Builders' a trifle obscure, renders many of his verses where he feels he is bound to be lucid, as incomprehensible as the wildest rhapsody of Mr. Swinburne. Enough, however, has been said upon all these matters to explain the objection without further illustration; and enough, also, I hope, to convince Mr. Kipling, should he chance to read them, that these are the words of

AN ADMIRER

31. Neil Munro on 'Mr. Rudyard Kipling'

1899

Signed article from *Good Words*, Vol. XL, pp. 261–5 (April 1899).

Neil Munro (1864–1930) was a popular Scottish novelist who did much to encourage the 'Celtic Revival' with his dialect stories, historical novels and Scots poems.

The past month has seen oceans of ink spilled in the recountment of Mr. Kipling's achievements, yet of the myriad commentators who made the novelist's sick-bed inspire their laudatory pens no one seems to have attempted an analysis of the man, and what, in our indispensable phrase, we call his message. It has been iterated to weariness that he writes with the star-gemmed quill of genius and the fiery exaltation of the patriot. These are the more obvious of his qualities, the abstract impressions created by his work, that would of themselves perhaps have left us cold because of their very commonness, for Providence flicks a brain-patch a little out of the normal in one or two skulls in every English Board School (with a double allowance for North Britain), and reverence for the Old Rag, the zest of the glory of going on and of being an Englishman, is thrust, with gas-pipe drill and the manual exercise, into multitudinous Boys' Brigades till pride of country exudes from every pore. The clanging patriotic note we have heard so much about in the past few weeks is, at least in its more arrogant note of Imperialism, by no means the most universally esteemed of Mr. Kipling's characteristics, nor is it new with him. Did not Campbell trumpet to our hearts in the sonorous call that finds its last lingering haunting note in the name of Elsinore; and did not Tennyson and Doyle and Swinburne, eminently among others, strike lustily on Britain's brass-bossed shield generations more or less before the refrains of Atkins and the Adventurers hummed through the century end?

And yet the application of the spectroscope to a star so new and dazzling is no trivial business, for directly of the star itself we have seen but little. We have biographical glimpses of an infant in Bombay, a school-boy at Westward Ho!, a reporter and sub-editor in India, but no intimate details of what went to the making of a personality matured marvellously at the age of twenty-one, and destined to become the most potent influence in English letters in his own generation, so far as it has gone. What we know of Mr. Kipling must be gathered from his work: him the interviewer has followed vainly, and the personal paragrapher has had to dish up for his patrons disappointing and more or less apocryphal scraps. We find revealed in those works a singular physical and mental vitality, 'a very strong man', as he has said himself of Tommy Atkins, with a great and exuberant zest in every aspect of life, with huge self-confidence, humour, irony, curiosity, and stoicism in a wonderful degree. That ever-apparent delight he has in the terminology of crafts, trades, and callings obviously outwith his direct experience, may be accepted as indicative not only of the common artistic appreciation for out-of-the-way and pregnant words or phrases, but of a real love for the teeming interests, the human activities they express. For generations our poets and romancers have cherished the old mechanical plant of their ancestors—loves, seasons, scenery, and (to a lamentable and indecent extent of late) the internals. Mr. Kipling, thrown by the caprice of fortune into a career oscillating between two worlds, began the business of his life by surrendering most of the old conventional inspirations and locutions, and used his eyes to look abroad upon the marvel of the modern world. Cortes and his men (or, more correctly, Balboa) saw from their peak in Darien but an empty, wind-blown ocean; Kipling had a greater cause for wild surmise as perhaps the very first—Whitman out of count—to behold the Seven Seas thrid by the traffic of man, so infinitely romantic, so infinitely eloquent of the irrepressible valour of the race. Lesser men it has left unmoved—unless they were underwriters—him it touched to great emotional issues. It has been so with him on land too. Tommy Atkins and Britain's pioneer work on vexed frontiers have inspired him, not primarily because he was an Englishman, but because he was a man moved profoundly by the persistence of his fellows in a world whose pathos and oft futility he has obviously at the same time understood. Man the artificer, 'the disease of the agglutinate dust, lifting alternate feet', Mr. Kipling has seen in the light of comprehensive humanity and brotherhood. Ships threshing the seas triumphant, armies combating ague, fever, heathendom, and bloody death; railways roaring over continents, hunters boldly venturing upon trails mysterious and forlorn, outposts of progress in raw new lands—the terrific yet magnificent significance of these human enterprises has impressed him. And all that he has observed he has seen with the philosophic eye, he has enveloped his every picture, his very sentiment with stoic calm, that, now we have emerged from the experiments of the problem—novelists and the didactic poets, is essentially the mood in which the century shall go out.

About a dozen books—a book a year for the years of his activity—provide us with the scope of Mr. Kipling's genius. If he wrote no more they were sufficient to establish his reputation as a man marking an epoch in English letters. We could indeed sacrifice some of his work without detracting in the smallest degree from his permanent reputation, though the loss might mean the surrender of many light and cheerful hours. *Under the Deodars*, for instance, that exposure in youthful sarcasm of domestic eccentricities in Anglo-Indian life, so often superficially flippant and smart, reveals nothing of the mature, reflecting Kipling; another generation will probably confess that it would part without a pang with these and other stories where the Hauksbee flourishes. 'Brugglesmith' and *Badalia Herodsfoot*, 'My Sunday at Home', and a few other caprices of his prose muse might also pass into the limbo unwept, unhousel'd, unanel'd. The marvel is that a writer so profuse and versatile should have made mistakes so few. The perfect remainder, speaking comparatively, charm by their novelty, their vitality, their indubitable genius, but most of all because of the man they reveal, as must be the case in all great works of literary art, Mr. Browning's doctrine of reticence to the contrary. In them we find the human affection that inspires good literature, the essential, but not too prominent, touch of pathos, the tolerance that says the charitable word for the weakling, yet bows the head to just punishment, for man is master of his fate. It may be that Mr. Kipling has sought after the artist's impartiality in limning such a portrait as that of Terence Mulvaney, surely one of the most permanent and lovable characters in fiction, but despite himself his personal predilections emerge in the portrait. We have in that erratic representative of our red-coat rule in India the most familiar type of his creator's heroes. Mulvaney borrows some of the black-guardism of d'Artagnan; he is a little of the bully, of the drunkard, the barrack-room Don Juan, with few claims upon our respect as sober Christians and decent citizens. Yet how humorous are his lovable attributes; his camaraderie shines on him like a cuirass, his response to his better man is frequent and convincing. Savagely sur-rounded, savagely descended, the bitter circumstances of his life con-spiring always to show the worst of him, we must be prizing, as his painter does, the occasions when he defies his destiny and laboriously acts the man. What sins are we not half ready to condone in a hero so speckled when, in 'With the Main Guard', having kept his heat-tortured comrades amused through the sleepless night with his story,

'Oh, Terence,' I said, 'it's you that have the tongue.'

He looked at me wearily, his eyes were sunk in his head, and his face was drawn and white. 'Ey, ey,' said he, 'I've blandandhared him through the night somehow, but can thim that hilps others hilp thimselves? Answer me that, sorr.'

Mulvaney is the composite Kipling hero. Unlike the musketeer of Louis XIII, he moves in an atmosphere, not a vacuum tube; we know not only what he is, but why he is what he is; he is a living person, not a marionette. This realism and this atmospheric envelopment distin-guish all the best of Mr. Kipling's creations. His women, whether they be camp heroines, dubious ladies of the married quarters, creatures of Simla intrigue, or common wives and mothers, stand upon their legs, move and have their being in their appropriate and native air, a phrase here and there, let slip as if it had no great relation to the matter at issue, telling all the history and ancestry of which the new novelist of heredity must have numerous chapters, doleful and melancholy chapters, to lay bare. Mrs. Hauksbee is not a heroine except to the tolerant artistic eye that beholds her wonderfully human and true to a life that has contradictions and complexities utterly beyond our un-ravelling. I have said we might part with her without a pang, and yet I doubt if we could; rather I should have said we could let go her attendant train of vapid and caddish followers, and forget the social life of which she is the centre. She herself is Mr. Kipling's strongest female character. He knows her past, he reveals all the ignominy of her present, but, carrying his tolerance further in her than in any other, he betrays what seems an admiration for her powerful personality.

In his first few books Mr. Kipling, with heroes and heroines more or less variant of the two named, made more populous the world about us of unforgettable men and women of the imagination. *Plain Tales from the Hills*, and the half-dozen booklets published first by Wheeler of Allahabad, in grey paper covers that yet to look upon is to experience a sense of boon friendships—these contain the work that he will find it difficult to improve upon. There we were made acquaint for the first time with the Terentian philosophy—

> For to admire and for to see
> For to be'old this world so wide;

the British soldier became for the first time something more than a Surrey-side melodramatic tinpot hero; our little wars with Pathan and Dacoit jumped into actuality, and were no longer occult suggestions, remote, far-off, incomprehensible in the brief telegraphic news of the morning papers. India itself, with its name redolent of romance from the days of Virgil, found its exponent for the modern man, and we became of a sudden familiar with a country where nothing had ever happened before but famines and mutinies; with its heats, its rains, its colour, its vast spaces, its commingling odours. The hot savage soil on the fringe of barbarian blackness turned up red to the coulter of civilisation. Whitechapel and the English areas where zymotic disease abounds wrestled for our glory with savage Orientals; we were in a new world, where, luckily, people, as in the days of Scott, were doing things eternally, and not simply whining at existence.

'The Drums of the Fore and Aft' and 'The Man Who Would Be King', these notably among the early essays in a new method of fiction stirred us by the vivid illusion they conveyed, by the vista they suggested of space and action, by the romance with which they were informed in every image, the wholesome manliness that throbbed in every sentiment. It is in the genre of which they are the best examples that Mr. Kipling is pre-eminent. In the superficial elements of many of his other stories there is much imitable though novel and ingenious, in those named and in the horror of 'The Mark of the Beast' and 'The End of the Passage', there is in inspiration of a much more rare and elusive kind, a quality that cannot be repeated by any other writer.

The gods were extravagantly good to Mr. Kipling, for with his gift of dramatic tale and a career to equip him for its expression, they gave him the gift of poetry, lacking which prose narrative is soulless and evanescent. It is the poetic insight that over and over again redeems brutal and even vulgar passages in his tales from our indifference or contempt; there he would have shown the poet if *Departmental Ditties*, *Barrack-room Ballads*, and *The Seven Seas* had never been written. But he has in his works of verse justified himself as the laureate of English endeavour. A brain-weary people, sick of abstruse sermons played upon dulcimers, have hailed with gladness a song and chorus accompanied by the banjo. Some of the strenuous young gentlemen who sing in pestilently unmusical and jerky measure of life, time, and early demise have an equipment Mr. Kipling cannot or does not boast of. They rejoice in vocabularies extensive and precious; they have a fastidiousness that keeps them clear of the cheap tune, the vulgar hero, the sentiment of the *Lion Comique*, the dialect that is unheard in drawing-rooms.They can write much that Mr. Kipling could not write to save his soul, but they cannot write so as to be read or listened to, which, cant aside, has been the first ambition of every ballad-maker since the days when Homer smote his lyre. Literature in prose or poetry is saved from eternal perdition by fresh starts; just when the material of conventional verse has been spread out thin to invisibility, and sheer intellect is going to upset our apple-cart, a lark soars into the heavens with a simple song for lesson, a man sheds the cerements of convention, steps back from the choir, and gives his natural voice a trial unafraid. Then, no matter what he sings—weariness and fret, the joy of life, passion, Spring or stars, if a robust individuality, a clean nature, a lyric lilt and cadence be his, we must be listening. His are the airs that the people find haunting; they may be even only temporary in appeal, but permanence is not, in spite of all we say to the contrary, the first and greatest essential of poetry. Wharton boasted that with 'Lillibulero' he had whistled a king out of three kingdoms; we have today forgotten that air that Uncle Toby so constantly dwelt on, but in the final balancing of things that have influenced, who can say that the forgotten 'Lillibulero' is not more weighty than studious measures in classic mould a few rare exclusive souls have sung for centuries?

With material entirely new, with a method novel, Kipling, in *Barrack-room Ballads* and *The Seven Seas*, has captured the general ear and touched the general heart. That, it may be retorted, was done aforetime by the Muse of Mr. Sims. Yet in this instance there is a great difference, though it seems sacrilege to hint the necessity of differentiation. It is not the music-hall audience alone that is impressed by the weird terror of 'Danny Deever', the sentiment of the majestic 'Ballad of East and West', the *élan* of the 'Sons of the Widow', and the cadence and wistfulness of 'Mandalay'. In these measures artists have found the lyric note no way abased. Good as *Barrack-room Ballads* were, the more recent *Seven Seas* was better. There we found Mr. Kipling still with 'the best words in the best order', as Coleridge defined poetry, but more profound in the hearts of man. A wider sweep of interests, a more mature valuation of the phenomena of life, a more opulent and canorous note peals in his lines, the man behind the instrument is more finely revealed. Any claim by any other living man than the author of 'A Song of the English', to be considered the laureate by divine right of English peoples would be ridiculous. But the Imperialism of the book is only one of its impressive features. The age of steam and telegraph, Hotchkiss guns and Saratoga trunks has found its balladist there, and he has found nothing common or unclean. The soldiers of the later military ballads, too, betray an ageing creator; they are still strumming on the banjo, but their songs have lost some of the shallow inspiration of the 'Alls; they lean upon homing bulwarks and reflect upon the sweet futilities that have stayed them here and there upon the sides of 'the 'appy roads that take you o'er the world'. And the seas cry in his work for the first time, not the played-out oceans of dhow and galley and picturesque but unwieldy three-deckers, but of the darting cruiser, the liner spurning leagues a day in every weather, the buffeting of the elements, and the engineer.

There are other works of Mr. Kipling than those I have named. The *Jungle Books* delight by their insight, almost magic, of the untamed wilds and all their residents; *Captains Courageous*, less felicitously inspired but yet original and unique, *Many Inventions* and *The Day's Work*, *Life's Handicap*, *The Light that Failed*, and *The Naulakha* have material fresh and strong. Taking either his prose or poetry in separate parts, testing by ordinary canons, it will happen that the writing seems often to be on a lower plane than the imaginative inspiration, and a sense of something wanting may ensue. But surveying the work of Mr. Kipling as a whole, the most fastidious must be impressed by the greatness of its genius, the scope and variety it displays, the essentially wholesome influence it creates.

32. Two Reviews of *Stalky & Co.*

1899

Anonymous reviews in the *Athenaeum*, No. 3755, pp. 515–16 and the *Academy*, No. 1432, pp. 421–2 (both 14 October 1899).

These are included to show the divergences of critical opinion about this the most controversial of Kipling's books.

I

Most English boys—and most Englishmen who have anything of the boy still in them—will rejoice in *Stalky & Co.* Boys will declare that the book is 'spiffing' and if they read it in school hours—a not impossible feat—will have to keep a handkerchief ready to stuff into their mouths to prevent their laughter attracting the attention of the formmaster. Mr. Kipling himself has every reason to feel proud of the success with which he has phonographed the English public-school boy's talk and sentiments.

Mr. Kipling knows his English boy, as he seems to know everything, outside and inside—especially outside. Most men have a vivid memory of their boyhood's days; but with most there is an idealizing halo round them which altogether alters the value of the picture. Mr. Kipling, with that marvellous memory of his, recalls his school days as in themselves they really were. He sees the British boy, with his infinite capacity for fun, his finite capacity for insubordination, his coarseness in word and act, modified by an ultra-sensitive delicacy of feeling in certain directions. *Stalky & Co.* is almost a complete treatise on the strategy and tactics of the British schoolboy—or perhaps one should say the British public-school boy. Reverence for the head authority and contempt for all other authority, respect for most aspects of physical training, and utter indifference towards the training of the intellect, underlie the whole *Stimmung* of the book. Mr. Kipling has taught his public how Matthew Arnold's Barbarians are trained.

Here he not only describes—he defends; the implications of the whole book is a glorification of the public-school method of training character, or perhaps we should qualify, and say training the character of the leading classes. Two of the stories are bracketed together as 'Slaves of the Lamp, I.', and 'Slaves of the Lamp, II.' (the last story of the book—a kind of epilogue), with the seeming intention of showing that the tricks boys play upon their form-masters come in usefully as training in strategy for frontier warfare. In the first of the stories Stalky 'scores off' the best-hated master by leading a drunken carrier to think that the said master had used a catapult against him, where-upon he resorts to reprisals, and the form-master's study is made to suffer. In the last story Stalky, now a lieutenant on the frontier, is defending a fort which is attacked by two native tribes that have for the moment sunk their feuds. Stalky steals out with a detachment to the rear of their encampments, and, when the attack takes place, peppers one of the tribes with shots, seemingly coming from the direc-tion of the other. Result, revival of the feud, and the form-master tribe is attacked by the carrier one. In short, these portions of the book are, in a measure, Mr. Kipling's answer to the question our neighbours are asking, *A quoi tient la supériorité des Anglo-Saxons?*

It is natural to compare *Stalky & Co.* with Mr. Kipling's other boys' book, *Captains Courageous*: one treats of the boy in his native and natural environment, the other of a boy in strange surroundings. Both are eminently didactic in tone, the chief lesson inculcated being that of the good effects of a sound whacking on a boy's character, even if the cane is applied with seemingly 'flagrant injustice'. In both cases the type of boy to be turned out is that of the military or commercial organizer. 'Save he serve, no man may rule'—not perhaps, a very subtle lesson, nor particularly one that needs insisting on, but it is brought home with all Mr. Kipling's astonishing force, and in *Stalky & Co.* is presented with even a certain amount of polemical intention.

Mr. Kipling evidently does not believe in what is known as appealing to a boy's higher feelings. One of the most subtle sections of the book is that entitled 'The Flag of their Country'. A blatant politician gives an address to the school, just after a volunteer cadet corps has been formed, and at the finish unfurls a cheap calico Union Jack, with the result that the corps is immediately disbanded, and, for the only time, Stalky, in the presence of his chums, bursts into tears. Here Mr. Kipling touches upon one of the profoundest traits in the English character, the abhorrence of English boys—and, for the matter of that, of English men—of having their most sacred feelings referred to publicly. Some slight hits (not in the very best taste) at Dr. Farrar's books are doubtless meant to emphasize the same moral. After all, is not the contrast between the military and clerical ideas of life? Mr. Kipling, here as elsewhere, is on the side of Tommy Atkins.

The interest of *Stalky & Co.* for 'grown-ups' will naturally be the pictures of English military school life presented in it, but it would be misleading to accept them as representing all English boarding schools, or even all English public schools. To complete the picture we need a description of the former, which, on the evidence of others, would not present so pleasant an aspect as Westward Ho! And here it may be noted that Westward Ho! is not perhaps a fair representative of English public schools. Mr. Kipling himself indicates as much by the stress he lays on the undesirable portion of the school which has been with the 'crammer' in town. Public-school boys in general will ask in surprise, Why were the assistants so rotten when the Head was so able? And is it usual for school chaplains to smoke in small boys' studies? The 'honour of the House' is satirized; but is it nothing, ought it to be nothing?

There is another aspect of *Stalky & Co.* which will interest all English people—the light it throws on Mr. Kipling's own school career, and the formative influences on his character. He scarcely disguises that he is the 'Beetle' of the story, and that, but for his early spectacles, he would have tried to emulate the deeds of Indian army subalterns which he takes such pleasure in describing. Rarely has a personal defect proved of such national advantage. The hint is also given that Mr. Kipling's journalistic career was due to the discernment of Mr. Cormell Price, the headmaster of the school.

To the students of Mr. Kipling's art his new book affords a number of interesting problems. His greatest skill has hitherto been shown in the *conte*—the rapid presentation of one 'action', with the appropriate characterization, which makes the action artistically inevitable. Here we have a series of school *contes*, but their total result is to work up into a tolerably complete picture of a certain school organism—a military preparatory school in North Devon. We find not only various types of schoolboys delineated (with the significant exception of the 'sap' or 'swot'), but also a tolerably complete series of portraits of assistant masters, including the rather improbable 'Padre', who has the boys' entire confidence; and then, in a class apart, 'the Head', whose penetrating influence throughout the school is most subtly indicated in every story. We have even the relations of the school indicated with the surrounding population, and occasional snapshots of visitors, parents and guardians, and Old Boys. In this way the seemingly disconnected series of stories makes up a tolerably complete picture of the school as an organic whole. This is true artistry, such as had not been displayed by Mr. Kipling in his previous efforts. His very keenness of vision has apparently prevented him from composing his work on a larger canvas.

It is somewhat difficult and misleading to quote specimens of work which thus depends for its higher qualities on general tone and treatment rather than upon details. Perhaps the following will, at any rate, indicate the absolute accuracy with which boys' words and doings are touched off by Mr. Kipling. Stalky & Co. meet a prefect, while out of bounds with permission:

[quotes 'The Last Term' *Stalky, & Co.*, p. 222, line 16, to p. 223, line 30]

Nothing could be more lifelike and convincing. For the manner in which this episode leads up to a disgraceful rout of the whole body of prefects the reader must be referred to the story itself.

The best test of a book of this kind is not to judge it by the canons of high art, but to get a boy to read it. *Stalky & Co.* comes triumphantly past this test, for the experiment has been tried. The boy in question, on being asked to put in order of merit the various stories which had caused him so many guffaws, expressed his preference for 'The Moral Reformers'; it has a touch of cruelty in it which appeals to the savage elements of that age; then came 'An Unsavoury Interlude', again an appeal to the primeval instincts. The two 'Slaves of the Lamp' were bracketed together next—a triumphant compliment to Mr. Kipling's skill; and the total verdict, in which the higher criticism can but acquiesce, was 'Spiffing!'

II

Whether or not Mr. Kipling claims to have set before us the whole boy, or only a special acquaintance of his own, we do not know; but if *Stalky & Co.*, as we half suspect, purports to tell the truth where *Eric*, Dean Farrar's famous story (and Mr. Kipling's bugbear), only romances, we must say at once that it comes short of that ambition. The impression of boy life conveyed by *Eric* is not more false than that given by *Stalky & Co.*, but the two pictures are the poles asunder. Dean Farrar's weakness for sentiment is quite equalled by Mr. Kipling's infatuation for might. One is as wrong as the other. The real boy comes somewhere between the two; you will find more of him in *Tom Brown* and *Tom Sawyer* than anywhere else. Mr. Kipling for once is caught tripping. In his endeavour to capture his youth he has remembered everything but youth's immaturity. The escapades of youth are here, the joy of living, the high spirits; but a cleverness beyond all credence has been superimposed. The attempt to make forcible dialogue and successful strategy has been too much for the author, and fidelity to the fact has gone overboard in the interests of the yarn. We cannot believe that even at Westward Ho!, Mr. Kipling's own school, three boys ever existed with so complete a theory of life, such rapid and accurate powers of deduction, such uncanny sagacity, such unwavering disregard of the feelings of others, and such brutal and unflagging wit, as Stalky, M'Turk, and Beetle. Mr. Kipling is entitled to idealise his puppets if he likes, and yet we have for so long come to look to him for genuine efforts to depict people as they are that it is with difficulty that the mind is adjusted to this new phase. We shall express the matter more clearly, perhaps, by saying that in these narratives of the adventures of three boys for the discomfiture of masters or other enemies, and the glorification of themselves, the thought, the arrangement, and the orderly accomplishment are adult, the conditions and language—and that only approximately—alone being boyish. Now although the child is the father of the man, and all the rest of it, there is yet a vast difference between a boy's ways and a man's ways. Mr. Kipling seems to us to have overlooked that difference altogether.

He has also so overdone the book that it has to be pronounced his least satisfactory work. There is a piling on of youthful brutality beyond all need, a lack of selective skill. Had *Stalky & Co.* been a whole-hearted attempt at realism, a genuine effort to portray the boy, we should make no such objections. But it is nothing of the kind: the whole boy, indeed, would no more bear setting down in black and white than the whole man. Realism being, then, out of the question, it remains that Mr. Kipling might have made a far better book. For the moment his instinct for the best stories has left him: he has let in a very flood of the second best. 'In Ambush' and 'A Little Prep.', the best things here (as good in their kind as one could wish), make some of their companions appear singularly unnecessary. 'An Unsavoury Interlude', 'The Impressionists', 'The Moral Reformers'—no one of these is worth the amount of spirit and literary power which Mr. Kipling has put into them. 'An Unsavoury Interlude' in particular is quite unworthy—a story which relates how the three heroes, having been accused of neglecting to wash themselves, retaliate by hiding a putrid cat in their traducers' house. Boys doubtless do such things, and for an oral yarn the incident would serve; but when a man of genius sits down to elaborate the affair we feel that he is expending himself wantonly. The thing does not matter, is not worth the doing, especially by the same hand that gave us the beautiful gravity of the *Jungle Books.* However, to balance the less worthy or unworthy chapters there are the two that we have named, which are of the first-class of boisterous school story. These, though often unnecessarily exuberant, justify themselves; and, if we had our way, Mr. Kipling's reputation as a delineator of boy life in a military nursery should rest on them alone. We quote from 'In Ambush' the passages describing part of the conversation of the three when confined to their dormitory for a crime they did not commit:

[quotes 'In Ambush', *Stalky & Co.*, p. 28, line 23, to p. 30, line 4, and 'subsequently their visit to the Head'—p. 34, line 25, to p. 35, line 22]

We have used the phrase, boy life in a military nursery, because it must be remembered that that is what Mr. Kipling has set out to paint. *Stalky & Co.* is the book of empire-makers in the making, a fact which must be kept steadily in mind if one is to come through to the last page without qualms, or, indeed, come through to the last page at all. For empires are not made in accordance with the precepts of the fifth chapter of Matthew, or even of the ordinary citizen of the world, and empire-makers are a kind of boy in whom the softer emotions have no place, and in whom any cultivation of the delicacies is discouraged. The qualities which are most needed on our frontiers are the qualities which Mr. Kipling holds up for admiration. It is not so much Young England that is represented here as Young Fighting England, in whom there cannot be too much of quickness of thought and swiftness of decisive action, and who is successful only in so far as he is also merciless, adamant, and domineering. Courageous, too; although, curiously, Mr. Kipling leaves us to form our own conclusions as to his heroes' personal valour. Their victories are for the most part victories of diplomacy and vicarious blows. Stalky, we know from the last story, became a worthy soldier; but at school the three despised cricket with all their hearts, avoided football except under compulsion, and, so far as their historian informs us, fought no fights. On the other hand they once ill-treated a cow (although Mr. Kipling has not included the account of the incident in this volume), and in the course of curing two bullies of bullying their own experiments in that art reached a point of horrible atrocity. Hence, although for soldiers this is one of the most congenial collections of yarns that they are likely to get for some time, and for Volunteers and the military-minded it is hardly less admirable, for the Czar and for peace-loving and all gentle-souled readers it will be well-nigh impossible. Mr. Kipling, as apostle of muscle and aggressive Imperialism, has uttered many battle-cries in his time; but this is his completest incitement to war, his crowning achievement as the supreme Recruiting Sergeant. Particularly so, since *Stalky & Co.* appeals to the young and plastic mind. Parents must please themselves as to whether they add the book to the holiday library; but we can only say that if it is to be read freely by impressionable boys, the sooner the curtain is rung down on the farce of Christianity the better; for there is hardly a precept of the Sermon on the Mount that is not joyously outraged in its pages.

What the book chiefly needs is some humanising relief. Throughout there is the same unerring metallic smartness, with hardly a hint of deeper feelings; the same torrent of brilliant slang. And this reminds us that besides other reasons for not handing this book to a boy, which will occur to every schoolmaster who happens to read it, there is also the objection that imitators of Stalky, M'Turk, and Beetle would be a very noxious race. For the originals we have admiration, albeit tempered by incredulity; but their derivatives will be appalling.

33. Robert Buchanan: 'The Voice of the Hooligan'

1899

Signed article from the *Contemporary Review*, Vol. LXXVI, pp. 774–89 (December 1899), published with Besant's answer and Buchanan's final retort in a small volume by The Tucker Publishing Company, New York, 1900.

Robert Williams Buchanan (1841–1901) was a soured and unsuccessful minor poet, novelist and dramatist, who had already won notoriety for his virulent attack on Rossetti, 'The Fleshly School of Poetry', also published in the *Contemporary Review* (October 1871).

Although some of the present diatribe is general in application, it is included here in its entirety as the first major attack on Kipling for brutality, warmongering and illiberalism—lines soon to be followed by many other so-called critics for reasons almost entirely divorced from literature.

As the years advance which 'bring the philosophic mind', or at least the mind which we fondly flatter ourselves is philosophic—in other words, as men of thought and feeling approach the latter end of their pilgrimage—there is a tendency among them to under-reckon the advance which the world has made in the course of their experience, and to discover in the far-off days of their youth a light which has almost ceased to shine on earthly things.

Laudatores temporis acti, they look askance at all the results of progress, and assert, more or less emphatically that men were wiser and better when they themselves were young. They forget, of course, that distance lends enchantment to the view, and that the very splendour in which the world once appeared came rather from within than from without; and, forgetting this, they do scant justice to the achievements of later generations. A little sober reflection, nevertheless, may convince them that the world *does* advance, though perhaps not so surely and satisfactorily as they would wish to believe; and that, even if there is some occasional retrogression, inevitable under the conditions of human development, it is only, after all, temporary, and due to causes which are inherent in our imperfect human nature. From time to time, however, the momentum towards a higher and more spiritual ideal seems suspended altogether, and we appear to be swept centuries back, by a great back-wave, as it were, in the direction of absolute barbarism.

Such a back-wave, it appears to me, has been at work during the last few decades, and the accompanying phenomena, in public life, in religion, in literature, have been extraordinary enough to fill even a fairly philosophical mind with something like despair. Closer contemplation and profounder meditation, however, may prove that in all possibility the retrogression is less real than superficial, that the advance forward of our civilization has only been hampered, not absolutely and finally hindered, and that in due time we may become stronger and wiser through the very lessons hardly learned during the painful period of delay.

It would be quite beyond the scope of the present article to point out in detail the divers ways in which modern society, in England particularly, has drifted little by little, and day by day, away from those humanitarian traditions which appeared to open up to men, in the time of my own boyhood, the prospect of a new heaven and a new earth. At that time, the influence of the great leaders of modern thought was still felt, both in politics and in literature; the gospel of humanity, as expressed in the language of poets like Wordsworth and Shelley, and in the deeds of men like Wilberforce and Mazzini, had purified the very air men breathed; and down lower, in the humbler spheres of duty and human endeavour, humanists like Dickens were translating the results of religious aspiration into such simple and happy speech as even the lowliest of students could understand. It was a time of immense activity in all departments, but its chief characteristic, perhaps, was the almost universal dominance, among educated men, of the sentiment of *philanthropy*, of belief in the inherent perfectibility of human nature, as well as of faith in ideals which bore at least the semblance of a celestial origin. Not quite in vain, it seemed, had Owen and Fourier laboured, and Hood sung, and John Leech wielded the pencil, and Dickens and Thackeray used the pen. The name of Arnold was still a living force in our English schools, and the name of Mazzini was being whispered in every English home. The first noticeable change came, perhaps, with the criminal crusade of the Crimean war; and from that hour to this, owing in no little degree to the rough-and-ready generalizations of popular science, and the consequent discrediting of all religious sanctions, the enthusiasm of humanity among the masses has gradually, but surely, died away. Sentiment has at last become thoroughly out of fashion, and humanitarianism is left to the care of eccentric and unauthoritative teachers. Thus, while a few despairing thinkers and dreamers have been trying vainly to substitute a new Ethos for the old religious sanctions, the world at large, repudiating the enthusiasm of humanity altogether, and exchanging it for the worship of physical force and commercial success in any and every form, has turned rapturously towards activities which need no sanction whatever, or which, at any rate, can be easily sanctified by the wanton will of the majority. Men no longer, in the great civic centres at least, ask themselves whether a particular course of conduct is right or wrong, but whether it is expedient, profitable, and certain of clamorous approval. Thanks to the newspaper press—that 'mighty engine', as Mr. Morley calls it, for 'keeping the public intelligence on a low level'—they are fed from day to day with hasty news and gossip, and with bogus views of affairs, concocted in the interests of the wealthy classes. Ephemeral and empirical books of all sorts take the place of serious literature; so that, while a great work like Mr. Spencer's *Justice* falls still-born from the press, a sophistical defence of the *status quo* like Mr. Balfour's *Foundations of Belief* is read by thousands. The aristocracy, impoverished by its own idleness and luxury, rushes wildly to join the middle-class in speculations which necessitate new conquests of territory and constant acts of aggression. The mob, promised a merry time by the governing classes, just as the old Roman mob was deluded by bread and pageants —*panem et circenses*—dances merrily to patriotic war-tunes, while that modern monstrosity and anachronism, the conservative working man, exchanges his birthright of freedom and free thought for a pat on the head from any little rump-fed lord that steps his way and spouts the platitudes of cockney patriotism. The established Church, deprived of the conscience which accompanied honest belief, supports nearly every infamy of the moment in the name of the Christianity which it has long ago shifted quietly overboard. [Footnote quoting verses by Archbishop Alexander. See Besant's answer, page 257]

There is an universal scramble for plunder, for excitement, for amusement, for speculation, and, above it all, the flag of a Hooligan

Imperialism is raised, with the proclamation that it is the sole mission of Anglo-Saxon England, forgetful of the task of keeping its own drains in order, to expand and extend its boundaries indefinitely, and, again in the name of the Christianity it has practically abandoned, to conquer and inherit the earth.

It may be replied that this is an exaggerated picture, and I will admit at once that there is justice in the reply, if it is granted at the same time that the picture is true so far as London itself and an enormous majority of Englishmen are concerned. Only if this is granted, can the present relapse back to barbarism of our public life, our society, our literature, be explained. Now that Mr. Gladstone has departed, we possess no politician, with the single exception of Mr. Morley (whose sanity and honesty are unquestionable, though he lacks, unfortunately, the daemonic influence), who demands for the discussion of public affairs any conscientious and unselfish sanction whatever; we possess, instead, a thousand pertinacious counsellors, cynics like Lord Salisbury or trimmers like Lord Rosebery, for whom no one in his heart of hearts feels the slightest respect. Our fashionable society is admittedly so rotten, root and branch, that not even the Queen's commanding influence can impart to it the faintest suggestion of purity, or even decency. As for our popular literature, it has been in many of its manifestations long past praying for; it has run to seed in fiction of the baser sort, seldom or never, with all its cleverness, touching the quick of human conscience; but its most extraordinary feature at this moment is the exaltation to a position of almost unexampled popularity of a writer who in his single person adumbrates, I think, all that is most deplorable, all that is most retrograde and savage, in the restless and uninstructed Hooliganism of the time.

The English public's first knowledge of Mr. Rudyard Kipling was gathered from certain brief anecdotal stories and occasional verses which began to be quoted about a decade ago in England, and which were speedily followed by cheap reprints of the originals, sold on every bookstall. They possessed one not inconsiderable attraction, in so far as they dealt with a naturally romantic country, looming very far off to English readers, and doubly interesting as one of our own great national possessions. We had had many works about India—works of description and works of fiction; and a passionate interest in them, and in all that pertained to things Anglo-Indian, had been awakened by the Mutiny; but few writers had dealt with the ignobler details of military and civilian life, with the gossip of the messroom and the scandal of the governmental departments. Mr. Kipling's little Kodak-glimpses, therefore, seemed unusually fresh and new; nor would it be just to deny them the merits if great liveliness, intimate personal knowledge, and a certain unmistakable, though obviously cockney, humour. Although they dealt almost entirely with the baser aspects of our civilization, being chiefly devoted to the affairs of idle military men, savage soldiers, frisky wives and widows, and flippant civilians, they were indubitably bright and clever, and in the background of them we perceived, faintly but distinctly, the shadow of the great and wonderful national life of India. At any rate, whatever their merits were—and I hold their merits to be indisputable—they became rapidly popular, especially with the newspaper press, which hailed the writer as a new and quite amazing force in literature. So far as the lazy public was concerned, they had the one delightful merit of extreme brevity; he that ran might read them, just as he read *Tit-bits* and the society newspapers, and then treat them like the rose in Browning's poem:

> Smell, kiss, wear it—at last throw away!

Two factors contributed to their vogue; first, the utter apathy of general readers, too idle and uninstructed to study works of any length or demanding any contribution of serious thought on the reader's part, and eager for any amusement which did not remind them of the eternal problems which once beset humanity; and, second, the rapid growth in every direction of the military or militant spirit, of the Primrose League, of aggression abroad, and indifference at home to all religious ideals—in a word, of Greater Englandism, or Imperialism. For a considerable time Mr. Kipling poured out a rapid succession of these little tales and smoking-room anecdotes, to the great satisfaction of those who loved to listen to banalities about the English flag, seasoned with strong suggestions of social impropriety, as revealed in camps and barracks and the boudoirs of officers' mistresses and wives. The things seemed harmless enough, if not very elevating or ennobling. Encouraged by his success, the author attempted longer flights, with very indifferent results; though in the *Jungle Books*, for example, he got near to a really imaginative presentment of fine material, and, if he had continued his work in that direction, criticism might have had little or nothing to say against him. But in an unfortunate moment, encouraged by the journalistic praise lavished on certain fragments of verse with which he had ornamented his prose effusions, he elected to

237

challenge criticism as a poet—as, indeed, the approved and authoritative poet of the British empire; and the first result of this election, or, as I prefer to call it, this delusion and hallucination, was the publication of the volume of poems, partly new and partly reprinted, called *Barrack-Room Ballads.*

I have said that Mr. Kipling's estimate of himself as a poet was a delusion; it was no delusion, however, so far as his faith in the public was concerned. The book was received with instantaneous and clamorous approval; and, once again, let me pause to admit that it contained, here and there, glimpses of a real verse-making faculty—a faculty which, had the writer been spiritually and intellectually equipped, might have led to the production of work entitled to be called 'poetry'. On the very first page, however, the note of insincerity was struck, in a dedication addressed to Mr. Wolcott Balestier, but recognized at once as having done duty for quite a different purpose—resembling in this respect the famous acrostic of Mr. Slum, which, although written to fit the name of 'Warren', became at a pinch 'a positive inspiration for Jarley'. This dedication, with its false feeling and utterly unsuitable imagery, suggests the remark *en passant* that Mr. Kipling's muse alternates between two extremes—the lowest cockney vulgarity and the very height of what Americans call 'high-falutin' '—so that, when it is not setting the teeth on edge with the vocabulary of the London Hooligan, it is raving in capital letters about the Seraphim and the Pit and the Maidens Nine and the Planets.

The *Ballads* thus introduced are twenty-one in number, of which the majority are descriptive of whatever is basest and most brutal in the character of the British mercenary. One deals, naturally enough, with the want of sympathy shown in public-houses to Tommy Atkins in time of peace, as contrasted with the enthusiasm for him in time of war; another, entitled 'Cells', begins as follows:

> I've a head like a concertina: I've a tongue like
> a button-stick:
> I've a mouth like an old potato, and I'm more than
> a little sick.
> But I've had my fun with the Corp'ral's Guard: I've
> made the cinders fly,
> And I'm here in the Clink for a thundering drink
> and blacking the Corp'ral's eye;

it is, in fact, the glorification of the familiar episode of 'drunk and resisting the guard'. In an equally sublime spirit is conceived the ballad called 'Loot', beginning:

> If you've ever stole a pheasant-egg be'ind the keeper's back
> If you've ever snigged the washin' from a line;
> If you've ever crammed a gander in your bloomin' 'aversack,
> You will understand this little song of mine;

and the verses are indeed, with their brutal violence and their hideous refrain, only too sadly understandable. Worse still, in its horrible savagery, is the piece called 'Belts', which is the apotheosis of the soldier who uses his belt in drunken fury to assault civilians in the streets, and which has this agreeable refrain:

> But it was: 'Belts, belts, belts, an' that's one for you!'
> An' it was 'Belts, belts, belts, an' that's done for you!'
> O buckle an' tongue
> Was the song that we sung
> From Harrison's down to the Park!

If it is suggested that the poems I have quoted are only incidental bits of local colour, interspersed among verses of a very different character, the reply is that those pieces, although they are certainly the least defensible, are quite in keeping with the other ballads, scarcely one of which reaches to the intellectual level of the lowest music-hall effusions. The best of them is a ballad called 'Mandalay', describing the feelings of a soldier who regrets the heroine of a little amour out in India, and it certainly possesses a real melody and a certain pathos. But in all the ballads, with scarcely an exception, the tone is one of absolute vulgarity and triviality, unredeemed by a touch of human tenderness and pity. Even the little piece called 'Soldier, Soldier', which begins quite naturally and tenderly, ends with the cynical suggestion that the lady who mourns her old love had better take up at once with the party who brings the news of his death:

> True love! new love!
> Best take 'im for a new love!
> The dead they cannot rise, an' you'd better dry your eyes,
> An' you'd best take 'im for your true love.

With such touching sweetness and tender verisimilitude are these ballads of the barrack filled from end to end. Seriously, the picture they present is one of unmitigated barbarism. The Tommy Atkins they introduce is a drunken, swearing, coarse-minded Hooligan, for whom, nevertheless, our sympathy is eagerly entreated. Yet these pieces were accepted on their publication, not as cruel libel on the British soldier, but as a perfect and splendid representation of the red-coated patriot on whom our national security chiefly depended, and who was spreading abroad in every country the glory of our Imperial flag!

That we might be in no doubt about the sort of thinker who was claiming our suffrages, Mr. Kipling printed at the end of his book certain other lyrics not specially devoted to the military. The best of these, the 'Ballad of the *Bolivar*', is put into the mouth of seven drunken sailors, 'rolling down the Ratcliffe Road drunk and raising Cain', and loudly proclaiming, with the true brag and bluster so characteristic of modern British heroism, how 'they took the (water-logged) *Bolivar* across the Bay'. It seems, by the way, a favourite condition with Mr. Kipling, when he celebrates acts of manly daring, that his subjects should be mad drunk, and, at any rate, as drunken in their language as possible. But this ballad may pass, that we may turn to the poem 'Cleared', in which Mr. Kipling spits all the venom of cockney ignorance on the Irish party, apropos of a certain Commission of which we have all heard, and, while saying nothing on the subject of forged letters and cowardly accusations, affirms that Irish patriots are naturally and distinctively murderers, because in the name of patriotism murders have now and then been done. He who loves blood and gore so much, who cannot even follow the soldier home into our streets without celebrating his drunken assaults and savageries, has only hate and loathing for the unhappy nation which has suffered untold wrong, and which, when all is said and done, has struck back so seldom. In the poem which follows, 'An Imperial Rescript', he protests with all his might against any bond of brotherhood among the sons of toil, pledging the strong to work for and help the weak. Here, as elsewhere, he is on the side of all that is ignorant, selfish, base, and brutal in the instincts of humanity.

Before proceeding further to estimate Mr. Kipling's contributions to literature, let me glance for a moment at his second book of verse, *The Seven Seas*, published a year or two ago. It may be granted at once that it was a distinct advance on its predecessor, more restrained, less vulgar, and much more varied; here and there, indeed, as in the opening 'Song of the English', it struck a note of distinct and absolute poetry. But, in spite of its unquestionable picturesqueness, and of a certain swing and lilt in the go-as-you-please rhythms, it was still characterized by the same indefinable quality of brutality and latent baseness. Many of the poems, such as the 'Song of the Banjo', were on the level of the cleverness to be found in the contributions of the poet of the *Sporting Times*, known to the occult as the 'Pink 'Un'. The large majority, indeed, were cockney in spirit, in language, and in inspiration, and one or two, such as 'The Ladies' and 'The Sergeant's Weddin'', with its refrain:

> Cheer for the Sergeant's weddin'—
> Give 'em one cheer more!
> Grey gun-'orses in the lando,
> And a rogue is married to *etc.*,

were frankly and brutally indecent. The army appeared again, in the same ignoble light as before, with the same disregard of all literary luxuries, even of grammar and the aspirate. God, too, loomed largely in these productions, a cockney 'Gawd' again, chiefly requisitioned for purposes of blasphemy and furious emphasis. There was no glimpse anywhere of sober and self-respecting human beings—only a wild carnival of drunken, bragging, boasting Hooligans in red coats and seamen's jackets, shrieking to the sound of the banjo and applauding the English flag.

Faint almost to inaudibility have been the protests awakened by these cockney caricatures in the ranks of the army itself. Here and there a mild voice has been heard, but no military man has declared authoritatively that effusions like those which I have quoted are a libel on the Service, if not on human nature. Are we to assume, then, that there are no refined gentlemen among our officers, and no honest self-respecting human beings among their men? Is the life of a soldier, abroad as at home, a succession of savage escapades, bestial amusements, fuddlings, tipplings, and intrigues with other men's wives, redeemed from time to time by acts of brute courage and of sang-froid in the presence of danger? Is the spirit of Gordon quite forgotten, in the service over which he shed the glory of his illustrious name? If this is really the case, there is surely very little in the Anglo-Saxon military prestige which offers us any security for the stormy times to come. That Englishmen are brave, and capable of brave deeds, is a truism of which we need no longer to be assured; but bravery and brave deeds are not national possessions—they are the prerogative of the militant classes all over the earth. Englishmen in times past were not merely brave, they could be noble and magnanimous; their courage was not only that of the bulldog, but of the patriot, the hero, and even the philanthropist: they had not yet begun to mingle the idea of a national Imperialism with the political game of brag. I am not contending for one moment that the spirit which inspired them then has altogether departed; I am sure, on the contrary, that it is living yet, and living most strongly and influentially in the heart of the army itself; but, if this is admitted and believed, it is certain that the Tommy Atkins of Mr. Rudyard Kipling deserves drumming out of all decent barracks as a monstrosity and a rogue.

The truth is, however, that these lamentable productions were concocted, not for sane men or self-respecting soldiers, not even for those who are merely ignorant and uninstructed, but for the 'mean whites' of our eastern civilization, the idle and loafing men in the street, and for such women, the well-dressed Doll Tearsheets of our cities, as shriek at their heels. Mr. Kipling's very vocabulary is a purely cockney vocabulary, even his Irishmen speaking a dialect which would cause amazement in the Emerald Isle, but is familiar enough in Seven Dials. Turning over the leaves of his poems, one is transported at once to the region of low-drinking dens and gin-palaces, of dirty dissipation and drunken brawls; and the voice we hear is always the voice of the soldier whose God is a cockney 'Gawd', and who is ignorant of the aspirate in either heaven or hell. Are there no Scotchmen in the ranks, no Highlanders, no men from Dublin or Tipperary, no Lancashire or Yorkshire men, no Welshmen, and no men of any kind who speak the Queen's English? It would seem not, if, the poet of 'The Sergeant's Weddin' ' is to be trusted. Nor have our mercenaries, from the ranks upwards, any one thing, except brute courage, to distinguish them from the beasts of the field. This, at least, appears to be Mr. Kipling's contention, and even in the Service itself it seems to be undisputed.

How then, are we to account for the extraordinary popularity of works so contemptible in spirit and so barbarous in execution? In the first place, even fairly educated readers were sick to death of the insincerities and affectations of the professional 'Poets', with one or two familiar exceptions, and, failing the advent of a popular singer like Burns, capable of setting to brisk music the simple joys and sorrows of humanity, they turned eagerly to any writer who wrote verse, doggerel even, which seemed thoroughly alive. They were amused, therefore, by the free-and-easy rattles, the jog-trot tunes, which had hitherto been heard only in the music-halls and read only in the sporting newspapers. In the second place, the spirit abroad today is the spirit of ephemeral journalism, and whatever accords with that spirit—its vulgarity, its flippancy, and its radical unintelligence—is certain to attain tremendous vogue. Anything that demands a moment's thought or a moment's severe attention, anything that is not thoroughly noisy, blatant, cocksure, and self-assertive, is caviare to that man in the street on whom cheap journalism depends, and who, it should be said *en passant*, is often a member of smart society. In the third place, Mr. Kipling had the good, or bad, fortune to come at the very moment when the wave of false Imperialism was cresting most strongly upward, and when even the great organs of opinion, organs which, like *The Times*, subsist entirely on the good or bad passions of the hour, were in sore need of a writer who could express in fairly readable numbers the secret yearnings and sympathies of the baser military and commercial spirit. Mr. Kipling, in a word, although not a poet at all in the true sense of the word, is as near an approach to a poet as can be tolerated by the ephemeral and hasty judgment of the day. His very incapacity of serious thought or deep feeling is in his favour. He represents, with more or less accuracy, what the mob is thinking, and for this very reason he is likely to be forgotten as swiftly and summarily as he has been applauded, nay, to be judged and condemned as mean and insignificant on grounds quite as hasty as those on which he has been hailed as important and high-minded. Savage animalism and ignorant vainglory being in the ascendant, he is hailed at every street-corner and crowned by every newspaper. To-morrow, when the wind changes, and the silly crowd is in another and possibly saner temper, he is certain to fare very differently. The misfortune is that his effusions have no real poetical quality to preserve them when their momentary purpose has been served. Of more than one poet of this generation it has been said that 'he uttered nothing base'. Of Mr. Kipling it may be said, so far at least as his verses are concerned, that he has scarcely on any single occasion uttered anything that does not suggest moral baseness, or hover dangerously near it.

However, that we might not entertain one lingering doubt as to the nature of the spirit which inspires his easy-going Muse, Mr. Kipling himself, with a candour for which we cannot be sufficiently thankful, has recently laid bare, in a prose work, the inmost springs of his inspiration; in other words, he has described to us, with fearless and shameless accuracy, in a record of English boyhood, his ideal of the human character in adolescence. Now, there is nothing which so clearly and absolutely represents the nature of a grown man's intelligence as the manner in which he contemplates, looking backward, the feelings and aspirations of youthful days.

'Heaven lies about us in our infancy,' says the author of the immortal Ode, and heaven is still with us very often as we more closely approach to manhood. In Goethe's reminiscences of his childhood, we discover, faintly developing, all that was wisest and most beautiful in a soul which was distinguished, despite many imperfections, by an inherent love of gentleness and wisdom; the eager intelligence, the vision, the curiosity, are all there, in every thought and act of an extraordinary child. When Dickens, in *David Copperfield*, described under a thin veil of fiction the joys and sorrows of his own boyhood and youth, there welled up out of his great heart a love, a tenderness, a humour which filled the eyes of all humanity with happy tears. When Thackeray touched the same chords, as he did more than once, he was no longer the glorified Jeames of latter-day fiction—he was as kindly, as tender, and as loving as even his great contemporary. Even George Eliot, with imaginative gifts so far inferior, reached the height of her artistic achievement when she went back to the emotions of her early days— when for example, she described the personal relations of Tom and Maggie Tulliver, or when, in the one real poem she ever wrote, she told in sonnet-sequence of the little 'Brother and Sister'. It would be cruel, even brutal, to talk of Mr. Rudyard Kipling in the same breath as fine artists like these; but all writers, great or little, must finally be judged by the same test—that of the truth and beauty, the sanity or the folly, of their representations of our manifold human nature. Mere truth is not sufficient for Art; the truth must be there, but it must be spiritualized and have become beautiful. In *Stalky & Co.* Mr. Kipling obviously aims at verisimilitude; the picture he draws is at any rate repulsive and disgusting enough to be true; yet I trust for England's sake that it is not—that it is, like nearly all his writings with which I am familiar, merely a savage caricature.

Only the spoiled child of an utterly brutalized public could possibly have written *Stalky & Co.* or, having written it, have dared to publish it. These are strong words, but they can be justified. The story ran originally through the pages of a cheap monthly magazine, and contained, I fancy, in its first form, certain passages which the writer himself was compelled in pure shame to suppress. Its purpose, almost openly avowed, is to furnish English readers with an antidote to what Mr. Kipling styles 'Ericism', by which label is meant the kind of 'sentiment' which was once made familiar to schoolboys by Farrar's *Eric, or, Little by Little*; or, to put the matter in other words, the truly ideal schoolboy is not a little sentimentalist, he is simply a little beast. The heroes of this deplorable book are three youths, dwelling in a training school near Westward Ho!; one of them, the Beetle, reads poetry and wears spectacles, the two others, Stalky and M'Turk, are his bosom companions. This trio are leagued together for purposes of offence and defence against their comrades; they join in no honest play or manly sports, they lounge about, they drink, they smoke, they curse and swear, not like boys at all, but like hideous little men. Owing to their determination to obey their own instincts, and their diabolic ingenuity in revenging themselves on any one who meddles with them, they become a terror to the school. It is quietly suggested, however, that the headmaster sympathizes with them, especially in their power to inflict pain wantonly and to bear it stoically, which appears to him the noblest attribute of a human being. It is simply impossible to show by mere quotations the horrible vileness of the book describing the lives of these three small fiends in human likeness; only a perusal of the whole work would convey to the reader its truly repulsive character, and to read the pages through, I fear, would sorely test the stomach of any sensitive reader. The nature of one of the longest and most important episodes may be gathered from the statement that the episode turns on the way in which the three young Hooligans revenge themselves on a number of their schoolmates who have offended them, by means of a dead and putrefying cat. And here is a sample of the dialogue:

[quotes, p. 86, lines 10–30]

Another equally charming episode is the one describing how a certain plebeian called 'Rabbits-Eggs', through the machinations of the trio, wrecked the room of one of the masters, King:

[quotes, p. 58, line 11, to p. 59, line 16]

As I have already said, however, the book cannot be represented by extracts. The vulgarity, the brutality, the savagery, reeks on every page. It may be noted as a minor peculiarity that everything, according to our young Hooligans, is 'beastly', or 'giddy', or 'blooming'; adjectives of this sort cropping up everywhere in their conversation, as in that of the savages of the London slums. And the moral of the book—for, of course, like all such banalities, it professes to have a moral—is that out of materials like these is fashioned the humanity which is to ennoble and preserve our Anglo-Saxon empire! 'India's full of Stalkies,' says the Beetle, 'Cheltenham and Haileybury and Marlborough chaps—that we don't know anything about, and *the surprises will begin when there is really a big row on!*'

Perhaps, after all, I am unjust to Mr. Kipling in forgetting for the moment to credit him with a poet's prophetic vision? For, if *Stalky & Co.* was written before and not after recent political developments, it certainly furnishes a foretaste of what has actually happened! The 'surprises *have* begun', although the 'rows' have not been very 'big' ones, and the souls of Stalky and his companions *have* been looming large in our empire. Studying certain latter-day records, indeed, listening to the voice of the Hooligan in politics, in literature, and journalism, is really very like reading *Stalky & Co.* Some of our battles, even, faithfully reproduce the 'blooming' and 'giddy' orgies of the schoolroom, and in not a few of our public affairs there is a 'stench' like that of 'the dead cat'. Yes, there *must* be Stalkies and M'Turks and Beetles working busily, after all, and representing the new spirit which appears to have begun in the time of Mr. Kipling's boyhood. But whether they really represent the true spirit of our civilization, and make for its salvation, is a question which I will leave my readers to decide.

So much, however, for the voice of the Hooligan, as reverberating in current literature. It is needless to say that it would hardly have been necessary to discuss seriously such literature, if the object was merely to protest on intellectual grounds against its popularity; one might well examine seriously the current contributions to *Answers* and the *Sporting Times*, or hold up to artistic execration the topical songs in a Drury Lane pantomime. But even a straw may indicate the direction in which the wind is blowing, and the vogue of Mr. Kipling, the cheerful acceptance of his banalities by even educated people, is so sure a sign of the times that it deserves and needs a passing consideration. Behind that vogue lies, first and foremost, the influence of the newspaper press, and I cannot do better than quote in this connection some pregnant words contained in a recent work by a writer of undoubted insight, Mr. George Gissing.

'A wise autocrat might well prohibit newspapers altogether, don't you think?' [says one of Mr. Gissing's characters]. 'They have done good, I suppose, but they are just as likely to do harm. When the next great war comes, newspapers will be the chief cause of it. And for mere profit, that's the worst! There are newspaper proprietors in every country who would slaughter half mankind for the pennies of the half who were left, without caring the fraction of a penny whether they had preached war for a truth or a lie.' 'But doesn't a newspaper,' demands another character, 'simply echo the opinions and feelings of the public?' 'I'm afraid,' is the reply, 'it manufactures opinions and stirs up feeling . . . The business of newspapers in general is to give a show of importance to what has no real importance at all, to prevent the world from living quietly, to arouse bitterness, when the natural man would be quite indifferent . . . I suppose I quarrel with them because they have such gigantic power and don't make anything like the best use of it.'

If this statement is accepted as true—and few readers who have studied the recent developments of journalism will be inclined to doubt it—it will be understood at once how the popularity of Mr. Kipling has been accelerated by 'that mighty engine', the newspaper press.

It is no purpose of mine, in the present paper, to touch on political questions, except so far as they illustrate the movements of that back-wave toward barbarism on which, as I have suggested, we are now struggling. I write neither as a Banjo-Imperialist nor as a Little Eng-lander, but simply as a citizen of a great nation, who loves his country, and would gladly see it honoured and respected wherever the English tongue is spoken. It will scarcely be denied, indeed it is frankly ad-mitted by all parties, that the Hooligan spirit of patriotism, the fierce and quasi-savage militant spirit as expressed in many London news-papers and in such literature as the writings of Mr. Kipling, has measurably lowered the affection and respect once felt for us among European nations. Nor will any honest thinker combat the assertion that we have exhibited lately, in our dealings with other nationalities, a greed of gain, a vainglory, a cruelty, and a boastful indifference to the rights of others, of which in days when the old philanthropic spirit was abroad we should simply have been incapable. But it is not here, in the region of politics and militarism, that I wish to linger. My chief object in writing this paper has been to express my sorrow that Hooliganism, not satisfied with invading our newspapers, should already threaten to corrupt the pure springs of our literature. These noisy strains and coarse importations from the music-hall should not be heard where the fountains of intellectual light and beauty once played, where Chaucer and Shakespeare once drank inspiration, and where Wordsworth, Hood, and Shelley found messages for the yearning hearts of men. Anywhere but there; anywhere but in the speech of those who loved and blessed their fellows. And let it be remembered that those fountains are not yet dry. Poets and dreamers are living yet, to resent the pollution. Only a little while ago the one living novelist who inherits the great human tradition tore out his very heart, figuratively speaking, in revolt against the spirit of savagery and cruelty which is abroad; though, when Thomas Hardy wrote *Jude the Obscure*, touching therein the very quick of divine pity, only a coarse laugh from the professional critics greeted his protest. Elsewhere, too, there are voices, not to be silenced by the clamour of the crowd; as near as our own shores, where Herbert Spencer is still dwelling, as far away as South Africa, where Olive Schreiner has sought and found human love in the dominion of dreams; and there are others, shrinking away in shame from the brazen idols of the mart, and praying that this great empire may yet be warned and saved. To one and all of these has been brought home the lesson—'Woe to you when the world speaks well of you!'—and they have elected to let the world speak ill of them, rather than bow down in homage to its calves of gold. For to speak the truth as we see it, to confront the evil and folly of the hour, is as dangerous today as when Socrates drank his hemlock-cup.

I have left myself no space, I find, to draw a final contrast between the coarse and soulless patriotism of the hour and that nobler Imperialism in which all true Englishmen, to whatever political camp they may belong for the time being, must still believe. In the federation of Great Britain and her colonies, and in the slow and sure spread of what is best and purest in our civilization, there was indeed hope and inspiration for our race, and a message of freedom for all the world. But true Imperialism has nothing in common with the mere lust of conquest, with the vulgar idea of mere expansion, or with the increase of the spirit of mercenary militarism; its object is to diffuse light, not to darken the sunshine; to feed the toiling millions, not to immolate them; to free man, not to enslave him; to consecrate, and not to desecrate, the great temple of humanity. Some of its ways, like the ways of nature herself, must inevitably be destructive; the weaker and baser races must sooner or later dissolve away; but the process of dissolution should be made as gentle and merciful as possible, not savage, pitiless, and cruel. True Imperialism should be strong, but the strength should be that of justice, of wisdom, of brotherly love and sympathy; for the power which is bred of a mere multitude equipped with the engines of slaughter will in the long run avail nothing against the eternal law which determines that the righteous only shall inherit the earth. We are a people still, though we seem for the time being to be forgetting the conditions on which we received our charter, and deep in the heart of England survives the sentiment of a world-wide nationality, as expressed in the passionate lines of a modern poet:

> Hands across the Sea!
> Feet on British ground!
> The Motherhood means Brotherhood the whole world round!
> From the parent root,
> Sap, and stem, and fruit
> Grow the same, or soil or name—
> Hands across the Sea!

There sounds the true Imperial feeling, which will survive, I think, long after the repulsive school of patriotism which I have called (for want of a better name) the Hooligan school, is silent and forgotten. Let me at least hope that it may be so—that Englishmen, after their present wild orgy of militant savagery, may become clothed and in their right minds. There is time to pause yet, although they are already paying the penalty, in blood, in tears, in shame. Let them take warning by the fate of France, let them try to remember the old sanctions and the old enthusiasms; for, if they continue to forget them, they are in danger of being swept back into the vortex of barbarism altogether.

34. Sir Walter Besant: 'Is it the Voice of the Hooligan?'

1900

Signed article from the *Contemporary Review*, Vol. LXXVII, pp. 27–39 (January, 1900). The first ten paragraphs are omitted, being taken up with general principles of criticism and literary good manners.

Sir Walter Besant (1836–1901) was a well-known and successful novelist, and the founder of The Society of Authors. Kipling owed much to Besant, both for the encouragement given him during a dark period in India by reading his *All in a Garden Fair* (1883), and for much kindly advice when they met in London at the end of 1889. (See *Something of Myself*, pp. 65–6 and 83–4.)

If a poet or a novelist is not necessarily a critic—is presumably less likely to possess the critical faculty than if he were not a poet—it behoves him to examine himself very carefully before he ventures to pose as the watch-dog of literature, lest he betray his incompetence by barking, and rending the friends, instead of the enemies, of the literary craft.

Mr. Robert Buchanan has thought fit to attack Mr. Rudyard Kipling after the ancient manner. I do not suppose that what he has written will cost the younger poet a single friend; nor do I suppose that anything I may say on the other side will advance his reputation. Nor, again, do I pretend, myself, to be a watch-dog of literature; nor do I profess to be endowed with the critical faculty. But I think that it may be useful to set forth briefly some of the reasons why one among the many millions of Kipling's readers finds him worthy of the deepest admiration, and, in so doing, to express the views and the judgments of a vast following which may not be critical, yet does not with one consent give its admiration and affection except for good and sufficient reasons.

Except in one point, that of the actual situation, I am not concerned to answer Mr. Buchanan. He has his views and has stated them. Very well, I have mine, and I propose to state them. They are exactly opposite to those of Mr. Buchanan. Why that should be the case is a question which needs no answer in this place.

As regards the situation, then. I read with wondering eyes that this generation has drifted away from the humanitarian teaching which forty years ago, or thereabouts 'opened up to men the prospect of a new heaven and a new earth'. Drifted away? Is the writer serious? Is he blind to the present? Why, if there is any characteristic note of the times at all, it is the new and practical application of that very humanitarian teaching of the past. This teaching has sunk deep into the national heart; it is producing fruits unlooked for, beyond all expectation. The exercise of practical charity by personal service which is remarkable everywhere is the natural result of that teaching and the proof that it has gone home. In all directions is visible the working of the most real philanthropic endeavour that the world has ever seen— the nearest approach to practical Christianity that has appeared, I believe, since the foundation of the Christian religion. What else is the meaning of free schools, free libraries, factory Acts, continuation schools, polytechnics? What else is the meaning of the settlements in which scholars and refined women give their whole strength with all their thoughts and all their soul to the help of the people round them? What else is the meaning of Toynbee Hall, of Mansfield Hall, of Browning Hall, or of Oxford House? What else is the meaning of the quickened life in the parishes with the flocking companies of those who work for nothing but the love of humanity? What else is meant by the long list of associations for the benefit and help, in every degree, of those who can be helped? Is it possible to live in such a time as this and to be so utterly out of touch with all that is attempted, as to speak of a 'drifting away' from the old humanitarian teaching? This said, I leave Mr. Buchanan, and proceed to consider those qualities which the world recognizes in Rudyard Kipling, assuming that, as an average man, my own recognitions are those of what we call the world.

The first essential in fiction is reality. The story must be real; the figures must be real; the dialogue must be real; the action must spring naturally from the situation. Affectations; straining after phrase; a style that suggests labour and repeated correction—these things destroy the interest: the story must be told with directness; it must be told with force; it must be told because the storyteller has to tell it—is constrained to tell it. We want to be carried out of our own environment; we are ready to surrender ourselves willingly to the magnetic force of the storyteller; if he has no magnetic power, we turn away; if he has, we allow him to play upon us as he pleases; we are like one who is mesmerized and does what he is told to do—he really feels the emotions that the storyteller puts into his mind; he laughs when his master bids him laugh; he cries when he is told to cry.

These conditions are all found in Kipling's work, and in full measure, without any reservations. He has this magnetic force; he compels us to listen; he tells his story with directness, force, and simplicity. So real is the story, with such an air of reality does he present it, that we see it as we see the moving pictures which the new photography throws upon the canvas.

It is in writing as in drawing. One man produces his effects with many strokes and careful elaboration; another produces the same effect with a single bold stroke or with the least possible curve or deflection of a line. The effect is produced in Kipling's work by the one bold stroke; without apparent effort the right word presents itself; the right phrase, which others seek, and seek in vain, without apparent hesitation takes its place; it belongs to the story.

He also believes his own story; that faith is necessary if he would make his hearers believe it. And because he believes it he is enabled to tell it simply and directly, without seeking to add the artificial stimulus of a laboured style.

These reasons for the popularity of a writer are elementary. Yet they have, in this case, to be set forth, as the best answer to any assailant. Another reason, not so obvious to the ordinary reader, is his enthusiasm for humanity. Probably Kipling never gave it, consciously, so fine a name—is ignorant, perhaps, that this attribute can be found in his work. Yet the thing is there. Always, in every character, he presents a man, not an actor—a man with the passions, emotions, weaknesses, and instincts of humanity. It is perhaps one of the Soldiers Three, or it is the Man who went into the mountains because he would be a King; or the man who sat in the lonely lighthouse till he saw streaks; always the real man whom the reader sees beneath the uniform and behind the drink and the blackguardism. It is the humanity in the writer which makes his voice tremulous at times with unspoken pity and silent sympathy; it is the tremor of his voice which touches the heart of his audience. And it is this power of touching the heart which causes men and women of all classes and of every rank to respond with a greater love for the writer than for any other writer living among us at the present moment.

Mr. Henry James, who is certainly a critic as well as a novelist, has called attention to Kipling's power of attracting all classes. It surprises him that, 'being so much the sort of figure that the hardened critic likes to meet, he should also be the sort of figure that inspires the multitude with confidence; for a complicated air is, in general, the last thing that does this'. Exactly; but it is the special note of genius that it should present men and women who are real to all who read, and so real that they come with a simple 'air' to the simple and un-cultivated mind and with a 'complicated air' to the scholar. It is not the complicated air that the multitude ask or comprehend. For them it is the simple lay, the plain song. To those who, like Mr. Henry James, are practised observers and students, who can read between the lines, the air is as complicated as any study of human nature by Browning or by Meredith.

Going on with his analysis, Mr. Henry James admirably illustrates the different effects produced on different minds by the case of Mul-vaney, the great Mulvaney. He says, speaking for the multitude, that the figure of Mulvaney is 'a piece of portraiture of the largest, vividest kind, growing and growing on the painter's hands without ever outgrowing them'. And, speaking for himself and those like unto himself, he says: 'Hasn't he the tongue of a hoarse siren, and hasn't he also mysteries and infinities almost Carlylese?' Not for the multitude; for them he is only 'a six-foot saturated Irish private'; but so clearly drawn, so strongly drawn, that not the most simple can fail to under-stand him after their own fashion.

Another reason why we who are not critics—the many millions—delight in Kipling is that he gives us short stories. Not that we demand, as has been asserted, everything to be in paragraphs and scraps—that is quite an unfair interpretation of the demand for short stories—it is that the short story affords endless opportunities of touching life—I again quote Henry James—'in a thousand different places, taking it up in innumerable pieces, each a specimen and an illustration'. In the long story we are occupied with one place, one sequence of events, one set of characters; perhaps we read for the sequence of events, perhaps for the study of the character. Within the space occupied by the long story Kipling's volume of short stories gives us twenty situations, twenty scenes, twenty groups, and twenty sets of characters. Mr. James's critical remarks, from which I quote, are written for the volume called *Mine Own People*, which contains, among other things, the stories called respectively 'At the End of the Passage', 'The Incarnation of Krishna Mulvaney', 'The Courting of Dinah Shadd', and 'The Man who Was'. Every one of these stories—characters, situation, and all—is burned into the memory as deeply as if it had been worked up to occupy a volume all to itself. And we would rather have the short story than a long one from our storyteller, because he gives us picture after picture, play after play, dozens of pictures and of plays, in the time generally occupied by one.

But the man who would become a teller of short stories must have a wealth of material which few have the opportunities of collecting. Kipling has had these opportunities; he knows the world—especially the Anglo-Saxon world—the world of our empire and the world of the American republic. He is one of those thrice blessed who have not only received the gifts of observations and of sympathy—the gift of storytelling with the dramatic instinct and the power of selection and grouping—but he has obtained the gift of opportunity; he has lived in lands where there are still adventures and the adventurous, where there are still tribes who love fighting and tribes who murder the Englishman, where there are still unknown mysteries of hills and forests; he has found mines of material diverse and new and marvellous, and he has worked these mines as they have never been worked before. Henry James has instanced the figure of Mulvaney as one of the most remarkable in Kipling's gallery of portraits. We may, perhaps, take the Soldiers Three as illustrating the 'humanity' of which we have spoken. He has the coarsest and the roughest materials to deal with—three private soldiers of the lower type, which is common enough in our army—and in every other army. The men are foul-mouthed and drunken and tricky. All this must be faced and set forth with no shrinking or false colouring. This has been done, and yet, such is the force of reality in fiction, the result is that we see the real men behind their vices, and that we understand Tommy Atkins as we never understood him before. Had the drawing and the colouring been conventional, there would have been found some, no doubt, to call attention to the artistic treatment of the soldier and the finish and polish of his language and his views. They are, however, not in the least conventional, and for the multitude they are real living men, as living as themselves.

I believe that I am not alone in giving the highest praise—at least for 'grip'—to the story of 'The Man who would be King'. While that story was told, there was not heard in the whole of the vast audience a sound, a whisper, a breath. In dead silence it was received; in dead silence it concluded—in dead silence save for the sigh which spoke of a tension almost too great to be borne. Perhaps that sigh might be taken for applause. Perhaps the storyteller himself took it for applause.

Another point. Kipling presents himself with no apologies, no conventional humility, but with a splendid audacity—a confidence in himself and his own powers which in itself commands admiration; he has the gallant bearing of a soldier, he laughs, knowing that we shall respond; he plunges into his story, knowing that we shall listen; he lets us understand that he has come to conquer the world, and that he means to conquer it. The most finished actor could not impose his part upon the theatre more successfully than Kipling imposes his real nature upon his readers.

These are some of the reasons why we—the many millions—follow after Kipling and listen when he speaks. Some there are who think differently; they have not been carried away; for most of us the reasons above indicated seem sufficient to account for the phenomenal admiration which is also almost universal. To the critic—Henry James's 'hardened critic'—we may leave the analysis of methods and style and art.

I have spoken of Kipling's audience. But what an audience it is! The people sit in a theatre of which the front seats are at the storyteller's feet and the farthest tiers are twelve thousand miles away. Never, in the history of literature, has storyteller, in his own lifetime, faced such an audience. Scott and Dickens enjoy, if they can still look on, the posthumous happiness of this unnumbered audience; in their lifetime the theatre was smaller; the people which even then seemed so great a crowd were much less in number than those who come to hear their successor. Other writers speak today to crowded houses, but none to such a house as assembles when Kipling speaks. Saul has followers by the thousand; David, by the hundred thousand: Rudyard Kipling is the first of storytellers to whom it has been granted to speak, while he still lives, to the hundred millions of those who read the Anglo-Saxon tongue. From east and west and north and south, wherever the Union Jack or the Stars and Stripes may float, they flock into the vast theatre to listen spellbound to a single voice, which reaches clear and distinct to the most distant tier where the white faces look up and listen while the story is told.

Let us consider him next as the poet, and especially as the poet of the empire. He is emphatically not a Londoner; he does not seek inspiration in the smoking-room of a West End club: he does not observe in Piccadilly: he does not evolve humanity out of an easy chair with the aid of a cigarette. He is a son of the empire; he has brought home to the understanding of the most parochial of Little Englanders the sense and knowledge of what the British empire means. What Seeley taught scholars, Kipling has taught the multitude. He is the poet of the empire. Not the Jingo rhymer; the poet with the deepest reverence for those who have built up the Empire, the deepest respect for the Empire, the most profound sense of responsibility.

> Fair is our lot. Oh! goodly is our heritage!
> (Humble ye, my people, and be fearful in your mirth!)
>> For the Lord our God most High,
>> He hath made the deep as dry,
> He hath smote for us a pathway to the ends of all the earth!
> Yea, though we sinned—and our rulers went from righteousness—
> Deep in all dishonour though we stained our garments' hem.
>> Oh! be ye not dismayed,
>> Though we stumbled and we strayed,
> We were led by evil counsellors—the Lord shall deal with them!

That is, I suppose, the 'Voice of the Hooligan'. Again, is it the Hooligan who sings of the Last Chantey to the text 'And there was no more sea'?

[quotes stanzas 1, 8 and 13, DV. pp. 160–2]

Again, what kind of poet—'not a poet at all', says his latest critic—is he who could write the following?

> Take up the White Man's Burden—
>> Send forth the best ye breed—
> Go, bind your sons to exile
>> To serve your captives' need:
> To wait in heavy harness,
>> On fluttered folk and wild—
> Your new-caught sullen peoples,
>> Half devil and half child.
>
> Take up the White Man's Burden—
>> No iron rule of kings,
> But toil of serf and sweeper—
>> The tale of common things.

> The ports ye shall not enter,
> The roads ye shall not tread;
> Go, make them with your living,
> And mark them with your dead!

It is unnecessary to quote the Recessional Hymn save to remind ourselves of how this poet, alone of poets or preachers, saw, as in a vision of inspiration, the one thing that needed to be said: We were drunk with the pageant of power and of glory. The empire and all it meant was represented in that long procession of 1897. The people, bewildered with pride, were ready to shout they knew not what—to go they knew not whither. And then the poet spoke, and his words rang true. I know of no poem in history so opportune, that so went home to all our hearts—that did its work and delivered its message with so much force.

[quotes stanzas 1, 3 and 4 of 'Recessional', DV. pp. 328–9]

One more note, and I have done. Kipling, in verse and in prose, is one to whom war is an ever-present possibility and an ever-present certainty. There is a time to speak of war and a time to speak of peace. At this moment it is well that some one who has a voice should speak of war. It seems that in the present stage of civilization, just as in the past, there falls upon the nations, from time to time, the restlessness which can only be pacified by war. The French nation, at this moment, seem to be restless to the highest degree under this obsession. We ourselves are in the throes of the biggest war since the Indian Mutiny. Two years ago, the most pacific country in the world, the great republic of North America, was seized with this restlessness, which it is still working off. A time may come when war will not be a necessity —but that time is not yet. For my own part, I entirely agree with Archbishop Alexander in the words quoted by Mr. Buchanan:

> And as I note how nobly natures form
> Under the war's red rain, I deem it true
> That He who made the earthquake and the storm
> Perchance made battles too.

There are worse evils than war. There are

> —the lust of Gold
> And love of a Peace that is full of wrongs and shames.

It is a threadbare commonplace to write that there are worse evils than war, but it must be said over and over again, especially when the horrors of war are upon us. The poisonous weeds that grow rank in times of peace corrupt the national blood; they deaden the sense of honour; they encourage the ruthless company promoter who trades upon the ignorance of the helpless; they lower the standards of honour; they enlarge the slough of indulgence and the unclean life. War does not kill these things, but it may restore the sense of duty, sacrifice, patriotism; it may bring back the nobler ideals; it may teach the world that there are better gods than the idols they have fashioned with their own hands; it may seize on the hearts of the young and preserve their instincts of generosity.

> Though many a light shall darken and many shall weep
> For those that are crushed in the clash of jarring claims . . .
> . . . And many a darkness into light shall leap,
> And shine in the sudden making of splendid names,
> And noble thought be freer under the sun,
> And the heart of the people beat with one desire.

This potency of war, these possibilities, this necessity of war when the cause is just, this ennobling of a people by war, are present in the mind of Kipling as much as in the mind of Tennyson. The time, indeed, has come again when we are called

> To wake to the higher aims
> Of a land that has lost for a little the lust of gold.

It is not on the side of those who are ruled and led by this lust that Kipling stands; nor is it for barbaric conquest and the subjugation of free peoples that he sings.

I have endeavoured to explain and to justify, to a certain extent, the extraordinary affection with which this writer is regarded by millions unnumbered among our own people and our own kin. As was confessed at the outset, nothing that I can say can increase that affection. I leave criticism to those who, being at least scholars, have the right to take upon themselves the work of criticism; it is for them to discuss methods and style. It is enough for me and for those unnumbered millions to know that here is one who has a message to deliver which concerns us all; that he has people to present to us among whom we walk daily, yet have remained hitherto in ignorance of their ways and thoughts and speech; that he has taught the people of the empire what the empire means; that he has shown us below their rough and coarse exterior the manhood of soldier and sailor, of engine-man and lighthouse-man and fisher-man. It is enough for us that he speaks as no other in his generation—these be reasons enough and to spare why he is loved by old and young in every class and in every country where his language is the language of the folk.

35. Edward Dowden on 'The Poetry of Mr. Kipling'

1901

Signed article from the *New Liberal Review*, Vol. xxxviii, pp. 53–61 (February 1901).

Edward Dowden (1843–1913), scholar and critic, Professor of English at Trinity College, Dublin 1867–1913, is best known for his works on Shakespeare. But he also wrote studies of Southey, Shelley, Browning and Montaigne.

Mr. Kipling ought to be pleased with the acoustic properties of our globe; his voice fills the building. To have something to say, no doubt, helps a voice to carry far; people cease from chatter and look up; and Mr. Kipling, especially perhaps in his verse, has things to say; he says them in no halting or hesitating manner, but 'after the use of the English', as he has himself described that use, 'in straight-flung words and few'.

It was long since a morsel of verse constituted an historical event of importance for two hemispheres; but this, without exaggeration, is what certain short poems of Mr. Kipling have been. They have served to evoke or guide the feelings of nations, and to determine action in great affairs. However we may explain it, such is the fact. And of all explanations the least tenable is that which represents Mr. Kipling as a music-hall singer, addressing a vulgar crowd in the vulgar tones which they expect for the coin they pay. La Bruyère has said some-where that the favour of a prince is no evidence of merit, but that also it indicates no deficiency of merit; the statement holds good of the favour of Prince Demos. It is true that Mr. Kipling sometimes twangs the banjo; and with its *tinka-tinka-tinka-tinka-tink* he has not done ignobly; as a satirist he has with it 'jeered the fatted soul of things'; he has with it gallantly mocked defeat, and sung the song of lost endeavour. But he has also touched the solemn organ-stops, and it is precisely to such a poem as 'Recessional', with its old prophetic strain, its warning against vain idols, and folly, and carnal pride, that the deepest response of our race is made.

Mr. Kipling's swift conquest of the people indicates of course that his inspiration is not private and solitary; it means also that he is not the poet of a coterie or *cénacle*. The poet of solitary inspiration may belong to all the world; striking deep into his own heart, he arrives at the common heart of humanity; but it often takes tedious years to bring the world over to his side. His desire is to reach many minds, and, supported by 'faith in the whispers of the lonely muse', after patient waiting he attains his desire. The poet of a coterie is commonly forced to convert his incapacity to move the public into a proof of superiority. Having really nothing to say, he conceals his emptiness by a legerde-main of caprices, a new doctrine in art, a vaporous obscurity, or a clumsy subtlety, which may induce the coterie to wonder with a foolish face of praise. He declares oracularly: 'If you do not understand me, so much the worse for *you*.' Mr. Kipling says: 'If you do not under-stand me, so much the worse for *me*.' For he is a maker of tribal lays, and if they do not speak for and to the tribe the lays fall dumb. The great good fortune of a maker of tribal lays comes when he divines the moment at which some public sentiment of Imperial power is about to announce or disclose itself and when by one hour he anticipates that moment in his song. Or should we not rather say that the gather-ing emotion finds in the poet the most sensitive nerve of the body politic, and through that nerve first thrills and finds expression? The singer then not only anticipates, but assists in the general outbreak; he moulds passions, and creates new combinations of feeling. He is the earliest ray of the rising sun, which falls upon the petals of a bud that is eager to be a blossom.

Such has been the good fortune of Mr. Kipling, and he has put his opportunity to wise uses. The sense of the brotherhood of the blood was stirring in many English hearts before he wrote, but it was one of the native-born who gave it a resonant utterance. His feeling for Empire is characterised by two chief features: first, it is based securely upon concrete fact; and, secondly, it rises at the summit to a solemn and even a religious sense of duty. The strength and volume of Edmund Burke's political passions came in great part from the circumstance that, through virtue of his all-absorbing, all-retaining intellect, and his imaginative grasp, they were fed by a multitude of vivid details. His eloquence, therefore, did not deal in vacuous abstractions, but resumed, under great principles, a mass of real and various things. It is so also with Mr. Kipling's Imperialism. This is not a flourish of rhetoric, nor intoxication with a doctrinaire theory, but is rather a gathering up of his myriad observations into an ideal unity. It has its origin in 'the little things a fellow cares about'; it clings much to kinship and to comradeship; it rises to civic loyalty and pride:

> Surely in toil or fray
> Under an alien sky,
> Comfort it is to say:
> 'Of no mean city am I.'

It passes from the city to the birth-land, knit by closest ties of sonship to the mother-country; it includes the shepherd on his hill, the ploughman drawing his furrow, the miner delving the ore, the white sails and long smoke trails on all the seas, where the swift shuttles of the great loom ply backward and forward; it embraces finally the whole congeries of thought, and dream, and deed which, below the North Star, the Southern Cross, make up the majestic unity of Empire, of which unity the flag serves as emblem; and at every stage of development the emotions are fed by sights, by sounds, by the very scents of East and West, of land-breeze and sea-breeze, by all brave memories and all tender associations.

But Mr. Kipling's feeling of Empire is solemnised by the weight of real things and by a knowledge of the cost of Empire. The 'Song of the English' includes, as part of the cantata, the 'Song of the Dead'. The sea-wife by the Northern Gate, who breeds her roving sons and sends them over sea, is in no mood of shallow exultation; only in the depth of her old heart she is proud that her sons have indeed been men. There is a wail in Tommy's chorus as he tumbles aboard the transport and sees in imagination the large birds of prey on the far horizon, keen-scented and expectant; but none the less Tommy falls in upon the troop-deck. The Widow of Windsor's party is not all cakes and jam, but you can't refuse the card when the Widow gives the party, and the end of the show is satisfactory to the Colonel:

> We broke a King and we built a road—
> A court-house stands where the reg'ment goed,
> And the river's clean where the raw blood flowed
> When the Widow give the party.

The price of admiralty is blood, and 'Lord God, we ha' paid in full'. But the whisper, and the vision that called the dreamers, whose dreams were prophecy, to go forth and leave their bones on the sand-drift, on the veldt-side, in the fern-scrub, still summon our gentleman adventurers, and the dead cry to us:

> Follow after, follow after! We have watered the root,
> And the bud has come to blossom that ripens for fruit.

It is no lust of territory or empty pride of power that can help us to sustain the white man's burden; we bear it because this also is in the day's work appointed for us by the Master of all good workmen:

> Keep ye the Law—be swift in all obedience—
> Clear the land of evil, drive the road and bridge the ford.
> Make ye sure to each his own
> That he reap where he hath sown;
> By the peace among Our peoples let men know we serve the Lord!

Such is the religious feeling for Empire. If the banjo is strummed, it seems as if a Puritan of the old Ironside breed were the minstrel. Cromwell, after the victory of Dunbar, addressed the Speaker in words which go to the same manly tune.

Even in *Departmental Ditties* which may have been a fillip of fun for jaded Anglo-Indians, though now they seem too precociously clever and not agreeably bitter-sweet, the solemn note was struck at least once, in the finest poem of the collection—'The Galley Slave'. The German has not perhaps yet written a treatise on the *Kiplingsche Weltanschauung*, and it may be worth while to show briefly how it is constituted, and how it is essentially a religious conception of things. Mr. Kipling, with his keen and wide perceptions, sees a world that is 'wondrous large', one that holds 'a vast of various kinds of men'; he is not fastidious— sinners male and female, the coward, the bully, the cheat, the brave, the strong, the weak, the cad, the gentleman, the vain pretender, the simple hero—all seem to have a place in this large world, where passion clashes with passion and deed wrestles with deed. Possessing an un-

wearied curiosity, he views this changeful spectacle, infinitely pleased
to observe 'the different ways that different things are done', of which
things, indeed, some are odd—'most awful odd'—yet, upon the whole,
this world is a highly interesting world to the intelligent spectator:

> Gawd bless this world! Whatever she 'ath done—
> Excep' when awful long—I've found it good
> So write before I die, 'E liked it all!

Mr. Kipling is not fastidious, but he does not sophisticate with good
and evil. In a certain transcendental sense he may tell us that 'sin is
vain', and may indulge a little in the amusements of those gallant
gentlemen of the halls of heaven, who, knowing the vanity of sin, can
fearlessly whistle the devil to make them sport. In general his feeling
is the devout one that it is his task to 'draw the Thing as he sees It for
the God of Things as They Are', or as he says with great dignity in
presenting to the Master a completed volume of his tales:

> One stone the more swings to her place
> In that dread Temple of Thy worth—
> It is enough that through Thy grace
> I saw nought common on Thy earth.

Nought common, however much that is unclean.

But above this turmoil of passions, above this scene of shames and
heroisms, of evil doing, weak doing, mean doing, brave doing, rises
the immutable Law; and that is best in life whether it be toil, or suffering, or sorrow, which brings men into obedience to this law, or
rather into active co-operation with it. Even the goose-step is a stage
in the evolution of order, for the young recruit is silly, keeping himself 'awful', much as he does his side-arms; and it is well for him that
he should be hammered: it is well that he should be put in the way of

> Gettin' clear o'dirtiness, gettin' done with mess,
> Gettin' shut o'doin' things rather-more-or-less.

Not Carlyle himself could more sternly condemn the folly of doing
things 'rather-more-or-less' than does Mr. Kipling; and, in the building
of a man, he especially honours *pukka* workmanship. On that awful
day when Tommy ran, squealing for quarter, and the major cursed his
Maker, and the colonel broke his sword, the root of evil lay in the fact
that 'we was never disci*plined*'; if an order was obeyed it was considered
a favour; every little drummer had his rights and wrongs. And in the
true beat and full power of his engine, with faithfulness in every crank

and rod, M'Andrew reads its lesson and his own: 'Law, Orderr, Duty an' Restraint, Obedience, Discipline!'

The law and order of the world, again, is presided over by the Lawgiver, the Maker of men, who is a somewhat Hebraic or Puritanical deity. Not that, at least in a genial fantasy, He may not appear as a good-humoured, and even as an amused Lord God. It is He who, at the tuneful petition of the souls of the jolly, jolly mariners, supported by the afflicted Judas and the stout apostle Paul, gives back their sea to the silly sailor folk, and permits them to hand in, with tarry fingers, the golden fiddles they had somewhat clumsily handled. Jehovah is not always so good-humoured; but He knows how to value an honest workman, and to a strong man whom death has purged of pride—for pride is the special danger of the strong—who has ever walked 'in simpleness and gentleness and honour and clean mirth', He will tell tales of His daily toil and of the new-made Edens. For us, labourers on His earth, He is the great Overseer, who insists on faithful work, giving at the same time strength to the workman, which shall enable him, even amid hunger and drought and hardship, to accomplish the task assigned:

> If there be good in what I wrought
> Thy hand compelled it, Master, Thine;
> Where I have failed to meet Thy thought,
> I know, through Thee, the blame is mine.

All things—even the fall of a rose upon the garden-path—were determined by His will before the worlds came into existence. Such is the lesson of Mr. Kipling's piece of Oriental Calvinism, 'The Answer'; and the battered rose is consoled by the thought that its ruin has been for ever involved in the divine law governing the entire cosmos.

Faust in his study, pondering the words of Scripture, could not accept the sentence, 'In the beginning was the Word,' and he finally emended the text to 'In the beginning was the Act'. Mr. Kipling's emendation would most probably be, 'In the beginning was the Dream,' but with him the dream is essentially a prophecy of the act, or of some word which is itself of the nature of an act. He is a poet not of contemplation but of action, of the emotions arising from, and also held in check by, action, and of the dreams which result in a deed. In *Werther* and in all creations of the Werther school we have studies of emotions sapping in upon the active powers of the soul. The 'reigning personage', to borrow Taine's happy expression, of Mr. Kipling's creations, is the man who has done something, of his own initiative (or of God's), if he be a man of genius; and if not a man of genius, then something which he finds, like the brave M'Andrew—and he is almost a man of genius—allotted or assigned to him as duty. Tomlinson, of Berkeley Square, is spurned by Peter from Heaven's Gate because he can only give a shuffling answer to one straight question:

'Ye have read, ye have heard, ye have thought,' he said, 'and the tale is
yet to run:
By the worth of the body that once ye had, give answer—what ha' ye
done?'

The devil in hell knows too accurately the price of good pitcoal to waste it on such a whimpering spirit that had not virtue enough to possess one genuine native vice; off with him, therefore, once more to Berkeley Square! And, in truth, compared with Tomlinson, one of the legion of the lost, a gentleman ranker damned from here to eternity, who has gone the pace and gone it blind, is in an enviable position; his lot is piteous but not contemptible.

There are many emotions, such as those arising from the contemplation of beauty, which do not tend to action; though indirectly, in helping to form character, they may influence our deeds. These, speaking generally, do not enter into Mr. Kipling's poetry. Once or twice his man of action is in the contemplative mood; he leans over the ship-side and looks across the sea, remembering all the past, or sits in clink without his boots, and under either set of conditions, neutral or unhappy, can fall to 'admirin' 'ow the world was made':

For to admire an' for to see,
For to be'old this world so wide—
It never done no good to me,
But I can't drop it if I tried.

Far more often what Mr. Kipling portrays—and portrays with power—are those hasty escapes of emotion which action cannot wholly suppress; the swift hiss of steam in its jet from the safety-valve indicates better than any rhetoric the pressure within. Such a tune goes manly. Danny must hang, for is he not the disgrace of nine hundred of his country? and yet Files-on-Parade cannot forget that he drank Danny Deever's beer a score of times. It is a tenderly passionate reminiscence. Three rounds blank are all the honours that remain for the dead comrade, and before starting it is as well to finish off the swipes, but—bitter memory!—it was only last week the comrades fought about a dog—

> An' I strook 'im cruel 'ard, an' I wish I 'adn't now,
> Which is just what a man can't do.

Perhaps there is as much pathos in this as in any eloquent 'He who hath bent him o'er the dead'. The driver as he whips the limber across a wounded brother's body to put him out of pain does not wail or beat the breast; he gives a little coughing grunt and swings his horses handsome when the command 'Forward' is given, knowing that if you want to win your battles you must work your guns. But the driver's grunt holds within it all Malcolm's heartening words: 'Dispute it like a man,' and all Macduff's apology: 'I shall do so; but I must also feel it as a man.'

Through reality Mr. Kipling reaches after romance. It may be asserted in a general way that there are two kinds of romance, which, with no touch of disrespect for either, may be distinguished as its masculine and feminine forms. The one flies from all things gross and common; it chooses to gaze at what may be beheld from some magic casement

> opening on the foam
> Of perilous seas, in faery lands forlorn.

Or it finds its natural haunt and home where the elf-girls flood with wings

> Valleys full of plaintive air;
> There breathe perfumes; there in rings
> Whirl the foam-bewildered springs;
> Siren there
> Winds her dizzy hair and sings.

Of course, it may be alleged that the great and abiding realities of the soul are best discovered by a retreat from that part of life which contains much that is drossy and much that is transitory and accidental. In the palace of Art there are many mansions, and romance feminine has a chamber, enriched like Christabel's with fair things 'for a lady's chamber meet', things that are all made out of the carver's brain. The artist, as Mr. Kipling conceives him, is an artist because he sees the fact and the whole fact more exactly than the rest of the tribe; and, seeing exactly, he can scratch on bone his picture of the aurochs or the mammoth which astonishes his fellow-tribesmen, and brings them a joy that must relieve itself by gifts. The primitive tribesman, Ung, is not yet a romanticist; but he is the forefather of the masters of romance masculine, and precisely because he sees things as they are. The French painter, Millet, was in truth one of Ung's children, and in the figure of his 'Sower' he has left an example of art nobly romantic because it is profoundly real. Mr. Kipling cannot often rival the achievement of Millet; too often he relies on a superficial realism, at times heaping on local colour to excess, abusing his mastery of technical terms (which yet affect our ignorance with a mysterious power like that of the blessed word 'Mesopotamia') and using the cheap realism of Tommy's dialect to verify the strangeness of Tommy's romance. A day may come when the bloom of 'bloomin'' will have departed, and though his dialect helps Mr. Kipling, not illegitimately, to certain comic and pathetic effects, a noble romantic poem in standard English, such as 'The Derelict', may better stand the wear and tear of time.

Mr. Kipling's masculine romance does not require any aid from our charming Irish acquaintances, the people of the faery hills. He does not think that romance died with the cave-men or the lake-folk; it is Romance which brings up the nine-fifteen train:

> His hand was on the lever laid,
> His oil-can soothed the worrying cranks,
> His whistle waked the snowbound grade,
> His fog-horn cut the reeking banks;
> By dock and deep and mine and mill
> The Boy-god reckless laboured still.

The Viscount loon who questioned M'Andrew as to whether steam did not spoil romance at sea is very summarily dismissed; it is feebleness of imagination which has no sense of the world-lifting joy that still comes to cheer man the artifex, and a dream, not of the past, not of hide-bound coracle or beaked trireme, but of the Perfect Ship still lures him on. Our miracles are those which subdue the waves, and fill with messages of fate the deep-sea levels, and read the storms before they thunder on our coast, and toss the miles aside with crank-throw and tail-rod. 'Gross modern materialism!' sighs the votary of romance feminine; and such it may be for him, but such it is not for those who with masculine imagination and passion can perceive that it is the dream of the artifex which subdues and organises and animates the iron and the steel. We may sell a creel of turf in a sordid and grasping spirit, and we may design a steam-ship with something like the enthusiasm of a poet.

And as with man's instruments and man's work, so with man's character. It is well to nourish our imagination with tales of ancient gods and heroes; but the true romance still lives in the souls of modern men who dream of things to be—who plan, and toil, and incarnate the dream in a deed. The passion for adventure, which drove Defoe's forlorn hero away from hearth and home, still lives in English hearts, and is still at one with Crusoe's practical inventiveness and wholesome temper of self-help. Let anyone who comes across a volume of 1866, *Two Months on the Tobique*, a volume posthumously published, and which deserves to be reprinted, read the vivid pages in which the writer records his experiences in wintry solitude amid Canadian forests, and he will find that Crusoe was alive in the midmost years of the nineteenth century, islanded by voluntary exile in the impenetrable pine-wood and cedar-swamp. Many impressive passages of Mr. Kipling's poetry tell of this fire in the heart of our race—a race old yet ever young, to whom still come the whisper and the vision:

> with the places of the dead quickly filled,
> Through the battle, through defeat, moving yet and never stopping,
> Pioneers! O pioneers!

The romance again of that spell of the immemorial East laid upon the spirit of the West, and the nostalgia of the wanderer who has responded to the invitation of the East, has never been expressed with more of genuine magic than by Mr. Kipling. There is another form of romance, vulgarised indeed by cheap examples yet part of 'the true romance', with which he has dealt successfully—the discovery of some one, hidden, green oasis in a soul turned into desert by the drifted sand and parching winds of a worldly life. John Bunyan's Mr. Badman died 'like a lamb', for sin had wholly indurated his soul, and God's judgement upon him was to leave him alone. Mr. Kipling's 'Sir Anthony Gloster', in his death-bed wanderings, mingles together piteously carnal pride and sensuality with the relics of an iron will; yet he is not wholly lost, for a spot of sea, 'Hundred and eighteen East, remember, and South just three' by the Little Paternosters, is still sacred for him, and it is there, where he dropped the body of the wife of his youth in fourteen fathoms, that his own body must seek the depths. Perhaps the poor romance of the oasis is better than any splendid romance of the mirage.

36. J. H. Millar reviews *Kim*

1901

Anonymous review of 'Recent Fiction' in *Blackwood's Magazine*, Vol. CLXX, pp. 793–5 (December 1901).

By J. H. Millar (see his full-scale review-article on Kipling in 1898—No. 29 above).

In discussing a few of the novels of the last six months or so, it is right and proper, on many accounts, which it were superfluous to specify, that due precedence should be awarded to Mr. Kipling. *Kim* is in some respects his most ambitious and elaborate work, and having, we confess, 'shied' at *Stalky & Co.*, we fell with a double portion of alacrity upon a 'new Kipling' which held out hopes of proving equal to the old ones. Nor have we been disappointed. Mr. Kipling has decidedly 'acquired merit' by this his latest essay. There is fascination, almost magic, in every page of the delightful volume, whose attractiveness is enhanced by illustrations of (to our mind) superlative excellence.

Kim, the eponymous hero, is a white boy, a *pukka* sahib: the son, in short, of Kimball O'Hara, late sergeant in the Mavericks, and his wife, once a nursery-maid in the colonel's family. Left an orphan at an early age, he has been brought up in the town of Lahore, nominally by a native woman of no character at all, and in reality, upon the educational principles which found so much favour with the elder Mr. Weller and find so little at the present day with many men less wise than he. Kim has thus, when we make his acquaintance, acquired a considerable knowledge of mankind and their ways, in addition to the nickname of 'Friend of all the world'. He is 'hand in glove with men who led lives stranger than anything Haroun Al Raschid dreamed of: and he lived in a life wild as that of the Arabian Nights, but missionaries and secretaries of charitable societies could not see the beauty of it.'

To him enter an aged lama from Tibet, on pilgrimage in quest of 'the river which washes away all taint of sin'. Kim forthwith becomes his *chela* or attendant (the word may or may not be at bottom identical with the Highland *gillie*), and they set out together *en route* for Benares, *via* Umballa, where Kim has been charged with a commission to perform by Mahbub Ali, an Afghan horse-dealer, who is in the pay of the Survey Department of the Indian Government. We cannot detail the incidents which mark the journey by rail and road of this singular pair of travellers. We can only note that they separate for a time, after Kim has fallen in with his father's old regiment, the colonel and chaplains of which are bent upon taking charge of him. The lama, however, insists upon paying for Kim's education. 'Education is greatest blessing if of best sorts. Otherwise no earthly use.' Such are his views, as tersely and sensibly expressed by a professional letter-writer, in Baboo English. Accordingly, Kim is sent to the school of St. Francis Xavier at Lucknow, there to accumulate such information as may be useful to him in after-life. For already he is practically destined by the powers that be to the playing of the Great Game—which, being interpreted, means the Secret Service of the Government. His schooling over, he is almost immediately launched upon his career, wherein, at the outset, he acquits himself, 'in a dam-tight place' (as Babu Hurree Chunder Mookerjee expresses it), with such sagacity and discretion as to please 'all the Department'. Having foregathered once more with the lama, he has much wandering in his company among the hills, with many exciting adventures, in which the fascinating Hurree plays a prominent part. The story concludes with Kim's recovery from a serious illness, brought on by over-fatigue, and with the successful issue of the lama's quest. In other words, the venerable priest falls into a brook, while in a brown study, and, having been with difficulty rescued from a watery grave, believes that he has at length been washed in the river of the Arrow which was the object of his search.

The character of Kim is from first to last a masterly conception. As a study of adolescence—of the progress from boyhood to youth, and from youth to early manhood—it is incomparably fresh and true: full of the delight of the artificer in the work of his hands, of the joy that comes from nothing so much as from the sense of successful achievement. The pride of the labourer in a task well performed has always been a congenial and favourite theme with Mr. Kipling; and we know of no other which, once duly appreciated, is likely to do so much for the maintenance of our Empire in all its manifold interests. Over and above Kim, there is a portrait-gallery of unusual extent and interest. Mahbub Ali, the old Ressaldar, the Rajah's widow, and Baboo Hurree, are the chief of those who find a place in it. And in the background there is always the impressive figure of the lama, whose mysterious apophthegms about the Wheel and the most Excellent Law form a deep and solemn accompaniment, as it were, to the music of the whole composition. You do not stop to inquire whether he or any one else is true to life. You *know* they are; you accept them all without question or reservation or cavil. That absolute perfection, however, may not be predicated of his work, Mr. Kipling has been obliging enough to throw in a couple of characters of whom so much cannot be said. Both Mr. Bennett, the Anglican, and Father Victor, the Roman Catholic chaplain, strike us as being conventional and commonplace—just the sort of personages whom we have learned to expect from Mr. Kipling's imitators.

But it is neither in the fable (exciting and ingenious though it be) nor in the portrayal of character (however skilful and convincing) that the charm of *Kim* consists. Its secret lies in the wonderful panorama it unrolls before us of the life of the great Peninsula over whose government England has now presided for more than a century. We despair of giving our readers any adequate conception of the glorious variety of the feast here spread before them. The kaleidoscopic quality, if we may venture so to call it, of Mr. Kipling's genius, has never before been displayed on so extensive a scale or to such great advantage. Turn to the description of the wayfarers on the Grand Trunk Road (too long, unfortunately, for transcription here), and consider for a moment the patient industry, the protracted observation, the thorough knowledge, which go to the making of these three pages. The thought is merely astounding; and one feels inclined in one's bewilderment to fall back upon the convenient and plausible theory that Mr. Kipling knows everything by instinct. That he knew much of native life we were aware already, but how much he knew we had not—perhaps have not yet—fathomed. Take one of the Strickland series of his stories: expand it, strengthen it, add indefinite multiplicity of detail to it; and you have the formula for producing a *Kim*. But let the adventurous aspirant see that his hand is well 'in' before he tries it.

37. A Review of *Just So Stories*

1902

Anonymous review under 'Juvenile Literature' in the *Athenaeum*,
No. 3910, pp. 447–8 (4 October 1902).

The *Just So Stories* (Macmillan), in which Mr. Kipling appears both as
author and illustrator, should regain the favour which he has lost in
some quarters by indifferent verse. Mr. Kipling is, at his best, the most
inspired teller of tales that we have; he understands young folk as few
writers do, and better than other mysteries which he has attempted to
tackle with expert haste. The result is that several of these stories—for
instance those concerning the invention of letter-writing and of the
alphabet by the daughter of a cave-dweller, the independence of the
domestic cat, the reason for the elephant's trunk—are perfect, told once
for all so that other tellers need not hope to compete. The stories being
for younger folk than the *Jungle Books*, deal a good deal in what is pure
nonsense to the child, and clever fooling with ornate words and phrases
to the adult—such writing, in fact, as the catalogues of remedies in
Kingsley's *Water Babies*. There is, we fancy, a touch too much of this
clever stuff in the earlier stories, but the main invention and the delightfully easy exposition, with feats of duplicated onomatopoeic adjectives
and the odd little details which children love aptly interfused, carry
one on triumphantly. That invention is not always good; Mr. Kipling
can do much better when he likes than assure us that the camel got his
hump because he said 'humph' instead of working. The pictures show
the author's real talent in a new line, though indeed we might expect
as much from his father's son. They recall in their style and the elaborately naïve exposition attached to them that genuine piece of nursery
lore *Animal Land*,[1] and in their use of dead black the most original of
modern illustrators. Some of them are rather messy, but generally they
are a distinct aid to the text. The whole forms an outstanding book,
which, though not so delightful as the *Jungle Books*, is yet enough to

[1] [*Animal Land Where There Are No People*, 1897. By Sybil Corbet (aged 4)]

have made a reputation for a new author. We are eager to read as much more in this vein as Mr. Kipling will give us.

38. G. K. Chesterton reviews *Just So Stories*

1902

Signed review from the *Bookman* (London), Vol. XXIII, pp. 57–8 (November 1902).

Gilbert Keith Chesterton (1874–1936), essayist, novelist and minor poet, best remembered for his Father Brown detective stories, was also a discerning critic and a master of epigram. The religious writings of his later life are only excelled by those of C. S. Lewis.

For his fuller study of Kipling in *Heretics* (1905) see No. 42 below.

Mr. Rudyard Kipling is a most extraordinary and bewildering genius. Some of us have recently had reason to protest against certain phases of his later development, and we protested because they were pert and cockney and cruel, and full of that precocious old age which is the worst thing in this difficult cosmos, a thing which combines the brutality of youth with the disillusionment of antiquity, which is old age without its charity and youth without its hope. This rapidly aging, rapidly cheapening force of modernity is everywhere and in all things, a veritable spiritual evil: it looks out of the starved faces of a million gutter-boys, and its name is Ortheris. And just as we are in the afterglow of a certain indignation against this stale, bitter modernity which had begun to appear in Mr. Kipling's work, we come upon this superb thing, the *Just-So Stories*; a great chronicle of primal fables, which might have been told by Adam to Cain, before murder (that artistic and decadent pastime) was known in the world.

For the character of the *Just-So Stories* is really unique. They are not fairy tales; they are legends. A fairy tale is a tale told in a morbid age to the only remaining sane person, a child. A legend is a fairy tale told to men when men were sane. We grant a child a fairy tale, just as some savage king might grant a missionary permission to wear clothes, not understanding what we give, not knowing that it would be infinitely valuable if we kept it to ourselves, but simply because we are too kind to refuse. The true man will not buy fairy tales because he is kind; he will buy them because he is selfish. If Uncle John who has just bought the *Just-So Stories* for his niece were truly human (which of course Uncle John is not) it is doubtful whether the niece would ever see the book. One of the most lurid and awful marks of human degeneration that the mind can conceive is the fact that it is considered kind to play with children.

But the peculiar splendour, as I say, of these new Kipling stories is the fact that they do not read like fairy tales told to children by the modern fireside, so much as like fairy tales told to men in the morning of the world. They see animals, for instance, as primeval men saw them; not as types and numbers in an elaborate biological scheme of knowledge, but as walking portents, things marked by extravagant and peculiar features. An elephant is a monstrosity with his tail between his eyes; a rhinoceros is a monstrosity with his horn balanced on his nose; a camel, a zebra, a tortoise are fragments of a fantastic dream, to see which is not seeing a scientific species, but like seeing a man with three legs or a bird with three wings, or men as trees walking. The whole opens a very deep question, the question of the relations between the old wonder and the new wonder, between knowledge and science. The hump of the camel is very likely not so much his characteristic from a scientific point of view as the third bone in the joint of his hind leg, but to the eyes of the child and the poet it remains his feature. And it is more important in this sense that it is more direct and certain: there is a relation between the human soul and the hump of a camel, which there is not between the human soul and the bone in his hind leg. The hump still remains and the bone vanishes, if all these physical phenomena are nothing but a grotesque shadow-show, constructed by a paternal deity to amuse an universe of children.

This is the admirable achievement of Kipling, that he has written new legends. We hear in these days of continual worship of old legends, but not of the making of new; which would be the real worship of legends. Just in the same way we hear of the worship of old ceremonies,

but never of the making of new ones. If men decided that Mr. Gladstone's hat was to be carried three times round the House of Commons
they would have offered the best tribute to the Eleusinian mysteries.
That is the tribute which 'How the Whale got his Throat' offers to the
story of Sigurd and Hercules.

39. 'Kipling and the Children'

1902

Article first published in *Anglo-American Magazine* (Toronto),
Vol. VIII, pp. 14–21 (December 1902) and reprinted in *English
Illustrated Magazine*, Vol. XXX, pp. 470–4 (January 1904). By
Agnes Deans Cameron (1863–1912).

Kipling has been considered in many aspects—as the Bard of Tommy
Atkins, the exponent of Anglo-Indian life, the Laureate of the Empire,
the Poet of Wheel and Axle, Lever and Screw, and a most compelling
Voice from the Jungle. Not with his soldiers, nor with his animals, nor
his engines would we now deal, but with his children.

At the first blush one would not think to discover in Kipling a
fertile field for paternal and pedagogical research, to find him bristling
with maxims for the training of the young. But send out a town crier,
a sort of Pied Piper of Hamelin searching for children through the
length and breadth of Kipling-land, and see the following he will get.

Of Kipling's long stories, *Stalky & Co.* deals entirely with children;
Captains Courageous is in intent the story of a boy, so is *Kim*. *The Light
That Failed*, in its first and best chapters, is a study of child-life; while
that wondrous thing *The Jungle Book*, stronger than Aesop and with
a witchery all its own, what is it but a sustained treatise on the claims
of the commonwealth and the development of the individual?

And as the Piper pipes, out from 'somewhere east of Suez', to answer to the roll-call, comes crowding such a goodly company, a feast here for the student of child-life and for the lover of children.

Let us stand aside and watch the procession pass: Wee Willie Winkie, and his Majesty the King; Muhammed Din, poor baby, from his garden of dust and dead leaves; and Tods of the Amendment. Round the corner we stumble upon the little Japs splashing in their half-sunk barrel and trying to hide one behind the other 'in a hundred poses of spankable chubbiness', with the little American monstrosity, 'who, when it has nothing else to do, will answer to the name of Albert'; across the line of vision reel 'The Drums of the Fore and Aft', followed by 'Baa, Baa, Blacksheep', and Strickland, the son of his Father; here comes William the Conqueror's long line of goats with the naked famine babies as running commentary, while out of the shadows mysterious and fascinating of No-Man's Land glides into our ken The Brushwood Boy; at his heels, 'under a man's helmet wid the chin-straps swingin' about her little stummick', Jhansi McKenna staggers, the Child of the Regiment.

Are they not all very human and very lovable? The Pied Piper, who called them forth, turns to us and says, 'Who is the happy man? He that sees in his own home little children crowned with dust, leaping and falling and crying' (Munichandra). A writer's best stories are always in part autobiographical, and to this rule *Kim* and *Stalky & Co.* are no exceptions. 'Master Gigadibs', the festive Beetle—in retreat in his lair among the furze bushes, waiting for the dead cat to begin to twine like a giddy honeysuckle, worshipping the Head, baiting King, and confiding in the Padre—is always and ever Beetle the inimitable. In the light of what Beetle and Bard has since given us we can scarcely regret that his gig-lamps and short-sightedness kept him out of the army.

Stalky & Co. recently formed the bone of contention in a ladies' literary club, and few were the friends it found. One mother objected to the slang, another to the 'absence of ideals', a third abjured it altogether, but said that her son revelled in it and her husband approved. The chief fault of the book lies, perhaps, in the fact that Kipling has portrayed the scrapes of the trio, and has given us no account of the long, arid stretches of dig, grind, and plodding which must have existed in order that those stiff exams should be passed.

For those blessed with a close understanding of the animal 'boy', the slang part has no power to shock. What is it that George Eliot makes Fred Vincy say? 'All choice of words is slang. It marks a class. Correct

English is the slang of prigs who write history and essays. And the strongest slang of all is the slang of poets.'

The second charge, that against the morale of the story, is a more serious one. Is the effect of *Stalky & Co.* on the mind of the schoolboy reader bad? Does it set before him a low moral standard, and is it lacking in ideals? Let us look at the situation fairly. The Three Incomprehensibles, Stalky, Beetle and McTurk, had a creed, to which they adhered with more consistency than we always do to ours. This creed or code of ethics was not angelic, but it was delightfully human. The Head and the Padre treated them openly and trusted them, and in return were to be met always 'on the level'. The House Masters, King and Foxy, neither gave nor asked for confidence; here the wits of the governing and the governed were pitted against each other in open warfare; the boys looked upon the contest as a fair game, and the other side acquiesced.

And at this we, some of us, cavil. Let us be honest. These boys were being trained for what? For just this sort of thing. As British officers they were to go to 'India's sunny clime', and there to do what? To outwit the wily strategy of Britain's foes. And by what means? Was the enemy to be brought to terms by a 'polite letter-writer' effusion presented on a silver salver, or by meeting wile with wile?

Stalky, the man, proved, we are told, a past grand-master in the art of diplomacy. Who were his foils when he studied the rudiments of primeval warfare and learned his trade? Answer, O King and Prout and Foxy.

The finest bit in the book is, perhaps, the Flag scene. The bare idea of 'teaching patriotism' to British boys is sickening. But the schools have patrons and committee-men and trustees, and when these wise ones give advice, what can the poor pedagogue do but squirm? The satisfaction of blandly referring these to 'a most interesting chapter in *Stalky & Co.* dealing with the subject' is great, and for this thanks are due.

There is proof, if proof is needed, that even while Beetle with his *confrères* were scornfully repudiating 'the jelly-bellied flag-flapper' (!) and his spurious oratory, deep down in the heart of the young Imperialist burned thus early the fires of an Empire-wide patriotism, *vide* his poem *'Ave Imperatrix'*, written from Westward Ho! College, on the occasion of the last attempt on the life of the great and good Queen, while Beetle was yet unknown to fame:

[quotes *'Ave Imperatrix'*, first 5 stanzas: DV. p. 169]

In 'Only a Subaltern', Kipling gives us another Flag incident; it is just a glimpse. The subaltern is Bobby Wick, just gazetted sub-lieutenant of 'The Tyneside Tail-Twisters'.

More than once, too, he came officially into contact with the regimental colours, which looked like the lining of a bricklayer's hat on the end of a chewed stick. Bobby did not kneel and worship them, because British subalterns are not constructed in that manner. Indeed, he condemned them for their weight at the very moment they were filling him with awe and other more noble sentiments.

Peace hath her victories no less renowned than war. This is the Bobby who day by day in the cholera camp 'played the giddy garden goat', and at night fought with Death for dirty Dormer till the grey dawn came, a few days later, to 'go out' himself, dying for all that the Flag stands for: 'Not only to enforce by command but to encourage by example the energetic discharge of duty and the steady endurance of the difficulties and privations inseparable from Military Service' (Bengal Army Regulations).

Kipling's dedication of *Stalky & Co.* to his old head master is among the very finest things he has written:

[quotes stanzas 5, 7, 11, 13 of 'A School Song': DV. pp. 556–8]

'The Head', who had kindliness and wise insight enough ('God's Own Commonsense') to know that a boy may be in mischiefs manifold, the hero of many scrapes, and remain pure, wholesome, and withal very lovable, would not be insensible to this tribute coming 'after many days'.

Kipling believed in public schools. In 'Thrown Away' he has this to say of the 'sheltered life system':

To rear a boy under what parents call the 'sheltered-life system' is, if the boy must go out into the world and fend for himself, not wise. Unless he be one in a thousand, he has certainly to pass through many unnecessary troubles; and may, possibly, come to extreme grief simply from ignorance of the proper proportion of things. Let a puppy eat the soap in the bath-room, or chew a newly-blacked boot. He chews and chuckles until by-and-by he finds out that blacking and old brown Windsor make him very sick; so he argues that soap and boots are not wholesome. Any old dog about the house will soon show him the unwisdom of biting big dog's ears. Being young, he remembers and goes abroad at six months, a well-mannered little beast with a chastened appetite. If he had been kept away from boots and soap and big dogs until he came to the maturity, full-grown, and with developed teeth, consider how fearfully sick and thrashed he would be.

Apply that notion to the sheltered life, and see how it works. As Kipling says, it does not sound pretty; but is it not most terribly true?

In the 'Jungle School', did not Mowgli the 'Man-cub', find a teacher who on Farne's beadroll of Dominies must take a place second only to Froebel and Arnold, and the great of old? Listen to the words of wisdom which fall from the shaggy lips of Baloo, the brown bear, 'Teacher of the Law', to the Seonee wolf-cubs:

> 'There is none like to me!' says the Cub
> in the pride of his earliest kill;
> But the Jungle is large, and the Cub he is
> small. Let him think and be still.

Hathi, the wild elephant, never does anything till the time comes, and that is one of the reasons why he lives so long.

One of the beauties of Jungle Law is that punishment settles all scores. There is no nagging afterwards.

Better he should be bruised from head to foot by me who loves him, than that he should come to harm through ignorance.

(The sheltered-life system found no exponent in old Baloo.)

A brave heart and a courteous tongue, they shall carry thee far through the Jungle, Manling.

> 'Now these are the Laws of the Jungle,
> and many and mighty are they;
> But the head and the hoof of the Law, and
> the haunch and the hump is—OBEY!'

The Seonee Cubs, who passed under Baloo's hard training, had experience of the dogma of 'Life's Handicap':

> Ride with an idle whip, ride with an unused heel,
> But once in a way there will come a day
> When the colt must be taught to feel
> The lash that falls, and the curb that galls,
> and the sting of the rowelled steel.

And yet was there ever the truest tenderness in the Old Bear's teaching.

Kipling, who went forth

> For to admire an' for to see,
> For to be'old this world so wide,

like a greedily-impressionable bit of blotting-paper, soaking up everything on the face of the earth, in 'From Sea to Sea' pays a warm
tribute to the American girl:

Sweet and comely are the maidens of Devonshire; delicate and of gracious
seeming those who live in the pleasant places of London; fascinating for all
their demureness the damsels of France, clinging closely to their mothers, and
with large eyes wondering at the wicked world; excellent in her own place,
and to those who understand her is the Anglo-Indian 'spin' in her second season;
but the girls of America are above and beyond them all. They are clever; they
can talk. They are original, and look you between the brows with unabashed
eyes as a sister might look at a brother. They are self-possessed without parting
with any tenderness that is their sex-right; they are superbly independent; they
understand.

A word, too, for the 'long, elastic, well-built California boy':

Him I love because he is devoid of fear, carries himself like a man, and has a
heart as big as his boots.

If I were asked to strike the keynote of all Kipling's teachings, I
should say it was 'The sacredness, the imperativeness, to each man, of
his own day's work'.

A man must throw his whole being into his task, 'gettin' shut o'doin'
things rather more or less'; and that man shall 'by the vision splendid,
be on his way attended'. It is the Apotheosis of Work. And, surely,
has he earned a right to speak on this subject, for, literally, while his
companions slept, he was 'toiling upward in the night'.

Kipling, in his own impressionable youth, had the inestimable
advantage of living in India just at the time when the old order was
giving place to the new. Around him was an empire in making, and
he saw the raw edges of the work. For years, out of sight of the English
press, did he work like a grub of genius in a remote corner, spinning,
in long, hot, dusty days, and in hotter nights, a golden web out of
which only stray strands floated into the world's ken. There is a
camaraderie, a sort of freemasonry, in work; had he not himself been
a worker, it would not have been given to him to meet at first hand all
manners of men.

As it is, he gets his facts in days spent in the huts of the hill-country,
in the engine-rooms of great liners, in the opium shops of Lahore, in
the busy marts of men, far off on lone hillsides and riverways, where
men toiling, sweating, planning, fighting, build walls and bridges,
lead forlorn hopes, and do things.

And through the best of Kipling's boy-stories shines ever the insistence of the Day's Work. This lesson, though delayed, must be learned (be it by a bear's blows or at the hard hands of a Cape Cod-fisher), and to him who throws himself headlong into his task the reward will not be lacking.

Kim, hugging himself in sheer intoxication with the love of life and of work, would seem to exclaim with Tommy Atkins:

> Gawd bless this world! Whatever she hath done—
> Excep' when awful long—I've found it good,
> So write, before I die, 'E liked it all.

And so it was that, casting aside conventions, with a this-one-thing-I-do intentness, whether hand in hand with Old Lama, childlike seeking The Way, or following 'The Great Game' off his own bat, he caught brief elusive glimpses of the 'light that never was on land or sea'.

Love of energy is the axis of Kipling's mind. But while it is true that he is no dreamer of Arcady, it is also true that one cannot read his child-sketches without discovering in them a sub-current, a minor note of almost womanly tenderness. It is a pathetic touch, and exquisitely delicate. Is there to be found any other 'mere man' who could have written 'Baa, Baa, Blacksheep' or 'His Majesty the King'?

And then there are the child chapters of *The Light that Failed*, and that rare thing 'The Brushwood Boy'. And which of us can follow to the grave (respectfully, and at a distance, that we may not intrude), little Muhammed Din and not gulp hard to keep back the tears? For we, too, have folded baby-fingers that made gardens of dust and dead flowers, and the heart of a child is the same on whichsoever shore of the Seven Seas he builds his sand-houses and to whatsoever grave we carry him.

Kipling knows his children as he knows his soldiers, his animals, his engines; and when he half startles us with a statement like this, 'The reserve of a boy is tenfold deeper than the reserve of a maid,' it is only the ignorant of us who laugh.

'Only women,' he says, 'understand children properly; but if a mere man keeps very quiet and humbles himself properly, and refrains from talking down to his superiors, the children will sometimes be good to him and let him see what they think about the world.'

40. F. York Powell on 'Rudyard Kipling'

1903

Signed article in the *English Illustrated Magazine*, Vol. XXX, pp. 295–8 (December 1903) preceding Bibliographical List—one of a series.

Frederick York Powell (1850–1904), scholar, man of letters, Professor of Modern History at Oxford and outstanding Scandinavian scholar (he edited the *Corpus Poeticum Boreale* in 1881).

Mr. Kipling is a force in politics as in letters. But this makes it harder to judge him fairly. Some of his least artistic work is wholly sound in feeling. 'Pay! Pay! Pay!' is not his best poem, but as an effectual piece of writing it had a deserved success, and helped many that would have fared ill but for such an appeal. For myself, I do not greatly admire his Hymns, and I find the talking ponies and machinery of the kind tiresome, but these Hymns and Animal stories and the less inspired *Just So* tales are favourites with many both young and old, and certainly the moral is excellent. As a teacher, indeed, Mr. Kipling is undeniably effective. I am profoundly grateful for many of his sermons, and gladly acknowledge the practical good he has done. We English cannot help preaching; it is one of our most notable characteristics to the foreigner's eye that we must be eternally giving advice, advice generally unasked. To my mind, Mr. Kipling is very English (if I may differ, as I regret to do, from Mr. Chesterton); he loves the didactic; he dallies gladly with allegory; he has, like Defoe, practical ends. He is an artist born, but also a born preacher, though it is only fair to say that he does not make himself a missionary, and his ministrations are confined to his own countrymen, who have need of his advice. He preaches Faith, Hope, and Charity. He has enforced, again and again, the necessary lesson of sympathy with everything that lives. He has made us feel that there is a common humanity between us and the most inscrutable 'native'. He has made us understand that there is an abiding interest in the thoughts and ways of the plain man and woman doing their daily work and rejoicing in it. He has got very close to the inwardness of the soldier and the sailor, the engineer, the civilian, and the fisherman. The whole life and mind of the newspaper man, whether editor, reporter, correspondent, compositor, or printer's devil, is open to him, and revealed by him to us.

He is a perpetual and patient and swift observer, ever on the look-out for the vital and distinctive among the mass of phenomena that surrounds us all. He has not a little of Maupassant's gift of giving the local colour and the personal impression without waste of words, though he was trained in a far less artistic studio, and was some time before he worked free of the tricks of the school of Dickens and Sala and the Kingsleys, and reached the higher simplicities of finished art. Dumas has influenced him, as he influenced Stevenson, wholly for good, in the spirit and not in the letter. He has the delight Gautier so often expressed for technical detail; he sees its importance; he knows what the engine is to the engineer and the ship to the sailor. He can paint moods by a very different method to that of Henry James, but one as legitimate, and more Meredithian, discovering the instinct by the act, marking the play of incident on the character. It is not his business to endeavour to trace out, according to the miraculous and unique method of the greatest of American novelists, the whole working of the tangled current of will as it is contorted by circumstance. His prose is straightforward, concise, untrammelled by useless ornament and as he develops less and less disturbed by the episodic appeal to the reader which Defoe disdained, but which spoils much of Thackeray's work. His reader is never unfairly dealt with by Mr. Kipling. If he cannot move him by a 'plain tale', he will not strive by such illegitimate efforts to stimulate his stolid brain and dull heart. With a fine descriptive gift, never sliding into the dangerous catalogue style (which, though it was nobly employed by Balzac, was not seldom abused by Zola) he gets his effect by a careful but spontaneous-looking selection of the touches that really tell. I often wonder whether he does not practise in letters the method Phil May used in design, and write into his first sketch much more than he means to have printed, cutting out all but the really significant lines and leaving them to speak out clearly, unhampered by those that would only fill up and dull the impression he has already secured. He can create characters that help to people the world that each of us has in his brain; a world where Falstaff and Mrs. Gamp are as real as one's flesh-and-blood acquaintance. Mrs. Hauksbee and Private Ortheris,

Dick and the red-haired girl, Terence and Dinah, the Engineer's wife and Kim's old bonze, The Infant, Strickland, Torpenhow, Badalia and Judson, Jakin and Dan, are not paper things, but move, and talk, and laugh, and suffer, and breathe, and bleed, as mere puppets never can. For plot and situation he has of course a most rare and singular gift; such tales as 'The Man Who Was', 'The Brushwood Boy', 'The Strange Ride', and a score more that might be named, attest this power to the full. He has had, of course, scores of imitators, and not a few that have been inspired by him to do good work of their own (like Mr. J. London, whose *Call of the Wild* is far the best book Mr. Kipling's beast-tales have brought into existence), but his imitators have not made the originals stale.

For his verse there is much that is imperfect in it. He has let far too many poems be printed and reprinted that do not fairly represent him, that are imperfect, immature, unbalanced, unfinished. He has not yet the heart to prune his verse as he prunes his prose. He is too easily content with labouring and re-labouring inside the same circles of thought and expression. He injured some of his best poems by leaving ugly flaws that could easily be removed, by imperfect rhymes, extra-metrical lines (a bad fault this because it irritates), jarring discords, superfluity of expression and, above all, by labouring the idea over-much as Victor Hugo continually did. This is the sin of Eli, and it is deadly if a man do not repent and forswear it. Prose may be 'let go at that', but not verse; it is not 'playing the game'. But when all is said, Mr. Kipling is a vigorous and sincere poet. His best verse has music in it, and there are wings to his words. He has learnt much from Mr. Swinburne's early work, but it is the more massive qualities of his Master's rhythm rather than the delicacies of his more elaborate crafts-manship that have chiefly pleased him. Mr. Kipling has the essential gift that the poet of children and the crowd must have, the gift of correct time and clear flow, but he has more than that: there is a soul as well as a body in his finer poems; they cling, they haunt the mind, as they satisfy the ear. Some of the scraps of verse set at the heads of chapters are in this kind admirable. He is also, as few modern English poets are, a real song writer: he makes verse that calls for a singer, that demands the barytone and the tinkle of the strings, and the full-mouthed chorus. What he has written in slang is wonderfully good, full of movement, and never commonplace, as so much dialect verse tends to be. These are excellent specimens: 'Piet', 'M.I.', and 'Me' in his last volume. He is exceptionally strong in allegory, a vein rarely touched of late, but which he has worked to purpose. 'The Galley', 'The Three-decker', 'The Truce of the Bear', 'The Dykes', and 'True Thomas', are notable examples. Neither Tennyson nor (as I think) Browning could write a good ballad, but Mr. Kipling can. 'Fisher's Boardinghouse', 'The Bolivar', 'The Last Suttee', and 'Danny Deever', for instance, are real 'little epics'. For the full, rich, rolling verse in which he excels, perhaps the best are: 'The Last Chantey', 'The Dirge of the Dead Sisters', *Et Dona Ferentes*, 'The Long Trail', 'The Jollies', 'The Anchor Song', though there are a fair number nearly as good in manner or matter. But if these alone existed Mr. Kipling would go down to posterity with 'a full and proper kit of song' to use his own words.

His limitations are obvious, and they are not elastic, but they are the consequence of his peculiar gifts, and we do not look to him to rival the work of thinkers like Mr. Meredith, to walk with the dreamers like Mr. Yeats or A.E., or to touch the poignant personal note of such poets as Mr. Blunt or the best verse of Messrs. Watson and T. E. Brown. Henley's finest work was much more subjective than Mr. Kipling's is or can be. But there are many mansions in the House of Apollo, and to one of these his title is writ clear enough.

It is pleasant to write about good work, but Mr. Kipling's work may safely be left to speak for itself. He is yet young and strong, and in full power; one may hope for more prose and more verse from him. He will never lack subjects. He evidently loves his work and, like the artists in heaven of his 'Envoy', he would do it for the pure pleasure of it were there neither fame nor reward in it. He has deserved well of England, and well of the Empire. He has never hesitated to speak plainly to his countrymen, and some of them, at least, have taken his lesson to heart. He has been faithful to Art also, and his devotion has not been thrown away. He has always been a learner, and though at first one feared that he could be too easily satisfied, the increasing finish of his prose style (for his verse does not improve perceptibly) shows that he has constantly striven for more perfect expression. His leniency towards his past work is, though regrettable, easy to understand.

Perhaps no English man of letters since Byron has seen his ideas and his manner of conveying them so widely welcomed among the reading public of his countrymen. Unlike Byron in most things, he resembles him in this, that he commands the attention of the public because he can be easily understood, because his manner is that which his age admires and recognises, because he has something new to say, which he must say plainly, and does say well.

41. George Moore on 'Kipling and Loti'

1904

Extracts from section five of *Avowals*, first published in *Pall Mall Magazine*, Vol. XXXIII, pp. 374–9 (July 1904); later published in book form 1919.

George Augustus Moore (1852–1933), Irish novelist once highly esteemed but later neglected. Notable for his interest in style and his break with the conventions of previous novelists.

Perhaps even more than railways and steamboats, modern education has thrown art from the general into the particular; every one understands the particular, but abstract sentiments are understood only by a few. The success of a picture or book is in proportion to the number of facts related, and the inferior artist is tempted by money, and popular appreciation and local colour bring him both. That is why there is so little in modern art of that beautiful mediocrity which we find in ancient art. Local colour is proof of education—it proves the painter has travelled: truth of effect raises him almost to the level of the scientist, and historical accuracy testifies that he spent a good deal of his time in a library as well as in his studio. . . . I am not writing in the hope of converting any one. Men will cease to believe in education as soon as it pleases them to do so. But will things be better then, when the educational folly has passed? Not a jot. We shall exchange one folly for another—that will be all. Painters, writers, and musicians who have no hold upon the eternal verities must seize upon local colour to give passing interest to their work; but why should

critics be enthusiastic about local colour? Critics—well, great critics—
can pursue their calling, whatever artistic fashion prevails. Yet local
colour has been the stumbling-block of criticism for one hundred years.
Great and small, every critic is duped; the artist has only to find out
some particular part of the country and to bring back some curious
notes of travel to dupe every one. It would appear that we learn
nothing that we did not know before. I wrote this phrase twenty years
ago in *Confessions of a Young Man*, and I write it again. Notwithstanding
Berlioz's mistake, there was not one critic in London who was not
deceived in the eighties, when Mr. Kipling came with his *Plain Tales
from the Hills*. His stories are filled with hookahs and elephants, parakeets and crocodiles; they are as amusing as the Zoological Gardens
with beer *ad lib*. All the dialects are there—Irish and Scotch and
Cockney. As the name of Beethoven was introduced when *Le Desert*
was being written about, the name of Shakespeare was introduced
apropos of Mr. Kipling. A critical mistake is soon forgotten; no author
can be held responsible for his critic's blunders; and it is to Mr. Kipling's
credit that he seems to have known more about himself than his
critics. We can only convict him of having made one mistake in those
perilous times—he once got off his camel. It was the editor of an
American magazine who persuaded Mr. Kipling to write a story the
greater part of which should be camel-less. There were a few camels
in the beginning of the story, but there were none afterwards—not as
the story appeared in the magazine; but the story was rewritten, and
the second version ended amid herds of camels. The hero of this story
is a special artist, who has done some sketches in the East; these sketches
(done certainly in wash) attracted a great deal of attention when they
were exhibited in England. A dealer wanted to buy up the whole lot,
but the special artist says: 'I know a trick worth two of that,' and he
determines to get a great deal of money for his sketches. The analogy
between Mr. Kipling and the artist is obvious. We think Mr. Kipling
much better than any special artist ever sent out on a war expedition—
we think that Mr. Kipling libelled himself; if so, it was himself who
did it. An attempt is made to show that Dick Heldar is something
more than a journalist; he is represented painting a picture of Melancholia. A poet may disguise himself as a beggar, but not as a special
artist—to do so shows a certain coarseness of fibre, a lack of sensibility;
and to represent him as painting a Melancholia is to make him ridiculous.

The phrase I have attributed to Dick Heldar may not have been used by him, but his whole personality suggests the words, 'I know a trick worth two of that,'—they are in a way an abridgment, a compendium of his attitude towards life; he browses like a horse in tether within the circle of 'I know a trick worth two of that.' 'I know a trick worth two of that' is the keynote of his mind. It is the key in which he always writes; he indulges in some modulations, but the key of 'I know a trick worth two of that' is never quite out of his ear, and if one were so minded one could trace it through all his prose and a good many poems. Nearly the whole of *Kim* is written in this key; now and then he modulates into the world and its shows, the Great Wheel, etc., but one knows that the terrible key 'I know a trick worth two of that' is never far off. And he delights in Kim, just as he delighted in Dick, and his admiration is so spontaneous that it is impossible to read *Kim* without saying to oneself: 'Kim is Mr. Kipling.' Kim is never taken in, and not to be taken in is in Mr. Kipling's eyes a sort of north star whereby one steers the bark of life. Kim is a spy, but spying is called the Great Game, and nothing matters so long as you are not taken in. Mr. Kipling's beast-kind is the same as his mankind: the animals in the *Jungle Books* that we are to admire are those that 'know a trick worth two of that'. He does not venture among godkind, but if he did, his gods would 'know a trick worth two of that'.

Now it is a moot question if an author's mind extend much beyond the characters he creates. Did not Baudelaire say that in Balzac even the porters had genius? Among Mr. Kipling's works there is a book called *The Gadsbys*, and the theme is that if a man wants to get on in the army he should not get married. This will seem to those who admire the book an unfair description of it; but we must not be deceived by the external form—we must, if we would appreciate a writer, take into account his attitude towards life, we must discover if his vision is mean or noble, spiritual or material, narrow or wide; for all things are in the eye that sees, things having no existence in themselves—the earliest and latest philosophy. In the eighties none knew what world Mr. Kipling was about to reveal; but now his world is before us, and 'noble' and 'beautiful' are not the adjectives that any one would choose wherewith to designate the world of Kipling. Rough, harsh, coarse-grained, come into our minds; Mr. Kipling's world is a barrack full of oaths and clatter of sabres; but his language is copious, rich, sonorous. One is tempted to say that none since the Elizabethans has written so copiously. Others have written more beautifully, but no one that I can call to mind at this moment has written so copiously. Shelley and Wordsworth, Landor and Pater, wrote with part of the language; but who else, except Whitman, has written with the whole language since the Elizabethans? 'The flannelled fool at the wicket, the muddied oaf at the goal' is wonderful language. He writes with the eye that appreciates all that the eye can see, but of the heart he knows nothing, for the heart cannot be observed; his characters are therefore external, and they are stationary. At first we are taken by Kim—he is so well seen, so well observed, so well copied; the Lama we can see as if he were before us—an old man in his long habit and his rosary, we hear his continuous mumbling; but very soon we perceive that Kim and the Lama are fixed—we have not read thirty pages before we see that those two will be the same at the end of the book as they were in the beginning.

The Lama has come from Tibet in search of a sacred river, and he meets a street Arab, precocious and vile in his every instinct, at the outset of his journey, and these two go off together. They are but pegs whereon Mr. Kipling intends to hang his descriptions of India. If they are but pegs I would prefer them to be a little plainer—they are a little too much carved; but let the carving be waived—something must be granted to every writer—the object is henceforth to describe India: we shall see how he does this, and Mr. Kipling shall be measured by our standard. Our standard is *how* much life does the writer evoke, and this standard is applicable whether the writer is describing a sunset or an old woman peeling onions, whether he is putting words into the mouth of a tramp or of a philosopher. Whatever the subject may be, our standard is the same—how much of the precious wine do we taste, and in what intensity while reading? This is our standard whether the art under consideration be literature or painting, whether the literature be prose or poetry; and having stated our standard of criticism, we will proceed with the measurement of Mr. Kipling:

They entered the fort-like railway station, black in the end of night; the electrics sizzling over the goods-yard, where they handle the heavy Northern grain-traffic.

How strong the rhythm, lacking perhaps in subtlety, like the tramp of policemen, but a splendid rhythm! And it is Mr. Kipling's own rhythm; he borrows from no man, and it is always a pleasure to read or hear unborrowed literature or music.

A little farther on we find ourselves in the middle of a spacious paragraph, the sentences moving to the same sonorous march measure:

Then it came out that in those wordly days he had been a master-hand at casting horoscopes and nativities, and the family priest led him on to describe his methods, each giving the planets names that the other could not understand, and pointing upwards as the big stars sailed across the dark. The children of the house tugged unrebuked at his rosary; and he clean forgot the Rule which forbids looking at women as he talked of enduring snows, landslips, blocked passes, the remote cliffs where men find sapphires and turquoise, and that wonderful upland road that leads at last into great China itself.

And how finely it ends, that long sentence stretching itself out like the 'upland road that leads at last into great China itself'!

In saying these things we are praising Mr. Kipling's technical excellence, and technical excellence is of no value for us except as a means through which life is revealed.

A few pages farther on we come upon a description of evening; and evening is one of the eternal subjects—men were sensible to the charm and beauty and the tenderness of evening ten thousand years ago, and ten thousand years hence they will be moved in the same way.

By this time the sun was driving broad golden spokes through the lower branches of the mango-trees; the parakeets and doves were coming home in their hundreds; the chattering, grey-backed Seven Sisters, talking over the day's adventures, walked back and forth in twos and threes almost under the feet of the travellers; the shufflings and scufflings in the branches showed that the bats were ready to go out on the night picket. Swiftly the light gathered itself together, painted for an instant the faces and the cartwheels and bullocks' horns as red as blood. Then the night fell, changing the touch of the air, drawing a low, even haze like a gossamer veil of blue across the face of the country, and bringing out, keen and distinct, the smell of wood-smoke and cattle and the good scent of wheaten cakes cooked on ashes. The evening patrol hurried out of the police-station with important coughings and reiterated orders; and a live charcoal ball in the cup of a wayside carter's hookah glowed red while Kim's eyes mechanically watched the last flicker of the sun on the brass tweezers.

No one will deny the perfection of the writing, of the strong masculine rhythm of every sentence, and of the accuracy of every observation. But it seems to us that Mr. Kipling has seen much more than he has felt; and we prefer feeling to seeing; and when we come to analyse the lines we find a touch of local colour not only in every sentence, but in each part, between each semicolon. 'The sun was driving golden spokes through the branches of the *mango* trees', 'the *parakeets*', 'the doves', 'the chattering grey-backed Seven Sisters', 'the bats ready to go out on the *night picket*', 'the *light painting* the faces and the car wheels and the *bullocks' horns'*. At last a sentence that does not carry any local colour: 'then the night fell, changing the touch of the air, drawing a low even haze like a gossamer veil of blue across the face of the country', but after the comma local colour begins again, 'bringing out, keen and distinct, the smell of *wood-smoke* and *cattle*', 'and the *cakes*', etc. Then there is the evening patrol and the live *charcoal ball*, and then Kim's eyes watching the flicker of the sun on the *brass tweezers*.

It would be difficult to find a passage in literature of the same length so profusely touched with local colour. Was it not a shame to observe that slender wistful hour so closely? Mr. Kipling seems to have followed it about like a detective employed in a divorce case—like Kim himself, who is a political spy. We prefer an evening by Pierre Loti; he experiences a sensation and his words transmit the sensation and remind us of many things that we have experienced at sunsetting. Loti's touch is perhaps a little superficial, a little facile, the feeling is perhaps genteel, even trite, but with all there is more wistfulness in Loti than in Kipling, and an evening that is not wistful is not evening.

But evening comes, evening with its magic, and we relinquish ourselves to the charm once more.

About our brave little encampment, about the rough horizon where all danger seems at present asleep, the twilight sky kindles an incomparable rose border, orange, then green, and then, rising by degrees to the zenith, it softens and quenches. It is the hour indecisive and charming, when amid limpidities which are neither day nor night our odorous fires begin to burn clearly, sending up their white smoke to the first stars; our camels, relieved of their burdens and their high saddles, sweep by the thin bushes, browsing on perfumed branches, like great fantastic sheep, of slow inoffensive demeanour. It is the hour when our Bedouins sit in a circle to tell stories and sing; the hour of rest, and the hour of dream, the delicious hour of nomadic life.

The Bedouins and camels tell us that the evening Loti is describing is an Eastern evening, but even these two touches of local colour, which were unavoidable, add nothing to the beauty of the passage; suppress them, turn the Bedouins into gipsies and the camels into horses, and it would be impossible to say whether the evening described had happened in England or Japan. Loti's intention was to describe something that is eternal in the heart of man, something that he has known always, that he knew ten thousand years before Nineveh, and that he will know ten thousand years hence. Mr. Kipling's intention is more ethnological than poetic. We learn from it that the parakeets and doves come home to the woods in the evening, we learn that the sun turns the faces and the bullocks' horns red as blood, and a variety of other things. From Loti's description we have learned nothing, but we have been moved, as we are moved when we look at a portrait by Rembrandt. Not for a moment must it be thought that I compare Loti with Rembrandt, Loti is a painter in water colours, his sentences flow fragile and transparent like flower blooms; but Rembrandt's intention and Loti's intention are the same—the intention is to interest us in things that always have been and always will be. But we envy Mr. Kipling his copious and sonorous vocabulary, especially his neologisms; he writes with the whole language, with the language of the Bible, and with the language of the streets. He can do this, for he possesses the ink-pot which turns the vilest tin idiom into gold. Last night, his description of the hills was for us a cup of mixed admiration and misery, and we repeat our impression that no one has written as well as this since the Elizabethans, since the Bible.

[quotes *Kim*, p. 334 to top of p. 336]

A miserable midnight is often succeeded by a sunny morning. It was a relief to awake forgetful of what I had read overnight. Envy! Of course! We're envious because we admire; the lay reader neither admires nor envies—art is for the artists. I was glad to awake forgetful of Mr. Kipling, thinking of Pierre Loti, of a book I had not seen for months. On looking into *Kim* again I found pages of dialogue, magnificently wrought, hard and breathless; a hardware shop with iron tulips hanging from the rafters and brass forget-me-nots on the counter. Loti is never hard. His attitude towards life is that of a child, of a blond ringleted child with bright blue eyes and hands full of flower-blooms, and a sensibility like that of a perverse child impelled to caresses.

. . . Mr. Kipling's prose goes to a marching rhythm, the trumpet's blare and the fife's shriek; there is the bass clarionet and the great bass tuba that emits a sound like the earth quaking fathoms deep or the cook shovelling coal in the coal-cellar. The band is playing variations: but variations on what theme? The theme will appear presently . . . Listen! There is the theme, the shoddy tune of the average man—'I know a trick worth two of that.'

42. G. K. Chesterton 'On Mr. Rudyard Kipling'

1905

Extract from the essay 'On Mr. Rudyard Kipling and Making the World Small', in *Heretics* (1905), pp. 38–53. The beginning of the essay is too general to include here, and the end wanders again: the extract from p. 42 to p. 51 gives all that Chesterton has to say about Kipling. For his review of *Just So Stories* see No. 38 (pp. 273–5) above.

. . . The first and fairest thing to say about Rudyard Kipling is that he has borne a brilliant part in recovering the lost provinces of poetry. He has not been frightened by that brutal materialistic air which clings only to words; he has pierced through to the romantic, imaginative matter of the things themselves. He has perceived the significance and philosophy of steam and of slang. Steam may be, if you like, a dirty by-product of science. Slang may be, if you like, a dirty by-product of language. But at least he has been among the few who saw the divine parentage of these things, and knew that where there is smoke there is fire—that is, that wherever there is the foulest of things, there also is the purest. Above all, he has had something to say, a definite view of things to utter, and that always means that a man is fearless and faces everything. For the moment we have a view of the universe, we possess it.

Now, the message of Rudyard Kipling, that upon which he has really concentrated, is the only thing worth worrying about in him or in any other man. He has often written bad poetry, like Wordsworth. He has often said silly things, like Plato. He has often given way to mere political hysteria, like Gladstone. But no one can reasonably doubt that he means steadily and sincerely to say something, and the only serious question is, what is that which he has tried to say? Perhaps the best way of stating this fairly will be to begin with that element which has been most insisted by himself and by his opponents—

I mean his interest in militarism. But when we are seeking for the real merits of a man it is unwise to go to his enemies, and much more foolish to go to himself.

Now, Mr. Kipling is certainly wrong in his worship of militarism, but his opponents are, generally speaking, quite as wrong as he. The evil of militarism, is not that it shows certain men to be fierce and haughty and excessively warlike. The evil of militarism is that it shows most men to be tame and timid and excessively peaceable. The professional soldier gains more and more power as the general courage of a community declines. Thus the Pretorian guard became more and more important in Rome as Rome became more and more luxurious and feeble. The military man gains the civil power in proportion as the civilian loses the military virtues. And as it was in ancient Rome so it is in contemporary Europe. There never was a time when nations were more militarist. There never was a time when men were less brave. All ages and all epics have sung of arms and the man; but we have effected simultaneously the deterioration of the man and the fantastic perfection of the arms. Militarism demonstrated the decadence of Rome, and it demonstrates the decadence of Prussia.

And unconsciously Mr. Kipling has proved this, and proved it admirably. For in so far as his work is earnestly understood the military trade does not by any means emerge as the most important or attractive. He has not written so well about soldiers as he has about railway men or bridge builders, or even journalists. The fact is that what attracts Mr. Kipling to militarism is not the idea of courage, but the idea of discipline. There was far more courage to the square mile in the Middle Ages, when no king had a standing army, but every man had a bow or sword. But the fascination of the standing army upon Mr. Kipling is not courage, which scarcely interests him, but discipline, which is, when all is said and done, his primary theme. The modern army is not a miracle of courage; it has not enough opportunities, owing to the cowardice of everybody else. But it is really a miracle of organization, and that is the truly Kiplingite ideal. Kipling's subject is not that valour which properly belongs to war, but that interdependence and efficiency which belongs quite as much to engineers, or sailors, or mules, or railway engines. And thus it is that when he writes of engineers, or sailors, or mules, or steam-engines, he writes at his best. The real poetry, the 'true-romance' which Mr. Kipling has taught, is the romance of the division of labour and the discipline of all the trades. He sings the arts of peace much more accurately than the arts of war. And his main contention is vital and valuable. Everything is military in the sense that everything depends upon obedience. There is no perfectly epicurean corner; there is no perfectly irresponsible place. Everywhere men have made the way for us with sweat and submission. We may fling ourselves into a hammock in a fit of divine carelessness. But we are glad that the net-maker did not make the hammock in a fit of divine carelessness. We may jump upon a child's rocking-horse for a joke. But we are glad that the carpenter did not leave the legs of it unglued for a joke. So far from having merely preached that a soldier cleaning his side-arm is to be adored because he is military, Kipling at his best and clearest has preached that the baker baking loaves and the tailor cutting coats is as military as anybody.

Being devoted to this multitudinous vision of duty, Mr. Kipling is naturally a cosmopolitan. He happens to find his examples in the British Empire, but almost any other empire would do as well, or, indeed, any other highly civilized country. That which he admires in the British Army he would find even more apparent in the German Army; that which he desires in the British police he would find flourishing in the French police. The ideal of discipline is not the whole of life, but it is spread over the whole of the world. And the worship of it tends to confirm in Mr. Kipling a certain note of worldly wisdom, of the experience of the wanderer, which is one of the genuine charms of his best work.

The great gap in his mind is what may be roughly called the lack of patriotism—that is to say, he lacks altogether the faculty of attaching himself to any cause or community finally and tragically; for all finality must be tragic. He admires England, but he does not love her; for we admire things with reasons, but love them without reasons. He admires England because she is strong, not because she is English. There is no harshness in saying this, for, to do him justice, he avows it with his usual picturesque candour. In a very interesting poem, he says that—

If England was what England seems

—that is, weak and inefficient; if England were not what (as he believes) she is—that is, powerful and practical—

How quick we'd chuck 'er! But she ain't!

He admits, that is, that his devotion is the result of a criticism, and this is quite enough to put it in another category altogether from the patriotism of the Boers, whom he hounded down in South Africa. In speaking of the really patriotic peoples, such as the Irish, he has some difficulty in keeping a shrill irritation out of his language. The frame of mind which he really describes with beauty and nobility is the frame of mind of the cosmopolitan man who has seen men and cities.

> For to admire and for to see,
> For to be'old this world so wide.

He is a perfect master of that light melancholy with which a man looks back on having been the citizen of many communities, of that light melancholy with which a man looks back on having been the lover of many women. He is the philanderer of the nations. But a man may have learnt much about women in flirtations, and still be ignorant of first love; a man may have known as many lands as Ulysses, and still be ignorant of patriotism.

Mr. Rudyard Kipling has asked in a celebrated epigram what they can know of England who know England only. It is a far deeper and sharper question to ask: 'What can they know of England who know only the world?' for the world does not include England any more than it includes the Church. The moment we care for anything deeply, the world—that is, all the other miscellaneous interests—becomes our enemy. Christians showed it when they talked of keeping one's self 'unspotted from the world'; but lovers talk of it just as much when they talk of the 'world well lost'. Astronomically speaking, I understand that England is situated on the world; similarly, I suppose that the Church was a part of the world, and even the lovers inhabitants of that orb. But they all felt a certain truth—the truth that the moment you love anything the world becomes your foe. Thus Mr. Kipling does certainly know the world; he is a man of the world, with all the narrowness that belongs to those imprisoned in that planet. He knows England as an intelligent English gentleman knows Venice. He has been to England a great many times; he has stopped there for long visits. But he does not belong to it, or to any place; and the proof of it is this, that he thinks of England as a place. The moment we are rooted in a place the place vanishes. We live like a tree with the whole strength of the universe.

The globe-trotter lives in a smaller world than the peasant. He is always breathing an air of locality. London is a place, to be compared to Chicago; Chicago is a place, to be compared to Timbuctoo. But Timbuctoo is not a place, since there, at least, live men who regard it as the

universe, and breathe, not an air of locality, but the winds of the world.
The man in the saloon steamer has seen all the races of men, and he is
thinking of the things that divide men—diet, dress, decorum, rings in
the nose as in Africa, or in the ears as in Europe, blue paint among the
ancients, or red paint among the modern Britons. The man in the
cabbage field has seen nothing at all; but he is thinking of the things
that unite men—hunger and babies, and the beauty of women, and
the promise or menace of the sky. Mr. Kipling, with all his merits, is
the globe-trotter; he has not the patience to become part of anything.
So great and genuine a man is not to be accused of a merely cynical
cosmopolitanism; still, his cosmopolitanism is his weakness. That weakness is splendidly expressed in one of his finest poems, 'The Sestina of
the Tramp Royal', in which a man declares that he can endure anything
in the way of hunger or horror, but not permanent presence in one
place. In this there is certainly danger. The more dead and dry and dusty
a thing is the more it travels about; dust is like this and the thistledown
and the High Commissioner in South Africa. Fertile things are somewhat
heavier, like the heavy fruit trees on the pregnant mud of the Nile. In
the heated idleness of youth we were all rather inclined to quarrel
with the implication of that proverb which says that a rolling stone
gathers no moss. We were inclined to ask: 'Who wants to gather moss,
except silly old ladies?' But for all that we begin to perceive that the
proverb is right. The rolling stone rolls echoing from rock to rock;
but the rolling stone is dead. The moss is silent because the moss is
alive . . .

43. Alfred Noyes on 'Kipling the Mystic'

1906

Signed review of *Puck of Pook's Hill* in the *Bookman* (London), Vol. XXXI, pp. 81–2 (November 1906).

Alfred Noyes (1880–1958) was a poet of some distinction, now unduly neglected. His *The Flower of Old Japan* (1903) and *The Forest of Wild Thyme* (1905) have been described as 'the finest fairy poetry since the Elizabethans', while several of his lyrics and ballads have become standard anthology pieces. He was Professor of Modern English Literature at Princeton (1914–23), and published a volume of critical essays, *Aspects of Modern Poetry* in 1924.

'Chops, more chops, bloody ones with gristle in them!'—the cry, of the baser sort of Imperialist—has gently subsided into a fat smile, a benevolent radiation of sweetness and light, since it dawned upon the Mafficking patriot that he must pay, pay, pay and yet again pay, for even his most sanguinary and most human chops with his own yellow coin. We have not much belief in the depth of either of these common moods; but we believe there are 'the makings of a blooming soul' somewhere behind them, and that these outward manifestations correspond to merely momentary circumstances. There are men on both sides, however, in whose deep-seated sincerity one is compelled to believe. There were heroes on opposite sides in the *Iliad*. There are heroes on opposite sides to-day. There would be no grandeur in life but for the fact that its opposites are mighty, and that all great sincerities, if they go deep enough, are rooted in imperishable unity. Whether hard words—traitor, card-sharper, brute and ghoul—break bones or not, they never impart one tremor to that steadfast plinth of things. Political hatreds are of the day, of the hour, of the moment. Death smooths out our troubles; Death—and Love. 'In fifty years,' declares the great Norman of Mr. Kipling's new book, as, with a kind of defiant fury, he sanctions the betrothal of a Saxon maid to another Norman, 'in fifty years there will be neither Norman nor

Saxon, but all English'. It will always be the 'plinth of things' with which true patriotic literature is concerned. Brutus falls; and—if only in the poet's dream—the Antony who drove him to his death must mourn over his body: 'This was the noblest Roman of them all.' We have small concern with the little irrelevancies of their mortal feud. If Caesar, *if* Caesar, we say, now lies ill at Highbury, we may be assured that the overwhelming Liberal majority is not altogether of the party of Cassius. It may be true that Caesar was ambitious; but if and if he were Caesar in very truth, then very certainly it must also be true, in nine cases out of ten, that Brutus is an honourable man who, below the surface of politics, loves not Caesar less, but Rome more. 'Many roads thou hast fashioned: all of them lead to the Light!' That is one of the lines in Mr. Kipling's 'Hymn to Mithras' in the Roman portion of his new book; and it is a very significant one. We see, in this book, signs of a great change in Mr. Kipling. It is not, perhaps, his best work; but it looks like the beginning of his best and greatest work. It would certainly be the most interesting of all his writings if it were not for the fact that it illuminates and makes his former work even more arresting than it was when he had 'a voice with which statesmen might have to reckon'. In his last book of poems there was one of great pathos called 'The Palace', which describes how a Master Builder cleared him ground for a house such as a king should build, and how—under the silt—he came on the wreck of another palace built by a forgotten king.

> There was no worth in the fashion—there was no wit in the plan—
> Hither and thither, aimless, the ruined footings ran—
> Masonry, brute, mishandled, but carven on every stone
> After me cometh a Builder. Tell him, I too have known.

So to his own well-planned ground-works he tumbled the old quoins and ashlars, cut and reset them anew, and, as the old builder had risen and pleaded, he strove to understand 'the form of the dream he had followed in the face of the thing he had planned'.

> When I was a King and a Mason—in the open noon of my pride,
> They sent me a Word from the Darkness—they whispered and called me
> aside.
> They said—'The end is forbidden.' They said—'Thy use is fulfilled,
> And thy palace shall stand as that other's—the spoil of a king who shall
> build.'
> I called my men from my trenches, my quarries, my wharves, and my
> shears.
> All I had wrought I abandoned to the faith of the faithless years.

Only I cut on the timber, only I carved on the stone:
After me cometh a Builder. Tell him, I, too, have known.

In *Puck of Pook's Hill* we suspect that Mr. Kipling has for the first time dug through the silt of modern Imperialism. He has gone back to the old ground-works and seen the inscription upon them. The scheme of the book is simple. Some children meet Puck, the fairy, who introduces them in separate, yet connected stories to Romans, Normans, Saxons, Picts and Englishmen from different periods of our history; and the chief of these characters tell their own stories—grim, humorous and pathetic, in a manner illustrating the respective period of each; and on each successive period one seems to find inscribed— *After me cometh a Builder!* We know no book in the guise of fiction that gives the pageant of our history with such breadth and nobility of feeling, and with so sure and easy a touch. There are few passages in modern fiction more beautiful than that which describes the chivalry of a Norman to a conquered Saxon woman, whom he falls in love with, and eventually, though at first she rails against him as an enemy, wins and weds. There are few passages in modern fiction more stoically grand than the farewell letter of the doomed Caesar to his two young captains on the Great Wall. And always the cry is, *After me cometh a Builder!* It is impossible to say how far we are justified in saying that Mr. Kipling sees the writing on a certain modern wall; but there seems to be a note of very deep pathos in the 'Hymn to Mithras':

> Mithras, God of the Noontide, the heather swims in the heat,
> Our helmets scorch our foreheads; our sandals burn our feet.
> Now, in the ungirt hour; now, ere we blink and drowse,
> Mithras, also a soldier, keep us true to our vows!

And also there is an unexpected note of a very noble humility in the children's final hymn:

> Teach us the strength that cannot seek,
> By deed or thought, to hurt the weak;
> That, under Thee, we may possess
> Man's strength to comfort man's distress.

Mr. Kipling was, at the high tide of popular Imperialism, one of the very few popular Imperialists who could either have written or echoed the feeling of his 'Recessional'. His cry to the true Romance was 'Thy face is far from this our war!' How deep this vein of mysticism goes in him it is impossible, at present, to judge. But let popular Imperialists beware of him. The day may come when he will turn and rend them as he turned and rent large masses of his devoted readers in that delightful onslaught which he called 'The Islanders'. Mystics are always dangerous—to materialists, at any rate; and Mr. Kipling has mysticism in his blood and in his bones. He is, moreover, taking much broader and larger views of cities and men than he did when he wrote his verses on Bombay, for instance. It is a far cry from those verses to this, in his *Puck of Pook's Hill*:

> Cities and Thrones and Powers
> Stand in Time's eye
> Almost as long as flowers
> Which daily die:
> But, as new buds put forth
> To glad new men,
> Out of the spent and unconsidered earth
> The Cities rise again.

If Mr. Kipling has really dug through the silt, as we suspect; if he has, indeed, discovered that all roads lead to the Light, and that the greatness of a people depends, eventually, on that finer strength of love, he is indeed at the beginning of his greatest work. He was never more 'the interpreter to the English-speaking peoples' than he is in this book. Puck occasionally drops even into American-isms! Certainly it is one of those works which hasten the fulness of that time when there will be less need to inscribe on our palaces, *After me cometh a builder.*

44. Conan Doyle on 'Kipling's Best Story'

1907

Extract from *Through the Magic Door* (1907), pp. 118–19. Originally published in *Cassell's Magazine* from November 1906 to November 1907. Only the first paragraph of the following extract appeared in the serial (Vol. XLIII, p. 696, April 1907)—the second was added in book form.

Sir Arthur Conan Doyle (1859–1930) was, in his own kind, one of the leading short-story writers of the period. He seldom indulged in literary criticism—but his comments on his own particular kind of literature are interesting. Besides Kipling, he chose stories by Scott, Poe, Stevenson, Lytton, with Hawthorne, Grant Allen, H. G. Wells and Quiller-Couch in a slightly lower class. He considered Poe 'the world's supreme short story writer', and put Maupassant second.

Which are the greatest short stories of the English language? . . . If it be not an impertinence to mention a contemporary I should certainly have a brace from Rudyard Kipling. His power, his compression, his dramatic sense, his way of glowing suddenly into a vivid flame, all mark him as a great master. But which are we to choose from that long and varied collection, many of which have claims to the highest? Speaking from memory, I should say that the stories of his which have impressed me most are 'The Drums of the Fore and Aft', 'The Man Who Would be King', 'The Man who Was', and 'The Brushwood Boy'. Perhaps, on the whole, it is the first two which I should choose to add to my list of masterpieces.

They are stories which invite criticism and yet defy it. The great batsman at cricket is the man who can play an unorthodox game, take every liberty which is denied to inferior players, and yet succeed brilliantly in the face of his disregard of law. So it is here. I should think the model of these stories is the most dangerous that any young writer could follow. There is digression, that most deadly fault in the short narrative; there is incoherence, there is want of proportion which makes the story stand still for pages and bound forward in a few sentences. But genius overrides all that, just as the great cricketer hooks the off ball and glides the straight one to leg. There is a dash, an exuberance, a full-blooded confident mastery which carries everything before it. Yes, no team of immortals would be complete which did not contain at least two representatives of Kipling.

45. Ford Madox Hueffer's 'Critical Attitude'

1911

Extracts from *The Critical Attitude* (1911) by Ford Madox Hueffer; pp. 4, 106 and 177.

Ford Madox Hueffer (1873–1939) later changed his surname to Ford, and became famous as a novelist. Before he changed his name he collaborated in two novels with Joseph Conrad, wrote children's books, and founded the *English Review*.

There is a considerable writer—once he wrote the best short stories that are to be found in English literature, now, alas! *il pontifie*—there is a certain writer who once said that he welcomed the coming of the motor-car because it would make the Englishman think. We confess to having always been unable to get at the inner significance of this phrase. One motor-car might take an Englishman to Brighton, but could ten thousand make him think? Assuredly not, for nothing could make him think; nothing could make him review his thoughts. PAGE 106 The most dismal instance of this last tendency [attempting to become a social reformer, etc.] is Mr. Rudyard Kipling. In him we have a writer of gifts almost as great as gifts could be. To read merely, let us say *Stalky & Co.* is to be almost overwhelmed by the cleverness in handling incident and in suggesting atmosphere. But at a certain stage of his career Mr. Kipling became instinct with the desire to be of importance, with the result that, using his monumental and semi-biblical language, alternating it with his matchless use of colloquialisms, Mr. Kipling set out to attack world problems from the point of view of the journalists' club smoking-room and with the ambitions of a sort of cross between the German Emperor of caricature and a fifth-form public-schoolboy. This is a lamentable record, for in Mr. Kipling we seem to have lost for good a poet of the highest vitality, a writer the most emotionally suggestive.

PAGE 177 There is only one poet living who has ever appealed to the British public with a sort of clarion note such as was the Tennyson's of 'Riflemen Form'. And it is characteristic that this poet, Mr. Kipling, appealed to the same set of emotions. This set of emotions—those of patriotism, of voluntary service, and of simple physical aggression—probably remain dormant and ready to the hand of any writer with sufficient technical skill to awaken them. Mr. Kipling came exceedingly near being a great poet. Moreover, he is so exceedingly near to a supreme verbal skill, and so exceedingly near to the power of using the rhythm of music as only a genius can, that Mr. Kipling may yet—for all I should care to dogmatise—stand out as the representatively national figure amongst a band of singers as numerous, and as intimately satisfactory, as were ever the minor Elizabethans and the early Jacobeans. Mr. Kipling as a poet has never been regarded with very much critical attention, though his popularity was at one time as unboundedly swelling as it now is, rather unreasonably, on the wane. He is to be commended as much for his boldness in the use of the vernacular, as for his skill and his boldness, too, in catching the rhythm of popular music, with its quaint and fascinating irregularities.

But, with the exception of Mr. Kipling, there is no poet today who attempts successfully to sing of patriotism or any of the other eternal verities. And it is characteristic of the age that the poetry upon which Mr. Kipling built the platform for verse of such bland popularity as 'The absent-minded Beggar'—the poetry which put him in a position to become a prophet, was poetry not of a patriotic or of a national character—was poetry not even of a military type, but was the poetry of intimacy. Thus 'On the Road to Mandalay' expressed not heroic resolve, not the determination to die for England, but the nostalgia of an individual.

46. H. G. Wells on Kipling

1911 : 1920

Quotations from (1) *The New Machiavelli* (1911), Book 1, Chap. 4, Section 6, pp. 128–30; and (2) *The Outline of History* (1920), pp. 521–2.

Herbert George Wells (1866–1946), potentially great novelist and writer of scientific fantasy until (in Chesterton's phrase) he 'sold his birthright for a pot of message', veered sharply in his opinion of Kipling when he appointed himself social reformer instead of imaginative writer. In *When the Sleeper Wakes* (1899) he described 'The Man Who Would be King' as 'one of the best stories in the world', but in his *Experiment in Autobiography* (1934) described Kipling as 'the most incomprehensible of my contemporaries, with phases of real largeness and splendour and lapses into the quality of those mucky little sadists *Stalky & Co.*'.

(1) The prevailing force in my undergraduate days was not Socialism but Kiplingism. Our set was quite exceptional in its socialistic professions. And we were all, you must understand, very distinctly Imperialists also, and professed a vivid sense of the 'White Man's Burden'. It is a little difficult now to get back to the feelings of that period; Kipling has since been so mercilessly and exhaustively mocked, criticized and torn to shreds—never was a man so violently exalted and then, himself assisting, so relentlessly called down. But in the middle nineties this spectacled and moustached little figure with its heavy chin and its general effect of vehement gesticulation, its wild shouts of boyish enthusiasm for effective force, its lyric delight in the sounds and colours, in the very odours of Empire, its wonderful discovery of machinery and cotton waste and the under-officer and the engineer, and 'shop' as a poetic dialect, became almost a national symbol. He got hold of us wonderfully, he filled us with tinkling and haunting quotations, he stirred Britten and myself to futile imitations, he

coloured the very idiom of our conversation. He rose to his climax with his 'Recessional', while I was still an undergraduate.

What did he give me exactly?

He helped to broaden my geographical sense immensely, and he provided phrases for just that desire for discipline and devotion and organized effort the Socialism of our time failed to express, that the current socialist movement still fails, I think, to express. The sort of thing that follows, for example, tore something out of my inmost nature and gave it a shape, and I took it back from him shaped and let much of the rest of him, the tumult and the bullying, the hysteria and the impatience, the incoherence and inconsistency, go uncriticized for the sake of it:

> Keep ye the Law—be swift in all obedience
> Clear the land of evil, drive the road and bridge the ford,
> Make ye sure to each his own
> That he reap where he hath sown;
> By the peace among Our peoples let men know we serve the
> Lord!

And then again, and for all our later criticism, this sticks in my mind, sticks there now as quintessential wisdom:

> The 'eathen in 'is blindness bows down to wood an' stone;
> 'E don't obey no orders unless they is 'is own;
> 'E keeps 'is side-arms awful: 'e leaves 'em all about,
> An' then comes up the regiment an' pokes the 'eathen out.
> All along o' dirtiness, all along o' mess,
> All along o' doing things rather-more-or-less,
> All along of *abby-nay*, *kul*, an *hazar-ho*,
> Mind you keep your rifle an' yourself just so!

It is after all a secondary matter that Kipling, not having been born and brought up in Bromstead and Penge, and the war in South Africa being yet in the womb of time, could quite honestly entertain the now remarkable delusion that England had her side-arms at that time kept anything but 'awful'. He learnt better, and we all learnt with him in the dark years of exasperating and humiliating struggle that followed, and I do not see that we fellow-learners are justified in turning resentfully upon him for a common ignorance and assumption.

(2) . . . It was quite characteristic of the times [the late nineties] that Mr. Kipling should lead the children of the middle and upper-class British public back to the Jungle, to learn 'the law', and that in his

book *Stalky & Co.* he should give an appreciative description of the torture of two boys by three others, who have by a subterfuge tied up their victims helplessly before revealing their hostile intentions.

It is worth while to give a little attention to this incident in *Stalky & Co.*, because it lights up the political psychology of the British Empire at the close of the nineteenth century very vividly. The history of the last half-century is not to be understood without an understanding of the mental twist which this story exemplifies. The two boys who are tortured are 'bullies', that is the excuse of their tormentors, and these latter have further been excited to this orgy by a clergyman. Nothing can restrain the gusto with which they (and Mr. Kipling) set about the job. Before resorting to torture, the teaching seems to be, see that you pump up a little justifiable moral indignation, and all will be well. If you have the authorities on your side, then you cannot be to blame. Such, apparently, is the simple doctrine of this typical imperialist. But every bully has to the best of his ability followed that doctrine since the human animal developed sufficient intelligence to be consciously cruel.

Another point in the story is very significant indeed. The headmaster and his clerical assistant are both represented as being privy to the affair. They want this bullying to occur. Instead of exercising their own authority, they use these boys, who are Mr. Kipling's heroes, to punish the two victims. Headmaster and clergyman turn a deaf ear to the complaints of an indignant mother. All this Mr. Kipling represents as a most desirable state of affairs. In this we have the key to the ugliest, most retrogressive, and finally fatal idea of modern imperialism; the idea of a *tacit conspiracy between the law and illegal violence* . . .

47. Dixon Scott on 'Rudyard Kipling'

1912

Signed article in the *Bookman* (London), Vol. XLIII, pp. 143–6 (December 1912). Later collected in the author's *Men of Letters* (1916), pp. 48–62.

Dixon Scott (1881–1915) was a critic of great promise whose early death cut short his achievement. Many of his reviews were collected after his death in *Men of Letters* (1916)—including this which, as 'The Meekness of Mr. Rudyard Kipling', occupies pages 48–62.

A writer's reputation is often a kind of premature ghost that stalks between him and his audience, blurring their vision; but in Mr. Kipling's case this *doppelgänger* has proved specially pobby and impervious and full of energy. The convincing autobiography it rattles off runs something like this: 'I came out of the East, a youngster of twenty, but wiser than your very oldest men. Life had told me her last secrets, I could do anything I liked with words, and I tossed you tales of twisted deaths and queer adulteries with the nonchalant neatness of a conjurer and an air of indulgent half-contempt. I was an uncanny mixture of bored pierrot and bland priest; and in my splendid insolence (I was only twenty, mind you), I made poetry learn slang and set her serving in canteens. "Born blasé," muttered one of your own writers, maddened—himself reckoned something of a prodigy. I was the cleverest young man of my day.

And then I came West to your dingy, cosy Babylon, and tasted fame and fleshpots: very good. And the brightness died out of my colours and the snap from my tunes. Your snug horizons hemmed me in, I lost my vision, I relied contentedly on tricks I'd learned before. I wrote a bad novel and it made a worse drama. I made money, I made speeches, I spoiled my paints with party politics. And now here I am, sir, the popular favourite—*Vide* Max—Seen the *Post*? 'Save the King!'

Well, the main desire of this article is to denounce all that as perjury

—force aside the phantom—gain a glimpse of the real man behind; to suggest, that, instead of depreciating, the quality of his work has constantly improved, that his technique has never been so amazing as now, nor his artistic integrity more Lutheran;—and that instead of immensely precocious and worldly-wise—'born blasé' as Barrie (it was Barrie) once said—this young poet has always been, far more than Barrie himself, one of those who never grow up, who are never quite at home in the world, but who wander through it, like Hawthorne or Poe, a little alien and wistful, a little elf-like—and that this quality of envy of 'the happy folk in housen', of the practical grown-ups and worldlings, is indeed the essential characteristic of the man and the key to and core of his work.

Now to get the first glimmer of the ghost, to follow this Jekyll-and-Hyding from the outset, it is necessary to go back to the days of the *Ditties*—so swiftly did the severance begin. Many readers, not yet aged, will no doubt still remember the stab and glitter of the first Kipling furore, and the way the critical raptures went rocketing up, breaking into a superior fire of epigrams, eager to announce the discovery. A new star had arisen, a rival to Loti, and the elect were at once in full song. Perhaps the hour was specially apt for such an overture. It was the hour of the eighties, the ineffable, amateur eighties, when a recondite vulgarity was the vogue; and aesthetic London was not at all unanxious to display its capacity for enjoying raw sensation. Hedonism had deserted the Oxford of Pater for 'The Oxford'[1] of Marie Lloyd and Walter Sickert. If you were a poet you were ashamed not to be seen in cabmen's shelters; and a little hashish was considered quite the thing. A superior hour! And so, when the rag-time chords of the *Departmental Ditties* flicked and snapped an introduction to the laconic patter of the *Tales*, and when the *Tales* themselves, with their parakeets and ivory, their barbaric chic and rubricated slang, proved a mixture of Persian print and music-hall, then the 'ten superior persons scattered through the universe', were persuaded that their hour had found its very voice, that they were listening to the last delicious insolence of aesthetics:

> 'Er petticoat was yaller and 'er little cap was green,
> An' 'er name was Supi-yaw-lat—jes' the same as
>   Theebaw's queen;
> An' I see 'er first a-smokin' of a whackin' white cheroot,

---

[1] ['The Oxford' was a London music hall]

An' a-wastin' Christian kisses on an 'eathen idol's foot:
Bloomin' idol made o' mud
Wot they called the great Gawd Budd
Plucky lot she cared for idols when I kissed her where she
stood.

More daring, this, than even lithographs of music-halls: bizarrerie of the best. The youngster was bracketed with Beardsley, was bracketed with 'Max'. Mr. John Lane began to collect his first editions; Mr. Richard Le Gallienne was told off to Bodley Head him. Mr. Gosse (this is perfectly true), Mr. Edmund Gosse spake publicly of 'the troubling thrill, the voluptuous and agitating sentiment', which these tales sent through his system. The little sun-baked books from Allahabad seemed if anything more golden than *The Yellow Book*. The proof of the literary epicure was his palate for the Kipling liqueur.

And then the exasperating fellow became popular.

What do you call the apostles of the Cubists? Cubicles? Very well then. Consider the consternation of the cubicles if the general public began to clamour for Picassos. Think even of Mr. Roger Fry's chagrin if we made a popular favourite of Matisse. A consternation not dissimilar, we may be sure, shuddered through the initiates of the nineties. Absurd, of course, to suggest that the paling of critical approval, the soft extinction of the starrier estimates, was entirely due to the widening blaze of popularity; but even critics are human, and it helped. It was impossible to watch their liqueur being drained like Bass without having doubts about its quality. They felt that the public's enjoyment of Kipling was too true to be good. They grew querulous, they qualified, they discovered defects.

The defects they discovered, the demands which they made, and the effect of all this hedging and shuffling on Mr. Kipling's development, we will consider in a moment. Remark, parenthetically, first, what an entirely wholesome and satisfactory thing that wider popularity was—and is. There is probably no living writer who is regarded, in England, with such widespread and unprompted veneration. It is the nearest thing we have nowadays to the reverence that used to be excited by the great literary figures of last century. It is touching, it is beautiful, it is altogether honest and good. Bank clerks and clerics, doctors, and drapers, journalists, joiners, engineers,—the average sinful jurymen and his usual daughters and wife, all speak of this man and his work much as another kind of people speak of Wagner. Only, honestly.

There is no priggishness about it, nor any desire to impress or be improved; and yet they find beauty in his work, they find magic, they find hints of strange forces and powers and constant reminders of something unimaginable beyond; they experience that delicious commotion of the blood we call romance, and are thrilled and shaken and renewed by it much as others of us are supposed to be renewed and thrilled by poetry. And at the same time, unlike so much of their 'romance', it is never a mere dallying with lotus-land sensations, a coloured refuge from the drudge of day. Its action is always to excite their zest for life, to send them back into reality more exultantly—not (of course) because of any policy it may preach, but because it so crisply handles, names, and sanctifies, the tools of each man's trade. Much has been written of Mr. Kipling's capacity for picking up knowledge from experts; far too little of the lessons the experts have learned from him. He has renewed the workman's pride in his work and restored their mystery to the crafts. He has done more than any man of his time to make the middle-classes less middle-class.

But all this the ten superior ones were in no position to foresee. Said they, *Yellow Book*?—we meant yellow press. Said they—but he *likes* the music-hall? And, to him—these little tales are very neat, very clever; but before we can take you seriously you must produce a full-length novel. This is striking—but is it Art?

And the real Rudyard Kipling? Had been meanwhile moved, one avers, as little by a desire to please the great public as by the desire to *épater* it. Essentially a dreamer, born in exile, he was oddly innocent of all the motives men ascribed to him—and it was an accident of environment, and a streak of sinful pride, and a sort of homely emulation, that really determined his first choice of tone and topic—the violent topics and the casual tone of those *Plain Tales from the Hills*. He had no notion of exalting the common soldier. He wanted rather the soldier to reverence the pen. His spur was the kind of half-resentment from which many writers suffer—the emotion that probably had a good deal to do with the making of 'Don Juan', and that is accountable for Mr. Shaw's affection of ferocity and that perhaps prompted Mr. Maurice Hewlett's early hectics. It is the artist's human retort to that intolerable tolerance with which the workers, doers, men of action, regard his anaemic indoor trade. It was Beetle's way of enforcing respect at Westward Ho! It was young Kipling's way of adjusting things at Simla. He would prove that ink is thicker than blood and the pen more masculine than the sword; and that a certain small spectacled sub-editor fond of poetry was not quite the lamb that he looked. And so he borrowed tales from the bazaars and the barracks, and Bret-Hartened them and pointed them with Poe; and wrote them out, with an infinite cunning, in a hand like an indifferent drawl. One of the ways of out-Heroding Herod is to yawn when the head is brought in. Mr. Kipling's yawn was a masterpiece. His make-up was perfect, the deception complete; the mess-rooms were duly impressed: it was another victory for the pen ...

But a mask is a dangerous thing; it often moulds the face beneath. Left alone with his soothing Simla success, quietly sheltered behind it, young Kipling might indeed now have softly discarded his make-up and let his instincts find their native expression. But there leapt out upon him from Europe our roar of applause, and that riveted him to his role. Even the dabs of deprecation, the raps from falling rocket sticks, perversely whipped him in the same direction. 'You can write these little tales,' said they, 'but are you knowing enough to write long ones?' He did not know enough: he was never meant to be a novelist—but even less was he adapted for letting taunts slip by unanswered, and so he set his teeth, took up the challenge, and produced *The Light that Failed*. It did fail; and the critics who were really its sponsors had their moment of mean triumph. But by now his pride was in pledge; he would write a brilliant novel if it broke him; and for ten years he fought out fresh perfections of technique, using his convention of violence to hammer out new details of equipment until at length by dint of sheer virtuosity he achieved the protracted tale called *Kim*. He himself, it is said, considers *Kim* his master-work. He might well view it as a second vindication; his work henceforward, if I see it aright, stands for one long attempt on the part of his relieved genius to loosen the bars it had built about itself, and to twist an alien and artificial technique into an instrument for its deeper desires.

For it is the books that followed *Kim*—it is *Traffics and Discoveries, Actions and Reactions, Puck of Pook's Hill, Rewards and Fairies,* and the concurrent verse—that betray to us most clearly this queer subterranean disharmony and feud. If a reader will take these four books and consider them apart; if he will let their characteristics form a picture in his mind, an image of the kind of man who wrote them; and if he will then apply this reagent to the books that came before *Kim*, he will see how it eats out their accidentals. The falsities fade, there is a linking up of lighter touches, certain qualities, unrecognised before, rise glittering like veins. This fundamental filigree, this clear resultant mesh, is a map of Kipling's mind.

Now of this fundamental Kipling the cardinal qualities are three. The first is a passion for definition—a spiritual horror, almost desperate, of vagueness—a hunger for certitude and system. The second is the imaginative instrument of the first: a prodigious mental faculty, namely, for enforcing design, compelling coherence, for stamping dream-stuff into shapes as clean-cut and decisive as minted metal discs. And the third, on the physical plane, is the almost manual counterpart of these: a craftsman's cunning and capacity for fitting these terse units into complex patterns, adjusting them like the works of a watch with an exquisite accuracy, achieving miracles of minute mechanical perfection.

These are the three faculties, often bitted and strained, that form everywhere the sinews. Take, first, because most obvious, the so-called technical elements of his style. 'There is a writer called Stevenson,' he once said, 'who makes the most delicate inlay-work in black-and-white and files out to the fraction of a hair.' Kipling's own work is no less free from fluff or haze or slackness. The rhythms run with a snap from stop to stop; every sentence is as straight as a string; each has its self-contained tune. Prise one of them out of its place and you feel it would fall with a clink, leaving a slot that would never close up as the holes do in woollier work. Replace it, and it locks back like type in a forme, fitting into the paragraph as the paragraph fits into the tale. There are no glides or grace-notes, or blown spray of sound. Most prose that loves rhythm yields its music like a mist, an emanation that forms a bloom on the page, softly blurring the partitions of the periods. Kipling's prose shrinks stiffly from this trustfulness. The rhythms must report themselves promptly, prove their validity, start afresh after the full-stop. Lack of faith, if you like—but, also, constant keenness of craftsmanship.

Turn next to the optical integers—the sudden scenes which stud his page like inlaid stones. '*The leisurely ocean all patterned with peacocks' eyes of foam.*' '*I swung the car to clear the turf, brushed along the edge of the wood, and turned in on the broad stone path to where the fountain-basin lay like one star-sapphire.*' '*When his feet touched that still water, it changed, with a rustle of unrolling maps, to nothing less than a sixth quarter of the globe, with islands coloured yellow and blue, their lettering strung across their faces.*' And these are no mere decorations. These tales are jewelled, as watches are; it is round these tense, irreducible details that the action revolves. What is the emotional axis of 'The Finest

313

Story in the World?' It is that '*silver wire laid along the bulwarks which I thought was never going to break*'. Are we to know that a man was struck dumb? Then '*just as the lightning shot two tongues that cut the sky into three pieces . . . something wiped his lips of speech as a mother wipes the milky lips of her child*'. The motive of all his tales, as of 'At the End of the Passage', is a picture seen in a lens. Even the shadowy outer influences that brood over Kim's life, the inscrutable Powers that move in its background, come to us first in shapes vivid as heraldry—as a red Bull on a Field, as a House of Many Pillars; and before the close are resolved into the two most definite, clean-cut, and systematic of all earthly organisations: the military mechanism of India and the precise apparatus of Freemasonry. Kipling must have pattern and precision—and he has the power as well as the will. He can crush the sea into a shape as sharp as a crystal, can compress the Himalayas into a little lacquer-like design, has even in 'The Night Mail'—that clean, adroit, contenting piece of craftsmanship—printed a pattern on the empty air. He is primarily a pattern-maker; and the little pieces thus obtained he builds into a larger picture still. As the sentence into the paragraph—as the paragraph into the page—so do these sharp-edged items click together to form a geometrical pattern called the plot.

'The pattern called the plot.' It is here that we come very close to the irony that has ruled and wrenched all his career. Switch this mapmaking, pattern-making faculty upon the third element in fiction, the element of human nature, and what is the inevitable result? Inevitably, there is the same sudden stiffening and formulation. The characters spring to attention like soldiers on parade; they respond briskly to a certain description; they wear a fixed suit of idiosyncrasies like a uniform. A mind like this must use types and set counters; it feels dissatisfied, unsafe, ineffective, unless it can reduce the fluid waverings of character, its flitting caprices and twilight desires, to some tangible system. His characters will not only be definite; they will be definitions. His heroes will be courage incarnate; his weak men will be unwaveringly weak; and those who are mixed will be mixed mathematically, with all their traits clearly related to and explained by some neat blend of blood and race and caste behind. Is not all this true of Kipling's characters? They are marked by a strange immobility. They strike certain attitudes and retain them. Mulvaney, Ortheris and Learoyd live long but never alter; Kim never grows up. And indeed it is this very fixity that makes the short stories so effective. Their maker took these frozen gestures, rigid faces and tense attitudes, and fitted them together to form his effect; and whilst the inflexibility was exactly what he needed for neat mosaic-work, for making the sudden star called the story, the vividness of the details ('life seen by lightning-flashes' someone called them) seemed to prove the piercing humanity of the writer. It was only when he tried to construct a novel with them that the stiffness of these details turned to obstinacy, and their numbness became a kind of death. A short tale can be told in tableau—but a novel is not a long short tale. The pattern of *The Light that Failed* is as neat as the most successful of the *contes*, but it is the static symmetry of decoration and stained glass. It is applied art—that is to say, misapplied art. Its logic is not that of life. The characters are stowed into the interstices of a design that relies upon their remaining fixed quantities.

Perceive then, the almost maddening position! The very qualities that made the first tales tell, that seemed to prove his supreme capacity for fiction, are exactly the qualities that cut him off from the ability to write novels. The novelist is essentially the explorer, the questioner, the opener of doors; and the only law of human nature he knows is that the exception is the rule. But Mr. Kipling's first word is obedience; he is all for rules and rivets; for regularity and a four-square plan. Born under the sign of the Balance, his emblem is the compass and the square—and it is not with tools like these that men's motives can be measured. His vision of the world, like the Lama's, is a Wheel of Life with a neat niche for the individual; and even his famous militarism, his worship of the apparatus of war, is nothing more, in essence, than a longing for quiet comeliness and order. It is the mind, if you like, of a martinet—incapable therefore of complete imaginative sympathy. Any lapse from efficiency fills his craftsman's nature with disgust, and the only characters he can handle with perfect satisfaction are the Stricklands, the Mowglis, the Kims, as unconquerably capable as machines. His voice indeed is never so tolerant and humane as when he is dealing with heroes and heroines that are not human at all—with beasts and ships and polo-ponies or those odd little half-animals called children. His *Jungle Books* are among his best because here a psychology as elementary as Aesop's serves to convey the sense of an unusual understanding. A like reason gives its race and richness to his dialogue the moment it takes refuge in a dialect. For dialect, in spite of all its air of ragged lawlessness, is wholly impersonal, typical, fixed, the code of a caste, not the voice of an individual. It is when the novelist sets his characters talking King's English that he really puts his sympathy for the unconventional and capricious to the strain. Mr. Kipling's plain conversations are markedly unreal. But honest craftsmanship and an ear for strong rhythms provide him with many suits of dialects. With these he dresses the talk till it seems to surge with character.

And so, in this way and in that, the actual words he wrote joined in the conspiracy to keep him toiling, still hopefully, after that *ignis fatuus* of fiction. Until at length he made his supreme effort, fitted all the lore he had gathered—the sharp-set scenes, the well-cut dialects, the crisp impressions of life—into a single zoetrope, set it whirling on one of the spindles of the Indian machine, the secret spindle called the Great Game, and so created that spirited illusion of a novel which we know as *Kim*.

Thenceforward his work in prose has been a wonderful attempt to make his qualities cure their natural defects—to make sharpness and bright neatness produce their natural opposites—depth and shimmer and bloom. And by dint of an incomparable dexterity he has succeeded. There is no space left me now to trace the process with completeness— but roughly it may be described as an attempt to superimpose, as when you furl a fan, all the elements which in *Kim* had been laid side by side. The best example is perhaps *Rewards and Fairies*. If the reader will turn back to those wise fairy-tales he will see that each is really four-fold; a composite tissue made up of a layer of sunlit story (Dan's and Una's plane), on a layer of moonlit magic (plane of Puck), on a layer of history-stuff (René's plane and Gloriana's), on a last foundation of delicately bedimmed but never doubtful allegory. And he will note, too, the exquisite precision of the correspondences, a kind of practical punning, so that the self-same object plays a different part in every plane. One instance will suffice. Puck kicks a bunch of scarlet toad-stools idly. Why? Simply so that the red colour may stain back through all the textures till it matches, in the third, with the name of Rufus. This is not the mere swagger of virtuosity. The result of these imposi-tions is a very beautiful imposture. It gives the tales an opalescence that had hitherto seemed foreign to his work. It gives them the milki-ness of a magic crystal and makes them the completest symbols of life he has yet produced. These fairy tales for children are far more realistic than the *Plain Tales from the Hills*. For half of life is moonlit, and the image that would copy it exactly must be vague.

Nor is this all. If there be any logic in the lines of effort we have traced it is not here they find their consummation: they leap forward through this magic haze, emerge beyond it strangely clarified; they make it impossible not to believe that this woven obscurity, this new delicate dimness, is indeed but a curtain—a mist—not of dusk, but of dawn—that will dissolve to reveal Kipling carving his true master-work. Released at last from the conventions thrust upon it by pride and accident and the impertinencies of criticism, his system-seeking genius can now openly take up its true task, the task it has hitherto attempted only intermittently, and begin the sustained practice of that colossal kind of craftsmanship for which it is so singularly suited. It will beat out for itself a new form of imaginative prose, as unclogged by characterisation as his verse. The devices of drama it will use no doubt, and some of the tricks of narration; but its true medium will be massed impersonal things—tangles of human effort—the thickets of pheno-mena—the slow movements of industry, so muffled to the average eye—the general surge and litter of sensation. What his genius can do with material of this kind we have already in some sort seen. Driving into the darkness that beleaguers us, swirling and thrusting like a searchlight in a forest, it could bring out the essential structure of events and display the soaring pillars of contemporary achievement. It might not be the perfect definition; it might tend too much to turn the tides into firm floors, the branching constellations into rafters; but it would be enormously exhilarating. It would give toil a con-scious habitation; like actual architecture, like statuary, like all firm material forms, it would create, instead of merely copying, the emo-tions it lacks power to reproduce.

48. Ian Hay on *Stalky & Co.*

1914

Extract from *The Lighter Side of School Life* (1914) by Ian Hay, p. 158.

'Ian Hay'—pseudonym of John Hay Beith (1876–1952) wrote several books about the First World War, and followed them by popular novels and plays of a humorous kind, notably *Housemaster* (1936).

[re School Stories] We have many to choose from—*Stalky*, for instance. *Stalky* has come in for a shower of abuse from certain quarters. He hits the sentimentalist hard. We are told that the book is vulgar, that the famous trio are 'little beasts'. (I think Mr. A. C. Benson said so.) Still, Mr. Kipling never touches any subject which he does not adorn, and in *Stalky* he brings out vividly some of the salient features of modern school life. He has drawn masters as they have never been drawn before: the portraits may be cruel, biassed, not sufficiently representative; but how they live! He has put the case for the un-athletic boy with convincing truth. He depicts, too, very faithfully, the curious camaraderie which prevails nowadays between boys and masters, and pokes mordant fun at the sycophancy which this state of things breeds in a certain type of boy—the 'Oh, sir!' and 'No, sir!' and 'Yes, sir!' and 'Please, sir!' brigade—and deals faithfully with the master who takes advantage of out-of-school intimacy to be familiar and offensive in school, addressing boys by their nicknames and making humorous references to extra-scholastic incidents. And above all, Mr. Kipling knows the heart of a boy. He understands, above all men, a boy's intense reserve upon matters that lie deepest within him, and his shrinking from and repugnance to unrestrained and blatant discussion of these things. Do you remember the story of the fat man—'the jelly-bellied flag-flapper'—who came down to lecture to the school on patriotism?

[quotes from 'The Flag of their Country', *Stalky & Co.* pp. 212–13]

It was a Union Jack, you will remember, suddenly unfurled by way of peroration. 'Happy thought! Perhaps he was drunk.' That is true, all through.

49. 'A Diversity of Creatures'

1917

Anonymous review in the *Athenaeum*, No. 4617, p. 240 (May 1917).

If we had any misgivings, strengthened by some recent excursions in journalism, that decadence had set in with Mr. Kipling, this new book puts them to rest. He has never shown himself a greater master of the art of storytelling, never combined creative imagination with more triumphant realism, or handled his own English prose with more ease, economy, and certainty of effect. The first of the fourteen, 'As Easy as A.B.C.', is perhaps the finest short story of the future ever written. A sort of sequel to 'With the Night Mail', it is dated A.D. 2065, and is an historical episode in a world that has passed through the most profound and complete of social revolutions. Politics have ceased. No human being takes any interest in government, for all things run smoothly and in perfect order under a small and unobtrusive Aerial Board of Control, which leaves absolute privacy and security to the individual. 'Transportation is Civilization. Democracy is Disease.' In such a world, crowds and the people are the one source of evil, and a sporadic outbreak of now obsolete and mediaeval democratic agitation in Chicago arouses a storm of agoraphobia, and brings about the events to be narrated. Mr. Kipling does not describe, but makes the reader's imagination vividly realize, the wonders of aerial navigation, the ground-circuits, and the destructive sound-vibrations and withering rays of light, which are the defences and the artillery of the future. He moves among these sensations as if they were the commonplace of existence, as if mankind had been used to them for generations. His is a realism that Swift might have envied.

Some artists excel in giving an air of the marvellous and stupendous to things that really exist. Such is Mr. Pennell in his romantic pictures of colossal buildings, engines, and machinery. Others, like Mr. Muirhead Bone, can make the most incredible structures and implements of war matters of everyday familiarity. Mr. Kipling can do both. He can make the ordinary ultra-romantic; he can let us feel at home in a world where everything is new, strange, and astounding. To him romance is a plaything, which he handles with the skill and ease of a tennis champion brandishing a racket. Though none of the other stories travels into the world of mechanical wonders, several, perhaps most, would in cold analysis seem quite as improbable. In three, 'The Dog Hervey', 'In the Same Boat', and 'Swept and Garnished', occult sympathies, some form of telepathic bond, or a faculty of seeing the invisible, are rendered more than credible by like realistic devices. There are farces, such as 'The Vortex', 'The Horse Marines', and 'The Village that voted the Earth was Flat', which pile situation on ludicrous situation, and climax on climax, long after it seems as if the final limit of extravagance had been reached. The last-named story is a piece of uproarious comedy that exceeds 'The Incarnation of Krishna Mulvaney', and has the advantage of being laid in the home counties, and enacted by local magnates, villagers, city men, and M.P.s such as we all know. The success with which the inventor brings off his daring complications of humorous circumstance is not a whit less amazing than that of his 'Easy as A.B.C.'.

It is, in fact, all as easy as A.B.C. to Mr. Kipling, and that is perhaps what chiefly enthrals the discriminating reader and seizes our admiration. For it is the manner, not the matter, of these latest masterpieces which challenges attention. Mr. Kipling offers nothing conspicuously new. Various as the contents are, we are well acquainted with their different kinds. He set the direction in every instance years ago. The only wonder is that he is able to proceed still farther in every one. True, there is nothing of the same kind of imagination as in 'They' or 'The Brushwood Boy'. This set contains no story having the fundamental seriousness of several earlier ones that cling to memory. But as a craftsman, and something higher than a craftsman, Mr. Kipling has gone on developing. Though he is not a novelist, his character-drawing is substantial enough to last out the different events of many stories. Stalky and Beetle reappear here, and the former has obviously lived. There are also some Sikhs and Goorkhas reminiscent of *Kim* and other Indian stories. Perhaps it is a result of the War that infractions of the sixth commandment are treated with such sang-froid and nonchalance in 'Friendly Brook' and 'The Edge of the Evening'. Each story is followed by a kind of epilogue in verse, which sometimes explains a rather cryptic meaning, or at least enforces its bearing as Mr. Kipling conceives it. 'The Land' is an excellent history of the British peasant, who was there when the Romans came, and still is in real possession, 'For whoever pays the taxes old Mus' Hobden owns the land.' But the average quality of the verse is low; some pieces, such as 'The Children', in spite of a Swinburnian measure and fluent double-rhyming, are merely consecutive lengths of prose.

We should like to have quoted from that charming comedy of schoolboy humours and howlers, *Regulus*, to show what Mr. Kipling can do in the way of Platonic as well as other dialogue. He is first-rate on the teaching of Latin and its effect on living. But to open the book anywhere is to see that he is a supreme master of style, in all its applications.

50. T. S. Eliot's 'Kipling Redivivus'

1919

Signed ('T. S. E.') review of *The Years Between* in the *Athenaeum* No. 4645, pp. 297–8 (9 May 1919).

Thomas Stearns Eliot (1888–1965), leading poet of his period and a distinguished critic, later edited *A Choice of Kipling's Verse* (1941) with a long critical introduction of judicious praise that was prelude to the serious study of Kipling's place in literature which is now taking place. Eliot balanced this short early appreciation of Kipling with another forty years later delivered before the Kipling Society in October 1958 and published in the *Kipling Journal* number 129 (March 1959) and reprinted in Elliot L. Gilbert's *Kipling and the Critics* (1965).

Mr. Kipling is a laureate without laurels. He is a neglected celebrity. The arrival of a new book of his verse is not likely to stir the slightest ripple on the surface of our conversational intelligentsia. He has not been crowned by the elder generation; malevolent fate has not even allowed him to be one of the four or five or six greatest living poets. A serious contemporary has remarked of the present volume that 'in nearly all our poetical coteries the poetry of Kipling has long been anathema, with field sports, Imperialism, and public schools'. This is wide of the mark. Mr. Kipling is not anathema; he is merely not discussed. Most of our discerning critics have no more an opinion on Mr. Kipling than they have on the poetry of Mr. John Oxenham. The mind is not sufficiently curious, sufficiently brave, to examine Mr. Kipling. Yet the admired creator of Bouvard and Pecuchet would not have overlooked the Kipling *dossier*.

Mr. Kipling has not been analysed. There are the many to whom he is a gospel; there are the few to whom he is a shout in the street, or a whisper in the ear of death, unheard. Both are mistaken. Mr. Kipling is not without antecedents; he has an affinity to Swinburne, even a likeness. There are, of course, qualities peculiar to Mr. Kipling; but several of the apparent differences are misconceptions, and several can be reduced to superficial differences of environment. Both are men of a few simple ideas, both are preachers, both have marked their styles by an abuse of the English Bible.

They are alike even in a likeness which would strike most people immediately as a difference; they are alike in their use of sound. It is true that Swinburne relies more exclusively upon the power of sound than does Mr. Kipling. But it is the same type of sound, and it is not the sound-value of music. Anyone who thinks so may compare Swinburne's 'songs' with verse which demands the voice and the instrument, with Shelley's 'Music when soft voices die' or Campion's 'Fairy Queen Prosperpina'. What emerges from the comparison is that Swinburne's sound like Mr. Kipling's, has the sound-value of oratory, not of music.

'When the hounds of spring are on winter's traces' arrives at similar effects to Mr. Kipling: ' "What are the bugles blowin' for?" said Files on Parade;' or in the present volume:

> There was no need of a steed nor [*sic*] a lance to pursue them;
> It was decreed their own deed, and not chance, should undo them.

It is, in fact, the poetry of oratory; it is music just as the words of orator or preacher are music; they persuade, not by reason, but by emphatic sound. Swinburne and Mr. Kipling have, like the public speaker, an idea to impose; and they impose it in the public speaker's way, by turning the idea into sound, and iterating the sound. And, like the public speaker's, their business is not to express, to lay before you, to *state*, but to propel, to impose on you the idea. And, like the orator, they are personal; not by revelation, but by throwing themselves in and gesturing the emotion of the moment. The emotion is not 'there' simply, coldly independent of the author, of the audience, there and for ever like Shakespeare's and Aeschylus' emotions: it is present so long only as the author is on the platform and compels you to feel it.

> I look down at his feet: but that's a fable.
> If that thou be'st a devil, I cannot kill thee

is there, cold and indifferent.

> Nothing is better, I well think
> Than love; the hidden well-water
> Is not so delicate a drink.
> This was well seen of me and her

(to take from one of Swinburne's poems which most nearly resembles a statement); or

> The end of it's sitting and thinking
> And dreaming hell-fires to see—

these are not statements of emotion, but ways of stimulating a particular response in the reader.

Both of the poets have a few simple ideas. If we deprecate any philosophical complications, we may be allowed to call Swinburne's Liberty and Mr. Kipling's Empire 'ideas'. They are at least abstract, and not material which emotion can feed long upon. And they are not (in passing) very dissimilar. Swinburne had the *Risorgimento*, and Garibaldi, and Mazzini, and the model of Shelley, and the recoil from Tennyson, and he produced Liberty. Mr. Kipling, the Anglo-Indian, had frontier welfare, and rebellions, and Khartoum, and he produced the Empire. And we remember Swinburne's sentiments toward the Boers; he wished to intern them all. Swinburne and Mr. Kipling have these and such concepts; some poets, like Shakespeare or Dante or Villon, and some novelists, like Mr. Conrad, have, in contrast to ideas or concepts, points of view, or 'worlds'—what are incorrectly called 'philosophies'. Mr. Conrad is very germane to the question, because he is in many ways the antithesis of Mr. Kipling. He is, for one thing, the antithesis of Empire (as well as of democracy); his characters are the denial of Empire, of Nation, of Race almost, they are fearfully alone with the Wilderness. Mr. Conrad has no ideas, but he has a point of view, a world; it can hardly be defined, but it pervades his work and is unmistakable. It could not be otherwise. Swinburne's and Mr. Kipling's ideas could be otherwise. Had Mr. Kipling taken Liberty and Swinburne the Empire, the alteration would be unimportant.

And this is why both Swinburne's and Mr. Kipling's verse, in spite of the positive manner which each presses to his service, appear to lack cohesion—to be, frankly, immature. There is no point of view to hold them together. What is the point of view, one man's experience of life, behind 'Mandalay', and 'Danny Deever', and 'MacAndrew', and the 'Recessional'? The volume in hand, at least, ought to be consistent with itself: the subjects are in sympathy with each other; they express Mr. Kipling's attitudes toward various aspects of the war. But the poems no more hang together than the verses of a schoolboy. This, in spite of Mr. Kipling's undeniable manner.

The manner itself, indeed, involves no discoveries in syntax or vocabulary; the structure reveals nothing unusual.

> The banked oars fell an hundred strong,
>   And backed and threshed and ground,
> But bitter was the rowers' song
>   As they brought the war-boat round.

The construction 'bitter was . . . as . . .' has a very familiar sound. The old order of words persists, not giving place to new. This is not, however, *the* manner. And we should not be positive that

> The Hun is at the gate! . . .
> Be well assured that on our side
> The abiding oceans fight . . .

(Mr. Conrad would hardly issue this opinion about the oceans) were by Mr. Kipling, though we could not associate them with any equally distinguished name. But when we peruse the following:

> A tinker out of Bedford
> A vagrant oft in quod . . .
> And Bunyan was his name! . . .

> They do not preach that their God will rouse them a little before the nuts
>   work loose.
> They do not preach that His Pity allows them to leave their work when
>   they damn-well choose . . .

> There is a gland at the back of the jaw
> And an answering lump by the collar-bone . . .

> When the Himalayan peasant meets the he-bear in his pride . . .

in all of these we have the true formula, with its touch of the newspapers, of Billy Sunday, and the Revised Version filtered through Rabbi Zeal-of-the-Land Busy. The Revised Version (substantially the same style as all the versions from Tindal) is excellent prose for its matter. It is often redundant and bombastic in the Prophets, who sometimes fell into these vices, and it is a model of firm and limpid style in the sayings of Jesus. But it is not a style into which any significant modern content can be shoved. Mr. Kipling is one of the Minor Prophets.

There is one more element in the style or manner of Mr. Kipling which demands attention. The eighteenth century was in part cynical and in part sentimental, but it never arrived at complete amalgamation of the two feelings. Whoever makes a study of the sentimentalism of the nineteenth and twentieth centuries will not neglect the peculiar cynical sentiment of Mr. Kipling. In a poem like Mr. Kipling's 'The Ladies' the fusion is triumphant. The sentiment of Tennyson and Mrs. Browning is obsolete, it is no longer a living force; it is superseded by Mr. Kipling's. Tennyson, we must insist, could never have written

> Love at first sight was her trouble,
> She didn't know what it were;
> But I wouldn't do such, 'cause I liked her too much—
> And I learned about women from 'er;

nor could he have written

> Gentlemen-rankers off on a spree,
> Damned from here to eternity.
> O God, have mercy on such as we:
> Ba Ba Ba.

Mr. Kipling may have winked at Tennyson down the road. But Tennyson did not wink back.

And yet Mr. Kipling is very nearly a great writer. There is an unconsciousness about him which, while it is one of the reasons why he is not an artist, is a kind of salvation. There is an echo of greatness in his naïve appeal to so large an audience as he addresses; something which makes him, like one or two other writers who are not or hardly artists, a lonely figure. And in *Plain Tales from the Hills* he has given the one perfect picture of a society of English, narrow, snobbish, spiteful, ignorant and vulgar, set down absurdly in a continent of which they are unconscious. What Mirza Murad Ali Beg's book[1] is to all other books of native life, so is Mr. Kipling's to all other books of Anglo-Indian life. It is wrong, of course, of Mr. Kipling to address a large audience; but it is a better thing than to address a small one. The only better thing is to address the one hypothetical Intelligent Man who does not exist and who is the audience of the Artist.

[1] [*Lalum the Beragun*, Bombay 1884. See *Plain Tales*, p. 333]

51. Richard Le Gallienne on 'Kipling's Place in Literature'

1919

Signed article in *Munsey's Magazine*, Vol. LXVIII, pp. 238–46 (November 1919), reprinted in *Around the World with Kipling* (New York, 1926), pp. 45–51.

Richard Le Gallienne (1866–1947), minor poet and essayist, is remembered best for *The Quest of the Golden Girl* (1896) and *The Romantic Nineties* (1926). He also wrote studies of Meredith (1890), Whitman (1898), and Kipling (1900)—the last, echoing the contemporary attack on Kipling for 'hooliganism', is in a very different vein from the more balanced and considered judgment of the following essay.

Henry James, in an early appreciation of Rudyard Kipling's writings, which was a striking illustration of his own literary catholicity, referred to 'the particular property that made us all so precipitately drop everything else to attend to him'. The phrase is vividly and truthfully descriptive of the manner in which, so to say, Mr. Kipling first hit literary London; for his sudden and swift arrival was a very unmistakable jolt to the literary fashions then prevailing.

The times were decidedly 'precious'. We were in the midst of a rather hectic aftermath of pre-Raphaelitism and the 'esthetic' movement. The labels 'decadent' and '*fin-de-siècle*' were the prevailing catchwords, and 'strange sins', and peculiar 'soul-states', and 'artistic temperaments' were in vogue. It was the heyday of Oscar Wilde and Aubrey Beardsley, of Paterian and Stevensonian prose. 'Style' and 'distinction' were our only wear. Also the cults of the poster, the music-hall, and the short story were at their height. *The Yellow Book* was being published in Vigo Street, and the Rhymers' Club was meeting at the Cheshire Cheese. In short, it was the eighteen-nineties.

It is not necessary to depreciate those stirring times, as surely I would be the last to do, in order to emphasize the singularity of Mr. Kipling's paradoxical arrival among them. There was a genuine artistic vitality in them, which has not only left behind some notable work, becoming more seriously recognized as time goes on, and the picturesque memories of certain ill-starred men of talent, if not genius, but which is, at the moment, perhaps too potently alive and influential in that new wave of 'preciousness' wherein we are at present engulfed. Indeed, the despised and rejected of the eighteen-nineties have become, it is to be feared, almost too much the chief corner-stones of contemporary movements and manifestoes.

However, 'that', as Mr. Kipling first taught us to say, 'is another story'. Mr. Kipling's influence has had a long innings. If those influences which he temporarily overwhelmed are now to have theirs—well, it takes all sorts to make a world. Of one thing we may be gladly certain—the iron and quinine with which he has so plentifully dosed us will remain in the blood of the younger generation, and will serve to correct any threatened fevers of luxurious 'hedonism'. No recent writer can so confidently apply Whitman's words to himself, in addressing his contemporaries, and say:

> You will hardly know who I am or what I mean,
> But I will be good health to you, nevertheless,
> And filter and fibre your blood.

Leaving artistic considerations aside for a moment, Mr. Kipling's moral influence on his day and generation has been of an importance which it is scarcely an exaggeration to call prophetic. Few writers have ever come so precisely in the nick of time. If a voice crying 'England hath need of thee' had summoned him, he could not have been more pat to the occasion. Wordsworth's 'stern daughter of the voice of God' has seldom been in greater need of a candid friend and servant. But how whimsically characteristic of the times it was, too, that that mouthpiece of the ancient verities should come in the guise of an Anglo-Indian teller of tales, the banjo-minstrel of Tommy Atkins and *Supi-yaw-lat!*

And surely, at first, no one dreamed what this cock-sure *enfant terrible* was to mean to the British Empire in particular, and to the morale of the world in general. His guise was certainly anything but prophetic, and his accents anything but reverential. Other-worldliness—of which he has essentially a great deal—was the last quality you would attribute to him. On the contrary, a queerly acrid worldliness, an omniscient cynicism, and a jarring brutality, made the peculiar tang of this strange, new fruit from the Tree of Knowledge. One's first reading of him was like one's first experience with olives. Some people never learn to like olives, and some people—lovers, too, of the best in literature—have never quite learned to like Rudyard Kipling. There is something in him that still frightens them.

But the fruit that Mr. Kipling brought us, even in that first astonishing volume of *Plain Tales from the Hills*, was more subtly blended in flavor than any olive. It had, indeed, every kind of flavor, and was not without an odd touch of the nectarine. Among all his other experiences, its author had not missed the honey of pre-Raphaelitism, was not unacquainted with the Lady Lilith, and could put Rossetti's 'Song of the Bower' into the mouth of his drunken acquaintance, McIntosh Jellaludin. And, while on one page we would find him lyrically celebrating 'the hunting of man', what exquisite tenderness we would find on another—lover-tenderness, mother-tenderness—and what noble and touching pity for the sorrows and frailties of his fellows! With all his uncanny and precocious knowledge of the world—so many different worlds—his somewhat overdone and distasteful knowingness, and along with his apparent cold-bloodedness of observation and accent, there went, in unaccustomed association, so deep a sense of the tears in mortal things that one soon realized that here was something more than a diabolically clever teller of tales, and that, in fact, we were safe in the hands of a deep and serious poet.

It need hardly be said that one of the first notes to be struck by Mr. Kipling, a note that has reverberated as from an iron string through all his subsequent writings, has been that an Englishman's first duty is his duty to England. 'Keep we the faith!' From first to last he has been an incorrigible Britisher, and in his case there seems never to have been a shadow of those Gilbertian temptations to belong to other nations. Least of all has he ever shown the smallest inclination to be an internationalist. In that famous envoi to *The Seven Seas*, in which he expresses his creed as an artist, he has told us that in the happy hereafter for artists, 'when the oldest colors have faded and the youngest critic has died'—

> ... Only the Master shall praise us, and only
> the Master shall blame;
> And no one shall work for money, and no one
> shall work for fame;

But each for the joy of the working, and each,
    in his separate star,
Shall draw the Thing as he sees It for the God
    of Things as They Are!

From first to last the God he has served, with a prayerful devotion which gives all his work a curious seriousness, even solemnity, has been the God of Things as They Are; and, when you come to think of it, what other god is there? Under another name, such was the deity of another modern writer who seems very different from Mr. Kipling, but from whom, I conjecture, he has drawn no little inspiration— George Meredith. 'Sacred Reality', Meredith called his divinity. 'Smite, Sacred Reality,' he cries in the anguish of *A Faith on Trial*; and when we can say that in sincerity, he adds, 'we have come of our faith's ordeal'. Meredith and Mr. Kipling alike are fiercely impatient, of sentimental evasions of the facts of existence, and though, perhaps, far from agreement on details, are alike intolerant of half-baked social and political panaceas, both having gone to school to that wise spirit which teaches us to discriminate between true idealism and its spurious, sophomoric imitations.

For this reason Mr. Kipling is by many regarded as a reactionary—a label, it is to be feared, which must be patiently accepted by all such who do not swallow wholesale those nostrums of contemporary lawlessness and disorder which parade variously under the names of progress and revolution.

Mr. Kipling has an old-fashioned belief in duty, and in the discipline which enforces it, and makes it second nature. 'He did not know,' he says of his Brushwood Boy, 'that he bore with him from school and college a character worth much fine gold.' Character—that is the old-fashioned quality which again and again he holds up for our admiration in his mute, inglorious heroes, and possibly he writes sometimes a little too much as if it were an exclusively British possession.

For, in spite of his having, in Barrie's phrase, swaggered in bad company over so many continents, he is the least cosmopolitan of writers. He is nothing if not patriotic—that antique virtue which our internationalists are doing their best to ridicule and destroy. It was already, in many intellectual quarters, being superciliously depreciated as insularity, and so forth, when Mr. Kipling first 'smote 'is bloomin' lyre'. Perhaps, for some, the recent war, with its fearful menace, may point an old-fashioned moral in Mr. Kipling's favor; and those who study it, and who are following, too, the recent developments among the various new peace-born nations, may hesitate before exchanging it for the blessings of the 'inter-nation'.

In fact, Mr. Kipling is, both by temperament and by conviction, a Tory. But it is not necessary to agree with the whole of a writer to be glad of him, and this is especially true of Mr. Kipling. One may, indeed, often violently, disagree with him, for his work is very much of a challenge to his time, yet admire and give thanks for him all the same. Perhaps as one grows older and better acquainted with the works and ways of his God of Things as They Are, one is inclined to agree with him more rather than less; nor need the doing so imply our senectitude, for we must recall that Mr. Kipling thought the same at twenty as he does now, that his young shoulders were born with a strangely old Tory head upon them. He saw the Thing as It Is from a very early age; and, when we say that, we must not forget that it was far from being only the seamy side of it that he saw. He saw that, indeed, with strangely precocious eyes, but it was as nothing in his vision compared with the power and the glory, the wonder and the mystery, which he also saw, and which no man of our time has seen with clearer, more passionate, or more worshipful seeing.

52. Edmund Blunden: Review of
The Irish Guards

1923

Extract from review of *The Irish Guards in the Great War* headed 'Mr. Kipling Reconstructs' published in the *Nation and Athenaeum*, Vol. XXXIII, pp. 122–3 (28 April 1923). The rest of the article deals generally with histories and descriptions of the War, and only the last paragraph is concerned directly with Kipling's book.

Edmund Charles Blunden (1896–   ) one of the leading poets and critics of his generation is also the author of the best volume of First War memories, *Undertones of War* (1929). He succeeded Kipling as literary adviser to the War Graves Commission.

The fact is that Mr. Kipling appears not perfectly to understand the pandemonium and nerve-strain of war; it seldom surges up in his pages of that appalling misery which brought seasoned men down in the shell holes beyond Thiepval, as they went up to relieve the Schwaben Redoubt, crying, and 'whacked to the wide'. He makes constant stern attempts at actuality; he constantly falls short, in expressions merely strained, in sheer want of comprehension. To those who were in the line, his technical phraseology will seem incongruous now and then; but the deeper defects may be exemplified by such expressions as—touching pill-box warfare—'the annoying fights and checks rounded the concreted machine gun posts'; or 'While they watched drowsily the descent and thickening of a fresh German shell-storm, preluding fresh infantry attacks . . .'; or again, 'what had been a Brigade ceased to exist—had soaked horribly into the ground'. Here mere languidness, these exaggerations, conflicts with memory; the Irish Guards have been chronicled with decision and skill, but as to the multitudinous enigma of war atmosphere, Mr. Kipling has not written much that convinces us.

53. Christopher Morley on 'Horace, Book Five'

1926

Signed review of 'Horace, Book Five' (and *Debits and Credits*) published in the *Saturday Review of Literature* (New York), Vol. III, p. 155 (2 October 1926).

Christopher Morley (1890–1957) was a well-known American novelist and essayist, highly regarded for his reviews. He is best remembered for *Thunder on the Left* (1925) and *The Seacoast of Bohemia* (1929).

With gay instinct for the painful and irrelevant, the editorial writers mostly agreed to pick upon the least important poem in Rudyard Kipling's new book, and wrote ponderous grievance about it. As a matter of fact not one but three of the poems are pretty straightly barbed against America; but the other two are too subtly led to be readily observable. The one on Prohibition would have been the one to quote, for an editor with a nostril for News.

But I did have to blink my eyes a little, finding in our gravest journals such remarks as this: 'The numerous poems which adorn *Debits and Credits* do not compel one to much comment . . . Frankness compels one to state that the original pieces composed for the present volume do not measure up.' What, do four new 'translations' from the Fifth Book of Horace's Odes compel no comment? Or are we to suppose that our reviewers don't know the joke about Horace's Fifth Book? I was brooding a bit morosely on this matter when, just in time to gruntle my heart somewhat, I met F.P.A.[1] coming out of the subway. It was a jocund coincidence, for he had under his arm the rare little *Carminum Liber Quintus* (*a Rudyardo Kipling et Carolo Graves Anglice Redditus*) which is also one of my treasures. We stood prating

---

[1] [Franklin Pierce Adams, popular American columnist and author, generally known by his initials, with which he signed his work.]

together in City Hall Park, two happy casuals, our erring bosoms full of homage to the man who, after nineteen centuries, recaptures the very voice.

The huge paradox of Kipling is never more apparent than when you read the reviews of a new book of his. This extraordinary writer, whom we are accustomed to see billed as speaking to the world's hugest fiction audience, is really the subtlest of highbrows. His finest things would bore the slackwit reader just as Shakespeare does. He would have been the greatest professor of English Literature that our tongue has ever known, because he has the violent and tragic sense of literature as the very perspiration on the brow of life. He writes a story ostensibly about big howitzers, and it is really a lover's tribute to Jane Austen. He writes a story apparently about wireless, and it means nothing save to a student of Keats. In this new volume the two Stalkies and the Jane Austen story coruscate with literary allusion and esoteric jape. 'The Propagation of Knowledge' might have been written specially to wring the withers of the Modern Language Association. His fragment on 'How Shakespeare Came to Write *The Tempest*', written in 1898 as a letter to the London *Spectator*, like all his marvellous side-glances into Elizabethan doings (have a look at his old poem 'The Craftsman') shows his understanding of how and where poetry is born. Only learned students, packed with curious and private lore, could properly trace the wild chameleon variation of his mind. How, with a hundred tints and shadings he has been able to take at will the color of any man from Horace to Mulvaney—and yet, in the core of the crystal, we see ever the identity of the egregious Beetle. When was there a more vast, wanton, irrepressible, furious, grotesque, and impossible fecundity? It is a silly thing to say—yet how much of literature consists in saying the silliest things possible—there is perhaps more of the specific and technical Shakespeare-gift in our well-loved Beetle than in any other man these times have seen. At his worst, God knows, he is as bad as Shakespeare ever was. At his best, he has looked upon pure flame. Those who know the color of naked fire will recognize it when they see,

> Rubies of every heat, where through we scan
> The fiercer and more fiery heart of man.

It was odd that 'The United Idolaters', perhaps the charmingest tribute of love ever paid to an American sanctity—Uncle Remus—hasn't been mentioned in the editorials. But that is not what editorials are for. They must leap upon the verses in which a man with tragedy in his heart ventures to say, and with mannerly disguise, some words that seem to him bitterly true. There are others in which the soul is opened so plainly that one keeps decent silence. And here and there, if you are on the air for these things, is that specific wavelength of Kipling genius, that is not always relished or understood but is uniquely itself. If anyone ever tells you it is a genius available for the million, I think you will be safe to contradict. I haven't yet read all the stories, but I didn't let the sun go down on any unread poems. With no right or permission whatever I'm going to quote from the addenda to Horace—

TO THE COMPANIONS
Horace, Ode 17, Bk. V

How comes it that, at even-tide,
  When level beams should show most truth,
Man, failing, takes unfailing pride
  In memories of his frolic youth?

Venus and Liber fill their hour,
  The games engage, the law-courts prove,
Till hardened life breeds love of power
  Or Avarice, Age's final love.

Yet at the end, these comfort not—
  Nor any triumph Fate decrees—
Compared with glorious, unforgot—
  ten innocent enormities

Of frontless days before the beard,
  When, instant on the casual jest,
The God Himself of Mirth appeared
  And snatched us to His heaving breast.

And we—not caring who He was
  But certain He would come again—
Accepted all He brought to pass
  As Gods accept the lives of men.

Then He withdrew from sight and speech,
  Nor left a shrine. How comes it now
While Charon's keel grates on the beach,
  He calls so clear: 'Rememberest thou?'

I've been interested to see that the *Literary Review* is conducting a symposium on whether authors care what the critics say about their work, and perhaps that topic is akin to the present matter. If any writer says he is not interested in the critics' comments he is probably either a liar or a genius. But as to reviews having any real effect, turning any of his inward valves, it seems to me inconceivable.

Long before a book reaches the reviewers, its author has made up his own mind about it. He knows bitterly well how nearly it represents his intentions. Praise from those he respects probably shames him and makes him eager to do better. Reproach usually stiffens his neck. But in his core and gizzard he is totally unmoved. I am told that some writers actually subscribe to clipping bureaus so as not to miss any of their 'notices'. The idea is incredible.

For printers' ink, chucked about at random, is so murderous to the finer delicacies that one is soon cured of any appetite for mere publicity. And if you ever had a notion to deal, a bit savagely, with some of the central realities and joys and horrors, you would probably be told that you are pleasantly whimsical. Also there will always be those who resent any man saying what he exactly thinks. To such resentment there can be no answer. Horace suggested in the Fifth Book—since he didn't write it—that silence is best.

54. Brander Matthews on 'Kipling's Deeper Note'

1926

Signed review of *Debits and Credits* in *Literary Digest International Book Review* (U.S.A.), Vol. IX, pp. 745-6 (November 1926) headed 'Mr. Kipling Strikes a Deeper Note'.

Brander Matthews (1852–1929) was a notable American essayist and dramatic critic of his period. He held Chairs in Literature at Columbia University from 1892 to 1924, and wrote more than forty books ranging from literary essays such as *Pen and Ink* (1888) and short stories such as *Tales of Fantasy and Fact* (1896) to such scholarly works as *Molière* (1910) and *Principles of Play-making* (1919).

It is pleasant to welcome this new collection of Rudyard Kipling's short stories, the first in ten years; and it is pleasant to know that his popularity is attested by the steady sale of his many volumes. His earliest books, those which gave him his sudden fame, *Plain Tales from the Hills*, *Soldiers Three*, and their companions, were not protected by copyright in this country when they first appeared; they were pirated by half-a-dozen publishers; and they were sold by tens of thousands. The international copyright act went into effect on the first of July, 1891; and Kipling has been able to profit by the books he has written in the past thirty-five years. To the courtesy of the publishers who have just issued *Debits and Credits*, I am indebted for the privilege of stating that since they took over the publication of Kipling's books they have sold more than two and a half million volumes. *Kim* and *Just So Stories* have each attained to a circulation of more than 150,000; and *The Day's Work* is not far behind.

There are signs, it is true, that Kipling is not now held in high esteem by the Little Group of Serious Thinkers, who are proud to style themselves 'Young Intellectuals'—altho' they are certainly not as juvenile as they act, and probably not as intellectual as they believe; Their dislike for the foremost figure in the contemporary literature of our language is easily explicable; they are vociferous in vaunting their revolt from all the conventions, all the traditions, and all the inheritances from the past; they assert with persistent violence the right of every man to 'express himself' and to 'live his own life' more or less regardless of the rights of every other man; and, therefore, they can not but be annoyed by Kipling's sobriety and sanity, by his regard for form, by his resolute self-control, by his freedom from freakishness, and by his insistence in holding fast to that which is true and of good report. Altho' he never preaches, there is a moral implicit in all his work. When I once exprest to him my appreciation of the Mowgli stories, he explained that they were easy enough: 'When I had once found the Law of the Jungle,' he said, 'then all the rest followed as a matter of course.' Obey the law, do your duty, play the game, be a man, and do the day's work—that is the moral which underlies the *Jungle Book* and *Captains Courageous* and *Kim* and the rest of that noble company. Perhaps it is in 'If' that this ethical code is most resonantly exprest; and probably there are few lyrics more distasteful than this to the Young Intellectuals, be the same more or less. As Mr. Paul Elmer More pointed out a few years ago, Mr. Kipling's sense of order and obedience 'rises into a pure feeling for righteousness that reminds one of the Hebrew prophets'—and yet he never goes up into the pulpit to inculcate a moral. If there are sermons in his songs and in his stories, the reader, young or old, must find them for himself.

Kipling is the only man of letters in our time who is equally esteemed as a singer of ballads in rime and as a teller of tales in prose. He is the only man of letters in our time who is revered by young and old alike. Only the mature, who have come to an understanding of life, can fully appreciate *Kim*, that prose Odyssey of Hindustan; and only they have experience enough to relish the rich savor of *Puck of Pook's Hill* and *Rewards and Fairies*, that incomparable pair of volumes in which Kipling (as Barrett Wendell put it) 'makes the past of English history live with such implicit learning as is the wonder of historians and such imaginative truth as is paralleled in literature only by the splendidly vagrant chronicle-histories of Shakespeare'. These books, ripe in wisdom, are for the elders; and the *Just So Stories* and the *Jungle Books*, equally beloved by the old, are more particularly for the youngsters. They have taken their place by the side of *Alice in Wonderland* and *Uncle Remus* as permanent additions to the books not to be denied to youth. If a boy or girl is not made familiar with them at the age when they are most appealing, he has been deprived of his heritage.

That Kipling is one of the supreme masters of the short story is, I take it, admitted by all who have dealt with the theory and the practise of that form of fiction. There are some, and they are not a few, who are tempted at times to declare that in some respects at least Kipling is more accomplished than any of his rivals in his art. And who are these rivals? Who are the short-story writers worthy to be set by his side? They are not many, a scant half-dozen at the most—Hawthorne and Poe, at the beginning of the list, Maupassant and Stevenson at the end. It is futile to attempt to set these makers of myths in the serried order of their achievement. Beyond all question, each of them is a master in his own fashion and in spite of his limitations. But it would not be presumptuous to maintain that Kipling, whatever his ultimate rank among them, is obviously more various and more multifarious. He has more masterpieces to his credit than any of these competitors; and these masterpieces of his are of more different kinds.

Hawthorne (and I yield to no one in acknowledging the value of his best work), has less than half-a-score of truly great short stories; and a few of his other tales are rather pallid apologs. Poe, in his turn, is purely intellectual; as Lowell said: 'the heart is squeezed out by the mind'; he lacks 'the ruddy drop of human blood'; and his marvelous narratives are not peopled by men and women like unto ourselves. Stevenson has left us one indisputable and (in its kind) incomparable short story, 'Markheim', in which we behold the insatiable artist (which Stevenson was) working in partnership with the Shorter Catechist (which Stevenson was also); but in most of his other short stories even his most ardent admirers admit a lack of ease and an ill-concealed artificiality; these tales are 'not inevitable enough'. Remains Maupassant, whose ease is almost his most evident quality; but he is—in his earlier short stories at least—unsympathetic, devoid of sentiment, hard and heartless. That most perfect specimen of narration, 'The Necklace', is cruel in its frigidity, not to call it inhuman. It is true that in his later novels Maupassant softened into sentiment, and lost that cold contempt for all mankind which is paraded in his earlier and briefer tales.

Kipling has a far wider range than any of his rivals. His masterpieces —and they are at least as many as any of these competitors can boast —are of many different kinds. Take 'Without Benefit of Clergy' (that simplest of stories, with a pathos as unforced as it is poignant), and set this by the side of 'An Habitation Enforced' (that lovely idyll of married life, exquisite in its unparaded sentiment). Take 'The Man Who Was' (that brief tenth act in an untold tragedy), and set this over against 'The Brushwood Boy' (one of the most perfect of love stories, as it is one of the most original in its invention and in its imagination). Compare 'They' (with its sheer poetry and its mystic penumbra) with the robust 'Courting of Dinah Shadd'. Once more, compare 'The Children of the Zodiac' (that cosmic fantasy, which is intensely and eternally human, altho' it seems to transcend time and space)—compare this with 'The Centurion on the Wall' (that martial tale which marches straight forward, keeping step boldly with the blare of the trumpets). Nor must we overlook the kaleidoscopic color of 'Krishna Mulvaney' or the rapid-fire action of any one of a dozen other adventures of *Soldiers Three*.

'When an author is yet living,' said Dr. Johnson, 'we estimate his powers by his worst performance, and when he is dead, by his best.' This seems to me an overstatement. I doubt if we really estimate a living writer by his worst performance; but we tend to judge him by his latest. Here, in *Debits and Credits*, we have Kipling's latest performance; and what is our estimate of it? Of course, the fourteen tales it contains are not equal in merit—a statement which might be made of any volume by any other writer of short stories. That is to say, some of these narratives are better than others; and it must be noted at once that several of them are very good indeed, even if no one of them is as indisputably supreme as 'They' or 'The Brushwood Boy' or 'An Habitation Enforced'. It needs to be said also that, taken as a whole, the collection is completely characteristic. There are here three or four tales that no other living writer could equal.

In his *Philosophy of Art*, Taine tells us that there is a certain quality in the work of a great artist which we may adorn with beautiful names:

we may call it genius or inspiration, which is right and proper; but if you wish to define it precisely, you must always verify therein the vivid, spontaneous suggestion which groups together the train of accessory ideas, and which masters them, fashions them, metamorphoses them and employs them in order to make itself manifest.

And in nearly every one of these new stories Kipling has given us this 'vivid, spontaneous suggestion'. He here delights us with the old mastery; he charms us with the old craftsmanship; and he moves us with the old magic. And it is magic, this essential quality of his. There is no other word for it—a magic made up of insight and understanding and imagination.

Two of the fourteen tales are, as it were, omitted chapters from *Stalky & Co.*, that intimate study of a boy's school, in which Kipling recovers the days of his youth, just as Mark Twain did when he wrote *Tom Sawyer*. Two others, 'Enemies to Each Other' and 'On the Gate', are fantasies not unrelated to 'The Children of the Zodiac'. A fifth, 'The Eye of Allah', is a resuscitation of the remote past with Roger Bacon for the central figure—a resuscitation which might easily have been included in *Puck of Pook's Hill* or *Rewards and Fairies*, and which is worthy of that companionship. A sixth, 'The Bull that Thought', is to be set by the side of 'The Maltese Cat', in that this new tale pictures for us a bull-fight as the earlier story presents a polo match; and the adventure of the thinking bull is richer in content and deeper in meaning than the exciting narrative wherein the quick-witted polo pony is the protagonist.

Half-a-dozen of the other tales have to do with the War, as the War was seen in retrospect by certain of the surviving combatants; and I know no other visions of actual fighting more illuminating than two or three of these, in which we are made to see the ghastly horrors of the days in the trenches and also to catch a glimpse—and often more than a glimpse—of the joy of the combat, the fleeting ecstasy of battle, the glorious hour of strife, which seemed for the moment to make fighting eternally worth while. One of the sequels to war's alarms, 'The Gardener', is a beautiful tale beautifully told; and in its spirit it is akin to 'They', as it has something of the same misty mysticism at the end, which leaves us wondering exactly what had happened and who the mysterious gardener might be. But those will pierce the veil who recall the memorable meeting of Mary Magdalen with 'one in the likeness of a gardener'.

In two of the tales, 'The Wish-House' and 'The Madonna of the Trenches', both stories of love enduring through life and even after death, I have been surprised to find a new note—the note of passion, of deep and dominating passion, not debased by the puerile salacity which is paraded in certain contemporary fictions falsely acclaimed as 'frank' and 'daring'. In these two stories of Kipling there is no leering lewdness, there is true passion, presented with manly reticence, but burning none the less and all the more fiercely because it is an inward fire, which never comes to the surface.

55. Bonamy Dobrée: 'Rudyard Kipling'

1927

Signed article from the *Monthly Criterion*, Vol. VI, pp. 499–515 (December 1927). This is the original article, which Professor Dobrée later rewrote and expanded in his *The Lamp and the Lute* (1929 and 1964)—and completely superseded by his admirable study *Rudyard Kipling : Realist and Fabulist* (1967).

Bonamy Dobrée, O.B.E. (1891–   ) was Professor of English Literature at Cairo 1926–9, and at the University of Leeds 1936–55. He is a leading authority on the literature of the Restoration and Augustan periods, and contributed the volume on *English Literature in The Early Eighteenth Century, 1700–1740* to the Oxford History of English Literature in 1959. He has written reviews and literary criticism for the *Criterion*, *Spectator*, *TLS* and other periodicals.

Mr. Kipling has so scrupulously winnowed the elements of his art, that his candour has deceived many into thinking him too near a simpleton to yield much that can be of use to them in exploring life. They are inclined to take too literally Mr. Max Beerbohm's vision of him dancing a jig with Britannia upon Hampstead Heath, and have thought her as much belittled by his hat, as he is made ridiculous by her helmet. Really it is only the high finish of his art which has made him seem to lack subtlety, for he does not display the workings of his mind, his doubts, and his gropings. He drives his thought to a conclusion, and only when it has reached the force of an intuition, of an assent in Newman's sense of the word, does he clothe it in symbols.

He is, perhaps, romantic by impulse, but he tries his romance seven times in the fire of actuality, and brings it to crystal clearness. Romance, for him, does not lie in yearning, but in fruition; it is not a vague beacon floating in a distant void. It may be

A veil to draw 'twixt God his Law
And Man's infirmity:

but that throwing up of the sponge, that beglamouring of facts, is not really to his taste. What is more to the credit of romance is that it brings up the nine-fifteen. Yet, if that were the end, romance itself would be a trivial thing to make such a pother about, even if bringing up the nine-fifteen stands also for building cities and conquering continents. For even these things are not, in themselves, of vast worth to Mr. Kipling; they are of value only in so far as they are the mechanism which brings action into play. For action is, on this scheme of things, of the first and final importance, since nothing else can make real for man what is no more than a dream in the mind of Brahma. So small a matter as

> . . . the everyday affair of business, meals and clothing
> Builds a Bulkhead 'twixt Despair and the Edge of Nothing,

for man is playing a Great Game of 'To be or not to be' in the face of an indifferent universe. Man must work, since, 'For the pain of the soul there is, outside God's Grace, but one drug; and that is a man's craft, learning, or other helpful motion of his own mind,' and by the last Mr. Kipling means action, because it is only through doing that thought is brought to completion.

The story, 'The Children of the Zodiac', seems most wholly to express Mr. Kipling's view; and there we read 'You cannot pull a plough,' said the bull, with a little touch of contempt. 'I can, and that prevents me thinking of the Scorpion,' namely death. But that is not running away from thinking, it is identifying oneself with the material of thought. But even so the problem is not so clear and shallow as to be solved so easily, for disillusion lurks even behind useful action, and the void may still be there:

> As Adam was a-working outside of Eden-Wall,
> He used the Earth, he used the Seas, he used the Air and all;
> > And out of black disaster
> > He arose to be the master
> > > Of Earth and Water, Air and Fire,
> > > But never reached his heart's desire!
> > > (The Apple Tree's cut down!)

It is plain that this disillusion must also be warded off, otherwise work will not take place; and the Children of the Zodiac did not succeed in warding it off until they had learnt to laugh. Therefore Mr. Kipling also laughs, sometimes to ease his bitterness in this way, but more often to do more than this, and he laughs, not the Bergsonian laughter of social adjustment, but the impassioned, defiant laughter of Nietzsche; not the rectifying laughter of comedy, but the healing laughter of farce. Whence 'Brugglesmith', 'The Village that Voted the Earth was Flat', and the immortal, the Puck-like Pyecroft. Man must laugh lest he perish, just as he must work if he is to exist at all.

Yet it must not be thought that by work Mr. Kipling means fuss and hurry; he will have nothing of 'indecent restlessness'. As to the battle of life, 'The God who sees us all die knows that there is far too much of that battle', and the man who created Kim's Lama is not blind to the possible vanity of his own means of defeating emptiness and evading the fear of death. There is a small rift somewhere, and Ganesh in *The Bridge Builders* may after all be right in regarding the toil of men but as 'dirt digging in the dirt'. There must then be something behind action, something which justifies it, and it is with a love of loyalty that Mr. Kipling reinforces his philosophy of action. First of all there is that of man to man, a loyalty born through understanding of a man's work, and the wholeness of his character. But personal loyalty, if infinitely valuable, is also horribly rare, and Mr. Kipling has not too great faith in it; he has come not to hope overmuch of man. 'The raw fact of life,' Pharaoh Akhenaton told him (why did he choose that particularly nauseating, pot-bellied king?), 'is that mankind is just a little lower than the angels, but if you begin by the convention that men are angels, they will assuredly become bigger beasts than ever.' And loyalty is an angelic quality.

This, we see, takes us a long way from the 'personal relation', the establishment of which figures so large in recent literature; and indeed, what distinguishes Mr. Kipling from so many present-day writers, is precisely that he does not attempt to break down man's loneliness, seeing only futility in the balm of the 'personal relation':

> Chase not with undesired largesse
> Of sympathy the heart
> Which, knowing her own bitterness
> Presumes to dwell apart.

That is why, when Mulvaney told him the story of 'The Courting of Dinah Shadd', Mr. Kipling said nothing; he gave him a hand, which can help, but not heal, for at the moment when a man's black hour descends upon him he has to fight it out alone. 'When I woke I saw Mulvaney, the night dew-gemming his moustache, leaning on his rifle at picket, lonely as Prometheus on his rock, with I know not what vultures tearing his liver.'

But since man is thus unavoidably lonely among men, there is another loyalty to serve as a spring of action, and this is a devotion to something each man must conceive of as bigger than himself. Power man has, yet

> It is not given
> For goods or gear,
> But for the Thing,

whatever the Thing may be. Mr. Kipling does not even admit the last infirmity of noble mind, for fame does not count. Thus more than sympathy, admiration and love, go out from him to obscure men with whom 'heroism, failure, doubt, despair, and self-abnegation' are daily matters, and about whom the official reports are silent. His heart is given at once to any person who strives to do a thing well, not for praise, but through sheer love of the craftsman. For him, as for Parolles, self-love is 'the most inhibited sin in the canon', and, after all, 'one must always risk one's life or one's soul, or one's peace—or some little thing'.

Here, already, we see the scale of Mr. Kipling's values. First it is essential to accept the world for what it is, to play the man while the odds are eternally and crushingly against you. It is hopeless to try to alter the world. Even if you are capable of adding to it, if yours is not the appointed time, your work will be sacrificed, as the priest in *Debits and Credits* had to smash his microscope, and the seaman in *Rewards and Fairies* had to abandon his idea of iron ships: the time was not yet. But man must not complain, nor ask for life's handicap to be reduced. 'My right!' Ortheris answered with deep scorn. 'My right! I ain't a recruity to go whining about my rights to this and my rights to that, just as if I couldn't look after myself. My rights! 'Strewth A'mighty! I'm a man.' It is that kind of individuality, that kind of integrity, proud and secure in its own fortress, which constitutes the aristocracy which alone is worth while, which alone can play the Great Game of actuality.

An aristocrat is, for Mr. Kipling, one who, of whatever race or caste or creed, has a full man within him: Ortheris, Tallantire of the frontier district, Mahbub Ali, M'Andrew—a whole host of them—all are aristocrats, as is Hobden the labourer, with his sardonic smile at the changes of landlords, and the unchangeableness of the world. They are aristocrats because they care little for themselves in comparison with what they stand for, because they are generous, and play the Great Game with laughter on their lips, seeking nobody's help, and claiming no reward. 'First a man must suffer, then he must learn his work, and the self-respect that that knowledge brings.' Never mind if he is a failure, a tramp or a drunkard, he may yet be an aristocrat if he keeps himself whole, and does not set an undue value upon his feelings. This band of chosen naturally hates the intriguers of Simla, or the Tomlinsons, who when they die in their houses in Berkeley Square, deserve neither heaven nor hell. It despises the self-styled 'intellectuals' who 'deal with people's insides from the point of view of men who have no stomachs'. It loathes the rabble which whimpers, and the elements which ruin the industrious hive, crying to the workers, 'Come here, you dear downy duck, and tell us all about your feelings.' The mob which denies the loneliness of man is hateful to it, for it has accomplished nothing, and always defiles what it does not understand. Thus Mr. Kipling's Utopia is one where privacy must not be violated, and where men slink away when they find themselves part of a crowd, loathing the claims of 'the People', who can be crueller than kings. Moreover, Mr. Kipling has only contempt for those who would marshal and pigeon-hole mankind, making it nicely tidy and neat; he feels they are ignorant of men, shallow in their analysis of motives, 'since the real reasons which make or break a man are too absurd or too obscene to be reached from outside'. For him 'social reform' is the selfish game of the idle.

And with this aristocratic preference there goes, as so often, a sense of some Divine Ruler, for to whom else is man to dedicate his work? But Mr. Kipling has no especial choice, he is no sectarian, believing that 'when a man has come to the turnstiles of Night, all the creeds in the world seem to him wonderfully alike and colourless'. He asks of a creed only that it shall give a man the virtues he admires. 'I tell you now that the faith that takes care that every man shall keep faith, even though he may save his soul by breaking faith, is the faith for a man to believe in.' He has small opinion of Christianity because it has not eliminated the fear of the end, so that the Western world 'clings to the dread of death more closely than to the hope of life'. However, he is very tender to other people's beliefs, for men, after all, need a respite. 'Those that faced the figures prayed more zealously than the others, so I judged that their troubles were the greater.' For when all has been written and acted, his own faith also may be subject to disillusion; with perfect consistency he can urge us 'be gentle while the heathen pray to Buddha at Kamakura'.

This, oddly enough, brings us back to Hampstead Heath, for once we speak of Mr. Kipling's religion, we speak of the British Empire. Mr. Beerbohm was cruel in his caricature, but also wittier than appears at first sight, for he made Mr. Kipling look a little unhappy at having thus blatantly to parade the lady of his homage. Yet one must agree that Mr. Kipling cannot be dissociated from the British Empire. It would almost seem that his mission was to bind it together in one blood-brotherhood, a purposive masonic lodge, whose business it is to clear the world of shoddy. Nor can he altogether escape the suspicion of being dazzled by it. He is enraptured by the vision of men clean of mind and thew, clear of eye and inward sight, spreading out over the earth, their lands bound by the ships which fly over the sea like shuttles, weaving the clan together. His is no mere picture of red on the map, since Britannia for him is a goddess. Not only is she a goddess by the fact of her being, but in her nature, for she exacts much toil from her votaries, much of the silent endurance, abnegation and loyalty that he loves. The Empire then is to be cherished, not so much because it is in itself an achievement, but because, like old Rome, it is the most superb instrument to enable man to outface the universe, assert himself against vacancy. Since it unifies the impulses needed to do this, it is Mr. Kipling's Catholic Church.

These things being, apparently, the basis of Mr. Kipling's thought (though the Empire is, strictly speaking, only an accident, an expression rather than a necessity), we may now ask ourselves, honestly facing the risk of being impudent and unduly probing, of what impulses this thought is the satisfaction. And at the foundation of his philosophic love of action we are tempted to find that pining for action men often have when, for one reason or another, it is denied them. He sometimes comes near to blaspheming his art, echoing James Thomson's

> Singing is sweet, but be sure of this;
> Lips only sing when they cannot kiss,

as though the mere act of writing were itself proof of impotence and frustration. This is not a final attitude, but it indicates what may lie behind Mr. Kipling's adoration of perfectly insufferable and not altogether real subalterns, and others who, in various degrees (so long as it is not from offices), handle the affairs of the world.

Yet, ultimately, he is far too good a craftsman, too whole an artist, not to see that God, or whatever other name He may be known by, is to be praised in more ways than the obvious. Nevertheless he now and then reaches out for support to the knowledge that he also is playing the great game, if not of the universe, at least of the world, and is as worthy of a number as Kim, Mahbub Ali, or Hurree Babu:

> Who once hath dealt in the widest game
>> That all of a man can play,
> No later love, no larger fame
>> Will lure him long away.
> As the war-horse smelleth the battle afar,
>> The entered Soul, no less
> He saith: 'Ha! Ha!' where the trumpets are
>> And the thunders of the Press.

Such an attitude permanently held would be much too jejune to produce the real intensity of vision we get from Mr. Kipling; and luckily for us he has at bottom that worship of his own craft he so much admires in others. Addressing his God, his subtilized Jehovah, who judges man by his deeds, he says:

> Who lest all thought of Eden fade
>> Bring'st Eden to the craftsman's brain,
> God-like to muse on his own trade
>> And Man-like stand with God again.

There he is the priest of the Mysterious Will, who causes all things to come in their own time, but one feels he sometimes needs to justify his work to himself. He finds it necessary to make plain that his stories are all parables. Thus:

> When all the world would have a matter hid,
>> Since Truth is seldom friend to any crowd,
> Men write in fable, as old Aesop did,
>> Jesting at that which none will name aloud.
> And this they needs must do, or it will fall
> Unless they please they are not heard at all.

It is plain that art, for Mr. Kipling, is not an escape: it is a precision of bare facts, which his art must make palatable.

Further, since the choice of a goddess does not altogether lie within a man's mental scope, we may seek in Mr. Kipling's impulses the reason for his profound satisfaction in the Empire, his need to assert it. Perhaps the most important of these is his desire to belong to something, a love, not of the 'little platoon', to use Burke's phrase, but of the large regiment. 'It must be pleasant to have a country of one's own to show off,' he remarks. Indeed, his craving for roots makes even the deck of a P. and O. British soil; British, because he is a citizen of the Empire, not of England alone, for if it were essential to be the latter, he would be partly dispossessed. Having spent so many of his early years in India, he is not wholly of England: indeed India is the place where he really belongs. When, for instance, in 1913 he visited Cairo, he wrote:

It is true that the call to prayer, the cadence of some of the street cries, and the cut of some of the garments differed a little from what I had been brought up to; but for the rest, the shadow on the dial had turned back twenty degrees for me, and I found myself saying, as perhaps the dead say when they have recovered their wits, 'This is my real world again!'

But he is not an Indian, he is an Englishman; therefore, to be an integral whole, he must at all costs make England and the Empire one.

Mr. Kipling's love of the Empire and his admiration for those virtues it brings out in men, make him apt to find qualities in Englishmen only, which really exist in all races, and this is part of the deformation Mr. Kipling the artist has at times undergone at the hands of Mr. Kipling the man of action, who found his weapon in the press and his altar in the British Empire. If there had been no daily, or weekly, or monthly papers he might have remained a priest; but in his middle days he fell into the encouraging hands of W. E. Henley, then, in 1893, editing the *National Observer*. Though this gave his talent scope, it meant that instead of speaking only to those who would understand his very special philosophy, he began to proselytise, and shout too loud into the deaf ear of Demos. His work suffered by the accidents of time and circumstance, by the mischance that he was born into an age of magazines and newspapers, when the listeners are the many, and not the aristocrats to whom he truly belongs. It took him, with his slightly unhappy expression, on to Hampstead Heath. A change came over his work, and the echo of the voice of Henley 'throwing a chest' (another man of action to whom action was denied) is ever and anon heard between the lines. In 1893 he published *Many Inventions*, a rich, varied and mature work, which might be singled out as the best volume of his stories, unless *Life's Handicap* be preferred: but from the year he joined Henley his writing took on a more obvious and didactic hue, and we have *The Day's Work*, such parables as 'A Walking Delegate', that tale of perfectly dutiful horses kicking the Trades-Union-Agitator horse, and later, the terrible jingo outbursts of the Boer War. In 1887, or thereabouts, he was writing those delightful

Letters of Marque, with their profound tolerance of India: in 1907 he wrote for the *Morning Post* those clangorous *Letters to the Family*. The man who had in earlier days remarked: 'He began to understand why Boondi does not encourage Englishmen,' could now complain 'Yet South Africa could even now be made a tourists' place—if only the railroad and steamship lines had faith.' That is shocking. It is true that he had always loved the Empire, but he had not loved it in the Hampstead Heath way; and surely it was the exigencies of this later didactic journalism which turned him from a priest into an advance-booking agent, and forced him into a too extravagant statement of 'British' qualities. He does not, however, in all his work feel that these are the monopoly of the British, for he awards his due to the Frenchman and the Sikh, and even to the Bengali, when he really gives rein to his profound instincts, and forgets the thunders of the press. Therefore the distortion does not matter in the long run, for time and again he gives us things of a breadth and a peculiar grip we get from no other writer of his generation.

The accidents, then, of Mr. Kipling's attitude may be dismissed, to allow us to return to his intuitions, and proceed to the next step in our analysis, namely a consideration of what symbols he has chosen to clothe his intuitions with. He has usually chosen men and women to body forth his notions, and his people, as is always the case in really creative art, are symbols of something else. They are not merely vehicles for an idle tale. Where he has chosen other material, as in 'The Mother Hive' or 'The Ship that Found Herself', he has failed, as anyone is bound to do. An apologue always smacks of the schoolroom, and it is worth noticing that these stories belong to his most didactic period. There he is not quite at his ease, his assent is a little forced, but where his intuition was whole, as in *Kim*, in which the artist conquers the moralist and buries him deep underground, he is nothing short of superb: his symbols clothe his intuition so that we take it for flesh and blood. That is, we work from life to the thought that created it, and not from the thought to life, as we do with lesser artists, who have ideas they wish to impose on life. Mr. Kipling's failures occur either when his shallower, demagogue nature takes charge, and we are conscious of didacticism; or where the intuition is uncompleted. It is uncompleted in two sets of circumstances: the first where women are concerned, whence Mrs. Hauksbee, Mrs. Gadsby and others, where the symbols are vulgar because the intuition is false (there is a reservation to be made in the case of the woman in the last story in *Debits and Credits*); the second is in the mysterious world of unreality which he feels about him, but which he has not resolved within himself: hence such failures—one must here defy popular opinion—as 'They' and 'The Brushwood Boy'. There the symbols are sentimental because the intuition is feeble.

So far an attempt has been made to define Mr. Kipling's philosophic apparatus; but without delight, a living sympathy, and perhaps an attitude of praise, there can be no great art in the grand manner, and these he has abundantly. *A Diversity of Creatures*; that is not only the title of a book, it is a phrase continually occurring in other of his volumes, and he often thanks God for the variety of His beings. He is an apt illustration of those who claim that only by adoring what is can one add to life. He revels in men so long as they are positive, since it is only by his deeds that a man can exist. Also, with a generous sensuality which rejects no physical sensation, he loves the 'good brown earth', especially the smells that it produces, West or East. With all these likes and keen senses, this recognition of adventures in life and his feeling for romance in works, his zestful following of men on their occasions lawful and unlawful, he has God's plenty within him.

Thus it is that his best symbols also have God's plenty within them. It is noticeable that they are not those of Tchekov, say, or Henry James, since different symbols correspond to different intuitions, and his are not theirs. Mr. Kipling's live close to the ground, and he has frequented the more primitive sort of men because 'all the earth is full of tales to him who listens and does not drive away the poor from his door. The poor are the best of tale-tellers, for they must lay their ear to the ground every night.' He met a hundred men on the road to Delhi, and they were all his brothers, since they were close to the earth, that is, to the actuality that can be handled. There were the people in *Kim*, there were Peachey Carnehan and Daniel Dravot ('The Man Who Would Be King'); there were forgotten toilers in out-stations; and above all there were Mulvaney, Ortheris, and Learoyd. Nor must it pass unnoticed that all his three soldiers had trodden paths of bitterness, and were at times subject to an overwhelming sorrow akin to madness, the sorrow of disillusion. They are of value as symbols precisely because they have outfaced much. They were none of them obviously successful, for Mr. Kipling despises success except that which consists in keeping one's soul intact. Whence his sympathy for those who are broken because they are too positive, such as the sometime Fellow of an Oxford college who had passed 'outside the pale', for the lighthouse man who went mad from the infernal streakiness of the tides, and even for Love o' Women. In such cases, where human beings seem wholly to live the life of the symbol, to exist as a quality, Mr. Kipling is content that men, himself included, should be no more than part of the earth; he is happy to be their interpreter, and give them their place as players of the Great Game.

If, at this point, we try to mark what it is that most distinguishes Mr. Kipling from the other writers to be treated of in this enquiry, we find that he shares with most the despondency of the day, but not its optimism as regards panaceas, and that his delight in the actuality of men, their proven virtues, gives him values instead of vague hopes. In his metaphysical scepticism, his belief in the void which surrounds existence, he is a child of his time, as modern as any of our literary nihilists who see, in Mr. Housman's phrase that, 'when men think they fasten their hands upon their hearts'. It is safe to say that at no modern period has the world seemed so empty a thing, the universe so indifferent, our values so factitious: and as we look back upon the centuries we can see that this attitude has been fatefully coming upon us. Yet, though Mr. Kipling manifests this attitude, he differs from his contemporaries, and it is because of his difference that he already seems to survive them. He is more enduring because something of the past three centuries clings to him.

For the Elizabethans and Jacobeans life gained its glamour largely from its nearness to the plague-pit; its values were determined and heightened by the vigorously expressed dogmas of a Church, which, for pulpit purposes at least, believed in hell; the metaphysical void was filled by the sense that life was given to man as a discipline and an adventure: this is still part of Mr. Kipling's belief. Indeed, if one were to have to choose one man from whom he descends rather than from another, one would say it was Jeremy Taylor. In *Holy Dying* we read:

Softness is for slaves and beasts, for minstrels, and useless persons, for such who cannot ascend higher than the state of a fair ox, or a servant entertained for vainer offices: but the man that designs his son for noble employments, to honours and to triumphs, to consular dignities and presidencies of councils, loves to see him pale with study, or panting with labour, hardened with sufferance, or eminent by dangers. And so God dresses us for heaven.

And in *Letters of Travel*:

I wonder sometimes whether any eminent novelist, philosopher, dramatist, or divine of today has to exercise half the pure imagination, not to mention insight, endurance and self-restraint, which is accepted without comment in what is called 'the material exploitation' of a new country. Take only the question of creating a new city at the juncture of two lines—all three in the air. The mere drama of it, the play of the human virtues, would fill a book. And when the work is finished, when the city is, when the new lines embrace a new belt of farms, and the tide of wheat has rolled North another unexpected degree, the men who did it break off, without compliments, to repeat the joke elsewhere.

The mind is the same, the matter only the difference of the centuries.

Then, with the advance of science and the retreat of the plague, man grew less concerned with himself, and more interested in the outer world, its marvels, its emerging order. Coupled with a somewhat flabby Deism, believing at the most in only a lukewarm hell, was the attitude of mind, best typified by John Evelyn, who, like Mr. Kipling, found naught common on the earth. Here Mr. Kipling largely stays, and with the introspective movement ushered in by Rousseau, with the hysterical subjective idealists whose only reality is their emotion, he will have nothing to do, and it is probable that Proust seems a dreary waste to him. He cannot away with men and women intent upon saving their souls, or who believe, even, that they have souls to save: it is typical that he should have described a man he disliked as 'fearing physical pain as some men fear sin'.

Yet the solipsist attitude still further weakened the idea of future punishment, and we are not surprised that in the century and a half which saw its development, an English Chief Justice, Lord Westbury, should, in a famous judgment, have 'dismissed Hell with costs, and taken away from orthodox members of the Church of England their last hope of everlasting damnation'. This was to have its effect, but habits of impulse do not change so fast, and if there was to be no hell, there was still to be service to God, and of this sense again Mr. Kipling has something, since, for the meaning alone, it might have been Browning who wrote:

> One instant's toil to Thee denied
> Stands all eternity's offence.

But soon it was realized that if there was to be no hell, the only heaven would have to be on earth, and if social reform began at least as early as Shaftesbury, not to go back to Shelburne, it is chiefly characteristic of the Edwardian period. Mr. Kipling, however, who cannot bear the flaccidity of social reform, still has a hope of hell, and agreeing that this world is sufficient for man, he places his hell upon earth. Thus he cannot accept our modern Utopias, so clean and hygienic, so free from temptation and sin and suffering—except, for him, the suffering of being forever in a crowd. Utopian perfection would be insipid and loathsome, and we may surmise that the final reason why the British Empire satisfies him is that it can contain both heaven and hell, at least as much as is good for any man.

Apart from delight, an important reservation, it is doubtful if the real value of any writer is apparent to his close contemporaries: his equals in age are more likely to seize upon what they already share with him, and with mankind's aversion for what is new in ideas, will reject what the next generation eagerly clutches at. As far as can be judged, the elements in Mr. Kipling's writings which have won him popularity, are the least important, the most ephemeral. It will only be possible to give him his rightful place when the political heats of his day have become coldly historical. But to us, the successive generation, he has a value that may well be permanent, apart from his language, which in itself deserves to live. He has indicated an attitude towards life, which to us, groping for a solid basis, may serve, if not for that basis itself, at least as a point of disagreement. He deals, after all, with the enduring problems of humanity, the problems out of which all religion, all real poetry, must arise. Moreover, he provides a solution, which those of his own cast of mind—and they are many, though most may be unaware of it—will greet with satisfaction, and even with that sense of glamour, of invigoration, which it is partly the function of literature to give.

56. R. Ellis Roberts: 'Rudyard Kipling'

1928

Signed article from the *Empire Review*, Vol. XLVII, pp. 184–93 (March 1928). Also collected in the author's *Reading for Pleasure, and Other Essays* (1928).

Richard Ellis Roberts (1879–1953), well-known critic and reviewer of the twenties and thirties.

We all know that Mr. Kipling began his career as a journalist. Some critics have realized that he was that rare thing, a great journalist. But I do not think anyone has realized how extraordinarily he has retained the great journalist's attitude to life. That attitude, like all attitudes of any value or truth, involves an apparent contradiction and a balance of opposites. The great journalist knows that almost nothing is really important, and that almost anything is news. He knows that just as a man forgets the contents of yesterday's paper, so the world forgets the events of last century; and he knows that something is always remembered, and that it is his business, if he wishes to be a good journalist, to learn how to 'spot' the events and the people which will be remembered. A good journalist always keeps his sense of proportion, and always appears to lose it; he must write of all news as if it were the most vital and exciting thing that has ever happened, and yet know in his heart that its interest is evanescent. Yet he must never be indifferent (cynicism is not indifference)—he must be excited about the transient; and the more deeply he believes that everything is transient the more eagerly and simply will he welcome the eternal news if it ever comes his way. The curse of the journalist is over-emphasis, adopted to impress both himself and others; his blessing is that he never suffers, as do the rest of the world, from that dreadful boredom which is the beginning of spiritual death. At the first symptom of accidie in his soul, the good journalist will start to analyse it; and he will make fresh news, late-press news out of the mere monotony of a repetitive universe.

How well Mr. Kipling has retained the great journalist's mind can be seen in the address he made when he was presented with the Gold Medal of the Royal Society of Literature in 1926. He spoke about the art of the novelist and literary fame:

All men are interested in reflections of themselves and their surroundings, whether in the pure heart of a crystal or in a muddy pool, and nearly every writer who supplies a reflection secretly desires a share of immortality for the pains he has been at in holding up the mirror—which also reflects himself. He may get his desire. Quite a dozen writers have achieved immortality in the past 2,500 years. From a bookmaker's—a real bookmaker's—point of view the odds are not attractive, but fiction is built on fiction. That is where it differs from the other arts.

Most of the arts admit the truth that it is not expedient to tell everyone everything. Fiction recognizes no such bar. There is no human emotion or mood which it is forbidden to assault—there is no canon of reserve or pity that need be respected—in fiction. Why should there be? The man, after all, is not telling the truth. He is only writing fiction. While he writes it, his world will extract from it just so much truth or pleasure as it requires for the moment. In time a little more, or much less, of the residue may be carried forward to the general account, and there, perhaps, diverted to ends of which the writer never dreamed.

Take a well-known instance. A man of overwhelming intellect and power goes scourged through life between the dread of insanity and the wrath of his own soul warring with a brutal age. He exhausts mind, heart, and brain in that battle; he consumes himself and perishes in utter desolation. Out of all his agony remains one little book, his dreadful testament against his fellow-kind, which today serves as a pleasant tale for the young under the title of *Gulliver's Travels*. That, and a faint recollection of some baby-talk in some love-letters, is as much as the world has chosen to retain of Jonathan Swift, Master of Irony. Think of it! It is like turning down the glare of a volcano to light a child to bed.

Mr. Kipling exhibits the traits of the great journalist which have served to make him the most popular, the most widely-read, the best-known of all living English authors who are also ranked high by the critics of literature. It is an odd accusation to make against the man who astonished us in the nineties by the *Barrack Room Ballads*, the *Plain Tales from the Hills*, and the collection of army and Indian stories —but I accuse Mr. Kipling, first, of modesty. All good journalists must be modest—they must believe, that is, that what they have to say, what they write about, is more important than themselves. There were many reasons for Mr. Kipling's extreme success; but it was really his modesty, in that age, which was mainly responsible.

He began to write at a time when authors all over Europe were bitten with the heresy of art for art's sake—a doctrine which soon resolves itself into art for the artist's sake. Two great schools had given support to this thesis. There was the aesthetic school, of which the head in England was not Wilde but Walter Pater, who found almost all the interest of their material in its effect on the personality of the artist. It was his nature, his temperament, his moods, his opinions which were of supreme importance: the world of experience only had such value as was given it by the artist's reactions and reflections. Secondly, there was the school—to which in a sense much of Mr. Kipling's earlier work in prose belonged—that followed the teachings of the great French naturalists. Zola, the Goncourts, Maupassant, the early Huysmans professed that the art of the novelist was the art of objective recording; and these men forgot that objectivity was in itself a subjective thing—or, in the modern cant, that extroversion is only a very limited kind of introversion—and that, could he do it, the novelist who did not select at all was, by his very refusal to select, exercising a choice as personal and arbitrary as the most eclectic writer. Both schools, then, attached an undue value to the will and the judgment of the novelist. Now Mr. Kipling, who began writing from a mind exceptionally well-stored from boyhood with many kinds of literature was, except in the matter of style, entirely free from literary *snobisme*. It is the secret of his popularity with men who care little for other modern books (except Mark Twain's, also very free from this weakness), engineers, travellers, businessmen, sailors, and others; and it is the reason why critics who can divest themselves of the fallacy that literature and the other arts are admittedly more important than any other avocations find Mr. Kipling's work some of the most tonic and delightful of our time.

In reading the bulk of Mr. Kipling's work in verse or prose two impressions are immediate and remain constant. The author is avidly curious of all aspects of life, and he has the power to see in any person or incident that unique value which does properly belong to it. In method and superficial manner his debt to Maupassant is evident in his early stories; but he has not Maupassant's deep-seated infidelity. Maupassant could be at times a little sentimental and slightly romantic; but we never believe in his romance nor his sentimentalism as we do in his cynicism and his realism. For Kipling the world of Mrs. Hauksbee, of the people in 'False Dawn', of the Gadsbys is as real as he makes it for us; but it is not more real than the world of 'Wee Willie Winkie', of 'The Brushwood Boy', and of 'They'. Kipling's place as an imaginative reporter is a greater than Maupassant's; no author since Robert

Browning has had quite so great an inquisitiveness into different kinds of life, quite so great a power of finding out the facts, or quite such a genius for telling us about the things he discovers. The early critics were so charmed or terrified by the young Kipling's diabolical cleverness, by his smartness, his air of cocksureness that they ignored his plain traditionalism. Really, as I said, Mr. Kipling is a modest author. He had, and still has at times, a cocksure, positive manner; but actually he is much less arrogant than such an author as Stevenson. For Mr. Kipling is cocksure not about what he thinks, nor what he believes, but about what he has been told. He annoys many people precisely because of the breadth of his interest, and here again he resembles Browning. Many people who are too mentally and imaginatively fatigued to read Browning sweep him aside because he makes them feel small and limited. Now that Mr. Kipling's smartness is not fresh, his manner no longer unfamiliar, we can ignore them and we find, if we read his work sympathetically, that what excites and pleases us is the author's excitement and pleasure in so many different kinds of people, in so dazzling a variety of scene as this world affords. We can apply to Kipling the lines Landor wrote to Robert Browning:

> Since Chaucer was alive and hale,
> No man hath walk'd along our roads with step
> So active, so inquiring eye, or tongue
> So varied in discourse.

This acute criticism of Browning is valuable because it recognizes the existence of a kind of artist too often confused with another class. Shakespeare, Dickens, Balzac, Tolstoy are men of great creative imagination; they do not only observe, they make—their people are often more real, that is nearer in our judgment to the truth of life, than the characters we meet. Chaucer, Browning, Kipling are not of that company. They are men of great invention and observant imagination. Their figures rarely—this is not true of Pompilia or the Pope in *The Ring and the Book*—have any reality greater than that of actual life, and they exist in the circumstances and conditions their creators make for them, and not outside these conditions. Take one of Mr. Kipling's best and most heartrending stories *The Record of Badalia Herodsfoot*. Badalia is dreadfully, poignantly alive. She is solid and three-dimensional. Mr. Kipling knows her every action, almost her every thought and aspiration, and can show them to us with a precision which not even Maupassant could excel. Badalia, Tom, and Jenny are as vivid as an author of genius can make them. How the speech of the 'second comforter' expresses the whole life of a woman in slum-land, if she lives with a blackguard:

Let 'er go an' dig for her bloomin' self. A man wears 'isself out to 'is bones shovin' meat down their mouths, while they sit at 'ome easy all day; an' the very fust time, mark you, you 'as a bit of a difference, an' very proper, too, for man as *is* a man, she ups an' 'as you out into the street, callin' you Gawd knows what all. What's the good o' that, I arx you?

It is the best story of slum-life in English, and it set a fashion both in England and America. Yet, if you turn from these three consummately drawn people, with every action and gesture right, to Charles Dickens' Bill Sikes and Nancy you are aware that you have passed into a higher realm of reality. Kipling's people are the more accurate, the more credible, far less tied to their creator's writing-table; but yet Bill and Nancy are more real. While Badalia, Jenny, and Tom are three-dimensional, Bill Sikes and Nancy and even the bull-terrier are four-dimensional. They exist outside the conditions of the story called *Oliver Twist*. They are free, and not determined. They are more 'types' than Mr. Kipling's people, and yet they are more individuals just because they are more typical. In the last part of Mr. Shaw's *Back to Methuselah*, Pygmalion makes two automata who are as human as human beings of today, though the people of A.D. 31,730 believe they are only dolls. They are consummately made, completely perfect, beautiful, splendid, and are, indeed, alive; they move and speak and feel. Then one of the Ancients touches them, and faintly into them flows the stream of that higher life after which it is man's destiny to strive. There is the difference between the works of the creative imagination and the inventive imagination. The creatures of the creative imagination may be clumsier, more ill-shaped, absurder, less lifelike than those of the inventive imagination; but they belong to a higher realm of reality. This distinction is to be found in all the arts—it is even clearer in painting, perhaps, than in literature—it separates Holbein from Rembrandt, Manet from Van Gogh, Hals from Velasquez, Raphael from Michaelangelo. It is not, let me insist again, that the creatures of the inventive imagination do not live, but they live on another level.

And on that level how alive they are, and what enormous pleasure they can give us. I am sorry for those who cannot appreciate the great company of artists whose work has this proximate reality. Sometimes their sheer craft is so great that their work passes into the other kind—

d'Artagnan sometimes, I think, goes riding with Falstaff, and I believe Mr. Pickwick watched, a little shocked, perhaps, as a certain police stretcher was pushed through the night and dawn to Brook Green, Hammersmith. But I neither understand nor respect the aesthetic Puritanism which will not allow us to enjoy any art which has not an immediate symbolic value. All the world's literatures contain specimens of the pure storyteller's art, and the man who is indifferent to the suggestion of the village fire, or the road to Canterbury, or that low room in which Scheherazade night after night postponed her death-sentence, seems to me to have mistaken his vocation if he writes, or, indeed, concerns himself about literature. There is, I believe, a moral and intellectual cowardice in his attitude. For the supreme storytellers, if they do not give us life as it is lived in the secret places of the heart, as it is in the dreams of the emancipated spirit, give us something inalienable and irreplaceable. They give us the spectacle of life. They give to those of us who cannot, through circumstance or character, have those adventures of the body and mind by the enduring of which man has learnt to desire the adventures of the imagination and the soul, a chance of experiencing what those pioneers experienced. To refuse to listen to them is to try to skip a step in our mental development. The man who despises those hazards which belong to the characters in the art of invention is never fit for those higher and more perilous hazards for the sake of which he pretends to belittle the others. Finally, if we are deaf to the cry of 'Let's pretend!' and 'Once upon a time', we are refusing to listen to an appeal on the response to which depended the very existence of that other art we profess so to value.

Of Mr. Kipling's supremacy of the story of invention I do not think there can be any question. Even Mr. Bennett's virtuosity, even Mr. Wells' intelligence seem a shade too careful, too considered beside Mr. Kipling's cool, unhurried, foolproof ease and skill. It is not possible to say in which tales the normal genius of Mr. Kipling is most obvious; there are too many which are so completely satisfying that they could not be altered without damage. 'The Finest Story in the World' is, perhaps, one in which may be seen at their highest the many and various aspects of his talent; but a critic would choose something less ambitious if he wished to expatiate on the direct force of Mr. Kipling's genius. Wonderful as are *Many Inventions* and *Life's Handicap*, I am not sure that it is not in *The Day's Work* that one can find the stories which display at its height the normal Kipling. 'William the Conqueror' and 'The Tomb of His Ancestors' have a mature mastery which it is difficult to match. If we add to these 'Without Benefit of Clergy' from *Life's Handicap*, 'An Habitation Enforced' from *Actions and Reactions*, we have then, I think, the tales by which an anthologist would represent Kipling's gift at its most characteristic.

Then there is the other Kipling. Some among the great artists of invention and imagination never seem aware of that other kingdom in which they are not masters. There is no hint in Dumas or in Rubens of a desire for any other world than that which they can control and so magnificently present. They are content that their art should be perfect, unheeding apparently the truth that perfection is something less as well as something more than human. Others, Chaucer is a notable instance, by sheer style carry us into that other country. Browning reached it in some poems by a power of sympathy as strong and more usual than the creative imagination of Keats or of Shelley. In his way, though one would not put him on a level with those poets, a similar event overcomes Mr. Kipling. If I may mis-apply the last sentence of 'The Brushwood Boy', it will stand as Mr. Kipling's question to himself as he records the spectacle of life. 'But—what shall I do when I see you in the light?' His question to himself is 'What shall I do when I see you in my dreams, in the night?' Very early the problem haunted him, often in grim and uncomfortable forms that resulted in stories of horror unequalled outside Poe, but often, especially in his later work, in stories of beauty and longing and a tender reverence which are not the less lovely for his boyishness of spirit. A great journalist, Mr. Kipling knows that there are countries the journalist cannot enter—that is the last lesson of journalism and is very rarely learnt; and so, when he is taken there by his spirit of love and curiosity, he abandons the journalist's method, even if he sometimes keeps the manner. He has stated his own attitude in a poem which is unfairly neglected by those who acclaim him as a party verse-maker, and a defender of the West against the East. Long before, in a brief chapter heading in *The Naulahka*, he had shown that he had, above most men, 'two different sides to his head'. It was no ignorant applauder of the *sahib* who wrote the damaging quatrain:

Now, it is not good for the Christian's health to hustle the Aryan brown,
For the Christian riles, and the Aryan smiles, and he weareth the Christian down;
And the end of the fight is a tombstone white, with the name of the late deceased,
And the epitaph drear: 'A fool lies here who tried to hustle the East.'

And it is the same spirit which is alive in that challenging verse:

> I'd not give way for an Emperor,
> I'd hold my road for a King—
> To the Triple Crown I would not bow down—
> But this is a different thing.
> I'll not fight with the Powers of the Air,
> Sentry, pass him through!
> Drawbridge let fall, 'tis the Lord of us all,
> The Dreamer whose dreams come true!

It is that Kipling who wrote a few poems of exquisite loveliness, certain stories of the beyond, and those strange tales of a further reality which force us to reconsider a classification which puts Kipling with those authors for whom the visible world and its inhabitants most supremely exist. 'The Brushwood Boy', 'The Miracle of Puran Bhagat'; most of *Kim*, 'Wireless', 'In the Same Boat', 'The Finest Story in the World', and 'They'—all these stories take me, at least, into the fourth dimension; so does most of the two *Jungle Books*, and at least one of Mr. Kipling's stupendous comedies. 'The Village that Voted the Earth was Flat', though it has in it a rather detestable taint of cruelty, is comedy of a kind which has not been written since Dickens. It has obvious affinities with that side of Mr. Wells' genius which gave us *Kipps* and *Mr. Polly*; it might be compared to some of Mr. Bennett's fantastic effects, but it has an unearthliness, a proper Aristophanic Rabelaisian quality which we cannot find in any other modern author, and only this time in Mr. Kipling. There is not a little of Mr. Kipling's work which shows how well acquainted he is with the men and manners of past time. In *Rewards and Fairies*, in *Puck of Pook's Hill*, I feel not that he has read about the remote days of the Roman occupation, nor of the days of Elizabeth, but that he has been there and comes back to tell us of them. So in 'The Eye of Allah' he writes with an ease which Miss Waddell might envy of the lore and the science of the Middle Ages. He is a supreme interviewer, for he asks his questions with that degree of sympathetic imagination which makes an answer inevitably right. And this gift which in his youth he applied chiefly to the men and women of today he has in later days exercised on the men and women of the past. In 'The Eye of Allah' the talk of the monks about medicine and science and art has a tang that brings the men back to their cloisters; and the final speech of the Abbot has, in brief, the same wry wisdom which Mr. Shaw found in the mediaeval scholastics who condemned St. Joan. In the same terms, for the same reason, the Abbot smashes the microscope and pronounces it idolatry:

He unscrewed the metal cylinder, laid it on the table, and with the dagger's hilt smashed some crystal to sparkling dust which he swept into a scooped hand and cast behind the hearth.

'It would seem,' he said, 'the choice lies between two sins. To deny the world a Light which is under our hand, or to enlighten the world before her time. What you have seen, I saw long since among the physicians of Cairo. And I know what doctrine they drew from it. Hast *thou* dreamed, Thomas? I also— with fuller knowledge. But this birth, my sons, is untimely. It will be but the mother of more death, more torture, more division, and greater darkness in this dark age. Therefore, I, who know both my world and the Church, take this Choice on my conscience. Go! It is finished.'

He thrust the wooden part of the compasses deep among the beech logs till all was burned.

But it is not this story which is the gem of his last volume. The primacy rests with 'the tale of 1916' called 'On the Gate'. It is a tale of the invasion of heaven by those who fell on the field of battle. All the characters are supernatural beings, or the souls of the great dead now in paradise, or the souls of the recently slain. I know no modern story in any language, not even in Russian, in which sacred and deeply moving things are handled at once with such daring and such reverence. I know no story in which Mr. Kipling's deep underlying pity, so often obscured by his cleverness of manner, is so well employed. The guardians of the gate are overworked and call in others to help against the angels of the pit who strive for the souls of the dead at the very bar of heaven. The extra pickets include Joan of Arc, Charles Bradlaugh, John Bunyan, John Calvin, Judas Iscariot, and William Shakespeare. Only a long quotation can do justice to the force and vision of the great scene of struggle:

[quotes *Debits and Credits*, p. 350, line 13, to p. 351, line 27—'Meantime, a sunken eyed Scots officer' to 'and compared notes']

I suppose the conventionally orthodox may be disturbed at Mr. Kipling's vision of the other world: it is not the mythology of the Middle Ages, for here Judas is out of hell and, with a bold return to the eschatology of Origen and the earlier Christian tradition, there is hope for the 'Lower Establishment'. I shall not be surprised if in the years to come this story may not be one of the greatest influences towards popularizing the modern idea of the meaning of eternity. The eternity of hell is not a matter of duration but of intensity; hell can be entered in this life, and its pains are eternal—that is, they have the same blazing quality of reality as the happiness of heaven. They touch all that is permanent and indestructible in the soul of man. And, just because they do that, they cannot be everlasting unless and except any soul insists for ever in remaining obdurate to all the pleadings of God within and without. 'On the Gate' has a wider scope, a deeper beauty than any other of Mr. Kipling's stories of the other world, and in it he justifies all his previous essays, whether in prose or verse, to snatch for a moment the veil from actual things and show to us the reality that alone supports and informs them.

57. Gilbert Frankau on Kipling

1928

Extract from signed article 'Rudyard Kipling' in the *London Magazine*, Vol. LXI, pp. 130–4 (August 1928).

Gilbert Frankau (1884–1952) was a popular novelist of the twenties, best known for *Peter Jackson, Cigar Merchant* (1919). He served in the Royal Field Artillery throughout the First World War, and wrote some of its best poetry in the form of ballads—following, but not imitating Kipling—in *The City of Fear, and Other Poems* (1917). His views on Kipling's work are typical of the general, unacademic appreciation of the period.

. . . All that I have in me of literary hero-worship was long ago given to the supreme present-day craftsman, and there remains.

I refer to Rudyard Kipling. And when I call him the supreme present-day craftsman, I do so in the perfect awareness that many a tight-lipped highbrow will rise up and disagree. For Rudyard Kipling has never pandered to the highbrow, and therein lies his main power. Nor—and may whatever gods there be bless him for it—has he ever pandered to Woman, who is the burden laid upon the shoulders of every mere novelist, and haunts him in his dreams.

We, the mere novelists of nowadays, are nearly all of us woman-ridden. The female reader with the library subscription (no English women *buy* books) either makes us or mars. And if we depict woman as the average male thinks of her, or talks of her in that which was once called 'the smoking-room', the marring is done swiftly. Thumbs down to the library girl! 'No; I don't think I'll take *that*, thank you, Miss Mudie. Haven't you got the new Marcel Harlene? Only for guaranteed subscribers? Oh dear; now isn't that too bad?'

But Kipling's women are—just women. From Mrs. Bathurst, who had 'It'—the phrase is R.K.'s, written twenty years ago, and whether Elinor Glyn stole 'It' or no is only Elinor Glyn's business—down to Badalia Herodsfoot, who loved the 'curick' and was kicked to death with 'the deadly intelligence born of whisky'. Kipling puts women in their place, whether the kitchen or the drawing-room. And because he does so, the woman who appreciates any but his stories of children is a rarity, to be either married or made a pal of, according to your temperament, as soon as found. Moreover, when Kipling, also the inconsequent, departs from this clear-eyed vision of the 'female of the species', he is apt to stumble, as even the best of craftsmen stumble, by the literary way.

Give Kipling a woman who is nurse, mate, mother, or old wife by the fireside, garrulous about lovers who are dead, and his picture comes away perfect, a marvel of pen-work, not to be denied. Give him woman as the women who read novels like to imagine themselves; that is to say creatures of romance, perpetually adored by perpetual Valentinos in an atmosphere which is one-third amorous excitement, one-third financial extravagance, and the rest sofa cushions—and Kipling jibs at her, as a wise horse jibs at a fence known too high. For Kipling, even as the good horse, knows his limitations. And the craftsman who has not learned that lesson, has not yet learned the rudiments of his craft.

He has other limitations, too, being as human as the rest of us. He can hate—which is no literary virtue. And his opponents' point of view is frequently anathema to him. But on the whole—compare him, let us say, with Galsworthy—his range is as wide as that Empire he loves with a devotion as rare, in these days of shoddy thought, shoddy sentences, and shoddy internationalism, as a poor tailor, or a rich journalist, or a man who won't take legal advantage of his Majesty's income-tax collectors if he gets the chance.

58. Harvey Darton on 'Kipling's Children's Books'

1932

Pp. 309–10 and 314–16 of F. J. Harvey Darton's *Children's Books in England* (1932).

F. J. Harvey Darton (1878–1936), a member of the family and firm that has published children's books for over two centuries, was a literary scholar and bibliographer, besides himself writing books for children. His *Children's Books in England* was the first, and still remains the greatest, work on the subject—though he gave relatively little space to the Golden Age of children's books in the reigns of Victoria and Edward VII. The paragraphs on Kipling show, however, the high and immediate place he took in this branch of Literature.

PAGES 309–10 The school story, however, bore in its very subject the explosive contradiction which was to kill it, or at least to blow away its layer of older readers. That contradiction was that its gradual perfection as a story took away any truth it had in relation to schools. The various kinds of boy, the obvious masters, the school servant, the townee friend or enemy, became all too soon stock actors. There was a mechanization like that of the earlier stage, when Congreve and Sheridan became Foote and Colman, and worse. It had come upon adult literature also, as writers once thought revolutionary perceived in the nineties. *Jude the Obscure, Plain Tales from the Hills, The Heavenly Twins, The Woman who Did,* to jumble a few names, were all books of the Diamond Jubilee decade; and the difference between *Erewhon* (1872) and *Erewhon Revisited* (1901) is more than a difference in the years of one man's life.

But the schoolboy readers, or those who chose books for them, were not conscious of this change in the national intellect. They overlooked the significance of the sub-title of F. Anstey's *Vice Versa* (1882)—

'A Lesson for Fathers'. A great part of that lesson was that many boys are by nature nasty little beasts (in the schoolboy sense), and that life in schools did not stand still, rooted in parental tradition. *Tom Brown* had become a lonely deserted rock in the distance. *Eric* was a kind of immovable moral jelly-fish left behind by the tide. Baines Reed and his imitators were the regular ripples in a smooth sea. No wonder that when *Stalky & Co.* appeared in 1899 there was an outcry. High—the highest —traditions seemed to be flouted and defiled by it. The academy represented—Westward Ho!, which there is reason to believe felt about the book much as King William's College felt about *Eric*—was said by unsympathetic persons not to be a public school at all, but an inferior place for inferior people, who not only spoke the wrong language, as all 'foreigners' do, but had the wrong code of life. It was not easily perceived that the code itself was under scrutiny, and that 'Beetle' was not meant to fit in with Tom Brown and Eric.

The book had in time many repercussions. It was read as general fiction, not only as a story for and about boys. The truth of its picture, in detail, though a matter of interest to persons immediately concerned is not here a question of importance. The significant thing is the absence of the old standards, on the one hand, and the merging of boy-and-man interests on the other. The masters are not stock types, any more than the pupils. Moral issues are largely ignored. The good or evil effect of the events described upon the characters is as irrelevant as the good or evil effect of the book upon the reader. The reader, in fact, was the reader of the average novel; and he was now son as well as father. The 'school story', for any 'young' public over about fourteen years of age, was dead, the public having grown up.

Stalky & Co. in that respect, became a precedent in adult fiction. It was the first of a number of school-life novels for the full-grown reader; later on, perhaps, for the full-blown. In the twentieth century these became common. Retaliation for *Stalky* came and was in turn retaliated upon. H. A. Vachell's *The Hill* (1905), produced in the stock form of a (then) six-shilling novel for the regular circulating library public, provoked the counterblast of Arnold Lunn's *The Harrovians* (1913). Much later, in 1917, Alec Waugh's *The Loom of Youth*, written when its author himself was only just out of school, set a second supply going, until it almost became a distinction for a public school not to have a novel all about itself under a thin disguise.

PAGES 314–16 The upper division of children, then, began in the last quarter of Victoria's reign to experience rapid 'materialistic' growth. Its temper of mind, the sum of little reflections from daily life which grow into an habitual outlook, was perceptibly affected by the mutations of practical progress. Whether there was an equally profound spiritual metabolism at work it is probably not yet time to say. We are still too near the World War and its emetic effects to be confident as to which new thing is symptom, which essence, which mere accident; and in that War many children of the nineties perished.

But in the world of younger children something very like a change of mental outlook was also becoming visible. 'Children', as now distinct from 'boys' and 'girls', were clearly unbabyish: old-fashioned people said more precocious. The simplicities and unquestioned make-believe of folk-lore were no longer quite adequate: even the youngest horizon was not the nursery wall. Rudyard Kipling, though not so devastating in this sphere, is once more a valuable index to what was happening. *Stalky* had been preceded by the two *Jungle Books* (1894 and 1895). Obviously animal study and human sociability for beasts was no new thing. The nurture of Mowgli had a legendary precedent in Roman history, and a vaguely historical one hinted at in the history of Peter the Wild Boy; while the philosophy of Uncle Remus now and then flickers up in gnomic comments on life. But the freshness of style, colour and vision was unmistakable. Even the occasional stridency of emphasis was a novel virtue. As for moral qualities, the Jungle Law was not an unfolding of the wonderful ways of Providence. It was what Life had reached by Social Evolution. Its results were a code of honour based on hard facts, with tooth and claw for its practical sanctions, but with a consciousness of responsibility which the Breed (white bipeds preferably English) felt even more exaltedly. Courage, endurance, observation, good faith, dexterity, physical and mental fitness—all these were transmuted from routine virtues into an eager inspiration. The *Jungle Books* were not romance, not fiction, even; they were young life conscious of itself and its extraordinarily stimulating world. And, while boys, girls and grown-ups could enjoy them, still younger readers could find them, after a little practice in the language (as *Uncle Remus* also had needed), enchanting fairy-tales. The two volumes were and are genuinely a modern children's book, with no predecessors in their kind.

Kim (1901, two years after *Stalky*) was more of a boys' and girls' book, in the new age-ratings, though, as it is the most serenely impersonal of all its author's longer stories, it is for all ages, like *Treasure*

Island and *King Solomon's Mines*. But unlike them, it is almost epic, and it is also instinct with a maturer wisdom. It comes nearest, perhaps, of all modern books in the form of fiction, to an intimacy with the strange association of East and West in India: to the sympathetic sensitiveness of good Imperialism. But it is all about a boy.

Similarly, though not quite so gently, the two 'Puck' books—*Puck of Pook's Hill* (1906) and *Rewards and Fairies* (1910)—come very near to an intimacy with England itself; the England of Bishop Corbet and William Churne of Staffordshire, 'Merlin's Isle of Gramarye'. They are good history and good fiction, both of a kind not common in 1906. Contrast them with the allegorical scraps of history in *The Water-Babies* or with the historical fiction of Harrison Ainsworth, or of Kingsley himself. It is a different voice speaking—it would have to be that, obviously; but it is speaking almost to a different race. The children of the stories, whom one can accept readily enough as true young contemporaries, are not like any that any earlier author had deliberately addressed; though you can conceive that Lewis Carroll really knew their language, and Catherine Sinclair a few words of it, and Stevenson a few more words, and that Shakespeare had heard both Autolycus and Mamilius using it to Puck.

And then in the crude avuncularity of the *Just-So Stories* (1902), the same author is observed to be after all only a conventional 'Victorian' brought up to date, with rather more insight in his jocularity than his grandfathers would usually have shown, but still only pretending to be young, like them: a performer for the occasion.

He is, at any rate, a writer who has influenced adult literature. In children's books he has been both symptomatic and an influence. His effect on the school story has been dealt with. The effect of the *Just-So Stories* has probably been infinitesimal, beyond the crystallizing of some animal attributes. But the other five volumes all contain two elements which have grown strong in the younger juvenile literature of the last thirty years—the qualities of unlimited range for the imagination (very evident in *Kim* and in isolated scenes in the others), and of packed comprehensive thoughtfulness. Mowgli and Kim are thinking hard and vitally throughout; and Puck is thinking for those to whom he is showing all the majesty and littleness of England. The children's story has got right outside its own self, and yet has preserved its identity. The author and the reader are as nearly as possible the same person, but infinitely more capacious—more prehensile and assimilative, perhaps—than ever before. Man and boy, woman and girl, can lawfully try, even hope, to comprehend anything and everything. Nature-study has become a kind of intimate romance, because man, the paragon of animals *is* Nature. The brute creation has been elevated to companionship with flowers and the stars and ourselves. We learn very early now that

> in a moment clouds may be
> Dead, and instinct with deity.

Those words were written before the Diamond Jubilee, nevertheless.

59. 'Stalky' on 'Kipling's India'

1933

Paper read to the Kipling Society on 20 June 1933 by L. C. Dunsterville and published in the *Kipling Journal*, No. 26, pp. 49–55 (June 1933).

Major-General Lionel Charles Dunsterville, C.B., C.S.I., I.A. (1865–1946) was the original of 'Stalky'. Kipling kept up his friendship throughout life, and his belief in Stalky's powers were triumphantly justified during the First World War when he led 'Dunster Force' through Persia. Dunsterville, the author of several books, is an excellent example of the well-read, thoughtful Regular Army Officer of the time—and this Paper is an epitome of the opinions of such a man speaking with the knowledge of one who had served in India throughout Kipling's period. Dunsterville was first President of The Kipling Society (founded 1927), and his paper was read to a gathering of more than 100 members —some of whose remarks are included in the brief note of the Discussion which followed it.

At the outset let me say that I recognise the Society as being divided into two distinct groups: (a) Those who read, enjoy, and admire the words of our great writer; (b) those who, in addition to the above, may justly be regarded as students of Kipling. The latter obviously get a double value out of their membership and might be asked for an enhanced subscription. I hasten to add that I belong to the former category. I feel sure that I can speak for Mr. Kipling, when I say that he likes my lot the better of the two. He doubtless fully appreciates the homage done to his genius by those who study, as well as merely enjoy, his works, but I gather that writers are a little shy of people who ask: 'What did he mean when he wrote so-and-so?' It is possible that if he ever replied—which he does not—to any such question, he would either say (a) 'I often wonder myself,' or (b) 'I meant what I said and there is no paraphrase.' Genius hits off a beautiful line in prose or poetry that is too unique to be capable of paraphrase. The writer knows what he means and can tell you no more. The inner circle of understanding readers also know what he means, but cannot tell the others. This is obviously true of all higher flights of genius.

Mr. Kipling rather looks askance at me in my capacity of Principal Operating Surgeon in the probings of the Kipling Society. He ought not to, because I am very careful and always say, like the dentist, 'Tell me if I'm hurting you'. But he should certainly bestow on me some mark of his favour because I am the only reader of his works who has not written either to him or to the papers to enquire how the 'old Moulmein Pagoda' looked 'eastward to the sea' and I am the only one who knows the answer, which in the author's own words might be, 'I never said it did. You can't read straight.' And now perhaps it is time I begin to tackle the subject announced in my paper.

Kipling, like all powerful writers, has had a great deal of adverse criticism. He has been such an unswerving advocate of what we call, for want of a better word, Imperialism, that every little-englander—and there are lots of them, I'm afraid—naturally rushes to the attack. The noble form of Kipling's Imperialism is distorted by these critics into 'Jingoism', a most foolish and unjust line of attack on the writer of 'Recessional'. He can, however, console himself by quoting his own lines—

> If you can bear to hear the truth you've spoken
> Twisted by knaves to make a trap for fools.

Among many modern critics it is usual to attack his outlook on Indians and Indian problems. His views may have passed muster in the days when his early works were appearing, over forty years ago, but they give us quite a false outlook at the present time. The 'Ballad of East and West' begins: 'Oh, East is East, and West is West, and never the twain shall meet'. But we are told that this is quite wrong; the East and West have met. A few Indian undergraduates at our universities walking arm-in-arm with their English friends proves to the eye the fact of East and West meeting.

So Kipling, you see, was wrong. Although the meeting of East and West is only typified by a hundred or so cases like the above, and the population of India is about 350,000,000, we must allow this fraction of one out of $3\frac{1}{2}$ millions to convince us of this 'meeting' of the races. There is no doubt about their having met, but one can meet in several different ways. You can meet by running up alongside, which sets up no disturbance, or you can meet head on, in the form of a collision. That is just how East and West do meet. Every single idea, every thread of heredity, of the oriental is—and it is right that it should be—diametrically opposed to the occidental mentality and heredity. The Indian way of thinking is perhaps—Mr. Gandhi thinks so—best for the Indians; whether it is best or not doesn't really matter—the fundamental difference is there and nothing will ever alter it. And this unalterable foundation of thought and character is utterly ignored by our politicians when they try to force on India a form of government adapted solely to our purely British and insular evolution. I wonder how the word 'constitution' is translated into Urdu; an assembly of the elders in a Punjab village discussing it would make a splendid theme for our great writer—on the lines of his earlier poems. The fundamental differences of East and West are never to be altered, and none can say that our Western culture is superior to that of the East—no comparison is possible between two opposites. In forcing our ideas on them we do both them and ourselves great harm. Because a certain system has been found to suit us, that is no reason why we should run about the world pressing our great gift on people who think that they are already in possession of something much better. We are like a man suffering from heart disease who says to another suffering from corns: 'This stuff has done my heart a lot of good; you must let me try it on your corns.'

Please do not think that I am trying to make a political speech. All this is merely to prove that the real India has not changed since the days when Kipling wrote, and that nothing can be more literally true than his line: 'Oh, East is East, and West is West, and never the twain shall meet.' I have not had time to analyse all Kipling's prose dealing with India, but have confined myself to his poems alone. He had not served for the best years of his life on the North–West frontier, of India, as many in this room have done. He was only twenty-four years old when he wrote this, and after schooldays most of his time had been spent in the office of a daily paper; yet he pens in these few lines the exact feeling that lies between frontier officers and the marauding tribes from whom they enlist their best soldiers. I could have expressed the same idea inadequately myself in prose, and it would have taken me much paper.

British rule in India may be an 'alien' rule, but India has had alien rulers throughout her long and bloody history. The Aryan rulers were alien invaders from the north, and the Moguls were equally 'alien', both to the Aryans and the aborigines. The only difference between our alien rule and that of our alien predecessors lies in the sense of responsibility which we feel and acknowledge towards the peoples we govern. This sense of responsibility is very hampering in the measures we pass for what we honestly believe to be the betterment of life conditions of the people we rule over. They don't thank us for it, but it is part of our make-up and we can rule in no other way. I can imagine an Indian peasant saying today: 'Not so much talk, please, about doing me good. This generally ends in doing me bad. Please just govern me and leave it at that. I don't want to be done good to. Let me understand that you really do rule me, that your orders are orders, that you mean what you say, and that you mean to be obeyed, and let me get on with my farming. And when you mean what you say, say something that means something. "Constitution" is a word I cannot pronounce and I shall never know what it means, so please don't worry me about it any more, and let's be friends as we used to be before you began all this *tamasha* about reforms.'

This underlying sense of responsibility towards the governed is splendidly expressed in *The White Man's Burden* written 34 years ago. The work we have done in India may have been to the ultimate gain of the Empire and its commercial interests, but the officers of the Executive, both Civil and Military, have reaped nothing, and have desired to reap nothing, of these benefits. I claim for them the honour of working for the love of the work and of the people among whom their lot is cast. When we are dead and gone, and history is written with a true perspective, generations not yet born—both Indians and British, but especially the former—will acclaim the nobility of our share in the evolution of this land of tangled races, religions and languages. If Kipling is out of date in his supposition that East and West can never meet—that is, on the mental and moral plane—then he was wrong when he wrote in 'One Viceroy Resigns':

> You'll never plumb the Oriental mind,
> And if you did it isn't worth the toil.
> Think of a sleek French priest in Canada;
> Divide by twenty half-breeds. Multiply
> By twice the Sphinx's silence. There's your East,
> And you're as wise as ever. So am I.

I can imagine no more lucid exposition of the way in which the Oriental mind works on lines that must forever baffle the Westerner—

that is, the Oriental mind as I knew it during my long service in India. But, like Kipling, I am out of date. I left India thirteen years ago and in those thirteen years the inherited mentality of the Indian family of Orientals has, after 4,000 years of petrifaction, undergone a complete change. At least so we are told. But what exactly will happen when complete freedom is bestowed on this unfortunate country, is prophetically narrated by Kipling in one of his early poems, 'What Happened'.

To sum up the chief points of Kipling's picture of the Indian: he portrays him as a loyal and devoted servant (Gunga Din), a brave soldier in some races, unreasoning and easily aroused by propaganda. Truth and impartiality are foreign to his nature. Sanitation and a regard for the underdog are repugnant to him. Before I leave this subject I must defend myself against a possible charge of blackening the Indian character. In regard to this I can say with truth that there is nothing that may be regarded as insulting to the Indian character in the above remarks that I have not heard from the lips of Indians themselves. And we may credit them with many virtues that we do not possess.

Now let us consider another charge frequently brought against Kipling: the types of the British soldier in *Soldiers Three* and *Barrack-Room Ballads* are untrue to life—there are no soldiers of this type and there never were. When the former was written, about 1887, Kipling was on the staff of the *Civil and Military Gazette* in Lahore, and was acquiring an intimate knowledge of the rank-and-file of the Northumberland Fusiliers and Royal Artillery who formed part of the Mian Mir garrison. We saw each other at intervals, but I never followed to see what he was up to, so I can give you no first-hand information as to what steps he took to ingratiate himself with the men, getting his unequalled insight into the character of the British soldier; it may be taken as a fact that the fiction that resulted from his researches is as near as the human mind can get to fact. As I had at that time more than the average knowledge of the soldier's character, I can speak with authority when I say that Kipling's types are literally men whom I have known in the flesh, and the language my men spoke was nearly word for word the language of his men.

As to the change between the men of those days and today, that is another matter. In those fifty years great changes have taken place; our soldiers were almost illiterate and were altogether a tough lot. Soldiers of today are men of considerable education and the Army attracts a less rough type of man. Crime and drunkenness have diminished, and language has been slightly sweetened. But the change is not really a very considerable one. I do a good deal of travelling by rail (third class and in a tweed suit that has seen better days, so there is little to distinguish me from any other citizen in the humbler walks of life); conversation reveals that 'I did my bit' in the war, so talk flows freely, and really I do not find the vocabulary and mode of expression of the soldier today differing greatly from what you will find in Kipling's early works. The hints on life in those most wise verses, 'The Young British Soldier', are not needed, we are told, by the present type. In this poem the young soldier gets advice from Kipling—a civilian aged about twenty-five—that might have come from an old soldier whose time was up, warning against insidious grog-sellers, the avoidance of cholera and sunstroke, guide to matrimony, treatment of an unfaithful wife, behaviour under fire, how to treat your rifle, what to fire at, how to act when all the odds are against you and when left wounded on the frontier—truly a comprehensive list and full of simple wisdom.

I could continue to quote from *Barrack-Room Ballads*, and repeat *ad nauseam* the question, 'Can it be that things are no longer like this?'—but you yourselves love the poems and many know them better than I do, so I will say no more. I hope at some later date that the Secretary will arrange for a converse to this Paper—a discussion on Kipling's India and the possibility of its having changed; and on the British soldier and his suggested tendency to ultra-refinement of deportment and language, written by an officer of about six years' service, in touch with India and the British soldier of today.

DISCUSSION

When inviting discussion on the lecture the Chairman called attention to its title and suggested that speakers should concentrate on Kipling's India and not be too political, however much they would like to be.

Mr. Bazley pleaded guilty to repeating something he had said at the previous meeting when there had also been some mention of India. General Dunsterville had quoted the poems, but he thought that the strongest testimony to British rule in India was found in 'On the City Wall', where it is shown how, 'year by year, England sends out fresh drafts for the first fighting line, which is officially called the Indian Civil Service; of these men, some die from overwork or worry, while some are killed; if all goes well, the native is praised—'if a failure occurs the Englishmen step forward and take the blame'. This extract presented the same idea as *The White Man's Burden* and these lines from the poem in *Stalky & Co.*

> Set to serve the lands they rule,
> (Save he serve no man may rule),
> Serve and love the lands they rule;
> Seeking praise nor guerdon.

Mr. J. O. Tyler raised the question as to whether or not *The White Man's Burden* had been addressed to the Americans in respect to the Philippine Islands as an exhortation to them to go and do there what the British had done in India, to which an affirmative answer was given.

Mr. J. H. C. Brooking (Founder) thought that, in regard to the question of India and this island, we ought to consider the parallel of Rome and England, which was then a pretty miserable country, and gave it some 500 years of happy rule; but after they left, panic and terror ensued for several hundred years. India now stood in danger; if we let go of her, she would go to the same depths of chaos. The Chairman was in complete agreement with this, and invited the original of 'McTurk' to speak.

Mr. G. C. Beresford began by citing a characteristic of the native villager which he had noticed during a two years' stay. He was always changing from a pro-British to an anti-British attitude, and back again, according as hurt pride or a realisation of the justice and even-handedness of British rule directed. He thought that a point that required emphasis at present was that we didn't (as was said) force our western institutions on the natives; the natives clamoured for them. Vocal India would willingly set aside all traditions; they clamoured for a dose of western medicine and we wouldn't give them a dose. To this point General Dunsterville agreed that 'vocal India does clamour', adding 'that is to say, one voice out of every million clamours!'

60. André Maurois:
'A French View of Kipling'

1934

Paper entitled 'Kipling and His Works from a French Point of View' by André Maurois, read before the Kipling Society on 18 April 1934 and published in the *Kipling Journal*, No. 30, pp. 42–7 (June 1934).

André Maurois, C.B.E., M.C. (1885–1967) [pseudonym of Emile Herzog] was a famous French novelist, essayist and biographer. He is best known in England for his *Ariel* (1923), a biography of Shelley and his *Prophets and Poets* (1935). He also wrote biographies of Byron, Disraeli, George Sand, Victor Hugo, Dumas and others.

He was an Honorary Vice-President of The Kipling Society before whom this paper was read to an audience of over 150, some of whose questions, with his answers are quoted from the Discussion which followed.

When I was asked to speak before you, I replied that my admiration for Kipling was such that I could not refuse, but that unfortunately I was quite unable to lecture in English and that the lecture would be in French. Colonel Bailey said that he thought the lecture would be more generally understood if it was in English; I was not quite so sure about that. I once gave in England a lecture in French which began with a quotation from Shakespeare in English; at the end of the lecture, the Chairman came to me and said: 'Well, your French is much better than I thought; I understood every word you said— except the first sentence!' So, from that day, I decided never to inflict again upon an English audience, a language which is not mine and which is not their own either!

Of course, I cannot possibly pretend to bring before the Kipling Society any new facts about Kipling, but I should like to try and show you, by recalling the memory of my childhood and youth, what Kipling's influence can be on young men who are not Englishmen. It has often been said of Kipling, that he is above all the poet of the British Empire, and it may seem strange at first, that he has given spiritual food to so many young Frenchmen. It is, however, a fact. When I was sixteen or seventeen, I read Kipling's tales of India, and *Kim* affected me more than any other book. I find that this is just as true today on questioning the generation of my sons, who are now 11 and 12. I should like tonight to say what it is that attracts the youth of all countries to Kipling. I think the reason is that they find in his books an heroic idea of life and it is of this idea that I am going to speak to you first—but in French.

[*Translation*] Kipling's heroic conception of life is not the peculiarity either of a country or of one set period of time. Nearly all men who have fought in wars, who have been leaders, who have done something worth doing, have held practically the same view, whether they were fine soldiers in the Trojan War, or fine soldiers in the Great War.

In human life, whatever the country or the century, men seem to have passed through three periods of similar type. First comes the time for the heroes—the big men who dominate their passions—constructors who lay the foundations for social life. Then follows the political period, when administrative methods maintain what has been created by the heroes. After this, when order has been firmly established, men always have the idea that virtues have ceased to be useful; they criticise what has been done and finally destroy society—and it begins all over again.

Kipling covers the three classes of men. The first type is to be found everywhere in his books; he had seen them in India; the men who lay the foundations. Sometimes they are officers, sometimes cotton-planters, but they are always men of very simple character who, during their work, think of nothing else but that work, and not of love or family ties. This kind of man has no confidence in any one replacing him, unless it be a man of his own type. Men of this type, men of action but younger than he, he treats as sons and works like slaves (but who work no harder than he himself); boys who must take his place later, but who would be horror-stricken if such a thing were suggested to them.

These men soon learn that action is not easy and that man is always having fierce struggles. The designing of a bridge is easy; the building very difficult. All kinds of opposition are to be met with: the river

o

itself, the current of the river, weather conditions, and the wrath of the gods. 'What is man against the wrath of Gods?' And this is never absent, for the Gods detest man's victories.

The true hero does not work for wealth or honour, but for love of service. I like so much the portrait of Scott who 'counted eight years' service in the Irrigation Department, and drew eight hundred rupees a month on the understanding that if he served the State faithfully for another twenty-two years, he could retire on a pension of some four hundred rupees a month.' It is the usual thing for such a man to learn, on completing an arduous duty, and at the moment of success, that another is to replace him.

In this same class, but after the leader, comes the subaltern, the young man who is destined one day to command, who is loved and worked hard by his chief. Then comes the sergeant, for whom the chief has a strong admiration (which I share) who rules because of his technical qualities, even as the hero rules because of his heroic qualities. At the bottom of the scale, lowest in rank but the most useful in emergency, follows the private—the worker. More than any other writer, Kipling understands his importance. To illustrate this point, I shall now ask the Baroness Van Heemstra to read Kipling's poem 'The Sons of Martha'. [DV. pp. 382-3.]

When the man who talks claims to control the man who *does*, Kipling becomes fiercely satirical, as in the case of Pagett, M.P., who talks lovingly, with tears in his eyes, of his home; who cannot appreciate any methods of doing which are not strictly of the administrative kind.

Sentimental talk and its consequences is seen in the story, 'The Mother Hive'. The young bees become contemptuous of the other bees who respect the Law, feed the Queen Bee and have a healthy fear of the Wax-moth. All this ends in the loss of the stored honey and the ruin of the hive. But it would be inaccurate to say that Kipling is anti-liberal minded. For him, liberty is essentially the daughter of Discipline and Law. The animals respect the Law; when the wolves forsook it because of the tiger, they met with disaster and begged for leadership again. The Law is the product of hundreds and thousands of years, and can only be changed by the wise and the strong; this view can be seen in 'As Easy as A.B.C.' and 'The Village That Voted the Earth was Flat'.

I must now make a few remarks on Kipling's work in respect to women. In the story of the two men who sought to be kings, all went well until the better of the two broke the contract made between them, and looked upon a woman. According to Kipling, woman kills the man of action and also the action itself. Captain Gadsby is thoroughly put out by his wife; and when Charlie Mears, who could reconstruct the life of pirates and re-live the past, placed before his friend the 'photograph of a girl with a curly head, and foolish slack mouth' it meant that he would write no more. Woman's disastrous effect on man's work is also shown in *The Light that Failed*.

But in contrast to this evil side of woman's sphere in the world, enters also the true wife of an heroic leader, who, like him, thinks of action and helps him to succeed in it. Thus is 'William the Conqueror', she who dealt with a famine, who can combine love and work; Kipling appreciates the wife of the soldier, who can tend the wounded, who knows how to wait and to be resigned. Nevertheless, even when admiring woman, Kipling cannot help thinking that they are mysterious and dangerous at bottom and have a sort of understanding between them, as in 'The Ladies'. [DV. pp. 442–3.]

I come to the question of the place accorded by this great artist in this world of heroes to artists. In my opinion, a writer who likes describing men of action is, to a great extent, a man of action who was frustrated and who feels of less account than the type he describes, even as Cleever felt touched and amazed at the admiration vouchsafed him by young boys who had seen 'dead men, and war, and power, and responsibility'. Did it ever arise that Kipling blasphemed his own Art, to be sorry for it in the morning, as did Cleever?

Kipling has no place in his world for the man who does not act; the wretched Tomlinson was refused place in both Heaven and Hell, because his sins were miserable crimes of which he had read and so non-existent. This does not mean that there is no hope for the artist. Kipling's view is that an artist can be a man of action without even moving from his own sphere but in this case his art must be treated as real work to be done in austere fashion—the technique thereof to be learned even as that of any other craft; he must respect his art—learn it conscientiously before attempting to express mere personal sentiments and, by talking of beauty, lose it.

[*Here the lecture was continued in English*] I promised to end as I began—with a few words in English. I wish to sum up my remarks as follows: Literary talent is very widely spread in the world. I have met in my life hundreds of talented men, but the impression of being face to face with genius is extremely unusual. What does it consist of? It is difficult to analyse. We find ourselves in the presence of a man, and we suddenly feel that he surpasses all others. He has a power of contact with nature, a wealth of invention, a sort of eternal youth that makes him entirely different.

I have had this strong impression only three times in my life. Once at school in the presence of one of my masters, a French philosopher, who, although quite unknown today, will sometime be as well-known as Socrates or Plato. Once in the presence of a soldier—Marè-chal Lyautey—whom I saw create a new country. The third time was in the presence of a writer. That writer was Rudyard Kipling.

Of course, I would not use the word 'genius' if Kipling himself were present. I can imagine him stopping me and saying, 'You must not say these things,' but, as he is not present I dare make a prediction that in a thousand years, or in two thousand years, men will still be reading Kipling and will find him still young. That is why your Society in devoting itself to this great writer, has chosen well and chosen the greatest. I thank you for giving me the opportunity of saying this, and for having listened with patience to this long speech in *two* foreign languages.

DISCUSSION

Mr. G. C. Beresford: 'I should like to ask Monsieur Maurois if he can explain why Bernard Shaw is the English author who is read on the East of the Rhine, and apparently Kipling on the West of the Rhine.'
M. Maurois: 'I think one might say that the main reason why Bernard Shaw is, I will not say unpopular in France (because many of his plays have been staged and acted there), but not an important author for us, is that we already had one Bernard Shaw—that is, Voltaire. What in Bernard Shaw may seem very new to you is not exactly new to us. He attacks things which in France are not to be attacked, because they do not exist. Now in the case of Kipling it is exactly the contrary. We needed Kipling because we have in France the "Kipling" type of man; we have a colonial Empire, and it has never been sung by our writers. They have never written about it, or very little. We have not got our Kipling, and that is why we need yours.'
Mr. Bazley (Hon. Editor) thanked M. Maurois very much, in French, for his lecture, which had been most interesting, and said that when one went through Kipling's works from the beginning one noticed his great and thorough understanding of French mentality.

In reply to a question as to whether Kipling had a parallel in Alfred de Vigny, M. Maurois said: 'I think it is a very apt point, because it is quite true that Vigny in "Servitude et Grandeur Militaire" is very near Kipling in his ideal of life but Vigny wrote 100 years ago and he has not dealt with the world of to-day. What is interesting to us in Kipling is that in his books we find the heroic point of view. What Kipling has done is to show that these qualities Vigny found in the officers of Napoleon, still exist now, not only among officers, but among engineers, workmen, sailors and men of all trades. He has shown us that the modern man is exactly the same man as the hero of other times. I once asked Kipling himself, because I had just read one of his stories about the Roman Wall in Scotland, how he managed to describe Roman officers and soldiers, and make them so true and alive. Was it not an extraordinary feat of literary skill? He replied: "No, it's very easy, I simply listened to the conversations of British officers in India, and gave them as the conversations of Roman officers and that did the trick." '

In the course of M. Maurois' lecture and at his request, the Baroness van Heemstra gave an excellent reading of the Kipling poems mentioned.

61. 'Rudyard Kipling's Place in English Literature'

25 January 1936

An anonymous obituary article published a week after Kipling's death in the *Times Literary Supplement* (25 January 1936). This seems to be about the best, fullest and most dispassionate of the obituary tributes; it is included here by kind permission of the Editor of the *Times Literary Supplement*. In accordance with the strict rule of anonymity, the author's name cannot be revealed.

Rudyard Kipling was a national institution . . . and regarded as such by all the world. His fame had been long established and his literary activity slight for many years. It was also the case that many had lost interest in him and many others had been repelled. Seldom had a famous national institution been the object of more hostile criticism; some of it, indeed, unfair and marred by lack of understanding, yet some of it damaging enough. There are veterans who were hostile from the first; there are today many thousands of young enthusiasts: but broadly speaking the vocal sections of two generations have been at variance regarding him. Now the time has come for a reckoning; not a final reckoning, for posterity will have its say, but for the verdict of this age, comprising the old and the young, sitting as the jury. The critic writing at the moment must try to assist the jury to find that verdict, not as advocate for or against—they have both been heard at length but, so far as he can and dare, as judge summing up. Conscious of his own limitations and mindful of the disasters of many who have assumed the role, he may also attempt a harder task: that of prophecy. Kipling in life and work alike was downright and decided, without hesitation as to goal or the road that led to it. Let us treat him as he would have chosen to be treated, without timidity or hedging. Let us venture not only to decide what shall be the verdict of our time upon him but to predict boldly what shall be his place in the annals of our letters.

We have to envisage him both as poet and writer of fiction, and in the former aspect our task is, it may be admitted, a difficult one. On the prose side the case is very different. There is, we believe, no heavy risk in the prophecy that Rudyard Kipling will live and be admired as one of the most virile and skilful of English masters of the short story; that if that art, in which we are weak, shows with us no great development in future, he will remain, in years to come, as he now is, unique; that if it goes forward and gives birth to new triumphs, he will still rank among the greatest of the pioneers.

The pioneer has always a special meed of honour, and that honour is Kipling's for more reasons than one. He won it alike for matter and manner. He was definitely the man of the hour, a milestone on the path of letters like Byron and Chateaubriand. He appeared at a moment when literature in this country was being sicklied o'er, not with the pale cast of thought but with the unnatural bloom of cosmetics. We can realize now more fully than was realized then that fine and enduring work was being done in the aesthetic nineties, outside the school of the aesthetes, even outside that of the two giants who had no relationship to that school, George Meredith and Thomas Hardy. Yet the general atmosphere was stale and scented, artistically as well as literally *fin-de-siècle*. There was an extraordinary preoccupation with the artificial, a delight, by no means assumed on the part of many of the 'yellow' world, in 'bought red mouths', 'parched flowers', pallid women, 'delicate' sins.

Before the nineties opened there had spread bruit of a young writer out in India who knew little of this world of opera-cloaks and gold-headed canes and scorned what he did know. Kipling was, as his acute French observer, M. André Chevrillon, remarked, English '*d'une façon simple, violente et, de plus, tres nouvelle*'; the world which he entered so violently, which he did more than any other to destroy, being, on the contrary, the pale and unsatisfying reflection of a phase in French literature. Kipling was indeed English, but in those early days he was the mouthpiece of classes and types that were not themselves vocal and had long lacked a chronicler. India, with its heat and dust, its diversities of creed and caste was suddenly brought to the door of the stay-at-home Englishman. He learned with a thrill how the more adventurous of his race, from private soldiers to governors of provinces, lived; how they fought and organized and ruled. For this precocious genius had not only observed and recorded for him a great number of interesting and astonishing facts and occurrences; he had also put at his disposal a marvellous power of catching an atmosphere, of summing up an impression of the scenes upon which the writer had looked. This was life indeed, exclaimed the reader in his armchair; this was life as it should be lived, this young seer in India was revealing the highest destiny of the Englishman. Soon it appeared that life could be lived elsewhere than in India. It could be lived in America, in Africa, in the ports of the world, at sea, whether in crack cargo-boats, rusty tramps or the fishing smacks on the Grand Bank, in the cab of a steam-engine; even, for those who knew how, in an unconventional public school. The same vigour, the same brilliant technique, the same power of making mechanism romantic marked each new effort and bound together the spell he had put upon the English public.

And then there came another phase. The worshipper of dangerous living, of physical excitement, of noise, some detractors averred, became entranced with the peaceful beauties and with the traditions of the English countryside, and touched upon them with as much originality as he had all the rest. Such are the broad lines of his literary career.

Rudyard Kipling is first of all master of the *conte*. He attempted full-length novels, achieving in *The Light that Failed* and *Captains Courageous* romances to which no adjective higher than 'successful' can be applied: in *The Naulahka* written in collaboration with his brother-in-law, not even that; and in *Kim* his one masterpiece in that province. But in the short story he has had few English rivals, even if we take the best work of others to match against his, and from his take any of forty or fifty which it is hard to separate from the point of view of merit. The short story was suited to his peculiar gifts of compression, of clarity, of characterization that needs no building up but is completed and fixed in a flash. In his stories he has used almost every kind of matter, though the love of the sexes plays a very much smaller part than with most writers. War, adventure of every type, machinery pure and simple, have been his familiar subjects. He has employed the grotesque, the horrible, and very often the eerie in his plots, looking with anxious but never credulous eyes at what may be distinguished or imagined 'at the end of the passage', in the half-world betwixt fact and dream. Nor has he neglected that form of short story which is almost an allegory, among which the Mowgli tales of *The Jungle Book* stand highest. In a great number of the early stories, in those of Mowgli above all, we seem to detect a form of idealism with as little historical justification as that of Rousseau. He sees the savage in man and that it is not far below the surface, and he is disposed to question the benefits of civilization.

The sentiment was perhaps with him no more than a phase, but those who study him closely can have little doubt that it existed. They will assuredly not regret the fact. For in the Mowgli stories Kipling achieved a rare feat: he invented a new form of expression. And these tales have a charm, a beauty, a boldness of imagination that we have not often seen equalled in our time. The animals are not, as are those of Kipling's numerous imitators in this vein, creatures with men's minds in the bodies of beasts. The sentiments of beasts may be inaccurately described; that we cannot tell, though we may suspect that their intelligence is exaggerated; but the whole affair is managed with such marvellous dexterity that we are convinced and willingly surrender to him our judgment. Can an animal find enjoyment in the thrill of danger, as many human beings can? Hear his answer and see if you can state the contrary opinion with equal plausibility?

To move down so cunningly that never a leaf stirred; to wade knee-deep in the roaring shallows that drown all noise from behind; to drink, looking backward over one shoulder, every muscle ready for the first desperate bound of keen terror; to roll on the sandy margin, and return, wet-muzzled and well plumped out, to the admiring herd, was a thing that all tall-antlered young bucks took a delight in, precisely because they knew that at any moment Bagheera or Shere Khan might leap upon them and bear them down.

That word plausibility, in fact, gives us the key to one of the chief secrets of his popularity. It also explains a certain impatience felt by those who caught him out. For, excellently documented as he was, he was not always correct—could hardly be so, seeing how wide was his range. But, right or wrong, he was always equally assured, cocksure said the less friendly of his critics. And yet, these slips apart, his plausibility is amazing. The finest of the stories, such as 'On Greenhow Hill', 'The Return of Imray', 'The Strange Ride of Morrowbie Jukes', 'The Man who would be King', 'Without Benefit of Clergy', 'The Mark of the Beast',—have the verisimilitude of chronicles. Let us say that chronicles they are indeed, the chronicles of an epoch of British administration in India, infused with the imagination of a great writer of fiction.

The poetry is another matter. Poetry demands a standard even higher than prose; that is to say, an infelicitous expression, a piece of loose thinking are in it more painfully apparent and bring their own condemnation more swiftly. In his early work in verse Kipling did not fly high. *Departmental Ditties* may have won him his earliest fame, but these popular ballads, parodies, society verses, satires, clever and witty as they are, do not warrant the bestowal of the title of poet. The elevation of Mr. Potiphar Gubbins, the transfer to Quetta of Jack Barrett, may take their place somewhere below the satiric verse of Marvell and above that of Churchill; the rest, if they live, will live because they are Kipling's. Yet on the last page of that volume came a poem, '*L'Envoi*', which few probably noticed, which a bold prophet might have seen as a cloud no bigger than a man's hand. Till that cloud has sailed up we continue in the arid heat of dexterity, of rhetoric, of admonition, of a sententiousness often grating. We are warmed and made happy by wit and humour, we recognize a master of metre, rhythm and onomatopoeia in a line like

'The heave and the halt and the hurl and the crash of the comber wind-hounded.'

But almost always we are either pulled up with a jar by a phrase which is definitely inappropriate, definitely no poetry; or, if we escape that, subsequent reflection seems to indicate a flaw in taste, a thought of which the expression begins well but is not sustained at the level of its early dignity and beauty. But the cloud was drawing nigher and swelling in size. There may be difference of opinions whether the later stories of the English countryside are the equals of the more brilliant exotic predecessors. There can be little doubt that in the lovely songs, strewn among them, buttercups and daisies amid rich green grass, Kipling reached his highest as a poet. The passionate patriotism which had often previously run riot, shocking and offending the weaker brethren, is here even more intense, but purified, purged of that note of brawling.

> Under their feet in the grasses
> My clinging magic runs.
> They shall return as strangers,
> They shall remain as sons.
>
> Scent of smoke in the evening.
> Smell of rain in the night,
> The hours, the days and the seasons,
> Order their souls aright.

In these songs, with their simplicity, their kindly and gracious philosophy, he reveals at last that lyric sweetness whereof we had had promise in '*L'Envoi*', and himself as not merely a satirist or humorist or master of the banjo ballad, but a lyric poet.

> Cities and Thrones and Powers,
>   Stand in Time's eye,
> Almost as long as flowers,
>   Which daily die:
> But, as new buds put forth
>   To glad new men
> Out of the spent and unconsidered Earth,
>   The Cities rise again.
>
> This season's Daffodil,
>   She never hears,
> What change, what chance, what chill,
>   Cut down last year's;
> But with bold countenance,
>   And knowledge small,
> Esteems her seven days' continuance
>   To be perpetual.

(Even in reading these lines we pause. Is there not something school-boyish in the irony of that 'almost as long'?)

Yet let us make no mistake. More of Kipling will go down to posterity than the fastidious literary critic is prepared to pass. The flaws are those of a great and original craftsman; in the most faulty productions there is power; one feels everywhere in them the grip of a strong hand. Often that which is not poetry is life itself. Take a poem such as 'If'; not poetry at all, some critics may declare. It may not be, yet it has been an inspiration to many thousands and those not the most ingenuous or limited in their appreciation of poetical merit. Its moral maxims are as clean-cut and forcible as those of Pope or Edward Young. Almost all the patriotic verse, though it may grate often upon the ears of those whom Kipling called, with rather less than strict fairness but a large measure of truth,

> Brittle intellectuals who crack beneath a strain,

and sometimes upon any critical ears, represents at least one side of England. 'Wordsworth,' wrote Lowell, 'never lets us long forget the deeply rooted stock from which he sprang—*vien ben da lui.*' The words may be applied with equal justice to Kipling. At his worst as at his best, the love of England breeds in him a passionate intensity and sincerity which ennoble even the verse marred by the shouting of party warfare or by extreme patriotic dogmatism, as by technical faults of like nature.

What verdict England of the future will pass upon England of the last years of Victoria and Edward VII, is uncertain, but it is incontestable that the age will always rank as one of the greatest in our history—great materially and great in national temper. And may one not dare to foresee that when, long hence, that age and its characteristics and products are called to mind, the name of Rudyard Kipling will come first to men's mouths when they talk of its most typical representatives? Is it not likely that then the lesser work will take its place with the greater, as all part of and symbolic of the country which he loved and celebrated?

It were not easy to imagine two writers more widely separated than Rudyard Kipling and Maurice Barrès, but their names are linked by the fact that as contemporaries, born within a few years of one another, each set up a philosophy of nationalism and each was assailed from a point of view in which the political mingled with the artistic. Each might have taken as motto the words of Disraeli: 'Now a nation is a work of art and a work of time;' and each tripped not seldom in the snares which arrogance sets for the feet of the nationalist. Hear them each, Barrès on his beloved Hill of Sion-Vaudemont:

Où sont les dames de Lorraine, sœurs, filles et femmes des Croisés, qui s'en venaient prier à Sion pendant que les hommes d'armes, là-bas, combattaient l'infidèle, et celles-là surtout qui, le lendemain de la bataille de Nicopolis, ignorantes encore, mais épouvantées par les rumeurs, montèrent ici intercéder pour des vivants qui étaient déjà des morts? Où la sainte princesse Philippe de Gueldre, à qui Notre-Dame de Sion découvrit, durant le temps de son sommeil, les desseins ambitieux des ennemis de la Lorraine? . . .

and Kipling on his Sussex Downs:

> See you the dimpled track that runs,
>   All hollow through the wheat?
> O that was where they hauled the guns
>   That smote King Philip's fleet.
>
> See you our stilly woods of oak,
>   And the dread ditch beside?
> O that was where the Saxons broke,
>   On the day that Harold died.

While Barrès, a mystic, heard 'the hushed and timid voices' of the gods of his ancestors at those spiritual points where, it seemed to him, the crust of the material world was thin and the poetry of great deeds and great lives came through it as in a vapour, Kipling, more realistically, conjured up upon the Downs his ancestors, themselves. *Puck of Pook's Hill, Rewards and Fairies*, have in them the very marrow of England. For them, at least, we may prophesy with assurance that death will not come quickly. In these entrancing volumes, in many another tale of the stamp of 'An Habitation Enforced', there is far more than merely the exquisite art of telling a story; there is the recreation of history, the essence of a nation's beginning and early development. The figures of De Aquila and Sir Richard Dalyngridge are not only great characters of fiction but pendants to the works of great historians. 'And so was England born.' The work of Kipling, as of Barrès, at its greatest moments is a flower of national art. It was fitting that the former should have known and loved and been honoured of France; and that the latter, though he said hard words of England, should have been the guest of our fleet in time of war and lauded its traditions to his countrymen.

We have hinted that the young men have less pleasure in the work of Kipling than those who reached manhood at any time between the publication of *Departmental Ditties* and that of *Kim*, though there is some doubt as to how far the young writers represent their generation in this. In any case there is in it nothing uncommon or prejudicial to his eventual fame. At Wordsworth's death, when subscriptions were being collected for a memorial to him Macaulay declared to Arnold that ten years earlier more money could have been raised to do him honour in Cambridge alone than was now raised all through the country. Thirty years later Arnold was bewailing that the diminution of Wordsworth's popularity was continuing, that, effaced first by Scott and Byron, he was now completely effaced by Tennyson. The selected poems of Wordsworth, which Arnold was then editing, to which the essay quoted was a preface, ran through thirteen editions between 1879 and the close of the century, and there have been many others. That which is popular today may be outmoded to-morrow, but if it has the stuff of life in it, it will assuredly not be dead the day after. Yet, where Kipling is concerned, it is improbable that there will ever be unanimity of opinion.

He was a man of strong prejudices, strong political views, with little tenderness for the opinions of others, and—though to lesser extent than now—he may always divide men into camps. So much granted, there will be, we are convinced, in years to come a general agreement upon the high merit of a great part of this man's work. The perfervid admirers will come to admit that there is dross—dross, why he threw it up in a heap about him as he worked, till at times we could scarce see him over the top of it! Those of the type of mind which is antagonized by a loud-voiced patriotism and Toryism will allow those English songs and stories which we last considered to be free from that offence, and will perhaps even pardon it elsewhere for the vigour and skill with which it is presented. Both will proclaim him a magician in the art of the short story, who raised it to a higher station in our literature than it had known before his coming. As novelist they will call him author of one, but one only, of the finest romances of his time. As a poet he will be remembered for a mass of vigorous, pithy, if faulty, work of the second order; for a patriotic hymn that had become part of every national ceremony; last, not least, as the singer of English country beauties and traditions. And if, amid the work he leaves behind him, those juries of the future contrive, to catch a glimpse of the man himself, as his own time knew him, they must add to their verdict a rider that this was a great man as well as a great wirter; and honourable and fearless and good.

Chronological Table

1865   Rudyard Kipling born in Bombay (30 December)

1871–7 At 'Lorne Lodge', 4 Campbell Road, Southsea [Capt. and Mrs. Pryse Agar Holloway]. (To day-school: 'Hope House', Somerset Place, Southsea)

1878–82 At United Services College, Westward Ho! Devon

1882–7 On the staff of the *Civil and Military Gazette*, Lahore

1886   *Departmental Ditties* [after appearing in *C. and M. Gazette* (1886); in the *Pioneer* (1884–6)]

1887–9 On the staff of the *Pioneer*, Allahabad

1888   *Plain Tales from the Hills* (January) [mostly from *C. and M. Gazette*, 1884–7]

1888   'The Indian Railway Library' paper backs: *Soldiers Three*, *The Story of the Gadsbys*, *In Black and White*, *Under the Deodars*, *The Phantom 'Rickshaw*, *Wee Willie Winkie* (mostly from the *Weeks News*, Allahabad: a few new)

1889   Left Allahabad 21 February, via Singapore, Hong Kong, Japan, U.S.A. Arrived Liverpool 5 October. 'Ballad of the King's Mercy', November, 'Ballad of East and West' and 'The Incarnation of Krishna Mulvaney' in *Macmillan's Magazine*, December

1890–1 *The Light that Failed* in *Lippincott's*, 1 January 1891, and complete form as book in March

1891   *Life's Handicap* (collected from various periodicals, mainly of 1890)

1892   Marriage. Settled at Brattleboro, Vermont, U.S.A. *Barrack-Room Ballads* (mainly from the *National Observer*), *The Naulahka* (serialized *Century Magazine*, November 1891–July 1892)

1893   *Many Inventions* (mainly from various magazines, 1890–2)

1894   *The Jungle Book* (from various magazines, 1893–4)

1895   *The Second Jungle Book* (mainly from *Pall Mall* and *St. Nicholas*, 1894–5)

1896   Returned to live in England. *The Seven Seas* (from various periodicals)

1897   Settled at Rottingdean. *Captains Courageous* (serialized in *McClure's Magazine*, November 1896–March 1897 and *Pearson's Magazine*, December 1896–April 1897). 'Recessional' in *The Times*, 17 July 1897

1898   *The Day's Work* (from various magazines, 1893–97)

1899   *Stalky & Co.* (mostly from *Windsor* and *McClure's Magazines*, January–June 1899)

1899 *From Sea to Sea* (from Indian papers, 1885–1890, previously issued in pirated or suppressed volumes)

1901 *Kim* (serialized *Cassell's* and *McClure's Magazines*, December 1900–October 1901)

1902 Settled for the rest of his life, at 'Bateman's', Burwash, Sussex. *Just So Stories for Little Children* (mostly from *St. Nicholas* 1897–8, *Ladies' Home Journal*, 1900–2)

1903 *The Five Nations* (from various periodicals)

1904 *Traffics and Discoveries* (from various magazines, 1901–4)

1906 *Puck of Pook's Hill* (serialized in the *Strand Magazine*, January–October 1906; divided between *McClure's* and *Ladies' Home Journal* in U.S.A.)

1907 Awarded Nobel Prize for Literature

1909 *Actions and Reactions* (mostly from magazines, 1899–1909)

1909 *Abaft the Funnel* (American 'pirate' collection of stories and sketches from Indian papers, 1888–90; not published in England until the 'Sussex Edition', 1938)

1910 *Rewards and Fairies* (mainly the *Delineator*, U.S.A., September 1909–August 1910; various in England)

1912–13 *Songs from Books* (1912 U.S.A., 1913 England: collected and expanded verses and poems from the prose volumes)

1917 *A Diversity of Creatures* (mainly from magazines, 1910–15)

1914–18 *The New Army in Training, Sea-Warfare, The Eyes of Asia* and other War pamphlets

1919 *The Years Between* (verse from various periodicals, etc.)

1920 *Letters of Travel* (from *The Times* and *New York Sun*, 1892; *Morning Post* and *Collier's Weekly*, 1908, and *Nash's Magazine* and the *Cosmopolitan*, 1914). *Brazilian Sketches*, from *Morning Post*, November–December 1927, added in 'Sussex Edition', 1938)

1920 *Q. Horatii Flacci Carminum Librer Quintus* (with C. L. Graves, A. D. Godley, A. B. Ramsay and R. A. Knox)

1923 *Land and Sea Tales for Scouts and Guides* (mostly from magazines, 1893–1910)

1923 *The Irish Guards in the Great War.* 2 vols.

1926 *Debits and Credits* (from magazines, 1915–26)

1928 *A Book of Words* (collected speeches 1906–1927. Later speeches in 'Sussex Edition', 1938

1930 *Thy Servant a Dog* (Two stories from *Cassell's Magazine*, 1930, and one new. With two extra stories 1938)

1932 *Limits and Renewals* (mostly from magazines, 1928–32)

1933 *Souvenirs of France*

1936 Rudyard Kipling died 18 January. Buried Westminster Abbey 23 January

1937   *Something of Myself: For My Friends Known and Unknown*
1937–9 *The 'Sussex Edition'* (35 vols). Complete edition of his acknowledged works, with many hitherto uncollected additions: prepared and signed by Kipling
1940   *Rudyard Kipling's Verse: Definitive Edition* (there had been many editions of *Collected Verse*, each containing more, since 1912)

Select Bibliography

This short select book list is of volumes containing collected criticism, critical or critical-plus-biographical volumes, and lists of criticism of Rudyard Kipling. For fuller lists see *English Literature in Transition* listed below, and *Cambridge Bibliography of English Literature*, new edition 1969.

A. CRITICAL ARTICLES

GERBER, HELMUT E. *et al.*, Rudyard Kipling: An Annotated Bibliography of Articles about him. *English Fiction in Transition*, Vol. 3, Numbers 3–5, 1960; and *English Literature in Transition*, Vol. 8, Numbers 3–4, 1965.

GILBERT, ELLIOT L., (Ed.), *Kipling and the Critics*, P. Owen, 1965. Reprinted essays, parodies and extracts by Andrew Lang, Oscar Wilde, Henry James, Robert Buchanan, Max Beerbohm, Bonamy Dobrée, Boris Ford, George Orwell, Lionel Trilling, C. S. Lewis, T. S. Eliot, J. M. S. Tompkins, Randall Jarrell, Steven Marcus and Elliot L. Gilbert.

GREEN, ROGER LANCELYN, (Ed.), the *Kipling Journal: Centenary Number*, December 1965. Articles specially written by Rosemary Sutcliff, Bonamy Dobrée, J. M. S. Tompkins, George Calvin Carter, Morton N. Cohen, Elliot L. Gilbert and Nevill Coghill. Reprinted articles by Andrew Lang and Charles Carrington. Centenary poem by Edmund Blunden.

POWELL, FREDERICK YORK, 'Rudyard Kipling—Bibliography'—*The English Illustrated Magazine*, Vol. XXX, pp. 430–2, December 1903.

RUTHERFORD, ANDREW, (Ed.), *Kipling's Mind and Art*, Oliver, 1964. Reprinted articles by W. L. Renwick, Edmund Wilson, George Orwell, Lionel Trilling and Noel Annan; and new articles by Mark Kinkeed-Weekes, J. H. Fenwick, W. W. Robson, George Shepperson, Alan Sandison and Andrew Rutherford.

B. CRITICAL AND CRITICAL-PLUS-BIOGRAPHICAL VOLUMES

BODELSON, C. A., *Aspects of Kipling's Art*, Manchester University Press, 1964.

BROWN, HILTON, *Rudyard Kipling: A New Appreciation*, Hamish Hamilton, 1945.

CARRINGTON, CHARLES, *Rudyard Kipling: His Life and Work*, Macmillan, 1955. [The authorized biography.]

COHEN, MORTON N., *Rudyard Kipling to Rider Haggard: The Record of a Friendship*, Hutchinson, 1965.

CORNELL, LOUIS L., *Kipling in India*, Macmillan, 1966.

DOBRÉE, BONAMY, *Rudyard Kipling: Realist and Fabulist*, Oxford University Press, 1967.

GREEN, ROGER LANCELYN, *Kipling and the Children*, Elek, 1965.

HARBORD, R. E. *et al.*, *The Reader's Guide to Rudyard Kipling's Works*, [Privately printed.] Vol. I, 1961; Vol. II, 1963; Vol. III, 1965; Vol. IV, 1966; Vol. V, 1969; [in progress] Vol. VI, 1970—to be completed in 10 vols.

LÉAUD, FRANÇOIS, *La Poétique de Rudyard Kipling*, Paris: Didier, 1958.

SHANKS, EDWARD, *Rudyard Kipling: A Study in Literature and Political Ideas*, Macmillan, 1940.

TOMPKINS, J. M. S., *The Art of Rudyard Kipling*, Methuen, 1959.

WEYGANDT, ANN M., *Kipling's Reading*, University of Pennsylvania Press, 1939.

C. IMPORTANT UNCOLLECTED CRITICAL ARTICLES

CHAUDHURI, NIRAD C., 'The Finest Story about India in English', [*Kim*], *Encounter*, April 1957.

DUNMAN, JACK, 'Kipling Re-estimated', *Marxism Today*, August 1965.

ELIOT, T. S., Introduction to *A Choice of Kipling's Verse*, Faber, 1941.

KIPLING JOURNAL, (Various), Published quarterly since 1927 by The Kipling Society, 18 Northumberland Avenue, London, W.C.2.

MAUGHAM, W. SOMERSET, Introduction to *A Choice of Kipling's Prose*, Macmillan, 1952.

ROWSE, A. L., 'Blowing Kipling's Trumpet', *Sunday Telegraph*, 19 December 1965.

STEWART, J. I. M., Section on Kipling in *Eight Modern Writers*, *Oxford History of English Literature*, Vol. XII, pp. 223–93, Oxford, 1963.

SUSSMAN, HERBERT L., Chapter on Kipling in *The Victorians and The Machine*, Oxford University Press, 1968.

Index

II TOPICS

MARK TWAIN

MARK TWAIN

THE INNOCENTS ABROAD
ROUGHING IT

THE LIBRARY OF AMERICA

Volume arrangement, notes, and chronology Copyright © 1984 by
Literary Classics of the United States, Inc., New York, N.Y.
All rights reserved.

Distributed to the trade in the United States
and Canada by the Viking Press.

Published outside North America by the Press Syndicate
of the University of Cambridge,
The Pitt Building, Trumpington Street, Cambridge CB2IRP, England
ISBN O 521 30097 5

Library of Congress Catalog Card Number: 84–11296
For Cataloging in Publication Data, see end of *Notes* section.
ISBN O—940450—25—9

First Printing

Manufactured in the United States of America

Grateful acknowledgement is made to the National Endowment for the Humanities and the Ford Foundation for their generous financial support of this series.

Contents

THE
INNOCENTS ABROAD,

OR

THE NEW PILGRIMS' PROGRESS;

BEING SOME ACCOUNT OF THE STEAMSHIP QUAKER
CITY'S PLEASURE EXCURSION TO EUROPE AND
THE HOLY LAND; WITH DESCRIPTIONS
OF COUNTRIES, NATIONS, INCIDENTS
AND ADVENTURES, AS THEY
APPEARED
TO THE
AUTHOR.

TO
MY MOST PATIENT READER
AND
MOST CHARITABLE CRITIC,
MY AGED MOTHER,
THIS VOLUME IS AFFECTIONATELY
INSCRIBED.

Preface

THIS BOOK is a record of a pleasure-trip. If it were a record of a solemn scientific expedition, it would have about it that gravity, that profundity, and that impressive incomprehensibility which are so proper to works of that kind, and withal so attractive. Yet notwithstanding it is only a record of a pic-nic, it has a purpose, which is, to suggest to the reader how *he* would be likely to see Europe and the East if he looked at them with his own eyes instead of the eyes of those who travelled in those countries before him. I make small pretence of showing any one how he *ought* to look at objects of interest beyond the sea—other books do that, and therefore, even if I were competent to do it, there is no need.

I offer no apologies for any departures from the usual style of travel-writing that may be charged against me—for I think I have seen with impartial eyes, and I am sure I have written at least honestly, whether wisely or not.

In this volume I have used portions of letters which I wrote for the *Daily Alta California*, of San Francisco, the proprietors of that journal having waived their rights and given me the necessary permission. I have also inserted portions of several letters written for the New York *Tribune* and the New York *Herald*.

THE AUTHOR.

SAN FRANCISCO, 1869.

3

Contents

Chapter I

F OR MONTHS the great Pleasure Excursion to Europe and the Holy Land was chatted about in the newspapers every where in America, and discussed at countless firesides. It was a novelty in the way of Excursions—its like had not been thought of before, and it compelled that interest which attractive novelties always command. It was to be a picnic on a gigantic scale. The participants in it, instead of freighting an ungainly steam ferry-boat with youth and beauty and pies and doughnuts, and paddling up some obscure creek to disembark upon a grassy lawn and wear themselves out with a long summer day's laborious frolicking under the impression that it was fun, were to sail away in a great steamship with flags flying and cannon pealing, and take a royal holiday beyond the broad ocean, in many a strange clime and in many a land renowned in history! They were to sail for months over the breezy Atlantic and the sunny Mediterranean; they were to scamper about the decks by day, filling the ship with shouts and laughter—or read novels and poetry in the shade of the smoke-stacks, or watch for the jelly-fish and the nautilus, over the side, and the shark, the whale, and other strange monsters of the deep; and at night they were to dance in the open air, on the upper deck, in the midst of a ball-room that stretched from horizon to horizon, and was domed by the bending heavens and lighted by no meaner lamps than the stars and the magnificent moon—dance, and promenade, and smoke, and sing, and make love, and search the skies for constellations that never associate with the "Big Dipper" they were so tired of; and they were to see the ships of twenty navies—the customs and costumes of twenty curious peoples—the great cities of half a world—they were to hob-nob with nobility and hold friendly converse with kings and princes, Grand Moguls, and the anointed lords of mighty empires!

It was a brave conception; it was the offspring of a most ingenious brain. It was well advertised, but it hardly needed it: the bold originality, the extraordinary character, the seductive nature, and the vastness of the enterprise provoked comment every where and advertised it in every household in the land. Who could read the programme of the excursion without longing to make one of the party? I will insert it here. It is almost as good as a map. As a text for this book, nothing could be better:

EXCURSION TO THE HOLY LAND, EGYPT, THE CRIMEA, GREECE, AND INTERMEDIATE POINTS OF INTEREST.

BROOKLYN, *February 1st, 1867.*

The undersigned will make an excursion as above during the coming season, and begs to submit to you the following programme:

A first-class steamer, to be under his own command, and capable of accommodating at least one hundred and fifty cabin passengers, will be selected, in which will be taken a select company, numbering not more than three-fourths of the ship's capacity. There is good reason to believe that this company can be easily made up in this immediate vicinity, of mutual friends and acquaintances.

The steamer will be provided with every necessary comfort, including library and musical instruments.

An experienced physician will be on board.

Leaving New York about June 1st, a middle and pleasant route will be taken across the Atlantic, and passing through the group of Azores, St. Michael will be reached in about ten days. A day or two will be spent here, enjoying the fruit and wild scenery of these islands, and the voyage continued, and Gibraltar reached in three or four days.

A day or two will be spent here in looking over the wonderful subterraneous fortifications, permission to visit these galleries being readily obtained.

From Gibraltar, running along the coasts of Spain and France, Marseilles will be reached in three days. Here ample time will be given not only to look over the city, which was founded six hundred years before the Christian era, and its artificial port, the finest of the kind in the Mediterranean, but to visit Paris during the Great Exhibition; and the beautiful city of Lyons, lying intermediate, from the heights of which, on a clear day, Mont Blanc and the Alps can be distinctly seen. Passengers who may wish to extend the time at Paris can do so, and, passing down through Switzerland, rejoin the steamer at Genoa.

From Marseilles to Genoa is a run of one night. The excursionists will have an opportunity to look over this, the "magnificent city of palaces," and visit the birth-place of Columbus, twelve miles off, over a beautiful road built by Napoleon I. From this point, excursions may be made to Milan, Lakes Como and Maggiore, or to Milan, Verona, (famous for its extraordinary fortifications,) Padua, and Venice. Or, if passengers desire to visit Parma (famous for Correggio's frescoes,) and Bologna, they can by rail go on to Florence, and rejoin the steamer at Leghorn, thus spending about three weeks amid the cities most famous for art in Italy.

From Genoa the run to Leghorn will be made along the coast in one night, and time appropriated to this point in which to visit Florence, its palaces and galleries; Pisa, its Cathedral and "Leaning Tower," and Lucca and its baths, and Roman amphitheatre; Florence, the most remote, being distant by rail about sixty miles.

From Leghorn to Naples, (calling at Civita Vecchia to land any who may prefer to go to Rome from that point,) the distance will be made in about thirty-six hours; the route will lay along the coast of Italy, close by Caprera, Elba, and Corsica. Arrangements have been made to take on board at Leghorn a pilot for Caprera, and, if practicable, a call will be made there to visit the home of Garibaldi.

Rome, [by rail] Herculaneum, Pompeii, Vesuvius, Virgil's tomb, and possibly, the ruins of Pæstum, can be visited, as well as the beautiful surroundings of Naples and its charming bay.

The next point of interest will be Palermo, the most beautiful city of Sicily, which will be reached in one night from Naples. A day will be spent here, and leaving in the evening, the course will be taken towards Athens.

Skirting along the north coast of Sicily, passing through the group of Æolian Isles, in sight of Stromboli and Vulcania, both active volcanoes, through the Straits of Messina, with "Scylla" on the one hand and "Charybdis" on the other, along the east coast of Sicily, and in sight of Mount Ætna, along the south coast of Italy, the west and south coast of Greece, in sight of ancient Crete, up Athens Gulf, and into the Piræus, Athens will be reached in two and a half or three days. After tarrying here awhile, the Bay of Salamis will be crossed, and a day given to Corinth, whence the voyage will be continued to Constantinople, passing on the way through the Grecian Archipelago, the Dardanelles, the Sea of Marmora, and the mouth of the Golden Horn, and arriving in about forty-eight hours from Athens.

After leaving Constantinople, the way will be taken out through the beautiful Bosphorus, across the Black Sea to Sebastopol and Balaklava, a run of about twenty-four hours. Here it is proposed to remain two days, visiting the harbors, fortifications, and battle-fields of the Crimea; thence back through the Bosphorus, touching at Constantinople to take in any who may have preferred to remain there; down through the Sea of Marmora and the Dardanelles, along the coasts of ancient Troy and Lydia in Asia, to Smyrna, which will be reached in two or two and a half days from Constantinople. A sufficient stay will be made here to give opportunity of visiting Ephesus, fifty miles distant by rail.

From Smyrna towards the Holy Land the course will lay through the Grecian Archipelago, close by the Isle of Patmos, along the coast of Asia, ancient Pamphylia, and the Isle of Cyprus. Beirout will be reached in three days. At Beirout time will be given to visit Damascus; after which the steamer will proceed to Joppa.

From Joppa, Jerusalem, the River Jordan, the Sea of Tiberias, Nazareth, Bethany, Bethlehem, and other points of interest in the Holy Land can be visited, and here those who may have preferred to make the journey from

Beirout *through* the country, passing through Damascus, Galilee, Capernaum, Samaria, and by the River Jordan and Sea of Tiberias, can rejoin the steamer.

Leaving Joppa, the next point of interest to visit will be Alexandria, which will be reached in twenty-four hours. The ruins of Cæsar's Palace, Pompey's Pillar, Cleopatra's Needle, the Catacombs, and ruins of ancient Alexandria, will be found worth the visit. The journey to Cairo, one hundred and thirty miles by rail, can be made in a few hours, and from which can be visited the site of ancient Memphis, Joseph's Granaries, and the Pyramids.

From Alexandria the route will be taken homeward, calling at Malta, Cagliari (in Sardinia,) and Parma (in Majorca,) all magnificent harbors, with charming scenery, and abounding in fruits.

A day or two will be spent at each place, and leaving Parma in the evening, Valencia in Spain will be reached the next morning. A few days will be spent in this, the finest city of Spain.

From Valencia, the homeward course will be continued, skirting along the coast of Spain. Alicant, Carthagena, Palos, and Malaga, will be passed but a mile or two distant, and Gibraltar reached in about twenty-four hours.

A stay of one day will be made here, and the voyage continued to Madeira, which will be reached in about three days. Captain Marryatt writes: "I do not know a spot on the globe which so much astonishes and delights upon first arrival as Madeira." A stay of one or two days will be made here, which, if time permits, may be extended, and passing on through the islands, and probably in sight of the Peak of Teneriffe, a southern track will be taken, and the Atlantic crossed within the latitudes of the Northeast trade winds, where mild and pleasant weather, and a smooth sea, can always be expected.

A call will be made at Bermuda, which lies directly in this route homeward, and will be reached in about ten days from Madeira, and after spending a short time with our friends the Bermudians, the final departure will be made for home, which will be reached in about three days.

Already, applications have been received from parties in Europe wishing to join the Excursion there.

The ship will at all times be a home, where the excursionists, if sick, will be surrounded by kind friends, and have all possible comfort and sympathy.

Should contagious sickness exist in any of the ports named in the programme, such ports will be passed, and others of interest substituted.

The price of passage is fixed at $1,250, currency, for each adult passenger. Choice of rooms and of seats at the tables apportioned in the order in which passages are engaged, and no passage considered engaged until ten per cent. of the passage money is deposited with the treasurer.

Passengers can remain on board of the steamer, at all ports, if they desire, without additional expense, and all boating at the expense of the ship.

All passages must be paid for when taken, in order that the most perfect arrangements be made for starting at the appointed time.

Applications for passage must be approved by the committee before tickets are issued, and can be made to the undersigned.

Articles of interest or curiosity, procured by the passengers during the voyage, may be brought home in the steamer free of charge.

Five dollars per day, in gold, it is believed, will be a fair calculation to make for *all* traveling expenses on shore, and at the various points where passengers may wish to leave the steamer for days at a time.

The trip can be extended, and the route changed, by *unanimous* vote of the passengers.

CHAS. C. DUNCAN,

117 WALL STREET, NEW YORK.

R. R. G******, Treasurer.

COMMITTEE ON APPLICATIONS.

J. T. H*****, ESQ.,   R. R. G*****, ESQ.,   C. C. DUNCAN.

COMMITTEE ON SELECTING STEAMER.

CAPT. W. W. S****. *Surveyor for Board of Underwriters.*

C. W. C******, *Consulting Engineer for U.S. and Canada.*

J. T. H*****, ESQ.

C. C. DUNCAN.

P. S.—The very beautiful and substantial side wheel steamship *"Quaker City"* has been chartered for the occasion, and will leave New York, June 8th. Letters have been issued by the government commending the party to courtesies abroad.

What was there lacking about that programme, to make it perfectly irresistible? Nothing, that any finite mind could discover. Paris, England, Scotland, Switzerland, Italy—Garibaldi! The Grecian archipelago! Vesuvius! Constantinople! Smyrna! The Holy Land! Egypt and "our friends the Bermudians!" People in Europe desiring to join the Excursion—contagious sickness to be avoided—boating at the expense of the ship—physician on board—the circuit of the globe to be made if the passengers unanimously desired it—the company to be rigidly selected by a pitiless "Committee on Applications"—the vessel to be as rigidly selected by as pitiless a "Committee on Selecting Steamer." Human nature could not withstand these bewildering temptations. I hurried to the Treasurer's office and deposited my ten per cent. I rejoiced to know that a few vacant state-rooms were still left. I *did* avoid a critical personal examination into my character, by that bowelless committee, but I referred to all the people of high standing I could think of in the community who would be least likely to know any thing about me.

Shortly a supplementary programme was issued which set

forth that the Plymouth Collection of Hymns would be used on board the ship. I then paid the balance of my passage money.

I was provided with a receipt, and duly and officially accepted as an excursionist. There was happiness in that, but it was tame compared to the novelty of being "select."

This supplementary programme also instructed the excursionists to provide themselves with light musical instruments for amusement in the ship; with saddles for Syrian travel; green spectacles and umbrellas; veils for Egypt; and substantial clothing to use in rough pilgrimizing in the Holy Land. Furthermore, it was suggested that although the ship's library would afford a fair amount of reading matter, it would still be well if each passenger would provide himself with a few guide-books, a Bible and some standard works of travel. A list was appended, which consisted chiefly of books relating to the Holy Land since the Holy Land was part of the excursion and seemed to be its main feature.

Rev. Henry Ward Beecher was to have accompanied the expedition, but urgent duties obliged him to give up the idea. There were other passengers who could have been spared better, and would have been spared more willingly. Lieut. Gen. Sherman was to have been of the party, also, but the Indian war compelled his presence on the plains. A popular actress had entered her name on the ship's books, but something interfered, and *she* couldn't go. The "Drummer Boy of the Potomac" deserted, and lo, we had never a celebrity left!

However, we were to have a "battery of guns" from the Navy Department, (as per advertisement,) to be used in answering royal salutes; and the document furnished by the Secretary of the Navy, which was to make "Gen. Sherman and party" welcome guests in the courts and camps of the old world, was still left to us, though both document and battery, I think, were shorn of somewhat of their original august proportions. However, had not we the seductive programme, still, with its Paris, its Constantinople, Smyrna, Jerusalem, Jericho, and "our friends the Bermudians?" What did we care?

Chapter II

O CCASIONALLY, during the following month, I dropped in at 117 Wall-street to inquire how the repairing and refurnishing of the vessel was coming on; how additions to the passenger list were averaging; how many people the committee were decreeing not "select," every day, and banishing in sorrow and tribulation. I was glad to know that we were to have a little printing-press on board and issue a daily newspaper of our own. I was glad to learn that our piano, our parlor organ and our melodeon were to be the best instruments of the kind that could be had in the market. I was proud to observe that among our excursionists were three ministers of the gospel, eight doctors, sixteen or eighteen ladies, several military and naval chieftains with sounding titles, an ample crop of "Professors" of various kinds, and a gentleman who had "COMMISSIONER OF THE UNITED STATES OF AMERICA TO EUROPE, ASIA, AND AFRICA" thundering after his name in one awful blast! I had carefully prepared myself to take rather a back seat in that ship, because of the uncommonly select material that would alone be permitted to pass through the camel's eye of that committee on credentials; I had schooled myself to expect an imposing array of military and naval heroes, and to have to set that back seat still further back in consequence of it, may be; but I state frankly that I was all unprepared for *this* crusher.

I fell under that titular avalanche a torn and blighted thing. I said that if that potentate *must* go over in our ship, why, I supposed he must—but that to my thinking, when the United States considered it necessary to send a dignitary of that tonnage across the ocean, it would be in better taste, and safer, to take him apart and cart him over in sections, in several ships.

Ah, if I had only known, then, that he was only a common mortal, and that his mission had nothing more overpowering about it than the collecting of seeds, and uncommon yams and extraordinary cabbages and peculiar bullfrogs for that poor, useless, innocent, mildewed old fossil, the Smithsonian Institute, I would have felt *so* much relieved.

During that memorable month I basked in the happiness of being for once in my life drifting with the tide of a great popular movement. Every body was going to Europe—I, too, was going to Europe. Every body was going to the famous Paris Exposition—I, too, was going to the Paris Exposition. The steamship lines were carrying Americans out of the various ports of the country at the rate of four or five thousand a week, in the aggregate. If I met a dozen individuals, during that month, who were not going to Europe shortly, I have no distinct remembrance of it now. I walked about the city a good deal with a young Mr. Blucher, who was booked for the excursion. He was confiding, good-natured, unsophisticated, companionable; but he was not a man to set the river on fire. He had the most extraordinary notions about this European exodus, and came at last to consider the whole nation as packing up for emigration to France. We stepped into a store in Broadway, one day, where he bought a handkerchief, and when the man could not make change, Mr. B. said:

"Never mind, I'll hand it to you in Paris."

"But I am not going to Paris."

"How is—what did I understand you to say?"

"I said I am not going to Paris."

"Not going to *Paris*! Not g—well then, where in the nation *are* you going to?"

"Nowhere at all."

"Not any where whatsoever?—not any place on earth but this?"

"Not any place at all but just this—stay here all summer."

My comrade took his purchase and walked out of the store without a word—walked out with an injured look upon his countenance. Up the street apiece he broke silence and said impressively: "It was a lie—that is my opinion of it!"

In the fullness of time the ship was ready to receive her passengers. I was introduced to the young gentleman who was to be my room mate, and found him to be intelligent, cheerful of spirit, unselfish, full of generous impulses, patient, considerate, and wonderfully good-natured. Not any passenger that sailed in the *Quaker City* will withhold his indorsement of what I have just said. We selected a state-room forward of the wheel, on the starboard side, "below decks." It had two berths in it, a dismal dead-light, a sink with a wash-bowl in it, and a long, sumptuously cushioned locker, which was to do service as a sofa—partly, and partly as a hiding-place for our things. Notwithstanding all this furniture, there was still room to turn around in, but not to swing a cat in, at least with entire security to the cat. However, the room was large, for a ship's state-room, and was in every way satisfactory.

The vessel was appointed to sail on a certain Saturday early in June.

A little after noon, on that distinguished Saturday, I reached the ship and went on board. All was bustle and confusion. [I have seen that remark before, somewhere.] The pier was crowded with carriages and men; passengers were arriving and hurrying on board; the vessel's decks were encumbered with trunks and valises; groups of excursionists, arrayed in unattractive traveling costumes, were moping about in a drizzling rain and looking as droopy and woe-begone as so many molting chickens. The gallant flag was up, but it was under the spell, too, and hung limp and disheartened by the mast. Altogether, it was the bluest, bluest spectacle! It was a pleasure excursion—there was no gainsaying that, because the programme said so—it was so nominated in the bond— but it surely hadn't the general aspect of one.

Finally, above the banging, and rumbling, and shouting and hissing of steam, rang the order to "cast off!"—a sudden rush to the gangways—a scampering ashore of visitors—a revolution of the wheels, and we were off—the pic-nic was begun! Two very mild cheers went up from the dripping crowd on the pier; we answered them gently from the slippery decks; the flag made an effort to wave, and failed; the "battery of guns" spake not—the ammunition was out.

We steamed down to the foot of the harbor and came to anchor. It was still raining. And not only raining, but storming. "Outside" we could see, ourselves, that there was a tremendous sea on. We must lie still, in the calm harbor, till the storm should abate. Our passengers hailed from fifteen States; only a few of them had ever been to sea before; manifestly it would not do to pit them against a full-blown tempest until they had got their sea-legs on. Toward evening the two steam-tugs that had accompanied us with a rollicking champagne-party of young New Yorkers on board who wished to bid farewell to one of our number in due and ancient form, departed, and we were alone on the deep. On deep five fathoms, and anchored fast to the bottom. And out in the solemn rain, at that. This was pleasuring with a vengeance.

It was an appropriate relief when the gong sounded for prayer meeting. The first Saturday night of any other pleasure excursion might have been devoted to whist and dancing; but I submit it to the unprejudiced mind if it would have been in good taste for *us* to engage in such frivolities, considering what we had gone through and the frame of mind we were in. We would have shone at a wake, but not at any thing more festive.

However, there is always a cheering influence about the sea; and in my berth, that night, rocked by the measured swell of the waves, and lulled by the murmur of the distant surf, I soon passed tranquilly out of all consciousness of the dreary experiences of the day and damaging premonitions of the future.

Chapter III

ALL DAY SUNDAY at anchor. The storm had gone down a great deal, but the sea had not. It was still piling its frothy hills high in air "outside," as we could plainly see with the glasses. We could not properly begin a pleasure excursion on Sunday; we could not offer untried stomachs to so pitiless a sea as that. We must lie still till Monday. And we did. But we had repetitions of church and prayer-meetings; and so, of course, we were just as eligibly situated as we could have been any where.

I was up early that Sabbath morning, and was early to breakfast. I felt a perfectly natural desire to have a good, long, unprejudiced look at the passengers, at a time when they should be free from self-consciousness—which is at breakfast, when such a moment occurs in the lives of human beings at all.

I was greatly surprised to see so many elderly people—I might almost say, so many venerable people. A glance at the long lines of heads was apt to make one think it was *all* gray. But it was not. There was a tolerably fair sprinkling of young folks, and another fair sprinkling of gentlemen and ladies who were non-committal as to age, being neither actually old or absolutely young.

The next morning, we weighed anchor and went to sea. It was a great happiness to get away, after this dragging, dispiriting delay. I thought there never was such gladness in the air before, such brightness in the sun, such beauty in the sea. I was satisfied with the picnic, then, and with all its belongings. All my malicious instincts were dead within me; and as America faded out of sight, I think a spirit of charity rose up in their place that was as boundless, for the time being, as the broad ocean that was heaving its billows about us. I wished to express my feelings—I wished to lift up my voice and sing; but I did not know any thing to sing, and so I was obliged to give up the idea. It was no loss to the ship though, perhaps.

It was breezy and pleasant, but the sea was still very rough. One could not promenade without risking his neck; at one moment the bowsprit was taking a deadly aim at the sun in mid-heaven, and at the next it was trying to harpoon a shark in the bottom of the ocean. What a weird sensation it is to feel the stern of a ship sinking swiftly from under you and see the bow climbing high away among the clouds! One's safest course, that day, was to clasp a railing and hang on; walking was too precarious a pastime.

By some happy fortune I was not seasick.—That was a thing to be proud of. I had not always escaped before. If there is one thing in the world that will make a man peculiarly and insufferably self-conceited, it is to have his stomach behave itself, the first day at sea, when nearly all his comrades are seasick. Soon, a venerable fossil, shawled to the chin and bandaged like a mummy, appeared at the door of the after deck-house, and the next lurch of the ship shot him into my arms. I said:

"Good-morning, Sir. It is a fine day."

He put his hand on his stomach and said, "*Oh*, my!" and then staggered away and fell over the coop of a skylight.

Presently another old gentleman was projected from the same door, with great violence. I said:

"Calm yourself, Sir—There is no hurry. It is a fine day, Sir."

He, also, put his hand on his stomach and said, "*Oh*, my!" and reeled away.

In a little while another veteran was discharged abruptly from the same door, clawing at the air for a saving support. I said:

"Good-morning, Sir. It is a fine day for pleasuring. You were about to say—"

"*Oh*, my!"

I thought so. I anticipated *him*, any how. I staid there and was bombarded with old gentlemen for an hour perhaps; and all I got out of any of them was "*Oh*, my!"

I went away, then, in a thoughtful mood. I said, this is a good pleasure excursion. I like it. The passengers are not garrulous, but still they are sociable. I like those old people, but somehow they all seem to have the "Oh, my" rather bad.

I knew what was the matter with them. They were seasick. And I was glad of it. We all like to see people seasick when we are not, ourselves. Playing whist by the cabin lamps when it is storming outside, is pleasant; walking the quarter-deck in the moonlight, is pleasant; smoking in the breezy foretop is pleasant, when one is not afraid to go up there; but these are all feeble and commonplace compared with the joy of seeing people suffering the miseries of seasickness.

I picked up a good deal of information during the afternoon. At one time I was climbing up the quarter-deck when the vessel's stern was in the sky; I was smoking a cigar and feeling passably comfortable. Somebody ejaculated:

"Come, now, *that* won't answer. Read the sign up there— No smoking abaft the wheel!"

It was Capt. Duncan, chief of the expedition. I went forward, of course. I saw a long spy-glass lying on a desk in one of the upper-deck state-rooms back of the pilot-house, and reached after it—there was a ship in the distance:

"Ah, ah—hands off! Come out of that!"

I came out of that. I said to a deck-sweep—but in a low voice:

"Who is that overgrown pirate with the whiskers and the discordant voice?"

"It's Capt. Bursley—executive officer—sailing-master."

I loitered about awhile, and then, for want of something better to do, fell to carving a railing with my knife. Somebody said, in an insinuating, admonitory voice:

"Now *say*—my friend—don't you know any better than to be whittling the ship all to pieces that way? *You* ought to know better than that."

I went back and found the deck-sweep:

"Who is that smooth-faced animated outrage yonder in the fine clothes?"

"That's Capt. L****, the owner of the ship—he's one of the main bosses."

In the course of time I brought up on the starboard side of the pilot-house, and found a sextant lying on a bench. Now, I said, they "take the sun" through this thing; I should think I might see that vessel through it. I had hardly got it to my eye when some one touched me on the shoulder and said, deprecatingly:

"I'll have to get you to give that to me, Sir. If there's any

thing you'd like to know about taking the sun, I'd as soon
tell you as not—but I don't like to trust any body with that
instrument. If you want any figuring done—Aye-aye, Sir!"

He was gone, to answer a call from the other side. I sought
the deck-sweep:

"Who is that spider-legged gorilla yonder with the sanctimonious countenance?"

"It's Capt. Jones, Sir—the chief mate."

"Well. This goes clear away ahead of any thing I ever heard
of before. Do you—now I ask you as a man and a brother—
do you think I could venture to throw a rock here in any
given direction without hitting a captain of this ship?"

"Well, Sir, I don't know—I think likely you'd fetch the
captain of the watch, may be, because he's a-standing right
yonder in the way."

I went below—meditating, and a little down-hearted. I
thought, if five cooks can spoil a broth, what may not five
captains do with a pleasure excursion.

Chapter IV

WE PLOWED ALONG bravely for a week or more, and without any conflict of jurisdiction among the captains worth mentioning. The passengers soon learned to accommodate themselves to their new circumstances, and life in the ship became nearly as systematically monotonous as the routine of a barrack. I do not mean that it was dull, for it was not entirely so by any means—but there was a good deal of sameness about it. As is always the fashion at sea, the passengers shortly began to pick up sailor terms—a sign that they were beginning to feel at home. Half-past six was no longer half-past six to these pilgrims from New England, the South, and the Mississippi Valley, it was "seven bells;" eight, twelve and four o'clock were "eight bells;" the captain did not take the longitude at nine o'clock, but at "two bells." They spoke glibly of the "after cabin," the "for'rard cabin," "port and starboard" and the "fo'castle."

At seven bells the first gong rang; at eight there was breakfast, for such as were not too seasick to eat it. After that all the well people walked arm-in-arm up and down the long promenade deck, enjoying the fine summer mornings, and the seasick ones crawled out and propped themselves up in the lee of the paddle-boxes and ate their dismal tea and toast, and looked wretched. From eleven o'clock until luncheon, and from luncheon until dinner at six in the evening, the employments and amusements were various. Some reading was done; and much smoking and sewing, though not by the same parties; there were the monsters of the deep to be looked after and wondered at; strange ships had to be scrutinized through opera-glasses, and sage decisions arrived at concerning them; and more than that, every body took a personal interest in seeing that the flag was run up and politely dipped three times in response to the salutes of those strangers; in the smoking-room there were always parties of gentlemen playing euchre, draughts and dominoes, especially dominoes, that delightfully harmless game; and down on the main deck, "for'rard"—for'rard of the chicken-coops and the cattle—we had what was called "horse-billiards." Horse-billiards is a fine game. It affords good, active exercise, hilarity, and consuming excitement. It is a mixture of "hop-scotch" and shuffle-board played with a crutch. A large hop-scotch diagram is marked out on the deck with chalk, and each compartment numbered. You stand off three or four steps, with some broad wooden disks before you on the deck, and these you send forward with a vigorous thrust of a long crutch. If a disk stops on a chalk line, it does not count any thing. If it stops in division No. 7, it counts 7; in 5, it counts 5, and so on. The game is 100, and four can play at a time. That game would be very simple, played on a stationary floor, but with us, to play it well required science. We had to allow for the reeling of the ship to the right or the left. Very often one made calculations for a heel to the right and the ship did not go that way. The consequence was that that disk missed the whole hop-scotch plan a yard or two, and then there was humiliation on one side and laughter on the other.

When it rained, the passengers had to stay in the house, of course—or at least the cabins—and amuse themselves with games, reading, looking out of the windows at the very familiar billows, and talking gossip.

By 7 o'clock in the evening, dinner was about over; an hour's promenade on the upper deck followed; then the gong sounded and a large majority of the party repaired to the after cabin (upper), a handsome saloon fifty or sixty feet long, for prayers. The unregenerated called this saloon the "Synagogue." The devotions consisted only of two hymns from the "Plymouth Collection," and a short prayer, and seldom occupied more than fifteen minutes. The hymns were accompanied by parlor organ music when the sea was smooth enough to allow a performer to sit at the instrument without being lashed to his chair.

After prayers the Synagogue shortly took the semblance of a writing-school. The like of that picture was never seen in a ship before. Behind the long dining-tables on either side of the saloon, and scattered from one end to the other of the latter, some twenty or thirty gentlemen and ladies sat them down under the swaying lamps, and for two or three hours wrote diligently in their journals. Alas! that journals so voluminously begun should come to so lame and impotent a conclusion as most of them did! I doubt if there is a single pilgrim of all that host but can show a hundred fair pages of journal concerning the first twenty days' voyaging in the Quaker City; and I am morally certain that not ten of the party can show twenty pages of journal for the succeeding twenty thousand miles of voyaging! At certain periods it becomes the dearest ambition of a man to keep a faithful record of his performances in a book; and he dashes at this work with an enthusiasm that imposes on him the notion that keeping a journal is the veriest pastime in the world, and the pleasantest. But if he only lives twenty-one days, he will find out that only those rare natures that are made up of pluck, endurance, devotion to duty for duty's sake, and invincible determination, may hope to venture upon so tremendous an enterprise as the keeping of a journal and not sustain a shameful defeat.

One of our favorite youths, Jack, a splendid young fellow with a head full of good sense, and a pair of legs that were a wonder to look upon in the way of length, and straightness, and slimness, used to report progress every morning in the most glowing and spirited way, and say:

"Oh, I'm coming along bully!" (he was a little given to slang, in his happier moods,) "I wrote ten pages in my journal last night—and you know I wrote nine the night before, and twelve the night before that. Why it's only fun!"

"What do you find to put in it, Jack?"

"Oh, every thing. Latitude and longitude, noon every day; and how many miles we made last twenty-four hours; and all the domino-games I beat, and horse-billiards; and whales and sharks and porpoises; and the text of the sermon, Sundays; (because that'll tell at home, you know,) and the ships we saluted and what nation they were; and which way the wind was, and whether there was a heavy sea, and what sail we carried, though we don't ever carry *any*, principally, going against a head wind always—wonder what is the reason of that?—and how many lies Moult has told—Oh, every thing! I've got every thing down. My father told me to keep that journal. Father wouldn't take a thousand dollars for it when I get it done."

"No, Jack; it will be worth more than a thousand dollars—when you get it done."

"Do you?—no, but do you think it will, though?"

"Yes, it will be worth at least as much as a thousand dollars—when you get it done. May be, more."

"Well, I about half think so, myself. It ain't no slouch of a journal."

But it shortly became a most lamentable "slouch of a journal." One night in Paris, after a hard day's toil in sight-seeing, I said:

"Now I'll go and stroll around the cafés awhile, Jack, and give you a chance to write up your journal, old fellow."

His countenance lost its fire. He said:

"Well, no, you needn't mind. I think I won't run that journal any more. It is awful tedious. Do you know—I reckon I'm as much as four thousand pages behind hand. I haven't got any France in it at all. First I thought I'd leave France out and start fresh. But that wouldn't do, *would* it? The governor would say, 'Hello, here—didn't see any thing in France?' *That* cat wouldn't fight, you know. First I thought I'd copy France out of the guide-book, like old Badger in the for'rard cabin who's writing a book, but there's more than three hundred pages of it. Oh, *I* don't think a journal's any use—do you? They're only a bother, *ain't* they?"

"Yes, a journal that is incomplete isn't of much use, but a journal properly kept, is worth a thousand dollars,—when you've got it done."

"A thousand!—well I should think so. *I* wouldn't finish it for a million."

His experience was only the experience of the majority of that industrious night-school in the cabin. If you wish to inflict a heartless and malignant punishment upon a young person, pledge him to keep a journal a year.

A good many expedients were resorted to to keep the excursionists amused and satisfied. A club was formed, of all the passengers, which met in the writing-school after prayers and read aloud about the countries we were approaching, and discussed the information so obtained.

Several times the photographer of the expedition brought out his transparent pictures and gave us a handsome magic lantern exhibition. His views were nearly all of foreign scenes, but there were one or two home pictures among them. He advertised that he would "open his performance in the after cabin at 'two bells,' (9, p. m.,) and show the passengers where they shall eventually arrive"—which was all very well, but by a funny accident the first picture that flamed out upon the canvas was a view of Greenwood Cemetery!

On several starlight nights we danced on the upper deck, under the awnings, and made something of a ball-room display of brilliancy by hanging a number of ship's lanterns to the stanchions. Our music consisted of the well-mixed strains of a melodeon which was a little asthmatic and apt to catch its breath where it ought to come out strong; a clarinet which was a little unreliable on the high keys and rather melancholy on the low ones; and a disreputable accordion that had a leak somewhere and breathed louder than it squawked—a more elegant term does not occur to me just now. However, the dancing was infinitely worse than the music. When the ship rolled to starboard the whole platoon of dancers came charging down to starboard with it, and brought up in mass at the rail; and when it rolled to port, they went floundering down to port with the same unanimity of sentiment. Waltzers spun around precariously for a matter of fifteen seconds and then went skurrying down to the rail as if they meant to go overboard. The Virginia reel, as performed on board the *Quaker City*, had more genuine reel about it than any reel I ever saw before, and was as full of interest to the spectator as it was full of desperate chances and hairbreadth escapes to the participant. We gave up dancing, finally.

We celebrated a lady's birthday anniversary, with toasts, speeches, a poem, and so forth. We also had a mock trial. No ship ever went to sea that hadn't a mock trial on board. The purser was accused of stealing an overcoat from state-room No. 10. A judge was appointed; also clerks, a crier of the court, constables, sheriffs; counsel for the State and for the defendant; witnesses were subpœnaed, and a jury empaneled after much challenging. The witnesses were stupid, and unreliable and contradictory, as witnesses always are. The counsel were eloquent, argumentative and vindictively abusive of each other, as was characteristic and proper. The case was at last submitted, and duly finished by the judge with an absurd decision and a ridiculous sentence.

The acting of charades was tried, on several evenings, by the young gentlemen and ladies, in the cabins, and proved the most distinguished success of all the amusement experiments.

An attempt was made to organize a debating club, but it was a failure. There was no oratorical talent in the ship.

We all enjoyed ourselves—I think I can safely say that, but it was in a rather quiet way. We very, very seldom played the piano; we played the flute and the clarinet together, and made good music, too, what there was of it, but we always played the same old tune; it was a very pretty tune—how well I remember it—I wonder when I shall ever get rid of it. We never played either the melodeon or the organ, except at devotions—but I am too fast: young Albert *did* know part of a tune—something about "O Something-Or-Other How Sweet it is to Know that he's his What's-his-Name," (I do not remember the exact title of it, but it was very plaintive, and full of sentiment;) Albert played that pretty much all the time, until we contracted with him to restrain himself. But nobody ever sang by moonlight on the upper deck, and the congregational singing at church and prayers was not of a superior order of architecture. I put up with it as long as I could, and then joined in and tried to improve it, but this encouraged young George to join in too, and that made a failure of it; because George's voice was just "turning," and when he was singing a dismal sort of base, it was apt to fly off the handle and startle every body with a most discordant cackle on the upper notes. George didn't know the tunes, either, which was also a drawback to his performances. I said:

"Come, now, George, *don't* improvise. It looks too egotistical. It will provoke remark. Just stick to 'Coronation,' like the others. It is a good tune—*you* can't improve it any, just off-hand, in this way."

"Why I'm not trying to improve it—and I *am* singing like the others—just as it is in the notes."

And he honestly thought he was, too; and so he had no one to blame but himself when his voice caught on the centre occasionally, and gave him the lockjaw.

There were those among the unregenerated who attributed the unceasing head-winds to our distressing choir-music. There were those who said openly that it was taking chances enough to have such ghastly music going on, even when it was at its best; and that to exaggerate the crime by letting George help, was simply flying in the face of Providence. These said that the choir would keep up their lacerating attempts at melody until they would bring down a storm some day that would sink the ship.

There were even grumblers at the prayers. The executive officer said the Pilgrims had no charity:

"There they are, down there every night at eight bells, praying for fair winds—when they know as well as I do that this is the only ship going east this time of the year, but there's a thousand coming west—what's a fair wind for us is a *head* wind to them—the Almighty's blowing a fair wind for a thousand vessels, and this tribe wants him to turn it clear around so as to accommodate *one*,—and she a steamship at that! It ain't good sense, it ain't good reason, it ain't good Christianity, it ain't common human charity. Avast with such nonsense!"

Chapter V

Taking it "by and large," as the sailors say, we had a pleasant ten days' run from New York to the Azores islands—not a fast run, for the distance is only twenty-four hundred miles—but a right pleasant one, in the main. True, we had head-winds *all* the time, and several stormy experiences which sent fifty per cent. of the passengers to bed, sick, and made the ship look dismal and deserted—stormy experiences that all will remember who weathered them on the tumbling deck, and caught the vast sheets of spray that every now and then sprang high in air from the weather bow and swept the ship like a thunder-shower; but for the most part we had balmy summer weather, and nights that were even finer than the days. We had the phenomenon of a full moon located just in the same spot in the heavens at the same hour every night. The reason of this singular conduct on the part of the moon did not occur to us at first, but it did afterward when we reflected that we were gaining about twenty minutes every day, because we were going east so fast—we gained just about enough every day to keep along with the moon. It was becoming an old moon to the friends we had left behind us, but to us Joshuas it stood still in the same place, and remained always the same.

Young Mr. Blucher, who is from the Far West, and is on his first voyage, was a good deal worried by the constantly changing "ship-time." He was proud of his new watch at first, and used to drag it out promptly when eight bells struck at noon, but he came to look after a while as if her were losing confidence in it. Seven days out from New York he came on deck, and said with great decision:

"This thing's a swindle!"

"What's a swindle?"

"Why, this watch. I bought her out in Illinois—gave $150 for her—and I thought she was good. And, by George, she *is* good on shore, but somehow she don't keep up her lick here on the water—gets seasick, may be. She skips; she runs along regular enough till half-past eleven, and then, all of a sudden, she lets down. I've set that old regulator up faster

and faster, till I've shoved it clear around, but it don't do any
good; she just distances every watch in the ship, and clatters
along in a way that's astonishing till it is noon, but them
eight bells always gets in about ten minutes ahead of her any
way. I don't know what to do with her now. She's doing all
she can—she's going her best gait, but it won't save her.
Now, don't you know, there ain't a watch in the ship that's
making better time than she is: but what does it signify?
When you hear them eight bells you'll find her just about ten
minutes short of her score, sure."

The ship was gaining a full hour every three days, and this
fellow was trying to make his watch go fast enough to keep
up to her. But, as he had said, he had pushed the regulator
up as far as it would go, and the watch was "on its best gait,"
and so nothing was left him but to fold his hands and see the
ship beat the race. We sent him to the captain, and he explained to him the mystery of "ship-time," and set his troubled mind at rest. This young man asked a great many
questions about seasickness before we left, and wanted to
know what its characteristics were, and how he was to tell
when he had it. He found out.

We saw the usual sharks, blackfish, porpoises, &c., of
course, and by and by large schools of Portuguese men-of-
war were added to the regular list of sea wonders. Some of
them were white and some of a brilliant carmine color. The
nautilus is nothing but a transparent web of jelly, that spreads
itself to catch the wind, and has fleshy-looking strings a foot
or two long dangling from it to keep it steady in the water.
It is an accomplished sailor, and has good sailor judgment. It
reefs its sail when a storm threatens or the wind blows pretty
hard, and furls it entirely and goes down when a gale blows.
Ordinarily it keeps its sail wet and in good sailing order by
turning over and dipping it in the water for a moment. Seamen say the nautilus is only found in these waters between
the 35th and 45th parallels of latitude.

At three o'clock on the morning of the 21st of June, we
were awakened and notified that the Azores islands were in
sight. I said I did not take any interest in islands at three
o'clock in the morning. But another persecutor came, and
then another and another, and finally believing that the gen-

eral enthusiasm would permit no one to slumber in peace, I got up and went sleepily on deck. It was five and a half o'clock now, and a raw, blustering morning. The passengers were huddled about the smoke-stacks and fortified behind ventilators, and all were wrapped in wintry costumes, and looking sleepy and unhappy in the pitiless gale and the drenching spray.

The island in sight was Flores. It seemed only a mountain of mud standing up out of the dull mists of the sea. But as we bore down upon it, the sun came out and made it a beautiful picture—a mass of green farms and meadows that swelled up to a height of fifteen hundred feet, and mingled its upper outlines with the clouds. It was ribbed with sharp, steep ridges, and cloven with narrow canons, and here and there on the heights, rocky upheavals shaped themselves into mimic battlements and castles; and out of rifted clouds came broad shafts of sunlight, that painted summit, and slope, and glen, with bands of fire, and left belts of sombre shade between. It was the aurora borealis of the frozen pole exiled to a summer land!

We skirted around two-thirds of the island, four miles from shore, and all the opera-glasses in the ship were called into requisition to settle disputes as to whether mossy spots on the uplands were groves of trees or groves of weeds, or whether the white villages down by the sea were really villages or only the clustering tombstones of cemeteries. Finally, we stood to sea and bore away for San Miguel, and Flores shortly became a dome of mud again, and sank down among the mists and disappeared. But to many a seasick passenger it was good to see the green hills again, and all were more cheerful after this episode than any body could have expected them to be, considering how sinfully early they had gotten up.

But we had to change our purpose about San Miguel, for a storm came up about noon that so tossed and pitched the vessel that common sense dictated a run for shelter. Therefore we steered for the nearest island of the group—Fayal, (the people there pronounce it Fy-all, and put the accent on the first syllable.) We anchored in the open roadstead of Horta, half a mile from the shore. The town has eight thousand to ten thousand inhabitants. Its snow-white houses nestle cosily in a sea of fresh green vegetation, and no village could look prettier or more attractive. It sits in the lap of an amphitheatre of hills which are three hundred to seven hundred feet high, and carefully cultivated clear to their summits—not a foot of soil left idle. Every farm and every acre is cut up into little square inclosures by stone walls, whose duty it is to protect the growing products from the destructive gales that blow there. These hundreds of green squares, marked by their black lava walls, make the hills look like vast checker-boards.

The islands belong to Portugal, and every thing in Fayal has Portuguese characteristics about it. But more of that anon. A swarm of swarthy, noisy, lying, shoulder-shrugging, gesticulating Portuguese boatmen, with brass rings in their ears, and fraud in their hearts, climbed the ship's sides, and various parties of us contracted with them to take us ashore at so much a head, silver coin of any country. We landed under the walls of a little fort, armed with batteries of twelve and thirty-two pounders, which Horta considered a most formidable institution, but if we were ever to get after it with one of our turreted monitors, they would have to move it out in the country if they wanted it where they could go and find it again when they needed it. The group on the pier was a rusty one—men and women, and boys and girls, all ragged, and barefoot, uncombed and unclean, and by instinct, education, and profession, beggars. They trooped after us, and never more, while we tarried in Fayal, did we get rid of them. We walked up the middle of the principal street, and these vermin surrounded us on all sides, and glared upon us; and every moment excited couples shot ahead of the procession to get a good look back, just as village boys do when they accompany the elephant on his advertising trip from street to street. It was very flattering to me to be part of the material for such a sensation. Here and there in the doorways we saw women, with fashionable Portuguese hoods on. This hood is of thick blue cloth, attached to a cloak of the same stuff, and is a marvel of ugliness. It stands up high, and spreads far abroad, and is unfathomably deep. It fits like a circus tent, and a woman's head is hidden away in it like the man's who prompts the singers from his tin shed in the stage of an opera. There is no particle of trimming about this monstrous *capote*, as they call it—it is just a plain, ugly dead-blue mass of sail, and a woman can't go within eight points of the wind with one of them on; she has to go before the wind or not at all. The general style of the capote is the same in all the islands, and will remain so for the next ten thousand years, but each island shapes its capotes just enough differently from the others to enable an observer to tell at a glance what particular island a lady hails from.

The Portuguese pennies or *reis* (pronounced rays) are prodigious. It takes one thousand reis to make a dollar, and all financial estimates are made in reis. We did not know this until after we had found it out through Blucher. Blucher said he was so happy and so grateful to be on solid land once more, that he wanted to give a feast—said he had heard it was a cheap land, and he was bound to have a grand banquet. He invited nine of us, and we ate an excellent dinner at the principal hotel. In the midst of the jollity produced by good cigars, good wine, and passable anecdotes, the landlord presented his bill. Blucher glanced at it and his countenance fell. He took another look to assure himself that his senses had not deceived him, and then read the items aloud, in a faltering voice, while the roses in his cheeks turned to ashes:

" 'Ten dinners, at 600 reis, 6,000 reis!' Ruin and desolation!"

" 'Twenty-five cigars, at 100 reis, 2,500 reis!' Oh, my sainted mother!"

" 'Eleven bottles of wine, at 1,200 reis, 13,200 reis!' Be with us all!"

" 'TOTAL, TWENTY ONE THOUSAND SEVEN HUNDRED REIS!' The suffering Moses!—there ain't money enough in the ship to pay that bill! Go—leave me to my misery, boys, I am a ruined community."

I think it was the blankest looking party I ever saw. No body could say a word. It was as if every soul had been stricken dumb. Wine-glasses descended slowly to the table, their contents untasted. Cigars dropped unnoticed from nerveless fingers. Each man sought his neighbor's eye, but found in it no ray of hope, no encouragement. At last the fearful silence was broken. The shadow of a desperate resolve settled upon Blucher's countenance like a cloud, and he rose up and said:

"Landlord, this is a low, mean swindle, and I'll never, never stand it. Here's a hundred and fifty dollars, Sir, and it's all you'll get—I'll swim in blood, before I'll pay a cent more."

Our spirits rose and the landlord's fell—at least we thought so; he was confused at any rate, notwithstanding he had not understood a word that had been said. He glanced from the little pile of gold pieces to Blucher several times, and then went out. He must have visited an American, for, when he returned, he brought back his bill translated into a language that a Christian could understand—thus:

10 dinners, 6,000 reis, or	$6.00
25 cigars, 2,500 reis, or	2.50
11 bottles wine, 13,200 reis, or	13.20
Total 21,700 reis, or	$21.70

Happiness reigned once more in Blucher's dinner party. More refreshments were ordered.

Chapter VI

I THINK the Azores must be very little known in America. Out of our whole ship's company there was not a solitary individual who knew any thing whatever about them. Some of the party, well read concerning most other lands, had no other information about the Azores than that they were a group of nine or ten small islands far out in the Atlantic, something more than half way between New York and Gibraltar. That was all. These considerations move me to put in a paragraph of dry facts just here.

The community is eminently Portuguese—that is to say, it is slow, poor, shiftless, sleepy, and lazy. There is a civil governor, appointed by the King of Portugal; and also a military governor, who can assume supreme control and suspend the civil government at his pleasure. The islands contain a population of about 200,000, almost entirely Portuguese. Every thing is staid and settled, for the country was one hundred years old when Columbus discovered America. The principal crop is corn, and they raise it and grind it just as their great-great-great-grandfathers did. They plow with a board slightly shod with iron; their trifling little harrows are drawn by men and women; small windmills grind the corn, ten bushels a day, and there is one assistant superintendent to feed the mill and a general superintendent to stand by and keep him from going to sleep. When the wind changes they hitch on some donkeys, and actually turn the whole upper half of the mill around until the sails are in proper position, instead of fixing the concern so that the sails could be moved instead of the mill. Oxen tread the wheat from the ear, after the fashion prevalent in the time of Methuselah. There is not a wheelbarrow in the land—they carry every thing on their heads, or on donkeys, or in a wicker-bodied cart, whose wheels are solid blocks of wood and whose axles turn with the wheel. There is not a modern plow in the islands, or a threshing-machine. All attempts to introduce them have failed. The good Catholic Portuguese crossed himself and prayed God to shield him from all blasphemous desire to know more than his father did before him. The climate is mild; they never have snow or ice, and I saw no chimneys in the town. The donkeys and the men, women and children of a family, all eat and sleep in the same room, and are unclean, are ravaged by vermin, and are truly happy. The people lie, and cheat the stranger, and are desperately ignorant, and have hardly any reverence for their dead. The latter trait shows how little better they are than the donkeys they eat and sleep with. The only well-dressed Portuguese in the camp are the half a dozen well-to-do families, the Jesuit priests and the soldiers of the little garrison. The wages of a laborer are twenty to twenty-four cents a day, and those of a good mechanic about twice as much. They count it in reis at a thousand to the dollar, and this makes them rich and contented. Fine grapes used to grow in the islands, and an excellent wine was made and exported. But a disease killed all the vines fifteen years ago, and since that time no wine has been made. The islands being wholly of volcanic origin, the soil is necessarily very rich. Nearly every foot of ground is under cultivation, and two or three crops a year of each article are produced, but nothing is exported save a few oranges—chiefly to England. Nobody comes here, and nobody goes away. News is a thing unknown in Fayal. A thirst for it is a passion equally unknown. A Portuguese of average intelligence inquired if our civil war was over? because, he said, somebody had told him it was— or at least it ran in his mind that somebody had told him something like that! And when a passenger gave an officer of the garrison copies of the *Tribune*, the *Herald*, and *Times*, he was surprised to find later news in them from Lisbon than he had just received by the little monthly steamer. He was told that it came by cable. He said he knew they had tried to lay a cable ten years ago, but it had been in his mind, somehow, that they hadn't succeeded!

It is in communities like this that Jesuit humbuggery flourishes. We visited a Jesuit cathedral nearly two hundred years old, and found in it a piece of the veritable cross upon which our Saviour was crucified. It was polished and hard, and in as excellent a state of preservation as if the dread tragedy on Calvary had occurred yesterday instead of eighteen centuries ago. But these confiding people believe in that piece of wood unhesitatingly.

In a chapel of the cathedral is an altar with facings of solid silver—at least they call it so, and I think myself it would go a couple of hundred to the ton (to speak after the fashion of the silver miners,) and before it is kept forever burning a small lamp. A devout lady who died, left money and contracted for unlimited masses for the repose of her soul, and also stipulated that this lamp should be kept lighted always, day and night. She did all this before she died, you understand. It is a very small lamp, and a very dim one, and it could not work her much damage, I think, if it went out altogether.

The great altar of the cathedral, and also three or four minor ones, are a perfect mass of gilt gimcracks and gingerbread. And they have a swarm of rusty, dusty, battered apostles standing around the filagree work, some on one leg and some with one eye out but a gamey look in the other, and some with two or three fingers gone, and some with not enough nose left to blow—all of them crippled and discouraged, and fitter subjects for the hospital than the cathedral.

The walls of the chancel are of porcelain, all pictured over with figures of almost life size, very elegantly wrought, and dressed in the fanciful costumes of two centuries ago. The design was a history of something or somebody, but none of us were learned enough to read the story. The old father, reposing under a stone close by, dated 1686, might have told us if he could have risen. But he didn't.

As we came down through the town, we encountered a squad of little donkeys ready saddled for use. The saddles were peculiar, to say the least. They consisted of a sort of sawbuck, with a small mattress on it, and this furniture covered about half the donkey. There were no stirrups, but really such supports were not needed—to use such a saddle was the next thing to riding a dinner table—there was ample support clear out to one's knee joints. A pack of ragged Portuguese muleteers crowded around us, offering their beasts at half a dollar an hour—more rascality to the stranger, for the market price is sixteen cents. Half a dozen of us mounted the ungainly affairs, and submitted to the indignity of making a ridiculous spectacle of ourselves through the principal streets of a town of 10,000 inhabitants.

We started. It was not a trot, a gallop, or a canter, but a

stampede, and made up of all possible or conceivable gaits. No spurs were necessary. There was a muleteer to every donkey and a dozen volunteers beside, and they banged the donkeys with their goad-sticks, and pricked them with their spikes, and shouted something that sounded like *"Sekki-yah!"* and kept up a din and a racket that was worse than Bedlam itself. These rascals were all on foot, but no matter, they were always up to time—they can outrun and outlast a donkey. Altogether ours was a lively and a picturesque procession, and drew crowded audiences to the balconies wherever we went.

Blucher could do nothing at all with his donkey. The beast scampered zigzag across the road and the others ran into him; he scraped Blucher against carts and the corners of houses; the road was fenced in with high stone walls, and the donkey gave him a polishing first on one side and then on the other, but never once took the middle; he finally came to the house he was born in and darted into the parlor, scraping Blucher off at the doorway. After remounting, Blucher said to the muleteer, "Now, that's enough, you know; you go slow hereafter." But the fellow knew no English and did not understand, so he simply said, *"Sekki-yah!"* and the donkey was off again like a shot. He turned a corner suddenly, and Blucher went over his head. And, to speak truly, every mule stumbled over the two, and the whole cavalcade was piled up in a heap. No harm done. A fall from one of those donkeys is of little more consequence than rolling off a sofa. The donkeys all stood still after the catastrophe, and waited for their dismembered saddles to be patched up and put on by the noisy muleteers. Blucher was pretty angry, and wanted to swear, but every time he opened his mouth his animal did so also, and let off a series of brays that drowned all other sounds.

It was fun, skurrying around the breezy hills and through the beautiful canons. There was that rare thing, novelty, about it; it was a fresh, new, exhilarating sensation, this donkey riding, and worth a hundred worn and threadbare home pleasures.

The roads were a wonder, and well they might be. Here was an island with only a handful of people in it—25,000—and yet such fine roads do not exist in the United States outside of Central Park. Every where you go, in any direction,

you find either a hard, smooth, level thoroughfare, just sprinkled with black lava sand, and bordered with little gutters
neatly paved with small smooth pebbles, or compactly paved
ones like Broadway. They talk much of the Russ pavement in
New York, and call it a new invention—yet here they have
been using it in this remote little isle of the sea for two
hundred years! Every street in Horta is handsomely paved
with the heavy Russ blocks, and the surface is neat and true
as a floor—not marred by holes like Broadway. And every
road is fenced in by tall, solid lava walls, which will last a
thousand years in this land where frost is unknown. They are
very thick, and are often plastered and whitewashed, and
capped with projecting slabs of cut stone. Trees from gardens
above hang their swaying tendrils down, and contrast their
bright green with the whitewash or the black lava of the
walls, and make them beautiful. The trees and vines stretch
across these narrow roadways sometimes, and so shut out the
sun that you seem to be riding through a tunnel. The pavements, the roads, and the bridges are all government work.

The bridges are of a single span—a single arch—of cut
stone, without a support, and paved on top with flags of lava
and ornamental pebble work. Every where are walls, walls,
walls,—and all of them tasteful and handsome—and eternally
substantial; and every where are those marvelous pavements,
so neat, so smooth, and so indestructible. And if ever roads
and streets, and the outsides of houses, were perfectly free
from any sign or semblance of dirt, or dust, or mud, or uncleanliness of any kind, it is Horta, it is Fayal. The lower
classes of the people, in their persons and their domicils, are
not clean—but there it stops—the town and the island are
miracles of cleanliness.

We arrived home again finally, after a ten-mile excursion,
and the irrepressible muleteers scampered at our heels
through the main street, goading the donkeys, shouting the
everlasting *"Sekki-yah,"* and singing "John Brown's Body" in
ruinous English.

When we were dismounted and it came to settling, the
shouting and jawing, and swearing and quarreling among the
muleteers and with us, was nearly deafening. One fellow
would demand a dollar an hour for the use of his donkey;

another claimed half a dollar for pricking him up, another a quarter for helping in that service, and about fourteen guides presented bills for showing us the way through the town and its environs; and every vagrant of them was more vociferous, and more vehement, and more frantic in gesture than his neighbor. We paid one guide, and paid for one muleteer to each donkey.

The mountains on some of the islands are very high. We sailed along the shore of the Island of Pico, under a stately green pyramid that rose up with one unbroken sweep from our very feet to an altitude of 7,613 feet, and thrust its summit above the white clouds like an island adrift in a fog!

We got plenty of fresh oranges, lemons, figs, apricots, etc. in these Azores, of course. But I will desist. I am not here to write Patent-Office reports.

We are on our way to Gibraltar, and shall reach there five or six days out from the Azores.

Chapter VII

A WEEK of buffeting a tempestuous and relentless sea; a week of seasickness and deserted cabins; of lonely quarter-decks drenched with spray—spray so ambitious that it even coated the smoke-stacks thick with a white crust of salt to their very tops; a week of shivering in the shelter of the life-boats and deck-houses by day, and blowing suffocating "clouds" and boisterously performing at dominoes in the smoking room at night.

And the last night of the seven was the stormiest of all. There was no thunder, no noise but the pounding bows of the ship, the keen whistling of the gale through the cordage, and the rush of the seething waters. But the vessel climbed aloft as if she would climb to heaven—then paused an instant that seemed a century, and plunged headlong down again, as from a precipice. The sheeted sprays drenched the decks like rain. The blackness of darkness was every where. At long intervals a flash of lightning clove it with a quivering line of fire, that revealed a heaving world of water where was nothing before, kindled the dusky cordage to glittering silver, and lit up the faces of the men with a ghastly lustre!

Fear drove many on deck that were used to avoiding the night-winds and the spray. Some thought the vessel could not live through the night, and it seemed less dreadful to stand out in the midst of the wild tempest and *see* the peril that threatened than to be shut up in the sepulchral cabins, under the dim lamps and imagine the horrors that were abroad on the ocean. And once out—once where they could see the ship struggling in the strong grasp of the storm—once where they could hear the shriek of the winds, and face the driving spray and look out upon the majestic picture the lightnings disclosed, they were prisoners to a fierce fascination they could not resist, and so remained. It was a wild night—and a very, very long one.

Every body was sent scampering to the deck at seven o'clock this lovely morning of the 30th of June with the glad news that land was in sight! It was a rare thing and a joyful, to see *all* the ship's family abroad once more, albeit the happiness that sat upon every countenance could only partly conceal the ravages which that long siege of storms had wrought there. But dull eyes soon sparkled with pleasure, pallid cheeks flushed again, and frames weakened by sickness gathered new life from the quickening influences of the bright, fresh morning. Yea, and from a still more potent influence: the worn castaways were to see the blessed land again!—and to see it was to bring back that mother-land that was in all their thoughts.

Within the hour we were fairly within the Straits of Gibraltar, the tall yellow-splotched hills of Africa on our right, with their bases veiled in a blue haze and their summits swathed in clouds—the same being according to Scripture, which says that "clouds and darkness are over the land." The words were spoken of this particular portion of Africa, I believe. On our left were the granite-ribbed domes of old Spain. The Strait is only thirteen miles wide in its narrowest part.

At short intervals, along the Spanish shore, were quaint-looking old stone towers—Moorish, we thought—but learned better afterwards. In former times the Morocco rascals used to coast along the Spanish Main in their boats till a safe opportunity seemed to present itself, and then dart in and capture a Spanish village, and carry off all the pretty women they could find. It was a pleasant business, and was very popular. The Spaniards built these watchtowers on the hills to enable them to keep a sharper lookout on the Moroccan speculators.

The picture on the other hand was very beautiful to eyes weary of the changeless sea, and bye and bye the ship's company grew wonderfully cheerful. But while we stood admiring the cloud-capped peaks and the lowlands robed in misty gloom, a finer picture burst upon us and chained every eye like a magnet—a stately ship, with canvas piled on canvas till she was one towering mass of bellying sail! She came speeding over the sea like a great bird. Africa and Spain were forgotten. All homage was for the beautiful stranger. While every body gazed, she swept superbly by and flung the Stars and Stripes to the breeze! Quicker than thought, hats and handkerchiefs flashed in the air, and a cheer went up! She was beautiful before—she was radiant now. Many a one on our

decks knew then for the first time how tame a sight his country's flag is at home compared to what it is in a foreign land.
To see it is to see a vision of home itself and all its idols, and
feel a thrill that would stir a very river of sluggish blood!

We were approaching the famed Pillars of Hercules, and
already the African one, "Ape's Hill," a grand old mountain
with summit streaked with granite ledges, was in sight. The
other, the great Rock of Gibraltar, was yet to come. The ancients considered the Pillars of Hercules the head of navigation and the end of the world. The information the ancients
didn't have was very voluminous. Even the prophets wrote
book after book and epistle after epistle, yet never once hinted
at the existence of a great continent on our side of the water;
yet they must have known it was there, I should think.

In a few moments a lonely and enormous mass of rock,
standing seemingly in the centre of the wide strait and apparently washed on all sides by the sea, swung magnificently into
view, and we needed no tedious traveled parrot to tell us it
was Gibraltar. There could not be two rocks like that in one
kingdom.

The Rock of Gibraltar is about a mile and a half long, I
should say, by 1,400 to 1,500 feet high, and a quarter of a mile
wide at its base. One side and one end of it come about as
straight up out of the sea as the side of a house, the other
end is irregular and the other side is a steep slant which an
army would find very difficult to climb. At the foot of this
slant is the walled town of Gibraltar—or rather the town occupies part of the slant. Every where—on hillside, in the
precipice, by the sea, on the heights,—every where you
choose to look, Gibraltar is clad with masonry and bristling
with guns. It makes a striking and lively picture, from whatsoever point you contemplate it. It is pushed out into the sea
on the end of a flat, narrow strip of land, and is suggestive of
a "gob" of mud on the end of a shingle. A few hundred yards
of this flat ground at its base belongs to the English, and
then, extending across the strip from the Atlantic to the Mediterranean, a distance of a quarter of a mile, comes the "Neutral Ground," a space two or three hundred yards wide, which
is free to both parties.

"Are you going through Spain to Paris?" That question was

bandied about the ship day and night from Fayal to Gibraltar, and I thought I never could get so tired of hearing any one combination of words again, or more tired of answering, "I don't know." At the last moment six or seven had sufficient decision of character to make up their minds to go, and did go, and I felt a sense of relief at once—it was forever too late, now, and I could make up my mind at my leisure, not to go. I must have a prodigious quantity of mind; it takes me as much as a week, sometimes, to make it up.

But behold how annoyances repeat themselves. We had no sooner gotten rid of the Spain distress than the Gibraltar guides started another—a tiresome repetition of a legend that had nothing very astonishing about it, even in the first place: "That high hill yonder is called the Queen's Chair; it is because one of the Queens of Spain placed her chair there when the French and Spanish troops were besieging Gibraltar, and said she would never move from the spot till the English flag was lowered from the fortresses. If the English hadn't been gallant enough to lower the flag for a few hours one day, she'd have had to break her oath or die up there."

We rode on asses and mules up the steep, narrow streets and entered the subterranean galleries the English have blasted out in the rock. These galleries are like spacious railway tunnels, and at short intervals in them great guns frown out upon sea and town through port-holes five or six hundred feet above the ocean. There is a mile or so of this subterranean work, and it must have cost a vast deal of money and labor. The gallery guns command the peninsula and the harbors of both oceans, but they might as well not be there, I should think, for an army could hardly climb the perpendicular wall of the rock any how. Those lofty port-holes afford superb views of the sea, though. At one place, where a jutting crag was hollowed out into a great chamber whose furniture was huge cannon and whose windows were port-holes, a glimpse was caught of a hill not far away, and a soldier said:

"That high hill yonder is called the Queen's Chair; it is because a queen of Spain placed her chair there, once, when the French and Spanish troops were besieging Gibraltar, and said she would never move from the spot till the English flag was lowered from the fortresses. If the English hadn't been gallant enough to lower the flag for a few hours, one day, she'd have had to break her oath or die up there."

On the topmost pinnacle of Gibraltar we halted a good while, and no doubt the mules were tired. They had a right to be. The military road was good, but rather steep, and there was a good deal of it. The view from the narrow ledge was magnificent; from it vessels seeming like the tiniest little toy-boats, were turned into noble ships by the telescopes; and other vessels that were fifty miles away, and even sixty, they said, and invisible to the naked eye, could be clearly distinguished through those same telescopes. Below, on one side, we looked down upon an endless mass of batteries, and on the other straight down to the sea.

While I was resting ever so comfortably on a rampart, and cooling my baking head in the delicious breeze, an officious guide belonging to another party came up and said:

"Senor, that high hill yonder is called the Queen's Chair"—

"Sir, I am a helpless orphan in a foreign land. Have pity on me. Don't—now *don't* inflict that most in-FERNAL old legend on me any more to-day!"

There—I had used strong language, after promising I would never do so again; but the provocation was more than human nature could bear. If you had been bored so, when you had the noble panorama of Spain and Africa and the blue Mediterranean, spread abroad at your feet, and wanted to gaze, and enjoy, and surfeit yourself with its beauty in silence, you might have even burst into stronger language than I did.

Gibraltar has stood several protracted sieges, one of them of nearly four years duration (it failed,) and the English only captured it by stratagem. The wonder is that any body should ever dream of trying so impossible a project as the taking it by assault—and yet it has been tried more than once.

The Moors held the place twelve hundred years ago, and a stanch old castle of theirs of that date still frowns from the middle of the town, with moss-grown battlements and sides well scarred by shots fired in battles and sieges that are forgotten now. A secret chamber, in the rock behind it, was discovered some time ago, which contained a sword of exquisite workmanship, and some quaint old armor of a fashion that antiquaries are not acquainted with, though it is supposed to be Roman. Roman armor and Roman relics, of various kinds, have been found in a cave in the sea extremity of Gibraltar; history says Rome held this part of the country about the Christian era, and these things seem to confirm the statement.

In that cave, also, are found human bones, crusted with a very thick, stony coating, and wise men have ventured to say that those men not only lived before the flood, but as much as ten thousand years before it. It may be true—it looks reasonable enough—but as long as those parties can't vote any more, the matter can be of no great public interest. In this cave, likewise, are found skeletons and fossils of animals that exist in every part of Africa, yet within memory and tradition have never existed in any portion of Spain save this lone peak of Gibraltar! So the theory is that the channel between Gibraltar and Africa was once dry land, and that the low, neutral neck between Gibraltar and the Spanish hills behind it was once ocean, and of course that these African animals, being over at Gibraltar (after rock, perhaps—there is plenty there,) got closed out when the great change occurred. The hills in Africa, across the channel, are full of apes, and there are now, and always have been, apes on the rock of Gibraltar—but not elsewhere in Spain! The subject is an interesting one.

There is an English garrison at Gibraltar of 6,000 or 7,000 men, and so uniforms of flaming red are plenty; and red and blue, and undress costumes of snowy white, and also the queer uniform of the bare-kneed Highlander; and one sees soft-eyed Spanish girls from San Roque, and veiled Moorish beauties (I suppose they are beauties) from Tarifa, and turbaned, sashed and trowsered Moorish merchants from Fez, and long-robed, bare-legged, ragged Mohammedan vagabonds from Tetouan and Tangier, some brown, some yellow and some as black as virgin ink—and Jews from all around, in gaberdine, skull-cap and slippers, just as they are in pictures and theatres, and just as they were three thousand years ago, no doubt. You can easily understand that a tribe (somehow our pilgrims suggest that expression, because they march in a straggling procession through these foreign places with such an Indian-like air of complacency and independence about them,) like ours, made up from fifteen or sixteen States of the

Union, found enough to stare at in this shifting panorama of fashion to-day.

Speaking of our pilgrims reminds me that we have one or two people among us who are sometimes an annoyance. However, I do not count the Oracle in that list. I will explain that the Oracle is an innocent old ass who eats for four and looks wiser than the whole Academy of France would have any right to look, and never uses a one-syllable word when he can think of a longer one, and never by any possible chance knows the meaning of any long word he uses, or ever gets it in the right place: yet he will serenely venture an opinion on the most abstruse subject, and back it up complacently with quotations from authors who never existed, and finally when cornered will slide to the other side of the question, say he has been there all the time, and come back at you with your own spoken arguments, only with the big words all tangled, and play them in your very teeth as original with himself. He reads a chapter in the guide-books, mixes the facts all up, with his bad memory, and then goes off to inflict the whole mess on somebody as wisdom which has been festering in his brain for years, and which he gathered in college from erudite authors who are dead, now, and out of print. This morning at breakfast he pointed out of the window, and said:

"Do you see that there hill out there on that African coast?—It's one of them Pillows of Herkewls, I should say—and there's the ultimate one alongside of it."

"The ultimate one—that is a good word—but the Pillars are not both on the same side of the strait." (I saw he had been deceived by a carelessly written sentence in the Guide Book.)

"Well, it ain't for you to say, nor for me. Some authors states it that way, and some states it different. Old Gibbons don't say nothing about it,—just shirks it complete—Gibbons always done that when he got stuck—but there is Rolampton, what does *he* say? Why, he says that they was both on the same side, and Trinculian, and Sobaster, and Syraccus, and Langomarganbl—"

"Oh, that will do—that's enough. If you have got your hand in for inventing authors and testimony, I have nothing more to say—let them *be* on the same side."

We don't mind the Oracle. We rather like him. We can tolerate the Oracle very easily; but we have a poet and a good-natured enterprising idiot on board, and they *do* distress the company. The one gives copies of his verses to Consuls, commanders, hotel keepers, Arabs, Dutch,—to any body, in fact, who will submit to a grievous infliction most kindly meant. His poetry is all very well on shipboard, notwithstanding when he wrote an "Ode to the Ocean in a Storm" in one half-hour, and an "Apostrophe to the Rooster in the Waist of the Ship" in the next, the transition was considered to be rather abrupt; but when he sends an invoice of rhymes to the Governor of Fayal and another to the commander-in-chief and other dignitaries in Gibraltar, with the compliments of the Laureate of the Ship, it is not popular with the passengers.

The other personage I have mentioned is young and green, and not bright, not learned and not wise. He will be, though, some day, if he recollects the answers to all his questions. He is known about the ship as the "Interrogation Point," and this by constant use has become shortened to "Interrogation." He has distinguished himself twice already. In Fayal they pointed out a hill and told him it was eight hundred feet high and eleven hundred feet long. And they told him there was a tunnel two thousand feet long and one thousand feet high running through the hill, from end to end. He believed it. He repeated it to every body, discussed it, and read it from his notes. Finally, he took a useful hint from this remark which a thoughtful old pilgrim made:

"Well, yes, it *is* a little remarkable—singular tunnel altogether—stands up out of the top of the hill about two hundred feet, and one end of it sticks out of the hill about nine hundred!"

Here in Gibraltar he corners these educated British officers and badgers them with braggadocio about America and the wonders she can perform. He told one of them a couple of our gunboats could come here and knock Gibraltar into the Mediterranean Sea!

At this present moment, half a dozen of us are taking a private pleasure excursion of our own devising. We form rather more than half the list of white passengers on board a small steamer bound for the venerable Moorish town of Tangier, Africa. Nothing could be more absolutely certain than that we are enjoying ourselves. One can not do otherwise who speeds over these sparkling waters, and breathes the soft atmosphere of this sunny land. Care can not assail us here. We are out of its jurisdiction.

We even steamed recklessly by the frowning fortress of Malabat, (a stronghold of the Emperor of Morocco,) without a twinge of fear. The whole garrison turned out under arms, and assumed a threatening attitude—yet still we did not fear. The entire garrison marched and counter-marched, within the rampart, in full view—yet notwithstanding even this, we never flinched.

I suppose we really do not know what fear is. I inquired the name of the garrison of the fortress of Malabat, and they said it was Mehemet Ali Ben Sancom. I said it would be a good idea to get some more garrisons to help him; but they said no; he had nothing to do but hold the place, and he was competent to do that; had done it two years already. That was evidence which one could not well refute. There is nothing like reputation.

Every now and then, my glove purchase in Gibraltar last night intrudes itself upon me. Dan and the ship's surgeon and I had been up to the great square, listening to the music of the fine military bands, and contemplating English and Spanish female loveliness and fashion, and, at 9 o'clock, were on our way to the theatre, when we met the General, the Judge, the Commodore, the Colonel, and the Commissioner of the United States of America to Europe, Asia, and Africa, who had been to the Club House, to register their several titles and impoverish the bill of fare; and they told us to go over to the little variety store, near the Hall of Justice, and buy some kid gloves. They said they were elegant, and very moderate in price. It seemed a stylish thing to go to the theatre in kid gloves, and we acted upon the hint. A very handsome young lady in the store offered me a pair of blue gloves. I did not want blue, but she said they would look very pretty on a hand like mine. The remark touched me tenderly. I glanced furtively at my hand, and somehow it did seem rather a comely member. I tried a glove on my left, and blushed a little.

Manifestly the size was too small for me. But I felt gratified when she said:

"Oh, it is just right!"—yet I knew it was no such thing.

I tugged at it diligently, but it was discouraging work. She said:

"Ah! I see *you* are accustomed to wearing kid gloves—but some gentlemen are *so* awkward about putting them on."

It was the last compliment I had expected. I only understand putting on the buckskin article perfectly. I made another effort, and tore the glove from the base of the thumb into the palm of the hand—and tried to hide the rent. She kept up her compliments, and I kept up my determination to deserve them or die:

"Ah, you have had experience!" [A rip down the back of the hand.] "They are just right for you—your hand is very small—if they tear you need not pay for them." [A rent across the middle.] "I can always tell when a gentleman understands putting on kid gloves. There is a grace about it that only comes with long practice." [The whole after-guard of the glove "fetched away," as the sailors say, the fabric parted across the knuckles, and nothing was left but a melancholy ruin.]

I was too much flattered to make an exposure, and throw the merchandise on the angel's hands. I was hot, vexed, confused, but still happy; but I hated the other boys for taking such an absorbing interest in the proceedings. I wished they were in Jericho. I felt exquisitely mean when I said cheerfully,—

"This one does very well; it fits elegantly. I like a glove that fits. No, never mind, ma'am, never mind; I'll put the other on in the street. It is warm here."

It *was* warm. It was the warmest place I ever was in. I paid the bill, and as I passed out with a fascinating bow, I thought I detected a light in the woman's eye that was gently ironical; and when I looked back from the street, and she was laughing all to herself about something or other, I said to myself, with withering sarcasm, "Oh, certainly; *you* know how to put on kid gloves, don't you?—a self-complacent ass, ready to be flattered out of your senses by every petticoat that chooses to take the trouble to do it!"

The silence of the boys annoyed me. Finally, Dan said, musingly:

"Some gentlemen don't know how to put on kid gloves at all; but some do."

And the doctor said (to the moon, I thought,)

"But it is always easy to tell when a gentleman is used to putting on kid gloves."

Dan soliloquized, after a pause:

"Ah, yes; there is a grace about it that only comes with long, very long practice."

"Yes, indeed, I've noticed that when a man hauls on a kid glove like he was dragging a cat out of an ash-hole by the tail, *he* understands putting on kid gloves; *he's* had ex—"

"Boys, enough of a thing 's enough! You think you are very smart, I suppose, but I don't. And if you go and tell any of those old gossips in the ship about this thing, I'll never forgive you for it; that's all."

They let me alone then, for the time being. We always let each other alone in time to prevent ill feeling from spoiling a joke. But they had bought gloves, too, as I did. We threw all the purchases away together this morning. They were coarse, unsubstantial, freckled all over with broad yellow splotches, and could neither stand wear nor public exhibition. We had entertained an angel unawares, but we did not take her in. She did that for us.

Tangier! A tribe of stalwart Moors are wading into the sea to carry us ashore on their backs from the small boats.

Chapter VIII

THIS IS ROYAL! Let those who went up through Spain make the best of it—these dominions of the Emperor of Morocco suit our little party well enough. We have had enough of Spain at Gibraltar for the present. Tangier is the spot we have been longing for all the time. Elsewhere we have found foreign-looking things and foreign-looking people, but always with things and people intermixed that we were familiar with before, and so the novelty of the situation lost a deal of its force. We wanted something thoroughly and uncompromisingly foreign—foreign from top to bottom—foreign from centre to circumference—foreign inside and outside and all around—nothing any where about it to dilute its foreignness—nothing to remind us of any other people or any other land under the sun. And lo! in Tangier we have found it. Here is not the slightest thing that ever we have seen save in pictures—and we always mistrusted the pictures before. We can not any more. The pictures used to seem exaggerations—they seemed too weird and fanciful for reality. But behold, they were not wild enough—they were not fanciful enough—they have not told half the story. Tangier is a foreign land if ever there was one; and the true spirit of it can never be found in any book save the Arabian Nights. Here are no white men visible, yet swarms of humanity are all about us. Here is a packed and jammed city inclosed in a massive stone wall which is more than a thousand years old. All the houses nearly are one and two-story; made of thick walls of stone; plastered outside; square as a dry-goods box; flat as a floor on top; no cornices; whitewashed all over—a crowded city of snowy tombs! And the doors are arched with the peculiar arch we see in Moorish pictures; the floors are laid in vari-colored diamond-flags; in tesselated many-colored porcelain squares wrought in the furnaces of Fez; in red tiles and broad bricks that time can not wear; there is no furniture in the rooms (of Jewish dwellings) save divans—what there is in Moorish ones no man may know; within their sacred walls no Christian dog can enter. And the streets are oriental—some of them three feet wide, some six, but only two

that are over a dozen; a man can blockade the most of them
by extending his body across them. Isn't it an oriental picture?

There are stalwart Bedouins of the desert here, and stately
Moors, proud of a history that goes back to the night of time;
and Jews, whose fathers fled hither centuries upon centuries
ago; and swarthy Riffians from the mountains—born cut-
throats—and original, genuine negroes, as black as Moses;
and howling dervishes, and a hundred breeds of Arabs—all
sorts and descriptions of people that are foreign and curious
to look upon.

And their dresses are strange beyond all description. Here
is a bronzed Moor in a prodigious white turban, curiously
embroidered jacket, gold and crimson sash, of many folds,
wrapped round and round his waist, trowsers that only come
a little below his knee, and yet have twenty yards of stuff in
them, ornamented scimetar, bare shins, stockingless feet, yellow slippers, and gun of preposterous length—a mere soldier!—I thought he was the Emperor at least. And here are
aged Moors with flowing white beards, and long white robes
with vast cowls; and Bedouins with long, cowled, striped
cloaks, and negroes and Riffians with heads clean-shaven, except a kinky scalp-lock back of the ear, or rather up on the
after corner of the skull, and all sorts of barbarians in all sorts
of weird costumes, and all more or less ragged. And here are
Moorish women who are enveloped from head to foot in
coarse white robes and whose sex can only be determined by
the fact that they only leave one eye visible, and never look at
men of their own race, or are looked at by them in public.
Here are five thousand Jews in blue gaberdines, sashes about
their waists, slippers upon their feet, little skull-caps upon the
backs of their heads, hair combed down on the forehead, and
cut straight across the middle of it from side to side—the
self-same fashion their Tangier ancestors have worn for I
don't know how many bewildering centuries. Their feet and
ankles are bare. Their noses are all hooked, and hooked alike.
They all resemble each other so much that one could almost
believe they were of one family. Their women are plump and
pretty, and do smile upon a Christian in a way which is in
the last degree comforting.

What a funny old town it is! It seems like profanation to

laugh, and jest, and bandy the frivolous chat of our day amid its hoary relics. Only the stately phraseology and the measured speech of the sons of the Prophet are suited to a venerable antiquity like this. Here is a crumbling wall that was old when Columbus discovered America; was old when Peter the Hermit roused the knightly men of the Middle Ages to arm for the first Crusade; was old when Charlemagne and his paladins beleaguered enchanted castles and battled with giants and genii in the fabled days of the olden time; was old when Christ and his disciples walked the earth; stood where it stands to-day when the lips of Memnon were vocal, and men bought and sold in the streets of ancient Thebes!

The Phœnicians, the Carthagenians, the English, Moors, Romans, all have battled for Tangier—all have won it and lost it. Here is a ragged, oriental-looking negro from some desert place in interior Africa, filling his goat-skin with water from a stained and battered fountain built by the Romans twelve hundred years ago. Yonder is a ruined arch of a bridge built by Julius Cæsar nineteen hundred years ago. Men who had seen the infant Saviour in the Virgin's arms, have stood upon it, may be.

Near it are the ruins of a dock-yard where Cæsar repaired his ships and loaded them with grain when he invaded Britain, fifty years before the Christian era.

Here, under the quiet stars, these old streets seem thronged with the phantoms of forgotten ages. My eyes are resting upon a spot where stood a monument which was seen and described by Roman historians less than two thousand years ago, whereon was inscribed:

"WE ARE THE CANAANITES. WE ARE THEY THAT HAVE BEEN DRIVEN OUT OF THE LAND OF CANAAN BY THE JEWISH ROBBER, JOSHUA."

Joshua drove them out, and they came here. Not many leagues from here is a tribe of Jews whose ancestors fled thither after an unsuccessful revolt against King David, and these their descendants are still under a ban and keep to themselves.

Tangier has been mentioned in history for three thousand years. And it was a town, though a queer one, when Hercules, clad in his lion-skin, landed here, four thousand years ago. In these streets he met Anitus, the king of the country, and brained him with his club, which was the fashion among gentlemen in those days. The people of Tangier (called Tingis, then,) lived in the rudest possible huts, and dressed in skins and carried clubs, and were as savage as the wild beasts they were constantly obliged to war with. But they were a gentlemanly race, and did no work. They lived·on the natural products of the land. Their king's country residence was at the famous Garden of Hesperides, seventy miles down the coast from here. The garden, with its golden apples, (oranges,) is gone now—no vestige of it remains. Antiquarians concede that such a personage as Hercules did exist in ancient times, and agree that he was an enterprising and energetic man, but decline to believe him a good, bona fide god, because that would be unconstitutional.

Down here at Cape Spartel is the celebrated cave of Hercules, where that hero took refuge when he was vanquished and driven out of the Tangier country. It is full of inscriptions in the dead languages, which fact makes me think Hercules could not have traveled much, else he would not have kept a journal.

Five days' journey from here—say two hundred miles—are the ruins of an ancient city, of whose history there is neither record nor tradition. And yet its arches, its columns, and its statues, proclaim it to have been built by an enlightened race.

The general size of a store in Tangier is about that of an ordinary shower-bath in a civilized land. The Mohammedan merchant, tinman, shoemaker, or vendor of trifles, sits cross-legged on the floor, and reaches after any article you may want to buy. You can rent a whole block of these pigeon-holes for fifty dollars a month. The market people crowd the market-place with their baskets of figs, dates, melons, apricots, etc., and among them file trains of laden asses, not much larger, if any, than a Newfoundland dog. The scene is lively, is picturesque, and smells like a police court. The Jewish money-changers have their dens close at hand; and all day long are counting bronze coins and transferring them from one bushel basket to another. They don't coin much money now-a-days, I think. I saw none but what was dated four or five hundred years back, and was badly worn and battered. These coins are not very valuable. Jack went out to get a Napoleon changed, so as to have money suited to the general cheapness of things, and came back and said he had "swamped the bank; had bought eleven quarts of coin, and the head of the firm had gone on the street to negotiate for the balance of the change." I bought nearly half a pint of their money for a shilling myself. I am not proud on account of having so much money, though. I care nothing for wealth.

The Moors have some small silver coins, and also some silver slugs worth a dollar each. The latter are exceedingly scarce—so much so that when poor ragged Arabs see one they beg to be allowed to kiss it.

They have also a small gold coin worth two dollars. And that reminds me of something. When Morocco is in a state of war, Arab couriers carry letters through the country, and charge a liberal postage. Every now and then they fall into the hands of marauding bands and get robbed. Therefore, warned by experience, as soon as they have collected two dollars' worth of money they exchange it for one of those little gold pieces, and when robbers come upon them, swallow it. The stratagem was good while it was unsuspected, but after that the marauders simply gave the sagacious United States mail an emetic and sat down to wait.

The Emperor of Morocco is a soulless despot, and the great officers under him are despots on a smaller scale. There is no regular system of taxation, but when the Emperor or the Bashaw want money, they levy on some rich man, and he has to furnish the cash or go to prison. Therefore, few men in Morocco dare to be rich. It is too dangerous a luxury. Vanity occasionally leads a man to display wealth, but sooner or later the Emperor trumps up a charge against him—any sort of one will do—and confiscates his property. Of course, there are many rich men in the empire, but their money is buried, and they dress in rags and counterfeit poverty. Every now and then the Emperor imprisons a man who is suspected of the crime of being rich, and makes things so uncomfortable for him that he is forced to discover where he has hidden his money.

Moors and Jews sometimes place themselves under the protection of the foreign consuls, and then they can flout their riches in the Emperor's face with impunity.

Chapter IX

ABOUT THE FIRST adventure we had yesterday afternoon, after landing here, came near finishing that heedless Blucher. We had just mounted some mules and asses, and started out under the guardianship of the stately, the princely, the magnificent Hadji Mohammed Lamarty, (may his tribe increase!) when we came upon a fine Moorish mosque, with tall tower, rich with checker-work of many-colored porcelain, and every part and portion of the edifice adorned with the quaint architecture of the Alhambra, and Blucher started to ride into the open door-way. A startling "Hi-hi!" from our camp-followers, and a loud "Halt!" from an English gentleman in the party checked the adventurer, and then we were informed that so dire a profanation is it for a Christian dog to set foot upon the sacred threshold of a Moorish mosque, that no amount of purification can ever make it fit for the faithful to pray in again. Had Blucher succeeded in entering the place, he would no doubt have been chased through the town and stoned; and the time has been, and not many years ago either, when a Christian would have been most ruthlessly slaughtered, if captured in a mosque. We caught a glimpse of the handsome tesselated pavements within, and of the devotees performing their ablutions at the fountains; but even that we took that glimpse was a thing not relished by the Moorish bystanders.

Some years ago the clock in the tower of the mosque got out of order. The Moors of Tangier have so degenerated that it has been long since there was an artificer among them capable of curing so delicate a patient as a debilitated clock. The great men of the city met in solemn conclave to consider how the difficulty was to be met. They discussed the matter thoroughly but arrived at no solution. Finally, a patriarch arose and said:

"Oh, children of the Prophet, it is known unto you that a Portuguee dog of a Christian clock-mender pollutes the city of Tangier with his presence. Ye know, also, that when mosques are builded, asses bear the stones and the cement, and cross the sacred threshold. Now, therefore, send the

Christian dog on all fours, and barefoot, into the holy place to mend the clock, and let him go as an ass!"

And in that way it was done. Therefore, if Blucher ever sees the inside of a mosque, he will have to cast aside his humanity and go in his natural character. We visited the jail, and found Moorish prisoners making mats and baskets. (This thing of utilizing crime savors of civilization.) Murder is punished with death. A short time ago, three murderers were taken beyond the city walls and shot. Moorish guns are not good, and neither are Moorish marksmen. In this instance, they set up the poor criminals at long range, like so many targets, and practiced on them—kept them hopping about and dodging bullets for half an hour before they managed to drive the centre.

When a man steals cattle, they cut off his right hand and left leg, and nail them up in the market-place as a warning to every body. Their surgery is not artistic. They slice around the bone a little; then break off the limb. Sometimes the patient gets well; but, as a general thing, he don't. However, the Moorish heart is stout. The Moors were always brave. These criminals undergo the fearful operation without a wince, without a tremor of any kind, without a groan! No amount of suffering can bring down the pride of a Moor, or make him shame his dignity with a cry.

Here, marriage is contracted by the parents of the parties to it. There are no valentines, no stolen interviews, no riding out, no courting in dim parlors, no lovers' quarrels and reconciliations—no nothing that is proper to approaching matrimony. The young man takes the girl his father selects for him, marries her, and after that she is unveiled, and he sees her for the first time. If, after due acquaintance, she suits him, he retains her; but if he suspects her purity, he bundles her back to her father; if he finds her diseased, the same; or if, after just and reasonable time is allowed her, she neglects to bear children, back she goes to the home of her childhood.

Mohammedans here, who can afford it, keep a good many wives on hand. They are called wives, though I believe the Koran only allows four genuine wives—the rest are concubines. The Emperor of Morocco don't know how many wives he has, but thinks he has five hundred. However, that is near enough—a dozen or so, one way or the other, don't matter.

Even the Jews in the interior have a plurality of wives.

I have caught a glimpse of the faces of several Moorish women, (for they are only human, and will expose their faces for the admiration of a Christian dog when no male Moor is by,) and I am full of veneration for the wisdom that leads them to cover up such atrocious ugliness.

They carry their children at their backs, in a sack, like other savages the world over.

Many of the negroes are held in slavery by the Moors. But the moment a female slave becomes her master's concubine her bonds are broken, and as soon as a male slave can read the first chapter of the Koran (which contains the creed,) he can no longer be held in bondage.

They have three Sundays a week in Tangier. The Mohammedan's comes on Friday, the Jew's on Saturday, and that of the Christian Consuls on Sunday. The Jews are the most radical. The Moor goes to his mosque about noon on his Sabbath, as on any other day, removes his shoes at the door, performs his ablutions, makes his salaams, pressing his forehead to the pavement time and again, says his prayers, and goes back to his work.

But the Jew shuts up shop; will not touch copper or bronze money at all; soils his fingers with nothing meaner than silver and gold; attends the synagogue devoutly; will not cook or have any thing to do with fire; and religiously refrains from embarking in any enterprise.

The Moor who has made a pilgrimage to Mecca is entitled to high distinction. Men call him Hadji, and he is thenceforward a great personage. Hundreds of Moors come to Tangier every year, and embark for Mecca. They go part of the way in English steamers; and the ten or twelve dollars they pay for passage is about all the trip costs. They take with them a quantity of food, and when the commissary department fails they "skirmish," as Jack terms it in his sinful, slangy way. From the time they leave till they get home again, they never wash, either on land or sea. They are usually gone from five to seven months, and as they do not change their clothes during all that time, they are totally unfit for the drawing-room when they get back.

Many of them have to rake and scrape a long time to gather together the ten dollars their steamer passage costs; and when one of them gets back he is a bankrupt forever after. Few Moors can ever build up their fortunes again in one short lifetime, after so reckless an outlay. In order to confine the dignity of Hadji to gentlemen of patrician blood and possessions, the Emperor decreed that no man should make the pilgrimage save bloated aristocrats who were worth a hundred dollars in specie. But behold how iniquity can circumvent the law! For a consideration, the Jewish money-changer lends the pilgrim one hundred dollars long enough for him to swear himself through, and then receives it back before the ship sails out of the harbor!

Spain is the only nation the Moors fear. The reason is, that Spain sends her heaviest ships of war and her loudest guns to astonish these Moslems; while America, and other nations, send only a little contemptible tub of a gun-boat occasionally. The Moors, like other savages, learn by what they see; not what they hear or read. We have great fleets in the Mediterranean, but they seldom touch at African ports. The Moors have a small opinion of England, France, and America, and put their representatives to a deal of red tape circumlocution before they grant them their common rights, let alone a favor. But the moment the Spanish Minister makes a demand, it is acceded to at once, whether it be just or not.

Spain chastised the Moors five or six years ago, about a disputed piece of property opposite Gibraltar, and captured the city of Tetouan. She compromised on an augmentation of her territory; twenty million dollars indemnity in money; and peace. And then she gave up the city. But she never gave it up until the Spanish soldiers had eaten up all the cats. They would not compromise as long as the cats held out. Spaniards are very fond of cats. On the contrary, the Moors reverence cats as something sacred. So the Spaniards touched them on a tender point that time. Their unfeline conduct in eating up all the Tetouan cats aroused a hatred toward them in the breasts of the Moors, to which even the driving them out of Spain was tame and passionless. Moors and Spaniards are foes forever now. France had a Minister here once who embittered the nation against him in the most innocent way. He killed a couple of battalions of cats (Tangier is full of them,) and made a parlor carpet out of their hides. He made his carpet in circles—first a circle of old gray tom-cats, with their tails all pointing towards the centre; then a circle of yellow cats; next a circle of black cats and a circle of white ones; then a circle of all sorts of cats; and, finally, a centre-piece of assorted kittens. It was very beautiful; but the Moors curse his memory to this day.

When we went to call on our American Consul-General, to-day, I noticed that all possible games for parlor amusement seemed to be represented on his centre-tables. I thought that hinted at lonesomeness. The idea was correct. His is the only American family in Tangier. There are many foreign Consuls in this place; but much visiting is not indulged in. Tangier is clear out of the world; and what is the use of visiting when people have nothing on earth to talk about? There is none. So each Consul's family stays at home chiefly, and amuses itself as best it can. Tangier is full of interest for one day, but after that it is a weary prison. The Consul-General has been here five years, and has got enough of it to do him for a century, and is going home shortly. His family seize upon their letters and papers when the mail arrives, read them over and over again for two days or three, talk them over and over again for two or three more, till they wear them out, and after that, for days together, they eat and drink and sleep, and ride out over the same old road, and see the same old tiresome things that even decades of centuries have scarcely changed, and say never a single word! They have literally nothing whatever to talk about. The arrival of an American man-of-war is a god-send to them. "Oh, Solitude, where are the charms which sages have seen in thy face?" It is the completest exile that I can conceive of. I would seriously recommend to the Government of the United States that when a man commits a crime so heinous that the law provides no adequate punishment for it, they make him Consul-General to Tangier.

I am glad to have seen Tangier—the second oldest town in the world. But I am ready to bid it good bye, I believe.

We shall go hence to Gibraltar this evening or in the morning; and doubtless the Quaker City will sail from that port within the next forty-eight hours.

Chapter X

WE PASSED the Fourth of July on board the Quaker City, in mid-ocean. It was in all respects a characteristic Mediterranean day—faultlessly beautiful. A cloudless sky; a refreshing summer wind; a radiant sunshine that glinted cheerily from dancing wavelets instead of crested mountains of water; a sea beneath us that was so wonderfully blue, so richly, brilliantly blue, that it overcame the dullest sensibilities with the spell of its fascination.

They even have fine sunsets on the Mediterranean—a thing that is certainly rare in most quarters of the globe. The evening we sailed away from Gibraltar, that hard-featured rock was swimming in a creamy mist so rich, so soft, so enchantingly vague and dreamy, that even the Oracle, that serene, that inspired, that overpowering humbug, scorned the dinner-gong and tarried to worship!

He said: "Well, that's gorgis, ain't it! They don't have none of them things in our parts, *do* they? I consider that them effects is on account of the superior refragability, as you may say, of the sun's diramic combination with the lymphatic forces of the perihelion of Jubiter. What should you think?"

"Oh, *go* to bed!" Dan said that, and went away.

"Oh, yes, it's all very well to say go to bed when a man makes an argument which another man can't answer. Dan don't never stand any chance in an argument with me. And he knows it, too. What should you say, Jack?"

"Now doctor, don't you come bothering around me with that dictionary bosh. I don't do you any harm, do I? Then you let *me* alone."

"He's gone, too. Well, them fellows have all tackled the old Oracle, as they say, but the old man's most too many for 'em. May be the Poet Lariat ain't satisfied with them deductions?"

The poet replied with a barbarous rhyme, and went below.

" 'Pears that *he* can't qualify, neither. Well, I didn't expect nothing out of *him*. I never see one of them poets yet that knowed any thing. He'll go down, now, and grind out about four reams of the awfullest slush about that old rock, and give it to a consul, or a pilot, or a nigger, or any body he comes across first which he can impose on. Pity but somebody'd take that poor old lunatic and dig all that poetry rubbage out of him. Why can't a man put his intellect onto things that's some value? Gibbons, and Hippocratus, and Sarcophagus, and all them old ancient philosophers was down on poets—"

"Doctor," I said, "you are going to invent authorities, now, and I'll leave you, too. I always enjoy your conversation, notwithstanding the luxuriance of your syllables, when the philosophy you offer rests on your own responsibility; but when you begin to soar—when you begin to support it with the evidence of authorities who are the creations of your own fancy, I lose confidence."

That was the way to flatter the doctor. He considered it a sort of acknowledgment on my part of a fear to argue with him. He was always persecuting the passengers with abstruse propositions framed in language that no man could understand, and they endured the exquisite torture a minute or two and then abandoned the field. A triumph like this, over half a dozen antagonists was sufficient for one day; from that time forward he would patrol the decks beaming blandly upon all comers, and so tranquilly, blissfully happy!

But I digress. The thunder of our two brave cannon announced the Fourth of July, at daylight, to all who were awake. But many of us got our information at a later hour, from the almanac. All the flags were sent aloft, except half a dozen that were needed to decorate portions of the ship below, and in a short time the vessel assumed a holiday appearance. During the morning, meetings were held and all manner of committees set to work on the celebration ceremonies. In the afternoon the ship's company assembled aft, on deck, under the awnings; the flute, the asthmatic melodeon, and the consumptive clarinet crippled the Star Spangled Banner, the choir chased it to cover, and George came in with a peculiarly lacerating screech on the final note and slaughtered it. Nobody mourned.

We carried out the corpse on three cheers (that joke was not intentional and I do not indorse it,) and then the President, throned behind a cable-locker with a national flag spread over it, announced the "Reader," who rose up and read that same old Declaration of Independence which we have all listened to so often without paying any attention to what it said; and after that the President piped the Orator of the Day to quarters and he made that same old speech about our national greatness which we so religiously believe and so fervently applaud. Now came the choir into court again, with the complaining instruments, and assaulted Hail Columbia; and when victory hung wavering in the scale, George returned with his dreadful wild-goose stop turned on and the choir won of course. A minister pronounced the benediction, and the patriotic little gathering disbanded. The Fourth of July was safe, as far as the Mediterranean was concerned.

At dinner in the evening, a well-written original poem was recited with spirit by one of the ship's captains, and thirteen regular toasts were washed down with several baskets of champagne. The speeches were bad—execrable, almost without exception. In fact, without *any* exception, but one. Capt. Duncan made a good speech; he made the only good speech of the evening. He said:

"LADIES AND GENTLEMEN:—May we all live to a green old age, and be prosperous and happy. Steward, bring up another basket of champagne."

It was regarded as a very able effort.

The festivities, so to speak, closed with another of those miraculous balls on the promenade deck. We were not used to dancing on an even keel, though, and it was only a questionable success. But take it altogether, it was a bright, cheerful, pleasant Fourth.

Toward nightfall, the next evening, we steamed into the great artificial harbor of this noble city of Marseilles, and saw the dying sunlight gild its clustering spires and ramparts, and flood its leagues of environing verdure with a mellow radiance that touched with an added charm the white villas that flecked the landscape far and near. [Copyright secured according to law.]

There were no stages out, and we could not get on the pier from the ship. It was annoying. We were full of enthusiasm— we wanted to see France! Just at nightfall our party of three contracted with a waterman for the privilege of using his boat as a bridge—its stern was at our companion ladder and its bow touched the pier. We got in and the fellow backed out into the harbor. I told him in French that all we wanted was to walk over his thwarts and step ashore, and asked him what he went away out there for? He said he could not understand me. I repeated. Still, he could not understand. He appeared to be very ignorant of French. The doctor tried him, but he could not understand the doctor. I asked this boatman to explain his conduct, which he did; and then I couldn't understand *him*. Dan said:

"Oh, go to the pier, you old fool—that's where we want to go!"

We reasoned calmly with Dan that it was useless to speak to this foreigner in English—that he had better let us conduct this business in the French language and not let the stranger see how uncultivated he was.

"Well, go on, go on," he said, "don't mind me. I don't wish to interfere. Only, if you go on telling him in your kind of French he never will find out where we want to go to. That is what I think about it."

We rebuked him severely for this remark, and said we never knew an ignorant person yet but was prejudiced. The Frenchman spoke again, and the doctor said:

"There, now, Dan, he says he is going to *allez* to the *douain*. Means he is going to the hotel. Oh, certainly—*we* don't know the French language."

This was a crusher, as Jack would say. It silenced further criticism from the disaffected member. We coasted past the sharp bows of a navy of great steamships, and stopped at last at a government building on a stone pier. It was easy to remember then, that the *douain* was the custom-house, and not the hotel. We did not mention it, however. With winning French politeness, the officers merely opened and closed our satchels, declined to examine our passports, and sent us on our way. We stopped at the first café we came to, and entered. An old woman seated us at a table and waited for orders. The doctor said:

"Avez vous du vin?"

The dame looked perplexed. The doctor said again, with elaborate distinctness of articulation:

"Avez-vous du—vin!"

The dame looked more perplexed than before. I said:

"Doctor, there is a flaw in your pronunciation somewhere. Let me try her. Madame, avez-vous du vin? It isn't any use, doctor—take the witness."

"Madame, avez-vous du vin—ou fromage—pain—pickled pigs' feet—beurre—des œfs—du beuf—horse-radish, sour-crout, hog and hominy—any thing, *any thing* in the world that can stay a Christian stomach!"

She said:

"Bless you, why didn't you speak English before?—I don't know any thing about your plagued French!"

The humiliating taunts of the disaffected member spoiled the supper, and we dispatched it in angry silence and got away as soon as we could. Here we were in beautiful France—in a vast stone house of quaint architecture—surrounded by all manner of curiously worded French signs—stared at by strangely-habited, bearded French people—every thing gradually and surely forcing upon us the coveted consciousness that at last, and beyond all question we *were* in beautiful France and absorbing its nature to the forgetfulness of every thing else, and coming to feel the happy romance of the thing in all its enchanting delightfulness—and to think of this skinny veteran intruding with her vile English, at such a moment, to blow the fair vision to the winds! It was exasperating.

We set out to find the centre of the city, inquiring the direction every now and then. We never did succeed in making any body understand just exactly what we wanted, and neither did we ever succeed in comprehending just exactly what they said in reply—but then they always pointed—they always did that, and we bowed politely and said "Merci, Monsieur," and so it was a blighting triumph over the disaffected member, any way. He was restive under these victories and often asked:

"What did that pirate say?"

"Why, he told us which way to go, to find the Grand Casino."

"Yes, but what did he *say?*"

"Oh, it don't matter what he said—*we* understood him. These are educated people—not like that absurd boatman."

"Well, I wish they were educated enough to tell a man a

direction that goes *some* where—for we've been going around in a circle for an hour—I've passed this same old drug store seven times."

We said it was a low, disreputable falsehood, (but we knew it was not.) It was plain that it would not do to pass that drug store again, though—we might go on asking directions, but we must cease from following finger-pointings if we hoped to check the suspicions of the disaffected member.

A long walk through smooth, asphaltum-paved streets bordered by blocks of vast new mercantile houses of cream-colored stone,—every house and every block precisely like all the other houses and all the other blocks for a mile, and all brilliantly lighted,—brought us at last to the principal thoroughfare. On every hand were bright colors, flashing constellations of gas-burners, gaily dressed men and women thronging the side-walks—hurry, life, activity, cheerfulness, conversation and laughter every where! We found the Grand Hotel du Louvre et de la Paix, and wrote down who we were, where we were born, what our occupations were, the place we came from last, whether we were married or single, how we liked it, how old we were, where we were bound for and when we expected to get there, and a great deal of information of similar importance—all for the benefit of the landlord and the secret police. We hired a guide and began the business of sight-seeing immediately. That first night on French soil was a stirring one. I can not think of half the places we went to, or what we particularly saw; we had no disposition to examine carefully into any thing at all—we only wanted to glance and go—to move, keep moving! The spirit of the country was upon us. We sat down, finally, at a late hour, in the great Casino, and called for unstinted champagne. It is so easy to be bloated aristocrats where it costs nothing of consequence! There were about five hundred people in that dazzling place, I suppose, though the walls being papered entirely with mirrors, so to speak, one could not really tell but that there were a hundred thousand. Young, daintily dressed exquisites and young, stylishly dressed women, and also old gentlemen and old ladies, sat in couples and groups about innumerable marble-topped tables, and ate fancy suppers, drank wine and kept up a chattering din of conversation that was dazing to the senses. There was a stage at the far end, and a large orchestra; and every now and then actors and actresses in preposterous comic dresses came out and sang the most extravagantly funny songs, to judge by their absurd actions; but that audience merely suspended its chatter, stared cynically, and never once smiled, never once applauded! I had always thought that Frenchmen were ready to laugh at any thing.

Chapter XI

WE ARE GETTING foreignized rapidly, and with facility. We are getting reconciled to halls and bed-chambers with unhomelike stone floors, and no carpets—floors that ring to the tread of one's heels with a sharpness that is death to sentimental musing. We are getting used to tidy, noiseless waiters, who glide hither and thither, and hover about your back and your elbows like butterflies, quick to comprehend orders, quick to fill them; thankful for a gratuity without regard to the amount; and always polite—never otherwise than polite. That is the strangest curiosity yet—a really polite hotel waiter who isn't an idiot. We are getting used to driving right into the central court of the hotel, in the midst of a fragrant circle of vines and flowers, and in the midst, also, of parties of gentlemen sitting quietly reading the paper and smoking. We are getting used to ice frozen by artificial process in ordinary bottles—the only kind of ice they have here. We are getting used to all these things; but we are *not* getting used to carrying our own soap. We are sufficiently civilized to carry our own combs and tooth-brushes; but this thing of having to ring for soap every time we wash is new to us, and not pleasant at all. We think of it just after we get our heads and faces thoroughly wet, or just when we think we have been in the bath-tub long enough, and then, of course, an annoying delay follows. These Marseillaise make Marseillaise hymns, and Marseilles vests, and Marseilles soap for all the world; but they never sing their hymns, or wear their vests, or wash with their soap themselves.

We have learned to go through the lingering routine of the table d'hote with patience, with serenity, with satisfaction. We take soup; then wait a few minutes for the fish; a few minutes more and the plates are changed, and the roast beef comes; another change and we take peas; change again and take lentils; change and take snail patties (I prefer grasshoppers;) change and take roast chicken and salad; then strawberry pie and ice cream; then green figs, pears, oranges, green almonds, &c.; finally coffee. Wine with every course, of course, being in France. With such a cargo on board, digestion is a slow process, and we must sit long in the cool chambers and smoke—and read French newspapers, which have a strange fashion of telling a perfectly straight story till you get to the "nub" of it, and then a word drops in that no man can translate, and that story is ruined. An embankment fell on some Frenchmen yesterday, and the papers are full of it to-day—but whether those sufferers were killed, or crippled, or bruised, or only scared, is more than I can possibly make out, and yet I would just give any thing to know.

We were troubled a little at dinner to-day, by the conduct of an American, who talked very loudly and coarsely, and laughed boisterously where all others were so quiet and well-behaved. He ordered wine with a royal flourish, and said: "I never dine without wine, sir," (which was a pitiful falsehood,) and looked around upon the company to bask in the admiration he expected to find in their faces. All these airs in a land where they would as soon expect to leave the soup out of the bill of fare as the wine!—in a land where wine is nearly as common among all ranks as water! This fellow said: "I am a free-born sovereign, sir, an American, sir, and I want every body to know it!" He did not mention that he was a lineal descendant of Balaam's ass; but every body knew that without his telling it.

We have driven in the Prado—that superb avenue bordered with patrician mansions and noble shade-trees—and have visited the Chateau Boarely and its curious museum. They showed us a miniature cemetery there—a copy of the first graveyard that was ever in Marseilles, no doubt. The delicate little skeletons were lying in broken vaults, and had their household gods and kitchen utensils with them. The original of this cemetery was dug up in the principal street of the city a few years ago. It had remained there, only twelve feet under ground, for a matter of twenty-five hundred years, or thereabouts. Romulus was here before he built Rome, and thought something of founding a city on this spot, but gave up the idea. He may have been personally acquainted with some of these Phœnicians whose skeletons we have been examining.

In the great Zoölogical Gardens, we found specimens of all the animals the world produces, I think, including a dromedary, a monkey ornamented with tufts of brilliant blue and

carmine hair—a very gorgeous monkey he was—a hippopot-
amus from the Nile, and a sort of tall, long-legged bird with
a beak like a powder-horn, and close-fitting wings like the
tails of a dress coat. This fellow stood up with his eyes shut
and his shoulders stooped forward a little, and looked as if he
had his hands under his coat tails. Such tranquil stupidity,
such supernatural gravity, such self-righteousness, and such
ineffable self-complacency as were in the countenance and attitude of that gray-bodied, dark-winged, bald-headed, and
preposterously uncomely bird! He was so ungainly, so pimply
about the head, so scaly about the legs; yet so serene, so unspeakably satisfied! He was the most comical looking creature
that can be imagined. It was good to hear Dan and the doctor
laugh—such natural and such enjoyable laughter had not
been heard among our excursionists since our ship sailed
away from America. This bird was a god-send to us, and I
should be an ingrate if I forgot to make honorable mention
of him in these pages. Ours was a pleasure excursion; therefore we stayed with that bird an hour, and made the most of
him. We stirred him up occasionally, but he only unclosed an
eye and slowly closed it again, abating no jot of his stately
piety of demeanor or his tremendous seriousness. He only
seemed to say, "Defile not Heaven's anointed with unsancti-
fied hands." We did not know his name, and so we called him
"The Pilgrim." Dan said:

"All he wants now is a Plymouth Collection."

The boon companion of the colossal elephant was a common cat! This cat had a fashion of climbing up the elephant's
hind legs, and roosting on his back. She would sit up there,
with her paws curved under her breast, and sleep in the sun
half the afternoon. It used to annoy the elephant at first, and
he would reach up and take her down, but she would go aft
and climb up again. She persisted until she finally conquered
the elephant's prejudices, and now they are inseparable
friends. The cat plays about her comrade's forefeet or his
trunk often, until dogs approach, and then she goes aloft out
of danger. The elephant has annihilated several dogs lately,
that pressed his companion too closely.

We hired a sail-boat and a guide and made an excursion to
one of the small islands in the harbor to visit the Castle d'If.

This ancient fortress has a melancholy history. It has been used as a prison for political offenders for two or three hundred years, and its dungeon walls are scarred with the rudely carved names of many and many a captive who fretted his life away here, and left no record of himself but these sad epitaphs wrought with his own hands. How thick the names were! And their long-departed owners seemed to throng the gloomy cells and corridors with their phantom shapes. We loitered through dungeon after dungeon, away down into the living rock below the level of the sea, it seemed. Names every where!—some plebeian, some noble, some even princely. Plebeian, prince, and noble, had one solicitude in common— they would not be forgotten! They could suffer solitude, inactivity, and the horrors of a silence that no sound ever disturbed; but they could not bear the thought of being utterly forgotten by the world. Hence the carved names. In one cell, where a little light penetrated, a man had lived twenty-seven years without seeing the face of a human being—lived in filth and wretchedness, with no companionship but his own thoughts, and they were sorrowful enough, and hopeless enough, no doubt. Whatever his jailers considered that he needed was conveyed to his cell by night, through a wicket. This man carved the walls of his prison-house from floor to roof with all manner of figures of men and animals, grouped in intricate designs. He had toiled there year after year, at his self-appointed task, while infants grew to boyhood—to vigorous youth—idled through school and college—acquired a profession—claimed man's mature estate—married and looked back to infancy as to a thing of some vague, ancient time, almost. But who shall tell how many ages it seemed to this prisoner? With the one, time flew sometimes; with the other, never—it crawled always. To the one, nights spent in dancing had seemed made of minutes instead of hours; to the other, those self-same nights had been like all other nights of dungeon life, and seemed made of slow, dragging weeks, instead of hours and minutes.

One prisoner of fifteen years had scratched verses upon his walls, and brief prose sentences—brief, but full of pathos. These spoke not of himself and his hard estate; but only of the shrine where his spirit fled the prison to worship—of home and the idols that were templed there. He never lived to see them.

The walls of these dungeons are as thick as some bed-chambers at home are wide—fifteen feet. We saw the damp, dismal cells in which two of Dumas' heroes passed their confinement—heroes of "Monte Christo." It was here that the brave Abbé wrote a book with his own blood; with a pen made of a piece of iron hoop, and by the light of a lamp made out of shreds of cloth soaked in grease obtained from his food; and then dug through the thick wall with some trifling instrument which he wrought himself out of a stray piece of iron or table cutlery, and freed Dantés from his chains. It was a pity that so many weeks of dreary labor should have come to naught at last.

They showed us the noisome cell where the celebrated "Iron Mask"—that ill-starred brother of a hard-hearted king of France—was confined for a season, before he was sent to hide the strange mystery of his life from the curious in the dungeons of St. Marguerite. The place had a far greater interest for us than it could have had if we had known beyond all question who the Iron Mask was, and what his history had been, and why this most unusual punishment had been meted out to him. Mystery! That was the charm. That speechless tongue, those prisoned features, that heart so freighted with unspoken troubles, and that breast so oppressed with its piteous secret, had been here. These dank walls had known the man whose dolorous story is a sealed book forever! There was fascination in the spot.

Chapter XII

WE HAVE COME five hundred miles by rail through the heart of France. What a bewitching land it is!—What a garden! Surely the leagues of bright green lawns are swept and brushed and watered every day and their grasses trimmed by the barber. Surely the hedges are shaped and measured and their symmetry preserved by the most architectural of gardeners. Surely the long straight rows of stately poplars that divide the beautiful landscape like the squares of a checker-board are set with line and plummet, and their uniform height determined with a spirit level. Surely the straight, smooth, pure white turnpikes are jack-planed and sandpapered every day. How else are these marvels of symmetry, cleanliness and order attained? It is wonderful. There are no unsightly stone walls, and never a fence of any kind. There is no dirt, no decay, no rubbish any where—nothing that even hints at untidiness—nothing that ever suggests neglect. All is orderly and beautiful—every thing is charming to the eye.

We had such glimpses of the Rhone gliding along between its grassy banks; of cosy cottages buried in flowers and shrubbery; of quaint old red-tiled villages with mossy mediæval cathedrals looming out of their midst; of wooded hills with ivy-grown towers and turrets of feudal castles projecting above the foliage; such glimpses of Paradise, it seemed to us, such visions of fabled fairy-land!

We knew, then, what the poet meant, when he sang of—

> "—thy cornfields green, and sunny vines,
> O pleasant land of France!"

And it *is* a pleasant land. No word describes it so felicitously as that one. They say there is no word for "home" in the French language. Well, considering that they have the article itself in such an attractive aspect, they ought to manage to get along without the word. Let us not waste too much pity on "homeless" France. I have observed that Frenchmen abroad seldom wholly give up the idea of going back to France some time or other. I am not surprised at it now.

We are not infatuated with these French railway cars, though. We took first class passage, not because we wished to attract attention by doing a thing which is uncommon in Europe, but because we could make our journey quicker by so doing. It is hard to make railroading pleasant, in any country. It is too tedious. Stage-coaching is infinitely more delightful. Once I crossed the plains and deserts and mountains of the West, in a stage-coach, from the Missouri line to California, and since then all my pleasure trips must be measured to that rare holiday frolic. Two thousand miles of ceaseless rush and rattle and clatter, by night and by day, and never a weary moment, never a lapse of interest! The first seven hundred miles a level continent, its grassy carpet greener and softer and smoother than any sea, and figured with designs fitted to its magnitude—the shadows of the clouds. Here were no scenes but summer scenes, and no disposition inspired by them but to lie at full length on the mail sacks, in the grateful breeze, and dreamily smoke the pipe of peace—what other, where all was repose and contentment? In cool mornings, before the sun was fairly up, it was worth a lifetime of city toiling and moiling, to perch in the foretop with the driver and see the six mustangs scamper under the sharp snapping of a whip that never touched them; to scan the blue distances of a world that knew no lords but us; to cleave the wind with uncovered head and feel the sluggish pulses rousing to the spirit of a speed that pretended to the resistless rush of a typhoon! Then thirteen hundred miles of desert solitudes; of limitless panoramas of bewildering perspective; of mimic cities, of pinnacled cathedrals, of massive fortresses, counterfeited in the eternal rocks and splendid with the crimson and gold of the setting sun; of dizzy altitudes among fog-wreathed peaks and never-melting snows, where thunders and lightnings and tempests warred magnificently at our feet and the storm-clouds above swung their shredded banners in our very faces!

But I forgot. I am in elegant France, now, and not skurrying through the great South Pass and the Wind River Mountains, among antelopes and buffaloes, and painted Indians on the war path. It is not meet that I should make too disparaging comparisons between hum-drum travel on a railway and that royal summer flight across a continent in a stage-coach. I meant in the beginning, to say that railway journey-ing is tedious and tiresome, and so it is—though at the time, I was thinking particularly of a dismal fifty-hour pilgrimage between New York and St. Louis. Of course our trip through France was not really tedious, because all its scenes and ex-periences were new and strange; but as Dan says, it had its "discrepancies."

The cars are built in compartments that hold eight persons each. Each compartment is partially subdivided, and so there are two tolerably distinct parties of four in it. Four face the other four. The seats and backs are thickly padded and cush-ioned and are very comfortable; you can smoke, if you wish; there are no bothersome peddlers; you are saved the infliction of a multitude of disagreeable fellow-passengers. So far, so well. But then the conductor locks you in when the train starts; there is no water to drink, in the car; there is no heat-ing apparatus for night travel; if a drunken rowdy should get in, you could not remove a matter of twenty seats from him, or enter another car; but above all, if you are worn out and must sleep, you must sit up and do it in naps, with cramped legs and in a torturing misery that leaves you withered and lifeless the next day—for behold they have not that culmina-tion of all charity and human kindness, a sleeping car, in all France. I prefer the American system. It has not so many grievous "discrepancies."

In France, all is clockwork, all is order. They make no mis-takes. Every third man wears a uniform, and whether he be a Marshal of the Empire or a brakeman, he is ready and per-fectly willing to answer all your questions with tireless polite-ness, ready to tell you which car to take, yea, and ready to go and put you into it to make sure that you shall not go astray. You can not pass into the waiting-room of the depot till you have secured your ticket, and you can not pass from its only exit till the train is at its threshold to receive you. Once on board, the train will not start till your ticket has been exam-ined—till every passenger's ticket has been inspected. This is chiefly for your own good. If by any possibility you have managed to take the wrong train, you will be handed over to a polite official who will take you whither you belong, and bestow you with many an affable bow. Your ticket will be inspected every now and then along the route, and when it is time to change cars you will know it. You are in the hands of officials who zealously study your welfare and your interest, instead of turning their talents to the invention of new methods of discommoding and snubbing you, as is very often the main employment of that exceedingly self-satisfied monarch, the railroad conductor of America.

But the happiest regulation in French railway government, is—thirty minutes to dinner! No five-minute boltings of flabby rolls, muddy coffee, questionable eggs, gutta-percha beef, and pies whose conception and execution are a dark and bloody mystery to all save the cook that created them! No; we sat calmly down—it was in old Dijon, which is so easy to spell and so impossible to pronounce, except when you civilize it and call it Demijohn—and poured out rich Burgundian wines and munched calmly through a long table d'hote bill of fare, snail-patties, delicious fruits and all, then paid the trifle it cost and stepped happily aboard the train again, without once cursing the railroad company. A rare experience, and one to be treasured forever.

They say they do not have accidents on these French roads, and I think it must be true. If I remember rightly, we passed high above wagon roads, or through tunnels under them, but never crossed them on their own level. About every quarter of a mile, it seemed to me, a man came out and held up a club till the train went by, to signify that every thing was safe ahead. Switches were changed a mile in advance, by pulling a wire rope that passed along the ground by the rail, from station to station. Signals for the day and signals for the night gave constant and timely notice of the position of switches.

No, they have no railroad accidents to speak of in France. But why? Because when one occurs, *somebody* has to hang for it!* Not hang, may be, but be punished at least with such vigor of emphasis as to make negligence a thing to be shuddered at by railroad officials for many a day thereafter. "No blame attached to the officers"—that lying and disaster-breeding verdict so common to our soft-hearted juries, is

*They go on the principle that it is better that one innocent man should suffer than five hundred.

seldom rendered in France. If the trouble occurred in the conductor's department, that officer must suffer if his subordinate can not be proven guilty; if in the engineer's department, and the case be similar, the engineer must answer.

The Old Travelers—those delightful parrots who have "been here before," and know more about the country than Louis Napoleon knows now or ever will know,—tell us these things, and we believe them because they are pleasant things to believe, and because they are plausible and savor of the rigid subjection to law and order which we behold about us every where.

But we love the Old Travelers. We love to hear them prate, and drivel and lie. We can tell them the moment we see them. They always throw out a few feelers; they never cast themselves adrift till they have sounded every individual and know that he has not traveled. Then they open their throttle-valves, and how they do brag, and sneer, and swell, and soar, and blaspheme the sacred name of Truth! Their central idea, their grand aim, is to subjugate you, keep you down, make you feel insignificant and humble in the blaze of their cosmopolitan glory! They will not let you know any thing. They sneer at your most inoffensive suggestions; they laugh unfeelingly at your treasured dreams of foreign lands; they brand the statements of your traveled aunts and uncles as the stupidest absurdities; they deride your most trusted authors and demolish the fair images they have set up for your willing worship with the pitiless ferocity of the fanatic iconoclast! But still I love the Old Travelers. I love them for their witless platitudes; for their supernatural ability to bore; for their delightful asinine vanity; for their luxuriant fertility of imagination; for their startling, their brilliant, their overwhelming mendacity!

By Lyons and the Saone (where we saw the lady of Lyons and thought little of her comeliness;) by Villa Franca, Tonnere, venerable Sens, Melun, Fontainebleau, and scores of other beautiful cities, we swept, always noting the absence of hog-wallows, broken fences, cowlots, unpainted houses and mud, and always noting, as well, the presence of cleanliness, grace, taste in adorning and beautifying, even to the disposition of a tree or the turning of a hedge, the marvel of roads in perfect repair, void of ruts and guiltless of even an inequality of surface—we bowled along, hour after hour, that brilliant summer day, and as nightfall approached we entered a wilderness of odorous flowers and shrubbery, sped through it, and then, excited, delighted, and half persuaded that we were only the sport of a beautiful dream, lo, we stood in magnificent Paris!

What excellent order they kept about that vast depot! There was no frantic crowding and jostling, no shouting and swearing, and no swaggering intrusion of services by rowdy hackmen. These latter gentry stood outside—stood quietly by their long line of vehicles and said never a word. A kind of hackman-general seemed to have the whole matter of transportation in his hands. He politely received the passengers and ushered them to the kind of conveyance they wanted, and told the driver where to deliver them. There was no "talking back," no dissatisfaction about overcharging, no grumbling about any thing. In a little while we were speeding through the streets of Paris, and delightfully recognizing certain names and places with which books had long ago made us familiar. It was like meeting an old friend when we read *"Rue de Rivoli"* on the street corner; we knew the genuine vast palace of the Louvre as well as we knew its picture; when we passed by the Column of July we needed no one to tell us what it was, or to remind us that on its site once stood the grim Bastile, that grave of human hopes and happiness, that dismal prison-house within whose dungeons so many young faces put on the wrinkles of age, so many proud spirits grew humble, so many brave hearts broke.

We secured rooms at the hotel, or rather, we had three beds put into one room, so that we might be together, and then we went out to a restaurant, just after lamp-lighting, and ate a comfortable, satisfactory, lingering dinner. It was a pleasure to eat where every thing was so tidy, the food so well cooked, the waiters so polite, and the coming and departing company so moustached, so frisky, so affable, so fearfully and wonderfully Frenchy! All the surroundings were gay and enlivening. Two hundred people sat at little tables on the sidewalk, sipping wine and coffee; the streets were thronged with light vehicles and with joyous pleasure seekers; there was music in the air, life and action all about us, and a conflagration of gaslight every where!

After dinner we felt like seeing such Parisian specialties as we might see without distressing exertion, and so we sauntered through the brilliant streets and looked at the dainty trifles in variety stores and jewelry shops. Occasionally, merely for the pleasure of being cruel, we put unoffending Frenchmen on the rack with questions framed in the incomprehensible jargon of their native language, and while they writhed, we impaled them, we peppered them, we scarified them, with their own vile verbs and participles.

We noticed that in the jewelry stores they had some of the articles marked "gold," and some labeled "imitation." We wondered at this extravagance of honesty, and inquired into the matter. We were informed that inasmuch as most people are not able to tell false gold from the genuine article, the government compels jewelers to have their gold work assayed and stamped officially according to its fineness, and their imitation work duly labeled with the sign of its falsity. They told us the jewelers would not dare to violate this law, and that whatever a stranger bought in one of their stores might be depended upon as being strictly what it was represented to be.—Verily, a wonderful land is France!

Then we hunted for a barber-shop. From earliest infancy it had been a cherished ambition of mine to be shaved some day in a palatial barber-shop of Paris. I wished to recline at full length in a cushioned invalid chair, with pictures about me, and sumptuous furniture; with frescoed walls and gilded arches above me, and vistas of Corinthian columns stretching far before me; with perfumes of Araby to intoxicate my senses, and the slumbrous drone of distant noises to soothe me to sleep. At the end of an hour I would wake up regretfully and find my face as smooth and as soft as an infant's. Departing, I would lift my hands above that barber's head and say, "Heaven bless you, my son!"

So we searched high and low, for a matter of two hours, but never a barber-shop could we see. We saw only wig-making establishments, with shocks of dead and repulsive hair bound upon the heads of painted waxen brigands who stared out from glass boxes upon the passer-by, with their stony

eyes, and scared him with the ghostly white of their countenances. We shunned these signs for a time, but finally we concluded that the wig-makers must of necessity be the barbers
as well, since we could find no single legitimate representative
of the fraternity. We entered and asked, and found that it was
even so.

I said I wanted to be shaved. The barber inquired where
my room was. I said, never mind where my room was, I
wanted to be shaved—there, on the spot. The doctor said he
would be shaved also. Then there was an excitement among
those two barbers! There was a wild consultation, and afterwards a hurrying to and for and a feverish gathering up of
razors from obscure places and a ransacking for soap. Next
they took us into a little mean, shabby back room; they got
two ordinary sitting-room chairs and placed us in them, with
our coats on. My old, old dream of bliss vanished into thin
air!

I sat bolt upright, silent, sad, and solemn. One of the wig-
making villains lathered my face for ten terrible minutes and
finished by plastering a mass of suds into my mouth. I ex-
pelled the nasty stuff with a strong English expletive and said,
"Foreigner, beware!" Then this outlaw strapped his razor on
his boot, hovered over me ominously for six fearful seconds,
and then swooped down upon me like the genius of destruction. The first rake of his razor loosened the very hide from
my face and lifted me out of the chair. I stormed and raved,
and the other boys enjoyed it. Their beards are not strong
and thick. Let us draw the curtain over this harrowing
scene. Suffice it that I submitted, and went through with
the cruel infliction of a shave by a French barber; tears of
exquisite agony coursed down my cheeks, now and then,
but I survived. Then the incipient assassin held a basin of
water under my chin and slopped its contents over my face,
and into my bosom, and down the back of my neck, with a
mean pretense of washing away the soap and blood. He
dried my features with a towel, and was going to comb my
hair; but I asked to be excused. I said, with withering
irony, that it was sufficient to be skinned—I declined to be
scalped.

I went away from there with my handkerchief about my

face, and never, never, never desired to dream of palatial
Parisian barber-shops any more. The truth is, as I believe I
have since found out, that they have no barber shops worthy
of the name, in Paris—and no barbers, either, for that matter.
The impostor who does duty as a barber, brings his pans and
napkins and implements of torture to your residence and deliberately skins you in your private apartments. Ah, I have
suffered, suffered, suffered, here in Paris, but never mind—
the time is coming when I shall have a dark and bloody revenge. Some day a Parisian barber will come to my room to
skin me, and from that day forth, that barber will never be
heard of more.

At eleven o'clock we alighted upon a sign which manifestly
referred to billiards. Joy! We had played billiards in the
Azores with balls that were not round, and on an ancient
table that was very little smoother than a brick pavement—
one of those wretched old things with dead cushions, and
with patches in the faded cloth and invisible obstructions that
made the balls describe the most astonishing and unsuspected
angles and perform feats in the way of unlooked-for and almost impossible "scratches," that were perfectly bewildering.
We had played at Gibraltar with balls the size of a walnut, on
a table like a public square—and in both instances we
achieved far more aggravation than amusement. We expected
to fare better here, but we were mistaken. The cushions were
a good deal higher than the balls, and as the balls had a fashion of always stopping under the cushions, we accomplished
very little in the way of caroms. The cushions were hard and
unelastic, and the cues were so crooked that in making a shot
you had to allow for the curve or you would infallibly put the
"English" on the wrong side of the ball. Dan was to mark
while the doctor and I played. At the end of an hour neither
of us had made a count, and so Dan was tired of keeping tally
with nothing to tally, and we were heated and angry and disgusted. We paid the heavy bill—about six cents—and said
we would call around some time when we had a week to
spend, and finish the game.

We adjourned to one of those pretty cafés and took supper
and tested the wines of the country, as we had been instructed
to do, and found them harmless and unexciting. They might

have been exciting, however, if we had chosen to drink a suf-ficiency of them.

To close our first day in Paris cheerfully and pleasantly, we now sought our grand room in the Grand Hotel du Louvre and climbed into our sumptuous bed, to read and smoke— but alas!

> It was pitiful,
> In a whole city-full,
> Gas we had none.

No gas to read by—nothing but dismal candles. It was a shame. We tried to map out excursions for the morrow; we puzzled over French "Guides to Paris;" we talked disjointedly, in a vain endeavor to make head or tail of the wild chaos of the day's sights and experiences; we subsided to indolent smoking; we gaped and yawned, and stretched—then feebly wondered if we were really and truly in renowned Paris, and drifted drowsily away into that vast mysterious void which men call sleep.

Chapter XIII

T HE NEXT MORNING we were up and dressed at ten o'clock. We went to the *commissionaire* of the hotel—I don't know what a *commissionaire* is, but that is the man we went to—and told him we wanted a guide. He said the great International Exposition had drawn such multitudes of Englishmen and Americans to Paris that it would be next to impossible to find a good guide unemployed. He said he usually kept a dozen or two on hand, but he only had three now. He called them. One looked so like a very pirate that we let him go at once. The next one spoke with a simpering precision of pronunciation that was irritating, and said:

"If ze zhentlemans will to me make ze grande honneur to me rattain in hees serveece, I shall show to him every sing zat is magnifique to look upon in ze beautiful Parree. I speaky ze Angleesh pairfaitemaw."

He would have done well to have stopped there, because he had that much by heart and said it right off without making a mistake. But his self-complacency seduced him into attempting a flight into regions of unexplored English, and the reckless experiment was his ruin. Within ten seconds he was so tangled up in a maze of mutilated verbs and torn and bleeding forms of speech that no human ingenuity could ever have gotten him out of it with credit. It was plain enough that he could not "speaky" the English quite as "pairfaitemaw" as he had pretended he could.

The third man captured us. He was plainly dressed, but he had a noticeable air of neatness about him. He wore a high silk hat which was a little old, but had been carefully brushed. He wore second-hand kid gloves, in good repair, and carried a small rattan cane with a curved handle—a female leg, of ivory. He stepped as gently and as daintily as a cat crossing a muddy street; and oh, he was urbanity; he was quiet, unobtrusive self-possession; he was deference itself! He spoke softly and guardedly; and when he was about to make a statement on his sole responsibility, or offer a suggestion, he weighed it by drachms and scruples first, with the crook of his little stick placed meditatively to his teeth. His opening speech was perfect. It was perfect in construction, in phraseology, in grammar, in emphasis, in pronunciation—everything. He spoke little and guardedly, after that. We were charmed. We were more than charmed—we were overjoyed. We hired him at once. We never even asked him his price. This man—our lackey, our servant, our unquestioning slave though he was, was still a gentleman—we could see that—while of the other two one was coarse and awkward, and the other was a born pirate. We asked our man Friday's name. He drew from his pocket-book a snowy little card, and passed it to us with a profound bow:

> A. BILLFINGER,
> Guide to Paris, France, Germany,
> Spain, &c., &c.,
> *Grande Hotel du Louvre.*

"Billfinger! Oh, carry me home to die!"

That was an "aside" from Dan. The atrocious name grated harshly on my ear, too. The most of us can learn to forgive, and even to like, a countenance that strikes us unpleasantly at first, but few of us, I fancy, become reconciled to a jarring name so easily. I was almost sorry we had hired this man, his name was so unbearable. However, no matter. We were impatient to start. Billfinger stepped to the door to call a carriage, and then the doctor said:

"Well, the guide goes with the barber-shop, with the billiard-table, with the gasless room, and may be with many another pretty romance of Paris. I expected to have a guide named Henri de Montmorency, or Armand de la Chartreuse, or something that would sound grand in letters to the villagers at home; but to think of a Frenchman by the name of Billfinger! Oh! this is absurd, you know. This will never do. We can't say Billfinger; it is nauseating. Name him over again: what had we better call him? Alexis du Caulaincourt?"

"Alphonse Henri Gustave de Hauteville," I suggested.

"Call him Ferguson," said Dan.

That was practical, unromantic good sense. Without de-

bate, we expunged Billfinger *as* Billfinger, and called him
Ferguson.

The carriage—an open barouche—was ready. Ferguson
mounted beside the driver, and we whirled away to breakfast.
As was proper, Mr. Ferguson stood by to transmit our orders
and answer questions. Bye and bye, he mentioned casually—
the artful adventurer—that he would go and get his breakfast
as soon as we had finished ours. He knew we could not get
along without him, and that we would not want to loiter
about and wait for him. We asked him to sit down and eat
with us. He begged, with many a bow, to be excused. It was
not proper, he said; he would sit at another table. We ordered
him peremptorily to sit down with us.

Here endeth the first lesson. It was a mistake.

As long as we had that fellow after that, he was always
hungry; he was always thirsty. He came early; he stayed late;
he could not pass a restaurant; he looked with a lecherous eye
upon every wine shop. Suggestions to stop, excuses to eat and
to drink were forever on his lips. We tried all we could to fill
him so full that he would have no room to spare for a fortnight; but it was a failure. He did not hold enough to
smother the cravings of his superhuman appetite.

He had another "discrepancy" about him. He was always
wanting us to buy things. On the shallowest pretenses, he
would inveigle us into shirt stores, boot stores, tailor shops,
glove shops—any where under the broad sweep of the heavens that there seemed a chance of our buying any thing. Any
one could have guessed that the shopkeepers paid him a per
centage on the sales; but in our blessed innocence we didn't,
until this feature of his conduct grew unbearably prominent.
One day, Dan happened to mention that he thought of buying three or four silk dress patterns for presents. Ferguson's
hungry eye was upon him in an instant. In the course of
twenty minutes, the carriage stopped.

"What's this?"

"Zis is ze finest silk magazin in Paris—ze most celebrate."

"What did you come here for? We told you to take us to
the palace of the Louvre."

"I suppose ze gentleman say he wish to buy some silk."

"You are not required to 'suppose' things for the party, Ferguson. We do not wish to tax your energies too much. We will bear some of the burden and heat of the day ourselves. We will endeavor to do such 'supposing' as is really necessary to be done. Drive on." So spake the doctor.

Within fifteen minutes the carriage halted again, and before another silk store. The doctor said:

"Ah, the palace of the Louvre: beautiful, beautiful edifice! Does the Emperor Napoleon live here now, Ferguson?"

"Ah, doctor! you do jest; zis is not ze palace; we come there directly. But since we pass right by zis store, where is such beautiful silk—"

"Ah! I see, I see. I meant to have told you that we did not wish to purchase any silks to-day; but in my absent-mindedness I forgot it. I also meant to tell you we wished to go directly to the Louvre; but I forgot that also. However, we will go there now. Pardon my seeming carelessness, Ferguson. Drive on."

Within the half hour, we stopped again—in front of another silk store. We were angry; but the doctor was always serene, always smooth-voiced. He said:

"At last! How imposing the Louvre is, and yet how small! how exquisitely fashioned! how charmingly situated!—Venerable, venerable pile—"

"Pairdon, doctor, zis is not ze Louvre—it is—"

"*What* is it?"

"I have ze idea—it come to me in a moment—zat ze silk in zis magazin—"

"Ferguson, how heedless I am. I fully intended to tell you that we did not wish to buy any silks to-day, and I also intended to tell you that we yearned to go immediately to the palace of the Louvre, but enjoying the happiness of seeing you devour four breakfasts this morning has so filled me with pleasurable emotions that I neglect the commonest interests of the time. However, we will proceed now to the Louvre, Ferguson."

"But doctor," (excitedly,) "it will take not a minute—not but one small minute! Ze gentleman need not to buy if he not wish to—but only *look* at ze silk—*look* at ze beautiful fabric." [Then pleadingly.] "*Sair*—just only one *leetle* moment!"

Dan said, "Confound the idiot! I don't want to see any silks to-day, and I *won't* look at them. Drive on."

And the doctor: "We need no silks now, Ferguson. Our hearts yearn for the Louvre. Let us journey on—let us journey on."

"But *doctor!* it is only one moment—one leetle moment. And ze time will be save—entirely save! Because zere is nothing to see, now—it is too late. It want ten minute to four and ze Louvre close at four—*only* one leetle moment, doctor!"

The treacherous miscreant! After four breakfasts and a gallon of champagne, to serve us such a scurvy trick. We got no sight of the countless treasures of art in the Louvre galleries that day, and our only poor little satisfaction was in the reflection that Ferguson sold not a solitary silk dress pattern.

I am writing this chapter partly for the satisfaction of abusing that accomplished knave, Billfinger, and partly to show whosoever shall read this how Americans fare at the hands of the Paris guides, and what sort of people Paris guides are. It need not be supposed that we were a stupider or an easier prey than our countrymen generally are, for we were not. The guides deceive and defraud every American who goes to Paris for the first time and sees its sights alone or in company with others as little experienced as himself. I shall visit Paris again some day, and then let the guides beware! I shall go in my war-paint—I shall carry my tomahawk along.

I think we have lost but little time in Paris. We have gone to bed every night tired out. Of course we visited the renowned International Exposition. All the world did that. We went there on our third day in Paris—and we stayed there *nearly two hours*. That was our first and last visit. To tell the truth, we saw at a glance that one would have to spend weeks—yea, even months—in that monstrous establishment, to get an intelligible idea of it. It was a wonderful show, but the moving masses of people of all nations we saw there were a still more wonderful show. I discovered that if I were to stay there a month, I should still find myself looking at the people instead of the inanimate objects on exhibition. I got a little interested in some curious old tapestries of the thirteenth century, but a party of Arabs came by, and their dusky faces and quaint costumes called my attention away at once. I watched a silver swan, which had a living grace about his movements, and a living intelligence in his eyes—watched him swimming about as comfortably and as unconcernedly as if he had been born in a morass instead of a jeweller's shop— watched him seize a silver fish from under the water and hold up his head and go through all the customary and elaborate motions of swallowing it—but the moment it disappeared down his throat some tattooed South Sea Islanders approached and I yielded to their attractions. Presently I found a revolving pistol several hundred years old which looked strangely like a modern Colt, but just then I heard that the Empress of the French was in another part of the building, and hastened away to see what she might look like. We heard martial music—we saw an unusual number of soldiers walking hurriedly about—there was a general movement among the people. We inquired what it was all about, and learned that the Emperor of the French and the Sultan of Turkey were about to review twenty-five thousand troops at the *Arc de l'Etoile*. We immediately departed. I had a greater anxiety to see these men than I could have had to see twenty Expositions.

We drove away and took up a position in an open space opposite the American Minister's house. A speculator bridged a couple of barrels with a board and we hired standing-places on it. Presently there was a sound of distant music; in another minute a pillar of dust came moving slowly toward us; a moment more, and then, with colors flying and a grand crash of military music, a gallant array of cavalrymen emerged from the dust and came down the street on a gentle trot. After them came a long line of artillery; then more cavalry, in splendid uniforms; and then their Imperial Majesties Napoleon III. and Abdul Aziz. The vast concourse of people swung their hats and shouted—the windows and house-tops in the wide vicinity burst into a snow-storm of waving handkerchiefs, and the wavers of the same mingled their cheers with those of the masses below. It was a stirring spectacle.

But the two central figures claimed all my attention. Was ever such a contrast set up before a multitude till then? Napoleon, in military uniform—a long-bodied, short-legged man, fiercely moustached, old, wrinkled, with eyes half closed, and *such* a deep, crafty, scheming expression about them!—Napoleon, bowing ever so gently to the loud plaudits, and watching every thing and every body with his cat-eyes from under his depressed hat-brim, as if to discover any sign that those cheers were not heartfelt and cordial.

Abdul Aziz, absolute lord of the Ottoman Empire,—clad in dark green European clothes, almost without ornament or insignia of rank; a red Turkish fez on his head—a short, stout, dark man, black-bearded, black-eyed, stupid, unprepossessing—a man whose whole appearance somehow suggested that if he only had a cleaver in his hand and a white apron on, one would not be at all surprised to hear him say: "A mutton-roast to-day, or will you have a nice porter-house steak?"

Napoleon III., the representative of the highest modern civilization, progress, and refinement; Abdul-Aziz, the representative of a people by nature and training filthy, brutish, ignorant, unprogressive, superstitious—and a government whose Three Graces are Tyranny, Rapacity, Blood. Here in brilliant Paris, under this majestic Arch of Triumph, the First Century greets the Nineteenth!

NAPOLEON III., Emperor of France! Surrounded by shouting thousands, by military pomp, by the splendors of his capital city, and companioned by kings and princes—this is the man who was sneered at, and reviled, and called Bastard—yet who was dreaming of a crown and an Empire all the while; who was driven into exile—but carried his dreams with him; who associated with the common herd in America, and ran foot-races for a wager—but still sat upon a throne, in fancy; who braved every danger to go to his dying mother—and grieved that she could not be spared to see him cast aside his plebeian vestments for the purple of royalty; who kept his faithful watch and walked his weary beat a common policeman of London—but dreamed the while of a coming night when he should tread the long-drawn corridors of the Tuileries; who made the miserable *fiasco* of Strasbourg; saw his poor, shabby eagle, forgetful of its lesson, refuse to perch upon his shoulder; delivered his carefully-prepared, sententious burst of eloquence, unto unsympathetic ears; found

himself a prisoner, the butt of small wits, a mark for the pitiless ridicule of all the world—yet went on dreaming of
coronations and splendid pageants, as before; who lay a forgotten captive in the dungeons of Ham—and still schemed
and planned and pondered over future glory and future
power; President of France at last! a *coup d'etat*, and surrounded by applauding armies, welcomed by the thunders of
cannon, he mounts a throne and waves before an astounded
world the sceptre of a mighty Empire! Who talks of the marvels of fiction? Who speaks of the wonders of romance? Who
prates of the tame achievements of Aladdin and the Magii of
Arabia?

ABDUL-AZIZ, Sultan of Turkey, Lord of the Ottoman Empire! Born to a throne; weak, stupid, ignorant, almost, as his
meanest slave; chief of a vast royalty, yet the puppet of his
Premier and the obedient child of a tyrannical mother; a man
who sits upon a throne—the beck of whose finger moves navies and armies—who holds in his hands the power of life
and death over millions—yet who sleeps, sleeps, eats, eats,
idles with his eight hundred concubines, and when he is surfeited with eating and sleeping and idling, and would rouse
up and take the reins of government and threaten to *be* a
Sultan, is charmed from his purpose by wary Fuad Pacha with
a pretty plan for a new palace or a new ship—charmed away
with a new toy, like any other restless child; a man who sees
his people robbed and oppressed by soulless tax-gatherers,
but speaks no word to save them; who believes in gnomes,
and genii and the wild fables of the Arabian Nights, but has
small regard for the mighty magicians of to-day, and is nervous in the presence of their mysterious railroads and steamboats and telegraphs; who would see undone in Egypt all that
great Mehemet Ali achieved, and would prefer rather to forget than emulate him; a man who found his great Empire a
blot upon the earth—a degraded, poverty-stricken, miserable,
infamous agglomeration of ignorance, crime, and brutality,
and will idle away the allotted days of his trivial life, and then
pass to the dust and the worms and leave it so!

Napoleon has augmented the commercial prosperity of
France, in ten years, to such a degree that figures can hardly
compute it. He has rebuilt Paris, and has partly rebuilt every

city in the State. He condemns a whole street at a time, assesses the damages, pays them and rebuilds superbly. Then speculators buy up the ground and sell, but the original owner is given the first choice by the government at a stated price before the speculator is permitted to purchase. But above all things, he has taken the sole control of the Empire of France into his hands, and made it a tolerably free land— for people who will not attempt to go too far in meddling with government affairs. No country offers greater security to life and property than France, and one has all the freedom he wants, but no license—no license to interfere with any body, or make any one uncomfortable.

As for the Sultan, one could set a trap any where and catch a dozen abler men in a night.

The bands struck up, and the brilliant adventurer, Napoleon III., the genius of Energy, Persistence, Enterprise; and the feeble Abdul-Aziz, the genius of Ignorance, Bigotry and Indolence, prepared for the Forward—March!

We saw the splendid review, we saw the white-moustached old Crimean soldier, Canrobert, Marshal of France, we saw— well, we saw every thing, and then we went home satisfied.

Chapter XIV

WE WENT to see the Cathedral of Notre Dame.—We had heard of it before. It surprises me, sometimes, to think how much we *do* know, and how intelligent we are. We recognized the brown old Gothic pile in a moment; it was like the pictures. We stood at a little distance and changed from one point of observation to another, and gazed long at its lofty square towers and its rich front, clustered thick with stony, mutilated saints who had been looking calmly down from their perches for ages. The Patriarch of Jerusalem stood under them in the old days of chivalry and romance, and preached the third Crusade, more than six hundred years ago; and since that day they have stood there and looked quietly down upon the most thrilling scenes, the grandest pageants, the most extraordinary spectacles that have grieved or delighted Paris. These battered and broken-nosed old fellows saw many and many a cavalcade of mail-clad knights come marching home from Holy Land; they heard the bells above them toll the signal for the St. Bartholomew's Massacre, and they saw the slaughter that followed; later, they saw the Reign of Terror, the carnage of the Revolution, the overthrow of a king, the coronation of two Napoleons, the christening of the young prince that lords it over a regiment of servants in the Tuileries to-day—and they may possibly continue to stand there until they see the Napoleon dynasty swept away and the banners of a great Republic floating above its ruins. I wish these old parties could speak. They could tell a tale worth the listening to.

They say that a pagan temple stood where Notre Dame now stands, in the old Roman days, eighteen or twenty centuries ago—remains of it are still preserved in Paris; and that a Christian church took its place about A. D. 300; another took the place of that in A. D. 500; and that the foundations of the present Cathedral were laid about A. D. 1100. The ground ought to be measurably sacred by this time, one would think. One portion of this noble old edifice is suggestive of the quaint fashions of ancient times. It was built by Jean Sans-Peur, Duke of Burgundy, to set his conscience at rest—he had assassinated the Duke of Orleans. Alas! those good old times are gone, when a murderer could wipe the stain from his name and soothe his troubles to sleep simply by getting out his bricks and mortar and building an addition to a church.

The portals of the great western front are bisected by square pillars. They took the central one away, in 1852, on the occasion of thanksgivings for the reinstitution of the Presidential power—but precious soon they had occasion to reconsider that motion and put it back again! And they did.

We loitered through the grand aisles for an hour or two, staring up at the rich stained glass windows embellished with blue and yellow and crimson saints and martyrs, and trying to admire the numberless great pictures in the chapels, and then we were admitted to the sacristy and shown the magnificent robes which the Pope wore when he crowned Napoleon I.; a wagon-load of solid gold and silver utensils used in the great public processions and ceremonies of the church; some nails of the true cross, a fragment of the cross itself, a part of the crown of thorns. We had already seen a large piece of the true cross in a church in the Azores, but no nails. They showed us likewise the bloody robe which that Archbishop of Paris wore who exposed his sacred person and braved the wrath of the insurgents of 1848, to mount the barricades and hold aloft the olive branch of peace in the hope of stopping the slaughter. His noble effort cost him his life. He was shot dead. They showed us a cast of his face, taken after death, the bullet that killed him, and the two vertebræ in which it lodged. These people have a somewhat singular taste in the matter of relics. Ferguson told us that the silver cross which the good Archbishop wore at his girdle was seized and thrown into the Seine, where it lay embedded in the mud for fifteen years, and then an angel appeared to a priest and told him where to dive for it; he *did* dive for it and got it, and now it is there on exhibition at Notre Dame, to be inspected by any body who feels an interest in inanimate objects of miraculous intervention.

Next we went to visit the Morgue, that horrible receptacle for the dead who die mysteriously and leave the manner of their taking off a dismal secret. We stood before a grating and looked through into a room which was hung all about with the clothing of dead men; coarse blouses, water-soaked; the delicate garments of women and children; patrician vestments, hacked and stabbed and stained with red; a hat that was crushed and bloody. On a slanting stone lay a drowned man, naked, swollen, purple; clasping the fragment of a broken bush with a grip which death had so petrified that human strength could not unloose it—mute witness of the last despairing effort to save the life that was doomed beyond all help. A stream of water trickled ceaselessly over the hideous face. We knew that the body and the clothing were there for identification by friends, but still we wondered if any body could love that repulsive object or grieve for its loss. We grew meditative and wondered if, some forty years ago, when the mother of that ghastly thing was dandling it upon her knee, and kissing it and petting it and displaying it with satisfied pride to the passers-by, a prophetic vision of this dread ending ever flitted through her brain. I half feared that the mother, or the wife or a brother of the dead man might come while we stood there, but nothing of the kind occurred. Men and women came, and some looked eagerly in, and pressed their faces against the bars; others glanced carelessly at the body, and turned away with a disappointed look—people, I thought, who live upon strong excitements, and who attend the exhibitions of the Morgue regularly, just as other people go to see theatrical spectacles every night. When one of these looked in and passed on, I could not help thinking—

"Now this don't afford you any satisfaction—a party with his head shot off is what *you* need."

One night we went to the celebrated *Jardin Mabille*, but only staid a little while. We wanted to see some of this kind of Paris life, however, and therefore, the next night we went to a similar place of entertainment in a great garden in the suburb of Asniéres. We went to the railroad depot, toward evening, and Ferguson got tickets for a second-class carriage. Such a perfect jam of people I have not often seen—but there was no noise, no disorder, no rowdyism. Some of the women and young girls that entered the train we knew to be of the *demi-monde*, but others we were not at all sure about.

The girls and women in our carriage behaved themselves

modestly and becomingly, all the way out, except that they smoked. When we arrived at the garden in Asniéres, we paid a franc or two admission, and entered a place which had flower-beds in it, and grass plats, and long, curving rows of ornamental shrubbery, with here and there a secluded bower convenient for eating ice-cream in. We moved along the sinuous gravel walks, with the great concourse of girls and young men, and suddenly a domed and filagreed white temple, starred over and over and over again with brilliant gas-jets, burst upon us like a fallen sun. Near by was a large, handsome house with its ample front illuminated in the same way, and above its roof floated the Star Spangled Banner of America.

"Well!" I said. "How is this?" It nearly took my breath away.

Ferguson said an American—a New Yorker—kept the place, and was carrying on quite a stirring opposition to the *Jardin Mabille*.

Crowds, composed of both sexes and nearly all ages, were frisking about the garden or sitting in the open air in front of the flag-staff and the temple, drinking wine and coffee, or smoking. The dancing had not begun, yet. Ferguson said there was to be an exhibition. The famous Blondin was going to perform on a tight-rope in another part of the garden. We went thither. Here the light was dim, and the masses of people were pretty closely packed together. And now I made a mistake which any donkey might make, but a sensible man never. I committed an error which I find myself repeating every day of my life.—Standing right before a young lady, I said—

"Dan, just look at this girl, how beautiful she is!"

"I thank you more for the evident sincerity of the compliment, sir, than for the extraordinary publicity you have given to it!" This in good, pure English.

We took a walk, but my spirits were very, very sadly dampened. I did not feel right comfortable for some time afterward. Why *will* people be so stupid as to suppose themselves the only foreigners among a crowd of ten thousand persons?

But Blondin came out shortly. He appeared on a stretched cable, far away above the sea of tossing hats and handkerchiefs, and in the glare of the hundreds of rockets that whizzed heavenward by him he looked like a wee insect. He balanced his pole and walked the length of his rope—two or three hundred feet; he came back and got a man and carried him across; he returned to the centre and danced a jig; next he performed some gymnastic and balancing feats too peril-ous to afford a pleasant spectacle; and he finished by fastening to his person a thousand Roman candles, Catherine wheels, serpents and rockets of all manner of brilliant colors, setting them on fire all at once and walking and waltzing across his rope again in a blinding blaze of glory that lit up the garden and the people's faces like a great conflagration at midnight.

The dance had begun, and we adjourned to the temple. Within it was a drinking saloon; and all around it was a broad circular platform for the dancers. I backed up against the wall of the temple, and waited. Twenty sets formed, the music struck up, and then—I placed my hands before my face for very shame. But I looked through my fingers. They were dancing the renowned *"Can-can."* A handsome girl in the set before me tripped forward lightly to meet the opposite gen-tleman—tripped back again, grasped her dresses vigorously on both sides with her hands, raised them pretty high, danced an extraordinary jig that had more activity and exposure about it than any jig I ever saw before, and then, drawing her clothes still higher, she advanced gaily to the centre and launched a vicious kick full at her *vis-a-vis* that must infallibly have removed his nose if he had been seven feet high. It was a mercy he was only six.

That is the *can-can*. The idea of it is to dance as wildly, as noisily, as furiously as you can; expose yourself as much as possible if you are a woman; and kick as high as you can, no matter which sex you belong to. There is no word of exag-geration in this. Any of the staid, respectable, aged people who were there that night can testify to the truth of that statement. There were a good many such people present. I suppose French morality is not of that straight-laced descrip-tion which is shocked at trifles.

I moved aside and took a general view of the *can-can*. Shouts, laughter, furious music, a bewildering chaos of dart-ing and intermingling forms, stormy jerking and snatching of gay dresses, bobbing heads, flying arms, lightning-flashes of white-stockinged calves and dainty slippers in the air, and then a grand final rush, riot, a terrific hubbub and a wild stampede! Heavens! Nothing like it has been seen on earth since trembling Tam O'Shanter saw the devil and the witches at their orgies that stormy night in "Alloway's auld haunted kirk."

We visited the Louvre, at a time when we had no silk purchases in view, and looked at its miles of paintings by the old masters. Some of them were beautiful, but at the same time they carried such evidences about them of the cringing spirit of those great men that we found small pleasure in examining them. Their nauseous adulation of princely patrons was more prominent to me and chained my attention more surely than the charms of color and expression which are claimed to be in the pictures. Gratitude for kindnesses is well, but it seems to me that some of those artists carried it so far that it ceased to be gratitude, and became worship. If there is a plausible excuse for the worship of men, then by all means let us forgive Rubens and his brethren.

But I will drop the subject, lest I say something about the old masters that might as well be left unsaid.

Of course we drove in the *Bois de Boulogne*, that limitless park, with its forests, its lakes, its cascades, and its broad avenues. There were thousands upon thousands of vehicles abroad, and the scene was full of life and gayety. There were very common hacks, with father and mother and all the children in them; conspicuous little open carriages with celebrated ladies of questionable reputation in them; there were Dukes and Duchesses abroad, with gorgeous footmen perched behind, and equally gorgeous outriders perched on each of the six horses; there were blue and silver, and green and gold, and pink and black, and all sorts and descriptions of stunning and startling liveries out, and I almost yearned to be a flunkey myself, for the sake of the fine clothes.

But presently the Emperor came along and he out-shone them all. He was preceded by a body guard of gentlemen on horseback in showy uniforms, his carriage-horses (there appeared to be somewhere in the remote neighborhood of a thousand of them,) were bestridden by gallant looking fellows, also in stylish uniforms, and after the carriage followed another detachment of body-guards. Every body got out of the way; every body bowed to the Emperor and his friend the Sultan, and they went by on a swinging trot and disappeared.

I will not describe the *Bois de Boulogne*. I can not do it. It is simply a beautiful, cultivated, endless, wonderful wilderness. It is an enchanting place. It is in Paris, now, one may say, but a crumbling old cross in one portion of it reminds one that it was not always so. The cross marks the spot where a celebrated troubadour was waylaid and murdered in the fourteenth century. It was in this park that that fellow with an unpronounceable name made the attempt upon the Russian Czar's life last spring with a pistol. The bullet struck a tree. Ferguson showed us the place. Now in America that interesting tree would be chopped down or forgotten within the next five years, but it will be treasured here. The guides will point it out to visitors for the next eight hundred years, and when it decays and falls down they will put up another there and go on with the same old story just the same.

Chapter XV

ONE OF OUR pleasantest visits was to Père la Chaise, the national burying-ground of France, the honored resting-place of some of her greatest and best children, the last home of scores of illustrious men and women who were born to no titles, but achieved fame by their own energy and their own genius. It is a solemn city of winding streets, and of miniature marble temples and mansions of the dead gleaming white from out a wilderness of foliage and fresh flowers. Not every city is so well peopled as this, or has so ample an area within its walls. Few palaces exist in any city, that are so exquisite in design, so rich in art, so costly in material, so graceful, so beautiful.

We had stood in the ancient church of St. Denis, where the marble effigies of thirty generations of kings and queens lay stretched at length upon the tombs, and the sensations invoked were startling and novel; the curious armor, the obsolete costumes, the placid faces, the hands placed palm to palm in eloquent supplication—it was a vision of gray antiquity. It seemed curious enough to be standing face to face, as it were, with old Dagobert I., and Clovis and Charlemagne, those vague, colossal heroes, those shadows, those myths of a thousand years ago! I touched their dust-covered faces with my finger, but Dagobert was deader than the sixteen centuries that have passed over him, Clovis slept well after his labor for Christ, and old Charlemagne went on dreaming of his paladins, of bloody Roncesvalles, and gave no heed to me.

The great names of Père la Chaise impress one, too, but differently. There the suggestion brought constantly to his mind is, that this place is sacred to a nobler royalty—the royalty of heart and brain. Every faculty of mind, every noble trait of human nature, every high occupation which men engage in seems represented by a famous name. The effect is a curious medley. Davoust and Massena, who wrought in many a battle-tragedy, are here, and so also is Rachel, of equal renown in mimic tragedy on the stage. The Abbé Sicard sleeps here—the first great teacher of the deaf and dumb—a man whose heart went out to every unfortunate, and whose life was given to kindly offices in their service; and not far off, in repose and peace at last, lies Marshal Ney, whose stormy spirit knew no music like the bugle call to arms. The man who originated public gas-lighting, and that other benefactor who introduced the cultivation of the potato and thus blessed millions of his starving countrymen, lie with the Prince of Masserano, and with exiled queens and princes of Further India. Gay-Lussac the chemist, Laplace the astronomer, Larrey the surgeon, de Séze the advocate, are here, and with them are Talma, Bellini, Rubini; de Balzac, Beaumarchais, Beranger; Molière and Lafontaine, and scores of other men whose names and whose worthy labors are as familiar in the remote by-places of civilization as are the historic deeds of the kings and princes that sleep in the marble vaults of St. Denis.

But among the thousands and thousands of tombs in Père la Chaise, there is one that no man, no woman, no youth of either sex, ever passes by without stopping to examine. Every visitor has a sort of indistinct idea of the history of its dead, and comprehends that homage is due there, but not one in twenty thousand clearly remembers the story of that tomb and its romantic occupants. This is the grave of Abelard and Heloise—a grave which has been more revered, more widely known, more written and sung about and wept over, for seven hundred years, than any other in Christendom, save only that of the Saviour. All visitors linger pensively about it; all young people capture and carry away keepsakes and mementoes of it; all Parisian youths and maidens who are disappointed in love come there to bail out when they are full of tears; yea, many stricken lovers make pilgrimages to this shrine from distant provinces to weep and wail and "grit" their teeth over their heavy sorrows, and to purchase the sympathies of the chastened spirits of that tomb with offerings of immortelles and budding flowers.

Go when you will, you find somebody snuffling over that tomb. Go when you will, you find it furnished with those bouquets and immortelles. Go when you will, you find a gravel-train from Marseilles arriving to supply the deficiencies caused by memento-cabbaging vandals whose affections have miscarried.

Yet who really knows the story of Abelard and Heloise?

Precious few people. The names are perfectly familiar to everybody, and that is about all. With infinite pains I have acquired a knowledge of that history, and I propose to narrate it here, partly for the honest information of the public and partly to show that public that they have been wasting a good deal of marketable sentiment very unnecessarily.

STORY OF ABELARD AND HELOISE.

Heloise was born seven hundred and sixty-six years ago. She may have had parents. There is no telling. She lived with her uncle Fulbert, a canon of the cathedral of Paris. I do not know what a canon of a cathedral is, but that is what he was. He was nothing more than a sort of a mountain howitzer, likely, because they had no heavy artillery in those days. Suffice it, then, that Heloise lived with her uncle the howitzer, and was happy.—She spent the most of her childhood in the convent of Argenteuil—never heard of Argenteuil before, but suppose there was really such a place. She then returned to her uncle, the old gun, or son of a gun, as the case may be, and he taught her to write and speak Latin, which was the language of literature and polite society at that period.

Just at this time, Pierre Abelard, who had already made himself widely famous as a rhetorician, came to found a school of rhetoric in Paris. The originality of his principles, his eloquence, and his great physical strength and beauty created a profound sensation. He saw Heloise, and was captivated by her blooming youth, her beauty and her charming disposition. He wrote to her; she answered. He wrote again, she answered again. He was now in love. He longed to know her—to speak to her face to face.

His school was near Fulbert's house. He asked Fulbert to allow him to call. The good old swivel saw here a rare opportunity: his niece, whom he so much loved, would absorb knowledge from this man, and it would not cost him a cent. Such was Fulbert—penurious.

Fulbert's first name is not mentioned by any author, which is unfortunate. However, George W. Fulbert will answer for him as well as any other. We will let him go at that. He asked Abelard to teach her.

Abelard was glad enough of the opportunity. He came

often and staid long. A letter of his shows in its very first sentence that he came under that friendly roof like a cold-hearted villain as he was, with the deliberate intention of debauching a confiding, innocent girl. This is the letter:

"I can not cease to be astonished at the simplicity of Fulbert; I was as much surprised as if he had placed a lamb in the power of a hungry wolf. Heloise and I, under pretext of study, gave ourselves up wholly to love, and the solitude that love seeks our studies procured for us. Books were open before us, but we spoke oftener of love than philosophy, and kisses came more readily from our lips than words."

And so, exulting over an honorable confidence which to his degraded instinct was a ludicrous "simplicity," this unmanly Abelard seduced the niece of the man whose guest he was. Paris found it out. Fulbert was told of it—told often—but refused to believe it. He could not comprehend how a man could be so depraved as to use the sacred protection and security of hospitality as a means for the commission of such a crime as that. But when he heard the rowdies in the streets singing the love-songs of Abelard to Heloise, the case was too plain—love-songs come not properly within the teachings of rhetoric and philosophy.

He drove Abelard from his house. Abelard returned secretly and carried Heloise away to Palais, in Brittany, his native country. Here, shortly afterward, she bore a son, who, from his rare beauty, was surnamed Astrolabe—William G. The girl's flight enraged Fulbert, and he longed for vengeance, but feared to strike lest retaliation visit Heloise—for he still loved her tenderly. At length Abelard offered to marry Heloise—but on a shameful condition: that the marriage should be kept secret from the world, to the end that (while her good name remained a wreck, as before,) his priestly reputation might be kept untarnished. It was like that miscreant. Fulbert saw his opportunity and consented. He would see the parties married, and then violate the confidence of the man who had taught him that trick; he would divulge the secret and so remove somewhat of the obloquy that attached to his niece's fame. But the niece suspected his scheme. She refused the marriage, at first; she said Fulbert would betray the secret to save her, and besides, she did not wish to drag down a lover who was so gifted, so honored by the world, and who had such a splendid career before him. It was noble, self-sacrificing love, and characteristic of the pure-souled Heloise, but it was not good sense.

But she was overruled, and the private marriage took place. Now for Fulbert! The heart so wounded should be healed at last; the proud spirit so tortured should find rest again; the humbled head should be lifted up once more. He proclaimed the marriage in the high places of the city, and rejoiced that dishonor had departed from his house. But lo! Abelard denied the marriage! Heloise denied it! The people, knowing the former circumstances, might have believed Fulbert, had only Abelard denied it, but when the person chiefly interested—the girl herself—denied it, they laughed despairing Fulbert to scorn.

The poor canon of the cathedral of Paris was spiked again. The last hope of repairing the wrong that had been done his house was gone. What next? Human nature suggested revenge. He compassed it. The historian says:

"Ruffians, hired by Fulbert, fell upon Abelard by night, and inflicted upon him a terrible and nameless mutilation."

I am seeking the last resting-place of those "ruffians." When I find it I shall shed some tears on it, and stack up some bouquets and immortelles and cart away from it some gravel whereby to remember that howsoever blotted by crime their lives may have been, these ruffians did one just deed, at any rate, albeit it was not warranted by the strict letter of the law.

Heloise entered a convent and gave good-bye to the world and its pleasures for all time. For twelve years she never heard of Abelard—never even heard his name mentioned. She had become prioress of Argenteuil, and led a life of complete seclusion. She happened one day to see a letter written by him, in which he narrated his own history. She cried over it, and wrote him. He answered, addressing her as his "sister in Christ." They continued to correspond, she in the unweighed language of unwavering affection, he in the chilly phraseology of the polished rhetorician. She poured out her heart in passionate, disjointed sentences; he replied with finished essays, divided deliberately into heads and sub-heads, premises and argument. She showered upon him the tenderest epithets that love could devise, he addressed her from the North Pole of his frozen heart as the "Spouse of Christ!" The abandoned villain!

On account of her too easy government of her nuns, some disreputable irregularities were discovered among them, and the Abbot of St. Denis broke up her establishment. Abelard was the official head of the monastery of St. Gildas de Ruys, at that time, and when he heard of her homeless condition a sentiment of pity was aroused in his breast (it is a wonder the unfamiliar emotion did not blow his head off,) and he placed her and her troop in the little oratory of the Paraclete, a religious establishment which he had founded. She had many privations and sufferings to undergo at first, but her worth and her gentle disposition won influential friends for her, and she built up a wealthy and flourishing nunnery. She became a great favorite with the heads of the church, and also the people, though she seldom appeared in public. She rapidly advanced in esteem, in good report and in usefulness, and Abelard as rapidly lost ground. The Pope so honored her that he made her the head of her order. Abelard, a man of splendid talents, and ranking as the first debater of his time, became timid, irresolute, and distrustful of his powers. He only needed a great misfortune to topple him from the high position he held in the world of intellectual excellence, and it came. Urged by kings and princes to meet the subtle St. Bernard in debate and crush him, he stood up in the presence of a royal and illustrious assemblage, and when his antagonist had finished he looked about him, and stammered a commencement; but his courage failed him, the cunning of his tongue was gone: with his speech unspoken, he trembled and sat down, a disgraced and vanquished champion.

He died a nobody, and was buried at Cluny, A. D., 1144. They removed his body to the Paraclete afterward, and when Heloise died, twenty years later, they buried her with him, in accordance with her last wish. He died at the ripe age of 64, and she at 63. After the bodies had remained entombed three hundred years, they were removed once more. They were removed again in 1800, and finally, seventeen years afterward, they were taken up and transferred to Père la Chaise, where they will remain in peace and quiet until it comes time for them to get up and move again.

History is silent concerning the last acts of the mountain howitzer. Let the world say what it will about him, *I*, at least, shall always respect the memory and sorrow for the abused trust, and the broken heart, and the troubled spirit of the old smooth-bore. Rest and repose be his!

Such is the story of Abelard and Heloise. Such is the history that Lamartine has shed such cataracts of tears over. But that man never could come within the influence of a subject in the least pathetic without overflowing his banks. He ought to be dammed—or leveed, I should more properly say. Such is the history—not as it is usually told, but as it is when stripped of the nauseous sentimentality that would enshrine for our loving worship a dastardly seducer like Pierre Abelard. I have not a word to say against the misused, faithful girl, and would not withhold from her grave a single one of those simple tributes which blighted youths and maidens offer to her memory, but I am sorry enough that I have not time and opportunity to write four or five volumes of my opinion of her friend the founder of the Parachute, or the Paraclete, or whatever it was.

The tons of sentiment I have wasted on that unprincipled humbug, in my ignorance! I shall throttle down my emotions hereafter, about this sort of people, until I have read them up and know whether they are entitled to any tearful attentions or not. I wish I had my immortelles back, now, and that bunch of radishes.

In Paris we often saw in shop windows the sign, *"English Spoken Here,"* just as one sees in the windows at home the sign, *"Ici on parle francaise."* We always invaded these places at once—and invariably received the information, framed in faultless French, that the clerk who did the English for the establishment had just gone to dinner and would be back in an hour—would Monsieur buy something? We wondered why those parties happened to take their dinners at such erratic and extraordinary hours, for we never called at a time when an exemplary Christian would be in the least likely to be abroad on such an errand. The truth was, it was a base fraud—a snare to trap the unwary—chaff to catch fledglings with. They had no English-murdering clerk. They trusted to the sign to inveigle foreigners into their lairs, and trusted to their own blandishments to keep them there till they bought something.

We ferreted out another French imposition—a frequent sign to this effect: "ALL MANNER OF AMERICAN DRINKS ARTISTICALLY PREPARED HERE." We procured the services of a gentleman experienced in the nomenclature of the American bar, and moved upon the works of one of these impostors. A bowing, aproned Frenchman skipped forward and said:

"Que voulez les messieurs?" I do not know what Que voulez les messieurs means, but such was his remark.

Our General said, "We will take a whisky-straight."

[A stare from the Frenchman.]

"Well, if you don't know what that is, give us a champagne cock-tail."

[A stare and a shrug.]

"Well, then, give us a sherry cobbler."

The Frenchman was checkmated. This was all Greek to him.

"Give us a brandy smash!"

The Frenchman began to back away, suspicious of the ominous vigor of the last order—began to back away, shrugging his shoulders and spreading his hands apologetically.

The General followed him up and gained a complete victory. The uneducated foreigner could not even furnish a Santa Cruz Punch, an Eye-Opener, a Stone-Fence, or an Earthquake. It was plain that he was a wicked impostor.

An acquaintance of mine said, the other day, that he was doubtless the only American visitor to the Exposition who had had the high honor of being escorted by the Emperor's body guard. I said with unobtrusive frankness that I was astonished that such a long-legged, lantern-jawed, unprepossessing looking spectre as he should be singled out for a distinction like that, and asked how it came about. He said he had attended a great military review in the *Champ de Mars*, some time ago, and while the multitude about him was growing thicker and thicker every moment, he observed an open space inside the railing. He left his carriage and went into it. He was the only person there, and so he had plenty of room, and the situation being central, he could see all the preparations going on about the field. By and by there was a sound of music, and soon the Emperor of the French and the Emperor of Austria, escorted by the famous *Cent Gardes*, entered the inclosure. They seemed not to observe him, but directly, in response to a sign from the commander of the Guard, a young lieutenant came toward him with a file of his men following, halted, raised his hand and gave the military salute, and then said in a low voice that he was sorry to have to disturb a stranger and a gentleman, but the place was sacred to royalty. Then this New Jersey phantom rose up and bowed and begged pardon, then with the officer beside him, the file of men marching behind him, and with every mark of respect, he was escorted to his carriage by the imperial *Cent Gardes*! The officer saluted again and fell back, the New Jersey sprite bowed in return and had presence of mind enough to pretend that he had simply called on a matter of private business with those emperors, and so waved them an adieu, and drove from the field!

Imagine a poor Frenchman ignorantly intruding upon a public rostrum sacred to some six-penny dignitary in America. The police would scare him to death, first, with a storm of their elegant blasphemy, and then pull him to pieces getting him away from there. We are measurably superior to the French in some things, but they are immeasurably our betters in others.

Enough of Paris for the present. We have done our whole duty by it. We have seen the Tuileries, the Napoleon Column, the Madeleine, that wonder of wonders the tomb of Napoleon, all the great churches and museums, libraries, imperial palaces, and sculpture and picture galleries, the Pantheon, *Jardin des Plantes*, the opera, the circus, the Legislative Body, the billiard-rooms, the barbers, the *grisettes*—

Ah, the *grisettes*! I had almost forgotten. They are another romantic fraud. They were (if you let the books of travel tell it,) always so beautiful—so neat and trim, so graceful—so naive and trusting—so gentle, so winning—so faithful to their shop duties, so irresistible to buyers in their prattling importunity—so devoted to their poverty-stricken students of the Latin Quarter—so light hearted and happy on their Sunday picnics in the suburbs—and oh, so charmingly, so delightfully immoral!

Stuff! For three or four days I was constantly saying:

"Quick, Ferguson! is that a *grisette*?"

And he always said "No."

He comprehended, at last, that I wanted to see a grisette. Then he showed me dozens of them. They were like nearly all the Frenchwomen I ever saw—homely. They had large hands, large feet, large mouths; they had pug noses as a general thing, and mustaches that not even good breeding could overlook; they combed their hair straight back without parting; they were ill-shaped, they were not winning, they were not graceful; I knew by their looks that they ate garlic and onions; and lastly and finally, to my thinking it would be base flattery to call them immoral.

Aroint thee, wench! I sorrow for the vagabond student of the Latin Quarter now, even more than formerly I envied him. Thus topples to earth another idol of my infancy.

We have seen every thing, and to-morrow we go to Versailles. We shall see Paris only for a little while as we come back to take up our line of march for the ship, and so I may as well bid the beautiful city a regretful farewell. We shall travel many thousands of miles after we leave here, and visit many great cities, but we shall find none so enchanting as this.

Some of our party have gone to England, intending to take a roundabout course and rejoin the vessel at Leghorn or Naples, several weeks hence. We came near going to Geneva, but have concluded to return to Marseilles and go up through Italy from Genoa.

I will conclude this chapter with a remark that I am sincerely proud to be able to make—and glad, as well, that my comrades cordially indorse it, to wit: by far the handsomest women we have seen in France were born and reared in America.

I feel, now, like a man who has redeemed a failing reputation and shed lustre upon a dimmed escutcheon, by a single just deed done at the eleventh hour.

Let the curtain fall, to slow music.

Chapter XVI

VERSAILLES! It is wonderfully beautiful! You gaze, and stare, and try to understand that it is real, that it is on the earth, that it is not the Garden of Eden—but your brain grows giddy, stupefied by the world of beauty around you, and you half believe you are the dupe of an exquisite dream. The scene thrills one like military music! A noble palace, stretching its ornamented front block upon block away, till it seemed that it would never end; a grand promenade before it, whereon the armies of an empire might parade; all about it rainbows of flowers, and colossal statues that were almost numberless, and yet seemed only scattered over the ample space; broad flights of stone steps leading down from the promenade to lower grounds of the park—stairways that whole regiments might stand to arms upon and have room to spare; vast fountains whose great bronze effigies discharged rivers of sparkling water into the air and mingled a hundred curving jets together in forms of matchless beauty; wide grass-carpeted avenues that branched hither and thither in every direction and wandered to seemingly interminable distances, walled all the way on either side with compact ranks of leafy trees whose branches met above and formed arches as faultless and as symmetrical as ever were carved in stone; and here and there were glimpses of sylvan lakes with miniature ships glassed in their surfaces. And every where—on the palace steps, and the great promenade, around the fountains, among the trees, and far under the arches of the endless avenues, hundreds and hundreds of people in gay costumes walked or ran or danced, and gave to the fairy picture the life and animation which was all of perfection it could have lacked.

It was worth a pilgrimage to see. Every thing is on so gigantic a scale. Nothing is small—nothing is cheap. The statues are all large; the palace is grand; the park covers a fair-sized county; the avenues are interminable. All the distances and all the dimensions about Versailles are vast. I used to think the pictures exaggerated these distances and these dimensions beyond all reason, and that they made Versailles more beautiful than it was possible for any place in the world to be. I know now that the pictures never came up to the subject in any respect, and that no painter could represent Versailles on canvas as beautiful as it is in reality. I used to abuse Louis XIV. for spending two hundred millions of dollars in creating this marvelous park, when bread was so scarce with some of his subjects; but I have forgiven him now. He took a tract of land sixty miles in circumference and set to work to make this park and build this palace and a road to it from Paris. He kept 36,000 men employed daily on it, and the labor was so unhealthy that they used to die and be hauled off by cart-loads every night. The wife of a nobleman of the time speaks of this as an *"inconvenience,"* but naively remarks that "it does not seem worthy of attention in the happy state of tranquillity we now enjoy."

I always thought ill of people at home, who trimmed their shrubbery into pyramids, and squares, and spires, and all manner of unnatural shapes, and when I saw the same thing being practiced in this great park I began to feel dissatisfied. But I soon saw the idea of the thing and the wisdom of it. They seek the *general* effect. We distort a dozen sickly trees into unaccustomed shapes in a little yard no bigger than a dining-room, and then surely they look absurd enough. But here they take two hundred thousand tall forest trees and set them in a double row; allow no sign of leaf or branch to grow on the trunk lower down than six feet above the ground; from that point the boughs begin to project, and very gradually they extend outward further and further till they meet overhead, and a faultless tunnel of foliage is formed. The arch is mathematically precise. The effect is then very fine. They make trees take fifty different shapes, and so these quaint effects are infinitely varied and picturesque. The trees in no two avenues are shaped alike, and consequently the eye is not fatigued with any thing in the nature of monotonous uniformity. I will drop this subject now, leaving it to others to determine how these people manage to make endless ranks of lofty forest trees grow to just a certain thickness of trunk (say a foot and two-thirds;) how they make them spring to precisely the same height for miles; how they make them grow so close together; how they compel one huge limb to spring from the same identical spot on each tree and form the main sweep of the arch; and how all these things are kept exactly in the same condition, and in the same exquisite shapeliness and symmetry month after month and year after year—for I have tried to reason out the problem, and have failed.

We walked through the great hall of sculpture and the one hundred and fifty galleries of paintings in the palace of Versailles, and felt that to be in such a place was useless unless one had a whole year at his disposal. These pictures are all battle-scenes, and only one solitary little canvas among them all treats of anything but great French victories. We wandered, also, through the Grand Trianon and the Petit Trianon, those monuments of royal prodigality, and with histories so mournful—filled, as it is, with souvenirs of Napoleon the First, and three dead Kings and as many Queens. In one sumptuous bed they had all slept in succession, but no one occupies it now. In a large dining-room stood the table at which Louis XIV. and his mistress, Madame Maintenon, and after them Louis XV., and Pompadour, had sat at their meals naked and unattended—for the table stood upon a trap-door, which descended with it to regions below when it was necessary to replenish its dishes. In a room of the Petit Trianon stood the furniture, just as poor Marie Antoinette left it when the mob came and dragged her and the King to Paris, never to return. Near at hand, in the stables, were prodigious carriages that showed no color but gold—carriages used by former Kings of France on state occasions, and never used now save when a kingly head is to be crowned, or an imperial infant christened. And with them were some curious sleighs, whose bodies were shaped like lions, swans, tigers, etc.—vehicles that had once been handsome with pictured designs and fine workmanship, but were dusty and decaying now. They had their history. When Louis XIV. had finished the Grand Trianon, he told Maintenon he had created a Paradise for her, and asked if she could think of any thing now to wish for. He said he wished the Trianon to be perfection— nothing less. She said she could think of but one thing—it was summer, and it was balmy France—yet she would like well to sleigh-ride in the leafy avenues of Versailles! The next morning found miles and miles of grassy avenues spread thick with snowy salt and sugar, and a procession of those quaint sleighs waiting to receive the chief concubine of the gayest and most unprincipled court that France has ever seen!

From sumptuous Versailles, with its palaces, its statues, its gardens and its fountains, we journeyed back to Paris and sought its antipodes—the Faubourg St. Antoine. Little, narrow streets; dirty children blockading them; greasy, slovenly women capturing and spanking them; filthy dens on first floors, with rag stores in them (the heaviest business in the Faubourg is the chiffonier's;) other filthy dens where whole suits of second and third-hand clothing are sold at prices that would ruin any proprietor who did not steal his stock; still other filthy dens where they sold groceries—sold them by the half-pennyworth—five dollars would buy the man out, good-will and all. Up these little crooked streets they will murder a man for seven dollars and dump the body in the Seine. And up some other of these streets—most of them, I should say—live lorettes.

All through this Faubourg St. Antoine, misery, poverty, vice and crime go hand in hand, and the evidences of it stare one in the face from every side. Here the people live who begin the revolutions. Whenever there is any thing of that kind to be done, they are always ready. They take as much genuine pleasure in building a barricade as they do in cutting a throat or shoving a friend into the Seine. It is these savage-looking ruffians who storm the splendid halls of the Tuileries, occasionally, and swarm into Versailles when a King is to be called to account.

But they will build no more barricades, they will break no more soldiers' heads with paving-stones. Louis Napoleon has taken care of all that. He is annihilating the crooked streets, and building in their stead noble boulevards as straight as an arrow—avenues which a cannon ball could traverse from end to end without meeting an obstruction more irresistible than the flesh and bones of men—boulevards whose stately edifices will never afford refuges and plotting-places for starving, discontented revolution-breeders. Five of these great thorough-fares radiate from one ample centre—a centre which is exceedingly well adapted to the accommodation of heavy artillery. The mobs used to riot there, but they must seek another rallying-place in future. And this ingenious Napoleon paves the streets of his great cities with a smooth, compact composition of asphaltum and sand. No more barricades of flag-stones—no more assaulting his Majesty's troops with cobbles. I can not feel friendly toward my quondam fellow-American, Napoleon III., especially at this time,* when in fancy I see his credulous victim, Maximilian, lying stark and stiff in Mexico, and his maniac widow watching eagerly from her French asylum for the form that will never come—but I do admire his nerve, his calm self-reliance, his shrewd good sense.

*July, 1867.

Chapter XVII

WE HAD A pleasant journey of it seaward again. We found that for the three past nights our ship had been in a state of war. The first night the sailors of a British ship, being happy with grog, came down on the pier and challenged our sailors to a free fight. They accepted with alacrity, repaired to the pier and gained—their share of a drawn battle. Several bruised and bloody members of both parties were carried off by the police, and imprisoned until the following morning. The next night the British boys came again to renew the fight, but our men had had strict orders to remain on board and out of sight. They did so, and the besieging party grew noisy, and more and more abusive as the fact became apparent (to them,) that our men were afraid to come out. They went away, finally, with a closing burst of ridicule and offensive epithets. The third night they came again, and were more obstreperous than ever. They swaggered up and down the almost deserted pier, and hurled curses, obscenity and stinging sarcasms at our crew. It was more than human nature could bear. The executive officer ordered our men ashore—with instructions not to fight. They charged the British and gained a brilliant victory. I probably would not have mentioned this war had it ended differently. But I travel to learn, and I still remember that they picture no French defeats in the battle-galleries of Versailles.

It was like home to us to step on board the comfortable ship again, and smoke and lounge about her breezy decks. And yet it was not altogether like home, either, because so many members of the family were away. We missed some pleasant faces which we would rather have found at dinner, and at night there were gaps in the euchre-parties which could not be satisfactorily filled. "Moult." was in England, Jack in Switzerland, Charley in Spain. Blucher was gone, none could tell where. But we were at sea again, and we had the stars and the ocean to look at, and plenty of room to meditate in.

In due time the shores of Italy were sighted, and as we stood gazing from the decks early in the bright summer morning, the stately city of Genoa rose up out of the sea and flung back the sunlight from her hundred palaces.

Here we rest, for the present—or rather, here we have been trying to rest, for some little time, but we run about too much to accomplish a great deal in that line.

I would like to remain here. I had rather not go any further. There may be prettier women in Europe, but I doubt it. The population of Genoa is 120,000; two-thirds of these are women, I think, and at least two-thirds of the women are beautiful. They are as dressy, and as tasteful and as graceful as they could possibly be without being angels. However, angels are not very dressy, I believe. At least the angels in pictures are not—they wear nothing but wings. But these Genoese women do look so charming. Most of the young demoiselles are robed in a cloud of white from head to foot, though many trick themselves out more elaborately. Nine-tenths of them wear nothing on their heads but a filmy sort of veil, which falls down their backs like a white mist. They are very fair, and many of them have blue eyes, but black and dreamy dark brown ones are met with oftenest.

The ladies and gentlemen of Genoa have a pleasant fashion of promenading in a large park on the top of a hill in the centre of the city, from six till nine in the evening, and then eating ices in a neighboring garden an hour or two longer. We went to the park on Sunday evening. Two thousand persons were present, chiefly young ladies and gentlemen. The gentlemen were dressed in the very latest Paris fashions, and the robes of the ladies glinted among the trees like so many snow-flakes. The multitude moved round and round the park in a great procession. The bands played, and so did the fountains; the moon and the gas lamps lit up the scene, and altogether it was a brilliant and an animated picture. I scanned every female face that passed, and it seemed to me that all were handsome. I never saw such a freshet of loveliness before. I do not see how a man of only ordinary decision of character could marry here, because, before he could get his mind made up he would fall in love with somebody else.

Never smoke any Italian tobacco. Never do it on any account. It makes me shudder to think what it must be made of. You can not throw an old cigar "stub" down any where, but some vagabond will pounce upon it on the instant. I like to smoke a good deal, but it wounds my sensibilities to see one of these stub-hunters watching me out of the corners of his hungry eyes and calculating how long my cigar will be likely to last. It reminded me too painfully of that San Francisco undertaker who used to go to sick-beds with his watch in his hand and time the corpse. One of these stub-hunters followed us all over the park last night, and we never had a smoke that was worth any thing. We were always moved to appease him with the stub before the cigar was half gone, because he looked so viciously anxious. He regarded us as his own legitimate prey, by right of discovery, I think, because he drove off several other professionals who wanted to take stock in us.

Now, they surely must chew up those old stubs, and dry and sell them for smoking-tobacco. Therefore, give your custom to other than Italian brands of the article.

"The Superb" and the "City of Palaces" are names which Genoa has held for centuries. She is full of palaces, certainly, and the palaces are sumptuous inside, but they are very rusty without, and make no pretensions to architectural magnificence. "Genoa, the Superb," would be a felicitous title if it referred to the women.

We have visited several of the palaces—immense thick-walled piles, with great stone staircases, tesselated marble pavements on the floors, (sometimes they make a mosaic work, of intricate designs, wrought in pebbles, or little fragments of marble laid in cement,) and grand *salons* hung with pictures by Rubens, Guido, Titian, Paul Veronese, and so on, and portraits of heads of the family, in plumed helmets and gallant coats of mail, and patrician ladies, in stunning costumes of centuries ago. But, of course, the folks were all out in the country for the summer, and might not have known enough to ask us to dinner if they had been at home, and so all the grand empty *salons*, with their resounding pavements, their grim pictures of dead ancestors, and tattered banners with the dust of bygone centuries upon them, seemed to brood solemnly of death and the grave, and our spirits ebbed away, and our cheerfulness passed from us. We never went up to the eleventh story. We always began to suspect ghosts.

There was always an undertaker-looking servant along, too, who handed us a programme, pointed to the picture that began the list of the *salon* he was in, and then stood stiff and stark and unsmiling in his petrified livery till we were ready to move on to the next chamber, whereupon he marched sadly ahead and took up another malignantly respectful position as before. I wasted so much time praying that the roof would fall in on these dispiriting flunkeys that I had but little left to bestow upon palace and pictures.

And besides, as in Paris, we had a guide. Perdition catch all the guides. This one said he was the most gifted linguist in Genoa, as far as English was concerned, and that only two persons in the city beside himself could talk the language at all. He showed us the birthplace of Christopher Columbus, and after we had reflected in silent awe before it for fifteen minutes, he said it was not the birthplace of Columbus, but of Columbus's grandmother! When we demanded an explanation of his conduct he only shrugged his shoulders and answered in barbarous Italian. I shall speak further of this guide in a future chapter. All the information we got out of him we shall be able to carry along with us, I think.

I have not been to church so often in a long time as I have in the last few weeks. The people in these old lands seem to make churches their specialty. Especially does this seem to be the case with the citizens of Genoa. I think there is a church every three or four hundred yards all over town. The streets are sprinkled from end to end with shovel-hatted, long-robed, well-fed priests, and the church bells by dozens are pealing all the day long, nearly. Every now and then one comes across a friar of orders gray, with shaven head, long, coarse robe, rope girdle and beads, and with feet cased in sandals or entirely bare. These worthies suffer in the flesh, and do penance all their lives, I suppose, but they look like consummate famine-breeders. They are all fat and serene.

The old Cathedral of San Lorenzo is about as notable a building as we have found in Genoa. It is vast, and has colonnades of noble pillars, and a great organ, and the customary pomp of gilded moldings, pictures, frescoed ceilings, and so forth. I can not describe it, of course—it would require a good many pages to do that. But it is a curious place. They said that half of it—from the front door half way down to the altar—was a Jewish Synagogue before the Saviour was born, and that no alteration had been made in it since that time. We doubted the statement, but did it reluctantly. We would much rather have believed it. The place looked in too perfect repair to be so ancient.

The main point of interest about the Cathedral is the little Chapel of St. John the Baptist. They only allow women to enter it on one day in the year, on account of the animosity they still cherish against the sex because of the murder of the Saint to gratify a caprice of Herodias. In this Chapel is a marble chest, in which, they told us, were the ashes of St. John; and around it was wound a chain, which, they said, had confined him when he was in prison. We did not desire to disbelieve these statements, and yet we could not feel certain that they were correct—partly because we could have broken that chain, and so could St. John, and partly because we had seen St. John's ashes before, in another Church. We could not bring ourselves to think St. John had two sets of ashes.

They also showed us a portrait of the Madonna which was painted by St. Luke, and it did not look half as old and smoky as some of the pictures by Rubens. We could not help admiring the Apostle's modesty in never once mentioning in his writings that he could paint.

But isn't this relic matter a little overdone? We find a piece of the true cross in every old church we go into, and some of the nails that held it together. I would not like to be positive, but I think we have seen as much as a keg of these nails. Then there is the crown of thorns; they have part of one in Sainte Chapelle, in Paris, and part of one, also, in Notre Dame. And as for bones of St. Denis, I feel certain we have seen enough of them to duplicate him, if necessary.

I only meant to write about the churches, but I keep wandering from the subject. I could say that the Church of the Annunciation is a wilderness of beautiful columns, of statues, gilded moldings, and pictures almost countless, but that would give no one an entirely perfect idea of the thing, and so where is the use? One family built the whole edifice, and have got money left. There is where the mystery lies. We had an idea at first that only a mint could have survived the expense.

These people here live in the heaviest, highest, broadest, darkest, solidest houses one can imagine. Each one might "laugh a siege to scorn." A hundred feet front and a hundred high is about the style, and you go up three flights of stairs before you begin to come upon signs of occupancy. Every thing is stone, and stone of the heaviest—floors, stairways, mantels, benches—every thing. The walls are four to five feet thick. The streets generally are four or five to eight feet wide and as crooked as a corkscrew. You go along one of these gloomy cracks, and look up and behold the sky like a mere ribbon of light, far above your head, where the tops of the tall houses on either side of the street bend almost together. You feel as if you were at the bottom of some tremendous abyss, with all the world far above you. You wind in and out and here and there, in the most mysterious way, and have no more idea of the points of the compass than if you were a blind man. You can never persuade yourself that these are actually streets, and the frowning, dingy, monstrous houses dwellings, till you see one of these beautiful, prettily dressed women emerge from them—see her emerge from a dark, dreary-looking den that looks dungeon all over, from the ground away half-way up to heaven. And then you wonder that such a charming moth could come from such a forbidding shell as that. The streets are wisely made narrow and the houses heavy and thick and stony, in order that the people may be cool in this roasting climate. And they are cool, and stay so. And while I think of it—the men wear hats and have very dark complexions, but the women wear no head-gear but a flimsy veil like a gossamer's web, and yet are exceedingly fair as a general thing. Singular, isn't it?

The huge palaces of Genoa are each supposed to be occupied by one family, but they could accommodate a hundred, I should think. They are relics of the grandeur of Genoa's palmy days—the days when she was a great commercial and maritime power several centuries ago. These houses, solid marble palaces though they be, are in many cases of a dull pinkish color, outside, and from pavement to eaves are pictured with Genoese battle-scenes, with monstrous Jupiters and Cupids and with familiar illustrations from Grecian mythology. Where the paint has yielded to age and exposure and is peeling off in flakes and patches, the effect is not happy. A noseless Cupid, or a Jupiter with an eye out, or a Venus with a fly-blister on her breast, are not attractive features in a picture. Some of these painted walls reminded me somewhat of the tall van, plastered with fanciful bills and posters, that follows the band-wagon of a circus about a country village. I have not read or heard that the outsides of the houses of any other European city are frescoed in this way.

I can not conceive of such a thing as Genoa in ruins. Such massive arches, such ponderous substructions as support these towering broad-winged edifices, we have seldom seen before; and surely the great blocks of stone of which these edifices are built can never decay; walls that are as thick as an ordinary American doorway is high, can not crumble.

The Republics of Genoa and Pisa were very powerful in the middle ages. Their ships filled the Mediterranean, and they carried on an extensive commerce with Constantinople and Syria. Their warehouses were the great distributing depots from whence the costly merchandise of the East was sent abroad over Europe. They were warlike little nations, and defied, in those days, governments that overshadow them now as mountains overshadow molehills. The Saracens captured and pillaged Genoa nine hundred years ago, but during the following century Genoa and Pisa entered into an offensive and defensive alliance and besieged the Saracen colonies in Sardinia and the Balearic Isles with an obstinacy that maintained its pristine vigor and held to its purpose for forty long years. They were victorious at last, and divided their conquests equably among their great patrician families. Descendants of some of those proud families still inhabit the palaces of Genoa, and trace in their own features a resemblance to the grim knights whose portraits hang in their stately halls, and to pictured beauties with pouting lips and merry eyes whose originals have been dust and ashes for many a dead and forgotten century.

The hotel we live in belonged to one of those great orders of knights of the Cross in the times of the Crusades, and its mailed sentinels once kept watch and ward in its massive turrets and woke the echoes of these halls and corridors with their iron heels.

But Genoa's greatness has degenerated into an unostentatious commerce in velvets and silver filagree work. They say that each European town has its specialty. These filagree things are Genoa's specialty. Her smiths take silver ingots and work them up into all manner of graceful and beautiful forms. They make bunches of flowers, from flakes and wires of silver, that counterfeit the delicate creations the frost weaves upon a window pane; and we were shown a miniature silver temple whose fluted columns, whose Corinthian capitals and rich entablatures, whose spire, statues, bells, and ornate lavishness of sculpture were wrought in polished silver, and with such matchless art that every detail was a fascinating study, and the finished edifice a wonder of beauty.

We are ready to move again, though we are not really tired, yet, of the narrow passages of this old marble cave. Cave is a good word—when speaking of Genoa under the stars. When we have been prowling at midnight through the gloomy crevices they call streets, where no foot falls but ours were echoing, where only ourselves were abroad, and lights appeared only at long intervals and at a distance, and mysteriously disappeared again, and the houses at our elbows seemed to stretch upward farther than ever toward the heavens, the memory of a cave I used to know at home was always in my mind, with its lofty passages, its silence and solitude, its shrouding gloom, its sepulchral echoes, its flitting lights, and more than all, its sudden revelations of branching crevices and corridors where we least expected them.

We are not tired of the endless processions of cheerful, chattering gossipers that throng these courts and streets all day long, either; nor of the coarse-robed monks; nor of the "Asti" wines, which that old doctor (whom we call the Oracle,) with customary felicity in the matter of getting every thing wrong, misterms "nasty." But we must go, nevertheless.

Our last sight was the cemetery, (a burial-place intended to accommodate 60,000 bodies,) and we shall continue to remember it after we shall have forgotten the palaces. It is a vast marble collonaded corridor extending around a great unoccupied square of ground; its broad floor is marble, and on every slab is an inscription—for every slab covers a corpse. On either side, as one walks down the middle of the passage, are monuments, tombs, and sculptured figures that are exquisitely wrought and are full of grace and beauty. They are new, and snowy; every outline is perfect, every feature guiltless of mutilation, flaw or blemish; and therefore, to us these far-reaching ranks of bewitching forms are a hundred fold more lovely than the damaged and dingy statuary they have saved from the wreck of ancient art and set up in the galleries of Paris for the worship of the world.

Well provided with cigars and other necessaries of life, we are now ready to take the cars for Milan.

Chapter XVIII

ALL DAY LONG we sped through a mountainous country whose peaks were bright with sunshine, whose hillsides were dotted with pretty villas sitting in the midst of gardens and shrubbery, and whose deep ravines were cool and shady, and looked ever so inviting from where we and the birds were winging our flight through the sultry upper air.

We had plenty of chilly tunnels wherein to check our perspiration, though. We timed one of them. We were twenty minutes passing through it, going at the rate of thirty to thirty-five miles an hour.

Beyond Alessandria we passed the battle-field of Marengo.

Toward dusk we drew near Milan, and caught glimpses of the city and the blue mountain peaks beyond. But we were not caring for these things—they did not interest us in the least. We were in a fever of impatience; we were dying to see the renowned Cathedral! We watched—in this direction and that—all around—every where. We needed no one to point it out—we did not wish any one to point it out—we would recognize it, even in the desert of the great Sahara.

At last, a forest of graceful needles, shimmering in the amber sunlight, rose slowly above the pigmy house-tops, as one sometimes sees, in the far horizon, a gilded and pinnacled mass of cloud lift itself above the waste of waves, at sea,—the Cathedral! We knew it in a moment.

Half of that night, and all of the next day, this architectural autocrat was our sole object of interest.

What a wonder it is! So grand, so solemn, so vast! And yet so delicate, so airy, so graceful! A very world of solid weight, and yet it seems in the soft moonlight only a fairy delusion of frost-work that might vanish with a breath! How sharply its pinnacled angles and its wilderness of spires were cut against the sky, and how richly their shadows fell upon its snowy roof! It was a vision!—a miracle!—an anthem sung in stone, a poem wrought in marble!

Howsoever you look at the great Cathedral, it is noble, it is beautiful! Wherever you stand in Milan, or within seven miles of Milan, it is visible—and when it is visible, no other object can chain your whole attention. Leave your eyes unfettered by your will but a single instant and they will surely turn to seek it. It is the first thing you look for when you rise in the morning, and the last your lingering gaze rests upon at night. Surely, it must be the princeliest creation that ever brain of man conceived.

At nine o'clock in the morning we went and stood before this marble colossus. The central one of its five great doors is bordered with a bas-relief of birds and fruits and beasts and insects, which have been so ingeniously carved out of the marble that they seem like living creatures—and the figures are so numerous and the design so complex, that one might study it a week without exhausting its interest. On the great steeple—surmounting the myriad of spires—inside of the spires—over the doors, the windows—in nooks and corners—every where that a niche or a perch can be found about the enormous building, from summit to base, there is a marble statue, and every statue is a study in itself! Raphael, Angelo, Canova—giants like these gave birth to the designs, and their own pupils carved them. Every face is eloquent with expression, and every attitude is full of grace. Away above, on the lofty roof, rank on rank of carved and fretted spires spring high in the air, and through their rich tracery one sees the sky beyond. In their midst the central steeple towers proudly up like the mainmast of some great Indiaman among a fleet of coasters.

We wished to go aloft. The sacristan showed us a marble stairway (of course it was marble, and of the purest and whitest—there is no other stone, no brick, no wood, among its building materials,) and told us to go up one hundred and eighty-two steps and stop till he came. It was not necessary to say stop—we should have done that any how. We were tired by the time we got there. This was the roof. Here, springing from its broad marble flagstones, were the long files of spires, looking very tall close at hand, but diminishing in the distance like the pipes of an organ. We could see, now, that the statue on the top of each was the size of a large man, though they all looked like dolls from the street. We could see, also, that from the inside of each and every one of these

hollow spires, from sixteen to thirty-one beautiful marble statues looked out upon the world below.

From the eaves to the comb of the roof stretched in endless
succession great curved marble beams, like the fore-and-aft
braces of a steamboat, and along each beam from end to end
stood up a row of richly carved flowers and fruits—each separate and distinct in kind, and over 15,000 species represented.
At a little distance these rows seem to close together like the
ties of a railroad track, and then the mingling together of the
buds and blossoms of this marble garden forms a picture that
is very charming to the eye.

We descended and entered. Within the church, long rows
of fluted columns, like huge monuments, divided the building into broad aisles, and on the figured pavement fell many
a soft blush from the painted windows above. I knew the
church was very large, but I could not fully appreciate its
great size until I noticed that the men standing far down by
the altar looked like boys, and seemed to glide, rather than
walk. We loitered about gazing aloft at the monster windows
all aglow with brilliantly colored scenes in the lives of the
Saviour and his followers. Some of these pictures are mosaics, and so artistically are their thousand particles of tinted
glass or stone put together that the work has all the smoothness and finish of a painting. We counted sixty panes of glass
in one window, and each pane was adorned with one of
these master achievements of genius and patience.

The guide showed us a coffee-colored piece of sculpture
which he said was considered to have come from the hand of
Phidias, since it was not possible that any other artist, of any
epoch, could have copied nature with such faultless accuracy.
The figure was that of a man without a skin; with every vein,
artery, muscle, every fibre and tendon and tissue of the human frame, represented in minute detail. It looked natural,
because somehow it looked as if it were in pain. A skinned
man would be likely to look that way, unless his attention
were occupied with some other matter. It was a hideous
thing, and yet there was a fascination about it some where. I
am very sorry I saw it, because I shall always see it, now. I
shall dream of it, sometimes. I shall dream that it is resting its
corded arms on the bed's head and looking down on me with

its dead eyes; I shall dream that it is stretched between the sheets with me and touching me with its exposed muscles and its stringy cold legs.

It is hard to forget repulsive things. I remember yet how I ran off from school once, when I was a boy, and then, pretty late at night, concluded to climb into the window of my father's office and sleep on a lounge, because I had a delicacy about going home and getting thrashed. As I lay on the lounge and my eyes grew accustomed to the darkness, I fancied I could see a long, dusky, shapeless thing stretched upon the floor. A cold shiver went through me. I turned my face to the wall. That did not answer. I was afraid that that thing would creep over and seize me in the dark. I turned back and stared at it for minutes and minutes—they seemed hours. It appeared to me that the lagging moonlight never, never would get to it. I turned to the wall and counted twenty, to pass the feverish time away. I looked—the pale square was nearer. I turned again and counted fifty—it was almost touching it. With desperate will I turned again and counted one hundred, and faced about, all in a tremble. A white human hand lay in the moonlight! Such an awful sinking at the heart—such a sudden gasp for breath! I felt—I can not tell *what* I felt. When I recovered strength enough, I faced the wall again. But no boy could have remained so, with that mysterious hand behind him. I counted again, and looked—the most of a naked arm was exposed. I put my hands over my eyes and counted till I could stand it no longer, and then—the pallid face of a man was there, with the corners of the mouth drawn down, and the eyes fixed and glassy in death! I raised to a sitting posture and glowered on that corpse till the light crept down the bare breast,—line by line—inch by inch—past the nipple,—and then it disclosed a ghastly stab!

I went away from there. I do not say that I went away in any sort of a hurry, but I simply went—that is sufficient. I went out at the window, and I carried the sash along with me. I did not need the sash, but it was handier to take it than it was to leave it, and so I took it.—I was not scared, but I was considerably agitated.

When I reached home, they whipped me, but I enjoyed it.

It seemed perfectly delightful. That man had been stabbed near the office that afternoon, and they carried him in there to doctor him, but he only lived an hour. I have slept in the same room with him often, since then—in my dreams.

Now we will descend into the crypt, under the grand altar of Milan Cathedral, and receive an impressive sermon from lips that have been silent and hands that have been gestureless for three hundred years.

The priest stopped in a small dungeon and held up his candle. This was the last resting-place of a good man, a warm-hearted, unselfish man; a man whose whole life was given to succoring the poor, encouraging the faint-hearted, visiting the sick; in relieving distress, whenever and wherever he found it. His heart, his hand and his purse were always open. With his story in one's mind he can almost see his benignant countenance moving calmly among the haggard faces of Milan in the days when the plague swept the city, brave where all others were cowards, full of compassion where pity had been crushed out of all other breasts by the instinct of self-preservation gone mad with terror, cheering all, praying with all, helping all, with hand and brain and purse, at a time when parents forsook their children, the friend deserted the friend, and the brother turned away from the sister while her pleadings were still wailing in his ears.

This was good St. Charles Borroméo, Bishop of Milan. The people idolized him; princes lavished uncounted treasures upon him. We stood in his tomb. Near by was the sarcophagus, lighted by the dripping candles. The walls were faced with bas-reliefs representing scenes in his life done in massive silver. The priest put on a short white lace garment over his black robe, crossed himself, bowed reverently, and began to turn a windlass slowly. The sarcophagus separated in two parts, lengthwise, and the lower part sank down and disclosed a coffin of rock crystal as clear as the atmosphere. Within lay the body, robed in costly habiliments covered with gold embroidery and starred with scintillating gems. The decaying head was black with age, the dry skin was drawn tight to the bones, the eyes were gone, there was a hole in the temple and another in the cheek, and the skinny lips were parted as in a ghastly smile! Over this dreadful face, its dust and decay, and its mocking grin, hung a crown sown thick with flashing brilliants; and upon the breast lay crosses and croziers of solid gold that were splendid with emeralds and diamonds.

How poor, and cheap, and trivial these gew-gaws seemed in presence of the solemnity, the grandeur, the awful majesty of Death! Think of Milton, Shakspeare, Washington, standing before a reverent world tricked out in the glass beads, the brass ear-rings and tin trumpery of the savages of the plains!

Dead Bartoloméo preached his pregnant sermon, and its burden was: You that worship the vanities of earth—you that long for worldly honor, worldly wealth, worldly fame—behold their worth!

To us it seemed that so good a man, so kind a heart, so simple a nature, deserved rest and peace in a grave sacred from the intrusion of prying eyes, and believed that he himself would have preferred to have it so, but peradventure our wisdom was at fault in this regard.

As we came out upon the floor of the church again, another priest volunteered to show us the treasures of the church. What, more? The furniture of the narrow chamber of death we had just visited, weighed six millions of francs in ounces and carats alone, without a penny thrown into the account for the costly workmanship bestowed upon them! But we followed into a large room filled with tall wooden presses like wardrobes. He threw them open, and behold, the cargoes of "crude bullion" of the assay offices of Nevada faded out of my memory. There were Virgins and bishops there, above their natural size, made of solid silver, each worth, by weight, from eight hundred thousand to two millions of francs, and bearing gemmed books in their hands worth eighty thousand; there were bas-reliefs that weighed six hundred pounds, carved in solid silver; croziers and crosses, and candlesticks six and eight feet high, all of virgin gold, and brilliant with precious stones; and beside these were all manner of cups and vases, and such things, rich in proportion. It was an Aladdin's palace. The treasures here, by simple weight, without counting workmanship, were valued at fifty millions of francs! If I could get the custody of them for a while, I fear me the market price of silver bishops would advance shortly, on account of their exceeding scarcity in the Cathedral of Milan.

The priests showed us two of St. Paul's fingers, and one of St. Peter's; a bone of Judas Iscariot, (it was black,) and also bones of all the other disciples; a handkerchief in which the Saviour had left the impression of his face. Among the most precious of the relics were a stone from the Holy Sepulchre, part of the crown of thorns, (they have a whole one at Notre Dame,) a fragment of the purple robe worn by the Saviour, a nail from the Cross, and a picture of the Virgin and Child painted by the veritable hand of St. Luke. This is the second of St. Luke's Virgins we have seen. Once a year all these holy relics are carried in procession through the streets of Milan.

I like to revel in the dryest details of the great cathedral. The building is five hundred feet long by one hundred and eighty wide, and the principal steeple is in the neighborhood of four hundred feet high. It has 7,148 marble statues, and will have upwards of three thousand more when it is finished. In addition, it has one thousand five hundred bas-reliefs. It has one hundred and thirty-six spires—twenty-one more are to be added. Each spire is surmounted by a statue six and a half feet high. Every thing about the church is marble, and all from the same quarry; it was bequeathed to the Archbishopric for this purpose centuries ago. So nothing but the mere workmanship costs; still that is expensive—the bill foots up six hundred and eighty-four millions of francs, thus far (considerably over a hundred millions of dollars,) and it is estimated that it will take a hundred and twenty years yet to finish the cathedral. It looks complete, but is far from being so. We saw a new statue put in its niche yesterday, alongside of one which had been standing these four hundred years, they said. There are four staircases leading up to the main steeple, each of which cost a hundred thousand dollars, with the four hundred and eight statues which adorn them. Marco Compioni was the architect who designed the wonderful structure more than five hundred years ago, and it took him forty-six years to work out the plan and get it ready to hand over to the builders. He is dead now. The building was begun a little less than five hundred years ago, and the third generation hence will not see it completed.

The building looks best by moonlight, because the older portions of it being stained with age, contrast unpleasantly with the newer and whiter portions. It seems somewhat too broad for its height, but may be familiarity with it might dissipate this impression.

They say that the Cathedral of Milan is second only to St. Peter's at Rome. I can not understand how it can be second to any thing made by human hands.

We bid it good-bye, now—possibly for all time. How surely, in some future day, when the memory of it shall have lost its vividness, shall we half believe we have seen it in a wonderful dream, but never with waking eyes!

Chapter XIX

"DO YOU wis zo haut can be?"

That was what the guide asked, when we were looking up at the bronze horses on the Arch of Peace. It meant, do you wish to go up there? I give it as a specimen of guide-English. These are the people that make life a burthen to the tourist. Their tongues are never still. They talk forever and forever, and that is the kind of billingsgate they use. Inspiration itself could hardly comprehend them. If they would only show you a masterpiece of art, or a venerable tomb, or a prison-house, or a battle-field, hallowed by touching memories or historical reminiscences, or grand traditions, and then step aside and hold still for ten minutes and let you think, it would not be so bad. But they interrupt every dream, every pleasant train of thought, with their tiresome cackling. Sometimes when I have been standing before some cherished old idol of mine that I remembered years and years ago in pictures in the geography at school, I have thought I would give a whole world if the human parrot at my side would suddenly perish where he stood and leave me to gaze, and ponder, and worship.

No, we did not "wis zo haut can be." We wished to go to La Scala, the largest theatre in the world, I think they call it. We did so. It was a large place. Seven separate and distinct masses of humanity—six great circles and a monster parquette.

We wished to go to the Ambrosian Library, and we did that also. We saw a manuscript of Virgil, with annotations in the handwriting of Petrarch, the gentleman who loved another man's Laura, and lavished upon her all through life a love which was a clear waste of the raw material. It was sound sentiment, but bad judgment. It brought both parties fame, and created a fountain of commiseration for them in sentimental breasts that is running yet. But who says a word in behalf of poor Mr. Laura? (I do not know his other name.) Who glorifies him? Who bedews him with tears? Who writes poetry about him? Nobody. How do you suppose *he* liked the state of things that has given the world so much pleasure?

How did he enjoy having another man following his wife every where and making her name a familiar word in every garlic-exterminating mouth in Italy with his sonnets to her pre-empted eyebrows? *They* got fame and sympathy—he got neither. This is a peculiarly felicitous instance of what is called poetical justice. It is all very fine; but it does not chime with my notions of right. It is too one-sided—too ungenerous. Let the world go on fretting about Laura and Petrarch if it will; but as for me, my tears and my lamentations shall be lavished upon the unsung defendant.

We saw also an autograph letter of Lucrezia Borgia, a lady for whom I have always entertained the highest respect, on account of her rare histrionic capabilities, her opulence in solid gold goblets made of gilded wood, her high distinction as an operatic screamer, and the facility with which she could order a sextuple funeral and get the corpses ready for it. We saw one single coarse yellow hair from Lucrezia's head, likewise. It awoke emotions, but we still live. In this same library we saw some drawings by Michael Angelo (these Italians call him Mickel Angelo,) and Leonardo da Vinci. (They spell it Vinci and pronounce it Vinchy; foreigners always spell better than they pronounce.) We reserve our opinion of these sketches.

In another building they showed us a fresco representing some lions and other beasts drawing chariots; and they seemed to project so far from the wall that we took them to be sculptures. The artist had shrewdly heightened the delusion by painting dust on the creatures' backs, as if it had fallen there naturally and properly. Smart fellow—if it be smart to deceive strangers.

Elsewhere we saw a huge Roman amphitheatre, with its stone seats still in good preservation. Modernized, it is now the scene of more peaceful recreations than the exhibition of a party of wild beasts with Christians for dinner. Part of the time, the Milanese use it for a race track, and at other seasons they flood it with water and have spirited yachting regattas there. The guide told us these things, and he would hardly try so hazardous an experiment as the telling of a falsehood, when it is all he can do to speak the truth in English without getting the lock-jaw.

In another place we were shown a sort of summer arbor, with a fence before it. We said that was nothing. We looked again, and saw, through the arbor, an endless stretch of garden, and shrubbery, and grassy lawn. We were perfectly willing to go in there and rest, but it could not be done. It was only another delusion—a painting by some ingenious artist with little charity in his heart for tired folk. The deception was perfect. No one could have imagined the park was not real. We even thought we smelled the flowers at first.

We got a carriage at twilight and drove in the shaded avenues with the other nobility, and after dinner we took wine and ices in a fine garden with the great public. The music was excellent, the flowers and shrubbery were pleasant to the eye, the scene was vivacious, every body was genteel and well-behaved, and the ladies were slightly moustached, and handsomely dressed, but very homely.

We adjourned to a café and played billiards an hour, and I made six or seven points by the doctor pocketing his ball, and he made as many by my pocketing my ball. We came near making a carom sometimes, but not the one we were trying to make. The table was of the usual European style—cushions dead and twice as high as the balls; the cues in bad repair. The natives play only a sort of pool on them. We have never seen any body playing the French three-ball game yet, and I doubt if there is any such game known in France, or that there lives any man mad enough to try to play it on one of these European tables. We had to stop playing, finally, because Dan got to sleeping fifteen minutes between the counts and paying no attention to his marking.

Afterward we walked up and down one of the most popular streets for some time, enjoying other people's comfort and wishing we could export some of it to our restless, driving, vitality-consuming marts at home. Just in this one matter lies the main charm of life in Europe—comfort. In America, we hurry—which is well; but when the day's work is done, we go on thinking of losses and gains, we plan for the morrow, we even carry our business cares to bed with us, and toss and worry over them when we ought to be restoring our racked bodies and brains with sleep. We burn up our energies with these excitements, and either die early or drop into a lean and mean old age at a time of life which they call a man's prime in Europe. When an acre of ground has produced long and well, we let it lie fallow and rest for a season; we take no man clear across the continent in the same coach he started in—the coach is stabled somewhere on the plains and its heated machinery allowed to cool for a few days; when a razor has seen long service and refuses to hold an edge, the barber lays it away for a few weeks, and the edge comes back of its own accord. We bestow thoughtful care upon inanimate objects, but none upon ourselves. What a robust people, what a nation of thinkers we might be, if we would only lay ourselves on the shelf occasionally and renew our edges!

I do envy these Europeans the comfort they take. When the work of the day is done, they forget it. Some of them go, with wife and children, to a beer hall, and sit quietly and genteelly drinking a mug or two of ale and listening to music; others walk the streets, others drive in the avenues; others assemble in the great ornamental squares in the early evening to enjoy the sight and the fragrance of flowers and to hear the military bands play—no European city being without its fine military music at eventide; and yet others of the populace sit in the open air in front of the refreshment houses and eat ices and drink mild beverages that could not harm a child. They go to bed moderately early, and sleep well. They are always quiet, always orderly, always cheerful, comfortable, and appreciative of life and its manifold blessings. One never sees a drunken man among them. The change that has come over our little party is surprising. Day by day we lose some of our restlessness and absorb some of the spirit of quietude and ease that is in the tranquil atmosphere about us and in the demeanor of the people. We grow wise apace. We begin to comprehend what life is for.

We have had a bath in Milan, in a public bath-house. They were going to put all three of us in one bath-tub, but we objected. Each of us had an Italian farm on his back. We could have felt affluent if we had been officially surveyed and fenced in. We chose to have three bath-tubs, and large ones—tubs suited to the dignity of aristocrats who had real estate, and brought it with them. After we were stripped and had taken the first chilly dash, we discovered that haunting atrocity that has embittered our lives in so many cities and villages of Italy and France—there was no soap. I called. A woman answered, and I barely had time to throw myself against the door—she would have been in, in another second. I said:

"Beware, woman! Go away from here—go away, now, or it will be the worse for you. I am an unprotected male, but I will preserve my honor at the peril of my life!"

These words must have frightened her, for she skurried away very fast.

Dan's voice rose on the air:

"Oh, bring some soap, why don't you!"

The reply was Italian. Dan resumed:

"Soap, you know—soap. That is what I want—soap. S-o-a-p, soap; s-o-p-e, soap; s-o-u-p, soap. Hurry up! I don't know how you Irish spell it, but I want it. Spell it to suit yourself, but fetch it. I'm freezing."

I heard the doctor say, impressively:

"Dan, how often have we told you that these foreigners can not understand English? Why will you not depend upon us? Why will you not tell *us* what you want, and let us ask for it in the language of the country? It would save us a great deal of the humiliation your reprehensible ignorance causes us. I will address this person in his mother tongue: 'Here, cospetto! corpo di Bacco! Sacramento! Solferino!—Soap, you son of a gun!' Dan, if you would let *us* talk for you, you would never expose your ignorant vulgarity."

Even this fluent discharge of Italian did not bring the soap at once, but there was a good reason for it. There was not such an article about the establishment. It is my belief that there never had been. They had to send far up town, and to several different places before they finally got it, so they said. We had to wait twenty or thirty minutes. The same thing had occurred the evening before, at the hotel. I think I have divined the reason for this state of things at last. The English know how to travel comfortably, and they carry soap with them; other foreigners do not use the article.

At every hotel we stop at we always have to send out for soap, at the last moment, when we are grooming ourselves for dinner, and they put it in the bill along with the candles and other nonsense. In Marseilles they make half the fancy toilet soap we consume in America, but the Marseillaise only have a vague theoretical idea of its use, which they have obtained from books of travel, just as they have acquired an uncertain notion of clean shirts, and the peculiarities of the gorilla, and other curious matters. This reminds me of poor Blucher's note to the landlord in Paris:

"PARIS, le 7 Juillet.

"*Monsieur le Landlord*—Sir: *Pourquoi* don't you *mettez* some *savon* in your bed-chambers? *Est-ce que vous pensez* I will steal it? *La nuit passée* you charged me *pour deux chandelles* when I only had one; *hier vous avez* charged me *avec glace* when I had none at all; *tout les jours* you are coming some fresh game or other on me, *mais vous ne pouvez pas* play this *savon* dodge on me twice. *Savon* is a necessary *de la vie* to any body but a Frenchman, *et je l'aurai hors de cet hôtel* or make trouble. You hear *me. Allons.*

BLUCHER."

I remonstrated against the sending of this note, because it was so mixed up that the landlord would never be able to make head or tail of it; but Blucher said he guessed the old man could read the French of it and average the rest.

Blucher's French is bad enough, but it is not much worse than the English one finds in advertisements all over Italy every day. For instance, observe the printed card of the hotel we shall probably stop at on the shores of Lake Como:

"NOTISH."

"This hotel which the best it is in Italy and most superb, is handsome locate on the best situation of the lake, with the most splendid view near the Villas Melzy, to the King of Belgian, and Serbelloni. This hotel have recently enlarge, do offer all commodities on moderate price, at the strangers gentlemen who whish spend the seasons on the Lake Como."

How is that, for a specimen? In the hotel is a handsome little chapel where an English clergyman is employed to preach to such of the guests of the house as hail from England and America, and this fact is also set forth in barbarous English in the same advertisement. Wouldn't you have supposed that the adventurous linguist who framed the card would have known enough to submit it to that clergyman before he sent it to the printer?

Here, in Milan, in an ancient tumble-down ruin of a church, is the mournful wreck of the most celebrated painting in the world—"The Last Supper," by Leonardo da Vinci. We are not infallible judges of pictures, but of course we went there to see this wonderful painting, once so beautiful, always so worshipped by masters in art, and forever to be famous in song and story. And the first thing that occurred was the infliction on us of a placard fairly reeking with wretched English. Take a morsel of it:

"Bartholomew (that is the first figure on the left hand side at the spectator,) uncertain and doubtful about what he thinks to have heard, and upon which he wants to be assured by himself at Christ and by no others."

Good, isn't it? And then Peter is described as "argumenting in a threatening and angrily condition at Judas Iscariot."

This paragraph recalls the picture. "The Last Supper" is painted on the dilapidated wall of what was a little chapel attached to the main church in ancient times, I suppose. It is battered and scarred in every direction, and stained and discolored by time, and Napoleon's horses kicked the legs off most the disciples when they (the horses, not the disciples,) were stabled there more than half a century ago.

I recognized the old picture in a moment—the Saviour with bowed head seated at the centre of a long, rough table with scattering fruits and dishes upon it, and six disciples on either side in their long robes, talking to each other—the picture from which all engravings and all copies have been made for three centuries. Perhaps no living man has ever known an attempt to paint the Lord's Supper differently. The world seems to have become settled in the belief, long ago, that it is not possible for human genius to outdo this creation of Da Vinci's. I suppose painters will go on copying it as long as any of the original is left visible to the eye. There were a dozen easels in the room, and as many artists transferring the great picture to their canvases. Fifty proofs of steel engravings and lithographs were scattered around, too. And as usual, I could not help noticing how superior the copies were to the original, that is, to my inexperienced eye. Wherever you find a Raphael, a Rubens, a Michael Angelo, a Caracci, or a Da Vinci (and we see them every day,) you find artists copying them, and the copies are always the handsomest. May be the originals were handsome when they were new, but they are not now.

This picture is about thirty feet long, and ten or twelve high, I should think, and the figures are at least life size. It is one of the largest paintings in Europe.

The colors are dimmed with age; the countenances are scaled and marred, and nearly all expression is gone from them; the hair is a dead blur upon the wall, and there is no life in the eyes. Only the attitudes are certain.

People come here from all parts of the world, and glorify this masterpiece. They stand entranced before it with bated breath and parted lips, and when they speak, it is only in the catchy ejaculations of rapture:

"O, wonderful!"

"Such expression!"

"Such grace of attitude!"

"Such dignity!"

"Such faultless drawing!"

"Such matchless coloring!"

"Such feeling!"

"What delicacy of touch!"

"What sublimity of conception!"

"A vision! a vision!"

I only envy these people; I envy them their honest admiration, if it be honest—their delight, if they feel delight. I harbor no animosity toward any of them. But at the same time the thought *will* intrude itself upon me, How can they see what is not visible? What would you think of a man who looked at some decayed, blind, toothless, pock-marked Cleopatra, and said: "What matchless beauty! What soul! What expression!" What would you think of a man who gazed upon a dingy, foggy sunset, and said: "What sublimity! what feeling! what richness of coloring!" What would you think of a man who stared in ecstacy upon a desert of stumps and said: "Oh, my soul, my beating heart, what a noble forest is here!"

You would think that those men had an astonishing talent for seeing things that had already passed away. It was what I thought when I stood before the Last Supper and heard men apostrophizing wonders, and beauties and perfections which had faded out of the picture and gone, a hundred years before they were born. We can imagine the beauty that was once in an aged face; we can imagine the forest if we see the stumps; but we can not absolutely *see* these things when they are not there. I am willing to believe that the eye of the practiced artist can rest upon the Last Supper and renew a lustre where only a hint of it is left, supply a tint that has faded away, restore an expression that is gone; patch, and color, and add, to the dull canvas until at last its figures shall stand before him aglow with the life, the feeling, the freshness, yea, with all the noble beauty that was theirs when first they came from the hand of the master. But *I* can not work this miracle. Can those other uninspired visitors do it, or do they only happily imagine they do?

After reading so much about it, I am satisfied that the Last Supper was a very miracle of art once. But it was three hundred years ago.

It vexes me to hear people talk so glibly of "feeling," "expression," "tone," and those other easily acquired and in-expensive technicalities of art that make such a fine show in conversations concerning pictures. There is not one man in seventy-five hundred that can tell *what* a pictured face is intended to express. There is not one man in five hundred that can go into a court-room and be sure that he will not mistake some harmless innocent of a juryman for the black-hearted assassin on trial. Yet such people talk of "character" and presume to interpret "expression" in pictures. There is an old story that Matthews, the actor, was once lauding the ability of the human face to express the passions and emotions hidden in the breast. He said the countenance could disclose what was passing in the heart plainer than the tongue could.

"Now," he said, "observe my face—what does it express?"

"Despair!"

"Bah, it expresses peaceful resignation! What does *this* express?"

"Rage!"

"Stuff! it means terror! *This!*"

"Imbecility!"

"Fool! It is smothered ferocity! Now *this!*"

"Joy!"

"Oh, perdition! *Any* ass can see it means insanity!"

Expression! People coolly pretend to read it who would think themselves presumptuous if they pretended to interpret the hieroglyphics on the obelisks of Luxor—yet they are fully as competent to do the one thing as the other. I have heard two very intelligent critics speak of Murillo's Immaculate Conception (now in the museum at Seville,) within the past few days. One said:

"Oh, the Virgin's face is full of the ecstasy of a joy that is complete—that leaves nothing more to be desired on earth!"

The other said:

"Ah, that wonderful face is so humble, so pleading—it says as plainly as words could say it: 'I fear; I tremble; I am unworthy. But Thy will be done; sustain Thou Thy servant!'"

The reader can see the picture in any drawing-room; it can be easily recognized: the Virgin (the only young and really beautiful Virgin that was ever painted by one of the old masters, some of us think,) stands in the crescent of the new moon, with a multitude of cherubs hovering about her, and more coming; her hands are crossed upon her breast, and upon her uplifted countenance falls a glory out of the heavens. The reader may amuse himself, if he chooses, in trying to determine which of these gentlemen read the Virgin's "expression" aright, or if either of them did it.

Any one who is acquainted with the old masters will comprehend how much the Last Supper is damaged when I say that the spectator can not really tell, now, whether the disciples are Hebrews or Italians. These ancient painters never succeeded in denationalizing themselves. The Italian artists painted Italian Virgins, the Dutch painted Dutch Virgins, the Virgins of the French painters were Frenchwomen—none of them ever put into the face of the Madonna that indescribable something which proclaims the Jewess, whether you find her in New York, in Constantinople, in Paris, Jerusalem, or in the Empire of Morocco. I saw in the Sandwich Islands, once, a picture, copied by a talented German artist from an engraving in one of the American illustrated papers. It was an allegory, representing Mr. Davis in the act of signing a secession act or some such document. Over him hovered the ghost of Washington in warning attitude, and in the background a troop of shadowy soldiers in Continental uniform were limping with shoeless, bandaged feet through a driving snow-storm. Valley Forge was suggested, of course. The copy seemed accurate, and yet there was a discrepancy somewhere. After a long examination I discovered what it was—the shadowy soldiers were all Germans! Jeff. Davis was a German! even the hovering ghost was a German ghost! The artist had unconsciously worked his nationality into the picture. To tell the truth, I am getting a little perplexed about John the Baptist and his portraits. In France I finally grew reconciled to him as a Frenchman; here he is unquestionably an Italian. What next? Can it be possible that the painters make John the Baptist a Spaniard in Madrid and an Irishman in Dublin?

We took an open barouche and drove two miles out of Milan to "see ze echo," as the guide expressed it. The road was smooth, it was bordered by trees, fields, and grassy meadows, and the soft air was filled with the odor of flowers. Troops of picturesque peasant girls, coming from work, hooted at us, shouted at us, made all manner of game of us, and entirely delighted me. My long-cherished judgment was confirmed. I always did think those frowsy, romantic, unwashed peasant girls I had read so much about in poetry were a glaring fraud.

We enjoyed our jaunt. It was an exhilarating relief from tiresome sight-seeing.

We distressed ourselves very little about the astonishing echo the guide talked so much about. We were growing accustomed to encomiums on wonders that too often proved no wonders at all. And so we were most happily disappointed to find in the sequel that the guide had even failed to rise to the magnitude of his subject.

We arrived at a tumble-down old rookery called the Palazzo Simonetti—a massive hewn-stone affair occupied by a family of ragged Italians. A good-looking young girl conducted us to a window on the second floor which looked out on a court

walled on three sides by tall buildings. She put her head out
at the window and shouted. The echo answered more times
than we could count. She took a speaking trumpet and
through it she shouted, sharp and quick, a single

"Ha!" The echo answered:

"Ha!——ha!——ha!——ha!—ha!—ha! ha! h-a-a-a-a-a!"
and finally went off into a rollicking convulsion of the jolliest
laughter that could be imagined. It was so joyful—so long
continued—so perfectly cordial and hearty, that every body
was forced to join in. There was no resisting it.

Then the girl took a gun and fired it. We stood ready to
count the astonishing clatter of reverberations. We could not
say one, two, three, fast enough, but we could dot our notebooks with our pencil points almost rapidly enough to take
down a sort of short-hand report of the result. My page revealed the following account. I could not keep up, but I did
as well as I could:

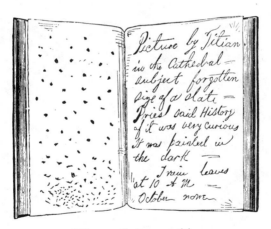

Picture by Titian—
in the Cathedral—
subject forgotten
size of a slate =
Priest said History
of it was very curious
It was painted in
the dark —
I rain leaves
at 10 A M =
October none =

Fifty-two distinct repetitions.

I set down fifty-two distinct repetitions, and then the echo
got the advantage of me. The doctor set down sixty-four, and
thenceforth the echo moved too fast for him, also. After the
separate concussions could no longer be noted, the reverberations dwindled to a wild, long-sustained clatter of sounds

such as a watchman's rattle produces. It is likely that this is the most remarkable echo in the world.

The doctor, in jest, offered to kiss the young girl, and was taken a little aback when she said he might for a franc! The commonest gallantry compelled him to stand by his offer, and so he paid the franc and took the kiss. She was a philosopher. She said a franc was a good thing to have, and she did not care any thing for one paltry kiss, because she had a million left. Then our comrade, always a shrewd business man, offered to take the whole cargo at thirty days, but that little financial scheme was a failure.

Chapter XX

WE LEFT MILAN by rail. The Cathedral six or seven miles behind us—vast, dreamy, blueish snow-clad mountains twenty miles in front of us,—these were the accented points in the scenery. The more immediate scenery consisted of fields and farm-houses outside the car and a monster-headed dwarf and a moustached woman inside it. These latter were not show-people. Alas, deformity and female beards are too common in Italy to attract attention.

We passed through a range of wild, picturesque hills, steep, wooded, cone-shaped, with rugged crags projecting here and there, and with dwellings and ruinous castles perched away up toward the drifting clouds. We lunched at the curious old town of Como, at the foot of the lake, and then took the small steamer and had an afternoon's pleasure excursion to this place,—Bellaggio.

When we walked ashore, a party of policemen (people whose cocked hats and showy uniforms would shame the finest uniform in the military service of the United States,) put us into a little stone cell and locked us in. We had the whole passenger list for company, but their room would have been preferable, for there was no light, there were no windows, no ventilation. It was close and hot. We were much crowded. It was the Black Hole of Calcutta on a small scale. Presently a smoke rose about our feet—a smoke that smelt of all the dead things of earth, of all the putrefaction and corruption imaginable.

We were there five minutes, and when we got out it was hard to tell which of us carried the vilest fragrance.

These miserable outcasts called that "fumigating" us, and the term was a tame one indeed. They fumigated us to guard themselves against the cholera, though we hailed from no infected port. We had left the cholera far behind us all the time. However, they must keep epidemics away somehow or other, and fumigation is cheaper than soap. They must either wash themselves or fumigate other people. Some of the lower classes had rather die than wash, but the fumigation of strangers causes them no pangs. They need no fumigation themselves. Their habits make it unnecessary. They carry their preventive with them; they sweat and fumigate all the day long. I trust I am a humble and a consistent Christian. I try to do what is right. I know it is my duty to "pray for them that despitefully use me;" and therefore, hard as it is, I shall still try to pray for these fumigating, maccaroni-stuffing organ grinders.

Our hotel sits at the water's edge—at least its front garden does—and we walk among the shrubbery and smoke at twilight; we look afar off at Switzerland and the Alps, and feel an indolent willingness to look no closer; we go down the steps and swim in the lake; we take a shapely little boat and sail abroad among the reflections of the stars; lie on the thwarts and listen to the distant laughter, the singing, the soft melody of flutes and guitars that comes floating across the water from pleasuring gondolas; we close the evening with exasperating billiards on one of those same old execrable tables. A midnight luncheon in our ample bed-chamber; a final smoke in its contracted veranda facing the water, the gardens and the mountains; a summing up of the day's events. Then to bed, with drowsy brains harassed with a mad panorama that mixes up pictures of France, of Italy, of the ship, of the ocean, of home, in grotesque and bewildering disorder. Then a melting away of familiar faces, of cities and of tossing waves, into a great calm of forgetfulness and peace.

After which, the nightmare.

Breakfast in the morning, and then the Lake.

I did not like it yesterday. I thought Lake Tahoe was *much* finer. I have to confess now, however, that my judgment erred somewhat, though not extravagantly. I always had an idea that Como was a vast basin of water, like Tahoe, shut in by great mountains. Well, the border of huge mountains is here, but the lake itself is not a basin. It is as crooked as any brook, and only from one-quarter to two-thirds as wide as the Mississippi. There is not a yard of low ground on either side of it—nothing but endless chains of mountains that spring abruptly from the water's edge, and tower to altitudes varying from a thousand to two thousand feet. Their craggy sides are clothed with vegetation, and white specks of houses peep out from the luxuriant foliage every where; they are even perched upon jutting and picturesque pinnacles a thousand feet above your head.

Again, for miles along the shores, handsome country seats, surrounded by gardens and groves, sit fairly in the water, sometimes in nooks carved by Nature out of the vine-hung precipices, and with no ingress or egress save by boats. Some have great broad stone staircases leading down to the water, with heavy stone balustrades ornamented with statuary and fancifully adorned with creeping vines and bright-colored flowers—for all the world like a drop-curtain in a theatre, and lacking nothing but long-waisted, high-heeled women and plumed gallants in silken tights coming down to go serenading in the splendid gondola in waiting.

A great feature of Como's attractiveness is the multitude of pretty houses and gardens that cluster upon its shores and on its mountain sides. They look so snug and so homelike, and at eventide when every thing seems to slumber, and the music of the vesper bells comes stealing over the water, one almost believes that nowhere else than on the Lake of Como can there be found such a paradise of tranquil repose.

From my window here in Bellaggio, I have a view of the other side of the lake now, which is as beautiful as a picture. A scarred and wrinkled precipice rises to a height of eighteen hundred feet; on a tiny bench half way up its vast wall, sits a little snow-flake of a church, no bigger than a martin-box, apparently; skirting the base of the cliff are a hundred orange groves and gardens, flecked with glimpses of the white dwellings that are buried in them; in front, three or four gondolas lie idle upon the water—and in the burnished mirror of the lake, mountain, chapel, houses, groves and boats are counterfeited so brightly and so clearly that one scarce knows where the reality leaves off and the reflection begins!

The surroundings of this picture are fine. A mile away, a grove-plumed promontory juts far into the lake and glasses its palace in the blue depths; in midstream a boat is cutting the shining surface and leaving a long track behind, like a ray of light; the mountains beyond are veiled in a dreamy purple haze; far in the opposite direction a tumbled mass of domes and verdant slopes and valleys bars the lake, and here indeed does distance lend enchantment to the view—for on this broad canvas, sun and clouds and the richest of atmospheres have blended a thousand tints together, and over its surface the filmy lights and shadows drift, hour after hour, and glorify it with a beauty that seems reflected out of Heaven itself. Beyond all question, this is the most voluptuous scene we have yet looked upon.

Last night the scenery was striking and picturesque. On the other side crags and trees and snowy houses were reflected in the lake with a wonderful distinctness, and streams of light from many a distant window shot far abroad over the still waters. On this side, near at hand, great mansions, white with moonlight, glared out from the midst of masses of foliage that lay black and shapeless in the shadows that fell from the cliff above—and down in the margin of the lake every feature of the weird vision was faithfully repeated.

To-day we have idled through a wonder of a garden attached to a ducal estate—but enough of description is enough, I judge. I suspect that this was the same place the gardener's son deceived the Lady of Lyons with, but I do not know. You may have heard of the passage somewhere:

> "A deep vale,
> Shut out by Alpine hills from the rude world,
> Near a clear lake margined by fruits of gold
> And whispering myrtles:
> Glassing softest skies, cloudless,
> Save with rare and roseate shadows;
> A palace, lifting to eternal heaven its marbled walls,
> From out a glossy bower of coolest foliage musical with
>   birds."

That is all very well, except the "clear" part of the lake. It certainly is clearer than a great many lakes, but how dull its waters are compared with the wonderful transparence of Lake Tahoe! I speak of the north shore of Tahoe, where one can count the scales on a trout at a depth of a hundred and eighty feet. I have tried to get this statement off at par here, but with no success; so I have been obliged to negotiate it at fifty per cent discount. At this rate I find some takers; perhaps the reader will receive it on the same terms—ninety feet instead of one hundred and eighty. But let it be remembered that those are forced terms—Sheriff's sale prices. As far as I am privately concerned, I abate not a jot of the original assertion that in those strangely magnifying waters one may count the scales on a trout (a trout of the large kind,) at a depth of a hundred and eighty feet—may see every pebble on the bottom—might even count a paper of dray-pins. People talk of the transparent waters of the Mexican Bay of Acapulco, but in my own experience I know they can not compare with those I am speaking of. I have fished for trout, in Tahoe, and at a measured depth of eighty-four feet I have seen them put their noses to the bait and I could see their gills open and shut. I could hardly have seen the trout themselves at that distance in the open air.

As I go back in spirit and recall that noble sea, reposing among the snow-peaks six thousand feet above the ocean, the conviction comes strong upon me again that Como would only seem a bedizened little courtier in that august presence.

Sorrow and misfortune overtake the Legislature that still from year to year permits Tahoe to retain its unmusical cognomen! Tahoe! It suggests no crystal waters, no picturesque shores, no sublimity. Tahoe for a sea in the clouds: a sea that has character, and asserts it in solemn calms, at times, at times in savage storms; a sea, whose royal seclusion is guarded by a cordon of sentinel peaks that lift their frosty fronts nine thousand feet above the level world; a sea whose every aspect is impressive, whose belongings are all beautiful, whose lonely majesty types the Deity!

Tahoe means grasshoppers. It means grasshopper soup. It is Indian, and suggestive of Indians. They say it is Pi-ute—possibly it is Digger. I am satisfied it was named by the Diggers—those degraded savages who roast their dead relatives, then mix the human grease and ashes of bones with tar, and "gaum" it thick all over their heads and foreheads and ears, and go caterwauling about the hills and call it *mourning*. *These* are the gentry that named the Lake.

People say that Tahoe means "Silver Lake"—"Limpid Water"—"Falling Leaf." Bosh. It means grasshopper soup, the favorite dish of the Digger tribe—and of the Pi-utes as well. It isn't worth while, in these practical times, for people to talk about Indian poetry—there never was any in them—except in the Fennimore Cooper Indians. But *they* are an extinct tribe that never existed. I know the Noble Red Man. I have camped with the Indians; I have been on the war-path with them, taken part in the chase with them—for grasshoppers; helped them steal cattle; I have roamed with them, scalped them, had them for breakfast. I would gladly eat the whole race if I had a chance.

But I am growing unreliable. I will return to my comparison of the Lakes. Como is a little deeper than Tahoe, if people here tell the truth. They say it is eighteen hundred feet deep at this point, but it does not look a dead enough blue for that. Tahoe is one thousand five hundred and twenty-five feet deep in the centre, by the State Geologist's measurement. They say the great peak opposite this town is five thousand feet high: but I feel sure that three thousand feet of that statement is a good honest lie. The lake is a mile wide, here, and maintains about that width from this point to its northern extremity—which is distant sixteen miles: from here to its southern extremity—say fifteen miles—it is not over half a mile wide in any place, I should think. Its snow-clad mountains one hears so much about are only seen occasionally, and then in the distance, the Alps. Tahoe is from ten to eighteen miles wide, and its mountains shut it in like a wall. Their summits are never free from snow the year round. One thing about it is very strange: it never has even a skim of ice upon its surface, although lakes in the same range of mountains, lying in a lower and warmer temperature, freeze over in winter.

It is cheerful to meet a shipmate in these out-of-the-way places and compare notes with him. We have found one of ours here—an old soldier of the war, who is seeking bloodless adventures and rest from his campaigns, in these sunny lands.*

---

*Col. J. HERON FOSTER, editor of a Pittsburgh journal, and a most estimable gentleman. As these sheets are being prepared for the press, I am pained to learn of his decease shortly after his return home.—M. T.

Chapter XXI

WE VOYAGED by steamer down the Lago di Lecco, through wild mountain scenery, and by hamlets and villas, and disembarked at the town of Lecco. They said it was two hours, by carriage to the ancient city of Bergamo, and that we would arrive there in good season for the railway train. We got an open barouche and a wild, boisterous driver, and set out. It was delightful. We had a fast team and a perfectly smooth road. There were towering cliffs on our left, and the pretty Lago di Lecco on our right, and every now and then it rained on us. Just before starting, the driver picked up, in the street, a stump of a cigar an inch long, and put it in his mouth. When he had carried it thus about an hour, I thought it would be only Christian charity to give him a light. I handed him my cigar, which I had just lit, and he put it in his mouth and returned his stump to his pocket! I never saw a more sociable man. At least I never saw a man who was more sociable on a short acquaintance.

We saw interior Italy, now. The houses were of solid stone, and not often in good repair. The peasants and their children were idle, as a general thing, and the donkeys and chickens made themselves at home in drawing-room and bed-chamber and were not molested. The drivers of each and every one of the slow-moving market-carts we met were stretched in the sun upon their merchandise, sound asleep. Every three or four hundred yards, it seemed to me, we came upon the shrine of some saint or other—a rude picture of him built into a huge cross or a stone pillar by the road-side.—Some of the pictures of the Saviour were curiosities in their way. They represented him stretched upon the cross, his countenance distorted with agony. From the wounds of the crown of thorns; from the pierced side; from the mutilated hands and feet; from the scourged body—from every hand-breadth of his person streams of blood were flowing! Such a gory, ghastly spectacle would frighten the children out of their senses, I should think. There were some unique auxiliaries to the painting which added to its spirited effect. These were genuine wooden and iron implements, and were prominently disposed round about the figure: a bundle of nails; the hammer to drive them; the sponge; the reed that supported it; the cup of vinegar; the ladder for the ascent of the cross; the spear that pierced the Saviour's side. The crown of thorns was made of real thorns, and was nailed to the sacred head. In some Italian church-paintings, even by the old masters, the Saviour and the Virgin wear silver or gilded crowns that are fastened to the pictured head with nails. The effect is as grotesque as it is incongruous.

Here and there, on the fronts of roadside inns, we found huge, coarse frescoes of suffering martyrs like those in the shrines. It could not have diminished their sufferings any to be so uncouthly represented. We were in the heart and home of priestcraft—of a happy, cheerful, contented ignorance, superstition, degradation, poverty, indolence, and everlasting unaspiring worthlessness. And we said fervently, It suits these people precisely; let them enjoy it, along with the other animals, and Heaven forbid that they be molested. *We* feel no malice toward these fumigators.

We passed through the strangest, funniest, undreampt-of old towns, wedded to the customs and steeped in the dreams of the elder ages, and perfectly unaware that the world turns round! And perfectly indifferent, too, as to whether it turns around or stands still. *They* have nothing to do but eat and sleep and sleep and eat, and toil a little when they can get a friend to stand by and keep them awake. *They* are not paid for thinking—*they* are not paid to fret about the world's concerns. They were not respectable people—they were not worthy people—they were not learned and wise and brilliant people—but in their breasts, all their stupid lives long, resteth a peace that passeth understanding! How can men, calling themselves men, consent to be so degraded and happy?

We whisked by many a gray old medieval castle, clad thick with ivy that swung its green banners down from towers and turrets where once some old Crusader's flag had floated. The driver pointed to one of these ancient fortresses, and said, (I translate):

"Do you see that great iron hook that projects from the wall just under the highest window in the ruined tower?"

We said we could not see it at such a distance, but had no doubt it was there.

"Well," he said, "there is a legend connected with that iron hook. Nearly seven hundred years ago, that castle was the property of the noble Count Luigi Gennaro Guido Alphonso di Genova—"

"What was his other name?" said Dan.

"He had no other name. The name I have spoken was all the name he had. He was the son of—"

"Poor but honest parents—that is all right—never mind the particulars—go on with the legend."

THE LEGEND.

Well, then, all the world, at that time, was in a wild excitement about the Holy Sepulchre. All the great feudal lords in Europe were pledging their lands and pawning their plate to fit out men-at-arms so that they might join the grand armies of Christendom and win renown in the Holy Wars. The Count Luigi raised money, like the rest, and one mild September morning, armed with battle-ax, portcullis and thundering culverin, he rode through the greaves and bucklers of his donjon-keep with as gallant a troop of Christian bandits as ever stepped in Italy. He had his sword, Excalibur, with him. His beautiful countess and her young daughter waved him a tearful adieu from the battering-rams and buttresses of the fortress, and he galloped away with a happy heart.

He made a raid on a neighboring baron and completed his outfit with the booty secured. He then razed the castle to the ground, massacred the family and moved on. They were hardy fellows in the grand old days of chivalry. Alas! those days will never come again.

Count Luigi grew high in fame in Holy Land. He plunged into the carnage of a hundred battles, but his good Excalibur always brought him out alive, albeit often sorely wounded. His face became browned by exposure to the Syrian sun in long marches; he suffered hunger and thirst; he pined in prisons, he languished in loathsome plague-hospitals. And many and many a time he thought of his loved ones at home, and wondered if all was well with them. But his heart said, Peace, is not thy brother watching over thy household?

Forty-two years waxed and waned; the good fight was won; Godfrey reigned in Jerusalem—the Christian hosts reared the banner of the cross above the Holy Sepulchre!

Twilight was approaching. Fifty harlequins, in flowing robes, approached this castle wearily, for they were on foot, and the dust upon their garments betokened that they had traveled far. They overtook a peasant, and asked him if it were likely they could get food and a hospitable bed there, for love of Christian charity, and if perchance, a moral parlor entertainment might meet with generous countenance—"for," said they, "this exhibition hath no feature that could offend the most fastidious taste."

"Marry," quoth the peasant, "an' it please your worships, ye had better journey many a good rood hence with your juggling circus than trust your bones in yonder castle."

"How now, sirrah!" exclaimed the chief monk, "explain thy ribald speech, or by'r Lady it shall go hard with thee."

"Peace, good mountebank, I did but utter the truth that was in my heart. San Paolo be my witness that did ye but find the stout Count Leonardo in his cups, sheer from the castle's topmost battlements would he hurl ye all! Alack-a-day, the good Lord Luigi reigns not here in these sad times."

"The good Lord Luigi?"

"Aye, none other, please your worship. In his day, the poor rejoiced in plenty and the rich he did oppress; taxes were not known, the fathers of the church waxed fat upon his bounty; travelers went and came, with none to interfere; and whosoever would, might tarry in his halls in cordial welcome, and eat his bread and drink his wine, withal. But woe is me! some two and forty years agone the good count rode hence to fight for Holy Cross, and many a year hath flown since word or token have we had of him. Men say his bones lie bleaching in the fields of Palestine."

"And now?"

"*Now!* God 'a mercy, the cruel Leonardo lords it in the castle. He wrings taxes from the poor; he robs all travelers that journey by his gates; he spends his days in feuds and murders, and his nights in revel and debauch; he roasts the fathers of the church upon his kitchen spits, and enjoyeth the same, calling it pastime. These thirty years Luigi's countess hath not been seen by any he in all this land, and many whisper that she pines in the dungeons of the castle for that she will not wed with Leonardo, saying her dear lord still liveth and that she will die ere she prove false to him. They whisper likewise that her daughter is a prisoner as well. Nay, good jugglers, seek ye refreshment other wheres. 'Twere better that ye perished in a Christian way than that ye plunged from off yon dizzy tower. Give ye good-day."

"God keep ye, gentle knave—farewell."

But heedless of the peasant's warning, the players moved straightway toward the castle.

Word was brought to Count Leonardo that a company of mountebanks besought his hospitality.

" 'Tis well. Dispose of them in the customary manner. Yet stay! I have need of them. Let them come hither. Later, cast them from the battlements—or—how many priests have ye on hand?"

"The day's results are meagre, good my lord. An abbot and a dozen beggarly friars is all we have."

"Hell and furies! Is the estate going to seed? Send hither the mountebanks. Afterward, broil them with the priests."

The robed and close-cowled harlequins entered. The grim Leonardo sate in state at the head of his council board. Ranged up and down the hall on either hand stood near a hundred men-at-arms.

"Ha, villains!" quoth the count. "What can ye do to earn the hospitality ye crave."

"Dread lord and mighty, crowded audiences have greeted our humble efforts with rapturous applause. Among our body count we the versatile and talented Ugolino; the justly celebrated Rodolpho; the gifted and accomplished Roderigo; the management have spared neither pains nor expense—"

"S'death! what can ye *do*? Curb thy prating tongue."

"Good my lord, in acrobatic feats, in practice with the dumb-bells, in balancing and ground and lofty tumbling are we versed—and sith your highness asketh me, I venture here to publish that in the truly marvelous and entertaining Zampillaerostation—"

"Gag him! throttle him! Body of Bacchus! am I a dog that

I am to be assailed with polysyllabled blasphemy like to this? But hold! Lucretia, Isabel, stand forth! Sirrah, behold this dame, this weeping wench. The first I marry, within the hour; the other shall dry her tears or feed the vultures. Thou and thy vagabonds shall crown the wedding with thy merry-makings. Fetch hither the priest!"

The dame sprang toward the chief player.

"O, save me!" she cried; "save me from a fate far worse than death! Behold these sad eyes, these sunken cheeks, this withered frame! See thou the wreck this fiend hath made, and let thy heart be moved with pity! Look upon this damosel; note her wasted form, her halting step, her bloomless cheeks where youth should blush and happiness exult in smiles! Hear us and have compassion. This monster was my husband's brother. He who should have been our shield against all harm, hath kept us shut within the noisome caverns of his donjon-keep for lo these thirty years. And for what crime? None other than that I would not belie my troth, root out my strong love for him who marches with the legions of the cross in Holy Land, (for O, he is not dead!) and wed with him! Save us, O, save thy persecuted suppliants!"

She flung herself at his feet and clasped his knees.

"Ha!-ha!-ha!" shouted the brutal Leonardo. "Priest, to thy work!" and he dragged the weeping dame from her refuge. "Say, once for all, *will* you be mine?—for by my halidome, that breath that uttereth thy refusal shall be thy last on earth!"

"NE-VER!"

"Then die!" and the sword leaped from its scabbard.

Quicker than thought, quicker than the lightning's flash, fifty monkish habits disappeared, and fifty knights in splendid armor stood revealed! fifty falchions gleamed in air above the men-at-arms, and brighter, fiercer than them all, flamed Excalibur aloft, and cleaving downward struck the brutal Leonardo's weapon from his grasp!

"A Luigi to the rescue! Whoop!"

"A Leonardo! tare an ouns!"

"Oh, God, Oh, God, my husband!"

"Oh, God, Oh, God, my wife!"

"My father!"

"My precious!" [Tableau.]

Count Luigi bound his usurping brother hand and foot. The practiced knights from Palestine made holyday sport of carving the awkward men-at-arms into chops and steaks. The victory was complete. Happiness reigned. The knights all married the daughter. Joy! wassail! finis!

"But what did they do with the wicked brother?"

"Oh nothing—only hanged him on that iron hook I was speaking of. By the chin."

"As how?"

"Passed it up through his gills into his mouth."

"Leave him there?"

"Couple of years."

"Ah—is—is he dead?"

"Six hundred and fifty years ago, or such a matter."

"Splendid legend—splendid lie—drive on."

We reached the quaint old fortified city of Bergamo, the renowned in history, some three-quarters of an hour before the train was ready to start. The place has thirty or forty thousand inhabitants and is remarkable for being the birthplace of harlequin. When we discovered that, that legend of our driver took to itself a new interest in our eyes.

Rested and refreshed, we took the rail happy and contented. I shall not tarry to speak of the handsome Lago di Gardi; its stately castle that holds in its stony bosom the secrets of an age so remote that even tradition goeth not back to it; the imposing mountain scenery that ennobles the landscape thereabouts; nor yet of ancient Padua or haughty Verona; nor of their Montagues and Capulets, their famous balconies and tombs of Juliet and Romeo *et al.*, but hurry straight to the ancient city of the sea, the widowed bride of the Adriatic. It was a long, long ride. But toward evening, as we sat silent and hardly conscious of where we were—subdued into that meditative calm that comes so surely after a conversational storm—some one shouted—

"Venice!"

And sure enough, afloat on the placid sea a league away, lay a great city, with its towers and domes and steeples drowsing in a golden mist of sunset.

Chapter XXII

THIS VENICE, which was a haughty, invincible, magnificent Republic for nearly fourteen hundred years; whose armies compelled the world's applause whenever and wherever they battled; whose navies well nigh held dominion of the seas, and whose merchant fleets whitened the remotest oceans with their sails and loaded these piers with the products of every clime, is fallen a prey to poverty, neglect and melancholy decay. Six hundred years ago, Venice was the Autocrat of Commerce; her mart was the great commercial centre, the distributing-house from whence the enormous trade of the Orient was spread abroad over the Western world. To-day her piers are deserted, her warehouses are empty, her merchant fleets are vanished, her armies and her navies are but memories. Her glory is departed, and with her crumbling grandeur of wharves and palaces about her she sits among her stagnant lagoons, forlorn and beggared, forgotten of the world. She that in her palmy days commanded the commerce of a hemisphere and made the weal or woe of nations with a beck of her puissant finger, is become the humblest among the peoples of the earth,—a peddler of glass beads for women, and trifling toys and trinkets for school-girls and children.

The venerable Mother of the Republics is scarce a fit subject for flippant speech or the idle gossiping of tourists. It seems a sort of sacrilege to disturb the glamour of old romance that pictures her to us softly from afar off as through a tinted mist, and curtains her ruin and her desolation from our view. One ought, indeed, to turn away from her rags, her poverty and her humiliation, and think of her only as she was when she sunk the fleets of Charlemagne; when she humbled Frederick Barbarossa or waved her victorious banners above the battlements of Constantinople.

We reached Venice at eight in the evening, and entered a hearse belonging to the Grand Hotel d'Europe. At any rate, it was more like a hearse than any thing else, though to speak by the card, it was a gondola. And this was the storied gondola of Venice!—the fairy boat in which the princely cavaliers of the olden time were wont to cleave the waters of the moonlit canals and look the eloquence of love into the soft eyes of patrician beauties, while the gay gondolier in silken doublet touched his guitar and sang as only gondoliers can sing! This the famed gondola and this the gorgeous gondolier!—the one an inky, rusty old canoe with a sable hearse-body clapped on to the middle of it, and the other a mangy, barefooted guttersnipe with a portion of his raiment on exhibition which should have been sacred from public scrutiny. Presently, as he turned a corner and shot his hearse into a dismal ditch between two long rows of towering, untenanted buildings, the gay gondolier began to sing, true to the traditions of his race. I stood it a little while. Then I said:

"Now, here, Roderigo Gonzales Michael Angelo, I'm a pilgrim, and I'm a stranger, but I am not going to have my feelings lacerated by any such caterwauling as that. If that goes on, one of us has got to take water. It is enough that my cherished dreams of Venice have been blighted forever as to the romantic gondola and the gorgeous gondolier; this system of destruction shall go no farther; I will accept the hearse, under protest, and you may fly your flag of truce in peace, but here I register a dark and bloody oath that you shan't sing. Another yelp, and overboard you go."

I began to feel that the old Venice of song and story had departed forever. But I was too hasty. In a few minutes we swept gracefully out into the Grand Canal, and under the mellow moonlight the Venice of poetry and romance stood revealed. Right from the water's edge rose long lines of stately palaces of marble; gondolas were gliding swiftly hither and thither and disappearing suddenly through unsuspected gates and alleys; ponderous stone bridges threw their shadows athwart the glittering waves. There was life and motion everywhere, and yet everywhere there was a hush, a stealthy sort of stillness, that was suggestive of secret enterprises of bravoes and of lovers; and clad half in moonbeams and half in mysterious shadows, the grim old mansions of the Republic seemed to have an expression about them of having an eye out for just such enterprises as these at that same moment. Music came floating over the waters—Venice was complete.

It was a beautiful picture—very soft and dreamy and beautiful. But what was this Venice to compare with the Venice of midnight? Nothing. There was a fête—a grand fête in honor of some saint who had been instrumental in checking the cholera three hundred years ago, and all Venice was abroad on the water. It was no common affair, for the Venetians did not know how soon they might need the saint's services again, now that the cholera was spreading every where. So in one vast space—say a third of a mile wide and two miles long—were collected two thousand gondolas, and every one of them had from two to ten, twenty and even thirty colored lanterns suspended about it, and from four to a dozen occupants. Just as far as the eye could reach, these painted lights were massed together—like a vast garden of many-colored flowers, except that these blossoms were never still; they were ceaselessly gliding in and out, and mingling together, and seducing you into bewildering attempts to follow their mazy evolutions. Here and there a strong red, green, or blue glare from a rocket that was struggling to get away, splendidly illuminated all the boats around it. Every gondola that swam by us, with its crescents and pyramids and circles of colored lamps hung aloft, and lighting up the faces of the young and the sweet-scented and lovely below, was a picture; and the reflections of those lights, so long, so slender, so numberless, so many-colored and so distorted and wrinkled by the waves, was a picture likewise, and one that was enchantingly beautiful. Many and many a party of young ladies and gentlemen had their state gondolas handsomely decorated, and ate supper on board, bringing their swallow-tailed, white-cravatted varlets to wait upon them, and having their tables tricked out as if for a bridal supper. They had brought along the costly globe lamps from their drawing-rooms, and the lace and silken curtains from the same places, I suppose. And they had also brought pianos and guitars, and they played and sang operas, while the plebeian paper-lanterned gondolas from the suburbs and the back alleys crowded around to stare and listen.

There was music every where—chorusses, string bands, brass bands, flutes, every thing. I was so surrounded, walled in, with music, magnificence and loveliness, that I became inspired with the spirit of the scene, and sang one tune myself. However, when I observed that the other gondolas had sailed away, and my gondolier was preparing to go overboard, I stopped.

The fête was magnificent. They kept it up the whole night long, and I never enjoyed myself better than I did while it lasted.

What a funny old city this Queen of the Adriatic is! Narrow streets, vast, gloomy marble palaces, black with the corroding damps of centuries, and all partly submerged; no dry land visible any where, and no sidewalks worth mentioning; if you want to go to church, to the theatre, or to the restaurant, you must call a gondola. It must be a paradise for cripples, for verily a man has no use for legs here.

For a day or two the place looked so like an overflowed Arkansas town, because of its currentless waters laving the very doorsteps of all the houses, and the cluster of boats made fast under the windows, or skimming in and out of the alleys and by-ways, that I could not get rid of the impression that there was nothing the matter here but a spring freshet, and that the river would fall in a few weeks and leave a dirty high-water mark on the houses, and the streets full of mud and rubbish.

In the glare of day, there is little poetry about Venice, but under the charitable moon her stained palaces are white again, their battered sculptures are hidden in shadows, and the old city seems crowned once more with the grandeur that was hers five hundred years ago. It is easy, then, in fancy, to people these silent canals with plumed gallants and fair ladies— with Shylocks in gaberdine and sandals, venturing loans upon the rich argosies of Venetian commerce—with Othellos and Desdemonas, with Iagos and Roderigos—with noble fleets and victorious legions returning from the wars. In the treacherous sunlight we see Venice decayed, forlorn, poverty-stricken, and commerceless—forgotten and utterly insignificant. But in the moonlight, her fourteen centuries of greatness fling their glories about her, and once more is she the princeliest among the nations of the earth.

> "There is a glorious city in the sea;
> The sea is in the broad, the narrow streets,
> Ebbing and flowing; and the salt-sea weed

Clings to the marble of her palaces.
No track of men, no footsteps to and fro,
Lead to her gates! The path lies o'er the sea,
Invisible: and from the land we went,
As to a floating city—steering in,
And gliding up her streets, as in a dream,
So smoothly, silently—by many a dome,
Mosque-like, and many a stately portico,
The statues ranged along an azure sky;
By many a pile, in more than Eastern pride,
Of old the residence of merchant kings;
The fronts of some, tho' time had shatter'd them,
Still glowing with the richest hues of art,
As tho' the wealth within them had run o'er."

What would one naturally wish to see first in Venice? The Bridge of Sighs, of course—and next the Church and the Great Square of St. Mark, the Bronze Horses, and the famous Lion of St. Mark.

We intended to go to the Bridge of Sighs, but happened into the Ducal Palace first—a building which necessarily figures largely in Venetian poetry and tradition. In the Senate Chamber of the ancient Republic we wearied our eyes with staring at acres of historical paintings by Tintoretto and Paul Veronese, but nothing struck us forcibly except the one thing that strikes *all* strangers forcibly—a black square in the midst of a gallery of portraits. In one long row, around the great hall, were painted the portraits of the Doges of Venice (venerable fellows, with flowing white beards, for of the three hundred Senators eligible to the office, the oldest was usually chosen Doge,) and each had its complimentary inscription attached—till you came to the place that should have had Marino Faliero's picture in it, and that was blank and black— blank, except that it bore a terse inscription, saying that the conspirator had died for his crime. It seemed cruel to keep that pitiless inscription still staring from the walls after the unhappy wretch had been in his grave five hundred years.

At the head of the Giant's Staircase, where Marino Faliero was beheaded, and where the Doges were crowned in ancient times, two small slits in the stone wall were pointed out—

two harmless, insignificant orifices that would never attract a
stranger's attention—yet these were the terrible Lions'
Mouths! The heads were gone (knocked off by the French
during their occupation of Venice,) but these were the
throats, down which went the anonymous accusation, thrust
in secretly at dead of night by an enemy, that doomed many
an innocent man to walk the Bridge of Sighs and descend
into the dungeon which none entered and hoped to see the
sun again. This was in the old days when the Patricians alone
governed Venice—the common herd had no vote and no
voice. There were one thousand five hundred Patricians; from
these, three hundred Senators were chosen; from the Senators
a Doge and a Council of Ten were selected, and by secret
ballot the Ten chose from their own number a Council of
Three. All these were Government spies, then, and every spy
was under surveillance himself—men spoke in whispers in
Venice, and no man trusted his neighbor—not always his
own brother. No man knew who the Council of Three
were—not even the Senate, not even the Doge; the members
of that dread tribunal met at night in a chamber to themselves, masked, and robed from head to foot in scarlet cloaks,
and did not even know each other, unless by voice. It was
their duty to judge heinous political crimes, and from their
sentence there was no appeal. A nod to the executioner was
sufficient. The doomed man was marched down a hall and
out at a door-way into the covered Bridge of Sighs, through
it and into the dungeon and unto his death. At no time in his
transit was he visible to any save his conductor. If a man had
an enemy in those old days, the cleverest thing he could do
was to slip a note for the Council of Three into the Lion's
mouth, saying "This man is plotting against the Government." If the awful Three found no proof, ten to one they
would drown him anyhow, because he was a deep rascal,
since his plots were unsolvable. Masked judges and masked
executioners, with unlimited power, and no appeal from their
judgments, in that hard, cruel age, were not likely to be le-
nient with men they suspected yet could not convict.

We walked through the hall of the Council of Ten, and
presently entered the infernal den of the Council of Three.

The table around which they had sat was there still, and

likewise the stations where the masked inquisitors and executioners formerly stood, frozen, upright and silent, till they received a bloody order, and then, without a word, moved off,
like the inexorable machines they were, to carry it out. The
frescoes on the walls were startlingly suited to the place. In
all the other saloons, the halls, the great state chambers of the
palace, the walls and ceilings were bright with gilding, rich
with elaborate carving, and resplendent with gallant pictures
of Venetian victories in war, and Venetian display in foreign
courts, and hallowed with portraits of the Virgin, the Savior
of men, and the holy saints that preached the Gospel of Peace
upon earth—but here, in dismal contrast, were none but pictures of death and dreadful suffering!—not a living figure but
was writhing in torture, not a dead one but was smeared with
blood, gashed with wounds, and distorted with the agonies
that had taken away its life!

From the palace to the gloomy prison is but a step—one
might almost jump across the narrow canal that intervenes.
The ponderous stone Bridge of Sighs crosses it at the second
story—a bridge that is a covered tunnel—you can not be
seen when you walk in it. It is partitioned lengthwise, and
through one compartment walked such as bore light sentences in ancient times, and through the other marched sadly
the wretches whom the Three had doomed to lingering misery and utter oblivion in the dungeons, or to sudden and
mysterious death. Down below the level of the water, by the
light of smoking torches, we were shown the damp, thick-
walled cells where many a proud patrician's life was eaten
away by the long-drawn miseries of solitary imprisonment—
without light, air, books; naked, unshaven, uncombed, covered with vermin; his useless tongue forgetting its office, with
none to speak to; the days and nights of his life no longer
marked, but merged into one eternal eventless night; far away
from all cheerful sounds, buried in the silence of a tomb; forgotten by his helpless friends, and his fate a dark mystery to
them forever; losing his own memory at last, and knowing no
more who he was or how he came there; devouring the loaf
of bread and drinking the water that were thrust into the cell
by unseen hands, and troubling his worn spirit no more with
hopes and fears and doubts and longings to be free; ceasing

to scratch vain prayers and complainings on walls where none, not even himself, could see them, and resigning himself to hopeless apathy, driveling childishness, lunacy! Many and many a sorrowful story like this these stony walls could tell if they could but speak.

In a little narrow corridor, near by, they showed us where many a prisoner, after lying in the dungeons until he was forgotten by all save his persecutors, was brought by masked executioners and garroted, or sewed up in a sack, passed through a little window to a boat, at dead of night, and taken to some remote spot and drowned.

They used to show to visitors the implements of torture wherewith the Three were wont to worm secrets out of the accused—villainous machines for crushing thumbs; the stocks where a prisoner sat immovable while water fell drop by drop upon his head till the torture was more than humanity could bear; and a devilish contrivance of steel, which inclosed a prisoner's head like a shell, and crushed it slowly by means of a screw. It bore the stains of blood that had trickled through its joints long ago, and on one side it had a projection whereon the torturer rested his elbow comfortably and bent down his ear to catch the moanings of the sufferer perishing within.

Of course we went to see the venerable relic of the ancient glory of Venice, with its pavements worn and broken by the passing feet of a thousand years of plebeians and patricians— The Cathedral of St. Mark. It is built entirely of precious marbles, brought from the Orient—nothing in its composition is domestic. Its hoary traditions make it an object of absorbing interest to even the most careless stranger, and thus far it had interest for me; but no further. I could not go into ecstacies over its coarse mosaics, its unlovely Byzantine architecture, or its five hundred curious interior columns from as many distant quarries. Every thing was worn out—every block of stone was smooth and almost shapeless with the polishing hands and shoulders of loungers who devoutly idled here in by-gone centuries and have died and gone to the dev—no, simply died, I mean.

Under the altar repose the ashes of St. Mark—and Matthew, Luke and John, too, for all I know. Venice reveres those relics above all things earthly. For fourteen hundred years St.

Mark has been her patron saint. Every thing about the city
seems to be named after him or so named as to refer to him
in some way—so named, or some purchase rigged in some
way to scrape a sort of hurrahing acquaintance with him.
That seems to be the idea. To be on good terms with St.
Mark, seems to be the very summit of Venetian ambition.
They say St. Mark had a tame lion, and used to travel with
him—and every where that St. Mark went, the lion was sure
to go. It was his protector, his friend, his librarian. And so
the Winged Lion of St. Mark, with the open Bible under his
paw, is a favorite emblem in the grand old city. It casts its
shadow from the most ancient pillar in Venice, in the Grand
Square of St. Mark, upon the throngs of free citizens below,
and has so done for many a long century. The winged lion is
found every where—and doubtless here, where the winged
lion is, no harm can come.

St. Mark died at Alexandria, in Egypt. He was martyred, I
think. However, that has nothing to do with my legend.
About the founding of the city of Venice—say four hundred
and fifty years after Christ—(for Venice is much younger
than any other Italian city,) a priest dreamed that an angel
told him that until the remains of St. Mark were brought to
Venice, the city could never rise to high distinction among
the nations; that the body must be captured, brought to the
city, and a magnificent church built over it; and that if ever
the Venetians allowed the Saint to be removed from his new
resting-place, in that day Venice would perish from off the
face of the earth. The priest proclaimed his dream, and forthwith Venice set about procuring the corpse of St. Mark. One
expedition after another tried and failed, but the project was
never abandoned during four hundred years. At last it was
secured by stratagem, in the year eight hundred and something. The commander of a Venetian expedition disguised
himself, stole the bones, separated them, and packed them in
vessels filled with lard. The religion of Mahomet causes its
devotees to abhor anything that is in the nature of pork, and
so when the Christian was stopped by the officers at the gates
of the city, they only glanced once into his precious baskets,
then turned up their noses at the unholy lard, and let him go.
The bones were buried in the vaults of the grand cathedral,

which had been waiting long years to receive them, and thus the safety and the greatness of Venice were secured. And to this day there be those in Venice who believe that if those holy ashes were stolen away, the ancient city would vanish like a dream, and its foundations be buried forever in the un-remembering sea.

Chapter XXIII

THE VENETIAN GONDOLA is as free and graceful, in its gliding movement, as a serpent. It is twenty or thirty feet long, and is narrow and deep, like a canoe; its sharp bow and stern sweep upward from the water like the horns of a crescent with the abruptness of the curve slightly modified.

The bow is ornamented with a steel comb with a battle-ax attachment which threatens to cut passing boats in two occasionally, but never does. The gondola is painted black because in the zenith of Venetian magnificence the gondolas became too gorgeous altogether, and the Senate decreed that all such display must cease, and a solemn, unembellished black be substituted. If the truth were known, it would doubtless appear that rich plebeians grew too prominent in their affectation of patrician show on the Grand Canal, and required a wholesome snubbing. Reverence for the hallowed Past and its traditions keeps the dismal fashion in force now that the compulsion exists no longer. So let it remain. It is the color of mourning. Venice mourns. The stern of the boat is decked over and the gondolier stands there. He uses a single oar—a long blade, of course, for he stands nearly erect. A wooden peg, a foot and a half high, with two slight crooks or curves in one side of it and one in the other, projects above the starboard gunwale. Against that peg the gondolier takes a purchase with his oar, changing it at intervals to the other side of the peg or dropping it into another of the crooks, as the steering of the craft may demand—and how in the world he can back and fill, shoot straight ahead, or flirt suddenly around a corner, and make the oar stay in those insignificant notches, is a problem to me and a never diminishing matter of interest. I am afraid I study the gondolier's marvelous skill more than I do the sculptured palaces we glide among. He cuts a corner so closely, now and then, or misses another gondola by such an imperceptible hair-breadth that I feel myself "scrooching," as the children say, just as one does when a buggy wheel grazes his elbow. But he makes all his calculations with the nicest precision, and goes darting in and out among a Broadway confusion of busy craft with the easy confidence of the educated hackman. He never makes a mistake.

Sometimes we go flying down the great canals at such a gait that we can get only the merest glimpses into front doors, and again, in obscure alleys in the suburbs, we put on a solemnity suited to the silence, the mildew, the stagnant waters, the clinging weeds, the deserted houses and the general lifelessness of the place, and move to the spirit of grave meditation.

The gondolier *is* a picturesque rascal for all he wears no satin harness, no plumed bonnet, no silken tights. His attitude is stately; he is lithe and supple; all his movements are full of grace. When his long canoe, and his fine figure, towering from its high perch on the stern, are cut against the evening sky, they make a picture that is very novel and striking to a foreign eye.

We sit in the cushioned carriage-body of a cabin, with the curtains drawn, and smoke, or read, or look out upon the passing boats, the houses, the bridges, the people, and enjoy ourselves much more than we could in a buggy jolting over our cobble-stone pavements at home. This is the gentlest, pleasantest locomotion we have ever known.

But it seems queer—ever so queer—to see a boat doing duty as a private carriage. We see business men come to the front door, step into a gondola, instead of a street car, and go off down town to the counting-room.

We see visiting young ladies stand on the stoop, and laugh, and kiss good-bye, and flirt their fans and say "Come soon— now *do*—you've been just as mean as ever you can be— mother's dying to see you—and we've moved into the new house, O such a love of a place!—so convenient to the post-office and the church, and the Young Men's Christian Association; and we do have such fishing, and such carrying on, and *such* swimming-matches in the back yard—Oh, you *must* come—no distance at all, and if you go down through by St. Mark's and the Bridge of Sighs, and cut through the alley and come up by the church of Santa Maria dei Frari, and into the Grand Canal, there isn't a *bit* of current—now *do* come, Sally Maria—by-bye!" and then the little humbug trips down the steps, jumps into the gondola, says, under her breath, "Disagreeable old thing, I hope she *won't!*" goes skimming away, round the corner; and the other girl slams the street door and says, "Well, *that* infliction's over, any way,—but I suppose I've got to go and see her—tiresome stuck-up thing!" Human nature appears to be just the same, all over the world. We see the diffident young man, mild of moustache, affluent of hair, indigent of brain, elegant of costume, drive up to *her* father's mansion, tell his hackman to bail out and wait, start fearfully up the steps and meet "the old gentleman" right on the threshold!—hear him ask what street the new British Bank is in—as if *that* were what he came for—and then bounce into his boat and skurry away with his coward heart in his boots!—see him come sneaking around the corner again, directly, with a crack of the curtain open toward the old gentleman's disappearing gondola, and out scampers his Susan with a flock of little Italian endearments fluttering from her lips, and goes to drive with him in the watery avenues down toward the Rialto.

We see the ladies go out shopping, in the most natural way, and flit from street to street and from store to store, just in the good old fashion, except that they leave the gondola, instead of a private carriage, waiting at the curbstone a couple of hours for them,—waiting while they make the nice young clerks pull down tons and tons of silks and velvets and moire antiques and those things; and then they buy a paper of pins and go paddling away to confer the rest of their disastrous patronage on some other firm. And they always have their purchases sent home just in the good old way. Human nature is *very* much the same all over the world; and it is *so* like my dear native home to see a Venetian lady go into a store and buy ten cents' worth of blue ribbon and have it sent home in a scow. Ah, it is these little touches of nature that move one to tears in these far-off foreign lands.

We see little girls and boys go out in gondolas with their nurses, for an airing. We see staid families, with prayer-book and beads, enter the gondola dressed in their Sunday best, and float away to church. And at midnight we see the theatre break up and discharge its swarm of hilarious youth and beauty; we hear the cries of the hackman-gondoliers, and behold the struggling crowd jump aboard, and the black multitude of boats go skimming down the moonlit avenues; we see them separate here and there, and disappear up divergent streets; we hear the faint sounds of laughter and of shouted farewells floating up out of the distance; and then, the strange pageant being gone, we have lonely stretches of glittering water—of stately buildings—of blotting shadows—of weird stone faces creeping into the moonlight—of deserted bridges—of motionless boats at anchor. And over all broods that mysterious stillness, that stealthy quiet, that befits so well this old dreaming Venice.

We have been pretty much every where in our gondola. We have bought beads and photographs in the stores, and wax matches in the Great Square of St. Mark. The last remark suggests a digression. Every body goes to this vast square in the evening. The military bands play in the centre of it and countless couples of ladies and gentlemen promenade up and down on either side, and platoons of them are constantly drifting away toward the old Cathedral, and by the venerable column with the Winged Lion of St. Mark on its top, and out to where the boats lie moored; and other platoons are as constantly arriving from the gondolas and joining the great throng. Between the promenaders and the side-walks are seated hundreds and hundreds of people at small tables, smoking and taking *granita*, (a first cousin to ice-cream;) on the side-walks are more employing themselves in the same way. The shops in the first floor of the tall rows of buildings that wall in three sides of the square are brilliantly lighted, the air is filled with music and merry voices, and altogether the scene is as bright and spirited and full of cheerfulness as any man could desire. We enjoy it thoroughly. Very many of the young women are exceedingly pretty and dress with rare good taste. We are gradually and laboriously learning the ill-manners of staring them unflinchingly in the face—not because such conduct is agreeable to us, but because it is the custom of the country and they say the girls like it. We wish to learn all the curious, outlandish ways of all the different countries, so that we can "show off" and astonish people when we get home. We wish to excite the envy of our untraveled friends with our strange foreign fashions which we can't shake off. All our passengers are paying strict attention to this thing, with the end in view which I have mentioned. The gentle reader will never, never know what a consummate ass he can become, until he goes abroad. I speak now, of course, in the supposition that the gentle reader has not been abroad, and therefore is not already a consummate ass. If the case be otherwise, I beg his pardon and extend to him the cordial hand of fellowship and call him brother. I shall always delight to meet an ass after my own heart when I shall have finished my travels.

On this subject let me remark that there are Americans abroad in Italy who have actually forgotten their mother tongue in three months—forgot it in France. They can not even write their address in English in a hotel register. I append these evidences, which I copied *verbatim* from the register of a hotel in a certain Italian city:

"John P. Whitcomb, *Etats Unis.*
"Wm. L. Ainsworth, *travailleur* (he meant traveler, I suppose,) *Etats Unis.*
"George P. Morton *et fils, d'Amerique.*
"Lloyd B. Williams, *et trois amis, ville de* Boston, *Amerique.*
"J. Ellsworth Baker, *tout de suite de France, place de naissance Amerique, destination la Grand Bretagne.*"

I love this sort of people. A lady passenger of ours tells of a fellow-citizen of hers who spent eight weeks in Paris and then returned home and addressed his dearest old bosom friend Herbert as Mr. "Er-bare!" He apologized, though, and said, " 'Pon my soul it is aggravating, but I cahn't help it—I have got so used to speaking nothing but French, my dear Erbare—damme there it goes again!—got so used to French pronunciation that I cahn't get rid of it—it is positively annoying, I assure you." This entertaining idiot, whose name was Gordon, allowed himself to be hailed three times in the street before he paid any attention, and then begged a thousand pardons and said he had grown so accustomed to hearing himself addressed as M'sieu Gor-r-*dong*," with a roll to the r, that he had forgotten the legitimate sound of his name! He wore a rose in his button-hole; he gave the French salutation—two flips of the hand in front of the face; he called

Paris *Pair-ree* in ordinary English conversation; he carried envelopes bearing foreign postmarks protruding from his breast-pocket; he cultivated a moustache and imperial, and did what else he could to suggest to the beholder his pet fancy that he resembled Louis Napoleon—and in a spirit of thankfulness which is entirely unaccountable, considering the slim foundation there was for it, he praised his Maker that he was *as* he was, and went on enjoying his little life just the same as if he really *had* been deliberately designed and erected by the great Architect of the Universe.

Think of our Whitcombs, and our Ainsworths and our Williamses writing themselves down in dilapidated French in foreign hotel registers! We laugh at Englishmen, when we are at home, for sticking so sturdily to their national ways and customs, but we look back upon it from abroad very forgivingly. It is not pleasant to see an American thrusting his nationality forward *obtrusively* in a foreign land, but Oh, it is pitiable to see him making of himself a thing that is neither male nor female, neither fish, flesh, nor fowl—a poor, miserable, hermaphrodite Frenchman!

Among a long list of churches, art galleries, and such things, visited by us in Venice, I shall mention only one—the church of Santa Maria dei Frari. It is about five hundred years old, I believe, and stands on twelve hundred thousand piles. In it lie the body of Canova and the heart of Titian, under magnificent monuments. Titian died at the age of almost one hundred years. A plague which swept away fifty thousand lives was raging at the time, and there is notable evidence of the reverence in which the great painter was held, in the fact that to him alone the state permitted a public funeral in all that season of terror and death.

In this church, also, is a monument to the doge Foscari, whose name a once resident of Venice, Lord Byron, has made permanently famous.

The monument to the doge Giovanni Pesaro, in this church, is a curiosity in the way of mortuary adornment. It is eighty feet high and is fronted like some fantastic pagan temple. Against it stand four colossal Nubians, as black as night, dressed in white marble garments. The black legs are bare, and through rents in sleeves and breeches, the skin, of shiny black marble, shows. The artist was as ingenious as his funeral designs were absurd. There are two bronze skeletons bearing scrolls, and two great dragons uphold the sarcophagus. On high, amid all this grotesqueness, sits the departed doge.

In the conventual buildings attached to this church are the state archives of Venice. We did not see them, but they are said to number millions of documents. "They are the records of centuries of the most watchful, observant and suspicious government that ever existed—in which every thing was written down and nothing spoken out." They fill nearly three hundred rooms. Among them are manuscripts from the archives of nearly two thousand families, monasteries and convents. The secret history of Venice for a thousand years is here—its plots, its hidden trials, its assassinations, its commissions of hireling spies and masked bravoes—food, ready to hand, for a world of dark and mysterious romances.

Yes, I think we have seen all of Venice. We have seen, in these old churches, a profusion of costly and elaborate sepulchre ornamentation such as we never dreampt of before. We have stood in the dim religious light of these hoary sanctuaries, in the midst of long ranks of dusty monuments and effigies of the great dead of Venice, until we seemed drifting back, back, back, into the solemn past, and looking upon the scenes and mingling with the peoples of a remote antiquity. We have been in a half-waking sort of dream all the time. I do not know how else to describe the feeling. A part of our being has remained still in the nineteenth century, while another part of it has seemed in some unaccountable way walking among the phantoms of the tenth.

We have seen famous pictures until our eyes are weary with looking at them and refuse to find interest in them any longer. And what wonder, when there are twelve hundred pictures by Palma the Younger in Venice and fifteen hundred by Tintoretto? And behold there are Titians and the works of other artists in proportion. We have seen Titian's celebrated Cain and Abel, his David and Goliah, his Abraham's Sacrifice. We have seen Tintoretto's monster picture, which is seventy-four feet long and I do not know how many feet high, and thought it a very commodious picture. We have seen pictures of martyrs enough, and saints enough, to regenerate the world. I ought not to confess it, but still, since one has no opportunity in America to acquire a critical judgment in art, and since I could not hope to become educated in it in Europe in a few short weeks, I may therefore as well acknowledge with such apologies as may be due, that to me it seemed that when I had seen one of these martyrs I had seen them all. They all have a marked family resemblance to each other, they dress alike, in coarse monkish robes and sandals, they are all bald headed, they all stand in about the same attitude, and without exception they are gazing heavenward with countenances which the Ainsworths, the Mortons and the Williamses, *et fils*, inform me are full of "expression." To me there is nothing tangible about these imaginary portraits, nothing that I can grasp and take a living interest in. If great Titian had only been gifted with prophecy, and had skipped a martyr, and gone over to England and painted a portrait of Shakspeare, even as a youth, which we could all have confidence in now, the world down to the latest generations would have forgiven him the lost martyr in the rescued seer. I think posterity could have spared one more martyr for the sake of a great historical picture of Titian's time and painted by his brush—such as Columbus returning in chains from the discovery of a world, for instance. The old masters did paint some Venetian historical pictures, and these we did not tire of looking at, notwithstanding representations of the formal introduction of defunct doges to the Virgin Mary in regions beyond the clouds clashed rather harshly with the proprieties, it seemed to us.

But humble as we are, and unpretending, in the matter of art, our researches among the painted monks and martyrs have not been wholly in vain. We have striven hard to learn. We have had some success. We have mastered some things, possibly of trifling import in the eyes of the learned, but to us they give pleasure, and we take as much pride in our little acquirements as do others who have learned far more, and we love to display them full as well. When we see a monk going about with a lion and looking tranquilly up to heaven, we know that that is St. Mark. When we see a monk with a book and a pen, looking tranquilly up to heaven, trying to think of a word, we know that that is St. Matthew. When we see a monk sitting on a rock, looking tranquilly up to heaven, with a human skull beside him, and without other baggage, we know that that is St. Jerome. Because we know that he always went flying light in the matter of baggage. When we see a party looking tranquilly up to heaven, unconscious that his body is shot through and through with arrows, we know that that is St. Sebastian. When we see other monks looking tranquilly up to heaven, but having no trade-mark, we always ask who those parties are. We do this because we humbly wish to learn. We have seen thirteen thousand St. Jeromes, and twenty-two thousand St. Marks, and sixteen thousand St. Matthews, and sixty thousand St. Sebastians, and four millions of assorted monks, undesignated, and we feel encouraged to believe that when we have seen some more of these various pictures, and had a larger experience, we shall begin to take an absorbing interest in them like our cultivated countrymen from *Amerique*.

Now it does give me real pain to speak in this almost unappreciative way of the old masters and their martyrs, because good friends of mine in the ship—friends who do thoroughly and conscientiously appreciate them and are in every way competent to discriminate between good pictures and inferior ones—have urged me for my own sake not to make public the fact that I lack this appreciation and this critical discrimination myself. I believe that what I have written and may still write about pictures will give them pain, and I am honestly sorry for it. I even promised that I would hide my uncouth sentiments in my own breast. But alas! I never could keep a promise. I do not blame myself for this weakness, because the fault must lie in my physical organization. It is likely that such a very liberal amount of space was given to the organ which enables me to *make* promises, that the organ which should enable me to keep them was crowded out. But I grieve not. I like no half-way things. I had rather have one faculty nobly developed than two faculties of mere ordinary capacity. I certainly meant to keep that promise, but I find I can not do it. It is impossible to travel through Italy without speaking of pictures, and can I see them through others' eyes?

If I did not so delight in the grand pictures that are spread before me every day of my life by that monarch of all the old masters, Nature, I should come to believe, sometimes, that I had in me no appreciation of the beautiful, whatsoever.

It seems to me that whenever I glory to think that for once I have discovered an ancient painting that is beautiful and worthy of all praise, the pleasure it gives me is an infallible proof that it is *not* a beautiful picture and not in any wise worthy of commendation. This very thing has occurred more times than I can mention, in Venice. In every single instance the guide has crushed out my swelling enthusiasm with the remark:

"It is nothing—it is of the *Renaissance*."

I did not know what in the mischief the Renaissance was, and so always I had to simply say,

"Ah! so it is—I had not observed it before."

I could not bear to be ignorant before a cultivated negro, the offspring of a South Carolina slave. But it occurred too often for even my self-complacency, did that exasperating "It is nothing—it is of the *Renaissance*." I said at last:

"*Who* is this Renaissance? Where did he come from? Who gave him permission to cram the Republic with his execrable daubs?"

We learned, then, that Renaissance was not a man; that *renaissance* was a term used to signify what was at best but an imperfect rejuvenation of art. The guide said that after Titian's time and the time of the other great names we had grown so familiar with, high art declined; then it partially rose again—an inferior sort of painters sprang up, and these shabby pictures were the work of their hands. Then I said, in my heat, that I "wished to goodness high art had declined five hundred years sooner." The Renaissance pictures suit me very well, though sooth to say its school were too much given to painting real men and did not indulge enough in martyrs.

The guide I have spoken of is the only one we have had yet who knew any thing. He was born in South Carolina, of slave parents. They came to Venice while he was an infant. He has grown up here. He is well educated. He reads, writes, and speaks English, Italian, Spanish, and French, with perfect facility; is a worshipper of art and thoroughly conversant with it; knows the history of Venice by heart and never tires of talking of her illustrious career. He dresses better than any of us, I think, and is daintily polite. Negroes are deemed as good as white people, in Venice, and so this man feels no desire to go back to his native land. His judgment is correct.

I have had another shave. I was writing in our front room this afternoon and trying hard to keep my attention on my work and refrain from looking out upon the canal. I was resisting the soft influences of the climate as well as I could, and endeavoring to overcome the desire to be indolent and happy. The boys sent for a barber. They asked me if I would be shaved. I reminded them of my tortures in Genoa, Milan, Como; of my declaration that I would suffer no more on Italian soil. I said "Not any for me, if you please."

I wrote on. The barber began on the doctor. I heard him say:

"Dan, this is the easiest shave I have had since we left the ship."

He said again, presently:

"Why Dan, a man could go to sleep with this man shaving him."

Dan took the chair. Then he said:

"Why this is Titian. This is one of the old masters."

I wrote on. Directly Dan said:

"Doctor, it is perfect luxury. The ship's barber isn't any thing to him."

My rough beard was distressing me beyond measure. The barber was rolling up his apparatus. The temptation was too strong. I said:

"Hold on, please. Shave me also."

I sat down in the chair and closed my eyes. The barber soaped my face, and then took his razor and gave me a rake that well nigh threw me into convulsions. I jumped out of the chair: Dan and the doctor were both wiping blood off their faces and laughing.

I said it was a mean, disgraceful fraud.

They said that the misery of this shave had gone so far beyond anything they had ever experienced before, that they could not bear the idea of losing such a chance of hearing a cordial opinion from me on the subject.

It was shameful. But there was no help for it. The skinning was begun and had to be finished. The tears flowed with every rake, and so did the fervent execrations. The barber grew confused, and brought blood every time. I think the boys enjoyed it better than any thing they have seen or heard since they left home.

We have seen the Campanile, and Byron's house and Balbi's the geographer, and the palaces of all the ancient dukes and doges of Venice, and we have seen their effeminate descendants airing their nobility in fashionable French attire in the Grand Square of St. Mark, and eating ices and drinking cheap wines, instead of wearing gallant coats of mail and destroying fleets and armies as their great ancestors did in the days of Venetian glory. We have seen no bravoes with poisoned stilettos, no masks, no wild carnival; but we have seen the ancient pride of Venice, the grim Bronze Horses that figure in a thousand legends. Venice may well cherish them, for they are the only horses she ever had. It is said there are hundreds of people in this curious city who never have seen a living horse in their lives. It is entirely true, no doubt.

And so, having satisfied ourselves, we depart to-morrow, and leave the venerable Queen of the Republics to summon her vanished ships, and marshal her shadowy armies, and know again in dreams the pride of her old renown.

Chapter XXIV

S OME OF THE Quaker City's passengers had arrived in
Venice from Switzerland and other lands before we left
there, and others were expected every day. We heard of no
casualties among them, and no sickness.

We were a little fatigued with sight seeing, and so we rattled through a good deal of country by rail without caring to
stop. I took few notes. I find no mention of Bologna in my
memorandum book, except that we arrived there in good season, but saw none of the sausages for which the place is so
justly celebrated.

Pistoia awoke but a passing interest.

Florence pleased us for a while. I think we appreciated the
great figure of David in the grand square, and the sculptured
group they call the Rape of the Sabines. We wandered
through the endless collections of paintings and statues of the
Pitti and Ufizzi galleries, of course. I make that statement in
self-defense; there let it stop. I could not rest under the im-
putation that I visited Florence and did not traverse its weary
miles of picture galleries. We tried indolently to recollect
something about the Guelphs and Ghibelines and the other
historical cut-throats whose quarrels and assassinations make
up so large a share of Florentine history, but the subject was
not attractive. We had been robbed of all the fine mountain
scenery on our little journey by a system of railroading that
had three miles of tunnel to a hundred yards of daylight, and
we were not inclined to be sociable with Florence. We had
seen the spot, outside the city somewhere, where these people
had allowed the bones of Galileo to rest in unconsecrated
ground for an age because his great discovery that the world
turned around was regarded as a damning heresy by the
church; and we know that long after the world had accepted
his theory and raised his name high in the list of its great
men, they had still let him rot there. That we had lived to see
his dust in honored sepulture in the church of Santa Croce
we owed to a society of *literati*, and not to Florence or her
rulers. We saw Danté's tomb in that church, also, but we were
glad to know that his body was not in it; that the ungrateful

city that had exiled him and persecuted him would give much to have it there, but need not hope to ever secure that high honor to herself. Medicis are good enough for Florence. Let her plant Medicis and build grand monuments over them to testify how gratefully she was wont to lick the hand that scourged her.

Magnanimous Florence! Her jewelry marts are filled with artists in mosaic. Florentine mosaics are the choicest in all the world. Florence loves to have that said. Florence is proud of it. Florence would foster this specialty of hers. She is grateful to the artists that bring to her this high credit and fill her coffers with foreign money, and so she encourages them with pensions. With pensions! Think of the lavishness of it. She knows that people who piece together the beautiful trifles die early, because the labor is so confining, and so exhausting to hand and brain, and so she has decreed that all these people who reach the age of sixty shall have a pension after that! I have not heard that any of them have called for their dividends yet. One man did fight along till he was sixty, and started after his pension, but it appeared that there had been a mistake of a year in his family record, and so he gave it up and died.

These artists will take particles of stone or glass no larger than a mustard seed, and piece them together on a sleeve button or a shirt stud, so smoothly and with such nice adjustment of the delicate shades of color the pieces bear, as to form a pigmy rose with stem, thorn, leaves, petals complete, and all as softly and as truthfully tinted as though Nature had builded it herself. They will counterfeit a fly, or a high-toned bug, or the ruined Coliseum, within the cramped circle of a breastpin, and do it so deftly and so neatly that any man might think a master painted it.

I saw a little table in the great mosaic school in Florence— a little trifle of a centre table—whose top was made of some sort of precious polished stone, and in the stone was inlaid the figure of a flute, with bell-mouth and a mazy complication of keys. No painting in the world could have been softer or richer; no shading out of one tint into another could have been more perfect; no work of art of any kind could have been more faultless than this flute, and yet to count the mul-

titude of little fragments of stone of which they swore it was
formed would bankrupt any man's arithmetic! I do not think
one could have seen where two particles joined each other
with eyes of ordinary shrewdness. Certainly *we* could detect
no such blemish. This table-top cost the labor of one man for
ten long years, so they said, and it was for sale for thirty-five
thousand dollars.

We went to the Church of Santa Croce, from time to time,
in Florence, to weep over the tombs of Michael Angelo, Raphael and Machiavelli, (I suppose they are buried there, but
it may be that they reside elsewhere and rent their tombs to
other parties—such being the fashion in Italy,) and between
times we used to go and stand on the bridges and admire the
Arno. It is popular to admire the Arno. It is a great historical
creek with four feet in the channel and some scows floating
around. It would be a very plausible river if they would pump
some water into it. They all call it a river, and they honestly
think it *is* a river, do these dark and bloody Florentines. They
even help out the delusion by building bridges over it. I do
not see why they are too good to wade.

How the fatigues and annoyances of travel fill one with
bitter prejudices sometimes! I might enter Florence under
happier auspices a month hence and find it all beautiful, all
attractive. But I do not care to think of it now, at all, nor of
its roomy shops filled to the ceiling with snowy marble and
alabaster copies of all the celebrated sculptures in Europe—
copies so enchanting to the eye that I wonder how they can
really be shaped like the dingy petrified nightmares they are
the portraits of. I got lost in Florence at nine o'clock, one
night, and staid lost in that labyrinth of narrow streets and
long rows of vast buildings that look all alike, until toward
three o'clock in the morning. It was a pleasant night and at
first there were a good many people abroad, and there were
cheerful lights about. Later, I grew accustomed to prowling
about mysterious drifts and tunnels and astonishing and interesting myself with coming around corners expecting to
find the hotel staring me in the face, and not finding it doing
any thing of the kind. Later still, I felt tired. I soon felt remarkably tired. But there was no one abroad, now—not even
a policeman. I walked till I was out of all patience, and very

hot and thirsty. At last, somewhere after one o'clock, I came unexpectedly to one of the city gates. I knew then that I was very far from the hotel. The soldiers thought I wanted to leave the city, and they sprang up and barred the way with their muskets. I said:

"Hotel d'Europe!"

It was all the Italian I knew, and I was not certain whether that was Italian or French. The soldiers looked stupidly at each other and at me, and shook their heads and took me into custody. I said I wanted to go home. They did not understand me. They took me into the guard-house and searched me, but they found no sedition on me. They found a small piece of soap (we carry soap with us, now,) and I made them a present of it, seeing that they regarded it as a curiosity. I continued to say Hotel d'Europe, and they continued to shake their heads, until at last a young soldier nodding in the corner roused up and said something. He said he knew where the hotel was, I suppose, for the officer of the guard sent him away with me. We walked a hundred or a hundred and fifty miles, it appeared to me, and then *he* got lost. He turned this way and that, and finally gave it up and signified that he was going to spend the remainder of the morning trying to find the city gate again. At that moment it struck me that there was something familiar about the house over the way. It was the hotel!

It was a happy thing for me that there happened to be a soldier there that knew even as much as he did; for they say that the policy of the government is to change the soldiery from one place to another constantly and from country to city, so that they can not become acquainted with the people and grow lax in their duties and enter into plots and conspiracies with friends. My experiences of Florence were chiefly unpleasant. I will change the subject.

At Pisa we climbed up to the top of the strangest structure the world has any knowledge of—the Leaning Tower. As every one knows, it is in the neighborhood of one hundred and eighty feet high—and I beg to observe that one hundred and eighty feet reach to about the height of four ordinary three-story buildings piled one on top of the other, and is a very considerable altitude for a tower of uniform thickness to aspire to, even when it stands upright—yet this one leans more than thirteen feet out of the perpendicular. It is seven hundred years old, but neither history or tradition say whether it was built as it is, purposely, or whether one of its sides has settled. There is no record that it ever stood straight up. It is built of marble. It is an airy and a beautiful structure, and each of its eight stories is encircled by fluted columns, some of marble and some of granite, with Corinthian capitals that were handsome when they were new. It is a bell tower, and in is top hangs a chime of ancient bells. The winding staircase within is dark, but one always knows which side of the tower he is on because of his naturally gravitating from one side to the other of the staircase with the rise or dip of the tower. Some of the stone steps are foot-worn only on one end; others only on the other end; others only in the middle. To look down into the tower from the top is like looking down into a tilted well. A rope that hangs from the centre of the top touches the wall before it reaches the bottom. Standing on the summit, one does not feel altogether comfortable when he looks down from the high side; but to crawl on your breast to the verge on the lower side and try to stretch your neck out far enough to see the base of the tower, makes your flesh creep, and convinces you for a single moment in spite of all your philosophy, that the building is falling. You handle yourself very carefully, all the time, under the silly impression that if it is *not* falling, your trifling weight will start it unless you are particular not to "bear down" on it.

The Duomo, close at hand, is one of the finest cathedrals in Europe. It is eight hundred years old. Its grandeur has outlived the high commercial prosperity and the political importance that made it a necessity, or rather a possibility. Surrounded by poverty, decay and ruin, it conveys to us a more tangible impression of the former greatness of Pisa than books could give us.

The Baptistery, which is a few years older than the Leaning Tower, is a stately rotunda, of huge dimensions, and was a costly structure. In it hangs the lamp whose measured swing suggested to Galileo the pendulum. It looked an insignificant thing to have conferred upon the world of science and mechanics such a mighty extension of their dominions as it has.

Pondering, in its suggestive presence, I seemed to see a crazy universe of swinging disks, the toiling children of this sedate parent. He appeared to have an intelligent expression about him of knowing that he was not a lamp at all; that he was a Pendulum; a pendulum disguised, for prodigious and inscrutable purposes of his own deep devising, and not a common pendulum either, but the old original patriarchal Pendulum—the Abraham Pendulum of the world.

This Baptistery is endowed with the most pleasing echo of all the echoes we have read of. The guide sounded two sonorous notes, about half an octave apart; the echo answered with the most enchanting, the most melodious, the richest blending of sweet sounds that one can imagine. It was like a long-drawn chord of a church organ, infinitely softened by distance. I may be extravagant in this matter, but if this be the case my ear is to blame—not my pen. I am describing a memory—and one that will remain long with me.

The peculiar devotional spirit of the olden time, which placed a higher confidence in outward forms of worship than in the watchful guarding of the heart against sinful thoughts and the hands against sinful deeds, and which believed in the protecting virtues of inanimate objects made holy by contact with holy things, is illustrated in a striking manner in one of the cemeteries of Pisa. The tombs are set in soil brought in ships from the Holy Land ages ago. To be buried in such ground was regarded by the ancient Pisans as being more potent for salvation than many masses purchased of the church and the vowing of many candles to the Virgin.

Pisa is believed to be about three thousand years old. It was one of the twelve great cities of ancient Etruria, that commonwealth which has left so many monuments in testimony of its extraordinary advancement, and so little history of itself that is tangible and comprehensible. A Pisan antiquarian gave me an ancient tear-jug which he averred was full four thousand years old. It was found among the ruins of one of the oldest of the Etruscan cities. He said it came from a tomb, and was used by some bereaved family in that remote age when even the Pyramids of Egypt were young, Damascus a village, Abraham a prattling infant and ancient Troy not yet dreampt of, to receive the tears wept for some lost idol of a household. It spoke to us in a language of its own; and with a pathos more tender than any words might bring, its mute eloquence swept down the long roll of the centuries with its tale of a vacant chair, a familiar footstep missed from the threshold, a pleasant voice gone from the chorus, a vanished form!—a tale which is always so new to us, so startling, so terrible, so benumbing to the senses, and behold how threadbare and old it is! No shrewdly-worded history could have brought the myths and shadows of that old dreamy age before us clothed with human flesh and warmed with human sympathies so vividly as did this poor little unsentient vessel of pottery.

Pisa was a republic in the middle ages, with a government of her own, armies and navies of her own and a great commerce. She was a warlike power, and inscribed upon her banners many a brilliant fight with Genoese and Turks. It is said that the city once numbered a population of four hundred thousand; but her sceptre has passed from her grasp, now, her ships and her armies are gone, her commerce is dead. Her battle-flags bear the mold and the dust of centuries, her marts are deserted, she has shrunken far within her crumbling walls, and her great population has diminished to twenty thousand souls. She has but one thing left to boast of, and that is not much, viz: she is the second city of Tuscany.

We reached Leghorn in time to see all we wished to see of it long before the city gates were closed for the evening, and then came on board the ship.

We felt as though we had been away from home an age. We never entirely appreciated, before, what a very pleasant den our state-room is; nor how jolly it is to sit at dinner in one's own seat in one's own cabin, and hold familiar conversation with friends in one's own language. Oh, the rare happiness of comprehending every single word that is said, and knowing that every word one says in return will be understood as well! We would talk ourselves to death, now, only there are only about ten passengers out of the sixty-five to talk to. The others are wandering, we hardly know where. We shall not go ashore in Leghorn. We are surfeited with Italian cities for the present, and much prefer to walk the familiar quarter-deck and view this one from a distance.

The stupid magnates of this Leghorn government can not understand that so large a steamer as ours could cross the broad Atlantic with no other purpose than to indulge a party of ladies and gentlemen in a pleasure excursion. It looks too improbable. It is suspicious, they think. Something more important must be hidden behind it all. They can not understand it, and they scorn the evidence of the ship's papers. They have decided at last that we are a battalion of incendiary, blood-thirsty Garibaldians in disguise! And in all seriousness they have set a gun-boat to watch the vessel night and day, with orders to close down on any revolutionary movement in a twinkling! Police boats are on patrol duty about us all the time, and it is as much as a sailor's liberty is worth to show himself in a red shirt. These policemen follow the executive officer's boat from shore to ship and from ship to shore and watch his dark maneuvres with a vigilant eye. They will arrest him yet unless he assumes an expression of countenance that shall have less of carnage, insurrection and sedition in it. A visit paid in a friendly way to General Garibaldi yesterday (by cordial invitation,) by some of our passengers, has gone far to confirm the dread suspicions the government harbors toward us. It is thought the friendly visit was only the cloak of a bloody conspiracy. These people draw near and watch us when we bathe in the sea from the ship's side. Do they think we are communing with a reserve force of rascals at the bottom?

It is said that we shall probably be quarantined at Naples. Two or three of us prefer not to run this risk. Therefore, when we are rested, we propose to go in a French steamer to Civita Vecchia, and from thence to Rome, and by rail to Naples. They do not quarantine the cars, no matter where they got their passengers from.

Chapter XXV

THERE ARE a good many things about this Italy which I do not understand—and more especially I can not understand how a bankrupt Government can have such palatial railroad depots and such marvels of turnpikes. Why, these latter are as hard as adamant, as straight as a line, as smooth as a floor, and as white as snow. When it is too dark to see any other object, one can still see the white turnpikes of France and Italy; and they are clean enough to eat from, without a table-cloth. And yet no tolls are charged.

As for the railways—we have none like them. The cars slide as smoothly along as if they were on runners. The depots are vast palaces of cut marble, with stately colonnades of the same royal stone traversing them from end to end, and with ample walls and ceilings richly decorated with frescoes. The lofty gateways are graced with statues, and the broad floors are all laid in polished flags of marble.

These things win me more than Italy's hundred galleries of priceless art treasures, because I can understand the one and am not competent to appreciate the other. In the turnpikes, the railways, the depots, and the new boulevards of uniform houses in Florence and other cities here, I see the genius of Louis Napoleon, or rather, I see the works of that statesman imitated. But Louis has taken care that in France there shall be a foundation for these improvements—money. He has always the wherewithal to back up his projects; they strengthen France and never weaken her. Her material prosperity is genuine. But here the case is different. This country is bankrupt. There is no real foundation for these great works. The prosperity they would seem to indicate is a pretence. There is no money in the treasury, and so they enfeeble her instead of strengthening. Italy has achieved the dearest wish of her heart and become an independent State—and in so doing she has drawn an elephant in the political lottery. She has nothing to feed it on. Inexperienced in government, she plunged into all manner of useless expenditure, and swamped her treasury almost in a day. She squandered millions of francs on a navy which she did not need, and the first time she took her new

CHAPTER XXV 201

toy into action she got it knocked higher than Gilderoy's kite—to use the language of the Pilgrims.

But it is an ill-wind that blows nobody good. A year ago, when Italy saw utter ruin staring her in the face and her greenbacks hardly worth the paper they were printed on, her Parliament ventured upon a *coup de main* that would have appalled the stoutest of her statesmen under less desperate circumstances. They, in a manner, confiscated the domains of the Church! This in priest-ridden Italy! This in a land which has groped in the midnight of priestly superstition for sixteen hundred years! It was a rare good fortune for Italy, the stress of weather that drove her to break from this prison-house.

They do not call it *confiscating* the church property. That would sound too harshly yet. But it amounts to that. There are thousands of churches in Italy, each with untold millions of treasures stored away in its closets, and each with its battalion of priests to be supported. And then there are the estates of the Church—league on league of the richest lands and the noblest forests in all Italy—all yielding immense revenues to the Church, and none paying a cent in taxes to the State. In some great districts the Church owns *all* the property—lands, watercourses, woods, mills and factories. They buy, they sell, they manufacture, and since they pay no taxes, who can hope to compete with them?

Well, the Government has seized all this in effect, and will yet seize it in rigid and unpoetical reality, no doubt. Something must be done to feed a starving treasury, and there is no other resource in all Italy—none but the riches of the Church. So the Government intends to take to itself a great portion of the revenues arising from priestly farms, factories, etc., and also intends to take possession of the churches and carry them on, after its own fashion and upon its own responsibility. In a few instances it will leave the establishments of great pet churches undisturbed, but in all others only a handful of priests will be retained to preach and pray, a few will be pensioned, and the balance turned adrift.

Pray glance at some of these churches and their embellishments, and see whether the Government is doing a righteous thing or not. In Venice, to-day, a city of a hundred thousand inhabitants, there are twelve hundred priests. Heaven only

knows how many there were before the Parliament reduced
their numbers. There was the great Jesuit Church. Under the
old regime it required sixty priests to engineer it—the Government does it with five, now, and the others are discharged
from service. All about that church wretchedness and poverty
abound. At its door a dozen hats and bonnets were doffed to
us, as many heads were humbly bowed, and as many hands
extended, appealing for pennies—appealing with foreign
words we could not understand, but appealing mutely, with
sad eyes, and sunken cheeks, and ragged raiment, that no
words were needed to translate. Then we passed within the
great doors, and it seemed that the riches of the world were
before us! Huge columns carved out of single masses of marble, and inlaid from top to bottom with a hundred intricate
figures wrought in costly verde antique; pulpits of the same
rich materials, whose draperies hung down in many a pictured fold, the stony fabric counterfeiting the delicate work
of the loom; the grand altar brilliant with polished facings
and balustrades of oriental agate, jasper, verde antique, and
other precious stones, whose names, even, we seldom hear—
and slabs of priceless lapis lazuli lavished every where as recklessly as if the church had owned a quarry of it. In the midst
of all this magnificence, the solid gold and silver furniture of
the altar seemed cheap and trivial. Even the floors and ceilings
cost a princely fortune.

Now, where is the use of allowing all those riches to lie
idle, while half of that community hardly know, from day to
day, how they are going to keep body and soul together?
And, where is the wisdom in permitting hundreds upon
hundreds of millions of francs to be locked up in the useless
trumpery of churches all over Italy, and the people ground to
death with taxation to uphold a perishing Government?

As far as I can see, Italy, for fifteen hundred years, has
turned all her energies, all her finances, and all her industry
to the building up of a vast array of wonderful church edifices, and starving half her citizens to accomplish it. She is to-
day one vast museum of magnificence and misery. All the
churches in an ordinary American city put together could
hardly buy the jeweled frippery in one of her hundred cathedrals. And for every beggar in America, Italy can show a

hundred—and rags and vermin to match. It is the wretched-est, princeliest land on earth.

Look at the grand Duomo of Florence—a vast pile that has been sapping the purses of her citizens for five hundred years, and is not nearly finished yet. Like all other men, I fell down and worshipped it, but when the filthy beggars swarmed around me the contrast was too striking, too suggestive, and I said, "O, sons of classic Italy, *is* the spirit of enterprise, of self-reliance, of noble endeavor, utterly dead within ye? Curse your indolent worthlessness, why don't you rob your church?"

Three hundred happy, comfortable priests are employed in that Cathedral.

And now that my temper is up, I may as well go on and abuse every body I can think of. They have a grand mauso-leum in Florence, which they built to bury our Lord and Sa-viour and the Medici family in. It sounds blasphemous, but it is true, and here they *act* blasphemy. The dead and damned Medicis who cruelly tyrannized over Florence and were her curse for over two hundred years, are salted away in a circle of costly vaults, and in their midst the Holy Sepulchre was to have been set up. The expedition sent to Jerusalem to seize it got into trouble and could not accomplish the burglary, and so the centre of the mausoleum is vacant now. They say the entire mausoleum was intended for the Holy Sepulchre, and was only turned into a family burying place after the Jerusa-lem expedition failed—but you will excuse me. Some of those Medicis would have smuggled themselves in sure.—What *they* had not the effrontery to do, was not worth doing. Why, they had their trivial, forgotten exploits on land and sea pic-tured out in grand frescoes (as did also the ancient Doges of Venice) with the Saviour and the Virgin throwing bouquets to them out of the clouds, and the Deity himself applauding from his throne in Heaven! And who painted these things? Why, Titian, Tintoretto, Paul Veronese, Raphael—none other than the world's idols, the "old masters."

Andrea del Sarto glorified his princes in pictures that must save them for ever from the oblivion they merited, and they let him starve. Served him right. Raphael pictured such in-fernal villains as Catherine and Marie de Medicis seated in heaven and conversing familiarly with the Virgin Mary and the angels, (to say nothing of higher personages,) and yet my friends abuse me because I am a little prejudiced against the old masters—because I fail sometimes to see the beauty that is in their productions. I can not help but see it, now and then, but I keep on protesting against the groveling spirit that could persuade those masters to prostitute their noble talents to the adulation of such monsters as the French, Venetian and Florentine Princes of two and three hundred years ago, all the same.

I am told that the old masters had to do these shameful things for bread, the princes and potentates being the only patrons of art. If a grandly gifted man may drag his pride and his manhood in the dirt for bread rather than starve with the nobility that is in him untainted, the excuse is a valid one. It would excuse theft in Washingtons and Wellingtons, and unchastity in women as well.

But somehow, I can not keep that Medici mausoleum out of my memory. It is as large as a church; its pavement is rich enough for the pavement of a King's palace; its great dome is gorgeous with frescoes; its walls are made of—what? Marble?—plaster?—wood?—paper? No. Red porphyry—verde antique—jasper—oriental agate—alabaster—mother-of-pearl—chalcedony—red coral—lapis lazuli! All the vast walls are made wholly of these precious stones, worked in, and in and in together in elaborate patterns and figures, and polished till they glow like great mirrors with the pictured splendors reflected from the dome overhead. And before a statue of one of those dead Medicis reposes a crown that blazes with diamonds and emeralds enough to buy a ship-of-the-line, almost. These are the things the Government has its evil eye upon, and a happy thing it will be for Italy when they melt away in the public treasury.

And now—. However, another beggar approaches. I will go out and destroy him, and then come back and write another chapter of vituperation.

Having eaten the friendless orphan—having driven away his comrades—having grown calm and reflective at length—I now feel in a kindlier mood. I feel that after talking so freely about the priests and the churches, justice demands that if I know any thing good about either I ought to say it. I *have* heard of many things that redound to the credit of the priesthood, but the most notable matter that occurs to me now is the devotion one of the mendicant orders showed during the prevalence of the cholera last year. I speak of the Dominican friars—men who wear a coarse, heavy brown robe and a cowl, in this hot climate, and go barefoot. They live on alms altogether, I believe. They must unquestionably love their religion, to suffer so much for it. When the cholera was raging in Naples; when the people were dying by hundreds and hundreds every day; when every concern for the public welfare was swallowed up in selfish private interest, and every citizen made the taking care of himself his sole object, these men banded themselves together and went about nursing the sick and burying the dead. Their noble efforts cost many of them their lives. They laid them down cheerfully, and well they might. Creeds mathematically precise, and hair-splitting niceties of doctrine, are absolutely necessary for the salvation of some kinds of souls, but surely the charity, the purity, the unselfishness that are in the hearts of men like these would save their souls though they were bankrupt in the true religion—which is ours.

One of these fat bare-footed rascals came here to Civita Vecchia with us in the little French steamer. There were only half a dozen of us in the cabin. He belonged in the steerage. He was the life of the ship, the bloody-minded son of the Inquisition! He and the leader of the marine band of a French man-of-war played on the piano and sang opera turn about; they sang duets together; they rigged impromptu theatrical costumes and gave us extravagant farces and pantomimes. We got along first-rate with the friar, and were excessively conversational, albeit he could not understand what we said, and certainly he never uttered a word that we could guess the meaning of.

This Civita Vecchia is the finest nest of dirt, vermin and ignorance we have found yet, except that African perdition they call Tangier, which is just like it. The people here live in alleys two yards wide, which have a smell about them which is peculiar but not entertaining. It is well the alleys are not wider, because they hold as much smell now as a person can stand, and of course, if they were wider they would hold more, and then the people would die. These alleys are paved with stone, and carpeted with deceased cats, and decayed rags, and decomposed vegetable-tops, and remnants of old boots, all soaked with dish-water, and the people sit around on stools and enjoy it. They are indolent, as a general thing, and yet have few pastimes. They work two or three hours at a time, but not hard, and then they knock off and catch flies. This does not require any talent, because they only have to grab—if they do not get the one they are after, they get another. It is all the same to them. They have no partialities. Whichever one they get is the one they want.

They have other kinds of insects, but it does not make them arrogant. They are very quiet, unpretending people. They have more of these kind of things than other communities, but they do not boast.

They are very uncleanly—these people—in face, in person and dress. When they see any body with a clean shirt on, it arouses their scorn. The women wash clothes, half the day, at the public tanks in the streets, but they are probably somebody else's. Or may be they keep one set to wear and another to wash; because they never put on any that have ever been washed. When they get done washing, they sit in the alleys and nurse their cubs. They nurse one ash-cat at a time, and the others scratch their backs against the door-post and are happy.

All this country belongs to the Papal States. They do not appear to have any schools here, and only one billiard table. Their education is at a very low stage. One portion of the men go into the military, another into the priesthood, and the rest into the shoe-making business.

They keep up the passport system here, but so they do in Turkey. This shows that the Papal States are as far advanced as Turkey. This fact will be alone sufficient to silence the tongues of malignant calumniators. I had to get my passport *vised* for Rome in Florence, and then they would not let me come ashore here until a policeman had examined it on the wharf and sent me a permit. They did not even dare to let me take my passport in my hands for twelve hours, I looked so formidable. They judged it best to let me cool down. They thought I wanted to take the town, likely. Little did they know me. I wouldn't have it. They examined my baggage at the depot. They took one of my ablest jokes and read it over carefully twice and then read it backwards. But it was too deep for them. They passed it around, and every body speculated on it awhile, but it mastered them all.

It was no common joke. At length a veteran officer spelled it over deliberately and shook his head three or four times and said that in his opinion it was seditious. That was the first time I felt alarmed. I immediately said I would explain the document, and they crowded around. And so I explained and explained and explained, and they took notes of all I said, but the more I explained the more they could not understand it, and when they desisted at last, I could not even understand it myself. They said they believed it was an incendiary document, leveled at the government. I declared solemnly that it was not, but they only shook their heads and would not be satisfied. Then they consulted a good while; and finally they confiscated it. I was very sorry for this, because I had worked a long time on that joke, and took a good deal of pride in it, and now I suppose I shall never see it any more. I suppose it will be sent up and filed away among the criminal archives of Rome, and will always be regarded as a mysterious infernal machine which would have blown up like a mine and scattered the good Pope all around, but for a miraculous providential interference. And I suppose that all the time I am in Rome the police will dog me about from place to place because they think I am a dangerous character.

It is fearfully hot in Civita Vecchia. The streets are made very narrow and the houses built very solid and heavy and high, as a protection against the heat. This is the first Italian town I have seen which does not appear to have a patron saint. I suppose no saint but the one that went up in the chariot of fire could stand the climate.

There is nothing here to see. They have not even a cathedral, with eleven tons of solid silver archbishops in the back room; and they do not show you any moldy buildings that are seven thousand years old; nor any smoke-dried old fire-screens which are *chef d'œuvres* of Reubens or Simpson, or Titian or Ferguson, or any of those parties; and they haven't any bottled fragments of saints, and not even a nail from the true cross. We are going to Rome. There is nothing to see here.

Chapter XXVI

WHAT IS IT that confers the noblest delight? What is that which swells a man's breast with pride above that which any other experience can bring to him? Discovery! To know that you are walking where none others have walked; that you are beholding what human eye has not seen before; that you are breathing a virgin atmosphere. To give birth to an idea—to discover a great thought—an intellectual nugget, right under the dust of a field that many a brain-plow had gone over before. To find a new planet, to invent a new hinge, to find the way to make the lightnings carry your messages. To be the *first*—that is the idea. To do something, say something, see something, before *any body* else—these are the things that confer a pleasure compared with which other pleasures are tame and commonplace, other ecstasies cheap and trivial. Morse, with his first message, brought by his servant, the lightning; Fulton, in that long-drawn century of suspense, when he placed his hand upon the throttle-valve and lo, the steamboat moved; Jenner, when his patient with the cow's virus in his blood, walked through the small-pox hospitals unscathed; Howe, when the idea shot through his brain that for a hundred and twenty generations the eye had been bored through the wrong end of the needle; the nameless lord of art who laid down his chisel in some old age that is forgotten, now, and gloated upon the finished Laocoon; Daguerre, when he commanded the sun, riding in the zenith, to print the landscape upon his insignificant silvered plate, and he obeyed; Columbus, in the Pinta's shrouds, when he swung his hat above a fabled sea and gazed abroad upon an unknown world! These are the men who have really *lived*—who have actually comprehended what pleasure is—who have crowded long lifetimes of ecstasy into a single moment.

What is there in Rome for me to see that others have not seen before me? What is there for me to touch that others have not touched? What is there for me to feel, to learn, to hear, to know, that shall thrill me before it pass to others? What can I discover?—Nothing. Nothing whatsoever. One charm of travel dies here. But if I were only a Roman!—If, added to my own I could be gifted with modern Roman sloth, modern Roman superstition, and modern Roman boundlessness of ignorance, what bewildering worlds of unsuspected wonders I would discover! Ah, if I were only a habitant of the Campagna five and twenty miles from Rome! *Then* I would travel.

I would go to America, and see, and learn, and return to the Campagna and stand before my countrymen an illustrious discoverer. I would say:

"I saw there a country which has no overshadowing Mother Church, and yet the people survive. I saw a government which never was protected by foreign soldiers at a cost greater than that required to carry on the government itself. I saw common men and common women who could read; I even saw small children of common country people reading from books; if I dared think you would believe it, I would say they could write, also. In the cities I saw people drinking a delicious beverage made of chalk and water, but never once saw goats driven through their Broadway or their Pennsylvania Avenue or their Montgomery street and milked at the doors of the houses. I saw real glass windows in the houses of even the commonest people. Some of the houses are not of stone, nor yet of bricks; I solemnly swear they are made of wood. Houses there will take fire and burn, sometimes—actually burn entirely down, and not leave a single vestige behind. I could state that for a truth, upon my death-bed. And as a proof that the circumstance is not rare, I aver that they have a thing which they call a fire-engine, which vomits forth great streams of water, and is kept always in readiness, by night and by day, to rush to houses that are burning. You would think one engine would be sufficient, but some great cities have a hundred; they keep men hired, and pay them by the month to do nothing but put out fires. For a certain sum of money other men will insure that your house shall not burn down; and if it burns they will pay you for it. There are hundreds and thousands of schools, and any body may go and learn to be wise, like a priest. In that singular country if a rich man dies a sinner, he is damned; he can not buy salvation with money for masses. There is really not much use in being rich, there. Not much use as far as the other world is concerned, but much, very much use, as concerns this; because there, if a man be rich, he is very greatly honored, and can become a legislator, a governor, a general, a senator, no matter how ignorant an ass he is—just as in our beloved Italy the nobles hold all the great places, even though sometimes they are born noble idiots. There, if a man be rich, they give him costly presents, they ask him to feasts, they invite him to drink complicated beverages; but if he be poor and in debt, they require him to do that which they term to "settle." The women put on a different dress almost every day; the dress is usually fine, but absurd in shape; the very shape and fashion of it changes twice in a hundred years; and did I but covet to be called an extravagant falsifier, I would say it changed even oftener. Hair does not grow upon the American women's heads; it is made for them by cunning workmen in the shops, and is curled and frizzled into scandalous and ungodly forms. Some persons wear eyes of glass which they see through with facility perhaps, else they would not use them; and in the mouths of some are teeth made by the sacrilegious hand of man. The dress of the men is laughably grotesque. They carry no musket in ordinary life, nor no long-pointed pole; they wear no wide green-lined cloak; they wear no peaked black felt hat, no leather gaiters reaching to the knee, no goat-skin breeches with the hair side out, no hob-nailed shoes, no prodigious spurs. They wear a conical hat termed a "nail-kag;" a coat of saddest black; a shirt which shows dirt so easily that it has to be changed every month, and is very troublesome; things called pantaloons, which are held up by shoulder straps, and on their feet they wear boots which are ridiculous in pattern and can stand no wear. Yet dressed in this fantastic garb, these people laughed at *my* costume. In that country, books are so common that it is really no curiosity to see one. Newspapers also. They have a great machine which prints such things by thousands every hour.

"I saw common men, there—men who were neither priests nor princes—who yet absolutely owned the land they tilled. It was not rented from the church, nor from the nobles. I am ready to take my oath of this. In that country you might fall from a third story window three several times, and not mash either a soldier or a priest.—The scarcity of such people is astonishing. In the cities you will see a dozen civilians for every soldier, and as many for every priest or preacher. Jews, there, are treated just like human beings, instead of dogs. They can work at any business they please; they can sell brand new goods if they want to; they can keep drug-stores; they can practice medicine among Christians; they can even shake hands with Christians if they choose; they can associate with them, just the same as one human being does with another human being; they don't have to stay shut up in one corner of the towns; they can live in any part of a town they like best; it is said they even have the privilege of buying land and houses, and owning them themselves, though I doubt that, myself; they never have had to run races naked through the public streets, against jackasses, to please the people in carnival time; there they never have been driven by the soldiers into a church every Sunday for hundreds of years to hear themselves and their religion especially and particularly cursed; at this very day, in that curious country, a Jew is allowed to vote, hold office, yea, get up on a rostrum in the public street and express his opinion of the government if the government don't suit him! Ah, it is wonderful. The common people there know a great deal; they even have the effrontery to complain if they are not properly governed, and to take hold and help conduct the government themselves; if they had laws like ours, which give one dollar of every three a crop produces to the government for taxes, they would have that law altered: instead of paying thirty-three dollars in taxes, out of every one hundred they receive, they complain if they have to pay seven. They are curious people. They do not know when they are well off. Mendicant priests do not prowl among them with baskets begging for the church and eating up their substance. One hardly ever sees a minister of the gospel going around there in his bare feet, with a basket, begging for subsistence. In that country the preachers are not like our mendicant orders of friars—they have two or three suits of clothing, and they wash sometimes. In that land are mountains far higher than the Alban mountains; the vast Roman Campagna, a hundred miles long and full forty broad, is really small compared to the United States of America; the Tiber, that celebrated river of ours, which stretches its mighty course almost two hundred miles, and which a lad can scarcely throw a stone across at Rome, is not so long, nor yet so wide, as the American Mississippi—nor yet the Ohio, nor even the Hudson. In America the people are absolutely wiser and know much more than their grandfathers did. *They* do not plow with a sharpened stick, nor yet with a three-cornered block of wood that merely scratches the top of the ground. We do that because our fathers did, three thousand years ago, I suppose. But those people have no holy reverence for their ancestors. They plow with a plow that is a sharp, curved blade of iron, and it cuts into the earth full five inches. And this is not all. They cut their grain with a horrid machine that mows down whole fields in a day. If I dared, I would say that sometimes they use a blasphemous plow that works by fire and vapor and tears up an acre of ground in a single hour—but—but—I see by your looks that you do not believe the things I am telling you. Alas, my character is ruined, and I am a branded speaker of untruths!"

Of course we have been to the monster Church of St. Peter, frequently. I knew its dimensions. I knew it was a prodigious structure. I knew it was just about the length of the capitol at Washington—say seven hundred and thirty feet. I knew it was three hundred and sixty-four feet wide, and consequently wider than the capitol. I knew that the cross on the top of the dome of the church was four hundred and thirty-eight feet above the ground, and therefore about a hundred or may be a hundred and twenty-five feet higher than the dome of the capitol.—Thus I had one gauge. I wished to come as near forming a correct idea of how it was going to look, as possible; I had a curiosity to see how much I would err. I erred considerably. St. Peter's did not look nearly so large as the capitol, and certainly not a twentieth part as beautiful, from the outside.

When we reached the door, and stood fairly within the church, it was impossible to comprehend that it was a *very* large building. I had to *cipher* a comprehension of it. I had to ransack my memory for some more similes. St. Peter's is bulky. Its height and size would represent two of the Washington capitol set one on top of the other—if the capitol were wider; or two blocks or two blocks and a half of ordi-

nary buildings set one on top of the other. St. Peter's *was*
that large, but it could and would not look so. The trouble
was that everything in it and about it was on such a scale of
uniform vastness that there were no contrasts to judge by—
none but the people, and I had not noticed them. They were
insects. The statues of children holding vases of holy water
were immense, according to the tables of figures, but so was
every thing else around them. The mosaic pictures in the
dome were huge, and were made of thousands and thousands
of cubes of glass as large as the end of my little finger, but
those pictures looked smooth, and gaudy of color, and in
good proportion to the dome. Evidently they would not answer to measure by. Away down toward the far end of the
church (I thought it was really clear at the far end, but discovered afterward that it was in the centre, under the dome,)
stood the thing they call the *baldacchino*—a great bronze py-
ramidal frame-work like that which upholds a mosquito bar.
It only looked like a considerably magnified bedstead—nothing more. Yet I knew it was a good deal more than half as
high as Niagara Falls. It was overshadowed by a dome so
mighty that its own height was snubbed. The four great
square piers or pillars that stand equidistant from each other
in the church, and support the roof, I could not work up to
their real dimensions by any method of comparison. I knew
that the faces of each were about the width of a very large
dwelling-house front, (fifty or sixty feet,) and that they were
twice as high as an ordinary three-story dwelling, but still
they looked small. I tried all the different ways I could think
of to compel myself to understand how large St. Peter's was,
but with small success. The mosaic portrait of an Apostle who
was writing with a pen six feet long seemed only an ordinary
Apostle.

But the people attracted my attention after a while. To
stand in the door of St. Peter's and look at men down toward
its further extremity, two blocks away, has a diminishing effect on them; surrounded by the prodigious pictures and statues, and lost in the vast spaces, they look very much smaller
than they would if they stood two blocks away in the open
air. I "averaged" a man as he passed me and watched him as
he drifted far down by the *baldacchino* and beyond—watched

him dwindle to an insignificant school-boy, and then, in the midst of the silent throng of human pigmies gliding about him, I lost him. The church had lately been decorated, on the occasion of a great ceremony in honor of St. Peter, and men were engaged, now, in removing the flowers and gilt paper from the walls and pillars. As no ladders could reach the great heights, the men swung themselves down from balustrades and the capitals of pilasters by ropes, to do this work. The upper gallery which encircles the inner sweep of the dome is two hundred and forty feet above the floor of the church— very few steeples in America could reach up to it. Visitors always go up there to look down into the church because one gets the best idea of some of the heights and distances from that point. While we stood on the floor one of the workmen swung loose from that gallery at the end of a long rope. I had not supposed, before, that a man *could* look so much like a spider. He was insignificant in size, and his rope seemed only a thread. Seeing that he took up so little space, I could believe the story, then, that ten thousand troops went to St. Peter's, once, to hear mass, and their commanding officer came after-ward, and not finding them, supposed they had not yet ar-rived. But they were in the church, nevertheless—they were in one of the transepts. Nearly fifty thousand persons assem-bled in St. Peter's to hear the publishing of the dogma of the Immaculate Conception. It is estimated that the floor of the church affords standing room for—for a large number of people; I have forgotten the exact figures. But it is no mat-ter—it is near enough.

They have twelve small pillars, in St. Peter's, which came from Solomon's Temple. They have, also—which was far more interesting to me—a piece of the true cross, and some nails, and a part of the crown of thorns.

Of course we ascended to the summit of the dome, and of course we also went up into the gilt copper ball which is above it.—There was room there for a dozen persons, with a little crowding, and it was as close and hot as an oven. Some of those people who are so fond of writing their names in prominent places had been there before us—a million or two, I should think. From the dome of St. Peter's one can see every notable object in Rome, from the Castle of St. Angelo to the Coliseum. He can discern the seven hills upon which Rome is built. He can see the Tiber, and the locality of the bridge which Horatius kept "in the brave days of old" when Lars Porsena attempted to cross it with his invading host. He can see the spot where the Horatii and the Curatii fought their famous battle. He can see the broad green Campagna, stretching away toward the mountains, with its scattered arches and broken aqueducts of the olden time, so picturesque in their gray ruin, and so daintily festooned with vines. He can see the Alban Mountains, the Appenines, the Sabine Hills, and the blue Mediterranean. He can see a panorama that is varied, extensive, beautiful to the eye, and more illustrious in history than any other in Europe.—About his feet is spread the remnant of a city that once had a population of four million souls; and among its massed edifices stand the ruins of temples, columns, and triumphal arches that knew the Cæsars, and the noonday of Roman splendor; and close by them, in unimpaired strength, is a drain of arched and heavy masonry that belonged to that older city which stood here before Romulus and Remus were born or Rome thought of. The Appian Way is here yet, and looking much as it did, perhaps, when the triumphal processions of the Emperors moved over it in other days bringing fettered princes from the confines of the earth. We can not see the long array of chariots and mail-clad men laden with the spoils of conquest, but we can imagine the pageant, after a fashion. We look out upon many objects of interest from the dome of St. Peter's; and last of all, almost at our feet, our eyes rest upon the building which was once the Inquisition. How times changed, between the older ages and the new! Some seventeen or eighteen centuries ago, the ignorant men of Rome were wont to put Christians in the arena of the Coliseum yonder, and turn the wild beasts in upon them for a show. It was for a lesson as well. It was to teach the people to abhor and fear the new doctrine the followers of Christ were teaching. The beasts tore the victims limb from limb and made poor mangled corpses of them in the twinkling of an eye. But when the Christians came into power, when the holy Mother Church became mistress of the barbarians, she taught them the error of their ways by no such means. No, she put them

in this pleasant Inquisition and pointed to the Blessed Redeemer, who was so gentle and so merciful toward all men,
and they urged the barbarians to love him; and they did all
they could to persuade them to love and honor him—first by
twisting their thumbs out of joint with a screw; then by nipping their flesh with pincers—red-hot ones, because they are
the most comfortable in cold weather; then by skinning them
alive a little, and finally by roasting them in public. They always convinced those barbarians. The true religion, properly
administered, as the good Mother Church used to administer
it, is very, very soothing. It is wonderfully persuasive, also.
There is a great difference between feeding parties to wild
beasts and stirring up their finer feelings in an Inquisition.
One is the system of degraded barbarians, the other of enlightened, civilized people. It is a great pity the playful Inquisition is no more.

I prefer not to describe St. Peter's. It has been done before.
The ashes of Peter, the disciple of the Saviour, repose in a
crypt under the *baldacchino*. We stood reverently in that place;
so did we also in the Mamertine Prison, where he was confined, where he converted the soldiers, and where tradition
says he caused a spring of water to flow in order that he
might baptize them. But when they showed us the print of
Peter's face in the hard stone of the prison wall and said he
made that by falling up against it, we doubted. And when,
also, the monk at the church of San Sebastian showed us a
paving-stone with two great footprints in it and said that Peter's feet made those, we lacked confidence again. Such things
do not impress one. The monk said that angels came and liberated Peter from prison by night, and he started away from
Rome by the Appian Way. The Saviour met him and told him
to go back, which he did. Peter left those footprints in the
stone upon which he stood at the time. It was not stated how
it was ever discovered whose footprints they were, seeing the
interview occurred secretly and at night. The print of the face
in the prison was that of a man of common size; the foot-
prints were those of a man ten or twelve feet high. The discrepancy confirmed our unbelief.

We necessarily visited the Forum, where Cæsar was assassinated, and also the Tarpeian Rock. We saw the Dying Glad-

iator at the Capitol, and I think that even we appreciated that wonder of art; as much, perhaps, as we did that fearful story wrought in marble, in the Vatican—the Laocoon. And then the Coliseum.

Every body knows the picture of the Coliseum; every body recognizes at once that "looped and windowed" band-box with a side bitten out. Being rather isolated, it shows to better advantage than any other of the monuments of ancient Rome. Even the beautiful Pantheon, whose pagan altars uphold the cross, now, and whose Venus, tricked out in consecrated gimcracks, does reluctant duty as a Virgin Mary to-day, is built about with shabby houses and its stateliness sadly marred. But the monarch of all European ruins, the Coliseum, maintains that reserve and that royal seclusion which is proper to majesty. Weeds and flowers spring from its massy arches and its circling seats, and vines hang their fringes from its lofty walls. An impressive silence broods over the monstrous structure where such multitudes of men and women were wont to assemble in other days. The butterflies have taken the places of the queens of fashion and beauty of eighteen centuries ago, and the lizards sun themselves in the sacred seat of the Emperor. More vividly than all the written histories, the Coliseum tells the story of Rome's grandeur and Rome's decay. It is the worthiest type of both that exists. Moving about the Rome of to-day, we might find it hard to believe in her old magnificence and her millions of population; but with this stubborn evidence before us that she was obliged to have a theatre with sitting room for eighty thousand persons and standing room for twenty thousand more, to accommodate such of her citizens as required amusement, we find belief less difficult. The Coliseum is over one thousand six hundred feet long, seven hundred and fifty wide, and one hundred and sixty-five high. Its shape is oval.

In America we make convicts useful at the same time that we punish them for their crimes. We farm them out and compel them to earn money for the State by making barrels and building roads. Thus we combine business with retribution, and all things are lovely. But in ancient Rome they combined religious duty with pleasure. Since it was necessary that the new sect called Christians should be exterminated, the people judged it wise to make this work profitable to the State at the same time, and entertaining to the public. In addition to the gladiatorial combats and other shows, they sometimes threw members of the hated sect into the arena of the Coliseum and turned wild beasts in upon them. It is estimated that seventy thousand Christians suffered martyrdom in this place. This has made the Coliseum holy ground, in the eyes of the followers of the Saviour. And well it might; for if the chain that bound a saint, and the footprints a saint has left upon a stone he chanced to stand upon, be holy, surely the spot where a man gave up his life for his faith is holy.

Seventeen or eighteen centuries ago this Coliseum was *the* theatre of Rome, and Rome was mistress of the world. Splendid pageants were exhibited here, in presence of the Emperor, the great ministers of State, the nobles, and vast audiences of citizens of smaller consequence. Gladiators fought with gladiators and at times with warrior prisoners from many a distant land. It was *the* theatre of Rome—of the world—and the man of fashion who could not let fall in a casual and unintentional manner something about "my private box at the Coliseum" could not move in the first circles. When the clothing-store merchant wished to consume the corner grocery man with envy, he bought secured seats in the front row and let the thing be known. When the irresistible dry goods clerk wished to blight and destroy, according to his native instinct, he got himself up regardless of expense and took some other fellow's young lady to the Coliseum, and then accented the affront by cramming her with ice cream between the acts, or by approaching the cage and stirring up the martyrs with his whalebone cane for her edification. The Roman swell was in his true element only when he stood up against a pillar and fingered his moustache unconscious of the ladies; when he viewed the bloody combats through an opera-glass two inches long; when he excited the envy of provincials by criticisms which showed that he had been to the Coliseum many and many a time and was long ago over the novelty of it; when he turned away with a yawn at last and said,

"*He* a star! handles his sword like an apprentice brigand! he'll do for the country, maybe, but he don't answer for the metropolis!"

Glad was the contraband that had a seat in the pit at the Saturday matinee, and happy the Roman street-boy who ate his peanuts and guyed the gladiators from the dizzy gallery.

For me was reserved the high honor of discovering among the rubbish of the ruined Coliseum the only playbill of that establishment now extant. There was a suggestive smell of mint-drops about it still, a corner of it had evidently been chewed, and on the margin, in choice Latin, these words were written in a delicate female hand:

"*Meet me on the Tarpeian Rock to-morrow evening, dear, at sharp seven. Mother will be absent on a visit to her friends in the Sabine Hills.*
CLAUDIA."

Ah, where is that lucky youth to-day, and where the little hand that wrote those dainty lines! Dust and ashes these seventeen hundred years!

Thus reads the bill:

ROMAN COLISEUM.

UNPARALLELED ATTRACTION!
NEW PROPERTIES! NEW LIONS! NEW GLADIATORS!

Engagement of the renowned

MARCUS MARCELLUS VALERIAN!
FOR SIX NIGHTS ONLY!

The management beg leave to offer to the public an entertainment surpassing in magnificence any thing that has heretofore been attempted on any stage. No expense has been spared to make the opening season one which shall be worthy the generous patronage which the management feel sure will crown their efforts. The management beg leave to state that they have succeeded in securing the services of a

GALAXY OF TALENT!

such as has not been beheld in Rome before.

The performance will commence this evening with a

GRAND BROADSWORD COMBAT!

between two young and promising amateurs and a celebrated Parthian gladiator who has just arrived a prisoner from the Camp of Verus.

This will be followed by a grand moral

BATTLE-AX ENGAGEMENT!

between the renowned Valerian (with one hand tied behind him,) and two gigantic savages from Britain.

After which the renowned Valerian (if he survive,) will fight with the broadsword,

LEFT-HANDED!

against six Sophomores and a Freshman from the Gladiatorial College!

A long series of brilliant engagements will follow, in which the finest talent of the Empire will take part.

After which the celebrated Infant Prodigy known as

"THE YOUNG ACHILLES,"

will engage four tiger whelps in combat, armed with no other weapon than his little spear!

The whole to conclude with a chaste and elegant

GENERAL SLAUGHTER!

In which thirteen African Lions and twenty-two Barbarian Prisoners will war with each other until all are exterminated.

BOX OFFICE NOW OPEN.

Dress Circle One Dollar; Children and Servants half price.

An efficient police force will be on hand to preserve order and keep the wild beasts from leaping the railings and discommoding the audience.

Doors open at 7: performance begins at 8.

POSITIVELY NO FREE LIST.

Diodorus Job Press.

It was as singular as it was gratifying that I was also so fortunate as to find among the rubbish of the arena, a stained and mutilated copy of the *Roman Daily Battle-Ax*, containing a critique upon this very performance. It comes to hand too late by many centuries to rank as news, and therefore I translate and publish it simply to show how very little the general style and phraseology of dramatic criticism has altered in the ages that have dragged their slow length along since the carriers laid this one damp and fresh before their Roman patrons:

"THE OPENING SEASON.—COLISEUM.—Notwithstanding the inclemency of the weather, quite a respectable number of the rank and fashion of the city assembled last night to witness the debut upon metropolitan boards of the young tragedian who has of late been winning such golden opinions in the amphitheatres of the provinces. Some sixty thousand persons were present, and but for the fact that the streets were almost impassable, it is fair to presume that the house would have been full. His august Majesty, the Emperor Aurelius, occupied the imperial box, and was the cynosure of all eyes. Many illustrious nobles and generals of the Empire graced the occasion with their presence, and not the least among them was the young patrician lieutenant whose laurels, won in the ranks of the "Thundering Legion," are still so green upon his brow. The cheer which greeted his entrance was heard beyond the Tiber!

"The late repairs and decorations add both to the comeliness and the comfort of the Coliseum. The new cushions are a great improvement upon the hard marble seats we have been so long accustomed to. The present management deserve well of the public. They have restored to the Coliseum the gilding, the rich upholstery and the uniform magnificence which old Coliseum frequenters tell us Rome was so proud of fifty years ago.

"The opening scene last night—the broadsword combat between two young amateurs and a famous Parthian gladiator who was sent here a prisoner—was very fine. The elder of the two young gentlemen handled his weapon with a grace that marked the possession of extraordinary talent. His feint of thrusting, followed instantly by a happily delivered blow which unhelmeted the Parthian, was received with hearty applause. He was not thoroughly up in the backhanded stroke, but it was very gratifying to his numerous friends to know that, in time, practice would have overcome this defect. However, he was killed. His sisters, who were present, expressed considerable regret. His mother left the Coliseum. The other youth maintained the contest with such spirit as to call forth enthusiastic bursts of applause. When at last he fell a corpse, his aged mother ran screaming, with hair disheveled and tears streaming from her eyes, and swooned away just as her hands were clutching at the railings of the arena. She was promptly removed by the police. Under the circumstances the woman's conduct was pardonable, perhaps, but we suggest that such exhibitions interfere with the decorum which should be preserved during the performances, and are highly improper in the presence of the Emperor. The Parthian prisoner fought bravely and well; and well he might, for he was fighting for both life and liberty. His wife and children were there to nerve his arm with their love, and to remind him of the old home he should see again if he conquered. When his second assailant fell, the woman clasped her children to her breast and wept for joy. But it was only a transient happiness. The captive staggered toward her and she saw that the liberty he had earned was earned too late. He was wounded unto death. Thus the first act closed in a manner which was entirely satisfactory. The manager was called before the curtain and returned his thanks for the honor done him, in a speech which was replete with wit and humor, and closed by hoping that his humble efforts to afford cheerful and instructive entertainment would continue to meet with the approbation of the Roman public.

"The star now appeared, and was received with vociferous applause and the simultaneous waving of sixty thousand handkerchiefs. Marcus Marcellus Valerian (stage name—his real name is Smith,) is a splendid specimen of physical development, and an artist of rare merit. His management of the battle-ax is wonderful. His gayety and his playfulness are irresistible, in his comic parts, and yet they are inferior to his sublime conceptions in the grave realm of tragedy. When his ax was describing fiery circles about the heads of the bewildered barbarians, in exact time with his springing body and his prancing legs, the audience gave way to uncontrollable bursts of laughter; but when the back of his weapon broke the skull of one and almost in the same instant its edge clove the other's body in twain, the howl of enthusiastic applause that shook the building, was the acknowledgment of a critical assemblage that he was a master of the noblest department of his profession. If he has a fault, (and we are sorry to even intimate that he has,) it is that of glancing at the audience, in the midst of the most exciting moments of the performance, as if seeking admiration. The pausing in a fight to bow when bouquets are thrown to him is also in bad taste. In the great left-handed combat he appeared to be looking at the audience half the time, instead of carving his adversaries; and when he had slain all the sophomores and was dallying with the freshman, he stooped and snatched a bouquet as it fell, and offered it to his adversary at a time when a blow was descending which promised favorably to be his death-warrant. Such levity is proper enough in the provinces, we make no doubt, but it ill suits the dignity of the metropolis. We trust our young friend will take these remarks in good part, for we mean them solely for his benefit. All who know us are aware that although we are at times justly severe upon tigers and martyrs, we never intentionally offend gladiators.

"The Infant Prodigy performed wonders. He overcame his four tiger whelps with ease, and with no other hurt than the loss of a portion of his scalp. The General Slaughter was rendered with a faithfulness to details which reflects the highest credit upon the late participants in it.

"Upon the whole, last night's performances shed honor not only upon the management but upon the city that encourages and sustains such wholesome and instructive entertainments. We would simply suggest that the practice of vulgar young boys in the gallery of shying peanuts and paper pellets at the tigers, and saying "Hi-yi!" and manifesting approbation or dissatisfaction by such observations as "Bully for the lion!" "Go it, Gladdy!" "Boots!" "Speech!" "Take a walk round the block!" and so on, are extremely reprehensible, when the Emperor is present, and ought to be stopped by the police. Several times last night, when the supernumeraries entered the arena to drag out the bodies, the young ruffians in the gallery shouted, "Supe! supe!" and also, "Oh, what a coat!" and "Why don't you pad them shanks?" and made use of various other remarks expressive of derision. These things are very annoying to the audience.

"A matinee for the little folks is promised for this afternoon, on which occasion several martyrs will be eaten by the tigers. The regular performance will continue every night till further notice. Material change of programme every evening. Benefit of Valerian, Tuesday, 29th, if he lives."

I have been a dramatic critic myself, in my time, and I was often surprised to notice how much more I knew about Hamlet than Forrest did; and it gratifies me to observe, now, how much better my brethren of ancient times knew how a broadsword battle ought to be fought than the gladiators.

Chapter XXVII

S O FAR, GOOD. If any man has a right to feel proud of himself, and satisfied, surely it is I. For I have written about the Coliseum, and the gladiators, the martyrs, and the lions, and yet have never once used the phrase "butchered to make a Roman holyday." I am the only free white man of mature age, who has accomplished this since Byron originated the expression.

Butchered to make a Roman holyday sounds well for the first seventeen or eighteen hundred thousand times one sees it in print, but after that it begins to grow tiresome. I find it in all the books concerning Rome—and here latterly it reminds me of Judge Oliver. Oliver was a young lawyer, fresh from the schools, who had gone out to the deserts of Nevada to begin life. He found that country, and our ways of life, there, in those early days, different from life in New England or Paris. But he put on a woollen shirt and strapped a navy revolver to his person, took to the bacon and beans of the country, and determined to do in Nevada as Nevada did. Oliver accepted the situation so completely that although he must have sorrowed over many of his trials, he never complained—that is, he never complained but once. He, two others, and myself, started to the new silver mines in the Humboldt mountains—he to be Probate Judge of Humboldt county, and we to mine. The distance was two hundred miles. It was dead of winter. We bought a two-horse wagon and put eighteen hundred pounds of bacon, flour, beans, blasting-powder, picks and shovels in it; we bought two sorry-looking Mexican "plugs," with the hair turned the wrong way and more corners on their bodies than there are on the mosque of Omar; we hitched up and started. It was a dreadful trip. But Oliver did not complain. The horses dragged the wagon two miles from town and then gave out. Then we three pushed the wagon seven miles, and Oliver moved ahead and pulled the horses after him by the bits. We complained, but Oliver did not. The ground was frozen, and it froze our backs while we slept; the wind swept across our faces and froze our noses. Oliver did not complain. Five days of pushing the wagon by day and freezing by night brought us to the bad part of the journey—the Forty Mile Desert, or the Great American Desert, if you please. Still, this mildest-mannered man that ever was, had not complained. We started across at eight in the morning, pushing through sand that had no bottom; toiling all day long by the wrecks of a thousand wagons, the skeletons of ten thousand oxen; by wagon-tires enough to hoop the Washington Monument to the top, and ox-chains enough to girdle Long Island; by human graves; with our throats parched always, with thirst; lips bleeding from the alkali dust; hungry, perspiring, and very, very weary—so weary that when we dropped in the sand every fifty yards to rest the horses, we could hardly keep from going to sleep—no complaints from Oliver: none the next morning at three o'clock, when we got across, tired to death. Awakened two or three nights afterward at midnight, in a narrow canon, by the snow falling on our faces, and appalled at the imminent danger of being "snowed in," we harnessed up and pushed on till eight in the morning, passed the "Divide" and knew we were saved. No complaints. Fifteen days of hardship and fatigue brought us to the end of the two hundred miles, and the Judge had not complained. We wondered if any thing *could* exasperate him. We built a Humboldt house. It is done in this way. You dig a square in the steep base of the mountain, and set up two uprights and top them with two joists. Then you stretch a great sheet of "cotton domestic" from the point where the joists join the hill-side down over the joists to the ground; this makes the roof and the front of the mansion; the sides and back are the dirt walls your digging has left. A chimney is easily made by turning up one corner of the roof. Oliver was sitting alone in this dismal den, one night, by a sage-brush fire, writing poetry; he was very fond of digging poetry out of himself—or blasting it out when it came hard. He heard an animal's footsteps close to the roof; a stone or two and some dirt came through and fell by him. He grew uneasy and said "Hi!—clear out from there, can't you!"—from time to time. But by and by he fell asleep where he sat, and pretty soon a mule fell down the chimney! The fire flew in every direction, and Oliver went over backwards. About ten nights after that, he recovered confidence enough to go to writing poetry again. Again he dozed off to sleep, and again a mule fell down the chimney. This time, about half of that side of the house came in with the mule. Struggling to get up, the mule kicked the candle out and smashed most of the kitchen furniture, and raised considerable dust. These violent awakenings must have been annoying to Oliver, but he never complained. He moved to a mansion on the opposite side of the canon, because he had noticed the mules did not go there. One night about eight o'clock he was endeavoring to finish his poem, when a stone rolled in—then a hoof appeared below the canvas—then part of a cow—the after part. He leaned back in dread, and shouted "Hooy! hooy! get out of this!" and the cow struggled manfully—lost ground steadily—dirt and dust streamed down, and before Oliver could get well away, the entire cow crashed through on to the table and made a shapeless wreck of every thing!

Then, for the first time in his life, I think, Oliver complained. He said,

"This thing is growing monotonous!"

Then he resigned his judgeship and left Humboldt county. "Butchered to make a Roman holyday" has grown monotonous to me.

In this connection I wish to say one word about Michael Angelo Buonarotti. I used to worship the mighty genius of Michael Angelo—that man who was great in poetry, painting, sculpture, architecture—great in every thing he undertook. But I do not want Michael Angelo for breakfast—for luncheon—for dinner—for tea—for supper—for between meals. I like a change, occasionally. In Genoa, he designed every thing; in Milan he or his pupils designed every thing; he designed the Lake of Como; in Padua, Verona, Venice, Bologna, who did we ever hear of, from guides, but Michael Angelo? In Florence, he painted every thing, designed every thing, nearly, and what he did not design he used to sit on a favorite stone and look at, and they showed us the stone. In Pisa he designed every thing but the old shot-tower, and they would have attributed that to him if it had not been so awfully out of the perpendicular. He designed the piers of Leghorn and the custom house regulations of Civita Vecchia. But, here—here it is frightful. He designed St. Peter's; he designed the Pope; he designed the Pantheon, the uniform of the Pope's soldiers, the Tiber, the Vatican, the Coliseum, the Capitol, the Tarpeian Rock, the Barberini Palace, St. John Lateran, the Campagna, the Appian Way, the Seven Hills, the Baths of Caracalla, the Claudian Aqueduct, the Cloaca Maxima—the eternal bore designed the Eternal City, and unless all men and books do lie, he painted every thing in it! Dan said the other day to the guide, "Enough, enough, enough! Say no more! Lump the whole thing! say that the Creator made Italy from designs by Michael Angelo!"

I never felt so fervently thankful, so soothed, so tranquil, so filled with a blessed peace, as I did yesterday when I learned that Michael Angelo was dead.

But we have taken it out of this guide. He has marched us through miles of pictures and sculpture in the vast corridors of the Vatican; and through miles of pictures and sculpture in twenty other palaces; he has shown us the great picture in the Sistine Chapel, and frescoes enough to frescoe the heavens— pretty much all done by Michael Angelo. So with him we have played that game which has vanquished so many guides for us—imbecility and idiotic questions. These creatures never suspect—they have no idea of a sarcasm.

He shows us a figure and says: "Statoo brunzo." (Bronze statue.)

We look at it indifferently and the doctor asks: "By Michael Angelo?"

"No—not know who."

Then he shows us the ancient Roman Forum. The doctor asks: "Michael Angelo?"

A stare from the guide. "No—thousan' year before he is born."

Then an Egyptian obelisk. Again: "Michael Angelo?"

"Oh, *mon dieu*, genteelmen! Zis is *two* thousan' year before he is born!"

He grows so tired of that unceasing question sometimes, that he dreads to show us any thing at all. The wretch has tried all the ways he can think of to make us comprehend that Michael Angelo is only responsible for the creation of a *part* of the world, but somehow he has not succeeded yet. Relief for overtasked eyes and brain from study and sight-seeing is necessary, or we shall become idiotic sure enough. Therefore this guide must continue to suffer. If he does not enjoy it, so much the worse for him. We do.

In this place I may as well jot down a chapter concerning those necessary nuisances, European guides. Many a man has wished in his heart he could do without his guide; but knowing he could not, has wished he could get some amusement out of him as a remuneration for the affliction of his society. We accomplished this latter matter, and if our experience can be made useful to others they are welcome to it.

Guides know about enough English to tangle every thing up so that a man can make neither head or tail of it. They know their story by heart—the history of every statue, painting, cathedral or other wonder they show you. They know it and tell it as a parrot would—and if you interrupt, and throw them off the track, they have to go back and begin over again. All their lives long, they are employed in showing strange things to foreigners and listening to their bursts of admiration. It is human nature to take delight in exciting admiration. It is what prompts children to say "smart" things, and do absurd ones, and in other ways "show off" when company is present. It is what makes gossips turn out in rain and storm to go and be the first to tell a startling bit of news. Think, then, what a passion it becomes with a guide, whose privilege it is, every day, to show to strangers wonders that throw them into perfect ecstasies of admiration! He gets so that he could not by any possibility live in a soberer atmosphere. After we discovered this, we *never* went into ecstasies any more—we never admired any thing—we never showed any but impassible faces and stupid indifference in the presence of the sublimest wonders a guide had to display. We had found their weak point. We have made good use of it ever since. We have made some of those people savage, at times, but we have never lost our own serenity.

The doctor asks the questions, generally, because he can keep his countenance, and look more like an inspired idiot, and throw more imbecility into the tone of his voice than any man that lives. It comes natural to him.

The guides in Genoa are delighted to secure an American party, because Americans so much wonder, and deal so much in sentiment and emotion before any relic of Columbus. Our guide there fidgeted about as if he had swallowed a spring mattrass. He was full of animation—full of impatience. He said:

"Come wis me, genteelmen!—come! I show you ze letter writing by Christopher Colombo!—write it himself!—write it wis his own hand!—come!"

He took us to the municipal palace. After much impressive fumbling of keys and opening of locks, the stained and aged document was spread before us. The guide's eyes sparkled. He danced about us and tapped the parchment with his finger:

"What I tell you, genteelmen! Is it not so! See! hand-writing Christopher Colombo!—write it himself!"

We looked indifferent—unconcerned. The doctor examined the document very deliberately, during a painful pause.—Then he said, without any show of interest:

"Ah—Ferguson—what—what did you say was the name of the party who wrote this?"

"Christopher Colombo! ze great Christopher Colombo!"

Another deliberate examination.

"Ah—did he write it himself, or—or how?"

"He write it himself!—Christopher Colombo! he's own hand-writing, write by himself!"

Then the doctor laid the document down and said:

"Why, I have seen boys in America only fourteen years old that could write better than that."

"But zis is ze great Christo—"

"I don't care who it is! It's the worst writing I ever saw. Now you musn't think you can impose on us because we are strangers. We are not fools, by a good deal. If you have got any specimens of penmanship of real merit, trot them out!—and if you haven't, drive on!"

We drove on. The guide was considerably shaken up, but he made one more venture. He had something which he thought would overcome us. He said:

"Ah, genteelmen, you come wis me! I show you beautiful, O, magnificent bust Christopher Colombo!—splendid, grand, magnificent!"

He brought us before the beautiful bust—for it *was* beautiful—and sprang back and struck an attitude:

"Ah, look, genteelmen!—beautiful, grand,—bust Christopher Colombo!—beautiful bust, beautiful pedestal!"

The doctor put up his eye-glass—procured for such occasions:

"Ah—what did you say this gentleman's name was?"

"Christopher Colombo!—ze great Christopher Colombo!"

"Christopher Colombo—the great Christopher Colombo. Well, what did *he* do?"

"Discover America!—discover America, Oh, ze devil!"

"Discover America. No—that statement will hardly wash. We are just from America ourselves. We heard nothing about it. Christopher Colombo—pleasant name—is—is he dead?"

"Oh, corpo di Baccho!—three hundred year!"

"What did he die of?"

"I do not know!—I can not tell."

"Small-pox, think?"

"I do not know, genteelmen!—I do not know *what* he die of!"

"Measles, likely?"

"May be—may be—I do *not* know—I think he die of somethings."

"Parents living?"

"Im-posseeble!"

"Ah—which is the bust and which is the pedestal?"

"Santa Maria!—*zis* ze bust!—*zis* ze pedestal!"

"Ah, I see, I see—happy combination—very happy combination, indeed. Is—is this the first time this gentleman was ever on a bust?"

That joke was lost on the foreigner—guides can not master the subtleties of the American joke.

We have made it interesting for this Roman guide. Yesterday we spent three or four hours in the Vatican, again, that wonderful world of curiosities. We came very near expressing interest, sometimes—even admiration—it was very hard to keep from it. We succeeded though. Nobody else ever did, in the Vatican museums. The guide was bewildered—nonplussed. He walked his legs off, nearly, hunting up extraordinary things, and exhausted all his ingenuity on us, but it was a failure; we never showed any interest in any thing. He had reserved what he considered to be his greatest wonder till the last—a royal Egyptian mummy, the best preserved in the world, perhaps. He took us there. He felt so sure, this time, that some of his old enthusiasm came back to him:

"See, genteelmen!—Mummy! Mummy!"

The eye-glass came up as calmly, as deliberately as ever.

"Ah,—Ferguson—what did I understand you to say the gentleman's name was?"

"Name?—he got no name!—Mummy!—'Gyptian mummy!"

"Yes, yes. Born here?"

"No! *'Gyptian* mummy!"

"Ah, just so. Frenchman, I presume?"

"No!— *not* Frenchman, not Roman!—born in Egypt!"

"Born in Egypt. Never heard of Egypta before. Foreign locality, likely. Mummy—mummy. How calm he is—how self-possessed. Is, ah—is he dead?"

"Oh, *sacre bleu*, been dead three thousan' year!"

The doctor turned on him savagely:

"Here, now, what do you mean by such conduct as this! Playing us for Chinamen because we are strangers and trying to learn! Trying to impose your vile second-hand carcasses on *us*!—thunder and lightning, I've a notion to—to—if you've got a nice *fresh* corpse, fetch him out!—or by George we'll brain you!"

We make it exceedingly interesting for this Frenchman. However, he has paid us back, partly, without knowing it. He came to the hotel this morning to ask if we were up, and he endeavored as well as he could to describe us, so that the landlord would know which persons he meant. He finished with the casual remark that we were lunatics. The observation was so innocent and so honest that it amounted to a very good thing for a guide to say.

There is one remark (already mentioned,) which never yet has failed to disgust these guides. We use it always, when we can think of nothing else to say. After they have exhausted their enthusiasm pointing out to us and praising the beauties of some ancient bronze image or broken-legged statue, we look at it stupidly and in silence for five, ten, fifteen minutes—as long as we can hold out, in fact—and then ask:

"Is—is he dead?"

That conquers the serenest of them. It is not what they are looking for—especially a new guide. Our Roman Ferguson is the most patient, unsuspecting, long-suffering subject we have had yet. We shall be sorry to part with him. We have enjoyed his society very much. We trust he has enjoyed ours, but we are harassed with doubts.

We have been in the catacombs. It was like going down into a very deep cellar, only it was a cellar which had no end to it. The narrow passages are roughly hewn in the rock, and on each hand as you pass along, the hollowed shelves are carved out, from three to fourteen deep; each held a corpse once. There are names, and Christian symbols, and prayers, or sentences expressive of Christian hopes, carved upon nearly every sarcophagus. The dates belong away back in the dawn of the Christian era, of course. Here, in these holes in the ground, the first Christians sometimes burrowed to escape persecution. They crawled out at night to get food, but remained under cover in the day time. The priest told us that St. Sebastian lived under ground for some time while he was being hunted; he went out one day, and the soldiery discovered and shot him to death with arrows. Five or six of the early Popes—those who reigned about sixteen hundred years ago—held their papal courts and advised with their clergy in the bowels of the earth. During seventeen years—from A. D. 235 to A. D. 252—the Popes did not appear above ground. Four were raised to the great office during that period. Four years apiece, or thereabouts. It is very suggestive of the unhealthiness of underground graveyards as places of residence. One Pope afterward spent his entire pontificate in the catacombs—eight years. Another was discovered in them and murdered in the episcopal chair. There was no satisfaction in being a Pope in those days. There were too many annoyances. There are one hundred and sixty catacombs under Rome, each with its maze of narrow passages crossing and recrossing each other and each passage walled to the top with scooped graves its entire length. A careful estimate makes the length of the passages of all the catacombs combined foot up nine hundred miles, and their graves number seven millions. We did not go through all the passages of all the catacombs. We were very anxious to do it, and made the necessary arrangements, but our too limited time obliged us to give up the idea. So we only groped through the dismal labyrinth of St. Callixtus, under the Church of St. Sebastian. In the various catacombs are small chapels rudely hewn in the stones, and here the early Christians often held their religious services by dim, ghostly lights. Think of mass and a sermon away down in those tangled caverns under ground!

In the catacombs were buried St. Cecilia, St. Agnes, and several other of the most celebrated of the saints. In the catacomb of St. Callixtus, St. Bridget used to remain long hours in holy contemplation, and St. Charles Borroméo was wont to spend whole nights in prayer there. It was also the scene of a very marvelous thing.

"Here the heart of St. Philip Neri was so inflamed with divine love as to burst his ribs."

I find that grave statement in a book published in New York in 1858, and written by "Rev. William H. Neligan, LL.D., M. A., Trinity College, Dublin; Member of the Archæological Society of Great Britain." Therefore, I believe it. Otherwise, I could not. Under other circumstances I should have felt a curiosity to know what Philip had for dinner.

This author puts my credulity on its mettle every now and then. He tells of one St. Joseph Calasanctius whose house in Rome he visited; he visited only the house—the priest has been dead two hundred years. He says the Virgin Mary appeared to this saint. Then he continues:

"His tongue and his heart, which were found after nearly a century to be whole, when the body was disinterred before his canonization, are still preserved in a glass case, and after two centuries the heart is still whole. When the French troops came to Rome, and when Pius VII. was carried away prisoner, blood dropped from it."

To read that in a book written by a monk far back in the Middle Ages, would surprise no one; it would sound natural and proper; but when it is seriously stated in the middle of the nineteenth century, by a man of finished education, an LL.D., M. A., and an Archæological magnate, it sounds strangely enough. Still, I would gladly change my unbelief for

Neligan's faith, and let him make the conditions as hard as he pleased.

The old gentleman's undoubting, unquestioning simplicity has a rare freshness about it in these matter-of-fact railroading and telegraphing days. Hear him, concerning the church of Ara Cœli:

"In the roof of the church, directly above the high altar, is engraved, '*Regina Cœli laetare Alleluia.*' In the sixth century Rome was visited by a fearful pestilence. Gregory the Great urged the people to do penance, and a general procession was formed. It was to proceed from Ara Cœli to St. Peter's. As it passed before the mole of Adrian, now the Castle of St. Angelo, the sound of heavenly voices was heard singing (it was Easter morn,) '*Regina Cœli, laetare! alleluia! quia quem meruisti portare, alleluia! resurrexit sicut dixit; alleluia!*' The Pontiff, carrying in his hands the portrait of the Virgin, (which is over the high altar and is said to have been painted by St. Luke,) answered, with the astonished people, '*Ora pro nobis Deum, alleluia!*' At the same time an angel was seen to put up a sword in a scabbard, and the pestilence ceased on the same day. There are four circumstances which *confirm** this miracle: the annual procession which takes place in the western church on the feast of St. Mark; the statue of St. Michael, placed on the mole of Adrian, which has since that time been called the Castle of St. Angelo; the antiphon Regina Cœli, which the Catholic church sings during paschal time; and the inscription in the church."

*The italics are mine.—M. T.

Chapter XXVIII

F ROM THE sanguinary sports of the Holy Inquisition; the slaughter of the Coliseum; and the dismal tombs of the Catacombs, I naturally pass to the picturesque horrors of the Capuchin Convent. We stopped a moment in a small chapel in the church to admire a picture of St. Michael vanquishing Satan—a picture which is so beautiful that I can not but think it belongs to the reviled *"Renaissance,"* notwithstanding I believe they told us one of the ancient old masters painted it—and then we descended into the vast vault underneath.

Here was a spectacle for sensitive nerves! Evidently the old masters had been at work in this place. There were six divisions in the apartment, and each division was ornamented with a style of decoration peculiar to itself—and these decorations were in every instance formed of human bones! There were shapely arches, built wholly of thigh bones; there were startling pyramids, built wholly of grinning skulls; there were quaint architectural structures of various kinds, built of shin bones and the bones of the arm; on the wall were elaborate frescoes, whose curving vines were made of knotted human vertebræ; whose delicate tendrils were made of sinews and tendons; whose flowers were formed of knee-caps and toe-nails. Every lasting portion of the human frame was represented in these intricate designs (they were by Michael Angelo, I think,) and there was a careful finish about the work, and an attention to details that betrayed the artist's love of his labors as well as his schooled ability. I asked the good-natured monk who accompanied us, who did this? And he said, *"We* did it"—meaning himself and his brethren up stairs. I could see that the old friar took a high pride in his curious show. We made him talkative by exhibiting an interest we never betrayed to guides.

"Who were these people?"

"We—up stairs—Monks of the Capuchin order—my brethren."

"How many departed monks were required to upholster these six parlors?"

"These are the bones of four thousand."

"It took a long time to get enough?"

"Many, many centuries."

"Their different parts are well separated—skulls in one room, legs in another, ribs in another—there would be stirring times here for a while if the last trump should blow. Some of the brethren might get hold of the wrong leg, in the confusion, and the wrong skull, and find themselves limping, and looking through eyes that were wider apart or closer together than they were used to. You can not tell any of these parties apart, I suppose?"

"Oh, yes, I know many of them."

He put his finger on a skull. "This was Brother Anselmo—dead three hundred years—a good man."

He touched another. "This was Brother Alexander—dead two hundred and eighty years. This was Brother Carlo—dead about as long."

Then he took a skull and held it in his hand, and looked reflectively upon it, after the manner of the grave-digger when he discourses of Yorick.

"This," he said, "was Brother Thomas. He was a young prince, the scion of a proud house that traced its lineage back to the grand old days of Rome well nigh two thousand years ago. He loved beneath his estate. His family persecuted him; persecuted the girl, as well. They drove her from Rome; he followed; he sought her far and wide; he found no trace of her. He came back and offered his broken heart at our altar and his weary life to the service of God. But look you. Shortly his father died, and likewise his mother. The girl returned, rejoicing. She sought every where for him whose eyes had used to look tenderly into hers out of this poor skull, but she could not find him. At last, in this coarse garb we wear, she recognized him in the street. He knew her. It was too late. He fell where he stood. They took him up and brought him here. He never spoke afterward. Within the week he died. You can see the color of his hair—faded, somewhat—by this thin shred that clings still to the temple. This," [taking up a thigh bone,] "was his. The veins of this leaf in the decorations over your head, were his finger-joints, a hundred and fifty years ago."

This business-like way of illustrating a touching story of the heart by laying the several fragments of the lover before us and naming them, was as grotesque a performance, and as ghastly, as any I ever witnessed. I hardly knew whether to smile or shudder. There are nerves and muscles in our frames whose functions and whose methods of working it seems a sort of sacrilege to describe by cold physiological names and surgical technicalities, and the monk's talk suggested to me something of this kind. Fancy a surgeon, with his nippers lifting tendons, muscles and such things into view, out of the complex machinery of a corpse, and observing, "Now this little nerve quivers—the vibration is imparted to this muscle—from here it is passed to this fibrous substance; here its ingredients are separated by the chemical action of the blood—one part goes to the heart and thrills it with what is popularly termed emotion, another part follows this nerve to the brain and communicates intelligence of a startling character—the third part glides along this passage and touches the spring connected with the fluid receptacles that lie in the rear of the eye. Thus, by this simple and beautiful process, the party is informed that his mother is dead, and he weeps." Horrible!

I asked the monk if all the brethren up stairs expected to be put in this place when they died. He answered quietly:

"We must all lie here at last."

See what one can accustom himself to.—The reflection that he must some day be taken apart like an engine or a clock, or like a house whose owner is gone, and worked up into arches and pyramids and hideous frescoes, did not distress this monk in the least. I thought he even looked as if he were thinking, with complacent vanity, that his own skull would look well on top of the heap and his own ribs add a charm to the frescoes which possibly they lacked at present.

Here and there, in ornamental alcoves, stretched upon beds of bones, lay dead and dried-up monks, with lank frames dressed in the black robes one sees ordinarily upon priests. We examined one closely. The skinny hands were clasped upon the breast; two lustreless tufts of hair stuck to the skull; the skin was brown and sunken; it stretched tightly over the cheek bones and made them stand out sharply; the crisp dead eyes were deep in the sockets; the nostrils were painfully prominent, the end of the nose being gone; the lips had shriveled away from the yellow teeth: and brought down to us through the circling years, and petrified there, was a weird laugh a full century old!

It was the jolliest laugh, but yet the most dreadful, that one can imagine. Surely, I thought, it must have been a most extraordinary joke this veteran produced with his latest breath, that he has not got done laughing at it yet. At this moment I saw that the old instinct was strong upon the boys, and I said we had better hurry to St. Peter's. They were trying to keep from asking, "Is—is he dead?"

It makes me dizzy, to think of the Vatican—of its wilderness of statues, paintings, and curiosities of every description and every age. The "old masters" (especially in sculpture,) fairly swarm, there. I can not write about the Vatican. I think I shall never remember any thing I saw there distinctly but the mummies, and the Transfiguration, by Raphael, and some other things it is not necessary to mention now. I shall remember the Transfiguration partly because it was placed in a room almost by itself; partly because it is acknowledged by all to be the first oil painting in the world; and partly because it was wonderfully beautiful. The colors are fresh and rich, the "expression," I am told, is fine, the "feeling" is lively, the "tone" is good, the "depth" is profound, and the width is about four and a half feet, I should judge. It is a picture that really holds one's attention; its beauty is fascinating. It is fine enough to be a *Renaissance*. A remark I made a while ago suggests a thought—and a hope. Is it not possible that the reason I find such charms in this picture is because it is out of the crazy chaos of the galleries? If some of the others were set apart, might not they be beautiful? If this were set in the midst of the tempest of pictures one finds in the vast galleries of the Roman palaces, would I think it so handsome? If, up to this time, I had seen only one "old master" in each palace, instead of acres and acres of walls and ceilings fairly papered with them, might I not have a more civilized opinion of the old masters than I have now? I think so. When I was a school-boy and was to have a new knife, I could not make up my mind as to which was the prettiest in the show-case, and I did not think any of them were particularly pretty; and so I chose with a heavy heart. But when I looked at my purchase, at home, where no glittering blades came into competition with it, I was astonished to see how handsome it was. To this day my new hats look better out of the shop than they did in it with other new hats. It begins to dawn upon me, now, that possibly, what I have been taking for uniform ugliness in the galleries may be uniform beauty after all. I honestly hope it is, to others, but certainly it is not to me. Perhaps the reason I used to enjoy going to the Academy of Fine Arts in New York was because there were but a few hundred paintings in it, and it did not surfeit me to go through the list. I suppose the Academy was bacon and beans in the Forty-Mile Desert, and a European gallery is a state dinner of thirteen courses. One leaves no sign after him of the one dish, but the thirteen frighten away his appetite and give him no satisfaction.

There is one thing I am certain of, though. With all the Michael Angelos, the Raphaels, the Guidos and the other old masters, the sublime history of Rome remains unpainted! They painted Virgins enough, and popes enough and saintly scarecrows enough, to people Paradise, almost, and these things are all they did paint. "Nero fiddling o'er burning Rome," the assassination of Cæsar, the stirring spectacle of a hundred thousand people bending forward with rapt interest, in the Coliseum, to see two skillful gladiators hacking away each others' lives, a tiger springing upon a kneeling martyr— these and a thousand other matters which we read of with a living interest, must be sought for only in books—not among the rubbish left by the old masters—who are no more, I have the satisfaction of informing the public.

They did paint, and they did carve in marble, one historical scene, and one only, (of any great historical consequence.) And what was it and why did they choose it, particularly? It was the Rape of the Sabines, and they chose it for the legs and busts.

I like to look at statues, however, and I like to look at pictures, also—even of monks looking up in sacred ecstacy, and monks looking down in meditation, and monks skirmishing for something to eat—and therefore I drop ill nature to thank the papal government for so jealously guarding and so industriously gathering up these things; and for permitting me, a stranger and not an entirely friendly one, to roam at will and unmolested among them, charging me nothing, and only requiring that I shall behave myself simply as well as I ought to behave in any other man's house. I thank the Holy Father right heartily, and I wish him long life and plenty of happiness.

The Popes have long been the patrons and preservers of art, just as our new, practical Republic is the encourager and upholder of mechanics. In their Vatican is stored up all that is curious and beautiful in art; in our Patent Office is hoarded all that is curious or useful in mechanics. When a man invents a new style of horse-collar or discovers a new and superior method of telegraphing, our government issues a patent to him that is worth a fortune; when a man digs up an ancient statue in the Campagna, the Pope gives him a fortune in gold coin. We can make something of a guess at a man's character by the style of nose he carries on his face. The Vatican and the Patent Office are governmental noses, and they bear a deal of character about them.

The guide showed us a colossal statue of Jupiter, in the Vatican, which he said looked so damaged and rusty—so like the God of the Vagabonds—because it had but recently been dug up in the Campagna. He asked how much we supposed this Jupiter was worth? I replied, with intelligent promptness, that he was probably worth about four dollars—may be four and a half. "A hundred thousand dollars!" Ferguson said. Ferguson said, further, that the Pope permits no ancient work of this kind to leave his dominions. He appoints a commission to examine discoveries like this and report upon the value; then the Pope pays the discoverer one-half of that assessed value and takes the statue. He said this Jupiter was dug from a field which had just been bought for thirty-six thousand dollars, so the first crop was a good one for the new farmer. I do not know whether Ferguson always tells the truth or not, but I suppose he does. I know that an exorbitant export duty is exacted upon all pictures painted by the old masters, in order to discourage the sale of those in the private collections. I am satisfied, also, that genuine old masters hardly exist at all, in America, because the cheapest and most insignificant of them are valued at the price of a fine farm. I proposed to buy a small trifle of a Raphael, myself, but the price of it was eighty thousand dollars, the export duty would have made it considerably over a hundred, and so I studied on it awhile and concluded not to take it.

I wish here to mention an inscription I have seen, before I forget it:

"Glory to God in the highest, peace on earth TO MEN OF GOOD WILL!" It is not good scripture, but it is sound Catholic and human nature.

This is in letters of gold around the apsis of a mosaic group at the side of the *scala santa*, church of St. John Lateran, the Mother and Mistress of all the Catholic churches of the world. The group represents the Saviour, St. Peter, Pope Leo, St. Silvester, Constantine and Charlemagne. Peter is giving the *pallium* to the Pope, and a standard to Charlemagne. The Saviour is giving the keys to St. Silvester, and a standard to Constantine. No prayer is offered to the Saviour, who seems to be of little importance any where in Rome; but an inscription below says, *"Blessed Peter, give life to Pope Leo and victory to King Charles."* It does not say, *"Intercede for us*, through the Saviour, with the Father, for this boon," but "Blessed Peter, *give it* us."

In all seriousness—without meaning to be frivolous— without meaning to be irreverent, and more than all, without meaning to be blasphemous,—I state as my simple deduction from the things I have seen and the things I have heard, that the Holy Personages rank thus in Rome:

First—"The Mother of God"—otherwise the Virgin Mary.

Second—The Deity.

Third—Peter.

Fourth—Some twelve or fifteen canonized Popes and martyrs.

Fifth—Jesus Christ the Saviour—(but always as an infant in arms.)

I may be wrong in this—my judgment errs often, just as is the case with other men's—but it *is* my judgment, be it good or bad.

Just here I will mention something that seems curious to me. There are no "Christ's Churches" in Rome, and no "Churches of the Holy Ghost," that I can discover. There are some four hundred churches, but about a fourth of them seem to be named for the Madonna and St. Peter. There are so many named for Mary that they have to be distinguished by all sorts of affixes, if I understand the matter rightly. Then we have churches of St. Louis; St. Augustine; St. Agnes; St. Calixtus; St. Lorenzo in Lucina; St. Lorenzo in Damaso; St. Cecilia; St. Athanasius; St. Philip Neri; St. Catherine, St. Dominico, and a multitude of lesser saints whose names are not familiar in the world—and away down, clear out of the list of the churches, comes a couple of hospitals: one of them is named for the Saviour and the other for the Holy Ghost!

Day after day and night after night we have wandered among the crumbling wonders of Rome; day after day and night after night we have fed upon the dust and decay of five-and-twenty centuries—have brooded over them by day and dreampt of them by night till sometimes we seemed moldering away ourselves, and growing defaced and cornerless, and liable at any moment to fall a prey to some antiquary and be patched in the legs, and "restored" with an unseemly nose, and labeled wrong and dated wrong, and set up in the Vatican for poets to drivel about and vandals to scribble their names on forever and forevermore.

But the surest way to stop writing about Rome is to stop. I wished to write a real "guide-book" chapter on this fascinating city, but I could not do it, because I have felt all the time like a boy in a candy-shop—there was every thing to choose from, and yet no choice. I have drifted along hopelessly for a hundred pages of manuscript without knowing where to commence. I will not commence at all. Our passports have been examined. We will go to Naples.

Chapter XXIX

Tʜᴇ sʜɪᴘ is lying here in the harbor of Naples—quarantined. She has been here several days and will remain several more. We that came by rail from Rome have escaped this misfortune. Of course no one is allowed to go on board the ship, or come ashore from her. She is a prison, now. The passengers probably spend the long, blazing days looking out from under the awnings at Vesuvius and the beautiful city—and in swearing. Think of ten days of this sort of pastime!—We go out every day in a boat and request them to come ashore. It soothes them. We lie ten steps from the ship and tell them how splendid the city is; and how much better the hotel fare is here than any where else in Europe; and how cool it is; and what frozen continents of ice cream there are; and what a time we are having cavorting about the country and sailing to the islands in the Bay. This tranquilizes them.

Ascent of Vesuvius.

I shall remember our trip to Vesuvius for many a day—partly because of its sight-seeing experiences, but chiefly on account of the fatigue of the journey. Two or three of us had been resting ourselves among the tranquil and beautiful scenery of the island of Ischia, eighteen miles out in the harbor, for two days; we called it "resting," but I do not remember now what the resting consisted of, for when we got back to Naples we had not slept for forty-eight hours. We were just about to go to bed early in the evening, and catch up on some of the sleep we had lost, when we heard of this Vesuvius expedition. There was to be eight of us in the party, and we were to leave Naples at midnight. We laid in some provisions for the trip, engaged carriages to take us to Annunciation, and then moved about the city, to keep awake, till twelve. We got away punctually, and in the course of an hour and a half arrived at the town of Annunciation. Annunciation is the very last place under the sun. In other towns in Italy the people lie around quietly and wait for you to ask them a question or do some overt act that can be charged for—but in Annunciation

they have lost even that fragment of delicacy; they seize a
lady's shawl from a chair and hand it to her and charge a
penny; they open a carriage door, and charge for it—shut it
when you get out, and charge for it; they help you to take
off a duster—two cents; brush your clothes and make them
worse than they were before—two cents; smile upon you—
two cents; bow, with a lick-spittle smirk, hat in hand—two
cents; they volunteer all information, such as that the mules
will arrive presently—two cents—warm day, sir—two
cents—take you four hours to make the ascent—two cents.
And so they go. They crowd you—infest you—swarm about
you, and sweat and smell offensively, and look sneaking and
mean, and obsequious. There is no office too degrading for
them to perform, for money. I have had no opportunity to
find out any thing about the upper classes by my own observation, but from what I hear said about them I judge that
what they lack in one or two of the bad traits the *canaille*
have, they make up in one or two others that are worse. How
the people beg!—many of them very well dressed, too.

I said I knew nothing against the upper classes by personal
observation. I must recall it! I had forgotten. What I saw
their bravest and their fairest do last night, the lowest multitude that could be scraped up out of the purlieus of Christendom would blush to do, I think. They assembled by
hundreds, and even thousands, in the great Theatre of San
Carlo, to do—what? Why, simply, to make fun of an old
woman—to deride, to hiss, to jeer at an actress they once
worshipped, but whose beauty is faded now and whose voice
has lost its former richness. Every body spoke of the rare
sport there was to be. They said the theatre would be
crammed, because Frezzolini was going to sing. It was said
she could not sing well, now, but then the people liked to see
her, anyhow. And so we went. And every time the woman
sang they hissed and laughed—the whole magnificent
house—and as soon as she left the stage they called her on
again with applause. Once or twice she was encored five and
six times in succession, and received with hisses when she appeared, and discharged with hisses and laughter when she had
finished—then instantly encored and insulted again! And
how the high-born knaves enjoyed it! White-kidded gentle-

men and ladies laughed till the tears came, and clapped their hands in very ecstacy when that unhappy old woman would come meekly out for the sixth time, with uncomplaining patience, to meet a storm of hisses! It was the cruelest exhibition—the most wanton, the most unfeeling. The singer would have conquered an audience of American rowdies by her brave, unflinching tranquillity (for she answered encore after encore, and smiled and bowed pleasantly, and sang the best she possibly could, and went bowing off, through all the jeers and hisses, without ever losing countenance or temper:) and surely in any other land than Italy her sex and her helplessness must have been an ample protection to her—she could have needed no other. Think what a multitude of small souls were crowded into that theatre last night. If the manager could have filled his theatre with Neapolitan souls alone, without the bodies, he could not have cleared less than ninety millions of dollars. What traits of character must a man have to enable him to help three thousand miscreants to hiss, and jeer, and laugh at one friendless old woman, and shamefully humiliate her? He must have *all* the vile, mean traits there are. My observation persuades me (I do not like to venture beyond my own personal observation,) that the upper classes of Naples possess those traits of character. Otherwise they may be very good people; I can not say.

ASCENT OF VESUVIUS—CONTINUED.

In this city of Naples, they believe in and support one of the wretchedest of all the religious impostures one can find in Italy—the miraculous liquefaction of the blood of St. Januarius. Twice a year the priests assemble all the people at the Cathedral, and get out this vial of clotted blood and let them see it slowly dissolve and become liquid—and every day for eight days, this dismal farce is repeated, while the priests go among the crowd and collect money for the exhibition. The first day, the blood liquefies in forty-seven minutes—the church is crammed, then, and time must be allowed the collectors to get around: after that it liquefies a little quicker and a little quicker, every day, as the houses grow smaller, till on the eighth day, with only a few dozens present to see the miracle, it liquefies in four minutes.

And here, also, they used to have a grand procession, of priests, citizens, soldiers, sailors, and the high dignitaries of the City Government, once a year, to shave the head of a made-up Madonna—a stuffed and painted image, like a milliner's dummy—whose hair miraculously grew and restored itself every twelve months. They still kept up this shaving procession as late as four or five years ago. It was a source of great profit to the church that possessed the remarkable effigy, and the ceremony of the public barbering of her was always carried out with the greatest possible eclat and display—the more the better, because the more excitement there was about it the larger the crowds it drew and the heavier the revenues it produced—but at last a day came when the Pope and his servants were unpopular in Naples, and the City Government stopped the Madonna's annual show.

There we have two specimens of these Neapolitans—two of the silliest possible frauds, which half the population religiously and faithfully believed, and the other half either believed also or else said nothing about, and thus lent themselves to the support of the imposture. I am very well satisfied to think the whole population believed in those poor, cheap miracles—a people who want two cents every time they bow to you, and who abuse a woman, are capable of it, I think.

Ascent of Vesuvius—Continued.

These Neapolitans always ask four times as much money as they intend to take, but if you give them what they first demand, they feel ashamed of themselves for aiming so low, and immediately ask more. When money is to be paid and received, there is always some vehement jawing and gesticulating about it. One can not buy and pay for two cents' worth of clams without trouble and a quarrel. One "course," in a two-horse carriage, costs a franc—that is law—but the hackman always demands more, on some pretence or other, and if he gets it he makes a new demand. It is said that a stranger took a one-horse carriage for a course—tariff, half a franc.

He gave the man five francs, by way of experiment. He demanded more, and received another franc. Again he demanded more, and got a franc—demanded more, and it was refused. He grew vehement—was again refused, and became noisy. The stranger said, "Well, give me the seven francs again, and I will see what I can do"—and when he got them, he handed the hackman half a franc, and he immediately asked for two cents to buy a drink with. It may be thought that I am prejudiced. Perhaps I am. I would be ashamed of myself if I were not.

Ascent of Vesuvius—Continued.

Well, as I was saying, we got our mules and horses, after an hour and a half of bargaining with the population of Annunciation, and started sleepily up the mountain, with a vagrant at each mule's tail who pretended to be driving the brute along, but was really holding on and getting himself dragged up instead. I made slow headway at first, but I began to get dissatisfied at the idea of paying my minion five francs to hold my mule back by the tail and keep him from going up the hill, and so I discharged him. I got along faster then.

We had one magnificent picture of Naples from a high point on the mountain side. We saw nothing but the gas lamps, of course—two-thirds of a circle, skirting the great Bay—a necklace of diamonds glinting up through the darkness from the remote distance—less brilliant than the stars overhead, but more softly, richly beautiful—and over all the great city the lights crossed and recrossed each other in many and many a sparkling line and curve. And back of the town, far around and abroad over the miles of level campagna, were scattered rows, and circles, and clusters of lights, all glowing like so many gems, and marking where a score of villages were sleeping. About this time, the fellow who was hanging on to the tail of the horse in front of me and practicing all sorts of unnecessary cruelty upon the animal, got kicked some fourteen rods, and this incident, together with the fairy spectacle of the lights far in the distance, made me serenely happy, and I was glad I started to Vesuvius.

ASCENT OF MOUNT VESUVIUS—CONTINUED.

This subject will be excellent matter for a chapter, and to-morrow or next day I will write it.

Chapter XXX

S EE NAPLES and die." Well, I do not know that one would necessarily die after merely seeing it, but to attempt to live there might turn out a little differently. To see Naples as we saw it in the early dawn from far up on the side of Vesuvius, is to see a picture of wonderful beauty. At that distance its dingy buildings looked white—and so, rank on rank of balconies, windows and roofs, they piled themselves up from the blue ocean till the colossal castle of St. Elmo topped the grand white pyramid and gave the picture symmetry, emphasis and completeness. And when its lilies turned to roses— when it blushed under the sun's first kiss—it was beautiful beyond all description. One might well say, then, "See Naples and die." The frame of the picture was charming, itself. In front, the smooth sea—a vast mosaic of many colors; the lofty islands swimming in a dreamy haze in the distance; at our end of the city the stately double peak of Vesuvius, and its strong black ribs and seams of lava stretching down to the limitless level campagna—a green carpet that enchants the eye and leads it on and on, past clusters of trees, and isolated houses, and snowy villages, until it shreds out in a fringe of mist and general vagueness far away. It is from the Hermitage, there on the side of Vesuvius, that one should "see Naples and die."

But do not go within the walls and look at it in detail. That takes away some of the romance of the thing. The people are filthy in their habits, and this makes filthy streets and breeds disagreeable sights and smells. There never was a community so prejudiced against the cholera as these Neapolitans are. But they have good reason to be. The cholera generally vanquishes a Neapolitan when it seizes him, because, you understand, before the doctor can dig through the dirt and get at the disease the man dies. The upper classes take a sea-bath every day, and are pretty decent.

The streets are generally about wide enough for one wagon, and how they do swarm with people! It is Broadway repeated in every street, in every court, in every alley! Such masses, such throngs, such multitudes of hurrying, bustling, struggling humanity! We never saw the like of it, hardly even in New York, I think. There are seldom any sidewalks, and when there are, they are not often wide enough to pass a man on without caroming on him. So everybody walks in the street—and where the street is wide enough, carriages are forever dashing along. Why a thousand people are not run over and crippled every day is a mystery that no man can solve.

But if there is an eighth wonder in the world, it must be the dwelling-houses of Naples. I honestly believe a good majority of them are a hundred feet high! And the solid brick walls are seven feet through. You go up nine flights of stairs before you get to the "first" floor. No, not nine, but there or thereabouts. There is a little bird-cage of an iron railing in front of every window clear away up, up, up, among the eternal clouds, where the roof is, and there is always somebody looking out of every window—people of ordinary size looking out from the first floor, people a shade smaller from the second, people that look a little smaller yet from the third—and from thence upward they grow smaller and smaller by a regularly graduated diminution, till the folks in the topmost windows seem more like birds in an uncommonly tall martin-box than any thing else. The perspective of one of these narrow cracks of streets, with its rows of tall houses stretching away till they come together in the distance like railway tracks; its clothes-lines crossing over at all altitudes and waving their bannered raggedness over the swarms of people below; and the white-dressed women perched in balcony railings all the way from the pavement up to the heavens—a perspective like that is really worth going into Neapolitan details to see.

ASCENT OF VESUVIUS—CONTINUED.

Naples, with its immediate suburbs, contains six hundred and twenty-five thousand inhabitants, but I am satisfied it covers no more ground than an American city of one hundred and fifty thousand. It reaches up into the air infinitely higher than three American cities, though, and there is where the secret of it lies. I will observe here, in passing, that the contrasts between opulence and poverty, and magnificence and misery, are more frequent and more striking in Naples than in Paris even. One must go to the Bois de Boulogne to see fashionable dressing, splendid equipages and stunning liveries, and to the Faubourg St. Antoine to see vice, misery, hunger, rags, dirt—but in the thoroughfares of Naples these things are all mixed together. Naked boys of nine years and the fancy-dressed children of luxury; shreds and tatters, and brilliant uniforms; jackass-carts and state-carriages; beggars, Princes and Bishops, jostle each other in every street. At six o'clock every evening, all Naples turns out to drive on the *Riviere di Chiaja*, (whatever that may mean;) and for two hours one may stand there and see the motliest and the worst mixed procession go by that ever eyes beheld. Princes (there are more Princes than policemen in Naples—the city is infested with them)—Princes who live up seven flights of stairs and don't own any principalities, will keep a carriage and go hungry; and clerks, mechanics, milliners and strumpets will go without their dinners and squander the money on a hack-ride in the Chiaja; the rag-tag and rubbish of the city stack themselves up, to the number of twenty or thirty, on a rickety little go-cart hauled by a donkey not much bigger than a cat, and *they* drive in the Chiaja; Dukes and bankers, in sumptuous carriages and with gorgeous drivers and footmen, turn out, also, and so the furious procession goes. For two hours rank and wealth, and obscurity and poverty clatter along side by side in the wild procession, and then go home serene, happy, covered with glory!

I was looking at a magnificent marble staircase in the King's palace, the other day, which, it was said, cost five million francs, and I suppose it did cost half a million, may be. I felt as if it must be a fine thing to live in a country where there was such comfort and such luxury as this. And then I stepped out musing, and almost walked over a vagabond who was eating his dinner on the curbstone—a piece of bread and a bunch of grapes. When I found that this mustang was clerking in a fruit establishment (he had the establishment along with him in a basket,) at two cents a day, and that he had no palace at home where he lived, I lost some of my enthusiasm concerning the happiness of living in Italy.

This naturally suggests to me a thought about wages here. Lieutenants in the army get about a dollar a day, and common soldiers a couple of cents. I only know one clerk—he gets four dollars a month. Printers get six dollars and a half a month, but I have heard of a foreman who gets thirteen. To be growing suddenly and violently rich, as this man is, naturally makes him a bloated aristocrat. The airs he puts on are insufferable.

And, speaking of wages, reminds me of prices of merchandise. In Paris you pay twelve dollars a dozen for Jouvin's best kid gloves; gloves of about as good quality sell here at three or four dollars a dozen. You pay five and six dollars apiece for fine linen shirts in Paris; here and in Leghorn you pay two and a half. In Marseilles you pay forty dollars for a first-class dress coat made by a good tailor, but in Leghorn you can get a full dress suit for the same money. Here you get handsome business suits at from ten to twenty dollars, and in Leghorn you can get an overcoat for fifteen dollars that would cost you seventy in New York. Fine kid boots are worth eight dollars in Marseilles and four dollars here. Lyons velvets rank higher in America than those of Genoa. Yet the bulk of Lyons velvets you buy in the States are made in Genoa and imported into Lyons, where they receive the Lyons stamp and are then exported to America. You can buy enough velvet in Genoa for twenty-five dollars to make a five hundred dollar cloak in New York—so the ladies tell me. Of course these things bring me back, by a natural and easy transition, to the

Ascent of Vesuvius—Continued.

And thus the wonderful Blue Grotto is suggested to me. It is situated on the Island of Capri, twenty-two miles from Naples. We chartered a little steamer and went out there. Of course, the police boarded us and put us through a health examination, and inquired into our politics, before they would let us land. The airs these little insect Governments put on are in the last degree ridiculous. They even put a policeman on board of our boat to keep an eye on us as long as we were in the Capri dominions. They thought we wanted to steal the grotto, I suppose. It was worth stealing. The entrance to the cave is four feet high and four feet wide, and is in the face of a lofty perpendicular cliff—the sea-wall. You enter in small boats—and a tight squeeze it is, too. You can not go in at all when the tide is up. Once within, you find yourself in an arched cavern about one hundred and sixty feet long, one hundred and twenty wide, and about seventy high. How deep it is no man knows. It goes down to the bottom of the ocean. The waters of this placid subterranean lake are the brightest, loveliest blue that can be imagined. They are as transparent as plate glass, and their coloring would shame the richest sky that ever bent over Italy. No tint could be more ravishing, no lustre more superb. Throw a stone into the water, and the myriad of tiny bubbles that are created flash out a brilliant glare like blue theatrical fires. Dip an oar, and its blade turns to splendid frosted silver, tinted with blue. Let a man jump in, and instantly he is cased in an armor more gorgeous than ever kingly Crusader wore.

Then we went to Ischia, but I had already been to that island and tired myself to death "resting" a couple of days and studying human villainy, with the landlord of the Grande Sentinelle for a model. So we went to Procida, and from thence to Pozzuoli, where St. Paul landed after he sailed from Samos. I landed at precisely the same spot where St. Paul landed, and so did Dan and the others. It was a remarkable coincidence. St. Paul preached to these people seven days before he started to Rome.

Nero's Baths, the ruins of Baiæ, the Temple of Serapis; Cumæ, where the Cumæn Sybil interpreted the oracles, the Lake Agnano, with its ancient submerged city still visible far down in its depths—these and a hundred other points of interest we examined with critical imbecility, but the Grotto of the Dog claimed our chief attention, because we had heard and read so much about it. Every body has written about the Grotto del Cane and its poisonous vapors, from Pliny down to Smith, and every tourist has held a dog over its floor by the legs to test the capabilities of the place. The dog dies in a minute and a half—a chicken instantly. As a general thing, strangers who crawl in there to sleep do not get up until they are called. And then they don't either. The stranger that ventures to sleep there takes a permanent contract. I longed to see this grotto. I resolved to take a dog and hold him myself; suffocate him a little, and time him; suffocate him some more and then finish him. We reached the grotto at about three in the afternoon, and proceeded at once to make the experiments. But now, an important difficulty presented itself. We had no dog.

ASCENT OF VESUVIUS—CONTINUED.

At the Hermitage we were about fifteen or eighteen hundred feet above the sea, and thus far a portion of the ascent had been pretty abrupt. For the next two miles the road was a mixture—sometimes the ascent was abrupt and sometimes it was not: but one characteristic it possessed all the time, without failure—without modification—it was all uncompromisingly and unspeakably infamous. It was a rough, narrow trail, and led over an old lava flow—a black ocean which was tumbled into a thousand fantastic shapes—a wild chaos of ruin, desolation, and barrenness—a wilderness of billowy upheavals, of furious whirlpools, of miniature mountains rent asunder—of gnarled and knotted, wrinkled and twisted masses of blackness that mimicked branching roots, great vines, trunks of trees, all interlaced and mingled together: and all these weird shapes, all this turbulent panorama, all this stormy, far-stretching waste of blackness, with its thrilling suggestiveness of life, of action, of boiling, surging, furious motion, was petrified!—all stricken dead and cold in the instant of its maddest rioting!—fettered, paralyzed, and left to glower at heaven in impotent rage for evermore!

Finally we stood in a level, narrow valley (a valley that had been created by the terrific march of some old time irruption) and on either hand towered the two steep peaks of Vesuvius. The one we had to climb—the one that contains the active volcano—seemed about eight hundred or one thousand feet high, and looked almost too straight-up-and-down for any man to climb, and certainly no mule could climb it with a

man on his back. Four of these native pirates will carry you
to the top in a sedan chair, if you wish it, but suppose they
were to slip and let you fall,—is it likely that you would ever
stop rolling? Not this side of eternity, perhaps. We left the
mules, sharpened our finger-nails, and began the ascent I have
been writing about so long, at twenty minutes to six in the
morning. The path led straight up a rugged sweep of loose
chunks of pumice-stone, and for about every two steps forward we took, we slid back one. It was so excessively steep
that we had to stop, every fifty or sixty steps, and rest a moment. To see our comrades, we had to look very nearly
straight up at those above us, and very nearly straight down
at those below. We stood on the summit at last—it had taken
an hour and fifteen minutes to make the trip.

What we saw there was simply a circular crater—a circular
ditch, if you please—about two hundred feet deep, and four
or five hundred feet wide, whose inner wall was about half a
mile in circumference. In the centre of the great circus ring
thus formed, was a torn and ragged upheaval a hundred feet
high, all snowed over with a sulphur crust of many and many
a brilliant and beautiful color, and the ditch inclosed this like
the moat of a castle, or surrounded it as a little river does a
little island, if the simile is better. The sulphur coating of that
island was gaudy in the extreme—all mingled together in the
richest confusion were red, blue, brown, black, yellow,
white—I do not know that there was a color, or shade of a
color, or combination of colors, unrepresented—and when
the sun burst through the morning mists and fired this tinted
magnificence, it topped imperial Vesuvius like a jeweled
crown!

The crater itself—the ditch—was not so variegated in coloring, but yet, in its softness, richness, and unpretentious elegance, it was more charming, more fascinating to the eye.
There was nothing "loud" about its well-bred and well-
dressed look. Beautiful? One could stand and look down
upon it for a week without getting tired of it. It had the
semblance of a pleasant meadow, whose slender grasses and
whose velvety mosses were frosted with a shining dust, and
tinted with palest green that deepened gradually to the darkest hue of the orange leaf, and deepened yet again into gravest

brown, then faded into orange, then into brightest gold, and culminated in the delicate pink of a new-blown rose. Where portions of the meadow had sunk, and where other portions had been broken up like an ice-floe, the cavernous openings of the one, and the ragged upturned edges exposed by the other, were hung with a lace-work of soft-tinted crystals of sulphur that changed their deformities into quaint shapes and figures that were full of grace and beauty.

The walls of the ditch were brilliant with yellow banks of sulphur and with lava and pumice-stone of many colors. No fire was visible any where, but gusts of sulphurous steam issued silently and invisibly from a thousand little cracks and fissures in the crater, and were wafted to our noses with every breeze. But so long as we kept our nostrils buried in our handkerchiefs, there was small danger of suffocation.

Some of the boys thrust long slips of paper down into holes and set them on fire, and so achieved the glory of lighting their cigars by the flames of Vesuvius, and others cooked eggs over fissures in the rocks and were happy.

The view from the summit would have been superb but for the fact that the sun could only pierce the mists at long intervals. Thus the glimpses we had of the grand panorama below were only fitful and unsatisfactory.

THE DESCENT.

The descent of the mountain was a labor of only four minutes. Instead of stalking down the rugged path we ascended, we chose one which was bedded knee-deep in loose ashes, and ploughed our way with prodigious strides that would almost have shamed the performance of him of the seven-league boots.

The Vesuvius of to-day is a very poor affair compared to the mighty volcano of Kilauea, in the Sandwich Islands, but I am glad I visited it. It was well worth it.

It is said that during one of the grand eruptions of Vesuvius it discharged massy rocks weighing many tons a thousand feet into the air, its vast jets of smoke and steam ascended thirty miles toward the firmament, and clouds of its ashes were wafted abroad and fell upon the decks of ships seven hundred and fifty miles at sea! I will take the ashes at a moderate discount, if any one will take the thirty miles of smoke, but I do not feel able to take a commanding interest in the whole story by myself.

Chapter XXXI

The Buried City of Pompeii.

They pronounce it Pom-*pay*-e. I always had an idea that you went down into Pompeii with torches, by the way of damp, dark stairways, just as you do in silver mines, and traversed gloomy tunnels with lava overhead and something on either hand like dilapidated prisons gouged out of the solid earth, that faintly resembled houses. But you do nothing of the kind. Fully one-half of the buried city, perhaps, is completely exhumed and thrown open freely to the light of day; and there stand the long rows of solidly-built brick houses (roofless) just as they stood eighteen hundred years ago, hot with the flaming sun; and there lie their floors, clean-swept, and not a bright fragment tarnished or wanting of the labored mosaics that pictured them with the beasts, and birds, and flowers which we copy in perishable carpets to-day; and there are the Venuses, and Bacchuses, and Adonises, making love and getting drunk in many-hued frescoes on the walls of saloon and bed-chamber; and there are the narrow streets and narrower sidewalks, paved with flags of good hard lava, the one deeply rutted with the chariot-wheels, and the other with the passing feet of the Pompeiians of by-gone centuries; and there are the bake-shops, the temples, the halls of justice, the baths, the theatres—all clean-scraped and neat, and suggesting nothing of the nature of a silver mine away down in the bowels of the earth. The broken pillars lying about, the doorless doorways and the crumbled tops of the wilderness of walls, were wonderfully suggestive of the "burnt district" in one of our cities, and if there had been any charred timbers, shattered windows, heaps of debris, and general blackness and smokiness about the place, the resemblance would have been perfect. But no—the sun shines as brightly down on old Pompeii to-day as it did when Christ was born in Bethlehem, and its streets are cleaner a hundred times than ever Pompeiian saw them in her prime. I know whereof I speak—for in the great, chief thoroughfares (Merchant street and the Street of Fortune) have I not seen with my own eyes how for two hundred years at least the pavements were not re-

paired!—how ruts five and even ten inches deep were worn
into the thick flag-stones by the chariot-wheels of generations
of swindled tax-payers? And do I not know by these signs
that Street Commissioners of Pompeii never attended to their
business, and that if they never mended the pavements they
never cleaned them? And, besides, is it not the inborn nature
of Street Commissioners to avoid their duty whenever they
get a chance? I wish I knew the name of the last one that held
office in Pompeii so that I could give him a blast. I speak with
feeling on this subject, because I caught my foot in one of
those ruts, and the sadness that came over me when I saw the
first poor skeleton, with ashes and lava sticking to it, was tempered by the reflection that may be that party was the Street
Commissioner.

No—Pompeii is no longer a buried city. It is a city of
hundreds and hundreds of roofless houses, and a tangled
maze of streets where one could easily get lost, without a
guide, and have to sleep in some ghostly palace that had
known no living tenant since that awful November night of
eighteen centuries ago.

We passed through the gate which faces the Mediterranean,
(called the "Marine Gate,") and by the rusty, broken image
of Minerva, still keeping tireless watch and ward over the possessions it was powerless to save, and went up a long street
and stood in the broad court of the Forum of Justice. The
floor was level and clean, and up and down either side was a
noble colonnade of broken pillars, with their beautiful Ionic
and Corinthian columns scattered about them. At the upper
end were the vacant seats of the Judges, and behind them we
descended into a dungeon where the ashes and cinders had
found two prisoners chained on that memorable November
night, and tortured them to death. How they must have
tugged at the pitiless fetters as the fierce fires surged around
them!

Then we lounged through many and many a sumptuous
private mansion which we could not have entered without a
formal invitation in incomprehensible Latin, in the olden
time, when the owners lived there—and we probably
wouldn't have got it. These people built their houses a good
deal alike. The floors were laid in fanciful figures wrought in

mosaics of many-colored marbles. At the threshold your eyes
fall upon a Latin sentence of welcome, sometimes, or a picture of a dog, with the legend "Beware of the Dog," and
sometimes a picture of a bear or a faun with no inscription at
all. Then you enter a sort of vestibule, where they used to
keep the hat-rack, I suppose; next a room with a large marble
basin in the midst and the pipes of a fountain; on either side
are bed-rooms; beyond the fountain is a reception-room, then
a little garden, dining-room, and so forth and so on. The
floors were all mosaic, the walls were stuccoed, or frescoed,
or ornamented with bas-reliefs, and here and there were statues, large and small, and little fish-pools, and cascades of sparkling water that sprang from secret places in the colonnade of
handsome pillars that surrounded the court, and kept the
flower-beds fresh and the air cool. Those Pompeiians were
very luxurious in their tastes and habits. The most exquisite
bronzes we have seen in Europe, came from the exhumed
cities of Herculaneum and Pompeii, and also the finest cameos and the most delicate engravings on precious stones; their
pictures, eighteen or nineteen centuries old, are often much
more pleasing than the celebrated rubbish of the old masters
of three centuries ago. They were well up in art. From the
creation of these works of the first, clear up to the eleventh
century, art seems hardly to have existed at all—at least no
remnants of it are left—and it was curious to see how far (in
some things, at any rate,) these old time pagans excelled the
remote generations of masters that came after them. The
pride of the world in sculptures seem to be the Laocoon and
the Dying Gladiator, in Rome. They are as old as Pompeii,
were dug from the earth like Pompeii; but their exact age or
who made them can only be conjectured. But worn, and
cracked, without a history, and with the blemishing stains of
numberless centuries upon them, they still mutely mock at all
efforts to rival their perfections.

It was a quaint and curious pastime, wandering through
this old silent city of the dead—lounging through utterly deserted streets where thousands and thousands of human
beings once bought and sold, and walked and rode, and made
the place resound with the noise and confusion of traffic and
pleasure. They were not lazy. They hurried in those days. We

had evidence of that. There was a temple on one corner, and it was a shorter cut to go between the columns of that temple from one street to the other than to go around—and behold that pathway had been worn deep into the heavy flag-stone floor of the building by generations of time-saving feet! They would not go around when it was quicker to go through. We do that way in our cities.

Every where, you see things that make you wonder how old these old houses were before the night of destruction came—things, too, which bring back those long dead inhabitants and place them living before your eyes. For instance: The steps (two feet thick—lava blocks) that lead up out of the school, and the same kind of steps that lead up into the dress circle of the principal theatre, are almost worn through! For ages the boys hurried out of that school, and for ages their parents hurried into that theatre, and the nervous feet that have been dust and ashes for eighteen centuries have left their record for us to read to-day. I imagined I could see crowds of gentlemen and ladies thronging into the theatre, with tickets for secured seats in their hands, and on the wall, I read the imaginary placard, in infamous grammar, "POSITIVELY NO FREE LIST, EXCEPT MEMBERS OF THE PRESS!" Hanging about the doorway (I fancied,) were slouchy Pompeiian street-boys uttering slang and profanity, and keeping a wary eye out for checks. I entered the theatre, and sat down in one of the long rows of stone benches in the dress circle, and looked at the place for the orchestra, and the ruined stage, and around at the wide sweep of empty boxes, and thought to myself, "This house won't pay." I tried to imagine the music in full blast, the leader of the orchestra beating time, and the "versatile" So-and-So (who had "just returned from a most successful tour in the provinces to play his last and farewell engagement of positively six nights only, in Pompeii, previous to his departure for Herculaneum,") charging around the stage and piling the agony mountains high—but I could not do it with such a "house" as that; those empty benches tied my fancy down to dull reality. I said, these people that ought to be here have been dead, and still, and moldering to dust for ages and ages, and will never care for the trifles and follies of life any more for ever—"Owing to circumstances, etc., etc., there will not be any performance to-night." Close down the curtain. Put out the lights.

And so I turned away and went through shop after shop and store after store, far down the long street of the merchants, and called for the wares of Rome and the East, but the tradesmen were gone, the marts were silent, and nothing was left but the broken jars all set in cement of cinders and ashes: the wine and the oil that once had filled them were gone with their owners.

In a bake-shop was a mill for grinding the grain, and the furnaces for baking the bread: and they say that here, in the same furnaces, the exhumers of Pompeii found nice, well baked loaves which the baker had not found time to remove from the ovens the last time he left his shop, because circumstances compelled him to leave in such a hurry.

In one house (the only building in Pompeii which no woman is now allowed to enter,) were the small rooms and short beds of solid masonry, just as they were in the old times, and on the walls were pictures which looked almost as fresh as if they were painted yesterday, but which no pen could have the hardihood to describe; and here and there were Latin inscriptions—obscene scintillations of wit, scratched by hands that possibly were uplifted to Heaven for succor in the midst of a driving storm of fire before the night was done.

In one of the principal streets was a ponderous stone tank, and a water-spout that supplied it, and where the tired, heated toilers from the Campagna used to rest their right hands when they bent over to put their lips to the spout, the thick stone was worn down to a broad groove an inch or two deep. Think of the countless thousands of hands that had pressed that spot in the ages that are gone, to so reduce a stone that is as hard as iron!

They had a great public bulletin board in Pompeii—a place where announcements for gladiatorial combats, elections, and such things, were posted—not on perishable paper, but carved in enduring stone. One lady, who, I take it, was rich and well brought up, advertised a dwelling or so to rent, with baths and all the modern improvements, and several hundred shops, stipulating that the dwellings should not be put to immoral purposes. You can find out who lived in many a house in Pompeii by the carved stone door-plates affixed to them: and in the same way you can tell who they were that occupy the tombs. Every where around are things that reveal to you something of the customs and history of this forgotten people. But what would a volcano leave of an American city, if it once rained its cinders on it? Hardly a sign or a symbol to tell its story.

In one of these long Pompeiian halls the skeleton of a man was found, with ten pieces of gold in one hand and a large key in the other. He had seized his money and started toward the door, but the fiery tempest caught him at the very threshold, and he sank down and died. One more minute of precious time would have saved him. I saw the skeletons of a man, a woman, and two young girls. The woman had her hands spread wide apart, as if in mortal terror, and I imagined I could still trace upon her shapeless face something of the expression of wild despair that distorted it when the heavens rained fire in these streets, so many ages ago. The girls and the man lay with their faces upon their arms, as if they had tried to shield them from the enveloping cinders. In one apartment eighteen skeletons were found, all in sitting postures, and blackened places on the walls still mark their shapes and show their attitudes, like shadows. One of them, a woman, still wore upon her skeleton throat a necklace, with her name engraved upon it—JULIE DI DIOMEDE.

But perhaps the most poetical thing Pompeii has yielded to modern research, was that grand figure of a Roman soldier, clad in complete armor; who, true to his duty, true to his proud name of a soldier of Rome, and full of the stern courage which had given to that name its glory, stood to his post by the city gate, erect and unflinching, till the hell that raged around him *burned out* the dauntless spirit it could not conquer.

We never read of Pompeii but we think of that soldier; we can not write of Pompeii without the natural impulse to grant to him the mention he so well deserves. Let us remember that he was a soldier—not a policeman—and so, praise him. Being a soldier, he staid,—because the warrior instinct forbade him to fly. Had he been a policeman he would have staid, also—because he would have been asleep.

There are not half a dozen flights of stairs in Pompeii, and no other evidences that the houses were more than one story high. The people did not live in the clouds, as do the Venetians, the Genoese and Neapolitans of to-day.

We came out from under the solemn mysteries of this city of the Venerable Past—this city which perished, with all its old ways and its quaint old fashions about it, remote centuries ago, when the Disciples were preaching the new religion, which is as old as the hills to us now—and went dreaming among the trees that grow over acres and acres of its still buried streets and squares, till a shrill whistle and the cry of *"All aboard—last train for Naples!"* woke me up and reminded me that I belonged in the nineteenth century, and was not a dusty mummy, caked with ashes and cinders, eighteen hundred years old. The transition was startling. The idea of a railroad train actually running to old dead Pompeii, and whistling irreverently, and calling for passengers in the most bustling and business-like way, was as strange a thing as one could imagine, and as unpoetical and disagreeable as it was strange.

Compare the cheerful life and the sunshine of this day with the horrors the younger Pliny saw here, the 9th of November, A. D. 79, when he was so bravely striving to remove his mother out of reach of harm, while she begged him, with all a mother's unselfishness, to leave her to perish and save himself.

"By this time the murky darkness had so increased that one might have believed himself abroad in a black and moonless night, or in a chamber where all the lights had been extinguished. On every hand was heard the complaints of women, the wailing of children, and the cries of men. One called his father, another his son, and another his wife, and only by their voices could they know each other. Many in their despair begged that death would come and end their distress.

"Some implored the gods to succor them, and some believed that this night was the last, the eternal night which should engulf the universe!

"Even so it seemed to me—and I consoled myself for the coming death with the reflection: BEHOLD, THE WORLD IS PASSING AWAY!"

*   *   *

After browsing among the stately ruins of Rome, of Baiæ, of Pompeii, and after glancing down the long marble ranks of battered and nameless imperial heads that stretch down the corridors of the Vatican, one thing strikes me with a force it never had before: the unsubstantial, unlasting character of fame. Men lived long lives, in the olden time, and struggled feverishly through them, toiling like slaves, in oratory, in generalship, or in literature, and then laid them down and died, happy in the possession of an enduring history and a deathless name. Well, twenty little centuries flutter away, and what is left of these things? A crazy inscription on a block of stone, which snuffy antiquaries bother over and tangle up and make nothing out of but a bare name (which they spell wrong)— no history, no tradition, no poetry—nothing that can give it even a passing interest. What may be left of General Grant's great name forty centuries hence? This—in the Encyclopedia for A. D. 5868, possibly:

"URIAH S. (or Z.) GRAUNT—popular poet of ancient times in the Aztec provinces of the United States of British America. Some authors say flourished about A. D. 742; but the learned Ah-ah Foofoo states that he was a contemporary of Scharkspyre, the English poet, and flourished about A. D. 1328, some three centuries *after* the Trojan war instead of before it. He wrote 'Rock me to Sleep, Mother.' "

These thoughts sadden me. I will to bed.

Chapter XXXII

HOME, AGAIN! For the first time, in many weeks, the ship's entire family met and shook hands on the quarter-deck. They had gathered from many points of the compass and from many lands, but not one was missing; there was no tale of sickness or death among the flock to dampen the pleasure of the reunion. Once more there was a full audience on deck to listen to the sailors' chorus as they got the anchor up, and to wave an adieu to the land as we sped away from Naples. The seats were full at dinner again, the domino parties were complete, and the life and bustle on the upper deck in the fine moonlight at night was like old times—old times that had been gone weeks only, but yet they were weeks so crowded with incident, adventure and excitement, that they seemed almost like years. There was no lack of cheerfulness on board the *Quaker City*. For once, her title was a misnomer.

At seven in the evening, with the western horizon all golden from the sunken sun, and specked with distant ships, the full moon sailing high over head, the dark blue of the sea under foot, and a strange sort of twilight affected by all these different lights and colors around us and about us, we sighted superb Stromboli. With what majesty the monarch held his lonely state above the level sea! Distance clothed him in a purple gloom, and added a veil of shimmering mist that so softened his rugged features that we seemed to see him through a web of silver gauze. His torch was out; his fires were smoldering; a tall column of smoke that rose up and lost itself in the growing moonlight was all the sign he gave that he was a living Autocrat of the Sea and not the spectre of a dead one.

At two in the morning we swept through the Straits of Messina, and so bright was the moonlight that Italy on the one hand and Sicily on the other seemed almost as distinctly visible as though we looked at them from the middle of a street we were traversing. The city of Messina, milk-white, and starred and spangled all over with gaslights, was a fairy spectacle. A great party of us were on deck smoking and making a noise, and waiting to see famous Scylla and Charybdis. And presently the Oracle stepped out with his eternal spy-glass and squared himself on the deck like another Colossus of Rhodes. It was a surprise to see him abroad at such an hour. Nobody supposed he cared any thing about an old fable like that of Scylla and Charybdis. One of the boys said:

"Hello, doctor, what are you doing up here at this time of night?—What do you want to see this place for?"

"What do *I* want to see this place for? Young man, little do you know me, or you wouldn't ask such a question. I wish to see *all* the places that's mentioned in the Bible."

"Stuff—this place isn't mentioned in the Bible."

"It ain't mentioned in the Bible!—*this* place ain't—well now, what place *is* this, since you know so much about it?"

"Why it's Scylla and Charybdis."

"Scylla and Cha—confound it, I thought it was Sodom and Gomorrah!"

And he closed up his glass and went below. The above is the ship story. Its plausibility is marred a little by the fact that the Oracle was not a biblical student, and did not spend much of his time instructing himself about Scriptural localities.— They say the Oracle complains, in this hot weather, lately, that the only beverage in the ship that is passable, is the butter. He did not mean butter, of course, but inasmuch as that article remains in a melted state now since we are out of ice, it is fair to give him the credit of getting one long word in the right place, anyhow, for once in his life. He said, in Rome, that the Pope was a noble-looking old man, but he never *did* think much of his Iliad.

We spent one pleasant day skirting along the Isles of Greece. They are very mountainous. Their prevailing tints are gray and brown, approaching to red. Little white villages surrounded by trees, nestle in the valleys or roost upon the lofty perpendicular sea-walls.

We had one fine sunset—a rich carmine flush that suffused the western sky and cast a ruddy glow far over the sea.—Fine sunsets seem to be rare in this part of the world—or at least, striking ones. They are soft, sensuous, lovely—they are exquisite, refined, effeminate, but we have seen no sunsets here yet like the gorgeous conflagrations that flame in the track of the sinking sun in our high northern latitudes.

But what were sunsets to us, with the wild excitement upon us of approaching the most renowned of cities! What cared we for outward visions, when Agamemnon, Achilles, and a thousand other heroes of the great Past were marching in ghostly procession through our fancies? What were sunsets to us, who were about to live and breathe and walk in actual Athens; yea, and go far down into the dead centuries and bid in person for the slaves, Diogenes and Plato, in the public market-place, or gossip with the neighbors about the siege of Troy or the splendid deeds of Marathon? We scorned to consider sunsets.

We arrived, and entered the ancient harbor of the Piræus at last. We dropped anchor within half a mile of the village. Away off, across the undulating Plain of Attica, could be seen a little square-topped hill with a something on it, which our glasses soon discovered to be the ruined edifices of the citadel of the Athenians, and most prominent among them loomed the venerable Parthenon. So exquisitely clear and pure is this wonderful atmosphere that every column of the noble structure was discernible through the telescope, and even the smaller ruins about it assumed some semblance of shape. This at a distance of five or six miles. In the valley, near the Acropolis, (the square-topped hill before spoken of,) Athens itself could be vaguely made out with an ordinary lorgnette. Every body was anxious to get ashore and visit these classic localities as quickly as possible. No land we had yet seen had aroused such universal interest among the passengers.

But bad news came. The commandant of the Piræus came in his boat, and said we must either depart or else get outside the harbor and remain imprisoned in our ship, under rigid quarantine, for eleven days! So we took up the anchor and moved outside, to lie a dozen hours or so, taking in supplies, and then sail for Constantinople. It was the bitterest disappointment we had yet experienced. To lie a whole day in sight of the Acropolis, and yet be obliged to go away without visiting Athens! Disappointment was hardly a strong enough word to describe the circumstances.

All hands were on deck, all the afternoon, with books and

maps and glasses, trying to determine which "narrow rocky ridge" was the Areopagus, which sloping hill the Pnyx, which elevation the Museum Hill, and so on. And we got things confused. Discussion became heated, and party spirit ran high. Church members were gazing with emotion upon a hill which they said was the one St. Paul preached from, and another faction claimed that that hill was Hymettus, and another that it was Pentelicon! After all the trouble, we could be certain of only one thing—the square-topped hill was the Acropolis, and the grand ruin that crowned it was the Parthenon, whose picture we knew in infancy in the school books.

We inquired of every body who came near the ship, whether there were guards in the Piræus, whether they were strict, what the chances were of capture should any of us slip ashore, and in case any of us made the venture and were caught, what would be probably done to us? The answers were discouraging: There was a strong guard or police force; the Piræus was a small town, and any stranger seen in it would surely attract attention—capture would be certain. The commandant said the punishment would be "heavy;" when asked "how heavy?" he said it would be "very severe"— that was all we could get out of him.

At eleven o'clock at night, when most of the ship's company were abed, four of us stole softly ashore in a small boat, a clouded moon favoring the enterprise, and started two and two, and far apart, over a low hill, intending to go clear around the Piræus, out of the range of its police. Picking our way so stealthily over that rocky, nettle-grown eminence, made me feel a good deal as if I were on my way somewhere to steal something. My immediate comrade and I talked in an undertone about quarantine laws and their penalties, but we found nothing cheering in the subject. I was posted. Only a few days before, I was talking with our captain, and he mentioned the case of a man who swam ashore from a quarantined ship somewhere, and got imprisoned six months for it; and when he was in Genoa a few years ago, a captain of a quarantined ship went in his boat to a departing ship, which was already outside of the harbor, and put a letter on board to be taken to his family, and the authorities imprisoned him three months for it, and then conducted him and his ship fairly to sea, and warned him never to show himself in that port again while he lived. This kind of conversation did no good, further than to give a sort of dismal interest to our quarantine-breaking expedition, and so we dropped it. We made the entire circuit of the town without seeing any body but one man, who stared at us curiously, but said nothing, and a dozen persons asleep on the ground before their doors, whom we walked among and never woke—but we woke up dogs enough, in all conscience—we always had one or two barking at our heels, and several times we had as many as ten and twelve at once. They made such a preposterous din that persons aboard our ship said they could tell how we were progressing for a long time, and where we were, by the bark-ing of the dogs. The clouded moon still favored us. When we had made the whole circuit, and were passing among the houses on the further side of the town, the moon came out splendidly, but we no longer feared the light. As we ap-proached a well, near a house, to get a drink, the owner merely glanced at us and went within. He left the quiet, slum-bering town at our mercy. I record it here proudly, that we didn't do any thing to it.

Seeing no road, we took a tall hill to the left of the distant Acropolis for a mark, and steered straight for it over all ob-structions, and over a little rougher piece of country than ex-ists any where else outside of the State of Nevada, perhaps. Part of the way it was covered with small, loose stones—we trod on six at a time, and they all rolled. Another part of it was dry, loose, newly-ploughed ground. Still another part of it was a long stretch of low grape-vines, which were tangle-some and troublesome, and which we took to be brambles. The Attic Plain, barring the grape-vines, was a barren, deso-late, unpoetical waste—I wonder what it was in Greece's Age of Glory, five hundred years before Christ?

In the neighborhood of one o'clock in the morning, when we were heated with fast walking and parched with thirst, Denny exclaimed, "Why, these weeds are grape-vines!" and in five minutes we had a score of bunches of large, white, delicious grapes, and were reaching down for more when a dark shape rose mysteriously up out of the shadows beside us and said "Ho!" And so we left.

In ten minutes more we struck into a beautiful road, and unlike some others we had stumbled upon at intervals, it led in the right direction. We followed it. It was broad, and smooth, and white—handsome and in perfect repair, and shaded on both sides for a mile or so with single ranks of trees, and also with luxuriant vineyards. Twice we entered and stole grapes, and the second time somebody shouted at us from some invisible place. Whereupon we left again. We speculated in grapes no more on that side of Athens.

Shortly we came upon an ancient stone aqueduct, built upon arches, and from that time forth we had ruins all about us—we were approaching our journey's end. We could not see the Acropolis now or the high hill, either, and I wanted to follow the road till we were abreast of them, but the others overruled me, and we toiled laboriously up the stony hill immediately in our front—and from its summit saw another—climbed it and saw another! It was an hour of exhausting work. Soon we came upon a row of open graves, cut in the solid rock—(for a while one of them served Socrates for a prison)—we passed around the shoulder of the hill, and the citadel, in all its ruined magnificence, burst upon us! We hurried across the ravine and up a winding road, and stood on the old Acropolis, with the prodigious walls of the citadel towering above our heads. We did not stop to inspect their massive blocks of marble, or measure their height, or guess at their extraordinary thickness, but passed at once through a great arched passage like a railway tunnel, and went straight to the gate that leads to the ancient temples. It was locked! So, after all, it seemed that we were not to see the great Parthenon face to face. We sat down and held a council of war. Result: the gate was only a flimsy structure of wood—we would break it down. It seemed like desecration, but then we had traveled far, and our necessities were urgent. We could not hunt up guides and keepers—we must be on the ship before daylight. So we argued. This was all very fine, but when we came to break the gate, we could not do it. We moved around an angle of the wall and found a low bas-tion—eight feet high without—ten or twelve within. Denny prepared to scale it, and we got ready to follow. By dint of hard scrambling he finally straddled the top, but some loose stones crumbled away and fell with a crash into the court within. There was instantly a banging of doors and a shout. Denny dropped from the wall in a twinkling, and we retreated in disorder to the gate. Xerxes took that mighty citadel four hundred and eighty years before Christ, when his five millions of soldiers and camp-followers followed him to Greece, and if we four Americans could have remained unmolested five minutes longer, we would have taken it too.

The garrison had turned out—four Greeks. We clamored at the gate, and they admitted us. [Bribery and corruption.]

We crossed a large court, entered a great door, and stood upon a pavement of purest white marble, deeply worn by foot-prints. Before us, in the flooding moonlight, rose the noblest ruins we had ever looked upon—the Propylæ; a small Temple of Minerva; the Temple of Hercules, and the grand Parthenon. [We got these names from the Greek guide, who didn't seem to know more than seven men ought to know.] These edifices were all built of the whitest Pentelic marble, but have a pinkish stain upon them now. Where any part is broken, however, the fracture looks like fine loaf sugar. Six caryatides, or marble women, clad in flowing robes, support the portico of the Temple of Hercules, but the porticos and colonnades of the other structures are formed of massive Doric and Ionic pillars, whose flutings and capitals are still measurably perfect, notwithstanding the centuries that have gone over them and the sieges they have suffered. The Parthenon, originally, was two hundred and twenty-six feet long, one hundred wide, and seventy high, and had two rows of great columns, eight in each, at either end, and single rows of seventeen each down the sides, and was one of the most graceful and beautiful edifices ever erected.

Most of the Parthenon's imposing columns are still standing, but the roof is gone. It was a perfect building two hundred and fifty years ago, when a shell dropped into the Venetian magazine stored here, and the explosion which followed wrecked and unroofed it. I remember but little about the Parthenon, and I have put in one or two facts and figures for the use of other people with short memories. Got them from the guide-book.

As we wandered thoughtfully down the marble-paved length of this stately temple, the scene about us was strangely impressive. Here and there, in lavish profusion, were gleaming white statues of men and women, propped against blocks of marble, some of them armless, some without legs, others headless—but all looking mournful in the moonlight, and startlingly human! They rose up and confronted the midnight intruder on every side—they stared at him with stony eyes from unlooked-for nooks and recesses; they peered at him over fragmentary heaps far down the desolate corridors; they barred his way in the midst of the broad forum, and solemnly pointed with handless arms the way from the sacred fane; and through the roofless temple the moon looked down, and banded the floor and darkened the scattered fragments and broken statues with the slanting shadows of the columns.

What a world of ruined sculpture was about us! Set up in rows—stacked up in piles—scattered broadcast over the wide area of the Acropolis—were hundreds of crippled statues of all sizes and of the most exquisite workmanship; and vast fragments of marble that once belonged to the entablatures, covered with bas-reliefs representing battles and sieges, ships of war with three and four tiers of oars, pageants and processions—every thing one could think of. History says that the temples of the Acropolis were filled with the noblest works of Praxiteles and Phidias, and of many a great master in sculpture besides—and surely these elegant fragments attest it.

We walked out into the grass-grown, fragment-strewn court beyond the Parthenon. It startled us, every now and then, to see a stony white face stare suddenly up at us out of the grass with its dead eyes. The place seemed alive with ghosts. I half expected to see the Athenian heroes of twenty centuries ago glide out of the shadows and steal into the old temple they knew so well and regarded with such boundless pride.

The full moon was riding high in the cloudless heavens, now. We sauntered carelessly and unthinkingly to the edge of the lofty battlements of the citadel, and looked down—a vision! And such a vision! Athens by moonlight! The prophet that thought the splendors of the New Jerusalem were revealed to him, surely saw this instead! It lay in the level plain right under our feet—all spread abroad like a picture—and we looked down upon it as we might have looked from a balloon. We saw no semblance of a street, but every house, every window, every clinging vine, every projection, was as distinct and sharply marked as if the time were noon-day; and yet there was no glare, no glitter, nothing harsh or repulsive—the noiseless city was flooded with the mellowest light that ever streamed from the moon, and seemed like some living creature wrapped in peaceful slumber. On its further side was a little temple, whose delicate pillars and ornate front glowed with a rich lustre that chained the eye like a spell; and nearer by, the palace of the king reared its creamy walls out of the midst of a great garden of shrubbery that was flecked all over with a random shower of amber lights—a spray of golden sparks that lost their brightness in the glory of the moon, and glinted softly upon the sea of dark foliage like the pallid stars of the milky-way. Overhead the stately columns, majestic still in their ruin—under foot the dreaming city—in the distance the silver sea—not on the broad earth is there another picture half so beautiful!

As we turned and moved again through the temple, I wished that the illustrious men who had sat in it in the remote ages could visit it again and reveal themselves to our curious eyes—Plato, Aristotle, Demosthenes, Socrates, Phocion, Pythagoras, Euclid, Pindar, Xenophon, Herodotus, Praxiteles and Phidias, Zeuxis the painter. What a constellation of celebrated names! But more than all, I wished that old Diogenes, groping so patiently with his lantern, searching so zealously for one solitary honest man in all the world, might meander along and stumble on our party. I ought not to say it, may be, but still I suppose he would have put out his light.

We left the Parthenon to keep its watch over old Athens, as it had kept it for twenty-three hundred years, and went and stood outside the walls of the citadel. In the distance was the ancient, but still almost perfect Temple of Theseus, and close by, looking to the west, was the Bema, from whence Demosthenes thundered his philippics and fired the wavering patriotism of his countrymen. To the right was Mars Hill, where the Areopagus sat in ancient times, and where St. Paul defined his position, and below was the market-place where he "disputed daily" with the gossip-loving Athenians. We climbed the stone steps St. Paul ascended, and stood in the square-cut place he stood in, and tried to recollect the Bible account of the matter—but for certain reasons, I could not recall the words. I have found them since:

"Now while Paul waited for them at Athens, his spirit was stirred in him, when he saw the city wholly given up to idolatry.

"Therefore disputed he in the synagogue with the Jews, and with the devout persons, and in the market daily with them that met with him.

*   *   *   *   *   *   *

"And they took him and brought him unto Areopagus, saying, May we know what this new doctrine whereof thou speakest is?

*   *   *   *   *   *   *

"Then Paul stood in the midst of Mars hill, and said, Ye men of Athens, I perceive that in all things ye are too superstitious;

"For as I passed by and beheld your devotions, I found an altar with this inscription: TO THE UNKNOWN GOD. Whom, therefore, ye ignorantly worship, him declare I unto you."—*Acts*, ch. xvii.

It occurred to us, after a while, that if we wanted to get home before daylight betrayed us, we had better be moving. So we hurried away. When far on our road, we had a parting view of the Parthenon, with the moonlight streaming through its open colonnades and touching its capitals with silver. As it looked then, solemn, grand, and beautiful, it will always remain in our memories.

As we marched along, we began to get over our fears, and ceased to care much about quarantine scouts or any body else. We grew bold and reckless; and once, in a sudden burst of courage, I even threw a stone at a dog. It was a pleasant reflection, though, that I did not hit him, because his master might just possibly have been a policeman. Inspired by this happy failure, my valor became utterly uncontrollable, and at intervals I absolutely whistled, though on a moderate key. But boldness breeds boldness, and shortly I plunged into a vineyard, in the full light of the moon, and captured a gallon of superb grapes, not even minding the presence of a peasant who rode by on a mule. Denny and Birch followed my example. Now I had grapes enough for a dozen, but then Jackson was all swollen up with courage, too, and he was obliged to enter a vineyard presently. The first bunch he seized brought trouble. A frowsy, bearded brigand sprang into the road with a shout, and flourished a musket in the light of the moon! We sidled toward the Piræus— not running, you understand, but only advancing with celerity. The brigand shouted again, but still we advanced. It was getting late, and we had no time to fool away on every ass that wanted to drivel Greek platitudes to us. We would just as soon have talked with him as not if we had not been in a hurry. Presently Denny said, "Those fellows are following us!"

We turned, and, sure enough, there they were—three fantastic pirates armed with guns. We slackened our pace to let them come up, and in the meantime I got out my cargo of grapes and dropped them firmly but reluctantly into the shadows by the wayside. But I was not afraid. I only felt that it was not right to steal grapes. And all the more so when the owner was around—and not only around, but with his friends around also. The villains came up and searched a bundle Dr. Birch had in his hand, and scowled upon him when they found it had nothing in it but some holy rocks from Mars Hill, and these were not contraband. They evidently suspected him of playing some wretched fraud upon them, and seemed half inclined to scalp the party. But finally they dismissed us with a warning, couched in excellent Greek, I suppose, and dropped tranquilly in our wake. When they had gone three hundred yards they stopped, and we went on rejoiced. But behold, another armed rascal came out of the shadows and took their place, and followed us two hundred yards. Then he delivered us over to another miscreant, who emerged from some mysterious place, and he in turn to another! For a mile and a half our rear was guarded all the while by armed men. I never traveled in so much state before in all my life.

It was a good while after that before we ventured to steal any more grapes, and when we did we stirred up another troublesome brigand, and then we ceased all further speculation in that line. I suppose that fellow that rode by on the mule posted all the sentinels, from Athens to the Piræus, about us.

Every field on that long route was watched by an armed sentinel, some of whom had fallen asleep, no doubt, but were on hand, nevertheless. This shows what sort of a country modern Attica is—a community of questionable characters. These men were not there to guard their possessions against strangers, but against each other; for strangers seldom visit Athens and the Piræus, and when they do, they go in daylight, and can buy all the grapes they want for a trifle. The modern inhabitants are confiscators and falsifiers of high repute, if gossip speaks truly concerning them, and I freely believe it does.

Just as the earliest tinges of the dawn flushed the eastern sky and turned the pillared Parthenon to a broken harp hung in the pearly horizon, we closed our thirteenth mile of weary, round-about marching, and emerged upon the sea-shore abreast the ships, with our usual escort of fifteen hundred Piræan dogs howling at our heels. We hailed a boat that was two or three hundred yards from shore, and discovered in a moment that it was a police-boat on the lookout for any quarantine-breakers that might chance to be abroad. So we dodged—we were used to that by this time—and when the scouts reached the spot we had so lately occupied, we were absent. They cruised along the shore, but in the wrong direction, and shortly our own boat issued from the gloom and took us aboard. They had heard our signal on the ship. We rowed noiselessly away, and before the police-boat came in sight again, we were safe at home once more.

Four more of our passengers were anxious to visit Athens, and started half an hour after we returned; but they had not been ashore five minutes till the police discovered and chased them so hotly that they barely escaped to their boat again, and that was all. They pursued the enterprise no further.

We set sail for Constantinople to-day, but some of us little care for that. We have seen all there was to see in the old city that had its birth sixteen hundred years before Christ was born, and was an old town before the foundations of Troy were laid—and saw it in its most attractive aspect. Wherefore, why should *we* worry?

Two other passengers ran the blockade successfully last night. So we learned this morning. They slipped away so quietly that they were not missed from the ship for several hours. They had the hardihood to march into the Piræus in the early dusk and hire a carriage. They ran some danger of adding two or three months' imprisonment to the other novelties of their Holy Land Pleasure Excursion. I admire "cheek."* But they went and came safely, and never walked a step.

*Quotation from the Pilgrims.

Chapter XXXIII

FROM ATHENS all through the islands of the Grecian Archipelago, we saw little but forbidding sea-walls and barren hills, sometimes surmounted by three or four graceful columns of some ancient temple, lonely and deserted—a fitting symbol of the desolation that has come upon all Greece in these latter ages. We saw no ploughed fields, very few villages, no trees or grass or vegetation of any kind, scarcely, and hardly ever an isolated house. Greece is a bleak, unsmiling desert, without agriculture, manufactures or commerce, apparently. What supports its poverty-stricken people or its Government, is a mystery.

I suppose that ancient Greece and modern Greece compared, furnish the most extravagant contrast to be found in history. George I., an infant of eighteen, and a scraggy nest of foreign office holders, sit in the places of Themistocles, Pericles, and the illustrious scholars and generals of the Golden Age of Greece. The fleets that were the wonder of the world when the Parthenon was new, are a beggarly handful of fishing-smacks now, and the manly people that performed such miracles of valor at Marathon are only a tribe of unconsidered slaves to-day. The classic Illyssus has gone dry, and so have all the sources of Grecian wealth and greatness. The nation numbers only eight hundred thousand souls, and there is poverty and misery and mendacity enough among them to furnish forty millions and be liberal about it. Under King Otho the revenues of the State were five millions of dollars—raised from a tax of *one-tenth* of all the agricultural products of the land (which tenth the farmer had to bring to the royal granaries on pack-mules any distance not exceeding six leagues) and from extravagant taxes on trade and commerce. Out of that five millions the small tyrant tried to keep an army of ten thousand men, pay all the hundreds of useless Grand Equerries in Waiting, First Grooms of the Bedchamber, Lord High Chancellors of the Exploded Exchequer, and all the other absurdities which these puppy-kingdoms indulge in, in imitation of the great monarchies; and in addition he set about building a white marble palace to cost about five millions itself. The result was, simply: ten into five goes no times and none over. All these things could not be done with five millions, and Otho fell into trouble.

The Greek throne, with its unpromising adjuncts of a ragged population of ingenious rascals who were out of employment eight months in the year because there was little for them to borrow and less to confiscate, and a waste of barren hills and weed-grown deserts, went begging for a good while. It was offered to one of Victoria's sons, and afterwards to various other younger sons of royalty who had no thrones and were out of business, but they all had the charity to decline the dreary honor, and veneration enough for Greece's ancient greatness to refuse to mock her sorrowful rags and dirt with a tinsel throne in this day of her humiliation—till they came to this young Danish George, and he took it. He has finished the splendid palace I saw in the radiant moonlight the other night, and is doing many other things for the salvation of Greece, they say.

We sailed through the barren Archipelago, and into the narrow channel they sometimes call the Dardanelles and sometimes the Hellespont. This part of the country is rich in historic reminiscences, and poor as Sahara in every thing else. For instance, as we approached the Dardanelles, we coasted along the Plains of Troy and past the mouth of the Scamander; we saw where Troy had stood (in the distance,) and where it does not stand now—a city that perished when the world was young. The poor Trojans are all dead, now. They were born too late to see Noah's ark, and died too soon to see our menagarie. We saw where Agamemnon's fleets rendezvoused, and away inland a mountain which the map said was Mount Ida. Within the Hellespont we saw where the original first shoddy contract mentioned in history was carried out, and the "parties of the second part" gently rebuked by Xerxes. I speak of the famous bridge of boats which Xerxes ordered to be built over the narrowest part of the Hellespont (where it is only two or three miles wide.) A moderate gale destroyed the flimsy structure, and the King, thinking that to publicly rebuke the contractors might have a good effect on the next set, called them out before the army and had them beheaded. In the next ten minutes he let a new contract for the bridge. It has been observed by ancient writers that the second bridge was a very good bridge. Xerxes crossed his host of five millions of men on it, and if it had not been purposely destroyed, it would probably have been there yet. If our Government would rebuke some of our shoddy contractors occasionally, it might work much good. In the Hellespont we saw where Leander and Lord Byron swam across, the one to see her upon whom his soul's affections were fixed with a devotion that only death could impair, and the other merely for a flyer, as Jack says. We had two noted tombs near us, too. On one shore slept Ajax, and on the other Hecuba.

We had water batteries and forts on both sides of the Hellespont, flying the crimson flag of Turkey, with its white crescent, and occasionally a village, and sometimes a train of camels; we had all these to look at till we entered the broad sea of Marmora, and then the land soon fading from view, we resumed euchre and whist once more.

We dropped anchor in the mouth of the Golden Horn at daylight in the morning. Only three or four of us were up to see the great Ottoman capital. The passengers do not turn out at unseasonable hours, as they used to, to get the earliest possible glimpse of strange foreign cities. They are well over that. If we were lying in sight of the Pyramids of Egypt, they would not come on deck until after breakfast, now-a-days.

The Golden Horn is a narrow arm of the sea, which branches from the Bosporus (a sort of broad river which connects the Marmora and Black Seas,) and, curving around, divides the city in the middle. Galata and Pera are on one side of the Bosporus, and the Golden Horn; Stamboul (ancient Byzantium) is upon the other. On the other bank of the Bosporus is Scutari and other suburbs of Constantinople. This great city contains a million inhabitants, but so narrow are its streets, and so crowded together are its houses, that it does not cover much more than half as much ground as New York City. Seen from the anchorage or from a mile or so up the Bosporus, it is by far the handsomest city we have seen. Its dense array of houses swells upward from the water's edge, and spreads over the domes of many hills; and the gardens that peep out here and there, the great globes of the mosques, and the countless minarets that meet the eye every where, invest the metropolis with the quaint Oriental aspect one dreams of when he reads books of eastern travel. Constantinople makes a noble picture.

But its attractiveness begins and ends with its picturesqueness. From the time one starts ashore till he gets back again, he execrates it. The boat he goes in is admirably miscalculated for the service it is built for. It is handsomely and neatly fitted up, but no man could handle it well in the turbulent currents that sweep down the Bosporus from the Black Sea, and few men could row it satisfactorily even in still water. It is a long, light canoe (caique,) large at one end and tapering to a knife blade at the other. They make that long sharp end the bow, and you can imagine how these boiling currents spin it about. It has two oars, and sometimes four, and no rudder. You start to go to a given point and you run in fifty different directions before you get there. First one oar is backing water, and then the other; it is seldom that both are going ahead at once. This kind of boating is calculated to drive an impatient man mad in a week. The boatmen are the awkwardest, the stupidest, and the most unscientific on earth, without question.

Ashore, it was—well, it was an eternal circus. People were thicker than bees, in those narrow streets, and the men were dressed in all the outrageous, outlandish, idolatrous, extravagant, thunder-and-lightning costumes that ever a tailor with the delirium tremens and seven devils could conceive of. There was no freak in dress too crazy to be indulged in; no absurdity too absurd to be tolerated; no frenzy in ragged diabolism too fantastic to be attempted. No two men were dressed alike. It was a wild masquerade of all imaginable costumes—every struggling throng in every street was a dissolving view of stunning contrasts. Some patriarchs wore awful turbans, but the grand mass of the infidel horde wore the fiery red skull-cap they call a fez. All the remainder of the raiment they indulged in was utterly indescribable.

The shops here are mere coops, mere boxes, bath-rooms, closets—any thing you please to call them—on the first floor. The Turks sit cross-legged in them, and work and trade and smoke long pipes, and smell like—like Turks. That covers the ground. Crowding the narrow streets in front of them are beggars, who beg forever, yet never collect any thing; and

wonderful cripples, distorted out of all semblance of humanity, almost; vagabonds driving laden asses; porters carrying
dry-goods boxes as large as cottages on their backs; peddlers
of grapes, hot corn, pumpkin seeds, and a hundred other
things, yelling like fiends; and sleeping happily, comfortably,
serenely, among the hurrying feet, are the famed dogs of
Constantinople; drifting noiselessly about are squads of Turkish women, draped from chin to feet in flowing robes, and
with snowy veils bound about their heads, that disclose only
the eyes and a vague, shadowy notion of their features. Seen
moving about, far away in the dim, arched aisles of the Great
Bazaar, they look as the shrouded dead must have looked
when they walked forth from their graves amid the storms
and thunders and earthquakes that burst upon Calvary that
awful night of the Crucifixion. A street in Constantinople is a
picture which one ought to see once—not oftener.

And then there was the goose-rancher—a fellow who
drove a hundred geese before him about the city, and tried to
sell them. He had a pole ten feet long, with a crook in the
end of it, and occasionally a goose would branch out from
the flock and make a lively break around the corner, with
wings half lifted and neck stretched to its utmost. Did the
goose-merchant get excited? No. He took his pole and
reached after that goose with unspeakable *sang froid*—took a
hitch round his neck, and "yanked" him back to his place in
the flock without an effort. He steered his geese with that
stick as easily as another man would steer a yawl. A few hours
afterward we saw him sitting on a stone at a corner, in the
midst of the turmoil, sound asleep in the sun, with his geese
squatting around him, or dodging out of the way of asses and
men. We came by again, within the hour, and he was taking
account of stock, to see whether any of his flock had strayed
or been stolen. The way he did it was unique. He put the end
of his stick within six or eight inches of a stone wall, and
made the geese march in single file between it and the wall.
He counted them as they went by. There was no dodging
that arrangement.

If you want dwarfs—I mean just a few dwarfs for a curiosity—go to Genoa. If you wish to buy them by the gross,
for retail, go to Milan. There are plenty of dwarfs all over

Italy, but it did seem to me that in Milan the crop was luxuriant. If you would see a fair average style of assorted cripples, go to Naples, or travel through the Roman States. But if you would see the very heart and home of cripples and human monsters, both, go straight to Constantinople. A beggar in Naples who can show a foot which has all run into one horrible toe, with one shapeless nail on it, has a fortune—but such an exhibition as that would not provoke any notice in Constantinople. The man would starve. Who would pay any attention to attractions like his among the rare monsters that throng the bridges of the Golden Horn and display their deformities in the gutters of Stamboul? O, wretched impostor! How could he stand against the three-legged woman, and the man with his eye in his cheek? How would he blush in presence of the man with fingers on his elbow? Where would he hide himself when the dwarf with seven fingers on each hand, no upper lip, and his under-jaw gone, came down in his majesty? Bismillah! The cripples of Europe are a delusion and a fraud. The truly gifted flourish only in the by-ways of Pera and Stamboul.

That three-legged woman lay on the bridge, with her stock in trade so disposed as to command the most striking effect—one natural leg, and two long, slender, twisted ones with feet on them like somebody else's fore-arm. Then there was a man further along who had no eyes, and whose face was the color of a fly-blown beefsteak, and wrinkled and twisted like a lava-flow—and verily so tumbled and distorted were his features that no man could tell the wart that served him for a nose from his cheek-bones. In Stamboul was a man with a prodigious head, an uncommonly long body, legs eight inches long and feet like snow-shoes. He traveled on those feet and his hands, and was as sway-backed as if the Colossus of Rhodes had been riding him. Ah, a beggar has to have exceedingly good points to make a living in Constantinople. A blue-faced man, who had nothing to offer except that he had been blown up in a mine, would be regarded as a rank impostor, and a mere damaged soldier on crutches would never make a cent. It would pay him to get a piece of his head taken off, and cultivate a wen like a carpet sack.

The Mosque of St. Sophia is the chief lion of Constantinople. You must get a firman and hurry there the first thing. We did that. We did not get a firman, but we took along four or five francs apiece, which is much the same thing.

I do not think much of the Mosque of St. Sophia. I suppose I lack appreciation. We will let it go at that. It is the rustiest old barn in heathendom. I believe all the interest that attaches to it comes from the fact that it was built for a Christian church and then turned into a mosque, without much alteration, by the Mohammedan conquerors of the land. They made me take off my boots and walk into the place in my stocking-feet. I caught cold, and got myself so stuck up with a complication of gums, slime and general corruption, that I wore out more than two thousand pair of boot-jacks getting my boots off that night, and even then some Christian hide peeled off with them. I abate not a single boot-jack.

St. Sophia is a colossal church, thirteen or fourteen hundred years old, and unsightly enough to be very, very much older. Its immense dome is said to be more wonderful than St. Peter's, but its dirt is much more wonderful than its dome, though they never mention it. The church has a hundred and seventy pillars in it, each a single piece, and all of costly marbles of various kinds, but they came from ancient temples at Baalbec, Heliopolis, Athens and Ephesus, and are battered, ugly and repulsive. They were a thousand years old when this church was new, and then the contrast must have been ghastly—if Justinian's architects did not trim them any. The inside of the dome is figured all over with a monstrous inscription in Turkish characters, wrought in gold mosaic, that looks as glaring as a circus bill; the pavements and the marble balustrades are all battered and dirty; the perspective is marred every where by a web of ropes that depend from the dizzy height of the dome, and suspend countless dingy, coarse oil lamps, and ostrich-eggs, six or seven feet above the floor. Squatting and sitting in groups, here and there and far and near, were ragged Turks reading books, hearing sermons, or receiving lessons like children, and in fifty places were more of the same sort bowing and straightening up, bowing again and getting down to kiss the earth, muttering prayers the while, and keeping up their gymnastics till they ought to have been tired, if they were not.

Every where was dirt, and dust, and dinginess, and gloom; every where were signs of a hoary antiquity, but with nothing touching or beautiful about it; every where were those groups of fantastic pagans; overhead the gaudy mosaics and the web of lamp-ropes—nowhere was there any thing to win one's love or challenge his admiration.

The people who go into ecstacies over St. Sophia must surely get them out of the guide-book (where every church is spoken of as being "considered by good judges to be the most marvelous structure, in many respects, that the world has ever seen.") Or else they are those old connoisseurs from the wilds of New Jersey who laboriously learn the difference between a fresco and a fire-plug and from that day forward feel privileged to void their critical bathos on painting, sculpture and architecture forever more.

We visited the Dancing Dervishes. There were twenty-one of them. They wore a long, light-colored loose robe that hung to their heels. Each in his turn went up to the priest (they were all within a large circular railing) and bowed profoundly and then went spinning away deliriously and took his appointed place in the circle, and continued to spin. When all had spun themselves to their places, they were about five or six feet apart—and so situated, the entire circle of spinning pagans spun itself three separate times around the room. It took twenty-five minutes to do it. They spun on the left foot, and kept themselves going by passing the right rapidly before it and digging it against the waxed floor. Some of them made incredible "time." Most of them spun around forty times in a minute, and one artist averaged about sixty-one times a minute, and kept it up during the whole twenty-five. His robe filled with air and stood out all around him like a balloon.

They made no noise of any kind, and most of them tilted their heads back and closed their eyes, entranced with a sort of devotional ecstacy. There was a rude kind of music, part of the time, but the musicians were not visible. None but spinners were allowed within the circle. A man had to either spin or stay outside. It was about as barbarous an exhibition as we have witnessed yet. Then sick persons came and lay down, and beside them women laid their sick children (one a babe at the breast,) and the patriarch of the Dervishes walked upon their bodies. He was supposed to cure their diseases by trampling upon their breasts or backs or standing on the back of their necks. This is well enough for a people who think all their affairs are made or marred by viewless spirits of the air—by giants, gnomes, and genii—and who still believe, to this day, all the wild tales in the Arabian Nights. Even so an intelligent missionary tells me.

We visited the Thousand and One Columns. I do not know what it was originally intended for, but they said it was built for a reservoir. It is situated in the centre of Constantinople. You go down a flight of stone steps in the middle of a barren place, and there you are. You are forty feet under ground, and in the midst of a perfect wilderness of tall, slender, granite columns, of Byzantine architecture. Stand where you would, or change your position as often as you pleased, you were always a centre from which radiated a dozen long archways and colonnades that lost themselves in distance and the sombre twilight of the place. This old dried-up reservoir is occupied by a few ghostly silk-spinners now, and one of them showed me a cross cut high up in one of the pillars. I suppose he meant me to understand that the institution was there before the Turkish occupation, and I thought he made a remark to that effect; but he must have had an impediment in his speech, for I did not understand him.

We took off our shoes and went into the marble mausoleum of the Sultan Mahmoud, the neatest piece of architecture, inside, that I have seen lately. Mahmoud's tomb was covered with a black velvet pall, which was elaborately embroidered with silver; it stood within a fancy silver railing; at the sides and corners were silver candlesticks that would weigh more than a hundred pounds, and they supported candles as large as a man's leg; on the top of the sarcophagus was a fez, with a handsome diamond ornament upon it, which an attendant said cost a hundred thousand pounds, and lied like a Turk when he said it. Mahmoud's whole family were comfortably planted around him.

We went to the great Bazaar in Stamboul, of course, and I shall not describe it further than to say it is a monstrous hive of little shops—thousands, I should say—all under one roof, and cut up into innumerable little blocks by narrow streets

which are arched overhead. One street is devoted to a particular kind of merchandise, another to another, and so on.
When you wish to buy a pair of shoes you have the swing of
the whole street—you do not have to walk yourself down
hunting stores in different localities. It is the same with silks,
antiquities, shawls, etc. The place is crowded with people all
the time, and as the gay-colored Eastern fabrics are lavishly
displayed before every shop, the great Bazaar of Stamboul is
one of the sights that are worth seeing. It is full of life, and
stir, and business, dirt, beggars, asses, yelling peddlers, porters, dervishes, high-born Turkish female shoppers, Greeks,
and weird-looking and weirdly dressed Mohammedans from
the mountains and the far provinces—and the only solitary
thing one does not smell when he is in the Great Bazaar, is
something which smells good.

Chapter XXXIV

MOSQUES ARE PLENTY, churches are plenty, graveyards are plenty, but morals and whiskey are scarce. The Koran does not permit Mohammedans to drink. Their natural instincts do not permit them to be moral. They say the Sultan has eight hundred wives. This almost amounts to bigamy. It makes our cheeks burn with shame to see such a thing permitted here in Turkey. We do not mind it so much in Salt Lake, however.

Circassian and Georgian girls are still sold in Constantinople by their parents, but not publicly. The great slave marts we have all read so much about—where tender young girls were stripped for inspection, and criticised and discussed just as if they were horses at an agricultural fair—no longer exist. The exhibition and the sales are private now. Stocks are up, just at present, partly because of a brisk demand created by the recent return of the Sultan's suite from the courts of Europe; partly on account of an unusual abundance of breadstuffs, which leaves holders untortured by hunger and enables them to hold back for high prices; and partly because buyers are too weak to bear the market, while sellers are amply prepared to bull it. Under these circumstances, if the American metropolitan newspapers were published here in Constantinople, their next commercial report would read about as follows, I suppose:

SLAVE GIRL MARKET REPORT.

"Best brands Circassians, crop of 1850, £200; 1852, £250; 1854, £300. Best brands Georgian, none in market; second quality, 1851, £180. Nineteen fair to middling Wallachian girls offered at £130 @ 150, but no takers; sixteen prime A 1 sold in small lots to close out—terms private.

"Sales of one lot Circassians, prime to good, 1852 to 1854, at £240 @ 242½, buyer 30; one forty-niner—damaged—at £23, seller ten, no deposit. Several Georgians, fancy brands, 1852, changed hands to fill orders. The Georgians now on hand are mostly last year's crop, which was unusually poor. The new crop is a little backward, but will be coming in shortly. As regards its quantity and quality, the accounts are most encouraging. In this connection we can safely say, also, that the new crop of Circassians is looking extremely well. His

Majesty the Sultan has already sent in large orders for his new harem, which will be finished within a fortnight, and this has naturally strengthened the market and given Circassian stock a strong upward tendency. Taking advantage of the inflated market, many of our shrewdest operators are selling short. There are hints of a "corner" on Wallachians.

"There is nothing new in Nubians. Slow sale.

"Eunuchs—None offering; however, large cargoes are expected from Egypt to-day."

I think the above would be about the style of the commercial report. Prices are pretty high now, and holders firm; but, two or three years ago, parents in a starving condition brought their young daughters down here and sold them for even twenty and thirty dollars, when they could do no better, simply to save themselves and the girls from dying of want. It is sad to think of so distressing a thing as this, and I for one am sincerely glad the prices are up again.

Commercial morals, especially, are bad. There is no gainsaying that. Greek, Turkish and Armenian morals consist only in attending church regularly on the appointed Sabbaths, and in breaking the ten commandments all the balance of the week. It comes natural to them to lie and cheat in the first place, and then they go on and improve on nature until they arrive at perfection. In recommending his son to a merchant as a valuable salesman, a father does not say he is a nice, moral, upright boy, and goes to Sunday School and is honest, but he says, "This boy is worth his weight in broad pieces of a hundred—for behold, he will cheat whomsoever hath dealings with him, and from the Euxine to the waters of Marmora there abideth not so gifted a liar!" How is that for a recommendation? The Missionaries tell me that they hear encomiums like that passed upon people every day. They say of a person they admire, "Ah, he is a charming swindler, and a most exquisite liar!"

Every body lies and cheats—every body who is in business, at any rate. Even foreigners soon have to come down to the custom of the country, and they do not buy and sell long in Constantinople till they lie and cheat like a Greek. I say like a Greek, because the Greeks are called the worst transgressors in this line. Several Americans long resident in Constanti-

nople contend that most Turks are pretty trustworthy, but
few claim that the Greeks have any virtues that a man can
discover—at least without a fire assay.

I am half willing to believe that the celebrated dogs of Constantinople have been misrepresented—slandered. I have always been led to suppose that they were so thick in the streets
that they blocked the way; that they moved about in organized companies, platoons and regiments, and took what they
wanted by determined and ferocious assault; and that at night
they drowned all other sounds with their terrible howlings.
The dogs I see here can not be those I have read of.

I find them every where, but not in strong force. The most
I have found together has been about ten or twenty. And
night or day a fair proportion of them were sound asleep.
Those that were not asleep always looked as if they wanted to
be. I never saw such utterly wretched, starving, sad-visaged,
broken-hearted looking curs in my life. It seemed a grim satire to accuse such brutes as these of taking things by force of
arms. They hardly seemed to have strength enough or ambition enough to walk across the street—I do not know that I
have seen one walk that far yet. They are mangy and bruised
and mutilated, and often you see one with the hair singed off
him in such wide and well defined tracts that he looks like a
map of the new Territories. They are the sorriest beasts that
breathe—the most abject—the most pitiful. In their faces is
a settled expression of melancholy, an air of hopeless despondency. The hairless patches on a scalded dog are preferred by
the fleas of Constantinople to a wider range on a healthier
dog; and the exposed places suit the fleas exactly. I saw a dog
of this kind start to nibble at a flea—a fly attracted his attention, and he made a snatch at him; the flea called for him
once more, and that forever unsettled him; he looked sadly at
his flea-pasture, then sadly looked at his bald spot. Then he
heaved a sigh and dropped his head resignedly upon his paws.
He was not equal to the situation.

The dogs sleep in the streets, all over the city. From one
end of the street to the other, I suppose they will average
about eight or ten to a block. Sometimes, of course, there are
fifteen or twenty to a block. They do not belong to any body,
and they seem to have no close personal friendships among

each other. But they district the city themselves, and the dogs of each district, whether it be half a block in extent, or ten blocks, have to remain within its bounds. Woe to a dog if he crosses the line! His neighbors would snatch the balance of his hair off in a second. So it is said. But they don't look it.

They sleep in the streets these days. They are my compass—my guide. When I see the dogs sleep placidly on, while men, sheep, geese, and all moving things turn out and go around them, I know I am not in the great street where the hotel is, and must go further. In the Grand Rue the dogs have a sort of air of being on the lookout—an air born of being obliged to get out of the way of many carriages every day—and that expression one recognizes in a moment. It does not exist upon the face of any dog without the confines of that street. All others sleep placidly and keep no watch. They would not move, though the Sultan himself passed by.

In one narrow street (but none of them are wide) I saw three dogs lying coiled up, about a foot or two apart. End to end they lay, and so they just bridged the street neatly, from gutter to gutter. A drove of a hundred sheep came along. They stepped right over the dogs, the rear crowding the front, impatient to get on. The dogs looked lazily up, flinched a little when the impatient feet of the sheep touched their raw backs—sighed, and lay peacefully down again. No talk could be plainer than that. So some of the sheep jumped over them and others scrambled between, occasionally chipping a leg with their sharp hoofs, and when the whole flock had made the trip, the dogs sneezed a little, in the cloud of dust, but never budged their bodies an inch. I thought I was lazy, but I am a steam-engine compared to a Constantinople dog. But was not that a singular scene for a city of a million inhabitants?

These dogs are the scavengers of the city. That is their official position, and a hard one it is. However, it is their protection. But for their usefulness in partially cleansing these terrible streets, they would not be tolerated long. They eat any thing and every thing that comes in their way, from melon rinds and spoiled grapes up through all the grades and species of dirt and refuse to their own dead friends and relatives—and yet they are always lean, always hungry, always despondent. The people are loath to kill them—do not kill them, in fact. The Turks have an innate antipathy to taking the life of any dumb animal, it is said. But they do worse. They hang and kick and stone and scald these wretched creatures to the very verge of death, and then leave them to live and suffer.

Once a Sultan proposed to kill off all the dogs here, and did begin the work—but the populace raised such a howl of horror about it that the massacre was stayed. After a while, he proposed to remove them all to an island in the Sea of Marmora. No objection was offered, and a ship-load or so was taken away. But when it came to be known that somehow or other the dogs never got to the island, but always fell overboard in the night and perished, another howl was raised and the transportation scheme was dropped.

So the dogs remain in peaceable possession of the streets. I do not say that they do not howl at night, nor that they do not attack people who have not a red fez on their heads. I only say that it would be mean for *me* to accuse them of these unseemly things who have not seen them do them with my own eyes or heard them with my own ears.

I was a little surprised to see Turks and Greeks playing newsboy right here in the mysterious land where the giants and genii of the Arabian Nights once dwelt—where winged horses and hydra-headed dragons guarded enchanted castles—where Princes and Princesses flew through the air on carpets that obeyed a mystic talisman—where cities whose houses were made of precious stones sprang up in a night under the hand of the magician, and where busy marts were suddenly stricken with a spell and each citizen lay or sat, or stood with weapon raised or foot advanced, just as he was, speechless and motionless, till time had told a hundred years!

It was curious to see newsboys selling papers in so dreamy a land as that. And, to say truly, it is comparatively a new thing here. The selling of newspapers had its birth in Constantinople about a year ago, and was a child of the Prussian and Austrian war.

There is one paper published here in the English language—*The Levant Herald*—and there are generally a number of Greek and a few French papers rising and falling, struggling up and falling again. Newspapers are not popular with the Sultan's Government. They do not understand journalism. The proverb says, "The unknown is always great." To the court, the newspaper is a mysterious and rascally institution. They know what a pestilence is, because they have one occasionally that thins the people out at the rate of two thousand a day, and they regard a newspaper as a mild form of pestilence. When it goes astray, they suppress it—pounce upon it without warning, and throttle it. When it don't go astray for a long time, they get suspicious and throttle it anyhow, because they think it is hatching deviltry. Imagine the Grand Vizier in solemn council with the magnates of the realm, spelling his way through the hated newspaper, and finally delivering his profound decision: "This thing means mischief—it is too darkly, too suspiciously inoffensive—suppress it! Warn the publisher that we can not have this sort of thing: put the editor in prison!"

The newspaper business has its inconveniences in Constantinople. Two Greek papers and one French one were suppressed here within a few days of each other. No victories of the Cretans are allowed to be printed. From time to time the Grand Vizier sends a notice to the various editors that the Cretan insurrection is entirely suppressed, and although that editor knows better, he still has to print the notice. The *Levant Herald* is too fond of speaking praisefully of Americans to be popular with the Sultan, who does not relish our sympathy with the Cretans, and therefore that paper has to be particularly circumspect in order to keep out of trouble. Once the editor, forgetting the official notice in his paper that the Cretans were crushed out, printed a letter of a very different tenor, from the American Consul in Crete, and was fined two hundred and fifty dollars for it. Shortly he printed another from the same source and was imprisoned three months for his pains. I think I could get the assistant editorship of the *Levant Herald*, but I am going to try to worry along without it.

To suppress a paper here involves the ruin of the publisher, almost. But in Naples I think they speculate on misfortunes of that kind. Papers are suppressed there every day, and spring up the next day under a new name. During the ten days or a fortnight we staid there one paper was murdered and resurrected twice. The newsboys are smart there, just as they are elsewhere. They take advantage of popular weaknesses. When they find they are not likely to sell out, they approach a citizen mysteriously, and say in a low voice— "Last copy, sir: double price; paper just been suppressed!" The man buys it, of course, and finds nothing in it. They do say—I do not vouch for it—but they do say that men sometimes print a vast edition of a paper, with a ferociously seditious article in it, distribute it quickly among the newsboys, and clear out till the Government's indignation cools. It pays well. Confiscation don't amount to any thing. The type and presses are not worth taking care of.

There is only one English newspaper in Naples. It has seventy subscribers. The publisher is getting rich very deliberately—very deliberately indeed.

I never shall want another Turkish lunch. The cooking apparatus was in the little lunch room, near the bazaar, and it was all open to the street. The cook was slovenly, and so was the table, and it had no cloth on it. The fellow took a mass of sausage-meat and coated it round a wire and laid it on a charcoal fire to cook. When it was done, he laid it aside and a dog walked sadly in and nipped it. He smelt it first, and probably recognized the remains of a friend. The cook took it away from him and laid it before us. Jack said, "I pass"— he plays euchre sometimes—and we all passed in turn. Then the cook baked a broad, flat, wheaten cake, greased it well with the sausage, and started towards us with it. It dropped in the dirt, and he picked it up and polished it on his breeches, and laid it before us. Jack said, "I pass." We all passed. He put some eggs in a frying pan, and stood pensively prying slabs of meat from between his teeth with a fork. Then he used the fork to turn the eggs with—and brought them along. Jack said "Pass again." All followed suit. We did not know what to do, and so we ordered a new ration of sausage. The cook got out his wire, apportioned a proper amount of sausage-meat, spat it on his hands and fell to work! This time, with one accord, we all passed out. We paid and left. That is all I learned about Turkish lunches. A Turkish lunch is good, no doubt, but it has its little drawbacks.

When I think how I have been swindled by books of Oriental travel, I want a tourist for breakfast. For years and years I have dreamed of the wonders of the Turkish bath; for years and years I have promised myself that I would yet enjoy one. Many and many a time, in fancy, I have lain in the marble bath, and breathed the slumbrous fragrance of Eastern spices that filled the air; then passed through a weird and complicated system of pulling and hauling, and drenching and scrubbing, by a gang of naked savages who loomed vast and vaguely through the steaming mists, like demons; then rested for a while on a divan fit for a king; then passed through another complex ordeal, and one more fearful than the first; and, finally, swathed in soft fabrics, been conveyed to a princely saloon and laid on a bed of eider down, where eunuchs, gorgeous of costume, fanned me while I drowsed and dreamed, or contentedly gazed at the rich hangings of the apartment, the soft carpets, the sumptuous furniture, the pictures, and drank delicious coffee, smoked the soothing narghili, and dropped, at the last, into tranquil repose, lulled by sensuous odors from unseen censers, by the gentle influence of the narghili's Persian tobacco, and by the music of fountains that counterfeited the pattering of summer rain.

That was the picture, just as I got it from incendiary books of travel. It was a poor, miserable imposture. The reality is no more like it than the Five Points are like the Garden of Eden. They received me in a great court, paved with marble slabs; around it were broad galleries, one above another, carpeted with seedy matting, railed with unpainted balustrades, and furnished with huge rickety chairs, cushioned with rusty old mattresses, indented with impressions left by the forms of nine successive generations of men who had reposed upon them. The place was vast, naked, dreary; its court a barn, its galleries stalls for human horses. The cadaverous, half nude varlets that served in the establishment had nothing of poetry in their appearance, nothing of romance, nothing of Oriental splendor. They shed no entrancing odors—just the contrary. Their hungry eyes and their lank forms continually suggested one glaring, unsentimental fact—they wanted what they term in California "a square meal."

I went into one of the racks and undressed. An unclean

starveling wrapped a gaudy table-cloth about his loins, and hung a white rag over my shoulders. If I had had a tub then, it would have come natural to me to take in washing. I was then conducted down stairs into the wet, slippery court, and the first things that attracted my attention were my heels. My fall excited no comment. They expected it, no doubt. It belonged in the list of softening, sensuous influences peculiar to this home of Eastern luxury. It was softening enough, certainly, but its application was not happy. They now gave me a pair of wooden clogs—benches in miniature, with leather straps over them to confine my feet (which they would have done, only I do not wear No. 13s.) These things dangled uncomfortably by the straps when I lifted up my feet, and came down in awkward and unexpected places when I put them on the floor again, and sometimes turned sideways and wrenched my ankles out of joint. However, it was all Oriental luxury, and I did what I could to enjoy it.

They put me in another part of the barn and laid me on a stuffy sort of pallet, which was not made of cloth of gold, or Persian shawls, but was merely the unpretending sort of thing I have seen in the negro quarters of Arkansas. There was nothing whatever in this dim marble prison but five more of these biers. It was a very solemn place. I expected that the spiced odors of Araby were going to steal over my senses now, but they did not. A copper-colored skeleton, with a rag around him, brought me a glass decanter of water, with a lighted tobacco pipe in the top of it, and a pliant stem a yard long, with a brass mouth-piece to it.

It was the famous "narghili" of the East—the thing the Grand Turk smokes in the pictures. This began to look like luxury. I took one blast at it, and it was sufficient; the smoke went in a great volume down into my stomach, my lungs, even into the uttermost parts of my frame. I exploded one mighty cough, and it was as if Vesuvius had let go. For the next five minutes I smoked at every pore, like a frame house that is on fire on the inside. Not any more narghili for me. The smoke had a vile taste, and the taste of a thousand infidel tongues that remained on that brass mouthpiece was viler still. I was getting discouraged. Whenever, hereafter, I see the cross-legged Grand Turk smoking his narghili, in pretended bliss, on the outside of a paper of Connecticut tobacco, I shall know him for the shameless humbug he is.

This prison was filled with hot air. When I had got warmed up sufficiently to prepare me for a still warmer temperature, they took me where it was—into a marble room, wet, slippery and steamy, and laid me out on a raised platform in the centre. It was very warm. Presently my man sat me down by a tank of hot water, drenched me well, gloved his hand with a coarse mitten, and began to polish me all over with it. I began to smell disagreeably. The more he polished the worse I smelt. It was alarming. I said to him:

"I perceive that I am pretty far gone. It is plain that I ought to be buried without any unnecessary delay. Perhaps you had better go after my friends at once, because the weather is warm, and I can not 'keep' long."

He went on scrubbing, and paid no attention. I soon saw that he was reducing my size. He bore hard on his mitten, and from under it rolled little cylinders, like maccaroni. It could not be dirt, for it was too white. He pared me down in this way for a long time. Finally I said:

"It is a tedious process. It will take hours to trim me to the size you want me; I will wait; go and borrow a jack-plane."

He paid no attention at all.

After a while he brought a basin, some soap, and something that seemed to be the tail of a horse. He made up a prodigious quantity of soap-suds, deluged me with them from head to foot, without warning me to shut my eyes, and then swabbed me viciously with the horse-tail. Then he left me there, a snowy statue of lather, and went away. When I got tired of waiting I went and hunted him up. He was propped against the wall, in another room, asleep. I woke him. He was not disconcerted. He took me back and flooded me with hot water, then turbaned my head, swathed me with dry table-cloths, and conducted me to a latticed chicken-coop in one of the galleries, and pointed to one of those Arkansas beds. I mounted it, and vaguely expected the odors of Araby again. They did not come.

The blank, unornamented coop had nothing about it of that oriental voluptuousness one reads of so much. It was more suggestive of the county hospital than any thing else.

The skinny servitor brought a narghili, and I got him to take it out again without wasting any time about it. Then he brought the world-renowned Turkish coffee that poets have sung so rapturously for many generations, and I seized upon it as the last hope that was left of my old dreams of Eastern luxury. It was another fraud. Of all the unchristian beverages that ever passed my lips, Turkish coffee is the worst. The cup is small, it is smeared with grounds; the coffee is black, thick, unsavory of smell, and execrable in taste. The bottom of the cup has a muddy sediment in it half an inch deep. This goes down your throat, and portions of it lodge by the way, and produce a tickling aggravation that keeps you barking and coughing for an hour.

Here endeth my experience of the celebrated Turkish bath, and here also endeth my dream of the bliss the mortal revels in who passes through it. It is a malignant swindle. The man who enjoys it is qualified to enjoy any thing that is repulsive to sight or sense, and he that can invest it with a charm of poetry is able to do the same with any thing else in the world that is tedious, and wretched, and dismal, and nasty.

Chapter XXXV

WE LEFT A dozen passengers in Constantinople, and sailed through the beautiful Bosporus and far up into the Black Sea. We left them in the clutches of the celebrated Turkish guide, "FAR-AWAY MOSES," who will seduce them into buying a ship-load of ottar of roses, splendid Turkish vestments, and all manner of curious things they can never have any use for. Murray's invaluable guide-books have mentioned Far-away Moses' name, and he is a made man. He rejoices daily in the fact that he is a recognized celebrity. However, we can not alter our established customs to please the whims of guides; we can not show partialities this late in the day. Therefore, ignoring this fellow's brilliant fame, and ignoring the fanciful name he takes such pride in, we called him Ferguson, just as we had done with all other guides. It has kept him in a state of smothered exasperation all the time. Yet we meant him no harm. After he has gotten himself up regardless of expense, in showy, baggy trowsers, yellow, pointed slippers, fiery fez, silken jacket of blue, voluminous waist-sash of fancy Persian stuff filled with a battery of silver-mounted horse-pistols, and has strapped on his terrible scimetar, he considers it an unspeakable humiliation to be called Ferguson. It can not be helped. All guides are Fergusons to us. We can not master their dreadful foreign names.

Sebastopol is probably the worst battered town in Russia or any where else. But we ought to be pleased with it, nevertheless, for we have been in no country yet where we have been so kindly received, and where we felt that to be Americans was a sufficient *visé* for our passports. The moment the anchor was down, the Governor of the town immediately dispatched an officer on board to inquire if he could be of any assistance to us, and to invite us to make ourselves at home in Sebastopol! If you know Russia, you know that this was a wild stretch of hospitality. They are usually so suspicious of strangers that they worry them excessively with the delays and aggravations incident to a complicated passport system. Had we come from any other country we could not have had permission to enter Sebastopol and leave again under three days—but as it was, we were at liberty to go and come when and where we pleased. Every body in Constantinople warned us to be very careful about our passports, see that they were strictly *en regle*, and never to mislay them for a moment: and they told us of numerous instances of Englishmen and others who were delayed days, weeks, and even months, in Sebastopol, on account of trifling informalities in their passports, and for which they were not to blame. I had lost my passport, and was traveling under my room-mate's, who stayed behind in Constantinople to await our return. To read the description of him in that passport and then look at me, any man could see that I was no more like him than I am like Hercules. So I went into the harbor of Sebastopol with fear and trembling—full of a vague, horrible apprehension that I was going to be found out and hanged. But all that time my true passport had been floating gallantly overhead—and behold it was only our flag. They never asked us for any other.

We have had a great many Russian and English gentlemen and ladies on board to-day, and the time has passed cheerfully away. They were all happy-spirited people, and I never heard our mother tongue sound so pleasantly as it did when it fell from those English lips in this far-off land. I talked to the Russians a good deal, just to be friendly, and they talked to me from the same motive; I am sure that both enjoyed the conversation, but never a word of it either of us understood. I did most of my talking to those English people though, and I am sorry we can not carry some of them along with us.

We have gone whithersoever we chose, to-day, and have met with nothing but the kindest attentions. Nobody inquired whether we had any passports or not.

Several of the officers of the Government have suggested that we take the ship to a little watering-place thirty miles from here, and pay the Emperor of Russia a visit. He is rusticating there. These officers said they would take it upon themselves to insure us a cordial reception. They said if we would go, they would not only telegraph the Emperor, but send a special courier overland to announce our coming. Our time is so short, though, and more especially our coal is so nearly out, that we judged it best to forego the rare pleasure of holding social intercourse with an Emperor.

Ruined Pompeii is in good condition compared to Sebastopol. Here, you may look in whatsoever direction you please, and your eye encounters scarcely any thing but ruin, ruin, ruin!—fragments of houses, crumbled walls, torn and ragged hills, devastation every where! It is as if a mighty earthquake had spent all its terrible forces upon this one little spot. For eighteen long months the storms of war beat upon the helpless town, and left it at last the saddest wreck that ever the sun has looked upon. Not one solitary house escaped unscathed—not one remained habitable, even. Such utter and complete ruin one could hardly conceive of. The houses had all been solid, dressed stone structures; most of them were ploughed through and through by cannon balls—unroofed and sliced down from eaves to foundation—and now a row of them, half a mile long, looks merely like an endless procession of battered chimneys. No semblance of a house remains in such as these. Some of the larger buildings had corners knocked off; pillars cut in two; cornices smashed; holes driven straight through the walls. Many of these holes are as round and as cleanly cut as if they had been made with an auger. Others are half pierced through, and the clean impression is there in the rock, as smooth and as shapely as if it were done in putty. Here and there a ball still sticks in a wall, and from it iron tears trickle down and discolor the stone.

The battle-fields were pretty close together. The Malakoff tower is on a hill which is right in the edge of the town. The Redan was within rifle-shot of the Malakoff; Inkerman was a mile away; and Balaklava removed but an hour's ride. The French trenches, by which they approached and invested the Malakoff were carried so close under its sloping sides that one might have stood by the Russian guns and tossed a stone into them. Repeatedly, during three terrible days, they swarmed up the little Malakoff hill, and were beaten back with terrible slaughter. Finally, they captured the place, and drove the Russians out, who then tried to retreat into the town, but the English had taken the Redan, and shut them off with a wall of flame; there was nothing for them to do but go back and retake the Malakoff or die under its guns. They did go back; they took the Malakoff and retook it two or three times, but their desperate valor could not avail, and they had to give up at last.

These fearful fields, where such tempests of death used to rage, are peaceful enough now; no sound is heard, hardly a living thing moves about them, they are lonely and silent—their desolation is complete.

There was nothing else to do, and so every body went to hunting relics. They have stocked the ship with them. They brought them from the Malakoff, from the Redan, Inkerman, Balaklava—every where. They have brought cannon balls, broken ramrods, fragments of shell—iron enough to freight a sloop. Some have even brought bones—brought them laboriously from great distances, and were grieved to hear the surgeon pronounce them only bones of mules and oxen. I knew Blucher would not lose an opportunity like this. He brought a sack full on board and was going for another. I prevailed upon him not to go. He has already turned his state-room into a museum of worthless trumpery, which he has gathered up in his travels. He is labeling his trophies, now. I picked up one a while ago, and found it marked "Fragment of a Russian General." I carried it out to get a better light upon it—it was nothing but a couple of teeth and part of the jaw-bone of a horse. I said with some asperity:

"Fragment of a Russian General! This is absurd. Are you never going to learn any sense?"

He only said: "Go slow—the old woman won't know any different." [His aunt.]

This person gathers mementoes with a perfect recklessness, now-a-days; mixes them all up together, and then serenely labels them without any regard to truth, propriety, or even plausibility. I have found him breaking a stone in two, and labeling half of it "Chunk busted from the pulpit of Demosthenes," and the other half "Darnick from the Tomb of Abelard and Heloise." I have known him to gather up a handful of pebbles by the roadside, and bring them on board ship and label them as coming from twenty celebrated localities five hundred miles apart. I remonstrate against these outrages upon reason and truth, of course, but it does no good. I get the same tranquil, unanswerable reply every time:

"It don't signify—the old woman won't know any different."

Ever since we three or four fortunate ones made the midnight trip to Athens, it has afforded him genuine satisfaction to give every body in the ship a pebble from the Mars-hill where St. Paul preached. He got all those pebbles on the sea-shore, abreast the ship, but professes to have gathered them from one of our party. However, it is not of any use for me to expose the deception—it affords him pleasure, and does no harm to any body. He says he never expects to run out of mementoes of St. Paul as long as he is in reach of a sand-bank. Well, he is no worse than others. I notice that all travelers supply deficiencies in their collections in the same way. I shall never have any confidence in such things again while I live.

Chapter XXXVI

W E HAVE GOT so far east, now—a hundred and fifty-five degrees of longitude from San Francisco—that my watch can not "keep the hang" of the time any more. It has grown discouraged, and stopped. I think it did a wise thing. The difference in time between Sebastopol and the Pacific coast is enormous. When it is six o'clock in the morning here, it is somewhere about week before last in California. We are excusable for getting a little tangled as to time. These distractions and distresses about the time have worried me so much that I was afraid my mind was so much affected that I never would have any appreciation of time again; but when I noticed how handy I was yet about comprehending when it was dinner-time, a blessed tranquillity settled down upon me, and I am tortured with doubts and fears no more.

Odessa is about twenty hours' run from Sebastopol, and is the most northerly port in the Black Sea. We came here to get coal, principally. The city has a population of one hundred and thirty-three thousand, and is growing faster than any other small city out of America. It is a free port, and is the great grain mart of this particular part of the world. Its roadstead is full of ships. Engineers are at work, now, turning the open roadstead into a spacious artificial harbor. It is to be almost inclosed by massive stone piers, one of which will extend into the sea over three thousand feet in a straight line.

I have not felt so much at home for a long time as I did when I "raised the hill" and stood in Odessa for the first time. It looked just like an American city; fine, broad streets, and straight as well; low houses, (two or three stories,) wide, neat, and free from any quaintness of architectural ornamentation; locust trees bordering the sidewalks (they call them acacias;) a stirring, business-look about the streets and the stores; fast walkers; a familiar *new* look about the houses and every thing; yea, and a driving and smothering cloud of dust that was so like a message from our own dear native land that we could hardly refrain from shedding a few grateful tears and execrations in the old time-honored American way. Look up the street or down the street, this way or that way, we saw only America! There was not one thing to remind us that we were in Russia. We walked for some little distance, reveling in this home vision, and then we came upon a church and a hack-driver, and presto! the illusion vanished! The church had a slender-spired dome that rounded inward at its base, and looked like a turnip turned upside down, and the hackman seemed to be dressed in a long petticoat without any hoops. These things were essentially foreign, and so were the carriages—but every body knows about these things, and there is no occasion for my describing them.

We were only to stay here a day and a night and take in coal; we consulted the guide-books and were rejoiced to know that there were no sights in Odessa to see; and so we had one good, untrammeled holyday on our hands, with nothing to do but idle about the city and enjoy ourselves. We sauntered through the markets and criticised the fearful and wonderful costumes from the back country; examined the populace as far as eyes could do it; and closed the entertainment with an ice-cream debauch. We do not get ice-cream every where, and so, when we do, we are apt to dissipate to excess. We never cared any thing about ice-cream at home, but we look upon it with a sort of idolatry now that it is so scarce in these red-hot climates of the East.

We only found two pieces of statuary, and this was another blessing. One was a bronze image of the Duc de Richelieu, grand-nephew of the splendid Cardinal. It stood in a spacious, handsome promenade, overlooking the sea, and from its base a vast flight of stone steps led down to the harbor— two hundred of them, fifty feet long, and a wide landing at the bottom of every twenty. It is a noble staircase, and from a distance the people toiling up it looked like insects. I mention this statue and this stairway because they have their story. Richelieu founded Odessa—watched over it with paternal care—labored with a fertile brain and a wise understanding for its best interests—spent his fortune freely to the same end—endowed it with a sound prosperity, and one which will yet make it one of the great cities of the Old World—built this noble stairway with money from his own private purse—and——. Well, the people for whom he had done so much, let him walk down these same steps, one day, unattended, old, poor, without a second coat to his back; and when, years afterwards, he died in Sebastopol in poverty and neglect, they called a meeting, subscribed liberally, and immediately erected this tasteful monument to his memory, and named a great street after him. It reminds me of what Robert Burns' mother said when they erected a stately monument to his memory: "Ah, Robbie, ye asked them for bread and they hae gi'en ye a stane."

The people of Odessa have warmly recommended us to go and call on the Emperor, as did the Sebastopolians. They have telegraphed his Majesty, and he has signified his willingness to grant us an audience. So we are getting up the anchors and preparing to sail to his watering-place. What a scratching around there will be, now! what a holding of important meetings and appointing of solemn committees!— and what a furbishing up of claw-hammer coats and white silk neck-ties! As this fearful ordeal we are about to pass through pictures itself to my fancy in all its dread sublimity, I begin to feel my fierce desire to converse with a genuine Emperor cooling down and passing away. What am I to do with my hands? What am I to do with my feet? What in the world am I to do with myself?

Chapter XXXVII

WE ANCHORED HERE at Yalta, Russia, two or three days ago. To me the place was a vision of the Sierras. The tall, gray mountains that back it, their sides bristling with pines—cloven with ravines—here and there a hoary rock towering into view—long, straight streaks sweeping down from the summit to the sea, marking the passage of some avalanche of former times—all these were as like what one sees in the Sierras as if the one were a portrait of the other. The little village of Yalta nestles at the foot of an amphitheatre which slopes backward and upward to the wall of hills, and looks as if it might have sunk quietly down to its present position from a higher elevation. This depression is covered with the great parks and gardens of noblemen, and through the mass of green foliage the bright colors of their palaces bud out here and there like flowers. It is a beautiful spot.

We had the United States Consul on board—the Odessa Consul. We assembled in the cabin and commanded him to tell us what we must do to be saved, and tell us quickly. He made a speech. The first thing he said fell like a blight on every hopeful spirit: he had never seen a court reception. (Three groans for the Consul.) But he said he had seen receptions at the Governor-General's in Odessa, and had often listened to people's experiences of receptions at the Russian and other courts, and believed he knew very well what sort of ordeal we were about to essay. (Hope budded again.) He said we were many; the summer-palace was small—a mere mansion; doubtless we should be received in summer fashion—in the garden; we would stand in a row, all the gentlemen in swallow-tail coats, white kids, and white neck-ties, and the ladies in light-colored silks, or something of that kind; at the proper moment—12 meridian—the Emperor, attended by his suite arrayed in splendid uniforms, would appear and walk slowly along the line, bowing to some, and saying two or three words to others. At the moment his Majesty appeared, a universal, delighted, enthusiastic smile ought to break out like a rash among the passengers—a smile of love, of gratification, of admiration—and with one accord, the party must begin to bow—not obsequiously, but respectfully, and with dignity; at the end of fifteen minutes the Emperor would go in the house, and we could run along home again. We felt immensely relieved. It seemed, in a manner, easy. There was not a man in the party but believed that with a little practice he could stand in a row, especially if there were others along; there was not a man but believed he could bow without tripping on his coat tail and breaking his neck; in a word, we came to believe we were equal to any item in the performance except that complicated smile. The Consul also said we ought to draft a little address to the Emperor, and present it to one of his aides-de-camp, who would forward it to him at the proper time. Therefore, five gentlemen were appointed to prepare the document, and the fifty others went sadly smiling about the ship—practicing. During the next twelve hours we had the general appearance, somehow, of being at a funeral, where every body was sorry the death had occurred, but glad it was over—where every body was smiling, and yet broken-hearted.

A committee went ashore to wait on his Excellency the Governor-General, and learn our fate. At the end of three hours of boding suspense, they came back and said the Emperor would receive us at noon the next day—would send carriages for us—would hear the address in person. The Grand Duke Michael had sent to invite us to his palace also. Any man could see that there was an intention here to show that Russia's friendship for America was so genuine as to render even her private citizens objects worthy of kindly attentions.

At the appointed hour we drove out three miles, and assembled in the handsome garden in front of the Emperor's palace.

We formed a circle under the trees before the door, for there was no one room in the house able to accommodate our three-score persons comfortably, and in a few minutes the imperial family came out bowing and smiling, and stood in our midst. A number of great dignitaries of the Empire, in undress uniforms, came with them. With every bow, his Majesty said a word of welcome. I copy these speeches. There is character in them—Russian character—which is politeness itself, and the genuine article. The French are polite, but it is often mere ceremonious politeness. A Russian imbues his polite things with a heartiness, both of phrase and expression, that compels belief in their sincerity. As I was saying, the Czar punctuated his speeches with bows:

"Good morning—I am glad to see you—I am gratified—I am delighted—I am happy to receive you!"

All took off their hats, and the Consul inflicted the address on him. He bore it with unflinching fortitude; then took the rusty-looking document and handed it to some great officer or other, to be filed away among the archives of Russia—in the stove. He thanked us for the address, and said he was very much pleased to see us, especially as such friendly relations existed between Russia and the United States. The Empress said the Americans were favorites in Russia, and she hoped the Russians were similarly regarded in America. These were all the speeches that were made, and I recommend them to parties who present policemen with gold watches, as models of brevity and point. After this the Empress went and talked sociably (for an Empress) with various ladies around the circle; several gentlemen entered into a disjointed general conversation with the Emperor; the Dukes and Princes, Admirals and Maids of Honor dropped into free-and-easy chat with first one and then another of our party, and whoever chose stepped forward and spoke with the modest little Grand Duchess Marie, the Czar's daughter. She is fourteen years old, light-haired, blue-eyed, unassuming and pretty. Every body talks English.

The Emperor wore a cap, frock coat and pantaloons, all of some kind of plain white drilling—cotton or linen—and sported no jewelry or any insignia whatever of rank. No costume could be less ostentatious. He is very tall and spare, and a determined-looking man, though a very pleasant-looking one, nevertheless. It is easy to see that he is kind and affectionate. There is something very noble in his expression when his cap is off. There is none of that cunning in his eye that all of us noticed in Louis Napoleon's.

The Empress and the little Grand Duchess wore simple suits of foulard (or foulard silk, I don't know which is proper,) with a small blue spot in it; the dresses were trimmed with blue; both ladies wore broad blue sashes about their waists; linen collars and clerical ties of muslin; low-crowned straw-hats trimmed with blue velvet; parasols and flesh-colored gloves. The Grand Duchess had no heels on her shoes. I do not know this of my own knowledge, but one of our ladies told me so. I was not looking at her shoes. I was glad to observe that she wore her own hair, plaited in thick braids against the back of her head, instead of the uncomely thing they call a waterfall, which is about as much like a waterfall as a canvas-covered ham is like a cataract. Taking the kind expression that is in the Emperor's face and the gentle-ness that is in his young daughter's into consideration, I won-dered if it would not tax the Czar's firmness to the utmost to condemn a supplicating wretch to misery in the wastes of Si-beria if she pleaded for him. Every time their eyes met, I saw more and more what a tremendous power that weak, diffident school-girl could wield if she chose to do it. Many and many a time she might rule the Autocrat of Russia, whose lightest word is law to seventy millions of human beings! She was only a girl, and she looked like a thousand others I have seen, but never a girl provoked such a novel and peculiar interest in me before. A strange, new sensation is a rare thing in this hum-drum life, and I had it here. There was nothing stale or worn out about the thoughts and feelings the situation and the circumstances created. It seemed strange—stranger than I can tell—to think that the central figure in the cluster of men and women, chatting here under the trees like the most ordi-nary individual in the land, was a man who could open his lips and ships would fly through the waves, locomotives would speed over the plains, couriers would hurry from vil-lage to village, a hundred telegraphs would flash the word to the four corners of an Empire that stretches its vast propor-tions over a seventh part of the habitable globe, and a count-less multitude of men would spring to do his bidding. I had a sort of vague desire to examine his hands and see if they were of flesh and blood, like other men's. Here was a man who could do this wonderful thing, and yet if I chose I could knock him down. The case was plain, but it seemed prepos-terous, nevertheless—as preposterous as trying to knock down a mountain or wipe out a continent. If this man sprained his ankle, a million miles of telegraph would carry the news over mountains—valleys—uninhabited deserts—under the trackless sea—and ten thousand newspapers would prate of it; if he were grievously ill, all the nations would know it before the sun rose again; if he dropped lifeless where he stood, his fall might shake the thrones of half a world! If I could have stolen his coat, I would have done it. When I meet a man like that, I want something to remember him by.

As a general thing, we have been shown through palaces by some plush-legged filagreed flunkey or other, who charged a franc for it; but after talking with the company half an hour, the Emperor of Russia and his family conducted us all through their mansion themselves. They made no charge. They seemed to take a real pleasure in it.

We spent half an hour idling through the palace, admiring the cosy apartments and the rich but eminently home-like appointments of the place, and then the Imperial family bade our party a kind good-bye, and proceeded to count the spoons.

An invitation was extended to us to visit the palace of the eldest son, the Crown Prince of Russia, which was near at hand. The young man was absent, but the Dukes and Countesses and Princes went over the premises with us as leisurely as was the case at the Emperor's, and conversation continued as lively as ever.

It was a little after one o'clock, now. We drove to the Grand Duke Michael's, a mile away, in response to his invitation, previously given.

We arrived in twenty minutes from the Emperor's. It is a lovely place. The beautiful palace nestles among the grand old groves of the park, the park sits in the lap of the picturesque crags and hills, and both look out upon the breezy ocean. In the park are rustic seats, here and there, in secluded nooks that are dark with shade; there are rivulets of crystal water; there are lakelets, with inviting, grassy banks; there are glimpses of sparkling cascades through openings in the wilderness of foliage; there are streams of clear water gushing from mimic knots on the trunks of forest trees; there are miniature marble temples perched upon gray old crags; there are airy lookouts whence one may gaze upon a broad expanse of landscape and ocean. The palace is modeled after the choicest forms of Grecian architecture, and its wide colonnades surround a central court that is banked with rare flowers that fill the place with their fragrance, and in their midst springs a fountain that cools the summer air, and may possibly breed mosquitoes, but I do not think it does.

The Grand Duke and his Duchess came out, and the presentation ceremonies were as simple as they had been at the Emperor's. In a few minutes, conversation was under way, as before. The Empress appeared in the verandah, and the little Grand Duchess came out into the crowd. They had beaten us there. In a few minutes, the Emperor came himself on horseback. It was very pleasant. You can appreciate it if you have ever visited royalty and felt occasionally that possibly you might be wearing out your welcome—though as a general thing, I believe, royalty is not scrupulous about discharging you when it is done with you.

The Grand Duke is the third brother of the Emperor, is about thirty-seven years old, perhaps, and is the princeliest figure in Russia. He is even taller than the Czar, as straight as an Indian, and bears himself like one of those gorgeous knights we read about in romances of the Crusades. He looks like a great-hearted fellow who would pitch an enemy into the river in a moment, and then jump in and risk his life fishing him out again. The stories they tell of him show him to be of a brave and generous nature. He must have been desirous of proving that Americans were welcome guests in the imperial palaces of Russia, because he rode all the way to Yalta and escorted our procession to the Emperor's himself, and kept his aids scurrying about, clearing the road and offering assistance wherever it could be needed. We were rather familiar with him then, because we did not know who he was. We recognized him now, and appreciated the friendly spirit that prompted him to do us a favor that any other Grand Duke in the world would have doubtless declined to do. He had plenty of servitors whom he could have sent, but he chose to attend to the matter himself.

The Grand Duke was dressed in the handsome and showy uniform of a Cossack officer. The Grand Duchess had on a white alpaca robe, with the seams and gores trimmed with black barb lace, and a little gray hat with a feather of the same color. She is young, rather pretty, modest and unpretending, and full of winning politeness.

Our party walked all through the house, and then the nobility escorted them all over the grounds, and finally brought them back to the palace about half-past two o'clock to breakfast. They called it breakfast, but we would have called it luncheon. It consisted of two kinds of wine; tea, bread, cheese, and cold meats, and was served on the centre-tables in the reception room and the verandahs—any where that was convenient; there was no ceremony. It was a sort of picnic. I had heard before that we were to breakfast there, but Blucher said he believed Baker's boy had suggested it to his Imperial Highness. I think not—though it would be like him. Baker's boy is the famine-breeder of the ship. He is always hungry. They say he goes about the state-rooms when the passengers are out, and eats up all the soap. And they say he eats oakum. They say he will eat any thing he can get between meals, but he prefers oakum. He does not like oakum for dinner, but he likes it for a lunch, at odd hours, or any thing that way. It makes him very disagreeable, because it makes his breath bad, and keeps his teeth all stuck up with tar. Baker's boy may have suggested the breakfast, but I hope he did not. It went off well, anyhow. The illustrious host moved about from place to place, and helped to destroy the provisions and keep the conversation lively, and the Grand Duchess talked with the verandah parties and such as had satisfied their appetites and straggled out from the reception room.

The Grand Duke's tea was delicious. They give one a lemon to squeeze into it, or iced milk, if he prefers it. The former is best. This tea is brought overland from China. It injures the article to transport it by sea.

When it was time to go, we bade our distinguished hosts good-bye, and they retired happy and contented to their apartments to count *their* spoons.

We had spent the best part of half a day in the home of royalty, and had been as cheerful and comfortable all the time as we could have been in the ship. I would as soon have thought of being cheerful in Abraham's bosom as in the palace of an Emperor. I supposed that Emperors were terrible

people. I thought they never did any thing but wear magnificent crowns and red velvet dressing-gowns with dabs of wool
sewed on them in spots, and sit on thrones and scowl at the
flunkies and the people in the parquette, and order Dukes and
Duchesses off to execution. I find, however, that when one is
so fortunate as to get behind the scenes and see them at home
and in the privacy of their firesides, they are strangely like
common mortals. They are pleasanter to look upon then than
they are in their theatrical aspect. It seems to come as natural
to them to dress and act like other people as it is to put a
friend's cedar pencil in your pocket when you are done using
it. But I can never have any confidence in the tinsel kings of
the theatre after this. It will be a great loss. I used to take
such a thrilling pleasure in them. But, hereafter, I will turn
me sadly away and say;

"This does not answer—this isn't the style of king that *I*
am acquainted with."

When they swagger around the stage in jeweled crowns
and splendid robes, I shall feel bound to observe that all the
Emperors that ever *I* was personally acquainted with wore
the commonest sort of clothes, and did not swagger. And
when they come on the stage attended by a vast body-guard
of supes in helmets and tin breastplates, it will be my duty as
well as my pleasure to inform the ignorant that no crowned
head of my acquaintance has a soldier any where about his
house or his person.

Possibly it may be thought that our party tarried too long,
or did other improper things, but such was not the case. The
company felt that they were occupying an unusually responsible position—they were representing the people of America, not the Government—and therefore they were careful to
do their best to perform their high mission with credit.

On the other hand, the Imperial families, no doubt, considered that in entertaining us they were more especially entertaining the people of America than they could by showering
attentions on a whole platoon of ministers plenipotentiary;
and therefore they gave to the event its fullest significance, as
an expression of good will and friendly feeling toward the
entire country. We took the kindnesses we received as attentions thus directed, of course, and not to ourselves as a party.

That we felt a personal pride in being received as the repre-sentatives of a nation, we do not deny; that we felt a national pride in the warm cordiality of that reception, can not be doubted.

Our poet has been rigidly suppressed, from the time we let go the anchor. When it was announced that we were going to visit the Emperor of Russia, the fountains of his great deep were broken up, and he rained ineffable bosh for four-and-twenty hours. Our original anxiety as to what we were going to do with ourselves, was suddenly transformed into anxiety about what we were going to do with our poet. The problem was solved at last. Two alternatives were offered him—he must either swear a dreadful oath that he would not issue a line of his poetry while he was in the Czar's dominions, or else remain under guard on board the ship until we were safe at Constantinople again. He fought the dilemma long, but yielded at last. It was a great deliverance. Perhaps the savage reader would like a specimen of his style. I do not mean this term to be offensive. I only use it because "the gentle reader" has been used so often that any change from it can not but be refreshing:

> "Save us and sanctify us, and finally, then,
>   See good provisions we enjoy while we journey to
>   Jerusa*lem*.
>   For so man proposes, which it is most true,
>   And time will wait for none, nor for us too."

The sea has been unusually rough all day. However, we have had a lively time of it, anyhow. We have had quite a run of visitors. The Governor-General came, and we received him with a salute of nine guns. He brought his family with him. I observed that carpets were spread from the pier-head to his carriage for him to walk on, though I have seen him walk there without any carpet when he was not on business. I thought may be he had what the accidental insurance people might call an extra-hazardous polish ("policy"—joke, but not above mediocrity,) on his boots, and wished to protect them, but I examined and could not see that they were blacked any better than usual. It may have been that he had forgotten his carpet, before, but he did not have it with him, anyhow. He was an exceedingly pleasant old gentleman; we all liked him, especially Blucher. When he went away, Blucher invited him to come again and fetch his carpet along.

Prince Dolgorouki and a Grand Admiral or two, whom we had seen yesterday at the reception, came on board also. I was a little distant with these parties, at first, because when I have been visiting Emperors I do not like to be too familiar with people I only know by reputation, and whose moral characters and standing in society I can not be thoroughly acquainted with. I judged it best to be a little offish, at first. I said to myself, Princes and Counts and Grand Admirals are very well, but they are not Emperors, and one can not be too particular about who he associates with.

Baron Wrangel came, also. He used to be Russian Ambassador at Washington. I told him I had an uncle who fell down a shaft and broke himself in two, as much as a year before that. That was a falsehood, but then I was not going to let any man eclipse me on surprising adventures, merely for the want of a little invention. The Baron is a fine man, and is said to stand high in the Emperor's confidence and esteem.

Baron Ungern-Sternberg, a boisterous, whole-souled old nobleman, came with the rest. He is a man of progress and enterprise—a representative man of the age. He is the Chief Director of the railway system of Russia—a sort of railroad king. In his line he is making things move along in this country. He has traveled extensively in America. He says he has tried convict labor on his railroads, and with perfect success. He says the convicts work well, and are quiet and peaceable. He observed that he employs nearly ten thousand of them now. This appeared to be another call on my resources. I was equal to the emergency. I said we had eighty thousand convicts employed on the railways in America—all of them under sentence of death for murder in the first degree. That closed *him* out.

We had General Todtleben (the famous defender of Sebastopol, during the siege,) and many inferior army and also navy officers, and a number of unofficial Russian ladies and gentlemen. Naturally, a champagne luncheon was in order, and was accomplished without loss of life. Toasts and jokes were discharged freely, but no speeches were made save one thanking the Emperor and the Grand Duke, through the Governor-General, for our hospitable reception, and one by the Governor-General in reply, in which he returned the Emperor's thanks for the speech, etc., etc.

Chapter XXXVIII

W E RETURNED to Constantinople, and after a day or two spent in exhausting marches about the city and voyages up the Golden Horn in *caiques*, we steamed away again. We passed through the Sea of Marmora and the Dardanelles, and steered for a new land—a new one to us, at least—Asia. We had as yet only acquired a bowing acquaintance with it, through pleasure excursions to Scutari and the regions round about.

We passed between Lemnos and Mytilene, and saw them as we had seen Elba and the Balearic Isles—mere bulky shapes, with the softening mists of distance upon them— whales in a fog, as it were. Then we held our course southward, and began to "read up" celebrated Smyrna.

At all hours of the day and night the sailors in the forecastle amused themselves and aggravated us by burlesquing our visit to royalty. The opening paragraph of our Address to the Emperor was framed as follows:

"We are a handful of private citizens of America, traveling simply for recreation—and unostentatiously, as becomes our unofficial state—and, therefore, we have no excuse to tender for presenting ourselves before your Majesty, save the desire of offering our grateful acknowledgments to the lord of a realm, which, through good and through evil report, has been the steadfast friend of the land we love so well."

The third cook, crowned with a resplendent tin basin and wrapped royally in a table-cloth mottled with grease-spots and coffee stains, and bearing a sceptre that looked strangely like a belaying-pin, walked upon a dilapidated carpet and perched himself on the capstan, careless of the flying spray; his tarred and weather-beaten Chamberlains, Dukes and Lord High Admirals surrounded him, arrayed in all the pomp that spare tarpaulins and remnants of old sails could furnish. Then the visiting "watch below," transformed into graceless ladies and uncouth pilgrims, by rude travesties upon waterfalls, hoopskirts, white kid gloves and swallow-tail coats, moved solemnly up the companion way, and bowing low, began a system of complicated and extraordinary smiling which few monarchs could look upon and live. Then the mock consul, a slush-plastered deck-sweep, drew out a soiled fragment of paper and proceeded to read, laboriously

"To His Imperial Majesty, Alexander II., Emperor of Russia:

"We are a handful of private citizens of America, traveling simply for recreation,—and unostentatiously, as becomes our unofficial state—and therefore, we have no excuse to tender for presenting ourselves before your Majesty—"

The Emperor—"Then what the devil did you come for?"

—"Save the desire of offering our grateful acknowledgments to the lord of a realm which—"

The Emperor—"Oh, d—n the Address!—read it to the police. Chamberlain, take these people over to my brother, the Grand Duke's, and give them a square meal. Adieu! I am happy—I am gratified—I am delighted—I am bored. Adieu, adieu—vamos the ranch! The First Groom of the Palace will proceed to count the portable articles of value belonging to the premises."

The farce then closed, to be repeated again with every change of the watches, and embellished with new and still more extravagant inventions of pomp and conversation.

At all times of the day and night the phraseology of that tiresome address fell upon our ears. Grimy sailors came down out of the foretop placidly announcing themselves as "a handful of private citizens of America, *traveling simply for recreation* and unostentatiously*," etc.; the coal passers moved to their duties in the profound depths of the ship, explaining the blackness of their faces and their uncouthness of dress, with the reminder that *they* were "a handful of private citizens, traveling simply for recreation," etc., and when the cry rang through the vessel at midnight: "EIGHT BELLS!—LARBOARD WATCH, TURN OUT!" the larboard watch came gaping and stretching out of their den, with the everlasting formula: "Aye-aye, sir! We are a handful of private citizens of America, traveling simply for recreation, and unostentatiously, as becomes our unofficial state!"

As I was a member of the committee, and helped to frame the Address, these sarcasms came home to me. I never heard a sailor proclaiming himself as a handful of American citizens traveling for recreation, but I wished he might trip and fall overboard, and so reduce his handful by one individual, at least. I never was so tired of any one phrase as the sailors made me of the opening sentence of the Address to the Emperor of Russia.

This seaport of Smyrna, our first notable acquaintance in Asia, is a closely packed city of one hundred and thirty thousand inhabitants, and, like Constantinople, it has no outskirts. It is as closely packed at its outer edges as it is in the centre, and then the habitations leave suddenly off and the plain beyond seems houseless. It is just like any other Oriental city. That is to say, its Moslem houses are heavy and dark, and as comfortless as so many tombs; its streets are crooked, rudely and roughly paved, and as narrow as an ordinary staircase; the streets uniformly carry a man to any other place than the one he wants to go to, and surprise him by landing him in the most unexpected localities; business is chiefly carried on in great covered bazaars, celled like a honeycomb with innumerable shops no larger than a common closet, and the whole hive cut up into a maze of alleys about wide enough to accommodate a laden camel, and well calculated to confuse a stranger and eventually lose him; every where there is dirt, every where there are fleas, every where there are lean, broken-hearted dogs; every alley is thronged with people; wherever you look, your eye rests upon a wild masquerade of extravagant costumes; the workshops are all open to the streets, and the workmen visible; all manner of sounds assail the ear, and over them all rings out the muezzin's cry from some tall minaret, calling the faithful vagabonds to prayer; and superior to the call to prayer, the noises in the streets, the interest of the costumes—superior to every thing, and claiming the bulk of attention first, last, and all the time—is a combination of Mohammedan stenches, to which the smell of even a Chinese quarter would be as pleasant as the roasting odors of the fatted calf to the nostrils of the returning Prodigal. Such is Oriental luxury—such is Oriental splendor! We read about it all our days, but we comprehend it not until we see it. Smyrna is a very old city. Its name occurs several times in the Bible, one or two of the disciples of Christ visited it, and here was located one of the original seven apocalyptic

churches spoken of in Revelations. These churches were sym-
bolized in the Scriptures as candlesticks, and on certain conditions there was a sort of implied promise that Smyrna
should be endowed with a "crown of life." She was to "be
faithful unto death"—those were the terms. She has not kept
up her faith straight along, but the pilgrims that wander
hither consider that she has come near enough to it to save
her, and so they point to the fact that Smyrna to-day wears
her crown of life, and is a great city, with a great commerce
and full of energy, while the cities wherein were located the
other six churches, and to which no crown of life was promised, have vanished from the earth. So Smyrna really still possesses her crown of life, in a business point of view. Her
career, for eighteen centuries, has been a chequered one, and
she has been under the rule of princes of many creeds, yet
there has been no season during all that time, as far as we
know, (and during such seasons as she was inhabited at all,)
that she has been without her little community of Christians
"faithful unto death." Hers was the only church against which
no threats were implied in the Revelations, and the only one
which survived.

With Ephesus, forty miles from here, where was located
another of the seven churches, the case was different. The
"candlestick" has been removed from Ephesus. Her light has
been put out. Pilgrims, always prone to find prophecies in the
Bible, and often where none exist, speak cheerfully and complacently of poor, ruined Ephesus as the victim of prophecy.
And yet there is no sentence that promises, without due qual-
ification, the destruction of the city. The words are:

"Remember, therefore, from whence thou art fallen and repent,
and do the first works; or else I will come unto thee quickly, and
will remove thy candlestick out of his place, except thou repent."

That is all; the other verses are singularly *complimentary* to
Ephesus. The threat is qualified. There is no history to show
that she did not repent. But the cruelest habit the modern
prophecy-savans have, is that one of coolly and arbitrarily fitting the prophetic shirt on to the wrong man. They do it
without regard to rhyme or reason. Both the cases I have just
mentioned are instances in point. Those "prophecies" are dis-

tinctly leveled at the "*churches* of Ephesus, Smyrna," etc., and yet the pilgrims invariably make them refer to the *cities* instead. No crown of life is promised to the town of Smyrna and its commerce, but to the handful of Christians who formed its "church." If *they* were "faithful unto death," they have their crown now—but no amount of faithfulness and legal shrewdness combined could legitimately drag the *city* into a participation in the promises of the prophecy. The stately language of the Bible refers to a crown of life whose lustre will reflect the day-beams of the endless ages of eternity, not the butterfly existence of a city built by men's hands, which must pass to dust with the builders and be forgotten even in the mere handful of centuries vouchsafed to the solid world itself between its cradle and its grave.

The fashion of delving out fulfillments of prophecy where that prophecy consists of mere "ifs," trenches upon the absurd. Suppose, a thousand years from now, a malarious swamp builds itself up in the shallow harbor of Smyrna, or something else kills the town; and suppose, also, that within that time the swamp that has filled the renowned harbor of Ephesus and rendered her ancient site deadly and uninhabitable to-day, becomes hard and healthy ground; suppose the natural consequence ensues, to wit: that Smyrna becomes a melancholy ruin, and Ephesus is rebuilt. What would the prophecy-savans say? They would coolly skip over our age of the world, and say: "Smyrna was not faithful unto death, and so her crown of life was denied her; Ephesus repented, and lo! her candlestick was not removed. Behold these evidences! How wonderful is prophecy!"

Smyrna has been utterly destroyed six times. If her crown of life had been an insurance policy, she would have had an opportunity to collect on it the first time she fell. But she holds it on sufferance and by a complimentary construction of language which does not refer to her. Six different times, however, I suppose some infatuated prophecy-enthusiast blundered along and said, to the infinite disgust of Smyrna and the Smyrniotes: "In sooth, here is astounding fulfillment of prophecy! Smyrna hath not been faithful unto death, and behold her crown of life is vanished from her head. Verily, these things be astonishing!"

Such things have a bad influence. They provoke worldly men into using light conversation concerning sacred subjects. Thick-headed commentators upon the Bible, and stupid preachers and teachers, work more damage to religion than sensible, cool-brained clergymen can fight away again, toil as they may. It is not good judgment to fit a crown of life upon a city which has been destroyed six times. That other class of wiseacres who twist prophecy in such a manner as to make it promise the destruction and desolation of the same city, use judgment just as bad, since the city is in a very flourishing condition now, unhappily for them. These things put arguments into the mouth of infidelity.

A portion of the city is pretty exclusively Turkish; the Jews have a quarter to themselves; the Franks another quarter; so, also, with the Armenians. The Armenians, of course, are Christians. Their houses are large, clean, airy, handsomely paved with black and white squares of marble, and in the centre of many of them is a square court, which has in it a luxuriant flower-garden and a sparkling fountain; the doors of all the rooms open on this. A very wide hall leads to the street door, and in this the women sit, the most of the day. In the cool of the evening they dress up in their best raiment and show themselves at the door. They are all comely of countenance, and exceedingly neat and cleanly; they look as if they were just out of a band-box. Some of the young ladies— many of them, I may say—are even very beautiful; they average a shade better than American girls—which treasonable words I pray may be forgiven me. They are very sociable, and will smile back when a stranger smiles at them, bow back when he bows, and talk back if he speaks to them. No introduction is required. An hour's chat at the door with a pretty girl one never saw before, is easily obtained, and is very pleasant. I have tried it. I could not talk any thing but English, and the girl knew nothing but Greek, or Armenian, or some such barbarous tongue, but we got along very well. I find that in cases like these, the fact that you can not comprehend each other isn't much of a drawback. In that Russian town of Yalta I danced an astonishing sort of dance an hour long, and one I had not heard of before, with a very pretty girl, and we talked incessantly, and laughed exhaustingly, and neither one ever knew what the other was driving at. But it was splendid. There were twenty people in the set, and the dance was very lively and complicated. It was complicated enough without me—with me it was more so. I threw in a figure now and then that surprised those Russians. But I have never ceased to think of that girl. I have written to her, but I can not direct the epistle because her name is one of those nine-jointed Russian affairs, and there are not letters enough in our alphabet to hold out. I am not reckless enough to try to pronounce it when I am awake, but I make a stagger at it in my dreams, and get up with the lockjaw in the morning. I am fading. I do not take my meals now, with any sort of regularity. Her dear name haunts me still in my dreams. It is awful on teeth. It never comes out of my mouth but it fetches an old snag along with it. And then the lockjaw closes down and nips off a couple of the last syllables—but they taste good.

Coming through the Dardanelles, we saw camel trains on shore with the glasses, but we were never close to one till we got to Smyrna. These camels are very much larger than the scrawny specimens one sees in the menagerie. They stride along these streets, in single file, a dozen in a train, with heavy loads on their backs, and a fancy-looking negro in Turkish costume, or an Arab, preceding them on a little donkey and completely overshadowed and rendered insignificant by the huge beasts. To see a camel train laden with the spices of Arabia and the rare fabrics of Persia come marching through the narrow alleys of the bazaar, among porters with their burdens, money-changers, lamp-merchants, Alnaschars in the glassware business, portly cross-legged Turks smoking the famous narghili, and the crowds drifting to and fro in the fanciful costumes of the East, is a genuine revelation of the Orient. The picture lacks nothing. It casts you back at once into your forgotten boyhood, and again you dream over the wonders of the Arabian Nights; again your companions are princes, your lord is the Caliph Haroun Al Raschid, and your servants are terrific giants and genii that come with smoke and lightning and thunder, and go as a storm goes when they depart!

Chapter XXXIX

WE INQUIRED, and learned that the lions of Smyrna consisted of the ruins of the ancient citadel, whose broken and prodigious battlements frown upon the city from a lofty hill just in the edge of the town—the Mount Pagus of Scripture, they call it; the site of that one of the Seven Apocalyptic Churches of Asia which was located here in the first century of the Christian era; and the grave and the place of martyrdom of the venerable Polycarp, who suffered in Smyrna for his religion some eighteen hundred years ago.

We took little donkeys and started. We saw Polycarp's tomb, and then hurried on.

The "Seven Churches"—thus they abbreviate it—came next on the list. We rode there—about a mile and a half in the sweltering sun—and visited a little Greek church which they said was built upon the ancient site; and we paid a small fee, and the holy attendant gave each of us a little wax candle as a remembrancer of the place, and I put mine in my hat and the sun melted it and the grease all ran down the back of my neck; and so now I have not any thing left but the wick, and it is a sorry and a wilted-looking wick at that.

Several of us argued as well as we could that the "church" mentioned in the Bible meant a party of Christians, and not a building; that the Bible spoke of them as being very poor— so poor, I thought, and so subject to persecution (as per Polycarp's martyrdom) that in the first place they probably could not have afforded a church edifice, and in the second would not have dared to build it in the open light of day if they could; and finally, that if they had had the privilege of building it, common judgment would have suggested that they build it somewhere near the town. But the elders of the ship's family ruled us down and scouted our evidences. However, retribution came to them afterward. They found that they had been led astray and had gone to the wrong place; they discovered that the accepted site is in the city.

Riding through the town, we could see marks of the six Smyrnas that have existed here and been burned up by fire or knocked down by earthquakes. The hills and the rocks are rent asunder in places, excavations expose great blocks of building-stone that have lain buried for ages, and all the mean houses and walls of modern Smyrna along the way are spotted white with broken pillars, capitals and fragments of sculptured marble that once adorned the lordly palaces that were the glory of the city in the olden time.

The ascent of the hill of the citadel is very steep, and we proceeded rather slowly. But there were matters of interest about us. In one place, five hundred feet above the sea, the perpendicular bank on the upper side of the road was ten or fifteen feet high, and the cut exposed three veins of oyster shells, just as we have seen quartz veins exposed in the cutting of a road in Nevada or Montana. The veins were about eighteen inches thick and two or three feet apart, and they slanted along downward for a distance of thirty feet or more, and then disappeared where the cut joined the road. Heaven only knows how far a man might trace them by "stripping." They were clean, nice oyster shells, large, and just like any other oyster shells. They were thickly massed together, and none were scattered above or below the veins. Each one was a well-defined lead by itself, and without a spur. My first instinct was to set up the usual—

NOTICE:
"We, the undersigned, claim five claims of two hundred feet each, (and one for discovery,) on this ledge or lode of oyster-shells, with all its dips, spurs, angles, variations and sinuosities, and fifty feet on each side of the same, to work it, etc., etc., according to the mining laws of Smyrna."

They were such perfectly natural-looking leads that I could hardly keep from "taking them up." Among the oyster-shells were mixed many fragments of ancient, broken crockery ware. Now how did those masses of oyster-shells get there? I can not determine. Broken crockery and oyster-shells are suggestive of restaurants—but then they could have had no such places away up there on that mountain side in our time, because nobody has lived up there. A restaurant would not pay in such a stony, forbidding, desolate place. And besides, there were no champagne corks among the shells. If there ever was a restaurant there, it must have been in Smyrna's palmy days, when the hills were covered with palaces. I could believe in one restaurant, on those terms; but then how about the three? Did they have restaurants there at three different periods of the world?—because there are two or three feet of solid earth between the oyster leads. Evidently, the restaurant solution will not answer.

The hill might have been the bottom of the sea, once, and been lifted up, with its oyster-beds, by an earthquake—but, then, how about the crockery? And moreover, how about *three* oyster beds, one above another, and thick strata of good honest earth between?

That theory will not do. It is just possible that this hill is Mount Ararat, and that Noah's Ark rested here, and he ate oysters and threw the shells overboard. But that will not do, either. There are the three layers again and the solid earth between—and, besides, there were only eight in Noah's family, and they could not have eaten all these oysters in the two or three months they staid on top of that mountain. The beasts—however, it is simply absurd to suppose he did not know any more than to feed the beasts on oyster suppers.

It is painful—it is even humiliating—but I am reduced at last to one slender theory: that the oysters climbed up there of their own accord. But what object could they have had in view?—what did they want up there? What could any oyster want to climb a hill for? To climb a hill must necessarily be fatiguing and annoying exercise for an oyster. The most natural conclusion would be that the oysters climbed up there to look at the scenery. Yet when one comes to reflect upon the nature of an oyster, it seems plain that he does not care for scenery. An oyster has no taste for such things; he cares nothing for the beautiful. An oyster is of a retiring disposition, and not lively—not even cheerful above the average, and never enterprising. But above all, an oyster does not take any interest in scenery—he scorns it. What have I arrived at now? Simply at the point I started from, namely, *those oyster shells are there*, in regular layers, five hundred feet above the sea, and no man knows how they got there. I have hunted up the guide-books, and the gist of what they say is this: "They are there, but how they got there is a mystery."

Twenty-five years ago, a multitude of people in America

put on their ascension robes, took a tearful leave of their friends, and made ready to fly up into heaven at the first blast of the trumpet. But the angel did not blow it. Miller's resurrection day was a failure. The Millerites were disgusted. I did not suspect that there were Millers in Asia Minor, but a gentleman tells me that they had it all set for the world to come to an end in Smyrna one day about three years ago. There was much buzzing and preparation for a long time previously, and it culminated in a wild excitement at the appointed time. A vast number of the populace ascended the citadel hill early in the morning, to get out of the way of the general destruction, and many of the infatuated closed up their shops and retired from all earthly business. But the strange part of it was that about three in the afternoon, while this gentleman and his friends were at dinner in the hotel, a terrific storm of rain, accompanied by thunder and lightning, broke forth and continued with dire fury for two or three hours. It was a thing unprecedented in Smyrna at that time of the year, and scared some of the most skeptical. The streets ran rivers and the hotel floor was flooded with water. The dinner had to be suspended. When the storm finished and left every body drenched through and through, and melancholy and half-drowned, the ascensionists came down from the mountain as dry as so many charity-sermons! They had been looking down upon the fearful storm going on below, and really believed that their proposed destruction of the world was proving a grand success.

A railway here in Asia—in the dreamy realm of the Orient—in the fabled land of the Arabian Nights—is a strange thing to think of. And yet they have one already, and are building another. The present one is well built and well conducted, by an English Company, but is not doing an immense amount of business. The first year it carried a good many passengers, but its freight list only comprised eight hundred pounds of figs!

It runs almost to the very gates of Ephesus—a town great in all ages of the world—a city familiar to readers of the Bible, and one which was as old as the very hills when the disciples of Christ preached in its streets. It dates back to the shadowy ages of tradition, and was the birthplace of gods renowned in Grecian mythology. The idea of a locomotive tearing through such a place as this, and waking the phantoms of its old days of romance out of their dreams of dead and gone centuries, is curious enough.

We journey thither to-morrow to see the celebrated ruins.

Chapter XL

THIS HAS BEEN a stirring day. The Superintendent of the railway put a train at our disposal, and did us the further kindness of accompanying us to Ephesus and giving to us his watchful care. We brought sixty scarcely perceptible donkeys in the freight cars, for we had much ground to go over. We have seen some of the most grotesque costumes, along the line of the railroad, that can be imagined. I am glad that no possible combination of words could describe them, for I might then be foolish enough to attempt it.

At ancient Ayassalook, in the midst of a forbidding desert, we came upon long lines of ruined aqueducts, and other remnants of architectural grandeur, that told us plainly enough we were nearing what had been a metropolis, once. We left the train and mounted the donkeys, along with our invited guests—pleasant young gentlemen from the officers' list of an American man-of-war.

The little donkeys had saddles upon them which were made very high in order that the rider's feet might not drag the ground. The preventative did not work well in the cases of our tallest pilgrims, however. There were no bridles—nothing but a single rope, tied to the bit. It was purely ornamental, for the donkey cared nothing for it. If he were drifting to starboard, you might put your helm down hard the other way, if it were any satisfaction to you to do it, but he would continue to drift to starboard all the same. There was only one process which could be depended on, and that was to get down and lift his rear around until his head pointed in the right direction, or take him under your arm and carry him to a part of the road which he could not get out of without climbing. The sun flamed down as hot as a furnace, and neckscarfs, veils and umbrellas seemed hardly any protection; they served only to make the long procession look more than ever fantastic—for be it known the ladies were all riding astride because they could not stay on the shapeless saddles sidewise, the men were perspiring and out of temper, their feet were banging against the rocks, the donkeys were capering in every direction but the right one and being belabored with clubs for it, and every now and then a broad umbrella would suddenly go down out of the cavalcade, announcing to all that one more pilgrim had bitten the dust. It was a wilder picture than those solitudes had seen for many a day. No donkeys ever existed that were as hard to navigate as these, I think, or that had so many vile, exasperating instincts. Occasionally we grew so tired and breathless with fighting them that we had to desist,—and immediately the donkey would come down to a deliberate walk. This, with the fatigue, and the sun, would put a man asleep; and as soon as the man was asleep, the donkey would lie down. My donkey shall never see his boyhood's home again. He has lain down once too often. He must die.

We all stood in the vast theatre of ancient Ephesus,—the stone-benched amphitheatre I mean—and had our picture taken. We looked as proper there as we would look any where, I suppose. We do not embellish the general desolation of a desert much. We add what dignity we can to a stately ruin with our green umbrellas and jackasses, but it is little. However, we mean well.

I wish to say a brief word of the aspect of Ephesus.

On a high, steep hill, toward the sea, is a gray ruin of ponderous blocks of marble, wherein, tradition says, St. Paul was imprisoned eighteen centuries ago. From these old walls you have the finest view of the desolate scene where once stood Ephesus, the proudest city of ancient times, and whose Temple of Diana was so noble in design, and so exquisite of workmanship, that it ranked high in the list of the Seven Wonders of the World.

Behind you is the sea; in front is a level green valley, (a marsh, in fact,) extending far away among the mountains; to the right of the front view is the old citadel of Ayassalook, on a high hill; the ruined Mosque of the Sultan Selim stands near it in the plain, (this is built over the grave of St. John, and was formerly a Christian Church;) further toward you is the hill of Pion, around whose front is clustered all that remains of the ruins of Ephesus that still stand; divided from it by a narrow valley is the long, rocky, rugged mountain of Coressus. The scene is a pretty one, and yet desolate—for in that wide plain no man can live, and in it is no human habitation.

But for the crumbling arches and monstrous piers and broken walls that rise from the foot of the hill of Pion, one could not believe that in this place once stood a city whose renown is older than tradition itself. It is incredible to reflect that things as familiar all over the world to-day as household words, belong in the history and in the shadowy legends of this silent, mournful solitude. We speak of Apollo and of Diana—they were born here; of the metamorphosis of Syrinx into a reed—it was done here; of the great god Pan—he dwelt in the caves of this hill of Coressus; of the Amazons—this was their best prized home; of Bacchus and Hercules—both fought the warlike women here; of the Cyclops—they laid the ponderous marble blocks of some of the ruins yonder; of Homer—this was one of his many birthplaces; of Cimon of Athens; of Alcibiades, Lysander, Agesilaus—they visited here; so did Alexander the Great; so did Hannibal and Antiochus, Scipio, Lucullus and Sylla; Brutus, Cassius, Pompey, Cicero, and Augustus; Antony was a judge in this place, and left his seat in the open court, while the advocates were speaking, to run after Cleopatra, who passed the door; from this city these two sailed on pleasure excursions, in galleys with silver oars and perfumed sails, and with companies of beautiful girls to serve them, and actors and musicians to amuse them; in days that seem almost modern, so remote are they from the early history of this city, Paul the Apostle preached the new religion here, and so did John, and here it is supposed the former was pitted against wild beasts, for in 1 Corinthians, xv. 32 he says:

"If after the manner of men I have fought with beasts at Ephesus," &c.,

when many men still lived who had seen the Christ; here Mary Magdalen died, and here the Virgin Mary ended her days with John, albeit Rome has since judged it best to locate her grave elsewhere; six or seven hundred years ago—almost yesterday, as it were—troops of mail-clad Crusaders thronged the streets; and to come down to trifles, we speak of meandering streams, and find a new interest in a common word when we discover that the crooked river Meander, in yonder valley, gave it to our dictionary. It makes me feel as old as these dreary hills to look down upon these moss-hung ruins, this historic desolation. One may read the Scriptures and believe, but he can not go and stand yonder in the ruined theatre and in imagination people it again with the vanished multitudes who mobbed Paul's comrades there and shouted, with one voice, "Great is Diana of the Ephesians!" The idea of a shout in such a solitude as this almost makes one shudder.

It was a wonderful city, this Ephesus. Go where you will about these broad plains, you find the most exquisitely sculptured marble fragments scattered thick among the dust and weeds; and protruding from the ground, or lying prone upon it, are beautiful fluted columns of porphyry and all precious marbles; and at every step you find elegantly carved capitals and massive bases, and polished tablets engraved with Greek inscriptions. It is a world of precious relics, a wilderness of marred and mutilated gems. And yet what are these things to the wonders that lie buried here under the ground? At Constantinople, at Pisa, in the cities of Spain, are great mosques and cathedrals, whose grandest columns came from the temples and palaces of Ephesus, and yet one has only to scratch the ground here to match them. We shall never know what magnificence is, until this imperial city is laid bare to the sun.

The finest piece of sculpture we have yet seen and the one that impressed us most, (for we do not know much about art and can not easily work up ourselves into ecstacies over it,) is one that lies in this old theatre of Ephesus which St. Paul's riot has made so celebrated. It is only the headless body of a man, clad in a coat of mail, with a Medusa head upon the breast-plate, but we feel persuaded that such dignity and such majesty were never thrown into a form of stone before.

What builders they were, these men of antiquity! The massive arches of some of these ruins rest upon piers that are fifteen feet square and built entirely of solid blocks of marble, some of which are as large as a Saratoga trunk, and some the size of a boarding-house sofa. They are not shells or shafts of stone filled inside with rubbish, but the whole pier is a mass of solid masonry. Vast arches, that may have been the gates of the city, are built in the same way. They have braved the storms and sieges of three thousand years, and have been shaken by many an earthquake, but still they stand. When they dig alongside of them, they find ranges of ponderous masonry that are as perfect in every detail as they were the day those old Cyclopian giants finished them. An English Company is going to excavate Ephesus—and then!

And now am I reminded of—

THE LEGEND OF THE SEVEN SLEEPERS.

In the Mount of Pion, yonder, is the Cave of the Seven Sleepers. Once upon a time, about fifteen hundred years ago, seven young men lived near each other in Ephesus, who belonged to the despised sect of the Christians. It came to pass that the good King Maximilianus, (I am telling this story for nice little boys and girls,) it came to pass, I say, that the good King Maximilianus fell to persecuting the Christians, and as time rolled on he made it very warm for them. So the seven young men said one to the other, let us get up and travel. And they got up and traveled. They tarried not to bid their fathers and mothers good-bye, or any friend they knew. They only took certain moneys which their parents had, and garments that belonged unto their friends, whereby they might remember them when far away; and they took also the dog Ketmehr, which was the property of their neighbor Malchus, because the beast did run his head into a noose which one of the young men was carrying carelessly, and they had not time to release him; and they took also certain chickens that seemed lonely in the neighboring coops, and likewise some bottles of curious liquors that stood near the grocer's window; and then they departed from the city. By-and-by they came to a marvelous cave in the Hill of Pion and entered into it and feasted, and presently they hurried on again. But they forgot the bottles of curious liquors, and left them behind. They traveled in many lands, and had many strange adventures. They were virtuous young men, and lost no opportunity that fell in their way to make their livelihood. Their motto was in these words, namely, "Procrastination is the thief of time." And so, whenever they did come upon a man who was alone, they said, Behold, this person hath the wherewithal—let us go through him. And they went through him. At the end of five years they had waxed tired of travel and adventure, and longed to revisit their old home again and hear the voices and see the faces that were dear unto their youth. Therefore they went through such parties as fell in their way where they sojourned at that time, and journeyed back toward Ephesus again. For the good King Maximilianus was become converted unto the new faith, and the Christians rejoiced because they were no longer persecuted. One day as the sun went down, they came to the cave in the Mount of Pion, and they said, each to his fellow, Let us sleep here, and go and feast and make merry with our friends when the morning cometh. And each of the seven lifted up his voice and said, It is a whiz. So they went in, and lo, where they had put them, there lay the bottles of strange liquors, and they judged that age had not impaired their excellence. Wherein the wanderers were right, and the heads of the same were level. So each of the young men drank six bottles, and behold they felt very tired, then, and lay down and slept soundly.

When they awoke, one of them, Johannes—surnamed Smithianus—said, We are naked. And it was so. Their raiment was all gone, and the money which they had gotten from a stranger whom they had proceeded through as they approached the city, was lying upon the ground, corroded and rusted and defaced. Likewise the dog Ketmehr was gone, and nothing save the brass that was upon his collar remained. They wondered much at these things. But they took the money, and they wrapped about their bodies some leaves, and came up to the top of the hill. Then were they perplexed. The wonderful temple of Diana was gone; many grand edifices they had never seen before stood in the city; men in strange garbs moved about the streets, and every thing was changed.

Johannes said, It hardly seems like Ephesus. Yet here is the great gymnasium; here is the mighty theatre, wherein I have seen seventy thousand men assembled; here is the Agora; there is the font where the sainted John the Baptist immersed the converts; yonder is the prison of the good St. Paul, where we all did use to go to touch the ancient chains that bound him and be cured of our distempers; I see the tomb of the disciple Luke, and afar off is the church wherein repose the ashes of the holy John, where the Christians of Ephesus go twice a year to gather the dust from the tomb, which is able to make bodies whole again that are corrupted by disease, and cleanse the soul from sin; but see how the wharves encroach upon the sea, and what multitudes of ships are anchored in the bay; see, also, how the city hath stretched abroad, far over the valley behind Pion, and even unto the walls of Ayassa-look; and lo, all the hills are white with palaces and ribbed with colonnades of marble. How mighty is Ephesus become!

And wondering at what their eyes had seen, they went down into the city and purchased garments and clothed themselves. And when they would have passed on, the merchant bit the coins which they had given him, with his teeth, and turned them about and looked curiously upon them, and cast them upon his counter, and listened if they rang; and then he said, These be bogus. And they said, Depart thou to Hades, and went their way. When they were come to their houses, they recognized them, albeit they seemed old and mean; and they rejoiced, and were glad. They ran to the doors, and knocked, and strangers opened, and looked inquiringly upon them. And they said, with great excitement, while their hearts beat high, and the color in their faces came and went, Where is my father? Where is my mother? Where are Dionysius and Serapion, and Pericles, and Decius? And the strangers that opened said, We know not these. The Seven said, How, you know them not? How long have ye dwelt here, and whither are they gone that dwelt here before ye? And the strangers said, Ye play upon us with a jest, young men; we and our fathers have sojourned under these roofs these six generations; the names ye utter rot upon the tombs, and they that bore them have run their brief race, have laughed and sung, have borne the sorrows and the weariness that were allotted them, and are at rest; for nine-score years the summers have come and gone, and the autumn leaves have fallen, since the roses faded out of their cheeks and they laid them to sleep with the dead.

Then the seven young men turned them away from their homes, and the strangers shut the doors upon them. The wanderers marveled greatly, and looked into the faces of all they met, as hoping to find one that they knew; but all were strange, and passed them by and spake no friendly word.

They were sore distressed and sad. Presently they spake unto a citizen and said, Who is King in Ephesus? And the citizen answered and said, Whence come ye that ye know not that great Laertius reigns in Ephesus? They looked one at the other, greatly perplexed, and presently asked again, Where, then, is the good King Maximilianus? The citizen moved him apart, as one who is afraid, and said, Verily these men be mad, and dream dreams, else would they know that the King whereof they speak is dead above two hundred years agone.

Then the scales fell from the eyes of the Seven, and one said, Alas, that we drank of the curious liquors. They have made us weary, and in dreamless sleep these two long centuries have we lain. Our homes are desolate, our friends are dead. Behold, the jig is up—let us die. And that same day went they forth and laid them down and died. And in that self-same day, likewise, the Seven-up did cease in Ephesus, for that the Seven that were up were down again, and departed and dead withal. And the names that be upon their tombs, even unto this time, are Johannes Smithianus, Trumps, Gift, High, and Low, Jack, and The Game. And with the sleepers lie also the bottles wherein were once the curious liquors; and upon them is writ, in ancient letters, such words as these— names of heathen gods of olden time, perchance: Rumpunch, Jinsling, Egnog.

Such is the story of the Seven Sleepers, (with slight varia- tions,) and I know it is true, because I have seen the cave myself.

Really, so firm a faith had the ancients in this legend, that as late as eight or nine hundred years ago, learned travelers held it in superstitious fear. Two of them record that they ventured into it, but ran quickly out again, not daring to tarry lest they should fall asleep and outlive their great grand- children a century or so. Even at this day the ignorant deni- zens of the neighboring country prefer not to sleep in it.

Chapter XLI

WHEN I LAST MADE a memorandum, we were at Ephesus. We are in Syria, now, encamped in the mountains of Lebanon. The interregnum has been long, both as to time and distance. We brought not a relic from Ephesus! After gathering up fragments of sculptured marbles and breaking ornaments from the interior work of the Mosques; and after bringing them at a cost of infinite trouble and fatigue, five miles on muleback to the railway depot, a government officer compelled all who had such things to disgorge! He had an order from Constantinople to *look out for our party*, and see that we carried nothing off. It was a wise, a just, and a well-deserved rebuke, but it created a sensation. I never resist a temptation to plunder a stranger's premises without feeling insufferably vain about it. This time I felt proud beyond expression. I was serene in the midst of the scoldings that were heaped upon the Ottoman government for its affront offered to a pleasuring party of entirely respectable gentlemen and ladies. I said, "We that have free souls, it touches us not." The shoe not only pinched our party, but it pinched hard; a principal sufferer discovered that the imperial order was inclosed in an envelop bearing the seal of the British Embassy at Constantinople, and therefore must have been inspired by the representative of the Queen. This was bad—very bad. Coming solely from the Ottomans, it might have signified only Ottoman hatred of Christians, and a vulgar ignorance as to genteel methods of expressing it; but coming from the Christianized, educated, politic British legation, it simply intimated that we were a sort of gentlemen and ladies who would bear watching! So the party regarded it, and were incensed accordingly. The truth doubtless was, that the same precautions would have been taken against *any* travelers, because the English Company who have acquired the right to excavate Ephesus, and have paid a great sum for that right, need to be protected, and deserve to be. They can not afford to run the risk of having their hospitality abused by travelers, especially since travelers are such notorious scorners of honest behavior.

We sailed from Smyrna, in the wildest spirit of expectancy, for the chief feature, the grand goal of the expedition, was near at hand—we were approaching the Holy Land! Such a burrowing into the hold for trunks that had lain buried for weeks, yes for months; such a hurrying to and fro above decks and below; such a riotous system of packing and unpacking; such a littering up of the cabins with shirts and skirts, and indescribable and unclassable odds and ends; such a making up of bundles, and setting apart of umbrellas, green spectacles and thick veils; such a critical inspection of saddles and bridles that had never yet touched horses; such a cleaning and loading of revolvers and examining of bowie-knives; such a half-soling of the seats of pantaloons with serviceable buckskin; then such a poring over ancient maps; such a reading up of Bibles and Palestine travels; such a marking out of routes; such exasperating efforts to divide up the company into little bands of congenial spirits who might make the long and arduous journey without quarreling; and morning, noon and night, such mass-meetings in the cabins, such speech-making, such sage suggesting, such worrying and quarreling, and such a general raising of the very mischief, was never seen in the ship before!

But it is all over now. We are cut up into parties of six or eight, and by this time are scattered far and wide. Ours is the only one, however, that is venturing on what is called "the long trip"—that is, out into Syria, by Baalbec to Damascus, and thence down through the full length of Palestine. It would be a tedious, and also a too risky journey, at this hot season of the year, for any but strong, healthy men, accustomed somewhat to fatigue and rough life in the open air. The other parties will take shorter journeys.

For the last two months we have been in a worry about one portion of this Holy Land pilgrimage. I refer to transportation service. We knew very well that Palestine was a country which did not do a large passenger business, and every man we came across who knew any thing about it gave us to understand that not half of our party would be able to get dragomen and animals. At Constantinople every body fell to telegraphing the American Consuls at Alexandria and Beirout to give notice that we wanted dragomen and transportation. We were desperate—would take horses, jackasses, cameleopards, kangaroos—any thing. At Smyrna, more telegraphing was done, to the same end. Also, fearing for the worst, we telegraphed for a large number of seats in the diligence for Damascus, and horses for the ruins of Baalbec.

As might have been expected, a notion got abroad in Syria and Egypt that the whole population of the Province of America (the Turks consider us a trifling little province in some unvisited corner of the world,) were coming to the Holy Land—and so, when we got to Beirout yesterday, we found the place full of dragomen and their outfits. We had all intended to go by diligence to Damascus, and switch off to Baalbec as we went along—because we expected to rejoin the ship, go to Mount Carmel, and take to the woods from there. However, when our own private party of eight found that it was possible, and proper enough, to make the "long trip," we adopted that programme. We have never been much trouble to a Consul before, but we have been a fearful nuisance to our Consul at Beirout. I mention this because I can not help admiring his patience, his industry, and his accommodating spirit. I mention it also, because I think some of our ship's company did not give him as full credit for his excellent services as he deserved.

Well, out of our eight, three were selected to attend to all business connected with the expedition. The rest of us had nothing to do but look at the beautiful city of Beirout, with its bright, new houses nestled among a wilderness of green shrubbery spread abroad over an upland that sloped gently down to the sea; and also at the mountains of Lebanon that environ it; and likewise to bathe in the transparent blue water that rolled its billows about the ship (we did not know there were sharks there.) We had also to range up and down through the town and look at the costumes. These are picturesque and fanciful, but not so varied as at Constantinople and Smyrna; the women of Beirout add an agony—in the two former cities the sex wear a thin veil which one can see through (and they often expose their ancles,) but at Beirout they cover their entire faces with dark-colored or black veils, so that they look like mummies, and then expose their breasts to the public. A young gentleman (I believe he was a Greek,) volunteered to show us around the city, and said it would afford him great pleasure, because he was studying English and wanted practice in that language. When we had finished the rounds, however, he called for remuneration—said he hoped the gentlemen would give him a trifle in the way of a few piastres (equivalent to a few five cent pieces.) We did so. The Consul was surprised when he heard it, and said he knew the young fellow's family very well, and that they were an old and highly respectable family and worth a hundred and fifty thousand dollars! Some people, so situated, would have been ashamed of the berth he had with us and his manner of crawling into it.

At the appointed time our business committee reported, and said all things were in readiness—that we were to start to-day, with horses, pack animals, and tents, and go to Baalbec, Damascus, the Sea of Tiberias, and thence southward by the way of the scene of Jacob's Dream and other notable Bible localities to Jerusalem—from thence probably to the Dead Sea, but possibly not—and then strike for the ocean and rejoin the ship three or four weeks hence at Joppa; terms, five dollars a day apiece, in gold, and every thing to be furnished by the dragoman. They said we would live as well as at a hotel. I had read something like that before, and did not shame my judgment by believing a word of it. I said nothing, however, but packed up a blanket and a shawl to sleep in, pipes and tobacco, two or three woollen shirts, a portfolio, a guide-book, and a Bible. I also took along a towel and a cake of soap, to inspire respect in the Arabs, who would take me for a king in disguise.

We were to select our horses at 3 P. M. At that hour Abraham, the dragoman, marshaled them before us. With all solemnity I set it down here, that those horses were the hardest lot I ever did come across, and their accoutrements were in exquisite keeping with their style. One brute had an eye out; another had his tail sawed off close, like a rabbit, and was proud of it; another had a bony ridge running from his neck to his tail, like one of those ruined aqueducts one sees about Rome, and had a neck on him like a bowsprit; they all limped, and had sore backs, and likewise raw places and old scales scattered about their persons like brass nails in a hair trunk; their gaits were marvelous to contemplate, and replete with variety—under way the procession looked like a fleet in a storm. It was fearful. Blucher shook his head and said:

"That dragon is going to get himself into trouble fetching these old crates out of the hospital the way they are, unless he has got a permit."

I said nothing. The display was exactly according to the guide-book, and were we not traveling by the guide-book? I selected a certain horse because I thought I saw him shy, and I thought that a horse that had spirit enough to shy was not to be despised.

At 6 o'clock P. M., we came to a halt here on the breezy summit of a shapely mountain overlooking the sea, and the handsome valley where dwelt some of those enterprising Phœnicians of ancient times we read so much about; all around us are what were once the dominions of Hiram, King of Tyre, who furnished timber from the cedars of these Lebanon hills to build portions of King Solomon's Temple with.

Shortly after six, our pack train arrived. I had not seen it before, and a good right I had to be astonished. We had nineteen serving men and twenty-six pack mules! It was a perfect caravan. It looked like one, too, as it wound among the rocks. I wondered what in the very mischief we wanted with such a vast turn-out as that, for eight men. I wondered awhile, but soon I began to long for a tin plate, and some bacon and beans. I had camped out many and many a time before, and knew just what was coming. I went off, without waiting for serving men, and unsaddled my horse, and washed such portions of his ribs and his spine as projected through his hide, and when I came back, behold five stately circus tents were up—tents that were brilliant, within, with blue, and gold, and crimson, and all manner of splendid adornment! I was speechless. Then they brought eight little iron bedsteads, and set them up in the tents; they put a soft mattress and pillows and good blankets and two snow-white sheets on each bed. Next, they rigged a table about the centre-pole, and on it placed pewter pitchers, basins, soap, and the whitest of towels—one set for each man; they pointed to pockets in the tent, and said we could put our small trifles in them for convenience, and if we needed pins or such things, they were sticking every where. Then came the finishing touch—they spread carpets on the floor! I simply said, "If you call this camping out, all right—but it isn't the style *I* am used to; my little baggage that I brought along is at a discount."

It grew dark, and they put candles on the tables—candles set in bright, new, brazen candlesticks. And soon the bell—a genuine, simon-pure bell—rang, and we were invited to "the saloon." I had thought before that we had a tent or so too many, but now here was one, at least, provided for; it was to be used for nothing but an eating-saloon. Like the others, it was high enough for a family of giraffes to live in, and was very handsome and clean and bright-colored within. It was a gem of a place. A table for eight, and eight canvas chairs; a table-cloth and napkins whose whiteness and whose fineness laughed to scorn the things we were used to in the great excursion steamer; knives and forks, soup-plates, dinner-plates—every thing, in the handsomest kind of style. It was wonderful! And they call *this* camping out. Those stately fellows in baggy trowsers and turbaned fezzes brought in a dinner which consisted of roast mutton, roast chicken, roast goose, potatoes, bread, tea, pudding, apples, and delicious grapes; the viands were better cooked than any we had eaten for weeks, and the table made a finer appearance, with its large German silver candlesticks and other finery, than any table we had sat down to for a good while, and yet that polite dragoman, Abraham, came bowing in and apologizing for the whole affair, on account of the unavoidable confusion of getting under way for a very long trip, and promising to do a great deal better in future!

It is midnight, now, and we break camp at six in the morning.

They call this camping out. At this rate it is a glorious privilege to be a pilgrim to the Holy Land.

Chapter XLII

W E ARE CAMPED near *Temnin-el-Foka*—a name which the boys have simplified a good deal, for the sake of convenience in spelling. They call it Jacksonville. It sounds a little strangely, here in the Valley of Lebanon, but it has the merit of being easier to remember than the Arabic name.

"COME LIKE SPIRITS, SO DEPART."

"The night shall be filled with music,
    And the cares that infest the day
Shall fold their tents like the Arabs,
    And as silently steal away."

I slept very soundly last night, yet when the dragoman's bell rang at half-past five this morning and the cry went abroad of "Ten minutes to dress for breakfast!" I heard both. It surprised me, because I have not heard the breakfast gong in the ship for a month, and whenever we have had occasion to fire a salute at daylight, I have only found it out in the course of conversation afterward. However, camping out, even though it be in a gorgeous tent, makes one fresh and lively in the morning—especially if the air you are breathing is the cool, fresh air of the mountains.

I was dressed within the ten minutes, and came out. The saloon tent had been stripped of its sides, and had nothing left but its roof; so when we sat down to table we could look out over a noble panorama of mountain, sea and hazy valley. And sitting thus, the sun rose slowly up and suffused the picture with a world of rich coloring.

Hot mutton chops, fried chicken, omelettes, fried potatoes and coffee—all excellent. This was the bill of fare. It was sauced with a savage appetite purchased by hard riding the day before, and refreshing sleep in a pure atmosphere. As I called for a second cup of coffee, I glanced over my shoulder, and behold our white village was gone—the splendid tents had vanished like magic! It was wonderful how quickly those Arabs had "folded their tents;" and it was wonderful, also, how quickly they had gathered the thousand odds and ends of the camp together and disappeared with them.

By half-past six we were under way, and all the Syrian world seemed to be under way also. The road was filled with mule trains and long processions of camels. This reminds me that we have been trying for some time to think what a camel looks like, and now we have made it out. When he is down on all his knees, flat on his breast to receive his load, he looks something like a goose swimming; and when he is upright he looks like an ostrich with an extra set of legs. Camels are not beautiful, and their long under lip gives them an exceedingly "gallus"* expression. They have immense, flat, forked cushions of feet, that make a track in the dust like a pie with a slice cut out of it. They are not particular about their diet. They would eat a tombstone if they could bite it. A thistle grows about here which has needles on it that would pierce through leather, I think; if one touches you, you can find relief in nothing but profanity. The camels eat these. They show by their actions that they enjoy them. I suppose it would be a real treat to a camel to have a keg of nails for supper.

While I am speaking of animals, I will mention that I have a horse now by the name of "Jericho." He is a mare. I have seen remarkable horses before, but none so remarkable as this. I wanted a horse that could shy, and this one fills the bill. I had an idea that shying indicated spirit. If I was correct, I have got the most spirited horse on earth. He shies at every thing he comes across, with the utmost impartiality. He appears to have a mortal dread of telegraph poles, especially; and it is fortunate that these are on both sides of the road, because as it is now, I never fall off twice in succession on the same side. If I fell on the same side always, it would get to be monotonous after a while. This creature has scared at every thing he has seen to-day, except a haystack. He walked up to that with an intrepidity and a recklessness that were astonishing. And it would fill any one with admiration to see how he preserves his self-possession in the presence of a barley sack. This dare-devil bravery will be the death of this horse some day.

*Excuse the slang—no other word will describe it.

He is not particularly fast, but I think he will get me through the Holy Land. He has only one fault. His tail has been chopped off or else he has sat down on it too hard, some time or other, and he has to fight the flies with his heels. This is all very well, but when he tries to kick a fly off the top of his head with his hind foot, it is too much variety. He is going to get himself into trouble that way some day. He reaches around and bites my legs too. I do not care particularly about that, only I do not like to see a horse too sociable.

I think the owner of this prize had a wrong opinion about him. He had an idea that he was one of those fiery, untamed steeds, but he is not of that character. I know the Arab had this idea, because when he brought the horse out for inspection in Beirout, he kept jerking at the bridle and shouting in Arabic, "Ho! will you? Do you want to run away, you ferocious beast, and break your neck?" when all the time the horse was not doing any thing in the world, and only looked like he wanted to lean up against something and think. Whenever he is not shying at things, or reaching after a fly, he wants to do that yet. How it would surprise his owner to know this.

We have been in a historical section of country all day. At noon we camped three hours and took luncheon at Mekseh, near the junction of the Lebanon Mountains and the Jebel el Kuneiyiseh, and looked down into the immense, level, garden-like Valley of Lebanon. To-night we are camping near the same valley, and have a very wide sweep of it in view. We can see the long, whale-backed ridge of Mount Hermon projecting above the eastern hills. The "dews of Hermon" are falling upon us now, and the tents are almost soaked with them.

Over the way from us, and higher up the valley, we can discern, through the glasses, the faint outlines of the wonderful ruins of Baalbec, the supposed Baal-Gad of Scripture. Joshua, and another person, were the two spies who were sent into this land of Canaan by the children of Israel to report upon its character—I mean they were the spies who reported favorably. They took back with them some specimens of the grapes of this country, and in the children's picture-books they are always represented as bearing one monstrous bunch swung to a pole between them, a respectable load for a pack-train. The Sunday-school books exaggerated it a little. The grapes are most excellent to this day, but the bunches are not as large as those in the pictures. I was surprised and hurt when I saw them, because those colossal bunches of grapes were one of my most cherished juvenile traditions.

Joshua reported favorably, and the children of Israel journeyed on, with Moses at the head of the general government, and Joshua in command of the army of six hundred thousand fighting men. Of women and children and civilians there was a countless swarm. Of all that mighty host, none but the two faithful spies ever lived to set their feet in the Promised Land. They and their descendants wandered forty years in the desert, and then Moses, the gifted warrior, poet, statesman and philosopher, went up into Pisgah and met his mysterious fate. Where he was buried no man knows—for

> " *   *   *   no man dug that sepulchre,
>   And no man saw it e'er—
>   For the Sons of God upturned the sod
>   And laid the dead man there!"

Then Joshua began his terrible raid, and from Jericho clear to this Baal-Gad, he swept the land like the Genius of Destruction. He slaughtered the people, laid waste their soil, and razed their cities to the ground. He wasted thirty-one kings also. One may call it that, though really it can hardly be called wasting them, because there were always plenty of kings in those days, and to spare. At any rate, he destroyed thirty-one kings, and divided up their realms among his Israelites. He divided up this valley stretched out here before us, and so it was once Jewish territory. The Jews have long since disappeared from it, however.

Back yonder, an hour's journey from here, we passed through an Arab village of stone dry-goods boxes (they look like that,) where Noah's tomb lies under lock and key. [Noah built the ark.] Over these old hills and valleys the ark that contained all that was left of a vanished world once floated.

I make no apology for detailing the above information. It will be news to some of my readers, at any rate.

Noah's tomb is built of stone, and is covered with a long

stone building. Bucksheesh let us in. The building had to be long, because the grave of the honored old navigator is two hundred and ten feet long itself! It is only about four feet high, though. He must have cast a shadow like a lightning-rod. The proof that this is the genuine spot where Noah was buried can only be doubted by uncommonly incredulous people. The evidence is pretty straight. Shem, the son of Noah, was present at the burial, and showed the place to his descendants, who transmitted the knowledge to their descendants, and the lineal descendants of these introduced themselves to us to-day. It was pleasant to make the acquaintance of members of so respectable a family. It was a thing to be proud of. It was the next thing to being acquainted with Noah himself.

Noah's memorable voyage will always possess a living interest for me, henceforward.

If ever an oppressed race existed, it is this one we see fettered around us under the inhuman tyranny of the Ottoman Empire. I wish Europe would let Russia annihilate Turkey a little—not much, but enough to make it difficult to find the place again without a divining-rod or a diving-bell. The Syrians are very poor, and yet they are ground down by a system of taxation that would drive any other nation frantic. Last year their taxes were heavy enough, in all conscience—but this year they have been increased by the addition of taxes that were forgiven them in times of famine in former years. On top of this the Government has levied a tax of *one-tenth* of the whole proceeds of the land. This is only half the story. The Pacha of a Pachalic does not trouble himself with appointing tax-collectors. He figures up what all these taxes ought to amount to in a certain district. Then he farms the collection out. He calls the rich men together, the highest bidder gets the speculation, pays the Pacha on the spot, and then sells out to smaller fry, who sell in turn to a piratical horde of still smaller fry. These latter compel the peasant to bring his little trifle of grain to the village, at his own cost. It must be weighed, the various taxes set apart, and the remainder returned to the producer. But the collector delays this duty day after day, while the producer's family are perishing for bread; at last the poor wretch, who can not but understand the game, says, "Take a quarter—take half—take two-thirds if you will, and let me go!" It is a most outrageous state of things.

These people are naturally good-hearted and intelligent, and with education and liberty, would be a happy and contented race. They often appeal to the stranger to know if the great world will not some day come to their relief and save them. The Sultan has been lavishing money like water in England and Paris, but his subjects are suffering for it now.

This fashion of camping out bewilders me. We have boot-jacks and a bath-tub, now, and yet all the mysteries the pack-mules carry are not revealed. What next?

Chapter XLIII

WE HAD A tedious ride of about five hours, in the sun, across the Valley of Lebanon. It proved to be not quite so much of a garden as it had seemed from the hill-sides. It was a desert, weed-grown waste, littered thickly with stones the size of a man's fist. Here and there the natives had scratched the ground and reared a sickly crop of grain, but for the most part the valley was given up to a handful of shepherds, whose flocks were doing what they honestly could to get a living, but the chances were against them. We saw rude piles of stones standing near the roadside, at intervals, and recognized the custom of marking boundaries which obtained in Jacob's time. There were no walls, no fences, no hedges—nothing to secure a man's possessions but these random heaps of stones. The Israelites held them sacred in the old patriarchal times, and these other Arabs, their lineal descendants, do so likewise. An American, of ordinary intelligence, would soon widely extend his property, at an outlay of mere manual labor, performed at night, under so loose a system of fencing as this.

The plows these people use are simply a sharpened stick, such as Abraham plowed with, and they still winnow their wheat as he did—they pile it on the house-top, and then toss it by shovel-fulls into the air until the wind has blown all the chaff away. They never invent any thing, never learn any thing.

We had a fine race, of a mile, with an Arab perched on a camel. Some of the horses were fast, and made very good time, but the camel scampered by them without any very great effort. The yelling and shouting, and whipping and galloping, of all parties interested, made it an exhilarating, exciting, and particularly boisterous race.

At eleven o'clock, our eyes fell upon the walls and columns of Baalbec, a noble ruin whose history is a sealed book. It has stood there for thousands of years, the wonder and admiration of travelers; but who built it, or when it was built, are questions that may never be answered. One thing is very sure, though. Such grandeur of design, and such grace of execution, as one sees in the temples of Baalbec, have not been equaled or even approached in any work of men's hands that has been built within twenty centuries past.

The great Temple of the Sun, the Temple of Jupiter, and several smaller temples, are clustered together in the midst of one of these miserable Syrian villages, and look strangely enough in such plebeian company. These temples are built upon massive substructions that might support a world, almost; the materials used are blocks of stone as large as an omnibus—very few, if any of them, are smaller than a carpenter's tool chest—and these substructions are traversed by tunnels of masonry through which a train of cars might pass. With such foundations as these, it is little wonder that Baalbec has lasted so long. The Temple of the Sun is nearly three hundred feet long and one hundred and sixty feet wide. It had fifty-four columns around it, but only six are standing now—the others lie broken at its base, a confused and picturesque heap. The six columns are perfect, as also are their bases, Corinthian capitals and entablature—and six more shapely columns do not exist. The columns and the entablature together are ninety feet high—a prodigious altitude for shafts of stone to reach, truly—and yet one only thinks of their beauty and symmetry when looking at them; the pillars look slender and delicate, the entablature, with its elaborate sculpture, looks like rich stucco-work. But when you have gazed aloft till your eyes are weary, you glance at the great fragments of pillars among which you are standing, and find that they are eight feet through; and with them lie beautiful capitals apparently as large as a small cottage; and also single slabs of stone, superbly sculptured, that are four or five feet thick, and would completely cover the floor of any ordinary parlor. You wonder where these monstrous things came from, and it takes some little time to satisfy yourself that the airy and graceful fabric that towers above your head is made up of their mates. It seems too preposterous.

The Temple of Jupiter is a smaller ruin than the one I have been speaking of, and yet is immense. It is in a tolerable state of preservation. One row of nine columns stands almost uninjured. They are sixty-five feet high and support a sort of porch or roof, which connects them with the roof of the building. This porch-roof is composed of tremendous slabs of stone, which are so finely sculptured on the under side that the work looks like a fresco from below. One or two of these slabs had fallen, and again I wondered if the gigantic masses of carved stone that lay about me were no larger than those above my head. Within the temple, the ornamentation was elaborate and colossal. What a wonder of architectural beauty and grandeur this edifice must have been when it was new! And what a noble picture it and its statelier companion, with the chaos of mighty fragments scattered about them, yet makes in the moonlight!

I can not conceive how those immense blocks of stone were ever hauled from the quarries, or how they were ever raised to the dizzy heights they occupy in the temples. And yet these sculptured blocks are trifles in size compared with the rough-hewn blocks that form the wide verandah or platform which surrounds the Great Temple. One stretch of that platform, two hundred feet long, is composed of blocks of stone as large, and some of them larger, than a street-car. They surmount a wall about ten or twelve feet high. I thought those were large rocks, but they sank into insignificance compared with those which formed another section of the platform. These were three in number, and I thought that each of them was about as long as three street cars placed end to end, though of course they are a third wider and a third higher than a street car. Perhaps two railway freight cars of the largest pattern, placed end to end, might better represent their size. In combined length these three stones stretch nearly two hundred feet; they are thirteen feet square; two of them are sixty-four feet long each, and the third is sixty-nine. They are built into the massive wall some twenty feet above the ground. They are there, but how they got there is the question. I have seen the hull of a steamboat that was smaller than one of those stones. All these great walls are as exact and shapely as the flimsy things we build of bricks in these days. A race of gods or of giants must have inhabited Baalbec many a century ago. Men like the men of our day could hardly rear such temples as these.

We went to the quarry from whence the stones of Baalbec were taken. It was about a quarter of a mile off, and down hill. In a great pit lay the mate of the largest stone in the ruins. It lay there just as the giants of that old forgotten time had left it when they were called hence—just as they had left it, to remain for thousands of years, an eloquent rebuke unto such as are prone to think slightingly of the men who lived before them. This enormous block lies there, squared and ready for the builders' hands—a solid mass fourteen feet by seventeen, and but a few inches less than seventy feet long! Two buggies could be driven abreast of each other, on its surface, from one end of it to the other, and leave room enough for a man or two to walk on either side.

One might swear that all the John Smiths and George Wilkinsons, and all the other pitiful nobodies between Kingdom Come and Baalbec would inscribe their poor little names upon the walls of Baalbec's magnificent ruins, and would add the town, the county and the State they came from—and swearing thus, be infallibly correct. It is a pity some great ruin does not fall in and flatten out some of these reptiles, and scare their kind out of ever giving their names to fame upon any walls or monuments again, forever.

Properly, with the sorry relics we bestrode, it was a three days' journey to Damascus. It was necessary that we should do it in less than two. It was necessary because our three pilgrims would not travel on the Sabbath day. We were all perfectly willing to keep the Sabbath day, but there are times when to keep the *letter* of a sacred law whose spirit is righteous, becomes a sin, and this was a case in point. We pleaded for the tired, ill-treated horses, and tried to show that their faithful service deserved kindness in return, and their hard lot compassion. But when did ever self-righteousness know the sentiment of pity? What were a few long hours added to the hardships of some over-taxed brutes when weighed against the peril of those human souls? It was not the most promising party to travel with and hope to gain a higher veneration for religion through the example of its devotees. We said the Saviour who pitied dumb beasts and taught that the ox must be rescued from the mire even on the Sabbath day, would not have counseled a forced march like this. We said the "long trip" was exhausting and therefore dangerous in the blistering heats of summer, even when the ordinary days' stages were traversed, and if we persisted in this hard march, some of us might be stricken down with the fevers of the country in consequence of it. Nothing could move the pilgrims. They *must* press on. Men might die, horses might die, but they must enter upon holy soil next week, with no Sabbath-breaking stain upon them. Thus they were willing to commit a sin against the spirit of religious law, in order that they might preserve the letter of it. It was not worth while to tell them "the letter kills." I am talking now about personal friends; men whom I like; men who are good citizens; who are honorable, upright, conscientious; but whose idea of the Saviour's religion seems to me distorted. They lecture our shortcomings unsparingly, and every night they call us together and read to us chapters from the Testament that are full of gentleness, of charity, and of tender mercy; and then all the next day they stick to their saddles clear up to the summits of these rugged mountains, and clear down again. Apply the Testament's gentleness, and charity, and tender mercy to a toiling, worn and weary horse?—Nonsense— these are for God's human creatures, not His dumb ones. What the pilgrims choose to do, respect for their almost sacred character demands that I should allow to pass—but I would so like to catch any other member of the party riding his horse up one of these exhausting hills once!

We have given the pilgrims a good many examples that might benefit them, but it is virtue thrown away. They have never heard a cross word out of our lips toward each other— but *they* have quarreled once or twice. We love to hear them at it, after they have been lecturing us. The very first thing they did, coming ashore at Beirout, was to quarrel in the boat. I have said I like them, and I do like them—but every time they read me a scorcher of a lecture I mean to talk back in print.

Not content with doubling the legitimate stages, they switched off the main road and went away out of the way to visit an absurd fountain called Figia, because Baalam's ass had drank there once. So we journeyed on, through the terrible hills and decerts and the roasting sun, and then far into the night, seeking the honored pool of Baalam's ass, the patron saint of all pilgrims like us. I find no entry but this in my note-book:

"Rode to-day, altogether, thirteen hours, through deserts, partly, and partly over barren, unsightly hills, and latterly through wild, rocky scenery, and camped at about eleven o'clock at night on the banks of a limpid stream, near a Syrian village. Do not know its name—do not wish to know it—want to go to bed. Two horses lame (mine and Jack's) and the others worn out. Jack and I walked three or four miles, over the hills, and led the horses. Fun—but of a mild type."

Twelve or thirteen hours in the saddle, even in a Christian land and a Christian climate, and on a good horse, is a tire-some journey; but in an oven like Syria, in a ragged spoon of a saddle that slips fore-and-aft, and "thort-ships," and every way, and on a horse that is tired and lame, and yet must be whipped and spurred with hardly a moment's cessation all day long, till the blood comes from his side, and your con-science hurts you every time you strike, if you are half a man,—it is a journey to be remembered in bitterness of spirit and execrated with emphasis for a liberal division of a man's lifetime.

Chapter XLIV

THE NEXT DAY was an outrage upon men and horses both. It was another thirteen-hour stretch (including an hour's "nooning.") It was over the barrenest chalk-hills and through the baldest canons that even Syria can show. The heat quivered in the air every where. In the canons we almost smothered in the baking atmosphere. On high ground, the reflection from the chalk-hills was blinding. It was cruel to urge the crippled horses, but it had to be done in order to make Damascus Saturday night. We saw ancient tombs and temples of fanciful architecture carved out of the solid rock high up in the face of precipices above our heads, but we had neither time nor strength to climb up there and examine them. The terse language of my note-book will answer for the rest of this day's experiences:

"Broke camp at 7 A. M., and made a ghastly trip through the Zeb Dana valley and the rough mountains—horses limping and that Arab screech-owl that does most of the singing and carries the water-skins, always a thousand miles ahead, of course, and no water to drink—will he *never* die? Beautiful stream in a chasm, lined thick with pomegranate, fig, olive and quince orchards, and nooned an hour at the celebrated Baalam's Ass Fountain of Figia, second in size in Syria, and the coldest water out of Siberia—guide-books do not say Baalam's ass ever drank there—somebody been imposing on the pilgrims, may be. Bathed in it—Jack and I. Only a second—ice-water. It is the principal source of the Abana river—only one-half mile down to where it joins. Beautiful place—giant trees all around—*so* shady and cool, if one could keep awake—vast stream gushes straight out from under the mountain in a torrent. Over it is a very ancient ruin, with no known history—supposed to have been for the worship of the deity of the fountain or Baalam's ass or somebody. Wretched nest of human vermin about the fountain—rags, dirt, sunken cheeks, pallor of sickness, sores, projecting bones, dull, aching misery in their eyes and ravenous hunger speaking from every eloquent fibre and muscle from head to foot. How they sprang upon a bone, how they crunched the bread we gave them! Such as these to swarm about one and watch every bite he takes, with greedy looks, and swallow unconsciously every time he swallows, as if they half fancied the precious morsel went down their own throats—

hurry up the caravan!—I never shall enjoy a meal in this distressful country. To think of eating three times every day under *such* circumstances for three weeks yet—it is worse punishment than riding all day in the sun. There are sixteen starving babies from one to six years old in the party, and their legs are no larger than broom handles. Left the fountain at 1 P. M. (the fountain took us at least two hours out of our way,) and reached Mahomet's lookout perch, over Damascus, in time to get a good long look before it was necessary to move on. Tired? Ask of the winds that far away with fragments strewed the sea."

As the glare of day mellowed into twilight, we looked down upon a picture which is celebrated all over the world. I think I have read about four hundred times that when Mahomet was a simple camel-driver he reached this point and looked down upon Damascus for the first time, and then made a certain renowned remark. He said man could enter only one paradise; he preferred to go to the one above. So he sat down there and feasted his eyes upon the earthly paradise of Damascus, and then went away without entering its gates. They have erected a tower on the hill to mark the spot where he stood.

Damascus *is* beautiful from the mountain. It is beautiful even to foreigners accustomed to luxuriant vegetation, and I can easily understand how unspeakably beautiful it must be to eyes that are only used to the God-forsaken barrenness and desolation of Syria. I should think a Syrian would go wild with ecstacy when such a picture bursts upon him for the first time.

From his high perch, one sees before him and below him, a wall of dreary mountains, shorn of vegetation, glaring fiercely in the sun; it fences in a level desert of yellow sand, smooth as velvet and threaded far away with fine lines that stand for roads, and dotted with creeping mites we know are camel-trains and journeying men; right in the midst of the desert is spread a billowy expanse of green foliage; and nestling in its heart sits the great white city, like an island of pearls and opals gleaming out of a sea of emeralds. This is the picture you see spread far below you, with distance to soften it, the sun to glorify it, strong contrasts to heighten the effects, and over it and about it a drowsing air of repose to spiritualize it and make it seem rather a beautiful estray from the mysterious worlds we visit in dreams than a substantial tenant of our coarse, dull globe. And when you think of the leagues of blighted, blasted, sandy, rocky, sun-burnt, ugly, dreary, infamous country you have ridden over to get here, you think it is the most beautiful, beautiful picture that ever human eyes rested upon in all the broad universe! If I were to go to Damascus again, I would camp on Mahomet's hill about a week, and then go away. There is no need to go inside the walls. The Prophet was wise without knowing it when he decided not to go down into the paradise of Damascus.

There is an honored old tradition that the immense garden which Damascus stands in was the Garden of Eden, and modern writers have gathered up many chapters of evidence tending to show that it really was the Garden of Eden, and that the rivers Pharpar and Abana are the "two rivers" that watered Adam's Paradise. It may be so, but it is not paradise now, and one would be as happy outside of it as he would be likely to be within. It is so crooked and cramped and dirty that one can not realize that he is in the splendid city he saw from the hill-top. The gardens are hidden by high mud-walls, and the paradise is become a very sink of pollution and uncomeliness. Damascus has plenty of clear, pure water in it, though, and this is enough, of itself, to make an Arab think it beautiful and blessed. Water is scarce in blistered Syria. We run railways by our large cities in America; in Syria they curve the roads so as to make them run by the meagre little puddles they call "fountains," and which are not found oftener on a journey than every four hours. But the "rivers" of Pharpar and Abana of Scripture (mere creeks,) run through Damascus, and so every house and every garden have their sparkling fountains and rivulets of water. With her forest of foliage and her abundance of water, Damascus must be a wonder of wonders to the Bedouin from the deserts. Damascus is simply an oasis—that is what it is. For four thousand years its waters have not gone dry or its fertility failed. Now we can understand why the city has existed so long. It could not die. So long as its waters remain to it away out there in the midst of that howling desert, so long will Damascus live to bless the sight of the tired and thirsty wayfarer.

"Though old as history itself, thou art fresh as the breath of spring, blooming as thine own rose-bud, and fragrant as thine own orange flower, O Damascus, pearl of the East!"

Damascus dates back anterior to the days of Abraham, and is the oldest city in the world. It was founded by Uz, the grandson of Noah. "The early history of Damascus is shrouded in the mists of a hoary antiquity." Leave the matters written of in the first eleven chapters of the Old Testament out, and no recorded event has occurred in the world but Damascus was in existence to receive the news of it. Go back as far as you will into the vague past, there was always a Damascus. In the writings of every century for more than four thousand years, its name has been mentioned and its praises sung. To Damascus, years are only moments, decades are only flitting trifles of time. She measures time, not by days and months and years, but by the empires she has seen rise, and prosper and crumble to ruin. She is a type of immortality. She saw the foundations of Baalbec, and Thebes, and Ephesus laid; she saw these villages grow into mighty cities, and amaze the world with their grandeur—and she has lived to see them desolate, deserted, and given over to the owls and the bats. She saw the Israelitish empire exalted, and she saw it annihilated. She saw Greece rise, and flourish two thousand years, and die. In her old age she saw Rome built; she saw it overshadow the world with its power; she saw it perish. The few hundreds of years of Genoese and Venetian might and splendor were, to grave old Damascus, only a trifling scintillation hardly worth remembering. Damascus has seen all that has ever occurred on earth, and still she lives. She has looked upon the dry bones of a thousand empires, and will see the tombs of a thousand more before she dies. Though another claims the name, old Damascus is by right the Eternal City.

We reached the city gates just at sundown. They do say that one can get into any walled city of Syria, after night, for bucksheesh, except Damascus. But Damascus, with its four thousand years of respectability in the world, has many old fogy notions. There are no street lamps there, and the law compels all who go abroad at night to carry lanterns, just as was the case in old days, when heroes and heroines of the

Arabian Nights walked the streets of Damascus, or flew away toward Bagdad on enchanted carpets.

It was fairly dark a few minutes after we got within the wall, and we rode long distances through wonderfully crooked streets, eight to ten feet wide, and shut in on either side by the high mud-walls of the gardens. At last we got to where lanterns could be seen flitting about here and there, and knew we were in the midst of the curious old city. In a little narrow street, crowded with our pack-mules and with a swarm of uncouth Arabs, we alighted, and through a kind of a hole in the wall entered the hotel. We stood in a great flagged court, with flowers and citron trees about us, and a huge tank in the centre that was receiving the waters of many pipes. We crossed the court and entered the rooms prepared to receive four of us. In a large marble-paved recess between the two rooms was a tank of clear, cool water, which was kept running over all the time by the streams that were pouring into it from half a dozen pipes. Nothing, in this scorching, desolate land could look so refreshing as this pure water flashing in the lamp-light; nothing could look so beautiful, nothing could sound so delicious as this mimic rain to ears long unaccustomed to sounds of such a nature. Our rooms were large, comfortably furnished, and even had their floors clothed with soft, cheerful-tinted carpets. It was a pleasant thing to see a carpet again, for if there is any thing drearier than the tomb-like, stone-paved parlors and bed-rooms of Europe and Asia, I do not know what it is. They make one think of the grave all the time. A very broad, gaily caparisoned divan, some twelve or fourteen feet long, extended across one side of each room, and opposite were single beds with spring mattrasses. There were great looking-glasses and marble-top tables. All this luxury was as grateful to systems and senses worn out with an exhausting day's travel, as it was unexpected—for one can not tell what to expect in a Turkish city of even a quarter of a million inhabitants.

I do not know, but I think they used that tank between the rooms to draw drinking water from; that did not occur to me, however, until I had dipped my baking head far down into its cool depths. I thought of it then, and superb as the bath was, I was sorry I had taken it, and was about to go and explain to the landlord. But a finely curled and scented poodle dog frisked up and nipped the calf of my leg just then, and before I had time to think, I had soused him to the bottom of the tank, and when I saw a servant coming with a pitcher I went off and left the pup trying to climb out and not succeeding very well. Satisfied revenge was all I needed to make me perfectly happy, and when I walked in to supper that first night in Damascus I was in that condition. We lay on those divans a long time, after supper, smoking narghilies and long-stemmed chibouks, and talking about the dreadful ride of the day, and I knew then what I had sometimes known before—that it is worth while to get tired out, because one so enjoys resting afterward.

In the morning we sent for donkeys. It is worthy of note that we had to *send* for these things. I said Damascus was an old fossil, and she is. Any where else we would have been assailed by a clamorous army of donkey-drivers, guides, peddlers and beggars—but in Damascus they so hate the very sight of a foreign Christian that they want no intercourse whatever with him; only a year or two ago, his person was not always safe in Damascus streets. It is the most fanatical Mohammedan purgatory out of Arabia. Where you see one green turban of a Hadji elsewhere (the honored sign that my lord has made the pilgrimage to Mecca,) I think you will see a dozen in Damascus. The Damascenes are the ugliest, wickedest looking villains we have seen. All the veiled women we had seen yet, nearly, left their eyes exposed, but numbers of these in Damascus completely hid the face under a close-drawn black veil that made the woman look like a mummy. If ever we caught an eye exposed it was quickly hidden from our contaminating Christian vision; the beggars actually passed us by without demanding bucksheesh; the merchants in the bazaars did not hold up their goods and cry out eagerly, "Hey, John!" or "Look this, Howajji!" On the contrary, they only scowled at us and said never a word.

The narrow streets swarmed like a hive with men and women in strange Oriental costumes, and our small donkeys knocked them right and left as we plowed through them, urged on by the merciless donkey-boys. These persecutors run after the animals, shouting and goading them for hours together; they keep the donkey in a gallop always, yet never get tired themselves or fall behind. The donkeys fell down and spilt us over their heads occasionally, but there was nothing for it but to mount and hurry on again. We were banged against sharp corners, loaded porters, camels, and citizens generally; and we were so taken up with looking out for collisions and casualties that we had no chance to look about us at all. We rode half through the city and through the famous "street which is called Straight" without seeing any thing, hardly. Our bones were nearly knocked out of joint, we were wild with excitement, and our sides ached with the jolting we had suffered. I do not like riding in the Damascus street-cars.

We were on our way to the reputed houses of Judas and Ananias. About eighteen or nineteen hundred years ago, Saul, a native of Tarsus, was particularly bitter against the new sect called Christians, and he left Jerusalem and started across the country on a furious crusade against them. He went forth "breathing threatenings and slaughter against the disciples of the Lord."

"And as he journeyed, he came near Damascus, and suddenly there shined round about him a light from heaven:

"And he fell to the earth and heard a voice saying unto him, 'Saul, Saul, why persecutest thou me?'

"And when he knew that it was Jesus that spoke to him he trembled, and was astonished, and said, 'Lord, what wilt thou have me to do?'"

He was told to arise and go into the ancient city and one would tell him what to do. In the meantime his soldiers stood speechless and awe-stricken, for they heard the mysterious voice but saw no man. Saul rose up and found that that fierce supernatural light had destroyed his sight, and he was blind, so "they led him by the hand and brought him to Damascus." He was converted.

Paul lay three days, blind, in the house of Judas, and during that time he neither ate nor drank.

There came a voice to a citizen of Damascus, named Ananias, saying, "Arise, and go into the street which is called Straight, and inquire at the house of Judas, for one called Saul, of Tarsus; for behold, he prayeth."

Ananias did not wish to go at first, for he had heard of Saul before, and he had his doubts about that style of a "chosen vessel" to preach the gospel of peace. However, in obedience to orders, he went into the "street called Straight" (how he ever found his way into it, and after he did, how he ever found his way out of it again, are mysteries only to be accounted for by the fact that he was acting under Divine inspiration.) He found Paul and restored him, and ordained him a preacher; and from this old house we had hunted up in the street which is miscalled Straight, he had started out on that bold missionary career which he prosecuted till his death. It was not the house of the disciple who sold the Master for thirty pieces of silver. I make this explanation in justice to Judas, who was a far different sort of man from the person just referred to. A very different style of man, and lived in a very good house. It is a pity we do not know more about him.

I have given, in the above paragraphs, some more information for people who will not read Bible history until they are defrauded into it by some such method as this. I hope that no friend of progress and education will obstruct or interfere with my peculiar mission.

The street called Straight is straighter than a corkscrew, but not as straight as a rainbow. St. Luke is careful not to commit himself; he does not say it is the street which *is* straight, but the "street which is *called* Straight." It is a fine piece of irony; it is the only facetious remark in the Bible, I believe. We traversed the street called Straight a good way, and then turned off and called at the reputed house of Ananias. There is small question that a part of the original house is there still; it is an old room twelve or fifteen feet under ground, and its masonry is evidently ancient. If Ananias did not live there in St. Paul's time, somebody else did, which is just as well. I took a drink out of Ananias' well, and singularly enough, the water was just as fresh as if the well had been dug yesterday.

We went out toward the north end of the city to see the place where the disciples let Paul down over the Damascus wall at dead of night—for he preached Christ so fearlessly in Damascus that the people sought to kill him, just as they would to-day for the same offense, and he had to escape and flee to Jerusalem.

Then we called at the tomb of Mahomet's children and at a tomb which purported to be that of St. George who killed the dragon, and so on out to the hollow place under a rock where Paul hid during his flight till his pursuers gave him up; and to the mausoleum of the five thousand Christians who were massacred in Damascus in 1861 by the Turks. They say those narrow streets ran blood for several days, and that men, women and children were butchered indiscriminately and left to rot by hundreds all through the Christian quarter; they say, further, that the stench was dreadful. All the Christians who could get away fled from the city, and the Mohammedans would not defile their hands by burying the "infidel dogs." The thirst for blood extended to the high lands of Hermon and Anti-Lebanon, and in a short time twenty-five thousand more Christians were massacred and their possessions laid waste. How they hate a Christian in Damascus!—and pretty much all over Turkeydom as well. And how they will pay for it when Russia turns her guns upon them again!

It is soothing to the heart to abuse England and France for interposing to save the Ottoman Empire from the destruction it has so richly deserved for a thousand years. It hurts my vanity to see these pagans refuse to eat of food that has been cooked for us; or to eat from a dish we have eaten from; or to drink from a goatskin which we have polluted with our Christian lips, except by filtering the water through a rag which they put over the mouth of it or through a sponge! I never disliked a Chinaman as I do these degraded Turks and Arabs, and when Russia is ready to war with them again, I hope England and France will not find it good breeding or good judgment to interfere.

In Damascus they think there are no such rivers in all the world as their little Abana and Pharpar. The Damascenes have always thought that way. In 2 Kings, chapter v., Naaman boasts extravagantly about them. That was three thousand years ago. He says: "Are not Abana and Pharpar, rivers of Damascus, better than all the waters of Israel? May I not wash in them and be clean?" But some of my readers have forgotten who Naaman was, long ago. Naaman was the commander of the Syrian armies. He was the favorite of the king and lived in great state. "He was a mighty man of valor, but he was a leper." Strangely enough, the house they point out to you now as his, has been turned into a leper hospital, and the inmates expose their horrid deformities and hold up their hands and beg for bucksheesh when a stranger enters.

One can not appreciate the horror of this disease until he looks upon it in all its ghastliness, in Naaman's ancient dwelling in Damascus. Bones all twisted out of shape, great knots protruding from face and body, joints decaying and dropping away—horrible!

Chapter XLV

THE LAST twenty-four hours we staid in Damascus I lay prostrate with a violent attack of cholera, or cholera morbus, and therefore had a good chance and a good excuse to lie there on that wide divan and take an honest rest. I had nothing to do but listen to the pattering of the fountains and take medicine and throw it up again. It was dangerous recreation, but it was pleasanter than traveling in Syria. I had plenty of snow from Mount Hermon, and as it would not stay on my stomach, there was nothing to interfere with my eating it—there was always room for more. I enjoyed myself very well. Syrian travel has its interesting features, like travel in any other part of the world, and yet to break your leg or have the cholera adds a welcome variety to it.

We left Damascus at noon and rode across the plain a couple of hours, and then the party stopped a while in the shade of some fig-trees to give me a chance to rest. It was the hottest day we had seen yet—the sun-flames shot down like the shafts of fire that stream out before a blow-pipe; the rays seemed to fall in a steady deluge on the head and pass downward like rain from a roof. I imagined I could distinguish between the floods of rays—I thought I could tell when each flood struck my head, when it reached my shoulders, and when the next one came. It was terrible. All the desert glared so fiercely that my eyes were swimming in tears all the time. The boys had white umbrellas heavily lined with dark green. They were a priceless blessing. I thanked fortune that I had one, too, notwithstanding it was packed up with the baggage and was ten miles ahead. It is madness to travel in Syria without an umbrella. They told me in Beirout (these people who always gorge you with advice) that it was madness to travel in Syria without an umbrella. It was on this account that I got one.

But, honestly, I think an umbrella is a nuisance any where when its business is to keep the sun off. No Arab wears a brim to his fez, or uses an umbrella, or any thing to shade his eyes or his face, and he always looks comfortable and proper in the sun. But of all the ridiculous sights I ever have seen,

our party of eight is the most so—they do cut such an outlandish figure. They travel single file; they all wear the endless
white rag of Constantinople wrapped round and round their
hats and dangling down their backs; they all wear thick green
spectacles, with side-glasses to them; they all hold white umbrellas, lined with green, over their heads; without exception
their stirrups are too short—they are the very worst gang of
horsemen on earth; their animals to a horse trot fearfully
hard—and when they get strung out one after the other;
glaring straight ahead and breathless; bouncing high and out
of turn, all along the line; knees well up and stiff, elbows
flapping like a rooster's that is going to crow, and the long
file of umbrellas popping convulsively up and down—when
one sees this outrageous picture exposed to the light of day,
he is amazed that the gods don't get out their thunderbolts
and destroy them off the face of the earth! I do—I wonder
at it. I wouldn't let any such caravan go through a country of
mine.

And when the sun drops below the horizon and the boys
close their umbrellas and put them under their arms, it is only
a variation of the picture, not a modification of its absurdity.

But may be you can not see the wild extravagance of my
panorama. You could if you were here. Here, you feel all the
time just as if you were living about the year 1200 before
Christ—or back to the patriarchs—or forward to the New
Era. The scenery of the Bible is about you—the customs of
the patriarchs are around you—the same people, in the same
flowing robes, and in sandals, cross your path—the same
long trains of stately camels go and come—the same impressive religious solemnity and silence rest upon the desert and
the mountains that were upon them in the remote ages of
antiquity, and behold, intruding upon a scene like this, comes
this fantastic mob of green-spectacled Yanks, with their flapping elbows and bobbing umbrellas! It is Daniel in the lion's
den with a green cotton umbrella under his arm, all over
again.

My umbrella is with the baggage, and so are my green
spectacles—and there they shall stay. I will not use them. I
will show some respect for the eternal fitness of things. It will
be bad enough to get sun-struck, without looking ridiculous

into the bargain. If I fall, let me fall bearing about me the semblance of a Christian, at least.

Three or four hours out from Damascus we passed the spot where Saul was so abruptly converted, and from this place we looked back over the scorching desert, and had our last glimpse of beautiful Damascus, decked in its robes of shining green. After nightfall we reached our tents, just outside of the nasty Arab village of Jonesborough. Of course the real name of the place is El something or other, but the boys still refuse to recognize the Arab names or try to pronounce them. When I say that that village is of the usual style, I mean to insinuate that all Syrian villages within fifty miles of Damascus are alike—so much alike that it would require more than human intelligence to tell wherein one differed from another. A Syrian village is a hive of huts one story high (the height of a man,) and as square as a dry-goods box; it is mud-plastered all over, flat roof and all, and generally whitewashed after a fashion. The same roof often extends over half the town, covering many of the *streets*, which are generally about a yard wide. When you ride through one of these villages at noon-day, you first meet a melancholy dog, that looks up at you and silently begs that you won't run over him, but he does not offer to get out of the way; next you meet a young boy without any clothes on, and he holds out his hand and says "Bucksheesh!"—he don't really expect a cent, but then he learned to say that before he learned to say mother, and now he can not break himself of it; next you meet a woman with a black veil drawn closely over her face, and her bust exposed; finally, you come to several sore-eyed children and children in all stages of mutilation and decay; and sitting humbly in the dust, and all fringed with filthy rags, is a poor devil whose arms and legs are gnarled and twisted like grape-vines. These are all the people you are likely to see. The balance of the population are asleep within doors, or abroad tending goats in the plains and on the hill-sides. The village is built on some consumptive little water-course, and about it is a little fresh-looking vegetation. Beyond this charmed circle, for miles on every side, stretches a weary desert of sand and gravel, which produces a gray bunchy shrub like sage-brush. A Syrian village is the sorriest sight in the world, and its surroundings are eminently in keeping with it.

I would not have gone into this dissertation upon Syrian villages but for the fact that Nimrod, the Mighty Hunter of Scriptural notoriety, is buried in Jonesborough, and I wished the public to know about how he is located. Like Homer, he is said to be buried in many other places, but this is the only true and genuine place his ashes inhabit.

When the original tribes were dispersed, more than four thousand years ago, Nimrod and a large party traveled three or four hundred miles, and settled where the great city of Babylon afterwards stood. Nimrod built that city. He also began to build the famous Tower of Babel, but circumstances over which he had no control put it out of his power to finish it. He ran it up eight stories high, however, and two of them still stand, at this day—a colossal mass of brickwork, rent down the centre by earthquakes, and seared and vitrified by the lightnings of an angry God. But the vast ruin will still stand for ages, to shame the puny labors of these modern generations of men. Its huge compartments are tenanted by owls and lions, and old Nimrod lies neglected in this wretched village, far from the scene of his grand enterprise.

We left Jonesborough very early in the morning, and rode forever and forever and forever, it seemed to me, over parched deserts and rocky hills, hungry, and with no water to drink. We had drained the goat-skins dry in a little while. At noon we halted before the wretched Arab town of El Yuba Dam, perched on the side of a mountain, but the dragoman said if we applied there for water we would be attacked by the whole tribe, for they did not love Christians. We had to journey on. Two hours later we reached the foot of a tall isolated mountain, which is crowned by the crumbling castle of Banias, the stateliest ruin of that kind on earth, no doubt. It is a thousand feet long and two hundred wide, all of the most symmetrical, and at the same time the most ponderous masonry. The massive towers and bastions are more than thirty feet high, and have been sixty. From the mountain's peak its broken turrets rise above the groves of ancient oaks and olives, and look wonderfully picturesque. It is of such high antiquity that no man knows who built it or when it was built. It is utterly inaccessible, except in one place, where a bridle-path winds upward among the solid rocks to the old portcullis. The horses' hoofs have bored holes in these rocks to the depth of six inches during the hundreds and hundreds of years that the castle was garrisoned. We wandered for three hours among the chambers and crypts and dungeons of the fortress, and trod where the mailed heels of many a knightly Crusader had rang, and where Phenician heroes had walked ages before them.

We wondered how such a solid mass of masonry could be affected even by an earthquake, and could not understand what agency had made Banias a ruin; but we found the destroyer, after a while, and then our wonder was increased ten-fold. Seeds had fallen in crevices in the vast walls; the seeds had sprouted; the tender, insignificant sprouts had hardened; they grew larger and larger, and by a steady, imperceptible pressure forced the great stones apart, and now are bringing sure destruction upon a giant work that has even mocked the earthquakes to scorn! Gnarled and twisted trees spring from the old walls every where, and beautify and overshadow the gray battlements with a wild luxuriance of foliage.

From these old towers we looked down upon a broad, far-reaching green plain, glittering with the pools and rivulets which are the sources of the sacred river Jordan. It was a grateful vision, after so much desert.

And as the evening drew near, we clambered down the mountain, through groves of the Biblical oaks of Bashan, (for we were just stepping over the border and entering the long-sought Holy Land,) and at its extreme foot, toward the wide valley, we entered this little execrable village of Banias and camped in a great grove of olive trees near a torrent of sparkling water whose banks are arrayed in fig-trees, pomegranates and oleanders in full leaf. Barring the proximity of the village, it is a sort of paradise.

The very first thing one feels like doing when he gets into camp, all burning up and dusty, is to hunt up a bath. We followed the stream up to where it gushes out of the mountain side, three hundred yards from the tents, and took a bath that was so icy that if I did not know this was the main source of the sacred river, I would expect harm to come of it. It was bathing at noonday in the chilly source of the Abana, "River of Damascus," that gave me the cholera, so Dr. B. said. However, it generally does give me the cholera to take a bath.

The incorrigible pilgrims have come in with their pockets full of specimens broken from the ruins. I wish this vandalism could be stopped. They broke off fragments from Noah's tomb; from the exquisite sculptures of the temples of Baalbec; from the houses of Judas and Ananias, in Damascus; from the tomb of Nimrod the Mighty Hunter in Jonesborough; from the worn Greek and Roman inscriptions set in the hoary walls of the Castle of Banias; and now they have been hacking and chipping these old arches here that Jesus looked upon in the flesh. Heaven protect the Sepulchre when this tribe invades Jerusalem!

The ruins here are not very interesting. There are the massive walls of a great square building that was once the citadel; there are many ponderous old arches that are so smothered with debris that they barely project above the ground; there are heavy-walled sewers through which the crystal brook of which Jordan is born still runs; in the hill-side are the substructions of a costly marble temple that Herod the Great built here—patches of its handsome mosaic floors still remain; there is a quaint old stone bridge that was here before Herod's time, may be; scattered every where, in the paths and in the woods, are Corinthian capitals, broken porphyry pillars, and little fragments of sculpture; and up yonder in the precipice where the fountain gushes out, are well-worn Greek inscriptions over niches in the rock where in ancient times the Greeks, and after them the Romans, worshipped the sylvan god Pan. But trees and bushes grow above many of these ruins now; the miserable huts of a little crew of filthy Arabs are perched upon the broken masonry of antiquity, the whole place has a sleepy, stupid, rural look about it, and one can hardly bring himself to believe that a busy, substantially built city once existed here, even two thousand years ago. The place was nevertheless the scene of an event whose effects have added page after page and volume after volume to the world's history. For in this place Christ stood when he said to Peter:

"Thou art Peter; and upon this rock will I build my church, and the gates of hell shall not prevail against it. And I will give unto thee the keys of the Kingdom of Heaven; and whatsoever thou shalt bind on earth shall be bound in heaven, and whatsoever thou shalt loose on earth shall be loosed in heaven."

On those little sentences have been built up the mighty edifice of the Church of Rome; in them lie the authority for the imperial power of the Popes over temporal affairs, and their godlike power to curse a soul or wash it white from sin. To sustain the position of "the only true Church," which Rome claims was thus conferred upon her, she has fought and labored and struggled for many a century, and will continue to keep herself busy in the same work to the end of time. The memorable words I have quoted give to this ruined city about all the interest it possesses to people of the present day.

It seems curious enough to us to be standing on ground that was once actually pressed by the feet of the Saviour. The situation is suggestive of a reality and a tangibility that seem at variance with the vagueness and mystery and ghostliness that one naturally attaches to the character of a god. I can not comprehend yet that I am sitting where a god has stood, and looking upon the brook and the mountains which that god looked upon, and am surrounded by dusky men and women whose ancestors saw him, and even talked with him, face to face, and carelessly, just as they would have done with any other stranger. I can not comprehend this; the gods of my understanding have been always hidden in clouds and very far away.

This morning, during breakfast, the usual assemblage of squalid humanity sat patiently without the charmed circle of the camp and waited for such crumbs as pity might bestow upon their misery. There were old and young, brown-skinned and yellow. Some of the men were tall and stalwart, (for one hardly sees any where such splendid-looking men as here in the East,) but all the women and children looked worn and sad, and distressed with hunger. They reminded me much of

Indians, did these people. They had but little clothing, but such as they had was fanciful in character and fantastic in its arrangement. Any little absurd gewgaw or gimcrack they had they disposed in such a way as to make it attract attention most readily. They sat in silence, and with tireless patience watched our every motion with that vile, uncomplaining impoliteness which is so truly Indian, and which makes a white man so nervous and uncomfortable and savage that he wants to exterminate the whole tribe.

These people about us had other peculiarities, which I have noticed in the noble red man, too: they were infested with vermin, and the dirt had caked on them till it amounted to bark.

The little children were in a pitiable condition—they all had sore eyes, and were otherwise afflicted in various ways. They say that hardly a native child in all the East is free from sore eyes, and that thousands of them go blind of one eye or both every year. I think this must be so, for I see plenty of blind people every day, and I do not remember seeing any children that hadn't sore eyes. And, would you suppose that an American mother could sit for an hour, with her child in her arms, and let a hundred flies roost upon its eyes all that time undisturbed? I see that every day. It makes my flesh creep. Yesterday we met a woman riding on a little jackass, and she had a little child in her arms; honestly, I thought the child had goggles on as we approached, and I wondered how its mother could afford so much style. But when we drew near, we saw that the goggles were nothing but a camp meeting of flies assembled around each of the child's eyes, and at the same time there was a detachment prospecting its nose. The flies were happy, the child was contented, and so the mother did not interfere.

As soon as the tribe found out that we had a doctor in our party, they began to flock in from all quarters. Dr. B., in the charity of his nature, had taken a child from a woman who sat near by, and put some sort of a wash upon its diseased eyes. That woman went off and started the whole nation, and it was a sight to see them swarm! The lame, the halt, the blind, the leprous—all the distempers that are bred of indolence, dirt, and iniquity—were represented in the Congress in ten minutes, and still they came! Every woman that had a sick baby brought it along, and every woman that hadn't, borrowed one. What reverent and what worshiping looks they bent upon that dread, mysterious power, the Doctor! They watched him take his phials out; they watched him measure the particles of white powder; they watched him add drops of one precious liquid, and drops of another; they lost not the slightest movement; their eyes were riveted upon him with a fascination that nothing could distract. I believe they thought he was gifted like a god. When each individual got his portion of medicine, his eyes were radiant with joy—notwithstanding by nature they are a thankless and impassive race—and upon his face was written the unquestioning faith that nothing on earth could prevent the patient from getting well now.

Christ knew how to preach to these simple, superstitious, disease-tortured creatures: He healed the sick. They flocked to our poor human doctor this morning when the fame of what he had done to the sick child went abroad in the land, and they worshiped him with their eyes while they did not know as yet whether there was virtue in his simples or not. The ancestors of these—people precisely like them in color, dress, manners, customs, simplicity—flocked in vast multitudes after Christ, and when they saw Him make the afflicted whole with a word, it is no wonder they worshiped Him. No wonder His deeds were the talk of the nation. No wonder the multitude that followed Him was so great that at one time—thirty miles from here—they had to let a sick man down through the roof because no approach could be made to the door; no wonder His audiences were so great at Galilee that He had to preach from a ship removed a little distance from the shore; no wonder that even in the desert places about Bethsaida, five thousand invaded His solitude, and He had to feed them by a miracle or else see them suffer for their confiding faith and devotion; no wonder when there was a great commotion in a city in those days, one neighbor explained it to another in words to this effect: "They say that Jesus of Nazareth is come!"

Well, as I was saying, the doctor distributed medicine as long as he had any to distribute, and his reputation is mighty in Galilee this day. Among his patients was the child of the Shiek's daughter—for even this poor, ragged handful of sores and sin has its royal Shiek—a poor old mummy that looked as if he would be more at home in a poor-house than in the Chief Magistracy of this tribe of hopeless, shirtless savages. The princess—I mean the Shiek's daughter—was only thirteen or fourteen years old, and had a very sweet face and a pretty one. She was the only Syrian female we have seen yet who was not so sinfully ugly that she couldn't smile after ten o'clock Saturday night without breaking the Sabbath. Her child was a hard specimen, though—there wasn't enough of it to make a pie, and the poor little thing looked so pleadingly up at all who came near it (as if it had an idea that now was its chance or never,) that we were filled with compassion which was genuine and not put on.

But this last new horse I have got is trying to break his neck over the tent-ropes, and I shall have to go out and anchor him. Jericho and I have parted company. The new horse is not much to boast of, I think. One of his hind legs bends the wrong way, and the other one is as straight and stiff as a tent-pole. Most of his teeth are gone, and he is as blind as a bat. His nose has been broken at some time or other, and is arched like a culvert now. His under lip hangs down like a camel's, and his ears are chopped off close to his head. I had some trouble at first to find a name for him, but I finally concluded to call him Baalbec, because he is such a magnificent ruin. I can not keep from talking about my horses, because I have a very long and tedious journey before me, and they naturally occupy my thoughts about as much as matters of apparently much greater importance.

We satisfied our pilgrims by making those hard rides from Baalbec to Damascus, but Dan's horse and Jack's were so crippled we had to leave them behind and get fresh animals for them. The dragoman says Jack's horse died. I swapped horses with Mohammed, the kingly-looking Egyptian who is our Ferguson's lieutenant. By Ferguson I mean our dragoman Abraham, of course. I did not take this horse on account of his personal appearance, but because I have not seen his back. I do not wish to see it. I have seen the backs of all the other horses, and found most of them covered with dreadful saddle-boils which I know have not been washed or doctored for years. The idea of riding all day long over such ghastly inquisitions of torture is sickening. My horse must be like the others, but I have at least the consolation of not knowing it to be so.

I hope that in future I may be spared any more sentimental praises of the Arab's idolatry of his horse. In boyhood I longed to be an Arab of the desert and have a beautiful mare, and call her Selim or Benjamin or Mohammed, and feed her with my own hands, and let her come into the tent, and teach her to caress me and look fondly upon me with her great tender eyes; and I wished that a stranger might come at such a time and offer me a hundred thousand dollars for her, so that I could do like the other Arabs—hesitate, yearn for the money, but overcome by my love for my mare, at last say, "Part with thee, my beautiful one! Never with my life! Away, tempter, I scorn thy gold!" and then bound into the saddle and speed over the desert like the wind!

But I recall those aspirations. If these Arabs be like the other Arabs, their love for their beautiful mares is a fraud. These of my acquaintance have no love for their horses, no sentiment of pity for them, and no knowledge of how to treat them or care for them. The Syrian saddle-blanket is a quilted mattrass two or three inches thick. It is never removed from the horse, day or night. It gets full of dirt and hair, and becomes soaked with sweat. It is bound to breed sores. These pirates never think of washing a horse's back. They do not shelter the horses in the tents, either; they must stay out and take the weather as it comes. Look at poor cropped and dilapidated "Baalbec," and weep for the sentiment that has been wasted upon the Selims of romance!

Chapter XLVI

A BOUT AN HOUR'S ride over a rough, rocky road, half
flooded with water, and through a forest of oaks of Bashan, brought us to Dan.

From a little mound here in the plain issues a broad stream
of limpid water and forms a large shallow pool, and then
rushes furiously onward, augmented in volume. This puddle
is an important source of the Jordan. Its banks, and those of
the brook are respectably adorned with blooming oleanders,
but the unutterable beauty of the spot will not throw a well-
balanced man into convulsions, as the Syrian books of travel
would lead one to suppose.

From the spot I am speaking of, a cannon-ball would carry
beyond the confines of Holy Land and light upon profane
ground three miles away. We were only one little hour's travel
within the borders of Holy Land—we had hardly begun to
appreciate yet that we were standing upon any different sort
of earth than that we had always been used to, and yet see
how the historic names began already to cluster! Dan—Bashan—Lake Huleh—the Sources of Jordan—the Sea of Galilee. They were all in sight but the last, and it was not far
away. The little township of Bashan was once the kingdom
so famous in Scripture for its bulls and its oaks. Lake Huleh
is the Biblical "Waters of Merom." Dan was the northern and
Beersheba the southern limit of Palestine—hence the expression "from Dan to Beersheba." It is equivalent to our phrases
"from Maine to Texas"—"from Baltimore to San Francisco."
Our expression and that of the Israelites both mean the
same—great distance. With their slow camels and asses, it
was about a seven days' journey from Dan to Beersheba—say
a hundred and fifty or sixty miles—it was the entire length of
their country, and was not to be undertaken without great
preparation and much ceremony. When the Prodigal traveled
to "a far country," it is not likely that he went more than
eighty or ninety miles. Palestine is only from forty to sixty
miles wide. The State of Missouri could be split into three
Palestines, and there would then be enough material left for
part of another—possibly a whole one. From Baltimore to

San Francisco is several thousand miles, but it will be only a seven days' journey in the cars when I am two or three years older.* If I live I shall necessarily have to go across the continent every now and then in those cars, but one journey from Dan to Beersheba will be sufficient, no doubt. It must be the most trying of the two. Therefore, if we chance to discover that from Dan to Beersheba seemed a mighty stretch of country to the Israelites, let us not be airy with them, but reflect that it *was* and *is* a mighty stretch when one can not traverse it by rail.

The small mound I have mentioned a while ago was once occupied by the Phenician city of Laish. A party of filibusters from Zorah and Eschol captured the place, and lived there in a free and easy way, worshiping gods of their own manufacture and stealing idols from their neighbors whenever they wore their own out. Jeroboam set up a golden calf here to fascinate his people and keep them from making dangerous trips to Jerusalem to worship, which might result in a return to their rightful allegiance. With all respect for those ancient Israelites, I can not overlook the fact that they were not always virtuous enough to withstand the seductions of a golden calf. Human nature has not changed much since then.

Some forty centuries ago the city of Sodom was pillaged by the Arab princes of Mesopotamia, and among other prisoners they seized upon the patriarch Lot and brought him here on their way to their own possessions. They brought him to Dan, and father Abraham, who was pursuing them, crept softly in at dead of night, among the whispering oleanders and under the shadows of the stately oaks, and fell upon the slumbering victors and startled them from their dreams with the clash of steel. He recaptured Lot and all the other plunder.

We moved on. We were now in a green valley, five or six miles wide and fifteen long. The streams which are called the sources of the Jordan flow through it to Lake Huleh, a shallow pond three miles in diameter, and from the southern extremity of the Lake the concentrated Jordan flows out. The Lake is surrounded by a broad marsh, grown with reeds. Between the marsh and the mountains which wall the valley is a

*The railroad has been completed, since the above was written.

respectable strip of fertile land; at the end of the valley, toward Dan, as much as half the land is solid and fertile, and
watered by Jordan's sources. There is enough of it to make a
farm. It almost warrants the enthusiasm of the spies of that
rabble of adventurers who captured Dan. They said: "We
have seen the land, and behold it is very good.   *   *   *   A
place where there is no want of any thing that is in the earth."

Their enthusiasm was at least warranted by the fact that
they had never seen a country as good as this. There was
enough of it for the ample support of their six hundred men
and their families, too.

When we got fairly down on the level part of the Danite
farm, we came to places where we could actually run our
horses. It was a notable circumstance.

We had been painfully clambering over interminable hills
and rocks for days together, and when we suddenly came
upon this astonishing piece of rockless plain, every man drove
the spurs into his horse and sped away with a velocity he
could surely enjoy to the utmost, but could never hope to
comprehend in Syria.

Here were evidences of cultivation—a rare sight in this
country—an acre or two of rich soil studded with last season's dead corn-stalks of the thickness of your thumb and
very wide apart. But in such a land it was a thrilling spectacle.
Close to it was a stream, and on its banks a great herd of
curious-looking Syrian goats and sheep were gratefully eating
gravel. I do not state this as a petrified fact—I only *suppose*
they were eating gravel, because there did not appear to be
any thing else for them to eat. The shepherds that tended
them were the very pictures of Joseph and his brethren I have
no doubt in the world. They were tall, muscular, and very
dark-skinned Bedouins, with inky black beards. They had firm
lips, unquailing eyes, and a kingly stateliness of bearing. They
wore the parti-colored half bonnet, half hood, with fringed
ends falling upon their shoulders, and the full, flowing robe
barred with broad black stripes—the dress one sees in all pictures of the swarthy sons of the desert. These chaps would
sell their younger brothers if they had a chance, I think. They
have the manners, the customs, the dress, the occupation and
the loose principles of the ancient stock. [They attacked our

camp last night, and I bear them no good will.] They had with them the pigmy jackasses one sees all over Syria and remembers in all pictures of the "Flight into Egypt," where Mary and the Young Child are riding and Joseph is walking alongside, towering high above the little donkey's shoulders.

But really, here the man rides and carries the child, as a general thing, and the woman walks. The customs have not changed since Joseph's time. We would not have in our houses a picture representing Joseph riding and Mary walking; we would see profanation in it, but a Syrian Christian would not. I know that hereafter the picture I first spoke of will look odd to me.

We could not stop to rest two or three hours out from our camp, of course, albeit the brook was beside us. So we went on an hour longer. We saw water, then, but nowhere in all the waste around was there a foot of shade, and we were scorching to death. "Like unto the shadow of a great rock in a weary land." Nothing in the Bible is more beautiful than that, and surely there is no place we have wandered to that is able to give it such touching expression as this blistering, naked, treeless land.

Here you do not stop just when you please, but when you can. We found water, but no shade. We traveled on and found a tree at last, but no water. We rested and lunched, and came on to this place, Ain Mellahah (the boys call it Baldwinsville.) It was a very short day's run, but the dragoman does not want to go further, and has invented a plausible lie about the country beyond this being infested by ferocious Arabs, who would make sleeping in their midst a dangerous pastime. Well, they ought to be dangerous. They carry a rusty old weather-beaten flintlock gun, with a barrel that is longer than themselves; it has no sights on it; it will not carry farther than a brickbat, and is not half so certain. And the great sash they wear in many a fold around their waists has two or three absurd old horse-pistols in it that are rusty from eternal disuse—weapons that would hang fire just about long enough for you to walk out of range, and then burst and blow the Arab's head off. Exceedingly dangerous these sons of the desert are.

It used to make my blood run cold to read Wm. C. Grimes'

hairbreadth escapes from Bedouins, but I think I could read them now without a tremor. He never said he was attacked by Bedouins, I believe, or was ever treated uncivilly, but then in about every other chapter he discovered them approaching, any how, and he had a blood-curdling fashion of working up the peril; and of wondering how his relations far away would feel could they see their poor wandering boy, with his weary feet and his dim eyes, in such fearful danger; and of thinking for the last time of the old homestead, and the dear old church, and the cow, and those things; and of finally straightening his form to its utmost height in the saddle, drawing his trusty revolver, and then dashing the spurs into "Mohammed" and sweeping down upon the ferocious enemy determined to sell his life as dearly as possible. True the Bedouins never did any thing to him when he arrived, and never had any intention of doing any thing to him in the first place, and wondered what in the mischief he was making all that to-do about; but still I could not divest myself of the idea, somehow, that a frightful peril had been escaped through that man's dare-devil bravery, and so I never could read about Wm. C. Grimes' Bedouins and sleep comfortably afterward. But I believe the Bedouins to be a fraud, now. I have seen the monster, and I can outrun him. I shall never be afraid of his daring to stand behind his own gun and discharge it.

About fifteen hundred years before Christ, this campground of ours by the Waters of Merom was the scene of one of Joshua's exterminating battles. Jabin, King of Hazor, (up yonder above Dan,) called all the shieks about him together, with their hosts, to make ready for Israel's terrible General who was approaching.

"And when all these Kings were met together, they came and pitched together by the Waters of Merom, to fight against Israel.

"And they went out, they and all their hosts with them, much people, even as the sand that is upon the sea-shore for multitude," etc.

But Joshua fell upon them and utterly destroyed them, root and branch. That was his usual policy in war. He never left any chance for newspaper controversies about who won the battle. He made this valley, so quiet now, a reeking slaughter-pen.

Somewhere in this part of the country—I do not know exactly where—Israel fought another bloody battle a hundred years later. Deborah, the prophetess, told Barak to take ten thousand men and sally forth against another King Jabin who had been doing something. Barak came down from Mount Tabor, twenty or twenty-five miles from here, and gave battle to Jabin's forces, who were in command of Sisera. Barak won the fight, and while he was making the victory complete by the usual method of exterminating the remnant of the defeated host, Sisera fled away on foot, and when he was nearly exhausted by fatigue and thirst, one Jael, a woman he seems to have been acquainted with, invited him to come into her tent and rest himself. The weary soldier acceded readily enough, and Jael put him to bed. He said he was very thirsty, and asked his generous preserver to get him a cup of water. She brought him some milk, and he drank of it gratefully and lay down again, to forget in pleasant dreams his lost battle and his humbled pride. Presently when he was asleep she came softly in with a hammer and drove a hideous tent-pen down through his brain!

"For he was fast asleep and weary. So he died." Such is the touching language of the Bible. "The Song of Deborah and Barak" praises Jael for the memorable service she had rendered, in an exultant strain:

"Blessed above women shall Jael the wife of Heber the Kenite be, blessed shall she be above women in the tent.

"He asked for water, and she gave him milk; she brought forth butter in a lordly dish.

"She put her hand to the nail, and her right hand to the workman's hammer; and with the hammer she smote Sisera, she smote off his head when she had pierced and stricken through his temples.

"At her feet he bowed, he fell, he lay down: at her feet he bowed, he fell: where he bowed, there he fell down dead."

Stirring scenes like these occur in this valley no more. There is not a solitary village throughout its whole extent—not for thirty miles in either direction. There are two or three small clusters of Bedouin tents, but not a single permanent habitation. One may ride ten miles, hereabouts, and not see ten human beings.

To this region one of the prophecies is applied:

"I will bring the land into desolation; and your enemies which dwell therein shall be astonished at it. And I will scatter you among the heathen, and I will draw out a sword after you; and your land shall be desolate and your cities waste."

No man can stand here by deserted Ain Mellahah and say the prophecy has not been fulfilled.

In a verse from the Bible which I have quoted above, occurs the phrase "all these kings." It attracted my attention in a moment, because it carries to my mind such a vastly different significance from what it always did at home. I can see easily enough that if I wish to profit by this tour and come to a correct understanding of the matters of interest connected with it, I must studiously and faithfully unlearn a great many things I have somehow absorbed concerning Palestine. I must begin a system of reduction. Like my grapes which the spies bore out of the Promised Land, I have got every thing in Palestine on too large a scale. Some of my ideas were wild enough. The word Palestine always brought to my mind a vague suggestion of a country as large as the United States. I do not know why, but such was the case. I suppose it was because I could not conceive of a small country having so large a history. I think I was a little surprised to find that the grand Sultan of Turkey was a man of only ordinary size. I must try to reduce my ideas of Palestine to a more reasonable shape. One gets large impressions in boyhood, sometimes, which he has to fight against all his life. "All these kings." When I used to read that in Sunday School, it suggested to me the several kings of such countries as England, France, Spain, Germany, Russia, etc., arrayed in splendid robes ablaze with jewels, marching in grave procession, with sceptres of gold in their hands and flashing crowns upon their heads. But here in Ain Mellahah, after coming through Syria, and after giving serious study to the character and customs of the country, the phrase "all these kings" loses its grandeur. It suggests only a parcel of petty chiefs—ill-clad and ill-conditioned savages much like our Indians, who lived in full sight of each other and whose "kingdoms" were large when they were five miles square and contained two thousand souls. The com-

bined monarchies of the thirty "kings" destroyed by Joshua
on one of his famous campaigns, only covered an area about
equal to four of our counties of ordinary size. The poor old
sheik we saw at Cesarea Philippi with his ragged band of a
hundred followers, would have been called a "king" in those
ancient times.

It is seven in the morning, and as we are in the country,
the grass ought to be sparkling with dew, the flowers enriching the air with their fragrance, and the birds singing in the
trees. But alas, there is no dew here, nor flowers, nor birds,
nor trees. There is a plain and an unshaded lake, and beyond
them some barren mountains. The tents are tumbling, the
Arabs are quarreling like dogs and cats, as usual, the campground is strewn with packages and bundles, the labor of
packing them upon the backs of the mules is progressing with
great activity, the horses are saddled, the umbrellas are out,
and in ten minutes we shall mount and the long procession
will move again. The white city of the Mellahah, resurrected
for a moment out of the dead centuries, will have disappeared
again and left no sign.

Chapter XLVII

WE TRAVERSED SOME miles of desolate country whose soil is rich enough, but is given over wholly to weeds—a silent, mournful expanse, wherein we saw only three persons—Arabs, with nothing on but a long coarse shirt like the "tow-linen" shirts which used to form the only summer garment of little negro boys on Southern plantations. Shepherds they were, and they charmed their flocks with the traditional shepherd's pipe—a reed instrument that made music as exquisitely infernal as these same Arabs create when they sing.

In their pipes lingered no echo of the wonderful music the shepherd forefathers heard in the Plains of Bethlehem what time the angels sang "Peace on earth, good will to men."

Part of the ground we came over was not ground at all, but rocks—cream-colored rocks, worn smooth, as if by water; with seldom an edge or a corner on them, but scooped out, honey-combed, bored out with eye-holes, and thus wrought into all manner of quaint shapes, among which the uncouth imitation of skulls was frequent. Over this part of the route were occasional remains of an old Roman road like the Appian Way, whose paving-stones still clung to their places with Roman tenacity.

Gray lizards, those heirs of ruin, of sepulchres and desolation, glided in and out among the rocks or lay still and sunned themselves. Where prosperity has reigned, and fallen; where glory has flamed, and gone out; where beauty has dwelt, and passed away; where gladness was, and sorrow is; where the pomp of life has been, and silence and death brood in its high places, there this reptile makes his home, and mocks at human vanity. His coat is the color of ashes: and ashes are the symbol of hopes that have perished, of aspirations that came to nought, of loves that are buried. If he could speak, he would say, Build temples: I will lord it in their ruins; build palaces: I will inhabit them; erect empires: I will inherit them; bury your beautiful: I will watch the worms at their work; and you, who stand here and moralize over me: I will crawl over *your* corpse at the last.

A few ants were in this desert place, but merely to spend the summer. They brought their provisions from Ain Mellahah—eleven miles.

Jack is not very well to-day, it is easy to see; but boy as he is, he is too much of a man to speak of it. He exposed himself to the sun too much yesterday, but since it came of his earnest desire to learn, and to make this journey as useful as the opportunities will allow, no one seeks to discourage him by fault-finding. We missed him an hour from the camp, and then found him some distance away, by the edge of a brook, and with no umbrella to protect him from the fierce sun. If he had been used to going without his umbrella, it would have been well enough, of course; but he was not. He was just in the act of throwing a clod at a mud-turtle which was sunning itself on a small log in the brook. We said:

"Don't do that, Jack. What do you want to harm him for? What has he done?"

"Well, then, I won't kill him, but I ought to, because he is a fraud."

We asked him why, but he said it was no matter. We asked him why, once or twice, as we walked back to the camp, but he still said it was no matter. But late at night, when he was sitting in a thoughtful mood on the bed, we asked him again and he said:

"Well, it don't matter; I don't mind it now, but I did not like it to-day, you know, because *I* don't tell any thing that isn't so, and I don't think the Colonel ought to, either. But he did; he told us at prayers in the Pilgrims' tent, last night, and he seemed as if he was reading it out of the Bible, too, about this country flowing with milk and honey, and about the voice of the turtle being heard in the land. I thought that was drawing it a little strong, about the turtles, any how, but I asked Mr. Church if it was so, and he said it was, and what Mr. Church tells me, I believe. But I sat there and watched that turtle nearly an hour to-day, and I almost burned up in the sun; but I never heard him sing. I believe I sweated a double handful of sweat—I *know* I did—because it got in my eyes, and it was running down over my nose all the time; and you know my pants are tighter than any body else's— Paris foolishness—and the buckskin seat of them got wet with sweat, and then got dry again and began to draw up and pinch and tear loose—it was awful—but I never heard him sing. Finally I said, This is a fraud—that is what it is, it is a fraud—and if I had had any sense I might have known a cursed mud-turtle couldn't sing. And then I said, I don't wish to be hard on this fellow, and I will just give him ten minutes to commence; ten minutes—and then if he don't, down goes his building. But he *didn't* commence, you know. I had staid there all that time, thinking may be he might, pretty soon, because he kept on raising his head up and letting it down, and drawing the skin over his eyes for a minute and then opening them out again, as if he was trying to study up something to sing, but just as the ten minutes were up and I was all beat out and blistered, he laid his blamed head down on a knot and went fast asleep."

"It *was* a little hard, after you had waited so long."

"I should think so. I said, Well, if you won't sing, you shan't sleep, any way; and if you fellows had let me alone I would have made him shin out of Galilee quicker than any turtle ever did yet. But it isn't any matter now—let it go. The skin is all off the back of my neck."

About ten in the morning we halted at Joseph's Pit. This is a ruined Khan of the Middle Ages, in one of whose side courts is a great walled and arched pit with water in it, and this pit, one tradition says, is the one Joseph's brethren cast him into. A more authentic tradition, aided by the geography of the country, places the pit in Dothan, some two days' journey from here. However, since there are many who believe in this present pit as the true one, it has its interest.

It is hard to make a choice of the most beautiful passage in a book which is so gemmed with beautiful passages as the Bible; but it is certain that not many things within its lids may take rank above the exquisite story of Joseph. Who taught those ancient writers their simplicity of language, their felicity of expression, their pathos, and above all, their faculty of sinking themselves entirely out of sight of the reader and making the narrative stand out alone and seem to tell itself? Shakspeare is always present when one reads his book; Macaulay is present when we follow the march of his stately sentences; but the Old Testament writers are hidden from view.

If the pit I have been speaking of is the right one, a scene transpired there, long ages ago, which is familiar to us all in pictures. The sons of Jacob had been pasturing their flocks near there. Their father grew uneasy at their long absence, and sent Joseph, his favorite, to see if any thing had gone wrong with them. He traveled six or seven days' journey; he was only seventeen years old, and, boy like, he toiled through that long stretch of the vilest, rockiest, dustiest country in Asia, arrayed in the pride of his heart, his beautiful claw-hammer coat of many colors. Joseph was the favorite, and that was one crime in the eyes of his brethren; he had dreamed dreams, and interpreted them to foreshadow his elevation far above all his family in the far future, and that was another; he was dressed well and had doubtless displayed the harmless vanity of youth in keeping the fact prominently before his brothers. These were crimes his elders fretted over among themselves and proposed to punish when the opportunity should offer. When they saw him coming up from the Sea of Galilee, they recognized him and were glad. They said, "Lo, here is this dreamer—let us kill him." But Reuben pleaded for his life, and they spared it. But they seized the boy, and stripped the hated coat from his back and pushed him into the pit. *They* intended to let him die there, but Reuben intended to liberate him secretly. However, while Reuben was away for a little while, the brethren sold Joseph to some Ishmaelitish merchants who were journeying towards Egypt. Such is the history of the pit. And the self-same pit is there in that place, even to this day; and there it will remain until the next detachment of image-breakers and tomb-desecraters arrives from the *Quaker City* excursion, and they will infallibly dig it up and carry it away with them. For behold in them is no reverence for the solemn monuments of the past, and whithersoever they go they destroy and spare not.

Joseph became rich, distinguished, powerful—as the Bible expresses it, "lord over all the land of Egypt." Joseph was the real king, the strength, the brain of the monarchy, though Pharaoh held the title. Joseph is one of the truly great men of the Old Testament. And he was the noblest and the manliest, save Esau. Why shall we not say a good word for the princely Bedouin? The only crime that can be brought against him is that he was unfortunate. Why must every body praise Joseph's great-hearted generosity to his cruel brethren, without stint of fervent language, and fling only a reluctant bone of praise to Esau for his still sublimer generosity to the brother who had wronged him? Jacob took advantage of Esau's consuming hunger to rob him of his birthright and the great honor and consideration that belonged to the position; by treachery and falsehood he robbed him of his father's blessing; he made of him a stranger in his home, and a wanderer. Yet after twenty years had passed away and Jacob met Esau and fell at his feet quaking with fear and begging piteously to be spared the punishment he knew he deserved, what did that magnificent savage do? He fell upon his neck and embraced him! When Jacob—who was incapable of comprehending nobility of character—still doubting, still fearing, insisted upon "finding grace with my lord" by the bribe of a present of cattle, what did the gorgeous son of the desert say?

"Nay, I have enough, my brother; keep that thou hast unto thyself!"

Esau found Jacob rich, beloved by wives and children, and traveling in state, with servants, herds of cattle and trains of camels—but he himself was still the uncourted outcast this brother had made him. After thirteen years of romantic mystery, the brethren who had wronged Joseph, came, strangers in a strange land, hungry and humble, to buy "a little food;" and being summoned to a palace, charged with crime, they beheld in its owner their wronged brother; they were trembling beggars—he, the lord of a mighty empire! What Joseph that ever lived would have thrown away such a chance to "show off?" Who stands first—outcast Esau forgiving Jacob in prosperity, or Joseph on a king's throne forgiving the ragged tremblers whose happy rascality placed him there?

Just before we came to Joseph's Pit, we had "raised" a hill, and there, a few miles before us, with not a tree or a shrub to interrupt the view, lay a vision which millions of worshipers in the far lands of the earth would give half their possessions to see—the sacred Sea of Galilee!

Therefore we tarried only a short time at the pit. We rested the horses and ourselves, and felt for a few minutes the blessed shade of the ancient buildings. We were out of water, but the two or three scowling Arabs, with their long guns, who were idling about the place, said they had none and that there was none in the vicinity. They knew there was a little brackish water in the pit, but they venerated a place made sacred by their ancestor's imprisonment too much to be willing to see Christian dogs drink from it. But Ferguson tied rags and handkerchiefs together till he made a rope long enough to lower a vessel to the bottom, and we drank and then rode on; and in a short time we dismounted on those shores which the feet of the Saviour have made holy ground.

At noon we took a swim in the Sea of Galilee—a blessed privilege in this roasting climate—and then lunched under a neglected old fig-tree at the fountain they call Ain-et-Tin, a hundred yards from ruined Capernaum. Every rivulet that gurgles out of the rocks and sands of this part of the world is dubbed with the title of "fountain," and people familiar with the Hudson, the great lakes and the Mississippi fall into transports of admiration over them, and exhaust their powers of composition in writing their praises. If all the poetry and nonsense that have been discharged upon the fountains and the bland scenery of this region were collected in a book, it would make a most valuable volume to burn.

During luncheon, the pilgrim enthusiasts of our party, who had been so light-hearted and happy ever since they touched holy ground that they did little but mutter incoherent rhapsodies, could scarcely eat, so anxious were they to "take shipping" and sail in very person upon the waters that had borne the vessels of the Apostles. Their anxiety grew and their excitement augmented with every fleeting moment, until my fears were aroused and I began to have misgivings that in their present condition they might break recklessly loose from all considerations of prudence and buy a whole fleet of ships to sail in instead of hiring a single one for an hour, as quiet folk are wont to do. I trembled to think of the ruined purses this day's performances might result in. I could not help reflecting bodingly upon the intemperate zeal with which middle-aged men are apt to surfeit themselves upon a seductive folly which they have tasted for the first time. And yet I did not feel that I had a right to be surprised at the state of things which was giving me so much concern. These men had been taught from infancy to revere, almost to worship, the holy places whereon their happy eyes were resting now. For many and many a year this very picture had visited their thoughts by day and floated through their dreams by night. To stand before it in the flesh—to see it as they saw it now—to sail upon the hallowed sea, and kiss the holy soil that compassed it about: these were aspirations they had cherished while a generation dragged its lagging seasons by and left its furrows in their faces and its frosts upon their hair. To look upon this picture, and sail upon this sea, they had forsaken home and its idols and journeyed thousands and thousands of miles, in weariness and tribulation. What wonder that the sordid lights of work-day prudence should pale before the glory of a hope like theirs in the full splendor of its fruition? Let them squander millions! I said—who speaks of money at a time like this?

In this frame of mind I followed, as fast as I could, the eager footsteps of the pilgrims, and stood upon the shore of the lake, and swelled, with hat and voice, the frantic hail they sent after the "ship" that was speeding by. It was a success. The toilers of the sea ran in and beached their barque. Joy sat upon every countenance.

"How much?—ask him how much, Ferguson!—how much to take us all—eight of us, and you—to Bethsaida, yonder, and to the mouth of Jordan, and to the place where the swine ran down into the sea—quick!—and we want to coast around every where—every where!—all day long!—*I* could sail a year in these waters!—and tell him we'll stop at Magdala and finish at Tiberias!—ask him how much?—any thing—any thing whatever!—tell him we don't care what the expense is!" [I said to myself, I knew how it would be.]

Ferguson—(interpreting)—"He says two Napoleons—eight dollars."

One or two countenances fell. Then a pause.

"Too much!—we'll give him one!"

I never shall know how it was—I shudder yet when I think how the place is given to miracles—but in a single instant of time, as it seemed to me, that ship was twenty paces from the shore, and speeding away like a frightened thing! Eight crest-fallen creatures stood upon the shore, and O, to think of it! this—this—after all that overmastering ecstacy! Oh, shameful, shameful ending, after such unseemly boasting! It was too much like "Ho! let me at him!" followed by a prudent "Two of you hold him—one can hold me!"

Instantly there was wailing and gnashing of teeth in the camp. The two Napoleons were offered—more if necessary—and pilgrims and dragoman shouted themselves hoarse with pleadings to the retreating boatmen to come back. But they sailed serenely away and paid no further heed to pilgrims who had dreamed all their lives of some day skimming over the sacred waters of Galilee and listening to its hallowed story in the whisperings of its waves, and had journeyed countless leagues to do it, and—and then concluded that the fare was too high. Impertinent Mohammedan Arabs, to think such things of gentlemen of another faith!

Well, there was nothing to do but just submit and forego the privilege of voyaging on Genessaret, after coming half around the globe to taste that pleasure. There was a time, when the Saviour taught here, that boats were plenty among the fishermen of the coasts—but boats and fishermen both are gone, now; and old Josephus had a fleet of men-of-war in these waters eighteen centuries ago—a hundred and thirty bold canoes—but they, also, have passed away and left no sign. They battle here no more by sea, and the commercial marine of Galilee numbers only two small ships, just of a pattern with the little skiffs the disciples knew. One was lost to us for good—the other was miles away and far out of hail. So we mounted the horses and rode grimly on toward Magdala, cantering along in the edge of the water for want of the means of passing over it.

How the pilgrims abused each other! Each said it was the other's fault, and each in turn denied it. No word was spoken by the sinners—even the mildest sarcasm might have been dangerous at such a time. Sinners that have been kept down and had examples held up to them, and suffered frequent lectures, and been so put upon in a moral way and in the matter of going slow and being serious and bottling up slang, and so crowded in regard to the matter of being proper and always and forever behaving, that their lives have become a burden to them, would not lag behind pilgrims at such a time as this, and wink furtively, and be joyful, and commit other such crimes—because it would not occur to them to do it. Otherwise they would. But they did do it, though—and it did them a world of good to hear the pilgrims abuse each other, too. We took an unworthy satisfaction in seeing them fall out, now and then, because it showed that they were only poor human people like us, after all.

So we all rode down to Magdala, while the gnashing of teeth waxed and waned by turns, and harsh words troubled the holy calm of Galilee.

Lest any man think I mean to be ill-natured when I talk about our pilgrims as I have been talking, I wish to say in all sincerity that I do not. I would not listen to lectures from men I did not like and could not respect; and none of these can say I ever took their lectures unkindly, or was restive under the infliction, or failed to try to profit by what they said to me. They are better men than I am; I can say that honestly; they are good friends of mine, too—and besides, if they did not wish to be stirred up occasionally in print, why in the mischief did they travel with me? They knew me. They knew my liberal way—that I like to give and take—when it is for me to give and other people to take. When one of them threatened to leave me in Damascus when I had the cholera, he had no real idea of doing it—I know his passionate nature and the good impulses that underlie it. And did I not overhear Church, another pilgrim, say he did not care who went or who staid, *he* would stand by me till I walked out of Damascus on my own feet or was carried out in a coffin, if it was a year? And do I not include Church every time I abuse the pilgrims—and would I be likely to speak ill-naturedly of him? I wish to stir them up and make them healthy; that is all.

We had left Capernaum behind us. It was only a shapeless ruin. It bore no semblance to a town, and had nothing about it to suggest that it had ever been a town. But all desolate and unpeopled as it was, it was illustrious ground. From it sprang that tree of Christianity whose broad arms overshadow so many distant lands to-day. After Christ was tempted of the devil in the desert, he came here and began his teachings; and during the three or four years he lived afterward, this place was his home almost altogether. He began

to heal the sick, and his fame soon spread so widely that sufferers came from Syria and beyond Jordan, and even from
Jerusalem, several days' journey away, to be cured of their
diseases. Here he healed the centurion's servant and Peter's
mother-in-law, and multitudes of the lame and the blind and
persons possessed of devils; and here, also, he raised Jairus's
daughter from the dead. He went into a ship with his disciples, and when they roused him from sleep in the midst of a
storm, he quieted the winds and lulled the troubled sea to
rest with his voice. He passed over to the other side, a few
miles away, and relieved two men of devils, which passed into
some swine. After his return he called Matthew from the receipt of customs, performed some cures, and created scandal
by eating with publicans and sinners. Then he went healing
and teaching through Galilee, and even journeyed to Tyre and
Sidon. He chose the twelve disciples, and sent them abroad
to preach the new gospel. He worked miracles in Bethsaida
and Chorazin—villages two or three miles from Capernaum.
It was near one of them that the miraculous draft of fishes is
supposed to have been taken, and it was in the desert places
near the other that he fed the thousands by the miracles of
the loaves and fishes. He cursed them both, and Capernaum
also, for not repenting, after all the great works he had done
in their midst, and prophesied against them. They are all in
ruins, now—which is gratifying to the pilgrims, for, as usual,
they fit the eternal words of gods to the evanescent things of
this earth; Christ, it is more probable, referred to the *people*,
not their shabby villages of wigwams: he said it would be sad
for them at "the day of judgment"—and what business have
mud-hovels at the Day of Judgment? it would not affect the
prophecy in the least—it would neither prove it or disprove
it—if these towns were splendid cities now instead of the
almost vanished ruins they are. Christ visited Magdala, which
is near by Capernaum, and he also visited Cesarea Philippi.
He went up to his old home at Nazareth, and saw his brothers Joses, and Judas, and James, and Simon—those persons
who, being own brothers to Jesus Christ, one would expect
to hear mentioned sometimes, yet who ever saw their names
in a newspaper or heard them from a pulpit? Who ever inquires what manner of youths they were; and whether they

slept with Jesus, played with him and romped about him; quarreled with him concerning toys and trifles; struck him in anger, not suspecting what he was? Who ever wonders what they thought when they saw him come back to Nazareth a celebrity, and looked long at his unfamiliar face to make sure, and then said, "It *is* Jesus?" Who wonders what passed in their minds when they saw this brother, (who was *only* a brother to them, however much he might be to others a mysterious stranger who was a god and had stood face to face with God above the clouds,) doing strange miracles with crowds of astonished people for witnesses? Who wonders if the brothers of Jesus asked him to come home with them, and said his mother and his sisters were grieved at his long absence, and would be wild with delight to see his face again? Who ever gives a thought to the sisters of Jesus at all?—yet he had sisters; and memories of them must have stolen into his mind often when he was ill-treated among strangers; when he was homeless and said he had not where to lay his head; when all deserted him, even Peter, and he stood alone among his enemies.

Christ did few miracles in Nazareth, and staid but a little while. The people said, "*This* the Son of God! Why, his father is nothing but a carpenter. We know the family. We see them every day. Are not his brothers named so and so, and his sisters so and so, and is not his mother the person they call Mary? This is absurd." He did not curse his home, but he shook its dust from his feet and went away.

Capernaum lies close to the edge of the little sea, in a small plain some five miles long and a mile or two wide, which is mildly adorned with oleanders which look all the better contrasted with the bald hills and the howling deserts which surround them, but they are not as deliriously beautiful as the books paint them. If one be calm and resolute he can look upon their comeliness and live.

One of the most astonishing things that have yet fallen under our observation is the exceedingly small portion of the earth from which sprang the now flourishing plant of Christianity. The longest journey our Saviour ever performed was from here to Jerusalem—about one hundred to one hundred and twenty miles. The next longest was from here to Sidon—

say about sixty or seventy miles. Instead of being wide apart—as American appreciation of distances would naturally suggest—the places made most particularly celebrated by the presence of Christ are nearly all right here in full view, and within cannon-shot of Capernaum. Leaving out two or three short journeys of the Saviour, he spent his life, preached his gospel, and performed his miracles within a compass no larger than an ordinary county in the United States. It is as much as I can do to comprehend this stupefying fact. How it wears a man out to have to read up a hundred pages of history every two or three miles—for verily the celebrated localities of Palestine occur that close together. How wearily, how bewilderingly they swarm about your path!

In due time we reached the ancient village of Magdala.

Chapter XLVIII

MAGDALA is not a beautiful place. It is thoroughly Syrian, and that is to say that it is thoroughly ugly, and cramped, squalid, uncomfortable, and filthy—just the style of cities that have adorned the country since Adam's time, as all writers have labored hard to prove, and have succeeded. The streets of Magdala are any where from three to six feet wide, and reeking with uncleanliness. The houses are from five to seven feet high, and all built upon one arbitrary plan—the ungraceful form of a dry-goods box. The sides are daubed with a smooth white plaster, and tastefully frescoed aloft and alow with disks of camel-dung placed there to dry. This gives the edifice the romantic appearance of having been riddled with cannon-balls, and imparts to it a very warlike aspect. When the artist has arranged his materials with an eye to just proportion—the small and the large flakes in alternate rows, and separated by carefully-considered intervals—I know of nothing more cheerful to look upon than a spirited Syrian fresco. The flat, plastered roof is garnished by picturesque stacks of fresco materials, which, having become thoroughly dried and cured, are placed there where it will be convenient. It is used for fuel. There is no timber of any consequence in Palestine—none at all to waste upon fires—and neither are there any mines of coal. If my description has been intelligible, you will perceive, now, that a square, flat-roofed hovel, neatly frescoed, with its wall-tops gallantly bastioned and turreted with dried camel-refuse, gives to a landscape a feature that is exceedingly festive and picturesque, especially if one is careful to remember to stick in a cat wherever, about the premises, there is room for a cat to sit. There are no windows to a Syrian hut, and no chimneys. When I used to read that they let a bed-ridden man down through the roof of a house in Capernaum to get him into the presence of the Saviour, I generally had a three-story brick in my mind, and marveled that they did not break his neck with the strange experiment. I perceive now, however, that they might have taken him by the heels and thrown him clear over the house without discommoding him very much. Palestine is not changed any since those days, in manners, customs, architecture, or people.

As we rode into Magdala not a soul was visible. But the ring of the horses' hoofs roused the stupid population, and they all came trooping out—old men and old women, boys and girls, the blind, the crazy, and the crippled, all in ragged, soiled and scanty raiment, and all abject beggars by nature, instinct and education. How the vermin-tortured vagabonds did swarm! How they showed their scars and sores, and piteously pointed to their maimed and crooked limbs, and begged with their pleading eyes for charity! We had invoked a spirit we could not lay. They hung to the horses's tails, clung to their manes and the stirrups, closed in on every side in scorn of dangerous hoofs—and out of their infidel throats, with one accord, burst an agonizing and most infernal chorus: "Howajji, bucksheesh! howajji, bucksheesh! howajji, bucksheesh! bucksheesh! bucksheesh!" I never was in a storm like that before.

As we paid the bucksheesh out to sore-eyed children and brown, buxom girls with repulsively tattooed lips and chins, we filed through the town and by many an exquisite fresco, till we came to a bramble-infested inclosure and a Roman-looking ruin which had been the veritable dwelling of St. Mary Magdalene, the friend and follower of Jesus. The guide believed it, and so did I. I could not well do otherwise, with the house right there before my eyes as plain as day. The pilgrims took down portions of the front wall for specimens, as is their honored custom, and then we departed.

We are camped in this place, now, just within the city walls of Tiberias. We went into the town before nightfall and looked at its people—we cared nothing about its houses. Its people are best examined at a distance. They are particularly uncomely Jews, Arabs, and negroes. Squalor and poverty are the pride of Tiberias. The young women wear their dower strung upon a strong wire that curves downward from the top of the head to the jaw—Turkish silver coins which they have raked together or inherited. Most of these maidens were not wealthy, but some few had been very kindly dealt with by

fortune. I saw heiresses there worth, in their own right—
worth, well, I suppose I might venture to say, as much as nine
dollars and a half. But such cases are rare. When you come
across one of these, she naturally puts on airs. She will not
ask for bucksheesh. She will not even permit of undue familiarity. She assumes a crushing dignity and goes on serenely
practicing with her fine-tooth comb and quoting poetry just
the same as if you were not present at all. Some people can
not stand prosperity.

They say that the long-nosed, lanky, dyspeptic-looking
body-snatchers, with the indescribable hats on, and a long
curl dangling down in front of each ear, are the old, familiar,
self-righteous Pharisees we read of in the Scriptures. Verily,
they look it. Judging merely by their general style, and
without other evidence, one might easily suspect that self-
righteousness was their specialty.

From various authorities I have culled information concerning Tiberias. It was built by Herod Antipas, the murderer
of John the Baptist, and named after the Emperor Tiberius.
It is believed that it stands upon the site of what must have
been, ages ago, a city of considerable architectural pretensions, judging by the fine porphyry pillars that are scattered
through Tiberias and down the lake shore southward. These
were fluted, once, and yet, although the stone is about as hard
as iron, the flutings are almost worn away. These pillars are
small, and doubtless the edifices they adorned were distinguished more for elegance than grandeur. This modern
town—Tiberias—is only mentioned in the New Testament;
never in the Old.

The Sanhedrim met here last, and for three hundred years
Tiberias was the metropolis of the Jews in Palestine. It is one
of the four holy cities of the Israelites, and is to them what
Mecca is to the Mohammedan and Jerusalem to the Christian.
It has been the abiding place of many learned and famous
Jewish rabbins. They lie buried here, and near them lie also
twenty-five thousand of their faith who traveled far to be near
them while they lived and lie with them when they died. The
great Rabbi Ben Israel spent three years here in the early part
of the third century. He is dead, now.

The celebrated Sea of Galilee is not so large a sea as Lake Tahoe* by a good deal—it is just about two-thirds as large. And when we come to speak of beauty, this sea is no more to be compared to Tahoe than a meridian of longitude is to a rainbow. The dim waters of this pool can not suggest the limpid brilliancy of Tahoe; these low, shaven, yellow hillocks of rocks and sand, so devoid of perspective, can not suggest the grand peaks that compass Tahoe like a wall, and whose ribbed and chasmed fronts are clad with stately pines that seem to grow small and smaller as they climb, till one might fancy them reduced to weeds and shrubs far upward, where they join the everlasting snows. Silence and solitude brood over Tahoe; and silence and solitude brood also over this lake of Genessaret. But the solitude of the one is as cheerful and fascinating as the solitude of the other is dismal and repellant.

In the early morning one watches the silent battle of dawn and darkness upon the waters of Tahoe with a placid interest; but when the shadows sulk away and one by one the hidden beauties of the shore unfold themselves in the full splendor of noon; when the still surface is belted like a rainbow with broad bars of blue and green and white, half the distance from circumference to centre; when, in the lazy summer afternoon, he lies in a boat, far out to where the dead blue of the deep water begins, and smokes the pipe of peace and idly winks at the distant crags and patches of snow from under his cap-brim; when the boat drifts shoreward to the white water, and he lolls over the gunwale and gazes by the hour down through the crystal depths and notes the colors of the pebbles and reviews the finny armies gliding in procession a hundred feet below; when at night he sees moon and stars, mountain ridges feathered with pines, jutting white capes, bold promontories, grand sweeps of rugged scenery topped with bald, glimmering peaks, all magnificently pictured in the polished mirror of the lake, in richest, softest detail, the tranquil interest that was born with the morning deepens and deepens, by

*I measure all lakes by Tahoe, partly because I am far more familiar with it than with any other, and partly because I have such a high admiration for it and such a world of pleasant recollections of it, that it is very nearly impossible for me to speak of lakes and not mention it.

sure degrees, till it culminates at last in resistless fascination!

It is solitude, for birds and squirrels on the shore and fishes in the water are all the creatures that are near to make it otherwise, but it is not the sort of solitude to make one dreary. Come to Galilee for that. If these unpeopled deserts, these rusty mounds of barrenness, that never, never, never do shake the glare from their harsh outlines, and fade and faint into vague perspective; that melancholy ruin of Capernaum; this stupid village of Tiberias, slumbering under its six funereal plumes of palms; yonder desolate declivity where the swine of the miracle ran down into the sea, and doubtless thought it was better to swallow a devil or two and get drowned into the bargain than have to live longer in such a place; this cloudless, blistering sky; this solemn, sailless, tintless lake, reposing within its rim of yellow hills and low, steep banks, and looking just as expressionless and unpoetical (when we leave its sublime history out of the question,) as any metropolitan reservoir in Christendom—if these things are not food for rock me to sleep, mother, none exist, I think.

But I should not offer the evidence for the prosecution and leave the defense unheard. Wm. C. Grimes deposes as follows:—

"We had taken ship to go over to the other side. The sea was not more than six miles wide. Of the beauty of the scene, however, I can not say enough, nor can I imagine where those travelers carried their eyes who have described the scenery of the lake as tame or uninteresting. The first great characteristic of it is the deep basin in which it lies. This is from three to four hundred feet deep on all sides except at the lower end, and the sharp slope of the banks, which are all of the richest green, is broken and diversified by the wâdys and water-courses which work their way down through the sides of the basin, forming dark chasms or light sunny valleys. Near Tiberias these banks are rocky, and ancient sepulchres open in them, with their doors toward the water. They selected grand spots, as did the Egyptians of old, for burial places, as if they designed that when the voice of God should reach the sleepers, they should walk forth and open their eyes on scenes of glorious beauty. On the east, the wild and desolate mountains contrast finely with the deep blue lake; and toward the north, sublime and majestic, Hermon looks down on the sea, lifting his white crown to heaven with the pride of a hill that has seen the departing footsteps of a hundred generations. On the north-east shore of the sea was a single tree, and this is the only tree of any size visible from the water of the lake, except a few lonely palms in the city of Tiberias, and by its solitary position attracts more attention than would a forest. The whole appearance of the scene is precisely what we would expect and desire the scenery of Genessaret to be, grand beauty, but quiet calm. The very mountains are calm."

It is an ingeniously written description, and well calculated to deceive. But if the paint and the ribbons and the flowers be stripped from it, a skeleton will be found beneath.

So stripped, there remains a lake six miles wide and neutral in color; with steep green banks, unrelieved by shrubbery; at one end bare, unsightly rocks, with (almost invisible) holes in them of no consequence to the picture; eastward, " wild and desolate mountains;" (low, desolate hills, he should have said;) in the north, a mountain called Hermon, with snow on it; peculiarity of the picture, "calmness;" its prominent feature, one tree.

No ingenuity could make such a picture beautiful—to one's actual vision.

I claim the right to correct misstatements, and have so corrected the color of the water in the above recapitulation. The waters of Genessaret are of an exceedingly mild blue, even from a high elevation and a distance of five miles. Close at hand (the witness was sailing on the lake,) it is hardly proper to call them blue at all, much less "deep" blue. I wish to state, also, not as a correction, but as matter of opinion, that Mount Hermon is not a striking or picturesque mountain by any means, being too near the height of its immediate neighbors to be so. That is all. I do not object to the witness dragging a mountain forty-five miles to help the scenery under consideration, because it is entirely proper to do it, and besides, the picture needs it.

"C. W. E.," (of "Life in the Holy Land,") deposes as follows:—

"A beautiful sea lies unbosomed among the Galilean hills, in the midst of that land once possessed by Zebulon and Naphtali, Asher and Dan. The azure of the sky penetrates the depths of the lake, and the waters are sweet and cool. On the west, stretch broad fertile plains; on the north the rocky shores rise step by step until in the far distance tower the snowy heights of Hermon; on the east through a misty veil are seen the high plains of Perea, which stretch away in rugged mountains leading the mind by varied paths toward Jerusalem the Holy. Flowers bloom in this terrestrial paradise, once beautiful and verdant with waving trees; singing birds enchant the ear; the turtle-dove soothes with its soft note; the crested lark sends up its song toward heaven, and the grave and stately stork inspires the mind with thought, and leads it on to meditation and repose. Life here was once idyllic, charming; here were once no rich, no poor, no high, no low. It was a world of ease, simplicity, and beauty; now it is a scene of desolation and misery."

This is not an ingenious picture. It is the worst I ever saw. It describes in elaborate detail what it terms a "terrestrial paradise," and closes with the startling information that this paradise is "a scene of *desolation and misery.*"

I have given two fair, average specimens of the character of the testimony offered by the majority of the writers who visit this region. One says, "Of the beauty of the scene I can not say enough," and then proceeds to cover up with a woof of glittering sentences a thing which, when stripped for inspection, proves to be only an unobtrusive basin of water, some mountainous desolation, and one tree. The other, after a conscientious effort to build a terrestrial paradise out of the same materials, with the addition of a "grave and stately stork," spoils it all by blundering upon the ghastly truth at the last.

Nearly every book concerning Galilee and its lake describes the scenery as beautiful. No—not always so straightforward as that. Sometimes the *impression* intentionally conveyed is that it is beautiful, at the same time that the author is careful not to *say* that it is, in plain Saxon. But a careful analysis of these descriptions will show that the materials of which they are formed are not individually beautiful and can not be wrought into combinations that are beautiful. The veneration and the affection which some of these men felt for the scenes they were speaking of, heated their fancies and biased their judgment; but the pleasant falsities they wrote were full of honest sincerity, at any rate. Others wrote as they did, because they feared it would be unpopular to write otherwise.

Others were hypocrites and deliberately meant to deceive. Any of them would say in a moment, if asked, that it was *always* right and always *best* to tell the truth. They would say that, at any rate, if they did not perceive the drift of the question.

But why should not the truth be spoken of this region? Is the truth harmful? Has it ever needed to hide its face? God made the Sea of Galilee and its surroundings as they are. Is it the province of Mr. Grimes to improve upon the work?

I am sure, from the tenor of books I have read, that many who have visited this land in years gone by, were Presbyterians, and came seeking evidences in support of their particular creed; they found a Presbyterian Palestine, and they had already made up their minds to find no other, though possibly they did not know it, being blinded by their zeal. Others were Baptists, seeking Baptist evidences and a Baptist Palestine. Others were Catholics, Methodists, Episcopalians, seeking evidences indorsing their several creeds, and a Catholic, a Methodist, an Episcopalian Palestine. Honest as these men's intentions may have been, they were full of partialities and prejudices, they entered the country with their verdicts already prepared, and they could no more write dispassionately and impartially about it than they could about their own wives and children. Our pilgrims have brought *their* verdicts with them. They have shown it in their conversation ever since we left Beirout. I can almost tell, in set phrase, what they will say when they see Tabor, Nazareth, Jericho and Jerusalem— *because I have the books they will "smouch" their ideas from*. These authors write pictures and frame rhapsodies, and lesser men follow and see with the author's eyes instead of their own, and speak with his tongue. What the pilgrims said at Cesarea Philippi surprised me with its wisdom. I found it afterwards in Robinson. What they said when Genessaret burst upon their vision, charmed me with its grace. I find it in Mr. Thompson's "Land and the Book." They have spoken often, in happily worded language which never varied, of how they mean to lay their weary heads upon a stone at Bethel, as Jacob did, and close their dim eyes, and dream, perchance, of angels descending out of heaven on a ladder. It was very pretty. But I have recognized the weary head and the dim eyes, finally. They borrowed the idea—and the words—and the construction—and the punctuation—from Grimes. The pilgrims will tell of Palestine, when they get home, not as it appeared to *them*, but as it appeared to Thompson and Robinson and Grimes—with the tints varied to suit each pilgrim's creed.

Pilgrims, sinners and Arabs are all abed, now, and the camp is still. Labor in loneliness is irksome. Since I made my last few notes, I have been sitting outside the tent for half an hour. Night is the time to see Galilee. Genessaret under these lustrous stars, has nothing repulsive about it. Genessaret with the glittering reflections of the constellations flecking its surface, almost makes me regret that I ever saw the rude glare of the day upon it. Its history and its associations are its chiefest charm, in any eyes, and the spells they weave are feeble in the searching light of the sun. *Then*, we scarcely feel the fetters. Our thoughts wander constantly to the practical concerns of life, and refuse to dwell upon things that seem vague and unreal. But when the day is done, even the most unimpressible must yield to the dreamy influences of this tranquil starlight. The old traditions of the place steal upon his memory and haunt his reveries, and then his fancy clothes all sights and sounds with the supernatural. In the lapping of the waves upon the beach, he hears the dip of ghostly oars; in the secret noises of the night he hears spirit voices; in the soft sweep of the breeze, the rush of invisible wings. Phantom ships are on the sea, the dead of twenty centuries come forth from the tombs, and in the dirges of the night wind the songs of old forgotten ages find utterance again.

In the starlight, Galilee has no boundaries but the broad compass of the heavens, and is a theatre meet for great events; meet for the birth of a religion able to save a world; and meet for the stately Figure appointed to stand upon its stage and proclaim its high decrees. But in the sunlight, one says: Is it for the deeds which were done and the words which were spoken in this little acre of rocks and sand eighteen centuries gone, that the bells are ringing to-day in the remote islands of the sea and far and wide over continents that clasp the circumference of the huge globe?

One can comprehend it only when night has hidden all incongruities and created a theatre proper for so grand a drama.

Chapter XLIX

WE TOOK ANOTHER swim in the Sea of Galilee at twilight yesterday, and another at sunrise this morning. We have not sailed, but three swims are equal to a sail, are they not? There were plenty of fish visible in the water, but we have no outside aids in this pilgrimage but "Tent Life in the Holy Land," "The Land and the Book," and other literature of like description—no fishing-tackle. There were no fish to be had in the village of Tiberias. True, we saw two or three vagabonds mending their nets, but never trying to catch anything with them.

We did not go to the ancient warm baths two miles below Tiberias. I had no desire in the world to go there. This seemed a little strange, and prompted me to try to discover what the cause of this unreasonable indifference was. It turned out to be simply because Pliny mentions them. I have conceived a sort of unwarrantable unfriendliness toward Pliny and St. Paul, because it seems as if I can never ferret out a place that I can have to myself. It always and eternally transpires that St. Paul has been to that place, and Pliny has "mentioned" it.

In the early morning we mounted and started. And then a weird apparition marched forth at the head of the procession—a pirate, I thought, if ever a pirate dwelt upon land. It was a tall Arab, as swarthy as an Indian; young—say thirty years of age. On his head he had closely bound a gorgeous yellow and red striped silk scarf, whose ends, lavishly fringed with tassels, hung down between his shoulders and dallied with the wind. From his neck to his knees, in ample folds, a robe swept down that was a very star-spangled banner of curved and sinuous bars of black and white. Out of his back, somewhere, apparently, the long stem of a chibouk projected, and reached far above his right shoulder. Athwart his back, diagonally, and extending high above his left shoulder, was an Arab gun of Saladin's time, that was splendid with silver plating from stock clear up to the end of its measureless stretch of barrel. About his waist was bound many and many a yard of elaborately figured but sadly tarnished stuff that came from sumptuous Persia, and among the baggy folds in front the sun-beams glinted from a formidable battery of old brass-mounted horse-pistols and the gilded hilts of blood-thirsty knives. There were holsters for more pistols appended to the wonderful stack of long-haired goat-skins and Persian carpets, which the man had been taught to regard in the light of a saddle; and down among the pendulous rank of vast tassels that swung from that saddle, and clanging against the iron shovel of a stirrup that propped the warrior's knees up toward his chin, was a crooked, silver-clad scimetar of such awful dimensions and such implacable expression that no man might hope to look upon it and not shudder. The fringed and bedizened prince whose privilege it is to ride the pony and lead the elephant into a country village is poor and naked compared to this chaos of paraphernalia, and the happy vanity of the one is the very poverty of satisfaction compared to the majestic serenity, the overwhelming complacency of the other.

"*Who* is this? *What* is this?" That was the trembling inquiry all down the line.

"Our guard! From Galilee to the birthplace of the Saviour, the country is infested with fierce Bedouins, whose sole happiness it is, in this life, to cut and stab and mangle and murder unoffending Christians. Allah be with us!"

"Then hire a regiment! Would you send us out among these desperate hordes, with no salvation in our utmost need but this old turret?"

The dragoman laughed—not at the facetiousness of the simile, for verily, that guide or that courier or that dragoman never yet lived upon earth who had in him the faintest appreciation of a joke, even though that joke were so broad and so ponderous that if it fell on him it would flatten him out like a postage stamp—the dragoman laughed, and then, emboldened by some thought that was in his brain, no doubt, proceeded to extremities and winked.

In straits like these, when a man laughs, it is encouraging; when he winks, it is positively reassuring. He finally intimated that one guard would be sufficient to protect us, but that that one was an absolute necessity. It was because of the moral weight his awful panoply would have with the Bedouins.

Then I said we didn't want any guard at all. If one fantastic vagabond could protect eight armed Christians and a pack of Arab servants from all harm, surely that detachment could protect themselves. He shook his head doubtfully. Then I said, just think of how it looks—think of how it would read, to self-reliant Americans, that we went sneaking through this deserted wilderness under the protection of this masquerading Arab, who would break his neck getting out of the country if a man that *was* a man ever started after him. It was a mean, low, degrading position. Why were we ever told to bring navy revolvers with us if we had to be protected at last by this infamous star-spangled scum of the desert? These appeals were vain—the dragoman only smiled and shook his head.

I rode to the front and struck up an acquaintance with King Solomon-in-all-his-glory, and got him to show me his lingering eternity of a gun. It had a rusty flint lock; it was ringed and barred and plated with silver from end to end, but it was as desperately out of the perpendicular as are the billiard cues of '49 that one finds yet in service in the ancient mining camps of California. The muzzle was eaten by the rust of centuries into a ragged filagree-work, like the end of a burnt-out stove-pipe. I shut one eye and peered within—it was flaked with iron rust like an old steamboat boiler. I borrowed the ponderous pistols and snapped them. They were rusty inside, too—had not been loaded for a generation. I went back, full of encouragement, and reported to the guide, and asked him to discharge this dismantled fortress. It came out, then. This fellow was a retainer of the Sheik of Tiberias. He was a source of Government revenue. He was to the Empire of Tiberias what the customs are to America. The Sheik imposed guards upon travelers and charged them for it. It is a lucrative source of emolument, and sometimes brings into the national treasury as much as thirty-five or forty dollars a year.

I knew the warrior's secret now; I knew the hollow vanity of his rusty trumpery, and despised his asinine complacency. I told on him, and with reckless daring the cavalcade rode straight ahead into the perilous solitudes of the desert, and scorned his frantic warnings of the mutilation and death that hovered about them on every side.

Arrived at an elevation of twelve hundred feet above the lake, (I ought to mention that the lake lies six hundred feet below the level of the Mediterranean—no traveler ever neglects to flourish that fragment of news in his letters,) as bald and unthrilling a panorama as any land can afford, perhaps, was spread out before us. Yet it was so crowded with historical interest, that if all the pages that have been written about it were spread upon its surface, they would flag it from horizon to horizon like a pavement. Among the localities comprised in this view, were Mount Hermon; the hills that border Cesarea Philippi, Dan, the Sources of the Jordan and the Waters of Merom; Tiberias; the Sea of Galilee; Joseph's Pit; Capernaum; Bethsaida; the supposed scenes of the Sermon on the Mount, the feeding of the multitudes and the miraculous draught of fishes; the declivity down which the swine ran to the sea; the entrance and the exit of the Jordan; Safed, "the city set upon a hill," one of the four holy cities of the Jews, and the place where they believe the real Messiah will appear when he comes to redeem the world; part of the battle-field of Hattin, where the knightly Crusaders fought their last fight, and in a blaze of glory passed from the stage and ended their splendid career forever; Mount Tabor, the traditional scene of the Lord's Transfiguration. And down toward the southeast lay a landscape that suggested to my mind a quotation (imperfectly remembered, no doubt:)

"The Ephraimites, not being called upon to share in the rich spoils of the Ammonitish war, assembled a mighty host to fight against Jeptha, Judge of Israel; who, being apprised of their approach, gathered together the men of Israel and gave them battle and put them to flight. To make his victory the more secure, he stationed guards at the different fords and passages of the Jordan, with instructions to let none pass who could not say Shibboleth. The Ephraimites, being of a different tribe, could not frame to pronounce the word aright, but called it Sibboleth, which proved them enemies and cost them their lives; wherefore, forty and two thousand fell at the different fords and passages of the Jordan that day."

We jogged along peacefully over the great caravan route from Damascus to Jerusalem and Egypt, past Lubia and other Syrian hamlets, perched, in the unvarying style, upon the summit of steep mounds and hills, and fenced round about with giant cactuses, (the sign of worthless land,) with prickly pears upon them like hams, and came at last to the battle-field of Hattin.

It is a grand, irregular plateau, and looks as if it might have been created for a battle-field. Here the peerless Saladin met the Christian host some seven hundred years ago, and broke their power in Palestine for all time to come. There had long been a truce between the opposing forces, but according to the Guide-Book, Raynauld of Chatillon, Lord of Kerak, broke it by plundering a Damascus caravan, and refusing to give up either the merchants or their goods when Saladin demanded them. This conduct of an insolent petty chieftain stung the Sultan to the quick, and he swore that he would slaughter Raynauld with his own hand, no matter how, or when, or where he found him. Both armies prepared for war. Under the weak King of Jerusalem was the very flower of the Christian chivalry. He foolishly compelled them to undergo a long, exhausting march, in the scorching sun, and then, without water or other refreshment, ordered them to encamp in this open plain. The splendidly mounted masses of Moslem soldiers swept round the north end of Genessaret, burning and destroying as they came, and pitched their camp in front of the opposing lines. At dawn the terrific fight began. Surrounded on all sides by the Sultan's swarming battalions, the Christian Knights fought on without a hope for their lives. They fought with desperate valor, but to no purpose; the odds of heat and numbers, and consuming thirst, were too great against them. Towards the middle of the day the bravest of their band cut their way through the Moslem ranks and gained the summit of a little hill, and there, hour after hour, they closed around the banner of the Cross, and beat back the charging squadrons of the enemy.

But the doom of the Christian power was sealed. Sunset found Saladin Lord of Palestine, the Christian chivalry strewn in heaps upon the field, and the King of Jerusalem, the Grand Master of the Templars, and Raynauld of Chatillon, captives in the Sultan's tent. Saladin treated two of the prisoners with princely courtesy, and ordered refreshments to be set before them. When the King handed an iced Sherbet to Chatillon, the Sultan said, "It is thou that givest it to him, not I." He remembered his oath, and slaughtered the hapless Knight of Chatillon with his own hand.

It was hard to realize that this silent plain had once resounded with martial music and trembled to the tramp of armed men. It was hard to people this solitude with rushing columns of cavalry, and stir its torpid pulses with the shouts of victors, the shrieks of the wounded, and the flash of banner and steel above the surging billows of war. A desolation is here that not even imagination can grace with the pomp of life and action.

We reached Tabor safely, and considerably in advance of that old iron-clad swindle of a guard. We never saw a human being on the whole route, much less lawless hordes of Bedouins. Tabor stands solitary and alone, a giant sentinel above the Plain of Esdraelon. It rises some fourteen hundred feet above the surrounding level, a green, wooden cone, symmetrical and full of grace—a prominent landmark, and one that is exceedingly pleasant to eyes surfeited with the repulsive monotony of desert Syria. We climbed the steep path to its summit, through breezy glades of thorn and oak. The view presented from its highest peak was almost beautiful. Below, was the broad, level plain of Esdraelon, checkered with fields like a chess-board, and full as smooth and level, seemingly; dotted about its borders with white, compact villages, and faintly penciled, far and near, with the curving lines of roads and trails. When it is robed in the fresh verdure of spring, it must form a charming picture, even by itself. Skirting its southern border rises "Little Hermon," over whose summit a glimpse of Gilboa is caught. Nain, famous for the raising of the widow's son, and Endor, as famous for the performances of her witch, are in view. To the eastward lies the Valley of the Jordan and beyond it the mountains of Gilead. Westward is Mount Carmel. Hermon in the north—the table-lands of Bashan—Safed, the holy city, gleaming white upon a tall spur of the mountains of Lebanon—a steel-blue corner of the Sea of Galilee—saddle-peaked Hattin, traditional "Mount of Beatitudes" and mute witness of the last brave fight of the Crusading host for Holy Cross—these fill up the picture.

To glance at the salient features of this landscape through

the picturesque framework of a ragged and ruined stone win-
dow-arch of the time of Christ, thus hiding from sight all that
is unattractive, is to secure to yourself a pleasure worth climbing the mountain to enjoy. One must stand on his head to
get the best effect in a fine sunset, and set a landscape in a
bold, strong framework that is very close at hand, to bring
out all its beauty. One learns this latter truth never more to
forget it, in that mimic land of enchantment, the wonderful
garden of my lord the Count Pallavicini, near Genoa. You go
wandering for hours among hills and wooded glens, artfully
contrived to leave the impression that Nature shaped them
and not man; following winding paths and coming suddenly
upon leaping cascades and rustic bridges; finding sylvan lakes
where you expected them not; loitering through battered
mediæval castles in miniature that seem hoary with age and
yet were built a dozen years ago; meditating over ancient
crumbling tombs, whose marble columns were marred and
broken purposely by the modern artist that made them; stumbling unawares upon toy palaces, wrought of rare and costly
materials, and again upon a peasant's hut, whose dilapidated
furniture would never suggest that it was made so to order;
sweeping round and round in the midst of a forest on an
enchanted wooden horse that is moved by some invisible
agency; traversing Roman roads and passing under majestic
triumphal arches; resting in quaint bowers where unseen spirits discharge jets of water on you from every possible direction, and where even the flowers you touch assail you with a
shower; boating on a subterranean lake among caverns and
arches royally draped with clustering stalactites, and passing
out into open day upon another lake, which is bordered with
sloping banks of grass and gay with patrician barges that
swim at anchor in the shadow of a miniature marble temple
that rises out of the clear water and glasses its white statues,
its rich capitals and fluted columns in the tranquil depths. So,
from marvel to marvel you have drifted on, thinking all the
time that the one last seen must be the chiefest. And, verily,
the chiefest wonder *is* reserved until the last, but you do not
see it until you step ashore, and passing through a wilderness
of rare flowers, collected from every corner of the earth, you
stand at the door of one more mimic temple. Right in this

place the artist taxed his genius to the utmost, and fairly opened the gates of fairy land. You look through an unpretending pane of glass, stained yellow; the first thing you see is a mass of quivering foliage, ten short steps before you, in the midst of which is a ragged opening like a gateway—a thing that is common enough in nature, and not apt to excite suspicions of a deep human design—and above the bottom of the gateway, project, in the most careless way, a few broad tropic leaves and brilliant flowers. All of a sudden, through this bright, bold gateway, you catch a glimpse of the faintest, softest, richest picture that ever graced the dream of a dying Saint, since John saw the New Jerusalem glimmering above the clouds of Heaven. A broad sweep of sea, flecked with careening sails; a sharp, jutting cape, and a lofty lighthouse on it; a sloping lawn behind it; beyond, a portion of the old "city of palaces," with its parks and hills and stately mansions; beyond these, a prodigious mountain, with its strong outlines sharply cut against ocean and sky; and over all, vagrant shreds and flakes of cloud, floating in a sea of gold. The ocean is gold, the city is gold, the meadow, the mountain, the sky— every thing is golden—rich, and mellow, and dreamy as a vision of Paradise. No artist could put upon canvas its entrancing beauty, and yet, without the yellow glass, and the carefully contrived accident of a framework that cast it into enchanted distance and shut out from it all unattractive features, it was not a picture to fall into ecstacies over. Such is life, and the trail of the serpent is over us all.

There is nothing for it now but to come back to old Tabor, though the subject is tiresome enough, and I can not stick to it for wandering off to scenes that are pleasanter to remember. I think I will skip, any how. There is nothing about Tabor (except we concede that it was the scene of the Transfiguration,) but some gray old ruins, stacked up there in all ages of the world from the days of stout Gideon and parties that flourished thirty centuries ago to the fresh yesterday of Crusading times. It has its Greek Convent, and the coffee there is good, but never a splinter of the true cross or bone of a hallowed saint to arrest the idle thoughts of worldlings and turn them into graver channels. A Catholic church is nothing to me that has no relics.

The plain of Esdraelon—"the battle-field of the nations"—only sets one to dreaming of Joshua, and Benhadad, and Saul, and Gideon; Tamerlane, Tancred, Cœur de Lion, and Saladin; the warrior Kings of Persia, Egypt's heroes, and Napoleon—for they all fought here. If the magic of the moonlight could summon from the graves of forgotten centuries and many lands the countless myriads that have battled on this wide, far-reaching floor, and array them in the thousand strange costumes of their hundred nationalities, and send the vast host sweeping down the plain, splendid with plumes and banners and glittering lances, I could stay here an age to see the phantom pageant. But the magic of the moonlight is a vanity and a fraud; and whoso putteth his trust in it shall suffer sorrow and disappointment.

Down at the foot of Tabor, and just at the edge of the storied Plain of Esdraelon, is the insignificant village of Deburieh, where Deborah, prophetess of Israel, lived. It is just like Magdala.

Chapter L

WE DESCENDED from Mount Tabor, crossed a deep ravine, and followed a hilly, rocky road to Nazareth—distant two hours. All distances in the East are measured by hours, not miles. A good horse will walk three miles an hour over nearly any kind of a road; therefore, an hour, here, always stands for three miles. This method of computation is bothersome and annoying; and until one gets thoroughly accustomed to it, it carries no intelligence to his mind until he has stopped and translated the pagan hours into Christian miles, just as people do with the spoken words of a foreign language they are acquainted with, but not familiarly enough to catch the meaning in a moment. Distances traveled by human feet are also estimated by hours and minutes, though I do not know what the base of the calculation is. In Constantinople you ask, "How far is it to the Consulate?" and they answer, "About ten minutes." "How far is it to the Lloyds' Agency?" "Quarter of an hour." "How far is it to the lower bridge?" "Four minutes." I can not be positive about it, but I think that there, when a man orders a pair of pantaloons, he says he wants them a quarter of a minute in the legs and nine seconds around the waist.

Two hours from Tabor to Nazareth—and as it was an uncommonly narrow, crooked trail, we necessarily met all the camel trains and jackass caravans between Jericho and Jacksonville in that particular place and nowhere else. The donkeys do not matter so much, because they are so small that you can jump your horse over them if he is an animal of spirit, but a camel is not jumpable. A camel is as tall as any ordinary dwelling-house in Syria—which is to say a camel is from one to two, and sometimes nearly three feet taller than a good-sized man. In this part of the country his load is oftenest in the shape of colossal sacks—one on each side. He and his cargo take up as much room as a carriage. Think of meeting this style of obstruction in a narrow trail. The camel would not turn out for a king. He stalks serenely along, bringing his cushioned stilts forward with the long, regular swing of a pendulum, and whatever is in the way must get out of the way peaceably, or be wiped out forcibly by the bulky sacks. It was a tiresome ride to us, and perfectly exhausting to the horses. We were compelled to jump over upwards of eighteen hundred donkeys, and only one person in the party was unseated less than sixty times by the camels. This seems like a powerful statement, but the poet has said, "Things are not what they seem." I can not think of any thing, now, more certain to make one shudder, than to have a soft-footed camel sneak up behind him and touch him on the ear with its cold, flabby under-lip. A camel did this for one of the boys, who was drooping over his saddle in a brown study. He glanced up and saw the majestic apparition hovering above him, and made frantic efforts to get out of the way, but the camel reached out and bit him on the shoulder before he accomplished it. This was the only pleasant incident of the journey.

At Nazareth we camped in an olive grove near the Virgin Mary's fountain, and that wonderful Arab "guard" came to collect some bucksheesh for his "services" in following us from Tiberias and warding off invisible dangers with the terrors of his armament. The dragoman had paid his master, but that counted as nothing—if you hire a man to sneeze for you, here, and another man chooses to help him, you have got to pay both. They do nothing whatever without pay. How it must have surprised these people to hear the way of salvation offered to them *"without money and without price."* If the manners, the people or the customs of this country have changed since the Saviour's time, the figures and metaphors of the Bible are not the evidences to prove it by.

We entered the great Latin Convent which is built over the traditional dwelling-place of the Holy Family. We went down a flight of fifteen steps below the ground level, and stood in a small chapel tricked out with tapestry hangings, silver lamps, and oil paintings. A spot marked by a cross, in the marble floor, under the altar, was exhibited as the place made forever holy by the feet of the Virgin when she stood up to receive the message of the angel. So simple, so unpretending a locality, to be the scene of so mighty an event! The very scene of the Annunciation—an event which has been commemorated by splendid shrines and august temples all over the civilized world, and one which the princes of art have made it their loftiest ambition to picture worthily on their canvas; a spot whose history is familiar to the very children of every house, and city, and obscure hamlet of the furthest lands of Christendom; a spot which myriads of men would toil across the breadth of a world to see, would consider it a priceless privilege to look upon. It was easy to think these thoughts. But it was not easy to bring myself up to the magnitude of the situation. I could sit off several thousand miles and imagine the angel appearing, with shadowy wings and lustrous countenance, and note the glory that streamed downward upon the Virgin's head while the message from the Throne of God fell upon her ears—any one can do that, beyond the ocean, but few can do it here. I saw the little recess from which the angel stepped, but could not fill its void. The angels that I know are creatures of unstable fancy—they will not fit in niches of substantial stone. Imagination labors best in distant fields. I doubt if any man can stand in the Grotto of the Annunciation and people with the phantom images of his mind its too tangible walls of stone.

They showed us a broken granite pillar, depending from the roof, which they said was hacked in two by the Moslem conquerors of Nazareth, in the vain hope of pulling down the sanctuary. But the pillar remained miraculously suspended in the air, and, unsupported itself, supported then and still supports the roof. By dividing this statement up among eight, it was found not difficult to believe it.

These gifted Latin monks never do any thing by halves. If they were to show you the Brazen Serpent that was elevated in the wilderness, you could depend upon it that they had on hand the pole it was elevated on also, and even the hole it stood in. They have got the "Grotto" of the Annunciation here; and just as convenient to it as one's throat is to his mouth, they have also the Virgin's Kitchen, and even her sitting-room, where she and Joseph watched the infant Saviour play with Hebrew toys eighteen hundred years ago. All under one roof, and all clean, spacious, comfortable "grottoes." It seems curious that personages intimately connected with the Holy Family always lived in grottoes—in Nazareth, in Bethlehem, in imperial Ephesus—and yet nobody else in their day and generation thought of doing any thing of the kind. If they ever did, their grottoes are all gone, and I suppose we ought to wonder at the peculiar marvel of the preservation of these I speak of. When the Virgin fled from Herod's wrath, she hid in a grotto in Bethlehem, and the same is there to this day. The slaughter of the innocents in Bethlehem was done in a grotto; the Saviour was born in a grotto—both are shown to pilgrims yet. It is exceedingly strange that these tremendous events all happened in grottoes—and exceedingly fortunate, likewise, because the strongest houses must crumble to ruin in time, but a grotto in the living rock will last forever. It is an imposture—this grotto stuff—but it is one that all men ought to thank the Catholics for. Wherever they ferret out a lost locality made holy by some Scriptural event, they straightway build a massive—almost imperishable—church there, and preserve the memory of that locality for the gratification of future generations. If it had been left to Protestants to do this most worthy work, we would not even know where Jerusalem is to-day, and the man who could go and put his finger on Nazareth would be too wise for this world. The world owes the Catholics its good will even for the happy rascality of hewing out these bogus grottoes in the rock; for it is infinitely more satisfactory to look at a grotto, where people have faithfully believed for centuries that the Virgin once lived, than to have to imagine a dwelling-place for her somewhere, any where, nowhere, loose and at large all over this town of Nazareth. There is too large a scope of country. The imagination can not work. There is no one particular spot to chain your eye, rivet your interest, and make you think. The memory of the Pilgrims can not perish while Plymouth Rock remains to us. The old monks are wise. They know how to drive a stake through a pleasant tradition that will hold it to its place forever.

We visited the places where Jesus worked for fifteen years as a carpenter, and where he attempted to teach in the synagogue and was driven out by a mob. Catholic chapels stand upon these sites and protect the little fragments of the ancient walls which remain. Our pilgrims broke off specimens. We visited, also, a new chapel, in the midst of the town, which is built around a boulder some twelve feet long by four feet thick; the priests discovered, a few years ago, that the disciples had sat upon this rock to rest, once, when they had walked up from Capernaum. They hastened to preserve the relic. Relics are very good property. Travelers are expected to pay for seeing them, and they do it cheerfully. We like the idea. One's conscience can never be the worse for the knowledge that he has paid his way like a man. Our pilgrims would have liked very well to get out their lampblack and stencil-plates and paint their names on that rock, together with the names of the villages they hail from in America, but the priests permit nothing of that kind. To speak the strict truth, however, our party seldom offend in that way, though we have men in the ship who never lose an opportunity to do it. Our pilgrims' chief sin is their lust for "specimens." I suppose that by this time they know the dimensions of that rock to an inch, and its weight to a ton; and I do not hesitate to charge that they will go back there to-night and try to carry it off.

This "Fountain of the Virgin" is the one which tradition says Mary used to get water from, twenty times a day, when she was a girl, and bear it away in a jar upon her head. The water streams through faucets in the face of a wall of ancient masonry which stands removed from the houses of the village. The young girls of Nazareth still collect about it by the dozen and keep up a riotous laughter and sky-larking. The Nazarene girls are homely. Some of them have large, lustrous eyes, but none of them have pretty faces. These girls wear a single garment, usually, and it is loose, shapeless, of undecided color; it is generally out of repair, too. They wear, from crown to jaw, curious strings of old coins, after the manner of the belles of Tiberias, and brass jewelry upon their wrists and in their ears. They wear no shoes and stockings. They are the most human girls we have found in the country yet, and the best natured. But there is no question that these pictur-esque maidens sadly lack comeliness.

A pilgrim—the "Enthusiast"—said: "See that tall, graceful girl! look at the Madonna-like beauty of her countenance!"

Another pilgrim came along presently and said: "Observe that tall, graceful girl; what queenly Madonna-like gracefulness of beauty is in her countenance."

I said: "She is not tall, she is short; she is not beautiful, she is homely; she is graceful enough, I grant, but she is rather boisterous."

The third and last pilgrim moved by, before long, and he said: "Ah, what a tall, graceful girl! what Madonna-like gracefulness of queenly beauty!"

The verdicts were all in. It was time, now, to look up the authorities for all these opinions. I found this paragraph, which follows. Written by whom? Wm. C. Grimes:

> "After we were in the saddle, we rode down to the spring to have a last look at the women of Nazareth, who were, as a class, much the prettiest that we had seen in the East. As we approached the crowd a tall girl of nineteen advanced toward Miriam and offered her a cup of water. Her movement was graceful and queenly. We exclaimed on the spot at the Madonna-like beauty of her countenance. Whitely was suddenly thirsty, and begged for water, and drank it slowly, with his eyes over the top of the cup, fixed on her large black eyes, which gazed on him quite as curiously as he on her. Then Moreright wanted water. She gave it to him and he managed to spill it so as to ask for another cup, and by the time she came to me she saw through the operation; her eyes were full of fun as she looked at me. I laughed outright, and she joined me in as gay a shout as ever country maiden in old Orange county. I wished for a picture of her. A Madonna, whose face was a portrait of that beautiful Nazareth girl, would be a 'thing of beauty' and 'a joy forever.'"

That is the kind of gruel which has been served out from Palestine for ages. Commend me to Fennimore Cooper to find beauty in the Indians, and to Grimes to find it in the Arabs. Arab men are often fine looking, but Arab women are not. We can all believe that the Virgin Mary was beautiful; it is not natural to think otherwise; but does it follow that it is our duty to find beauty in these present women of Nazareth?

I love to quote from Grimes, because he is so dramatic. And because he is so romantic. And because he seems to care but little whether he tells the truth or not, so he scares the reader or excites his envy or his admiration.

He went through this peaceful land with one hand forever on his revolver, and the other on his pocket-handkerchief. Always, when he was not on the point of crying over a holy place, he was on the point of killing an Arab. More surprising things happened to him in Palestine than ever happened to any traveler here or elsewhere since Munchausen died.

At Beit Jin, where nobody had interfered with him, he crept out of his tent at dead of night and shot at what he took to be an Arab lying on a rock, some distance away, planning evil. The ball killed a wolf. Just before he fired, he makes a dramatic picture of himself—as usual, to scare the reader:

"Was it imagination, or did I see a moving object on the surface of the rock? If it were a man, why did he not now drop me? He had a beautiful shot as I stood out in my black boornoose against the white tent. I had the sensation of an entering bullet in my throat, breast, brain."

Reckless creature!

Riding toward Genessaret, they saw two Bedouins, and "we looked to our pistols and loosened them quietly in our shawls," etc. Always cool.

In Samaria, he charged up a hill, in the face of a volley of stones; he fired into the crowd of men who threw them. He says:

"*I never lost an opportunity* of impressing the Arabs with the perfection of American and English weapons, and the danger of attacking any one of the armed Franks. I think the lesson of that ball not lost."

At Beitin he gave his whole band of Arab muleteers a piece of his mind, and then—

"I contented myself with a solemn assurance that if there occurred another instance of disobedience to orders, I would thrash the responsible party as he never dreamed of being thrashed, and if I could not find who was responsible, I would whip them all, from first to last, whether there was a governor at hand to do it or I had to do it myself."

Perfectly fearless, this man.

He rode down the perpendicular path in the rocks, from the Castle of Banias to the oak grove, at a flying gallop, his horse striding "thirty feet" at every bound. I stand prepared to bring thirty reliable witnesses to prove that Putnam's famous feat at Horseneck was insignificant compared to this.

Behold him—always theatrical—looking at Jerusalem—

this time, by an oversight, with his hand off his pistol for once.

"I stood in the road, my hand on my horse's neck, and with my dim eyes sought to trace the outlines of the holy places which I had long before fixed in my mind, but the fast-flowing tears forbade my succeeding. There were our Mohammedan servants, a Latin monk, two Armenians and a Jew in our cortege, and all alike gazed with overflowing eyes."

If Latin monks and Arabs cried, I know to a moral certainty that the horses cried also, and so the picture is complete.

But when necessity demanded, he could be firm as adamant. In the Lebanon Valley an Arab youth—a Christian; he is particular to explain that Mohammedans do not steal—robbed him of a paltry ten dollars' worth of powder and shot. He convicted him before a sheik and looked on while he was punished by the terrible bastinado. Hear him:

"He (Mousa) was on his back in a twinkling, howling, shouting, screaming, but he was carried out to the piazza before the door, where we could see the operation, and laid face down. One man sat on his back and one on his legs, the latter holding up his feet, while a third laid on the bare soles a rhinoceros-hide koorbash* that whizzed through the air at every stroke. Poor Moreright was in agony, and Nama and Nama the Second (mother and sister of Mousa,) were on their faces begging and wailing, now embracing my knees and now Whitely's, while the brother, outside, made the air ring with cries louder than Mousa's. Even Yusef came and asked me on his knees to relent, and last of all, Betuni—the rascal had lost a feedbag in their house and had been loudest in his denunciations that morning—besought the Howajji to have mercy on the fellow."

But not he! The punishment was "suspended," at the *fifteenth blow*, to hear the confession. Then Grimes and his party rode away, and left the entire Christian family to be fined and as severely punished as the *Mohammedan sheik* should deem proper.

*"A Koorbash is Arabic for cowhide, the cow being a rhinoceros. It is the most cruel whip known to fame. Heavy as lead, and flexible as India-rubber, usually about forty inches long and tapering gradually from an inch in diameter to a point, it administers a blow which *leaves its mark for time*."— *Scow Life in Egypt*, by the same author.

"As I mounted, Yusef once more begged me to interfere and have mercy on them, but I looked around at the dark faces of the crowd, and I couldn't find one drop of pity in my heart for them."

He closes his picture with a rollicking burst of humor which contrasts finely with the grief of the mother and her children.

One more paragraph:

"Then once more I bowed my head. It is no shame to have wept in Palestine. I wept, when I saw Jerusalem, I wept when I lay in the starlight at Bethlehem, I wept on the blessed shores of Galilee. My hand was no less firm on the rein, my finger did not tremble on the trigger of my pistol when I rode with it in my right hand along the shore of the blue sea" (weeping.) "My eye was not dimmed by those tears nor my heart in aught weakened. Let him who would sneer at my emotion close this volume here, for he will find little to his taste in my journeyings through Holy Land."

He never bored but he struck water.

I am aware that this is a pretty voluminous notice of Mr. Grimes' book. However, it is proper and legitimate to speak of it, for "Nomadic Life in Palestine" is a representative book—the representative of a *class* of Palestine books—and a criticism upon it will serve for a criticism upon them all. And since I am treating it in the comprehensive capacity of a representative book, I have taken the liberty of giving to both book and author fictitious names. Perhaps it is in better taste, any how, to do this.

Chapter LI

NAZARETH is wonderfully interesting because the town has an air about it of being precisely as Jesus left it, and one finds himself saying, all the time, "The boy Jesus has stood in this doorway—has played in that street—has touched these stones with his hands—has rambled over these chalky hills." Whoever shall write the Boyhood of Jesus ingeniously, will make a book which will possess a vivid interest for young and old alike. I judge so from the greater interest we found in Nazareth than any of our speculations upon Capernaum and the Sea of Galilee gave rise to. It was not possible, standing by the Sea of Galilee, to frame more than a vague, far-away idea of the majestic Personage who walked upon the crested waves as if they had been solid earth, and who touched the dead and they rose up and spoke. I read among my notes, now, with a new interest, some sentences from an edition of 1621 of the Apocryphal New Testament. [Extract.]

"Christ, kissed by a bride made dumb by sorcerers, cures her. A leprous girl cured by the water in which the infant Christ was washed, and becomes the servant of Joseph and Mary. The leprous son of a Prince cured in like manner.

"A young man who had been bewitched and turned into a mule, miraculously cured by the infant Saviour being put on his back, and is married to the girl who had been cured of leprosy. Whereupon the bystanders praise God.

"Chapter 16. Christ miraculously widens or contracts gates, milk-pails, sieves or boxes, not properly made by Joseph, he not being skillful at his carpenter's trade. The King of Jerusalem gives Joseph an order for a throne. Joseph works on it for two years and makes it two spans too short. The King being angry with him, Jesus comforts him—commands him to pull one side of the throne while he pulls the other, and brings it to its proper dimensions.

"Chapter 19. Jesus, charged with throwing a boy from the roof of a house, miraculously causes the dead boy to speak and acquit him; fetches water for his mother, breaks the pitcher and miraculously gathers the water in his mantle and brings it home.

"Sent to a schoolmaster, refuses to tell his letters, and the schoolmaster going to whip him, his hand withers."

Further on in this quaint volume of rejected gospels is an epistle of St. Clement to the Corinthians, which was used in the churches and considered genuine fourteen or fifteen hundred years ago. In it this account of the fabled phœnix occurs:

"1. Let us consider that wonderful type of the resurrection, which is seen in the Eastern countries, that is to say, in Arabia.

"2. There is a certain bird called a phœnix. Of this there is never but one at a time, and that lives five hundred years. And when the time of its dissolution draws near, that it must die, it makes itself a nest of frankincense, and myrrh, and other spices, into which, when its time is fulfilled, it enters and dies.

"3. But its flesh, putrefying, breeds a certain worm, which, being nourished by the juice of the dead bird, brings forth feathers; and when it is grown to a perfect state, it takes up the nest in which the bones of its parent lie, and carries it from Arabia into Egypt, to a city called Heliopolis:

"4. And flying in open day in the sight of all men, lays it upon the altar of the sun, and so returns from whence it came.

"5. The priests then search into the records of the time, and find that it returned precisely at the end of five hundred years."

Business is business, and there is nothing like punctuality, especially in a phœnix.

The few chapters relating to the infancy of the Saviour contain many things which seem frivolous and not worth preserving. A large part of the remaining portions of the book read like good Scripture, however. There is one verse that ought not to have been rejected, because it so evidently prophetically refers to the general run of Congresses of the United States:

"199. They carry themselves high, and as prudent men; and though they are fools, yet would seem to be teachers."

I have set these extracts down, as I found them. Every where, among the cathedrals of France and Italy, one finds traditions of personages that do not figure in the Bible, and of miracles that are not mentioned in its pages. But they are all in this Apocryphal New Testament, and though they have been ruled out of our modern Bible, it is claimed that they were accepted gospel twelve or fifteen centuries ago, and ranked as high in credit as any. One needs to read this book before he visits those venerable cathedrals, with their treasures of tabooed and forgotten tradition.

They imposed another pirate upon us at Nazareth—another invincible Arab guard. We took our last look at the city, clinging like a whitewashed wasp's nest to the hill-side, and at eight o'clock in the morning, departed. We dismounted and drove the horses down a bridle-path which I think was fully as crooked as a corkscrew; which I know to be as steep as the downward sweep of a rainbow, and which I believe to be the worst piece of road in the geography, except one in the Sandwich Islands, which I remember painfully, and possibly one or two mountain trails in the Sierra Nevadas. Often, in this narrow path, the horse had to poise himself nicely on a rude stone step and then drop his fore-feet over the edge and down something more than half his own height. This brought his nose near the ground, while his tail pointed up toward the sky somewhere, and gave him the appearance of preparing to stand on his head. A horse can not look dignified in this position. We accomplished the long descent at last, and trotted across the great Plain of Esdraelon.

Some of us will be shot before we finish this pilgrimage. The pilgrims read "Nomadic Life" and keep themselves in a constant state of Quixotic heroism. They have their hands on their pistols all the time, and every now and then, when you least expect it, they snatch them out and take aim at Bedouins who are not visible, and draw their knives and make savage passes at other Bedouins who do not exist. I am in deadly peril always, for these spasms are sudden and irregular, and of course I can not tell when to be getting out of the way. If I am accidentally murdered, some time, during one of these romantic frenzies of the pilgrims, Mr. Grimes must be rigidly held to answer as an accessory before the fact. If the pilgrims would take deliberate aim and shoot at a man, it would be all right and proper—because that man would not be in any danger; but these random assaults are what I object to. I do not wish to see any more places like Esdraelon, where the ground is level and people can gallop. It puts melodramatic nonsense into the pilgrims' heads. All at once, when one is jogging along stupidly in the sun, and thinking about something ever so far away, here they come, at a stormy gallop, spurring and whooping at those ridgy old sore-backed plugs till their heels fly higher than their heads, and as they whiz by, out comes a little potato-gun of a revolver, there is a startling little pop, and a small pellet goes singing through the air. Now that I have begun this pilgrimage, I intend to go through with it, though sooth to say, nothing but the most desperate valor has kept me to my purpose up to the present time. I do not mind Bedouins,—I am not afraid of them; because neither Bedouins nor ordinary Arabs have shown any disposition to harm us, but I *do* feel afraid of my own comrades.

Arriving at the furthest verge of the Plain, we rode a little way up a hill and found ourselves at Endor, famous for its witch. Her descendants are there yet. They were the wildest horde of half-naked savages we have found thus far. They swarmed out of mud bee-hives; out of hovels of the dry-goods box pattern; out of gaping caves under shelving rocks; out of crevices in the earth. In five minutes the dead solitude and silence of the place were no more, and a begging, screeching, shouting mob were struggling about the horses' feet and blocking the way. "Bucksheesh! bucksheesh! bucksheesh! howajji, bucksheesh!" It was Magdala over again, only here the glare from the infidel eyes was fierce and full of hate. The population numbers two hundred and fifty, and more than half the citizens live in caves in the rock. Dirt, degradation and savagery are Endor's specialty. We say no more about Magdala and Deburieh now. Endor heads the list. It is worse than any Indian *campoodie*. The hill is barren, rocky, and forbidding. No sprig of grass is visible, and only one tree. This is a fig-tree, which maintains a precarious footing among the rocks at the mouth of the dismal cavern once occupied by the veritable Witch of Endor. In this cavern, tradition says, Saul, the King, sat at midnight, and stared and trembled, while the earth shook, the thunders crashed among the hills, and out of the midst of fire and smoke the spirit of the dead prophet rose up and confronted him. Saul had crept to this place in the darkness, while his army slept, to learn what fate awaited him in the morrow's battle. He went away a sad man, to meet disgrace and death.

A spring trickles out of the rock in the gloomy recesses of the cavern, and we were thirsty. The citizens of Endor objected to our going in there. They do not mind dirt; they do not mind rags; they do not mind vermin; they do not mind barbarous ignorance and savagery; they do not mind a reasonable degree of starvation, but they *do* like to be pure and holy before their god, whoever he may be, and therefore they shudder and grow almost pale at the idea of Christian lips polluting a spring whose waters must descend into their sanctified gullets. We had no wanton desire to wound even *their* feelings or trample upon their prejudices, but we were out of water, thus early in the day, and were burning up with thirst. It was at this time, and under these circumstances, that I framed an aphorism which has already become celebrated. I said: "Necessity knows no law." We went in and drank.

We got away from the noisy wretches, finally, dropping them in squads and couples as we filed over the hills—the aged first, the infants next, the young girls further on; the strong men ran beside us a mile, and only left when they had secured the last possible piastre in the way of bucksheesh.

In an hour, we reached Nain, where Christ raised the widow's son to life. Nain is Magdala on a small scale. It has no population of any consequence. Within a hundred yards of it is the original graveyard, for aught I know; the tombstones lie flat on the ground, which is Jewish fashion in Syria. I believe the Moslems do not allow them to have upright tombstones. A Moslem grave is usually roughly plastered over and whitewashed, and has at one end an upright projection which is shaped into exceedingly rude attempts at ornamentation. In the cities, there is often no appearance of a grave at all; a tall, slender marble tombstone, elaborately lettred, gilded and painted, marks the burial place, and this is surmounted by a turban, so carved and shaped as to signify the dead man's rank in life.

They showed a fragment of ancient wall which they said was one side of the gate out of which the widow's dead son was being brought so many centuries ago when Jesus met the procession:

"Now when he came nigh to the gate of the city, behold there was a dead man carried out, the only son of his mother, and she was a widow: and much people of the city was with her.

"And when the Lord saw her, he had compassion on her, and said, Weep not.

"And he came and touched the bier: and they that bare him stood still. And he said, Young man, I say unto thee, arise.

"And he that was dead sat up, and began to speak. And he delivered him to his mother.

"And there came a fear on all. And they glorified God, saying, That a great prophet is risen up among us; and That God hath visited his people."

A little mosque stands upon the spot which tradition says was occupied by the widow's dwelling. Two or three aged Arabs sat about its door. We entered, and the pilgrims broke specimens from the foundation walls, though they had to touch, and even step, upon the "praying carpets" to do it. It was almost the same as breaking pieces from the hearts of those old Arabs. To step rudely upon the sacred praying mats, with booted feet—a thing not done by any Arab—was to inflict pain upon men who had not offended us in any way. Suppose a party of armed foreigners were to enter a village church in America and break ornaments from the altar railings for curiosities, and climb up and walk upon the Bible and the pulpit cushions? However, the cases are different. One is the profanation of a temple of our faith—the other only the profanation of a pagan one.

We descended to the Plain again, and halted a moment at a well—of Abraham's time, no doubt. It was in a desert place. It was walled three feet above ground with squared and heavy blocks of stone, after the manner of Bible pictures. Around it some camels stood, and others knelt. There was a group of sober little donkeys with naked, dusky children clambering about them, or sitting astride their rumps, or pulling their tails. Tawny, black-eyed, barefooted maids, arrayed in rags and adorned with brazen armlets and pinchbeck earrings, were poising water-jars upon their heads, or drawing water from the well. A flock of sheep stood by, waiting for the shepherds to fill the hollowed stones with water, so that they might drink—stones which, like those that walled the well, were worn smooth and deeply creased by the chafing chins of a hundred generations of thirsty animals. Picturesque Arabs sat upon the ground, in groups, and solemnly smoked their long-stemmed chibouks. Other Arabs were filling black hog-skins with water—skins which, well filled, and distended with water till the short legs projected painfully out of the proper line, looked like the corpses of hogs bloated by drowning. Here was a grand Oriental picture which I had worshiped a thousand times in soft, rich steel engravings! But in the engraving there was no desolation; no dirt; no rags; no fleas; no ugly features; no sore eyes; no feasting flies; no besotted ignorance in the countenances; no raw places on the donkeys' backs; no disagreeable jabbering in unknown tongues; no stench of camels; no suggestion that a couple of tons of powder placed under the party and touched off would heighten the effect and give to the scene a genuine interest and a charm which it would always be pleasant to recall, even though a man lived a thousand years.

Oriental scenes look best in steel engravings. I can not be imposed upon any more by that picture of the Queen of Sheba visiting Solomon. I shall say to myself, You look fine, Madam, but your feet are not clean, and you smell like a camel.

Presently a wild Arab in charge of a camel train recognized an old friend in Ferguson, and they ran and fell upon each other's necks and kissed each other's grimy, bearded faces upon both cheeks. It explained instantly a something which had always seemed to me only a far-fetched Oriental figure of speech. I refer to the circumstance of Christ's rebuking a Pharisee, or some such character, and reminding him that from him he had received no "kiss of welcome." It did not seem reasonable to me that men should kiss each other, but I am aware, now, that they did. There was reason in it, too. The custom was natural and proper; because people must kiss, and a man would not be likely to kiss one of the women of this country of his own free will and accord. One must travel, to learn. Every day, now, old Scriptural phrases that never possessed any significance for me before, take to themselves a meaning.

We journeyed around the base of the mountain—"Little

Hermon,"—past the old Crusaders' castle of El Fuleh, and arrived at Shunem. This was another Magdala, to a fraction, frescoes and all. Here, tradition says, the prophet Samuel was born, and here the Shunamite woman built a little house upon the city wall for the accommodation of the prophet Elisha. Elisha asked her what she expected in return. It was a perfectly natural question, for these people are and were in the habit of proffering favors and services and then expecting and begging for pay. Elisha knew them well. He could not comprehend that any body should build for him that humble little chamber for the mere sake of old friendship, and with no selfish motive whatever. It used to seem a very impolite, not to say a rude question, for Elisha to ask the woman, but it does not seem so to me now. The woman said she expected nothing. Then for her goodness and her unselfishness, he rejoiced her heart with the news that she should bear a son. It was a high reward—but she would not have thanked him for a daughter—daughters have always been unpopular here. The son was born, grew, waxed strong, died. Elisha restored him to life in Shunem.

We found here a grove of lemon trees—cool, shady, hung with fruit. One is apt to overestimate beauty when it is rare, but to me this grove seemed very beautiful. It *was* beautiful. I do not overestimate it. I must always remember Shunem gratefully, as a place which gave to us this leafy shelter after our long, hot ride. We lunched, rested, chatted, smoked our pipes an hour, and then mounted and moved on.

As we trotted across the Plain of Jezreel, we met half a dozen Digger Indians (Bedouins) with very long spears in their hands, cavorting around on old crowbait horses, and spearing imaginary enemies; whooping, and fluttering their rags in the wind, and carrying on in every respect like a pack of hopeless lunatics. At last, here were the " wild, free sons of the desert, speeding over the plain like the wind, on their beautiful Arabian mares" we had read so much about and longed so much to see! Here were the "picturesque costumes!" This was the "gallant spectacle!" Tatterdemalion vagrants—cheap braggadocio—"Arabian mares" spined and necked like the ichthyosaurus in the museum, and humped and cornered like a dromedary! To glance at the genuine son of the desert is to take the romance out of him forever—to behold his steed is to long in charity to strip his harness off and let him fall to pieces.

Presently we came to a ruinous old town on a hill, the same being the ancient Jezreel.

Ahab, King of Samaria, (this was a very vast kingdom, for those days, and was very nearly half as large as Rhode Island) dwelt in the city of Jezreel, which was his capital. Near him lived a man by the name of Naboth, who had a vineyard. The King asked him for it, and when he would not give it, offered to buy it. But Naboth refused to sell it. In those days it was considered a sort of crime to part with one's inheritance at any price—and even if a man did part with it, it reverted to himself or his heirs again at the next jubilee year. So this spoiled child of a King went and lay down on the bed with his face to the wall, and grieved sorely. The Queen, a notorious character in those days, and whose name is a by-word and a reproach even in these, came in and asked him wherefore he sorrowed, and he told her. Jezebel said she could secure the vineyard; and she went forth and forged letters to the nobles and wise men, in the King's name, and ordered them to proclaim a fast and set Naboth on high before the people, and suborn two witnesses to swear that he had blasphemed. They did it, and the people stoned the accused by the city wall, and he died. Then Jezebel came and told the King, and said, Behold, Naboth is no more—rise up and seize the vineyard. So Ahab seized the vineyard, and went into it to possess it. But the Prophet Elijah came to him there and read his fate to him, and the fate of Jezebel; and said that in the place where dogs licked the blood of Naboth, dogs should also lick his blood—and he said, likewise, the dogs should eat Jezebel by the wall of Jezreel. In the course of time, the King was killed in battle, and when his chariot wheels were washed in the pool of Samaria, the dogs licked the blood. In after years, Jehu, who was King of Israel, marched down against Jezreel, by order of one of the Prophets, and administered one of those convincing rebukes so common among the people of those days: he killed many kings and their subjects, and as he came along he saw Jezebel, painted and finely dressed, looking out of a window, and ordered that she be thrown down to him. A servant did it, and Jehu's horse trampled her under foot. Then Jehu went in and sat down to dinner; and presently he said, Go and bury this cursed woman, for she is a King's daughter. The spirit of charity came upon him too late, however, for the prophecy had already been fulfilled—the dogs had eaten her, and they "found no more of her than the skull, and the feet, and the palms of her hands."

Ahab, the late King, had left a helpless family behind him, and Jehu killed seventy of the orphan sons. Then he killed all the relatives, and teachers, and servants and friends of the family, and rested from his labors, until he was come near to Samaria, where he met forty-two persons and asked them who they were; they said they were brothers of the King of Judah. He killed them. When he got to Samaria, he said he would show his zeal for the Lord; so he gathered all the priests and people together that worshiped Baal, pretending that he was going to adopt that worship and offer up a great sacrifice; and when they were all shut up where they could not defend themselves, he caused every person of them to be killed. Then Jehu, the good missionary, rested from his labors once more.

We went back to the valley, and rode to the Fountain of Ain Jelüd. They call it the Fountain of Jezreel, usually. It is a pond about one hundred feet square and four feet deep, with a stream of water trickling into it from under an overhanging ledge of rocks. It is in the midst of a great solitude. Here Gideon pitched his camp in the old times; behind Shunem lay the "Midianites, the Amalekites, and the Children of the East," who were "as grasshoppers for multitude; both they and their camels were without number, as the sand by the sea-side for multitude." Which means that there were one hundred and thirty-five thousand men, and that they had transportation service accordingly.

Gideon, with only three hundred men, surprised them in the night, and stood by and looked on while they butchered each other until a hundred and twenty thousand lay dead on the field.

We camped at Jenin before night, and got up and started again at one o'clock in the morning. Somewhere towards daylight we passed the locality where the best authenticated tradition locates the pit into which Joseph's brethren threw him, and about noon, after passing over a succession of mountain tops, clad with groves of fig and olive trees, with the Mediterranean in sight some forty miles away, and going by many ancient Biblical cities whose inhabitants glowered savagely upon our Christian procession, and were seemingly inclined to practice on it with stones, we came to the singularly terraced and unlovely hills that betrayed that we were out of Galilee and into Samaria at last.

We climbed a high hill to visit the city of Samaria, where the woman may have hailed from who conversed with Christ at Jacob's Well, and from whence, no doubt, came also the celebrated Good Samaritan. Herod the Great is said to have made a magnificent city of this place, and a great number of coarse limestone columns, twenty feet high and two feet through, that are almost guiltless of architectural grace of shape and ornament, are pointed out by many authors as evidence of the fact. They would not have been considered handsome in ancient Greece, however.

The inhabitants of this camp are particularly vicious, and stoned two parties of our pilgrims a day or two ago who brought about the difficulty by showing their revolvers when they did not intend to use them—a thing which is deemed bad judgment in the Far West, and ought certainly to be so considered any where. In the new Territories, when a man puts his hand on a weapon, he knows that he must use it; he must use it instantly or expect to be shot down where he stands. Those pilgrims had been reading Grimes.

There was nothing for us to do in Samaria but buy handfuls of old Roman coins at a franc a dozen, and look at a dilapidated church of the Crusaders and a vault in it which once contained the body of John the Baptist. This relic was long ago carried away to Genoa.

Samaria stood a disastrous siege, once, in the days of Elisha, at the hands of the King of Syria. Provisions reached such a figure that "an ass' head was sold for eighty pieces of silver and the fourth part of a cab of dove's dung for five pieces of silver."

An incident recorded of that heavy time will give one a very good idea of the distress that prevailed within these crumbling walls. As the King was walking upon the battlements one day, "a woman cried out, saying, Help, my lord, O King! And the King said, What aileth thee? and she answered, This woman said unto me, Give thy son, that we may eat him to-day, and we will eat my son to-morrow. So we boiled my son, and did eat him; and I said unto her on the next day, Give thy son that we may eat him; and she hath hid her son."

The prophet Elisha declared that within four and twenty hours the prices of food should go down to nothing, almost, and it was so. The Syrian army broke camp and fled, for some cause or other, the famine was relieved from without, and many a shoddy speculator in dove's dung and ass's meat was ruined.

We were glad to leave this hot and dusty old village and hurry on. At two o'clock we stopped to lunch and rest at ancient Shechem, between the historic Mounts of Gerizim and Ebal where in the old times the books of the law, the curses and the blessings, were read from the heights to the Jewish multitudes below.

Chapter LII

THE NARROW CANON in which Nablous, or Shechem, is situated, is under high cultivation, and the soil is exceedingly black and fertile. It is well watered, and its affluent vegetation gains effect by contrast with the barren hills that tower on either side. One of these hills is the ancient Mount of Blessings and the other the Mount of Curses; and wise men who seek for fulfillments of prophecy think they find here a wonder of this kind—to wit, that the Mount of Blessings is strangely fertile and its mate as strangely unproductive. We could not see that there was really much difference between them in this respect, however.

Shechem is distinguished as one of the residences of the patriarch Jacob, and as the seat of those tribes that cut themselves loose from their brethren of Israel and propagated doctrines not in conformity with those of the original Jewish creed. For thousands of years this clan have dwelt in Shechem under strict *tabu*, and having little commerce or fellowship with their fellow men of any religion or nationality. For generations they have not numbered more than one or two hundred, but they still adhere to their ancient faith and maintain their ancient rites and ceremonies. Talk of family and old descent! Princes and nobles pride themselves upon lineages they can trace back some hundreds of years. What is this trifle to this handful of old first families of Shechem, who can name their fathers straight back without a flaw for thousands—straight back to a period so remote that men reared in a country where the days of two hundred years ago are called "ancient" times grow dazed and bewildered when they try to comprehend it! Here is respectability for you—here is "family"—here is high descent worth talking about. This sad, proud remnant of a once mighty community still hold themselves aloof from all the world; they still live as their fathers lived, labor as their fathers labored, think as they did, feel as they did, worship in the same place, in sight of the same landmarks, and in the same quaint, patriarchal way their ancestors did more than thirty centuries ago. I found myself gazing at any straggling scion of this strange race with a riveted fascination, just as one would stare at a living mastodon, or a megatherium that had moved in the grey dawn of creation and seen the wonders of that mysterious world that was before the flood.

Carefully preserved among the sacred archives of this curious community is a MSS. copy of the ancient Jewish law, which is said to be the oldest document on earth. It is written on vellum, and is some four or five thousand years old. Nothing but bucksheesh can purchase a sight. Its fame is somewhat dimmed in these latter days, because of the doubts so many authors of Palestine travels have felt themselves privileged to cast upon it. Speaking of this MSS. reminds me that I procured from the high-priest of this ancient Samaritan community, at great expense, a secret document of still higher antiquity and far more extraordinary interest, which I propose to publish as soon as I have finished translating it.

Joshua gave his dying injunction to the children of Israel at Shechem, and buried a valuable treasure secretly under an oak tree there about the same time. The superstitious Samaritans have always been afraid to hunt for it. They believe it is guarded by fierce spirits invisible to men.

About a mile and a half from Shechem we halted at the base of Mount Ebal, before a little square area, inclosed by a high stone wall, neatly whitewashed. Across one end of this inclosure is a tomb built after the manner of the Moslems. It is the tomb of Joseph. No truth is better authenticated than this.

When Joseph was dying he prophesied that exodus of the Israelites from Egypt which occurred four hundred years afterwards. At the same time he exacted of his people an oath that when they journeyed to the land of Canaan, they would bear his bones with them and bury them in the ancient inheritance of his fathers. The oath was kept.

"And the bones of Joseph, which the children of Israel brought up out of Egypt, buried they in Shechem, in a parcel of ground which Jacob bought of the sons of Hamor the father of Shechem, for a hundred pieces of silver."

Few tombs on earth command the veneration of so many races and men of divers creeds as this of Joseph. "Samaritan and Jew, Moslem and Christian alike, revere it, and honor it with their visits. The tomb of Joseph, the dutiful son, the affectionate, forgiving brother, the virtuous man, the wise Prince and ruler. Egypt felt his influence—the world knows his history."

In this same "parcel of ground" which Jacob bought of the sons of Hamor for a hundred pieces of silver, is Jacob's celebrated well. It is cut in the solid rock, and is nine feet square and ninety feet deep. The name of this unpretending hole in the ground, which one might pass by and take no notice of, is as familiar as household words to even the children and the peasants of many a far-off country. It is more famous than the Parthenon; it is older than the Pyramids.

It was by this well that Jesus sat and talked with a woman of that strange, antiquated Samaritan community I have been speaking of, and told her of the mysterious water of life. As descendants of old English nobles still cherish in the traditions of their houses how that this king or that king tarried a day with some favored ancestor three hundred years ago, no doubt the descendants of the woman of Samaria, living there in Shechem, still refer with pardonable vanity to this conversation of their ancestor, held some little time gone by, with the Messiah of the Christians. It is not likely that they undervalue a distinction such as this. Samaritan nature is human nature, and human nature remembers contact with the illustrious, always.

For an offense done to the family honor, the sons of Jacob exterminated all Shechem once.

We left Jacob's Well and traveled till eight in the evening, but rather slowly, for we had been in the saddle nineteen hours, and the horses were cruelly tired. We got so far ahead of the tents that we had to camp in an Arab village, and sleep on the ground. We could have slept in the largest of the houses; but there were some little drawbacks: it was populous with vermin, it had a dirt floor, it was in no respect cleanly, and there was a family of goats in the only bedroom, and two donkeys in the parlor. Outside there were no inconveniences, except that the dusky, ragged, earnest-eyed villagers of both sexes and all ages grouped themselves on their haunches all around us, and discussed us and criticised us with noisy tongues till midnight. We did not mind the noise, being tired, but, doubtless, the reader is aware that it is almost an impossible thing to go to sleep when you know that people are looking at you. We went to bed at ten, and got up again at two and started once more. Thus are people persecuted by dragomen, whose sole ambition in life is to get ahead of each other.

About daylight we passed Shiloh, where the Ark of the Covenant rested three hundred years, and at whose gates good old Eli fell down and "brake his neck" when the messenger, riding hard from the battle, told him of the defeat of his people, the death of his sons, and, more than all, the capture of Israel's pride, her hope, her refuge, the ancient Ark her forefathers brought with them out of Egypt. It is little wonder that under circumstances like these he fell down and brake his neck. But Shiloh had no charms for us. We were so cold that there was no comfort but in motion, and so drowsy we could hardly sit upon the horses.

After a while we came to a shapeless mass of ruins, which still bears the name of Beth-el. It was here that Jacob lay down and had that superb vision of angels flitting up and down a ladder that reached from the clouds to earth, and caught glimpses of their blessed home through the open gates of Heaven.

The pilgrims took what was left of the hallowed ruin, and we pressed on toward the goal of our crusade, renowned Jerusalem.

The further we went the hotter the sun got, and the more rocky and bare, repulsive and dreary the landscape became. There could not have been more fragments of stone strewn broadcast over this part of the world, if every ten square feet of the land had been occupied by a separate and distinct stone-cutter's establishment for an age. There was hardly a tree or a shrub any where. Even the olive and the cactus, those fast friends of a worthless soil, had almost deserted the country. No landscape exists that is more tiresome to the eye than that which bounds the approaches to Jerusalem. The only difference between the roads and the surrounding country, perhaps, is that there are rather more rocks in the roads than in the surrounding country.

We passed Ramah, and Beroth, and on the right saw the tomb of the prophet Samuel, perched high upon a commanding eminence. Still no Jerusalem came in sight. We hurried on impatiently. We halted a moment at the ancient Fountain of Beira, but its stones, worn deeply by the chins of thirsty animals that are dead and gone centuries ago, had no interest for us—we longed to see Jerusalem. We spurred up hill after hill, and usually began to stretch our necks minutes before we got to the top—but disappointment always followed:—more stupid hills beyond—more unsightly landscape—no Holy City.

At last, away in the middle of the day, ancient bits of wall and crumbling arches began to line the way—we toiled up one more hill, and every pilgrim and every sinner swung his hat on high! Jerusalem!

Perched on its eternal hills, white and domed and solid, massed together and hooped with high gray walls, the venerable city gleamed in the sun. So small! Why, it was no larger than an American village of four thousand inhabitants, and no larger than an ordinary Syrian city of thirty thousand. Jerusalem numbers only fourteen thousand people.

We dismounted and looked, without speaking a dozen sentences, across the wide intervening valley for an hour or more; and noted those prominent features of the city that pictures make familiar to all men from their school days till their death. We could recognize the Tower of Hippicus, the Mosque of Omar, the Damascus Gate, the Mount of Olives, the Valley of Jehoshaphat, the Tower of David, and the Garden of Gethsemane—and dating from these landmarks could tell very nearly the localities of many others we were not able to distinguish.

I record it here as a notable but not discreditable fact that not even our pilgrims wept. I think there was no individual in the party whose brain was not teeming with thoughts and images and memories invoked by the grand history of the venerable city that lay before us, but still among them all was no "voice of them that wept."

There was no call for tears. Tears would have been out of place. The thoughts Jerusalem suggests are full of poetry, sublimity, and more than all, dignity. Such thoughts do not find their appropriate expression in the emotions of the nursery.

Just after noon we entered these narrow, crooked streets, by the ancient and the famed Damascus Gate, and now for several hours I have been trying to comprehend that I am actually in the illustrious old city where Solomon dwelt, where Abraham held converse with the Deity, and where walls still stand that witnessed the spectacle of the Crucifixion.

Chapter LIII

A FAST WALKER could go outside the walls of Jerusalem and walk entirely around the city in an hour. I do not know how else to make one understand how small it is. The appearance of the city is peculiar. It is as knobby with countless little domes as a prison door is with bolt-heads. Every house has from one to half a dozen of these white plastered domes of stone, broad and low, sitting in the centre of, or in a cluster upon, the flat roof. Wherefore, when one looks down from an eminence, upon the compact mass of houses (so closely crowded together, in fact, that there is no appearance of streets at all, and so the city looks solid,) he sees the knobbiest town in the world, except Constantinople. It looks as if it might be roofed, from centre to circumference, with inverted saucers. The monotony of the view is interrupted only by the great Mosque of Omar, the Tower of Hippicus, and one or two other buildings that rise into commanding prominence.

The houses are generally two stories high, built strongly of masonry, whitewashed or plastered outside, and have a cage of wooden lattice-work projecting in front of every window. To reproduce a Jerusalem street, it would only be necessary to up-end a chicken-coop and hang it before each window in an alley of American houses.

The streets are roughly and badly paved with stone, and are tolerably crooked—enough so to make each street appear to close together constantly and come to an end about a hundred yards ahead of a pilgrim as long as he chooses to walk in it. Projecting from the top of the lower story of many of the houses is a very narrow porch-roof or shed, without supports from below; and I have several times seen cats jump across the street from one shed to the other when they were out calling. The cats could have jumped double the distance without extraordinary exertion. I mention these things to give an idea of how narrow the streets are. Since a cat can jump across them without the least inconvenience, it is hardly necessary to state that such streets are too narrow for carriages. These vehicles can not navigate the Holy City.

The population of Jerusalem is composed of Moslems, Jews, Greeks, Latins, Armenians, Syrians, Copts, Abyssinians, Greek Catholics, and a handful of Protestants. One hundred of the latter sect are all that dwell now in this birthplace of Christianity. The nice shades of nationality comprised in the above list, and the languages spoken by them, are altogether too numerous to mention. It seems to me that all the races and colors and tongues of the earth must be represented among the fourteen thousand souls that dwell in Jerusalem. Rags, wretchedness, poverty and dirt, those signs and symbols that indicate the presence of Moslem rule more surely than the crescent-flag itself, abound. Lepers, cripples, the blind, and the idiotic, assail you on every hand, and they know but one word of but one language apparently—the eternal "bucksheesh." To see the numbers of maimed, malformed and diseased humanity that throng the holy places and obstruct the gates, one might suppose that the ancient days had come again, and that the angel of the Lord was expected to descend at any moment to stir the waters of Bethesda. Jerusalem is mournful, and dreary, and lifeless. I would not desire to live here.

One naturally goes first to the Holy Sepulchre. It is right in the city, near the western gate; it and the place of the Crucifixion, and, in fact, every other place intimately connected with that tremendous event, are ingeniously massed together and covered by one roof—the dome of the Church of the Holy Sepulchre.

Entering the building, through the midst of the usual assemblage of beggars, one sees on his left a few Turkish guards—for Christians of different sects will not only quarrel, but fight, also, in this sacred place, if allowed to do it. Before you is a marble slab, which covers the Stone of Unction, whereon the Saviour's body was laid to prepare it for burial. It was found necessary to conceal the real stone in this way in order to save it from destruction. Pilgrims were too much given to chipping off pieces of it to carry home. Near by is a circular railing which marks the spot where the Virgin stood when the Lord's body was anointed.

Entering the great Rotunda, we stand before the most sacred locality in Christendom—the grave of Jesus. It is in the centre of the church, and immediately under the great dome. It is inclosed in a sort of little temple of yellow and white stone, of fanciful design. Within the little temple is a portion of the very stone which was rolled away from the door of the Sepulchre, and on which the angel was sitting when Mary came thither "at early dawn." Stooping low, we enter the vault—the Sepulchre itself. It is only about six feet by seven, and the stone couch on which the dead Saviour lay extends from end to end of the apartment and occupies half its width. It is covered with a marble slab which has been much worn by the lips of pilgrims. This slab serves as an altar, now. Over it hang some fifty gold and silver lamps, which are kept always burning, and the place is otherwise scandalized by trumpery gewgaws and tawdry ornamentation.

All sects of Christians (except Protestants,) have chapels under the roof of the Church of the Holy Sepulchre, and each must keep to itself and not venture upon another's ground. It has been proven conclusively that they can not worship together around the grave of the Saviour of the World in peace. The chapel of the Syrians is not handsome; that of the Copts is the humblest of them all. It is nothing but a dismal cavern, roughly hewn in the living rock of the Hill of Calvary. In one side of it two ancient tombs are hewn, which are claimed to be those in which Nicodemus and Joseph of Aramathea were buried.

As we moved among the great piers and pillars of another part of the church, we came upon a party of black-robed, animal-looking Italian monks, with candles in their hands, who were chanting something in Latin, and going through some kind of religious performance around a disk of white marble let into the floor. It was there that the risen Saviour appeared to Mary Magdalen in the likeness of a gardener. Near by was a similar stone, shaped like a star—here the Magdalen herself stood, at the same time. Monks were performing in this place also. They perform every where—all over the vast building, and at all hours. Their candles are always flitting about in the gloom, and making the dim old church more dismal than there is any necessity that it should be, even though it is a tomb.

We were shown the place where our Lord appeared to His

mother after the Resurrection. Here, also, a marble slab marks the place where St. Helena, the mother of the Emperor Constantine, found the crosses about three hundred years after the Crucifixion. According to the legend, this great discovery elicited extravagant demonstrations of joy. But they were of short duration. The question intruded itself: "Which bore the blessed Saviour, and which the thieves?" To be in doubt, in so mighty a matter as this—to be uncertain which one to adore—was a grievous misfortune. It turned the public joy to sorrow. But when lived there a holy priest who could not set so simple a trouble as this at rest? One of these soon hit upon a plan that would be a certain test. A noble lady lay very ill in Jerusalem. The wise priests ordered that the three crosses be taken to her bedside one at a time. It was done. When her eyes fell upon the first one, she uttered a scream that was heard beyond the Damascus Gate, and even upon the Mount of Olives, it was said, and then fell back in a deadly swoon. They recovered her and brought the second cross. Instantly she went into fearful convulsions, and it was with the greatest difficulty that six strong men could hold her. They were afraid, now, to bring in the third cross. They began to fear that possibly they had fallen upon the wrong crosses, and that the true cross was not with this number at all. However, as the woman seemed likely to die with the convulsions that were tearing her, they concluded that the third could do no more than put her out of her misery with a happy dispatch. So they brought it, and behold, a miracle! The woman sprang from her bed, smiling and joyful, and perfectly restored to health. When we listen to evidence like this, we can not but believe. We would be ashamed to doubt, and properly, too. Even the very part of Jerusalem where this all occurred is there yet. So there is really no room for doubt.

The priests tried to show us, through a small screen, a fragment of the genuine Pillar of Flagellation, to which Christ was bound when they scourged him. But we could not see it, because it was dark inside the screen. However, a baton is kept here, which the pilgrim thrusts through a hole in the screen, and then he no longer doubts that the true Pillar of Flagellation is in there. He can not have any excuse to doubt it, for he can feel it with the stick. He can feel it as distinctly as he could feel any thing.

Not far from here was a niche where they used to preserve a piece of the True Cross, but it is gone, now. This piece of the cross was discovered in the sixteenth century. The Latin priests say it was stolen away, long ago, by priests of another sect. That seems like a hard statement to make, but we know very well that it *was* stolen, because we have seen it ourselves in several of the cathedrals of Italy and France.

But the relic that touched us most was the plain old sword of that stout Crusader, Godfrey of Bulloigne—King Godfrey of Jerusalem. No blade in Christendom wields such enchantment as this—no blade of all that rust in the ancestral halls of Europe is able to invoke such visions of romance in the brain of him who looks upon it—none that can prate of such chivalric deeds or tell such brave tales of the warrior days of old. It stirs within a man every memory of the Holy Wars that has been sleeping in his brain for years, and peoples his thoughts with mail-clad images, with marching armies, with battles and with sieges. It speaks to him of Baldwin, and Tancred, the princely Saladin, and great Richard of the Lion Heart. It was with just such blades as these that these splendid heroes of romance used to segregate a man, so to speak, and leave the half of him to fall one way and the other half the other. This very sword has cloven hundreds of Saracen Knights from crown to chin in those old times when Godfrey wielded it. It was enchanted, then, by a genius that was under the command of King Solomon. When danger approached its master's tent it always struck the shield and clanged out a fierce alarm upon the startled ear of night. In times of doubt, or in fog or darkness, if it were drawn from its sheath it would point instantly toward the foe, and thus reveal the way—and it would also attempt to start after them of its own accord. A Christian could not be so disguised that it would not know him and refuse to hurt him—nor a Moslem so disguised that it would not leap from its scabbard and take his life. These statements are all well authenticated in many legends that are among the most trustworthy legends the good old Catholic monks preserve. I can never forget old Godfrey's sword, now. I tried it on a Moslem, and clove him in twain like a doughnut. The spirit of Grimes was upon me, and if I had had a graveyard I would have destroyed all the infidels in Jerusalem. I wiped the blood off the old sword and handed it back to the priest—I did not want the fresh gore to obliterate those sacred spots that crimsoned its brightness one day six hundred years ago and thus gave Godfrey warning that before the sun went down his journey of life would end.

Still moving through the gloom of the Church of the Holy Sepulchre we came to a small chapel, hewn out of the rock—a place which has been known as "The Prison of Our Lord" for many centuries. Tradition says that here the Saviour was confined just previously to the crucifixion. Under an altar by the door was a pair of stone stocks for human legs. These things are called the "Bonds of Christ," and the use they were once put to has given them the name they now bear.

The Greek Chapel is the most roomy, the richest and the showiest chapel in the Church of the Holy Sepulchre. Its altar, like that of all the Greek churches, is a lofty screen that extends clear across the chapel, and is gorgeous with gilding and pictures. The numerous lamps that hang before it are of gold and silver, and cost great sums.

But the feature of the place is a short column that rises from the middle of the marble pavement of the chapel, and marks the exact *centre of the earth*. The most reliable traditions tell us that this was known to be the earth's centre, ages ago, and that when Christ was upon earth he set all doubts upon the subject at rest forever, by stating with his own lips that the tradition was correct. Remember, He said that that particular column stood upon the centre of the world. If the centre of the world changes, the column changes its position accordingly. This column has moved three different times, of its own accord. This is because, in great convulsions of nature, at three different times, masses of the earth—whole ranges of mountains, probably—have flown off into space, thus lessening the diameter of the earth, and changing the exact locality of its centre by a point or two. This is a very curious and interesting circumstance, and is a withering rebuke to those philosophers who would make us believe that it is not possible for any portion of the earth to fly off into space.

To satisfy himself that this spot was really the centre of the earth, a sceptic once paid well for the privilege of ascending to the dome of the church to see if the sun gave him a shadow at noon. He came down perfectly convinced. The day was very cloudy and the sun threw no shadows at all; but the man was satisfied that if the sun had come out and made shadows it could not have made any for him. Proofs like these are not to be set aside by the idle tongues of cavilers. To such as are not bigoted, and are willing to be convinced, they carry a conviction that nothing can ever shake.

If even greater proofs than those I have mentioned are wanted, to satisfy the headstrong and the foolish that this is the genuine centre of the earth, they are here. The greatest of them lies in the fact that from under this very column was taken the *dust from which Adam was made*. This can surely be regarded in the light of a settler. It is not likely that the original first man would have been made from an inferior quality of earth when it was entirely convenient to get first quality from the world's centre. This will strike any reflecting mind forcibly. That Adam was formed of dirt procured in this very spot is amply proven by the fact that in six thousand years no man has ever been able to prove that the dirt was *not* procured here whereof he was made.

It is a singular circumstance that right under the roof of this same great church, and not far away from that illustrious column, Adam himself, the father of the human race, lies buried. There is no question that he is actually buried in the grave which is pointed out as his—there can be none—because it has never yet been proven that that grave is not the grave in which he is buried.

The tomb of Adam! How touching it was, here in a land of strangers, far away from home, and friends, and all who cared for me, thus to discover the grave of a blood relation. True, a distant one, but still a relation. The unerring instinct of nature thrilled its recognition. The fountain of my filial affection was stirred to its profoundest depths, and I gave way to tumultuous emotion. I leaned upon a pillar and burst into tears. I deem it no shame to have wept over the grave of my poor dead relative. Let him who would sneer at my emotion close this volume here, for he will find little to his taste in my journeyings through Holy Land. Noble old man—he did not live to see me—he did not live to see his child. And I—I—alas, I did not live to see *him*. Weighed down by sorrow and disappointment, he died before I was born—six thousand brief summers before I was born. But let us try to bear it with fortitude. Let us trust that he is better off, where he is. Let us take comfort in the thought that his loss is our eternal gain.

The next place the guide took us to in the holy church was an altar dedicated to the Roman soldier who was of the military guard that attended at the crucifixion to keep order, and who—when the vail of the Temple was rent in the awful darkness that followed; when the rock of Golgotha was split asunder by an earthquake; when the artillery of heaven thundered, and in the baleful glare of the lightnings the shrouded dead flitted about the streets of Jerusalem—shook with fear and said, "Surely this was the Son of God!" Where this altar stands now, that Roman soldier stood then, in full view of the crucified Saviour—in full sight and hearing of all the marvels that were transpiring far and wide about the circumference of the Hill of Calvary. And in this self-same spot the priests of the Temple beheaded him for those blasphemous words he had spoken.

In this altar they used to keep one of the most curious relics that human eyes ever looked upon—a thing that had power to fascinate the beholder in some mysterious way and keep him gazing for hours together. It was nothing less than the copper plate Pilate put upon the Saviour's cross, and upon which he wrote, "This is the King of the Jews." I think St. Helena, the mother of Constantine, found this wonderful memento when she was here in the third century. She traveled all over Palestine, and was always fortunate. Whenever the good old enthusiast found a thing mentioned in her Bible, Old or New, she would go and search for that thing, and never stop until she found it. If it was Adam, she would find Adam; if it was the Ark, she would find the Ark; if it was Goliah, or Joshua, she would find *them*. She found the inscription here that I was speaking of, I think. She found it in this very spot, close to where the martyred Roman soldier stood. That copper plate is in one of the churches in Rome, now. Any one can see it there. The inscription is very distinct.

We passed along a few steps and saw the altar built over the very spot where the good Catholic priests say the soldiers divided the raiment of the Saviour.

Then we went down into a cavern which cavilers say was once a cistern. It is a chapel, now, however—the Chapel of St. Helena. It is fifty-one feet long by forty-three wide. In it is a marble chair which Helena used to sit in while she superintended her workmen when they were digging and delving for the True Cross. In this place is an altar dedicated to St. Dimas, the penitent thief. A new bronze statue is here—a statue of St. Helena. It reminded us of poor Maximilian, so lately shot. He presented it to this chapel when he was about to leave for his throne in Mexico.

From the cistern we descended twelve steps into a large roughly-shaped grotto, carved wholly out of the living rock. Helena blasted it out when she was searching for the true cross. She had a laborious piece of work, here, but it was richly rewarded. Out of this place she got the crown of thorns, the nails of the cross, the true cross itself, and the cross of the penitent thief. When she thought she had found every thing and was about to stop, she was told in a dream to continue a day longer. It was very fortunate. She did so, and found the cross of the other thief.

The walls and roof of this grotto still weep bitter tears in memory of the event that transpired on Calvary, and devout pilgrims groan and sob when these sad tears fall upon them from the dripping rock. The monks call this apartment the "Chapel of the Invention of the Cross"—a name which is unfortunate, because it leads the ignorant to imagine that a tacit acknowledgment is thus made that the tradition that Helena found the true cross here is a fiction—an invention. It is a happiness to know, however, that intelligent people do not doubt the story in any of its particulars.

Priests of any of the chapels and denominations in the Church of the Holy Sepulchre can visit this sacred grotto to weep and pray and worship the gentle Redeemer. Two different congregations are not allowed to enter at the same time, however, because they always fight.

Still marching through the venerable Church of the Holy Sepulchre, among chanting priests in coarse long robes and sandals; pilgrims of all colors and many nationalities, in all sorts of strange costumes; under dusky arches and by dingy piers and columns; through a sombre cathedral gloom freighted with smoke and incense, and faintly starred with scores of candles that appeared suddenly and as suddenly disappeared, or drifted mysteriously hither and thither about the distant aisles like ghostly jack-o'-lanterns—we came at last to a small chapel which is called the "Chapel of the Mocking." Under the altar was a fragment of a marble column; this was the seat Christ sat on when he was reviled, and mockingly made King, crowned with a crown of thorns and sceptred with a reed. It was here that they blindfolded him and struck him, and said in derision, "Prophesy who it is that smote thee." The tradition that this is the identical spot of the mocking is a very ancient one. The guide said that Saewulf was the first to mention it. I do not know Saewulf, but still, I can not well refuse to receive his evidence—none of us can.

They showed us where the great Godfrey and his brother Baldwin, the first Christian Kings of Jerusalem, once lay buried by that sacred sepulchre they had fought so long and so valiantly to wrest from the hands of the infidel. But the niches that had contained the ashes of these renowned crusaders were empty. Even the coverings of their tombs were gone— destroyed by devout members of the Greek Church, because Godfrey and Baldwin were Latin princes, and had been reared in a Christian faith whose creed differed in some unimportant respects from theirs.

We passed on, and halted before the tomb of Melchisedek! You will remember Melchisedek, no doubt; he was the King who came out and levied a tribute on Abraham the time that he pursued Lot's captors to Dan, and took all their property from them. That was about four thousand years ago, and Melchisedek died shortly afterward. However, his tomb is in a good state of preservation.

When one enters the Church of the Holy Sepulchre, the Sepulchre itself is the first thing he desires to see, and really is almost the first thing he does see. The next thing he has a strong yearning to see is the spot where the Saviour was crucified. But this they exhibit last. It is the crowning glory of the place. One is grave and thoughtful when he stands in the little Tomb of the Saviour—he could not well be otherwise in such a place—but he has not the slightest possible belief that ever the Lord lay there, and so the interest he feels in the spot is very, very greatly marred by that reflection. He looks at the place where Mary stood, in another part of the church, and where John stood, and Mary Magdalen; where the mob derided the Lord; where the angel sat; where the crown of thorns was found, and the true cross; where the risen Saviour appeared—he looks at all these places with interest, but with the same conviction he felt in the case of the Sepulchre, that there is nothing genuine about them, and that they are imaginary holy places created by the monks. But the place of the Crucifixion affects him differently. He fully believes that he is looking upon the very spot where the Saviour gave up his life. He remembers that Christ was very celebrated, long before he came to Jerusalem; he knows that his fame was so great that crowds followed him all the time; he is aware that his entry into the city produced a stirring sensation, and that his reception was a kind of ovation; he can not overlook the fact that when he was crucified there were very many in Jerusalem who believed that he was the true Son of God. To publicly execute such a personage was sufficient in itself to make the locality of the execution a memorable place for ages; added to this, the storm, the darkness, the earthquake, the rending of the vail of the Temple, and the untimely waking of the dead, were events calculated to fix the execution and the scene of it in the memory of even the most thoughtless witness. Fathers would tell their sons about the strange affair, and point out the spot; the sons would transmit the story to their children, and thus a period of three hundred years would easily be spanned*—at which time Helena came and built a church upon Calvary to commemorate the death and burial of the Lord and preserve the sacred place in the memories of men; since that time there has always been a church there. It is not possible that there can be any mistake about the locality of the Crucifixion. Not half a dozen persons knew

*The thought is Mr. Prime's, not mine, and is full of good sense. I borrowed it from his "Tent Life."—M. T.

where they buried the Saviour, perhaps, and a burial is not a
startling event, any how; therefore, we can be pardoned for
unbelief in the Sepulchre, but not in the place of the Crucifixion. Five hundred years hence there will be no vestige of
Bunker Hill Monument left, but America will still know
where the battle was fought and where Warren fell. The crucifixion of Christ was too notable an event in Jerusalem, and
the Hill of Calvary made too celebrated by it, to be forgotten
in the short space of three hundred years. I climbed the stairway in the church which brings one to the top of the small
inclosed pinnacle of rock, and looked upon the place where
the true cross once stood, with a far more absorbing interest
than I had ever felt in any thing earthly before. I could not
believe that the three holes in the top of the rock were the
actual ones the crosses stood in, but I felt satisfied that those
crosses had stood so near the place now occupied by them,
that the few feet of possible difference were a matter of no
consequence.

When one stands where the Saviour was crucified, he finds
it all he can do to keep it strictly before his mind that Christ
was not crucified in a Catholic Church. He must remind himself every now and then that the great event transpired in the
open air, and not in a gloomy, candle-lighted cell in a little
corner of a vast church, up-stairs—a small cell all bejeweled
and bespangled with flashy ornamentation, in execrable taste.

Under a marble altar like a table, is a circular hole in the
marble floor, corresponding with the one just under it in
which the true cross stood. The first thing every one does is
to kneel down and take a candle and examine this hole. He
does this strange prospecting with an amount of gravity that
can never be estimated or appreciated by a man who has not
seen the operation. Then he holds his candle before a richly
engraved picture of the Saviour, done on a massy slab of
gold, and wonderfully rayed and starred with diamonds,
which hangs above the hole within the altar, and his solemnity changes to lively admiration. He rises and faces the finely
wrought figures of the Saviour and the malefactors uplifted
upon their crosses behind the altar, and bright with a metallic
lustre of many colors. He turns next to the figures close to
them of the Virgin and Mary Magdalen; next to the rift in

the living rock made by the earthquake at the time of the Crucifixion, and an extension of which he had seen before in the wall of one of the grottoes below; he looks next at the show-case with a figure of the Virgin in it, and is amazed at the princely fortune in precious gems and jewelry that hangs so thickly about the form as to hide it like a garment almost. All about the apartment the gaudy trappings of the Greek Church offend the eye and keep the mind on the rack to remember that this is the Place of the Crucifixion—Golgotha—the Mount of Calvary. And the last thing he looks at is that which was also the first—the place where the true cross stood. That will chain him to the spot and compel him to look once more, and once again, after he has satisfied all curiosity and lost all interest concerning the other matters pertaining to the locality.

And so I close my chapter on the Church of the Holy Sepulchre—the most sacred locality on earth to millions and millions of men, and women, and children, the noble and the humble, bond and free. In its history from the first, and in its tremendous associations, it is the most illustrious edifice in Christendom. With all its clap-trap side-shows and unseemly impostures of every kind, it is still grand, reverend, venerable—for a god died there; for fifteen hundred years its shrines have been wet with the tears of pilgrims from the earth's remotest confines; for more than two hundred, the most gallant knights that ever wielded sword wasted their lives away in a struggle to seize it and hold it sacred from infidel pollution. Even in our own day a war, that cost millions of treasure and rivers of blood, was fought because two rival nations claimed the sole right to put a new dome upon it. History is full of this old Church of the Holy Sepulchre—full of blood that was shed because of the respect and the veneration in which men held the last resting-place of the meek and lowly, the mild and gentle, Prince of Peace!

Chapter LIV

W E WERE STANDING in a narrow street, by the Tower of Antonio. "On these stones that are crumbling away," the guide said, "the Saviour sat and rested before taking up the cross. This is the beginning of the Sorrowful Way, or the Way of Grief." The party took note of the sacred spot, and moved on. We passed under the "Ecce Homo Arch," and saw the very window from which Pilate's wife warned her husband to have nothing to do with the persecution of the Just Man. This window is in an excellent state of preservation, considering its great age. They showed us where Jesus rested the second time, and where the mob refused to give him up, and said, "Let his blood be upon our heads, and upon our children's children forever." The French Catholics are building a church on this spot, and with their usual veneration for historical relics, are incorporating into the new such scraps of ancient walls as they have found there. Further on, we saw the spot where the fainting Saviour fell under the weight of his cross. A great granite column of some ancient temple lay there at the time, and the heavy cross struck it such a blow that it broke in two in the middle. Such was the guide's story when he halted us before the broken column.

We crossed a street, and came presently to the former residence of St. Veronica. When the Saviour passed there, she came out, full of womanly compassion, and spoke pitying words to him, undaunted by the hootings and the threatenings of the mob, and wiped the perspiration from his face with her handkerchief. We had heard so much of St. Veronica, and seen her picture by so many masters, that it was like meeting an old friend unexpectedly to come upon her ancient home in Jerusalem. The strangest thing about the incident that has made her name so famous, is, that when she wiped the perspiration away, the print of the Saviour's face remained upon the handkerchief, a perfect portrait, and so remains unto this day. We knew this, because we saw this handkerchief in a cathedral in Paris, in another in Spain, and in two others in Italy. In the Milan cathedral it costs five francs to see it, and at St. Peter's, at Rome, it is almost im-

possible to see it at any price. No tradition is so amply verified as this of St. Veronica and her handkerchief.

At the next corner we saw a deep indention in the hard
stone masonry of the corner of a house, but might have gone
heedlessly by it but that the guide said it was made by the
elbow of the Saviour, who stumbled here and fell. Presently
we came to just such another indention in a stone wall. The
guide said the Saviour fell here, also, and made this depression with his elbow.

There were other places where the Lord fell, and others
where he rested; but one of the most curious landmarks of
ancient history we found on this morning walk through the
crooked lanes that lead toward Calvary, was a certain stone
built into a house—a stone that was so seamed and scarred
that it bore a sort of grotesque resemblance to the human
face. The projections that answered for cheeks were worn
smooth by the passionate kisses of generations of pilgrims
from distant lands. We asked "Why?" The guide said it was
because this was one of "the very stones of Jerusalem" that
Christ mentioned when he was reproved for permitting the
people to cry "Hosannah!" when he made his memorable entry into the city upon an ass. One of the pilgrims said, "But
there is no evidence that the stones *did* cry out—Christ said
that if the people stopped from shouting Hosannah, the very
stones *would* do it." The guide was perfectly serene. He said,
calmly, "This is one of the stones that *would* have cried out."
It was of little use to try to shake this fellow's simple faith—
it was easy to see that.

And so we came at last to another wonder, of deep and
abiding interest—the veritable house where the unhappy
wretch once lived who has been celebrated in song and story
for more than eighteen hundred years as the Wandering Jew.
On the memorable day of the Crucifixion he stood in this old
doorway with his arms akimbo, looking out upon the struggling mob that was approaching, and when the weary Saviour
would have sat down and rested him a moment, pushed him
rudely away and said, "Move on!" The Lord said, "Move on,
thou, likewise," and the command has never been revoked
from that day to this. All men know how that the miscreant
upon whose head that just curse fell has roamed up and down

the wide world, for ages and ages, seeking rest and never finding it—courting death but always in vain—longing to stop, in city, in wilderness, in desert solitudes, yet hearing always that relentless warning to march—march on! They say—do these hoary traditions—that when Titus sacked Jerusalem and slaughtered eleven hundred thousand Jews in her streets and by-ways, the Wandering Jew was seen always in the thickest of the fight, and that when battle-axes gleamed in the air, he bowed his head beneath them; when swords flashed their deadly lightnings, he sprang in their way; he bared his breast to whizzing javelins, to hissing arrows, to any and to every weapon that promised death and forgetfulness, and rest. But it was useless—he walked forth out of the carnage without a wound. And it is said that five hundred years afterward he followed Mahomet when he carried destruction to the cities of Arabia, and then turned against him, hoping in this way to win the death of a traitor. His calculations were wrong again. No quarter was given to any living creature but one, and that was the only one of all the host that did not want it. He sought death five hundred years later, in the wars of the Crusades, and offered himself to famine and pestilence at Ascalon. He escaped again—he could not die. These repeated annoyances could have at last but one effect—they shook his confidence. Since then the Wandering Jew has carried on a kind of desultory toying with the most promising of the aids and implements of destruction, but with small hope, as a general thing. He has speculated some in cholera and railroads, and has taken almost a lively interest in infernal machines and patent medicines. He is old, now, and grave, as becomes an age like his; he indulges in no light amusements save that he goes sometimes to executions, and is fond of funerals.

There is one thing he can not avoid; go where he will about the world, he must never fail to report in Jerusalem every fiftieth year. Only a year or two ago he was here for the thirty-seventh time since Jesus was crucified on Calvary. They say that many old people, who are here now, saw him then, and had seen him before. He looks always the same—old, and withered, and hollow-eyed, and listless, save that there is about him something which seems to suggest that he is looking for some one, expecting some one—the friends of his youth, perhaps. But the most of them are dead, now. He always pokes about the old streets looking lonesome, making his mark on a wall here and there, and eyeing the oldest buildings with a sort of friendly half interest; and he sheds a few tears at the threshold of his ancient dwelling, and bitter, bitter tears they are. Then he collects his rent and leaves again. He has been seen standing near the Church of the Holy Sepulchre on many a starlight night, for he has cherished an idea for many centuries that if he could only enter there, he could rest. But when he approaches, the doors slam to with a crash, the earth trembles, and all the lights in Jerusalem burn a ghastly blue! He does this every fifty years, just the same. It is hopeless, but then it is hard to break habits one has been eighteen hundred years accustomed to. The old tourist is far away on his wanderings, now. How he must smile to see a pack of blockheads like us, galloping about the world, and looking wise, and imagining we are finding out a good deal about it! He must have a consuming contempt for the ignorant, complacent asses that go skurrying about the world in these railroading days and call it traveling.

When the guide pointed out where the Wandering Jew had left his familiar mark upon a wall, I was filled with astonishment. It read:

"S. T. — 1860 — X."

All I have revealed about the Wandering Jew can be amply proven by reference to our guide.

The mighty Mosque of Omar, and the paved court around it, occupy *a fourth part* of Jerusalem. They are upon Mount Moriah, where King Solomon's Temple stood. This Mosque is the holiest place the Mohammedan knows, outside of Mecca. Up to within a year or two past, no Christian could gain admission to it or its court for love or money. But the prohibition has been removed, and we entered freely for bucksheesh.

I need not speak of the wonderful beauty and the exquisite grace and symmetry that have made this Mosque so celebrated — because I did not see them. One can not see such things at an instant glance — one frequently only finds out how really beautiful a really beautiful woman is after considerable acquaintance with her; and the rule applies to Niagara Falls, to majestic mountains and to mosques—especially to mosques.

The great feature of the Mosque of Omar is the prodigious rock in the centre of its rotunda. It was upon this rock that Abraham came so near offering up his son Isaac—this, at least, is authentic—it is very much more to be relied on than most of the traditions, at any rate. On this rock, also, the angel stood and threatened Jerusalem, and David persuaded him to spare the city. Mahomet was well acquainted with this stone. From it he ascended to heaven. The stone tried to follow him, and if the angel Gabriel had not happened by the merest good luck to be there to seize it, it would have done it. Very few people have a grip like Gabriel—the prints of his monstrous fingers, two inches deep, are to be seen in that rock to-day.

This rock, large as it is, is suspended in the air. It does not touch any thing at all. The guide said so. This is very wonderful. In the place on it where Mahomet stood, he left his foot-prints in the solid stone. I should judge that he wore about eighteens. But what I was going to say, when I spoke of the rock being suspended, was, that in the floor of the cavern under it they showed us a slab which they said covered a hole which was a thing of extraordinary interest to all Mohammedans, because that hole leads down to perdition, and every soul that is transferred from thence to Heaven must pass up through this orifice. Mahomet stands there and lifts them out by the hair. All Mohammedans shave their heads, but they are careful to leave a lock of hair for the Prophet to take hold of. Our guide observed that a good Mohammedan would consider himself doomed to stay with the damned forever if he were to lose his scalp-lock and die before it grew again. The most of them that I have seen ought to stay with the damned, any how, without reference to how they were barbered.

For several ages no woman has been allowed to enter the cavern where that important hole is. The reason is that one of the sex was once caught there blabbing every thing she knew about what was going on above ground, to the rapscallions in the infernal regions down below. She carried her gossiping to such an extreme that nothing could be kept private—nothing could be done or said on earth but every body in perdition knew all about it before the sun went down. It was about time to suppress this woman's telegraph, and it was promptly done. Her breath subsided about the same time.

The inside of the great mosque is very showy with variegated marble walls and with windows and inscriptions of elaborate mosaic. The Turks have their sacred relics, like the Catholics. The guide showed us the veritable armor worn by the great son-in-law and successor of Mahomet, and also the buckler of Mahomet's uncle. The great iron railing which surrounds the rock was ornamented in one place with a thousand rags tied to its open work. These are to remind Mahomet not to forget the worshipers who placed them there. It is considered the next best thing to tying threads around his finger by way of reminders.

Just outside the mosque is a miniature temple, which marks the spot where David and Goliah used to sit and judge the people.*

Every where about the Mosque of Omar are portions of pillars, curiously wrought altars, and fragments of elegantly carved marble—precious remains of Solomon's Temple. These have been dug from all depths in the soil and rubbish of Mount Moriah, and the Moslems have always shown a disposition to preserve them with the utmost care. At that portion of the ancient wall of Solomon's Temple which is called the Jew's Place of Wailing, and where the Hebrews assemble every Friday to kiss the venerated stones and weep over the fallen greatness of Zion, any one can see a part of the unquestioned and undisputed Temple of Solomon, the same consisting of three or four stones lying one upon the other, each of which is about twice as long as a seven-octave piano, and about as thick as such a piano is high. But, as I have remarked before, it is only a year or two ago that the ancient edict prohibiting Christian rubbish like ourselves to *enter* the Mosque of Omar and see the costly marbles that once

*A pilgrim informs me that it was not David and Goliah, but David and Saul. I stick to my own statement—the guide told me, and he ought to know.

adorned the inner Temple was annulled. The designs wrought upon these fragments are all quaint and peculiar, and so the charm of novelty is added to the deep interest they naturally inspire. One meets with these venerable scraps at every turn, especially in the neighboring Mosque el Aksa, into whose inner walls a very large number of them are carefully built for preservation. These pieces of stone, stained and dusty with age, dimly hint at a grandeur we have all been taught to regard as the princeliest ever seen on earth; and they call up pictures of a pageant that is familiar to all imaginations—camels laden with spices and treasure—beautiful slaves, presents for Solomon's harem—a long cavalcade of richly caparisoned beasts and warriors—and Sheba's Queen in the van of this vision of "Oriental magnificence." These elegant fragments bear a richer interest than the solemn vastness of the stones the Jews kiss in the Place of Wailing can ever have for the heedless sinner.

Down in the hollow ground, underneath the olives and the orange-trees that flourish in the court of the great Mosque, is a wilderness of pillars—remains of the ancient Temple; they supported it. There are ponderous archways down there, also, over which the destroying "plough" of prophecy passed harmless. It is pleasant to know we are disappointed, in that we never dreamed we might see portions of the actual Temple of Solomon, and yet experience no shadow of suspicion that they were a monkish humbug and a fraud.

We are surfeited with sights. Nothing has any fascination for us, now, but the Church of the Holy Sepulchre. We have been there every day, and have not grown tired of it; but we are weary of every thing else. The sights are too many. They swarm about you at every step; no single foot of ground in all Jerusalem or within its neighborhood seems to be without a stirring and important history of its own. It is a very relief to steal a walk of a hundred yards without a guide along to talk unceasingly about every stone you step upon and drag you back ages and ages to the day when it achieved celebrity.

It seems hardly real when I find myself leaning for a moment on a ruined wall and looking *listlessly* down into the historic pool of Bethesda. I did not think such things *could* be so crowded together as to diminish their interest. But in serious truth, we have been drifting about, for several days, using our eyes and our ears more from a sense of duty than any higher and worthier reason. And too often we have been glad when it was time to go home and be distressed no more about illustrious localities.

Our pilgrims compress too much into one day. One can gorge sights to repletion as well as sweetmeats. Since we breakfasted, this morning, we have seen enough to have furnished us food for a year's reflection if we could have seen the various objects in comfort and looked upon them deliberately. We visited the pool of Hezekiah, where David saw Uriah's wife coming from the bath and fell in love with her.

We went out of the city by the Jaffa gate, and of course were told many things about its Tower of Hippicus.

We rode across the Valley of Hinnom, between two of the Pools of Gihon, and by an aqueduct built by Solomon, which still conveys water to the city. We ascended the Hill of Evil Counsel, where Judas received his thirty pieces of silver, and we also lingered a moment under the tree a venerable tradition says he hanged himself on.

We descended to the canon again, and then the guide began to give name and history to every bank and boulder we came to: "This was the Field of Blood; these cuttings in the rocks were shrines and temples of Moloch; here they sacrificed children; yonder is the Zion Gate; the Tyropean Valley; the Hill of Ophel; here is the junction of the Valley of Jehoshaphat—on your right is the Well of Job." We turned up Jehoshaphat. The recital went on. "This is the Mount of Olives; this is the Hill of Offense; the nest of huts is the Village of Siloam; here, yonder, every where, is the King's Garden; under this great tree Zacharias, the high priest, was murdered; yonder is Mount Moriah and the Temple wall; the tomb of Absalom; the tomb of St. James; the tomb of Zacharias; beyond, are the Garden of Gethsemane and the tomb of the Virgin Mary; here is the Pool of Siloam, and—"

We said we would dismount, and quench our thirst, and rest. We were burning up with the heat. We were failing under the accumulated fatigue of days and days of ceaseless marching. All were willing.

The Pool is a deep, walled ditch, through which a clear

stream of water runs, that comes from under Jerusalem some-where, and passing through the Fountain of the Virgin, or being supplied from it, reaches this place by way of a tunnel of heavy masonry. The famous pool looked exactly as it looked in Solomon's time, no doubt, and the same dusky, Oriental women, came down in their old Oriental way, and carried off jars of the water on their heads, just as they did three thousand years ago, and just as they will do fifty thousand years hence if any of them are still left on earth.

We went away from there and stopped at the Fountain of the Virgin. But the water was not good, and there was no comfort or peace any where, on account of the regiment of boys and girls and beggars that persecuted us all the time for bucksheesh. The guide wanted us to give them some money, and we did it; but when he went on to say that they were starving to death we could not but feel that we had done a great sin in throwing obstacles in the way of such a desirable consummation, and so we tried to collect it back, but it could not be done.

We entered the Garden of Gethsemane, and we visited the Tomb of the Virgin, both of which we had seen before. It is not meet that I should speak of them now. A more fitting time will come.

I can not speak now of the Mount of Olives or its view of Jerusalem, the Dead Sea and the mountains of Moab; nor of the Damascus Gate or the tree that was planted by King God-frey of Jerusalem. One ought to feel pleasantly when he talks of these things. I can not say any thing about the stone column that projects over Jehoshaphat from the Temple wall like a cannon, except that the Moslems believe Mahomet will sit astride of it when he comes to judge the world. It is a pity he could not judge it from some roost of his own in Mecca, without trespassing on *our* holy ground. Close by is the Golden Gate, in the Temple wall—a gate that was an elegant piece of sculpture in the time of the Temple, and is even so yet. From it, in ancient times, the Jewish High Priest turned loose the scapegoat and let him flee to the wilderness and bear away his twelve-month load of the sins of the people. If they were to turn one loose now, he would not get as far as the Garden of Gethsemane, till these miserable vagabonds here would gobble him up,* sins and all. *They* wouldn't care. Mutton-chops and sin is good enough living for them. The Moslems watch the Golden Gate with a jealous eye, and an anxious one, for they have an honored tradition that when it falls, Islamism will fall, and with it the Ottoman Empire. It did not grieve me any to notice that the old gate was getting a little shaky.

We are at home again. We are exhausted. The sun has roasted us, almost.

We have full comfort in one reflection, however. Our experiences in Europe have taught us that in time this fatigue will be forgotten; the heat will be forgotten; the thirst, the tiresome volubility of the guide, the persecutions of the beggars—and then, all that will be left will be pleasant memories of Jerusalem, memories we shall call up with always increasing interest as the years go by, memories which some day will become all beautiful when the last annoyance that incumbers them shall have faded out of our minds never again to return. School-boy days are no happier than the days of after life, but we look back upon them regretfully because we have forgotten our punishments at school, and how we grieved when our marbles were lost and our kites destroyed—because we have forgotten all the sorrows and privations of that canonized epoch and remember only its orchard robberies, its wooden sword pageants and its fishing holydays. We are satisfied. We can wait. Our reward will come. To us, Jerusalem and to-day's experiences will be an enchanted memory a year hence—a memory which money could not buy from us.

*Favorite pilgrim expression.

Chapter LV

W E CAST UP the account. It footed up pretty fairly. There was nothing more at Jerusalem to be seen, except the traditional houses of Dives and Lazarus of the parable, the Tombs of the Kings, and those of the Judges; the spot where they stoned one of the disciples to death, and beheaded another; the room and the table made celebrated by the Last Supper; the fig-tree that Jesus withered; a number of historical places about Gethsemane and the Mount of Olives, and fifteen or twenty others in different portions of the city itself.

We were approaching the end. Human nature asserted itself, now. Overwork and consequent exhaustion began to have their natural effect. They began to master the energies and dull the ardor of the party. Perfectly secure now, against failing to accomplish any detail of the pilgrimage, they felt like drawing in advance upon the holyday soon to be placed to their credit. They grew a little lazy. They were late to breakfast and sat long at dinner. Thirty or forty pilgrims had arrived from the ship, by the short routes, and much swapping of gossip had to be indulged in. And in hot afternoons, they showed a strong disposition to lie on the cool divans in the hotel and smoke and talk about pleasant experiences of a month or so gone by—for even thus early do episodes of travel which were sometimes annoying, sometimes exasperating and full as often of no consequence at all when they transpired, begin to rise above the dead level of monotonous reminiscences and become shapely landmarks in one's memory. The fog-whistle, smothered among a million of trifling sounds, is not noticed a block away, in the city, but the sailor hears it far at sea, whither none of those thousands of trifling sounds can reach. When one is in Rome, all the domes are alike; but when he has gone away twelve miles, the city fades utterly from sight and leaves St. Peter's swelling above the level plain like an anchored balloon. When one is traveling in Europe, the daily incidents seem all alike; but when he has placed them all two months and two thousand miles behind him, those that were worthy of being remembered are prominent, and those that were really insignificant have vanished.

This disposition to smoke, and idle and talk, was not well. It was plain that it must not be allowed to gain ground. A diversion must be tried, or demoralization would ensue. The Jordan, Jericho and the Dead Sea were suggested. The remainder of Jerusalem must be left unvisited, for a little while. The journey was approved at once. New life stirred in every pulse. In the saddle—abroad on the plains—sleeping in beds bounded only by the horizon: fancy was at work with these things in a moment.—It was painful to note how readily these town-bred men had taken to the free life of the camp and the desert. The nomadic instinct is a human instinct; it was born with Adam and transmitted through the patriarchs, and after thirty centuries of steady effort, civilization has not educated it entirely out of us yet. It has a charm which, once tasted, a man will yearn to taste again. The nomadic instinct can not be educated out of an Indian at all.

The Jordan journey being approved, our dragoman was notified.

At nine in the morning the caravan was before the hotel door and we were at breakfast. There was a commotion about the place. Rumors of war and bloodshed were flying every where. The lawless Bedouins in the Valley of the Jordan and the deserts down by the Dead Sea were up in arms, and were going to destroy all comers. They had had a battle with a troop of Turkish cavalry and defeated them; several men killed. They had shut up the inhabitants of a village and a Turkish garrison in an old fort near Jericho, and were besieging them. They had marched upon a camp of our excursionists by the Jordan, and the pilgrims only saved their lives by stealing away and flying to Jerusalem under whip and spur in the darkness of the night. Another of our parties had been fired on from an ambush and then attacked in the open day. Shots were fired on both sides. Fortunately there was no bloodshed. We spoke with the very pilgrim who had fired one of the shots, and learned from his own lips how, in this imminent deadly peril, only the cool courage of the pilgrims, their strength of numbers and imposing display of war material, had saved them from utter destruction. It was reported that the Consul had requested that no more of our pilgrims should go to the Jordan while this state of things lasted; and further, that he was unwilling that any more should go, at least without an unusually strong military guard. Here was trouble. But with the horses at the door and every body aware of what they were there for, what would *you* have done? Acknowledged that you were afraid, and backed shamefully out? Hardly. It would not be human nature, where there were so many women. You would have done as we did: said you were not afraid of a million Bedouins—and made your will and proposed quietly to yourself to take up an unostentatious position in the rear of the procession.

I think we must all have determined upon the same line of tactics, for it did seem as if we never would get to Jericho. I had a notoriously slow horse, but somehow I could not keep him in the rear, to save my neck. He was forever turning up in the lead. In such cases I trembled a little, and got down to fix my saddle. But it was not of any use. The others all got down to fix their saddles, too. I never saw such a time with saddles. It was the first time any of them had got out of order in three weeks, and now they had all broken down at once. I tried walking, for exercise—I had not had enough in Jerusalem searching for holy places. But it was a failure. The whole mob were suffering for exercise, and it was not fifteen minutes till they were all on foot and I had the lead again. It was very discouraging.

This was all after we got beyond Bethany. We stopped at the village of Bethany, an hour out from Jerusalem. They showed us the tomb of Lazarus. I had rather live in it than in any house in the town. And they showed us also a large "Fountain of Lazarus," and in the centre of the village the ancient dwelling of Lazarus. Lazarus appears to have been a man of property. The legends of the Sunday Schools do him great injustice; they give one the impression that he was poor. It is because they get him confused with that Lazarus who had no merit but his virtue, and virtue never has been as respectable as money. The house of Lazarus is a three-story edifice, of stone masonry, but the accumulated rubbish of ages has buried all of it but the upper story. We took candles and descended to the dismal cell-like chambers where Jesus sat at meat with Martha and Mary, and conversed with them about their brother. We could not but look upon these old dingy apartments with a more than common interest.

We had had a glimpse, from a mountain top, of the Dead Sea, lying like a blue shield in the plain of the Jordan, and now we were marching down a close, flaming, rugged, desolate defile, where no living creature could enjoy life, except, perhaps, a salamander. It was such a dreary, repulsive, horrible solitude! It was the " wilderness" where John preached, with camel's hair about his loins—raiment enough—but he never could have got his locusts and wild honey here. We were moping along down through this dreadful place, every man in the rear. Our guards—two gorgeous young Arab sheiks, with cargoes of swords, guns, pistols and daggers on board—were loafing ahead.

"Bedouins!"

Every man shrunk up and disappeared in his clothes like a mud-turtle. My first impulse was to dash forward and destroy the Bedouins. My second was to dash to the rear to see if there were any coming in that direction. I acted on the latter impulse. So did all the others. If any Bedouins had approached us, then, from that point of the compass, they would have paid dearly for their rashness. We all remarked that, afterwards. There would have been scenes of riot and bloodshed there that no pen could describe. I know that, because each man told what he would have done, individually; and such a medley of strange and unheard-of inventions of cruelty you could not conceive of. One man said he had calmly made up his mind to perish where he stood, if need be, but never yield an inch; he was going to wait, with deadly patience, till he could count the stripes upon the first Bedouin's jacket, and then count them and let him have it. Another was going to sit still till the first lance reached within an inch of his breast, and then dodge it and seize it. I forbear to tell what he was going to do to that Bedouin that owned it. It makes my blood run cold to think of it. Another was going to scalp such Bedouins as fell to his share, and take his bald-headed sons of the desert home with him alive for trophies. But the wild-eyed pilgrim rhapsodist was silent. His orbs gleamed with a deadly light, but his lips moved not. Anxiety grew, and he was questioned. If he had got a Bedouin, what would he have done with him—shot him? He smiled a smile of grim contempt and shook his head. Would he have stabbed him? Another shake. Would he have quartered him—flayed him? More shakes. Oh! horror, what *would* he have done?

"Eat him!"

Such was the awful sentence that thundered from his lips. What was grammar to a desperado like that? I was glad in my heart that I had been spared these scenes of malignant carnage. No Bedouins attacked our terrible rear. And none attacked the front. The new-comers were only a reinforcement of cadaverous Arabs, in shirts and bare legs, sent far ahead of us to brandish rusty guns, and shout and brag, and carry on like lunatics, and thus scare away all bands of marauding Bedouins that might lurk about our path. What a shame it is that armed white Christians must travel under guard of vermin like this as a protection against the prowling vagabonds of the desert—those sanguinary outlaws who are always going to do something desperate, but never do it. I may as well mention here that on our whole trip we saw no Bedouins, and had no more use for an Arab guard than we could have had for patent leather boots and white kid gloves. The Bedouins that attacked the other parties of pilgrims so fiercely were provided for the occasion by the Arab guards of those parties, and shipped from Jerusalem for temporary service as Bedouins. They met together in full view of the pilgrims, after the battle, and took lunch, divided the bucksheesh extorted in the season of danger, and then accompanied the cavalcade home to the city! The nuisance of an Arab guard is one which is created by the Sheiks and the Bedouins together, for mutual profit, it is said, and no doubt there is a good deal of truth in it.

We visited the fountain the prophet Elisha sweetened (it is sweet yet;) where he remained some time and was fed by the ravens.

Ancient Jericho is not very picturesque as a ruin. When Joshua marched around it seven times, some three thousand years ago, and blew it down with his trumpet, he did the work so well and so completely that he hardly left enough of the city to cast a shadow. The curse pronounced against the rebuilding of it, has never been removed. One King, holding the curse in light estimation, made the attempt, but was stricken sorely for his presumption. Its site will always remain unoccupied; and yet it is one of the very best locations for a town we have seen in all Palestine.

At two in the morning they routed us out of bed—another piece of unwarranted cruelty—another stupid effort of our dragoman to get ahead of a rival. It was not two hours to the Jordan. However, we were dressed and under way before any one thought of looking to see what time it was, and so we drowsed on through the chill night air and dreamed of camp fires, warm beds, and other comfortable things.

There was no conversation. People do not talk when they are cold, and wretched, and sleepy. We nodded in the saddle, at times, and woke up with a start to find that the procession had disappeared in the gloom. Then there was energy and attention to business until its dusky outlines came in sight again. Occasionally the order was passed in a low voice down the line: "Close up—close up! Bedouins lurk here, every where!" What an exquisite shudder it sent shivering along one's spine!

We reached the famous river before four o'clock, and the night was so black that we could have ridden into it without seeing it. Some of us were in an unhappy frame of mind. We waited and waited for daylight, but it did not come. Finally we went away in the dark and slept an hour on the ground, in the bushes, and caught cold. It was a costly nap, on that account, but otherwise it was a paying investment because it brought unconsciousness of the dreary minutes and put us in a somewhat fitter mood for a first glimpse of the sacred river.

With the first suspicion of dawn, every pilgrim took off his clothes and waded into the dark torrent, singing:

> "On Jordan's stormy banks I stand,
>   And cast a wistful eye
> To Canaan's fair and happy land,
>   Where my possessions lie."

But they did not sing long. The water was so fearfully cold that they were obliged to stop singing and scamper out again.

Then they stood on the bank shivering, and so chagrined and so grieved, that they merited honest compassion. Because another dream, another cherished hope, had failed. They had promised themselves all along that they would cross the Jordan where the Israelites crossed it when they entered Canaan from their long pilgrimage in the desert. They would cross where the twelve stones were placed in memory of that great event. While they did it they would picture to themselves that vast army of pilgrims marching through the cloven waters, bearing the hallowed ark of the covenant and shouting hosannahs, and singing songs of thanksgiving and praise. Each had promised himself that he would be the first to cross. They were at the goal of their hopes at last, but the current was too swift, the water was too cold!

It was then that Jack did them a service. With that engaging recklessness of consequences which is natural to youth, and so proper and so seemly, as well, he went and led the way across the Jordan, and all was happiness again. Every individual waded over, then, and stood upon the further bank. The water was not quite breast deep, any where. If it had been more, we could hardly have accomplished the feat, for the strong current would have swept us down the stream, and we would have been exhausted and drowned before reaching a place where we could make a landing. The main object compassed, the drooping, miserable party sat down to wait for the sun again, for all wanted to see the water as well as feel it. But it was too cold a pastime. Some cans were filled from the holy river, some canes cut from its banks, and then we mounted and rode reluctantly away to keep from freezing to death. So we saw the Jordan very dimly. The thickets of bushes that bordered its banks threw their shadows across its shallow, turbulent waters ("stormy," the hymn makes them, which is rather a complimentary stretch of fancy,) and we could not judge of the width of the stream by the eye. We knew by our wading experience, however, that many streets in America are double as wide as the Jordan.

Daylight came, soon after we got under way, and in the course of an hour or two we reached the Dead Sea. Nothing grows in the flat, burning desert around it but weeds and the Dead Sea apple the poets say is beautiful to the eye, but crumbles to ashes and dust when you break it. Such as we found were not handsome, but they were bitter to the taste. They yielded no dust. It was because they were not ripe, perhaps.

The desert and the barren hills gleam painfully in the sun, around the Dead Sea, and there is no pleasant thing or living creature upon it or about its borders to cheer the eye. It is a scorching, arid, repulsive solitude. A silence broods over the scene that is depressing to the spirits. It makes one think of funerals and death.

The Dead Sea is small. Its waters are very clear, and it has a pebbly bottom and is shallow for some distance out from the shores. It yields quantities of asphaltum; fragments of it lie all about its banks; this stuff gives the place something of an unpleasant smell.

All our reading had taught us to expect that the first plunge into the Dead Sea would be attended with distressing results—our bodies would feel as if they were suddenly pierced by millions of red-hot needles; the dreadful smarting would continue for hours; we might even look to be blistered from head to foot, and suffer miserably for many days. We were disappointed. Our eight sprang in at the same time that another party of pilgrims did, and nobody screamed once. None of them ever did complain of any thing more than a slight pricking sensation in places where their skin was abraded, and then only for a short time. My face smarted for a couple of hours, but it was partly because I got it badly sun-burned while I was bathing, and staid in so long that it became plastered over with salt.

No, the water did not blister us; it did not cover us with a slimy ooze and confer upon us an atrocious fragrance; it was not very slimy; and I could not discover that we smelt really any worse than we have always smelt since we have been in Palestine. It was only a different kind of smell, but not conspicuous on that account, because we have a great deal of variety in that respect. We didn't smell, there on the Jordan, the same as we do in Jerusalem; and we don't smell in Jerusalem just as we did in Nazareth, or Tiberias, or Cesarea Philippi, or any of those other ruinous ancient towns in Galilee. No, we change all the time, and generally for the worse. We do our own washing.

It was a funny bath. We could not sink. One could stretch himself at full length on his back, with his arms on his breast, and all of his body above a line drawn from the corner of his jaw past the middle of his side, the middle of his leg and through his ancle bone, would remain out of water. He could lift his head clear out, if he chose. No position can be retained long; you lose your balance and whirl over, first on your back and then on your face, and so on. You can lie comfortably, on your back, with your head out, and your legs out from your knees down, by steadying yourself with your hands. You can sit, with your knees drawn up to your chin and your arms clasped around them, but you are bound to turn over presently, because you are top-heavy in that position. You can stand up straight in water that is over your head, and from the middle of your breast upward you will not be wet. But you can not remain so. The water will soon float your feet to the surface. You can not swim on your back and make any progress of any consequence, because your feet stick away above the surface, and there is nothing to propel yourself with but your heels. If you swim on your face, you kick up the water like a stern-wheel boat. You make no headway. A horse is so top-heavy that he can neither swim nor stand up in the Dead Sea. He turns over on his side at once. Some of us bathed for more than an hour, and then came out coated with salt till we shone like icicles. We scrubbed it off with a coarse towel and rode off with a splendid brand-new smell, though it was one which was not any more disagreeable than those we have been for several weeks enjoying. It was the variegated villainy and novelty of it that charmed us. Salt crystals glitter in the sun about the shores of the lake. In places they coat the ground like a brilliant crust of ice.

When I was a boy I somehow got the impression that the river Jordan was four thousand miles long and thirty-five miles wide. It is only ninety miles long, and so crooked that a man does not know which side of it he is on half the time. In going ninety miles it does not get over more than fifty miles of ground. It is not any wider than Broadway in New York. There is the Sea of Galilee and this Dead Sea—neither of them twenty miles long or thirteen wide. And yet when I was in Sunday School I thought they were sixty thousand miles in diameter.

Travel and experience mar the grandest pictures and rob us of the most cherished traditions of our boyhood. Well, let them go. I have already seen the Empire of King Solomon diminish to the size of the State of Pennsylvania; I suppose I can bear the reduction of the seas and the river.

We looked every where, as we passed along, but never saw grain or crystal of Lot's wife. It was a great disappointment. For many and many a year we had known her sad story, and taken that interest in her which misfortune always inspires. But she was gone. Her picturesque form no longer looms above the desert of the Dead Sea to remind the tourist of the doom that fell upon the lost cities.

I can not describe the hideous afternoon's ride from the Dead Sea to Mars Saba. It oppresses me yet, to think of it. The sun so pelted us that the tears ran down our cheeks once or twice. The ghastly, treeless, grassless, breathless canons smothered us as if we had been in an oven. The sun had positive *weight* to it, I think. Not a man could sit erect under it. All drooped low in the saddles. John preached in this "Wilderness!" It must have been exhausting work. What a very heaven the massy towers and ramparts of vast Mars Saba looked to us when we caught a first glimpse of them!

We staid at this great convent all night, guests of the hospitable priests. Mars Saba, perched upon a crag, a human nest stuck high up against a perpendicular mountain wall, is a world of grand masonry that rises, terrace upon terrace away above your head, like the terraced and retreating colonnades one sees in fanciful pictures of Belshazzar's Feast and the palaces of the ancient Pharaohs. No other human dwelling is near. It was founded many ages ago by a holy recluse who lived at first in a cave in the rock—a cave which is inclosed in the convent walls, now, and was reverently shown to us by the priests. This recluse, by his rigorous torturing of his flesh, his diet of bread and water, his utter withdrawal from all society and from the vanities of the world, and his constant prayer and saintly contemplation of a skull, inspired an emulation that brought about him many disciples. The precipice on the opposite side of the canon is well perforated with the

small holes they dug in the rock to live in. The present occupants of Mars Saba, about seventy in number, are all hermits.
They wear a coarse robe, an ugly, brimless stove-pipe of a hat,
and go without shoes. They eat nothing whatever but bread
and salt; they drink nothing but water. As long as they live
they can never go outside the walls, or look upon a woman—
for no woman is permitted to enter Mars Saba, upon any
pretext whatsoever.

Some of those men have been shut up there for thirty years.
In all that dreary time they have not heard the laughter of a
child or the blessed voice of a woman; they have seen no
human tears, no human smiles; they have known no human
joys, no wholesome human sorrows. In their hearts are no
memories of the past, in their brains no dreams of the future.
All that is lovable, beautiful, worthy, they have put far away
from them; against all things that are pleasant to look upon,
and all sounds that are music to the ear, they have barred
their massive doors and reared their relentless walls of stone
forever. They have banished the tender grace of life and left
only the sapped and skinny mockery. Their lips are lips that
never kiss and never sing; their hearts are hearts that never
hate and never love; their breasts are breasts that never swell
with the sentiment, "I have a country and a flag." They are
dead men who walk.

I set down these first thoughts because they are natural—
not because they are just or because it is right to set them
down. It is easy for book-makers to say "I thought so and so
as I looked upon such and such a scene"—when the truth is,
they thought all those fine things afterwards. One's first
thought is not likely to be strictly accurate, yet it is no crime
to think it and none to write it down, subject to modification
by later experience. These hermits *are* dead men, in several
respects, but not in all; and it is not proper, that, thinking ill
of them at first, I should go on doing so, or, speaking ill of
them I should reiterate the words and stick to them. No, they
treated us too kindly for that. There is something human
about them somewhere. They knew we were foreigners and
Protestants, and not likely to feel admiration or much friendliness toward them. But their large charity was above considering such things. They simply saw in us men who were

hungry, and thirsty, and tired, and that was sufficient. They opened their doors and gave us welcome. They asked no questions, and they made no self-righteous display of their hospitality. They fished for no compliments. They moved quietly about, setting the table for us, making the beds, and bringing water to wash in, and paid no heed when we said it was wrong for them to do that when we had men whose business it was to perform such offices. We fared most comfortably, and sat late at dinner. We walked all over the building with the hermits afterward, and then sat on the lofty battlements and smoked while we enjoyed the cool air, the wild scenery and the sunset. One or two chose cosy bedrooms to sleep in, but the nomadic instinct prompted the rest to sleep on the broad divan that extended around the great hall, because it seemed like sleeping out of doors, and so was more cheery and inviting. It was a royal rest we had.

When we got up to breakfast in the morning, we were new men. For all this hospitality no strict charge was made. We could give something if we chose; we need give nothing, if we were poor or if we were stingy. The pauper and the miser are as free as any in the Catholic Convents of Palestine. I have been educated to enmity toward every thing that is Catholic, and sometimes, in consequence of this, I find it much easier to discover Catholic faults than Catholic merits. But there is one thing I feel no disposition to overlook, and no disposition to forget: and that is, the honest gratitude I and all pilgrims owe, to the Convent Fathers in Palestine. Their doors are always open, and there is always a welcome for any worthy man who comes, whether he comes in rags or clad in purple. The Catholic Convents are a priceless blessing to the poor. A pilgrim without money, whether he be a Protestant or a Catholic, can travel the length and breadth of Palestine, and in the midst of her desert wastes find wholesome food and a clean bed every night, in these buildings. Pilgrims in better circumstances are often stricken down by the sun and the fevers of the country, and then their saving refuge is the Convent. Without these hospitable retreats, travel in Palestine would be a pleasure which none but the strongest men could dare to undertake. Our party, pilgrims and all, will always be ready and always willing, to touch glasses and drink health, prosperity and long life to the Convent Fathers of Palestine.

So, rested and refreshed, we fell into line and filed away over the barren mountains of Judea, and along rocky ridges and through sterile gorges, where eternal silence and solitude reigned. Even the scattering groups of armed shepherds we met the afternoon before, tending their flocks of long-haired goats, were wanting here. We saw but two living creatures. They were gazelles, of "soft-eyed" notoriety. They looked like very young kids, but they annihilated distance like an express train. I have not seen animals that moved faster, unless I might say it of the antelopes of our own great plains.

At nine or ten in the morning we reached the Plain of the Shepherds, and stood in a walled garden of olives where the shepherds were watching their flocks by night, eighteen centuries ago, when the multitude of angels brought them the tidings that the Saviour was born. A quarter of a mile away was Bethlehem of Judea, and the pilgrims took some of the stone wall and hurried on.

The Plain of the Shepherds is a desert, paved with loose stones, void of vegetation, glaring in the fierce sun. Only the music of the angels it knew once could charm its shrubs and flowers to life again and restore its vanished beauty. No less potent enchantment could avail to work this miracle.

In the huge Church of the Nativity, in Bethlehem, built fifteen hundred years ago by the inveterate St. Helena, they took us below ground, and into a grotto cut in the living rock. This was the "manger" where Christ was born. A silver star set in the floor bears a Latin inscription to that effect. It is polished with the kisses of many generations of worshiping pilgrims. The grotto was tricked out in the usual tasteless style observable in all the holy places of Palestine. As in the Church of the Holy Sepulchre, envy and uncharitableness were apparent here. The priests and the members of the Greek and Latin Churches can not come by the same corridor to kneel in the sacred birthplace of the Redeemer, but are compelled to approach and retire by different avenues, lest they quarrel and fight on this holiest ground on earth.

I have no "meditations," suggested by this spot where the very first "Merry Christmas!" was uttered in all the world, and from whence the friend of my childhood, Santa Claus, departed on his first journey, to gladden and continue to gladden roaring firesides on wintry mornings in many a distant land forever and forever. I touch, with reverent finger, the actual spot where the infant Jesus lay, but I think—nothing.

You *can not* think in this place any more than you can in any other in Palestine that would be likely to inspire reflection. Beggars, cripples and monks compass you about, and make you think only of bucksheesh when you would rather think of something more in keeping with the character of the spot.

I was glad to get away, and glad when we had walked through the grottoes where Eusebius wrote, and Jerome fasted, and Joseph prepared for the flight into Egypt, and the dozen other distinguished grottoes, and knew we were done. The Church of the Nativity is almost as well packed with exceeding holy places as the Church of the Holy Sepulchre itself. They even have in it a grotto wherein twenty thousand children were slaughtered by Herod when he was seeking the life of the infant Saviour.

We went to the Milk Grotto, of course—a cavern where Mary hid herself for a while before the flight into Egypt. Its walls were black before she entered, but in suckling the Child, a drop of her milk fell upon the floor and instantly changed the darkness of the walls to its own snowy hue. We took many little fragments of stone from here, because it is well known in all the East that a barren woman hath need only to touch her lips to one of these and her failing will depart from her. We took many specimens, to the end that we might confer happiness upon certain households that we wot of.

We got away from Bethlehem and its troops of beggars and relic-peddlers in the afternoon, and after spending some little time at Rachel's tomb, hurried to Jerusalem as fast as possible. I never was *so* glad to get home again before. I never have enjoyed rest as I have enjoyed it during these last few hours. The journey to the Dead Sea, the Jordan and Bethlehem was short, but it was an exhausting one. Such roasting heat, such oppressive solitude, and such dismal desolation can not surely exist elsewhere on earth. And *such* fatigue!

The commonest sagacity warns me that I ought to tell the

customary pleasant lie, and say I tore myself reluctantly away from every noted place in Palestine. Every body tells that, but with as little ostentation as I may, I doubt the word of every he who tells it. I could take a dreadful oath that I have never heard any one of our forty pilgrims say any thing of the sort, and they are as worthy and as sincerely devout as any that come here. They will say it when they get home, fast enough, but why should they not? They do not wish to array themselves against all the Lamartines and Grimeses in the world. It does not stand to reason that men are reluctant to leave places where the very life is almost badgered out of them by importunate swarms of beggars and peddlers who hang in strings to one's sleeves and coat-tails and shriek and shout in his ears and horrify his vision with the ghastly sores and malformations they exhibit. One is *glad* to get away. I have heard shameless people say they were glad to get away from Ladies' Festivals where they were importuned to buy by bevies of lovely young ladies. Transform those houris into dusky hags and ragged savages, and replace their rounded forms with shrunken and knotted distortions, their soft hands with scarred and hideous deformities, and the persuasive music of their voices with the discordant din of a hated language, and *then* see how much lingering reluctance to leave could be mustered. No, it is the neat thing to say you were reluctant, and then append the profound thoughts that "struggled for utterance," in your brain; but it is the true thing to say you were not reluctant, and found it impossible to think at all— though in good sooth it is not respectable to say it, and not poetical, either.

We do not think, in the holy places; we think in bed, afterwards, when the glare, and the noise, and the confusion are gone, and in fancy we revisit alone, the solemn monuments of the past, and summon the phantom pageants of an age that has passed away.

Chapter LVI

W E VISITED ALL the holy places about Jerusalem which we had left unvisited when we journeyed to the Jordan, and then, about three o'clock one afternoon, we fell into procession and marched out at the stately Damascus gate, and the walls of Jerusalem shut us out forever. We paused on the summit of a distant hill and took a final look and made a final farewell to the venerable city which had been such a good home to us.

For about four hours we traveled down hill constantly. We followed a narrow bridle-path which traversed the beds of the mountain gorges, and when we could we got out of the way of the long trains of laden camels and asses, and when we could not we suffered the misery of being mashed up against perpendicular walls of rock and having our legs bruised by the passing freight. Jack was caught two or three times, and Dan and Moult as often. One horse had a heavy fall on the slippery rocks, and the others had narrow escapes. However, this was as good a road as we had found in Palestine, and possibly even the best, and so there was not much grumbling.

Sometimes, in the glens, we came upon luxuriant orchards of figs, apricots, pomegranates, and such things, but oftener the scenery was rugged, mountainous, verdureless and forbidding. Here and there, towers were perched high up on acclivities which seemed almost inaccessible. This fashion is as old as Palestine itself and was adopted in ancient times for security against enemies.

We crossed the brook which furnished David the stone that killed Goliath, and no doubt we looked upon the very ground whereon that noted battle was fought. We passed by a picturesque old gothic ruin whose stone pavements had rung to the armed heels of many a valorous Crusader, and we rode through a piece of country which we were told once knew Samson as a citizen.

We staid all night with the good monks at the convent of Ramleh, and in the morning got up and galloped the horses a good part of the distance from there to Jaffa, or Joppa, for the plain was as level as a floor and free from stones, and besides this was our last march in Holy Land. These two or three hours finished, we and the tired horses could have rest and sleep as long as we wanted it. This was the plain of which Joshua spoke when he said, "Sun, stand thou still on Gibeon, and thou moon in the valley of Ajalon." As we drew near to Jaffa, the boys spurred up the horses and indulged in the excitement of an actual race—an experience we had hardly had since we raced on donkeys in the Azores islands.

We came finally to the noble grove of orange-trees in which the Oriental city of Jaffa lies buried; we passed through the walls, and rode again down narrow streets and among swarms of animated rags, and saw other sights and had other experiences we had long been familiar with. We dismounted, for the last time, and out in the offing, riding at anchor, we saw the ship! I put an exclamation point there because we felt one when we saw the vessel. The long pilgrimage was ended, and somehow we seemed to feel glad of it.

[For description of Jaffa, see Universal Gazetteer.] Simon the Tanner formerly lived here. We went to his house. All the pilgrims visit Simon the Tanner's house. Peter saw the vision of the beasts let down in a sheet when he lay upon the roof of Simon the Tanner's house. It was from Jaffa that Jonah sailed when he was told to go and prophesy against Nineveh, and no doubt it was not far from the town that the whale threw him up when he discovered that he had no ticket. Jonah was disobedient, and of a fault-finding, complaining disposition, and deserves to be lightly spoken of, almost. The timbers used in the construction of Solomon's temple were floated to Jaffa in rafts, and the narrow opening in the reef through which they passed to the shore is not an inch wider or a shade less dangerous to navigate than it was then. Such is the sleepy nature of the population Palestine's only good sea-port has now and always had. Jaffa has a history and a stirring one. It will not be discovered any where in this book. If the reader will call at the circulating library and mention my name, he will be furnished with books which will afford him the fullest information concerning Jaffa.

So ends the pilgrimage. We ought to be glad that we did not make it for the purpose of feasting our eyes upon fascinating aspects of nature, for we should have been disappointed—at least at this season of the year. A writer in "Life in the Holy Land" observes:

"Monotonous and uninviting as much of the Holy Land will appear to persons accustomed to the almost constant verdure of flowers, ample streams and varied surface of our own country, we must remember that its aspect to the Israelites after the weary march of forty years through the desert must have been very different."

Which all of us will freely grant. But it truly *is* "monotonous and uninviting," and there is no sufficient reason for describing it as being otherwise.

Of all the lands there are for dismal scenery, I think Palestine must be the prince. The hills are barren, they are dull of color, they are unpicturesque in shape. The valleys are unsightly deserts fringed with a feeble vegetation that has an expression about it of being sorrowful and despondent. The Dead Sea and the Sea of Galilee sleep in the midst of a vast stretch of hill and plain wherein the eye rests upon no pleasant tint, no striking object, no soft picture dreaming in a purple haze or mottled with the shadows of the clouds. Every outline is harsh, every feature is distinct, there is no perspective—distance works no enchantment here. It is a hopeless, dreary, heart-broken land.

Small shreds and patches of it must be very beautiful in the full flush of spring, however, and all the more beautiful by contrast with the far-reaching desolation that surrounds them on every side. I would like much to see the fringes of the Jordan in spring-time, and Shechem, Esdraelon, Ajalon and the borders of Galilee—but even then these spots would seem mere toy gardens set at wide intervals in the waste of a limitless desolation.

Palestine sits in sackcloth and ashes. Over it broods the spell of a curse that has withered its fields and fettered its energies. Where Sodom and Gomorrah reared their domes and towers, that solemn sea now floods the plain, in whose bitter waters no living thing exists—over whose waveless surface the blistering air hangs motionless and dead—about whose borders nothing grows but weeds, and scattering tufts of cane, and that treacherous fruit that promises refreshment to parching lips, but turns to ashes at the touch. Nazareth is forlorn; about that ford of Jordan where the hosts of Israel entered the Promised Land with songs of rejoicing, one finds only a squalid camp of fantastic Bedouins of the desert; Jericho the accursed, lies a moldering ruin, to-day, even as Joshua's miracle left it more than three thousand years ago; Bethlehem and Bethany, in their poverty and their humiliation, have nothing about them now to remind one that they once knew the high honor of the Saviour's presence; the hallowed spot where the shepherds watched their flocks by night, and where the angels sang Peace on earth, good will to men, is untenanted by any living creature, and unblessed by any feature that is pleasant to the eye. Renowned Jerusalem itself, the stateliest name in history, has lost all its ancient grandeur, and is become a pauper village; the riches of Solomon are no longer there to compel the admiration of visiting Oriental queens; the wonderful temple which was the pride and the glory of Israel, is gone, and the Ottoman crescent is lifted above the spot where, on that most memorable day in the annals of the world, they reared the Holy Cross. The noted Sea of Galilee, where Roman fleets once rode at anchor and the disciples of the Saviour sailed in their ships, was long ago deserted by the devotees of war and commerce, and its borders are a silent wilderness; Capernaum is a shapeless ruin; Magdala is the home of beggared Arabs; Bethsaida and Chorazin have vanished from the earth, and the "desert places" round about them where thousands of men once listened to the Saviour's voice and ate the miraculous bread, sleep in the hush of a solitude that is inhabited only by birds of prey and skulking foxes.

Palestine is desolate and unlovely. And why should it be otherwise? Can the *curse* of the Deity beautify a land?

Palestine is no more of this work-day world. It is sacred to poetry and tradition—it is dream-land.

Chapter LVII

IT WAS WORTH a kingdom to be at sea again. It was a relief to drop all anxiety whatsoever—all questions as to where we should go; how long we should stay; whether it were worth while to go or not; all anxieties about the condition of the horses; all such questions as "Shall we *ever* get to water?" "Shall we *ever* lunch?" "Ferguson, how many *more* million miles have we got to creep under this awful sun before we camp?" It was a relief to cast all these torturing little anxieties far away—ropes of steel they were, and every one with a separate and distinct strain on it—and feel the temporary contentment that is born of the banishment of all care and responsibility. We did not look at the compass: we did not care, now, where the ship went to, so that she went out of sight of land as quickly as possible. When I travel again, I wish to go in a pleasure ship. No amount of money could have purchased for us, in a strange vessel and among unfamiliar faces, the perfect satisfaction and the sense of being *at home* again which we experienced when we stepped on board the "Quaker City,"—*our own ship*—after this wearisome pilgrimage. It is a something we have felt always when we returned to her, and a something we had no desire to sell.

We took off our blue woollen shirts, our spurs, and heavy boots, our sanguinary revolvers and our buckskin-seated pantaloons, and got shaved and came out in Christian costume once more. All but Jack, who changed all other articles of his dress, but clung to his traveling pantaloons. They still preserved their ample buckskin seat intact; and so his short peajacket and his long, thin legs assisted to make him a picturesque object whenever he stood on the forecastle looking abroad upon the ocean over the bows. At such times his father's last injunction suggested itself to me. He said:

"Jack, my boy, you are about to go among a brilliant company of gentlemen and ladies, who are refined and cultivated, and thoroughly accomplished in the manners and customs of good society. Listen to their conversation, study their habits of life, and learn. Be polite and obliging to all, and considerate towards every one's opinions, failings and prejudices.

487

Command the just respect of all your fellow-voyagers, even though you fail to win their friendly regard. And Jack—don't you ever dare, while you live, appear in public on those decks in fair weather, in a costume unbecoming your mother's drawing-room!"

It would have been worth any price if the father of this hopeful youth could have stepped on board some time, and seen him standing high on the fore-castle, pea-jacket, tasseled red fez, buckskin patch and all,—placidly contemplating the ocean—a rare spectacle for any body's drawing-room.

After a pleasant voyage and a good rest, we drew near to Egypt and out of the mellowest of sunsets we saw the domes and minarets of Alexandria rise into view. As soon as the anchor was down, Jack and I got a boat and went ashore. It was night by this time, and the other passengers were content to remain at home and visit ancient Egypt after breakfast. It was the way they did at Constantinople. They took a lively interest in new countries, but their school-boy impatience had worn off, and they had learned that it was wisdom to take things easy and go along comfortably—these old countries do not go away in the night; they stay till after breakfast.

When we reached the pier we found an army of Egyptian boys with donkeys no larger than themselves, waiting for passengers—for donkeys are the omnibuses of Egypt. We preferred to walk, but we could not have our own way. The boys crowded about us, clamored around us, and slewed their donkeys exactly across our path, no matter which way we turned. They were good-natured rascals, and so were the donkeys. We mounted, and the boys ran behind us and kept the donkeys in a furious gallop, as is the fashion at Damascus. I believe I would rather ride a donkey than any beast in the world. He goes briskly, he puts on no airs, he is docile, though opinionated. Satan himself could not scare him, and he is convenient—very convenient. When you are tired riding you can rest your feet on the ground and let him gallop from under you.

We found the hotel and secured rooms, and were happy to know that the Prince of Wales had stopped there once. They had it every where on signs. No other princes had stopped there since, till Jack and I came. We went abroad through the town, then, and found it a city of huge commercial buildings, and broad, handsome streets brilliant with gas-light. By night it was a sort of reminiscence of Paris. But finally Jack found an ice-cream saloon, and that closed investigations for that evening. The weather was very hot, it had been many a day since Jack had seen ice-cream, and so it was useless to talk of leaving the saloon till it shut up.

In the morning the lost tribes of America came ashore and infested the hotels and took possession of all the donkeys and other open barouches that offered. They went in picturesque procession to the American Consul's; to the great gardens; to Cleopatra's Needles; to Pompey's Pillar; to the palace of the Viceroy of Egypt; to the Nile; to the superb groves of date-palms. One of our most inveterate relic-hunters had his hammer with him, and tried to break a fragment off the upright Needle and could not do it; he tried the prostrate one and failed; he borrowed a heavy sledge hammer from a mason and failed again. He tried Pompey's Pillar, and this baffled him. Scattered all about the mighty monolith were sphinxes of noble countenance, carved out of Egyptian granite as hard as blue steel, and whose shapely features the wear of five thousand years had failed to mark or mar. The relic-hunter battered at these persistently, and sweated profusely over his work. He might as well have attempted to deface the moon. They regarded him serenely with the stately smile they had worn so long, and which seemed to say, "Peck away, poor insect; we were not made to fear such as you; in ten-score dragging ages we have seen more of your kind than there are sands at your feet: have they left a blemish upon us?"

But I am forgetting the Jaffa Colonists. At Jaffa we had taken on board some forty members of a very celebrated community. They were male and female; babies, young boys and young girls; young married people, and some who had passed a shade beyond the prime of life. I refer to the "Adams Jaffa Colony." Others had deserted before. We left in Jaffa Mr. Adams, his wife, and fifteen unfortunates who not only had no money but did not know where to turn or whither to go. Such was the statement made to us. Our forty were miserable enough in the first place, and they lay about the decks seasick all the voyage, which about completed their misery, I take it. However, one or two young men remained upright, and by constant persecution we wormed out of them some little information. They gave it reluctantly and in a very fragmentary condition, for, having been shamefully humbugged by their prophet, they felt humiliated and unhappy. In such circumstances people do not like to talk.

The colony was a complete *fiasco*. I have already said that such as could get away did so, from time to time. The prophet Adams—once an actor, then several other things, afterward a Mormon and a missionary, always an adventurer—remains at Jaffa with his handful of sorrowful subjects. The forty we brought away with us were chiefly destitute, though not all of them. They wished to get to Egypt. What might become of them then they did not know and probably did not care—any thing to get away from hated Jaffa. They had little to hope for. Because after many appeals to the sympathies of New England, made by strangers of Boston, through the newspapers, and after the establishment of an office there for the reception of moneyed contributions for the Jaffa colonists, One Dollar was subscribed. The consul-general for Egypt showed me the newspaper paragraph which mentioned the circumstance and mentioned also the discontinuance of the effort and the closing of the office. It was evident that practical New England was not sorry to be rid of such visionaries and was not in the least inclined to hire any body to bring them back to her. Still, to get to Egypt, was something, in the eyes of the unfortunate colonists, hopeless as the prospect seemed of ever getting further.

Thus circumstanced, they landed at Alexandria from our ship. One of our passengers, Mr. Moses S. Beach, of the New York *Sun*, inquired of the consul-general what it would cost to send these people to their home in Maine by the way of Liverpool, and he said fifteen hundred dollars in gold would do it. Mr. Beach gave his check for the money and so the troubles of the Jaffa colonists were at an end.*

Alexandria was too much like a European city to be novel,

---

*It was an unselfish act of benevolence; it was done without any ostentation, and has never been mentioned in any newspaper, I think. Therefore it is refreshing to learn now, several months after the above narrative was written, that another man received all the credit of this rescue of the colonists. Such is life.

and we soon tired of it. We took the cars and came up here to ancient Cairo, which *is* an Oriental city and of the completest pattern. There is little about it to disabuse one's mind of the error if he should take it into his head that he was in the heart of Arabia. Stately camels and dromedaries, swarthy Egyptians, and likewise Turks and black Ethiopians, turbaned, sashed, and blazing in a rich variety of Oriental costumes of all shades of flashy colors, are what one sees on every hand crowding the narrow streets and the honeycombed bazaars. We are stopping at Shepherd's Hotel, which is the worst on earth except the one I stopped at once in a small town in the United States. It is pleasant to read this sketch in my note-book, now, and know that I can stand Shepherd's Hotel, sure, because I have been in one just like it in America and survived:

I stopped at the Benton House. It used to be a good hotel, but that proves nothing—I used to be a good boy, for that matter. Both of us have lost character of late years. The Benton is not a good hotel. The Benton lacks a very great deal of being a good hotel. Perdition is full of better hotels than the Benton.

It was late at night when I got there, and I told the clerk I would like plenty of lights, because I wanted to read an hour or two. When I reached No. 15 with the porter (we came along a dim hall that was clad in ancient carpeting, faded, worn out in many places, and patched with old scraps of oil cloth—a hall that sank under one's feet, and creaked dismally to every footstep,) he struck a light—two inches of sallow, sorrowful, consumptive tallow candle, that burned blue, and sputtered, and got discouraged and went out. The porter lit it again, and I asked if that was all the light the clerk sent. He said, "Oh no, I've got another one here," and he produced another couple of inches of tallow candle. I said, "Light them both—I'll have to have one to see the other by." He did it, but the result was drearier than darkness itself. He was a cheery, accommodating rascal. He said he would go "somewheres" and steal a lamp. I abetted and encouraged him in his criminal design. I heard the landlord get after him in the hall ten minutes afterward.

"Where are you going with that lamp?"

"Fifteen wants it, sir."

"Fifteen! why he's got a double lot of candles—does the man want to illuminate the house?—does he want to get up a torch-light procession?—what *is* he up to, any how?"

"He don't like them candles—says he wants a lamp."

"Why what in the nation does—why I never heard of such a thing? What on earth can he want with that lamp?"

"Well, he only wants to read—that's what he says."

"Wants to read, does he?—ain't satisfied with a thousand candles, but has to have a lamp!—I do wonder what the devil that fellow wants that lamp for? Take him another candle, and then if——"

"But he wants the lamp—says he'll burn the d——d old house down if he don't get a lamp!" (a remark which I never made.)

"I'd like to see him at it once. Well, you take it along—but I swear it beats *my* time, though—and see if you can't find out what in the very nation he *wants* with that lamp."

And he went off growling to himself and still wondering and wondering over the unaccountable conduct of No. 15. The lamp was a good one, but it revealed some disagreeable things—a bed in the suburbs of a desert of room—a bed that had hills and valleys in it, and you'd have to accommodate your body to the impression left in it by the man that slept there last, before you could lie comfortably; a carpet that had seen better days; a melancholy washstand in a remote corner, and a dejected pitcher on it sorrowing over a broken nose; a looking-glass split across the centre, which chopped your head off at the chin, and made you look like some dreadful unfinished monster or other; the paper peeling in shreds from the walls.

I sighed and said: "This is charming; and now don't you think you could get me something to read?"

The porter said, "Oh, certainly; the old man's got dead loads of books;" and he was gone before I could tell him what sort of literature I would rather have. And yet his countenance expressed the utmost confidence in his ability to execute the commission with credit to himself. The old man made a descent on him.

"What are you going to do with that pile of books?"

"Fifteen wants 'em, sir."

"Fifteen, is it? He'll want a warming-pan, next—he'll want a nurse! Take him every thing there is in the house—take him the barkeeper—take him the baggage-wagon—take him a chamber-maid! Confound me, I never saw any thing like it. What did he say he wants with those books?"

"Wants to read 'em, like enough; it ain't likely he wants to eat 'em, I don't reckon."

"Wants to read 'em—wants to read 'em this time of night, the infernal lunatic! Well, he can't have them."

"But he says he's mor'ly bound to have 'em; he says he'll just go a-rairin' and a-chargin' through this house and raise more——well, there's no tellin' what he won't do if he don't get 'em; because he's drunk and crazy and desperate, and nothing'll soothe him down but them cussed books." [I had not made any threats, and was not in the condition ascribed to me by the porter.]

"Well, go on; but I will be around when he goes to rairing and charging, and the first rair he makes I'll make him rair out of the window." And then the old gentleman went off, growling as before.

The genius of that porter was something wonderful. He put an armful of books on the bed and said "Good night" as confidently as if he knew perfectly well that those books were exactly my style of reading matter. And well he might. His selection covered the whole range of legitimate literature. It comprised "The Great Consummation," by Rev. Dr. Cummings—theology; "Revised Statutes of the State of Missouri"—law; "The Complete Horse-Doctor"—medicine; "The Toilers of the Sea," by Victor Hugo—romance; "The works of William Shakspeare"—poetry. I shall never cease to admire the tact and the intelligence of that gifted porter.

But all the donkeys in Christendom, and most of the Egyptian boys, I think, are at the door, and there is some noise going on, not to put it in stronger language.—We are about starting to the illustrious Pyramids of Egypt, and the donkeys for the voyage are under inspection. I will go and select one before the choice animals are all taken.

Chapter LVIII

THE DONKEYS WERE all good, all handsome, all strong and in good condition, all fast and all willing to prove it. They were the best we had found any where, and the most *recherche*. I do not know what *recherche* is, but that is what these donkeys were, anyhow. Some were of a soft mouse-color, and the others were white, black, and vari-colored. Some were close-shaven, all over, except that a tuft like a paint-brush was left on the end of the tail. Others were so shaven in fanciful landscape garden patterns, as to mark their bodies with curving lines, which were bounded on one side by hair and on the other by the close plush left by the shears. They had all been newly barbered, and were exceedingly stylish. Several of the white ones were barred like zebras with rainbow stripes of blue and red and yellow paint. These were indescribably gorgeous. Dan and Jack selected from this lot because they brought back Italian reminiscences of the "old masters." The saddles were the high, stuffy, frog-shaped things we had known in Ephesus and Smyrna. The donkey-boys were lively young Egyptian rascals who could follow a donkey and keep him in a canter half a day without tiring. We had plenty of spectators when we mounted, for the hotel was full of English people bound overland to India and officers getting ready for the African campaign against the Abyssinian King Theodorus. We were not a very large party, but as we charged through the streets of the great metropolis, we made noise for five hundred, and displayed activity and created excitement in proportion. Nobody can steer a donkey, and some collided with camels, dervishes, effendis, asses, beggars and every thing else that offered to the donkeys a reasonable chance for a collision. When we turned into the broad avenue that leads out of the city toward Old Cairo, there was plenty of room. The walls of stately date-palms that fenced the gardens and bordered the way, threw their shadows down and made the air cool and bracing. We rose to the spirit of the time and the race became a wild rout, a stampede, a terrific panic. I wish to live to enjoy it again.

Somewhere along this route we had a few startling exhibitions of Oriental simplicity. A girl apparently thirteen years of age came along the great thoroughfare dressed like Eve before the fall. We would have called her thirteen at home; but here girls who look thirteen are often not more than nine, in reality. Occasionally we saw stark-naked men of superb build, bathing, and making no attempt at concealment. However, an hour's acquaintance with this cheerful custom reconciled the pilgrims to it, and then it ceased to occasion remark. Thus easily do even the most startling novelties grow tame and spiritless to these sight-surfeited wanderers.

Arrived at Old Cairo, the camp-followers took up the donkeys and tumbled them bodily aboard a small boat with a lateen sail, and we followed and got under way. The deck was closely packed with donkeys and men; the two sailors had to climb over and under and through the wedged mass to work the sails, and the steersman had to crowd four or five donkeys out of the way when he wished to swing his tiller and put his helm hard-down. But what were their troubles to us? We had nothing to do; nothing to do but enjoy the trip; nothing to do but shove the donkeys off our corns and look at the charming scenery of the Nile.

On the island at our right was the machine they call the Nilometer, a stone-column whose business it is to mark the rise of the river and prophecy whether it will reach only thirty-two feet and produce a famine, or whether it will properly flood the land at forty and produce plenty, or whether it will rise to forty-three and bring death and destruction to flocks and crops—but how it does all this they could not explain to us so that we could understand. On the same island is still shown the spot where Pharaoh's daughter found Moses in the bulrushes. Near the spot we sailed from, the Holy Family dwelt when they sojourned in Egypt till Herod should complete his slaughter of the innocents. The same tree they rested under when they first arrived, was there a short time ago, but the Viceroy of Egypt sent it to the Empress Eugenie lately. He was just in time, otherwise our pilgrims would have had it.

The Nile at this point is muddy, swift and turbid, and does not lack a great deal of being as wide as the Mississippi.

We scrambled up the steep bank at the shabby town of Ghi-
zeh, mounted the donkeys again, and scampered away. For
four or five miles the route lay along a high embankment
which they say is to be the bed of a railway the Sultan means
to build for no other reason than that when the Empress of
the French comes to visit him she can go to the Pyramids in
comfort. This is true Oriental hospitality. I am very glad it is
our privilege to have donkeys instead of cars.

At the distance of a few miles the Pyramids rising above
the palms, looked very clean-cut, very grand and imposing,
and very soft and filmy, as well. They swam in a rich haze
that took from them all suggestions of unfeeling stone, and
made them seem only the airy nothings of a dream—structures which might blossom into tiers of vague arches, or ornate colonnades, may be, and change and change again, into
all graceful forms of architecture, while we looked, and then
melt deliciously away and blend with the tremulous atmosphere.

At the end of the levee we left the mules and went in a sail-
boat across an arm of the Nile or an overflow, and landed
where the sands of the Great Sahara left their embankment,
as straight as a wall, along the verge of the alluvial plain of
the river. A laborious walk in the flaming sun brought us to
the foot of the great Pyramid of Cheops. It was a fairy vision
no longer. It was a corrugated, unsightly mountain of stone.
Each of its monstrous sides was a wide stairway which rose
upward, step above step, narrowing as it went, till it tapered
to a point far aloft in the air. Insect men and women—pilgrims from the *Quaker City*—were creeping about its dizzy
perches, and one little black swarm were waving postage
stamps from the airy summit—handkerchiefs will be understood.

Of course we were besieged by a rabble of muscular Egyptians and Arabs who wanted the contract of dragging us to
the top—all tourists are. Of course you could not hear your
own voice for the din that was around you. Of course the
Sheiks said *they* were the only responsible parties; that all
contracts must be made with them, all moneys paid over to
them, and none exacted from us by any but themselves alone.
Of course they contracted that the varlets who dragged us up

should not mention bucksheesh once. For such is the usual routine. Of course we contracted with them, paid them, were delivered into the hands of the draggers, dragged up the Pyramids, and harried and be-deviled for bucksheesh from the foundation clear to the summit. We paid it, too, for we were purposely spread very far apart over the vast side of the Pyramid. There was no help near if we called, and the Herculeses who dragged us had a way of asking sweetly and flatteringly for bucksheesh, which was seductive, and of looking fierce and threatening to throw us down the precipice, which was persuasive and convincing.

Each step being full as high as a dinner-table; there being very, very many of the steps; an Arab having hold of each of our arms and springing upward from step to step and snatching us with them, forcing us to lift our feet as high as our breasts every time, and do it rapidly and keep it up till we were ready to faint, who shall say it is not lively, exhilarating, lacerating, muscle-straining, bone-wrenching and perfectly excruciating and exhausting pastime, climbing the Pyramids? I beseeched the varlets not to twist *all* my joints asunder; I iterated, reiterated, even *swore* to them that I did not wish to beat any body to the top; did all I could to convince them that if I got there the last of all I would feel blessed above men and grateful to them forever; I begged them, prayed them, pleaded with them to let me stop and rest a moment— only one little moment: and they only answered with some more frightful springs, and an unenlisted volunteer behind opened a bombardment of determined boosts with his head which threatened to batter my whole political economy to wreck and ruin.

Twice, for one minute, they let me rest while they extorted bucksheesh, and then continued their maniac flight up the Pyramid. They wished to beat the other parties. It was nothing to them that I, a stranger, must be sacrificed upon the altar of their unholy ambition. But in the midst of sorrow, joy blooms. Even in this dark hour I had a sweet consolation. For I knew that except these Mohammedans repented they would go straight to perdition some day. And *they* never repent—they never forsake their paganism. This thought calmed me, cheered me, and I sank down, limp and exhausted, upon the summit, but happy, *so* happy and serene within.

On the one hand, a mighty sea of yellow sand stretched away toward the ends of the earth, solemn, silent, shorn of vegetation, its solitude uncheered by any forms of creature life; on the other, the Eden of Egypt was spread below us— a broad green floor, cloven by the sinuous river, dotted with villages, its vast distances measured and marked by the diminishing stature of receding clusters of palms. It lay asleep in an enchanted atmosphere. There was no sound, no motion. Above the date-plumes in the middle distance, swelled a domed and pinnacled mass, glimmering through a tinted, exquisite mist; away toward the horizon a dozen shapely pyramids watched over ruined Memphis: and at our feet the bland impassible Sphynx looked out upon the picture from her throne in the sands as placidly and pensively as she had looked upon its like full fifty lagging centuries ago.

We suffered torture no pen can describe from the hungry appeals for bucksheesh that gleamed from Arab eyes and poured incessantly from Arab lips. Why try to call up the traditions of vanished Egyptian grandeur; why try to fancy Egypt following dead Rameses to his tomb in the Pyramid, or the long multitude of Israel departing over the desert yonder? Why try to think at all? The thing was impossible. One must bring his meditations cut and dried, or else cut and dry them afterward.

The traditional Arab proposed, in the traditional way, to run down Cheops, cross the eighth of a mile of sand intervening between it and the tall pyramid of Cephron, ascend to Cephron's summit and return to us on the top of Cheops— all in nine minutes by the watch, and the whole service to be rendered for a single dollar. In the first flush of irritation, I said let the Arab and his exploits go to the mischief. But stay. The upper third of Cephron was coated with dressed marble, smooth as glass. A blessed thought entered my brain. He must infallibly break his neck. Close the contract with dispatch, I said, and let him go. He started. We watched. He went bounding down the vast broadside, spring after spring, like an ibex. He grew small and smaller till he became a bobbing pigmy, away down toward the bottom—then disappeared. We turned and peered over the other side—forty seconds—eighty seconds—a hundred—happiness, he is dead already!—two minutes—and a quarter—"There he goes!" Too true—it was too true. He was very small, now. Gradually, but surely, he overcame the level ground. He began to spring and climb again. Up, up, up—at last he reached the smooth coating—now for it. But he clung to it with toes and fingers, like a fly. He crawled this way and that—away to the right, slanting upward—away to the left, still slanting upward—and stood at last, a black peg on the summit, and waved his pigmy scarf! Then he crept downward to the raw steps again, then picked up his agile heels and flew. We lost him presently. But presently again we saw him under us, mounting with undiminished energy. Shortly he bounded into our midst with a gallant war-whoop. Time, eight minutes, forty-one seconds. He had won. His bones were intact. It was a failure. I reflected. I said to myself, he is tired, and must grow dizzy. I will risk another dollar on him.

He started again. Made the trip again. Slipped on the smooth coating—I almost had him. But an infamous crevice saved him. He was with us once more—perfectly sound. Time, eight minutes, forty-six seconds.

I said to Dan, "Lend me a dollar—I can beat this game, yet."

Worse and worse. He won again. Time, eight minutes, forty-eight seconds. I was out of all patience, now. I was desperate.—Money was no longer of any consequence. I said, "Sirrah, I will give you a hundred dollars to jump off this pyramid head first. If you do not like the terms, name your bet. I scorn to stand on expenses now. I will stay right here and risk money on you as long as Dan has got a cent."

I was in a fair way to win, now, for it was a dazzling opportunity for an Arab. He pondered a moment, and would have done it, I think, but his mother arrived, then, and interfered. Her tears moved me—I never can look upon the tears of woman with indifference—and I said I would give her a hundred to jump off, too.

But it was a failure. The Arabs are too high-priced in Egypt. They put on airs unbecoming to such savages.

We descended, hot and out of humor. The dragoman lit

candles, and we all entered a hole near the base of the pyramid, attended by a crazy rabble of Arabs who thrust their services upon us uninvited. They dragged us up a long inclined chute, and dripped candle-grease all over us. This chute was not more than twice as wide and high as a Saratoga trunk, and was walled, roofed and floored with solid blocks of Egyptian granite as wide as a wardrobe, twice as thick and three times as long. We kept on climbing, through the oppressive gloom, till I thought we ought to be nearing the top of the pyramid again, and then came to the "Queen's Chamber," and shortly to the Chamber of the King. These large apartments were tombs. The walls were built of monstrous masses of smoothed granite, neatly joined together. Some of them were nearly as large square as an ordinary parlor. A great stone sarcophagus like a bath-tub stood in the centre of the King's Chamber. Around it were gathered a picturesque group of Arab savages and soiled and tattered pilgrims, who held their candles aloft in the gloom while they chattered, and the winking blurs of light shed a dim glory down upon one of the irrepressible memento-seekers who was pecking at the venerable sarcophagus with his sacrilegious hammer.

We struggled out to the open air and the bright sunshine, and for the space of thirty minutes received ragged Arabs by couples, dozens and platoons, and paid them bucksheesh for services they swore and proved by each other that they had rendered, but which we had not been aware of before—and as each party was paid, they dropped into the rear of the procession and in due time arrived again with a newly-invented delinquent list for liquidation.

We lunched in the shade of the pyramid, and in the midst of this encroaching and unwelcome company, and then Dan and Jack and I started away for a walk. A howling swarm of beggars followed us—surrounded us—almost headed us off. A sheik, in flowing white bournous and gaudy head-gear, was with them. He wanted more bucksheesh. But we had adopted a new code—it was millions for defense, but not a cent for bucksheesh. I asked him if he could persuade the others to depart if we paid him. He said yes—for ten francs. We accepted the contract, and said—

"Now persuade your vassals to fall back."

He swung his long staff round his head and three Arabs bit the dust. He capered among the mob like a very maniac. His blows fell like hail, and wherever one fell a subject went down. We had to hurry to the rescue and tell him it was only necessary to damage them a little, he need not kill them.—In two minutes we were alone with the sheik, and remained so. The persuasive powers of this illiterate savage were remarkable.

Each side of the Pyramid of Cheops is about as long as the Capitol at Washington, or the Sultan's new palace on the Bosporus, and is longer than the greatest depth of St. Peter's at Rome—which is to say that each side of Cheops extends seven hundred and some odd feet. It is about seventy-five feet higher than the cross on St. Peter's. The first time I ever went down the Mississippi, I thought the highest bluff on the river between St. Louis and New Orleans—it was near Selma, Missouri—was probably the highest mountain in the world. It is four hundred and thirteen feet high. It still looms in my memory with undiminished grandeur. I can still see the trees and bushes growing smaller and smaller as I followed them up its huge slant with my eye, till they became a feathery fringe on the distant summit. This symmetrical Pyramid of Cheops—this solid mountain of stone reared by the patient hands of men—this mighty tomb of a forgotten monarch—dwarfs my cherished mountain. For it is four hundred and eighty feet high. In still earlier years than those I have been recalling, Holliday's Hill, in our town, was to me the noblest work of God. It appeared to pierce the skies. It was nearly three hundred feet high. In those days I pondered the subject much, but I never could understand why it did not swathe its summit with never-failing clouds, and crown its majestic brow with everlasting snows. I had heard that such was the custom of great mountains in other parts of the world. I remembered how I worked with another boy, at odd afternoons stolen from study and paid for with stripes, to undermine and start from its bed an immense boulder that rested upon the edge of that hill-top; I remembered how, one Saturday afternoon, we gave three hours of honest effort to the task, and saw at last that our reward was at hand; I remembered how we sat down, then, and wiped the perspiration away, and waited to let a picnic party get out of the way in the road below—and then we started the boulder. It was splendid. It went crashing down the hill-side, tearing up saplings, mowing bushes down like grass, ripping and crushing and smashing every thing in its path—eternally splintered and scattered a wood pile at the foot of the hill, and then sprang from the high bank clear over a dray in the road—the negro glanced up once and dodged—and the next second it made infinitesimal mince-meat of a frame cooper-shop, and the coopers swarmed out like bees. Then we said it was perfectly magnificent, and left. Because the coopers were starting up the hill to inquire.

Still, that mountain, prodigious as it was, was nothing to the Pyramid of Cheops. I could conjure up no comparison that would convey to my mind a satisfactory comprehension of the magnitude of a pile of monstrous stones that covered thirteen acres of ground and stretched upward four hundred and eighty tiresome feet, and so I gave it up and walked down to the Sphynx.

After years of waiting, it was before me at last. The great face was so sad, so earnest, so longing, so patient. There was a dignity not of earth in its mien, and in its countenance a benignity such as never any thing human wore. It was stone, but it seemed sentient. If ever image of stone thought, it was thinking. It was looking toward the verge of the landscape, yet looking *at* nothing—nothing but distance and vacancy. It was looking over and beyond everything of the present, and far into the past. It was gazing out over the ocean of Time—over lines of century-waves which, further and further receding, closed nearer and nearer together, and blended at last into one unbroken tide, away toward the horizon of remote antiquity. It was thinking of the wars of departed ages; of the empires it had seen created and destroyed; of the nations whose birth it had witnessed, whose progress it had watched, whose annihilation it had noted; of the joy and sorrow, the life and death, the grandeur and decay, of five thousand slow revolving years. It was the type of an attribute of man—of a faculty of his heart and brain. It was MEMORY—RETROSPECTION—wrought into visible, tangible form. All who know what pathos there is in memories of days that are

accomplished and faces that have vanished—albeit only a trifling score of years gone by—will have some appreciation of
the pathos that dwells in these grave eyes that look so steadfastly back upon the things they knew before History was
born—before Tradition had being—things that were, and
forms that moved, in a vague era which even Poetry and Romance scarce know of—and passed one by one away and left
the stony dreamer solitary in the midst of a strange new age,
and uncomprehended scenes.

The Sphynx is grand in its loneliness; it is imposing in its
magnitude; it is impressive in the mystery that hangs over its
story. And there is that in the overshadowing majesty of this
eternal figure of stone, with its accusing memory of the deeds
of all ages, which reveals to one something of what he shall
feel when he shall stand at last in the awful presence of God.

There are some things which, for the credit of America,
should be left unsaid, perhaps; but these very things happen
sometimes to be the very things which, for the real benefit of
Americans, ought to have prominent notice. While we stood
looking, a wart, or an excrescence of some kind, appeared on
the jaw of the Sphynx. We heard the familiar clink of a hammer, and understood the case at once. One of our well-meaning reptiles—I mean relic-hunters—had crawled up there
and was trying to break a "specimen" from the face of this
the most majestic creation the hand of man has wrought. But
the great image contemplated the dead ages as calmly as ever,
unconscious of the small insect that was fretting at its jaw.
Egyptian granite that has defied the storms and earthquakes
of all time has nothing to fear from the tack-hammers of ignorant excursionists—highwaymen like this specimen. He
failed in his enterprise. We sent a sheik to arrest him if he had
the authority, or to warn him, if he had not, that by the laws
of Egypt the crime he was attempting to commit was punishable with imprisonment or the bastinado. Then he desisted
and went away.

The Sphynx: a hundred and twenty-five feet long, sixty feet
high, and a hundred and two feet around the head, if I remember rightly—carved out of one solid block of stone
harder than any iron. The block must have been as large as
the Fifth Avenue Hotel before the usual waste (by the neces-

sities of sculpture) of a fourth or a half of the original mass
was begun. I only set down these figures and these remarks
to suggest the prodigious labor the carving of it so elegantly,
so symmetrically, so faultlessly, must have cost. This species
of stone is so hard that figures cut in it remain sharp and
unmarred after exposure to the weather for two or three
thousand years. Now did it take a hundred years of patient
toil to carve the Sphynx? It seems probable.

Something interfered, and we did not visit the Red Sea and
walk upon the sands of Arabia. I shall not describe the great
mosque of Mehemet Ali, whose entire inner walls are built of
polished and glistening alabaster; I shall not tell how the little
birds have built their nests in the globes of the great chande-
liers that hang in the mosque, and how they fill the whole
place with their music and are not afraid of any body because
their audacity is pardoned, their rights are respected, and nobody is allowed to interfere with them, even though the
mosque be thus doomed to go unlighted; I certainly shall not
tell the hackneyed story of the massacre of the Mamelukes,
because I am glad the lawless rascals were massacred, and I
do not wish to get up any sympathy in their behalf; I shall
not tell how that one solitary Mameluke jumped his horse a
hundred feet down from the battlements of the citadel and
escaped, because I do not think much of that—I could have
done it myself; I shall not tell of Joseph's well which he dug
in the solid rock of the citadel hill and which is still as good
as new, nor how the same mules he bought to draw up the
water (with an endless chain) are still at it yet and are getting
tired of it, too; I shall not tell about Joseph's granaries which
he built to store the grain in, what time the Egyptian brokers
were "selling short," unwitting that there would be no corn
in all the land when it should be time for them to deliver; I
shall not tell any thing about the strange, strange city of Cairo,
because it is only a repetition, a good deal intensified and
exaggerated, of the Oriental cities I have already spoken of; I
shall not tell of the Great Caravan which leaves for Mecca
every year, for I did not see it; nor of the fashion the people
have of prostrating themselves and so forming a long human
pavement to be ridden over by the chief of the expedition on
its return, to the end that their salvation may be thus secured,

for I did not see that either; I shall not speak of the railway, for it is like any other railway—I shall only say that the fuel they use for the locomotive is composed of mummies three thousand years old, purchased by the ton or by the graveyard for that purpose, and that sometimes one hears the profane engineer call out pettishly, "D—n these plebeians, they don't burn worth a cent—pass out a King;"* I shall not tell of the groups of mud cones stuck like wasps' nests upon a thousand mounds above high water-mark the length and breadth of Egypt—villages of the lower classes; I shall not speak of the boundless sweep of level plain, green with luxuriant grain, that gladdens the eye as far as it can pierce through the soft, rich atmosphere of Egypt; I shall not speak of the vision of the Pyramids seen at a distance of five and twenty miles, for the picture is too ethereal to be limned by an uninspired pen; I shall not tell of the crowds of dusky women who flocked to the cars when they stopped a moment at a station, to sell us a drink of water or a ruddy, juicy pomegranate; I shall not tell of the motley multitudes and wild costumes that graced a fair we found in full blast at another barbarous station; I shall not tell how we feasted on fresh dates and enjoyed the pleasant landscape all through the flying journey; nor how we thundered into Alexandria, at last, swarmed out of the cars, rowed aboard the ship, left a comrade behind, (who was to return to Europe, thence home,) raised the anchor, and turned our bows homeward finally and forever from the long voyage; nor how, as the mellow sun went down upon the oldest land on earth, Jack and Moult assembled in solemn state in the smoking-room and mourned over the lost comrade the whole night long, and would not be comforted. I shall not speak a word of any of these things, or write a line. They shall be as a sealed book. I do not know what a sealed book is, because I never saw one, but a sealed book is the expression to use in this connection, because it is popular.

We were glad to have seen the land which was the mother of civilization—which taught Greece her letters, and through Greece Rome, and through Rome the world; the land which could have humanized and civilized the hapless children of

*Stated to me for a fact. I only tell it as I got it. I am willing to believe it. I can believe any thing.

Israel, but allowed them to depart out of her borders little better than savages. We were glad to have seen that land which had an enlightened religion with future eternal rewards and punishment in it, while even Israel's religion contained no promise of a hereafter. We were glad to have seen that land which had glass three thousand years before England had it, and could paint upon it as none of us can paint now; that land which knew, three thousand years ago, well nigh all of medicine and surgery which science has *discovered* lately; which had all those curious surgical instruments which science has *invented* recently; which had in high excellence a thousand luxuries and necessities of an advanced civilization which we have gradually contrived and accumulated in modern times and claimed as things that were new under the sun; that had paper untold centuries before we dreampt of it— and waterfalls before our women thought of them; that had a perfect system of common schools so long before we boasted of our achievements in that direction that it seems forever and forever ago; that so embalmed the dead that flesh was made almost immortal—which we can not do; that built temples which mock at destroying time and smile grimly upon our lauded little prodigies of architecture; that old land that knew all which we know now, perchance, and more; that walked in the broad highway of civilization in the gray dawn of creation, ages and ages before we were born; that left the impress of exalted, cultivated Mind upon the eternal front of the Sphynx to confound all scoffers who, when all her other proofs had passed away, might seek to persuade the world that imperial Egypt, in the days of her high renown, had groped in darkness.

Chapter LIX

WE WERE AT sea now, for a very long voyage—we were to pass through the entire length of the Levant; through the entire length of the Mediterranean proper, also, and then cross the full width of the Atlantic—a voyage of several weeks. We naturally settled down into a very slow, stay-at-home manner of life, and resolved to be quiet, exemplary people, and roam no more for twenty or thirty days. No more, at least, than from stem to stern of the ship. It was a very comfortable prospect, though, for we were tired and needed a long rest.

We were all lazy and satisfied, now, as the meager entries in my note-book (that sure index, to me, of my condition,) prove. What a stupid thing a note-book gets to be at sea, any way. Please observe the style:

"*Sunday*—Services, as usual, at four bells. Services at night, also. No cards.

"*Monday*—Beautiful day, but rained hard. The cattle purchased at Alexandria for beef ought to be shingled. Or else fattened. The water stands in deep puddles in the depressions forward of their after shoulders. Also here and there all over their backs. It is well they are not cows—it would soak in and ruin the milk. The poor devil eagle* from Syria looks miserable and droopy in the rain, perched on the forward capstan. He appears to have his own opinion of a sea voyage, and if it were put into language and the language solidified, it would probably essentially dam the widest river in the world.

"*Tuesday*—Somewhere in the neighborhood of the island of Malta. Can not stop there. Cholera. Weather very stormy. Many passengers seasick and invisible.

"*Wednesday*—Weather still very savage. Storm blew two land birds to sea, and they came on board. A hawk was blown off, also. He circled round and round the ship, wanting to light, but afraid of the people. He was so tired, though, that he had to light, at last, or perish. He stopped in the foretop, repeatedly, and was as often blown away by the wind. At last Harry caught him. Sea full of flying-fish. They rise in flocks of three hundred and flash along above the tops of the waves a distance of two or three hundred feet, then fall and disappear.

*Afterwards presented to the Central Park.

"*Thursday*—Anchored off Algiers, Africa. Beautiful city, beautiful green hilly landscape behind it. Staid half a day and left. Not permitted to land, though we showed a clean bill of health. They were afraid of Egyptian plague and cholera.

"*Friday*—Morning, dominoes. Afternoon, dominoes. Evening, promenading the deck. Afterwards, charades.

"*Saturday*—Morning, dominoes. Afternoon, dominoes. Evening, promenading the decks. Afterwards, dominoes.

"*Sunday*—Morning service, four bells. Evening service, eight bells. Monotony till midnight.—Whereupon, dominoes.

"*Monday*—Morning, dominoes. Afternoon, dominoes. Evening, promenading the decks. Afterward, charades and a lecture from Dr. C. Dominoes.

"*No date*—Anchored off the picturesque city of Cagliari, Sardinia. Staid till midnight, but not permitted to land by these infamous foreigners. They smell inodorously—they do not wash—they dare not risk cholera.

"*Thursday*—Anchored off the beautiful cathedral city of Malaga, Spain.—Went ashore in the captain's boat—not ashore, either, for they would not let us land. Quarantine. Shipped my newspaper correspondence, which they took with tongs, dipped it in sea water, clipped it full of holes, and then fumigated it with villainous vapors till it smelt like a Spaniard. Inquired about chances to run the blockade and visit the Alhambra at Granada. Too risky—they might hang a body. Set sail—middle of afternoon.

"And so on, and so on, and so forth, for several days. Finally, anchored off Gibraltar, which looks familiar and home-like."

It reminds me of the journal I opened with the New Year, once, when I was a boy and a confiding and a willing prey to those impossible schemes of reform which well-meaning old maids and grandmothers set for the feet of unwary youths at that season of the year—setting oversized tasks for them, which, necessarily failing, as infallibly weaken the boy's strength of will, diminish his confidence in himself and injure his chances of success in life. Please accept of an extract:

"*Monday*—Got up, washed, went to bed.
"*Tuesday*—Got up, washed, went to bed.
"*Wednesday*—Got up, washed, went to bed.
"*Thursday*—Got up, washed, went to bed.
"*Friday*—Got up, washed, went to bed.
"*Next Friday*—Got up, washed, went to bed.

"*Friday fortnight*—Got up, washed, went to bed.
"*Following month*—Got up, washed, went to bed."

I stopped, then, discouraged. Startling events appeared to be too rare, in my career, to render a diary necessary. I still reflect with pride, however, that even at that early age I washed when I got up. That journal finished me. I never have had the nerve to keep one since. My loss of confidence in myself in that line was permanent.

The ship had to stay a week or more at Gibraltar to take in coal for the home voyage.

It would be very tiresome staying here, and so four of us ran the quarantine blockade and spent seven delightful days in Seville, Cordova, Cadiz, and wandering through the pleasant rural scenery of Andalusia, the garden of Old Spain. The experiences of that cheery week were too varied and numerous for a short chapter and I have not room for a long one. Therefore I shall leave them all out.

Chapter LX

TEN OR ELEVEN O'CLOCK found us coming down to breakfast one morning in Cadiz. They told us the ship had been lying at anchor in the harbor two or three hours. It was time for us to bestir ourselves. The ship could wait only a little while because of the quarantine. We were soon on board, and within the hour the white city and the pleasant shores of Spain sank down behind the waves and passed out of sight. We had seen no land fade from view so regretfully.

It had long ago been decided in a noisy public meeting in the main cabin that we could not go to Lisbon, because we must surely be quarantined there. We did every thing by mass-meeting, in the good old national way, from swapping off one empire for another on the programme of the voyage down to complaining of the cookery and the scarcity of napkins. I am reminded, now, of one of these complaints of the cookery made by a passenger. The coffee had been steadily growing more and more execrable for the space of three weeks, till at last it had ceased to be coffee altogether and had assumed the nature of mere discolored water—so this person said. He said it was so weak that it was transparent an inch in depth around the edge of the cup. As he approached the table one morning he saw the transparent edge—by means of his extraordinary vision—long before he got to his seat. He went back and complained in a high-handed way to Capt. Duncan. He said the coffee was disgraceful. The Captain showed his. It seemed tolerably good. The incipient mutineer was more outraged than ever, then, at what he denounced as the partiality shown the captain's table over the other tables in the ship. He flourished back and got his cup and set it down triumphantly, and said:

"Just try that mixture once, Captain Duncan."

He smelt it—tasted it—smiled benignantly—then said:

"It *is* inferior—for *coffee*—but it is pretty fair *tea*."

The humbled mutineer smelt it, tasted it, and returned to his seat. He had made an egregious ass of himself before the whole ship. He did it no more. After that he took things as they came. That was me.

510

The old-fashioned ship-life had returned, now that we were no longer in sight of land. For days and days it continued just the same, one day being exactly like another, and, to me, every one of them pleasant. At last we anchored in the open roadstead of Funchal, in the beautiful islands we call the Madeiras.

The mountains looked surpassingly lovely, clad as they were in living green; ribbed with lava ridges; flecked with white cottages; riven by deep chasms purple with shade; the great slopes dashed with sunshine and mottled with shadows flung from the drifting squadrons of the sky, and the superb picture fitly crowned by towering peaks whose fronts were swept by the trailing fringes of the clouds.

But we could not land. We staid all day and looked, we abused the man who invented quarantine, we held half a dozen mass-meetings and crammed them full of interrupted speeches, motions that fell still-born, amendments that came to nought and resolutions that died from sheer exhaustion in trying to get before the house. At night we set sail.

We averaged four mass-meetings a week for the voyage—we seemed always in labor in this way, and yet so often fallaciously that whenever at long intervals we were safely delivered of a resolution, it was cause for public rejoicing, and we hoisted the flag and fired a salute.

Days passed—and nights; and then the beautiful Bermudas rose out of the sea, we entered the tortuous channel, steamed hither and thither among the bright summer islands, and rested at last under the flag of England and were welcome. We were not a nightmare here, where were civilization and intelligence in place of Spanish and Italian superstition, dirt and dread of cholera. A few days among the breezy groves, the flower gardens, the coral caves, and the lovely vistas of blue water that went curving in and out, disappearing and anon again appearing through jungle walls of brilliant foliage, restored the energies dulled by long drowsing on the ocean, and fitted us for our final cruise—our little run of a thousand miles to New York—America—HOME.

We bade good-bye to "our friends the Bermudians," as our programme hath it—the majority of those we were most intimate with were negroes—and courted the great deep again.

I said the majority. We knew more negroes than white people, because we had a deal of washing to be done, but we made some most excellent friends among the whites, whom it will be a pleasant duty to hold long in grateful remembrance.

We sailed, and from that hour all idling ceased. Such another system of overhauling, general littering of cabins and packing of trunks we had not seen since we let go the anchor in the harbor of Beirout. Every body was busy. Lists of all purchases had to be made out, and values attached, to facilitate matters at the custom-house. Purchases bought by bulk in partnership had to be equitably divided, outstanding debts canceled, accounts compared, and trunks, boxes and packages labeled. All day long the bustle and confusion continued.

And now came our first accident. A passenger was running through a gangway, between decks, one stormy night, when he caught his foot in the iron staple of a door that had been heedlessly left off a hatchway, and the bones of his leg broke at the ancle. It was our first serious misfortune. We had traveled much more than twenty thousand miles, by land and sea, in many trying climates, without a single hurt, without a serious case of sickness and without a death among five and sixty passengers. Our good fortune had been wonderful. A sailor had jumped overboard at Constantinople one night, and was seen no more, but it was suspected that his object was to desert, and there was a slim chance, at least, that he reached the shore. But the passenger list was complete. There was no name missing from the register.

At last, one pleasant morning, we steamed up the harbor of New York, all on deck, all dressed in Christian garb—by special order, for there was a latent disposition in some quarters to come out as Turks—and amid a waving of handkerchiefs from welcoming friends, the glad pilgrims noted the shiver of the decks that told that ship and pier had joined hands again and the long, strange cruise was over. Amen.

Chapter LXI

IN THIS PLACE I will print an article which I wrote for the New York *Herald* the night we arrived. I do it partly because my contract with my publishers makes it compulsory; partly because it is a proper, tolerably accurate, and exhaustive summing up of the cruise of the ship and the performances of the pilgrims in foreign lands; and partly because some of the passengers have abused me for writing it, and I wish the public to see how thankless a task it is to put one's self to trouble to glorify unappreciative people. I was charged with "rushing into print" with these compliments. I did not rush. I had written news letters to the *Herald* sometimes, but yet when I visited the office that day I did not say any thing about writing a valedictory. I did go to the *Tribune* office to see if such an article was wanted, because I belonged on the regular staff of that paper and it was simply a duty to do it. The managing editor was absent, and so I thought no more about it. At night when the *Herald's* request came for an article, I did not "rush." In fact, I demurred for a while, because I did not feel like writing compliments then, and therefore was afraid to speak of the cruise lest I might be betrayed into using other than complimentary language. However, I reflected that it would be a just and righteous thing to go down and write a kind word for the Hadjis—Hadjis are people who have made the pilgrimage—because parties not interested could not do it so feelingly as I, a fellow-Hadji, and so I penned the valedictory. I have read it, and read it again; and if there is a sentence in it that is not fulsomely complimentary to captain, ship and passengers, *I* can not find it. If it is not a chapter that any company might be proud to have a body write about them, my judgment is fit for nothing. With these remarks I confidently submit it to the unprejudiced judgment of the reader:

RETURN OF THE HOLY LAND EXCURSIONISTS—
THE STORY OF THE CRUISE.

TO THE EDITOR OF THE HERALD:
  The steamer Quaker City has accomplished at last her ex-

traordinary voyage and returned to her old pier at the foot of Wall street. The expedition was a success in some respects, in some it was not. Originally it was advertised as a "pleasure excursion." Well, perhaps, it was a pleasure excursion, but certainly it did not look like one; certainly it did not act like one. Any body's and every body's notion of a pleasure excursion is that the parties to it will of a necessity be young and giddy and somewhat boisterous. They will dance a good deal, sing a good deal, make love, but sermonize very little. Any body's and every body's notion of a well conducted funeral is that there must be a hearse and a corpse, and chief mourners and mourners by courtesy, many old people, much solemnity, no levity, and a prayer and a sermon withal. Three-fourths of the Quaker City's passengers were between forty and seventy years of age! There was a picnic crowd for you! It may be supposed that the other fourth was composed of young girls. But it was not. It was chiefly composed of rusty old bachelors and a child of six years. Let us average the ages of the Quaker City's pilgrims and set the figure down as fifty years. Is any man insane enough to imagine that this picnic of patriarchs sang, made love, danced, laughed, told anecdotes, dealt in ungodly levity? In my experience they sinned little in these matters. No doubt it was presumed here at home that these frolicsome veterans laughed and sang and romped all day, and day after day, and kept up a noisy excitement from one end of the ship to the other; and that they played blind-man's buff or danced quadrilles and waltzes on moon-light evenings on the quarter-deck; and that at odd moments of unoccupied time they jotted a laconic item or two in the journals they opened on such an elaborate plan when they left home, and then skurried off to their whist and euchre labors under the cabin lamps. If these things were presumed, the presumption was at fault. The venerable excursionists were not gay and frisky. They played no blind-man's buff; they dealt not in whist; they shirked not the irksome journal, for alas! most of them were even writing books. They never romped, they talked but little, they never sang, save in the nightly prayer-meeting. The pleasure ship was a synagogue, and the pleasure trip was a funeral excursion without a corpse. (There is nothing exhilarating about a funeral excursion without a corpse.)

A free, hearty laugh was a sound that was not heard oftener than once in seven days about those decks or in those cabins, and when it was heard it met with precious little sympathy. The excursionists danced, on three separate evenings, long, long ago, (it seems an age,) quadrilles, of a single set, made up of three ladies and five gentlemen, (the latter with hand-kerchiefs around their arms to signify their sex,) who timed their feet to the solemn wheezing of a melodeon; but even this melancholy orgie was voted to be sinful, and dancing was discontinued.

The pilgrims played dominoes when too much Josephus or Robinson's Holy Land Researches, or book-writing, made recreation necessary—for dominoes is about as mild and sin-less a game as any in the world, perhaps, excepting always the ineffably insipid diversion they call croquet, which is a game where you don't pocket any balls and don't carom on any thing of any consequence, and when you are done nobody has to pay, and there are no refreshments to saw off, and, consequently, there isn't any satisfaction whatever about it— they played dominoes till they were rested, and then they blackguarded each other privately till prayer-time. When they were not seasick they were uncommonly prompt when the dinner-gong sounded. Such was our daily life on board the ship—solemnity, decorum, dinner, dominoes, devotions, slander. It was not lively enough for a pleasure trip; but if we had only had a corpse it would have made a noble funeral excursion. It is all over now; but when I look back, the idea of these venerable fossils skipping forth on a six months' pic-nic, seems exquisitely refreshing. The advertised title of the expedition—"The Grand Holy Land Pleasure Excursion"— was a misnomer. "The Grand Holy Land Funeral Procession" would have been better—much better.

Wherever we went, in Europe, Asia, or Africa, we made a sensation, and, I suppose I may add, created a famine. None of us had ever been any where before; we all hailed from the interior; travel was a wild novelty to us, and we conducted ourselves in accordance with the natural instincts that were in us, and trammeled ourselves with no ceremonies, no conven-tionalities. We always took care to make it understood that we were Americans—Americans! When we found that a good many foreigners had hardly ever heard of America, and that a good many more knew it only as a barbarous province away off somewhere, that had lately been at war with somebody, we pitied the ignorance of the Old World, but abated no jot of our importance. Many and many a simple community in the Eastern hemisphere will remember for years the incursion of the strange horde in the year of our Lord 1867, that called themselves Americans, and seemed to imagine in some unaccountable way that they had a right to be proud of it. We generally created a famine, partly because the coffee on the Quaker City was unendurable, and sometimes the more substantial fare was not strictly first class; and partly because one naturally tires of sitting long at the same board and eating from the same dishes.

The people of those foreign countries are very, very ignorant. They looked curiously at the costumes we had brought from the wilds of America. They observed that we talked loudly at table sometimes. They noticed that we looked out for expenses, and got what we conveniently could out of a franc, and wondered where in the mischief we came from. In Paris they just simply opened their eyes and stared when we spoke to them in French! We never did succeed in making those idiots understand their own language. One of our passengers said to a shopkeeper, in reference to a proposed return to buy a pair of gloves, *"Allong restay trankeel—may be ve coom Moonday;"* and would you believe it, that shopkeeper, a born Frenchman, had to ask what it was that had been said. Sometimes it seems to me, somehow, that there must be a difference between Parisian French and Quaker City French.

The people stared at us every where, and we stared at them. We generally made them feel rather small, too, before we got done with them, because we bore down on them with America's greatness until we crushed them. And yet we took kindly to the manners and customs, and especially to the fashions of the various people we visited. When we left the Azores, we wore awful capotes and used fine tooth combs—successfully. When we came back from Tangier, in Africa, we were topped with fezzes of the bloodiest hue, hung with tassels like an Indian's scalp-lock. In France and

Spain we attracted some attention in these costumes. In Italy they naturally took us for distempered Garibaldians, and set a gunboat to look for any thing significant in our changes of uniform. We made Rome howl. We could have made any place howl when we had all our clothes on. We got no fresh raiment in Greece—they had but little there of any kind. But at Constantinople, how we turned out! Turbans, scimetars, fezzes, horse-pistols, tunics, sashes, baggy trowsers, yellow slippers—Oh, we were gorgeous! The illustrious dogs of Constantinople barked their under jaws off, and even then failed to do us justice. They are all dead by this time. They could not go through such a run of business as we gave them and survive.

And then we went to see the Emperor of Russia. We just called on him as comfortably as if we had known him a century or so, and when we had finished our visit we variegated ourselves with selections from Russian costumes and sailed away again more picturesque than ever. In Smyrna we picked up camel's hair shawls and other dressy things from Persia; but in Palestine—ah, in Palestine—our splendid career ended. They didn't wear any clothes, there to speak of. We were satisfied, and stopped. We made no experiments. We did not try their costume. But we astonished the natives of that country. We astonished them with such eccentricities of dress as we could muster. We prowled through the Holy Land, from Cesarea Philippi to Jerusalem and the Dead Sea, a weird procession of pilgrims, gotten up regardless of expense, solemn, gorgeous, green-spectacled, drowsing under blue umbrellas, and astride of a sorrier lot of horses, camels and asses than those that came out of Noah's ark, after eleven months of seasickness and short rations. If ever those children of Israel in Palestine forget when Gideon's Band went through there from America, they ought to be cursed once more and finished. It was the rarest spectacle that ever astounded mortal eyes, perhaps.

Well, we were at home in Palestine. It was easy to see that that was the grand feature of the expedition. We had cared nothing much about Europe. We galloped through the Louvre, the Pitti, the Ufizzi, the Vatican—all the galleries—and through the pictured and frescoed churches of Venice,

Naples, and the cathedrals of Spain; some of us said that certain of the great works of the old masters were glorious creations of genius, (we found it out in the guide-book, though we got hold of the wrong picture sometimes,) and the others said they were disgraceful old daubs. We examined modern and ancient statuary with a critical eye in Florence, Rome, or any where we found it, and praised it if we saw fit, and if we didn't we said we preferred the wooden Indians in front of the cigar stores of America. But the Holy Land brought out all our enthusiasm. We fell into raptures by the barren shores of Galilee; we pondered at Tabor and at Nazareth; we exploded into poetry over the questionable loveliness of Esdraelon; we meditated at Jezreel and Samaria over the missionary zeal of Jehu; we rioted—fairly rioted among the holy places of Jerusalem; we bathed in Jordan and the Dead Sea, reckless whether our accident-insurance policies were extra-hazardous or not, and brought away so many jugs of precious water from both places that all the country from Jericho to the mountains of Moab will suffer from drouth this year, I think. Yet, the pilgrimage part of the excursion was its pet feature—there is no question about that. After dismal, smileless Palestine, beautiful Egypt had few charms for us. We merely glanced at it and were ready for home.

They wouldn't let us land at Malta—quarantine; they would not let us land in Sardinia; nor at Algiers, Africa; nor at Malaga, Spain, nor Cadiz, nor at the Madeira islands. So we got offended at all foreigners and turned our backs upon them and came home. I suppose we only stopped at the Bermudas because they were in the programme. We did not care any thing about any place at all. We wanted to go home. Homesickness was abroad in the ship—it was epidemic. If the authorities of New York had known how badly we had it, they would have quarantined us here.

The grand pilgrimage is over. Good-bye to it, and a pleasant memory to it, I am able to say in all kindness. I bear no malice, no ill-will toward any individual that was connected with it, either as passenger or officer. Things I did not like at all yesterday I like very well to-day, now that I am at home, and always hereafter I shall be able to poke fun at the whole gang if the spirit so moves me to do, without ever saying a malicious word. The expedition accomplished all that its pro-gramme promised that it should accomplish, and we ought all to be satisfied with the management of the matter, certainly. Bye-bye!

MARK TWAIN

I call that complimentary. It *is* complimentary; and yet I never have received a word of thanks for it from the Hadjis; on the contrary I speak nothing but the serious truth when I say that many of them even took exceptions to the article. In endeavoring to please them I slaved over that sketch for two hours, and had my labor for my pains. I never will do a gen-erous deed again.

Conclusion

NEARLY one year has flown since this notable pilgrimage was ended; and as I sit here at home in San Francisco thinking, I am moved to confess that day by day the mass of my memories of the excursion have grown more and more pleasant as the disagreeable incidents of travel which encumbered them flitted one by one out of my mind—and now, if the *Quaker City* were weighing her anchor to sail away on the very same cruise again, nothing could gratify me more than to be a passenger. With the same captain and even the same pilgrims, the same sinners. I was on excellent terms with eight or nine of the excursionists (they are my staunch friends yet,) and was even on speaking terms with the rest of the sixty-five. I have been at sea quite enough to know that that was a very good average. Because a long sea-voyage not only brings out all the mean traits one has, and exaggerates them, but raises up others which he never suspected he possessed, and even creates new ones. A twelve months' voyage at sea would make of an ordinary man a very miracle of meanness. On the other hand, if a man has good qualities, the spirit seldom moves him to exhibit them on shipboard, at least with any sort of emphasis. Now I am satisfied that our pilgrims are pleasant old people on shore; I am also satisfied that at sea on a second voyage they would be pleasanter, somewhat, than they were on our grand excursion, and so I say without hesitation that I would be glad enough to sail with them again. I could at least enjoy life with my handful of old friends. They could enjoy life with *their* cliques as well—passengers invariably divide up into cliques, on *all* ships.

And I will say, here, that I would rather travel with an excursion party of Methuselahs than have to be changing ships and comrades constantly, as people do who travel in the ordinary way. Those latter are always grieving over some *other* ship they have known and lost, and over *other* comrades whom diverging routes have separated from them. They learn to love a ship just in time to change it for another, and they become attached to a pleasant traveling companion only to lose him. They have that most dismal experience of being in a strange vessel, among strange people who care nothing about them, and of undergoing the customary bullying by strange officers and the insolence of strange servants, repeated over and over again within the compass of every month. They have also that other misery of packing and unpacking trunks—of running the distressing gauntlet of custom-houses—of the anxieties attendant upon getting a mass of baggage from point to point on land in safety. I had rather sail with a whole brigade of patriarchs than suffer so. We never packed our trunks but twice—when we sailed from New York, and when we returned to it. Whenever we made a land journey, we estimated how many days we should be gone and what amount of clothing we should need, figured it down to a mathematical nicety, packed a valise or two accordingly, and left the trunks on board. We chose our comrades from among our old, tried friends, and started. We were never dependent upon strangers for companionship. We often had occasion to pity Americans whom we found traveling drearily among strangers with no friends to exchange pains and pleasures with. Whenever we were coming back from a land journey, our eyes sought one thing in the distance first—the ship—and when we saw it riding at anchor with the flag apeak, we felt as a returning wanderer feels when he sees his home. When we stepped on board, our cares vanished, our troubles were at an end—for the ship was home to us. We always had the same familiar old state-room to go to, and feel safe and at peace and comfortable again.

I have no fault to find with the manner in which our excursion was conducted. Its programme was faithfully carried out—a thing which surprised me, for great enterprises usually promise vastly more than they perform. It would be well if such an excursion could be gotten up every year and the system regularly inaugurated. Travel is fatal to prejudice, bigotry and narrow-mindedness, and many of our people need it sorely on these accounts. Broad, wholesome, charitable views of men and things can not be acquired by vegetating in one little corner of the earth all one's lifetime.

The Excursion is ended, and has passed to its place among the things that were. But its varied scenes and its manifold incidents will linger pleasantly in our memories for many a year to come. Always on the wing, as we were, and merely pausing a moment to catch fitful glimpses of the wonders of half a world, we could not hope to receive or retain vivid impressions of all it was our fortune to see. Yet our holyday flight has not been in vain—for above the confusion of vague recollections, certain of its best prized pictures lift themselves and will still continue perfect in tint and outline after their surroundings shall have faded away.

We shall remember something of pleasant France; and something also of Paris, though it flashed upon us a splendid meteor, and was gone again, we hardly knew how or where. We shall remember, always, how we saw majestic Gibraltar glorified with the rich coloring of a Spanish sunset and swimming in a sea of rainbows. In fancy we shall see Milan again, and her stately Cathedral with its marble wilderness of graceful spires. And Padua—Verona—Como, jeweled with stars; and patrician Venice, afloat on her stagnant flood—silent, desolate, haughty—scornful of her humbled state—wrapping herself in memories of her lost fleets, of battle and triumph, and all the pageantry of a glory that is departed.

We can not forget Florence—Naples—nor the foretaste of heaven that is in the delicious atmosphere of Greece—and surely not Athens and the broken temples of the Acropolis. Surely not venerable Rome—nor the green plain that compasses her round about, contrasting its brightness with her gray decay—nor the ruined arches that stand apart in the plain and clothe their looped and windowed raggedness with vines. We shall remember St. Peter's: not as one sees it when he walks the streets of Rome and fancies all her domes are just alike, but as he sees it leagues away, when every meaner edifice has faded out of sight and that one dome looms superbly up in the flush of sunset, full of dignity and grace, strongly outlined as a mountain.

We shall remember Constantinople and the Bosporus—the colossal magnificence of Baalbec—the Pyramids of Egypt—the prodigious form, the benignant countenance of the Sphynx—Oriental Smyrna—sacred Jerusalem—Damascus, the "Pearl of the East," the pride of Syria, the fabled Garden of Eden, the home of princes and genii of the Arabian Nights, the oldest metropolis on earth, the one city in all the world that has kept its name and held its place and looked serenely on while the Kingdoms and Empires of four thousand years have risen to life, enjoyed their little season of pride and pomp, and then vanished and been forgotten!

ROUGHING IT

TO

CALVIN H. HIGBIE,

Of California,

An Honest Man, a Genial Comrade, and a Steadfast Friend,

THIS BOOK IS INSCRIBED

By the Author,

In Memory of the Curious Time

When We Two

WERE MILLIONAIRES FOR TEN DAYS.

Prefatory

THIS BOOK is merely a personal narrative, and not a pretentious history or a philosophical dissertation. It is a record of several years of variegated vagabondizing, and its object is rather to help the resting reader while away an idle hour than afflict him with metaphysics, or goad him with science. Still, there is information in the volume; information concerning an interesting episode in the history of the Far West, about which no books have been written by persons who were on the ground in person, and saw the happenings of the time with their own eyes. I allude to the rise, growth and culmination of the silver-mining fever in Nevada—a curious episode, in some respects; the only one, of its peculiar kind, that has occurred in the land; and the only one, indeed, that is likely to occur in it.

Yes, take it all around, there is quite a good deal of information in the book. I regret this very much; but really it could not be helped: information appears to stew out of me naturally, like the precious ottar of roses out of the otter. Sometimes it has seemed to me that I would give worlds if I could retain my facts; but it cannot be. The more I calk up the sources, and the tighter I get, the more I leak wisdom. Therefore, I can only claim indulgence at the hands of the reader, not justification.

THE AUTHOR.

Contents

Chapter I

My brother had just been appointed Secretary of Nevada Territory—an office of such majesty that it concentrated in itself the duties and dignities of Treasurer, Comptroller, Secretary of State, and Acting Governor in the Governor's absence. A salary of eighteen hundred dollars a year and the title of "Mr. Secretary," gave to the great position an air of wild and imposing grandeur. I was young and ignorant, and I envied my brother. I coveted his distinction and his financial splendor, but particularly and especially the long, strange journey he was going to make, and the curious new world he was going to explore. He was going to travel! I never had been away from home, and that word "travel" had a seductive charm for me. Pretty soon he would be hundreds and hundreds of miles away on the great plains and deserts, and among the mountains of the Far West, and would see buffaloes and Indians, and prairie dogs, and antelopes, and have all kinds of adventures, and may be get hanged or scalped, and have ever such a fine time, and write home and tell us all about it, and be a hero. And he would see the gold mines and the silver mines, and maybe go about of an afternoon when his work was done, and pick up two or three pailfuls of shining slugs, and nuggets of gold and silver on the hillside. And by and by he would become very rich, and return home by sea, and be able to talk as calmly about San Francisco and the ocean, and "the isthmus" as if it was nothing of any consequence to have seen those marvels face to face. What I suffered in contemplating his happiness, pen cannot describe. And so, when he offered me, in cold blood, the sublime position of private secretary under him, it appeared to me that the heavens and the earth passed away, and the firmament was rolled together as a scroll! I had nothing more to desire. My contentment was complete. At the end of an hour or two I was ready for the journey. Not much packing up was necessary, because we were going in the overland stage from the Missouri frontier to Nevada, and passengers were only allowed a small quantity of baggage apiece. There was no Pacific railroad in those fine times of ten or twelve years ago—not a single rail of it.

I only proposed to stay in Nevada three months—I had no thought of staying longer than that. I meant to see all I could that was new and strange, and then hurry home to business. I little thought that I would not see the end of that three-month pleasure excursion for six or seven uncommonly long years!

I dreamed all night about Indians, deserts, and silver bars, and in due time, next day, we took shipping at the St. Louis wharf on board a steamboat bound up the Missouri River.

We were six days going from St. Louis to "St. Jo."—a trip that was so dull, and sleepy, and eventless that it has left no more impression on my memory than if its duration had been six minutes instead of that many days. No record is left in my mind, now, concerning it, but a confused jumble of savage-looking snags, which we deliberately walked over with one wheel or the other; and of reefs which we butted and butted, and then retired from and climbed over in some softer place; and of sand-bars which we roosted on occasionally, and rested, and then got out our crutches and sparred over. In fact, the boat might almost as well have gone to St. Jo. by land, for she was walking most of the time, anyhow—climbing over reefs and clambering over snags patiently and laboriously all day long. The captain said she was a "bully" boat, and all she wanted was more "shear" and a bigger wheel. I thought she wanted a pair of stilts, but I had the deep sagacity not to say so.

Chapter II

THE FIRST THING we did on that glad evening that landed us at St. Joseph was to hunt up the stage-office, and pay a hundred and fifty dollars apiece for tickets per overland coach to Carson City, Nevada.

The next morning, bright and early, we took a hasty breakfast, and hurried to the starting-place. Then an inconvenience presented itself which we had not properly appreciated before, namely, that one cannot make a heavy traveling trunk stand for twenty-five pounds of baggage—because it weighs a good deal more. But that was all we could take—twenty-five pounds each. So we had to snatch our trunks open, and make a selection in a good deal of a hurry. We put our lawful twenty-five pounds apiece all in one valise, and shipped the trunks back to St. Louis again. It was a sad parting, for now we had no swallow-tail coats and white kid gloves to wear at Pawnee receptions in the Rocky Mountains, and no stovepipe hats nor patent-leather boots, nor anything else necessary to make life calm and peaceful. We were reduced to a war-footing. Each of us put on a rough, heavy suit of clothing, woolen army shirt and "stogy" boots included; and into the valise we crowded a few white shirts, some under-clothing and such things. My brother, the Secretary, took along about four pounds of United States statutes and six pounds of Unabridged Dictionary; for we did not know—poor innocents—that such things could be bought in San Francisco on one day and received in Carson City the next. I was armed to the teeth with a pitiful little Smith & Wesson's seven-shooter, which carried a ball like a homœopathic pill, and it took the whole seven to make a dose for an adult. But I thought it was grand. It appeared to me to be a dangerous weapon. It only had one fault—you could not hit anything with it. One of our "conductors" practiced awhile on a cow with it, and as long as she stood still and behaved herself she was safe; but as soon as she went to moving about, and he got to shooting at other things, she came to grief. The Secretary had a small-sized Colt's revolver strapped around him for protection against the Indians, and to guard against accidents he carried it uncapped. Mr. George Bemis was dismally formidable. George Bemis was our fellow-traveler. We had never seen him before. He wore in his belt an old original "Allen" revolver, such as irreverent people called a "pepper-box." Simply drawing the trigger back, cocked and fired the pistol. As the trigger came back, the hammer would begin to rise and the barrel to turn over, and presently down would drop the hammer, and away would speed the ball. To aim along the turning barrel and hit the thing aimed at was a feat which was probably never done with an "Allen" in the world. But George's was a reliable weapon, nevertheless, because, as one of the stage-drivers afterward said, "If she didn't get what she went after, she would fetch something else." And so she did. She went after a deuce of spades nailed against a tree, once, and fetched a mule standing about thirty yards to the left of it. Bemis did not want the mule; but the owner came out with a double-barreled shot-gun and persuaded him to buy it, anyhow. It was a cheerful weapon—the "Allen." Sometimes all its six barrels would go off at once, and then there was no safe place in all the region round about, but behind it.

We took two or three blankets for protection against frosty weather in the mountains. In the matter of luxuries we were modest—we took none along but some pipes and five pounds of smoking tobacco. We had two large canteens to carry water in, between stations on the Plains, and we also took with us a little shot-bag of silver coin for daily expenses in the way of breakfasts and dinners.

By eight o'clock everything was ready, and we were on the other side of the river. We jumped into the stage, the driver cracked his whip, and we bowled away and left "the States" behind us. It was a superb summer morning, and all the landscape was brilliant with sunshine. There was a freshness and breeziness, too, and an exhilarating sense of emancipation from all sorts of cares and responsibilities, that almost made us feel that the years we had spent in the close, hot city, toiling and slaving, had been wasted and thrown away. We were spinning along through Kansas, and in the course of an hour and a half we were fairly abroad on the great Plains. Just here the land was rolling—a grand sweep of regular elevations and depressions as far as the eye could reach—like the stately heave and swell of the ocean's bosom after a storm. And everywhere were cornfields, accenting with squares of deeper green, this limitless expanse of grassy land. But presently this sea upon dry ground was to lose its "rolling" character and stretch away for seven hundred miles as level as a floor!

Our coach was a great swinging and swaying stage, of the most sumptuous description—an imposing cradle on wheels. It was drawn by six handsome horses, and by the side of the driver sat the "conductor," the legitimate captain of the craft; for it was his business to take charge and care of the mails, baggage, express matter, and passengers. We three were the only passengers, this trip. We sat on the back seat, inside. About all the rest of the coach was full of mail bags—for we had three days' delayed mails with us. Almost touching our knees, a perpendicular wall of mail matter rose up to the roof. There was a great pile of it strapped on top of the stage, and both the fore and hind boots were full. We had twenty-seven hundred pounds of it aboard, the driver said—"a little for Brigham, and Carson, and 'Frisco, but the heft of it for the Injuns, which is powerful troublesome 'thout they get plenty of truck to read." But as he just then got up a fearful convulsion of his countenance which was suggestive of a wink being swallowed by an earthquake, we guessed that his remark was intended to be facetious, and to mean that we would unload the most of our mail matter somewhere on the Plains and leave it to the Indians, or whosoever wanted it.

We changed horses every ten miles, all day long, and fairly flew over the hard, level road. We jumped out and stretched our legs every time the coach stopped, and so the night found us still vivacious and unfatigued.

After supper a woman got in, who lived about fifty miles further on, and we three had to take turns at sitting outside with the driver and conductor. Apparently she was not a talkative woman. She would sit there in the gathering twilight and fasten her steadfast eyes on a mosquito rooting into her arm, and slowly she would raise her other hand till she had got his range, and then she would launch a slap at him that would have jolted a cow; and after that she would sit and contemplate the corpse with tranquil satisfaction—for she never missed her mosquito; she was a dead shot at short range. She never removed a carcase, but left them there for bait. I sat by this grim Sphynx and watched her kill thirty or forty mosquitoes—watched her, and waited for her to say something, but she never did. So I finally opened the conversation myself. I said:

"The mosquitoes are pretty bad, about here, madam."

"You bet!"

"What did I understand you to say, madam?"

"You BET!"

Then she cheered up, and faced around and said:

"Danged if I didn't begin to think you fellers was deef and dumb. I did, b' gosh. Here I've sot, and sot, and sot, a-bust'n muskeeters and wonderin' what was ailin' ye. Fust I thot you was deef and dumb, then I thot you was sick or crazy, or suthin', and then by and by I begin to reckon you was a passel of sickly fools that couldn't think of nothing to say. Wher'd ye come from?"

The Sphynx was a Sphynx no more! The fountains of her great deep were broken up, and she rained the nine parts of speech forty days and forty nights, metaphorically speaking, and buried us under a desolating deluge of trivial gossip that left not a crag or pinnacle of rejoinder projecting above the tossing waste of dislocated grammar and decomposed pronunciation!

How we suffered, suffered, suffered! She went on, hour after hour, till I was sorry I ever opened the mosquito question and gave her a start. She never did stop again until she got to her journey's end toward daylight; and then she stirred us up as she was leaving the stage (for we were nodding, by that time), and said:

"Now you git out at Cottonwood, you fellers, and lay over a couple o' days, and I'll be along some time to-night, and if I can do ye any good by edgin' in a word now and then, I'm right thar. Folks 'll tell you 't I've always ben kind o' offish and partic'lar for a gal that's raised in the woods, and I *am*, with the rag-tag and bob-tail, and a gal *has* to be, if she wants to *be* anything, but when people comes along which is my equals, I reckon I'm a pretty sociable heifer after all."

We resolved not to "lay by at Cottonwood."

Chapter III

ABOUT AN HOUR and a half before daylight we were bowling along smoothly over the road—so smoothly that our cradle only rocked in a gentle, lulling way, that was gradually soothing us to sleep, and dulling our consciousness—when something gave away under us! We were dimly aware of it, but indifferent to it. The coach stopped. We heard the driver and conductor talking together outside, and rummaging for a lantern, and swearing because they could not find it—but we had no interest in whatever had happened, and it only added to our comfort to think of those people out there at work in the murky night, and we snug in our nest with the curtains drawn. But presently, by the sounds, there seemed to be an examination going on, and then the driver's voice said:

"By George, the thoroughbrace is broke!"

This startled me broad awake—as an undefined sense of calamity is always apt to do. I said to myself: "Now, a thoroughbrace is probably part of a horse; and doubtless a vital part, too, from the dismay in the driver's voice. Leg, maybe—and yet how could he break his leg waltzing along such a road as this? No, it can't be his leg. That is impossible, unless he was reaching for the driver. Now, what can be the thoroughbrace of a horse, I wonder? Well, whatever comes, I shall not air my ignorance in this crowd, anyway."

Just then the conductor's face appeared at a lifted curtain, and his lantern glared in on us and our wall of mail matter. He said:

"Gents, you'll have to turn out a spell. Thoroughbrace is broke."

We climbed out into a chill drizzle, and felt ever so homeless and dreary. When I found that the thing they called a "thoroughbrace" was the massive combination of belts and springs which the coach rocks itself in, I said to the driver:

"I never saw a thoroughbrace used up like that, before, that I can remember. How did it happen?"

"Why, it happened by trying to make one coach carry three days' mail—that's how it happened," said he. "And right here is the very direction which is wrote on all the newspaper-bags which was to be put out for the Injuns for to keep 'em quiet. It's most uncommon lucky, becuz it's so nation dark I should 'a' gone by unbeknowns if that air thoroughbrace hadn't broke."

I knew that he was in labor with another of those winks of his, though I could not see his face, because he was bent down at work; and wishing him a safe delivery, I turned to and helped the rest get out the mail-sacks. It made a great pyramid by the roadside when it was all out. When they had mended the thoroughbrace we filled the two boots again, but put no mail on top, and only half as much inside as there was before. The conductor bent all the seat-backs down, and then filled the coach just half full of mail-bags from end to end. We objected loudly to this, for it left us no seats. But the conductor was wiser than we, and said a bed was better than seats, and moreover, this plan would protect his thorough-braces. We never wanted any seats after that. The lazy bed was infinitely preferable. I had many an exciting day, subsequently, lying on it reading the statutes and the dictionary, and wondering how the characters would turn out.

The conductor said he would send back a guard from the next station to take charge of the abandoned mail-bags, and we drove on.

It was now just dawn; and as we stretched our cramped legs full length on the mail sacks, and gazed out through the windows across the wide wastes of greensward clad in cool, powdery mist, to where there was an expectant look in the eastern horizon, our perfect enjoyment took the form of a tranquil and contented ecstasy. The stage whirled along at a spanking gait, the breeze flapping curtains and suspended coats in a most exhilarating way; the cradle swayed and swung luxuriously, the pattering of the horses' hoofs, the cracking of the driver's whip, and his "Hi-yi! g'lang!" were music; the spinning ground and the waltzing trees appeared to give us a mute hurrah as we went by, and then slack up and look after us with interest, or envy, or something; and as we lay and smoked the pipe of peace and compared all this luxury with the years of tiresome city life that had gone before it, we felt that there was only one complete and satisfying happiness in the world, and we had found it.

After breakfast, at some station whose name I have forgotten, we three climbed up on the seat behind the driver, and let the conductor have our bed for a nap. And by and by, when the sun made me drowsy, I lay down on my face on top of the coach, grasping the slender iron railing, and slept for an hour or more. That will give one an appreciable idea of those matchless roads. Instinct will make a sleeping man grip a fast hold of the railing when the stage jolts, but when it only swings and sways, no grip is necessary. Overland drivers and conductors used to sit in their places and sleep thirty or forty minutes at a time, on good roads, while spinning along at the rate of eight or ten miles an hour. I saw them do it, often. There was no danger about it; a sleeping man *will* seize the irons in time when the coach jolts. These men were hard worked, and it was not possible for them to stay awake all the time.

By and by we passed through Marysville, and over the Big Blue and Little Sandy; thence about a mile, and entered Nebraska. About a mile further on, we came to the Big Sandy—one hundred and eighty miles from St. Joseph.

As the sun was going down, we saw the first specimen of an animal known familiarly over two thousand miles of mountain and desert—from Kansas clear to the Pacific Ocean—as the "jackass rabbit." He is well named. He is just like any other rabbit, except that he is from one third to twice as large, has longer legs in proportion to his size, and has the most preposterous ears that ever were mounted on any creature *but* a jackass. When he is sitting quiet, thinking about his sins, or is absent-minded or unapprehensive of danger, his majestic ears project above him conspicuously; but the breaking of a twig will scare him nearly to death, and then he tilts his ears back gently and starts for home. All you can see, then, for the next minute, is his long gray form stretched out straight and "streaking it" through the low sage-brush, head erect, eyes right, and ears just canted a little to the rear, but showing you where the animal is, all the time, the same as if he carried a jib. Now and then he makes a marvelous spring with his long legs, high over the stunted sage-brush, and scores a leap that would make a horse envious. Presently he comes down to a long, graceful "lope," and shortly he mysteriously disappears. He has crouched behind a sage-bush, and will sit there and listen and tremble until you get within six feet of him, when he will get under way again. But one must shoot at this creature once, if he wishes to see him throw his heart into his heels, and do the best he knows how. He is frightened clear through, now, and he lays his long ears down on his back, straightens himself out like a yard-stick every spring he makes, and scatters miles behind him with an easy indifference that is enchanting.

Our party made this specimen "hump himself," as the conductor said. The secretary started him with a shot from the Colt; I commenced spitting at him with my weapon; and all in the same instant the old "Allen's" whole broadside let go with a rattling crash, and it is not putting it too strong to say that the rabbit was frantic! He dropped his ears, set up his tail, and left for San Francisco at a speed which can only be described as a flash and a vanish! Long after he was out of sight we could hear him whiz.

I do not remember where we first came across "sage-brush," but as I have been speaking of it I may as well describe it. This is easily done, for if the reader can imagine a gnarled and venerable live oak-tree reduced to a little shrub two feet high, with its rough bark, its foliage, its twisted boughs, all complete, he can picture the "sage-brush" exactly. Often, on lazy afternoons in the mountains, I have lain on the ground with my face under a sage-bush, and entertained myself with fancying that the gnats among its foliage were liliputian birds, and that the ants marching and countermarching about its base were liliputian flocks and herds, and myself some vast loafer from Brobdignag waiting to catch a little citizen and eat him.

It is an imposing monarch of the forest in exquisite miniature, is the "sage-brush." Its foliage is a grayish green, and gives that tint to desert and mountain. It smells like our domestic sage, and "sage-tea" made from it tastes like the sage-tea which all boys are so well acquainted with. The sage-brush is a singularly hardy plant, and grows right in the midst of deep sand, and among barren rocks, where nothing else in the vegetable world would try to grow, except "bunch-grass."* The sage-bushes grow from three to six or seven feet apart, all over the mountains and deserts of the Far West, clear to the borders of California. There is not a tree of any kind in the deserts, for hundreds of miles—there is no vegetation at all in a regular desert, except the sage-brush and its cousin the "greasewood," which is so much like the sage-brush that the difference amounts to little. Camp-fires and hot suppers in the deserts would be impossible but for the friendly sage-brush. Its trunk is as large as a boy's wrist (and from that up to a man's arm), and its crooked branches are half as large as its trunk—all good, sound, hard wood, very like oak.

When a party camps, the first thing to be done is to cut sage-brush; and in a few minutes there is an opulent pile of it ready for use. A hole a foot wide, two feet deep, and two feet long, is dug; and sage-brush chopped up and burned in it till it is full to the brim with glowing coals. Then the cooking begins, and there is no smoke, and consequently no swearing. Such a fire will keep all night, with very little replenishing; and it makes a very sociable camp-fire, and one around which the most impossible reminiscences sound plausible, instructive, and profoundly entertaining.

Sage-brush is very fair fuel, but as a vegetable it is a distinguished failure. Nothing can abide the taste of it but the jackass and his illegitimate child the mule. But their testimony to its nutritiousness is worth nothing, for they will eat pine knots, or anthracite coal, or brass filings, or lead pipe, or old bottles, or anything that comes handy, and then go off looking as grateful as if they had had oysters for dinner. Mules and donkeys and camels have appetites that anything will relieve temporarily, but nothing satisfy. In Syria, once, at the head-waters of the Jordan, a camel took charge of my overcoat while the tents were being pitched, and examined it with a critical eye, all over, with as much interest as if he had an

---

*"Bunch-grass" grows on the bleak mountain-sides of Nevada and neighboring territories, and offers excellent feed for stock, even in the dead of winter, wherever the snow is blown aside and exposes it; notwithstanding its unpromising home, bunch-grass is a better and more nutritious diet for cattle and horses than almost any other hay or grass that is known—so stock-men say.

idea of getting one made like it; and then, after he was done figuring on it as an article of apparel, he began to contemplate it as an article of diet. He put his foot on it, and lifted one of the sleeves out with his teeth, and chewed and chewed at it, gradually taking it in, and all the while opening and closing his eyes in a kind of religious ecstasy, as if he had never tasted anything as good as an overcoat before, in his life. Then he smacked his lips once or twice, and reached after the other sleeve. Next he tried the velvet collar, and smiled a smile of such contentment that it was plain to see that he regarded that as the daintiest thing about an overcoat. The tails went next, along with some percussion caps and cough candy, and some fig-paste from Constantinople. And then my newspaper correspondence dropped out, and he took a chance in that— manuscript letters written for the home papers. But he was treading on dangerous ground, now. He began to come across solid wisdom in those documents that was rather weighty on his stomach; and occasionally he would take a joke that would shake him up till it loosened his teeth; it was getting to be perilous times with him, but he held his grip with good courage and hopefully, till at last he began to stumble on statements that not even a camel could swallow with impunity. He began to gag and gasp, and his eyes to stand out, and his forelegs to spread, and in about a quarter of a minute he fell over as stiff as a carpenter's work-bench, and died a death of indescribable agony. I went and pulled the manuscript out of his mouth, and found that the sensitive creature had choked to death on one of the mildest and gentlest statements of fact that I ever laid before a trusting public.

I was about to say, when diverted from my subject, that occasionally one finds sage-bushes five or six feet high, and with a spread of branch and foliage in proportion, but two or two and a half feet is the usual height.

Chapter IV

As the sun went down and the evening chill came on, we made preparation for bed. We stirred up the hard leather letter-sacks, and the knotty canvas bags of printed matter (knotty and uneven because of projecting ends and corners of magazines, boxes and books). We stirred them up and redisposed them in such a way as to make our bed as level as possible. And we *did* improve it, too, though after all our work it had an upheaved and billowy look about it, like a little piece of a stormy sea. Next we hunted up our boots from odd nooks among the mail-bags where they had settled, and put them on. Then we got down our coats, vests, pantaloons and heavy woolen shirts, from the arm-loops where they had been swinging all day, and clothed ourselves in them—for, there being no ladies either at the stations or in the coach, and the weather being hot, we had looked to our comfort by stripping to our underclothing, at nine o'clock in the morning. All things being now ready, we stowed the uneasy Dictionary where it would lie as quiet as possible, and placed the water-canteens and pistols where we could find them in the dark. Then we smoked a final pipe, and swapped a final yarn; after which, we put the pipes, tobacco and bag of coin in snug holes and caves among the mail-bags, and then fastened down the coach curtains all around, and made the place as "dark as the inside of a cow," as the conductor phrased it in his picturesque way. It was certainly as dark as any place could be—nothing was even dimly visible in it. And finally, we rolled ourselves up like silk-worms, each person in his own blanket, and sank peacefully to sleep.

Whenever the stage stopped to change horses, we would wake up, and try to recollect where we were—and succeed— and in a minute or two the stage would be off again, and we likewise. We began to get into country, now, threaded here and there with little streams. These had high, steep banks on each side, and every time we flew down one bank and scrambled up the other, our party inside got mixed somewhat. First we would all be down in a pile at the forward end of the stage, nearly in a sitting posture, and in a second we would shoot to the other end, and stand on our heads. And we would sprawl and kick, too, and ward off ends and corners of mail-bags that came lumbering over us and about us; and as the dust rose from the tumult, we would all sneeze in chorus, and the majority of us would grumble, and probably say some hasty thing, like: "Take your elbow out of my ribs!—can't you quit crowding?"

Every time we avalanched from one end of the stage to the other, the Unabridged Dictionary would come too; and every time it came it damaged somebody. One trip it "barked" the Secretary's elbow; the next trip it hurt me in the stomach, and the third it tilted Bemis's nose up till he could look down his nostrils—he said. The pistols and coin soon settled to the bottom, but the pipes, pipe-stems, tobacco and canteens clattered and floundered after the Dictionary every time it made an assault on us, and aided and abetted the book by spilling tobacco in our eyes, and water down our backs.

Still, all things considered, it was a very comfortable night. It wore gradually away, and when at last a cold gray light was visible through the puckers and chinks in the curtains, we yawned and stretched with satisfaction, shed our cocoons, and felt that we had slept as much as was necessary. By and by, as the sun rose up and warmed the world, we pulled off our clothes and got ready for breakfast. We were just pleasantly in time, for five minutes afterward the driver sent the weird music of his bugle winding over the grassy solitudes, and presently we detected a low hut or two in the distance. Then the rattling of the coach, the clatter of our six horses' hoofs, and the driver's crisp commands, awoke to a louder and stronger emphasis, and we went sweeping down on the station at our smartest speed. It was fascinating—that old overland stage-coaching.

We jumped out in undress uniform. The driver tossed his gathered reins out on the ground, gaped and stretched complacently, drew off his heavy buckskin gloves with great deliberation and insufferable dignity—taking not the slightest notice of a dozen solicitous inquiries after his health, and humbly facetious and flattering accostings, and obsequious tenders of service, from five or six hairy and half-civilized station-keepers and hostlers who were nimbly unhitching our steeds and bringing the fresh team out of the stables—for in the eyes of the stage-driver of that day, station-keepers and hostlers were a sort of good enough low creatures, useful in their place, and helping to make up a world, but not the kind of beings which a person of distinction could afford to concern himself with; while, on the contrary, in the eyes of the station-keeper and the hostler, the stage-driver was a hero—a great and shining dignitary, the world's favorite son, the envy of the people, the observed of the nations. When they spoke to him they received his insolent silence meekly, and as being the natural and proper conduct of so great a man; when he opened his lips they all hung on his words with admiration (he never honored a particular individual with a remark, but addressed it with a broad generality to the horses, the stables, the surrounding country *and* the human underlings); when he discharged a facetious insulting personality at a hostler, that hostler was happy for the day; when he uttered his one jest—old as the hills, coarse, profane, witless, and inflicted on the same audience, in the same language, every time his coach drove up there—the varlets roared, and slapped their thighs, and swore it was the best thing they'd ever heard in all their lives. And how they would fly around when he wanted a basin of water, a gourd of the same, or a light for his pipe!—but they would instantly insult a passenger if he so far forgot himself as to crave a favor at their hands. They could do that sort of insolence as well as the driver they copied it from—for, let it be borne in mind, the overland driver had but little less contempt for his passengers than he had for his hostlers.

The hostlers and station-keepers treated the really powerful *conductor* of the coach merely with the best of what was their idea of civility, but the *driver* was the only being they bowed down to and worshipped. How admiringly they would gaze up at him in his high seat as he gloved himself with lingering deliberation, while some happy hostler held the bunch of reins aloft, and waited patiently for him to take it! And how they would bombard him with glorifying ejaculations as he cracked his long whip and went careering away.

The station buildings were long, low huts, made of sun-dried, mud-colored bricks, laid up without mortar (*adobes*, the Spaniards call these bricks, and Americans shorten it to *'dobies*). The roofs, which had no slant to them worth speaking of, were thatched and then sodded or covered with a thick layer of earth, and from this sprung a pretty rank growth of weeds and grass. It was the first time we had ever seen a man's front yard on top of his house. The buildings consisted of barns, stable-room for twelve or fifteen horses, and a hut for an eating-room for passengers. This latter had bunks in it for the station-keeper and a hostler or two. You could rest your elbow on its eaves, and you had to bend in order to get in at the door. In place of a window there was a square hole about large enough for a man to crawl through, but this had no glass in it. There was no flooring, but the ground was packed hard. There was no stove, but the fire-place served all needful purposes. There were no shelves, no cupboards, no closets. In a corner stood an open sack of flour, and nestling against its base were a couple of black and venerable tin coffee-pots, a tin tea-pot, a little bag of salt, and a side of bacon.

By the door of the station-keeper's den, outside, was a tin wash-basin, on the ground. Near it was a pail of water and a piece of yellow bar soap, and from the eaves hung a hoary blue woolen shirt, significantly—but this latter was the station-keeper's private towel, and only two persons in all the party might venture to use it—the stage-driver and the conductor. The latter would not, from a sense of decency; the former would not, because he did not choose to encourage the advances of a station-keeper. We had towels—in the valise; they might as well have been in Sodom and Gomorrah. We (and the conductor), used our handkerchiefs, and the driver his pantaloons and sleeves. By the door, inside, was fastened a small old-fashioned looking-glass frame, with two little fragments of the original mirror lodged down in one corner of it. This arrangement afforded a pleasant double-barreled portrait of you when you looked into it, with one half of your head set up a couple of inches above the other half. From the glass frame hung the half of a comb by a string—but if I had to describe that patriarch or die, I believe I would order some sample coffins. It had come down from Esau and Samson, and had been accumulating hair ever since—along with certain impurities. In one corner of the room stood three or four rifles and muskets, together with horns and pouches of ammunition. The station-men wore pantaloons of coarse, country-woven stuff, and into the seat and the inside of the legs were sewed ample additions of buckskin, to do duty in place of leggings, when the man rode horseback—so the pants were half dull blue and half yellow, and unspeakably picturesque. The pants were stuffed into the tops of high boots, the heels whereof were armed with great Spanish spurs, whose little iron clogs and chains jingled with every step. The man wore a huge beard and mustachios, an old slouch hat, a blue woolen shirt, no suspenders, no vest, no coat—in a leathern sheath in his belt, a great long "navy" revolver (slung on right side, hammer to the front), and projecting from his boot a horn-handled bowie-knife. The furniture of the hut was neither gorgeous nor much in the way. The rocking-chairs and sofas were not present, and never had been, but they were represented by two three-legged stools, a pine-board bench four feet long, and two empty candleboxes. The table was a greasy board on stilts, and the table-cloth and napkins had not come—and they were not looking for them, either. A battered tin platter, a knife and fork, and a tin pint cup, were at each man's place, and the driver had a queens-ware saucer that had seen better days. Of course this duke sat at the head of the table. There was one isolated piece of table furniture that bore about it a touching air of grandeur in misfortune. This was the caster. It was German silver, and crippled and rusty, but it was so preposterously out of place there that it was suggestive of a tattered exiled king among barbarians, and the majesty of its native position compelled respect even in its degradation. There was only one cruet left, and that was a stopperless, fly-specked, broken-necked thing, with two inches of vinegar in it, and a dozen preserved flies with their heels up and looking sorry they had invested there.

The station-keeper up-ended a disk of last week's bread, of the shape and size of an old-time cheese, and carved some slabs from it which were as good as Nicholson pavement, and tenderer.

He sliced off a piece of bacon for each man, but only the experienced old hands made out to eat it, for it was condemned army bacon which the United States would not feed

to its soldiers in the forts, and the stage company had bought
it cheap for the sustenance of their passengers and employes.
We may have found this condemned army bacon further out
on the plains than the section I am locating it in, but we
found it—there is no gainsaying that.

Then he poured for us a beverage which he called *"Slumgullion,"* and it is hard to think he was not inspired when he
named it. It really pretended to be tea, but there was too
much dish-rag, and sand, and old bacon-rind in it to deceive
the intelligent traveler. He had no sugar and no milk—not
even a spoon to stir the ingredients with.

We could not eat the bread or the meat, nor drink the
"slumgullion." And when I looked at that melancholy vine-
gar-cruet, I thought of the anecdote (a very, very old one,
even at that day) of the traveler who sat down to a table
which had nothing on it but a mackerel and a pot of mustard.
He asked the landlord if this was all. The landlord said:

"*All!* Why, thunder and lightning, I should think there was
mackerel enough there for six."

"But I don't like mackerel."

"Oh—then help yourself to the mustard."

In other days I had considered it a good, a very good, anecdote, but there was a dismal plausibility about it, here, that
took all the humor out of it.

Our breakfast was before us, but our teeth were idle.

I tasted and smelt, and said I would take coffee, I believed.
The station-boss stopped dead still, and glared at me speechless. At last, when he came to, he turned away and said, as
one who communes with himself upon a matter too vast to
grasp:

"*Coffee!* Well, if that don't go clean ahead of me, I'm
d——d!"

We could not eat, and there was no conversation among
the hostlers and herdsmen—we all sat at the same board. At
least there was no conversation further than a single hurried
request, now and then, from one employe to another. It was
always in the same form, and always gruffly friendly. Its western freshness and novelty startled me, at first, and interested
me; but it presently grew monotonous, and lost its charm. It
was:

"Pass the bread, you son of a skunk!" No, I forget—skunk was not the word; it seems to me it was still stronger than that; I know it was, in fact, but it is gone from my memory, apparently. However, it is no matter—probably it was too strong for print, anyway. It is the landmark in my memory which tells me where I first encountered the vigorous new vernacular of the occidental plains and mountains.

We gave up the breakfast, and paid our dollar apiece and went back to our mail-bag bed in the coach, and found comfort in our pipes. Right here we suffered the first diminution of our princely state. We left our six fine horses and took six mules in their place. But they were wild Mexican fellows, and a man had to stand at the head of each of them and hold him fast while the driver gloved and got himself ready. And when at last he grasped the reins and gave the word, the men sprung suddenly away from the mules' heads and the coach shot from the station as if it had issued from a cannon. How the frantic animals did scamper! It was a fierce and furious gallop—and the gait never altered for a moment till we reeled off ten or twelve miles and swept up to the next collection of little station-huts and stables.

So we flew along all day. At 2 P.M. the belt of timber that fringes the North Platte and marks its windings through the vast level floor of the Plains came in sight. At 4 P.M. we crossed a branch of the river, and at 5 P.M. we crossed the Platte itself, and landed at Fort Kearney, *fifty-six hours out from St. Joe*—THREE HUNDRED MILES!

Now that was stage-coaching on the great overland, ten or twelve years ago, when perhaps not more than ten men in America, all told, expected to live to see a railroad follow that route to the Pacific. But the railroad is there, now, and it pictures a thousand odd comparisons and contrasts in my mind to read the following sketch, in the New York *Times*, of a recent trip over almost the very ground I have been describing. I can scarcely comprehend the new state of things:

ACROSS THE CONTINENT.

"At 4.20 P.M., Sunday, we rolled out of the station at Omaha, and started westward on our long jaunt. A couple of hours out, dinner

was announced—an "event" to those of us who had yet to experience what it is to eat in one of Pullman's hotels on wheels; so, stepping into the car next forward of our sleeping palace, we found
ourselves in the dining-car. It was a revelation to us, that first dinner
on Sunday. And though we continued to dine for four days, and
had as many breakfasts and suppers, our whole party never ceased to
admire the perfection of the arrangements, and the marvelous results
achieved. Upon tables covered with snowy linen, and garnished with
services of solid silver, Ethiop waiters, flitting about in spotless
white, placed as by magic a repast at which Delmonico himself could
have had no occasion to blush; and, indeed, in some respects it
would be hard for that distinguished *chef* to match our *menu*; for,
in addition to all that ordinarily makes up a first-chop dinner, had
we not our antelope steak (the gormand who has not experienced
this—bah! what does he know of the feast of fat things?) our delicious mountain-brook trout, and choice fruits and berries, and
(sauce piquant and unpurchasable!) our sweet-scented, appetite-
compelling air of the prairies? You may depend upon it, we all did
justice to the good things, and as we washed them down with
bumpers of sparkling Krug, whilst we sped along at the rate of thirty
miles an hour, agreed it was the *fastest* living we had ever experienced. (We beat that, however, two days afterward when we made
twenty-seven miles in twenty-seven minutes, while our Champagne
glasses filled to the brim spilled not a drop!) After dinner we repaired to our drawing-room car, and, as it was Sabbath eve, intoned
some of the grand old hymns—"Praise God from whom," etc.;
"Shining Shore," "Coronation," etc.—the voices of the men singers
and of the women singers blending sweetly in the evening air, while
our train, with its great, glaring Polyphemus eye, lighting up long
vistas of prairie, rushed into the night and the Wild. Then to bed in
luxurious couches, where we slept the sleep of the just and only
awoke the next morning (Monday) at eight o'clock, to find ourselves
at the crossing of the North Platte, three hundred miles from
Omaha—*fifteen hours and forty minutes out.*"

Chapter V

ANOTHER NIGHT of alternate tranquillity and turmoil. But morning came, by and by. It was another glad awakening to fresh breezes, vast expanses of level greensward, bright sunlight, an impressive solitude utterly without visible human beings or human habitations, and an atmosphere of such amazing magnifying properties that trees that seemed close at hand were more than three miles away. We resumed undress uniform, climbed a-top of the flying coach, dangled our legs over the side, shouted occasionally at our frantic mules, merely to see them lay their ears back and scamper faster, tied our hats on to keep our hair from blowing away, and leveled an outlook over the world-wide carpet about us for things new and strange to gaze at. Even at this day it thrills me through and through to think of the life, the gladness and the wild sense of freedom that used to make the blood dance in my veins on those fine overland mornings!

Along about an hour after breakfast we saw the first prairie-dog villages, the first antelope, and the first wolf. If I remember rightly, this latter was the regular *cayote* (pronounced ky-o-te) of the farther deserts. And if it *was*, he was not a pretty creature or respectable either, for I got well acquainted with his race afterward, and can speak with confidence. The cayote is a long, slim, sick and sorry-looking skeleton, with a gray wolf-skin stretched over it, a tolerably bushy tail that forever sags down with a despairing expression of forsakenness and misery, a furtive and evil eye, and a long, sharp face, with slightly lifted lip and exposed teeth. He has a general slinking expression all over. The cayote is a living, breathing allegory of Want. He is *always* hungry. He is always poor, out of luck and friendless. The meanest creatures despise him, and even the fleas would desert him for a velocipede. He is so spiritless and cowardly that even while his exposed teeth are pretending a threat, the rest of his face is apologizing for it. And he is *so* homely!—so scrawny, and ribby, and coarse-haired, and pitiful. When he sees you he lifts his lip and lets a flash of his teeth out, and then turns a little out of the course he was pursuing, depresses his head a bit, and strikes a long, soft-footed trot through the sage-brush; glancing over his shoulder at you, from time to time till he is about out of easy pistol range, and then he stops and takes a deliberate survey of you; he will trot fifty yards and stop again—another fifty and stop again; and finally the gray of his gliding body blends with the gray of the sage-brush, and he disappears. All this is when you make no demonstration against him; but if you do, he develops a livelier interest in his journey, and instantly electrifies his heels and puts such a deal of real estate between himself and your weapon, that by the time you have raised the hammer you see that you need a minie rifle, and by the time you have got him in line you need a rifled cannon, and by the time you have "drawn a bead" on him you see well enough that nothing but an unusually long-winded streak of lightning could reach him where he is now. But if you start a swift-footed dog after him, you will enjoy it ever so much—especially if it is a dog that has a good opinion of himself, and has been brought up to think he knows something about speed. The cayote will go swinging gently off on that deceitful trot of his, and every little while he will smile a fraudful smile over his shoulder that will fill that dog entirely full of encouragement and worldly ambition, and make him lay his head still lower to the ground, and stretch his neck further to the front, and pant more fiercely, and stick his tail out straighter behind, and move his furious legs with a yet wilder frenzy, and leave a broader and broader, and higher and denser cloud of desert sand smoking behind, and marking his long wake across the level plain! And all this time the dog is only a short twenty feet behind the cayote, and to save the soul of him he cannot understand why it is that he cannot get perceptibly closer; and he begins to get aggravated, and it makes him madder and madder to see how gently the cayote glides along and never pants or sweats or ceases to smile; and he grows still more and more incensed to see how shamefully he has been taken in by an entire stranger, and what an ignoble swindle that long, calm, soft-footed trot is; and next he notices that he is getting fagged, and that the cayote actually has to slacken speed a little to keep from running away from him—and *then* that town-dog is mad in earnest, and he begins to strain and weep and swear, and paw the sand higher than ever, and reach for the cayote with concentrated and desperate energy. This "spurt" finds him six feet behind the gliding enemy, and two miles from his friends. And then, in the instant that a wild new hope is lighting up his face, the cayote turns and smiles blandly upon him once more, and with a something about it which seems to say: "Well, I shall have to tear myself away from you, bub—business is business, and it will not do for me to be fooling along this way all day"— and forthwith there is a rushing sound, and the sudden splitting of a long crack through the atmosphere, and behold that dog is solitary and alone in the midst of a vast solitude!

It makes his head swim. He stops, and looks all around; climbs the nearest sand-mound, and gazes into the distance; shakes his head reflectively, and then, without a word, he turns and jogs along back to his train, and takes up a humble position under the hindmost wagon, and feels unspeakably mean, and looks ashamed, and hangs his tail at half-mast for a week. And for as much as a year after that, whenever there is a great hue and cry after a cayote, that dog will merely glance in that direction without emotion, and apparently observe to himself, "I believe I do not wish any of the pie."

The cayote lives chiefly in the most desolate and forbidding deserts, along with the lizard, the jackass-rabbit and the raven, and gets an uncertain and precarious living, and earns it. He seems to subsist almost wholly on the carcases of oxen, mules and horses that have dropped out of emigrant trains and died, and upon windfalls of carrion, and occasional legacies of offal bequeathed to him by white men who have been opulent enough to have something better to butcher than condemned army bacon. He will eat anything in the world that his first cousins, the desert-frequenting tribes of Indians will, and they will eat anything they can bite. It is a curious fact that these latter are the only creatures known to history who will eat nitro-glycerine and ask for more if they survive.

The cayote of the deserts beyond the Rocky Mountains has a peculiarly hard time of it, owing to the fact that his relations, the Indians, are just as apt to be the first to detect a seductive scent on the desert breeze, and follow the fragrance to the late ox it emanated from, as he is himself; and when this occurs he has to content himself with sitting off at a little

distance watching those people strip off and dig out everything edible, and walk off with it. Then he and the waiting
ravens explore the skeleton and polish the bones. It is considered that the cayote, and the obscene bird, and the Indian of
the desert, testify their blood kinship with each other in that
they live together in the waste places of the earth on terms of
perfect confidence and friendship, while hating all other creatures and yearning to assist at their funerals. He does not
mind going a hundred miles to breakfast, and a hundred and
fifty to dinner, because he is sure to have three or four days
between meals, and he can just as well be traveling and looking at the scenery as lying around doing nothing and adding
to the burdens of his parents.

We soon learned to recognize the sharp, vicious bark of the
cayote as it came across the murky plain at night to disturb
our dreams among the mail-sacks; and remembering his forlorn aspect and his hard fortune, made shift to wish him the
blessed novelty of a long day's good luck and a limitless larder
the morrow.

Chapter VI

O UR NEW CONDUCTOR (just shipped) had been without sleep for twenty hours. Such a thing was very frequent. From St. Joseph, Missouri, to Sacramento, California, by stage-coach, was nearly nineteen hundred miles, and the trip was often made in fifteen days (the cars do it in four and a half, now), but the time specified in the mail contracts, and required by the schedule, was eighteen or nineteen days, if I remember rightly. This was to make fair allowance for winter storms and snows, and other unavoidable causes of detention. The stage company had everything under strict discipline and good system. Over each two hundred and fifty miles of road they placed an agent or superintendent, and invested him with great authority. His beat or jurisdiction of two hundred and fifty miles was called a "division." He purchased horses, mules, harness, and food for men and beasts, and distributed these things among his stage stations, from time to time, according to his judgment of what each station needed. He erected station buildings and dug wells. He attended to the paying of the station-keepers, hostlers, drivers and blacksmiths, and discharged them whenever he chose. He was a very, very great man in his "division"—a kind of Grand Mogul, a Sultan of the Indies, in whose presence common men were modest of speech and manner, and in the glare of whose greatness even the dazzling stage-driver dwindled to a penny dip. There were about eight of these kings, all told, on the overland route.

Next in rank and importance to the division-agent came the "conductor." His beat was the same length as the agent's— two hundred and fifty miles. He sat with the driver, and (when necessary) rode that fearful distance, night and day, without other rest or sleep than what he could get perched thus on top of the flying vehicle. Think of it! He had absolute charge of the mails, express matter, passengers and stage-coach, until he delivered them to the next conductor, and got his receipt for them. Consequently he had to be a man of intelligence, decision and considerable executive ability. He was usually a quiet, pleasant man, who attended closely to his duties, and was a good deal of a gentleman. It was not absolutely necessary that the division-agent should be a gentleman, and occasionally he wasn't. But he was always a general in administrative ability, and a bull-dog in courage and determination—otherwise the chieftainship over the lawless underlings of the overland service would never in any instance have been to him anything but an equivalent for a month of insolence and distress and a bullet and a coffin at the end of it. There were about sixteen or eighteen conductors on the overland, for there was a daily stage each way, and a conductor on every stage.

Next in *real* and official rank and importance, *after* the conductor, came my delight, the driver—next in real but not in *apparent* importance—for we have seen that in the eyes of the common herd the driver was to the conductor as an admiral is to the captain of the flag-ship. The driver's beat was pretty long, and his sleeping-time at the stations pretty short, sometimes; and so, but for the grandeur of his position his would have been a sorry life, as well as a hard and a wearing one. We took a new driver every day or every night (for they drove backward and forward over the same piece of road all the time), and therefore we never got as well acquainted with them as we did with the conductors; and besides, they would have been above being familiar with such rubbish as passengers, anyhow, as a general thing. Still, we were always eager to get a sight of each and every new driver as soon as the watch changed, for each and every day we were either anxious to get rid of an unpleasant one, or loath to part with a driver we had learned to like and had come to be sociable and friendly with. And so the first question we asked the conductor whenever we got to where we were to exchange drivers, was always, "Which is him?" The grammar was faulty, maybe, but we could not know, then, that it would go into a book some day. As long as everything went smoothly, the overland driver was well enough situated, but if a fellow driver got sick suddenly it made trouble, for the coach *must* go on, and so the potentate who was about to climb down and take a luxurious rest after his long night's siege in the midst of wind and rain and darkness, had to stay where he was and do the sick man's work. Once, in the Rocky Mountains, when I found a driver sound asleep on the box, and the mules going at the usual break-neck pace, the conductor said never mind him, there was no danger, and he was doing double duty—had driven seventy-five miles on one coach, and was now going back over it on this without rest or sleep. A hundred and fifty miles of holding back of six vindictive mules and keeping them from climbing the trees! It sounds incredible, but I remember the statement well enough.

The station-keepers, hostlers, etc., were low, rough characters, as already described; and from western Nebraska to Nevada a considerable sprinkling of them might be fairly set down as outlaws—fugitives from justice, criminals whose best security was a section of country which was without law and without even the pretence of it. When the "division-agent" issued an order to one of these parties he did it with the full understanding that he might have to enforce it with a navy six-shooter, and so he always went "fixed" to make things go along smoothly. Now and then a division-agent was really obliged to shoot a hostler through the head to teach him some simple matter that he could have taught him with a club if his circumstances and surroundings had been different. But they were snappy, able men, those division-agents, and when they tried to teach a subordinate anything, that subordinate generally "got it through his head."

A great portion of this vast machinery—these hundreds of men and coaches, and thousands of mules and horses—was in the hands of Mr. Ben Holliday. All the western half of the business was in his hands. This reminds me of an incident of Palestine travel which is pertinent here, and so I will transfer it just in the language in which I find it set down in my Holy Land note-book:

No doubt everybody has heard of Ben Holliday—a man of prodigious energy, who used to send mails and passengers flying across the continent in his overland stage-coaches like a very whirlwind—two thousand long miles in fifteen days and a half, by the watch! But this fragment of history is not about Ben Holliday, but about a young New York boy by the name of Jack, who traveled with our small party of pilgrims in the Holy Land (and who had traveled to California in Mr. Holliday's overland coaches three years before, and had by no means forgotten it or lost his gushing admiration of

Mr. H.) Aged nineteen. Jack was a good boy—a good-hearted and always well-meaning boy, who had been reared in the city of New York, and although he was bright and knew a great many useful things, his Scriptural education had been a good deal neglected—to such a degree, indeed, that all Holy Land history was fresh and new to him, and all Bible names mysteries that had never disturbed his virgin ear. Also in our party was an elderly pilgrim who was the reverse of Jack, in that he was learned in the Scriptures and an enthusiast concerning them. He was our encyclopedia, and we were never tired of listening to his speeches, nor he of making them. He never passed a celebrated locality, from Bashan to Bethlehem, without illuminating it with an oration. One day, when camped near the ruins of Jericho, he burst forth with something like this:

"Jack, do you see that range of mountains over yonder that bounds the Jordan valley? The mountains of Moab, Jack! Think of it, my boy—the actual mountains of Moab—renowned in Scripture history! We are actually standing face to face with those illustrious crags and peaks—and for all we know" [dropping his voice impressively], "*our eyes may be resting at this very moment upon the spot* WHERE LIES THE MYSTERIOUS GRAVE OF MOSES! Think of it, Jack!"

"Moses *who*?" (falling inflection).

"Moses *who*! Jack, you ought to be ashamed of yourself—you ought to be ashamed of such criminal ignorance. Why, Moses, the great guide, soldier, poet, lawgiver of ancient Israel! Jack, from this spot where we stand, to Egypt, stretches a fearful desert three hundred miles in extent—and across that desert that wonderful man brought the children of Israel!—guiding them with unfailing sagacity for forty years over the sandy desolation and among the obstructing rocks and hills, and landed them at last, safe and sound, within sight of this very spot; and where we now stand they entered the Promised Land with anthems of rejoicing! It was a wonderful, wonderful thing to do, Jack! Think of it!"

"*Forty years? Only three hundred miles?* Humph! Ben Holliday would have fetched them through in thirty-six hours!"

The boy meant no harm. He did not know that he had said anything that was wrong or irreverent. And so no one scolded him or felt offended with him—and nobody *could* but some ungenerous spirit incapable of excusing the heedless blunders of a boy.

At noon on the fifth day out, we arrived at the "Crossing of the South Platte," *alias* "Julesburg," *alias* "Overland City," four hundred and seventy miles from St. Joseph—the strangest, quaintest, funniest frontier town that our untraveled eyes had ever stared at and been astonished with.

Chapter VII

IT DID SEEM strange enough to see a town again after what appeared to us such a long acquaintance with deep, still, almost lifeless and houseless solitude! We tumbled out into the busy street feeling like meteoric people crumbled off the corner of some other world, and wakened up suddenly in this. For an hour we took as much interest in Overland City as if we had never seen a town before. The reason we had an hour to spare was because we had to change our stage (for a less sumptuous affair, called a "mud-wagon") and transfer our freight of mails.

Presently we got under way again. We came to the shallow, yellow, muddy South Platte, with its low banks and its scattering flat sand-bars and pigmy islands—a melancholy stream straggling through the centre of the enormous flat plain, and only saved from being impossible to find with the naked eye by its sentinel rank of scattering trees standing on either bank. The Platte was "up," they said—which made me wish I could see it when it was down, if it could look any sicker and sorrier. They said it was a dangerous stream to cross, now, because its quicksands were liable to swallow up horses, coach and passengers if an attempt was made to ford it. But the mails had to go, and we made the attempt. Once or twice in midstream the wheels sunk into the yielding sands so threateningly that we half believed we had dreaded and avoided the sea all our lives to be shipwrecked in a "mud-wagon" in the middle of a desert at last. But we dragged through and sped away toward the setting sun.

Next morning, just before dawn, when about five hundred and fifty miles from St. Joseph, our mud-wagon broke down. We were to be delayed five or six hours, and therefore we took horses, by invitation, and joined a party who were just starting on a buffalo hunt. It was noble sport galloping over the plain in the dewy freshness of the morning, but our part of the hunt ended in disaster and disgrace, for a wounded buffalo bull chased the passenger Bemis nearly two miles, and then he forsook his horse and took to a lone tree. He was very sullen about the matter for some twenty-four hours, but at last he began to soften little by little, and finally he said:

"Well, it was not funny, and there was no sense in those gawks making themselves so facetious over it. I tell you I was angry in earnest for awhile. I should have shot that long gangly lubber they called Hank, if I could have done it without crippling six or seven other people—but of course I couldn't, the old 'Allen's' so confounded comprehensive. I wish those loafers had been up in the tree; they wouldn't have wanted to laugh so. If I had had a horse worth a cent—but no, the minute he saw that buffalo bull wheel on him and give a bellow, he raised straight up in the air and stood on his heels. The saddle began to slip, and I took him round the neck and laid close to him, and began to pray. Then he came down and stood up on the other end awhile, and the bull actually stopped pawing sand and bellowing to contemplate the inhuman spectacle. Then the bull made a pass at him and uttered a bellow that sounded perfectly frightful, it was so close to me, and that seemed to literally prostrate my horse's reason, and make a raving distracted maniac of him, and I wish I may die if he didn't stand on his head for a quarter of a minute and shed tears. He was absolutely out of his mind—he was, as sure as truth itself, and he really didn't know what he was doing. Then the bull came charging at us, and my horse dropped down on all fours and took a fresh start—and then for the next ten minutes he would actually throw one hand-spring after another so fast that the bull began to get unsettled, too, and didn't know where to start in—and so he stood there sneezing, and shovelling dust over his back, and bellowing every now and then, and thinking he had got a fifteen-hundred dollar circus horse for breakfast, certain. Well, I was first out on his neck—the horse's, not the bull's—and then underneath, and next on his rump, and sometimes head up, and sometimes heels—but I tell you it seemed solemn and awful to be ripping and tearing and carrying on so in the presence of death, as you might say. Pretty soon the bull made a snatch for us and brought away some of my horse's tail (I suppose, but do not know, being pretty busy at the time), but *something* made him hungry for solitude and suggested to him to get up and hunt for it. And then you ought to have seen that spider-legged old skeleton go! and you ought to have seen the bull cut out after him, too—head down, tongue out, tail up, bellowing like everything, and actually mowing down the weeds, and tearing up the earth, and boosting up the sand like a whirlwind! By George, it was a hot race! I and the saddle were back on the rump, and I had the bridle in my teeth and holding on to the pommel with both hands. First we left the dogs behind; then we passed a jackass rabbit; then we overtook a cayote, and were gaining on an antelope when the rotten girth let go and threw me about thirty yards off to the left, and as the saddle went down over the horse's rump he gave it a lift with his heels that sent it more than four hundred yards up in the air, I wish I may die in a minute if he didn't. I fell at the foot of the only solitary tree there was in nine counties adjacent (as any creature could see with the naked eye), and the next second I had hold of the bark with four sets of nails and my teeth, and the next second after that I was astraddle of the main limb and blaspheming my luck in a way that made my breath smell of brimstone. I *had* the bull, now, if he did not think of *one* thing. But that one thing I dreaded. I dreaded it very seriously. There was a possibility that the bull might not think of it, but there were greater chances that he would. I made up my mind what I would do in case he did. It was a little over forty feet to the ground from where I sat. I cautiously unwound the lariat from the pommel of my saddle—"

"Your *saddle*? Did you take your saddle up in the tree with you?"

"Take it up in the tree with me? Why, how you talk. Of course I didn't. No man could do that. It *fell* in the tree when it came down."

"Oh—exactly."

"Certainly. I unwound the lariat, and fastened one end of it to the limb. It was the very best green raw-hide, and capable of sustaining tons. I made a slip-noose in the other end, and then hung it down to see the length. It reached down twenty-two feet—half way to the ground. I then loaded every barrel of the Allen with a double charge. I felt satisfied. I said to myself, if he never thinks of that one thing that I dread, all right—but if he does, all right anyhow—I am fixed for him.

But don't you know that the very thing a man dreads is the thing that always happens? Indeed it is so. I watched the bull, now, with anxiety—anxiety which no one can conceive of who has not been in such a situation and felt that at any moment death might come. Presently a thought came into the bull's eye. I knew it! said I—if my nerve fails now, I am lost. Sure enough, it was just as I had dreaded, he started in to climb the tree—"

"What, the bull?"

"Of course—who else?"

"But a bull can't climb a tree."

"He can't, can't he? Since you know so much about it, did you ever see a bull try?"

"No! I never dreamt of such a thing."

"Well, then, what is the use of your talking that way, then? Because you never saw a thing done, is that any reason why it can't be done?"

"Well, all right—go on. What did you do?"

"The bull started up, and got along well for about ten feet, then slipped and slid back. I breathed easier. He tried it again—got up a little higher—slipped again. But he came at it once more, and this time he was careful. He got gradually higher and higher, and my spirits went down more and more. Up he came—an inch at a time—with his eyes hot, and his tongue hanging out. Higher and higher—hitched his foot over the stump of a limb, and looked up, as much as to say, 'You are my meat, friend.' Up again—higher and higher, and getting more excited the closer he got. He was within ten feet of me! I took a long breath,—and then said I, 'It is now or never.' I had the coil of the lariat all ready; I paid it out slowly, till it hung right over his head; all of a sudden I let go of the slack, and the slip-noose fell fairly round his neck! Quicker than lightning I out with the Allen and let him have it in the face. It was an awful roar, and must have scared the bull out of his senses. When the smoke cleared away, there he was, dangling in the air, twenty foot from the ground, and going out of one convulsion into another faster than you could count! I didn't stop to count, anyhow—I shinned down the tree and shot for home."

"Bemis, is all that true, just as you have stated it?"

"I wish I may rot in my tracks and die the death of a dog if it isn't."

"Well, we can't refuse to believe it, and we don't. But if there were some proofs—"

"Proofs! Did I bring back my lariat?"

"No."

"Did I bring back my horse?"

"No."

"Did you ever see the bull again?"

"No."

"Well, then, what more do you want? I never saw anybody as particular as you are about a little thing like that."

I made up my mind that if this man was not a liar he only missed it by the skin of his teeth. This episode reminds me of an incident of my brief sojourn in Siam, years afterward. The European citizens of a town in the neighborhood of Bangkok had a prodigy among them by the name of Eckert, an Englishman—a person famous for the number, ingenuity and imposing magnitude of his lies. They were always repeating his most celebrated falsehoods, and always trying to "draw him out" before strangers; but they seldom succeeded. Twice he was invited to the house where I was visiting, but nothing could seduce him into a specimen lie. One day a planter named Bascom, an influential man, and a proud and sometimes irascible one, invited me to ride over with him and call on Eckert. As we jogged along, said he:

"Now, do you know where the fault lies? It lies in putting Eckert on his guard. The minute the boys go to pumping at Eckert he knows perfectly well what they are after, and of course he shuts up his shell. Anybody might know he would. But when we get there, we must play him finer than that. Let him shape the conversation to suit himself—let him drop it or change it whenever he wants to. Let him see that nobody is trying to draw him out. Just let him have his own way. He will soon forget himself and begin to grind out lies like a mill. Don't get impatient—just keep quiet, and let me play him. I will make him lie. It does seem to me that the boys must be blind to overlook such an obvious and simple trick as that."

Eckert received us heartily—a pleasant-spoken, gentle-mannered creature. We sat in the veranda an hour, sipping

English ale, and talking about the king, and the sacred white elephant, the Sleeping Idol, and all manner of things; and I noticed that my comrade never led the conversation himself or shaped it, but simply followed Eckert's lead, and betrayed no solicitude and no anxiety about anything. The effect was shortly perceptible. Eckert began to grow communicative; he grew more and more at his ease, and more and more talkative and sociable. Another hour passed in the same way, and then all of a sudden Eckert said:

"Oh, by the way! I came near forgetting. I have got a thing here to astonish you. Such a thing as neither you nor any other man ever heard of—I've got a cat that will eat cocoanut! Common green cocoanut—and not only eat the meat, but drink the milk. It is so—I'll swear to it."

A quick glance from Bascom—a glance that I understood—then:

"Why, bless my soul, I never heard of such a thing. Man, it is impossible."

"I knew you would say it. I'll fetch the cat."

He went in the house. Bascom said:

"There—what did I tell you? Now, that is the way to handle Eckert. You see, I have petted him along patiently, and put his suspicions to sleep. I am glad we came. You tell the boys about it when you go back. Cat eat a cocoanut—oh, my! Now, that is just his way, exactly—he will tell the absurdest lie, and trust to luck to get out of it again. Cat eat a cocoanut—the innocent fool!"

Eckert approached with his cat, sure enough.

Bascom smiled. Said he:

"I'll hold the cat—you bring a cocoanut."

Eckert split one open, and chopped up some pieces. Bascom smuggled a wink to me, and proffered a slice of the fruit to puss. She snatched it, swallowed it ravenously, and asked for more!

We rode our two miles in silence, and wide apart. At least I was silent, though Bascom cuffed his horse and cursed him a good deal, notwithstanding the horse was behaving well enough. When I branched off homeward, Bascom said:

"Keep the horse till morning. And—you need not speak of this——foolishness to the boys."

Chapter VIII

IN A LITTLE WHILE all interest was taken up in stretching our necks and watching for the "pony-rider"—the fleet messenger who sped across the continent from St. Joe to Sacramento, carrying letters nineteen hundred miles in eight days! Think of that for perishable horse and human flesh and blood to do! The pony-rider was usually a little bit of a man, brimful of spirit and endurance. No matter what time of the day or night his watch came on, and no matter whether it was winter or summer, raining, snowing, hailing, or sleeting, or whether his "beat" was a level straight road or a crazy trail over mountain crags and precipices, or whether it led through peaceful regions or regions that swarmed with hostile Indians, he must be always ready to leap into the saddle and be off like the wind! There was no idling-time for a pony-rider on duty. He rode fifty miles without stopping, by daylight, moonlight, starlight, or through the blackness of darkness— just as it happened. He rode a splendid horse that was born for a racer and fed and lodged like a gentleman; kept him at his utmost speed for ten miles, and then, as he came crashing up to the station where stood two men holding fast a fresh, impatient steed, the transfer of rider and mail-bag was made in the twinkling of an eye, and away flew the eager pair and were out of sight before the spectator could get hardly the ghost of a look. Both rider and horse went "flying light." The rider's dress was thin, and fitted close; he wore a "roundabout," and a skull-cap, and tucked his pantaloons into his boot-tops like a race-rider. He carried no arms—he carried nothing that was not absolutely necessary, for even the postage on his literary freight was worth *five dollars a letter*. He got but little frivolous correspondence to carry—his bag had business letters in it, mostly. His horse was stripped of all unnecessary weight, too. He wore a little wafer of a racing-saddle, and no visible blanket. He wore light shoes, or none at all. The little flat mail-pockets strapped under the rider's thighs would each hold about the bulk of a child's primer. They held many and many an important business chapter and newspaper letter, but these were written on paper as airy and thin as gold-leaf, nearly, and thus bulk and weight were economized. The stage-coach traveled about a hundred to a hundred and twenty-five miles a day (twenty-four hours), the pony-rider about two hundred and fifty. There were about eighty pony-riders in the saddle all the time, night and day, stretching in a long, scattering procession from Missouri to California, forty flying eastward, and forty toward the west, and among them making four hundred gallant horses earn a stirring livelihood and see a deal of scenery every single day in the year.

We had had a consuming desire, from the beginning, to see a pony-rider, but somehow or other all that passed us and all that met us managed to streak by in the night, and so we heard only a whiz and a hail, and the swift phantom of the desert was gone before we could get our heads out of the windows. But now we were expecting one along every moment, and would see him in broad daylight. Presently the driver exclaims:

"HERE HE COMES!"

Every neck is stretched further, and every eye strained wider. Away across the endless dead level of the prairie a black speck appears against the sky, and it is plain that it moves. Well, I should think so! In a second or two it becomes a horse and rider, rising and falling, rising and falling— sweeping toward us nearer and nearer—growing more and more distinct, more and more sharply defined—nearer and still nearer, and the flutter of the hoofs comes faintly to the ear—another instant a whoop and a hurrah from our upper deck, a wave of the rider's hand, but no reply, and man and horse burst past our excited faces, and go winging away like a belated fragment of a storm!

So sudden is it all, and so like a flash of unreal fancy, that but for the flake of white foam left quivering and perishing on a mail-sack after the vision had flashed by and disappeared, we might have doubted whether we had seen any actual horse and man at all, maybe.

We rattled through Scott's Bluffs Pass, by and by. It was along here somewhere that we first came across genuine and unmistakable alkali water in the road, and we cordially hailed it as a first-class curiosity, and a thing to be mentioned with eclat in letters to the ignorant at home. This water gave the road a soapy appearance, and in many places the ground looked as if it had been whitewashed. I think the strange alkali water excited us as much as any wonder we had come upon yet, and I know we felt very complacent and conceited, and better satisfied with life after we had added it to our list of things which *we* had seen and some other people had not. In a small way we were the same sort of simpletons as those who climb unnecessarily the perilous peaks of Mont Blanc and the Matterhorn, and derive no pleasure from it except the reflection that it isn't a common experience. But once in a while one of those parties trips and comes darting down the long mountain-crags in a sitting posture, making the crusted snow smoke behind him, flitting from bench to bench, and from terrace to terrace, jarring the earth where he strikes, and still glancing and flitting on again, sticking an iceberg into himself every now and then, and tearing his clothes, snatching at things to save himself, taking hold of trees and fetching them along with him, roots and all, starting little rocks now and then, then big boulders, then acres of ice and snow and patches of forest, gathering and still gathering as he goes, adding and still adding to his massed and sweeping grandeur as he nears a three thousand-foot precipice, till at last he waves his hat magnificently and rides into eternity on the back of a raging and tossing avalanche!

This is all very fine, but let us not be carried away by excitement, but ask calmly, how does this person feel about it in his cooler moments next day, with six or seven thousand feet of snow and stuff on top of him?

We crossed the sand hills near the scene of the Indian mail robbery and massacre of 1856, wherein the driver and conductor perished, and also all the passengers but one, it was supposed; but this must have been a mistake, for at different times afterward on the Pacific coast I was personally acquainted with a hundred and thirty-three or four people who were wounded during that massacre, and barely escaped with their lives. There was no doubt of the truth of it—I had it from their own lips. One of these parties told me that he kept coming across arrow-heads in his system for nearly seven years after the massacre; and another of them told me that he was stuck so literally full of arrows that after the Indians were gone and he could raise up and examine himself, he could not restrain his tears, for his clothes were completely ruined.

The most trustworthy tradition avers, however, that only one man, a person named Babbitt, survived the massacre, and he was desperately wounded. He dragged himself on his hands and knee (for one leg was broken) to a station several miles away. He did it during portions of two nights, lying concealed one day and part of another, and for more than forty hours suffering unimaginable anguish from hunger, thirst and bodily pain. The Indians robbed the coach of everything it contained, including quite an amount of treasure.

Chapter IX

W<small>E</small> <small>PASSED</small> Fort Laramie in the night, and on the seventh morning out we found ourselves in the Black Hills, with Laramie Peak at our elbow (apparently) looming vast and solitary—a deep, dark, rich indigo blue in hue, so portentously did the old colossus frown under his beetling brows of storm-cloud. He was thirty or forty miles away, in reality, but he only seemed removed a little beyond the low ridge at our right. We breakfasted at Horse-Shoe Station, six hundred and seventy-six miles out from St. Joseph. We had now reached a hostile Indian country, and during the afternoon we passed Laparelle Station, and enjoyed great discomfort all the time we were in the neighborhood, being aware that many of the trees we dashed by at arm's length concealed a lurking Indian or two. During the preceding night an ambushed savage had sent a bullet through the pony-rider's jacket, but he had ridden on, just the same, because pony-riders were not allowed to stop and inquire into such things except when killed. As long as they had life enough left in them they had to stick to the horse and ride, even if the Indians had been waiting for them a week, and were entirely out of patience. About two hours and a half before we arrived at Laparelle Station, the keeper in charge of it had fired four times at an Indian, but he said with an injured air that the Indian had "skipped around so's to spile everything—and ammunition's blamed skurse, too." The most natural inference conveyed by his manner of speaking was, that in "skipping around," the Indian had taken an unfair advantage. The coach we were in had a neat hole through its front—a reminiscence of its last trip through this region. The bullet that made it wounded the driver slightly, but he did not mind it much. He said the place to keep a man "huffy" was down on the Southern Overland, among the Apaches, before the company moved the stage-line up on the northern route. He said the Apaches used to annoy him all the time down there, and that he came as near as anything to starving to death in the midst of abundance, because they kept him so leaky with bullet holes that he "couldn't hold his vittles." This person's statements were not generally believed.

We shut the blinds down very tightly that first night in the hostile Indian country, and lay on our arms. We slept on them some, but most of the time we only lay on them. We did not talk much, but kept quiet and listened. It was an inky-black night, and occasionally rainy. We were among woods and rocks, hills and gorges—so shut in, in fact, that when we peeped through a chink in a curtain, we could discern nothing. The driver and conductor on top were still, too, or only spoke at long intervals, in low tones, as is the way of men in the midst of invisible dangers. We listened to rain-drops pattering on the roof; and the grinding of the wheels through the muddy gravel; and the low wailing of the wind; and all the time we had that absurd sense upon us, inseparable from travel at night in a close-curtained vehicle, the sense of remaining perfectly still in one place, notwithstanding the jolting and swaying of the vehicle, the trampling of the horses, and the grinding of the wheels. We listened a long time, with intent faculties and bated breath; every time one of us would relax, and draw a long sigh of relief and start to say something, a comrade would be sure to utter a sudden "Hark!" and instantly the experimenter was rigid and listening again. So the tiresome minutes and decades of minutes dragged away, until at last our tense forms filmed over with a dulled consciousness, and we slept, if one might call such a condition by so strong a name—for it was a sleep set with a hair-trigger. It was a sleep seething and teeming with a weird and distressful confusion of shreds and fag-ends of dreams—a sleep that was a chaos. Presently, dreams and sleep and the sullen hush of the night were startled by a ringing report, and cloven by *such* a long, wild, agonizing shriek! Then we heard—ten steps from the stage—

"Help! help! help!" [It was our driver's voice.]

"Kill him! Kill him like a dog!"

"I'm being murdered! Will no man lend me a pistol?"

"Look out! head him off! head him off!"

[Two pistol shots; a confusion of voices and the trampling of many feet, as if a crowd were closing and surging together around some object; several heavy, dull blows, as with a club; a voice that said appealingly, "Don't, gentlemen, please don't—I'm a dead man!" Then a fainter groan, and another blow, and away sped the stage into the darkness, and left the grisly mystery behind us.]

What a startle it was! Eight seconds would amply cover the time it occupied—maybe even five would do it. We only had time to plunge at a curtain and unbuckle and unbutton part of it in an awkward and hindering flurry, when our whip cracked sharply overhead, and we went rumbling and thundering away, down a mountain "grade."

We fed on that mystery the rest of the night—what was left of it, for it was waning fast. It had to remain a present mystery, for all we could get from the conductor in answer to our hails was something that sounded, through the clatter of the wheels, like "Tell you in the morning!"

So we lit our pipes and opened the corner of a curtain for a chimney, and lay there in the dark, listening to each other's story of how he first felt and how many thousand Indians he first thought had hurled themselves upon us, and what his remembrance of the subsequent sounds was, and the order of their occurrence. And we theorized, too, but there was never a theory that would account for our driver's voice being out there, not yet account for his Indian murderers talking such good English, if they *were* Indians.

So we chatted and smoked the rest of the night comfortably away, our boding anxiety being somehow marvelously dissipated by the real presence of something to be anxious *about*.

We never did get much satisfaction about that dark occurrence. All that we could make out of the odds and ends of the information we gathered in the morning, was that the disturbance occurred at a station; that we changed drivers there, and that the driver that got off there had been talking roughly about some of the outlaws that infested the region ("for there wasn't a man around there but had a price on his head and didn't dare show himself in the settlements," the conductor said); he had talked roughly about these characters, and ought to have "drove up there with his pistol cocked and

ready on the seat alongside of him, and begun business himself, because any softy would know they would be laying for
him."

That was all we could gather, and we could see that neither
the conductor nor the new driver were much concerned
about the matter. They plainly had little respect for a man
who would deliver offensive opinions of people and then be
so simple as to come into their presence unprepared to "back
his judgment," as they pleasantly phrased the killing of any
fellow-being who did not like said opinions. And likewise
they plainly had a contempt for the man's poor discretion in
venturing to rouse the wrath of such utterly reckless wild
beasts as those outlaws—and the conductor added:

"I tell you it's as much as Slade himself wants to do!"

This remark created an entire revolution in my curiosity. I
cared nothing now about the Indians, and even lost interest
in the murdered driver. There was such magic in that name,
SLADE! Day or night, now, I stood always ready to drop any
subject in hand, to listen to something new about Slade and
his ghastly exploits. Even before we got to Overland City, we
had begun to hear about Slade and his "division" (for he was
a "division-agent") on the Overland; and from the hour we
had left Overland City we had heard drivers and conductors
talk about only three things—"Californy," the Nevada silver
mines, and this desperado Slade. And a deal the most of the
talk was about Slade. We had gradually come to have a realizing sense of the fact that Slade was a man whose heart and
hands and soul were steeped in the blood of offenders against
his dignity; a man who awfully avenged all injuries, affronts,
insults or slights, of whatever kind—on the spot if he could,
years afterward if lack of earlier opportunity compelled it; a
man whose hate tortured him day and night till vengeance
appeased it—and not an ordinary vengeance either, but his
enemy's absolute death—nothing less; a man whose face
would light up with a terrible joy when he surprised a foe
and had him at a disadvantage. A high and efficient servant
of the Overland, an outlaw among outlaws and yet their relentless scourge, Slade was at once the most bloody, the most
dangerous and the most valuable citizen that inhabited the
savage fastnesses of the mountains.

Chapter X

REALLY AND TRULY, two thirds of the talk of drivers and conductors had been about this man Slade, ever since the day before we reached Julesburg. In order that the eastern reader may have a clear conception of what a Rocky Mountain desperado is, in his highest state of development, I will reduce all this mass of overland gossip to one straightforward narrative, and present it in the following shape:

Slade was born in Illinois, of good parentage. At about twenty-six years of age he killed a man in a quarrel and fled the country. At St. Joseph, Missouri, he joined one of the early California-bound emigrant trains, and was given the post of train-master. One day on the plains he had an angry dispute with one of his wagon-drivers, and both drew their revolvers. But the driver was the quicker artist, and had his weapon cocked first. So Slade said it was a pity to waste life on so small a matter, and proposed that the pistols be thrown on the ground and the quarrel settled by a fist-fight. The unsuspecting driver agreed, and threw down his pistol—whereupon Slade laughed at his simplicity, and shot him dead!

He made his escape, and lived a wild life for awhile, dividing his time between fighting Indians and avoiding an Illinois sheriff, who had been sent to arrest him for his first murder. It is said that in one Indian battle he killed three savages with his own hand, and afterward cut their ears off and sent them, with his compliments, to the chief of the tribe.

Slade soon gained a name for fearless resolution, and this was sufficient merit to procure for him the important post of overland division-agent at Julesburg, in place of Mr. Jules, removed. For some time previously, the company's horses had been frequently stolen, and the coaches delayed, by gangs of outlaws, who were wont to laugh at the idea of any man's having the temerity to resent such outrages. Slade resented them promptly. The outlaws soon found that the new agent was a man who did not fear anything that breathed the breath of life. He made short work of all offenders. The result was that delays ceased, the company's property was let alone, and no matter what happened or who suffered, Slade's coaches went through, every time! True, in order to bring about this wholesome change, Slade had to kill several men—some say three, others say four, and others six—but the world was the richer for their loss. The first prominent difficulty he had was with the ex-agent Jules, who bore the reputation of being a reckless and desperate man himself. Jules hated Slade for supplanting him, and a good fair occasion for a fight was all he was waiting for. By and by Slade dared to employ a man whom Jules had once discharged. Next, Slade seized a team of stage-horses which he accused Jules of having driven off and hidden somewhere for his own use. War was declared, and for a day or two the two men walked warily about the streets, seeking each other, Jules armed with a double-barreled shot gun, and Slade with his history-creating revolver. Finally, as Slade stepped into a store, Jules poured the contents of his gun into him from behind the door. Slade was pluck, and Jules got several bad pistol wounds in return. Then both men fell, and were carried to their respective lodgings, both swearing that better aim should do deadlier work next time. Both were bed-ridden a long time, but Jules got on his feet first, and gathering his possessions together, packed them on a couple of mules, and fled to the Rocky Mountains to gather strength in safety against the day of reckoning. For many months he was not seen or heard of, and was gradually dropped out of the remembrance of all save Slade himself. But Slade was not the man to forget him. On the contrary, common report said that Slade kept a reward standing for his capture, dead or alive!

After awhile, seeing that Slade's energetic administration had restored peace and order to one of the worst divisions of the road, the overland stage company transferred him to the Rocky Ridge division in the Rocky Mountains, to see if he could perform a like miracle there. It was the very paradise of outlaws and desperadoes. There was absolutely no semblance of law there. Violence was the rule. Force was the only recognized authority. The commonest misunderstandings were settled on the spot with the revolver or the knife. Murders were done in open day, and with sparkling frequency, and nobody thought of inquiring into them. It was considered that the parties who did the killing had their private reasons for it; for other people to meddle would have been looked upon as indelicate. After a murder, all that Rocky Mountain etiquette required of a spectator was, that he should help the gentleman bury his game—otherwise his churlishness would surely be remembered against him the first time he killed a man himself and needed a neighborly turn in interring him.

Slade took up his residence sweetly and peacefully in the midst of this hive of horse-thieves and assassins, and the very first time one of them aired his insolent swaggerings in his presence he shot him dead! He began a raid on the outlaws, and in a singularly short space of time he had completely stopped their depredations on the stage stock, recovered a large number of stolen horses, killed several of the worst desperadoes of the district, and gained such a dread ascendancy over the rest that they respected him, admired him, feared him, obeyed him! He wrought the same marvelous change in the ways of the community that had marked his administration at Overland City. He captured two men who had stolen overland stock, and with his own hands he hanged them. He was supreme judge in his district, and he was jury and executioner likewise—and not only in the case of offences against his employers, but against passing emigrants as well. On one occasion some emigrants had their stock lost or stolen, and told Slade, who chanced to visit their camp. With a single companion he rode to a ranch, the owners of which he suspected, and opening the door, commenced firing, killing three, and wounding the fourth.

From a bloodthirstily interesting little Montana book* I take this paragraph:

While on the road, Slade held absolute sway. He would ride down to a station, get into a quarrel, turn the house out of windows, and maltreat the occupants most cruelly. The unfortunates had no means of redress, and were compelled to recuperate as best they could. On one of these occasions, it is said he killed the father of the fine little half-breed boy Jemmy, whom he adopted, and who lived with his widow after his execution. Stories of Slade's hanging men, and of innumerable assaults, shootings, stabbings and beatings, in which he was a principal actor, form part of the legends of the stage line. As

*"The Vigilantes of Montana," by Prof. Thos. J. Dimsdale.

for minor quarrels and shootings, it is absolutely certain that a minute history of Slade's life would be one long record of such practices.

Slade was a matchless marksman with a navy revolver. The
legends say that one morning at Rocky Ridge, when he was
feeling comfortable, he saw a man approaching who had offended him some days before—observe the fine memory he
had for matters like that—and, "Gentlemen," said Slade,
drawing, "it is a good twenty-yard shot—I'll clip the third
button on his coat!" Which he did. The bystanders all admired it. And they all attended the funeral, too.

On one occasion a man who kept a little whisky-shelf at the
station did something which angered Slade—and went and
made his will. A day or two afterward Slade came in and
called for some brandy. The man reached under the counter
(ostensibly to get a bottle—possibly to get something else),
but Slade smiled upon him that peculiarly bland and satisfied
smile of his which the neighbors had long ago learned to recognize as a death-warrant in disguise, and told him to "none
of that!—pass out the high-priced article." So the poor bar-
keeper had to turn his back and get the high-priced brandy
from the shelf; and when he faced around again he was looking into the muzzle of Slade's pistol. "And the next instant,"
added my informant, impressively, "he was one of the deadest
men that ever lived."

The stage-drivers and conductors told us that sometimes
Slade would leave a hated enemy wholly unmolested, unnoticed and unmentioned, for weeks together—had done it
once or twice at any rate. And some said they believed he did
it in order to lull the victims into unwatchfulness, so that he
could get the advantage of them, and others said they believed he saved up an enemy that way, just as a schoolboy
saves up a cake, and made the pleasure go as far as it would
by gloating over the anticipation. One of these cases was that
of a Frenchman who had offended Slade. To the surprise of
everybody Slade did not kill him on the spot, but let him
alone for a considerable time. Finally, however, he went to
the Frenchman's house very late one night, knocked, and
when his enemy opened the door, shot him dead—pushed
the corpse inside the door with his foot, set the house on fire

and burned up the dead man, his widow and three children! I heard this story from several different people, and they evidently believed what they were saying. It may be true, and it may not. "Give a dog a bad name," etc.

Slade was captured, once, by a party of men who intended to lynch him. They disarmed him, and shut him up in a strong log-house, and placed a guard over him. He prevailed on his captors to send for his wife, so that he might have a last interview with her. She was a brave, loving, spirited woman. She jumped on a horse and rode for life and death. When she arrived they let her in without searching her, and before the door could be closed she whipped out a couple of revolvers, and she and her lord marched forth defying the party. And then, under a brisk fire, they mounted double and galloped away unharmed!

In the fulness of time Slade's myrmidons captured his ancient enemy Jules, whom they found in a well-chosen hiding-place in the remote fastnesses of the mountains, gaining a precarious livelihood with his rifle. They brought him to Rocky Ridge, bound hand and foot, and deposited him in the middle of the cattle-yard with his back against a post. It is said that the pleasure that lit Slade's face when he heard of it was something fearful to contemplate. He examined his enemy to see that he was securely tied, and then went to bed, content to wait till morning before enjoying the luxury of killing him. Jules spent the night in the cattle-yard, and it is a region where warm nights are never known. In the morning Slade practised on him with his revolver, nipping the flesh here and there, and occasionally clipping off a finger, while Jules begged him to kill him outright and put him out of his misery. Finally Slade reloaded, and walking up close to his victim, made some characteristic remarks and then dispatched him. The body lay there half a day, nobody venturing to touch it without orders, and then Slade detailed a party and assisted at the burial himself. But he first cut off the dead man's ears and put them in his vest pocket, where he carried them for some time with great satisfaction. That is the story as I have frequently heard it told and seen it in print in California newspapers. It is doubtless correct in all essential particulars.

In due time we rattled up to a stage-station, and sat down to breakfast with a half-savage, half-civilized company of armed and bearded mountaineers, ranchmen and station employees. The most gentlemanly-appearing, quiet and affable officer we had yet found along the road in the Overland Company's service was the person who sat at the head of the table, at my elbow. Never youth stared and shivered as I did when I heard them call him SLADE!

Here was romance, and I sitting face to face with it!— looking upon it—touching it—hobnobbing with it, as it were! Here, right by my side, was the actual ogre who, in fights and brawls and various ways, *had taken the lives of twenty-six human beings*, or all men lied about him! I suppose I was the proudest stripling that ever traveled to see strange lands and wonderful people.

He was so friendly and so gentle-spoken that I warmed to him in spite of his awful history. It was hardly possible to realize that this pleasant person was the pitiless scourge of the outlaws, the raw-head-and-bloody-bones the nursing mothers of the mountains terrified their children with. And to this day I can remember nothing remarkable about Slade except that his face was rather broad across the cheek bones, and that the cheek bones were low and the lips peculiarly thin and straight. But that was enough to leave something of an effect upon me, for since then I seldom see a face possessing those characteristics without fancying that the owner of it is a dangerous man.

The coffee ran out. At least it was reduced to one tin-cupful, and Slade was about to take it when he saw that my cup was empty. He politely offered to fill it, but although I wanted it, I politely declined. I was afraid he had not killed anybody that morning, and might be needing diversion. But still with firm politeness he insisted on filling my cup, and said I had traveled all night and better deserved it than he— and while he talked he placidly poured the fluid, to the last drop. I thanked him and drank it, but it gave me no comfort, for I could not feel sure that he would not be sorry, presently, that he had given it away, and proceed to kill me to distract his thoughts from the loss. But nothing of the kind occurred. We left him with only twenty-six dead people to account for, and I felt a tranquil satisfaction in the thought that in so judiciously taking care of No. 1 at that breakfast-table I had pleasantly escaped being No. 27. Slade came out to the coach and saw us off, first ordering certain reärrangements of the mail-bags for our comfort, and then we took leave of him, satisfied that we should hear of him again, some day, and wondering in what connection.

Chapter XI

AND SURE ENOUGH, two or three years afterward, we did hear of him again. News came to the Pacific coast that the Vigilance Committee in Montana (whither Slade had removed from Rocky Ridge) had hanged him. I find an account of the affair in the thrilling little book I quoted a paragraph from in the last chapter—"The Vigilantes of Montana; being a Reliable Account of the Capture, Trial and Execution of Henry Plummer's Notorious Road Agent Band: By Prof. Thos. J. Dimsdale, Virginia City, M. T." Mr. Dimsdale's chapter is well worth reading, as a specimen of how the people of the frontier deal with criminals when the courts of law prove inefficient. Mr. Dimsdale makes two remarks about Slade, both of which are accurately descriptive, and one of which is exceedingly picturesque: "Those who saw him in his natural state only, would pronounce him to be a kind husband, a most hospitable host and a courteous gentleman; on the contrary, those who met him when maddened with liquor and surrounded by a gang of armed roughs, would pronounce him a fiend incarnate." And this: "From Fort Kearney, west, he was feared *a great deal more than the Almighty*." For compactness, simplicity and vigor of expression, I will "back" that sentence against anything in literature. Mr. Dimsdale's narrative is as follows. In all places where italics occur, they are mine:

After the execution of the five men on the 14th of January, the Vigilantes considered that their work was nearly ended. They had freed the country of highwaymen and murderers to a great extent, and they determined that in the absence of the regular civil authority they would establish a People's Court where all offenders should be tried by judge and jury. This was the nearest approach to social order that the circumstances permitted, and, though strict legal authority was wanting, yet the people were firmly determined to maintain its efficiency, and to enforce its decrees. It may here be mentioned that the overt act which was the last round on the fatal ladder leading to the scaffold on which Slade perished, *was the tearing in pieces and stamping upon a writ of this court, followed by his arrest of the Judge, Alex. Davis, by authority of a presented Derringer, and with his own hands.*

J. A. Slade was himself, we have been informed, a Vigilante; he openly boasted of it, and said he knew all that they knew. He was never accused, or even suspected, of either murder or robbery, committed in this Territory (the latter crime was never laid to his charge, in any place); but that he had killed several men in other localities was notorious, and his bad reputation in this respect was a most powerful argument in determining his fate, when he was finally arrested for the offence above mentioned. On returning from Milk River he became more and more addicted to drinking, until at last it was a common feat for him and his friends to "take the town." He and a couple of his dependents might often be seen on one horse, galloping through the streets, shouting and yelling, firing revolvers, etc. On many occasions he would ride his horse into stores, break up bars, toss the scales out of doors and use most insulting language to parties present. Just previous to the day of his arrest, he had given a fearful beating to one of his followers; but such was his influence over them that the man wept bitterly at the gallows, and begged for his life with all his power. *It had become quite common, when Slade was on a spree, for the shop-keepers and citizens to close the stores and put out all the lights*; being fearful of some outrage at his hands. For his wanton destruction of goods and furniture, he was always ready to pay, when sober, if he had money; but there were not a few who regarded payment as small satisfaction for the outrage, and these men were his personal enemies.

From time to time Slade received warnings from men that he well knew would not deceive him, of the certain end of his conduct. There was not a moment, for weeks previous to his arrest, in which the public did not expect to hear of some bloody outrage. The dread of his very name, and the presence of the armed band of hangers-on who followed him alone prevented a resistance which must certainly have ended in the instant murder or mutilation of the opposing party.

Slade was frequently arrested by order of the court whose organization we have described, and had treated it with respect by paying one or two fines and promising to pay the rest when he had money; but in the transaction that occurred at this crisis, he forgot even this caution, and goaded by passion and the hatred of restraint, he sprang into the embrace of death.

Slade had been drunk and "cutting up" all night. He and his companions had made the town a perfect hell. In the morning, J. M. Fox, the sheriff, met him, arrested him, took him into court and commenced reading a warrant that he had for his arrest, by way or arraignment. He became uncontrollably furious, and *seizing the writ, he tore it up, threw it on the ground and stamped upon it.* The clicking of the locks of his companions' revolvers was instantly heard, and a crisis was expected. The sheriff did not attempt his retention; but being at least as prudent as he was valiant, he succumbed, leaving Slade the *master of the situation and the conqueror and ruler of the courts, law and law-makers.* This was a declaration of war, and was so accepted. The Vigilance Committee now felt that the question of social order and the preponderance of the law-abiding citizens had then and there to be decided. They knew the character of Slade, and they were well aware that they must submit to his rule without murmur, or else that he must be dealt with in such fashion as would prevent his being able to wreak his vengeance on the committee, who could never have hoped to live in the Territory secure from outrage or death, and who could never leave it without encountering his friends, whom his victory would have emboldened and stimulated to a pitch that would have rendered them reckless of consequences. The day previous he had ridden into Dorris's store, and on being requested to leave, he drew his revolver and threatened to kill the gentleman who spoke to him. Another saloon he had led his horse into, and buying a bottle of wine, he tried to make the animal drink it. This was not considered an uncommon performance, as he had often entered saloons and commenced firing at the lamps, causing a wild stampede.

A leading member of the committee met Slade, and informed him in the quiet, earnest manner of one who feels the importance of what he is saying: "Slade, get your horse at once, and go home, or there will be —— to pay." Slade started and took a long look, with his dark and piercing eyes, at the gentleman. "What do you mean?" said he. "You have no right to ask me what I mean," was the quiet reply, "get your horse at once, and remember what I tell you." After a short pause he promised to do so, and actually got into the saddle; but, being still intoxicated, he began calling aloud to one after another of his friends, and at last seemed to have forgotten the warning he had received and became again uproarious, shouting the name of a well-known courtezan in company with those of two men whom he considered heads of the committee, as a sort of challenge; perhaps, however, as a simple act of bravado. It seems probable that the intimation of personal danger he had received had not been forgotten entirely; though fatally for him, he took a foolish way of showing his remembrance of it. He sought out Alexander Davis, the Judge of the Court, and drawing a cocked Derringer, he presented it at his head, and told him that he should hold him as a hostage for his own safety. As the judge stood perfectly quiet, and offered no resistance to his captor, no further outrage followed on this score. Previous to this, on account of the critical state of affairs, the committee had met, and at last resolved to arrest him. His execution had not been agreed upon, and, at that time, would have been negatived, most assuredly. A messenger rode down to Nevada to inform the leading men of what was on hand, as it was desirable to show that there was a feeling of unanimity on the subject, all along the gulch.

The miners turned out almost *en masse*, leaving their work and forming in solid column, about six hundred strong, armed to the teeth, they marched up to Virginia. The leader of the body well knew the temper of his men on the subject. He spurred on ahead of them, and hastily called a meeting of the executive, he told them plainly that the miners meant "business," and that, if they came up, they would not stand in the street to be shot down by Slade's friends; but that they would take him and hang him. The meeting was small, as the Virginia men were loath to act at all. This momentous announcement of the feeling of the Lower Town was made to a cluster of men, who were deliberating behind a wagon, at the rear of a store on Main street.

The committee were most unwilling to proceed to extremities. All the duty they had ever performed seemed as nothing to the task before them; but they had to decide, and that quickly. It was finally agreed that if the whole body of the miners were of the opinion that he should be hanged, that the committee left it in their hands to deal with him. Off, at hot speed, rode the leader of the Nevada men to join his command.

Slade had found out what was intended, and the news sobered him instantly. He went into P. S. Pfouts' store, where Davis was, and apologized for his conduct, saying that he would take it all back.

The head of the column now wheeled into Wallace street and marched up at quick time. Halting in front of the store, the executive officer of the committee stepped forward and arrested Slade, who was at once informed of his doom, and inquiry was made as to whether he had any business to settle. Several parties spoke to him on the subject; but to all such inquiries he turned a deaf ear, being entirely absorbed in the terrifying reflections on his own awful position. He never ceased his entreaties for life, and to see his dear wife. The unfortunate lady referred to, between whom and Slade there existed a warm affection, was at this time living at their ranch on the Madison. She was possessed of considerable personal attractions; tall, well-formed, of graceful carriage, pleasing manners, and was, withal, an accomplished horsewoman.

A messenger from Slade rode at full speed to inform her of her husband's arrest. In an instant she was in the saddle, and with all the energy that love and despair could lend to an ardent temperament and a strong physique, she urged her fleet charger over the twelve miles of rough and rocky ground that intervened between her and the object of her passionate devotion.

Meanwhile a party of volunteers had made the necessary preparations for the execution, in the valley traversed by the branch. Beneath the site of Pfouts and Russell's stone building there was a corral, the gate-posts of which were strong and high. Across the top was laid a beam, to which the rope was fastened, and a dry-goods box served for the platform. To this place Slade was marched, surrounded by a guard, composing the best armed and most numerous force that has ever appeared in Montana Territory.

The doomed man had so exhausted himself by tears, prayers and lamentations, that he had scarcely strength left to stand under the fatal beam. He repeatedly exclaimed, "My God! my God! must I die? Oh, my dear wife!"

On the return of the fatigue party, they encountered some friends of Slade, staunch and reliable citizens and members of the committee, but who were personally attached to the condemned. On hearing of his sentence, one of them, a stout-hearted man, pulled out his handkerchief and walked away, weeping like a child. Slade still begged to see his wife, most piteously, and it seemed hard to deny his request; but the bloody consequences that were sure to follow the inevitable attempt at a rescue, that her presence and entreaties would have certainly incited, forbade the granting of his request. Several gentlemen were sent for to see him, in his last moments, one of whom (Judge Davis) made a short address to the people; but in such low tones as to be inaudible, save to a few in his immediate vicinity. One of his friends, after exhausting his powers of entreaty, threw off his coat and declared that the prisoner could not be hanged until he himself was killed. A hundred guns were instantly leveled at him; whereupon he turned and fled; but, being brought back, he was compelled to resume his coat, and to give a promise of future peaceable demeanor.

Scarcely a leading man in Virginia could be found, though numbers of the citizens joined the ranks of the guard when the arrest was made. All lamented the stern necessity which dictated the execution.

Everything being ready, the command was given, "Men, do your duty," and the box being instantly slipped from beneath his feet, he died almost instantaneously.

The body was cut down and carried to the Virginia Hotel, where, in a darkened room, it was scarcely laid out, when the unfortunate and bereaved companion of the deceased arrived, at headlong speed, to find that all was over, and that she was a widow. Her grief and heart-piercing cries were terrible evidences of the depth of her attachment for her lost husband, and a considerable period elapsed before she could regain the command of her excited feelings.

There is something about the desperado-nature that is wholly unaccountable—at least it looks unaccountable. It is this. The true desperado is gifted with splendid courage, and yet he will take the most infamous advantage of his enemy; armed and free, he will stand up before a host and fight until he is shot all to pieces, and yet when he is under the gallows and helpless he will cry and plead like a child. Words are cheap, and it is easy to call Slade a coward (all executed men who do not "die game" are promptly called cowards by unreflecting people), and when we read of Slade that he "had so exhausted himself by tears, prayers and lamentations, that he had scarcely strength left to stand under the fatal beam," the disgraceful word suggests itself in a moment—yet in frequently defying and inviting the vengeance of banded Rocky Mountain cut-throats by shooting down their comrades and leaders, and never offering to hide or fly, Slade showed that he was a man of peerless bravery. No coward would dare that. Many a notorious coward, many a chicken-livered poltroon, coarse, brutal, degraded, has made his dying speech without a quaver in his voice and been swung into eternity with what looked liked the calmest fortitude, and so we are justified in believing, from the low intellect of such a creature, that it was not *moral* courage that enabled him to do it. Then, if moral courage is not the requisite quality, what could it have been that this stout-hearted Slade lacked?—this bloody, desperate, kindly-mannered, urbane gentleman, who never hesitated to warn his most ruffianly enemies that he would kill them whenever or wherever he came across them next! I think it is a conundrum worth investigating.

Chapter XII

J UST BEYOND the breakfast-station we overtook a Mormon
emigrant train of thirty-three wagons; and tramping
wearily along and driving their herd of loose cows, were dozens of coarse-clad and sad-looking men, women and children,
who had walked as they were walking now, day after day for
eight lingering weeks, and in that time had compassed the
distance our stage had come in *eight days and three hours*—
seven hundred and ninety-eight miles! They were dusty and
uncombed, hatless, bonnetless and ragged, and they did look
so tired!

After breakfast, we bathed in Horse Creek, a (previously)
limpid, sparkling stream—an appreciated luxury, for it was
very seldom that our furious coach halted long enough for an
indulgence of that kind. We changed horses ten or twelve
times in every twenty-four hours—changed mules, rather—
six mules—and did it nearly every time in *four minutes*. It was
lively work. As our coach rattled up to each station six harnessed mules stepped gayly from the stable; and in the twinkling of an eye, almost, the old team was out, and the new
one in and we off and away again.

During the afternoon we passed Sweetwater Creek, Independence Rock, Devil's Gate and the Devil's Gap. The latter
were wild specimens of rugged scenery, and full of interest—
we were in the heart of the Rocky Mountains, now. And we also
passed by "Alkali" or "Soda Lake," and we woke up to the
fact that our journey had stretched a long way across the
world when the driver said that the Mormons often came
there from Great Salt Lake City to haul away saleratus. He
said that a few days gone by they had shoveled up enough
pure saleratus from the ground (it was a *dry* lake) to load two
wagons, and that when they got these two wagon-loads of a
drug that cost them nothing, to Salt Lake, they could sell it
for twenty-five cents a pound.

In the night we sailed by a most notable curiosity, and one
we had been hearing a good deal about for a day or two, and
were suffering to see. This was what might be called a natural
ice-house. It was August, now, and sweltering weather in the

daytime, yet at one of the stations the men could scrape the soil on the hill-side under the lee of a range of boulders, and at a depth of six inches cut out pure blocks of ice—hard, compactly frozen, and clear as crystal!

Toward dawn we got under way again, and presently as we sat with raised curtains enjoying our early-morning smoke and contemplating the first splendor of the rising sun as it swept down the long array of mountain peaks, flushing and gilding crag after crag and summit after summit, as if the invisible Creator reviewed his gray veterans and they saluted with a smile, we hove in sight of South Pass City. The hotel-keeper, the postmaster, the blacksmith, the mayor, the constable, the city marshal and the principal citizen and property holder, all came out and greeted us cheerily, and we gave him good day. He gave us a little Indian news, and a little Rocky Mountain news, and we gave him some Plains information in return. He then retired to his lonely grandeur and we climbed on up among the bristling peaks and the ragged clouds. South Pass City consisted of four log cabins, one of which was unfinished, and the gentleman with all those offices and titles was the chiefest of the ten citizens of the place. Think of hotel-keeper, postmaster, blacksmith, mayor, constable, city marshal and principal citizen all condensed into one person and crammed into one skin. Bemis said he was "a perfect Allen's revolver of dignities." And he said that if he were to die as postmaster, or as blacksmith, or as postmaster and blacksmith both, the people might stand it; but if he were to die all over, it would be a frightful loss to the community.

Two miles beyond South Pass City we saw for the first time that mysterious marvel which all Western untraveled boys have heard of and fully believe in, but are sure to be astounded at when they see it with their own eyes, nevertheless—banks of snow in dead summer time. We were now far up toward the sky, and knew all the time that we must presently encounter lofty summits clad in the "eternal snow" which was so common-place a matter of mention in books, and yet when I did see it glittering in the sun on stately domes in the distance and knew the month was August and that my coat was hanging up because it was too warm to wear it, I was full as much amazed as if I never had heard of snow in August before. Truly, "seeing is believing"—and many a man lives a long life through, *thinking* he believes certain universally received and well established things, and yet never suspects that if he were confronted by those things once, he would discover that he did not *really* believe them before, but only thought he believed them.

In a little while quite a number of peaks swung into view with long claws of glittering snow clasping them; and with here and there, in the shade, down the mountain side, a little solitary patch of snow looking no larger than a lady's pocket-handkerchief, but being in reality as large as a "public square."

And now, at last, we were fairly in the renowned SOUTH PASS, and whirling gayly along high above the common world. We were perched upon the extreme summit of the great range of the Rocky Mountains, toward which we had been climbing, patiently climbing, ceaselessly climbing, for days and nights together—and about us was gathered a convention of Nature's kings that stood ten, twelve, and even thirteen thousand feet high—grand old fellows who would have to stoop to see Mount Washington, in the twilight. We were in such an airy elevation above the creeping populations of the earth, that now and then when the obstructing crags stood out of the way it seemed that we could look around and abroad and contemplate the whole great globe, with its dissolving views of mountains, seas and continents stretching away through the mystery of the summer haze.

As a general thing the Pass was more suggestive of a valley than a suspension bridge in the clouds—but it strongly suggested the latter at one spot. At that place the upper third of one or two majestic purple domes projected above our level on either hand and gave us a sense of a hidden great deep of mountains and plains and valleys down about their bases which we fancied we might see if we could step to the edge and look over. These Sultans of the fastnesses were turbaned with tumbled volumes of cloud, which shredded away from time to time and drifted off fringed and torn, trailing their continents of shadow after them; and catching presently on an intercepting peak, wrapped it about and brooded there—then shredded away again and left the purple peak, as they had left the purple domes, downy and white with new-laid snow. In passing, these monstrous rags of cloud hung low and swept along right over the spectator's head, swinging their tatters so nearly in his face that his impulse was to shrink when they came closest. In the one place I speak of, one could look below him upon a world of diminishing crags and canyons leading down, down, and away to a vague plain with a thread in it which was a road, and bunches of feathers in it which were trees,—a pretty picture sleeping in the sunlight— but with a darkness stealing over it and glooming its features deeper and deeper under the frown of a coming storm; and then, while no film or shadow marred the noon brightness of his high perch, he could watch the tempest break forth down there and see the lightnings leap from crag to crag and the sheeted rain drive along the canyon-sides, and hear the thunders peal and crash and roar. We had this spectacle; a familiar one to many, but to us a novelty.

We bowled along cheerily, and presently, at the very summit (though it had been all summit to us, and all equally level, for half an hour or more), we came to a spring which spent its water through two outlets and sent it in opposite directions. The conductor said that one of those streams which we were looking at, was just starting on a journey westward to the Gulf of California and the Pacific Ocean, through hundreds and even thousands of miles of desert solitudes. He said that the other was just leaving its home among the snow-peaks on a similar journey eastward—and we knew that long after we should have forgotten the simple rivulet it would still be plodding its patient way down the mountain sides, and canyon-beds, and between the banks of the Yellowstone; and by and by would join the broad Missouri and flow through unknown plains and deserts and unvisited wildernesses; and add a long and troubled pilgrimage among snags and wrecks and sand-bars; and enter the Mississippi, touch the wharves of St. Louis and still drift on, traversing shoals and rocky channels, then endless chains of bottomless and ample bends, walled with unbroken forests, then mysterious byways and secret passages among woody islands, then the chained bends again, bordered with wide levels of shining sugar-cane in place of the sombre forests; then by New Orleans and still other chains of bends—and finally, after two long months of daily and nightly harassment, excitement, enjoyment, adventure, and awful peril of parched throats, pumps and evaporation, pass the Gulf and enter into its rest upon the bosom of the tropic sea, never to look upon its snow-peaks again or regret them.

I freighted a leaf with a mental message for the friends at home, and dropped it in the stream. But I put no stamp on it and it was held for postage somewhere.

On the summit we overtook an emigrant train of many wagons, many tired men and women, and many a disgusted sheep and cow. In the wofully dusty horseman in charge of the expedition I recognized John ——. Of all persons in the world to meet on top of the Rocky Mountains thousands of miles from home, he was the last one I should have looked for. We were school-boys together and warm friends for years. But a boyish prank of mine had disruptured this friendship and it had never been renewed. The act of which I speak was this. I had been accustomed to visit occasionally an editor whose room was in the third story of a building and overlooked the street. One day this editor gave me a watermelon which I made preparations to devour on the spot, but chancing to look out of the window, I saw John standing directly under it and an irresistible desire came upon me to drop the melon on his head, which I immediately did. I was the loser, for it spoiled the melon, and John never forgave me and we dropped all intercourse and parted, but now met again under these circumstances.

We recognized each other simultaneously, and hands were grasped as warmly as if no coldness had ever existed between us, and no allusion was made to any. All animosities were buried and the simple fact of meeting a familiar face in that isolated spot so far from home, was sufficient to make us forget all things but pleasant ones, and we parted again with sincere "good-byes" and "God bless you" from both.

We had been climbing up the long shoulders of the Rocky Mountains for many tedious hours—we started *down* them, now. And we went spinning away at a round rate too.

We left the snowy Wind River Mountains and Uinta Mountains behind, and sped away, always through splendid

scenery but occasionally through long ranks of white skeletons of mules and oxen—monuments of the huge emigration
of other days—and here and there were up-ended boards or
small piles of stones which the driver said marked the resting-
place of more precious remains. It was the loneliest land for
a grave! A land given over to the cayote and the raven—
which is but another name for desolation and utter solitude.
On damp, murky nights, these scattered skeletons gave forth
a soft, hideous glow, like very faint spots of moonlight star-
ring the vague desert. It was because of the phosphorus in
the bones. But no scientific explanation could keep a body
from shivering when he drifted by one of those ghostly lights
and knew that a skull held it.

At midnight it began to rain, and I never saw anything like
it—indeed, I did not even see this, for it was too dark. We
fastened down the curtains and even caulked them with clothing, but the rain streamed in in twenty places, notwithstanding. There was no escape. If one moved his feet out of a
stream, he brought his body under one; and if he moved his
body he caught one somewhere else. If he struggled out of
the drenched blankets and sat up, he was bound to get one
down the back of his neck. Meantime the stage was wandering about a plain with gaping gullies in it, for the driver could
not see an inch before his face nor keep the road, and the
storm pelted so pitilessly that there was no keeping the horses
still. With the first abatement the conductor turned out with
lanterns to look for the road, and the first dash he made was
into a chasm about fourteen feet deep, his lantern following
like a meteor. As soon as he touched bottom he sang out
frantically:

"Don't come here!"

To which the driver, who was looking over the precipice
where he had disappeared, replied, with an injured air:
"Think I'm a dam fool?"

The conductor was more than an hour finding the road—
a matter which showed us how far we had wandered and
what chances we had been taking. He traced our wheel-tracks
to the imminent verge of danger, in two places. I have always
been glad that we were not killed that night. I do not know
any particular reason, but I have always been glad.

In the morning, the tenth day out, we crossed Green River, a fine, large, limpid stream—stuck in it, with the water just up to the top of our mail-bed, and waited till extra teams were put on to haul us up the steep bank. But it was nice cool water, and besides it could not find any fresh place on us to wet.

At the Green River station we had breakfast—hot biscuits, fresh antelope steaks, and coffee—the only decent meal we tasted between the United States and Great Salt Lake City, and the only one we were ever really thankful for. Think of the monotonous execrableness of the thirty that went before it, to leave this one simple breakfast looming up in my memory like a shot-tower after all these years have gone by!

At five P.M. we reached Fort Bridger, one hundred and seventeen miles from the South Pass, and one thousand and twenty-five miles from St. Joseph. Fifty-two miles further on, near the head of Echo Canyon, we met sixty United States soldiers from Camp Floyd. The day before, they had fired upon three hundred or four hundred Indians, whom they supposed gathered together for no good purpose. In the fight that had ensued, four Indians were captured, and the main body chased four miles, but nobody killed. This looked like business. We had a notion to get out and join the sixty soldiers, but upon reflecting that there were four hundred of the Indians, we concluded to go on and join the Indians.

Echo Canyon is twenty miles long. It was like a long, smooth, narrow street, with a gradual descending grade, and shut in by enormous perpendicular walls of coarse conglomerate, four hundred feet high in many places, and turreted like mediæval castles. This was the most faultless piece of road in the mountains, and the driver said he would "let his team out." He did, and if the Pacific express trains whiz through there now any faster than we did then in the stage-coach, I envy the passengers the exhilaration of it. We fairly seemed to pick up our wheels and fly—and the mail matter was lifted up free from everything and held in solution! I am not given to exaggeration, and when I say a thing I mean it.

However, time presses. At four in the afternoon we arrived on the summit of Big Mountain, fifteen miles from Salt Lake City, when all the world was glorified with the setting sun, and the most stupendous panorama of mountain peaks yet encountered burst on our sight. We looked out upon this sublime spectacle from under the arch of a brilliant rainbow! Even the overland stage-driver stopped his horses and gazed!

Half an hour or an hour later, we changed horses, and took supper with a Mormon "Destroying Angel." "Destroying Angels," as I understand it, are Latter-Day Saints who are set apart by the Church to conduct permanent disappearances of obnoxious citizens. I had heard a deal about these Mormon Destroying Angels and the dark and bloody deeds they had done, and when I entered this one's house I had my shudder all ready. But alas for all our romances, he was nothing but a loud, profane, offensive, old blackguard! He was murderous enough, possibly, to fill the bill of a Destroyer, but would you have *any* kind of an Angel devoid of dignity? Could you abide an Angel in an unclean shirt and no suspenders? Could you respect an Angel with a horse-laugh and a swagger like a buccaneer?

There were other blackguards present—comrades of this one. And there was one person that looked like a gentleman—Heber C. Kimball's son, tall and well made, and thirty years old, perhaps. A lot of slatternly women flitted hither and thither in a hurry, with coffee-pots, plates of bread, and other appurtenances to supper, and these were said to be the wives of the Angel—or some of them, at least. And of course they were; for if they had been hired "help" they would not have let an angel from above storm and swear at them as he did, let alone one from the place this one hailed from.

This was our first experience of the western "peculiar institution," and it was not very prepossessing. We did not tarry long to observe it, but hurried on to the home of the Latter-Day Saints, the stronghold of the prophets, the capital of the only absolute monarch in America—Great Salt Lake City. As the night closed in we took sanctuary in the Salt Lake House and unpacked our baggage.

Chapter XIII

WE HAD a fine supper, of the freshest meats and fowls and vegetables—a great variety and as great abundance. We walked about the streets some, afterward, and glanced in at shops and stores; and there was fascination in surreptitiously staring at every creature we took to be a Mormon. This was fairy-land to us, to all intents and purposes—a land of enchantment, and goblins, and awful mystery. We felt a curiosity to ask every child how many mothers it had, and if it could tell them apart; and we experienced a thrill every time a dwelling-house door opened and shut as we passed, disclosing a glimpse of human heads and backs and shoulders—for we so longed to have a good satisfying look at a Mormon family in all its comprehensive ampleness, disposed in the customary concentric rings of its home circle.

By and by the Acting Governor of the Territory introduced us to other "Gentiles," and we spent a sociable hour with them. "Gentiles" are people who are not Mormons. Our fellow-passenger, Bemis, took care of himself, during this part of the evening, and did not make an overpowering success of it, either, for he came into our room in the hotel about eleven o'clock, full of cheerfulness, and talking loosely, disjointedly and indiscriminately, and every now and then tugging out a ragged word by the roots that had more hiccups than syllables in it. This, together with his hanging his coat on the floor on one side of a chair, and his vest on the floor on the other side, and piling his pants on the floor just in front of the same chair, and then contemplating the general result with superstitious awe, and finally pronouncing it "too many for *him*" and going to bed with his boots on, led us to fear that something he had eaten had not agreed with him.

But we knew afterward that it was something he had been drinking. It was the exclusively Mormon refresher, "valley tan." Valley tan (or, at least, one form of valley tan) is a kind of whisky, or first cousin to it; is of Mormon invention and manufactured only in Utah. Tradition says it is made of (imported) fire and brimstone. If I remember rightly no public drinking saloons were allowed in the kingdom by Brigham

Young, and no private drinking permitted among the faithful, except they confined themselves to "valley tan."

Next day we strolled about everywhere through the broad, straight, level streets, and enjoyed the pleasant strangeness of a city of fifteen thousand inhabitants with no loafers perceptible in it; and no visible drunkards or noisy people; a limpid stream rippling and dancing through every street in place of a filthy gutter; block after block of trim dwellings, built of "frame" and sunburned brick—a great thriving orchard and garden behind every one of them, apparently—branches from the street stream winding and sparkling among the garden beds and fruit trees—and a grand general air of neatness, repair, thrift and comfort, around and about and over the whole. And everywhere were workshops, factories, and all manner of industries; and intent faces and busy hands were to be seen wherever one looked; and in one's ears was the ceaseless clink of hammers, the buzz of trade and the contented hum of drums and fly-wheels.

The armorial crest of my own State consisted of two dissolute bears holding up the head of a dead and gone cask between them and making the pertinent remark, "UNITED, WE STAND—and—DIVIDED, WE FALL." It was always too figurative for the author of this book. But the Mormon crest was easy. And it was simple, unostentatious, and fitted like a glove. It was a representation of a GOLDEN BEEHIVE, with the bees all at work!

The city lies in the edge of a level plain as broad as the State of Connecticut, and crouches close down to the ground under a curving wall of mighty mountains whose heads are hidden in the clouds, and whose shoulders bear relics of the snows of winter all the summer long. Seen from one of these dizzy heights, twelve or fifteen miles off, Great Salt Lake City is toned down and diminished till it is suggestive of a child's toy-village reposing under the majestic protection of the Chinese wall.

On some of those mountains, to the southwest, it had been raining every day for two weeks, but not a drop had fallen in the city. And on hot days in late spring and early autumn the citizens could quit fanning and growling and go out and cool off by looking at the luxury of a glorious snow-storm going on in the mountains. They could enjoy it at a distance, at those seasons, every day, though no snow would fall in their streets, or anywhere near them.

Salt Lake City was healthy—an extremely healthy city. They declared there was only one physician in the place and he was arrested every week regularly and held to answer under the vagrant act for having "no visible means of support." [They always give you a good substantial article of truth in Salt Lake, and good measure and good weight, too. Very often, if you wished to weigh one of their airiest little commonplace statements you would want the hay scales.]

We desired to visit the famous inland sea, the American "Dead Sea," the great Salt Lake—seventeen miles, horseback, from the city—for we had dreamed about it, and thought about it, and talked about it, and yearned to see it, all the first part of our trip; but now when it was only arm's length away it had suddenly lost nearly every bit of its interest. And so we put it off, in a sort of general way, till next day—and that was the last we ever thought of it. We dined with some hospitable Gentiles; and visited the foundation of the prodigious temple; and talked long with that shrewd Connecticut Yankee, Heber C. Kimball (since deceased), a saint of high degree and a mighty man of commerce. We saw the "Tithing-House," and the "Lion House," and I do not know or remember how many more church and government buildings of various kinds and curious names. We flitted hither and thither and enjoyed every hour, and picked up a great deal of useful information and entertaining nonsense, and went to bed at night satisfied.

The second day, we made the acquaintance of Mr. Street (since deceased) and put on white shirts and went and paid a state visit to the king. He seemed a quiet, kindly, easy-mannered, dignified, self-possessed old gentleman of fifty-five or sixty, and had a gentle craft in his eye that probably belonged there. He was very simply dressed and was just taking off a straw hat as we entered. He talked about Utah, and the Indians, and Nevada, and general American matters and questions, with our secretary and certain government officials who came with us. But he never paid any attention to me, notwithstanding I made several attempts to "draw him out" on federal politics and his high handed attitude toward Congress. I thought some of the things I said were rather fine. But he merely looked around at me, at distant intervals, something as I have seen a benignant old cat look around to see which kitten was meddling with her tail. By and by I subsided into an indignant silence, and so sat until the end, hot and flushed, and execrating him in my heart for an ignorant savage. But he was calm. His conversation with those gentlemen flowed on as sweetly and peacefully and musically as any summer brook. When the audience was ended and we were retiring from the presence, he put his hand on my head, beamed down on me in an admiring way and said to my brother:

"Ah—your child, I presume? Boy, or girl?"

Chapter XIV

M<small>R. STREET</small> was very busy with his telegraphic matters—
and considering that he had eight or nine hundred
miles of rugged, snowy, uninhabited mountains, and water-
less, treeless, melancholy deserts to traverse with his wire, it
was natural and needful that he should be as busy as possible.
He could not go comfortably along and cut his poles by the
road-side, either, but they had to be hauled by ox teams
across those exhausting deserts—and it was two days' journey
from water to water, in one or two of them. Mr. Street's
contract was a vast work, every way one looked at it; and yet
to comprehend what the vague words "eight hundred miles
of rugged mountains and dismal deserts" mean, one must go
over the ground in person—pen and ink descriptions cannot
convey the dreary reality to the reader. And after all, Mr. S.'s
mightiest difficulty turned out to be one which he had never
taken into the account at all. Unto Mormons he had sub-let
the hardest and heaviest half of his great undertaking, and all
of a sudden they concluded that they were going to make
little or nothing, and so they tranquilly threw their poles
overboard in mountain or desert, just as it happened when
they took the notion, and drove home and went about their
customary business! They were under written contract to Mr.
Street, but they did not care anything for that. They said they
would "admire" to see a "Gentile" force a Mormon to fulfil a
losing contract in Utah! And they made themselves very
merry over the matter. Street said—for it was he that told us
these things:

"I was in dismay. I was under heavy bonds to complete my
contract in a given time, and this disaster looked very much
like ruin. It was an astounding thing; it was such a wholly
unlooked-for difficulty, that I was entirely nonplussed. I am a
business man—have always been a business man—do not
know anything *but* business—and so you can imagine how
like being struck by lightning it was to find myself in a country where *written contracts were worthless!*—that main security,
that sheet-anchor, that absolute necessity, of business. My
confidence left me. There was no use in making new con-

tracts—that was plain. I talked with first one prominent citizen and then another. They all sympathized with me, first rate, but they did not know how to help me. But at last a Gentile said, 'Go to Brigham Young!—these small fry cannot do you any good.' I did not think much of the idea, for if the *law* could not help me, what could an individual do who had not even anything to do with either making the laws or executing them? He might be a very good patriarch of a church and preacher in its tabernacle, but something sterner than religion and moral suasion was needed to handle a hundred refractory, half-civilized sub-contractors. But what was a man to do? I thought if Mr. Young could not do anything else, he might probably be able to give me some advice and a valuable hint or two, and so I went straight to him and laid the whole case before him. He said very little, but he showed strong interest all the way through. He examined all the papers in detail, and whenever there seemed anything like a hitch, either in the papers or my statement, he would go back and take up the thread and follow it patiently out to an intelligent and satisfactory result. Then he made a list of the contractors' names. Finally he said:

" 'Mr. Street, this is all perfectly plain. These contracts are strictly and legally drawn, and are duly signed and certified. These men manifestly entered into them with their eyes open. I see no fault or flaw anywhere.'

"Then Mr. Young turned to a man waiting at the other end of the room and said: 'Take this list of names to So-and-so, and tell him to have these men here at such-and-such an hour.'

"They were there, to the minute. So was I. Mr. Young asked them a number of questions, and their answers made my statement good. Then he said to them:

" 'You signed these contracts and assumed these obligations of your own free will and accord?'

" 'Yes.'

" 'Then carry them out to the letter, if it makes paupers of you! Go!'

"And they *did* go, too! They are strung across the deserts now, working like bees. And I never hear a word out of them. There is a batch of governors, and judges, and other officials here, shipped from Washington, and they maintain the semblance of a republican form of government—but the petrified truth is that Utah is an absolute monarchy and Brigham Young is king!"

Mr. Street was a fine man, and I believe his story. I knew him well during several years afterward in San Francisco.

Our stay in Salt Lake City amounted to only two days, and therefore we had no time to make the customary inquisition into the workings of polygamy and get up the usual statistics and deductions preparatory to calling the attention of the nation at large once more to the matter. I had the will to do it. With the gushing self-sufficiency of youth I was feverish to plunge in headlong and achieve a great reform here—until I saw the Mormon women. Then I was touched. My heart was wiser than my head. It warmed toward these poor, ungainly and pathetically "homely" creatures, and as I turned to hide the generous moisture in my eyes, I said, "No—the man that marries one of them has done an act of Christian charity which entitles him to the kindly applause of mankind, not their harsh censure—and the man that marries sixty of them has done a deed of open-handed generosity so sublime that the nations should stand uncovered in his presence and worship in silence."*

*For a brief sketch of Mormon history, and the noted Mountain Meadow massacre, see Appendices A and B.

Chapter XV

IT IS A luscious country for thrilling evening stories about assassinations of intractable Gentiles. I cannot easily conceive of anything more cosy than the night in Salt Lake which we spent in a Gentile den, smoking pipes and listening to tales of how Burton galloped in among the pleading and defenceless "Morisites" and shot them down, men and women, like so many dogs. And how Bill Hickman, a Destroying Angel, shot Drown and Arnold dead for bringing suit against him for a debt. And how Porter Rockwell did this and that dreadful thing. And how heedless people often come to Utah and make remarks about Brigham, or polygamy, or some other sacred matter, and the very next morning at daylight such parties are sure to be found lying up some back alley, contentedly waiting for the hearse.

And the next most interesting thing is to sit and listen to these Gentiles talk about polygamy; and how some portly old frog of an elder, or a bishop, marries a girl—likes her, marries her sister—likes her, marries another sister—likes her, takes another—likes her, marries her mother—likes her, marries her father, grandfather, great grandfather, and then comes back hungry and asks for more. And how the pert young thing of eleven will chance to be the favorite wife and her own venerable grandmother have to rank away down toward D 4 in their mutual husband's esteem, and have to sleep in the kitchen, as like as not. And how this dreadful sort of thing, this hiving together in one foul nest of mother and daughters, and the making a young daughter superior to her own mother in rank and authority, are things which Mormon women submit to because their religion teaches them that the more wives a man has on earth, and the more children he rears, the higher the place they will all have in the world to come—and the warmer, maybe, though they do not seem to say anything about that.

According to these Gentile friends of ours, Brigham Young's harem contains twenty or thirty wives. They said that some of them had grown old and gone out of active service, but were comfortably housed and cared for in the henery—

or the Lion House, as it is strangely named. Along with each wife were her children—fifty altogether. The house was perfectly quiet and orderly, when the children were still. They all took their meals in one room, and a happy and home-like sight it was pronounced to be. None of our party got an opportunity to take dinner with Mr. Young, but a Gentile by the name of Johnson professed to have enjoyed a sociable breakfast in the Lion House. He gave a preposterous account of the "calling of the roll," and other preliminaries, and the carnage that ensued when the buckwheat cakes came in. But he embellished rather too much. He said that Mr. Young told him several smart sayings of certain of his "two-year-olds," observing with some pride that for many years he had been the heaviest contributor in that line to one of the Eastern magazines; and then he wanted to show Mr. Johnson one of the pets that had said the last good thing, but he could not find the child. He searched the faces of the children in detail, but could not decide which one it was. Finally he gave it up with a sigh and said:

"I thought I would know the little cub again but I don't." Mr. Johnson said further, that Mr. Young observed that life was a sad, sad thing—"because the joy of every new marriage a man contracted was so apt to be blighted by the inopportune funeral of a less recent bride." And Mr. Johnson said that while he and Mr. Young were pleasantly conversing in private, one of the Mrs. Youngs came in and demanded a breast-pin, remarking that she had found out that he had been giving a breast-pin to No. 6, and *she*, for one, did not propose to let this partiality go on without making a satisfactory amount of trouble about it. Mr. Young reminded her that there was a stranger present. Mrs. Young said that if the state of things inside the house was not agreeable to the stranger, he could find room outside. Mr. Young promised the breast-pin, and she went away. But in a minute or two another Mrs. Young came in and demanded a breast-pin. Mr. Young began a remonstrance, but Mrs. Young cut him short. She said No. 6 had got one, and No. 11 was promised one, and it was "no use for him to try to impose on her—she hoped she knew her rights." He gave his promise, and she went. And presently three Mrs. Youngs entered in a body and opened on their

husband a tempest of tears, abuse, and entreaty. They had
heard all about No. 6, No. 11, and No. 14. Three more breast-
pins were promised. They were hardly gone when nine more
Mrs. Youngs filed into the presence, and a new tempest burst
forth and raged round about the prophet and his guest. Nine
breast-pins were promised, and the weird sisters filed out
again. And in came eleven more, weeping and wailing and
gnashing their teeth. Eleven promised breast-pins purchased
peace once more.

"That is a specimen," said Mr. Young. "You see how it is.
You see what a life I lead. A man *can't* be wise all the time.
In a heedless moment I gave my darling No. 6—excuse my
calling her thus, as her other name has escaped me for the
moment—a breast-pin. It was only worth twenty-five dollars—that is, *apparently* that was its whole cost—but its ultimate cost was inevitably bound to be a good deal more. You
yourself have seen it climb up to six hundred and fifty dollar—and alas, even that is not the end! For I have wives all
over this Territory of Utah. I have dozens of wives whose
numbers, even, I do not know without looking in the family
Bible. They are scattered far and wide among the mountains
and valleys of my realm. And mark you, every solitary one of
them will hear of this wretched breast-pin, and every last one
of them will have one or die. No. 6's breast pin will cost me
twenty-five hundred dollars before I see the end of it. And
these creatures will compare these pins together, and if one is
a shade finer than the rest, they will all be thrown on my
hands, and I will have to order a new lot to keep peace in the
family. Sir, you probably did not know it, but all the time
you were present with my children your every movement was
watched by vigilant servitors of mine. If you had offered to
give a child a dime, or a stick of candy, or any trifle of the
kind, you would have been snatched out of the house instantly, provided it could be done before your gift left your
hand. Otherwise it would be absolutely necessary for you to
make an exactly similar gift to all my children—and knowing
by experience the importance of the thing, I would have
stood by and seen to it myself that you did it, and did it
thoroughly. Once a gentleman gave one of my children a tin
whistle—a veritable invention of Satan, sir, and one which I

have an unspeakable horror of, and so would you if you had eighty or ninety children in your house. But the deed was done—the man escaped. I knew what the result was going to be, and I thirsted for vengeance. I ordered out a flock of Destroying Angels, and they hunted the man far into the fastnesses of the Nevada mountains. But they never caught him. I am not cruel, sir—I am not vindictive except when sorely outraged—but if I had caught him, sir, so help me Joseph Smith, I would have locked him into the nursery till the brats whistled him to death. By the slaughtered body of St. Parley Pratt (whom God assoil!) there was never anything on this earth like it! *I* knew who gave the whistle to the child, but I could not make those jealous mothers believe me. They believed *I* did it, and the result was just what any man of reflection could have foreseen: I had to order a hundred and ten whistles—I think we had a hundred and ten children in the house then, but some of them are off at college now—I had to order a hundred and ten of those shrieking things, and I wish I may never speak another word if we didn't have to talk on our fingers entirely, from that time forth until the children got tired of the whistles. And if ever another man gives a whistle to a child of mine and I get my hands on him, I will hang him higher than Haman! That is the word with the bark on it! Shade of Nephi! *You* don't know anything about married life. I am rich, and everybody knows it. I am benevolent, and everybody takes advantage of it. I have a strong fatherly instinct and all the foundlings are foisted on me. Every time a woman wants to do well by her darling, she puzzles her brain to cipher out some scheme for getting it into my hands. Why, sir, a woman came here once with a child of a curious lifeless sort of complexion (and so had the woman), and swore that the child was mine and she my wife—that I had married her at such-and-such a time in such-and-such a place, but she had forgotten her number, and of course I could not remember her name. Well, sir, she called my attention to the fact that the child looked like me, and really it did seem to resemble me—a common thing in the Territory—and, to cut the story short, I put it in my nursery, and she left. And by the ghost of Orson Hyde, when they came to wash the paint off that child it was an Injun! Bless my soul, you don't know anything about married life. It is a perfect dog's life, sir—a perfect dog's life. You can't economize. It isn't possible. I have tried keeping one set of bridal attire for all occasions. But it is of no use. First you'll marry a combination of calico and consumption that's as thin as a rail, and next you'll get a creature that's nothing more than the dropsy in disguise, and then you've got to eke out that bridal dress with an old balloon. That is the way it goes. And think of the wash-bill—(excuse these tears)—nine hundred and eighty-four pieces a week! No, sir, there is no such a thing as economy in a family like mine. Why, just the one item of cradles—think of it! And vermifuge! Soothing syrup! Teething rings! And 'papa's watches' for the babies to play with! And things to scratch the furniture with! And lucifer matches for them to eat, and pieces of glass to cut themselves with! The item of glass alone would support *your* family, I venture to say, sir. Let me scrimp and squeeze all I can, I still can't get ahead as fast as I feel I ought to, with my opportunities. Bless you, sir, at a time which I had seventy-two wives in this house, I groaned under the pressure of keeping thousands of dollars tied up in seventy-two bedsteads when the money ought to have been out at interest; and I just sold out the whole stock, sir, at a sacrifice, and built a bedstead seven feet long and ninety-six feet wide. But it was a failure, sir. I could *not* sleep. It appeared to me that the whole seventy-two women snored at once. The roar was deafening. And then the danger of it! That was what I was looking at. They would all draw in their breath at once, and you could actually see the walls of the house suck in—and then they would all exhale their breath at once, and you could see the walls swell out, and strain, and hear the rafters crack, and the shingles grind together. My friend, take an old man's advice, and *don't* encumber yourself with a large family—mind, I tell you, don't do it. In a small family, and in a small family only, you will find that comfort and that peace of mind which are the best at last of the blessings this world is able to afford us, and for the lack of which no accumulation of wealth, and no acquisition of fame, power, and greatness can ever compensate us. Take my word for it, ten or eleven wives is all you need—never go over it."

Some instinct or other made me set this Johnson down as

being unreliable. And yet he was a very entertaining person, and I doubt if some of the information he gave us could have been acquired from any other source. He was a pleasant contrast to those reticent Mormons.

Chapter XVI

ALL MEN have heard of the Mormon Bible, but few except the "elect" have seen it, or, at least, taken the trouble to read it. I brought away a copy from Salt Lake. The book is a curiosity to me, it is such a pretentious affair, and yet so "slow," so sleepy; such an insipid mess of inspiration. It is chloroform in print. If Joseph Smith composed this book, the act was a miracle—keeping awake while he did it was, at any rate. If he, according to tradition, merely translated it from certain ancient and mysteriously-engraved plates of copper, which he declares he found under a stone, in an out-of-the-way locality, the work of translating was equally a miracle, for the same reason.

The book seems to be merely a prosy detail of imaginary history, with the Old Testament for a model; followed by a tedious plagiarism of the New Testament. The author labored to give his words and phrases the quaint, old-fashioned sound and structure of our King James's translation of the Scriptures; and the result is a mongrel—half modern glibness, and half ancient simplicity and gravity. The latter is awkward and constrained; the former natural, but grotesque by the contrast. Whenever he found his speech growing too modern—which was about every sentence or two—he ladled in a few such Scriptural phrases as "exceeding sore," "and it came to pass," etc., and made things satisfactory again. "And it came to pass" was his pet. If he had left that out, his Bible would have been only a pamphlet.

The title-page reads as follows:

THE BOOK OF MORMON: AN ACCOUNT WRITTEN BY THE HAND OF MORMON, UPON PLATES TAKEN FROM THE PLATES OF NEPHI.

Wherefore it is an abridgment of the record of the people of Nephi, and also of the Lamanites; written to the Lamanites, who are a remnant of the House of Israel; and also to Jew and Gentile; written by way of commandment, and also by the spirit of prophecy and of revelation. Written and sealed up, and hid up unto the Lord, that they might not be destroyed; to come forth by the gift and power of God unto the interpretation thereof; sealed by the hand of Moroni, and hid up unto the Lord, to come forth in due time by the way of Gentile; the interpretation thereof by the gift of God. An abridgment taken from the Book of Ether also; which is a record of the people of Jared; who were scattered at the time the Lord confounded the language of the people when they were building a tower to get to Heaven.

"Hid up" is good. And so is "wherefore"—though why "wherefore"? Any other word would have answered as well —though in truth it would not have sounded so Scriptural.

Next comes

THE TESTIMONY OF THREE WITNESSES.

Be it known unto all nations, kindreds, tongues, and people unto whom this work shall come, that we, through the grace of God the Father, and our Lord Jesus Christ, have seen the plates which contain this record, which is a record of the people of Nephi, and also of the Lamanites, their brethren, and also of the people of Jared, who came from the tower of which hath been spoken; and we also know that they have been translated by the gift and power of God, for His voice hath declared it unto us; wherefore we know of a surety that the work is true. And we also testify that we have seen the engravings which are upon the plates; and they have been shown unto us by the power of God, and not of man. And we declare with words of soberness, that an angel of God came down from heaven, and he brought and laid before our eyes, that we beheld and saw the plates, and the engravings thereon; and we know that it is by the grace of God the Father, and our Lord Jesus Christ, that we beheld and bear record that these things are true; and it is marvellous in our eyes; nevertheless the voice of the Lord commanded us that we should bear record of it; wherefore, to be obedient unto the commandments of God, we bear testimony of these things. And we know that if we are faithful in Christ, we shall rid our garments of the blood of all men, and be found spotless before the judgment-seat of Christ, and shall dwell with Him eternally in the heavens. And the honor be to the Father, and to the Son, and to the Holy Ghost, which is one God. Amen.

OLIVER COWDERY,
DAVID WHITMER,
MARTIN HARRIS.

Some people have to have a world of evidence before they can come anywhere in the neighborhood of believing anything; but for me, when a man tells me that he has "seen the engravings which are upon the plates," and not only that, but an angel was there at the time, and saw him see them, and probably took his receipt for it, I am very far on the road to conviction, no matter whether I ever heard of that man before or not, and even if I do not know the name of the angel, or his nationality either.

Next is this:

AND ALSO THE TESTIMONY OF EIGHT WITNESSES.

Be it known unto all nations, kindreds, tongues, and people unto whom this work shall come, that Joseph Smith, Jr., the translator of this work, has shown unto us the plates of which hath been spoken, which have the appearance of gold; and as many of the leaves as the said Smith has translated, we did handle with our hands; and we also saw the engravings thereon, all of which has the appearance of ancient work, and of curious workmanship. And this we bear record with words of soberness, that the said Smith has shown unto us, for we have seen and hefted, and know of a surety that the said Smith has got the plates of which we have spoken. And we give our names unto the world, to witness unto the world that which we have seen; and we lie not, God bearing witness of it.

CHRISTIAN WHITMER,	HIRAM PAGE,
JACOB WHITMER,	JOSEPH SMITH, SR.,
PETER WHITMER, JR.,	HYRUM SMITH,
JOHN WHITMER,	SAMUEL H. SMITH.

And when I am far on the road to conviction, and eight men, be they grammatical or otherwise, come forward and tell me that they have seen the plates too; and not only seen those plates but "hefted" them, I *am* convinced. I could not feel more satisfied and at rest if the entire Whitmer family had testified.

The Mormon Bible consists of fifteen "books"—being the books of Jacob, Enos, Jarom, Omni, Mosiah, Zeniff, Alma, Helaman, Ether, Moroni, two "books" of Mormon, and three of Nephi.

In the first book of Nephi is a plagiarism of the Old Testament, which gives an account of the exodus from Jerusalem of the "children of Lehi"; and it goes on to tell of their wanderings in the wilderness, during eight years, and their supernatural protection by one of their number, a party by the name of Nephi. They finally reached the land of "Bountiful," and camped by the sea. After they had remained there "for the space of many days"—which is more Scriptural than definite—Nephi was commanded from on high to build a ship wherein to "carry the people across the waters." He travestied Noah's ark—but he obeyed orders in the matter of the plan. He finished the ship *in a single day*, while his brethren stood by and made fun of it—and of him, too—"saying, our brother is a fool, for he thinketh that he can build a ship." They did not wait for the timbers to dry, but the whole tribe or nation sailed the next day. Then a bit of genuine nature cropped out, and is revealed by outspoken Nephi with Scriptural frankness—they all got on a spree! They, "and also their wives, began to make themselves merry, insomuch that they began to dance, and to sing, and to speak with much rudeness; yea, they were lifted up unto exceeding rudeness."

Nephi tried to stop these scandalous proceedings; but they tied him neck and heels, and went on with their lark. But observe how Nephi the prophet circumvented them by the aid of the invisible powers:

And it came to pass that after they had bound me, insomuch that I could not move, the compass, which had been prepared of the Lord, did cease to work; wherefore, they knew not whither they should steer the ship, insomuch that there arose a great storm, yea, a great and terrible tempest, and we were driven back upon the waters for the space of three days; and they began to be frightened exceedingly, lest they should be drowned in the sea; nevertheless they did not loose me. And on the fourth day, which we had been driven back, the tempest began to be exceeding sore.

And it came to pass that we were about to be swallowed up in the depths of the sea.

Then they untied him.

And it came to pass after they had loosed me, behold, I took the compass, and it did work whither I desired it. And it came to pass that I prayed unto the Lord; and after I had prayed, the winds did cease, and the storm did cease, and there was a great calm.

Equipped with their compass, these ancients appear to have had the advantage of Noah.

Their voyage was toward a "promised land"—the only name they give it. They reached it in safety.

Polygamy is a recent feature in the Mormon religion, and was added by Brigham Young after Joseph Smith's death. Before that, it was regarded as an "abomination." This verse from the Mormon Bible occurs in Chapter II. of the book of Jacob:

For behold, thus saith the Lord, this people begin to wax in iniquity; they understand not the Scriptures; for they seek to excuse themselves in committing whoredoms, because of the things which were written concerning David, and Solomon his son. Behold, David and Solomon truly had many wives and concubines, which thing was abominable before me, saith the Lord; wherefore, thus saith the Lord, I have led this people forth out of the land of Jerusalem, by the power of mine arm, that I might raise up unto me a righteous branch from the fruit of the loins of Joseph. Wherefore, I the Lord God, will not suffer that this people shall do like unto them of old.

However, the project failed—or at least the modern Mormon end of it—for Brigham "suffers" it. This verse is from the same chapter:

Behold, the Lamanites your brethren, whom ye hate, because of their filthiness and the cursings which hath come upon their skins, are more righteous than you; for they have not forgotten the commandment of the Lord, which was given unto our fathers, that they should have, save it were one wife; and concubines they should have none.

The following verse (from Chapter IX. of the Book of Nephi) appears to contain information not familiar to everybody:

And now it came to pass that when Jesus had ascended into heaven, the multitude did disperse, and every man did take his wife and his children, and did return to his own home.

And it came to pass that on the morrow, when the multitude was gathered together, behold, Nephi and his brother whom he had raised from the dead, whose name was Timothy, and also his son, whose name was Jonas, and also Mathoni, and Mathonihah, his brother, and Kumen, and Kumenonhi, and Jeremiah, and Shemnon, and Jonas, and Zedekiah, and Isaiah; now these were the names of the disciples whom Jesus had chosen.

In order that the reader may observe how much more grandeur and picturesqueness (as seen by these Mormon twelve)

accompanied one of the tenderest episodes in the life of our
Saviour than other eyes seem to have been aware of, I quote
the following from the same "book"—Nephi:

> And it came to pass that Jesus spake unto them, and bade them
> arise. And they arose from the earth, and He said unto them, Blessed
> are ye because of your faith. And now behold, My joy is full. And
> when He had said these words, He wept, and the multitude bear
> record of it, and He took their little children, one by one, and
> blessed them, and prayed unto the Father for them. And when He
> had done this He wept again, and He spake unto the multitude, and
> saith unto them, Behold your little ones. And as they looked to be-
> hold, they cast their eyes toward heaven, and they saw the heavens
> open, and they saw angels descending out of heaven as it were, in
> the midst of fire; and they came down and encircled those little ones
> about, and they were encircled about with fire; and the angels did
> minister unto them, and the multitude did see and hear and bear
> record; and they know that their record is true, for they all of them
> did see and hear, every man for himself; and they were in number
> about two thousand and five hundred souls; and they did consist of
> men, women, and children.

And what else would they be likely to consist of?

The Book of Ether is an incomprehensible medley of "history," much of it relating to battles and sieges among peoples
whom the reader has possibly never heard of; and who inhabited a country which is not set down in the geography. There
was a King with the remarkable name of Coriantumr, and he
warred with Shared, and Lib, and Shiz, and others, in the
"plains of Heshlon"; and the "valley of Gilgal"; and the " wilderness of Akish"; and the "land of Moran"; and the "plains
of Agosh"; and "Ogath," and "Ramah," and the "land of
Corihor," and the "hill Comnor," by "the waters of Ripli-
ancum," etc., etc., etc. "And it came to pass," after a deal of
fighting, that Coriantumr, upon making calculation of his
losses, found that "there had been slain two millions of
mighty men, and also their wives and their children"—say
5,000,000 or 6,000,000 in all—"and he began to sorrow in
his heart." Unquestionably it was time. So he wrote to Shiz,
asking a cessation of hostilities, and offering to give up his
kingdom to save his people. Shiz declined, except upon condition that Coriantumr would come and let him cut his head

off first—a thing which Coriantumr would not do. Then there was more fighting for a season; then *four years* were devoted to gathering the forces for a final struggle—after which ensued a battle, which, I take it, is the most remarkable set forth in history,—except, perhaps, that of the Kilkenny cats, which it resembles in some respects. This is the account of the gathering and the battle:

7. And it came to pass that they did gather together all the people, upon all the face of the land, who had not been slain, save it was Ether. And it came to pass that Ether did behold all the doings of the people; and he beheld that the people who were for Coriantumr, were gathered together to the army of Coriantumr; and the people who were for Shiz, were gathered together to the army of Shiz; wherefore they were for the space of four years gathering together the people, that they might get all who were upon the face of the land, and that they might receive all the strength which it was possible that they could receive. And it came to pass that when they were all gathered together, every one to the army which he would, with their wives and their children; both men, women, and children being armed with weapons of war, having shields, and breast-plates, and head-plates, and being clothed after the manner of war, they did march forth one against another, to battle; and they fought all that day, and conquered not. And it came to pass that when it was night they were weary, and retired to their camps; and after they had retired to their camps, they took up a howling and a lamentation for the loss of the slain of their people; and so great were their cries, their howlings and lamentations, that it did rend the air exceedingly. And it came to pass that on the morrow they did go again to battle, and great and terrible was that day; nevertheless they conquered not, and when the night came again, they did rend the air with their cries, and their howlings, and their mournings, for the loss of the slain of their people.

8. And it came to pass that Coriantumr wrote again an epistle unto Shiz, desiring that he would not come again to battle, but that he would take the kingdom, and spare the lives of the people. But behold, the Spirit of the Lord had ceased striving with them, and Satan had full power over the hearts of the people, for they were given up unto the hardness of their hearts, and the blindness of their minds that they might be destroyed; wherefore they went again to battle. And it came to pass that they fought all that day, and when the night came they slept upon their swords; and on the morrow they fought even until the night came; and when the night came

they were drunken with anger, even as a man who is drunken with wine; and they slept again upon their swords; and on the morrow they fought again; and when the night came they had all fallen by the sword save it were fifty and two of the people of Coriantumr, and sixty and nine of the people of Shiz. And it came to pass that they slept upon their swords that night, and on the morrow they fought again, and they contended in their mights with their swords, and with their shields, all that day; and when the night came there were thirty and two of the people of Shiz, and twenty and seven of the people of Coriantumr.

9. And it came to pass that they ate and slept, and prepared for death on the morrow. And they were large and mighty men, as to the strength of men. And it came to pass that they fought for the space of three hours, and they fainted with the loss of blood. And it came to pass that when the men of Coriantumr had received sufficient strength, that they could walk, they were about to flee for their lives, but behold, Shiz arose, and also his men, and he swore in his wrath that he would slay Coriantumr, or he would perish by the sword: wherefore he did pursue them, and on the morrow he did overtake them; and they fought again with the sword. And it came to pass that when they had all fallen by the sword, save it were Coriantumr and Shiz, behold Shiz had fainted with loss of blood. And it came to pass that when Coriantumr had leaned upon his sword, that he rested a little, he smote off the head of Shiz. And it came to pass that after he had smote off the head of Shiz, that Shiz raised upon his hands and fell; and after that he had struggled for breath, he died. And it came to pass that Coriantumr fell to the earth, and became as if he had no life. And the Lord spake unto Ether, and said unto him, go forth. And he went forth, and beheld that the words of the Lord had all been fulfilled; and he finished his record; and the hundredth part I have not written.

It seems a pity he did not finish, for after all his dreary former chapters of commonplace, he stopped just as he was in danger of becoming interesting.

The Mormon Bible is rather stupid and tiresome to read, but there is nothing vicious in its teachings. Its code of morals is unobjectionable—it is "smouched"* from the New Testament and no credit given.

*Milton.

Chapter XVII

AT THE END of our two days' sojourn, we left Great Salt Lake City hearty and well fed and happy—physically superb but not so very much wiser, as regards the "Mormon question," than we were when we arrived, perhaps. We had a deal more "information" than we had before, of course, but we did not know what portion of it was reliable and what was not—for it all came from acquaintances of a day—strangers, strictly speaking. We were told, for instance, that the dreadful "Mountain Meadows Massacre" was the work of the Indians entirely, and that the Gentiles had meanly tried to fasten it upon the Mormons; we were told, likewise, that the Indians were to blame, partly, and partly the Mormons; and we were told, likewise, and just as positively, that the Mormons were almost if not wholly and completely responsible for that most treacherous and pitiless butchery. We got the story in all these different shapes, but it was not till several years afterward that Mrs. Waite's book, "The Mormon Prophet," came out with Judge Cradlebaugh's trial of the accused parties in it and revealed the truth that the latter version was the correct one and that the Mormons *were* the assassins. All our "information" had three sides to it, and so I gave up the idea that I could settle the "Mormon question" in two days. Still I have seen newspaper correspondents do it in one.

I left Great Salt Lake a good deal confused as to what state of things existed there—and sometimes even questioning in my own mind whether a state of things existed there at all or not. But presently I remembered with a lightening sense of relief that we had learned two or three trivial things there which we could be certain of; and so the two days were not wholly lost. For instance, we had learned that we were at last in a pioneer land, in absolute and tangible reality. The high prices charged for trifles were eloquent of high freights and bewildering distances of freightage. In the east, in those days, the smallest moneyed denomination was a penny and it represented the smallest purchasable quantity of any commodity. West of Cincinnati the smallest coin in use was the silver five-cent piece and no smaller quantity of an article could be bought than "five cents' worth." In Overland City the lowest coin appeared to be the ten-cent piece; but in Salt Lake there did not seem to be any money in circulation smaller than a quarter, or any smaller quantity purchasable of any commodity than twenty-five cents' worth. We had always been used to half dimes and "five cents' worth" as the minimum of financial negotiations; but in Salt Lake if one wanted a cigar, it was a quarter; if he wanted a chalk pipe, it was a quarter; if he wanted a peach, or a candle, or a newspaper, or a shave, or a little Gentile whiskey to rub on his corns to arrest indigestion and keep him from having the toothache, twenty-five cents was the price, every time. When we looked at the shot-bag of silver, now and then, we seemed to be wasting our substance in riotous living, but if we referred to the expense account we could see that we had not been doing anything of the kind. But people easily get reconciled to big money and big prices, and fond and vain of both—it is a descent to little coins and cheap prices that is hardest to bear and slowest to take hold upon one's toleration. After a month's acquaintance with the twenty-five cent minimum, the average human being is ready to blush every time he thinks of his despicable five-cent days. How sunburnt with blushes I used to get in gaudy Nevada, every time I thought of my first financial experience in Salt Lake. It was on this wise (which is a favorite expression of great authors, and a very neat one, too, but I never hear anybody *say* on this wise when they are talking). A young half-breed with a complexion like a yellow-jacket asked me if I would have my boots blacked. It was at the Salt Lake House the morning after we arrived. I said yes, and he blacked them. Then I handed him a silver five-cent piece, with the benevolent air of a person who is conferring wealth and blessedness upon poverty and suffering. The yellow-jacket took it with what I judged to be suppressed emotion, and laid it reverently down in the middle of his broad hand. Then he began to contemplate it, much as a philosopher contemplates a gnat's ear in the ample field of his microscope. Several mountaineers, teamsters, stage-drivers, etc., drew near and dropped into the tableau and fell to surveying the money with that attractive indifference to formality which is noticeable in the hardy pioneer. Presently the yellow-jacket handed the half dime back to me and told me I ought to keep my money in my pocket-book instead of in my soul, and then I wouldn't get it cramped and shriveled up so!

What a roar of vulgar laughter there was! I destroyed the mongrel reptile on the spot, but I smiled and smiled all the time I was detaching his scalp, for the remark he made *was* good for an "Injun."

Yes, we had learned in Salt Lake to be charged great prices without letting the inward shudder appear on the surface— for even already we had overheard and noted the tenor of conversations among drivers, conductors, and hostlers, and finally among citizens of Salt Lake, until we were well aware that these superior beings despised "emigrants." We permitted no tell-tale shudders and winces in our countenances, for we wanted to seem pioneers, or Mormons, half-breeds, teamsters, stage-drivers, Mountain Meadow assassins—anything in the world that the plains and Utah respected and admired—but we were wretchedly ashamed of being "emigrants," and sorry enough that we had white shirts and could not swear in the presence of ladies without looking the other way.

And many a time in Nevada, afterwards, we had occasion to remember with humiliation that we were "emigrants," and consequently a low and inferior sort of creatures. Perhaps the reader has visited Utah, Nevada, or California, even in these latter days, and while communing with himself upon the sorrowful banishment of those countries from what he considers "the world," has had his wings clipped by finding that *he* is the one to be pitied, and that there are entire populations around him ready and willing to do it for him—yea, who are complacently doing it for him already, wherever he steps his foot. Poor thing, they are making fun of his hat; and the cut of his New York coat; and his conscientiousness about his grammar; and his feeble profanity; and his consumingly ludicrous ignorance of ores, shafts, tunnels, and other things which he never saw before, and never felt enough interest in to read about. And all the time that he is thinking what a sad fate it is to be exiled to that far country, that lonely land, the citizens around him are looking down on him with a blighting compassion because he is an "emigrant" instead of that proudest and blessedest creature that exists on all the earth, a "FORTY-NINER."

The accustomed coach life began again, now, and by midnight it almost seemed as if we never had been out of our snuggery among the mail sacks at all. We had made one alteration, however. We had provided enough bread, boiled ham and hard boiled eggs to last double the six hundred miles of staging we had still to do.

And it was comfort in those succeeding days to sit up and contemplate the majestic panorama of mountains and valleys spread out below us and eat ham and hard boiled eggs while our spiritual natures revelled alternately in rainbows, thunderstorms, and peerless sunsets. Nothing helps scenery like ham and eggs. Ham and eggs, and after these a pipe—an old, rank, delicious pipe—ham and eggs and scenery, a "down grade," a flying coach, a fragrant pipe and a contented heart—these make happiness. It is what all the ages have struggled for.

Chapter XVIII

A T EIGHT in the morning we reached the remnant and ruin of what had been the important military station of "Camp Floyd," some forty-five or fifty miles from Salt Lake City. At four P.M. we had doubled our distance and were ninety or a hundred miles from Salt Lake. And now we entered upon one of that species of deserts whose concentrated hideousness shames the diffused and diluted horrors of Sahara—an "*alkali*" desert. For sixty-eight miles there was but one break in it. I do not remember that this was really a break; indeed it seems to me that it was nothing but a watering depot *in the midst* of the stretch of sixty-eight miles. If my memory serves me, there was no well or spring at this place, but the water was hauled there by mule and ox teams from the further side of the desert. There was a stage station there. It was forty-five miles from the beginning of the desert, and twenty-three from the end of it.

We plowed and dragged and groped along, the whole live-long night, and at the end of this uncomfortable twelve hours we finished the forty-five-mile part of the desert and got to the stage station where the imported water was. The sun was just rising. It was easy enough to cross a desert in the night while we were asleep; and it was pleasant to reflect, in the morning, that we in actual person *had* encountered an absolute desert and could always speak knowingly of deserts in presence of the ignorant thenceforward. And it was pleasant also to reflect that this was not an obscure, back country desert, but a very celebrated one, the metropolis itself, as you may say. All this was very well and very comfortable and satisfactory—but now we were to cross a desert in *daylight*. This was fine—novel—romantic—dramatically adventurous—*this*, indeed, was worth living for, worth traveling for! We would write home all about it.

This enthusiasm, this stern thirst for adventure, wilted under the sultry August sun and did not last above one hour. One poor little hour—and then we were ashamed that we had "gushed" so. The poetry was all in the anticipation—there is none in the reality. Imagine a vast, waveless ocean stricken dead and turned to ashes; imagine this solemn waste tufted with ash-dusted sage-bushes; imagine the lifeless silence and solitude that belong to such a place; imagine a coach, creeping like a bug through the midst of this shoreless level, and sending up tumbled volumes of dust as if it were a bug that went by steam; imagine this aching monotony of toiling and plowing kept up hour after hour, and the shore still as far away as ever, apparently; imagine team, driver, coach and passengers so deeply coated with ashes that they are all one colorless color; imagine ash-drifts roosting above moustaches and eyebrows like snow accumulations on boughs and bushes. This is the reality of it.

The sun beats down with dead, blistering, relentless malignity; the perspiration is welling from every pore in man and beast, but scarcely a sign of it finds its way to the surface—it is absorbed before it gets there; there is not the faintest breath of air stirring; there is not a merciful shred of cloud in all the brilliant firmament; there is not a living creature visible in any direction whither one searches the blank level that stretches its monotonous miles on every hand; there is not a sound—not a sigh—not a whisper—not a buzz, or a whir of wings, or distant pipe of bird—not even a sob from the lost souls that doubtless people that dead air. And so the occasional sneezing of the resting mules, and the champing of the bits, grate harshly on the grim stillness, not dissipating the spell but accenting it and making one feel more lonesome and forsaken than before.

The mules, under violent swearing, coaxing and whip-cracking, would make at stated intervals a "spurt," and drag the coach a hundred or may be two hundred yards, stirring up a billowy cloud of dust that rolled back, enveloping the vehicle to the wheel-tops or higher, and making it seem afloat in a fog. Then a rest followed, with the usual sneezing and bit-champing. Then another "spurt" of a hundred yards and another rest at the end of it. All day long we kept this up, without water for the mules and without ever changing the team. At least we kept it up ten hours, which, I take it, is a day, and a pretty honest one, in an alkali desert. It was from four in the morning till two in the afternoon. And it was so hot! and so close! and our water canteens went dry in the middle of the day and we got so thirsty! It was so stupid and tiresome and dull! and the tedious hours did lag and drag and limp along with such a cruel deliberation! It was so trying to give one's watch a good long undisturbed spell and then take it out and find that it had been fooling away the time and not trying to get ahead any! The alkali dust cut through our lips, it persecuted our eyes, it ate through the delicate membranes and made our noses bleed and *kept* them bleeding—and truly and seriously the romance all faded far away and disappeared, and left the desert trip nothing but a harsh reality—a thirsty, sweltering, longing, hateful reality!

Two miles and a quarter an hour for ten hours—that was what we accomplished. It was hard to bring the comprehension away down to such a snail-pace as that, when we had been used to making eight and ten miles an hour. When we reached the station on the farther verge of the desert, we were glad, for the first time, that the dictionary was along, because we never could have found language to tell how glad we were, in any sort of dictionary but an unabridged one with pictures in it. But there could not have been found in a whole library of dictionaries language sufficient to tell how tired those mules were after their twenty-three mile pull. To try to give the reader an idea of how *thirsty* they were, would be to "gild refined gold or paint the lily."

Somehow, now that it is there, the quotation does not seem to fit—but no matter, let it stay, anyhow. I think it is a graceful and attractive thing, and therefore have tried time and time again to work it in where it *would* fit, but could not succeed. These efforts have kept my mind distracted and ill at ease, and made my narrative seem broken and disjointed, in places. Under these circumstances it seems to me best to leave it in, as above, since this will afford at least a temporary respite from the wear and tear of trying to "lead up" to this really apt and beautiful quotation.

Chapter XIX

ON THE MORNING of the sixteenth day out from St. Joseph we arrived at the entrance of Rocky Canyon, two hundred and fifty miles from Salt Lake. It was along in this wild country somewhere, and far from any habitation of white men, except the stage stations, that we came across the wretchedest type of mankind I have ever seen, up to this writing. I refer to the Goshoot Indians. From what we could see and all we could learn, they are very considerably inferior to even the despised Digger Indians of California; inferior to all races of savages on our continent; inferior to even the Terra del Fuegans; inferior to the Hottentots, and actually inferior in some respects to the Kytches of Africa. Indeed, I have been obliged to look the bulky volumes of Wood's "Uncivilized Races of Men" clear through in order to find a savage tribe degraded enough to take rank with the Goshoots. I find but one people fairly open to that shameful verdict. It is the Bosjesmans (Bushmen) of South Africa. Such of the Goshoots as we saw, along the road and hanging about the stations, were small, lean, "scrawny" creatures; in complexion a dull black like the ordinary American negro; their faces and hands bearing dirt which they had been hoarding and accumulating for months, years, and even generations, according to the age of the proprietor; a silent, sneaking, treacherous looking race; taking note of everything, covertly, like all the other "Noble Red Men" that we (do not) read about, and betraying no sign in their countenances; indolent, everlastingly patient and tireless, like all other Indians; prideless beggars—for if the beggar instinct were left out of an Indian he would not "go," any more than a clock without a pendulum; hungry, always hungry, and yet never refusing anything that a hog would eat, though often eating what a hog would decline; hunters, but having no higher ambition than to kill and eat jackass rabbits, crickets and grasshoppers, and embezzle carrion from the buzzards and cayotes; savages who, when asked if they have the common Indian belief in a Great Spirit show a something which almost amounts to emotion, thinking whiskey is referred to; a thin, scattering race of almost naked black children, these Goshoots are, who produce nothing at all, and have no villages, and no gatherings together into strictly defined tribal communities—a people whose only shelter is a rag cast on a bush to keep off a portion of the snow, and yet who inhabit one of the most rocky, wintry, repulsive wastes that our country or any other can exhibit.

The Bushmen and our Goshoots are manifestly descended from the self-same gorilla, or kangaroo, or Norway rat, whichever animal-Adam the Darwinians trace them to.

One would as soon expect the rabbits to fight as the Goshoots, and yet they used to live off the offal and refuse of the stations a few months and then come some dark night when no mischief was expected, and burn down the buildings and kill the men from ambush as they rushed out. And once, in the night, they attacked the stage-coach when a District Judge, of Nevada Territory, was the only passenger, and with their first volley of arrows (and a bullet or two) they riddled the stage curtains, wounded a horse or two and mortally wounded the driver. The latter was full of pluck, and so was his passenger. At the driver's call Judge Mott swung himself out, clambered to the box and seized the reins of the team, and away they plunged, through the racing mob of skeletons and under a hurtling storm of missiles. The stricken driver had sunk down on the boot as soon as he was wounded, but had held on to the reins and said he would manage to keep hold of them until relieved. And after they were taken from his relaxing grasp, he lay with his head between Judge Mott's feet, and tranquilly gave directions about the road; he said he believed he could live till the miscreants were outrun and left behind, and that if he managed that, the main difficulty would be at an end, and then if the Judge drove so and so (giving directions about bad places in the road, and general course) he would reach the next station without trouble. The Judge distanced the enemy and at last rattled up to the station and knew that the night's perils were done; but there was no comrade-in-arms for him to rejoice with, for the soldierly driver was dead.

Let us forget that we have been saying harsh things about the Overland drivers, now. The disgust which the Goshoots gave me, a disciple of Cooper and a worshipper of the Red

Man—even of the scholarly savages in the "Last of the Mohicans" who are fittingly associated with backwoodsmen who divide each sentence into two equal parts: one part critically grammatical, refined and choice of language, and the other part just such an attempt to talk like a hunter or a mountaineer, as a Broadway clerk might make after eating an edition of Emerson Bennett's works and studying frontier life at the Bowery Theatre a couple of weeks—I say that the nausea which the Goshoots gave me, an Indian worshipper, set me to examining authorities, to see if perchance I had been overestimating the Red Man while viewing him through the mellow moonshine of romance. The revelations that came were disenchanting. It was curious to see how quickly the paint and tinsel fell away from him and left him treacherous, filthy and repulsive—and how quickly the evidences accumulated that wherever one finds an Indian tribe he has only found Goshoots more or less modified by circumstances and surroundings—but Goshoots, after all. They deserve pity, poor creatures; and they can have mine—at this distance. Nearer by, they never get anybody's.

There is an impression abroad that the Baltimore and Washington Railroad Company and many of its employés are Goshoots; but it is an error. There is only a plausible resemblance, which, while it is apt enough to mislead the ignorant, cannot deceive parties who have contemplated both tribes. But seriously, it was not only poor wit, but very wrong to start the report referred to above; for however innocent the motive may have been, the necessary effect was to injure the reputation of a class who have a hard enough time of it in the pitiless deserts of the Rocky Mountains, Heaven knows! If we cannot find it in our hearts to give those poor naked creatures our Christian sympathy and compassion, in God's name let us at least not throw mud at them.

Chapter XX

O N THE SEVENTEENTH DAY we passed the highest mountain peaks we had yet seen, and although the day was very warm the night that followed upon its heels was wintry cold and blankets were next to useless.

On the eighteenth day we encountered the eastward-bound telegraph-constructors at Reese River station and sent a message to his Excellency Gov. Nye at Carson City (distant one hundred and fifty-six miles).

On the nineteenth day we crossed the Great American Desert—forty memorable miles of bottomless sand, into which the coach wheels sunk from six inches to a foot. We worked our passage most of the way across. That is to say, we got out and walked. It was a dreary pull and a long and thirsty one, for we had no water. From one extremity of this desert to the other, the road was white with the bones of oxen and horses. It would hardly be an exaggeration to say that we could have walked the forty miles and set our feet on a bone at every step! The desert was one prodigious graveyard. And the log-chains, wagon tyres, and rotting wrecks of vehicles were almost as thick as the bones. I think we saw log-chains enough rusting there in the desert, to reach across any State in the Union. Do not these relics suggest something of an idea of the fearful suffering and privation the early emigrants to California endured?

At the border of the Desert lies Carson Lake, or The "Sink" of the Carson, a shallow, melancholy sheet of water some eighty or a hundred miles in circumference. Carson River empties into it and is lost—sinks mysteriously into the earth and never appears in the light of the sun again—for the lake has no outlet whatever.

There are several rivers in Nevada, and they all have this mysterious fate. They end in various lakes or "sinks," and that is the last of them. Carson Lake, Humboldt Lake, Walker Lake, Mono Lake, are all great sheets of water without any visible outlet. Water is always flowing into them; none is ever seen to flow out of them, and yet they remain always level full, neither receding nor overflowing. What they do with their surplus is only known to the Creator.

On the western verge of the Desert we halted a moment at Ragtown. It consisted of one log-house and is not set down on the map.

This reminds me of a circumstance. Just after we left Julesburg, on the Platte, I was sitting with the driver, and he said:

"I can tell you a most laughable thing indeed, if you would like to listen to it. Horace Greeley went over this road once. When he was leaving Carson City he told the driver, Hank Monk, that he had an engagement to lecture at Placerville and was very anxious to go through quick. Hank Monk cracked his whip and started off at an awful pace. The coach bounced up and down in such a terrific way that it jolted the buttons all off of Horace's coat, and finally shot his head clean through the roof of the stage, and then he yelled at Hank Monk and begged him to go easier—said he warn't in as much of a hurry as he was awhile ago. But Hank Monk said, 'Keep your seat, Horace, and I'll get you there on time'—and you bet you he did, too, what was left of him!"

A day or two after that we picked up a Denver man at the cross roads, and he told us a good deal about the country and the Gregory Diggings. He seemed a very entertaining person and a man well posted in the affairs of Colorado. By and by he remarked:

"I can tell you a most laughable thing indeed, if you would like to listen to it. Horace Greeley went over this road once. When he was leaving Carson City he told the driver, Hank Monk, that he had an engagement to lecture at Placerville and was very anxious to go through quick. Hank Monk cracked his whip and started off at an awful pace. The coach bounced up and down in such a terrific way that it jolted the buttons all off of Horace's coat, and finally shot his head clean through the roof of the stage, and then he yelled at Hank Monk and begged him to go easier—said he warn't in as much of a hurry as he was awhile ago. But Hank Monk said, 'Keep your seat, Horace, and I'll get you there on time!'—and you bet you he did, too, what was left of him!"

At Fort Bridger, some days after this, we took on board a cavalry sergeant, a very proper and soldierly person indeed. From no other man during the whole journey, did we gather such a store of concise and well-arranged military information. It was surprising to find in the desolate wilds of our country a man so thoroughly acquainted with everything useful to know in his line of life, and yet of such inferior rank and unpretentious bearing. For as much as three hours we listened to him with unabated interest. Finally he got upon the subject of trans-continental travel, and presently said:

"I can tell you a very laughable thing indeed, if you would like to listen to it. Horace Greeley went over this road once. When he was leaving Carson City he told the driver, Hank Monk, that he had an engagement to lecture at Placerville and was very anxious to go through quick. Hank Monk cracked his whip and started off at an awful pace. The coach bounced up and down in such a terrific way that it jolted the buttons all off of Horace's coat, and finally shot his head clean through the roof of the stage, and then he yelled at Hank Monk and begged him to go easier—said he warn't in as much of a hurry as he was awhile ago. But Hank Monk said, 'Keep your seat, Horace, and I'll get you there on time!'— and you bet you he did, too, what was left of him!"

When we were eight hours out from Salt Lake City a Mormon preacher got in with us at a way station—a gentle, soft-spoken, kindly man, and one whom any stranger would warm to at first sight. I can never forget the pathos that was in his voice as he told, in simple language, the story of his people's wanderings and unpitied sufferings. No pulpit eloquence was ever so moving and so beautiful as this outcast's picture of the first Mormon pilgrimage across the plains, struggling sorrowfully onward to the land of its banishment and marking its desolate way with graves and watering it with tears. His words so wrought upon us that it was a relief to us all when the conversation drifted into a more cheerful channel and the natural features of the curious country we were in came under treatment. One matter after another was pleasantly discussed, and at length the stranger said:

"I can tell you a most laughable thing indeed, if you would like to listen to it. Horace Greeley went over this road once. When he was leaving Carson City he told the driver, Hank Monk, that he had an engagement to lecture in Placerville, and was very anxious to go through quick. Hank Monk cracked his whip and started off at an awful pace. The coach bounced up and down in such a terrific way that it jolted the buttons all off of Horace's coat, and finally shot his head clean through the roof of the stage, and then he yelled at Hank Monk and begged him to go easier—said he warn't in as much of a hurry as he was awhile ago. But Hank Monk said, 'Keep your seat, Horace, and I'll get you there on time!'— and you bet you he did, too, what was left of him!"

Ten miles out of Ragtown we found a poor wanderer who had lain down to die. He had walked as long as he could, but his limbs had failed him at last. Hunger and fatigue had conquered him. It would have been inhuman to leave him there. We paid his fare to Carson and lifted him into the coach. It was some little time before he showed any very decided signs of life; but by dint of chafing him and pouring brandy between his lips we finally brought him to a languid consciousness. Then we fed him a little, and by and by he seemed to comprehend the situation and a grateful light softened his eye. We made his mail-sack bed as comfortable as possible, and constructed a pillow for him with our coats. He seemed very thankful. Then he looked up in our faces, and said in a feeble voice that had a tremble of honest emotion in it:

"Gentlemen, I know not who you are, but you have saved my life; and although I can never be able to repay you for it, I feel that I can at least make one hour of your long journey lighter. I take it you are strangers to this great thoroughfare, but I am entirely familiar with it. In this connection I can tell you a most laughable thing indeed, if you would like to listen to it. Horace Greeley—"

I said, impressively:

"Suffering stranger, proceed at your peril. You see in me the melancholy wreck of a once stalwart and magnificent manhood. What has brought me to this? That thing which you are about to tell. Gradually but surely, that tiresome old anecdote has sapped my strength, undermined my constitution, withered my life. Pity my helplessness. Spare me only just this once, and tell me about young George Washington and his little hatchet for a change."

We were saved. But not so the invalid. In trying to retain

the anecdote in his system he strained himself and died in our arms.

I am aware, now, that I ought not to have asked of the sturdiest citizen of all that region, what I asked of that mere shadow of a man; for, after seven years' residence on the Pacific coast, I know that no passenger or driver on the Overland ever corked that anecdote in, when a stranger was by, and survived. Within a period of six years I crossed and re-crossed the Sierras between Nevada and California thirteen times by stage and listened to that deathless incident four hundred and eighty-one or eighty-two times. I have the list somewhere. Drivers always told it, conductors told it, landlords told it, chance passengers told it, the very Chinamen and vagrant Indians recounted it. I have had the same driver tell it to me two or three times in the same afternoon. It has come to me in all the multitude of tongues that Babel bequeathed to earth, and flavored with whiskey, brandy, beer, cologne, sozodont, tobacco, garlic, onions, grasshoppers—everything that has a fragrance to it through all the long list of things that are gorged or guzzled by the sons of men. I never have smelt any anecdote as often as I have smelt that one; never have smelt any anecdote that smelt so variegated as that one. And you never could learn to know it by its smell, because every time you thought you had learned the smell of it, it would turn up with a different smell. Bayard Taylor has written about this hoary anecdote, Richardson has published it; so have Jones, Smith, Johnson, Ross Browne, and every other correspondence-inditing being that ever set his foot upon the great overland road anywhere between Julesburg and San Francisco; and I have heard that it is in the Talmud. I have seen it in print in nine different foreign languages; I have been told that it is employed in the inquisition in Rome; and I now learn with regret that it is going to be set to music. I do not think that such things are right.

Stage-coaching on the Overland is no more, and stage drivers are a race defunct. I wonder if they bequeathed that baldheaded anecdote to their successors, the railroad brakemen and conductors, and if these latter still persecute the helpless passenger with it until he concludes, as did many a tourist of other days, that the real grandeurs of the Pacific coast are not Yo Semite and the Big Trees, but Hank Monk and his adventure with Horace Greeley.*

*And what makes that worn anecdote the more aggravating, is, that the adventure it celebrates *never occurred*. If it were a good anecdote, that seeming demerit would be its chiefest virtue, for creative power belongs to greatness; but what ought to be done to a man who would wantonly contrive so flat a one as this? If *I* were to suggest what ought to be done to him, I should be called extravagant—but what does the thirteenth chapter of Daniel say? Aha!

Chapter XXI

WE WERE APPROACHING the end of our long journey. It was the morning of the twentieth day. At noon we would reach Carson City, the capital of Nevada Territory. We were not glad, but sorry. It had been a fine pleasure trip; we had fed fat on wonders every day; we were now well accustomed to stage life, and very fond of it; so the idea of coming to a stand-still and settling down to a humdrum existence in a village was not agreeable, but on the contrary depressing.

Visibly our new home was a desert, walled in by barren, snow-clad mountains. There was not a tree in sight. There was no vegetation but the endless sage-brush and greasewood. All nature was gray with it. We were plowing through great deeps of powdery alkali dust that rose in thick clouds and floated across the plain like smoke from a burning house. We were coated with it like millers; so were the coach, the mules, the mail-bags, the driver—we and the sage-brush and the other scenery were all one monotonous color. Long trains of freight wagons in the distance enveloped in ascending masses of dust suggested pictures of prairies on fire. These teams and their masters were the only life we saw. Otherwise we moved in the midst of solitude, silence and desolation. Every twenty steps we passed the skeleton of some dead beast of burthen, with its dust-coated skin stretched tightly over its empty ribs. Frequently a solemn raven sat upon the skull or the hips and contemplated the passing coach with meditative serenity.

By and by Carson City was pointed out to us. It nestled in the edge of a great plain and was a sufficient number of miles away to look like an assemblage of mere white spots in the shadow of a grim range of mountains overlooking it, whose summits seemed lifted clear out of companionship and consciousness of earthly things.

We arrived, disembarked, and the stage went on. It was a "wooden" town; its population two thousand souls. The main street consisted of four or five blocks of little white frame stores which were too high to sit down on, but not too high for various other purposes; in fact, hardly high enough.

They were packed close together, side by side, as if room were scarce in that mighty plain. The sidewalk was of boards that were more or less loose and inclined to rattle when walked upon. In the middle of the town, opposite the stores, was the "plaza" which is native to all towns beyond the Rocky Mountains—a large, unfenced, level vacancy, with a liberty pole in it, and very useful as a place for public auctions, horse trades, and mass meetings, and likewise for teamsters to camp in. Two other sides of the plaza were faced by stores, offices and stables. The rest of Carson City was pretty scattering.

We were introduced to several citizens, at the stage-office and on the way up to the Governor's from the hotel—among others, to a Mr. Harris, who was on horseback; he began to say something, but interrupted himself with the remark:

"I'll have to get you to excuse me a minute; yonder is the witness that swore I helped to rob the California coach—a piece of impertinent intermeddling, sir, for I am not even acquainted with the man."

Then he rode over and began to rebuke the stranger with a six-shooter, and the stranger began to explain with another. When the pistols were emptied, the stranger resumed his work (mending a whip-lash), and Mr. Harris rode by with a polite nod, homeward bound, with a bullet through one of his lungs, and several in his hips; and from them issued little rivulets of blood that coursed down the horse's sides and made the animal look quite picturesque. I never saw Harris shoot a man after that but it recalled to mind that first day in Carson.

This was all we saw that day, for it was two o'clock, now, and according to custom the daily "Washoe Zephyr" set in; a soaring dust-drift about the size of the United States set up edgewise came with it, and the capital of Nevada Territory disappeared from view. Still, there were sights to be seen which were not wholly uninteresting to new comers; for the vast dust cloud was thickly freckled with things strange to the upper air—things living and dead, that flitted hither and thither, going and coming, appearing and disappearing among the rolling billows of dust—hats, chickens and parasols sailing in the remote heavens; blankets, tin signs, sage-brush and shingles a shade lower; door-mats and buffalo robes lower still; shovels and coal scuttles on the next grade; glass doors, cats and little children on the next; disrupted lumber yards, light buggies and wheelbarrows on the next; and down only thirty or forty feet above ground was a scurrying storm of emigrating roofs and vacant lots.

It was something to see that much. I could have seen more, if I could have kept the dust out of my eyes.

But seriously a Washoe wind is by no means a trifling matter. It blows flimsy houses down, lifts shingle roofs occasionally, rolls up tin ones like sheet music, now and then blows a stage coach over and spills the passengers; and tradition says the reason there are so many bald people there, is, that the wind blows the hair off their heads while they are looking skyward after their hats. Carson streets seldom look inactive on Summer afternoons, because there are so many citizens skipping around their escaping hats, like chambermaids trying to head off a spider.

The "Washoe Zephyr" (Washoe is a pet nickname for Nevada) is a peculiarly Scriptural wind, in that no man knoweth "whence it cometh." That is to say, where it *originates*. It comes right over the mountains from the West, but when one crosses the ridge he does not find any of it on the other side! It probably is manufactured on the mountain-top for the occasion, and starts from there. It is a pretty regular wind, in the summer time. Its office hours are from two in the afternoon till two the next morning; and anybody venturing abroad during those twelve hours needs to allow for the wind or he will bring up a mile or two to leeward of the point he is aiming at. And yet the first complaint a Washoe visitor to San Francisco makes, is that the sea winds blow so, there! There is a good deal of human nature in that.

We found the state palace of the Governor of Nevada Territory to consist of a white frame one-story house with two small rooms in it and a stanchion supported shed in front— for grandeur—it compelled the respect of the citizen and inspired the Indians with awe. The newly arrived Chief and Associate Justices of the Territory, and other machinery of the government, were domiciled with less splendor. They were boarding around privately, and had their offices in their bedrooms.

The Secretary and I took quarters in the "ranch" of a worthy French lady by the name of Bridget O'Flannigan, a camp follower of his Excellency the Governor. She had known him in his prosperity as commander-in-chief of the Metropolitan Police of New York, and she would not desert him in his adversity as Governor of Nevada. Our room was on the lower floor, facing the plaza, and when we had got our bed, a small table, two chairs, the government fire-proof safe, and the Unabridged Dictionary into it, there was still room enough left for a visitor—may be two, but not without straining the walls. But the walls could stand it—at least the partitions could, for they consisted simply of one thickness of white "cotton domestic" stretched from corner to corner of the room. This was the rule in Carson—any other kind of partition was the rare exception. And if you stood in a dark room and your neighbors in the next had lights, the shadows on your canvas told queer secrets sometimes! Very often these partitions were made of old flour sacks basted together; and then the difference between the common herd and the aristocracy was, that the common herd had unornamented sacks, while the walls of the aristocrat were overpowering with rudimental fresco—*i. e.*, red and blue mill brands on the flour sacks. Occasionally, also, the better classes embellished their canvas by pasting pictures from *Harper's Weekly* on them. In many cases, too, the wealthy and the cultured rose to spittoons and other evidences of a sumptuous and luxurious taste.* We had a carpet and a genuine queen's-ware washbowl. Consequently we were hated without reserve by the other tenants of the O'Flannigan "ranch." When we added a painted oil-cloth window curtain, we simply took our lives into our own hands. To prevent bloodshed I removed up stairs and took up quarters with the untitled plebeians in one of the fourteen white pine cot-bedsteads that stood in two long ranks in the one sole room of which the second story consisted.

It was a jolly company, the fourteen. They were principally

---

*Washoe people take a joke so hard that I must explain that the above description was only the rule; there were many honorable exceptions in Carson—plastered ceilings and houses that had considerable furniture in them.—M. T.

voluntary camp-followers of the Governor, who had joined his retinue by their own election at New York and San Francisco and came along, feeling that in the scuffle for little territorial crumbs and offices they could not make their condition more precarious than it was, and might reasonably expect to make it better. They were popularly known as the "Irish Brigade," though there were only four or five Irishmen among all the Governor's retainers. His good-natured Excellency was much annoyed at the gossip his henchmen created—especially when there arose a rumor that they were paid assassins of his, brought along to quietly reduce the democratic vote when desirable!

Mrs. O'Flannigan was boarding and lodging them at ten dollars a week apiece, and they were cheerfully giving their notes for it. They were perfectly satisfied, but Bridget presently found that notes that could not be discounted were but a feeble constitution for a Carson boarding-house. So she began to harry the Governor to find employment for the "Brigade." Her importunities and theirs together drove him to a gentle desperation at last, and he finally summoned the Brigade to the presence. Then, said he:

"Gentlemen, I have planned a lucrative and useful service for you—a service which will provide you with recreation amid noble landscapes, and afford you never ceasing opportunities for enriching your minds by observation and study. I want you to survey a railroad from Carson City westward to a certain point! When the legislature meets I will have the necessary bill passed and the remuneration arranged."

"What, a railroad over the Sierra Nevada Mountains?"

"Well, then, survey it eastward to a certain point!"

He converted them into surveyors, chain-bearers and so on, and turned them loose in the desert. It was "recreation" with a vengeance! Recreation on foot, lugging chains through sand and sage-brush, under a sultry sun and among cattle bones, cayotes and tarantulas. "Romantic adventure" could go no further. They surveyed very slowly, very deliberately, very carefully. They returned every night during the first week, dusty, footsore, tired, and hungry, but very jolly. They brought in great store of prodigious hairy spiders—tarantulas—and imprisoned them in covered tumblers up stairs in the "ranch." After the first week, they had to camp on the field, for they were getting well eastward. They made a good many inquiries as to the location of that indefinite "certain point," but got no information. At last, to a peculiarly urgent inquiry of "How far eastward?" Governor Nye telegraphed back:

"To the Atlantic Ocean, blast you!—and then bridge it and go on!"

This brought back the dusty toilers, who sent in a report and ceased from their labors. The Governor was always comfortable about it; he said Mrs. O'Flannigan would hold him for the Brigade's board anyhow, and he intended to get what entertainment he could out of the boys; he said, with his old-time pleasant twinkle, that he meant to survey them into Utah and then telegraph Brigham to hang them for trespass!

The surveyors brought back more tarantulas with them, and so we had quite a menagerie arranged along the shelves of the room. Some of these spiders could straddle over a common saucer with their hairy, muscular legs, and when their feelings were hurt, or their dignity offended, they were the wickedest-looking desperadoes the animal world can furnish. If their glass prison-houses were touched ever so lightly they were up and spoiling for a fight in a minute. Starchy?—proud? Indeed, they would take up a straw and pick their teeth like a member of Congress. There was as usual a furious "zephyr" blowing the first night of the brigade's return, and about midnight the roof of an adjoining stable blew off, and a corner of it came crashing through the side of our ranch. There was a simultaneous awakening, and a tumultuous muster of the brigade in the dark, and a general tumbling and sprawling over each other in the narrow aisle between the bed-rows. In the midst of the turmoil, Bob H—— sprung up out of a sound sleep, and knocked down a shelf with his head. Instantly he shouted:

"Turn out, boys—the tarantulas is loose!"

No warning ever sounded so dreadful. Nobody tried, any longer, to leave the room, lest he might step on a tarantula. Every man groped for a trunk or a bed, and jumped on it. Then followed the strangest silence—a silence of grisly suspense it was, too—waiting, expectancy, fear. It was as dark as pitch, and one had to imagine the spectacle of those four-teen scant-clad men roosting gingerly on trunks and beds, for not a thing could be seen. Then came occasional little inter-ruptions of the silence, and one could recognize a man and tell his locality by his voice, or locate any other sound a suf-ferer made by his gropings or changes of position. The occa-sional voices were not given to much speaking—you simply heard a gentle ejaculation of "Ow!" followed by a solid thump, and you knew the gentleman had felt a hairy blanket or something touch his bare skin and had skipped from a bed to the floor. Another silence. Presently you would hear a gasping voice say:

"Su-su-something's crawling up the back of my neck!"

Every now and then you could hear a little subdued scram-ble and a sorrowful "O Lord!" and then you knew that some-body was getting away from something he took for a tarantula, and not losing any time about it, either. Directly a voice in the corner rang out wild and clear:

"I've got him! I've got him!" [Pause, and probable change of circumstances.] "No, he's got me! Oh, ain't they *never* going to fetch a lantern!"

The lantern came at that moment, in the hands of Mrs. O'Flannigan, whose anxiety to know the amount of damage done by the assaulting roof had not prevented her waiting a judicious interval, after getting out of bed and lighting up, to see if the wind was done, now, up stairs, or had a larger contract.

The landscape presented when the lantern flashed into the room was picturesque, and might have been funny to some people, but was not to us. Although we were perched so strangely upon boxes, trunks and beds, and so strangely at-tired, too, we were too earnestly distressed and too genuinely miserable to see any fun about it, and there was not the sem-blance of a smile anywhere visible. I know I am not capable of suffering more than I did during those few minutes of sus-pense in the dark, surrounded by those creeping, bloody-minded tarantulas. I had skipped from bed to bed and from box to box in a cold agony, and every time I touched any-thing that was furzy I fancied I felt the fangs. I had rather go to war than live that episode over again. Nobody was hurt.

The man who thought a tarantula had "got him" was mistaken—only a crack in a box had caught his finger. Not one of those escaped tarantulas was ever seen again. There were ten or twelve of them. We took candles and hunted the place high and low for them, but with no success. Did we go back to bed then? We did nothing of the kind. Money could not have persuaded us to do it. We sat up the rest of the night playing cribbage and keeping a sharp lookout for the enemy.

Chapter XXII

I T WAS THE end of August, and the skies were cloudless and the weather superb. In two or three weeks I had grown wonderfully fascinated with the curious new country, and concluded to put off my return to "the States" awhile. I had grown well accustomed to wearing a damaged slouch hat, blue woolen shirt, and pants crammed into boot-tops, and gloried in the absence of coat, vest and braces. I felt rowdyish and "bully," (as the historian Josephus phrases it, in his fine chapter upon the destruction of the Temple). It seemed to me that nothing could be so fine and so romantic. I had become an officer of the government, but that was for mere sublimity. The office was an unique sinecure. I had nothing to do and no salary. I was private Secretary to his majesty the Secretary and there was not yet writing enough for two of us. So Johnny K—— and I devoted our time to amusement. He was the young son of an Ohio nabob and was out there for recreation. He got it. We had heard a world of talk about the marvellous beauty of Lake Tahoe, and finally curiosity drove us thither to see it. Three or four members of the Brigade had been there and located some timber lands on its shores and stored up a quantity of provisions in their camp. We strapped a couple of blankets on our shoulders and took an axe apiece and started—for we intended to take up a wood ranch or so ourselves and become wealthy. We were on foot. The reader will find it advantageous to go horseback. We were told that the distance was eleven miles. We tramped a long time on level ground, and then toiled laboriously up a mountain about a thousand miles high and looked over. No lake there. We descended on the other side, crossed the valley and toiled up another mountain three or four thousand miles high, apparently, and looked over again. No lake yet. We sat down tired and perspiring, and hired a couple of Chinamen to curse those people who had beguiled us. Thus refreshed, we presently resumed the march with renewed vigor and determination. We plodded on, two or three hours longer, and at last the Lake burst upon us—a noble sheet of blue water lifted six thousand three hundred feet above the level of the sea, and walled in by a rim of snow-clad mountain peaks that towered aloft full three thousand feet higher still! It was a vast oval, and one would have to use up eighty or a hundred good miles in traveling around it. As it lay there with the shadows of the mountains brilliantly photographed upon its still surface I thought it must surely be the fairest picture the whole earth affords.

We found the small skiff belonging to the Brigade boys, and without loss of time set out across a deep bend of the lake toward the landmarks that signified the locality of the camp. I got Johnny to row—not because I mind exertion myself, but because it makes me sick to ride backwards when I am at work. But I steered. A three-mile pull brought us to the camp just as the night fell, and we stepped ashore very tired and wolfishly hungry. In a "cache" among the rocks we found the provisions and the cooking utensils, and then, all fatigued as I was, I sat down on a boulder and superintended while Johnny gathered wood and cooked supper. Many a man who had gone through what I had, would have wanted to rest.

It was a delicious supper—hot bread, fried bacon, and black coffee. It was a delicious solitude we were in, too. Three miles away was a saw-mill and some workmen, but there were not fifteen other human beings throughout the wide circumference of the lake. As the darkness closed down and the stars came out and spangled the great mirror with jewels, we smoked meditatively in the solemn hush and forgot our troubles and our pains. In due time we spread our blankets in the warm sand between two large boulders and soon fell asleep, careless of the procession of ants that passed in through rents in our clothing and explored our persons. Nothing could disturb the sleep that fettered us, for it had been fairly earned, and if our consciences had any sins on them they had to adjourn court for that night, any way. The wind rose just as we were losing consciousness, and we were lulled to sleep by the beating of the surf upon the shore.

It is always very cold on that lake shore in the night, but we had plenty of blankets and were warm enough. We never moved a muscle all night, but waked at early dawn in the original positions, and got up at once, thoroughly refreshed, free from soreness, and brim full of friskiness. There is no end of wholesome medicine in such an experience. That morning we could have whipped ten such people as we were the day before—sick ones at any rate. But the world is slow, and people will go to "water cures" and "movement cures" and to foreign lands for health. Three months of camp life on Lake Tahoe would restore an Egyptian mummy to his pristine vigor, and give him an appetite like an alligator. I do not mean the oldest and driest mummies, of course, but the fresher ones. The air up there in the clouds is very pure and fine, bracing and delicious. And why shouldn't it be?—it is the same the angels breathe. I think that hardly any amount of fatigue can be gathered together that a man cannot sleep off in one night on the sand by its side. Not under a roof, but under the sky; it seldom or never rains there in the summer time. I know a man who went there to die. But he made a failure of it. He was a skeleton when he came, and could barely stand. He had no appetite, and did nothing but read tracts and reflect on the future. Three months later he was sleeping out of doors regularly, eating all he could hold, three times a day, and chasing game over mountains three thousand feet high for recreation. And he was a skeleton no longer, but weighed part of a ton. This is no fancy sketch, but the truth. His disease was consumption. I confidently commend his experience to other skeletons.

I superintended again, and as soon as we had eaten breakfast we got in the boat and skirted along the lake shore about three miles and disembarked. We liked the appearance of the place, and so we claimed some three hundred acres of it and stuck our "notices" on a tree. It was yellow pine timber land—a dense forest of trees a hundred feet high and from one to five feet through at the butt. It was necessary to fence our property or we could not hold it. That is to say, it was necessary to cut down trees here and there and make them fall in such a way as to form a sort of enclosure (with pretty wide gaps in it). We cut down three trees apiece, and found it such heart-breaking work that we decided to "rest our case" on those; if they held the property, well and good; if they didn't, let the property spill out through the gaps and go; it was no use to work ourselves to death merely to save a few acres of land. Next day we came back to build a house—for a house was also necessary, in order to hold the property. We decided to build a substantial log-house and excite the envy of the Brigade boys; but by the time we had cut and trimmed the first log it seemed unnecessary to be so elaborate, and so we concluded to build it of saplings. However, two saplings, duly cut and trimmed, compelled recognition of the fact that a still modester architecture would satisfy the law, and so we concluded to build a "brush" house. We devoted the next day to this work, but we did so much "sitting around" and discussing, that by the middle of the afternoon we had achieved only a half-way sort of affair which one of us had to watch while the other cut brush, lest if both turned our backs we might not be able to find it again, it had such a strong family resemblance to the surrounding vegetation. But we were satisfied with it.

We were land owners now, duly seized and possessed, and within the protection of the law. Therefore we decided to take up our residence on our own domain and enjoy that large sense of independence which only such an experience can bring. Late the next afternoon, after a good long rest, we sailed away from the Brigade camp with all the provisions and cooking utensils we could carry off—borrow is the more accurate word—and just as the night was falling we beached the boat at our own landing.

Chapter XXIII

IF THERE IS any life that is happier than the life we led on our timber ranch for the next two or three weeks, it must be a sort of life which I have not read of in books or experienced in person. We did not see a human being but ourselves during the time, or hear any sounds but those that were made by the wind and the waves, the sighing of the pines, and now and then the far-off thunder of an avalanche. The forest about us was dense and cool, the sky above us was cloudless and brilliant with sunshine, the broad lake before us was glassy and clear, or rippled and breezy, or black and storm-tossed, according to Nature's mood; and its circling border of mountain domes, clothed with forests, scarred with land-slides, cloven by cañons and valleys, and helmeted with glittering snow, fitly framed and finished the noble picture. The view was always fascinating, bewitching, entrancing. The eye was never tired of gazing, night or day, in calm or storm; it suffered but one grief, and that was that it could not look always, but must close sometimes in sleep.

We slept in the sand close to the water's edge, between two protecting boulders, which took care of the stormy night-winds for us. We never took any paregoric to make us sleep. At the first break of dawn we were always up and running foot-races to tone down excess of physical vigor and exuberance of spirits. That is, Johnny was—but I held his hat. While smoking the pipe of peace after breakfast we watched the sentinel peaks put on the glory of the sun, and followed the conquering light as it swept down among the shadows, and set the captive crags and forests free. We watched the tinted pictures grow and brighten upon the water till every little detail of forest, precipice and pinnacle was wrought in and finished, and the miracle of the enchanter complete. Then to "business."

That is, drifting around in the boat. We were on the north shore. There, the rocks on the bottom are sometimes gray, sometimes white. This gives the marvelous transparency of the water a fuller advantage than it has elsewhere on the lake. We usually pushed out a hundred yards or so from shore, and then lay down on the thwarts, in the sun, and let the boat drift by the hour whither it would. We seldom talked. It interrupted the Sabbath stillness, and marred the dreams the luxurious rest and indolence brought. The shore all along was indented with deep, curved bays and coves, bordered by narrow sand-beaches; and where the sand ended, the steep mountain-sides rose right up aloft into space—rose up like a vast wall a little out of the perpendicular, and thickly wooded with tall pines.

So singularly clear was the water, that where it was only twenty or thirty feet deep the bottom was so perfectly distinct that the boat seemed floating in the air! Yes, where it was even *eighty* feet deep. Every little pebble was distinct, every speckled trout, every hand's-breadth of sand. Often, as we lay on our faces, a granite boulder, as large as a village church, would start out of the bottom apparently, and seem climbing up rapidly to the surface, till presently it threatened to touch our faces, and we could not resist the impulse to seize an oar and avert the danger. But the boat would float on, and the boulder descend again, and then we could see that when we had been exactly above it, it must still have been twenty or thirty feet below the surface. Down through the transparency of these great depths, the water was not *merely* transparent, but dazzlingly, brilliantly so. All objects seen through it had a bright, strong vividness, not only of outline, but of every minute detail, which they would not have had when seen simply through the same depth of atmosphere. So empty and airy did all spaces seem below us, and so strong was the sense of floating high aloft in mid-nothingness, that we called these boat-excursions "balloon-voyages."

We fished a good deal, but we did not average one fish a week. We could see trout by the thousand winging about in the emptiness under us, or sleeping in shoals on the bottom, but they would not bite—they could see the line too plainly, perhaps. We frequently selected the trout we wanted, and rested the bait patiently and persistently on the end of his nose at a depth of eighty feet, but he would only shake it off with an annoyed manner, and shift his position.

We bathed occasionally, but the water was rather chilly, for all it looked so sunny. Sometimes we rowed out to the "blue water," a mile or two from shore. It was as dead blue as indigo there, because of the immense depth. By official measurement the lake in its centre is one thousand five hundred and twenty-five feet deep!

Sometimes, on lazy afternoons, we lolled on the sand in camp, and smoked pipes and read some old well-worn novels. At night, by the camp-fire, we played euchre and seven-up to strengthen the mind—and played them with cards so greasy and defaced that only a whole summer's acquaintance with them could enable the student to tell the ace of clubs from the jack of diamonds.

We never slept in our "house." It never recurred to us, for one thing; and besides, it was built to hold the ground, and that was enough. We did not wish to strain it.

By and by our provisions began to run short, and we went back to the old camp and laid in a new supply. We were gone all day, and reached home again about night-fall, pretty tired and hungry. While Johnny was carrying the main bulk of the provisions up to our "house" for future use, I took the loaf of bread, some slices of bacon, and the coffee-pot, ashore, set them down by a tree, lit a fire, and went back to the boat to get the frying-pan. While I was at this, I heard a shout from Johnny, and looking up I saw that my fire was galloping all over the premises!

Johnny was on the other side of it. He had to run through the flames to get to the lake shore, and then we stood helpless and watched the devastation.

The ground was deeply carpeted with dry pine-needles, and the fire touched them off as if they were gunpowder. It was wonderful to see with what fierce speed the tall sheet of flame traveled! My coffee-pot was gone, and everything with it. In a minute and a half the fire seized upon a dense growth of dry manzanita chapparal six or eight feet high, and then the roaring and popping and crackling was something terrific. We were driven to the boat by the intense heat, and there we remained, spell-bound.

Within half an hour all before us was a tossing, blinding tempest of flame! It went surging up adjacent ridges—surmounted them and disappeared in the cañons beyond—burst into view upon higher and farther ridges, presently—shed a grander illumination abroad, and dove again—flamed out again, directly, higher and still higher up the mountain-side—threw out skirmishing parties of fire here and there, and sent them trailing their crimson spirals away among remote ramparts and ribs and gorges, till as far as the eye could reach the lofty mountain-fronts were webbed as it were with a tangled network of red lava streams. Away across the water the crags and domes were lit with a ruddy glare, and the firmament above was a reflected hell!

Every feature of the spectacle was repeated in the glowing mirror of the lake! Both pictures were sublime, both were beautiful; but that in the lake had a bewildering richness about it that enchanted the eye and held it with the stronger fascination.

We sat absorbed and motionless through four long hours. We never thought of supper, and never felt fatigue. But at eleven o'clock the conflagration had traveled beyond our range of vision, and then darkness stole down upon the landscape again.

Hunger asserted itself now, but there was nothing to eat. The provisions were all cooked, no doubt, but we did not go to see. We were homeless wanderers again, without any property. Our fence was gone, our house burned down; no insurance. Our pine forest was well scorched, the dead trees all burned up, and our broad acres of manzanita swept away. Our blankets were on our usual sand-bed, however, and so we lay down and went to sleep. The next morning we started back to the old camp, but while out a long way from shore, so great a storm came up that we dared not try to land. So I baled out the seas we shipped, and Johnny pulled heavily through the billows till we had reached a point three or four miles beyond the camp. The storm was increasing, and it became evident that it was better to take the hazard of beaching the boat than go down in a hundred fathoms of water; so we ran in, with tall white-caps following, and I sat down in the stern-sheets and pointed her head-on to the shore. The instant the bow struck, a wave came over the stern that washed crew and cargo ashore, and saved a deal of trouble. We shivered in the lee of a boulder all the rest of the day, and froze all the night through. In the morning the tempest had gone

down, and we paddled down to the camp without any unnecessary delay. We were so starved that we ate up the rest of the
Brigade's provisions, and then set out to Carson to tell them
about it and ask their forgiveness. It was accorded, upon payment of damages.

We made many trips to the lake after that, and had many a
hair-breadth escape and blood-curdling adventure which will
never be recorded in any history.

Chapter XXIV

I RESOLVED to have a horse to ride. I had never seen such wild, free, magnificent horsemanship outside of a circus as these picturesquely-clad Mexicans, Californians and Mexicanized Americans displayed in Carson streets every day. How they rode! Leaning just gently forward out of the perpendicular, easy and nonchalant, with broad slouch-hat brim blown square up in front, and long *riata* swinging above the head, they swept through the town like the wind! The next minute they were only a sailing puff of dust on the far desert. If they trotted, they sat up gallantly and gracefully, and seemed part of the horse; did not go jiggering up and down after the silly Miss-Nancy fashion of the riding-schools. I had quickly learned to tell a horse from a cow, and was full of anxiety to learn more. I was resolved to buy a horse.

While the thought was rankling in my mind, the auctioneer came skurrying through the plaza on a black beast that had as many humps and corners on him as a dromedary, and was necessarily uncomely; but he was "going, going, at twenty-two!—horse, saddle and bridle at twenty-two dollars, gentlemen!" and I could hardly resist.

A man whom I did not know (he turned out to be the auctioneer's brother) noticed the wistful look in my eye, and observed that that was a very remarkable horse to be going at such a price; and added that the saddle alone was worth the money. It was a Spanish saddle, with ponderous *tapidaros*, and furnished with the ungainly sole-leather covering with the unspellable name. I said I had half a notion to bid. Then this keen-eyed person appeared to me to be "taking my measure"; but I dismissed the suspicion when he spoke, for his manner was full of guileless candor and truthfulness. Said he:

"I know that horse—know him well. You are a stranger, I take it, and so you might think he was an American horse, maybe, but I assure you he is not. He is nothing of the kind; but—excuse my speaking in a low voice, other people being near—he is, without the shadow of a doubt, a Genuine Mexican Plug!"

I did not know what a Genuine Mexican Plug was, but

there was something about this man's way of saying it, that made me swear inwardly that I would own a Genuine Mexican Plug, or die.

"Has he any other—er—advantages?" I inquired, suppressing what eagerness I could.

He hooked his forefinger in the pocket of my army-shirt, led me to one side, and breathed in my ear impressively these words:

"He can out-buck anything in America!"

"Going, going, going—at *twent-ty*-four dollars and a half, gen—"

"Twenty-seven!" I shouted, in a frenzy.

"And sold!" said the auctioneer, and passed over the Genuine Mexican Plug to me.

I could scarcely contain my exultation. I paid the money, and put the animal in a neighboring livery-stable to dine and rest himself.

In the afternoon I brought the creature into the plaza, and certain citizens held him by the head, and others by the tail, while I mounted him. As soon as they let go, he placed all his feet in a bunch together, lowered his back, and then suddenly arched it upward, and shot me straight into the air a matter of three or four feet! I came as straight down again, lit in the saddle, went instantly up again, came down almost on the high pommel, shot up again, and came down on the horse's neck—all in the space of three or four seconds. Then he rose and stood almost straight up on his hind feet, and I, clasping his lean neck desperately, slid back into the saddle, and held on. He came down, and immediately hoisted his heels into the air, delivering a vicious kick at the sky, and stood on his forefeet. And then down he came once more, and began the original exercise of shooting me straight up again. The third time I went up I heard a stranger say:

"Oh, *don't* he buck, though!"

While I was up, somebody struck the horse a sounding thwack with a leathern strap, and when I arrived again the Genuine Mexican Plug was not there. A Californian youth chased him up and caught him, and asked if he might have a ride. I granted him that luxury. He mounted the Genuine, got lifted into the air once, but sent his spurs home as he descended, and the horse darted away like a telegram. He soared over three fences like a bird, and disappeared down the road toward the Washoe Valley.

I sat down on a stone, with a sigh, and by a natural impulse one of my hands sought my forehead, and the other the base of my stomach. I believe I never appreciated, till then, the poverty of the human machinery—for I still needed a hand or two to place elsewhere. Pen cannot describe how I was jolted up. Imagination cannot conceive how disjointed I was—how internally, externally and universally I was unsettled, mixed up and ruptured. There was a sympathetic crowd around me, though.

One elderly-looking comforter said:

"Stranger, you've been taken in. Everybody in this camp knows that horse. Any child, any Injun, could have told you that he'd buck; he is the very worst devil to buck on the continent of America. You hear *me*. I'm Curry. *Old* Curry. Old *Abe* Curry. And moreover, he is a simon-pure, out-and-out, genuine d—d Mexican plug, and an uncommon mean one at that, too. Why, you turnip, if you had laid low and kept dark, there's chances to buy an *American* horse for mighty little more than you paid for that bloody old foreign relic."

I gave no sign; but I made up my mind that if the auctioneer's brother's funeral took place while I was in the Territory I would postpone all other recreations and attend it.

After a gallop of sixteen miles the Californian youth and the Genuine Mexican Plug came tearing into town again, shedding foam-flakes like the spume-spray that drives before a typhoon, and, with one final skip over a wheelbarrow and a Chinaman, cast anchor in front of the "ranch."

Such panting and blowing! Such spreading and contracting of the red equine nostrils, and glaring of the wild equine eye! But was the imperial beast subjugated? Indeed he was not. His lordship the Speaker of the House thought he was, and mounted him to go down to the Capitol; but the first dash the creature made was over a pile of telegraph poles half as high as a church; and his time to the Capitol—one mile and three quarters—remains unbeaten to this day. But then he took an advantage—he left out the mile, and only did the three quarters. That is to say, he made a straight cut across lots, preferring fences and ditches to a crooked road; and when the Speaker got to the Capitol he said he had been in the air so much he felt as if he had made the trip on a comet.

In the evening the Speaker came home afoot for exercise, and got the Genuine towed back behind a quartz wagon. The next day I loaned the animal to the Clerk of the House to go down to the Dana silver mine, six miles, and *he* walked back for exercise, and got the horse towed. Everybody I loaned him to always walked back; they never could get enough exercise any other way. Still, I continued to loan him to anybody who was willing to borrow him, my idea being to get him crippled, and throw him on the borrower's hands, or killed, and make the borrower pay for him. But somehow nothing ever happened to him. He took chances that no other horse ever took and survived, but he always came out safe. It was his daily habit to try experiments that had always before been considered impossible, but he always got through. Sometimes he miscalculated a little, and did not get his rider through intact, but *he* always got through himself. Of course I had tried to sell him; but that was a stretch of simplicity which met with little sympathy. The auctioneer stormed up and down the streets on him for four days, dispersing the populace, interrupting business, and destroying children, and never got a bid—at least never any but the eighteen-dollar one he hired a notoriously substanceless bummer to make. The people only smiled pleasantly, and restrained their desire to buy, if they had any. Then the auctioneer brought in his bill, and I withdrew the horse from the market. We tried to trade him off at private vendue next, offering him at a sacrifice for second-hand tombstones, old iron, temperance tracts—any kind of property. But holders were stiff, and we retired from the market again. I never tried to ride the horse any more. Walking was good enough exercise for a man like me, that had nothing the matter with him except ruptures, internal injuries, and such things. Finally I tried to *give* him away. But it was a failure. Parties said earthquakes were handy enough on the Pacific coast—they did not wish to own one. As a last resort I offered him to the Governor for the use of the "Brigade." His face lit up eagerly at first, but toned down again, and he said the thing would be too palpable.

Just then the livery stable man brought in his bill for six weeks' keeping—stall-room for the horse, fifteen dollars; hay for the horse, two hundred and fifty! The Genuine Mexican Plug had eaten a ton of the article, and the man said he would have eaten a hundred if he had let him.

I will remark here, in all seriousness, that the regular price of hay during that year and a part of the next was really two hundred and fifty dollars a ton. During a part of the previous year it had sold at five hundred a ton, in gold, and during the winter before that there was such scarcity of the article that in several instances small quantities had brought eight hundred dollars a ton in coin! The consequence might be guessed without my telling it: peopled turned their stock loose to starve, and before the spring arrived Carson and Eagle valleys were almost literally carpeted with their carcases! Any old settler there will verify these statements.

I managed to pay the livery bill, and that same day I gave the Genuine Mexican Plug to a passing Arkansas emigrant whom fortune delivered into my hand. If this ever meets his eye, he will doubtless remember the donation.

Now whoever has had the luck to ride a real Mexican plug will recognize the animal depicted in this chapter, and hardly consider him exaggerated—but the uninitiated will feel justified in regarding his portrait as a fancy sketch, perhaps.

Chapter XXV

ORIGINALLY, Nevada was a part of Utah and was called Carson county; and a pretty large county it was, too. Certain of its valleys produced no end of hay, and this attracted small colonies of Mormon stock-raisers and farmers to them. A few orthodox Americans straggled in from California, but no love was lost between the two classes of colonists. There was little or no friendly intercourse; each party staid to itself. The Mormons were largely in the majority, and had the additional advantage of being peculiarly under the protection of the Mormon government of the Territory. Therefore they could afford to be distant, and even peremptory toward their neighbors. One of the traditions of Carson Valley illustrates the condition of things that prevailed at the time I speak of. The hired girl of one of the American families was Irish, and a Catholic; yet it was noted with surprise that she was the only person outside of the Mormon ring who could get favors from the Mormons. She asked kindnesses of them often, and always got them. It was a mystery to every body. But one day as she was passing out at the door, a large bowie knife dropped from under her apron, and when her mistress asked for an explanation she observed that she was going out to "borry a wash-tub from the Mormons!"

In 1858 silver lodes were discovered in "Carson County," and then the aspect of things changed. Californians began to flock in, and the American element was soon in the majority. Allegiance to Brigham Young and Utah was renounced, and a temporary territorial government for "Washoe" was instituted by the citizens. Governor Roop was the first and only chief magistrate of it. In due course of time Congress passed a bill to organize "Nevada Territory," and President Lincoln sent out Governor Nye to supplant Roop.

At this time the population of the Territory was about twelve or fifteen thousand, and rapidly increasing. Silver mines were being vigorously developed and silver mills erected. Business of all kinds was active and prosperous and growing more so day by day.

The people were glad to have a legitimately constituted

government, but did not particularly enjoy having strangers from distant States put in authority over them—a sentiment that was natural enough. They thought the officials should have been chosen from among themselves—from among prominent citizens who had earned a right to such promotion, and who would be in sympathy with the populace and likewise thoroughly acquainted with the needs of the Territory. They were right in viewing the matter thus, without doubt. The new officers were "emigrants," and that was no title to anybody's affection or admiration either.

The new government was received with considerable coolness. It was not only a foreign intruder, but a poor one. It was not even worth plucking—except by the smallest of small fry office-seekers and such. Everybody knew that Congress had appropriated only twenty thousand dollars a year in greenbacks for its support—about money enough to run a quartz mill a month. And everybody knew, also, that the first year's money was still in Washington, and that the getting hold of it would be a tedious and difficult process. Carson City was too wary and too wise to open up a credit account with the imported bantling with anything like indecent haste.

There is something solemnly funny about the struggles of a new-born Territorial government to get a start in this world. Ours had a trying time of it. The Organic Act and the "instructions" from the State Department commanded that a legislature should be elected at such-and-such a time, and its sittings inaugurated at such-and-such a date. It was easy to get legislators, even at three dollars a day, although board was four dollars and fifty cents, for distinction has its charm in Nevada as well as elsewhere, and there were plenty of patriotic souls out of employment; but to get a legislative hall for them to meet in was another matter altogether. Carson blandly declined to give a room rent-free, or let one to the government on credit.

But when Curry heard of the difficulty, he came forward, solitary and alone, and shouldered the Ship of State over the bar and got her afloat again. I refer to "Curry—*Old* Curry— Old *Abe* Curry." But for him the legislature would have been obliged to sit in the desert. He offered his large stone

building just outside the capital limits, rent-free, and it was
gladly accepted. Then he built a horse-railroad from town to
the capitol, and carried the legislators gratis. He also furnished pine benches and chairs for the legislature, and covered the floors with clean saw-dust by way of carpet and
spittoon combined. But for Curry the government would
have died in its tender infancy. A canvas partition to separate
the Senate from the House of Representatives was put up by
the Secretary, at a cost of three dollars and forty cents, but
the United States declined to pay for it. Upon being reminded that the "instructions" permitted the payment of a
liberal rent for a legislative hall, and that money was
saved to the country by Mr. Curry's generosity, the United
States said that did not alter the matter, and the three dollars
and forty cents would be subtracted from the Secretary's
eighteen hundred dollar salary—and it *was!*

The matter of printing was from the beginning an interesting feature of the new government's difficulties. The Secretary was sworn to obey his volume of written "instructions,"
and these commanded him to do two certain things without
fail, viz.:

1. Get the House and Senate journals printed; and,

2. For this work, pay one dollar and fifty cents per "thousand" for composition, and one dollar and fifty cents per "token" for press-work, in greenbacks.

It was easy to swear to do these two things, but it was
entirely impossible to do more than one of them. When
greenbacks had gone down to forty cents on the dollar, the
prices regularly charged everybody by printing establishments
were one dollar and fifty cents per "thousand" and one dollar
and fifty cents per "token," in *gold*. The "instructions" commanded that the Secretary regard a paper dollar issued by the
government as equal to any other dollar issued by the government. Hence the printing of the journals was discontinued.
Then the United States sternly rebuked the Secretary for dis-
regarding the "instructions," and warned him to correct his
ways. Wherefore he got some printing done, forwarded the
bill to Washington with full exhibits of the high prices of
things in the Territory, and called attention to a printed market report wherein it would be observed that even hay was

two hundred and fifty dollars a ton. The United States responded by subtracting the printing-bill from the Secretary's suffering salary—and moreover remarked with dense gravity that he would find nothing in his "instructions" requiring him to purchase hay!

Nothing in this world is palled in such impenetrable obscurity as a U. S. Treasury Comptroller's understanding. The very fires of the hereafter could get up nothing more than a fitful glimmer in it. In the days I speak of he never could be made to comprehend why it was that twenty thousand dollars would not go as far in Nevada, where all commodities ranged at an enormous figure, as it would in the other Territories, where exceeding cheapness was the rule. He was an officer who looked out for the little expenses all the time. The Secretary of the Territory kept his office in his bedroom, as I before remarked; and he charged the United States no rent, although his "instructions" provided for that item and he could have justly taken advantage of it (a thing which I would have done with more than lightning promptness if I had been Secretary myself). But the United States never applauded this devotion. Indeed, I think my country was ashamed to have so improvident a person in its employ.

Those "instructions" (we used to read a chapter from them every morning, as intellectual gymnastics, and a couple of chapters in Sunday school every Sabbath, for they treated of all subjects under the sun and had much valuable religious matter in them along with the other statistics) those "instructions" commanded that pen-knives, envelopes, pens and writing-paper be furnished the members of the legislature. So the Secretary made the purchase and the distribution. The knives cost three dollars apiece. There was one too many, and the Secretary gave it to the Clerk of the House of Representatives. The United States said the Clerk of the House was not a "member" of the legislature, and took that three dollars out of the Secretary's salary, as usual.

White men charged three or four dollars a "load" for sawing up stove-wood. The Secretary was sagacious enough to know that the United States would never pay any such price as that; so he got an Indian to saw up a load of office wood at one dollar and a half. He made out the usual voucher, but signed no name to it—simply appended a note explaining that an Indian had done the work, and had done it in a very capable and satisfactory way, but could not sign the voucher owing to lack of ability in the necessary direction. The Secretary had to pay that dollar and a half. He thought the United States would admire both his economy and his honesty in getting the work done at half price and not putting a pretended Indian's signature to the voucher, but the United States did not see it in that light. The United States was too much accustomed to employing dollar-and-a-half thieves in all manner of official capacities to regard his explanation of the voucher as having any foundation in fact.

But the next time the Indian sawed wood for us I taught him to make a cross at the bottom of the voucher—it looked like a cross that had been drunk a year—and then I "witnessed" it and it went through all right. The United States never said a word. I was sorry I had not made the voucher for a thousand loads of wood instead of one. The government of my country snubs honest simplicity but fondles artistic villainy, and I think I might have developed into a very capable pickpocket if I had remained in the public service a year or two.

That was a fine collection of sovereigns, that first Nevada legislature. They levied taxes to the amount of thirty or forty thousand dollars and ordered expenditures to the extent of about a million. Yet they had their little periodical explosions of economy like all other bodies of the kind. A member proposed to save three dollars a day to the nation by dispensing with the Chaplain. And yet that short-sighted man needed the Chaplain more than any other member, perhaps, for he generally sat with his feet on his desk, eating raw turnips, during the morning prayer.

The legislature sat sixty days, and passed private toll-road franchises all the time. When they adjourned it was estimated that every citizen owned about three franchises, and it was believed that unless Congress gave the Territory another degree of longitude there would not be room enough to accommodate the toll-roads. The ends of them were hanging over the boundary line everywhere like a fringe.

The fact is, the freighting business had grown to such important proportions that there was nearly as much excitement over suddenly acquired toll-road fortunes as over the wonderful silver mines.

Chapter XXVI

B Y AND BY I was smitten with the silver fever. "Prospecting parties" were leaving for the mountains every day, and discovering and taking possession of rich silver-bearing lodes and ledges of quartz. Plainly this was the road to fortune. The great "Gould and Curry" mine was held at three or four hundred dollars a foot when we arrived; but in two months it had sprung up to eight hundred. The "Ophir" had been worth only a mere trifle, a year gone by, and now it was selling at nearly *four thousand dollars a foot!* Not a mine could be named that had not experienced an astonishing advance in value within a short time. Everybody was talking about these marvels. Go where you would, you heard nothing else, from morning till far into the night. Tom So-and-So had sold out of the "Amanda Smith" for $40,000—hadn't a cent when he "took up" the ledge six months ago. John Jones had sold half his interest in the "Bald Eagle and Mary Ann" for $65,000, gold coin, and gone to the States for his family. The widow Brewster had "struck it rich" in the "Golden Fleece" and sold ten feet for $18,000—hadn't money enough to buy a crape bonnet when Sing-Sing Tommy killed her husband at Baldy Johnson's wake last spring. The "Last Chance" had found a "clay casing" and knew they were "right on the ledge"—consequence, "feet" that went begging yesterday were worth a brick house apiece to-day, and seedy owners who could not get trusted for a drink at any bar in the country yesterday were roaring drunk on champagne to-day and had hosts of warm personal friends in a town where they had forgotten how to bow or shake hands from long-continued want of practice. Johnny Morgan, a common loafer, had gone to sleep in the gutter and waked up worth a hundred thousand dollars, in consequence of the decision in the "Lady Franklin and Rough and Ready" lawsuit. And so on—day in and day out the talk pelted our ears and the excitement waxed hotter and hotter around us.

I would have been more or less than human if I had not gone mad like the rest. Cart-loads of solid silver bricks, as large as pigs of lead, were arriving from the mills every day, and such sights as that gave substance to the wild talk about me. I succumbed and grew as frenzied as the craziest.

Every few days news would come of the discovery of a bran-new mining region; immediately the papers would teem with accounts of its richness, and away the surplus population would scamper to take possession. By the time I was fairly inoculated with the disease, "Esmeralda" had just had a run and "Humboldt" was beginning to shriek for attention. "Humboldt! Humboldt!" was the new cry, and straightway Humboldt, the newest of the new, the richest of the rich, the most marvellous of the marvellous discoveries in silver-land, was occupying two columns of the public prints to "Esmeralda's" one. I was just on the point of starting to Esmeralda, but turned with the tide and got ready for Humboldt. That the reader may see what moved me, and what would as surely have moved him had he been there, I insert here one of the newspaper letters of the day. It and several other letters from the same calm hand were the main means of converting me. I shall not garble the extract, but put it in just as it appeared in the *Daily Territorial Enterprise*:

But what about our mines? I shall be candid with you. I shall express an honest opinion, based upon a thorough examination. Humboldt county is the richest mineral region upon God's footstool. Each mountain range is gorged with the precious ores. Humboldt is the true Golconda.

The other day an assay of mere *croppings* yielded exceeding *four thousand dollars to the ton*. A week or two ago an assay of just such surface developments made returns of *seven thousand* dollars to the ton. Our mountains are full of rambling prospectors. Each day and almost every hour reveals new and more startling evidences of the profuse and intensified wealth of our favored county. The metal is not silver alone. There are distinct ledges of auriferous ore. A late discovery plainly evinces cinnabar. The coarser metals are in gross abundance. Lately evidences of bituminous coal have been detected. My theory has ever been that coal is a ligneous formation. I told Col. Whitman, in times past, that the neighborhood of Dayton (Nevada) betrayed no present or previous manifestations of a ligneous foundation, and that hence I had no confidence in his lauded coal mines. I repeated the same doctrine to the exultant coal discoverers of Humboldt. I talked with my friend Captain Burch on the subject. My pyrhanism vanished upon his statement that in the very region referred to he had seen petrified trees of the length of two hundred feet. Then is the fact established that huge forests once cast their grim shadows over this remote section. I am firm in the coal faith. Have no fears of the mineral resources of Humboldt county. They are immense—incalculable.

Let me state one or two things which will help the reader to better comprehend certain items in the above. At this time, our near neighbor, Gold Hill, was the most successful silver mining locality in Nevada. It was from there that more than half the daily shipments of silver bricks came. "Very rich" (and scarce) Gold Hill ore yielded from $100 to $400 to the ton; but the usual yield was only $20 to $40 per ton—that is to say, each hundred pounds of ore yielded from one dollar to two dollars. But the reader will perceive by the above extract, that in Humboldt from one fourth to nearly half the mass was silver! That is to say, every one hundred pounds of the ore had from *two hundred* dollars up to about *three hundred and fifty* in it. Some days later this same correspondent wrote:

I have spoken of the vast and almost fabulous wealth of this region—it is incredible. The intestines of our mountains are gorged with precious ore to plethora. I have said that nature has so shaped our mountains as to furnish most excellent facilities for the working of our mines. I have also told you that the country about here is pregnant with the finest mill sites in the world. But what is the mining history of Humboldt? The Sheba mine is in the hands of energetic San Francisco capitalists. It would seem that the ore is combined with metals that render it difficult of reduction with our imperfect mountain machinery. The proprietors have combined the capital and labor hinted at in my exordium. They are toiling and probing. Their tunnel has reached the length of one hundred feet. From primal assays alone, coupled with the development of the mine and public confidence in the continuance of effort, the stock had reared itself to eight hundred dollars market value. I do not know that one ton of the ore has been converted into current metal. I do know that there are many lodes in this section that surpass the Sheba in primal assay value. Listen a moment to the calculations of the Sheba operators. They purpose transporting the ore concentrated to Europe. The conveyance from Star City (its locality) to Virginia City will cost seventy dollars per ton; from Virginia to San Francisco, forty dollars per ton; from thence to Liverpool, its destination, ten dollars per ton. Their idea is that its conglomerate metals will reimburse them their cost of original extraction, the price of transportation, and the expense of reduction, and that then a ton of the raw ore will net them twelve hundred dollars. The estimate may be extravagant. Cut it in twain, and the product is enormous, far transcending any previous developments of our racy Territory.

A very common calculation is that many of our mines will yield five hundred dollars to the ton. Such fecundity throws the Gould & Curry, the Ophir and the Mexican, of your neighborhood, in the darkest shadow. I have given you the estimate of the value of a single developed mine. Its richness is indexed by its market valuation. The people of Humboldt county are *feet* crazy. As I write, our towns are near deserted. They look as languid as a consumptive girl. What has become of our sinewy and athletic fellow-citizens? They are coursing through ravines and over mountain tops. Their tracks are visible in every direction. Occasionally a horseman will dash among us. His steed betrays hard usage. He alights before his adobe dwelling, hastily exchanges courtesies with his townsmen, hurries to an assay office and from thence to the District Recorder's. In the morning, having renewed his provisional supplies, he is off again on his wild and unbeaten route. Why, the fellow numbers already his feet by the thousands. He is the horse-leech. He has the craving stomach of the shark or anaconda. He would conquer metallic worlds.

This was enough. The instant we had finished reading the above article, four of us decided to go to Humboldt. We commenced getting ready at once. And we also commenced upbraiding ourselves for not deciding sooner—for we were in terror lest all the rich mines would be found and secured before we got there, and we might have to put up with ledges that would not yield more than two or three hundred dollars a ton, maybe. An hour before, I would have felt opulent if I had owned ten feet in a Gold Hill mine whose ore produced twenty-five dollars to the ton; now I was already annoyed at the prospect of having to put up with mines the poorest of which would be a marvel in Gold Hill.

Chapter XXVII

Hurry, was the word! We wasted no time. Our party consisted of four persons—a blacksmith sixty years of age, two young lawyers, and myself. We bought a wagon and two miserable old horses. We put eighteen hundred pounds of provisions and mining tools in the wagon and drove out of Carson on a chilly December afternoon. The horses were so weak and old that we soon found that it would be better if one or two of us got out and walked. It was an improvement. Next, we found that it would be better if a third man got out. That was an improvement also. It was at this time that I volunteered to drive, although I had never driven a harnessed horse before and many a man in such a position would have felt fairly excused from such a responsibility. But in a little while it was found that it would be a fine thing if the driver got out and walked also. It was at this time that I resigned the position of driver, and never resumed it again. Within the hour, we found that it would not only be better, but was absolutely necessary, that we four, taking turns, two at a time, should put our hands against the end of the wagon and push it through the sand, leaving the feeble horses little to do but keep out of the way and hold up the tongue. Perhaps it is well for one to know his fate at first, and get reconciled to it. We had learned ours in one afternoon. It was plain that we had to walk through the sand and shove that wagon and those horses two hundred miles. So we accepted the situation, and from that time forth we never rode. More than that, we stood regular and nearly constant watches pushing up behind.

We made seven miles, and camped in the desert. Young Clagett (now member of Congress from Montana) unharnessed and fed and watered the horses; Oliphant and I cut sage-brush, built the fire and brought water to cook with; and old Mr. Ballou the blacksmith did the cooking. This division of labor, and this appointment, was adhered to throughout the journey. We had no tent, and so we slept under our blankets in the open plain. We were so tired that we slept soundly.

We were fifteen days making the trip—two hundred miles;

thirteen, rather, for we lay by a couple of days, in one place, to let the horses rest. We could really have accomplished the journey in ten days if we had towed the horses behind the wagon, but we did not think of that until it was too late, and so went on shoving the horses and the wagon too when we might have saved half the labor. Parties who met us, occasionally, advised us to put the horses *in* the wagon, but Mr. Ballou, through whose iron-clad earnestness no sarcasm could pierce, said that that would not do, because the provisions were exposed and would suffer, the horses being "bituminous from long deprivation." The reader will excuse me from translating. What Mr. Ballou customarily meant, when he used a long word, was a secret between himself and his Maker. He was one of the best and kindest hearted men that ever graced a humble sphere of life. He was gentleness and simplicity itself—and unselfishness, too. Although he was more than twice as old as the eldest of us, he never gave himself any airs, privileges, or exemptions on that account. He did a *young* man's share of the work; and did his share of conversing and entertaining from the general stand-point of *any* age—not from the arrogant, overawing summit-height of sixty years. His one striking peculiarity was his Partingtonian fashion of loving and using big words *for their own sakes*, and independent of any bearing they might have upon the thought he was purposing to convey. He always let his ponderous syllables fall with an easy unconsciousness that left them wholly without offensiveness. In truth his air was so natural and so simple that one was always catching himself accepting his stately sentences as meaning something, when they really meant nothing in the world. If a word was long and grand and resonant, that was sufficient to win the old man's love, and he would drop that word into the most out-of-the-way place in a sentence or a subject, and be as pleased with it as if it were perfectly luminous with meaning.

We four always spread our common stock of blankets together on the frozen ground, and slept side by side; and finding that our foolish, long-legged hound pup had a deal of animal heat in him, Oliphant got to admitting him to the bed, between himself and Mr. Ballou, hugging the dog's warm back to his breast and finding great comfort in it. But in the night the pup would get stretchy and brace his feet against the old man's back and shove, grunting complacently the while; and now and then, being warm and snug, grateful and happy, he would paw the old man's back simply in excess of comfort; and at yet other times he would dream of the chase and in his sleep tug at the old man's back hair and bark in his ear. The old gentleman complained mildly about these familiarities, at last, and when he got through with his statement he said that such a dog as that was not a proper animal to admit to bed with tired men, because he was "so meretricious in his movements and so organic in his emotions." We turned the dog out.

It was a hard, wearing, toilsome journey, but it had its bright side; for after each day was done and our wolfish hunger appeased with a hot supper of fried bacon, bread, molasses and black coffee, the pipe-smoking, song-singing and yarn-spinning around the evening camp-fire in the still solitudes of the desert was a happy, care-free sort of recreation that seemed the very summit and culmination of earthly luxury. It is a kind of life that has a potent charm for all men, whether city or country-bred. We are descended from desert-lounging Arabs, and countless ages of growth toward perfect civilization have failed to root out of us the nomadic instinct. We all confess to a gratified thrill at the thought of "camping out."

Once we made twenty-five miles in a day, and once we made forty miles (through the Great American Desert), and ten miles beyond—fifty in all—in twenty-three hours, without halting to eat, drink or rest. To stretch out and go to sleep, even on stony and frozen ground, after pushing a wagon and two horses fifty miles, is a delight so supreme that for the moment it almost seems cheap at the price.

We camped two days in the neighborhood of the "Sink of the Humboldt." We tried to use the strong alkaline water of the Sink, but it would not answer. It was like drinking lye, and not weak lye, either. It left a taste in the mouth bitter and every way execrable, and a burning in the stomach that was very uncomfortable. We put molasses in it, but that helped it very little; we added a pickle, yet the alkali was the prominent taste, and so it was unfit for drinking. The coffee we made of this water was the meanest compound man has yet invented. It was really viler to the taste than the unameliorated water itself. Mr. Ballou, being the architect and builder of the beverage felt constrained to endorse and uphold it, and so drank half a cup, by little sips, making shift to praise it faintly the while, but finally threw out the remainder, and said frankly it was "too technical for *him*."

But presently we found a spring of fresh water, convenient, and then, with nothing to mar our enjoyment, and no stragglers to interrupt it, we entered into our rest.

Chapter XXVIII

AFTER LEAVING the Sink, we traveled along the Humboldt river a little way. People accustomed to the monster mile-wide Mississippi, grow accustomed to associating the term "river" with a high degree of watery grandeur. Consequently, such people feel rather disappointed when they stand on the shores of the Humboldt or the Carson and find that a "river" in Nevada is a sickly rivulet which is just the counterpart of the Erie canal in all respects save that the canal is twice as long and four times as deep. One of the pleasantest and most invigorating exercises one can contrive is to run and jump across the Humboldt river till he is overheated, and then drink it dry.

On the fifteenth day we completed our march of two hundred miles and entered Unionville, Humboldt county, in the midst of a driving snow-storm. Unionville consisted of eleven cabins and a liberty-pole. Six of the cabins were strung along one side of a deep canyon, and the other five faced them. The rest of the landscape was made up of bleak mountain walls that rose so high into the sky from both sides of the canyon that the village was left, as it were, far down in the bottom of a crevice. It was always daylight on the mountain tops a long time before the darkness lifted and revealed Unionville.

We built a small, rude cabin in the side of the crevice and roofed it with canvas, leaving a corner open to serve as a chimney, through which the cattle used to tumble occasionally, at night, and mash our furniture and interrupt our sleep. It was very cold weather and fuel was scarce. Indians brought brush and bushes several miles on their backs; and when we could catch a laden Indian it was well—and when we could not (which was the rule, not the exception), we shivered and bore it.

I confess, without shame, that I expected to find masses of silver lying all about the ground. I expected to see it glittering in the sun on the mountain summits. I said nothing about this, for some instinct told me that I might possibly have an exaggerated idea about it, and so if I betrayed my thought I

677

might bring derision upon myself. Yet I was as perfectly satisfied in my own mind as I could be of anything, that I was
going to gather up, in a day or two, or at furthest a week or
two, silver enough to make me satisfactorily wealthy—and so
my fancy was already busy with plans for spending this
money. The first opportunity that offered, I sauntered carelessly away from the cabin, keeping an eye on the other boys,
and stopping and contemplating the sky when they seemed
to be observing me; but as soon as the coast was manifestly
clear, I fled away as guiltily as a thief might have done and
never halted till I was far beyond sight and call. Then I began
my search with a feverish excitement that was brimful of expectation—almost of certainty. I crawled about the ground,
seizing and examining bits of stone, blowing the dust from
them or rubbing them on my clothes, and then peering at
them with anxious hope. Presently I found a bright fragment
and my heart bounded! I hid behind a boulder and polished
it and scrutinized it with a nervous eagerness and a delight
that was more pronounced than absolute certainty itself could
have afforded. The more I examined the fragment the more I
was convinced that I had found the door to fortune. I marked
the spot and carried away my specimen. Up and down the
rugged mountain side I searched, with always increasing interest and always augmenting gratitude that I had come to
Humboldt and come in time. Of all the experiences of my
life, this secret search among the hidden treasures of silverland was the nearest to unmarred ecstasy. It was a delirious
revel. By and by, in the bed of a shallow rivulet, I found a
deposit of shining yellow scales, and my breath almost forsook me! A gold mine, and in my simplicity I had been content with vulgar silver! I was so excited that I half believed
my overwrought imagination was deceiving me. Then a fear
came upon me that people might be observing me and would
guess my secret. Moved by this thought, I made a circuit of
the place, and ascended a knoll to reconnoiter. Solitude. No
creature was near. Then I returned to my mine, fortifying
myself against possible disappointment, but my fears were
groundless—the shining scales were still there. I set about
scooping them out, and for an hour I toiled down the windings of the stream and robbed its bed. But at last the descend-

ing sun warned me to give up the quest, and I turned homeward laden with wealth. As I walked along I could not help smiling at the thought of my being so excited over my fragment of silver when a nobler metal was almost under my nose. In this little time the former had so fallen in my estimation that once or twice I was on the point of throwing it away.

The boys were as hungry as usual, but I could eat nothing. Neither could I talk. I was full of dreams and far away. Their conversation interrupted the flow of my fancy somewhat, and annoyed me a little, too. I despised the sordid and commonplace things they talked about. But as they proceeded, it began to amuse me. It grew to be rare fun to hear them planning their poor little economies and sighing over possible privations and distresses when a gold mine, all our own, lay within sight of the cabin and I could point it out at any moment. Smothered hilarity began to oppress me, presently. It was hard to resist the impulse to burst out with exultation and reveal everything; but I did resist. I said within myself that I would filter the great news through my lips calmly and be serene as a summer morning while I watched its effect in their faces. I said:

"Where have you all been?"

"Prospecting."

"What did you find?"

"Nothing."

"Nothing? What do you think of the country?"

"Can't tell, yet," said Mr. Ballou, who was an old gold miner, and had likewise had considerable experience among the silver mines.

"Well, haven't you formed any sort of opinion?"

"Yes, a sort of a one. It's fair enough here, may be, but overrated. Seven thousand dollar ledges are scarce, though. That Sheba may be rich enough, but we don't own it; and besides, the rock is so full of base metals that all the science in the world can't work it. We'll not starve, here, but we'll not get rich, I'm afraid."

"So you think the prospect is pretty poor?"

"No name for it!"

"Well, we'd better go back, hadn't we?"

"Oh, not yet—of course not. We'll try it a riffle, first."

"Suppose, now—this is merely a supposition, you know—suppose you could find a ledge that would yield, say, a hundred and fifty dollars a ton—would that satisfy you?"

"Try us once!" from the whole party.

"Or suppose—merely a supposition, of course—suppose you were to find a ledge that would yield two thousand dollars a ton—would *that* satisfy you?"

"Here—what do you mean? What are you coming at? Is there some mystery behind all this?"

"Never mind. I am not saying anything. You know perfectly well there are no rich mines here—of course you do. Because you have been around and examined for yourselves. Anybody would know that, that had been around. But just for the sake of argument, suppose—in a kind of general way—suppose some person were to tell you that two-thousand-dollar ledges were simply contemptible—contemptible, understand—and that right yonder in sight of this very cabin there were piles of pure gold and pure silver—oceans of it—enough to make you all rich in twenty-four hours! Come!"

"I should say he was as crazy as a loon!" said old Ballou, but wild with excitement, nevertheless.

"Gentlemen," said I, "I don't say anything—*I* haven't been around, you know, and of course don't know anything—but all I ask of you is to cast your eye on *that*, for instance, and tell me what you think of it!" and I tossed my treasure before them.

There was an eager scramble for it, and a closing of heads together over it under the candle-light. Then old Ballou said:

"Think of it? I think it is nothing but a lot of granite rubbish and nasty glittering mica that isn't worth ten cents an acre!"

So vanished my dream. So melted my wealth away. So toppled my airy castle to the earth and left me stricken and forlorn.

Moralizing, I observed, then, that "all that glitters is not gold."

Mr. Ballou said I could go further than that, and lay it up among my treasures of knowledge, that *nothing* that glitters is gold. So I learned then, once for all, that gold in its native state is but dull, unornamental stuff, and that only low-born metals excite the admiration of the ignorant with an ostentatious glitter. However, like the rest of the world, I still go on underrating men of gold and glorifying men of mica. Commonplace human nature cannot rise above that.

Chapter XXIX

Tᴿᴜᴇ ᴋɴᴏᴡʟᴇᴅɢᴇ of the nature of silver mining came fast enough. We went out "prospecting" with Mr. Ballou. We climbed the mountain sides, and clambered among sage-brush, rocks and snow till we were ready to drop with exhaustion, but found no silver—nor yet any gold. Day after day we did this. Now and then we came upon holes burrowed a few feet into the declivities and apparently abandoned; and now and then we found one or two listless men still burrowing. But there was no appearance of silver. These holes were the beginnings of tunnels, and the purpose was to drive them hundreds of feet into the mountain, and some day tap the hidden ledge where the silver was. Some day! It seemed far enough away, and very hopeless and dreary. Day after day we toiled, and climbed and searched, and we younger partners grew sicker and still sicker of the promiseless toil. At last we halted under a beetling rampart of rock which projected from the earth high upon the mountain. Mr. Ballou broke off some fragments with a hammer, and examined them long and attentively with a small eye-glass; threw them away and broke off more; said this rock was quartz, and quartz was the sort of rock that contained silver. *Contained* it! I had thought that at least it would be caked on the outside of it like a kind of veneering. He still broke off pieces and critically examined them, now and then wetting the piece with his tongue and applying the glass. At last he exclaimed:

"We've got it!"

We were full of anxiety in a moment. The rock was clean and white, where it was broken, and across it ran a ragged thread of blue. He said that that little thread had silver in it, mixed with base metals, such as lead and antimony, and other rubbish, and that there was a speck or two of gold visible. After a great deal of effort we managed to discern some little fine yellow specks, and judged that a couple of tons of them massed together might make a gold dollar, possibly. We were not jubilant, but Mr. Ballou said there were worse ledges in the world than that. He saved what he called the "richest" piece of the rock, in order to determine its value by the process called the "fire-assay." Then we named the mine "Monarch of the Mountains" (modesty of nomenclature is not a prominent feature in the mines), and Mr. Ballou wrote out and struck up the following "notice," preserving a copy to be entered upon the books in the mining recorder's office in the town.

"NOTICE."

"We the undersigned claim three claims, of three hundred feet each (and one for discovery), on this silver-bearing quartz lead or lode, extending north and south from this notice, with all its dips, spurs, and angles, variations and sinuosities, together with fifty feet of ground on either side for working the same."

We put our names to it and tried to feel that our fortunes were made. But when we talked the matter all over with Mr. Ballou, we felt depressed and dubious. He said that this surface quartz was not all there was of our mine; but that the wall or ledge of rock called the "Monarch of the Mountains," extended down hundreds and hundreds of feet into the earth—he illustrated by saying it was like a curb-stone, and maintained a nearly uniform thickness—say twenty feet—away down into the bowels of the earth, and was perfectly distinct from the casing rock on each side of it; and that it kept to itself, and maintained its distinctive character always, no matter how deep it extended into the earth or how far it stretched itself through and across the hills and valleys. He said it might be a mile deep and ten miles long, for all we knew; and that wherever we bored into it above ground or below, we would find gold and silver in it, but no gold or silver in the meaner rock it was cased between. And he said that down in the great depths of the ledge was its richness, and the deeper it went the richer it grew. Therefore, instead of working here on the surface, we must either bore down into the rock with a shaft till we came to where it was rich—say a hundred feet or so—or else we must go down into the valley and bore a long tunnel into the mountain side and tap the ledge far under the earth. To do either was plainly the labor of months; for we could blast and bore only a few feet a day—some five or six. But this was not all. He said that after we got the ore out it must be hauled in wagons to a distant silver-mill, ground up, and the silver extracted by a tedious and costly process. Our fortune seemed a century away!

But we went to work. We decided to sink a shaft. So, for a week we climbed the mountain, laden with picks, drills, gads, crowbars, shovels, cans of blasting powder and coils of fuse and strove with might and main. At first the rock was broken and loose and we dug it up with picks and threw it out with shovels, and the hole progressed very well. But the rock became more compact, presently, and gads and crowbars came into play. But shortly nothing could make an impression but blasting powder. That was the weariest work! One of us held the iron drill in its place and another would strike with an eight-pound sledge—it was like driving nails on a large scale. In the course of an hour or two the drill would reach a depth of two or three feet, making a hole a couple of inches in diameter. We would put in a charge of powder, insert half a yard of fuse, pour in sand and gravel and ram it down, then light the fuse and run. When the explosion came and the rocks and smoke shot into the air, we would go back and find about a bushel of that hard, rebellious quartz jolted out. Nothing more. One week of this satisfied me. I resigned. Claggett and Oliphant followed. Our shaft was only twelve feet deep. We decided that a tunnel was the thing we wanted.

So we went down the mountain side and worked a week; at the end of which time we had blasted a tunnel about deep enough to hide a hogshead in, and judged that about nine hundred feet more of it would reach the ledge. I resigned again, and the other boys only held out one day longer. We decided that a tunnel was not what we wanted. We wanted a ledge that was already "developed." There were none in the camp.

We dropped the "Monarch" for the time being.

Meantime the camp was filling up with people, and there was a constantly growing excitement about our Humboldt mines. We fell victims to the epidemic and strained every nerve to acquire more "feet." We prospected and took up new claims, put "notices" on them and gave them grandiloquent names. We traded some of our "feet" for "feet" in other people's claims. In a little while we owned largely in the "Gray Eagle," the "Columbiana," the "Branch Mint," the "Maria

Jane," the "Universe," the "Root-Hog-or-Die," the "Samson and Delilah," the "Treasure Trove," the "Golconda," the "Sultana," the "Boomerang," the "Great Republic," the "Grand Mogul," and fifty other "mines" that had never been molested by a shovel or scratched with a pick. We had not less than thirty thousand "feet" apiece in the "richest mines on earth" as the frenzied cant phrased it—and were in debt to the butcher. We were stark mad with excitement—drunk with happiness—smothered under mountains of prospective wealth—arrogantly compassionate toward the plodding millions who knew not our marvellous canyon—but our credit was not good at the grocer's.

It was the strangest phase of life one can imagine. It was a beggars' revel. There was nothing doing in the district—no mining—no milling—no productive effort—no income—and not enough money in the entire camp to buy a corner lot in an eastern village, hardly; and yet a stranger would have supposed he was walking among bloated millionaires. Prospecting parties swarmed out of town with the first flush of dawn, and swarmed in again at nightfall laden with spoil—rocks. Nothing but rocks. Every man's pockets were full of them; the floor of his cabin was littered with them; they were disposed in labeled rows on his shelves.

Chapter XXX

I MET MEN at every turn who owned from one thousand to thirty thousand "feet" in undeveloped silver mines, every single foot of which they believed would shortly be worth from fifty to a thousand dollars—and as often as any other way they were men who had not twenty-five dollars in the world. Every man you met had his new mine to boast of, and his "specimens" ready; and if the opportunity offered, he would infallibly back you into a corner and offer as a favor to *you*, not to *him*, to part with just a few feet in the "Golden Age," or the "Sarah Jane," or some other unknown stack of croppings, for money enough to get a "square meal" with, as the phrase went. And you were never to reveal that he had made you the offer at such a ruinous price, for it was only out of friendship for you that he was willing to make the sacrifice. Then he would fish a piece of rock out of his pocket, and after looking mysteriously around as if he feared he might be waylaid and robbed if caught with such wealth in his possession, he would dab the rock against his tongue, clap an eye-glass to it, and exclaim:

"Look at that! Right there in that red dirt! See it? See the specks of gold? And the streak of silver? That's from the 'Uncle Abe.' There's a hundred thousand tons like that in sight! Right in sight, mind you! And when we get down on it and the ledge comes in solid, it will be the richest thing in the world! Look at the assay! I don't want you to believe *me*— look at the assay!"

Then he would get out a greasy sheet of paper which showed that the portion of rock assayed had given evidence of containing silver and gold in the proportion of so many hundreds or thousands of dollars to the ton. I little knew, then, that the custom was to hunt out the *richest* piece of rock and get it assayed! Very often, that piece, the size of a filbert, was the only fragment in a ton that had a particle of metal in it—and yet the assay made it pretend to represent the average value of the ton of rubbish it came from!

On such a system of assaying as that, the Humboldt world had gone crazy. On the authority of such assays its newspaper correspondents were frothing about rock worth four and seven thousand dollars a ton!

And does the reader remember, a few pages back, the calculations, of a quoted correspondent, whereby the ore is to be mined and shipped all the way to England, the metals extracted, and the gold and silver contents received back by the miners as clear profit, the copper, antimony and other things in the ore being sufficient to pay all the expenses incurred? Everybody's head was full of such "calculations" as those— such raving insanity, rather. Few people took *work* into their calculations—or outlay of money either; except the work and expenditures of other people.

We never touched our tunnel or our shaft again. Why? Because we judged that we had learned the *real* secret of success in silver mining—which was, *not* to mine the silver ourselves by the sweat of our brows and the labor of our hands, but to *sell* the ledges to the dull slaves of toil and let them do the mining!

Before leaving Carson, the Secretary and I had purchased "feet" from various Esmeralda stragglers. We had expected immediate returns of bullion, but were only afflicted with regular and constant "assessments" instead—demands for money wherewith to develop the said mines. These assessments had grown so oppressive that it seemed necessary to look into the matter personally. Therefore I projected a pilgrimage to Carson and thence to Esmeralda. I bought a horse and started, in company with Mr. Ballou and a gentleman named Ollendorff, a Prussian—not the party who has inflicted so much suffering on the world with his wretched foreign grammars, with their interminable repetitions of questions which never have occurred and are never likely to occur in any conversation among human beings. We rode through a snow-storm for two or three days, and arrived at "Honey Lake Smith's," a sort of isolated inn on the Carson river. It was a two-story log house situated on a small knoll in the midst of the vast basin or desert through which the sickly Carson winds its melancholy way. Close to the house were the Overland stage stables, built of sun-dried bricks. There was not another building within several leagues of the place. Towards sunset about twenty hay-wagons arrived and camped around the house and all the teamsters came in to supper—a very, very rough set. There were one or two Overland stage drivers there, also, and half a dozen vagabonds and stragglers; consequently the house was well crowded.

We walked out, after supper, and visited a small Indian camp in the vicinity. The Indians were in a great hurry about something, and were packing up and getting away as fast as they could. In their broken English they said, "By'm-by, heap water!" and by the help of signs made us understand that in their opinion a flood was coming. The weather was perfectly clear, and this was not the rainy season. There was about a foot of water in the insignificant river—or maybe two feet; the stream was not wider than a back alley in a village, and its banks were scarcely higher than a man's head. So, where was the flood to come from? We canvassed the subject awhile and then concluded it was a ruse, and that the Indians had some better reason for leaving in a hurry than fears of a flood in such an exceedingly dry time.

At seven in the evening we went to bed in the second story—with our clothes on, as usual, and all three in the same bed, for every available space on the floors, chairs, etc., was in request, and even then there was barely room for the housing of the inn's guests. An hour later we were awakened by a great turmoil, and springing out of bed we picked our way nimbly among the ranks of snoring teamsters on the floor and got to the front windows of the long room. A glance revealed a strange spectacle, under the moonlight. The crooked Carson was full to the brim, and its waters were raging and foaming in the wildest way—sweeping around the sharp bends at a furious speed, and bearing on their surface a chaos of logs, brush and all sorts of rubbish. A depression, where its bed had once been, in other times, was already filling, and in one or two places the water was beginning to wash over the main bank. Men were flying hither and thither, bringing cattle and wagons close up to the house, for the spot of high ground on which it stood extended only some thirty feet in front and about a hundred in the rear. Close to the old river bed just spoken of, stood a little log stable, and in this our horses were lodged. While we looked, the waters increased so fast in this place that in a few minutes a torrent was roaring by the little stable and its margin encroaching steadily on the logs. We suddenly realized that this flood was not a mere holiday spectacle, but meant damage—and not only to the small log stable but to the Overland buildings close to the main river, for the waves had now come ashore and were creeping about the foundations and invading the great hay-corral adjoining. We ran down and joined the crowd of excited men and frightened animals. We waded knee-deep into the log stable, unfastened the horses and waded out almost *waist*-deep, so fast the waters increased. Then the crowd rushed in a body to the hay-corral and began to tumble down the huge stacks of baled hay and roll the bales up on the high ground by the house. Meantime it was discovered that Owens, an overland driver, was missing, and a man ran to the large stable, and wading in, boot-top deep, discovered him asleep in his bed, awoke him, and waded out again. But Owens was drowsy and resumed his nap; but only for a minute or two, for presently he turned in his bed, his hand dropped over the side and came in contact with the cold water! It was up level with the mattrass! He waded out, breast-deep, almost, and the next moment the sun-burned bricks melted down like sugar and the big building crumbled to a ruin and was washed away in a twinkling.

At eleven o'clock only the roof of the little log stable was out of water, and our inn was on an island in mid-ocean. As far as the eye could reach, in the moonlight, there was no desert visible, but only a level waste of shining water. The Indians were true prophets, but how did they get their information? I am not able to answer the question.

We remained cooped up eight days and nights with that curious crew. Swearing, drinking and card playing were the order of the day, and occasionally a fight was thrown in for variety. Dirt and vermin—but let us forget those features; their profusion is simply inconceivable—it is better that they remain so.

There were two men—however, this chapter is long enough.

Chapter XXXI

THERE WERE two men in the company who caused me particular discomfort. One was a little Swede, about twenty-five years old, who knew only one song, and he was forever singing it. By day we were all crowded into one small, stifling bar-room, and so there was no escaping this person's music. Through all the profanity, whisky-guzzling, "old sledge" and quarreling, his monotonous song meandered with never a variation in its tiresome sameness, and it seemed to me, at last, that I would be content to die, in order to be rid of the torture. The other man was a stalwart ruffian called "Arkansas," who carried two revolvers in his belt and a bowie knife projecting from his boot, and who was always drunk and always suffering for a fight. But he was so feared, that nobody would accommodate him. He would try all manner of little wary ruses to entrap somebody into an offensive remark, and his face would light up now and then when he fancied he was fairly on the scent of a fight, but invariably his victim would elude his toils and then he would show a disappointment that was almost pathetic. The landlord, Johnson, was a meek, well-meaning fellow, and Arkansas fastened on him early, as a promising subject, and gave him no rest day or night, for awhile. On the fourth morning, Arkansas got drunk and sat himself down to wait for an opportunity. Presently Johnson came in, just comfortably sociable with whisky, and said:

"I reckon the Pennsylvania 'lection—"

Arkansas raised his finger impressively and Johnson stopped. Arkansas rose unsteadily and confronted him. Said he:

"Wha-what do you know a-about Pennsylvania? Answer me that. Wha-what do you know 'bout Pennsylvania?"

"I was only goin' to say—"

"You was only goin' to *say*. *You* was! You was only goin' to say —*what* was you goin' to say? That's it! That's what *I* want to know. *I* want to know wha-what you (*'ic*) what you know about Pennsylvania, since you're makin' yourself so d—d free. Answer me that!"

"Mr. Arkansas, if you'd only let me—"

"Who's a henderin' you? Don't you insinuate nothing agin me!—don't you do it. Don't you come in here bullyin' around, and cussin' and goin' on like a lunatic—don't you do it. 'Coz I won't *stand* it. If fight's what you want, out with it! I'm your man! Out with it!"

Said Johnson, backing into a corner, Arkansas following, menacingly:

"Why, *I* never said nothing, Mr. Arkansas. You don't give a man no chance. I was only goin' to say that Pennsylvania was goin' to have an election next week—that was all—that was everything I was goin' to say—I wish I may never stir if it wasn't."

"Well then why d'n't you say it? What did you come swellin' around that way for, and tryin' to raise trouble?"

"Why *I* didn't come swellin' around, Mr. Arkansas—I just—"

"I'm a liar am I! Ger-reat Cæsar's ghost—"

"Oh, please, Mr. Arkansas, I never meant such a thing as that, I wish I may die if I did. All the boys will tell you that I've always spoke well of you, and respected you more'n any man in the house. Ask Smith. Ain't it so, Smith? Didn't I say, no longer ago than last night, that for a man that was a gentleman *all* the time and every way you took him, give me Arkansas? I'll leave it to any gentleman here if them warn't the very words I used. Come, now, Mr. Arkansas, le's take a drink—le's shake hands and take a drink. Come up—everybody! It's my treat. Come up, Bill, Tom, Bob, Scotty—come up. I want you all to take a drink with me and Arkansas—*old* Arkansas, I call him—bully old Arkansas. Gimme your hand agin. Look at him, boys—just take a *look* at him. Thar stands the whitest man in America!—and the man that denies it has got to fight *me*, that's all. Gimme that old flipper agin!"

They embraced, with drunken affection on the landlord's part and unresponsive toleration on the part of Arkansas, who, bribed by a drink, was disappointed of his prey once more. But the foolish landlord was so happy to have escaped butchery, that he went on talking when he ought to have marched himself out of danger. The consequence was that Arkansas shortly began to glower upon him dangerously, and presently said:

"Lan'lord, will you p-please make that remark over agin if you please?"

"I was a-sayin' to Scotty that my father was up'ards of eighty year old when he died."

"Was that *all* that you said?"

"Yes, that was all."

"Didn't say nothing but that?"

"No—nothing."

Then an uncomfortable silence.

Arkansas played with his glass a moment, lolling on his elbows on the counter. Then he meditatively scratched his left shin with his right boot, while the awkward silence continued. But presently he loafed away toward the stove, looking dissatisfied; roughly shouldered two or three men out of a comfortable position; occupied it himself, gave a sleeping dog a kick that sent him howling under a bench, then spread his long legs and his blanket-coat tails apart and proceeded to warm his back. In a little while he fell to grumbling to himself, and soon he slouched back to the bar and said:

"Lan'lord, what's your idea for rakin' up old personalities and blowin' about your father? Ain't this company agreeable to you? Ain't it? If this company ain't agreeable to you, p'r'aps we'd better leave. Is that your idea? Is that what you're coming at?"

"Why bless your soul, Arkansas, I warn't thinking of such a thing. My father and my mother—"

"Lan'lord, *don't* crowd a man! Don't do it. If nothing'll do you but a disturbance, out with it like a man (*'ic*)—but *don't* rake up old bygones and fling 'em in the teeth of a passel of people that wants to be peaceable if they could git a chance. What's the matter with you this mornin', anyway? I never see a man carry on so."

"Arkansas, I reely didn't mean no harm, and I won't go on with it if it's onpleasant to you. I reckon my licker's got into my head, and what with the flood, and havin' so many to feed and look out for—"

"So *that's* what's a-ranklin' in your heart, is it? You want us to leave do you? There's too many on us. You want us to pack up and swim. Is that it? Come!"

"Please be reasonable, Arkansas. Now *you* know that I ain't the man to—"

"Are you a threatenin' me? Are you? By George, the man don't live that can skeer me! Don't you try to come that game, my chicken—'cuz I can stand a good deal, but I won't stand that. Come out from behind that bar till I clean you! You want to drive us out, do you, you sneakin' underhanded hound! Come out from behind that bar! *I'll* learn you to bully and badger and browbeat a gentleman that's forever trying to befriend you and keep you out of trouble!"

"Please, Arkansas, please don't shoot! If there's got to be bloodshed—"

"Do you hear that, gentlemen? Do you hear him talk about bloodshed? So it's blood you want, is it, you ravin' desperado! You'd made up your mind to murder somebody this mornin'—I knowed it perfectly well. I'm the man, am I? It's me you're goin' to murder, is it? But you can't do it 'thout I get one chance first, you thievin' black-hearted, white-livered son of a nigger! Draw your weepon!"

With that, Arkansas began to shoot, and the landlord to clamber over benches, men and every sort of obstacle in a frantic desire to escape. In the midst of the wild hubbub the landlord crashed through a glass door, and as Arkansas charged after him the landlord's wife suddenly appeared in the doorway and confronted the desperado with a pair of scissors! Her fury was magnificent. With head erect and flashing eye she stood a moment and then advanced, with her weapon raised. The astonished ruffian hesitated, and then fell back a step. She followed. She backed him step by step into the middle of the bar-room, and then, while the wondering crowd closed up and gazed, she gave him such another tongue-lashing as never a cowed and shamefaced braggart got before, perhaps! As she finished and retired victorious, a roar of applause shook the house, and every man ordered "drinks for the crowd" in one and the same breath.

The lesson was entirely sufficient. The reign of terror was over, and the Arkansas domination broken for good. During the rest of the season of island captivity, there was one man who sat apart in a state of permanent humiliation, never mixing in any quarrel or uttering a boast, and never resenting the insults the once cringing crew now constantly leveled at him, and that man was "Arkansas."

By the fifth or sixth morning the waters had subsided from the land, but the stream in the old river bed was still high and swift and there was no possibility of crossing it. On the eighth it was still too high for an entirely safe passage, but life in the inn had become next to insupportable by reason of the dirt, drunkenness, fighting, etc., and so we made an effort to get away. In the midst of a heavy snow-storm we embarked in a canoe, taking our saddles aboard and towing our horses after us by their halters. The Prussian, Ollendorff, was in the bow, with a paddle, Ballou paddled in the middle, and I sat in the stern holding the halters. When the horses lost their footing and began to swim, Ollendorff got frightened, for there was great danger that the horses would make our aim uncertain, and it was plain that if we failed to land at a certain spot the current would throw us off and almost surely cast us into the main Carson, which was a boiling torrent, now. Such a catastrophe would be death, in all probability, for we would be swept to sea in the "Sink" or overturned and drowned. We warned Ollendorff to keep his wits about him and handle himself carefully, but it was useless; the moment the bow touched the bank, he made a spring and the canoe whirled upside down in ten-foot water. Ollendorff seized some brush and dragged himself ashore, but Ballou and I had to swim for it, encumbered with our overcoats. But we held on to the canoe, and although we were washed down nearly to the Carson, we managed to push the boat ashore and make a safe landing. We were cold and water-soaked, but safe. The horses made a landing, too, but our saddles were gone, of course. We tied the animals in the sage-brush and there they had to stay for twenty-four hours. We baled out the canoe and ferried over some food and blankets for them, but we slept one more night in the inn before making another venture on our journey.

The next morning it was still snowing furiously when we got away with our new stock of saddles and accoutrements. We mounted and started. The snow lay so deep on the ground that there was no sign of a road perceptible, and the snow-fall was so thick that we could not see more than a hundred yards ahead, else we could have guided our course by the mountain ranges. The case looked dubious, but Ollendorff said his instinct was as sensitive as any compass, and that he could "strike a bee-line" for Carson city and never diverge from it. He said that if he were to straggle a single point out of the true line his instinct would assail him like an outraged conscience. Consequently we dropped into his wake happy and content. For half an hour we poked along warily enough, but at the end of that time we came upon a fresh trail, and Ollendorff shouted proudly:

"I knew I was as dead certain as a compass, boys! Here we are, right in somebody's tracks that will hunt the way for us without any trouble. Let's hurry up and join company with the party."

So we put the horses into as much of a trot as the deep snow would allow, and before long it was evident that we were gaining on our predecessors, for the tracks grew more distinct. We hurried along, and at the end of an hour the tracks looked still newer and fresher—but what surprised us was, that the *number* of travelers in advance of us seemed to steadily increase. We wondered how so large a party came to be traveling at such a time and in such a solitude. Somebody suggested that it must be a company of soldiers from the fort, and so we accepted that solution and jogged along a little faster still, for they could not be far off now. But the tracks still multiplied, and we began to think the platoon of soldiers was miraculously expanding into a regiment—Ballou said they had already increased to five hundred! Presently he stopped his horse and said:

"Boys, these are our own tracks, and we've actually been circussing round and round in a circle for more than two hours, out here in this blind desert! By George this is perfectly hydraulic!"

Then the old man waxed wroth and abusive. He called Ollendorff all manner of hard names—said he never saw such a lurid fool as he was, and ended with the peculiarly venomous opinion that he "did not know as much as a logarythm!"

We certainly had been following our own tracks. Ollendorff and his "mental compass" were in disgrace from that moment. After all our hard travel, here we were on the bank of the stream again, with the inn beyond dimly outlined through the driving snow-fall. While we were considering what to do, the young Swede landed from the canoe and took his pedestrian way Carson-wards, singing his same tiresome song about his "sister and his brother" and "the child in the grave with its mother," and in a short minute faded and disappeared in the white oblivion. He was never heard of again. He no doubt got bewildered and lost, and Fatigue delivered him over to Sleep and Sleep betrayed him to Death. Possibly he followed our treacherous tracks till he became exhausted and dropped.

Presently the Overland stage forded the now fast receding stream and started toward Carson on its first trip since the flood came. We hesitated no longer, now, but took up our march in its wake, and trotted merrily along, for we had good confidence in the driver's bump of locality. But our horses were no match for the fresh stage team. We were soon left out of sight; but it was no matter, for we had the deep ruts the wheels made for a guide. By this time it was three in the afternoon, and consequently it was not very long before night came—and not with a lingering twilight, but with a sudden shutting down like a cellar door, as is its habit in that country. The snow-fall was still as thick as ever, and of course we could not see fifteen steps before us; but all about us the white glare of the snow-bed enabled us to discern the smooth sugar-loaf mounds made by the covered sage-bushes, and just in front of us the two faint grooves which we knew were the steadily filling and slowly disappearing wheel-tracks.

Now those sage-bushes were all about the same height—three or four feet; they stood just about seven feet apart, all over the vast desert; each of them was a mere snow-mound, now; in *any* direction that you proceeded (the same as in a well laid out orchard) you would find yourself moving down a distinctly defined avenue, with a row of these snow-mounds on either side of it—an avenue the customary width of a road, nice and level in its breadth, and rising at the sides in the most natural way, by reason of the mounds. But we had not thought of this. Then imagine the chilly thrill that shot through us when it finally occurred to us, far in the night, that since the last faint trace of the wheel-tracks had long ago been buried from sight, we might now be wandering down a mere sage-brush avenue, miles away from the road and diverging further and further away from it all the time. Having a cake of ice slipped down one's back is placid comfort compared to it. There was a sudden leap and stir of blood that had been asleep for an hour, and as sudden a rousing of all the drowsing activities in our minds and bodies. We were alive and awake at once—and shaking and quaking with consternation, too. There was an instant halting and dismounting, a bending low and an anxious scanning of the road-bed. Useless, of course; for if a faint depression could not be discerned from an altitude of four or five feet above it, it certainly could not with one's nose nearly against it.

Chapter XXXII

WE SEEMED to be in a road, but that was no proof. We tested this by walking off in various directions—the regular snow-mounds and the regular avenues between them convinced each man that *he* had found the true road, and that the others had found only false ones. Plainly the situation was desperate. We were cold and stiff and the horses were tired. We decided to build a sage-brush fire and camp out till morning. This was wise, because if we were wandering from the right road and the snow-storm continued another day our case would be the next thing to hopeless if we kept on.

All agreed that a camp fire was what would come nearest to saving us, now, and so we set about building it. We could find no matches, and so we tried to make shift with the pistols. Not a man in the party had ever tried to do such a thing before, but not a man in the party doubted that it *could* be done, and without any trouble—because every man in the party had read about it in books many a time and had naturally come to believe it, with trusting simplicity, just as he had long ago accepted and believed *that other* common book-fraud about Indians and lost hunters making a fire by rubbing two dry sticks together.

We huddled together on our knees in the deep snow, and the horses put their noses together and bowed their patient heads over us; and while the feathery flakes eddied down and turned us into a group of white statuary, we proceeded with the momentous experiment. We broke twigs from a sage bush and piled them on a little cleared place in the shelter of our bodies. In the course of ten or fifteen minutes all was ready, and then, while conversation ceased and our pulses beat low with anxious suspense, Ollendorff applied his revolver, pulled the trigger and blew the pile clear out of the county! It was the flattest failure that ever was.

This was distressing, but it paled before a greater horror—the horses were gone! I had been appointed to hold the bridles, but in my absorbing anxiety over the pistol experiment I had unconsciously dropped them and the released animals had walked off in the storm. It was useless to try to follow them, for their footfalls could make no sound, and one could pass within two yards of the creatures and never see them. We gave them up without an effort at recovering them, and cursed the lying books that said horses would stay by their masters for protection and companionship in a distressful time like ours.

We were miserable enough, before; we felt still more forlorn, now. Patiently, but with blighted hope, we broke more sticks and piled them, and once more the Prussian shot them into annihilation. Plainly, to light a fire with a pistol was an art requiring practice and experience, and the middle of a desert at midnight in a snow-storm was not a good place or time for the acquiring of the accomplishment. We gave it up and tried the other. Each man took a couple of sticks and fell to chafing them together. At the end of half an hour we were thoroughly chilled, and so were the sticks. We bitterly execrated the Indians, the hunters and the books that had betrayed us with the silly device, and wondered dismally what was next to be done. At this critical moment Mr. Ballou fished out four matches from the rubbish of an overlooked pocket. To have found four gold bars would have seemed poor and cheap good luck compared to this. One cannot think how good a match looks under such circumstances—or how lovable and precious, and sacredly beautiful to the eye. This time we gathered sticks with high hopes; and when Mr. Ballou prepared to light the first match, there was an amount of interest centred upon him that pages of writing could not describe. The match burned hopefully a moment, and then went out. It could not have carried more regret with it if it had been a human life. The next match simply flashed and died. The wind puffed the third one out just as it was on the imminent verge of success. We gathered together closer than ever, and developed a solicitude that was rapt and painful, as Mr. Ballou scratched our last hope on his leg. It lit, burned blue and sickly, and then budded into a robust flame. Shading it with his hands, the old gentleman bent gradually down and every heart went with him—everybody, too, for that matter—and blood and breath stood still. The flame touched the sticks at last, took gradual hold upon them—hesitated—took a stronger hold—hesitated again—held its breath five heart-breaking seconds, then gave a sort of human gasp and went out.

Nobody said a word for several minutes. It was a solemn sort of silence; even the wind put on a stealthy, sinister quiet, and made no more noise than the falling flakes of snow. Finally a sad-voiced conversation began, and it was soon apparent that in each of our hearts lay the conviction that this was our last night with the living. I had so hoped that I was the only one who felt so. When the others calmly acknowledged their conviction, it sounded like the summons itself. Ollendorff said:

"Brothers, let us die together. And let us go without one hard feeling towards each other. Let us forget and forgive bygones. I know that you have felt hard towards me for turning over the canoe, and for knowing too much and leading you round and round in the snow—but I meant well; forgive me. I acknowledge freely that I have had hard feelings against Mr. Ballou for abusing me and calling me a logarythm, which is a thing I do not know what, but no doubt a thing considered disgraceful and unbecoming in America, and it has scarcely been out of my mind and has hurt me a great deal—but let it go; I forgive Mr. Ballou with all my heart, and—"

Poor Ollendorff broke down and the tears came. He was not alone, for I was crying too, and so was Mr. Ballou. Ollendorff got his voice again and forgave me for things I had done and said. Then he got out his bottle of whisky and said that whether he lived or died he would never touch another drop. He said he had given up all hope of life, and although ill-prepared, was ready to submit humbly to his fate; that he wished he could be spared a little longer, not for any selfish reason, but to make a thorough reform in his character, and by devoting himself to helping the poor, nursing the sick, and pleading with the people to guard themselves against the evils of intemperance, make his life a beneficent example to the young, and lay it down at last with the precious reflection that it had not been lived in vain. He ended by saying that his reform should begin at this moment, even here in the presence of death, since no longer time was to be vouchsafed wherein to prosecute it to men's help and benefit—and with that he threw away the bottle of whisky.

Mr. Ballou made remarks of similar purport, and began the reform he could not live to continue, by throwing away the ancient pack of cards that had solaced our captivity during the flood and made it bearable. He said he never gambled, but still was satisfied that the meddling with cards in any way was immoral and injurious, and no man could be wholly pure and blemishless without eschewing them. "And therefore," continued he, "in doing this act I already feel more in sympathy with that spiritual saturnalia necessary to entire and obsolete reform." These rolling syllables touched him as no intelligible eloquence could have done, and the old man sobbed with a mournfulness not unmingled with satisfaction.

My own remarks were of the same tenor as those of my comrades, and I know that the feelings that prompted them were heartfelt and sincere. We were all sincere, and all deeply moved and earnest, for we were in the presence of death and without hope. I threw away my pipe, and in doing it felt that at last I was free of a hated vice and one that had ridden me like a tyrant all my days. While I yet talked, the thought of the good I might have done in the world and the still greater good I might *now* do, with these new incentives and higher and better aims to guide me if I could only be spared a few years longer, overcame me and the tears came again. We put our arms about each other's necks and awaited the warning drowsiness that precedes death by freezing.

It came stealing over us presently, and then we bade each other a last farewell. A delicious dreaminess wrought its web about my yielding senses, while the snow-flakes wove a winding sheet about my conquered body. Oblivion came. The battle of life was done.

Chapter XXXIII

I DO NOT know how long I was in a state of forgetfulness, but it seemed an age. A vague consciousness grew upon me by degrees, and then came a gathering anguish of pain in my limbs and through all my body. I shuddered. The thought flitted through my brain, "this is death—this is the here-after."

Then came a white upheaval at my side, and a voice said, with bitterness:

"Will some gentleman be so good as to kick me behind?"

It was Ballou—at least it was a towzled snow image in a sitting posture, with Ballou's voice.

I rose up, and there in the gray dawn, not fifteen steps from us, were the frame buildings of a stage station, and under a shed stood our still saddled and bridled horses!

An arched snow-drift broke up, now, and Ollendorff emerged from it, and the three of us sat and stared at the houses without speaking a word. We really had nothing to say. We were like the profane man who could not "do the subject justice," the whole situation was so painfully ridiculous and humiliating that words were tame and we did not know where to commence anyhow.

The joy in our hearts at our deliverance was poisoned; well-nigh dissipated, indeed. We presently began to grow pettish by degrees, and sullen; and then, angry at each other, angry at ourselves, angry at everything in general, we moodily dusted the snow from our clothing and in unsociable single file plowed our way to the horses, unsaddled them, and sought shelter in the station.

I have scarcely exaggerated a detail of this curious and absurd adventure. It occurred almost exactly as I have stated it. We actually went into camp in a snow-drift in a desert, at midnight in a storm, forlorn and hopeless, within fifteen steps of a comfortable inn.

For two hours we sat apart in the station and ruminated in disgust. The mystery was gone, now, and it was plain enough why the horses had deserted us. Without a doubt they were under that shed a quarter of a minute after they had left us, and they must have overheard and enjoyed all our confessions and lamentations.

After breakfast we felt better, and the zest of life soon came back. The world looked bright again, and existence was as dear to us as ever. Presently an uneasiness came over me—grew upon me—assailed me without ceasing. Alas, my regeneration was not complete—I wanted to smoke! I resisted with all my strength, but the flesh was weak. I wandered away alone and wrestled with myself an hour. I recalled my promises of reform and preached to myself persuasively, upbraidingly, exhaustively. But it was all vain, I shortly found myself sneaking among the snow-drifts hunting for my pipe. I discovered it after a considerable search, and crept away to hide myself and enjoy it. I remained behind the barn a good while, asking myself how I would feel if my braver, stronger, truer comrades should catch me in my degradation. At last I lit the pipe, and no human being can feel meaner and baser than I did then. I was ashamed of being in my own pitiful company. Still dreading discovery, I felt that perhaps the further side of the barn would be somewhat safer, and so I turned the corner. As I turned the one corner, smoking, Ollendorff turned the other with his bottle to his lips, and between us sat unconscious Ballou deep in a game of "solitaire" with the old greasy cards!

Absurdity could go no farther. We shook hands and agreed to say no more about "reform" and "examples to the rising generation."

The station we were at was at the verge of the Twenty-six-Mile Desert. If we had approached it half an hour earlier the night before, we must have heard men shouting there and firing pistols; for they were expecting some sheep drovers and their flocks and knew that they would infallibly get lost and wander out of reach of help unless guided by sounds. While we remained at the station, three of the drovers arrived, nearly exhausted with their wanderings, but two others of their party were never heard of afterward.

We reached Carson in due time, and took a rest. This rest, together with preparations for the journey to Esmeralda, kept us there a week, and the delay gave us the opportunity to be present at the trial of the great land-slide case of Hyde *vs.*

Morgan—an episode which is famous in Nevada to this day. After a word or two of necessary explanation, I will set down the history of this singular affair just as it transpired.

Chapter XXXIV

THE MOUNTAINS are very high and steep about Carson, Eagle and Washoe Valleys—very high and very steep, and so when the snow gets to melting off fast in the Spring and the warm surface-earth begins to moisten and soften, the disastrous land-slides commence. The reader cannot know what a land-slide is, unless he has lived in that country and seen the whole side of a mountain taken off some fine morning and deposited down in the valley, leaving a vast, treeless, unsightly scar upon the mountain's front to keep the circumstance fresh in his memory all the years that he may go on living within seventy miles of that place.

General Buncombe was shipped out to Nevada in the invoice of Territorial officers, to be United States Attorney. He considered himself a lawyer of parts, and he very much wanted an opportunity to manifest it—partly for the pure gratification of it and partly because his salary was Territorially meagre (which is a strong expression). Now the older citizens of a new territory look down upon the rest of the world with a calm, benevolent compassion, as long as it keeps out of the way—when it gets in the way they snub it. Sometimes this latter takes the shape of a practical joke.

One morning Dick Hyde rode furiously up to General Buncombe's door in Carson city and rushed into his presence without stopping to tie his horse. He seemed much excited. He told the General that he wanted him to conduct a suit for him and would pay him five hundred dollars if he achieved a victory. And then, with violent gestures and a world of profanity, he poured out his griefs. He said it was pretty well known that for some years he had been farming (or ranching as the more customary term is) in Washoe District, and making a successful thing of it, and furthermore it was known that his ranch was situated just in the edge of the valley, and that Tom Morgan owned a ranch immediately above it on the mountain side. And now the trouble was, that one of those hated and dreaded land-slides had come and slid Morgan's ranch, fences, cabins, cattle, barns and everything down on top of *his* ranch and exactly covered up every single vestige of his property, to a depth of about thirty-eight feet. Morgan was in possession and refused to vacate the premises—said he was occupying his own cabin and not interfering with anybody else's—and said the cabin was standing on the same dirt and same ranch it had always stood on, and he would like to see anybody make him vacate.

"And when I reminded him," said Hyde, weeping, "that it was on top of my ranch and that he was trespassing, he had the infernal meanness to ask me why didn't I *stay* on my ranch and hold possession when I see him a-coming! Why didn't I *stay* on it, the blathering lunatic—by George, when I heard that racket and looked up that hill it was just like the whole world was a-ripping and a-tearing down that mountain side—splinters, and cord-wood, thunder and lightning, hail and snow, odds and ends of hay stacks, and awful clouds of dust!—trees going end over end in the air, rocks as big as a house jumping 'bout a thousand feet high and busting into ten million pieces, cattle turned inside out and a-coming head on with their tails hanging out between their teeth!—and in the midst of all that wrack and destruction sot that cussed Morgan on his gate-post, a-wondering why I didn't *stay and hold possession!* Laws bless me, I just took one glimpse, General, and lit out'n the county in three jumps exactly.

"But what grinds me is that that Morgan hangs on there and won't move off'n that ranch—says it's his'n and he's going to keep it—likes it better'n he did when it was higher up the hill. Mad! Well, I've been so mad for two days I couldn't find my way to town—been wandering around in the brush in a starving condition—got anything here to drink, General? But I'm here *now*, and I'm a-going to law. You hear *me!*"

Never in all the world, perhaps, were a man's feelings so outraged as were the General's. He said he had never heard of such high-handed conduct in all his life as this Morgan's. And he said there was no use in going to law—Morgan had no shadow of right to remain where he was—nobody in the wide world would uphold him in it, and no lawyer would take his case and no judge listen to it. Hyde said that right there was where he was mistaken—everybody in town sustained Morgan; Hal Brayton, a very smart lawyer, had taken his case; the courts being in vacation, it was to be tried before a referee, and ex-Governor Roop had already been appointed to that office and would open his court in a large public hall near the hotel at two that afternoon.

The General was amazed. He said he had suspected before that the people of that Territory were fools, and now he knew it. But he said rest easy, rest easy and collect the witnesses, for the victory was just as certain as if the conflict were already over. Hyde wiped away his tears and left.

At two in the afternoon referee Roop's Court opened, and Roop appeared throned among his sheriffs, the witnesses, and spectators, and wearing upon his face a solemnity so awe-inspiring that some of his fellow-conspirators had misgivings that maybe he had not comprehended, after all, that this was merely a joke. An unearthly stillness prevailed, for at the slightest noise the judge uttered sternly the command:

"Order in the Court!"

And the sheriffs promptly echoed it. Presently the General elbowed his way through the crowd of spectators, with his arms full of law-books, and on his ears fell an order from the judge which was the first respectful recognition of his high official dignity that had ever saluted them, and it trickled pleasantly through his whole system:

"Way for the United States Attorney!"

The witnesses were called—legislators, high government officers, ranchmen, miners, Indians, Chinamen, negroes. Three fourths of them were called by the defendant Morgan, but no matter, their testimony invariably went in favor of the plaintiff Hyde. Each new witness only added new testimony to the absurdity of a man's claiming to own another man's property because his farm had slid down on top of it. Then the Morgan lawyers made their speeches, and seemed to make singularly weak ones—they did really nothing to help the Morgan cause. And now the General, with exultation in his face, got up and made an impassioned effort; he pounded the table, he banged the law-books, he shouted, and roared, and howled, he quoted from everything and everybody, poetry, sarcasm, statistics, history, pathos, bathos, blasphemy, and wound up with a grand war-whoop for free speech, freedom of the press, free schools, the Glorious Bird of America and the principles of eternal justice! [Applause.]

When the General sat down, he did it with the conviction that if there was anything in good strong testimony, a great speech and believing and admiring countenances all around, Mr. Morgan's case was killed. Ex-Governor Roop leant his head upon his hand for some minutes, thinking, and the still audience waited for his decision. Then he got up and stood erect, with bended head, and thought again. Then he walked the floor with long, deliberate strides, his chin in his hand, and still the audience waited. At last he returned to his throne, seated himself, and began, impressively:

"Gentlemen, I feel the great responsibility that rests upon me this day. This is no ordinary case. On the contrary it is plain that it is the most solemn and awful that ever man was called upon to decide. Gentlemen, I have listened attentively to the evidence, and have perceived that the weight of it, the overwhelming weight of it, is in favor of the plaintiff Hyde. I have listened also to the remarks of counsel, with high interest—and especially will I commend the masterly and irrefutable logic of the distinguished gentleman who represents the plaintiff. But gentlemen, let us beware how we allow mere human testimony, human ingenuity in argument and human ideas of equity, to influence us at a moment so solemn as this. Gentlemen, it ill becomes us, worms as we are, to meddle with the decrees of Heaven. It is plain to me that Heaven, in its inscrutable wisdom, has seen fit to move this defendant's ranch for a purpose. We are but creatures, and we must submit. If Heaven has chosen to favor the defendant Morgan in this marked and wonderful manner; and if Heaven, dissatisfied with the position of the Morgan ranch upon the mountain side, has chosen to remove it to a position more eligible and more advantageous for its owner, it ill becomes us, insects as we are, to question the legality of the act or inquire into the reasons that prompted it. No—Heaven created the ranches and it is Heaven's prerogative to rearrange them, to experiment with them, to shift them around at its pleasure. It is for us to submit, without repining. I warn you that this thing which has happened is a thing with which the sacrilegious hands and brains and tongues of men must not meddle.

Gentlemen, it is the verdict of this court that the plaintiff, Richard Hyde, has been deprived of his ranch by the visitation of God! And from this decision there is no appeal."

Buncombe seized his cargo of law-books and plunged out of the court-room frantic with indignation. He pronounced Roop to be a miraculous fool, an inspired idiot. In all good faith he returned at night and remonstrated with Roop upon his extravagant decision, and implored him to walk the floor and think for half an hour, and see if he could not figure out some sort of modification of the verdict. Roop yielded at last and got up to walk. He walked two hours and a half, and at last his face lit up happily and he told Buncombe it had occurred to him that the ranch underneath the new Morgan ranch still belonged to Hyde, that his title to the ground was just as good as it had ever been, and therefore he was of opinion that Hyde had a right to dig it out from under there and—

The General never waited to hear the end of it. He was always an impatient and irascible man, that way. At the end of two months the fact that he had been played upon with a joke had managed to bore itself, like another Hoosac Tunnel, through the solid adamant of his understanding.

Chapter XXXV

WHEN WE FINALLY left for Esmeralda, horseback, we had an addition to the company in the person of Capt. John Nye, the Governor's brother. He had a good memory, and a tongue hung in the middle. This is a combination which gives immortality to conversation. Capt. John never suffered the talk to flag or falter once during the hundred and twenty miles of the journey. In addition to his conversational powers, he had one or two other endowments of a marked character. One was a singular "handiness" about doing anything and everything, from laying out a railroad or organizing a political party, down to sewing on buttons, shoeing a horse, or setting a broken leg, or a hen. Another was a spirit of accommodation that prompted him to take the needs, difficulties and perplexities of anybody and everybody upon his own shoulders at any and all times, and dispose of them with admirable facility and alacrity—hence he always managed to find vacant beds in crowded inns, and plenty to eat in the emptiest larders. And finally, wherever he met a man, woman or child, in camp, inn or desert, he either knew such parties personally or had been acquainted with a relative of the same. Such another traveling comrade was never seen before. I cannot forbear giving a specimen of the way in which he overcame difficulties. On the second day out, we arrived, very tired and hungry, at a poor little inn in the desert, and were told that the house was full, no provisions on hand, and neither hay nor barley to spare for the horses—we must move on. The rest of us wanted to hurry on while it was yet light, but Capt. John insisted on stopping awhile. We dismounted and entered. There was no welcome for us on any face. Capt. John began his blandishments, and within twenty minutes he had accomplished the following things, viz.: found old acquaintances in three teamsters; discovered that he used to go to school with the landlord's mother; recognized his wife as a lady whose life he had saved once in California, by stopping her runaway horse; mended a child's broken toy and won the favor of its mother, a guest of the inn; helped the hostler bleed a horse, and prescribed for another horse that had the "heaves"; treated the entire party three times at the landlord's bar; produced a later paper than anybody had seen for a week and sat himself down to read the news to a deeply interested audience. The result, summed up, was as follows: The hostler found plenty of feed for our horses; we had a trout supper, an exceedingly sociable time after it, good beds to sleep in, and a surprising breakfast in the morning—and when we left, we left lamented by all! Capt. John had some bad traits, but he had some uncommonly valuable ones to offset them with.

Esmeralda was in many respects another Humboldt, but in a little more forward state. The claims we had been paying assessments on were entirely worthless, and we threw them away. The principal one cropped out of the top of a knoll that was fourteen feet high, and the inspired Board of Directors were running a tunnel under that knoll to strike the ledge. The tunnel would have to be seventy feet long, and would then strike the ledge at the same depth that a *shaft* twelve feet deep would have reached! The Board were living on the "assessments." [N. B.—This hint comes too late for the enlightenment of New York silver miners; they have already learned all about this neat trick by experience.] The Board had no desire to strike the ledge, knowing that it was as barren of silver as a curbstone. This reminiscence calls to mind Jim Townsend's tunnel. He had paid assessments on a mine called the "Daley" till he was well-nigh penniless. Finally an assessment was levied to run a tunnel two hundred and fifty feet on the Daley, and Townsend went up on the hill to look into matters. He found the Daley cropping out of the apex of an exceedingly sharp-pointed peak, and a couple of men up there "facing" the proposed tunnel. Townsend made a calculation. Then he said to the men:

"So you have taken a contract to run a tunnel into this hill two hundred and fifty feet to strike this ledge?"

"Yes, sir."

"Well, do you know that you have got one of the most expensive and arduous undertakings before you that was ever conceived by man?"

"Why no—how is that?"

"Because this hill is only twenty-five feet through from side to side; and so you have got to build two hundred and twenty-five feet of your tunnel on trestle-work!"

The ways of silver mining Boards are exceedingly dark and sinuous.

We took up various claims, and *commenced* shafts and tunnels on them, but never finished any of them. We had to do a certain amount of work on each to "hold" it, else other parties could seize our property after the expiration of ten days. We were always hunting up new claims and doing a little work on them and then waiting for a buyer—who never came. We never found any ore that would yield more than fifty dollars a ton; and as the mills charged fifty dollars a ton for *working* ore and extracting the silver, our pocket-money melted steadily away and none returned to take its place. We lived in a little cabin and cooked for ourselves; and altogether it was a hard life, though a hopeful one—for we never ceased to expect fortune and a customer to burst upon us some day.

At last, when flour reached a dollar a pound, and money could not be borrowed on the best security at less than *eight per cent a month* (I being without the security, too), I abandoned mining and went to milling. That is to say, I went to work as a common laborer in a quartz mill, at ten dollars a week and board.

Chapter XXXVI

I HAD ALREADY learned how hard and long and dismal a task it is to burrow down into the bowels of the earth and get out the coveted ore; and now I learned that the burrowing was only half the work; and that to get the silver out of the ore was the dreary and laborious other half of it. We had to turn out at six in the morning and keep at it till dark. This mill was a six-stamp affair, driven by steam. Six tall, upright rods of iron, as large as a man's ankle, and heavily shod with a mass of iron and steel at their lower ends, were framed together like a gate, and these rose and fell, one after the other, in a ponderous dance, in an iron box called a "battery." Each of these rods or stamps weighed six hundred pounds. One of us stood by the battery all day long, breaking up masses of silver-bearing rock with a sledge and shoveling it into the battery. The ceaseless dance of the stamps pulverized the rock to powder, and a stream of water that trickled into the battery turned it to a creamy paste. The minutest particles were driven through a fine wire screen which fitted close around the battery, and were washed into great tubs warmed by super-heated steam—amalgamating pans, they are called. The mass of pulp in the pans was kept constantly stirred up by revolving "mullers." A quantity of quicksilver was kept always in the battery, and this seized some of the liberated gold and silver particles and held on to them; quicksilver was shaken in a fine shower into the pans, also, about every half hour, through a buckskin sack. Quantities of coarse salt and sulphate of copper were added, from time to time to assist the amalgamation by destroying base metals which coated the gold and silver and would not let it unite with the quicksilver. All these tiresome things we had to attend to constantly. Streams of dirty water flowed always from the pans and were carried off in broad wooden troughs to the ravine. One would not suppose that atoms of gold and silver would float on top of six inches of water, but they did; and in order to catch them, coarse blankets were laid in the troughs, and little obstructing "riffles" charged with quicksilver were placed here and there across the troughs also. These riffles had to be cleaned and the blankets washed out every evening, to get their precious accumulations—and after all this eternity of trouble one third of the silver and gold in a ton of rock would find its way to the end of the troughs in the ravine at last and have to be worked over again some day. There is nothing so aggravating as silver milling. There never was any idle time in that mill. There was always something to do. It is a pity that Adam could not have gone straight out of Eden into a quartz mill, in order to understand the full force of his doom to "earn his bread by the sweat of his brow." Every now and then, during the day, we had to scoop some pulp out of the pans, and tediously "wash" it in a horn spoon—wash it little by little over the edge till at last nothing was left but some little dull globules of quicksilver in the bottom. If they were soft and yielding, the pan needed some salt or some sulphate of copper or some other chemical rubbish to assist digestion; if they were crisp to the touch and would retain a dint, they were freighted with all the silver and gold they could seize and hold, and consequently the pans needed a fresh charge of quicksilver. When there was nothing else to do, one could always "screen tailings." That is to say, he could shovel up the dried sand that had washed down to the ravine through the troughs and dash it against an upright wire screen to free it from pebbles and prepare it for working over. The process of amalgamation differed in the various mills, and this included changes in style of pans and other machinery, and a great diversity of opinion existed as to the best in use, but none of the methods employed, involved the principle of milling ore without "screening the tailings." Of all recreations in the world, screening tailings on a hot day, with a long-handled shovel, is the most undesirable.

At the end of the week the machinery was stopped and we "cleaned up." That is to say, we got the pulp out of the pans and batteries, and washed the mud patiently away till nothing was left but the long accumulating mass of quicksilver, with its imprisoned treasures. This we made into heavy, compact snow-balls, and piled them up in a bright, luxurious heap for inspection. Making these snow-balls cost me a fine gold ring—that and ignorance together; for the quicksilver invaded the ring with the same facility with which water saturates a sponge—separated its particles and the ring crumbled to pieces.

We put our pile of quicksilver balls into an iron retort that had a pipe leading from it to a pail of water, and then applied a roasting heat. The quicksilver turned to vapor, escaped through the pipe into the pail, and the water turned it into good wholesome quicksilver again. Quicksilver is very costly, and they never waste it. On opening the retort, there was our week's work—a lump of pure white, frosty looking silver, twice as large as a man's head. Perhaps a fifth of the mass was gold, but the color of it did not show—would not have shown if two thirds of it had been gold. We melted it up and made a solid brick of it by pouring it into an iron brick-mould.

By such a tedious and laborious process were silver bricks obtained. This mill was but one of many others in operation at the time. The first one in Nevada was built at Egan Canyon and was a small insignificant affair and compared most unfavorably with some of the immense establishments afterwards located at Virginia City and elsewhere.

From our bricks a little corner was chipped off for the "fire-assay"—a method used to determine the proportions of gold, silver and base metals in the mass. This is an interesting process. The chip is hammered out as thin as paper and weighed on scales so fine and sensitive that if you weigh a two-inch scrap of paper on them and then write your name on the paper with a coarse, soft pencil and weigh it again, the scales will take marked notice of the addition. Then a little lead (also weighed) is rolled up with the flake of silver and the two are melted at a great heat in a small vessel called a cupel, made by compressing bone ashes into a cup-shape in a steel mold. The base metals oxidize and are absorbed with the lead into the pores of the cupel. A button or globule of perfectly pure gold and silver is left behind, and by weighing it and noting the loss, the assayer knows the proportion of base metal the brick contains. He has to separate the gold from the silver now. The button is hammered out flat and thin, put in the furnace and kept some time at a red heat; after cooling it off it is rolled up like a quill and heated in a glass vessel containing nitric acid; the acid dissolves the silver and leaves the gold pure and ready to be weighed on its own merits. Then salt water is poured into the vessel containing the dissolved silver and the silver returns to palpable form again and sinks to the bottom. Nothing now remains but to weigh it; then the proportions of the several metals contained in the brick are known, and the assayer stamps the value of the brick upon its surface.

The sagacious reader will know now, without being told, that the speculative miner, in getting a "fire-assay" made of a piece of rock from his mine (to help him sell the same), was not in the habit of picking out the least valuable fragment of rock on his dump-pile, but quite the contrary. I have seen men hunt over a pile of nearly worthless quartz for an hour, and at last find a little piece as large as a filbert, which was rich in gold and silver—and this was reserved for a fire-assay! Of course the fire-assay would demonstrate that a ton of such rock would yield hundreds of dollars—and on such assays many an utterly worthless mine was sold.

Assaying was a good business, and so some men engaged in it, occasionally, who were not strictly scientific and capable. One assayer got such rich results out of all specimens brought to him that in time he acquired almost a monopoly of the business. But like all men who achieve success, he became an object of envy and suspicion. The other assayers entered into a conspiracy against him, and let some prominent citizens into the secret in order to show that they meant fairly. Then they broke a little fragment off a carpenter's grindstone and got a stranger to take it to the popular scientist and get it assayed. In the course of an hour the result came—whereby it appeared that a ton of that rock would yield $1,284.40 in silver and $366.36 in gold!

Due publication of the whole matter was made in the paper, and the popular assayer left town "between two days."

I will remark, in passing, that I only remained in the milling business one week. I told my employer I could not stay longer without an advance in my wages; that I liked quartz milling, indeed was infatuated with it; that I had never before grown so tenderly attached to an occupation in so short a time; that nothing, it seemed to me, gave such scope to intellectual activity as feeding a battery and screening tailings, and nothing so stimulated the moral attributes as retorting bullion and washing blankets—still, I felt constrained to ask an increase of salary.

He said he was paying me ten dollars a week, and thought it a good round sum. How much did I want?

I said about four hundred thousand dollars a month, and board, was about all I could reasonably ask, considering the hard times.

I was ordered off the premises! And yet, when I look back to those days and call to mind the exceeding hardness of the labor I performed in that mill, I only regret that I did not ask him seven hundred thousand.

Shortly after this I began to grow crazy, along with the rest of the population, about the mysterious and wonderful "cement mine," and to make preparations to take advantage of any opportunity that might offer to go and help hunt for it.

Chapter XXXVII

IT WAS SOMEWHERE in the neighborhood of Mono Lake that the marvellous Whiteman cement mine was supposed to lie. Every now and then it would be reported that Mr. W. had passed stealthily through Esmeralda at dead of night, in disguise, and then we would have a wild excitement—because he must be steering for his secret mine, and now was the time to follow him. In less than three hours after daylight all the horses and mules and donkeys in the vicinity would be bought, hired or stolen, and half the community would be off for the mountains, following in the wake of Whiteman. But W. would drift about through the mountain gorges for days together, in a purposeless sort of way, until the provisions of the miners ran out, and they would have to go back home. I have known it reported at eleven at night, in a large mining camp, that Whiteman had just passed through, and in two hours the streets, so quiet before, would be swarming with men and animals. Every individual would be trying to be very secret, but yet venturing to whisper to just one neighbor that W. had passed through. And long before daylight—this in the dead of Winter—the stampede would be complete, the camp deserted, and the whole population gone chasing after W.

The tradition was that in the early immigration, more than twenty years ago, three young Germans, brothers, who had survived an Indian massacre on the Plains, wandered on foot through the deserts, avoiding all trails and roads, and simply holding a westerly direction and hoping to find California before they starved, or died of fatigue. And in a gorge in the mountains they sat down to rest one day, when one of them noticed a curious vein of cement running along the ground, shot full of lumps of dull yellow metal. They saw that it was gold, and that here was a fortune to be acquired in a single day. The vein was about as wide as a curbstone, and fully two thirds of it was pure gold. Every pound of the wonderful cement was worth well-nigh $200. Each of the brothers loaded himself with about twenty-five pounds of it, and then they covered up all traces of the vein, made a rude drawing of the locality and the principal landmarks in the vicinity, and started westward again. But troubles thickened about them. In their wanderings one brother fell and broke his leg, and the others were obliged to go on and leave him to die in the wilderness. Another, worn out and starving, gave up by and by, and laid down to die, but after two or three weeks of incredible hardships, the third reached the settlements of California exhausted, sick, and his mind deranged by his sufferings. He had thrown away all his cement but a few fragments, but these were sufficient to set everybody wild with excitement. However, he had had enough of the cement country, and nothing could induce him to lead a party thither. He was entirely content to work on a farm for wages. But he gave Whiteman his map, and described the cement region as well as he could, and thus transferred the curse to that gentleman—for when I had my one accidental glimpse of Mr. W. in Esmeralda he had been hunting for the lost mine, in hunger and thirst, poverty and sickness, for twelve or thirteen years. Some people believed he had found it, but most people believed he had not. I saw a piece of cement as large as my fist which was said to have been given to Whiteman by the young German, and it was of a seductive nature. Lumps of virgin gold were as thick in it as raisins in a slice of fruit cake. The privilege of working such a mine one week would be sufficient for a man of reasonable desires.

A new partner of ours, a Mr. Higbie, knew Whiteman well by sight, and a friend of ours, a Mr. Van Dorn, was well acquainted with him, and not only that, but had Whiteman's promise that he should have a private hint in time to enable him to join the next cement expedition. Van Dorn had promised to extend the hint to us. One evening Higbie came in greatly excited, and said he felt certain he had recognized Whiteman, up town, disguised and in a pretended state of intoxication. In a little while Van Dorn arrived and confirmed the news; and so we gathered in our cabin and with heads close together arranged our plans in impressive whispers.

We were to leave town quietly, after midnight, in two or three small parties, so as not to attract attention, and meet at dawn on the "divide" overlooking Mono Lake, eight or nine miles distant. We were to make no noise after starting, and not speak above a whisper under any circumstances. It was believed that for once Whiteman's presence was unknown in the town and his expedition unsuspected. Our conclave broke up at nine o'clock, and we set about our preparations diligently and with profound secrecy. At eleven o'clock we saddled our horses, hitched them with their long *riatas* (or lassos), and then brought out a side of bacon, a sack of beans, a small sack of coffee, some sugar, a hundred pounds of flour in sacks, some tin cups and a coffee pot, frying pan and some few other necessary articles. All these things were "packed" on the back of a led horse—and whoever has not been taught, by a Spanish adept, to pack an animal, let him never hope to do the thing by natural smartness. That is impossible. Higbie had had some experience, but was not perfect. He put on the pack saddle (a thing like a saw-buck), piled the property on it and then wound a rope all over and about it and under it, "every which way," taking a hitch in it every now and then, and occasionally surging back on it till the horse's sides sunk in and he gasped for breath—but every time the lashings grew tight in one place they loosened in another. We never did get the load tight all over, but we got it so that it would do, after a fashion, and then we started, in single file, close order, and without a word. It was a dark night. We kept the middle of the road, and proceeded in a slow walk past the rows of cabins, and whenever a miner came to his door I trembled for fear the light would shine on us and excite curiosity. But nothing happened. We began the long winding ascent of the canyon, toward the "divide," and presently the cabins began to grow infrequent, and the intervals between them wider and wider, and then I began to breathe tolerably freely and feel less like a thief and a murderer. I was in the rear, leading the pack horse. As the ascent grew steeper he grew proportionately less satisfied with his cargo, and began to pull back on his *riata* occasionally and delay progress. My comrades were passing out of sight in the gloom. I was getting anxious. I coaxed and bullied the pack horse till I presently got him into a trot, and then the tin cups and pans strung about his person frightened him and he ran. His *riata* was wound around the pummel of my saddle, and so, as he went by he dragged me from my horse and the two animals traveled briskly on without me. But I was not alone—the loosened cargo tumbled overboard from the pack horse and fell close to me. It was abreast of almost the last cabin. A miner came out and said:

"Hello!"

I was thirty steps from him, and knew he could not see me, it was so very dark in the shadow of the mountain. So I lay still. Another head appeared in the light of the cabin door, and presently the two men walked toward me. They stopped within ten steps of me, and one said:

" 'St! Listen."

I could not have been in a more distressed state if I had been escaping justice with a price on my head. Then the miners appeared to sit down on a boulder, though I could not see them distinctly enough to be very sure what they did. One said:

"I heard a noise, as plain as I ever heard anything. It seemed to be about there—"

A stone whizzed by my head. I flattened myself out in the dust like a postage stamp, and thought to myself if he mended his aim ever so little he would probably hear another noise. In my heart, now, I execrated secret expeditions. I promised myself that this should be my last, though the Sierras were ribbed with cement veins. Then one of the men said:

"I'll tell you what! Welch knew what he was talking about when he said he saw Whiteman to-day. I heard horses—that was the noise. I am going down to Welch's, right away."

They left and I was glad. I did not care whither they went, so they went. I was willing they should visit Welch, and the sooner the better.

As soon as they closed their cabin door my comrades emerged from the gloom; they had caught the horses and were waiting for a clear coast again. We remounted the cargo on the pack horse and got under way, and as day broke we reached the "divide" and joined Van Dorn. Then we journeyed down into the valley of the Lake, and feeling secure, we halted to cook breakfast, for we were tired and sleepy and hungry. Three hours later the rest of the population filed over the "divide" in a long procession, and drifted off out of sight around the borders of the Lake!

Whether or not my accident had produced this result we never knew, but at least one thing was certain—the secret was out and Whiteman would not enter upon a search for the cement mine this time. We were filled with chagrin.

We held a council and decided to make the best of our misfortune and enjoy a week's holiday on the borders of the curious Lake. Mono, it is sometimes called, and sometimes the "Dead Sea of California." It is one of the strangest freaks of Nature to be found in any land, but it is hardly ever mentioned in print and very seldom visited, because it lies away off the usual routes of travel and besides is so difficult to get at that only men content to endure the roughest life will consent to take upon themselves the discomforts of such a trip. On the morning of our second day, we traveled around to a remote and particularly wild spot on the borders of the Lake, where a stream of fresh, ice-cold water entered it from the mountain side, and then we went regularly into camp. We hired a large boat and two shot-guns from a lonely ranchman who lived some ten miles further on, and made ready for comfort and recreation. We soon got thoroughly acquainted with the Lake and all its peculiarities.

Chapter XXXVIII

MONO LAKE lies in a lifeless, treeless, hideous desert, eight thousand feet above the level of the sea, and is guarded by mountains two thousand feet higher, whose summits are always clothed in clouds. This solemn, silent, sailless sea—this lonely tenant of the loneliest spot on earth—is little graced with the picturesque. It is an unpretending expanse of grayish water, about a hundred miles in circumference, with two islands in its centre, mere upheavals of rent and scorched and blistered lava, snowed over with gray banks and drifts of pumice-stone and ashes, the winding sheet of the dead volcano, whose vast crater the lake has seized upon and occupied.

The lake is two hundred feet deep, and its sluggish waters are so strong with alkali that if you only dip the most hopelessly soiled garment into them once or twice, and wring it out, it will be found as clean as if it had been through the ablest of washerwomen's hands. While we camped there our laundry work was easy. We tied the week's washing astern of our boat, and sailed a quarter of a mile, and the job was complete, all to the wringing out. If we threw the water on our heads and gave them a rub or so, the white lather would pile up three inches high. This water is not good for bruised places and abrasions of the skin. We had a valuable dog. He had raw places on him. He had more raw places on him than sound ones. He was the rawest dog I almost ever saw. He jumped overboard one day to get away from the flies. But it was bad judgment. In his condition, it would have been just as comfortable to jump into the fire. The alkali water nipped him in all the raw places simultaneously, and he struck out for the shore with considerable interest. He yelped and barked and howled as he went—and by the time he got to the shore there was no bark to him—for he had barked the bark all out of his inside, and the alkali water had cleaned the bark all off his outside, and he probably wished he had never embarked in any such enterprise. He ran round and round in a circle, and pawed the earth and clawed the air, and threw double somersaults, sometimes backward and sometimes forward, in the most extraordinary manner. He was not a demonstrative dog, as a general thing, but rather of a grave and serious turn of mind, and I never saw him take so much interest in anything before. He finally struck out over the mountains, at a gait which we estimated at about two hundred and fifty miles an hour, and he is going yet. This was about nine years ago. We look for what is left of him along here every day.

A white man cannot drink the water of Mono Lake, for it is nearly pure lye. It is said that the Indians in the vicinity drink it sometimes, though. It is not improbable, for they are among the purest liars I ever saw. [There will be no additional charge for this joke, except to parties requiring an explanation of it. This joke has received high commendation from some of the ablest minds of the age.]

There are no fish in Mono Lake—no frogs, no snakes, no polliwigs—nothing, in fact, that goes to make life desirable. Millions of wild ducks and sea-gulls swim about the surface, but no living thing exists *under* the surface, except a white feathery sort of worm, one half an inch long, which looks like a bit of white thread frayed out at the sides. If you dip up a gallon of water, you will get about fifteen thousand of these. They give to the water a sort of grayish-white appearance. Then there is a fly, which looks something like our house fly. These settle on the beach to eat the worms that wash ashore—and any time, you can see there a belt of flies an inch deep and six feet wide, and this belt extends clear around the lake—a belt of flies one hundred miles long. If you throw a stone among them, they swarm up so thick that they look dense, like a cloud. You can hold them under water as long as you please—they do not mind it—they are only proud of it. When you let them go, they pop up to the surface as dry as a patent office report, and walk off as unconcernedly as if they had been educated especially with a view to affording instructive entertainment to man in that particular way. Providence leaves nothing to go by chance. All things have their uses and their part and proper place in Nature's economy: the ducks eat the flies—the flies eat the worms—the Indians eat all three—the wild cats eat the Indians—the white folks eat the wild cats—and thus all things are lovely.

Mono Lake is a hundred miles in a straight line from the ocean—and between it and the ocean are one or two ranges of mountains—yet thousands of sea-gulls go there every season to lay their eggs and rear their young. One would as soon expect to find sea-gulls in Kansas. And in this connection let us observe another instance of Nature's wisdom. The islands in the lake being merely huge masses of lava, coated over with ashes and pumice-stone, and utterly innocent of vegetation or anything that would burn; and sea-gulls' eggs being entirely useless to anybody unless they be cooked, Nature has provided an unfailing spring of boiling water on the largest island, and you can put your eggs in there, and in four minutes you can boil them as hard as any statement I have made during the past fifteen years. Within ten feet of the boiling spring is a spring of pure cold water, sweet and wholesome. So, in that island you get your board and washing free of charge—and if nature had gone further and furnished a nice American hotel clerk who was crusty and disobliging, and didn't know anything about the time tables, or the railroad routes—or—anything—and was proud of it—I would not wish for a more desirable boarding-house.

Half a dozen little mountain brooks flow into Mono Lake, but *not a stream of any kind flows out of it*. It neither rises nor falls, apparently, and what it does with its surplus water is a dark and bloody mystery.

There are only two seasons in the region round about Mono Lake—and these are, the breaking up of one Winter and the beginning of the next. More than once (in Esmeralda) I have seen a perfectly blistering morning open up with the thermometer at ninety degrees at eight o'clock, and seen the snow fall fourteen inches deep and that same identical thermometer go down to forty-four degrees under shelter, before nine o'clock at night. Under favorable circumstances it snows at least once in every single month in the year, in the little town of Mono. So uncertain is the climate in Summer that a lady who goes out visiting cannot hope to be prepared for all emergencies unless she takes her fan under one arm and her snow shoes under the other. When they have a Fourth of July procession it generally snows on them, and they do say that as a general thing when a man calls for a brandy toddy there, the bar keeper chops it off with a hatchet and wraps it up in a paper, like maple sugar. And it is further reported that the old soakers haven't any teeth—wore them out eating gin cocktails and brandy punches. I do not endorse that statement—I simply give it for what it is worth—and it is worth—well, I should say, millions, to any man who can believe it without straining himself. But I do endorse the snow on the Fourth of July—because I know that to be true.

Chapter XXXIX

ABOUT SEVEN O'CLOCK one blistering hot morning—for it was now dead summer time—Higbie and I took the boat and started on a voyage of discovery to the two islands. We had often longed to do this, but had been deterred by the fear of storms; for they were frequent, and severe enough to capsize an ordinary row-boat like ours without great difficulty—and once capsized, death would ensue in spite of the bravest swimming, for that venomous water would eat a man's eyes out like fire, and burn him out inside, too, if he shipped a sea. It was called twelve miles, straight out to the islands—a long pull and a warm one—but the morning was so quiet and sunny, and the lake so smooth and glassy and dead, that we could not resist the temptation. So we filled two large tin canteens with water (since we were not acquainted with the locality of the spring said to exist on the large island), and started. Higbie's brawny muscles gave the boat good speed, but by the time we reached our destination we judged that we had pulled nearer fifteen miles than twelve.

We landed on the big island and went ashore. We tried the water in the canteens, now, and found that the sun had spoiled it; it was so brackish that we could not drink it; so we poured it out and began a search for the spring—for thirst augments fast as soon as it is apparent that one has no means at hand of quenching it. The island was a long, moderately high hill of ashes—nothing but gray ashes and pumice-stone, in which we sunk to our knees at every step—and all around the top was a forbidding wall of scorched and blasted rocks. When we reached the top and got within the wall, we found simply a shallow, far-reaching basin, carpeted with ashes, and here and there a patch of fine sand. In places, picturesque jets of steam shot up out of crevices, giving evidence that although this ancient crater had gone out of active business, there was still some fire left in its furnaces. Close to one of these jets of steam stood the only tree on the island—a small pine of most graceful shape and most faultless symmetry; its color was a brilliant green, for the steam drifted unceasingly through its branches and kept them always moist.

It contrasted strangely enough, did this vigorous and beautiful outcast, with its dead and dismal surroundings. It was like
a cheerful spirit in a mourning household.

We hunted for the spring everywhere, traversing the full
length of the island (two or three miles), and crossing it
twice—climbing ash-hills patiently, and then sliding down
the other side in a sitting posture, plowing up smothering
volumes of gray dust. But we found nothing but solitude,
ashes and a heart-breaking silence. Finally we noticed that the
wind had risen, and we forgot our thirst in a solicitude of
greater importance; for, the lake being quiet, we had not
taken pains about securing the boat. We hurried back to a
point overlooking our landing place, and then—but mere
words cannot describe our dismay—the boat was gone! The
chances were that there was not another boat on the entire
lake. The situation was not comfortable—in truth, to speak
plainly, it was frightful. We were prisoners on a desolate island, in aggravating proximity to friends who were for the
present helpless to aid us; and what was still more uncomfortable was the reflection that we had neither food nor water. But presently we sighted the boat. It was drifting along,
leisurely, about fifty yards from shore, tossing in a foamy sea.
It drifted, and continued to drift, but at the same safe distance
from land, and we walked along abreast it and waited for
fortune to favor us. At the end of an hour it approached a
jutting cape, and Higbie ran ahead and posted himself on the
utmost verge and prepared for the assault. If we failed there,
there was no hope for us. It was driving gradually shoreward
all the time, now; but whether it was driving fast enough to
make the connection or not was the momentous question.
When it got within thirty steps of Higbie I was so excited
that I fancied I could hear my own heart beat. When, a little
later, it dragged slowly along and seemed about to go by,
only one little yard out of reach, it seemed as if my heart
stood still; and when it was exactly abreast him and began to
widen away, and he still standing like a watching statue, I
knew my heart did stop. But when he gave a great spring, the
next instant, and lit fairly in the stern, I discharged a war-
whoop that woke the solitudes!

But it dulled my enthusiasm, presently, when he told me

he had not been caring whether the boat came within jumping distance or not, so that it passed within eight or ten yards of him, for he had made up his mind to shut his eyes and mouth and swim that trifling distance. Imbecile that I was, I had not thought of that. It was only a long swim that could be fatal.

The sea was running high and the storm increasing. It was growing late, too—three or four in the afternoon. Whether to venture toward the mainland or not, was a question of some moment. But we were so distressed by thirst that we decided to try it, and so Higbie fell to work and I took the steering-oar. When we had pulled a mile, laboriously, we were evidently in serious peril, for the storm had greatly augmented; the billows ran very high and were capped with foaming crests, the heavens were hung with black, and the wind blew with great fury. We would have gone back, now, but we did not dare to turn the boat around, because as soon as she got in the trough of the sea she would upset, of course. Our only hope lay in keeping her head-on to the seas. It was hard work to do this, she plunged so, and so beat and belabored the billows with her rising and falling bows. Now and then one of Higbie's oars would trip on the top of a wave, and the other one would snatch the boat half around in spite of my cumbersome steering apparatus. We were drenched by the sprays constantly, and the boat occasionally shipped water. By and by, powerful as my comrade was, his great exertions began to tell on him, and he was anxious that I should change places with him till he could rest a little. But I told him this was impossible; for if the steering oar were dropped a moment while we changed, the boat would slue around into the trough of the sea, capsize, and in less than five minutes we would have a hundred gallons of soap-suds in us and be eaten up so quickly that we could not even be present at our own inquest.

But things cannot last always. Just as the darkness shut down we came booming into port, head on. Higbie dropped his oars to hurrah—I dropped mine to help—the sea gave the boat a twist, and over she went!

The agony that alkali water inflicts on bruises, chafes and blistered hands, is unspeakable, and nothing but greasing all over will modify it—but we ate, drank and slept well, that night, notwithstanding.

In speaking of the peculiarities of Mono Lake, I ought to have mentioned that at intervals all around its shores stand picturesque turret-looking masses and clusters of a whitish, coarse-grained rock that resembles inferior mortar dried hard; and if one breaks off fragments of this rock he will find perfectly shaped and thoroughly petrified gulls' eggs deeply imbedded in the mass. How did they get there? I simply state the fact—for it is a fact—and leave the geological reader to crack the nut at his leisure and solve the problem after his own fashion.

At the end of a week we adjourned to the Sierras on a fishing excursion, and spent several days in camp under snowy Castle Peak, and fished successfully for trout in a bright, miniature lake whose surface was between ten and eleven thousand feet above the level of the sea; cooling ourselves during the hot August noons by sitting on snow banks ten feet deep, under whose sheltering edges *fine grass and dainty flowers flourished luxuriously*; and at night entertaining ourselves by almost freezing to death. Then we returned to Mono Lake, and finding that the cement excitement was over for the present, packed up and went back to Esmeralda. Mr. Ballou reconnoitred awhile, and not liking the prospect, set out alone for Humboldt.

About this time occurred a little incident which has always had a sort of interest to me, from the fact that it came so near "instigating" my funeral. At a time when an Indian attack had been expected, the citizens hid their gunpowder where it would be safe and yet convenient to hand when wanted. A neighbor of ours hid six cans of rifle powder in the bake-oven of an old discarded cooking stove which stood on the open ground near a frame out-house or shed, and from and after that day never thought of it again. We hired a half-tamed Indian to do some washing for us, and he took up quarters under the shed with his tub. The ancient stove reposed within six feet of him, and before his face. Finally it occurred to him that hot water would be better than cold, and he went out and fired up under that forgotten powder magazine and set on a kettle of water. Then he returned to his tub. I entered the shed presently and threw down some more clothes, and was about to speak to him when the stove blew up with a prodigious crash, and disappeared, leaving not a splinter behind. Fragments of it fell in the streets full two hundred yards away. Nearly a third of the shed roof over our heads was destroyed, and one of the stove lids, after cutting a small stanchion half in two in front of the Indian, whizzed between us and drove partly through the weather-boarding beyond. I was as white as a sheet and as weak as a kitten and speechless. But the Indian betrayed no trepidation, no distress, not even discomfort. He simply stopped washing, leaned forward and surveyed the clean, blank ground a moment, and then remarked:

"Mph! Dam stove heap gone!"—and resumed his scrubbing as placidly as if it were an entirely customary thing for a stove to do. I will explain, that "heap" is "Injun-English" for "very much." The reader will perceive the exhaustive expressiveness of it in the present instance.

Chapter XL

I NOW COME to a curious episode—the most curious, I think, that had yet accented my slothful, valueless, heedless career. Out of a hillside toward the upper end of the town, projected a wall of reddish looking quartz-croppings, the exposed comb of a silver-bearing ledge that extended deep down into the earth, of course. It was owned by a company entitled the "Wide West." There was a shaft sixty or seventy feet deep on the under side of the croppings, and everybody was acquainted with the rock that came from it—and tolerably rich rock it was, too, but nothing extraordinary. I will remark here, that although to the inexperienced stranger all the quartz of a particular "district" looks about alike, an old resident of the camp can take a glance at a mixed pile of rock, separate the fragments and tell you which mine each came from, as easily as a confectioner can separate and classify the various kinds and qualities of candy in a mixed heap of the article.

All at once the town was thrown into a state of extraordinary excitement. In mining parlance the Wide West had "struck it rich!" Everybody went to see the new developments, and for some days there was such a crowd of people about the Wide West shaft that a stranger would have supposed there was a mass meeting in session there. No other topic was discussed but the rich strike, and nobody thought or dreamed about anything else. Every man brought away a specimen, ground it up in a hand mortar, washed it out in his horn spoon, and glared speechless upon the marvelous result. It was not hard rock, but black, decomposed stuff which could be crumbled in the hand like a baked potato, and when spread out on a paper exhibited a thick sprinkling of gold and particles of "native" silver. Higbie brought a handful to the cabin, and when he had washed it out his amazement was beyond description. Wide West stock soared skywards. It was said that repeated offers had been made for it at a thousand dollars a foot, and promptly refused. We have all had the "blues"—the mere sky-blues—but mine were indigo, now—because I did not own in the Wide West. The world seemed hollow to me, and existence a grief. I lost my appetite, and ceased to take an interest in anything. Still I had to stay, and listen to other people's rejoicings, because I had no money to get out of the camp with.

The Wide West company put a stop to the carrying away of "specimens," and well they might, for every handful of the ore was worth a sum of some consequence. To show the exceeding value of the ore, I will remark that a sixteen-hundred-pounds parcel of it was sold, just as it lay, at the mouth of the shaft, at *one dollar a pound*; and the man who bought it "packed" it on mules a hundred and fifty or two hundred miles, over the mountains, to San Francisco, satisfied that it would yield at a rate that would richly compensate him for his trouble. The Wide West people also commanded their foreman to refuse any but their own operatives permission to enter the mine at any time or for any purpose. I kept up my "blue" meditations and Higbie kept up a deal of thinking, too, but of a different sort. He puzzled over the "rock," examined it with a glass, inspected it in different lights and from different points of view, and after each experiment delivered himself, in soliloquy, of one and the same unvarying opinion in the same unvarying formula:

"It is *not* Wide West rock!"

He said once or twice that he meant to have a look into the Wide West shaft if he got shot for it. I was wretched, and did not care whether he got a look into it or not. He failed that day, and tried again at night; failed again; got up at dawn and tried, and failed again. Then he lay in ambush in the sage brush hour after hour, waiting for the two or three hands to adjourn to the shade of a boulder for dinner; made a start once, but was premature—one of the men came back for something; tried it again, but when almost at the mouth of the shaft, another of the men rose up from behind the boulder as if to reconnoitre, and he dropped on the ground and lay quiet; presently he crawled on his hands and knees to the mouth of the shaft, gave a quick glance around, then seized the rope and slid down the shaft. He disappeared in the gloom of a "side drift" just as a head appeared in the mouth of the shaft and somebody shouted "Hello!"—which he did not answer. He was not disturbed any more. An hour later he entered the cabin, hot, red, and ready to burst with smothered excitement, and exclaimed in a stage whisper:

"I knew it! We are rich! It's A BLIND LEAD!"

I thought the very earth reeled under me. Doubt—conviction—doubt again—exultation—hope, amazement, belief, unbelief—every emotion imaginable swept in wild procession through my heart and brain, and I could not speak a word. After a moment or two of this mental fury, I shook myself to rights, and said:

"Say it again!"

"It's a blind lead!"

"Cal., let's—let's burn the house—or kill somebody! Let's get out where there's room to hurrah! But what is the use? It is a hundred times too good to be true."

"It's a blind lead, for a million!—hanging wall—foot wall—clay casings—everything complete!" He swung his hat and gave three cheers, and I cast doubt to the winds and chimed in with a will. For I was worth a million dollars, and did not care " whether school kept or not!"

But perhaps I ought to explain. A "blind lead" is a lead or ledge that does not "crop out" above the surface. A miner does not know where to look for such leads, but they are often stumbled upon by accident in the course of driving a tunnel or sinking a shaft. Higbie knew the Wide West rock perfectly well, and the more he had examined the new developments the more he was satisfied that the ore could not have come from the Wide West vein. And so had it occurred to him alone, of all the camp, that there was a blind lead down in the shaft, and that even the Wide West people themselves did not suspect it. He was right. When he went down the shaft, he found that the blind lead held its independent way through the Wide West vein, cutting it diagonally, and that it was enclosed in its own well-defined casing-rocks and clay. Hence it was public property. Both leads being perfectly well defined, it was easy for any miner to see which one belonged to the Wide West and which did not.

We thought it well to have a strong friend, and therefore we brought the foreman of the Wide West to our cabin that night and revealed the great surprise to him. Higbie said:

"We are going to take possession of this blind lead, record

it and establish ownership, and then forbid the Wide West company to take out any more of the rock. You cannot help your company in this matter—nobody can help them. I will go into the shaft with you and prove to your entire satisfaction that it *is* a blind lead. Now we propose to take you in with us, and claim the blind lead in our three names. What do you say?"

What could a man say who had an opportunity to simply stretch forth his hand and take possession of a fortune without risk of any kind and without wronging any one or attaching the least taint of dishonor to his name? He could only say, "Agreed."

The notice was put up that night, and duly spread upon the recorder's books before ten o'clock. We claimed two hundred feet each—six hundred feet in all—the smallest and compactest organization in the district, and the easiest to manage.

No one can be so thoughtless as to suppose that we slept, that night. Higbie and I went to bed at midnight, but it was only to lie broad awake and think, dream, scheme. The floorless, tumble-down cabin was a palace, the ragged gray blankets silk, the furniture rosewood and mahogany. Each new splendor that burst out of my visions of the future whirled me bodily over in bed or jerked me to a sitting posture just as if an electric battery had been applied to me. We shot fragments of conversation back and forth at each other. Once Higbie said:

"When are you going home—to the States?"

"To-morrow!"—with an evolution or two, ending with a sitting position. "Well—no—but next month, at furthest."

"We'll go in the same steamer."

"Agreed."

A pause.

"Steamer of the 10th?"

"Yes. No, the 1st."

"All right."

Another pause.

"Where are you going to live?" said Higbie.

"San Francisco."

"That's me!"

Pause.

"Too high—too much climbing"—from Higbie.

"What is?"

"I was thinking of Russian Hill—building a house up there."

"Too much climbing? Shan't you keep a carriage?"

"Of course. I forgot that."

Pause.

"Cal., what kind of a house are you going to build?"

"I was thinking about that. Three-story and an attic."

"But what *kind*?"

"Well, I don't hardly know. Brick, I suppose."

"Brick—bosh."

"Why? What is your idea?"

"Brown stone front—French plate glass—billiard-room off the dining-room—statuary and paintings—shrubbery and two-acre grass plat—greenhouse—iron dog on the front stoop—gray horses—landau, and a coachman with a bug on his hat!"

"By George!"

A long pause.

"Cal., when are you going to Europe?"

"Well—I hadn't thought of that. When are you?"

"In the Spring."

"Going to be gone all summer?"

"All summer! I shall remain there three years."

"No—but are you in earnest?"

"Indeed I am."

"I will go along too."

"Why of course you will."

"What part of Europe shall you go to?"

"All parts. France, England, Germany—Spain, Italy, Switzerland, Syria, Greece, Palestine, Arabia, Persia, Egypt—all over—everywhere."

"I'm agreed."

"All right."

"Won't it be a swell trip!"

"We'll spend forty or fifty thousand dollars trying to make it one, anyway."

Another long pause.

"Higbie, we owe the butcher six dollars, and he has been threatening to stop our—"

"Hang the butcher!"

"Amen."

And so it went on. By three o'clock we found it was no use, and so we got up and played cribbage and smoked pipes till sunrise. It was my week to cook. I always hated cooking—now, I abhorred it.

The news was all over town. The former excitement was great—this one was greater still. I walked the streets serene and happy. Higbie said the foreman had been offered two hundred thousand dollars for his third of the mine. I said I would like to see myself selling for any such price. My ideas were lofty. My figure was a million. Still, I honestly believe that if I had been offered it, it would have had no other effect than to make me hold off for more.

I found abundant enjoyment in being rich. A man offered me a three-hundred-dollar horse, and wanted to take my simple, unendorsed note for it. That brought the most realizing sense I had yet had that I was actually rich, beyond shadow of doubt. It was followed by numerous other evidences of a similar nature—among which I may mention the fact of the butcher leaving us a double supply of meat and saying nothing about money.

By the laws of the district, the "locators" or claimants of a ledge were obliged to do a fair and reasonable amount of work on their new property within ten days after the date of the location, or the property was forfeited, and anybody could go and seize it that chose. So we determined to go to work the next day. About the middle of the afternoon, as I was coming out of the post office, I met a Mr. Gardiner, who told me that Capt. John Nye was lying dangerously ill at his place (the "Nine-Mile Ranch"), and that he and his wife were not able to give him nearly as much care and attention as his case demanded. I said if he would wait for me a moment, I would go down and help in the sick room. I ran to the cabin to tell Higbie. He was not there, but I left a note on the table for him, and a few minutes later I left town in Gardiner's wagon.

Chapter XLI

CAPTAIN NYE was very ill indeed, with spasmodic rheumatism. But the old gentleman was himself—which is to say, he was kind-hearted and agreeable when comfortable, but a singularly violent wild-cat when things did not go well. He would be smiling along pleasantly enough, when a sudden spasm of his disease would take him and he would go out of his smile into a perfect fury. He would groan and wail and howl with the anguish, and fill up the odd chinks with the most elaborate profanity that strong convictions and a fine fancy could contrive. With fair opportunity he could swear very well and handle his adjectives with considerable judgment; but when the spasm was on him it was painful to listen to him, he was so awkward. However, I had seen him nurse a sick man himself and put up patiently with the inconveniences of the situation, and consequently I was willing that he should have full license now that his own turn had come. He could not disturb me, with all his raving and ranting, for my mind had work on hand, and it labored on diligently, night and day, whether my hands were idle or employed. I was altering and amending the plans for my house, and thinking over the propriety of having the billiard-room in the attic, instead of on the same floor with the dining-room; also, I was trying to decide between green and blue for the upholstery of the drawing-room, for, although my preference was blue I feared it was a color that would be too easily damaged by dust and sunlight; likewise while I was content to put the coachman in a modest livery, I was uncertain about a footman—I needed one, and was even resolved to have one, but wished he could properly appear and perform his functions out of livery, for I somewhat dreaded so much show; and yet, inasmuch as my late grandfather had had a coachman and such things, but no liveries, I felt rather drawn to beat him;—or beat his ghost, at any rate; I was also systematizing the European trip, and managed to get it all laid out, as to route and length of time to be devoted to it—everything, with one exception—namely, whether to cross the desert from Cairo to Jerusalem per camel, or go by sea to Beirut, and thence down through the country per caravan. Meantime I was writing to the friends at home every day, instructing them concerning all my plans and intentions, and directing them to look up a handsome homestead for my mother and agree upon a price for it against my coming, and also directing them to sell my share of the Tennessee land and tender the proceeds to the widows' and orphans' fund of the typographical union of which I had long been a member in good standing. [This Tennessee land had been in the possession of the family many years, and promised to confer high fortune upon us some day; it still promises it, but in a less violent way.]

When I had been nursing the Captain nine days he was somewhat better, but very feeble. During the afternoon we lifted him into a chair and gave him an alcoholic vapor bath, and then set about putting him on the bed again. We had to be exceedingly careful, for the least jar produced pain. Gardiner had his shoulders and I his legs; in an unfortunate moment I stumbled and the patient fell heavily on the bed in an agony of torture. I never heard a man swear so in my life. He raved like a maniac, and tried to snatch a revolver from the table—but I got it. He ordered me out of the house, and swore a world of oaths that he would kill me wherever he caught me when he got on his feet again. It was simply a passing fury, and meant nothing. I knew he would forget it in an hour, and maybe be sorry for it, too; but it angered me a little, at the moment. So much so, indeed, that I determined to go back to Esmeralda. I thought he was able to get along alone, now, since he was on the war path. I took supper, and as soon as the moon rose, began my nine-mile journey, on foot. Even millionaires needed no horses, in those days, for a mere nine-mile jaunt without baggage.

As I "raised the hill" overlooking the town, it lacked fifteen minutes of twelve. I glanced at the hill over beyond the canyon, and in the bright moonlight saw what appeared to be about half the population of the village massed on and around the Wide West croppings. My heart gave an exulting bound, and I said to myself, "They have made a new strike to-night—and struck it richer than ever, no doubt." I started over there, but gave it up. I said the "strike" would keep, and

I had climbed hills enough for one night. I went on down through the town, and as I was passing a little German bakery, a woman ran out and begged me to come in and help her. She said her husband had a fit. I went in, and judged she was right—he appeared to have a hundred of them, compressed into one. Two Germans were there, trying to hold him, and not making much of a success of it. I ran up the street half a block or so and routed out a sleeping doctor, brought him down half dressed, and we four wrestled with the maniac, and doctored, drenched and bled him, for more than an hour, and the poor German woman did the crying. He grew quiet, now, and the doctor and I withdrew and left him to his friends.

It was a little after one o'clock. As I entered the cabin door, tired but jolly, the dingy light of a tallow candle revealed Higbie, sitting by the pine table gazing stupidly at my note, which he held in his fingers, and looking pale, old, and haggard. I halted, and looked at him. He looked at me, stolidly. I said:

"Higbie, what—what is it?"

"We're ruined—we didn't do the work—THE BLIND LEAD'S RELOCATED!"

It was enough. I sat down sick, grieved—broken-hearted, indeed. A minute before, I was rich and brimful of vanity; I was a pauper now, and very meek. We sat still an hour, busy with thought, busy with vain and useless self-upbraidings, busy with "Why *didn't* I do this, and why *didn't* I do that," but neither spoke a word. Then we dropped into mutual explanations, and the mystery was cleared away. It came out that Higbie had depended on me, as I had on him, and as both of us had on the foreman. The folly of it! It was the first time that ever staid and steadfast Higbie had left an important matter to chance or failed to be true to his full share of a responsibility.

But he had never seen my note till this moment, and this moment was the first time he had been in the cabin since the day he had seen me last. He, also, had left a note for me, on that same fatal afternoon—had ridden up on horse-back, and looked through the window, and being in a hurry and not seeing me, had tossed the note into the cabin through a broken pane. Here it was, on the floor, where it had remained undisturbed for nine days:

"Don't fail to do the work before the ten days expire. W. has passed through and given me notice. I am to join him at Mono Lake, and we shall go on from there to-night. He says he will find it this time, sure. CAL."

"W." meant Whiteman, of course. That thrice accursed "cement!"

That was the way of it. An old miner, like Higbie, could no more withstand the fascination of a mysterious mining excitement like this "cement" foolishness, than he could refrain from eating when he was famishing. Higbie had been dreaming about the marvelous cement for months; and now, against his better judgment, he had gone off and "taken the chances" on my keeping secure a mine worth a million undiscovered cement veins. They had not been followed this time. His riding out of town in broad daylight was such a common-place thing to do that it had not attracted any attention. He said they prosecuted their search in the fastnesses of the mountains during nine days, without success; they could not find the cement. Then a ghastly fear came over him that something might have happened to prevent the doing of the necessary work to hold the blind lead (though indeed he thought such a thing hardly possible), and forthwith he started home with all speed. He would have reached Esmeralda in time, but his horse broke down and he had to walk a great part of the distance. And so it happened that as he came into Esmeralda by one road, I entered it by another. His was the superior energy, however, for he went straight to the Wide West, instead of turning aside as I had done—and he arrived there about five or ten minutes too late! The "notice" was already up, the "relocation" of our mine completed beyond recall, and the crowd rapidly dispersing. He learned some facts before he left the ground. The foreman had not been seen about the streets since the night we had located the mine—a telegram had called him to California on a matter of life and death, it was said. At any rate he had done no work and the watchful eyes of the community were taking note of the fact. At midnight of this woful tenth day, the ledge would be "relocatable," and by eleven o'clock the hill was black with men prepared to do the relocating. That was the crowd I had seen when I fancied a new "strike" had been made—idiot that I was. [We three had the same right to relocate the lead that other people had, provided we were quick enough.] As midnight was announced, fourteen men, duly armed and ready to back their proceedings, put up their "notice" and proclaimed their ownership of the blind lead, under the new name of the "Johnson." But A. D. Allen our partner (the foreman) put in a sudden appearance about that time, with a cocked revolver in his hand, and said his name must be added to the list, or he would "thin out the Johnson company some." He was a manly, splendid, determined fellow, and known to be as good as his word, and therefore a compromise was effected. They put in his name for a hundred feet, reserving to themselves the customary two hundred feet each. Such was the history of the night's events, as Higbie gathered from a friend on the way home.

Higbie and I cleared out on a new mining excitement the next morning, glad to get away from the scene of our sufferings, and after a month or two of hardship and disappointment, returned to Esmeralda once more. Then we learned that the Wide West and the Johnson companies had consolidated; that the stock, thus united, comprised five thousand feet, or shares; that the foreman, apprehending tiresome litigation, and considering such a huge concern unwieldy, had sold his hundred feet for ninety thousand dollars in gold and gone home to the States to enjoy it. If the stock was worth such a gallant figure, with five thousand shares in the corporation, it makes me dizzy to think what it would have been worth with only our original six hundred in it. It was the difference between six hundred men owning a house and five thousand owning it. We would have been millionaires if we had only worked with pick and spade one little day on our property and so secured our ownership!

It reads like a wild fancy sketch, but the evidence of many witnesses, and likewise that of the official records of Esmeralda District, is easily obtainable in proof that it is a true history. I can always have it to say that I was absolutely and unquestionably worth a million dollars, once, for ten days.

A year ago my esteemed and in every way estimable old millionaire partner, Higbie, wrote me from an obscure little mining camp in California that after nine or ten years of buffetings and hard striving, he was at last in a position where he could command twenty-five hundred dollars, and said he meant to go into the fruit business in a modest way. How such a thought would have insulted him the night we lay in our cabin planning European trips and brown stone houses on Russian Hill!

Chapter XLII

WHAT to do next?

It was a momentous question. I had gone out into the world to shift for myself, at the age of thirteen (for my father had endorsed for friends; and although he left us a sumptuous legacy of pride in his fine Virginian stock and its national distinction, I presently found that I could not live on that alone without occasional bread to wash it down with). I had gained a livelihood in various vocations, but had not dazzled anybody with my successes; still the list was before me, and the amplest liberty in the matter of choosing, provided I wanted to work—which I did not, after being so wealthy. I had once been a grocery clerk, for one day, but had consumed so much sugar in that time that I was relieved from further duty by the proprietor; said he wanted me outside, so that he could have my custom. I had studied law an entire week, and then given it up because it was so prosy and tiresome. I had engaged briefly in the study of blacksmithing, but wasted so much time trying to fix the bellows so that it would blow itself, that the master turned me adrift in disgrace, and told me I would come to no good. I had been a bookseller's clerk for awhile, but the customers bothered me so much I could not read with any comfort, and so the proprietor gave me a furlough and forgot to put a limit to it. I had clerked in a drug store part of a summer, but my prescriptions were unlucky, and we appeared to sell more stomach pumps than soda water. So I had to go. I had made of myself a tolerable printer, under the impression that I would be another Franklin some day, but somehow had missed the connection thus far. There was no berth open in the Esmeralda *Union*, and besides I had always been such a slow compositor that I looked with envy upon the achievements of apprentices of two years' standing; and when I took a "take," foremen were in the habit of suggesting that it would be wanted "some time during the year." I was a good average St. Louis and New Orleans pilot and by no means ashamed of my abilities in that line; wages were two hundred and fifty dollars a month and no board to pay, and I did long to stand behind a wheel again and never roam any more—but I had been making such an ass of myself lately in grandiloquent letters home about my blind lead and my European excursion that I did what many and many a poor disappointed miner had done before; said "It is all over with me now, and I will never go back home to be pitied—and snubbed." I had been a private secretary, a silver miner and a silver mill operative, and amounted to less than nothing in each, and now—

What to do next?

I yielded to Higbie's appeals and consented to try the mining once more. We climbed far up on the mountain side and went to work on a little rubbishy claim of ours that had a shaft on it eight feet deep. Higbie descended into it and worked bravely with his pick till he had loosened up a deal of rock and dirt and then I went down with a long-handled shovel (the most awkward invention yet contrived by man) to throw it out. You must brace the shovel forward with the side of your knee till it is full, and then, with a skilful toss, throw it backward over your left shoulder. I made the toss and landed the mess just on the edge of the shaft and it all came back on my head and down the back of my neck. I never said a word, but climbed out and walked home. I inwardly resolved that I would starve before I would make a target of myself and shoot rubbish at it with a long-handled shovel. I sat down, in the cabin, and gave myself up to solid misery—so to speak. Now in pleasanter days I had amused myself with writing letters to the chief paper of the Territory, the Virginia *Daily Territorial Enterprise*, and had always been surprised when they appeared in print. My good opinion of the editors had steadily declined; for it seemed to me that they might have found something better to fill up with than my literature. I had found a letter in the post office as I came home from the hill side, and finally I opened it. Eureka! [I never did know what Eureka meant, but it seems to be as proper a word to heave in as any when no other that sounds pretty offers.] It was a deliberate offer to me of Twenty-Five Dollars a week to come up to Virginia and be city editor of the *Enterprise*.

I would have challenged the publisher in the "blind lead" days—I wanted to fall down and worship him, now. Twenty-

Five Dollars a week—it looked like bloated luxury—a fortune—a sinful and lavish waste of money. But my transports cooled when I thought of my inexperience and consequent unfitness for the position—and straightway, on top of this, my long array of failures rose up before me. Yet if I refused this place I must presently become dependent upon somebody for my bread, a thing necessarily distasteful to a man who had never experienced such a humiliation since he was thirteen years old. Not much to be proud of, since it is so common—but then it was all I had to *be* proud of. So I was scared into being a city editor. I would have declined, otherwise. Necessity is the mother of "taking chances." I do not doubt that if, at that time, I had been offered a salary to translate the Talmud from the original Hebrew, I would have accepted—albeit with diffidence and some misgivings—and thrown as much variety into it as I could for the money.

I went up to Virginia and entered upon my new vocation. I was a rusty looking city editor, I am free to confess—coatless, slouch hat, blue woolen shirt, pantaloons stuffed into boot-tops, whiskered half down to the waist, and the universal navy revolver slung to my belt. But I secured a more Christian costume and discarded the revolver. I had never had occasion to kill anybody, nor ever felt a desire to do so, but had worn the thing in deference to popular sentiment, and in order that I might not, by its absence, be offensively conspicuous, and a subject of remark. But the other editors, and all the printers, carried revolvers. I asked the chief editor and proprietor (Mr. Goodman, I will call him, since it describes him as well as any name could do) for some instructions with regard to my duties, and he told me to go all over town and ask all sorts of people all sorts of questions, make notes of the information gained, and write them out for publication. And he added:

"Never say 'We learn' so-and-so, or 'It is reported,' or 'It is rumored,' or 'We understand' so-and-so, but go to headquarters and get the absolute facts, and then speak out and say 'It *is* so-and-so.' Otherwise, people will not put confidence in your news. Unassailable certainty is the thing that gives a newspaper the firmest and most valuable reputation."

It was the whole thing in a nut-shell; and to this day when

I find a reporter commencing his article with "We understand," I gather a suspicion that he has not taken as much pains to inform himself as he ought to have done. I moralize well, but I did not always practise well when I was a city editor; I let fancy get the upper hand of fact too often when there was a dearth of news. I can never forget my first day's experience as a reporter. I wandered about town questioning everybody, boring everybody, and finding out that nobody knew anything. At the end of five hours my note-book was still barren. I spoke to Mr. Goodman. He said:

"Dan used to make a good thing out of the hay wagons in a dry time when there were no fires or inquests. Are there no hay wagons in from the Truckee? If there are, you might speak of the renewed activity and all that sort of thing, in the hay business, you know. It isn't sensational or exciting, but it fills up and looks business like."

I canvassed the city again and found one wretched old hay truck dragging in from the country. But I made affluent use of it. I multiplied it by sixteen, brought it into town from sixteen different directions, made sixteen separate items out of it, and got up such another sweat about hay as Virginia City had never seen in the world before.

This was encouraging. Two nonpareil columns had to be filled, and I was getting along. Presently, when things began to look dismal again, a desperado killed a man in a saloon and joy returned once more. I never was so glad over any mere trifle before in my life. I said to the murderer:

"Sir, you are a stranger to me, but you have done me a kindness this day which I can never forget. If whole years of gratitude can be to you any slight compensation, they shall be yours. I was in trouble and you have relieved me nobly and at a time when all seemed dark and drear. Count me your friend from this time forth, for I am not a man to forget a favor."

If I did not really say that to him I at least felt a sort of itching desire to do it. I wrote up the murder with a hungry attention to details, and when it was finished experienced but one regret—namely, that they had not hanged my benefactor on the spot, so that I could work him up too.

Next I discovered some emigrant wagons going into camp

on the plaza and found that they had lately come through the hostile Indian country and had fared rather roughly. I made the best of the item that the circumstances permitted, and felt that if I were not confined within rigid limits by the presence of the reporters of the other papers I could add particulars that would make the article much more interesting. However, I found one wagon that was going on to California, and made some judicious inquiries of the proprietor. When I learned, through his short and surly answers to my cross-questioning, that he was certainly going on and would not be in the city next day to make trouble, I got ahead of the other papers, for I took down his list of names and added his party to the killed and wounded. Having more scope here, I put this wagon through an Indian fight that to this day has no parallel in history.

My two columns were filled. When I read them over in the morning I felt that I had found my legitimate occupation at last. I reasoned within myself that news, and stirring news, too, was what a paper needed, and I felt that I was peculiarly endowed with the ability to furnish it. Mr. Goodman said that I was as good a reporter as Dan. I desired no higher commendation. With encouragement like that, I felt that I could take my pen and murder all the immigrants on the plains if need be and the interests of the paper demanded it.

Chapter XLIII

HOWEVER, as I grew better acquainted with the business and learned the run of the sources of information I ceased to require the aid of fancy to any large extent, and became able to fill my columns without diverging noticeably from the domain of fact.

I struck up friendships with the reporters of the other journals, and we swapped "regulars" with each other and thus economized work. "Regulars" are permanent sources of news, like courts, bullion returns, "clean-ups" at the quartz mills, and inquests. Inasmuch as everybody went armed, we had an inquest about every day, and so this department was naturally set down among the "regulars." We had lively papers in those days. My great competitor among the reporters was Boggs of the *Union*. He was an excellent reporter. Once in three or four months he would get a little intoxicated, but as a general thing he was a wary and cautious drinker although always ready to tamper a little with the enemy. He had the advantage of me in one thing; he could get the monthly public school report and I could not, because the principal hated the *Enterprise*. One snowy night when the report was due, I started out sadly wondering how I was going to get it. Presently, a few steps up the almost deserted street I stumbled on Boggs and asked him where he was going.

"After the school report."

"I'll go along with you."

"No, *sir*. I'll excuse you."

"Just as you say."

A saloon-keeper's boy passed by with a steaming pitcher of hot punch, and Boggs snuffed the fragrance gratefully. He gazed fondly after the boy and saw him start up the *Enterprise* stairs. I said:

"I wish you could help me get that school business, but since you can't, I must run up to the *Union* office and see if I can get them to let me have a proof of it after they have set it up, though I don't begin to suppose they will. Good night."

"Hold on a minute. I don't mind getting the report and

sitting around with the boys a little, while you copy it, if you're willing to drop down to the principal's with me."

"Now you talk like a rational being. Come along."

We plowed a couple of blocks through the snow, got the report and returned to our office. It was a short document and soon copied. Meantime Boggs helped himself to the punch. I gave the manuscript back to him and we started out to get an inquest, for we heard pistol shots near by. We got the particulars with little loss of time, for it was only an inferior sort of bar-room murder, and of little interest to the public, and then we separated. Away at three o'clock in the morning, when we had gone to press and were having a relaxing concert as usual—for some of the printers were good singers and others good performers on the guitar and on that atrocity the accordeon—the proprietor of the *Union* strode in and desired to know if anybody had heard anything of Boggs or the school report. We stated the case, and all turned out to help hunt for the delinquent. We found him standing on a table in a saloon, with an old tin lantern in one hand and the school report in the other, haranguing a gang of intoxicated Cornish miners on the iniquity of squandering the public moneys on education " when hundreds and hundreds of honest hard-working men are literally starving for whiskey." [Riotous applause.] He had been assisting in a regal spree with those parties for hours. We dragged him away and put him to bed.

Of course there was no school report in the *Union*, and Boggs held me accountable, though I was innocent of any intention or desire to compass its absence from that paper and was as sorry as any one that the misfortune had occurred.

But we were perfectly friendly. The day that the school report was next due, the proprietor of the "Genessee" mine furnished us a buggy and asked us to go down and write something about the property—a very common request and one always gladly acceded to when people furnished buggies, for we were as fond of pleasure excursions as other people. In due time we arrived at the "mine"—nothing but a hole in the ground ninety feet deep, and no way of getting down into it but by holding on to a rope and being lowered with a windlass. The workmen had just gone off somewhere to dinner. I was not strong enough to lower Boggs's bulk; so I took an unlighted candle in my teeth, made a loop for my foot in the end of the rope, implored Boggs not to go to sleep or let the windlass get the start of him, and then swung out over the shaft. I reached the bottom muddy and bruised about the elbows, but safe. I lit the candle, made an examination of the rock, selected some specimens and shouted to Boggs to hoist away. No answer. Presently a head appeared in the circle of daylight away aloft, and a voice came down:

"Are you all set?"

"All set—hoist away."

"Are you comfortable?"

"Perfectly."

"Could you wait a little?"

"Oh certainly—no particular hurry."

"Well—good by."

"Why? Where are you going?"

"After the school report!"

And he did. I staid down there an hour, and surprised the workmen when they hauled up and found a man on the rope instead of a bucket of rock. I walked home, too—five miles— up hill. We had no school report next morning; but the *Union* had.

Six months after my entry into journalism the grand "flush times" of Silverland began, and they continued with unabated splendor for three years. All difficulty about filling up the "local department" ceased, and the only trouble now was how to make the lengthened columns hold the world of incidents and happenings that came to our literary net every day. Virginia had grown to be the "livest" town, for its age and population, that America had ever produced. The sidewalks swarmed with people—to such an extent, indeed, that it was generally no easy matter to stem the human tide. The streets themselves were just as crowded with quartz wagons, freight teams and other vehicles. The procession was endless. So great was the pack, that buggies frequently had to wait half an hour for an opportunity to cross the principal street. Joy sat on every countenance, and there was a glad, almost fierce, intensity in every eye, that told of the money-getting schemes that were seething in every brain and the high hope that held

sway in every heart. Money was as plenty as dust; every individual considered himself wealthy, and a melancholy countenance was nowhere to be seen. There were military
companies, fire companies, brass bands, banks, hotels, theatres, "hurdy-gurdy houses," wide-open gambling palaces,
political pow-wows, civic processions, street fights, murders,
inquests, riots, a whiskey mill every fifteen steps, a Board of
Aldermen, a Mayor, a City Surveyor, a City Engineer, a Chief
of the Fire Department, with First, Second and Third Assistants, a Chief of Police, City Marshal and a large police force,
two Boards of Mining Brokers, a dozen breweries and half a
dozen jails and station-houses in full operation, and some talk
of building a church. The "flush times" were in magnificent
flower! Large fire-proof brick buildings were going up in the
principal streets, and the wooden suburbs were spreading out
in all directions. Town lots soared up to prices that were
amazing.

The great "Comstock lode" stretched its opulent length
straight through the town from north to south, and every
mine on it was in diligent process of development. One of
these mines alone employed six hundred and seventy-five
men, and in the matter of elections the adage was, "as the
'Gould and Curry' goes, so goes the city." Laboring men's
wages were four and six dollars a day, and they worked in
three "shifts" or gangs, and the blasting and picking and
shoveling went on without ceasing, night and day.

The "city" of Virginia roosted royally midway up the steep
side of Mount Davidson, seven thousand two hundred feet
above the level of the sea, and in the clear Nevada atmosphere
was visible from a distance of fifty miles! It claimed a population of fifteen thousand to eighteen thousand, and all day
long half of this little army swarmed the streets like bees and
the other half swarmed among the drifts and tunnels of the
"Comstock," hundreds of feet down in the earth directly under those same streets. Often we felt our chairs jar, and heard
the faint boom of a blast down in the bowels of the earth
under the office.

The mountain side was so steep that the entire town had a
slant to it like a roof. Each street was a terrace, and from each
to the next street below the descent was forty or fifty feet.

The fronts of the houses were level with the street they faced, but their rear first floors were propped on lofty stilts; a man could stand at a rear first floor window of a C street house and look down the chimneys of the row of houses below him facing D street. It was a laborious climb, in that thin atmosphere, to ascend from D to A street, and you were panting and out of breath when you got there; but you could turn around and go down again like a house a-fire—so to speak. The atmosphere was so rarified, on account of the great altitude, that one's blood lay near the surface always, and the scratch of a pin was a disaster worth worrying about, for the chances were that a grievous erysipelas would ensue. But to offset this, the thin atmosphere seemed to carry healing to gunshot wounds, and therefore, to simply shoot your adversary through both lungs was a thing not likely to afford you any permanent satisfaction, for he would be nearly certain to be around looking for you within the month, and not with an opera glass, either.

From Virginia's airy situation one could look over a vast, far-reaching panorama of mountain ranges and deserts; and whether the day was bright or overcast, whether the sun was rising or setting, or flaming in the zenith, or whether night and the moon held sway, the spectacle was always impressive and beautiful. Over your head Mount Davidson lifted its gray dome, and before and below you a rugged canyon clove the battlemented hills, making a sombre gateway through which a soft-tinted desert was glimpsed, with the silver thread of a river winding through it, bordered with trees which many miles of distance diminished to a delicate fringe; and still further away the snowy mountains rose up and stretched their long barrier to the filmy horizon—far enough beyond a lake that burned in the desert like a fallen sun, though that, itself, lay fifty miles removed. Look from your window where you would, there was fascination in the picture. At rare intervals—but very rare—there were clouds in our skies, and then the setting sun would gild and flush and glorify this mighty expanse of scenery with a bewildering pomp of color that held the eye like a spell and moved the spirit like music.

Chapter XLIV

M Y SALARY was increased to forty dollars a week. But I seldom drew it. I had plenty of other resources, and what were two broad twenty-dollar gold pieces to a man who had his pockets full of such and a cumbersome abundance of bright half dollars besides? [Paper money has never come into use on the Pacific coast.] Reporting was lucrative, and every man in the town was lavish with his money and his "feet." The city and all the great mountain side were riddled with mining shafts. There were more mines than miners. True, not ten of these mines were yielding rock worth hauling to a mill, but everybody said, "Wait till the shaft gets down where the ledge comes in solid, and then you will see!" So nobody was discouraged. These were nearly all "wild cat" mines, and wholly worthless, but nobody believed it then. The "Ophir," the "Gould & Curry," the "Mexican," and other great mines on the Comstock lead in Virginia and Gold Hill were turning out huge piles of rich rock every day, and every man believed that his little wild cat claim was as good as any on the "main lead" and would infallibly be worth a thousand dollars a foot when he "got down where it came in solid." Poor fellow, he was blessedly blind to the fact that he never would see that day. So the thousand wild cat shafts burrowed deeper and deeper into the earth day by day, and all men were beside themselves with hope and happiness. How they labored, prophesied, exulted! Surely nothing like it was ever seen before since the world began. Every one of these wild cat mines—not mines, but holes in the ground over imaginary mines—was incorporated and had handsomely engraved "stock" and the stock was salable, too. It was bought and sold with a feverish avidity in the boards every day. You could go up on the mountain side, scratch around and find a ledge (there was no lack of them), put up a "notice" with a grandiloquent name in it, start a shaft, get your stock printed, and with nothing whatever to prove that your mine was worth a straw, you could put your stock on the market and sell out for hundreds and even thousands of dollars. To make money, and make it fast, was as easy as it was to eat your dinner.

Every man owned "feet" in fifty different wild cat mines and considered his fortune made. Think of a city with not one solitary poor man in it! One would suppose that when month after month went by and still not a wild cat mine (by wild cat I mean, in general terms, *any* claim not located on the mother vein, *i. e.*, the "Comstock") yielded a ton of rock worth crushing, the people would begin to wonder if they were not putting too much faith in their prospective riches; but there was not a thought of such a thing. They burrowed away, bought and sold, and were happy.

New claims were taken up daily, and it was the friendly custom to run straight to the newspaper offices, give the reporter forty or fifty "feet," and get them to go and examine the mine and publish a notice of it. They did not care a fig what you said about the property so you said something. Consequently we generally said a word or two to the effect that the "indications" were good, or that the ledge was "six feet wide," or that the rock "resembled the Comstock" (and so it did—but as a general thing the resemblance was not startling enough to knock you down). If the rock was moderately promising, we followed the custom of the country, used strong adjectives and frothed at the mouth as if a very marvel in silver discoveries had transpired. If the mine was a "developed" one, and had no pay ore to show (and of course it hadn't), we praised the tunnel; said it was one of the most infatuating tunnels in the land; driveled and driveled about the tunnel till we ran entirely out of ecstasies—but never said a word about the rock. We would squander half a column of adulation on a shaft, or a new wire rope, or a dressed pine windlass, or a fascinating force pump, and close with a burst of admiration of the "gentlemanly and efficient Superintendent" of the mine—but never utter a whisper about the rock. And those people were always pleased, always satisfied. Occasionally we patched up and varnished our reputation for discrimination and stern, undeviating accuracy, by giving some old abandoned claim a blast that ought to have made its dry bones rattle—and then somebody would seize it and sell it on the fleeting notoriety thus conferred upon it.

There was *nothing* in the shape of a mining claim that was not salable. We received presents of "feet" every day. If we needed a hundred dollars or so, we sold some; if not, we hoarded it away, satisfied that it would ultimately be worth a thousand dollars a foot. I had a trunk about half full of "stock." When a claim made a stir in the market and went up to a high figure, I searched through my pile to see if I had any of its stock—and generally found it.

The prices rose and fell constantly; but still a fall disturbed us little, because a thousand dollars a foot was our figure, and so we were content to let it fluctuate as much as it pleased till it reached it. My pile of stock was not all given to me by people who wished their claims "noticed." At least half of it was given me by persons who had no thought of such a thing, and looked for nothing more than a simple verbal "thank you;" and you were not even obliged by law to furnish that. If you are coming up the street with a couple of baskets of apples in your hands, and you meet a friend, you naturally invite him to take a few. That describes the condition of things in Virginia in the "flush times." Every man had his pockets full of stock, and it was the actual *custom* of the country to part with small quantities of it to friends without the asking. Very often it was a good idea to close the transaction instantly, when a man offered a stock present to a friend, for the offer was only good and binding at that moment, and if the price went to a high figure shortly afterward the procrastination was a thing to be regretted. Mr. Stewart (Senator, now, from Nevada) one day told me he would give me twenty feet of "Justis" stock if I would walk over to his office. It was worth five or ten dollars a foot. I asked him to make the offer good for next day, as I was just going to dinner. He said he would not be in town; so I risked it and took my dinner instead of the stock. Within the week the price went up to seventy dollars and afterward to a hundred and fifty, but nothing could make that man yield. I suppose he sold that stock of mine and placed the guilty proceeds in his own pocket. [My revenge will be found in the accompanying portrait.] I met three friends one afternoon, who said they had been buying "Overman" stock at auction at eight dollars a foot. One said if I would come up to his office he would give me fifteen feet; another said he would add fifteen; the third said he would do the same. But I was going after an inquest and could not stop. A few weeks afterward they sold all their "Overman" at six hundred dollars a foot and generously came around to tell me about it—and also to urge me to accept of the next forty-five feet of it that people tried to force on me. These are actual facts, and I could make the list a long one and still confine myself strictly to the truth. Many a time friends gave us as much as twenty-five feet of

PORTRAIT OF MR. STEWART

stock that was selling at twenty-five dollars a foot, and they thought no more of it than they would of offering a guest a cigar. These were "flush times" indeed! I thought they were going to last always, but somehow I never was much of a prophet.

To show what a wild spirit possessed the mining brain of the community, I will remark that "claims" were actually "located" in excavations for cellars, where the pick had exposed what seemed to be quartz veins—and not cellars in the suburbs, either, but in the very heart of the city; and forthwith stock would be issued and thrown on the market. It was small matter who the cellar belonged to—the "ledge" belonged to the finder, and unless the United States government interfered (inasmuch as the government holds the primary right to mines of the noble metals in Nevada—or at least did then), it was considered to be his privilege to work it. Imagine a stranger staking out a mining claim among the costly shrubbery in your front yard and calmly proceeding to lay waste the ground with pick and shovel and blasting powder! It has been often done in California. In the middle of one of the principal business streets of Virginia, a man "located" a mining claim and began a shaft on it. He gave me a hundred feet of the stock and I sold it for a fine suit of clothes because I was afraid somebody would fall down the shaft and sue for damages. I owned in another claim that was located in the middle of another street; and to show how absurd people can be, that "East India" stock (as it was called) sold briskly although there was an ancient tunnel running directly under the claim and any man could go into it and see that it did not cut a quartz ledge or anything that remotely resembled one.

One plan of acquiring sudden wealth was to "salt" a wild cat claim and sell out while the excitement was up. The process was simple. The schemer located a worthless ledge, sunk a shaft on it, bought a wagon load of rich "Comstock" ore, dumped a portion of it into the shaft and piled the rest by its side, above ground. Then he showed the property to a simpleton and sold it to him at a high figure. Of course the wagon load of rich ore was all that the victim ever got out of his purchase. A most remarkable case of "salting" was that of the "North Ophir." It was claimed that this vein was a remote "extension" of the original "Ophir," a valuable mine on the "Comstock." For a few days everybody was talking about the rich developments in the North Ophir. It was said that it yielded perfectly pure silver in small, solid lumps. I went to the place with the owners, and found a shaft six or eight feet deep, in the bottom of which was a badly shattered vein of dull, yellowish, unpromising rock. One would as soon expect to find silver in a grindstone. We got out a pan of the rubbish and washed it in a puddle, and sure enough, among the sediment we found half a dozen black, bullet-looking pellets of unimpeachable "native" silver. Nobody had ever heard of such a thing before; science could not account for such a queer novelty. The stock rose to sixty-five dollars a foot, and at this figure the world-renowned tragedian, McKean Buchanan, bought a commanding interest and prepared to quit the stage once more—he was always doing that. And then it transpired that the mine had been "salted"—and not in any hackneyed way, either, but in a singularly bold, barefaced and peculiarly original and outrageous fashion. On one of the lumps of "native" silver was discovered the minted legend, "TED STATES OF," and then it was plainly apparent that the mine had been "salted" with melted half-dollars! The lumps thus obtained had been blackened till they resembled native silver, and were then mixed with the shattered rock in the bottom of the shaft. It is literally true. Of course the price of the stock at once fell to nothing, and the tragedian was ruined. But for this calamity we might have lost McKean Buchanan from the stage.

Chapter XLV

T HE "FLUSH TIMES" held bravely on. Something over two
years before, Mr. Goodman and another journeyman
printer, had borrowed forty dollars and set out from San
Francisco to try their fortunes in the new city of Virginia.
They found the *Territorial Enterprise*, a poverty-stricken
weekly journal, gasping for breath and likely to die. They
bought it, type, fixtures, good-will and all, for a thousand
dollars, on long time. The editorial sanctum, news-room,
press-room, publication office, bed-chamber, parlor, and
kitchen were all compressed into one apartment and it was a
small one, too. The editors and printers slept on the floor, a
Chinaman did their cooking, and the "imposing-stone" was
the general dinner table. But now things were changed. The
paper was a great daily, printed by steam; there were five editors and twenty-three compositors; the subscription price
was sixteen dollars a year; the advertising rates were exorbitant, and the columns crowded. The paper was clearing from
six to ten thousand dollars a month, and the "Enterprise
Building" was finished and ready for occupation—a stately
fire-proof brick. Every day from five all the way up to eleven
columns of "live" advertisements were left out or crowded
into spasmodic and irregular "supplements."

The "Gould & Curry" company were erecting a monster
hundred-stamp mill at a cost that ultimately fell little short of
a million dollars. Gould & Curry stock paid heavy dividends—a rare thing, and an experience confined to the dozen
or fifteen claims located on the "main lead," the "Comstock."
The Superintendent of the Gould & Curry lived, rent free, in
a fine house built and furnished by the company. He drove a
fine pair of horses which were a present from the company,
and his salary was twelve thousand dollars a year. The superintendent of another of the great mines traveled in grand
state, had a salary of twenty-eight thousand dollars a year, and
in a law suit in after days claimed that he was to have had
one per cent. on the gross yield of the bullion likewise.

Money was wonderfully plenty. The trouble was, not how
to get it,—but how to spend it, how to lavish it, get rid of

it, squander it. And so it was a happy thing that just at this juncture the news came over the wires that a great United States Sanitary Commission had been formed and money was wanted for the relief of the wounded sailors and soldiers of the Union languishing in the Eastern hospitals. Right on the heels of it came word that San Francisco had responded superbly before the telegram was half a day old. Virginia rose as one man! A Sanitary Committee was hurriedly organized, and its chairman mounted a vacant cart in C street and tried to make the clamorous multitude understand that the rest of the committee were flying hither and thither and working with all their might and main, and that if the town would only wait an hour, an office would be ready, books opened, and the Commission prepared to receive contributions. His voice was drowned and his information lost in a ceaseless roar of cheers, and demands that the money be received *now*— they swore they would not wait. The chairman pleaded and argued, but, deaf to all entreaty, men plowed their way through the throng and rained checks of gold coin into the cart and skurried away for more. Hands clutching money, were thrust aloft out of the jam by men who hoped this eloquent appeal would cleave a road their strugglings could not open. The very Chinamen and Indians caught the excitement and dashed their half dollars into the cart without knowing or caring what it was all about. Women plunged into the crowd, trimly attired, fought their way to the cart with their coin, and emerged again, by and by, with their apparel in a state of hopeless dilapidation. It was the wildest mob Virginia had ever seen and the most determined and ungovernable; and when at last it abated its fury and dispersed, it had not a penny in its pocket. To use its own phraseology, it came there "flush" and went away "busted."

After that, the Commission got itself into systematic working order, and for weeks the contributions flowed into its treasury in a generous stream. Individuals and all sorts of organizations levied upon themselves a regular weekly tax for the sanitary fund, graduated according to their means, and there was not another grand universal outburst till the famous "Sanitary Flour Sack" came our way. Its history is peculiar and interesting. A former schoolmate of mine, by the name of Reuel Gridley, was living at the little city of Austin, in the Reese river country, at this time, and was the Democratic candidate for mayor. He and the Republican candidate made an agreement that the defeated man should be publicly presented with a fifty-pound sack of flour by the successful one, and should carry it home on his shoulder. Gridley was defeated. The new mayor gave him the sack of flour, and he shouldered it and carried it a mile or two, from Lower Austin to his home in Upper Austin, attended by a band of music and the whole population. Arrived there, he said he did not need the flour, and asked what the people thought he had better do with it. A voice said:

"Sell it to the highest bidder, for the benefit of the Sanitary fund."

The suggestion was greeted with a round of applause, and Gridley mounted a dry-goods box and assumed the role of auctioneer. The bids went higher and higher, as the sympathies of the pioneers awoke and expanded, till at last the sack was knocked down to a mill man at two hundred and fifty dollars, and his check taken. He was asked where he would have the flour delivered, and he said:

"Nowhere—sell it again."

Now the cheers went up royally, and the multitude were fairly in the spirit of the thing. So Gridley stood there and shouted and perspired till the sun went down; and when the crowd dispersed he had sold the sack to three hundred different people, and had taken in eight thousand dollars in gold. And still the flour sack was in his possession.

The news came to Virginia, and a telegram went back:

"Fetch along your flour sack!"

Thirty-six hours afterward Gridley arrived, and an afternoon mass meeting was held in the Opera House, and the auction began. But the sack had come sooner than it was expected; the people were not thoroughly aroused, and the sale dragged. At nightfall only five thousand dollars had been secured, and there was a crestfallen feeling in the community. However, there was no disposition to let the matter rest here and acknowledge vanquishment at the hands of the village of Austin. Till late in the night the principal citizens were at work arranging the morrow's campaign, and when they went to bed they had no fears for the result. At eleven the next morning a procession of open carriages, attended by clamorous bands of music and adorned with a moving display of flags, filed along C street and was soon in danger of blockade by a huzzaing multitude of citizens. In the first carriage sat Gridley, with the flour sack in prominent view, the latter splendid with bright paint and gilt lettering; also in the same carriage sat the mayor and the recorder. The other carriages contained the Common Council, the editors and reporters, and other people of imposing consequence. The crowd pressed to the corner of C and Taylor streets, expecting the sale to begin there, but they were disappointed, and also unspeakably surprised; for the cavalcade moved on as if Virginia had ceased to be of importance, and took its way over the "divide," toward the small town of Gold Hill. Telegrams had gone ahead to Gold Hill, Silver City and Dayton, and those communities were at fever heat and rife for the conflict. It was a very hot day, and wonderfully dusty. At the end of a short half hour we descended into Gold Hill with drums beating and colors flying, and enveloped in imposing clouds of dust. The whole population—men, women and children, Chinamen and Indians, were massed in the main street, all the flags in town were at the mast head, and the blare of the bands was drowned in cheers. Gridley stood up and asked who would make the first bid for the National Sanitary Flour Sack. Gen. W. said:

"The Yellow Jacket silver mining company offers a thousand dollars, coin!"

A tempest of applause followed. A telegram carried the news to Virginia, and fifteen minutes afterward that city's population was massed in the streets devouring the tidings—for it was part of the programme that the bulletin boards should do a good work that day. Every few minutes a new dispatch was bulletined from Gold Hill, and still the excitement grew. Telegrams began to return to us from Virginia beseeching Gridley to bring back the flour sack; but such was not the plan of the campaign. At the end of an hour Gold Hill's small population had paid a figure for the flour sack that awoke all the enthusiasm of Virginia when the grand total was displayed upon the bulletin boards. Then the

Gridley cavalcade moved on, a giant refreshed with new lager beer and plenty of it—for the people brought it to the carriages without waiting to measure it—and within three hours more the expedition had carried Silver City and Dayton by storm and was on its way back covered with glory. Every move had been telegraphed and bulletined, and as the procession entered Virginia and filed down C street at half past eight in the evening the town was abroad in the thoroughfares, torches were glaring, flags flying, bands playing, cheer on cheer cleaving the air, and the city ready to surrender at discretion. The auction began, every bid was greeted with bursts of applause, and at the end of two hours and a half a population of fifteen thousand souls had paid in coin for a fifty-pound sack of flour a sum equal to forty thousand dollars in greenbacks! It was at a rate in the neighborhood of three dollars for each man, woman and child of the population. The grand total would have been twice as large, but the streets were very narrow, and hundreds who wanted to bid could not get within a block of the stand, and could not make themselves heard. These grew tired of waiting and many of them went home long before the auction was over. This was the greatest day Virginia ever saw, perhaps.

Gridley sold the sack in Carson city and several California towns; also in San Francisco. Then he took it east and sold it in one or two Atlantic cities, I think. I am not sure of that, but I know that he finally carried it to St. Louis, where a monster Sanitary Fair was being held, and after selling it there for a large sum and helping on the enthusiasm by displaying the portly silver bricks which Nevada's donation had produced, he had the flour baked up into small cakes and retailed them at high prices.

It was estimated that when the flour sack's mission was ended it had been sold for a grand total of a hundred and fifty thousand dollars in greenbacks! This is probably the only instance on record where common family flour brought three thousand dollars a pound in the public market.

It is due to Mr. Gridley's memory to mention that the expenses of his sanitary flour sack expedition of fifteen thousand miles, going and returning, were paid in large part, if not entirely, out of his own pocket. The time he gave to it was not less than three months. Mr. Gridley was a soldier in the Mexican war and a pioneer Californian. He died at Stockton, California, in December, 1870, greatly regretted.

Chapter XLVI

THERE WERE NABOBS in those days—in the "flush times," I mean. Every rich strike in the mines created one or two. I call to mind several of these. They were careless, easy-going fellows, as a general thing, and the community at large was as much benefited by their riches as they were themselves—possibly more, in some cases.

Two cousins, teamsters, did some hauling for a man and had to take a small segregated portion of a silver mine in lieu of $300 cash. They gave an outsider a third to open the mine, and they went on teaming. But not long. Ten months afterward the mine was out of debt and paying each owner $8,000 to $10,000 a month—say $100,000 a year.

One of the earliest nabobs that Nevada was delivered of wore $6,000 worth of diamonds in his bosom, and swore he was unhappy because he could not spend his money as fast as he made it.

Another Nevada nabob boasted an income that often reached $16,000 a month; and he used to love to tell how he had worked in the very mine that yielded it, for five dollars a day, when he first came to the country.

The silver and sage-brush State has knowledge of another of these pets of fortune—lifted from actual poverty to affluence almost in a single night—who was able to offer $100,000 for a position of high official distinction, shortly afterward, and did offer it—but failed to get it, his politics not being as sound as his bank account.

Then there was John Smith. He was a good, honest, kindhearted soul, born and reared in the lower ranks of life, and miraculously ignorant. He drove a team, and owned a small ranch—a ranch that paid him a comfortable living, for although it yielded but little hay, what little it did yield was worth from $250 to $300 in gold per ton in the market. Presently Smith traded a few acres of the ranch for a small undeveloped silver mine in Gold Hill. He opened the mine and built a little unpretending ten-stamp mill. Eighteen months afterward he retired from the hay business, for his mining income had reached a most comfortable figure. Some people said it was $30,000 a month, and others said it was $60,000. Smith was very rich at any rate.

And then he went to Europe and traveled. And when he came back he was never tired of telling about the fine hogs he had seen in England, and the gorgeous sheep he had seen in Spain, and the fine cattle he had noticed in the vicinity of Rome. He was full of the wonders of the old world, and advised everybody to travel. He said a man never imagined what surprising things there were in the world till he had traveled.

One day, on board ship, the passengers made up a pool of $500, which was to be the property of the man who should come nearest to guessing the run of the vessel for the next twenty-four hours. Next day, toward noon, the figures were all in the purser's hands in sealed envelopes. Smith was serene and happy, for he had been bribing the engineer. But another party won the prize! Smith said:

"Here, that won't do! He guessed two miles wider of the mark than I did."

The purser said, "Mr. Smith, you missed it further than any man on board. We traveled two hundred and eight miles yesterday."

"Well, sir," said Smith, "that's just where I've got you, for I guessed two hundred and nine. If you'll look at my figgers again you'll find a 2 and two o's, which stands for 200, don't it?—and after 'em you'll find a 9 (2009), which stands for two hundred and nine. I reckon I'll take that money, if you please."

The Gould & Curry claim comprised twelve hundred feet, and it all belonged originally to the two men whose names it bears. Mr. Curry owned two thirds of it—and he said that he sold it out for twenty-five hundred dollars in cash, and an old plug horse that ate up his market value in hay and barley in seventeen days by the watch. And he said that Gould sold out for a pair of second-hand government blankets and a bottle of whisky that killed nine men in three hours, and that an unoffending stranger that smelt the cork was disabled for life. Four years afterward the mine thus disposed of was worth in the San Francisco market seven millions six hundred thousand dollars in gold coin.

In the early days a poverty-stricken Mexican who lived in a canyon directly back of Virginia City, had a stream of water as large as a man's wrist trickling from the hill-side on his premises. The Ophir Company segregated a hundred feet of their mine and traded it to him for the stream of water. The hundred feet proved to be the richest part of the entire mine; four years after the swap, its market value (including its mill) was $1,500,000.

An individual who owned twenty feet in the Ophir mine before its great riches were revealed to men, traded it for a horse, and a very sorry looking brute he was, too. A year or so afterward, when Ophir stock went up to $3,000 a foot, this man, who had not a cent, used to say he was the most startling example of magnificence and misery the world had ever seen—because he was able to ride a sixty-thousand-dollar horse—yet could not scrape up cash enough to buy a saddle, and was obliged to borrow one or ride bareback. He said if fortune were to give him another sixty-thousand-dollar horse it would ruin him.

A youth of nineteen, who was a telegraph operator in Virginia on a salary of a hundred dollars a month, and who, when he could not make out German names in the list of San Francisco steamer arrivals, used to ingeniously select and supply substitutes for them out of an old Berlin city directory, made himself rich by watching the mining telegrams that passed through his hands and buying and selling stocks accordingly, through a friend in San Francisco. Once when a private dispatch was sent from Virginia announcing a rich strike in a prominent mine and advising that the matter be kept secret till a large amount of the stock could be secured, he bought forty "feet" of the stock at twenty dollars a foot, and afterward sold half of it at eight hundred dollars a foot and the rest at double that figure. Within three months he was worth $150,000, and had resigned his telegraphic position.

Another telegraph operator who had been discharged by the company for divulging the secrets of the office, agreed with a moneyed man in San Francisco to furnish him the result of a great Virginia mining lawsuit within an hour after its private reception by the parties to it in San Francisco. For

this he was to have a large percentage of the profits on purchases and sales made on it by his fellow-conspirator. So he
went, disguised as a teamster, to a little wayside telegraph
office in the mountains, got acquainted with the operator,
and sat in the office day after day, smoking his pipe, complaining that his team was fagged out and unable to travel—
and meantime listening to the dispatches as they passed clicking through the machine from Virginia. Finally the private
dispatch announcing the result of the lawsuit sped over the
wires, and as soon as he heard it he telegraphed his friend in
San Francisco:

"Am tired waiting. Shall sell the team and go home."

It was the signal agreed upon. The word "waiting" left
out, would have signified that the suit had gone the other
way. The mock teamster's friend picked up a deal of the mining stock, at low figures, before the news became public, and
a fortune was the result.

For a long time after one of the great Virginia mines had
been incorporated, about fifty feet of the original location
were still in the hands of a man who had never signed the
incorporation papers. The stock became very valuable, and
every effort was made to find this man, but he had disappeared. Once it was heard that he was in New York, and one
or two speculators went east but failed to find him. Once the
news came that he was in the Bermudas, and straightway a
speculator or two hurried east and sailed for Bermuda—but
he was not there. Finally he was heard of in Mexico, and a
friend of his, a bar-keeper on a salary, scraped together a little
money and sought him out, bought his "feet" for a hundred
dollars, returned and sold the property for $75,000.

But why go on? The traditions of Silverland are filled with
instances like these, and I would never get through enumer-
ating them were I to attempt to do it. I only desired to give
the reader an idea of a peculiarity of the "flush times" which
I could not present so strikingly in any other way, and which
some mention of was necessary to a realizing comprehension
of the time and the country.

I was personally acquainted with the majority of the nabobs I have referred to, and so, for old acquaintance sake, I
have shifted their occupations and experiences around in such

a way as to keep the Pacific public from recognizing these once notorious men. No longer notorious, for the majority of them have drifted back into poverty and obscurity again.

In Nevada there used to be current the story of an adventure of two of her nabobs, which may or may not have occurred. I give it for what it is worth:

Col. Jim had seen somewhat of the world, and knew more or less of its ways; but Col. Jack was from the back settlements of the States, had led a life of arduous toil, and had never seen a city. These two, blessed with sudden wealth, projected a visit to New York,—Col. Jack to see the sights, and Col. Jim to guard his unsophistication from misfortune. They reached San Francisco in the night, and sailed in the morning. Arrived in New York, Col. Jack said:

"I've heard tell of carriages all my life, and now I mean to have a ride in one; I don't care what it costs. Come along."

They stepped out on the sidewalk, and Col. Jim called a stylish barouche. But Col. Jack said:

"*No*, sir! None of your cheap-John turn-outs for me. I'm here to have a good time, and money ain't any object. I mean to have the nobbiest rig that's going. Now here comes the very trick. Stop that yaller one with the pictures on it—don't you fret—I'll stand all the expenses myself."

So Col. Jim stopped an empty omnibus, and they got in. Said Col. Jack:

"Ain't it gay, though? Oh, no, I reckon not! Cushions, and windows, and pictures, till you can't rest. What would the boys say if they could see us cutting a swell like this in New York? By George, I wish they *could* see us."

Then he put his head out of the window, and shouted to the driver:

"Say, Johnny, this suits *me!*—suits yours truly, you bet, you! I want this shebang all day. I'm *on* it, old man! Let 'em out! Make 'em go! We'll make it all right with *you*, sonny!"

The driver passed his hand through the strap-hole, and tapped for his fare—it was before the gongs came into common use. Col. Jack took the hand, and shook it cordially. He said:

"You twig me, old pard! All right between gents. Smell of *that*, and see how you like it!"

And he put a twenty-dollar gold piece in the driver's hand. After a moment the driver said he could not make change.

"Bother the change! Ride it out. Put it in your pocket."

Then to Col. Jim, with a sounding slap on his thigh:

"*Ain't* it style, though? Hanged if I don't hire this thing every day for a week."

The omnibus stopped, and a young lady got in. Col. Jack stared a moment, then nudged Col. Jim with his elbow:

"Don't say a word," he whispered. "Let her ride, if she wants to. Gracious, there's room enough."

The young lady got out her porte-monnaie, and handed her fare to Col. Jack.

"What's this for?" said he.

"Give it to the driver, please."

"Take back your money, madam. We can't allow it. You're welcome to ride here as long as you please, but this shebang's chartered, and we can't let you pay a cent."

The girl shrunk into a corner, bewildered. An old lady with a basket climbed in, and proffered her fare.

"Excuse me," said Col. Jack. "You're perfectly welcome here, madam, but we can't allow you to pay. Set right down there, mum, and don't you be the least uneasy. Make yourself just as free as if you was in your own turn-out."

Within two minutes, three gentlemen, two fat women, and a couple of children, entered.

"Come right along, friends," said Col. Jack; "don't mind *us*. This is a free blow-out." Then he whispered to Col. Jim, "New York ain't no sociable place, I don't reckon—it ain't no *name* for it!"

He resisted every effort to pass fares to the driver, and made everybody cordially welcome. The situation dawned on the people, and they pocketed their money, and delivered themselves up to covert enjoyment of the episode. Half a dozen more passengers entered.

"Oh, there's *plenty* of room," said Col. Jack. "Walk right in, and make yourselves at home. A blow-out ain't worth any-thing *as* a blow-out, unless a body has company." Then in a whisper to Col. Jim: "But *ain't* these New Yorkers friendly? And ain't they cool about it, too? Icebergs ain't anywhere. I reckon they'd tackle a hearse, if it was going their way."

More passengers got in; more yet, and still more. Both seats were filled, and a file of men were standing up, holding on to the cleats overhead. Parties with baskets and bundles were climbing up on the roof. Half-suppressed laughter rippled up from all sides.

"Well, for clean, cool, out-and-out cheek, if this don't bang anything that ever I saw, I'm an Injun!" whispered Col. Jack.

A Chinaman crowded his way in.

"I weaken!" said Col. Jack. "Hold on, driver! Keep your seats, ladies and gents. Just make yourselves free—everything's paid for. Driver, rustle these folks around as long as they're a mind to go—friends of ours, you know. Take them everywheres—and if you want more money, come to the St. Nicholas, and we'll make it all right. Pleasant journey to you, ladies and gents—go it just as long as you please—it shan't cost you a cent!"

The two comrades got out, and Col. Jack said:

"Jimmy, it's the sociablest place *I* ever saw. The Chinaman waltzed in as comfortable as anybody. If we'd staid awhile, I reckon we'd had some niggers. B' George, we'll have to barricade our doors to-night, or some of these ducks will be trying to sleep with us."

Chapter XLVII

SOMEBODY HAS SAID that in order to know a community, one must observe the style of its funerals and know what manner of men they bury with most ceremony. I cannot say which class we buried with most eclat in our "flush times," the distinguished public benefactor or the distinguished rough—possibly the two chief grades or grand divisions of society honored their illustrious dead about equally; and hence, no doubt the philosopher I have quoted from would have needed to see two representative funerals in Virginia before forming his estimate of the people.

There was a grand time over Buck Fanshaw when he died. He was a representative citizen. He had "killed his man"—not in his own quarrel, it is true, but in defence of a stranger unfairly beset by numbers. He had kept a sumptuous saloon. He had been the proprietor of a dashing helpmeet whom he could have discarded without the formality of a divorce. He had held a high position in the fire department and been a very Warwick in politics. When he died there was great lamentation throughout the town, but especially in the vast bottom-stratum of society.

On the inquest it was shown that Buck Fanshaw, in the delirium of a wasting typhoid fever, had taken arsenic, shot himself through the body, cut his throat, and jumped out of a four-story window and broken his neck—and after due deliberation, the jury, sad and tearful, but with intelligence unblinded by its sorrow, brought in a verdict of death "by the visitation of God." What could the world do without juries?

Prodigious preparations were made for the funeral. All the vehicles in town were hired, all the saloons put in mourning, all the municipal and fire-company flags hung at half-mast, and all the firemen ordered to muster in uniform and bring their machines duly draped in black. Now—let us remark in parenthesis—as all the peoples of the earth had representative adventurers in the Silverland, and as each adventurer had brought the slang of his nation or his locality with him, the combination made the slang of Nevada the richest and the most infinitely varied and copious that had ever existed anywhere in the world, perhaps, except in the mines of California in the "early days." Slang was the language of Nevada. It was hard to preach a sermon without it, and be understood. Such phrases as "You bet!" "Oh, no, I reckon not!" "No Irish need apply," and a hundred others, became so common as to fall from the lips of a speaker unconsciously—and very often when they did not touch the subject under discussion and consequently failed to mean anything.

After Buck Fanshaw's inquest, a meeting of the short-haired brotherhood was held, for nothing can be done on the Pacific coast without a public meeting and an expression of sentiment. Regretful resolutions were passed and various committees appointed; among others, a committee of one was deputed to call on the minister, a fragile, gentle, spirituel new fledgling from an Eastern theological seminary, and as yet unacquainted with the ways of the mines. The committee-man, "Scotty" Briggs, made his visit; and in after days it was worth something to hear the minister tell about it. Scotty was a stalwart rough, whose customary suit, when on weighty official business, like committee work, was a fire helmet, flaming red flannel shirt, patent leather belt with spanner and revolver attached, coat hung over arm, and pants stuffed into boot tops. He formed something of a contrast to the pale theological student. It is fair to say of Scotty, however, in passing, that he had a warm heart, and a strong love for his friends, and never entered into a quarrel when he could reasonably keep out of it. Indeed, it was commonly said that whenever one of Scotty's fights was investigated, it always turned out that it had originally been no affair of his, but that out of native goodheartedness he had dropped in of his own accord to help the man who was getting the worst of it. He and Buck Fanshaw were bosom friends, for years, and had often taken adventurous "pot-luck" together. On one occasion, they had thrown off their coats and taken the weaker side in a fight among strangers, and after gaining a hard-earned victory, turned and found that the men they were helping had deserted early, and not only that, but had stolen their coats and made off with them! But to return to Scotty's visit to the minister. He was on a sorrowful mission, now, and his face was the picture of woe. Being admitted to the presence he sat

down before the clergyman, placed his fire-hat on an unfinished manuscript sermon under the minister's nose, took
from it a red silk handkerchief, wiped his brow and heaved a
sigh of dismal impressiveness, explanatory of his business. He
choked, and even shed tears; but with an effort he mastered
his voice and said in lugubrious tones:

"Are you the duck that runs the gospel-mill next door?"

"Am I the—pardon me, I believe I do not understand?"

With another sigh and a half-sob, Scotty rejoined:

"Why you see we are in a bit of trouble, and the boys
thought maybe you would give us a lift, if we'd tackle you—
that is, if I've got the rights of it and you are the head clerk
of the doxology-works next door."

"I am the shepherd in charge of the flock whose fold is next
door."

"The which?"

"The spiritual adviser of the little company of believers
whose sanctuary adjoins these premises."

Scotty scratched his head, reflected a moment, and then
said:

"You ruther hold over me, pard. I reckon I can't call that
hand. Ante and pass the buck."

"How? I beg pardon. What did I understand you to say?"

"Well, you've ruther got the bulge on me. Or maybe we've
both got the bulge, somehow. You don't smoke me and I
don't smoke you. You see, one of the boys has passed in his
checks and we want to give him a good send-off, and so the
thing I'm on now is to roust out somebody to jerk a little
chin-music for us and waltz him through handsome."

"My friend, I seem to grow more and more bewildered.
Your observations are wholly incomprehensible to me. Cannot you simplify them in some way? At first I thought perhaps I understood you, but I grope now. Would it not
expedite matters if you restricted yourself to categorical statements of fact unencumbered with obstructing accumulations
of metaphor and allegory?"

Another pause, and more reflection. Then, said Scotty:

"I'll have to pass, I judge."

"How?"

"You've raised me out, pard."

"I still fail to catch your meaning."

"Why, that last lead of yourn is too many for me—that's
the idea. I can't neither trump nor follow suit."

The clergyman sank back in his chair perplexed. Scotty
leaned his head on his hand and gave himself up to thought.
Presently his face came up, sorrowful but confident.

"I've got it now, so's you can savvy," he said. "What we
want is a gospel-sharp. See?"

"A what?"

"Gospel-sharp. Parson."

"Oh! Why did you not say so before? I am a clergyman—
a parson."

"Now you talk! You see my blind and straddle it like a man.
Put it there!"—extending a brawny paw, which closed over
the minister's small hand and gave it a shake indicative of
fraternal sympathy and fervent gratification.

"Now we're all right, pard. Let's start fresh. Don't you
mind my snuffling a little—becuz we're in a power of trouble. You see, one of the boys has gone up the flume—"

"Gone where?"

"Up the flume—throwed up the sponge, you understand."

"Thrown up the sponge?"

"Yes—kicked the bucket—"

"Ah—has departed to that mysterious country from whose
bourne no traveler returns."

"Return! I reckon not. Why pard, he's *dead!*"

"Yes, I understand."

"Oh, you do? Well I thought maybe you might be getting
tangled some more. Yes, you see he's dead again—"

"*Again?* Why, has he ever been dead before?"

"Dead before? No! Do you reckon a man has got as many
lives as a cat? But you bet you he's awful dead now, poor old
boy, and I wish I'd never seen this day. I don't want no better
friend than Buck Fanshaw. I knowed him by the back; and
when I know a man and like him, I freeze to him—you hear
me. Take him all round, pard, there never was a bullier man
in the mines. No man ever knowed Buck Fanshaw to go back
on a friend. But it's all up, you know, it's all up. It ain't no
use. They've scooped him."

"Scooped him?"

"Yes—death has. Well, well, well, we've got to give him up. Yes indeed. It's a kind of a hard world, after all, *ain't* it? But pard, he was a rustler! You ought to seen him get started once. He was a bully boy with a glass eye! Just spit in his face and give him room according to his strength, and it was just beautiful to see him peel and go in. He was the worst son of a thief that ever drawed breath. Pard, he was *on* it! He was on it bigger than an Injun!"

"On it? On what?"

"On the shoot. On the shoulder. On the fight, you understand. *He* didn't give a continental for *any*body. *Beg* your pardon, friend, for coming so near saying a cuss-word—but you see I'm on an awful strain, in this palaver, on account of having to cramp down and draw everything so mild. But we've got to give him up. There ain't any getting around that, I don't reckon. Now if we can get you to help plant him—"

"Preach the funeral discourse? Assist at the obsequies?"

"Obs'quies is good. Yes. That's it—that's our little game. We are going to get the thing up regardless, you know. He was always nifty himself, and so you bet you his funeral ain't going to be no slouch—solid silver door-plate on his coffin, six plumes on the hearse, and a nigger on the box in a biled shirt and a plug hat—how's that for high? And we'll take care of *you*, pard. We'll fix you all right. There'll be a kerridge for you; and whatever you want, you just 'scape out and we'll 'tend to it. We've got a shebang fixed up for you to stand behind, in No. 1's house, and don't you be afraid. Just go in and toot your horn, if you don't sell a clam. Put Buck through as bully as you can, pard, for anybody that knowed him will tell you that he was one of the whitest men that was ever in the mines. You can't draw it too strong. He never could stand it to see things going wrong. He's done more to make this town quiet and peaceable than any man in it. I've seen him lick four Greasers in eleven minutes, myself. If a thing wanted regulating, *he* warn't a man to go browsing around after somebody to do it, but he would prance in and regulate it himself. He warn't a Catholic. Scasely. He was down on 'em. His word was, 'No Irish need apply!' But it didn't make no difference about that when it came down to what a man's rights was—and so, when some roughs jumped the Catholic bone-yard and started in to stake out town-lots in it he *went* for 'em! And he *cleaned* 'em, too! I was there, pard, and I seen it myself."

"That was very well indeed—at least the impulse was—whether the act was strictly defensible or not. Had deceased any religious convictions? That is to say, did he feel a dependence upon, or acknowledge allegiance to a higher power?"

More reflection.

"I reckon you've stumped me again, pard. Could you say it over once more, and say it slow?"

"Well, to simplify it somewhat, was he, or rather had he ever been connected with any organization sequestered from secular concerns and devoted to self-sacrifice in the interests of morality?"

"All down but nine—set 'em up on the other alley, pard."

"What did I understand you to say?"

"Why, you're most too many for me, you know. When you get in with your left I hunt grass every time. Every time you draw, you fill; but I don't seem to have any luck. Lets have a new deal."

"How? Begin again?"

"That's it."

"Very well. Was he a good man, and—"

"There—I see that; don't put up another chip till I look at my hand. A good man, says you? Pard, it ain't no name for it. He was the best man that ever—pard, you would have doted on that man. He could lam any galoot of his inches in America. It was him that put down the riot last election before it got a start; and everybody said he was the only man that could have done it. He waltzed in with a spanner in one hand and a trumpet in the other, and sent fourteen men home on a shutter in less than three minutes. He had that riot all broke up and prevented nice before anybody ever got a chance to strike a blow. He was always for peace, and he would *have* peace—he could not stand disturbances. Pard, he was a great loss to this town. It would please the boys if you could chip in something like that and do him justice. Here once when the Micks got to throwing stones through the Methodis' Sunday school windows, Buck Fanshaw, all of his own notion, shut up his saloon and took a couple of six-shooters and mounted guard over the Sunday school. Says he, 'No Irish need apply!' And they didn't. He was the bulliest man in the mountains, pard! He could run faster, jump higher, hit harder, and hold more tangle-foot whisky without spilling it than any man in seventeen counties. Put that in, pard—it'll please the boys more than anything you could say. And you can say, pard, that he never shook his mother."

"Never shook his mother?"

"That's it—any of the boys will tell you so."

"Well, but why *should* he shake her?"

"That's what *I* say—but some people does."

"Not people of any repute?"

"Well, some that averages pretty so-so."

"In my opinion the man that would offer personal violence to his own mother, ought to—"

"Cheese it, pard; you've banked your ball clean outside the string. What I was a drivin' at, was, that he never *throwed off* on his mother—don't you see? No indeedy. He give her a house to live in, and town lots, and plenty of money; and he looked after her and took care of her all the time; and when she was down with the small-pox I'm d—d if he didn't set up nights and nuss her himself! *Beg* your pardon for saying it, but it hopped out too quick for yours truly. You've treated me like a gentleman, pard, and I ain't the man to hurt your feelings intentional. I think you're white. I think you're a square man, pard. I like you, and I'll lick any man that don't. I'll lick him till he can't tell himself from a last year's corpse! Put it *there!*" [Another fraternal handshake—and exit.]

The obsequies were all that "the boys" could desire. Such a marvel of funeral pomp had never been seen in Virginia. The plumed hearse, the dirge-breathing brass bands, the closed marts of business, the flags drooping at half mast, the long, plodding procession of uniformed secret societies, military battalions and fire companies, draped engines, carriages of officials, and citizens in vehicles and on foot, attracted multitudes of spectators to the sidewalks, roofs and windows; and for years afterward, the degree of grandeur attained by any civic display in Virginia was determined by comparison with Buck Fanshaw's funeral.

Scotty Briggs, as a pall-bearer and a mourner, occupied a

prominent place at the funeral, and when the sermon was finished and the last sentence of the prayer for the dead man's soul ascended, he responded, in a low voice, but with feeling:

"AMEN. No Irish need apply."

As the bulk of the response was without apparent relevancy, it was probably nothing more than a humble tribute to the memory of the friend that was gone; for, as Scotty had once said, it was "his word."

Scotty Briggs, in after days, achieved the distinction of becoming the only convert to religion that was ever gathered from the Virginia roughs; and it transpired that the man who had it in him to espouse the quarrel of the weak out of inborn nobility of spirit was no mean timber whereof to construct a Christian. The making him one did not warp his generosity or diminish his courage; on the contrary it gave intelligent direction to the one and a broader field to the other. If his Sunday-school class progressed faster than the other classes, was it matter for wonder? I think not. He talked to his pioneer small-fry in a language they understood! It was my large privilege, a month before he died, to hear him tell the beautiful story of Joseph and his brethren to his class " without looking at the book." I leave it to the reader to fancy what it was like, as it fell, riddled with slang, from the lips of that grave, earnest teacher, and was listened to by his little learners with a consuming interest that showed that they were as unconscious as he was that any violence was being done to the sacred proprieties!

Chapter XLVIII

THE FIRST TWENTY-SIX graves in the Virginia cemetery were occupied by *murdered* men. So everybody said, so everybody believed, and so they will always say and believe. The reason why there was so much slaughtering done, was, that in a new mining district the rough element predominates, and a person is not respected until he has "killed his man." That was the very expression used.

If an unknown individual arrived, they did not inquire if he was capable, honest, industrious, but—had he killed his man? If he had not, he gravitated to his natural and proper position, that of a man of small consequence; if he had, the cordiality of his reception was graduated according to the number of his dead. It was tedious work struggling up to a position of influence with bloodless hands; but when a man came with the blood of half a dozen men on his soul, his worth was recognized at once and his acquaintance sought.

In Nevada, for a time, the lawyer, the editor, the banker, the chief desperado, the chief gambler, and the saloon keeper, occupied the same level in society, and it was the highest. The cheapest and easiest way to become an influential man and be looked up to by the community at large, was to stand behind a bar, wear a cluster-diamond pin, and sell whisky. I am not sure but that the saloon-keeper held a shade higher rank than any other member of society. His opinion had weight. It was his privilege to say how the elections should go. No great movement could succeed without the countenance and direction of the saloon-keepers. It was a high favor when the chief saloon-keeper consented to serve in the legislature or the board of aldermen. Youthful ambition hardly aspired so much to the honors of the law, or the army and navy as to the dignity of proprietorship in a saloon.

To be a saloon-keeper and kill a man was to be illustrious. Hence the reader will not be surprised to learn that more than one man was killed in Nevada under hardly the pretext of provocation, so impatient was the slayer to achieve reputation and throw off the galling sense of being held in indifferent repute by his associates. I knew two youths who tried to "kill their men" for no other reason—and got killed themselves for their pains. "There goes the man that killed Bill Adams" was higher praise and a sweeter sound in the ears of this sort of people than any other speech that admiring lips could utter.

The men who murdered Virginia's original twenty-six cemetery-occupants were never punished. Why? Because Alfred the Great, when he invented trial by jury, and knew that he had admirably framed it to secure justice in his age of the world, was not aware that in the nineteenth century the condition of things would be so entirely changed that unless he rose from the grave and altered the jury plan to meet the emergency, it would prove the most ingenious and infallible agency for *defeating* justice that human wisdom could contrive. For how could he imagine that we simpletons would go on using his jury plan after circumstances had stripped it of its usefulness, any more than he could imagine that we would go on using his candle-clock after we had invented chronometers? In his day news could not travel fast, and hence he could easily find a jury of honest, intelligent men who had not heard of the case they were called to try—but in our day of telegraphs and newspapers his plan compels us to swear in juries composed of fools and rascals, because the system rigidly excludes honest men and men of brains.

I remember one of those sorrowful farces, in Virginia, which we call a jury trial. A noted desperado killed Mr. B., a good citizen, in the most wanton and cold-blooded way. Of course the papers were full of it, and all men capable of reading, read about it. And of course all men not deaf and dumb and idiotic, talked about it. A jury-list was made out, and Mr. B. L., a prominent banker and a valued citizen, was questioned precisely as he would have been questioned in any court in America:

"Have you heard of this homicide?"

"Yes."

"Have you held conversations upon the subject?"

"Yes."

"Have you formed or expressed opinions about it?"

"Yes."

"Have you read the newspaper accounts of it?"

"Yes."

"We do not want you."

A minister, intelligent, esteemed, and greatly respected; a merchant of high character and known probity; a mining superintendent of intelligence and unblemished reputation; a quartz mill owner of excellent standing, were all questioned in the same way, and all set aside. Each said the public talk and the newspaper reports had not so biased his mind but that sworn testimony would overthrow his previously formed opinions and enable him to render a verdict without prejudice and in accordance with the facts. But of course such men could not be trusted with the case. Ignoramuses alone could mete out unsullied justice.

When the peremptory challenges were all exhausted, a jury of twelve men was impaneled—a jury who swore they had neither heard, read, talked about nor expressed an opinion concerning a murder which the very cattle in the corrals, the Indians in the sage-brush and the stones in the streets were cognizant of! It was a jury composed of two desperadoes, two low beer-house politicians, three bar-keepers, two ranchmen who could not read, and three dull, stupid, human donkeys! It actually came out afterward, that one of these latter thought that incest and arson were the same thing.

The verdict rendered by this jury was, Not Guilty. What else could one expect?

The jury system puts a ban upon intelligence and honesty, and a premium upon ignorance, stupidity and perjury. It is a shame that we must continue to use a worthless system because it *was* good a thousand years ago. In this age, when a gentleman of high social standing, intelligence and probity, swears that testimony given under solemn oath will outweigh, with him, street talk and newspaper reports based upon mere hearsay, he is worth a hundred jurymen who will swear to their own ignorance and stupidity, and justice would be far safer in his hands than in theirs. Why could not the jury law be so altered as to give men of brains and honesty an *equal chance* with fools and miscreants? Is it right to show the present favoritism to one class of men and inflict a disability on another, in a land whose boast is that all its citizens are free and equal? I am a candidate for the legislature. I desire to tamper with the jury law. I wish to so alter it as to put a

premium on intelligence and character, and close the jury box
against idiots, blacklegs, and people who do not read newspapers. But no doubt I shall be defeated—every effort I make
to save the country "misses fire."

My idea, when I began this chapter, was to say something
about desperadoism in the "flush times" of Nevada. To attempt a portrayal of that era and that land, and leave out the
blood and carnage, would be like portraying Mormondom
and leaving out polygamy. The desperado stalked the streets
with a swagger graded according to the number of his homicides, and a nod of recognition from him was sufficient to
make a humble admirer happy for the rest of the day. The
deference that was paid to a desperado of wide reputation,
and who "kept his private graveyard," as the phrase went, was
marked, and cheerfully accorded. When he moved along the
sidewalk in his excessively long-tailed frock-coat, shiny stump-
toed boots, and with dainty little slouch hat tipped over left
eye, the small-fry roughs made room for his majesty; when
he entered the restaurant, the waiters deserted bankers and
merchants to overwhelm him with obsequious service; when
he shouldered his way to a bar, the shouldered parties
wheeled indignantly, recognized him, and—apologized. They
got a look in return that froze their marrow, and by that time
a curled and breast-pinned bar keeper was beaming over the
counter, proud of the established acquaintanceship that permitted such a familiar form of speech as:

"How 're ye, Billy, old fel? Glad to see you. What 'll you
take—the old thing?"

The "old thing" meant his customary drink, of course.

The best known names in the Territory of Nevada were
those belonging to these long-tailed heroes of the revolver.
Orators, Governors, capitalists and leaders of the legislature
enjoyed a degree of fame, but it seemed local and meagre
when contrasted with the fame of such men as Sam Brown,
Jack Williams, Billy Mulligan, Farmer Pease, Sugarfoot Mike,
Pock-Marked Jake, El Dorado Johnny, Jack McNabb, Joe
McGee, Jack Harris, Six-fingered Pete, etc., etc. There was a
long list of them. They were brave, reckless men, and traveled
with their lives in their hands. To give them their due, they
did their killing principally among themselves, and seldom

molested peaceable citizens, for they considered it small credit
to add to their trophies so cheap a bauble as the death of a
man who was "not on the shoot," as they phrased it. They
killed each other on slight provocation, and hoped and expected to be killed themselves—for they held it almost shame
to die otherwise than " with their boots on," as they expressed
it.

I remember an instance of a desperado's contempt for such
small game as a private citizen's life. I was taking a late supper
in a restaurant one night, with two reporters and a little
printer named—Brown, for instance—any name will do.
Presently a stranger with a long-tailed coat on came in, and
not noticing Brown's hat, which was lying in a chair, sat
down on it. Little Brown sprang up and became abusive in a
moment. The stranger smiled, smoothed out the hat, and offered it to Brown with profuse apologies couched in caustic
sarcasm, and begged Brown not to destroy him. Brown threw
off his coat and challenged the man to fight—abused him,
threatened him, impeached his courage, and urged and even
implored him to fight; and in the meantime the smiling
stranger placed himself under our protection in mock distress.
But presently he assumed a serious tone, and said:

"Very well, gentlemen, if we must fight, we must, I suppose. But don't rush into danger and then say I gave you no
warning. I am more than a match for all of you when I get
started. I will give you proofs, and then if my friend here still
insists, I will try to accommodate him."

The table we were sitting at was about five feet long, and
unusually cumbersome and heavy. He asked us to put our
hands on the dishes and hold them in their places a moment—one of them was a large oval dish with a portly roast
on it. Then he sat down, tilted up one end of the table, set
two of the legs on his knees, took the end of the table between his teeth, took his hands away, and pulled down with
his teeth till the table came up to a level position, dishes and
all! He said he could lift a keg of nails with his teeth. He
picked up a common glass tumbler and bit a semi-circle out
of it. Then he opened his bosom and showed us a net-work
of knife and bullet scars; showed us more on his arms and
face, and said he believed he had bullets enough in his body

to make a pig of lead. He was armed to the teeth. He closed
with the remark that he was Mr. —— of Cariboo—a celebrated name whereat we shook in our shoes. I would publish
the name, but for the suspicion that he might come and carve
me. He finally inquired if Brown still thirsted for blood.
Brown turned the thing over in his mind a moment, and
then—asked him to supper.

With the permission of the reader, I will group together,
in the next chapter, some samples of life in our small mountain village in the old days of desperadoism. I was there at
the time. The reader will observe peculiarities in our *official*
society; and he will observe also, an instance of how, in new
countries, murders breed murders.

Chapter XLIX

AN EXTRACT or two from the newspapers of the day will furnish a photograph that can need no embellishment:

FATAL SHOOTING AFFRAY.—An affray occurred, last evening, in a billiard saloon on C street, between *Deputy Marshal Jack Williams* and Wm. Brown, which resulted in the immediate death of the latter. There had been some difficulty between the parties for several months.

An inquest was immediately held, and the following testimony adduced:

Officer GEO. BIRDSALL, sworn, says:—I was told Wm. Brown was drunk and was looking for Jack Williams; so soon as I heard that I started for the parties to prevent a collision; went into the billiard saloon; saw Billy Brown running around, saying if anybody had anything against him to show cause; he was talking in a boisterous manner, and officer Perry took him to the other end of the room to talk to him; Brown came back to me; remarked to me that he thought he was as good as anybody, and knew how to take care of himself; he passed by me and went to the bar; don't know whether he drank or not; Williams was at the end of the billiard-table, next to the stairway; Brown, after going to the bar, came back and said he was as good as any man in the world; he had then walked out to the end of the first billiard-table from the bar; I moved closer to them, supposing there would be a fight; as Brown drew his pistol I caught hold of it; he had fired one shot at Williams; don't know the effect of it; caught hold of him with one hand, and took hold of the pistol and turned it up; think he fired once after I caught hold of the pistol; I wrenched the pistol from him; walked to the end of the billiard-table and told a party that I had Brown's pistol, and to stop shooting; I think four shots were fired in all; after walking out, Mr. Foster remarked that Brown was shot dead.

Oh, there was no excitement about it—he merely "remarked" the small circumstance!

Four months later the following item appeared in the same paper (the *Enterprise*). In this item the name of one of the city officers above referred to (*Deputy Marshal Jack Williams*) occurs again:

ROBBERY AND DESPERATE AFFRAY.—On Tuesday night, a German named Charles Hurtzal, engineer in a mill at Silver City, came to this place, and visited the hurdy-gurdy house on B street. The music, dancing and Teutonic maidens awakened memories of Fader-land until our German friend was carried away with rapture. He evidently had money, and was spending it freely. Late in the evening Jack Williams and Andy Blessington invited him down stairs to take a cup of coffee. Williams proposed a game of cards and went up stairs to procure a deck, but not finding any returned. On the stair-way he met the German, and drawing his pistol knocked him down and rifled his pockets of some seventy dollars. Hurtzal dared give no alarm, as he was told, with a pistol at his head, if he made any noise or exposed them, they would blow his brains out. So effectually was he frightened that he made no complaint, until his friends forced him. Yesterday a warrant was issued, but the culprits had disap-peared.

This efficient city officer, Jack Williams, had the common reputation of being a burglar, a highwayman and a desper-ado. It was said that he had several times drawn his revolver and levied money contributions on citizens at dead of night in the public streets of Virginia.

Five months after the above item appeared, Williams was assassinated while sitting at a card table one night; a gun was thrust through the crack of the door and Williams dropped from his chair riddled with balls. It was said, at the time, that Williams had been for some time aware that a party of his own sort (desperadoes) had sworn away his life; and it was generally believed among the people that Williams's friends and enemies would make the assassination memorable—and useful, too—by a wholesale destruction of each other.*

*However, one prophecy was verified, at any rate. It was asserted by the desperadoes that one of their brethren (Joe McGee, *a special policeman*) was known to be the conspirator chosen by lot to assassinate Williams; and they also asserted that doom had been pronounced against McGee, and that he would be assassinated in exactly the same manner that had been adopted for the destruction of Williams—a prophecy which came true a year later. After twelve months of distress (for McGee saw a fancied assassin in every man that approached him), he made the last of many efforts to get out of the country unwatched. He went to Carson and sat down in a saloon to wait for the stage—it would leave at four in the morning. But as the night waned and the crowd thinned, he grew uneasy, and told the bar-keeper that assassins were on his track. The bar-keeper told him to stay in the middle of the room, then, and not go near the door, or the window by the stove. But a fatal fascination seduced him to the neighborhood of the stove every now and

It did not so happen, but still, times were not dull during the next twenty-four hours, for within that time a woman was killed by a pistol shot, a man was brained with a slung shot, and a man named Reeder was also disposed of permanently. Some matters in the *Enterprise* account of the killing of Reeder are worth noting—especially the accommodating complaisance of a Virginia justice of the peace. The italics in the following narrative are mine:

MORE CUTTING AND SHOOTING.—The devil seems to have again broken loose in our town. Pistols and guns explode and knives gleam in our streets as in early times. When there has been a long season of quiet, people are slow to wet their hands in blood; but once blood is spilled, cutting and shooting come easy. Night before last Jack Williams was assassinated, and yesterday forenoon we had more bloody work, growing out of the killing of Williams, and on the same street in which he met his death. It appears that Tom Reeder, a friend of Williams, and George Gumbert were talking, at the meat market of the latter, about the killing of Williams the previous night, when Reeder said it was a most cowardly act to shoot a man in such a way, giving him "no show." Gumbert said that Williams had "as good a show as he gave Billy Brown," meaning the man killed by Williams last March. Reeder said it was a d—d lie, that Williams had no show at all. At this, Gumbert drew a knife and stabbed Reeder, cutting him in two places in the back. One stroke of the knife cut into the sleeve of Reeder's coat and passed downward in a slanting direction through his clothing, and entered his body at the small of the back; another blow struck more squarely, and made a much more dangerous wound. Gumbert gave himself up to the officers of justice, and was shortly after discharged by Justice Atwill, *on his own recognizance*, to appear for trial at six o'clock in the evening. In the meantime Reeder had been taken into the office of Dr. Owens, where his wounds were properly dressed. *One of his wounds was considered quite dangerous, and it was thought by*

---

then, and repeatedly the bar-keeper brought him back to the middle of the room and warned him to remain there. But he could not. At three in the morning he again returned to the stove and sat down by a stranger. Before the bar-keeper could get to him with another warning whisper, some one outside fired through the window and riddled McGee's breast with slugs, killing him almost instantly. By the same discharge the stranger at McGee's side also received attentions which proved fatal in the course of two or three days.

many that it would prove fatal. But being considerably under the influ-
ence of liquor, Reeder did not feel his wounds as he otherwise would, and
he got up and went into the street. He went to the meat market and
renewed his quarrel with Gumbert, threatening his life. Friends tried
to interfere to put a stop to the quarrel and get the parties away
from each other. In the Fashion Saloon Reeder made threats against
the life of Gumbert, saying he would kill him, and it is said that *he*
requested the officers not to arrest Gumbert, as he intended to kill him.
After these threats Gumbert went off and procured a double-barreled shot gun, loaded with buck-shot or revolver balls, and went
after Reeder. Two or three persons were assisting him along the
street, trying to get him home, and had him just in front of the store
of Klopstock & Harris, when Gumbert came across toward him
from the opposite side of the street with his gun. He came up within
about ten or fifteen feet of Reeder, and called out to those with him
to "look out! get out of the way!" and they had only time to heed
the warning, when he fired. Reeder was at the time attempting to
screen himself behind a large cask, which stood against the awning
post of Klopstock & Harris's store, but some of the balls took effect
in the lower part of his breast, and he reeled around forward and fell
in front of the cask. Gumbert then raised his gun and fired the second barrel, which missed Reeder and entered the ground. At the
time that this occurred, there were a great many persons on the
street in the vicinity, and a number of them called out to Gumbert,
when they saw him raise his gun, to "hold on," and "don't shoot!"
The cutting took place about ten o'clock and the shooting about
twelve. After the shooting the street was instantly crowded with the
inhabitants of that part of the town, some appearing much excited
and laughing—declaring that it looked like the "good old times of
'60." Marshal Perry and officer Birdsall were near when the shooting
occurred, and Gumbert was immediately arrested and his gun taken
from him, when he was marched off to jail. Many persons who were
attracted to the spot where this bloody work had just taken place,
looked bewildered and seemed to be asking themselves what was to
happen next, appearing in doubt as to whether the killing mania had
reached its climax, or whether we were to turn in and have a grand
killing spell, shooting whoever might have given us offence. It was
whispered around that it was not all over yet—five or six more were
to be killed before night. Reeder was taken to the Virginia City
Hotel, and doctors called in to examine his wounds. They found that
two or three balls had entered his right side; one of them appeared
to have passed through the substance of the lungs, while another
passed into the liver. Two balls were also found to have struck one

of his legs. As some of the balls struck the cask, the wounds in Reeder's leg were probably from these, glancing downwards, though they might have been caused by the second shot fired. After being shot, Reeder said when he got on his feet—smiling as he spoke—"It will take better shooting than that to kill me." The doctors consider it almost impossible for him to recover, but as he has an excellent constitution he may survive, notwithstanding the number and dangerous character of the wounds he has received. The town appears to be perfectly quiet at present, as though the late stormy times had cleared our moral atmosphere; but who can tell in what quarter clouds are lowering or plots ripening?

Reeder—or at least what was left of him—survived his wounds two days! Nothing was ever done with Gumbert.

Trial by jury is the palladium of our liberties. I do not know what a palladium is, having never seen a palladium, but it is a good thing no doubt at any rate. Not less than a hundred men have been murdered in Nevada—perhaps I would be within bounds if I said three hundred—and as far as I can learn, only two persons have suffered the death penalty there. However, four or five who had no money and no political influence have been punished by imprisonment—one languished in prison as much as eight months, I think. However, I do not desire to be extravagant—it may have been less.

Chapter L

THESE MURDER and jury statistics remind me of a certain very extraordinary trial and execution of twenty years ago; it is a scrap of history familiar to all old Californians, and worthy to be known by other peoples of the earth that love simple, straightforward justice unencumbered with nonsense. I would apologize for this digression but for the fact that the information I am about to offer is apology enough in itself. And since I digress constantly anyhow, perhaps it is as well to eschew apologies altogether and thus prevent their growing irksome.

Capt. Ned Blakely—that name will answer as well as any other fictitious one (for he was still with the living at last accounts, and may not desire to be famous)—sailed ships out of the harbor of San Francisco for many years. He was a stalwart, warm-hearted, eagle-eyed veteran, who had been a sailor nearly fifty years—a sailor from early boyhood. He was a rough, honest creature, full of pluck, and just as full of hard-headed simplicity, too. He hated trifling conventionalities—"business" was the word, with him. He had all a sailor's vindictiveness against the quips and quirks of the law, and steadfastly believed that the first and last aim and object of the law and lawyers was to defeat justice.

He sailed for the Chincha Islands in command of a guano ship. He had a fine crew, but his negro mate was his pet—on him he had for years lavished his admiration and esteem. It was Capt. Ned's first voyage to the Chinchas, but his fame had gone before him—the fame of being a man who would fight at the dropping of a handkerchief, when imposed upon, and would stand no nonsense. It was a fame well earned. Arrived in the islands, he found that the staple of conversation was the exploits of one Bill Noakes, a bully, the mate of a trading ship. This man had created a small reign of terror there. At nine o'clock at night, Capt. Ned, all alone, was pacing his deck in the starlight. A form ascended the side, and approached him. Capt. Ned said:

"Who goes there?"

"I'm Bill Noakes, the best man in the islands."

"What do you want aboard this ship?"

"I've heard of Capt. Ned Blakely, and one of us is a better man than 'tother—I'll know which, before I go ashore."

"You've come to the right shop—I'm your man. I'll learn you to come aboard this ship without an *invite*."

He seized Noakes, backed him against the mainmast, pounded his face to a pulp, and then threw him overboard.

Noakes was not convinced. He returned the next night, got the pulp renewed, and went overboard head first, as before. He was satisfied.

A week after this, while Noakes was carousing with a sailor crowd on shore, at noonday, Capt. Ned's colored mate came along, and Noakes tried to pick a quarrel with him. The negro evaded the trap, and tried to get away. Noakes followed him up; the negro began to run; Noakes fired on him with a revolver and killed him. Half a dozen sea-captains witnessed the whole affair. Noakes retreated to the small after-cabin of his ship, with two other bullies, and gave out that death would be the portion of any man that intruded there. There was no attempt made to follow the villains; there was no disposition to do it, and indeed very little thought of such an enterprise. There were no courts and no officers; there was no government; the islands belonged to Peru, and Peru was far away; she had no official representative on the ground; and neither had any other nation.

However, Capt. Ned was not perplexing his head about such things. They concerned him not. He was boiling with rage and furious for justice. At nine o'clock at night he loaded a double-barreled gun with slugs, fished out a pair of hand-cuffs, got a ship's lantern, summoned his quartermaster, and went ashore. He said:

"Do you see that ship there at the dock?"

"Ay-ay, sir."

"It's the Venus."

"Ay-ay, sir."

"You—you know *me*."

"Ay-ay, sir."

"Very well, then. Take the lantern. Carry it just under your chin. I'll walk behind you and rest this gun-barrel on your shoulder, p'inting forward—so. Keep your lantern well up, so's I can see things ahead of you good. I'm going to march in on Noakes—and take him—and jug the other chaps. If you flinch—well, you know *me*."

"Ay-ay, sir."

In this order they filed aboard softly, arrived at Noakes's den, the quartermaster pushed the door open, and the lantern revealed the three desperadoes sitting on the floor. Capt. Ned said:

"I'm Ned Blakely. I've got you under fire. Don't you move without orders—any of you. You two kneel down in the corner; faces to the wall—now. Bill Noakes, put these handcuffs on; now come up close. Quartermaster, fasten 'em. All right. Don't stir, sir. Quartermaster, put the key in the outside of the door. Now, men, I'm going to lock you two in; and if you try to burst through this door—well, you've heard of *me*. Bill Noakes, fall in ahead, and march. All set. Quartermaster, lock the door."

Noakes spent the night on board Blakely's ship, a prisoner under strict guard. Early in the morning Capt. Ned called in all the sea-captains in the harbor and invited them, with nautical ceremony, to be present on board his ship at nine o'clock to witness the hanging of Noakes at the yard-arm!

"What! The man has not been tried."

"Of course he hasn't. But didn't he kill the nigger?"

"Certainly he did; but you are not thinking of hanging him without a trial?"

"*Trial!* What do I want to try him for, if he killed the nigger?"

"Oh, Capt. Ned, this will *never* do. Think how it will sound."

"Sound be hanged! *Didn't he kill the nigger?*"

"Certainly, certainly, Capt. Ned,—nobody denies that,—but—"

"Then I'm going to *hang* him, that's all. Everybody I've talked to talks just the same way you do. Everybody says he killed the nigger, everybody knows he killed the nigger, and yet every lubber of you wants him *tried* for it. I don't understand such bloody foolishness as that. *Tried!* Mind you, I don't object to trying him, if it's got to be done to give satisfaction; and I'll be there, and chip in and help, too; but put it off till afternoon—put it off till afternoon, for I'll have my hands middling full till after the burying—"

"Why, what do you mean? Are you going to hang him *any how*—and try him afterward?"

"Didn't I *say* I was going to hang him? I never saw such people as you. What's the difference? You ask a favor, and then you ain't satisfied when you get it. Before or after's all one—*you* know how the trial will go. He killed the nigger. Say—I must be going. If your mate would like to come to the hanging, fetch him along. I like him."

There was a stir in the camp. The captains came in a body and pleaded with Capt. Ned not to do this rash thing. They promised that they would create a court composed of captains of the best character; they would empanel a jury; they would conduct everything in a way becoming the serious nature of the business in hand, and give the case an impartial hearing and the accused a fair trial. And they said it would be murder, and punishable by the American courts if he persisted and hung the accused on his ship. They pleaded hard. Capt. Ned said:

"Gentlemen, I'm not stubborn and I'm not unreasonable. I'm always willing to do just as near right as I can. How long will it take?"

"Probably only a little while."

"And can I take him up the shore and hang him as soon as you are done?"

"If he is proven guilty he shall be hanged without unnecessary delay."

"*If* he's proven guilty. Great Neptune, *ain't* he guilty? This beats my time. Why you all *know* he's guilty."

But at last they satisfied him that they were projecting nothing underhanded. Then he said:

"Well, all right. You go on and try him and I'll go down and overhaul his conscience and prepare him to go—like enough he needs it, and I don't want to send him off without a show for hereafter."

This was another obstacle. They finally convinced him that it was necessary to have the accused in court. Then they said they would send a guard to bring him.

"No, sir, I prefer to fetch him myself—he don't get out of

my hands. Besides, I've got to go to the ship to get a rope, anyway."

The court assembled with due ceremony, empaneled a jury, and presently Capt. Ned entered, leading the prisoner with one hand and carrying a Bible and a rope in the other. He seated himself by the side of his captive and told the court to "up anchor and make sail." Then he turned a searching eye on the jury, and detected Noakes's friends, the two bullies. He strode over and said to them confidentially:

"You're here to interfere, you see. Now you vote right, do you hear?—or else there 'll be a double-barreled inquest here when this trial's off, and your remainders will go home in a couple of baskets."

The caution was not without fruit. The jury was a unit—the verdict, "Guilty."

Capt. Ned sprung to his feet and said:

"Come along—you're my meat *now*, my lad, anyway. Gentlemen you've done yourselves proud. I invite you all to come and see that I do it all straight. Follow me to the canyon, a mile above here."

The court informed him that a sheriff had been appointed to do the hanging, and—

Capt. Ned's patience was at an end. His wrath was boundless. The subject of a sheriff was judiciously dropped.

When the crowd arrived at the canyon, Capt. Ned climbed a tree and arranged the halter, then came down and noosed his man. He opened his Bible, and laid aside his hat. Selecting a chapter at random, he read it through, in a deep bass voice and with sincere solemnity. Then he said:

"Lad, you are about to go aloft and give an account of yourself; and the lighter a man's manifest is, as far as sin's concerned, the better for him. Make a clean breast, man, and carry a log with you that 'll bear inspection. You killed the nigger?"

No reply. A long pause.

The captain read another chapter, pausing, from time to time, to impress the effect. Then he talked an earnest, persuasive sermon to him, and ended by repeating the question:

"Did you kill the nigger?"

No reply—other than a malignant scowl. The captain now

read the first and second chapters of Genesis, with deep feeling—paused a moment, closed the book reverently, and said with a perceptible savor of satisfaction:

"There. Four chapters. There's few that would have took the pains with you that I have."

Then he swung up the condemned, and made the rope fast; stood by and timed him half an hour with his watch, and then delivered the body to the court. A little after, as he stood contemplating the motionless figure, a doubt came into his face; evidently he felt a twinge of conscience—a misgiving—and he said with a sigh:

"Well, p'raps I ought to burnt him, maybe. But I was trying to do for the best."

When the history of this affair reached California (it was in the "early days") it made a deal of talk, but did not diminish the captain's popularity in any degree. It increased it, indeed. California had a population then that "inflicted" justice after a fashion that was simplicity and primitiveness itself, and could therefore admire appreciatively when the same fashion was followed elsewhere.

Chapter LI

VICE FLOURISHED luxuriantly during the hey-day of our "flush times." The saloons were overburdened with custom; so were the police courts, the gambling dens, the brothels and the jails—unfailing signs of high prosperity in a mining region—in any region for that matter. Is it not so? A crowded police court docket is the surest of all signs that trade is brisk and money plenty. Still, there is one other sign; it comes last, but when it does come it establishes beyond cavil that the "flush times" are at the flood. This is the birth of the "literary" paper. The *Weekly Occidental*, "devoted to literature," made its appearance in Virginia. All the literary people were engaged to write for it. Mr. F. was to edit it. He was a felicitous skirmisher with a pen, and a man who could say happy things in a crisp, neat way. Once, while editor of the *Union*, he had disposed of a labored, incoherent, two-column attack made upon him by a cotemporary, with a single line, which, at first glance, seemed to contain a solemn and tremendous compliment—viz.: "THE LOGIC OF OUR ADVERSARY RESEMBLES THE PEACE OF GOD,"—and left it to the reader's memory and after-thought to invest the remark with another and "more different" meaning by supplying for himself and at his own leisure the rest of the Scripture—"*in that it passeth understanding.*" He once said of a little, half-starved, wayside community that had no subsistence except what they could get by preying upon chance passengers who stopped over with them a day when traveling by the overland stage, that in their Church service they had altered the Lord's Prayer to read: "Give us this day our daily stranger!"

We expected great things of the *Occidental*. Of course it could not get along without an original novel, and so we made arrangements to hurl into the work the full strength of the company. Mrs. F. was an able romancist of the ineffable school—I know no other name to apply to a school whose heroes are all dainty and all perfect. She wrote the opening chapter, and introduced a lovely blonde simpleton who talked nothing but pearls and poetry and who was virtuous to the verge of eccentricity. She also introduced a young French

Duke of aggravated refinement, in love with the blonde. Mr. F. followed next week, with a brilliant lawyer who set about getting the Duke's estates into trouble, and a sparkling young lady of high society who fell to fascinating the Duke and impairing the appetite of the blonde. Mr. D., a dark and bloody editor of one of the dailies, followed Mr. F., the third week, introducing a mysterious Roscicrucian who transmuted metals, held consultations with the devil in a cave at dead of night, and cast the horoscope of the several heroes and heroines in such a way as to provide plenty of trouble for their future careers and breed a solemn and awful public interest in the novel. He also introduced a cloaked and masked melodramatic miscreant, put him on a salary and set him on the midnight tract of the Duke with a poisoned dagger. He also created an Irish coachman with a rich brogue and placed him in the service of the society-young-lady with an ulterior mission to carry billet-doux to the Duke.

About this time there arrived in Virginia a dissolute stranger with a literary turn of mind—rather seedy he was, but very quiet and unassuming; almost diffident, indeed. He was so gentle, and his manners were so pleasing and kindly, whether he was sober or intoxicated, that he made friends of all who came in contact with him. He applied for literary work, offered conclusive evidence that he wielded an easy and practiced pen, and so Mr. F. engaged him at once to help write the novel. His chapter was to follow Mr. D.'s, and mine was to come next. Now what does this fellow do but go off and get drunk and then proceed to his quarters and set to work with his imagination in a state of chaos, and that chaos in a condition of extravagant activity. The result may be guessed. He scanned the chapters of his predecessors, found plenty of heroes and heroines already created, and was satisfied with them; he decided to introduce no more; with all the confidence that whisky inspires and all the easy complacency it gives to its servant, he then launched himself lovingly into his work: he married the coachman to the society-young-lady for the sake of the scandal; married the Duke to the blonde's stepmother, for the sake of the sensation; stopped the desperado's salary; created a misunderstanding between the devil and the Roscicrucian; threw the Duke's property into the

wicked lawyer's hands; made the lawyer's upbraiding conscience drive him to drink, thence to *delirium tremens*, thence
to suicide; broke the coachman's neck; let his widow succumb
to contumely, neglect, poverty and consumption; caused the
blonde to drown herself, leaving her clothes on the bank with
the customary note pinned to them forgiving the Duke and
hoping he would be happy; revealed to the Duke, by means
of the usual strawberry mark on left arm, that he had married
his own long-lost mother and destroyed his long-lost sister;
instituted the proper and necessary suicide of the Duke and
the Duchess in order to compass poetical justice; opened the
earth and let the Roscicrucian through, accompanied with the
accustomed smoke and thunder and smell of brimstone, and
finished with the promise that in the next chapter, after holding a general inquest, he would take up the surviving character of the novel and tell what became of the devil!

It read with singular smoothness, and with a "dead" earnestness that was funny enough to suffocate a body. But there
was war when it came in. The other novelists were furious.
The mild stranger, not yet more than half sober, stood there,
under a scathing fire of vituperation, meek and bewildered,
looking from one to another of his assailants, and wondering
what he could have done to invoke such a storm. When a lull
came at last, he said his say gently and appealingly—said he
did not rightly remember what he had written, but was sure
he had tried to do the best he could, and knew his object had
been to make the novel not only pleasant and plausible but
instructive and—

The bombardment began again. The novelists assailed his
ill-chosen adjectives and demolished them with a storm of de-
nunciation and ridicule. And so the siege went on. Every time
the stranger tried to appease the enemy he only made matters
worse. Finally he offered to rewrite the chapter. This arrested
hostilities. The indignation gradually quieted down, peace
reigned again and the sufferer retired in safety and got him to
his own citadel.

But on the way thither the evil angel tempted him and he
got drunk again. And again his imagination went mad. He
led the heroes and heroines a wilder dance than ever; and yet
all through it ran that same convincing air of honesty and

earnestness that had marked his first work. He got the characters into the most extraordinary situations, put them through the most surprising performances, and made them talk the strangest talk! But the chapter cannot be described. It was symmetrically crazy; it was artistically absurd; and it had explanatory footnotes that were fully as curious as the text. I remember one of the "situations," and will offer it as an example of the whole. He altered the character of the brilliant lawyer, and made him a great-hearted, splendid fellow; gave him fame and riches, and set his age at thirty-three years. Then he made the blonde discover, through the help of the Roscicrucian and the melodramatic miscreant, that while the Duke loved her money ardently and wanted it, he secretly felt a sort of leaning toward the society-young-lady. Stung to the quick, she tore her affections from him and bestowed them with tenfold power upon the lawyer, who responded with consuming zeal. But the parents would none of it. What they wanted in the family was a Duke; and a Duke they were determined to have; though they confessed that next to the Duke the lawyer had their preference. Necessarily the blonde now went into a decline. The parents were alarmed. They pleaded with her to marry the Duke, but she steadfastly refused, and pined on. Then they laid a plan. They told her to wait a year and a day, and if at the end of that time she still felt that she could not marry the Duke, she might marry the lawyer with their full consent. The result was as they had foreseen: gladness came again, and the flush of returning health. Then the parents took the next step in their scheme. They had the family physician recommend a long sea voyage and much land travel for the thorough restoration of the blonde's strength; and they invited the Duke to be of the party. They judged that the Duke's constant presence and the lawyer's protracted absence would do the rest—for they did not invite the lawyer.

So they set sail in a steamer for America—and the third day out, when their sea-sickness called truce and permitted them to take their first meal at the public table, behold there sat the lawyer! The Duke and party made the best of an awkward situation; the voyage progressed, and the vessel neared America. But, by and by, two hundred miles off New Bedford, the ship took fire; she burned to the water's edge; of all her crew and passengers, only thirty were saved. They floated about the sea half an afternoon and all night long. Among them were our friends. The lawyer, by superhuman exertions, had saved the blonde and her parents, swimming back and forth two hundred yards and bringing one each time—(the girl first). The Duke had saved himself. In the morning two whale ships arrived on the scene and sent their boats. The weather was stormy and the embarkation was attended with much confusion and excitement. The lawyer did his duty like a man; helped his exhausted and insensible blonde, her parents and some others into a boat (the Duke helped himself in); then a child fell overboard at the other end of the raft and the lawyer rushed thither and helped half a dozen people fish it out, under the stimulus of its mother's screams. Then he ran back—a few seconds too late—the blonde's boat was under way. So he had to take the other boat, and go to the other ship. The storm increased and drove the vessels out of sight of each other—drove them whither it would. When it calmed, at the end of three days, the blonde's ship was seven hundred miles north of Boston and the other about seven hundred south of that port. The blonde's captain was bound on a whaling cruise in the North Atlantic and could not go back such a distance or make a port without orders; such being nautical law. The lawyer's captain was to cruise in the North Pacific, and *he* could not go back or make a port without orders. All the lawyer's money and baggage were in the blonde's boat and went to the blonde's ship—so his captain made him work his passage as a common sailor. When both ships had been cruising nearly a year, the one was off the coast of Greenland and the other in Behring's Strait. The blonde had long ago been well-nigh persuaded that her lawyer had been washed overboard and lost just before the whale ships reached the raft, and now, under the pleadings of her parents and the Duke she was at last beginning to nerve herself for the doom of the covenant, and prepare for the hated marriage. But she would not yield a day before the date set. The weeks dragged on, the time narrowed, orders were given to deck the ship for the wedding—a wedding at sea among icebergs and walruses. Five days more and all would be over.

So the blonde reflected, with a sigh and a tear. Oh where was her true love—and why, why did he not come and save her? At that moment he was lifting his harpoon to strike a whale in Behring's Strait, five thousand miles away, by the way of the Arctic Ocean, or twenty thousand by the way of the Horn—that was the reason. He struck, but not with perfect aim—his foot slipped and he fell in the whale's mouth and went down his throat. He was insensible five days. Then he came to himself and heard voices; daylight was streaming through a hole cut in the whale's roof. He climbed out and astonished the sailors who were hoisting blubber up a ship's side. He recognized the vessel, flew aboard, surprised the wedding party at the altar and exclaimed:

"Stop the proceedings—I'm here! Come to my arms, my own!"

There were foot-notes to this extravagant piece of literature wherein the author endeavored to show that the whole thing was within the possibilities; he said he got the incident of the whale traveling from Behring's Strait to the coast of Greenland, five thousand miles in five days, through the Arctic Ocean, from Charles Reade's "Love Me Little Love Me Long," and considered that that established the fact that the thing could be done; and he instanced Jonah's adventure as proof that a man could live in a whale's belly, and added that if a preacher could stand it three days a lawyer could surely stand it five!

There was a fiercer storm than ever in the editorial sanctum now, and the stranger was peremptorily discharged, and his manuscript flung at his head. But he had already delayed things so much that there was not time for some one else to rewrite the chapter, and so the paper came out without any novel in it. It was but a feeble, struggling, stupid journal, and the absence of the novel probably shook public confidence; at any rate, before the first side of the next issue went to press, the *Weekly Occidental* died as peacefully as an infant.

An effort was made to resurrect it, with the proposed advantage of a telling new title, and Mr. F. said that *The Phenix* would be just the name for it, because it would give the idea of a resurrection from its dead ashes in a new and undreamed of condition of splendor; but some low-priced smarty on one of the dailies suggested that we call it the *Lazarus*; and inasmuch as the people were not profound in Scriptural matters but thought the resurrected Lazarus and the dilapidated mendicant that begged in the rich man's gateway were one and the same person, the name became the laughing stock of the town, and killed the paper for good and all.

I was sorry enough, for I was very proud of being connected with a literary paper—prouder than I have ever been of anything since, perhaps. I had written some rhymes for it—poetry I considered it—and it was a great grief to me that the production was on the "first side" of the issue that was not completed, and hence did not see the light. But time brings its revenges—I can put it in here; it will answer in place of a tear dropped to the memory of the lost *Occidental*. The idea (not the chief idea, but the vehicle that bears it) was probably suggested by the old song called "The Raging Canal," but I cannot remember now. I do remember, though, that at that time I thought my doggerel was one of the ablest poems of the age:

THE AGED PILOT MAN.

On the Erie Canal, it was,
    All on a summer's day,
I sailed forth with my parents
    Far away to Albany.

From out the clouds at noon that day
    There came a dreadful storm,
That piled the billows high about,
    And filled us with alarm.

A man came rushing from a house,
    Saying, "Snub up* your boat I pray,
Snub up your boat, snub up, alas,
    Snub up while yet you may."

Our captain cast one glance astern,
    Then forward glanced he,

---

*The customary canal technicality for "tie up."

And said, "My wife and little ones
   I never more shall see."

Said Dollinger the pilot man,
   In noble words, but few,—
"Fear not, but lean on Dollinger,
   And he will fetch you through."

The boat drove on, the frightened mules
   Tore through the rain and wind,
And bravely still, in danger's post,
   The whip-boy strode behind.

"Come 'board, come 'board," the captain cried,
   "Nor tempt so wild a storm;"
But still the raging mules advanced,
   And still the boy strode on.

Then said the captain to us all,
   "Alas, 'tis plain to me,
The greater danger is not there,
   But here upon the sea.

So let us strive, while life remains,
   To save all souls on board,
And then if die at last we must,
   Let . . . . I *cannot* speak the word!"

Said Dollinger the pilot man,
   Tow'ring above the crew,
"Fear not, but trust in Dollinger,
   And he will fetch you through."

"Low bridge! low bridge!" all heads went down,
   The laboring bark sped on;
A mill we passed, we passed a church,
   Hamlets, and fields of corn;
And all the world came out to see,
   And chased along the shore

Crying, "Alas, alas, the sheeted rain,
   The wind, the tempest's roar!
Alas, the gallant ship and crew,
   Can *nothing* help them more?"

And from our deck sad eyes looked out
   Across the stormy scene:
The tossing wake of billows aft,
   The bending forests green,
The chickens sheltered under carts
   In lee of barn the cows,
The skurrying swine with straw in mouth,
   The wild spray from our bows!

   "She balances!
    She wavers!
Now let her go about!
   If she misses stays and broaches to,
We're all"—[then with a shout,]
   "Huray! huray!
    Avast! belay!
    Take in more sail!
    Lord, what a gale!
Ho, boy, haul taut on the hind mule's tail!"

"Ho! lighten ship! ho! man the pump!
   Ho, hostler, heave the lead!
And count ye all, both great and small,
   As numbered with the dead!
For mariner for forty year,
   On Erie, boy and man,
I never yet saw such a storm,
   Or one 't with it began!"

So overboard a keg of nails
   And anvils three we threw,
Likewise four bales of gunny-sacks,
   Two hundred pounds of glue,
Two sacks of corn, four ditto wheat,

A box of books, a cow,
A violin, Lord Byron's works,
  A rip-saw and a sow.

A curve! a curve! the dangers grow!
  "Labbord!—stabbord!—s-t-e-a-d-y!—so!—
Hard-a-port, Dol!—hellum-a-lee!
  Haw the head mule!—the aft one gee!
Luff!—bring her to the wind!"

"A quarter-three!—'tis shoaling fast!
  Three feet large!—t-h-r-e-e feet!—
Three feet scant!" I cried in fright
  "Oh, is there *no* retreat?"

Said Dollinger, the pilot man,
  As on the vessel flew,
"Fear not, but trust in Dollinger,
  And he will fetch you through."

A panic struck the bravest hearts,
  The boldest cheek turned pale;
For plain to all, this shoaling said
A leak had burst the ditch's bed!
And, straight as bolt from crossbow sped,
Our ship swept on, with shoaling lead,
  Before the fearful gale!

"Sever the tow-line! Cripple the mules!"
  Too late! . . . . . There comes a shock!
*   *   *   *   *   *
Another length, and the fated craft
  Would have swum in the saving lock!

Then gathered together the shipwrecked crew
  And took one last embrace,
While sorrowful tears from despairing eyes
  Ran down each hopeless face;
And some did think of their little ones
  Whom they never more might see,

And others of waiting wives at home,
    And mothers that grieved would be.

But of all the children of misery there
    On that poor sinking frame,
But one spake words of hope and faith,
    And I worshipped as they came:
Said Dollinger the pilot man,—
    (O brave heart, strong and true!)—
"Fear not, but trust in Dollinger,
    For he will fetch you through."

Lo! scarce the words have passed his lips
    The dauntless prophet say'th,
When every soul about him seeth
    A wonder crown his faith!

For straight a farmer brought a plank,—
    (Mysteriously inspired)—
And laying it unto the ship,
    In silent awe retired.

Then every sufferer stood amazed
    That pilot man before;
A moment stood. Then wondering turned,
    And speechless walked ashore.

Chapter LII

S INCE I DESIRE, in this chapter, to say an instructive word or two about the silver mines, the reader may take this fair warning and skip, if he chooses. The year 1863 was perhaps the very top blossom and culmination of the "flush times." Virginia swarmed with men and vehicles to that degree that the place looked like a very hive—that is when one's vision could pierce through the thick fog of alkali dust that was generally blowing in summer. I will say, concerning this dust, that if you drove ten miles through it, you and your horses would be coated with it a sixteenth of an inch thick and present an outside appearance that was a uniform pale yellow color, and your buggy would have three inches of dust in it, thrown there by the wheels. The delicate scales used by the assayers were inclosed in glass cases intended to be airtight, and yet some of this dust was so impalpable and so invisibly fine that it would get in, somehow, and impair the accuracy of those scales.

Speculation ran riot, and yet there was a world of substantial business going on, too. All freights were brought over the mountains from California (150 miles) by pack-train partly, and partly in huge wagons drawn by such long mule teams that each team amounted to a procession, and it did seem, sometimes, that the grand combined procession of animals stretched unbroken from Virginia to California. Its long route was traceable clear across the deserts of the Territory by the writhing serpent of dust it lifted up. By these wagons, freights over that hundred and fifty miles were $200 a ton for small lots (same price for all express matter brought by stage), and $100 a ton for full loads. One Virginia firm received one hundred tons of freight a month, and paid $10,000 a month freightage. In the winter the freights were much higher. All the bullion was shipped in bars by stage to San Francisco (a bar was usually about twice the size of a pig of lead and contained from $1,500 to $3,000 according to the amount of gold mixed with the silver), and the freight on it (when the shipment was large) was one and a quarter per cent. of its intrinsic value. So, the freight on these bars probably averaged something more than $25 each. Small shippers paid two per cent. There were three stages a day, each way, and I have seen the out-going stages carry away a third of a ton of bullion each, and more than once I saw them divide a two-ton lot and take it off. However, these were extraordinary events.*

Two tons of silver bullion would be in the neighborhood of forty bars, and the freight on it over $1,000. Each coach always carried a deal of ordinary express matter beside, and also from fifteen to twenty passengers at from $25 to $30 a head. With six stages going all the time, Wells, Fargo and Co.'s Virginia City business was important and lucrative.

All along under the centre of Virginia and Gold Hill, for a couple of miles, ran the great Comstock silver lode—a vein of ore from fifty to eighty feet thick between its solid walls of rock—a vein as wide as some of New York's streets. I will

---

*Mr. Valentine, Wells Fargo's agent, has handled all the bullion shipped through the Virginia office for many a month. To his memory—which is excellent—we are indebted for the following exhibit of the company's business in the Virginia office since the first of January, 1862: From January 1st to April 1st, about $270,000 worth of bullion passed through that office; during the next quarter, $570,000; next quarter, $800,000; next quarter, $956,000; next quarter, $1,275,000; and for the quarter ending on the 30th of last June, about $1,600,000. Thus in a year and a half, the Virginia office only shipped $5,330,000 in bullion. During the year 1862 they shipped $2,615,000, so we perceive the average shipments have more than doubled in the last six months. This gives us room to promise for the Virginia office $500,000 a month for the year 1863 (though perhaps, judging by the steady increase in the business, we are under estimating, somewhat). This gives us $6,000,000 for the year. Gold Hill and Silver City together can beat us—we will give them $10,000,000. To Dayton, Empire City, Ophir and Carson City, we will allow an aggregate of $8,000,000, which is not over the mark, perhaps, and may possibly be a little under it. To Esmeralda we give $4,000,000. To Reese River and Humboldt $2,000,000, which is liberal now, but may not be before the year is out. So we prognosticate that the yield of bullion this year will be about $30,000,000. Placing the number of mills in the Territory at one hundred, this gives to each the labor of producing $300,000 in bullion during the twelve months. Allowing them to run three hundred days in the year (which none of them more than do), this makes their work average $1,000 a day. Say the mills average twenty tons of rock a day and this rock worth $50 as a general thing, and you have the actual work of our one hundred mills figured down "to a spot"—$1,000 a day each, and $30,000,000 a year in the aggregate.—*Enterprise*.

[A considerable over estimate.—M. T.]

remind the reader that in Pennsylvania a coal vein only eight feet wide is considered ample.

Virginia was a busy city of streets and houses above ground. Under it was another busy city, down in the bowels of the earth, where a great population of men thronged in and out among an intricate maze of tunnels and drifts, flitting hither and thither under a winking sparkle of lights, and over their heads towered a vast web of interlocking timbers that held the walls of the gutted Comstock apart. These timbers were as large as a man's body, and the framework stretched upward so far that no eye could pierce to its top through the closing gloom. It was like peering up through the clean-picked ribs and bones of some colossal skeleton. Imagine such a framework two miles long, sixty feet wide, and higher than any church spire in America. Imagine this stately lattice-work stretching down Broadway, from the St. Nicholas to Wall street, and a Fourth of July procession, reduced to pigmies, parading on top of it and flaunting their flags, high above the pinnacle of Trinity steeple. One can imagine that, but he cannot well imagine what that forest of timbers cost, from the time they were felled in the pineries beyond Washoe Lake, hauled up and around Mount Davidson at atrocious rates of freightage, then squared, let down into the deep maw of the mine and built up there. Twenty ample fortunes would not timber one of the greatest of those silver mines. The Spanish proverb says it requires a gold mine to "run" a silver one, and it is true. A beggar with a silver mine is a pitiable pauper indeed if he cannot sell.

I spoke of the underground Virginia as a city. The Gould and Curry is only one single mine under there, among a great many others; yet the Gould and Curry's streets of dismal drifts and tunnels were five miles in extent, altogether, and its population five hundred miners. Taken as a whole, the underground city had some thirty miles of streets and a population of five or six thousand. In this present day some of those populations are at work from twelve to sixteen hundred feet under Virginia and Gold Hill, and the signal-bells that tell them what the superintendent above ground desires them to do are struck by telegraph as we strike a fire alarm. Sometimes men fall down a shaft, there, a thousand feet deep. In such cases, the usual plan is to hold an inquest.

If you wish to visit one of those mines, you may walk through a tunnel about half a mile long if you prefer it, or you may take the quicker plan of shooting like a dart down a shaft, on a small platform. It is like tumbling down through an empty steeple, feet first. When you reach the bottom, you take a candle and tramp through drifts and tunnels where throngs of men are digging and blasting; you watch them send up tubs full of great lumps of stone—silver ore; you select choice specimens from the mass, as souvenirs; you admire the world of skeleton timbering; you reflect frequently that you are buried under a mountain, a thousand feet below daylight; being in the bottom of the mine you climb from "gallery" to "gallery," up endless ladders that stand straight up and down; when your legs fail you at last, you lie down in a small box-car in a cramped "incline" like a half-up-ended sewer and are dragged up to daylight feeling as if you are crawling through a coffin that has no end to it. Arrived at the top, you find a busy crowd of men receiving the ascending cars and tubs and dumping the ore from an elevation into long rows of bins capable of holding half a dozen tons each; under the bins are rows of wagons loading from chutes and trap-doors in the bins, and down the long street is a procession of these wagons wending toward the silver mills with their rich freight. It is all "done," now, and there you are. You need never go down again, for you have seen it all. If you have forgotten the process of reducing the ore in the mill and making the silver bars, you can go back and find it again in my Esmeralda chapters if so disposed.

Of course these mines cave in, in places, occasionally, and then it is worth one's while to take the risk of descending into them and observing the crushing power exerted by the pressing weight of a settling mountain. I published such an experience in the *Enterprise*, once, and from it I will take an extract:

An Hour in the Caved Mines.—We journeyed down into the Ophir mine, yesterday, to see the earthquake. We could not go down the deep incline, because it still has a propensity to cave in places. Therefore we traveled through the long tunnel which enters the hill above the Ophir office, and then by means of a series of long ladders, climbed away down from the first to the fourth gallery. Traversing a drift, we came to the Spanish line, passed five sets of timbers still uninjured, and found the earthquake. Here was as complete a chaos as ever was seen—vast masses of earth and splintered and broken timbers piled confusedly together, with scarcely an aperture left large enough for a cat to creep through. Rubbish was still falling at intervals from above, and one timber which had braced others earlier in the day, was *now* crushed down out of its former position, showing that the caving and settling of the tremendous mass was still going on. We were in that portion of the Ophir known as the "north mines." Returning to the surface, we entered a tunnel leading into the Central, for the purpose of getting into the main Ophir. Descending a long incline in this tunnel, we traversed a drift or so, and then went down a deep shaft from whence we proceeded into the fifth gallery of the Ophir. From a side-drift we crawled through a small hole and got into the midst of the earthquake again—earth and broken timbers mingled together without regard to grace or symmetry. A large portion of the second, third and fourth galleries had caved in and gone to destruction—the two latter at seven o'clock on the previous evening.

At the turn-table, near the northern extremity of the fifth gallery, two big piles of rubbish had forced their way through from the fifth gallery, and from the looks of the timbers, more was about to come. These beams are solid—eighteen inches square; first, a great beam is laid on the floor, then upright ones, five feet high, stand on it, supporting another horizontal beam, and so on, square above square, like the framework of a window. The superincumbent weight was sufficient to mash the ends of those great upright beams fairly into the solid wood of the horizontal ones three inches, compressing and bending the upright beam till it curved like a bow. Before the Spanish caved in, some of their twelve-inch horizontal timbers were compressed in this way until they were only five inches thick! Imagine the power it must take to squeeze a solid log together in that way. Here, also, was a range of timbers, for a distance of twenty feet, tilted six inches out of the perpendicular by the weight resting upon them from the caved galleries above. You could hear things cracking and giving way, and it was not pleasant to know that the world overhead was slowly and silently sinking down upon you. The men down in the mine do not mind it, however.

Returning along the fifth gallery, we struck the safe part of the Ophir incline, and went down it to the sixth; but we found ten inches of water there, and had to come back. In repairing the damage done to the incline, the pump had to be stopped for two hours, and in the meantime the water gained about a foot. However, the pump was at work again, and the flood-water was decreasing. We climbed up to the fifth gallery again and sought a deep shaft, whereby we might descend to another part of the sixth, out of reach of the water, but suffered disappointment, as the men had gone to dinner, and there was no one to man the windlass. So, having seen the earthquake, we climbed out at the Union incline and tunnel, and adjourned, all dripping with candle grease and perspiration, to lunch at the Ophir office.

During the great flush year of 1863, Nevada [claims to have] produced $25,000,000 in bullion—almost, if not quite, a round million to each thousand inhabitants, which is very well, considering that she was without agriculture and manufactures.* Silver mining was her sole productive industry.

*Since the above was in type, I learn from an official source that the above figure is too high, and that the yield for 1863 did not exceed $20,000,000. However, the day for large figures is approaching; the Sutro Tunnel is to plow through the Comstock lode from end to end, at a depth of two thousand feet, and then mining will be easy and comparatively inexpensive; and the momentous matters of drainage, and hoisting and hauling of ore will cease to be burdensome. This vast work will absorb many years, and millions of dollars, in its completion; but it will early yield money, for that desirable epoch will begin as soon as it strikes the first end of the vein. The tunnel will be some eight miles long, and will develop astonishing riches. Cars will carry the ore through the tunnel and dump it in the mills and thus do away with the present costly system of double handling and transportation by mule teams. The water from the tunnel will furnish the motive power for the mills. Mr. Sutro, the originator of this prodigious enterprise, is one of the few men in the world who is gifted with the pluck and perseverance necessary to follow up and hound such an undertaking to its completion. He has converted several obstinate Congresses to a deserved friendliness toward his important work, and has gone up and down and to and fro in Europe until he has enlisted a great moneyed interest in it there.

Chapter LIII

EVERY NOW and then, in these days, the boys used to tell me I ought to get one Jim Blaine to tell me the stirring story of his grandfather's old ram—but they always added that I must not mention the matter unless Jim was drunk at the time—just comfortably and sociably drunk. They kept this up until my curiosity was on the rack to hear the story. I got to haunting Blaine; but it was of no use, the boys always found fault with his condition; he was often moderately but never satisfactorily drunk. I never watched a man's condition with such absorbing interest, such anxious solicitude; I never so pined to see a man uncompromisingly drunk before. At last, one evening I hurried to his cabin, for I learned that this time his situation was such that even the most fastidious could find no fault with it—he was tranquilly, serenely, symmetrically drunk—not a hiccup to mar his voice, not a cloud upon his brain thick enough to obscure his memory. As I entered, he was sitting upon an empty powder-keg, with a clay pipe in one hand and the other raised to command silence. His face was round, red, and very serious; his throat was bare and his hair tumbled; in general appearance and costume he was a stalwart miner of the period. On the pine table stood a candle, and its dim light revealed "the boys" sitting here and there on bunks, candle-boxes, powder-kegs, etc. They said:

"Sh—! Don't speak—he's going to commence."

THE STORY OF THE OLD RAM.

I found a seat at once, and Blaine said:

"I don't reckon them times will ever come again. There never was a more bullier old ram than what he was. Grandfather fetched him from Illinois—got him of a man by the name of Yates—Bill Yates—maybe you might have heard of him; his father was a deacon—Baptist—and he was a rustler, too; a man had to get up ruther early to get the start of old Thankful Yates; it was him that put the Greens up to jining teams with my grandfather when he moved west. Seth Green

was prob'ly the pick of the flock; he married a Wilkerson—
Sarah Wilkerson—good cretur, she was—one of the likeliest
heifers that was ever raised in old Stoddard, everybody said
that knowed her. She could heft a bar'l of flour as easy as I
can flirt a flapjack. And spin? Don't mention it! Independent?
Humph! When Sile Hawkins come a browsing around her,
she let him know that for all his tin he couldn't trot in harness
alongside of *her*. You see, Sile Hawkins was—no, it warn't
Sile Hawkins, after all—it was a galoot by the name of Fil-
kins—I disremember his first name; but he *was* a stump—
come into pra'r meeting drunk, one night, hooraying for
Nixon, becuz he thought it was a primary; and old deacon
Ferguson up and scooted him through the window and he lit
on old Miss Jefferson's head, poor old filly. She was a good
soul—had a glass eye and used to lend it to old Miss Wagner,
that hadn't any, to receive company in; it warn't big enough,
and when Miss Wagner warn't noticing, it would get twisted
around in the socket, and look up, maybe, or out to one side,
and every which way, while t' other one was looking as
straight ahead as a spy-glass. Grown people didn't mind it,
but it most always made the children cry, it was so sort of
scary. She tried packing it in raw cotton, but it wouldn't
work, somehow—the cotton would get loose and stick out
and look so kind of awful that the children couldn't stand it
no way. She was always dropping it out, and turning up her
old dead-light on the company empty, and making them on-
comfortable, becuz *she* never could tell when it hopped out,
being blind on that side, you see. So somebody would have
to hunch her and say, "Your game eye has fetched loose, Miss
Wagner dear"—and then all of them would have to sit and
wait till she jammed it in again—wrong side before, as a general thing, and green as a bird's egg, being a bashful cretur
and easy sot back before company. But being wrong side before warn't much difference, anyway, becuz her own eye was
sky-blue and the glass one was yaller on the front side, so
whichever way she turned it it didn't match nohow. Old Miss
Wagner was considerable on the borrow, she was. When she
had a quilting, or Dorcas S'iety at her house she gen'ally borrowed Miss Higgins's wooden leg to stump around on; it was
considerable shorter than her other pin, but much *she* minded

that. She said she couldn't abide crutches when she had company, becuz they were so slow; said when she had company
and things had to be done, she wanted to get up and hump
herself. She was as bald as a jug, and so she used to borrow
Miss Jacops's wig—Miss Jacops was the coffin-peddler's
wife—a ratty old buzzard, he was, that used to go roosting
around where people was sick, waiting for 'em; and there that
old rip would sit all day, in the shade, on a coffin that he
judged would fit the can'idate; and if it was a slow customer
and kind of uncertain, he'd fetch his rations and a blanket
along and sleep in the coffin nights. He was anchored out
that way, in frosty weather, for about three weeks, once, before old Robbins's place, waiting for him; and after that, for
as much as two years, Jacops was not on speaking terms with
the old man, on account of his disapp'inting him. He got one
of his feet froze, and lost money, too, becuz old Robbins
took a favorable turn and got well. The next time Robbins
got sick, Jacops tried to make up with him, and varnished up
the same old coffin and fetched it along; but old Robbins was
too many for him; he had him in, and 'peared to be powerful
weak; he bought the coffin for ten dollars and Jacops was to
pay it back and twenty-five more besides if Robbins didn't
like the coffin after he'd tried it. And then Robbins died, and
at the funeral he bursted off the lid and riz up in his shroud
and told the parson to let up on the performances, becuz he
could *not* stand such a coffin as that. You see he had been in
a trance once before, when he was young, and he took the
chances on another, cal'lating that if he made the trip it was
money in his pocket, and if he missed fire he couldn't lose a
cent. And by George he sued Jacops for the rhino and got
jedgment; and he set up the coffin in his back parlor and said
he 'lowed to take his time, now. It was always an aggravation
to Jacops, the way that miserable old thing acted. He moved
back to Indiany pretty soon—went to Wellsville—Wellsville
was the place the Hogadorns was from. Mighty fine family.
Old Maryland stock. Old Squire Hogadorn could carry
around more mixed licker, and cuss better than most any man
I ever see. His second wife was the widder Billings—she that
was Becky Martin; her dam was deacon Dunlap's first wife.
Her oldest child, Maria, married a missionary and died in

grace—et up by the savages. They et *him*, too, poor feller—
biled him. It warn't the custom, so they say, but they explained to friends of his'n that went down there to bring
away his things, that they'd tried missionaries every other
way and never could get any good out of 'em—and so it
annoyed all his relations to find out that that man's life was
fooled away just out of a dern'd experiment, so to speak. But
mind you, there ain't anything ever reely lost; everything that
people can't understand and don't see the reason of does
good if you only hold on and give it a fair shake; Prov'dence
don't fire no blank ca'tridges, boys. That there missionary's
substance, unbeknowns to himself, actu'ly converted every
last one of them heathens that took a chance at the barbacue.
Nothing ever fetched them but that. Don't tell *me* it was an
accident that he was biled. There ain't no such a thing as an
accident. When my uncle Lem was leaning up agin a scaffold-
ing once, sick, or drunk, or suthin, an Irishman with a hod
full of bricks fell on him out of the third story and broke the
old man's back in two places. People said it was an accident.
Much accident there was about that. He didn't know what he
was there for, but he was there for a good object. If he hadn't
been there the Irishman would have been killed. Nobody can
ever make me believe anything different from that. Uncle
Lem's dog was there. Why didn't the Irishman fall on the
dog? Becuz the dog would a seen him a coming and stood
from under. That's the reason the dog warn't appinted. A
dog can't be depended on to carry out a special providence.
Mark my words it was a put-up thing. Accidents don't happen, boys. Uncle Lem's dog—I wish you could a seen that
dog. He was a reglar shepherd—or ruther he was part bull
and part shepherd—splendid animal; belonged to parson Hagar before Uncle Lem got him. Parson Hagar belonged to the
Western Reserve Hagars; prime family; his mother was a Watson; one of his sisters married a Wheeler; they settled in Morgan county, and he got nipped by the machinery in a carpet
factory and went through in less than a quarter of a minute;
his widder bought the piece of carpet that had his remains
wove in, and people come a hundred mile to 'tend the funeral. There was fourteen yards in the piece. She wouldn't let
them roll him up, but planted him just so—full length. The

church was middling small where they preached the funeral, and they had to let one end of the coffin stick out of the window. They didn't bury him—they planted one end, and let him stand up, same as a monument. And they nailed a sign on it and put—put on—put on it—sacred to—the m-e-m-o-r-y—of fourteen y-a-r-d-s—of three-ply—car - - - pet—containing all that was—m-o-r-t-a-l—of—of—W-i-l-l-i-a-m—W-h-e—"

Jim Blaine had been growing gradually drowsy and drows-ier—his head nodded, once, twice, three times—dropped peacefully upon his breast, and he fell tranquilly asleep. The tears were running down the boys' cheeks—they were suffo-cating with suppressed laughter—and had been from the start, though I had never noticed it. I perceived that I was "sold." I learned then that Jim Blaine's peculiarity was that whenever he reached a certain stage of intoxication, no hu-man power could keep him from setting out, with impressive unction, to tell about a wonderful adventure which he had once had with his grandfather's old ram—and the mention of the ram in the first sentence was as far as any man had ever heard him get, concerning it. He always maundered off, in-terminably, from one thing to another, till his whisky got the best of him and he fell asleep. What the thing was that hap-pened to him and his grandfather's old ram is a dark mystery to this day, for nobody has ever yet found out.

Chapter LIV

O F COURSE there was a large Chinese population in Virginia—it is the case with every town and city on the Pacific coast. They are a harmless race when white men either let them alone or treat them no worse than dogs; in fact they are almost entirely harmless anyhow, for they seldom think of resenting the vilest insults or the cruelest injuries. They are quiet, peaceable, tractable, free from drunkenness, and they are as industrious as the day is long. A disorderly Chinaman is rare, and a lazy one does not exist. So long as a Chinaman has strength to use his hands he needs no support from anybody; white men often complain of want of work, but a Chinaman offers no such complaint; he always manages to find something to do. He is a great convenience to everybody—even to the worst class of white men, for he bears the most of their sins, suffering fines for their petty thefts, imprisonment for their robberies, and death for their murders. Any white man can swear a Chinaman's life away in the courts, but no Chinaman can testify against a white man. Ours is the "land of the free"—nobody denies that—nobody challenges it. [Maybe it is because we won't let other people testify.] As I write, news comes that in broad daylight in San Francisco, some boys have stoned an inoffensive Chinaman to death, and that although a large crowd witnessed the shameful deed, no one interfered.

There are seventy thousand (and possibly one hundred thousand) Chinamen on the Pacific coast. There were about a thousand in Virginia. They were penned into a "Chinese quarter"—a thing which they do not particularly object to, as they are fond of herding together. Their buildings were of wood; usually only one story high, and set thickly together along streets scarcely wide enough for a wagon to pass through. Their quarter was a little removed from the rest of the town. The chief employment of Chinamen in towns is to wash clothing. They always send a bill, like this below, pinned to the clothes.

It is mere ceremony, for it does not enlighten the customer much. Their price for washing was $2.50 per dozen—rather cheaper than white people could afford to wash for at that time. A very common sign on the Chinese houses was: "See Yup, Washer and Ironer"; "Hong Wo, Washer"; "Sam Sing & Ah Hop, Washing." The house servants, cooks, etc., in California and Nevada, were chiefly Chinamen. There were few white servants and no China-women so employed. Chinamen make good house servants, being quick, obedient, patient, quick to learn and tirelessly industrious. They do not need to be taught a thing twice, as a general thing. They are imitative. If a Chinaman were to see his master break up a centre table, in a passion, and kindle a fire with it, that Chinaman would be likely to resort to the furniture for fuel forever afterward.

All Chinamen can read, write and cipher with easy facility—pity but all our petted *voters* could. In California they rent little patches of ground and do a deal of gardening. They will raise surprising crops of vegetables on a sand pile. They waste nothing. What is rubbish to a Christian, a Chinaman carefully preserves and makes useful in one way or another. He gathers up all the old oyster and sardine cans that white people throw away, and procures marketable tin and solder from them by melting. He gathers up old bones and turns them into manure. In California he gets a living out of old mining claims that white men have abandoned as exhausted and worthless—and then the officers come down on him once a month with an exorbitant swindle to which the legislature has given the broad, general name of "foreign" mining tax, but it is usually inflicted on no foreigners but Chinamen. This swindle has in some cases been repeated once or twice on the same victim in the course of the same month—but the public treasury was not additionally enriched by it, probably.

Chinamen hold their dead in great reverence—they worship their departed ancestors, in fact. Hence, in China, a man's front yard, back yard, or any other part of his premises, is made his family burying ground, in order that he may visit the graves at any and all times. Therefore that huge empire is one mighty cemetery; it is ridged and wringled from its centre to its circumference with graves—and inasmuch as every foot of ground must be made to do its utmost, in China, lest the swarming population suffer for food, the very graves are cultivated and yield a harvest, custom holding this to be no dishonor to the dead. Since the departed are held in such worshipful reverence, a Chinaman cannot bear that any indignity be offered the places where they sleep. Mr. Burlingame said that herein lay China's bitter opposition to railroads; a road could not be built anywhere in the empire without disturbing the graves of their ancestors or friends.

A Chinaman hardly believes he could enjoy the hereafter except his body lay in his beloved China; also, he desires to receive, himself, after death, that worship with which he has honored his dead that preceded him. Therefore, if he visits a foreign country, he makes arrangements to have his bones returned to China in case he dies; if he hires to go to a foreign country on a labor contract, there is always a stipulation that his body shall be taken back to China if he dies; if the government sells a gang of Coolies to a foreigner for the usual five-year term, it is specified in the contract that their bodies shall be restored to China in case of death. On the Pacific coast the Chinamen all belong to one or another of several great companies or organizations, and these companies keep track of their members, register their names, and ship their bodies home when they die. The See Yup Company is held to be the largest of these. The Ning Yeong Company is next, and numbers eighteen thousand members on the coast. Its headquarters are at San Francisco, where it has a costly temple, several great officers (one of whom keeps regal state in seclusion and cannot be approached by common humanity), and a numerous priesthood. In it I was shown a register of its members, with the dead and the date of their shipment to China duly marked. Every ship that sails from San Francisco carries away a heavy freight of Chinese corpses—or did, at least, until the legislature, with an ingenious refinement of Christian cruelty, forbade the shipments, as a neat underhanded way of deterring Chinese immigration. The bill was offered, whether it passed or not. It is my impression that it passed. There was another bill—it became a law—compelling every incoming Chinaman to be vaccinated on the wharf and pay a duly appointed quack (no decent doctor would defile himself with such legalized robbery) ten dollars for it. As few importers of Chinese would want to go to an expense like that, the law-makers thought this would be another heavy blow to Chinese immigration.

What the Chinese quarter of Virginia was like—or, indeed, what the Chinese quarter of any Pacific coast town was and is like—may be gathered from this item which I printed in the *Enterprise* while reporting for that paper:

CHINATOWN.—Accompanied by a fellow reporter, we made a trip through our Chinese quarter the other night. The Chinese have built their portion of the city to suit themselves; and as they keep neither carriages nor wagons, their streets are not wide enough, as a general thing, to admit of the passage of vehicles. At ten o'clock at night the Chinaman may be seen in all his glory. In every little cooped-up, dingy cavern of a hut, faint with the odor of burning Josh-lights and with nothing to see the gloom by save the sickly, guttering tallow candle, were two or three yellow, long-tailed vagabonds, coiled up on a sort of short truckle-bed, smoking opium, motionless and with their lustreless eyes turned inward from excess of satisfaction—or rather the recent smoker looks thus, immediately after having passed the pipe to his neighbor—for opium-smoking is a comfortless operation, and requires constant attention. A lamp sits on the bed, the length of the long pipe-stem from the smoker's mouth; he puts a pellet of opium on the end of a wire, sets it on fire, and plasters it into the pipe much as a Christian would fill a hole with putty; then he applies the bowl to the lamp and proceeds to smoke—and the stewing and frying of the drug and the gurgling of the juices in the stem would wellnigh turn the stomach of a statue. John likes it, though; it soothes him, he takes about two dozen whiffs, and then rolls over to dream, Heaven only knows what, for we could not imagine by looking at the soggy creature. Possibly in his visions he travels far away from the gross world and his regular washing, and feasts on succulent rats and birds'-nests in Paradise.

Mr. Ah Sing keeps a general grocery and provision store at No. 13 Wang street. He lavished his hospitality upon our party in the friendliest way. He had various kinds of colored and colorless wines and brandies, with unpronounceable names, imported from China in little crockery jugs, and which he offered to us in dainty little miniature wash-basins of porcelain. He offered us a mess of birds'-nests; also, small, neat sausages, of which we could have swallowed several yards if we had chosen to try, but we suspected that each link contained the corpse of a mouse, and therefore refrained. Mr. Sing had in his store a thousand articles of merchandise, curious to behold, impossible to imagine the uses of, and beyond our ability to describe.

His ducks, however, and his eggs, we could understand; the former were split open and flattened out like codfish, and came from China in that shape, and the latter were plastered over with some kind of paste which kept them fresh and palatable through the long voyage.

We found Mr. Hong Wo, No. 87 Chow-chow street, making up a lottery scheme—in fact we found a dozen others occupied in the same way in various parts of the quarter, for about every third Chinaman runs a lottery, and the balance of the tribe "buck" at it. "Tom," who speaks faultless English, and used to be chief and only cook to the *Territorial Enterprise*, when the establishment kept bachelor's hall two years ago, said that "Sometime Chinaman buy ticket one dollar hap, ketch um two tree hundred, sometime no ketch um anyting; lottery like one man fight um seventy—may-be he whip, may-be he get whip heself, welly good." However, the percentage being sixty-nine against him, the chances are, as a general thing, that "he get whip heself." We could not see that these lotteries differed in any respect from our own, save that the figures being Chinese, no ignorant white man might ever hope to succeed in telling "t'other from which;" the manner of drawing is similar to ours.

Mr. See Yup keeps a fancy store on Live Fox street. He sold us fans of white feathers, gorgeously ornamented; perfumery that smelled like Limburger cheese, Chinese pens, and watch-charms made of a stone unscratchable with steel instruments, yet polished and tinted like the inner coat of a sea-shell.* As tokens of his esteem, See Yup presented the party with gaudy plumes made of gold tinsel and trimmed with peacocks' feathers.

We ate chow-chow with chop-sticks in the celestial restaurants; our comrade chided the moon-eyed damsels in front of the houses for their want of feminine reserve; we received protecting Josh-lights from our hosts and "dickered" for a pagan God or two. Finally, we were impressed with the genius of a Chinese book-keeper; he figured up his accounts on a machine like a grid-iron with buttons strung on its bars; the different rows represented units, tens, hundreds and thousands. He fingered them with incredible rapidity—in fact, he

---

*A peculiar species of the "jade-stone"—to a Chinaman peculiarly precious.

pushed them from place to place as fast as a musical professor's fingers travel over the keys of a piano.

They are a kindly disposed, well-meaning race, and are respected and well treated by the upper classes, all over the Pacific coast. No Californian *gentleman or lady* ever abuses or oppresses a Chinaman, under any circumstances, an explanation that seems to be much needed in the East. Only the scum of the population do it—they and their children; they, and, naturally and consistently, the policemen and politicians, likewise, for these are the dust-licking pimps and slaves of the scum, there as well as elsewhere in America.

Chapter LV

I BEGAN to get tired of staying in one place so long. There was no longer satisfying variety in going down to Carson to report the proceedings of the legislature once a year, and horse-races and pumpkin-shows once in three months; (they had got to raising pumpkins and potatoes in Washoe Valley, and of course one of the first achievements of the legislature was to institute a ten-thousand-dollar Agricultural Fair to show off forty dollars' worth of those pumpkins in—however, the territorial legislature was usually spoken of as the "asylum"). I wanted to see San Francisco. I wanted to go somewhere. I wanted—I did not know *what* I wanted. I had the "spring fever" and wanted a change, principally, no doubt. Besides, a convention had framed a State Constitution; nine men out of every ten wanted an office; I believed that these gentlemen would "treat" the moneyless and the irresponsible among the population into adopting the constitution and thus wellnigh killing the country (it could not well carry such a load as a State government, since it had nothing to tax that could stand a tax, for undeveloped mines could not, and there were not fifty developed ones in the land, there was but little realty to tax, and it did seem as if nobody was ever going to think of the simple salvation of inflicting a money penalty on murder). I believed that a State government would destroy the "flush times," and I wanted to get away. I believed that the mining stocks I had on hand would soon be worth $100,000, and thought if they reached that before the Constitution was adopted, I would sell out and make myself secure from the crash the change of government was going to bring. I considered $100,000 sufficient to go home with decently, though it was but a small amount compared to what I had been expecting to return with. I felt rather down-hearted about it, but I tried to comfort myself with the reflection that with such a sum I could not fall into want. About this time a schoolmate of mine whom I had not seen since boyhood, came tramping in on foot from Reese River, a very allegory of Poverty. The son of wealthy parents, here he was, in a strange land, hungry, bootless, mantled in an ancient horse-blanket, roofed with a brimless hat, and so generally and so extravagantly dilapidated that he could have "taken the shine out of the Prodigal Son himself," as he pleasantly remarked. He wanted to borrow forty-six dollars—twenty-six to take him to San Francisco, and twenty for something else; to buy some soap with, maybe, for he needed it. I found I had but little more than the amount wanted, in my pocket; so I stepped in and borrowed forty-six dollars of a banker (on twenty days' time, without the formality of a note), and gave it him, rather than walk half a block to the office, where I had some specie laid up. If anybody had told me that it would take me two years to pay back that forty-six dollars to the banker (for I did not expect it of the Prodigal, and was not disappointed), I would have felt injured. And so would the banker.

I wanted a change. I wanted variety of some kind. It came. Mr. Goodman went away for a week and left me the post of chief editor. It destroyed me. The first day, I wrote my "leader" in the forenoon. The second day, I had no subject and put it off till the afternoon. The third day I put it off till evening, and then copied an elaborate editorial out of the "American Cyclopedia," that steadfast friend of the editor, all over this land. The fourth day I "fooled around" till midnight, and then fell back on the Cyclopedia again. The fifth day I cudgeled my brain till midnight, and then kept the press waiting while I penned some bitter personalities on six different people. The sixth day I labored in anguish till far into the night and brought forth—nothing. The paper went to press without an editorial. The seventh day I resigned. On the eighth, Mr. Goodman returned and found six duels on his hands—my personalities had borne fruit.

Nobody, except he has tried it, knows what it is to be an editor. It is easy to scribble local rubbish, with the facts all before you; it is easy to clip selections from other papers; it is easy to string out a correspondence from any locality; but it is unspeakable hardship to write editorials. *Subjects* are the trouble—the dreary lack of them, I mean. Every day, it is drag, drag, drag—think, and worry and suffer—all the world is a dull blank, and yet the editorial columns *must* be filled. Only give the editor a *subject*, and his work is done—it is no trouble to write it up; but fancy how you would feel if you had to pump your brains dry every day in the week, fifty-two weeks in the year. It makes one low spirited simply to think of it. The matter that each editor of a daily paper in America writes in the course of a year would fill from four to eight bulky volumes like this book! Fancy what a library an editor's work would make, after twenty or thirty years' service. Yet people often marvel that Dickens, Scott, Bulwer, Dumas, etc., have been able to produce so many books. If these authors had wrought as voluminously as newspaper editors do, the result would be something to marvel at, indeed. How editors can continue this tremendous labor, this exhausting consumption of brain fibre (for their work is creative, and not a mere mechanical laying-up of facts, like reporting), day after day and year after year, is incomprehensible. Preachers take two months' holiday in midsummer, for they find that to produce two sermons a week is wearing, in the long run. In truth it must be so, and is so; and therefore, how an editor can take from ten to twenty texts and build upon them from ten to twenty painstaking editorials a week and keep it up all the year round, is farther beyond comprehension than ever. Ever since I survived my week as editor, I have found at least one pleasure in any newspaper that comes to my hand; it is in admiring the long columns of editorial, and wondering to myself how in the mischief he did it!

Mr. Goodman's return relieved me of employment, unless I chose to become a reporter again. I could not do that; I could not serve in the ranks after being General of the army. So I thought I would depart and go abroad into the world somewhere. Just at this juncture, Dan, my associate in the reportorial department, told me, casually, that two citizens had been trying to persuade him to go with them to New York and aid in selling a rich silver mine which they had discovered and secured in a new mining district in our neighborhood. He said they offered to pay his expenses and give him one third of the proceeds of the sale. He had refused to go. It was the very opportunity I wanted. I abused him for keeping so quiet about it, and not mentioning it sooner. He said it had not occurred to him that I would like to go, and so he had recommended them to apply to Marshall, the reporter of the other paper. I asked Dan if it was a good, honest mine, and no swindle. He said the men had shown him nine tons of the rock, which they had got out to take to New York, and he could cheerfully say that he had seen but little rock in Nevada that was richer; and moreover, he said that they had secured a tract of valuable timber and a mill-site, near the mine. My first idea was to kill Dan. But I changed my mind, notwithstanding I was so angry, for I thought maybe the chance was not yet lost. Dan said it was by no means lost; that the men were absent at the mine again, and would not be in Virginia to leave for the East for some ten days; that they had requested him to do the talking to Marshall, and he had promised that he would either secure Marshall or somebody else for them by the time they got back; he would now say nothing to anybody till they returned, and then fulfil his promise by furnishing me to them.

It was splendid. I went to bed all on fire with excitement; for nobody had yet gone East to sell a Nevada silver mine, and the field was white for the sickle. I felt that such a mine as the one described by Dan would bring a princely sum in New York, and sell without delay or difficulty. I could not sleep, my fancy so rioted through its castles in the air. It was the "blind lead" come again.

Next day I got away, on the coach, with the usual eclat attending departures of old citizens,—for if you have only half a dozen friends out there they will make noise for a hundred rather than let you seem to go away neglected and unregretted—and Dan promised to keep strict watch for the men that had the mine to sell.

The trip was signalized but by one little incident, and that occurred just as we were about to start. A very seedy looking vagabond passenger got out of the stage a moment to wait till the usual ballast of silver bricks was thrown in. He was standing on the pavement, when an awkward express employé, carrying a brick weighing a hundred pounds, stumbled and let it fall on the bummer's foot. He instantly dropped on the ground and began to howl in the most heart-breaking way. A sympathizing crowd gathered around and were going to pull his boot off; but he screamed louder than ever and they desisted; then he fell to gasping, and between the gasps ejaculated "Brandy! for Heaven's sake, brandy!" They poured half a pint down him, and it wonderfully restored and comforted him. Then he begged the people to assist him to the stage, which was done. The express people urged him to have a doctor at their expense, but he declined, and said that if he only had a little brandy to take along with him, to soothe his paroxysms of pain when they came on, he would be grateful and content. He was quickly supplied with two bottles, and we drove off. He was so smiling and happy after that, that I could not refrain from asking him how he could possibly be so comfortable with a crushed foot.

"Well," said he, "I hadn't had a drink for twelve hours, and hadn't a cent to my name. I was most perishing—and so, when that duffer dropped that hundred-pounder on my foot, I see my chance. Got a cork leg, you know!" and he pulled up his pantaloons and proved it.

He was as drunk as a lord all day long, and full of chucklings over his timely ingenuity.

One drunken man necessarily reminds one of another. I once heard a gentleman tell about an incident which he witnessed in a Californian bar-room. He entitled it "Ye Modest Man Taketh a Drink." It was nothing but a bit of acting, but it seemed to me a perfect rendering, and worthy of Toodles himself. The modest man, tolerably far gone with beer and other matters, enters a saloon (twenty-five cents is the price for anything and everything, and specie the only money used) and lays down a half dollar; calls for whiskey and drinks it; the bar-keeper makes change and lays the quarter in a wet place on the counter; the modest man fumbles at it with nerveless fingers, but it slips and the water holds it; he contemplates it, and tries again; same result; observes that people are interested in what he is at, blushes; fumbles at the quarter again—blushes—puts his forefinger carefully, slowly down, to make sure of his aim—pushes the coin toward the bar keeper, and says with a sigh:

"('ic!) Gimme a cigar!"

Naturally, another gentleman present told about another drunken man. He said he reeled toward home late at night; made a mistake and entered the wrong gate; thought he saw a dog on the stoop; and it was—an iron one. He stopped and considered; wondered if it was a dangerous dog; ventured to say "Be (hic) begone!" No effect. Then he approached warily, and adopted conciliation; pursed up his lips and tried to whistle, but failed; still approached, saying, "Poor dog!—doggy, doggy, doggy!—poor doggy-dog!" Got up on the stoop, still petting with fond names; till master of the advantages; then exclaimed, "Leave, you thief!"—planted a vindictive kick in his ribs, and went head-over-heels overboard, of course. A pause; a sigh or two of pain, and then a remark in a reflective voice:

"Awful solid dog. What could he ben eating? ('ic!) Rocks, p'raps. Such animals is dangerous. 'At's what *I* say—they're dangerous. If a man—('ic!)—if a man wants to feed a dog on rocks, let him *feed* him on rocks; 'at's all right; but let him keep him at *home*—not have him layin' round promiscuous, where ('ic!) where people's liable to stumble over him when they ain't noticin'!"

It was not without regret that I took a last look at the tiny flag (it was thirty-five feet long and ten feet wide) fluttering like a lady's handkerchief from the topmost peak of Mount Davidson, two thousand feet above Virginia's roofs, and felt that doubtless I was bidding a permanent farewell to a city which had afforded me the most vigorous enjoyment of life I had ever experienced. And this reminds me of an incident which the dullest memory Virginia could boast at the time it happened must vividly recall, at times, till its possessor dies. Late one summer afternoon we had a rain shower. That was astonishing enough, in itself, to set the whole town buzzing, for it only rains (during a week or two weeks) in the winter in Nevada, and even then not enough at a time to make it worth while for any merchant to keep umbrellas for sale. But the rain was not the chief wonder. It only lasted five or ten minutes; while the people were still talking about it all the heavens gathered to themselves a dense blackness as of midnight. All the vast eastern front of Mount Davidson, overlooking the city, put on such a funereal gloom that only the nearness and solidity of the mountain made its outlines even faintly distinguishable from the dead blackness of the heavens they rested against. This unaccustomed sight turned all eyes toward the mountain; and as they looked, a little tongue of rich golden flame was seen waving and quivering in the heart of the midnight, away up on the extreme summit! In a few minutes the streets were packed with people, gazing with hardly an uttered word, at the one brilliant mote in the brooding world of darkness. It flicked like a candle-flame, and looked no larger; but with such a background it was wonderfully bright, small as it was. It was the flag!—though no one suspected it at first, it seemed so like a supernatural visitor of some kind—a mysterious messenger of good tidings, some were fain to believe. It was the nation's emblem transfigured by the departing rays of a sun that was entirely palled from view; and on no other object did the glory fall, in all the broad panorama of mountain ranges and deserts. Not even upon the staff of the flag—for that, a needle in the distance at any time, was now untouched by the light and undistinguishable in the gloom. For a whole hour the weird visitor winked and burned in its lofty solitude, and still the thousands of uplifted eyes watched it with fascinated interest. How the people were wrought up! The superstition grew apace that this was a mystic courier come with great news from the war—the poetry of the idea excusing and commending it—and on it spread, from heart to heart, from lip to lip and from street to street, till there was a general impulse to have out the military and welcome the bright waif with a salvo of artillery!

And all that time one sorely tired man, the telegraph operator sworn to official secrecy, had to lock his lips and chain his tongue with a silence that was like to rend them; for he, and he only, of all the speculating multitude, knew the great things this sinking sun had seen that day in the east—Vicksburg fallen, and the Union arms victorious at Gettysburg!

But for the journalistic monopoly that forbade the slightest revealment of eastern news till a day after its publication in the California papers, the glorified flag on Mount Davidson would have been saluted and re-saluted, that memorable evening, as long as there was a charge of powder to thunder with; the city would have been illuminated, and every man that had any respect for himself would have got drunk,—as was the custom of the country on all occasions of public moment. Even at this distant day I cannot think of this needlessly marred supreme opportunity without regret. What a time we might have had!

Chapter LVI

W ᴇ ʀᴜᴍʙʟᴇᴅ over the plains and valleys, climbed the Sierras to the clouds, and looked down upon summer-clad California. And I will remark here, in passing, that all scenery in California requires *distance* to give it its highest charm. The mountains are imposing in their sublimity and their majesty of form and altitude, from any point of view—but one must have distance to soften their ruggedness and enrich their tintings; a Californian forest is best at a little distance, for there is a sad poverty of variety in species, the trees being chiefly of one monotonous family—redwood, pine, spruce, fir—and so, at a near view there is a wearisome sameness of attitude in their rigid arms, stretched downward and outward in one continued and reiterated appeal to all men to "Sh!—don't say a word!—you might disturb somebody!" Close at hand, too, there is a reliefless and relentless smell of pitch and turpentine; there is a ceaseless melancholy in their sighing and complaining foliage; one walks over a soundless carpet of beaten yellow bark and dead spines of the foliage till he feels like a wandering spirit bereft of a footfall; he tires of the endless tufts of needles and yearns for substantial, shapely leaves; he looks for moss and grass to loll upon, and finds none, for where there is no bark there is naked clay and dirt, enemies to pensive musing and clean apparel. Often a grassy plain in California, is what it should be, but often, too, it is best contemplated at a distance, because although its grass blades are tall, they stand up vindictively straight and self-sufficient, and are unsociably wide apart, with uncomely spots of barren sand between.

One of the queerest things I know of, is to hear tourists from "the States" go into ecstasies over the loveliness of "ever-blooming California." And they always do go into that sort of ecstasies. But perhaps they would modify them if they knew how old Californians, with the memory full upon them of the dust-covered and questionable summer greens of Californian "verdure," stand astonished, and filled with worshipping admiration, in the presence of the lavish richness, the brilliant green, the infinite freshness, the spend-thrift variety

834

of form and species and foliage that make an Eastern land-scape a vision of Paradise itself. The idea of a man falling into raptures over grave and sombre California, when that man has seen New England's meadow-expanses and her maples, oaks and cathedral-windowed elms decked in summer attire, or the opaline splendors of autumn descending upon her forests, comes very near being funny—would be, in fact, but that it is so pathetic. No land with an unvarying climate can be very beautiful. The tropics are not, for all the sentiment that is wasted on them. They seem beautiful at first, but sameness impairs the charm by and by. *Change* is the handmaiden Nature requires to do her miracles with. The land that has four well-defined seasons, cannot lack beauty, or pall with monotony. Each season brings a world of enjoyment and interest in the watching of its unfolding, its gradual, harmonious development, its culminating graces—and just as one begins to tire of it, it passes away and a radical change comes, with new witcheries and new glories in its train. And I think that to one in sympathy with nature, each season, in its turn, seems the loveliest.

San Francisco, a truly fascinating city to live in, is stately and handsome at a fair distance, but close at hand one notes that the architecture is mostly old-fashioned, many streets are made up of decaying, smoke-grimed, wooden houses, and the barren sand-hills toward the outskirts obtrude themselves too prominently. Even the kindly climate is sometimes pleasanter when read about than personally experienced, for a lovely, cloudless sky wears out its welcome by and by, and then when the longed for rain does come it *stays*. Even the playful earthquake is better contemplated at a dis—

However there are varying opinions about that.

The climate of San Francisco is mild and singularly equable. The thermometer stands at about seventy degrees the year round. It hardly changes at all. You sleep under one or two light blankets Summer and Winter, and never use a mosquito bar. Nobody ever wears Summer clothing. You wear black broadcloth—if you have it—in August and January, just the same. It is no colder, and no warmer, in the one month than the other. You do not use overcoats and you do not use fans. It is as pleasant a climate as could well be contrived, take it all around, and is doubtless the most unvarying in the whole world. The wind blows there a good deal in the Summer months, but then you can go over to Oakland, if you choose—three or four miles away—it does not blow there. It has only snowed twice in San Francisco in nineteen years, and then it only remained on the ground long enough to astonish the children, and set them to wondering what the feathery stuff was.

During eight months of the year, straight along, the skies are bright and cloudless, and never a drop of rain falls. But when the other four months come along, you will need to go and steal an umbrella. Because you will require it. Not just one day, but one hundred and twenty days in hardly varying succession. When you want to go visiting, or attend church, or the theatre, you never look up at the clouds to see whether it is likely to rain or not—you look at the almanac. If it is Winter, it will *rain*—and if it is Summer, it *won't* rain, and you cannot help it. You never need a lightning-rod, because it never thunders and it never lightens. And after you have listened for six or eight weeks, every night, to the dismal monotony of those quiet rains, you will wish in your heart the thunder *would* leap and crash and roar along those drowsy skies once, and make everything alive—you will wish the prisoned lightnings *would* cleave the dull firmament asunder and light it with a blinding glare for *one* little instant. You would give *anything* to hear the old familiar thunder again and see the lightning strike somebody. And along in the Summer, when you have suffered about four months of lustrous, pitiless sunshine, you are ready to go down on your knees and plead for rain—hail—snow—thunder and lightning—anything to break the monotony—you will take an earthquake, if you cannot do any better. And the chances are that you'll get it, too.

San Francisco is built on sand hills, but they are prolific sand hills. They yield a generous vegetation. All the rare flowers which people in "the States" rear with such patient care in parlor flower-pots and green-houses, flourish luxuriantly in the open air there all the year round. Calla lilies, all sorts of geraniums, passion flowers, moss roses—I do not know the names of a tenth part of them. I only know that while New

Yorkers are burdened with banks and drifts of snow, Californians are burdened with banks and drifts of flowers, if they only keep their hands off and let them grow. And I have heard that they have also that rarest and most curious of all the flowers, the beautiful *Espiritu Santo*, as the Spaniards call it—or flower of the Holy Spirit—though I thought it grew only in Central America—down on the Isthmus. In its cup is the daintiest little fac-simile of a dove, as pure as snow. The Spaniards have a superstitious reverence for it. The blossom has been conveyed to the States, submerged in ether; and the bulb has been taken thither also, but every attempt to make it bloom after it arrived, has failed.

I have elsewhere spoken of the endless Winter of Mono, California, and but this moment of the eternal Spring of San Francisco. Now if we travel a hundred miles in a straight line, we come to the eternal Summer of Sacramento. One never sees Summer-clothing or mosquitoes in San Francisco—but they can be found in Sacramento. Not always and unvaryingly, but about one hundred and forty-three months out of twelve years, perhaps. Flowers bloom there, always, the reader can easily believe—people suffer and sweat, and swear, morning, noon and night, and wear out their stanchest energies fanning themselves. It gets hot there, but if you go down to Fort Yuma you will find it hotter. Fort Yuma is probably the hottest place on earth. The thermometer stays at one hundred and twenty in the shade there all the time—except when it varies and goes higher. It is a U. S. military post, and its occupants get so used to the terrific heat that they suffer without it. There is a tradition (attributed to John Phenix*) that a very, very wicked soldier died there, once, and of course, went straight to the hottest corner of perdition,—and the next day he *telegraphed back for his blankets*. There is no doubt about the truth of this statement—there can be no doubt about it. I have seen the place where that soldier used to board. In Sacramento it is fiery Summer always, and you can gather roses, and eat strawberries and ice-cream, and wear white linen clothes, and pant and perspire, at eight or nine o'clock in the morning, and then take the cars, and at noon

*It has been purloined by fifty different scribblers who were too poor to invent a fancy but not ashamed to steal one.—M. T.

put on your furs and your skates, and go skimming over frozen Donner Lake, seven thousand feet above the valley, among snow banks fifteen feet deep, and in the shadow of grand mountain peaks that lift their frosty crags ten thousand feet above the level of the sea. There is a transition for you! Where will you find another like it in the Western hemisphere? And some of us have swept around snow-walled curves of the Pacific Railroad in that vicinity, six thousand feet above the sea, and looked down as the birds do, upon the deathless Summer of the Sacramento Valley, with its fruitful fields, its feathery foliage, its silver streams, all slumbering in the mellow haze of its enchanted atmosphere, and all infinitely softened and spiritualized by distance—a dreamy, exquisite glimpse of fairyland, made all the more charming and striking that it was caught through a forbidden gateway of ice and snow, and savage crags and precipices.

Chapter LVII

IT WAS IN this Sacramento Valley, just referred to, that a deal of the most lucrative of the early gold mining was done, and you may still see, in places, its grassy slopes and levels torn and guttered and disfigured by the avaricious spoilers of fifteen and twenty years ago. You may see such disfigurements far and wide over California—and in some such places, where only meadows and forests are visible—not a living creature, not a house, no stick or stone or remnant of a ruin, and not a sound, not even a whisper to disturb the Sabbath stillness—you will find it hard to believe that there stood at one time a fiercely-flourishing little city, of two thousand or three thousand souls, with its newspaper, fire company, brass band, volunteer militia, bank, hotels, noisy Fourth of July processions and speeches, gambling hells crammed with tobacco smoke, profanity, and rough-bearded men of all nations and colors, with tables heaped with gold dust sufficient for the revenues of a German principality—streets crowded and rife with business—town lots worth four hundred dollars a front foot—labor, laughter, music, dancing, swearing, fighting, shooting, stabbing—a bloody inquest and a man for breakfast every morning—*everything* that delights and adorns existence—all the appointments and appurtenances of a thriving and prosperous and promising young city,—and *now* nothing is left of it all but a lifeless, homeless solitude. The men are gone, the houses have vanished, even the *name* of the place is forgotten. In no other land, in modern times, have towns so absolutely died and disappeared, as in the old mining regions of California.

It was a driving, vigorous, restless population in those days. It was a *curious* population. It was the *only* population of the kind that the world has ever seen gathered together, and it is not likely that the world will ever see its like again. For, observe, it was an assemblage of two hundred thousand *young* men—not simpering, dainty, kid-gloved weaklings, but stalwart, muscular, dauntless young braves, brimful of push and energy, and royally endowed with every attribute that goes to make up a peerless and magnificent manhood—the very pick and choice of the world's glorious ones. No women, no children, no gray and stooping veterans,—none but erect, bright-eyed, quick-moving, strong-handed young giants—the strangest population, the finest population, the most gallant host that ever trooped down the startled solitudes of an unpeopled land. And where are they now? Scattered to the ends of the earth—or prematurely aged and decrepit—or shot or stabbed in street affrays—or dead of disappointed hopes and broken hearts—all gone, or nearly all—victims devoted upon the altar of the golden calf—the noblest holocaust that ever wafted its sacrificial incense heavenward. It is pitiful to think upon.

It was a splendid population—for all the slow, sleepy, sluggish-brained sloths staid at home—you never find that sort of people among pioneers—you cannot build pioneers out of that sort of material. It was that population that gave to California a name for getting up astounding enterprises and rushing them through with a magnificent dash and daring and a recklessness of cost or consequences, which she bears unto this day—and when she projects a new surprise, the grave world smiles as usual, and says "Well, that is California all over."

But they were rough in those times! They fairly reveled in gold, whisky, fights, and fandangoes, and were unspeakably happy. The honest miner raked from a hundred to a thousand dollars out of his claim a day, and what with the gambling dens and the other entertainments, he hadn't a cent the next morning, if he had any sort of luck. They cooked their own bacon and beans, sewed on their own buttons, washed their own shirts—blue woollen ones; and if a man wanted a fight on his hands without any annoying delay, all he had to do was to appear in public in a white shirt or a stove-pipe hat, and he would be accommodated. For those people hated aristocrats. They had a particular and malignant animosity toward what they called a "biled shirt."

It was a wild, free, disorderly, grotesque society! *Men*— only swarming hosts of stalwart *men*—nothing juvenile, nothing feminine, visible anywhere!

In those days miners would flock in crowds to catch a glimpse of that rare and blessed spectacle, a woman! Old inhabitants tell how, in a certain camp, the news went abroad early in the morning that a woman was come! They had seen a calico dress hanging out of a wagon down at the camping-ground—sign of emigrants from over the great plains. Everybody went down there, and a shout went up when an actual, bona fide dress was discovered fluttering in the wind! The male emigrant was visible. The miners said:

"Fetch her out!"

He said: "It is my wife, gentlemen—she is sick—we have been robbed of money, provisions, everything, by the Indians—we want to rest."

"Fetch her out! We've got to see her!"

"But, gentlemen, the poor thing, she—"

"FETCH HER OUT!"

He "fetched her out," and they swung their hats and sent up three rousing cheers and a tiger; and they crowded around and gazed at her, and touched her dress, and listened to her voice with the look of men who listened to a *memory* rather than a present reality—and then they collected twenty-five hundred dollars in gold and gave it to the man, and swung their hats again and gave three more cheers, and went home satisfied.

Once I dined in San Francisco with the family of a pioneer, and talked with his daughter, a young lady whose first experience in San Francisco was an adventure, though she herself did not remember it, as she was only two or three years old at the time. Her father said that, after landing from the ship, they were walking up the street, a servant leading the party with the little girl in her arms. And presently a huge miner, bearded, belted, spurred, and bristling with deadly weapons—just down from a long campaign in the mountains, evidently—barred the way, stopped the servant, and stood gazing, with a face all alive with gratification and astonishment. Then he said, reverently:

"Well, if it ain't a child!" And then he snatched a little leather sack out of his pocket and said to the servant:

"There's a hundred and fifty dollars in dust, there, and I'll give it to you to let me kiss the child!"

That anecdote is *true*.

But see how things change. Sitting at that dinner-table,

listening to that anecdote, if I had offered double the money for the privilege of kissing the same child, I would have been refused. Seventeen added years have far more than doubled the price.

And while upon this subject I will remark that once in Star City, in the Humboldt Mountains, I took my place in a sort of long, post-office single file of miners, to patiently await my chance to peep through a crack in the cabin and get a sight of the splendid new sensation—a genuine, live Woman! And at the end of half of an hour my turn came, and I put my eye to the crack, and there she was, with one arm akimbo, and tossing flap-jacks in a frying-pan with the other. And she was one hundred and sixty-five* years old, and hadn't a tooth in her head.

*Being in calmer mood, now, I voluntarily knock off a hundred from that.—M. T.

Chapter LVIII

For a few months I enjoyed what to me was an entirely new phase of existence—a butterfly idleness; nothing to do, nobody to be responsible to, and untroubled with financial uneasiness. I fell in love with the most cordial and sociable city in the Union. After the sage-brush and alkali deserts of Washoe, San Francisco was Paradise to me. I lived at the best hotel, exhibited my clothes in the most conspicuous places, infested the opera, and learned to seem enraptured with music which oftener afflicted my ignorant ear than enchanted it, if I had had the vulgar honesty to confess it. However, I suppose I was not greatly worse than the most of my countrymen in that. I had longed to be a butterfly, and I was one at last. I attended private parties in sumptuous evening dress, simpered and aired my graces like a born beau, and polked and schottisched with a step peculiar to myself—and the kangaroo. In a word, I kept the due state of a man worth a hundred thousand dollars (prospectively,) and likely to reach absolute affluence when that silver-mine sale should be ultimately achieved in the East. I spent money with a free hand, and meantime watched the stock sales with an interested eye and looked to see what might happen in Nevada.

Something very important happened. The property holders of Nevada voted against the State Constitution; but the folks who had nothing to lose were in the majority, and carried the measure over their heads. But after all it did not immediately look like a disaster, though unquestionably it was one. I hesitated, calculated the chances, and then concluded not to sell. Stocks went on rising; speculation went mad; bankers, merchants, lawyers, doctors, mechanics, laborers, even the very washerwomen and servant girls, were putting up their earnings on silver stocks, and every sun that rose in the morning went down on paupers enriched and rich men beggared. What a gambling carnival it was! Gould and Curry soared to six thousand three hundred dollars a foot! And then—all of a sudden, out went the bottom and everything and everybody went to ruin and destruction! The wreck was complete. The bubble scarcely left a microscopic moisture behind it. I was an early beggar and a thorough one. My hoarded stocks were not worth the paper they were printed on. I threw them all away. I, the cheerful idiot that had been squandering money like water, and thought myself beyond the reach of misfortune, had not now as much as fifty dollars when I gathered together my various debts and paid them. I removed from the hotel to a very private boarding house. I took a reporter's berth and went to work. I was not entirely broken in spirit, for I was building confidently on the sale of the silver mine in the east. But I could not hear from Dan. My letters miscarried or were not answered.

One day I did not feel vigorous and remained away from the office. The next day I went down toward noon as usual, and found a note on my desk which had been there twenty-four hours. It was signed "Marshall"—the Virginia reporter—and contained a request that I should call at the hotel and see him and a friend or two that night, as they would sail for the east in the morning. A postscript added that their errand was a big mining speculation! I was hardly ever so sick in my life. I abused myself for leaving Virginia and entrusting to another man a matter I ought to have attended to myself; I abused myself for remaining away from the office on the one day of all the year that I should have been there. And thus berating myself I trotted a mile to the steamer wharf and arrived just in time to be too late. The ship was in the stream and under way.

I comforted myself with the thought that may be the speculation would amount to nothing—poor comfort at best—and then went back to my slavery, resolved to put up with my thirty-five dollars a week and forget all about it.

A month afterward I enjoyed my first earthquake. It was one which was long called the "great" earthquake, and is doubtless so distinguished till this day. It was just after noon, on a bright October day. I was coming down Third street. The only objects in motion anywhere in sight in that thickly built and populous quarter, were a man in a buggy behind me, and a street car wending slowly up the cross street. Otherwise, all was solitude and a Sabbath stillness. As I turned the corner, around a frame house, there was a great rattle and jar, and it occurred to me that here was an item!—no doubt a fight in that house. Before I could turn and seek the door, there came a really terrific shock; the ground seemed to roll under me in waves, interrupted by a violent joggling up and down, and there was a heavy grinding noise as of brick houses rubbing together. I fell up against the frame house and hurt my elbow. I knew what it was, now, and from mere reportorial instinct, nothing else, took out my watch and noted the time of day; at that moment a third and still severer shock came, and as I reeled about on the pavement trying to keep my footing, I saw a sight! The entire front of a tall four-story brick building in Third street sprung outward like a door and fell sprawling across the street, raising a dust like a great volume of smoke! And here came the buggy—over-board went the man, and in less time than I can tell it the vehicle was distributed in small fragments along three hundred yards of street. One could have fancied that some-body had fired a charge of chair-rounds and rags down the thoroughfare. The street car had stopped, the horses were rearing and plunging, the passengers were pouring out at both ends, and one fat man had crashed half way through a glass window on one side of the car, got wedged fast and was squirming and screaming like an impaled madman. Every door, of every house, as far as the eye could reach, was vom-iting a stream of human beings; and almost before one could execute a wink and begin another, there was a massed multi-tude of people stretching in endless procession down every street my position commanded. Never was solemn solitude turned into teeming life quicker.

Of the wonders wrought by "the great earthquake," these were all that came under my eye; but the tricks it did, else-where, and far and wide over the town, made toothsome gos-sip for nine days. The destruction of property was trifling— the injury to it was wide-spread and somewhat serious.

The "curiosities" of the earthquake were simply endless. Gentlemen and ladies who were sick, or were taking a siesta, or had dissipated till a late hour and were making up lost sleep, thronged into the public streets in all sorts of queer apparel, and some without any at all. One woman who had been washing a naked child, ran down the street holding it by the ankles as if it were a dressed turkey. Prominent citizens who were supposed to keep the Sabbath strictly, rushed out of saloons in their shirt-sleeves, with billiard cues in their hands. Dozens of men with necks swathed in napkins, rushed from barber-shops, lathered to the eyes or with one cheek clean shaved and the other still bearing a hairy stubble. Horses broke from stables, and a frightened dog rushed up a short attic ladder and out on to a roof, and when his scare was over had not the nerve to go down again the same way he had gone up. A prominent editor flew down stairs, in the principal hotel, with nothing on but one brief undergarment—met a chambermaid, and exclaimed:

"Oh, what *shall* I do! Where shall I go!"

She responded with naive serenity:

"If you have no choice, you might try a clothing-store!"

A certain foreign consul's lady was the acknowledged leader of fashion, and every time she appeared in anything new or extraordinary, the ladies in the vicinity made a raid on their husbands' purses and arrayed themselves similarly. One man who had suffered considerably and growled accordingly, was standing at the window when the shocks came, and the next instant the consul's wife, just out of the bath, fled by with no other apology for clothing than—a bath-towel! The sufferer rose superior to the terrors of the earthquake, and said to his wife:

"Now *that* is something *like*! Get out your towel my dear!"

The plastering that fell from ceilings in San Francisco that day, would have covered several acres of ground. For some days afterward, groups of eyeing and pointing men stood about many a building, looking at long zig-zag cracks that extended from the eaves to the ground. Four feet of the tops of three chimneys on one house were broken square off and turned around in such a way as to completely stop the draft. A crack a hundred feet long gaped open six inches wide in the middle of one street and then shut together again with such force, as to ridge up the meeting earth like a slender grave. A lady sitting in her rocking and quaking parlor, saw the wall part at the ceiling, open and shut twice, like a mouth, and then drop the end of a brick on the floor like a tooth. She was a woman easily disgusted with foolishness, and she arose and went out of there. One lady who was coming down stairs was astonished to see a bronze Hercules lean forward on its pedestal as if to strike her with its club. They both reached the bottom of the flight at the same time,—the woman insensible from the fright. Her child, born some little time afterward, was club-footed. However—on second thought,—if the reader sees any coincidence in this, he must do it at his own risk.

The first shock brought down two or three huge organ-pipes in one of the churches. The minister, with uplifted hands, was just closing the services. He glanced up, hesitated, and said:

"However, we will omit the benediction!"—and the next instant there was a vacancy in the atmosphere where he had stood.

After the first shock, an Oakland minister said:

"Keep your seats! There is no better place to die than this"—

And added, after the third:

"But outside is good enough!" He then skipped out at the back door.

Such another destruction of mantel ornaments and toilet bottles as the earthquake created, San Francisco never saw before. There was hardly a girl or a matron in the city but suffered losses of this kind. Suspended pictures were thrown down, but oftener still, by a curious freak of the earthquake's humor, they were whirled completely around with their faces to the wall! There was great difference of opinion, at first, as to the course or direction the earthquake traveled, but water that splashed out of various tanks and buckets settled that. Thousands of people were made so sea-sick by the rolling and pitching of floors and streets that they were weak and bed-ridden for hours, and some few for even days afterward.—Hardly an individual escaped nausea entirely.

The queer earthquake—episodes that formed the staple of San Francisco gossip for the next week would fill a much larger book than this, and so I will diverge from the subject.

By and by, in the due course of things, I picked up a copy of the *Enterprise* one day, and fell under this cruel blow:

NEVADA MINES IN NEW YORK.—G. M. Marshall, Sheba Hurst and Amos H. Rose, who left San Francisco last July for New York City, with ores from mines in Pine Wood District, Humboldt County, and on the Reese River range, have disposed of a mine containing six thousand feet and called the Pine Mountains Consolidated, for the sum of $3,000,000. The stamps on the deed, which is now on its way to Humboldt County, from New York, for record, amounted to $3,000, which is said to be the largest amount of stamps ever placed on one document. A working capital of $1,000,000 has been paid into the treasury, and machinery has already been purchased for a large quartz mill, which will be put up as soon as possible. The stock in this company is all full paid and entirely unassessable. The ores of the mines in this district somewhat resemble those of the Sheba mine in Humboldt. Sheba Hurst, the discoverer of the mines, with his friends corralled all the best leads and all the land and timber they desired before making public their whereabouts. Ores from there, assayed in this city, showed them to be exceedingly rich in silver and gold—silver predominating. There is an abundance of wood and water in the District. We are glad to know that New York capital has been enlisted in the development of the mines of this region. Having seen the ores and assays, we are satisfied that the mines of the District are very valuable—anything but wild-cat.

Once more native imbecility had carried the day, and I had lost a million! It was the "blind lead" over again.

Let us not dwell on this miserable matter. If I were inventing these things, I could be wonderfully humorous over them; but they are too true to be talked of with hearty levity, even at this distant day.* Suffice it that I so lost heart, and so yielded myself up to repinings and sighings and foolish regrets, that I neglected my duties and became about worthless, as a reporter for a brisk newspaper. And at last one of the proprietors took me aside, with a charity I still remember with considerable respect, and gave me an opportunity to resign my berth and so save myself the disgrace of a dismissal.

*True, and yet not exactly as given in the above figures, possibly. I saw Marshall, months afterward, and although he had plenty of money he did not claim to have captured an entire *million*. In fact I gathered that he had not then received $50,000. Beyond that figure his fortune appeared to consist of uncertain vast expectations rather than prodigious certainties. However, when the above item appeared in print I put full faith in it, and incontinently wilted and went to seed under it.

Chapter LIX

For a time I wrote literary screeds for the *Golden Era*. C. H. Webb had established a very excellent literary weekly called the *Californian*, but high merit was no guaranty of success; it languished, and he sold out to three printers, and Bret Harte became editor at $20 a week, and I was employed to contribute an article a week at $12. But the journal still languished, and the printers sold out to Captain Ogden, a rich man and a pleasant gentleman who chose to amuse himself with such an expensive luxury without much caring about the cost of it. When he grew tired of the novelty, he re-sold to the printers, the paper presently died a peaceful death, and I was out of work again. I would not mention these things but for the fact that they so aptly illustrate the ups and downs that characterize life on the Pacific coast. A man could hardly stumble into such a variety of queer vicissitudes in any other country.

For two months my sole occupation was avoiding acquaintances; for during that time I did not earn a penny, or buy an article of any kind, or pay my board. I became a very adept at "slinking." I slunk from back street to back street, I slunk away from approaching faces that looked familiar, I slunk to my meals, ate them humbly and with a mute apology for every mouthful I robbed my generous landlady of, and at midnight, after wanderings that were but slinkings away from cheerfulness and light, I slunk to my bed. I felt meaner, and lowlier and more despicable than the worms. During all this time I had but one piece of money—a silver ten cent piece— and I held to it and would not spend it on any account, lest the consciousness coming strong upon me that I was *entirely* penniless, might suggest suicide. I had pawned every thing but the clothes I had on; so I clung to my dime desperately, till it was smooth with handling.

However, I am forgetting. I did have one other occupation beside that of "slinking." It was the entertaining of a collector (and being entertained by him,) who had in his hands the Virginia banker's bill for the forty-six dollars which I had loaned my schoolmate, the "Prodigal." This man used to call regularly once a week and dun me, and sometimes oftener. He did it from sheer force of habit, for he knew he could get nothing. He would get out his bill, calculate the interest for me, at five per cent a month, and show me clearly that there was no attempt at fraud in it and no mistakes; and then plead, and argue and dun with all his might for any sum—any little trifle—even a dollar—even half a dollar, on account. Then his duty was accomplished and his conscience free. He immediately dropped the subject there always; got out a couple of cigars and divided, put his feet in the window, and then we would have a long, luxurious talk about everything and everybody, and he would furnish me a world of curious dunning adventures out of the ample store in his memory. By and by he would clap his hat on his head, shake hands and say briskly:

"Well, business is business—can't stay with you always!"— and was off in a second.

The idea of pining for a dun! And yet I used to long for him to come, and would get as uneasy as any mother if the day went by without his visit, when I was expecting him. But he never collected that bill, at last nor any part of it. I lived to pay it to the banker myself.

Misery loves company. Now and then at night, in out-of-the-way, dimly lighted places, I found myself happening on another child of misfortune. He looked so seedy and forlorn, so homeless and friendless and forsaken, that I yearned toward him as a brother. I wanted to claim kinship with him and go about and enjoy our wretchedness together. The drawing toward each other must have been mutual; at any rate we got to falling together oftener, though still seemingly by accident; and although we did not speak or evince any recognition, I think the dull anxiety passed out of both of us when we saw each other, and then for several hours we would idle along contentedly, wide apart, and glancing furtively in at home lights and fireside gatherings, out of the night shadows, and very much enjoying our dumb companionship.

Finally we spoke, and were inseparable after that. For our woes were identical, almost. He had been a reporter too, and lost his berth, and this was his experience, as nearly as I can recollect it. After losing his berth, he had gone down, down,

down, with never a halt: from a boarding house on Russian Hill to a boarding house in Kearney street; from thence to Dupont; from thence to a low sailor den; and from thence to lodgings in goods boxes and empty hogsheads near the wharves. Then, for a while, he had gained a meagre living by sewing up bursted sacks of grain on the piers; when that failed he had found food here and there as chance threw it in his way. He had ceased to show his face in daylight, now, for a reporter knows everybody, rich and poor, high and low, and cannot well avoid familiar faces in the broad light of day.

This mendicant Blucher—I call him that for convenience— was a splendid creature. He was full of hope, pluck and philosophy; he was well read and a man of cultivated taste; he had a bright wit and was a master of satire; his kindliness and his generous spirit made him royal in my eyes and changed his curb-stone seat to a throne and his damaged hat to a crown.

He had an adventure, once, which sticks fast in my memory as the most pleasantly grotesque that ever touched my sympathies. He had been without a penny for two months. He had shirked about obscure streets, among friendly dim lights, till the thing had become second nature to him. But at last he was driven abroad in daylight. The cause was sufficient; *he had not tasted food for forty-eight hours*, and he could not endure the misery of his hunger in idle hiding. He came along a back street, glowering at the loaves in bake-shop windows, and feeling that he could trade his life away for a morsel to eat. The sight of the bread doubled his hunger; but it was good to look at it, any how, and imagine what one might do if one only had it. Presently, in the middle of the street he saw a shining spot—looked again—did not, and could not, believe his eyes—turned away, to try them, then looked again. It was a verity—no vain, hunger-inspired delusion—it was a silver dime! He snatched it—gloated over it; doubted it—bit it—found it genuine—choked his heart down, and smothered a halleluiah. Then he looked around—saw that nobody was looking at him—threw the dime down where it was before—walked away a few steps, and approached again, pretending he did not know it was there, so that he could re-enjoy the luxury of finding it. He walked around it, viewing it from different points; then sauntered about with his hands in his pockets, looking up at the signs and now and then glancing at it and feeling the old thrill again. Finally he took it up, and went away, fondling it in his pocket. He idled through unfrequented streets, stopping in doorways and corners to take it out and look at it. By and by he went home to his lodgings—an empty queensware hogshead,—and employed himself till night trying to make up his mind what to buy with it. But it was hard to do. To get the most for it was the idea. He knew that at the Miner's Restaurant he could get a plate of beans and a piece of bread for ten cents; or a fish-ball and some few trifles, but they gave "no bread with one fish-ball" there. At French Pete's he could get a veal cutlet, plain, and some radishes and bread, for ten cents; or a cup of coffee—a pint at least—and a slice of bread; but the slice was not thick enough by the eighth of an inch, and sometimes they were still more criminal than that in the cutting of it. At seven o'clock his hunger was wolfish; and still his mind was not made up. He turned out and went up Merchant street, still ciphering; and chewing a bit of stick, as is the way of starving men. He passed before the lights of Martin's restaurant, the most aristocratic in the city, and stopped. It was a place where he had often dined, in better days, and Martin knew him well. Standing aside, just out of the range of the light, he worshiped the quails and steaks in the show window, and imagined that may be the fairy times were not gone yet and some prince in disguise would come along presently and tell him to go in there and take whatever he wanted. He chewed his stick with a hungry interest as he warmed to his subject. Just at this juncture he was conscious of some one at his side, sure enough; and then a finger touched his arm. He looked up, over his shoulder, and saw an apparition—a very allegory of Hunger! It was a man six feet high, gaunt, unshaven, hung with rags; with a haggard face and sunken cheeks, and eyes that pleaded piteously. This phantom said:

"Come with me—please."

He locked his arm in Blucher's and walked up the street to where the passengers were few and the light not strong, and then facing about, put out his hands in a beseeching way, and said:

"Friend—stranger—look at me! Life is easy to you—you go about, placid and content, as I did once, in my day—you have been in there, and eaten your sumptuous supper, and picked your teeth, and hummed your tune, and thought your pleasant thoughts, and said to yourself it is a good world—but you've never *suffered*! You don't know what trouble is—you don't know what misery is—nor hunger! Look at me! Stranger have pity on a poor friendless, homeless dog! As God is my judge, I have not tasted food for eight and forty hours!—look in my eyes and see if I lie! Give me the least trifle in the world to keep me from starving—anything—twenty-five cents! Do it, stranger—do it, *please*. It will be nothing to you, but life to me. Do it, and I will go down on my knees and lick the dust before you! I will kiss your foot-prints—I will worship the very ground you walk on! Only twenty-five cents! I am famishing—perishing—starving by inches! For God's sake don't desert me!"

Blucher was bewildered—and touched, too—stirred to the depths. He reflected. Thought again. Then an idea struck him, and he said:

"Come with me."

He took the outcast's arm, walked him down to Martin's restaurant, seated him at a marble table, placed the bill of fare before him, and said:

"Order what you want, friend. Charge it to me, Mr. Martin."

"All right, Mr. Blucher," said Martin.

Then Blucher stepped back and leaned against the counter and watched the man stow away cargo after cargo of buck-wheat cakes at seventy-five cents a plate; cup after cup of cof-fee, and porter house steaks worth two dollars apiece; and when six dollars and a half's worth of destruction had been accomplished, and the stranger's hunger appeased, Blucher went down to French Pete's, bought a veal cutlet plain, a slice of bread, and three radishes, with his dime, and set to and feasted like a king!

Take the episode all around, it was as odd as any that can be culled from the myriad curiosities of Californian life, perhaps.

Chapter LX

B Y AND BY, an old friend of mine, a miner, came down from one of the decayed mining camps of Tuolumne, California, and I went back with him. We lived in a small cabin on a verdant hillside, and there were not five other cabins in view over the wide expanse of hill and forest. Yet a flourishing city of two or three thousand population had occupied this grassy dead solitude during the flush times of twelve or fifteen years before, and where our cabin stood had once been the heart of the teeming hive, the centre of the city. When the mines gave out the town fell into decay, and in a few years wholly disappeared—streets, dwellings, shops, everything—and left no sign. The grassy slopes were as green and smooth and desolate of life as if they had never been disturbed. The mere handful of miners still remaining, had seen the town spring up, spread, grow and flourish in its pride; and they had seen it sicken and die, and pass away like a dream. With it their hopes had died, and their zest of life. They had long ago resigned themselves to their exile, and ceased to correspond with their distant friends or turn longing eyes toward their early homes. They had accepted banishment, forgotten the world and been forgotten of the world. They were far from telegraphs and railroads, and they stood, as it were, in a living grave, dead to the events that stirred the globe's great populations, dead to the common interests of men, isolated and outcast from brotherhood with their kind. It was the most singular, and almost the most touching and melancholy exile that fancy can imagine.—One of my associates in this locality, for two or three months, was a man who had had a university education; but now for eighteen years he had decayed there by inches, a bearded, rough-clad, clay-stained miner, and at times, among his sighings and soliloquizings, he unconsciously interjected vaguely remembered Latin and Greek sentences—dead and musty tongues, meet vehicles for the thoughts of one whose dreams were all of the past, whose life was a failure; a tired man, burdened with the present, and indifferent to the future; a man without ties, hopes, interests, waiting for rest and the end.

In that one little corner of California is found a species of mining which is seldom or never mentioned in print. It is called "pocket mining" and I am not aware that any of it is done outside of that little corner. The gold is not evenly distributed through the surface dirt, as in ordinary placer mines, but is collected in little spots, and they are very wide apart and exceedingly hard to find, but when you do find one you reap a rich and sudden harvest. There are not now more than twenty pocket miners in that entire little region. I think I know every one of them personally. I have known one of them to hunt patiently about the hill-sides every day for eight months without finding gold enough to make a snuff-box— his grocery bill running up relentlessly all the time—and then find a pocket and take out of it two thousand dollars in two dips of his shovel. I have known him to take out three thousand dollars in two hours, and go and pay up every cent of his indebtedness, then enter on a dazzling spree that finished the last of his treasure before the night was gone. And the next day he bought his groceries on credit as usual, and shouldered his pan and shovel and went off to the hills hunting pockets again happy and content. This is the most fascinating of all the different kinds of mining, and furnishes a very handsome percentage of victims to the lunatic asylum.

Pocket hunting is an ingenious process. You take a spadeful of earth from the hill-side and put it in a large tin pan and dissolve and wash it gradually away till nothing is left but a teaspoonful of fine sediment. Whatever gold was in that earth has remained, because, being the heaviest, it has sought the bottom. Among the sediment you will find half a dozen yellow particles no larger than pin-heads. You are delighted. You move off to one side and wash another pan. If you find gold again, you move to one side further, and wash a third pan. If you find *no* gold this time, you are delighted again, because you know you are on the right scent. You lay an imaginary plan, shaped like a fan, with its handle up the hill—for just where the end of the handle is, you argue that the rich deposit lies hidden, whose vagrant grains of gold have escaped and been washed down the hill, spreading farther and farther apart as they wandered. And so you proceed up the hill, washing the earth and narrowing your lines every time the

absence of gold in the pan shows that you are outside the
spread of the fan; and at last, twenty yards up the hill your
lines have converged to a point—a single foot from that
point you cannot find any gold. Your breath comes short and
quick, you are feverish with excitement; the dinner-bell may
ring its clapper off, you pay no attention; friends may die,
weddings transpire, houses burn down, they are nothing to
you; you sweat and dig and delve with a frantic interest—
and all at once you strike it! Up comes a spadeful of earth
and quartz that is all lovely with soiled lumps and leaves and
sprays of gold. Sometimes that one spadeful is all—$500.
Sometimes the nest contains $10,000, and it takes you three
or four days to get it all out. The pocket-miners tell of one
nest that yielded $60,000 and two men exhausted it in two
weeks, and then sold the ground for $10,000 to a party who
never got $300 out of it afterward.

The hogs are good pocket hunters. All the summer they
root around the bushes, and turn up a thousand little piles of
dirt, and then the miners long for the rains; for the rains beat
upon these little piles and wash them down and expose the
gold, possibly right over a pocket. Two pockets were found
in this way by the same man in one day. One had $5,000 in
it and the other $8,000. That man could appreciate it, for he
hadn't had a cent for about a year.

In Tuolumne lived two miners who used to go to the
neighboring village in the afternoon and return every night
with household supplies. Part of the distance they traversed a
trail, and nearly always sat down to rest on a great boulder
that lay beside the path. In the course of thirteen years they
had worn that boulder tolerably smooth, sitting on it. By and
by two vagrant Mexicans came along and occupied the seat.
They began to amuse themselves by chipping off flakes from
the boulder with a sledge-hammer. They examined one of
these flakes and found it rich with gold. That boulder paid
them $800 afterward. But the aggravating circumstance was
that these "Greasers" knew that there must be more gold
where that boulder came from, and so they went panning up
the hill and found what was probably the richest pocket that
region has yet produced. It took three months to exhaust it,
and it yielded $120,000. The two American miners who used

to sit on the boulder are poor yet, and they take turn about in getting up early in the morning to curse those Mexicans—and when it comes down to pure ornamental cursing, the native American is gifted above the sons of men.

I have dwelt at some length upon this matter of pocket mining because it is a subject that is seldom referred to in print, and therefore I judged that it would have for the reader that interest which naturally attaches to novelty.

Chapter LXI

 O NE OF MY comrades there—another of those victims of eighteen years of unrequited toil and blighted hopes—was one of the gentlest spirits that ever bore its patient cross in a weary exile: grave and simple Dick Baker, pocket-miner of Dead-House Gulch.—He was forty-six, gray as a rat, earnest, thoughtful, slenderly educated, slouchily dressed and clay-soiled, but his heart was finer metal than any gold his shovel ever brought to light—than any, indeed, that ever was mined or minted.

Whenever he was out of luck and a little down-hearted, he would fall to mourning over the loss of a wonderful cat he used to own (for where women and children are not, men of kindly impulses take up with pets, for they must love something). And he always spoke of the strange sagacity of that cat with the air of a man who believed in his secret heart that there was something human about it—may be even supernatural.

I heard him talking about this animal once. He said:

"Gentlemen, I used to have a cat here, by the name of Tom Quartz, which you'd a took an interest in I reckon—most any body would. I had him here eight year—and he was the remarkablest cat *I* ever see. He was a large gray one of the Tom specie, an' he had more hard, natchral sense than any man in this camp—'n' a *power* of dignity—he wouldn't let the Gov'ner of Californy be familiar with him. He never ketched a rat in his life—'peared to be above it. He never cared for nothing but mining. He knowed more about mining, that cat did, than any man *I* ever, ever see. You couldn't tell *him* noth'n' 'bout placer diggin's—'n' as for pocket mining, why he was just born for it. He would dig out after me an' Jim when we went over the hills prospect'n', and he would trot along behind us for as much as five mile, if we went so fur. An' he had the best judgment about mining ground—why you never see anything like it. When we went to work, he'd scatter a glance around, 'n' if he didn't think much of the indications, he would give a look as much as to say, 'Well, I'll have to get you to excuse *me*,' 'n' without another word he'd hyste his nose into the air 'n' shove for home. But if the ground suited him, he would lay low 'n' keep dark till the first pan was washed, 'n' then he would sidle up 'n' take a look, an' if there was about six or seven grains of gold *he* was satisfied—he didn't want no better prospect 'n' that—'n' then he would lay down on our coats and snore like a steamboat till we'd struck the pocket, an' then get up 'n' superintend. He was nearly lightnin' on superintending.

"Well, bye an' bye, up comes this yer quartz excitement. Every body was into it—every body was pick'n' 'n' blast'n' instead of shovelin' dirt on the hill side—every body was put'n' down a shaft instead of scrapin' the surface. Noth'n' would do Jim, but *we* must tackle the ledges, too, 'n' so we did. We commenced put'n' down a shaft, 'n' Tom Quartz he begin to wonder what in the Dickens it was all about. *He* hadn't ever seen any mining like that before, 'n' he was all upset, as you may say—he couldn't come to a right understanding of it no way—it was too many for *him*. He was down on it, too, you bet you—he was down on it powerful—'n' always appeared to consider it the cussedest foolishness out. But that cat, you know, was *always* agin new fangled arrangements—somehow he never could abide 'em. *You* know how it is with old habits. But by an' by Tom Quartz begin to git sort of reconciled a little, though he never *could* altogether understand that eternal sinkin' of a shaft an' never pannin' out any thing. At last he got to comin' down in the shaft, hisself, to try to cipher it out. An' when he'd git the blues, 'n' feel kind o' scruffy, 'n' aggravated 'n' disgusted—knowin' as he did, that the bills was runnin' up all the time an' we warn't makin' a cent—he would curl up on a gunny sack in the corner an' go to sleep. Well, one day when the shaft was down about eight foot, the rock got so hard that we had to put in a blast—the first blast'n' we'd ever done since Tom Quartz was born. An' then we lit the fuse 'n' clumb out 'n' got off 'bout fifty yards—'n' forgot 'n' left Tom Quartz sound asleep on the gunny sack. In 'bout a minute we seen a puff of smoke bust up out of the hole, 'n' then everything let go with an awful crash, 'n' about four million ton of rocks 'n' dirt 'n' smoke 'n' splinters shot up 'bout a mile an' a half into the air, an' by George, right in the dead centre of it was old Tom Quartz a goin' end over end, an' a snortin' an' a sneez'n', an' a clawin' an' a reachin' for things like all possessed. But it warn't no use, you know, it warn't no use. An' that was the last we see of *him* for about two minutes 'n' a half, an' then all of a sudden it begin to rain rocks and rubbage, an' directly he come down ker-whop about ten foot off f'm where we stood. Well, I reckon he was p'raps the orneriest lookin' beast you ever see. One ear was sot back on his neck, 'n' his tail was stove up, 'n' his eye-winkers was swinged off, 'n' he was all blacked up with powder an' smoke, an' all sloppy with mud 'n' slush f'm one end to the other. Well sir, it warn't no use to try to apologize—we couldn't say a word. He took a sort of a disgusted look at hisself, 'n' then he looked at us—an' it was just exactly the same as if he had said—'Gents, may be *you* think it's smart to take advantage of a cat that 'ain't had no experience of quartz minin', but *I* think *different*'—an' then he turned on his heel 'n' marched off home without ever saying another word.

"That was jest his style. An' may be you won't believe it, but after that you never see a cat so prejudiced agin quartz mining as what he was. An' by an' bye when he *did* get to goin' down in the shaft agin, you'd 'a been astonished at his sagacity. The minute we'd tetch off a blast 'n' the fuse'd begin to sizzle, he'd give a look as much as to say: 'Well, I'll have to git you to excuse *me*,' an' it was surpris'n' the way he'd shin out of that hole 'n' go f'r a tree. Sagacity? It ain't no name for it. 'Twas *inspiration*!"

I said, "Well, Mr. Baker, his prejudice against quartz-mining *was* remarkable, considering how he came by it. Couldn't you ever cure him of it?"

"*Cure him!* No! When Tom Quartz was sot once, he was *always* sot—and you might a blowed him up as much as three million times 'n' you'd never a broken him of his cussed prejudice agin quartz mining."

The affection and the pride that lit up Baker's face when he delivered this tribute to the firmness of his humble friend of other days, will always be a vivid memory with me.

At the end of two months we had never "struck" a pocket. We had panned up and down the hillsides till they looked plowed like a field; we could have put in a crop of grain, then, but there would have been no way to get it to market. We got many good "prospects," but when the gold gave out in the pan and we dug down, hoping and longing, we found only emptiness—the pocket that should have been there was as barren as our own.—At last we shouldered our pans and shovels and struck out over the hills to try new localities. We prospected around Angel's Camp, in Calaveras county, during three weeks, but had no success. Then we wandered on foot among the mountains, sleeping under the trees at night, for the weather was mild, but still we remained as centless as the last rose of summer. That is a poor joke, but it is in pathetic harmony with the circumstances, since we were so poor ourselves. In accordance with the custom of the country, our door had always stood open and our board welcome to tramping miners—they drifted along nearly every day, dumped their paust shovels by the threshold and took "pot luck" with us—and now on our own tramp we never found cold hospitality.

Our wanderings were wide and in many directions; and now I could give the reader a vivid description of the Big Trees and the marvels of the Yo Semite—but what has this reader done to me that I should persecute him? I will deliver him into the hands of less conscientious tourists and take his blessing. Let me be charitable, though I fail in all virtues else.

Some of the phrases in the above are mining technicalities, purely, and may be a little obscure to the general reader. In *"placer diggings"* the gold is scattered all through the surface dirt; in *"pocket"* diggings it is concentrated in one little spot; in *"quartz"* the gold is in a solid, continuous vein of rock, enclosed between distinct walls of some other kind of stone—and this is the most laborious and expensive of all the different kinds of mining. *"Prospecting"* is hunting for a *"placer"*; *"indications"* are signs of its presence; *"panning out"* refers to the washing process by which the grains of gold are separated from the dirt; a *"prospect"* is what one finds in the first panful of dirt—and its value determines whether it is a good or a bad prospect, and whether it is worth while to tarry there or seek further.

Chapter LXII

AFTER A THREE months' absence, I found myself in San Francisco again, without a cent. When my credit was about exhausted, (for I had become too mean and lazy, now, to work on a morning paper, and there were no vacancies on the evening journals,) I was created San Francisco correspondent of the *Enterprise*, and at the end of five months I was out of debt, but my interest in my work was gone; for my correspondence being a daily one, without rest or respite, I got unspeakably tired of it. I wanted another change. The vagabond instinct was strong upon me. Fortune favored and I got a new berth and a delightful one. It was to go down to the Sandwich Islands and write some letters for the Sacramento *Union*, an excellent journal and liberal with employés.

We sailed in the propeller *Ajax*, in the middle of winter. The almanac called it winter, distinctly enough, but the weather was a compromise between spring and summer. Six days out of port, it became summer altogether. We had some thirty passengers; among them a cheerful soul by the name of Williams, and three sea-worn old whaleship captains going down to join their vessels. These latter played euchre in the smoking room day and night, drank astonishing quantities of raw whisky without being in the least affected by it, and were the happiest people I think I ever saw. And then there was "the old Admiral—" a retired whaleman. He was a roaring, terrific combination of wind and lightning and thunder, and earnest, whole-souled profanity. But nevertheless he was tender-hearted as a girl. He was a raving, deafening, devastating typhoon, laying waste the cowering seas but with an unvexed refuge in the centre where all comers were safe and at rest. Nobody could know the "Admiral" without liking him; and in a sudden and dire emergency I think no friend of his would know which to choose—to be cursed by him or prayed for by a less efficient person.

His title of "Admiral" was more strictly "official" than any ever worn by a naval officer before or since, perhaps—for it was the voluntary offering of a whole nation, and came direct from the *people* themselves without any intermediate red tape—the people of the Sandwich Islands. It was a title that came to him freighted with affection, and honor, and appreciation of his unpretending merit. And in testimony of the genuineness of the title it was publicly ordained that an exclusive flag should be devised for him and used solely to welcome his coming and wave him God-speed in his going. From that time forth, whenever his ship was signaled in the offing, or he catted his anchor and stood out to sea, that ensign streamed from the royal halliards on the parliament house and the nation lifted their hats to it with spontaneous accord.

Yet he had never fired a gun or fought a battle in his life. When I knew him on board the *Ajax*, he was seventy-two years old and had plowed the salt water sixty-one of them. For sixteen years he had gone in and out of the harbor of Honolulu in command of a whaleship, and for sixteen more had been captain of a San Francisco and Sandwich Island passenger packet and had never had an accident or lost a vessel. The simple natives knew him for a friend who never failed them, and regarded him as children regard a father. It was a dangerous thing to oppress them when the roaring Admiral was around.

Two years before I knew the Admiral, he had retired from the sea on a competence, and had sworn a colossal nine-jointed oath that he would "never go within *smelling* distance of the salt water again as long as he lived." And he had conscientiously kept it. That is to say, *he* considered he had kept it, and it would have been more than dangerous to suggest to him, even in the gentlest way, that making eleven long sea voyages, as a passenger, during the two years that had transpired since he "retired," was only keeping the general spirit of it and not the strict letter.

The Admiral knew only one narrow line of conduct to pursue in any and all cases where there was a fight, and that was to shoulder his way straight in without an inquiry as to the rights or the merits of it, and take the part of the weaker side.—And this was the reason why he was always sure to be present at the trial of any universally execrated criminal to oppress and intimidate the jury with a vindictive pantomime of what he would do to them if he ever caught them out of the box. And this was why harried cats and outlawed dogs that knew him confidently took sanctuary under his chair in time of trouble. In the beginning he was the most frantic and bloodthirsty Union man that drew breath in the shadow of the Flag; but the instant the Southerners began to go down before the sweep of the Northern armies, he ran up the Confederate colors and from that time till the end was a rampant and inexorable secessionist.

He hated intemperance with a more uncompromising animosity than any individual I have ever met, of either sex; and he was never tired of storming against it and beseeching friends and strangers alike to be wary and drink with moderation. And yet if any creature had been guileless enough to intimate that his absorbing nine gallons of "straight" whisky during our voyage was any fraction short of rigid or inflexible abstemiousness, in that self-same moment the old man would have spun him to the uttermost parts of the earth in the whirlwind of his wrath. Mind, I am not saying his whisky ever affected his head or his legs, for it did not, in even the slightest degree. He was a capacious container, but he did not hold enough for that. He took a level tumblerful of whisky every morning before he put his clothes on—"to sweeten his bilgewater," he said.—He took another after he got the most of his clothes on, "to settle his mind and give him his bearings." He then shaved, and put on a clean shirt; after which he recited the Lord's Prayer in a fervent, thundering bass that shook the ship to her kelson and suspended all conversation in the main cabin. Then, at this stage, being invariably "by the head," or "by the stern," or "listed to port or starboard," he took one more to "put him on an even keel so that he would mind his hellum and not miss stays and go about, every time he came up in the wind."—And now, his stateroom door swung open and the sun of his benignant face beamed redly out upon men and women and children, and he roared his "Shipmets a'hoy!" in a way that was calculated to wake the dead and precipitate the final resurrection; and forth he strode, a picture to look at and a presence to enforce attention. Stalwart and portly; not a gray hair; broad-brimmed slouch hat; semi-sailor toggery of blue navy flannel—roomy and ample; a stately expanse of shirt-front and a liberal amount of black silk neck-cloth tied with a sailor knot; large chain and imposing seals impending from his fob; awe-inspiring feet, and "a hand like the hand of Providence," as his whaling brethren expressed it; wrist-bands and sleeves pushed back half way to the elbow, out of respect for the warm weather, and exposing hairy arms, gaudy with red and blue anchors, ships, and goddesses of liberty tattooed in India ink. But these details were only secondary matters—his face was the lodestone that chained the eye. It was a sultry disk, glowing determinedly out through a weather beaten mask of mahogany, and studded with warts, seamed with scars, "blazed" all over with unfailing fresh slips of the razor; and with cheery eyes, under shaggy brows, contemplating the world from over the back of a gnarled crag of a nose that loomed vast and lonely out of the undulating immensity that spread away from its foundations. At his heels frisked the darling of his bachelor estate, his terrier "Fan," a creature no larger than a squirrel. The main part of his daily life was occupied in looking after "Fan," in a motherly way, and doctoring her for a hundred ailments which existed only in his imagination.

The Admiral seldom read newspapers; and when he did he never believed anything they said. He read nothing, and believed in nothing, but "The Old Guard," a secession periodical published in New York. He carried a dozen copies of it with him, always, and referred to them for all required information. If it was not there, he supplied it himself, out of a bountiful fancy, inventing history, names, dates, and every thing else necessary to make his point good in an argument. Consequently he was a formidable antagonist in a dispute. Whenever he swung clear of the record and began to create history, the enemy was helpless and had to surrender. Indeed, the enemy could not keep from betraying some little spark of indignation at his manufactured history—and when it came to indignation, that was the Admiral's very "best hold." He was always ready for a political argument, and if nobody started one he would do it himself. With his third retort his temper would begin to rise, and within five minutes he would be blowing a gale, and within fifteen his smoking-room audience would be utterly stormed away and the old man left solitary and alone, banging the table with his fist, kicking the chairs, and roaring a hurricane of profanity. It got so, after a while, that whenever the Admiral approached, with politics in his eye, the passengers would drop out with quiet accord, afraid to meet him; and he would camp on a deserted field.

But he found his match at last, and before a full company. At one time or another, everybody had entered the lists against him and been routed, except the quiet passenger Williams. He had never been able to get an expression of opinion out of him on politics. But now, just as the Admiral drew near the door and the company were about to slip out, Williams said:

"Admiral, are you *certain* about that circumstance concerning the clergymen you mentioned the other day?"—referring to a piece of the Admiral's manufactured history.

Every one was amazed at the man's rashness. The idea of deliberately inviting annihilation was a thing incomprehensible. The retreat came to a halt; then everybody sat down again wondering, to await the upshot of it. The Admiral himself was as surprised as any one. He paused in the door, with his red handkerchief half raised to his sweating face, and contemplated the daring reptile in the corner.

"*Certain* of it? Am I *certain* of it? Do you think I've been lying about it? What do you take me for? Anybody that don't know that circumstance, don't know anything; a child ought to know it. Read up your history! Read it up —— —— —— ——, and don't come asking a man if he's *certain* about a bit of A B C stuff that the very southern niggers know all about."

Here the Admiral's fires began to wax hot, the atmosphere thickened, the coming earthquake rumbled, he began to thunder and lighten. Within three minutes his volcano was in full irruption and he was discharging flames and ashes of indignation, belching black volumes of foul history aloft, and vomiting red-hot torrents of profanity from his crater. Meantime Williams sat silent, and apparently deeply and earnestly interested in what the old man was saying. By and by, when the lull came, he said in the most deferential way, and with the gratified air of a man who has had a mystery cleared up which had been puzzling him uncomfortably:

"*Now* I understand it. I always thought I knew that piece of history well enough, but was still afraid to trust it, because there was not that convincing particularity about it that one likes to have in history; but when you mentioned every name, the other day, and every date, and every little circumstance, in their just order and sequence, I said to myself, *this* sounds something like—*this* is history—*this* is putting it in a shape that gives a man confidence; and I said to myself afterward, I will just ask the Admiral if he is perfectly certain about the details, and if he is I will come out and thank him for clearing this matter up for me. And that is what I want to do now— for until you set that matter right it was nothing but just a confusion in my mind, without head or tail to it."

Nobody ever saw the Admiral look so mollified before, and so pleased. Nobody had ever received his bogus history as gospel before; its genuineness had always been called in question either by words or looks; but here was a man that not only swallowed it all down, but was grateful for the dose. He was taken aback; he hardly knew what to say; even his profanity failed him. Now, Williams continued, modestly and earnestly:

"But Admiral, in saying that this was the first stone thrown, and that this precipitated the war, you have overlooked a circumstance which you are perfectly familiar with, but which has escaped your memory. Now I grant you that what you have stated is correct in every detail—to wit: that on the 16th of October, 1860, two Massachusetts clergymen, named Waite and Granger, went in disguise to the house of John Moody, in Rockport, at dead of night, and dragged forth two southern women and their two little children, and after tarring and feathering them conveyed them to Boston and burned them alive in the State House square; and I also grant your proposition that this deed is what led to the secession of South Carolina on the 20th of December following. Very well." [Here the company were pleasantly surprised to hear Williams proceed to come back at the Admiral with his own invincible weapon—clean, pure, *manufactured history*, without a word of truth in it.] "Very well, I say. But Admiral, why overlook the Willis and Morgan case in South Carolina? You are too well informed a man not to know all about that circumstance. Your arguments and your conversations have shown you to be intimately conversant with every detail of

this national quarrel. You develop matters of history every day
that show plainly that you are no smatterer in it, content to
nibble about the surface, but a man who has searched the
depths and possessed yourself of everything that has a bearing
upon the great question. Therefore, let me just recall to your
mind that Willis and Morgan case—though I see by your face
that the whole thing is already passing through your memory
at this moment. On the 12th of August, 1860, *two months* before the Waite and Granger affair, two South Carolina clergymen, named John H. Morgan and Winthrop L. Willis, one
a Methodist and the other an Old School Baptist, disguised
themselves, and went at midnight to the house of a planter
named Thompson—Archibald F. Thompson, Vice President
under Thomas Jefferson,—and took thence, at midnight, his
widowed aunt, (a Northern woman,) and her adopted child,
an orphan named Mortimer Highie, afflicted with epilepsy
and suffering at the time from white swelling on one of his
legs, and compelled to walk on crutches in consequence; and
the two ministers, in spite of the pleadings of the victims,
dragged them to the bush, tarred and feathered them, and
afterward burned them at the stake in the city of Charleston.
You remember perfectly well what a stir it made; you remember perfectly well that even the Charleston *Courier* stigma-
tized the act as being unpleasant, of questionable propriety,
and scarcely justifiable, and likewise that it would not be matter of surprise if retaliation ensued. And you remember also,
that this thing was the *cause* of the Massachusetts outrage.
Who, indeed, were the two Massachusetts ministers? and who
were the two Southern women they burned? I do not need
to remind *you*, Admiral, with your intimate knowledge of history, that Waite was the nephew of the woman burned in
Charleston; that Granger was her cousin in the second degree, and that the woman they burned in Boston was the wife
of John H. Morgan, and the still loved but divorced wife of
Winthrop L. Willis. Now, Admiral, it is only fair that you
should acknowledge that the first provocation came from the
Southern preachers and that the Northern ones were justified
in retaliating. In your arguments you never yet have shown
the least disposition to withhold a just verdict or be in any-
wise unfair, when authoritative history condemned your

position, and therefore I have no hesitation in asking you to take the original blame from the Massachusetts ministers, in this matter, and transfer it to the South Carolina clergymen where it justly belongs."

The Admiral was conquered. This sweet spoken creature who swallowed his fraudulent history as if it were the bread of life; basked in his furious blasphemy as if it were generous sunshine; found only calm, even-handed justice in his rampart partisanship; and flooded him with invented history so sugar-coated with flattery and deference that there was no rejecting it, was "too many" for him. He stammered some awkward, profane sentences about the ——— ——— ——— ——— Willis and Morgan business having escaped his memory, but that he "re-membered it now," and then, under pretence of giving Fan some medicine for an imaginary cough, drew out of the battle and went away, a vanquished man. Then cheers and laughter went up, and Williams, the ship's benefactor was a hero. The news went about the vessel, champagne was ordered, an en-thusiastic reception instituted in the smoking room, and ev-erybody flocked thither to shake hands with the conqueror. The wheelsman said afterward, that the Admiral stood up be-hind the pilot house and "ripped and cursed all to himself" till he loosened the smoke-stack guys and becalmed the main-sail.

The Admiral's power was broken. After that, if he began an argument, somebody would bring Williams, and the old man would grow weak and begin to quiet down at once. And as soon as he was done, Williams in his dulcet, insinuating way, would invent some history (referring for proof, to the old man's own excellent memory and to copies of "The Old Guard" known not to be in his possession) that would turn the tables completely and leave the Admiral all abroad and helpless. By and by he came to so dread Williams and his gilded tongue that he would stop talking when he saw him approach, and finally ceased to mention politics altogether, and from that time forward there was entire peace and seren-ity in the ship.

Chapter LXIII

O N A CERTAIN bright morning the Islands hove in sight, lying low on the lonely sea, and everybody climbed to the upper deck to look. After two thousand miles of watery solitude the vision was a welcome one. As we approached, the imposing promontory of Diamond Head rose up out of the ocean its rugged front softened by the hazy distance, and presently the details of the land began to make themselves manifest: first the line of beach; then the plumed cocoanut trees of the tropics; then cabins of the natives; then the white town of Honolulu, said to contain between twelve and fifteen thousand inhabitants spread over a dead level; with streets from twenty to thirty feet wide, solid and level as a floor, most of them straight as a line and few as crooked as a cork-screw.

The further I traveled through the town the better I liked it. Every step revealed a new contrast—disclosed something I was unaccustomed to. In place of the grand mud-colored brown fronts of San Francisco, I saw dwellings built of straw, adobies, and cream-colored pebble-and-shell-conglomerated coral, cut into oblong blocks and laid in cement; also a great number of neat white cottages, with green window-shutters; in place of front yards like billiard-tables with iron fences around them, I saw these homes surrounded by ample yards, thickly clad with green grass, and shaded by tall trees, through whose dense foliage the sun could scarcely penetrate; in place of the customary geranium, calla lily, etc., languishing in dust and general debility, I saw luxurious banks and thickets of flowers, fresh as a meadow after a rain, and glowing with the richest dyes; in place of the dingy horrors of San Francisco's pleasure grove, the "Willows," I saw huge-bodied, wide-spreading forest trees, with strange names and stranger appearance—trees that cast a shadow like a thunder-cloud, and were able to stand alone without being tied to green poles; in place of gold fish, wiggling around in glass globes, assuming countless shades and degrees of distortion through the magnifying and diminishing qualities of their transparent prison houses, I saw cats—Tom-cats, Mary Ann cats, long-tailed cats, bob-tailed cats, blind cats, one-eyed cats, wall-eyed cats, cross-eyed cats, gray cats, black cats, white cats, yellow cats, striped cats, spotted cats, tame cats, wild cats, singed cats, individual cats, groups of cats, platoons of cats, companies of cats, regiments of cats, armies of cats, multitudes of cats, millions of cats, and all of them sleek, fat, lazy and sound asleep.

I looked on a multitude of people, some white, in white coats, vests, pantaloons, even white cloth shoes, made snowy with chalk duly laid on every morning; but the majority of the people were almost as dark as negroes—women with comely features, fine black eyes, rounded forms, inclining to the voluptuous, clad in a single bright red or white garment that fell free and unconfined from shoulder to heel, long black hair falling loose, gypsy hats, encircled with wreaths of natural flowers of a brilliant carmine tint; plenty of dark men in various costumes, and some with nothing on but a battered stove-pipe hat tilted on the nose, and a very scant breech-clout;—certain smoke-dried children were clothed in nothing but sunshine—a very neat fitting and picturesque apparel indeed.

In place of roughs and rowdies staring and blackguarding on the corners, I saw long-haired, saddle-colored Sandwich Island maidens sitting on the ground in the shade of corner houses, gazing indolently at whatever or whoever happened along; instead of wretched cobble-stone pavements, I walked on a firm foundation of coral, built up from the bottom of the sea by the absurd but persevering insect of that name, with a light layer of lava and cinders overlying the coral, belched up out of fathomless perdition long ago through the seared and blackened crater that stands dead and harmless in the distance now; instead of cramped and crowded street-cars, I met dusky native women sweeping by, free as the wind, on fleet horses and astride, with gaudy riding-sashes, streaming like banners behind them; instead of the combined stenches of Chinadom and Brannan street slaughter-houses, I breathed the balmy fragrance of jessamine, oleander, and the Pride of India; in place of the hurry and bustle and noisy confusion of San Francisco, I moved in the midst of a Summer calm as tranquil as dawn in the Garden of Eden; in place of the

Golden City's skirting sand hills and the placid bay, I saw on the one side a frame-work of tall, precipitous mountains close at hand, clad in refreshing green, and cleft by deep, cool, chasm-like valleys—and in front the grand sweep of the ocean: a brilliant, transparent green near the shore, bound and bordered by a long white line of foamy spray dashing against the reef, and further out the dead blue water of the deep sea, flecked with "white caps," and in the far horizon a single, lonely sail—a mere accent-mark to emphasize a slumberous calm and a solitude that were without sound or limit. When the sun sunk down—the one intruder from other realms and persistent in suggestions of them—it was tranced luxury to sit in the perfumed air and forget that there was any world but these enchanted islands.

It was such ecstacy to dream, and dream—till you got a bite. A scorpion bite. Then the first duty was to get up out of the grass and kill the scorpion; and the next to bathe the bitten place with alcohol or brandy; and the next to resolve to keep out of the grass in future. Then came an adjournment to the bed-chamber and the pastime of writing up the day's journal with one hand and the destruction of mosquitoes with the other—a whole community of them at a slap. Then, observing an enemy approaching,—a hairy tarantula on stilts—why not set the spittoon on him? It is done, and the projecting ends of his paws give a luminous idea of the magnitude of his reach. Then to bed and become a promenade for a centipede with forty-two legs on a side and every foot hot enough to burn a hole through a raw-hide. More soaking with alcohol, and a resolution to examine the bed before entering it, in future. Then wait, and suffer, till all the mosquitoes in the neighborhood have crawled in under the bar, then slip out quickly, shut them in and sleep peacefully on the floor till morning. Meantime it is comforting to curse the tropics in occasional wakeful intervals.

We had an abundance of fruit in Honolulu, of course. Oranges, pine-apples, bananas, strawberries, lemons, limes, mangoes, guavas, melons, and a rare and curious luxury called the chirimoya, which is deliciousness itself. Then there is the tamarind. I thought tamarinds were made to eat, but that was probably not the idea. I ate several, and it seemed to me that they were rather sour that year. They pursed up my lips, till they resembled the stem-end of a tomato, and I had to take my sustenance through a quill for twenty-four hours. They sharpened my teeth till I could have shaved with them, and gave them a " wire edge" that I was afraid would stay; but a citizen said "no, it will come off when the enamel does"— which was comforting, at any rate. I found, afterward, that only strangers eat tamarinds—but they only eat them once.

Chapter LXIV

I N MY DIARY of our third day in Honolulu, I find this: I am probably the most sensitive man in Hawaii to-night—especially about sitting down in the presence of my betters. I have ridden fifteen or twenty miles on horse-back since 5 P.M. and to tell the honest truth, I have a delicacy about sitting down at all.

An excursion to Diamond Head and the King's Cocoanut Grove was planned to-day—time, 4:30 P.M.—the party to consist of half a dozen gentlemen and three ladies. They all started at the appointed hour except myself. I was at the Government prison, (with Captain Fish and another whaleship-skipper, Captain Phillips,) and got so interested in its examination that I did not notice how quickly the time was passing. Somebody remarked that it was twenty minutes past five o'clock, and that woke me up. It was a fortunate circumstance that Captain Phillips was along with his "turn out," as he calls a top-buggy that Captain Cook brought here in 1778, and a horse that was here when Captain Cook came. Captain Phillips takes a just pride in his driving and in the speed of his horse, and to his passion for displaying them I owe it that we were only sixteen minutes coming from the prison to the American Hotel—a distance which has been estimated to be over half a mile. But it took some fearful driving. The Captain's whip came down fast, and the blows started so much dust out of the horse's hide that during the last half of the journey we rode through an impenetrable fog, and ran by a pocket compass in the hands of Captain Fish, a whaler of twenty-six years experience, who sat there through the perilous voyage as self-possessed as if he had been on the euchre-deck of his own ship, and calmly said, "Port your helm—port," from time to time, and "Hold her a little free—steady—so-o," and "Luff—hard down to starboard!" and never once lost his presence of mind or betrayed the least anxiety by voice or manner. When we came to anchor at last, and Captain Phillips looked at his watch and said, "Sixteen minutes—I told you it was in her! that's over three miles an hour!" I could see he felt entitled to a compliment, and so I said I had never seen lightning go like that horse. And I never had.

The landlord of the American said the party had been gone nearly an hour, but that he could give me my choice of several horses that could overtake them. I said, never mind—I preferred a safe horse to a fast one—I would like to have an excessively gentle horse—a horse with no spirit whatever—a lame one, if he had such a thing. Inside of five minutes I was mounted, and perfectly satisfied with my outfit. I had no time to label him "This is a horse," and so if the public took him for a sheep I cannot help it. I was satisfied, and that was the main thing. I could see that he had as many fine points as any man's horse, and so I hung my hat on one of them, behind the saddle, and swabbed the perspiration from my face and started. I named him after this island, "Oahu" (pronounced O-waw-hee). The first gate he came to he started in; I had neither whip nor spur, and so I simply argued the case with him. He resisted argument, but ultimately yielded to insult and abuse. He backed out of that gate and steered for another one on the other side of the street. I triumphed by my former process. Within the next six hundred yards he crossed the street fourteen times and attempted thirteen gates, and in the meantime the tropical sun was beating down and threatening to cave the top of my head in, and I was literally dripping with perspiration. He abandoned the gate business after that and went along peaceably enough, but absorbed in meditation. I noticed this latter circumstance, and it soon began to fill me with apprehension. I said to myself, this creature is planning some new outrage, some fresh deviltry or other— no horse ever thought over a subject so profoundly as this one is doing just for nothing. The more this thing preyed upon my mind the more uneasy I became, until the suspense became almost unbearable and I dismounted to see if there was anything wild in his eye—for I had heard that the eye of this noblest of our domestic animals is very expressive. I cannot describe what a load of anxiety was lifted from my mind when I found that he was only asleep. I woke him up and started him into a faster walk, and then the villainy of his nature came out again. He tried to climb over a stone wall, five or six feet high. I saw that I must apply force to this horse, and that I might as well begin first as last. I plucked a stout switch from a tamarind tree, and the moment he saw it, he surrendered. He broke into a convulsive sort of a canter, which had three short steps in it and one long one, and reminded me alternately of the clattering shake of the great earthquake, and the sweeping plunging of the Ajax in a storm.

And now there can be no fitter occasion than the present to pronounce a left-handed blessing upon the man who invented the American saddle. There is no seat to speak of about it—one might as well sit in a shovel—and the stirrups are nothing but an ornamental nuisance. If I were to write down here all the abuse I expended on those stirrups, it would make a large book, even without pictures. Sometimes I got one foot so far through, that the stirrup partook of the nature of an anklet; sometimes both feet were through, and I was handcuffed by the legs; and sometimes my feet got clear out and left the stirrups wildly dangling about my shins. Even when I was in proper position and carefully balanced upon the balls of my feet, there was no comfort in it, on account of my nervous dread that they were going to slip one way or the other in a moment. But the subject is too exasperating to write about.

A mile and a half from town, I came to a grove of tall cocoa-nut trees, with clean, branchless stems reaching straight up sixty or seventy feet and topped with a spray of green foliage sheltering clusters of cocoa-nuts—not more picturesque than a forest of colossal ragged parasols, with bunches of magnified grapes under them, would be. I once heard a grouty northern invalid say that a cocoa-nut tree might be poetical, possibly it was; but it looked like a feather-duster struck by lightning. I think that describes it better than a picture—and yet, without any question, there is something fascinating about a cocoa-nut tree—and graceful, too.

About a dozen cottages, some frame and the others of native grass, nestled sleepily in the shade here and there. The grass cabins are of a grayish color, are shaped much like our own cottages, only with higher and steeper roofs usually, and are made of some kind of weed strongly bound together in bundles. The roofs are very thick, and so are the walls; the latter have square holes in them for windows. At a little distance these cabins have a furry appearance, as if they might be made of bear skins. They are very cool and pleasant inside. The King's flag was flying from the roof of one of the cottages, and His Majesty was probably within. He owns the whole concern thereabouts, and passes his time there frequently, on sultry days "laying off." The spot is called "The King's Grove."

Near by is an interesting ruin—the meagre remains of an ancient heathen temple—a place where human sacrifices were offered up in those old bygone days when the simple child of nature, yielding momentarily to sin when sorely tempted, acknowledged his error when calm reflection had shown it him, and came forward with noble frankness and offered up his grandmother as an atoning sacrifice—in those old days when the luckless sinner could keep on cleansing his conscience and achieving periodical happiness as long as his relations held out; long, long before the missionaries braved a thousand privations to come and make them permanently miserable by telling them how beautiful and how blissful a place heaven is, and how nearly impossible it is to get there; and showed the poor native how dreary a place perdition is and what unnecessarily liberal facilities there are for going to it; showed him how, in his ignorance he had gone and fooled away all his kinfolks to no purpose; showed him what rapture it is to work all day long for fifty cents to buy food for next day with, as compared with fishing for pastime and lolling in the shade through eternal Summer, and eating of the bounty that nobody labored to provide but Nature. How sad it is to think of the multitudes who have gone to their graves in this beautiful island and never knew there was a hell!

This ancient temple was built of rough blocks of lava, and was simply a roofless inclosure a hundred and thirty feet long and seventy wide—nothing but naked walls, very thick, but not much higher than a man's head. They will last for ages no doubt, if left unmolested. Its three altars and other sacred appurtenances have crumbled and passed away years ago. It is said that in the old times thousands of human beings were slaughtered here, in the presence of naked and howling savages. If these mute stones could speak, what tales they could tell, what pictures they could describe, of fettered victims writhing under the knife; of massed forms straining forward out of the gloom, with ferocious faces lit up by the sacrificial fires; of the background of ghostly trees; of the dark pyramid of Diamond Head standing sentinel over the uncanny scene, and the peaceful moon looking down upon it through rifts in the cloud-rack!

When Kamehameha (pronounced Ka-may-ha-may-ah) the Great—who was a sort of a Napoleon in military genius and uniform success—invaded this island of Oahu three quarters of a century ago, and exterminated the army sent to oppose him, and took full and final possession of the country, he searched out the dead body of the King of Oahu, and those of the principal chiefs, and impaled their heads on the walls of this temple.

Those were savage times when this old slaughter-house was in its prime. The King and the chiefs ruled the common herd with a rod of iron; made them gather all the provisions the masters needed; build all the houses and temples; stand all the expenses, of whatever kind; take kicks and cuffs for thanks; drag out lives well flavored with misery, and then suffer death for trifling offences or yield up their lives on the sacrificial altars to purchase favors from the gods for their hard rulers. The missionaries have clothed them, educated them, broken up the tyrannous authority of their chiefs, and given them freedom and the right to enjoy whatever their hands and brains produce with equal laws for all, and punishment for all alike who transgress them. The contrast is so strong—the benefit conferred upon this people by the missionaries is so prominent, so palpable and so unquestionable, that the frankest compliment I can pay them, and the best, is simply to point to the condition of the Sandwich Islanders of Captain Cook's time, and their condition to-day. Their work speaks for itself.

Chapter LXV

B Y AND BY, after a rugged climb, we halted on the summit of a hill which commanded a far-reaching view. The moon rose and flooded mountain and valley and ocean with a mellow radiance, and out of the shadows of the foliage the distant lights of Honolulu glinted like an encampment of fire-flies. The air was heavy with the fragrance of flowers. The halt was brief.—Gayly laughing and talking, the party galloped on, and I clung to the pommel and cantered after. Presently we came to a place where no grass grew—a wide expanse of deep sand. They said it was an old battle ground. All around everywhere, not three feet apart, the bleached bones of men gleamed white in the moonlight. We picked up a lot of them for mementoes. I got quite a number of arm bones and leg bones—of great chiefs, may be, who had fought savagely in that fearful battle in the old days, when blood flowed like wine where we now stood—and wore the choicest of them out on Oahu afterward, trying to make him go. All sorts of bones could be found except skulls; but a citizen said, irreverently, that there had been an unusual number of "skull-hunters" there lately—a species of sportsmen I had never heard of before.

Nothing whatever is known about this place—its story is a secret that will never be revealed. The oldest natives make no pretense of being possessed of its history. They say these bones were here when they were children. They were here when their grandfathers were children—but how they came here, they can only conjecture. Many people believe this spot to be an ancient battle-ground, and it is usual to call it so; and they believe that these skeletons have lain for ages just where their proprietors fell in the great fight. Other people believe that Kamehameha I. fought his first battle here. On this point, I have heard a story, which may have been taken from one of the numerous books which have been written concerning these islands—I do not know where the narrator got it. He said that when Kamehameha (who was at first merely a subordinate chief on the island of Hawaii), landed here, he brought a large army with him, and encamped at Waikiki. The

Oahuans marched against him, and so confident were they of success that they readily acceded to a demand of their priests that they should draw a line where these bones now lie, and take an oath that, if forced to retreat at all, they would never retreat beyond this boundary. The priests told them that death and everlasting punishment would overtake any who violated the oath, and the march was resumed. Kamehameha drove them back step by step; the priests fought in the front rank and exhorted them both by voice and inspiriting example to remember their oath—to die, if need be, but never cross the fatal line. The struggle was manfully maintained, but at last the chief priest fell, pierced to the heart with a spear, and the unlucky omen fell like a blight upon the brave souls at his back; with a triumphant shout the invaders pressed forward—the line was crossed—the offended gods deserted the despairing army, and, accepting the doom their perjury had brought upon them, they broke and fled over the plain where Honolulu stands now—up the beautiful Nuuanu Valley—paused a moment, hemmed in by precipitous mountains on either hand and the frightful precipice of the Pari in front, and then were driven over—a sheer plunge of six hundred feet!

The story is pretty enough, but Mr. Jarves' excellent history says the Oahuans were intrenched in Nuuanu Valley; that Kamehameha ousted them, routed them, pursued them up the valley and drove them over the precipice. He makes no mention of our bone-yard at all in his book.

Impressed by the profound silence and repose that rested over the beautiful landscape, and being, as usual, in the rear, I gave voice to my thoughts. I said:

"What a picture is here slumbering in the solemn glory of the moon! How strong the rugged outlines of the dead volcano stand out against the clear sky! What a snowy fringe marks the bursting of the surf over the long, curved reef! How calmly the dim city sleeps yonder in the plain! How soft the shadows lie upon the stately mountains that border the dream-haunted Mauoa Valley! What a grand pyramid of billowy clouds towers above the storied Pari! How the grim warriors of the past seem flocking in ghostly squadrons to their ancient battlefield again—how the wails of the dying well up from the——"

At this point the horse called Oahu sat down in the sand. Sat down to listen, I suppose. Never mind what he heard, I stopped apostrophising and convinced him that I was not a man to allow contempt of Court on the part of a horse. I broke the back-bone of a Chief over his rump and set out to join the cavalcade again.

Very considerably fagged out we arrived in town at 9 o'clock at night, myself in the lead—for when my horse finally came to understand that he was homeward bound and hadn't far to go, he turned his attention strictly to business.

This is a good time to drop in a paragraph of information. There is no regular livery stable in Honolulu, or, indeed, in any part of the kingdom of Hawaii; therefore unless you are acquainted with wealthy residents (who all have good horses), you must hire animals of the wretchedest description from the Kanakas. (i. e. natives.) Any horse you hire, even though it be from a white man, is not often of much account, because it will be brought in for you from some ranch, and has necessarily been leading a hard life. If the Kanakas who have been caring for him (inveterate riders they are) have not ridden him half to death every day themselves, you can depend upon it they have been doing the same thing by proxy, by clandestinely hiring him out. At least, so I am informed. The result is, that no horse has a chance to eat, drink, rest, recuperate, or look well or feel well, and so strangers go about the Islands mounted as I was to-day.

In hiring a horse from a Kanaka, you must have all your eyes about you, because you can rest satisfied that you are dealing with a shrewd unprincipled rascal. You may leave your door open and your trunk unlocked as long as you please, and he will not meddle with your property; he has no important vices and no inclination to commit robbery on a large scale; but if he can get ahead of you in the horse business, he will take a genuine delight in doing it. This trait is characteristic of horse jockeys, the world over, is it not? He will overcharge you if he can; he will hire you a fine-looking horse at night (anybody's—may be the King's, if the royal steed be in convenient view), and bring you the mate to my Oahu in the morning, and contend that it is the same animal. If you make trouble, he will get out by saying it was not

himself who made the bargain with you, but his brother,
"who went out in the country this morning." They have always got a "brother" to shift the responsibility upon. A victim said to one of these fellows one day:

"But I know I hired the horse of you, because I noticed
that scar on your cheek."

The reply was not bad: "Oh, yes—yes—my brother all
same—we twins!"

A friend of mine, J. Smith, hired a horse yesterday, the
Kanaka warranting him to be in excellent condition. Smith
had a saddle and blanket of his own, and he ordered the Kanaka to put these on the horse. The Kanaka protested that he
was perfectly willing to trust the gentleman with the saddle
that was already on the animal, but Smith refused to use it.
The change was made; then Smith noticed that the Kanaka
had only changed the saddles, and had left the original blanket on the horse; he said he forgot to change the blankets,
and so, to cut the bother short, Smith mounted and rode
away. The horse went lame a mile from town, and afterward
got to cutting up some extraordinary capers. Smith got down
and took off the saddle, but the blanket stuck fast to the horse
—glued to a procession of raw places. The Kanaka's mysterious conduct stood explained.

Another friend of mine bought a pretty good horse from a
native, a day or two ago, after a tolerably thorough examination of the animal. He discovered to-day that the horse was
as blind as a bat, in one eye. He meant to have examined that
eye, and came home with a general notion that he had done
it; but he remembers now that every time he made the
attempt his attention was called to something else by his
victimizer.

One more instance, and then I will pass to something else.
I am informed that when a certain Mr. L., a visiting stranger,
was here, he bought a pair of very respectable-looking match
horses from a native. They were in a little stable with a partition through the middle of it—one horse in each apartment. Mr. L. examined one of them critically through a
window (the Kanaka's "brother" having gone to the country
with the key), and then went around the house and examined
the other through a window on the other side. He said it was

the neatest match he had ever seen, and paid for the horses on the spot. Whereupon the Kanaka departed to join his brother in the country. The fellow had shamefully swindled L. There was only one "match" horse, and he had examined his starboard side through one window and his port side through another! I decline to believe this story, but I give it because it is worth something as a fanciful illustration of a fixed fact—namely, that the Kanaka horse-jockey is fertile in invention and elastic in conscience.

You can buy a pretty good horse for forty or fifty dollars, and a good enough horse for all practical purposes for two dollars and a half. I estimate "Oahu" to be worth somewhere in the neighborhood of thirty-five cents. A good deal better animal than he is was sold here day before yesterday for a dollar and seventy-five cents, and sold again to-day for two dollars and twenty-five cents; Williams bought a handsome and lively little pony yesterday for ten dollars; and about the best common horse on the island (and he is a really good one) sold yesterday, with Mexican saddle and bridle, for seventy dollars—a horse which is well and widely known, and greatly respected for his speed, good disposition and everlasting bottom. You give your horse a little grain once a day; it comes from San Francisco, and is worth about two cents a pound; and you give him as much hay as he wants; it is cut and brought to the market by natives, and is not very good; it is baled into long, round bundles, about the size of a large man; one of them is stuck by the middle on each end of a six-foot pole, and the Kanaka shoulders the pole and walks about the streets between the upright bales in search of customers. These hay bales, thus carried, have a general resemblance to a colossal capital H.

The hay-bundles cost twenty-five cents apiece, and one will last a horse about a day. You can get a horse for a song, a week's hay for another song, and you can turn your animal loose among the luxuriant grass in your neighbor's broad front yard without a song at all—you do it at midnight, and stable the beast again before morning. You have been at no expense thus far, but when you come to buy a saddle and bridle they will cost you from twenty to thirty-five dollars. You can hire a horse, saddle and bridle at from seven to ten dollars a week, and the owner will take care of them at his own expense.

It is time to close this day's record—bed time. As I prepare for sleep, a rich voice rises out of the still night, and, far as this ocean rock is toward the ends of the earth, I recognize a familiar home air. But the words seem somewhat out of joint:

"Waikiki lantoni œ Kaa hooly hooly wawhoo."

Translated, that means "When we were marching through Georgia."

Chapter LXVI

PASSING THROUGH the market place we saw that feature of Honolulu under its most favorable auspices—that is, in the full glory of Saturday afternoon, which is a festive day with the natives. The native girls by twos and threes and parties of a dozen, and sometimes in whole platoons and companies, went cantering up and down the neighboring streets astride of fleet but homely horses, and with their gaudy riding habits streaming like banners behind them. Such a troop of free and easy riders, in their natural home, the saddle, makes a gay and graceful spectacle. The riding habit I speak of is simply a long, broad scarf, like a tavern table cloth brilliantly colored, wrapped around the loins once, then apparently passed between the limbs and each end thrown backward over the same, and floating and flapping behind on both sides beyond the horse's tail like a couple of fancy flags; then, slipping the stirrup-irons between her toes, the girl throws her chest forward, sits up like a Major General and goes sweeping by like the wind.

The girls put on all the finery they can on Saturday afternoon—fine black silk robes; flowing red ones that nearly put your eyes out; others as white as snow; still others that discount the rainbow; and they wear their hair in nets, and trim their jaunty hats with fresh flowers, and encircle their dusky throats with home-made necklaces of the brilliant vermillion-tinted blossom of the *ohia*; and they fill the markets and the adjacent streets with their bright presences, and smell like a rag factory on fire with their offensive cocoanut oil.

Occasionally you see a heathen from the sunny isles away down in the South Seas, with his face and neck tattooed till he looks like the customary mendicant from Washoe who has been blown up in a mine. Some are tattooed a dead blue color down to the upper lip—masked, as it were—leaving the natural light yellow skin of Micronesia unstained from thence down; some with broad marks drawn down from hair to neck, on both sides of the face, and a strip of the original yellow skin, two inches wide, down the center—a gridiron with a spoke broken out; and some with the entire face discolored with the popular mortification tint, relieved only by one or two thin, wavy threads of natural yellow running across the face from ear to ear, and eyes twinkling out of this darkness, from under shadowing hat-brims, like stars in the dark of the moon.

Moving among the stirring crowds, you come to the poi merchants, squatting in the shade on their hams, in true native fashion, and surrounded by purchasers. (The Sandwich Islanders always squat on their hams, and who knows but they may be the old original "ham sandwiches?" The thought is pregnant with interest.) The poi looks like common flour paste, and is kept in large bowls formed of a species of gourd, and capable of holding from one to three or four gallons. Poi is the chief article of food among the natives, and is prepared from the *taro* plant. The taro root looks like a thick, or, if you please, a corpulent sweet potato, in shape, but is of a light purple color when boiled. When boiled it answers as a passable substitute for bread. The buck Kanakas bake it under ground, then mash it up well with a heavy lava pestle, mix water with it until it becomes a paste, set it aside and let it ferment, and then it is poi—and an unseductive mixture it is, almost tasteless before it ferments and too sour for a luxury afterward. But nothing is more nutritious. When solely used, however, it produces acrid humors, a fact which sufficiently accounts for the humorous character of the Kanakas. I think there must be as much of a knack in handling poi as there is in eating with chopsticks. The forefinger is thrust into the mess and stirred quickly round several times and drawn as quickly out, thickly coated, just as if it were poulticed; the head is thrown back, the finger inserted in the mouth and the delicacy stripped off and swallowed—the eye closing gently, meanwhile, in a languid sort of ecstasy. Many a different finger goes into the same bowl and many a different kind of dirt and shade and quality of flavor is added to the virtues of its contents.

Around a small shanty was collected a crowd of natives buying the *awa* root. It is said that but for the use of this root the destruction of the people in former times by certain imported diseases would have been far greater than it was, and by others it is said that this is merely a fancy. All agree that poi will rejuvenate a man who is used up and his vitality almost annihilated by hard drinking, and that in some kinds of diseases it will restore health after all medicines have failed; but all are not willing to allow to the *awa* the virtues claimed for it. The natives manufacture an intoxicating drink from it which is fearful in its effects when persistently indulged in. It covers the body with dry, white scales, inflames the eyes, and causes premature decrepitude. Although the man before whose establishment we stopped has to pay a Government license of eight hundred dollars a year for the exclusive right to sell *awa* root, it is said that he makes a small fortune every twelve-month; while saloon keepers, who pay a thousand dollars a year for the privilege of retailing whiskey, etc., only make a bare living.

We found the fish market crowded; for the native is very fond of fish, and *eats the article raw and alive!* Let us change the subject.

In old times here Saturday was a grand gala day indeed. All the native population of the town forsook their labors, and those of the surrounding country journeyed to the city. Then the white folks had to stay indoors, for every street was so packed with charging cavaliers and cavalieresses that it was next to impossible to thread one's way through the cavalcades without getting crippled.

At night they feasted and the girls danced the lascivious *hula hula*—a dance that is said to exhibit the very perfection of educated motion of limb and arm, hand, head and body, and the exactest uniformity of movement and accuracy of "time." It was performed by a circle of girls with no raiment on them to speak of, who went through an infinite variety of motions and figures without prompting, and yet so true was their "time," and in such perfect concert did they move that when they were placed in a straight line, hands, arms, bodies, limbs and heads waved, swayed, gesticulated, bowed, stooped, whirled, squirmed, twisted and undulated as if they were part and parcel of a single individual; and it was difficult to believe they were not moved in a body by some exquisite piece of mechanism.

Of late years, however, Saturday has lost most of its quondam gala features. This weekly stampede of the natives interfered too much with labor and the interests of the white folks, and by sticking in a law here, and preaching a sermon there, and by various other means, they gradually broke it up. The demoralizing *hula hula* was forbidden to be performed, save at night, with closed doors, in presence of few spectators, and only by permission duly procured from the authorities and the payment of ten dollars for the same. There are few girls now-a-days able to dance this ancient national dance in the highest perfection of the art.

The missionaries have christianized and educated all the natives. They all belong to the Church, and there is not one of them, above the age of eight years, but can read and write with facility in the native tongue. It is the most universally educated race of people outside of China. They have any quantity of books, printed in the Kanaka language, and all the natives are fond of reading. They are inveterate church-goers—nothing can keep them away. All this ameliorating cultivation has at last built up in the native women a profound respect for chastity—in other people. Perhaps that is enough to say on that head. The national sin will die out when the race does, but perhaps not earlier.—But doubtless this purifying is not far off, when we reflect that contact with civilization and the whites has reduced the native population from *four hundred thousand* (Captain Cook's estimate,) to *fifty-five thousand* in something over eighty years!

Society is a queer medley in this notable missionary, whaling and governmental centre. If you get into conversation with a stranger and experience that natural desire to know what sort of ground you are treading on by finding out what manner of man your stranger is, strike out boldly and address him as "Captain." Watch him narrowly, and if you see by his countenance that you are on the wrong tack, ask him where he preaches. It is a safe bet that he is either a missionary or captain of a whaler. I am now personally acquainted with seventy-two captains and ninety-six missionaries. The captains and ministers form one-half of the population; the third fourth is composed of common Kanakas and mercantile foreigners and their families, and the final fourth is made up of high officers of the Hawaiian Government. And there are just about cats enough for three apiece all around.

A solemn stranger met me in the suburbs the other day, and said:

"Good morning, your reverence. Preach in the stone church yonder, no doubt?"

"No, I don't. I'm not a preacher."

"Really, I beg your pardon, Captain. I trust you had a good season. How much oil"—

"Oil? What do you take me for? I'm not a whaler."

"Oh, I beg a thousand pardons, your Excellency. Major General in the household troops, no doubt? Minister of the Interior, likely? Secretary of war? First Gentleman of the Bed-chamber? Commissioner of the Royal"—

"Stuff! I'm no official. I'm not connected in any way with the Government."

"Bless my life! Then, who the mischief are you? what the mischief are you? and how the mischief did you get here, and where in thunder did you come from?"

"I'm only a private personage—an unassuming stranger—lately arrived from America."

"No? Not a missionary! Not a whaler! not a member of his Majesty's Government! not even Secretary of the Navy! Ah, Heaven! it is too blissful to be true; alas, I do but dream. And yet that noble, honest countenance—those oblique, in-genuous eyes—that massive head, incapable of—of—any-thing; your hand; give me your hand, bright waif. Excuse these tears. For sixteen weary years I have yearned for a mo-ment like this, and"—

Here his feelings were too much for him, and he swooned away. I pitied this poor creature from the bottom of my heart. I was deeply moved. I shed a few tears on him and kissed him for his mother. I then took what small change he had and "shoved."

Chapter LXVII

I STILL quote from my journal:

I found the national Legislature to consist of half a dozen white men and some thirty or forty natives. It was a dark assemblage. The nobles and Ministers (about a dozen of them altogether) occupied the extreme left of the hall, with David Kalakaua (the King's Chamberlain) and Prince William at the head. The President of the Assembly, His Royal Highness M. Kekuanaoa,* and the Vice President (the latter a white man,) sat in the pulpit, if I may so term it.

The President is the King's father. He is an erect, strongly built, massive featured, white-haired, tawny old gentleman of eighty years of age or thereabouts. He was simply but well dressed, in a blue cloth coat and white vest, and white pantaloons, without spot, dust or blemish upon them. He bears himself with a calm, stately dignity, and is a man of noble presence. He was a young man and a distinguished warrior under that terrific fighter, Kamehameha I., more than half a century ago. A knowledge of his career suggested some such thought as this: "This man, naked as the day he was born, and war-club and spear in hand, has charged at the head of a horde of savages against other hordes of savages more than a generation and a half ago, and reveled in slaughter and carnage; has worshipped wooden images on his devout knees; has seen hundreds of his race offered up in heathen temples as sacrifices to wooden idols, at a time when no missionary's foot had ever pressed this soil, and he had never heard of the white man's God; has believed his enemy could secretly pray him to death; has seen the day, in his childhood, when it was a crime punishable by death for a man to eat with his wife, or for a plebeian to let his shadow fall upon the King—and now look at him; an educated Christian; neatly and handsomely dressed; a high-minded, elegant gentleman; a traveler, in some degree, and one who has been the honored guest of royalty in Europe; a man practiced in holding the reins of an enlightened government, and well versed in the politics of his country and in general, practical information. Look at him,

*Since dead.

sitting there presiding over the deliberations of a legislative body, among whom are white men—a grave, dignified, statesmanlike personage, and as seemingly natural and fitted to the place as if he had been born in it and had never been out of it in his life time. How the experiences of this old man's eventful life shame the cheap inventions of romance!"

Kekuanaoa is not of the blood royal. He derives his princely rank from his wife, who was a daughter of Kamehameha the Great. Under other monarchies the male line takes precedence of the female in tracing genealogies, but here the opposite is the case—the female line takes precedence. Their reason for this is exceedingly sensible, and I recommend it to the aristocracy of Europe: They say it is easy to know who a man's mother was, but, etc., etc.

The christianizing of the natives has hardly even weakened some of their barbarian superstitions, much less destroyed them. I have just referred to one of these. It is still a popular belief that if your enemy can get hold of any article belonging to you he can get down on his knees over it and *pray you to death*. Therefore many a native gives up and dies merely because he *imagines* that some enemy is putting him through a course of damaging prayer. This praying an individual to death seems absurd enough at a first glance, but then when we call to mind some of the pulpit efforts of certain of our own ministers the thing looks plausible.

In former times, among the Islanders, not only a plurality of wives was customary, but a *plurality of husbands* likewise. Some native women of noble rank had as many as six husbands. A woman thus supplied did not reside with all her husbands at once, but lived several months with each in turn. An understood sign hung at her door during these months. When the sign was taken down, it meant "NEXT."

In those days woman was rigidly taught to "know her place." Her place was to do all the work, take all the cuffs, provide all the food, and content herself with what was left after her lord had finished his dinner. She was not only forbidden, by ancient law, and under penalty of death, to eat with her husband or enter a canoe, but was debarred, under the same penalty, from eating bananas, pine-apples, oranges and other choice fruits at any time or in any place. She had to confine herself pretty strictly to "poi" and hard work. These poor ignorant heathen seem to have had a sort of groping idea of what came of woman eating fruit in the garden of Eden, and they did not choose to take any more chances. But the missionaries broke up this satisfactory arrangement of things. They liberated woman and made her the equal of man.

The natives had a romantic fashion of burying some of their children alive when the family became larger than necessary. The missionaries interfered in this matter too, and stopped it.

To this day the natives are able to *lie down and die whenever they want to*, whether there is anything the matter with them or not. If a Kanaka takes a notion to die, that is the end of him; nobody can persuade him to hold on; all the doctors in the world could not save him.

A luxury which they enjoy more than anything else, is a large funeral. If a person wants to get rid of a troublesome native, it is only necessary to promise him a fine funeral and name the hour and he will be on hand to the minute—at least his remains will.

All the natives are Christians, now, but many of them still desert to the Great Shark God for temporary succor in time of trouble. An irruption of the great volcano of Kilauea, or an earthquake, always brings a deal of latent loyalty to the Great Shark God to the surface. It is common report that the King, educated, cultivated and refined Christian gentleman as he undoubtedly is, still turns to the idols of his fathers for help when disaster threatens. A planter caught a shark, and one of his christianized natives testified his emancipation from the thrall of ancient superstition by assisting to dissect the shark after a fashion forbidden by his abandoned creed. But remorse shortly began to torture him. He grew moody and sought solitude; brooded over his sin, refused food, and finally said he must die and ought to die, for he had sinned against the Great Shark God and could never know peace any more. He was proof against persuasion and ridicule, and in the course of a day or two took to his bed and died, although he showed no symptom of disease. His young daughter followed his lead and suffered a like fate within the week. Superstition is ingrained in the native blood and bone and it is only natural that it should crop out in time of distress. Wherever one goes in the Islands, he will find small piles of stones by the wayside, covered with leafy offerings, placed there by the natives to appease evil spirits or honor local deities belonging to the mythology of former days.

In the rural districts of any of the Islands, the traveler hourly comes upon parties of dusky maidens bathing in the streams or in the sea without any clothing on and exhibiting no very intemperate zeal in the matter of hiding their nakedness. When the missionaries first took up their residence in Honolulu, the native women would pay their families frequent friendly visits, day by day, not even clothed with a blush. It was found a hard matter to convince them that this was rather indelicate. Finally the missionaries provided them with long, loose calico robes, and that ended the difficulty— for the women would troop through the town, stark naked, with their robes folded under their arms, march to the missionary houses and then proceed to dress!—The natives soon manifested a strong proclivity for clothing, but it was shortly apparent that they only wanted it for grandeur. The missionaries imported a quantity of hats, bonnets, and other male and female wearing apparel, instituted a general distribution, and begged the people not to come to church naked, next Sunday, as usual. And they did not; but the national spirit of unselfishness led them to divide up with neighbors who were not at the distribution, and next Sabbath the poor preachers could hardly keep countenance before their vast congregations. In the midst of the reading of a hymn a brown, stately dame would sweep up the aisle with a world of airs, with nothing in the world on but a "stovepipe" hat and a pair of cheap gloves; another dame would follow, tricked out in a man's shirt, and nothing else; another one would enter with a flourish, with simply the sleeves of a bright calico dress tied around her waist and the rest of the garment dragging behind like a peacock's tail off duty; a stately "buck" Kanaka would stalk in with a woman's bonnet on, wrong side before—only this, and nothing more; after him would stride his fellow, with the legs of a pair of pantaloons tied around his neck, the rest of his person untrammeled; in his rear would come another gentleman simply gotten up in a fiery neck-tie and a

striped vest. The poor creatures were beaming with complacency and wholly unconscious of any absurdity in their appearance. They gazed at each other with happy admiration,
and it was plain to see that the young girls were taking note
of what each other had on, as naturally as if they had always
lived in a land of Bibles and knew what churches were made
for; here was the evidence of a dawning civilization. The spectacle which the congregation presented was so extraordinary
and withal so moving, that the missionaries found it difficult
to keep to the text and go on with the services; and by and
by when the simple children of the sun began a general swapping of garments in open meeting and produced some irre-
sistibly grotesque effects in the course of re-dressing, there
was nothing for it but to cut the thing short with the benediction and dismiss the fantastic assemblage.

In our country, children play "keep house;" and in the
same high-sounding but miniature way the grown folk here,
with the poor little material of slender territory and meagre
population, play "empire." There is his royal Majesty the
King, with a New York detective's income of thirty or thirty-
five thousand dollars a year from the "royal civil list" and the
"royal domain." He lives in a two-story frame "palace."

And there is the "royal family"—the customary hive of
royal brothers, sisters, cousins and other noble drones and
vagrants usual to monarchy,—all with a spoon in the national
pap-dish, and all bearing such titles as his or her Royal Highness the Prince or Princess So-and-so. Few of them can carry
their royal splendors far enough to ride in carriages, however;
they sport the economical Kanaka horse or "hoof it"* with
the plebeians.

Then there is his Excellency the "royal Chamberlain"—a
sinecure, for his majesty dresses himself with his own hands,
except when he is ruralizing at Waikiki and then he requires
no dressing.

Next we have his Excellency the Commander-in-chief of
the Household Troops, whose forces consist of about the
number of soldiers usually placed under a corporal in other
lands.

*Missionary phrase.

Next comes the royal Steward and the Grand Equerry in Waiting—high dignitaries with modest salaries and little to do.

Then we have his Excellency the First Gentleman of the Bed-chamber—an office as easy as it is magnificent.

Next we come to his Excellency the Prime Minister, a renegade American from New Hampshire, all jaw, vanity, bombast and ignorance, a lawyer of "shyster" calibre, a fraud by nature, a humble worshiper of the sceptre above him, a reptile never tired of sneering at the land of his birth or glorifying the ten-acre kingdom that has adopted him—salary, $4,000 a year, vast consequence, and no perquisites.

Then we have his Excellency the Imperial Minister of Finance, who handles a million dollars of public money a year, sends in his annual "budget" with great ceremony, talks prodigiously of "finance," suggests imposing schemes for paying off the "national debt" (of $150,000,) and does it all for $4,000 a year and unimaginable glory.

Next we have his Excellency the Minister of War, who holds sway over the royal armies—they consist of two hundred and thirty uniformed Kanakas, mostly Brigadier Generals, and if the country ever gets into trouble with a foreign power we shall probably hear from them. I knew an American whose copper-plate visiting card bore this impressive legend: "Lieutenant-Colonel in the Royal Infantry." To say that he was proud of this distinction is stating it but tamely. The Minister of War has also in his charge some venerable swivels on Punch-Bowl Hill wherewith royal salutes are fired when foreign vessels of war enter the port.

Next comes his Excellency the Minister of the Navy—a nabob who rules the "royal fleet," (a steam-tug and a sixty-ton schooner.)

And next comes his Grace the Lord Bishop of Honolulu, the chief dignitary of the "Established Church"—for when the American Presbyterian missionaries had completed the reduction of the nation to a compact condition of Christianity, native royalty stepped in and erected the grand dignity of an "Established (Episcopal) Church" over it, and imported a cheap ready-made Bishop from England to take charge. The chagrin of the missionaries has never been comprehensively expressed, to this day, profanity not being admissible.

Next comes his Excellency the Minister of Public Instruction.

Next, their Excellencies the Governors of Oahu, Hawaii, etc., and after them a string of High Sheriffs and other small fry too numerous for computation.

Then there are their Excellencies the Envoy Extraordinary and Minister Plenipotentiary of his Imperial Majesty the Emperor of the French; her British Majesty's Minister; the Minister Resident, of the United States; and some six or eight representatives of other foreign nations, all with sounding titles, imposing dignity and prodigious but economical state.

Imagine all this grandeur in a play-house "kingdom" whose population falls absolutely short of sixty thousand souls!

The people are so accustomed to nine-jointed titles and colossal magnates that a foreign prince makes very little more stir in Honolulu than a Western Congressman does in New York.

And let it be borne in mind that there is a strictly defined "court costume" of so "stunning" a nature that it would make the clown in a circus look tame and commonplace by comparison; and each Hawaiian official dignitary has a gorgeous vari-colored, gold-laced uniform peculiar to his office—no two of them are alike, and it is hard to tell which one is the "loudest." The King had a "drawing-room" at stated intervals, like other monarchs, and when these varied uniforms congregate there weak-eyed people have to contemplate the spectacle through smoked glass. Is there not a gratifying contrast between this latter-day exhibition and the one the ancestors of some of these magnates afforded the missionaries the Sunday after the old-time distribution of clothing? Behold what religion and civilization have wrought!

Chapter LXVIII

WHILE I was in Honolulu I witnessed the ceremonious funeral of the King's sister, her Royal Highness the Princess Victoria. According to the royal custom, the remains had lain in state at the palace *thirty days*, watched day and night by a guard of honor. And during all that time a great multitude of natives from the several islands had kept the palace grounds well crowded and had made the place a pandemonium every night with their howlings and wailings, beating of tom-toms and dancing of the (at other times) forbidden "hula-hula" by half-clad maidens to the music of songs of questionable decency chanted in honor of the deceased. The printed programme of the funeral procession interested me at the time; and after what I have just said of Hawaiian grandiloquence in the matter of "playing empire," I am persuaded that a perusal of it may interest the reader:

After reading the long list of dignitaries, etc., and remembering the sparseness of the population, one is almost inclined to wonder where the material for that portion of the procession devoted to "Hawaiian Population Generally" is going to be procured:

Undertaker.

Royal School. Kawaiahao School. Roman Catholic School.

Miæmæ School.

Honolulu Fire Department.

Mechanics' Benefit Union.

Attending Physicians.

Konohikis (Superintendents) of the Crown Lands, Konohikis of the Private Lands of His Majesty, Konohikis of Private Lands of Her late Royal Highness.

Governor of Oahu and Staff.

Hulumanu (Military Company).

Household Troops.

The Prince of Hawaii's Own (Military Company).

The King's household servants.

Servants of Her late Royal Highness.

Protestant Clergy. The Clergy of the Roman Catholic Church.

His Lordship Louis Maigret, The Right Rev. Bishop of Arathea, Vicar-Apostolic of the Hawaiian Islands.

The Clergy of the Hawaiian Reformed Catholic Church.

His Lordship the Right Rev. Bishop of Honolulu.

Escort Hawaiian Cavalry.
Large Kahilis. *
Small Kahilis.
Pall Bearers.

[HEARSE.]

Escort Hawaiian Cavalry.
Large Kahilis.
Small Kahilis.
Pall Bearers.

Her Majesty Queen Emma's Carriage.
His Majesty's Staff.
Carriage of Her late Royal Highness.
Carriage of Her Majesty the Queen Dowager.
The King's Chancellor.
Cabinet Ministers.
His Excellency the Minister Resident of the United States.
H. I. M's Commissioner.
H. B. M's Acting Commissioner.
Judges of Supreme Court.
Privy Councillors.
Members of Legislative Assembly.
Consular Corps.
Circuit Judges.
Clerks of Government Departments.
Members of the Bar.
Collector General, Custom-house Officers and
Officers of the Customs.
Marshal and Sheriffs of the different Islands.
King's Yeomanry.
Foreign Residents.
Ahahui Kaahumanu.
Hawaiian Population Generally.
Hawaiian Cavalry.
Police Force.

I resume my journal at the point where the procession arrived at the royal mausoleum:

*Ranks of long-handled mops made of gaudy feathers—sacred to royalty.
They are stuck in the ground around the tomb and left there.

As the procession filed through the gate, the military deployed handsomely to the right and left and formed an avenue through which the long column of mourners passed to the tomb. The coffin was borne through the door of the mausoleum, followed by the King and his chiefs, the great officers of the kingdom, foreign Consuls, Embassadors and distinguished guests (Burlingame and General Van Valkenburgh). Several of the kahilis were then fastened to a frame-work in front of the tomb, there to remain until they decay and fall to pieces, or, forestalling this, until another scion of royalty dies. At this point of the proceedings the multitude set up such a heart-broken wailing as I hope never to hear again. The soldiers fired three volleys of musketry—the wailing being previously silenced to permit of the guns being heard. His Highness Prince William, in a showy military uniform (the "true prince," this—scion of the house over-thrown by the present dynasty—he was formerly betrothed to the Princess but was not allowed to marry her), stood guard and paced back and forth within the door. The privileged few who followed the coffin into the mausoleum remained sometime, but the King soon came out and stood in the door and near one side of it. A stranger could have guessed his rank (although he was so simply and unpretentiously dressed) by the profound deference paid him by all persons in his vicinity; by seeing his high officers receive his quiet orders and suggestions with bowed and uncovered heads; and by observing how careful those persons who came out of the mausoleum were to avoid "crowding" him (although there was room enough in the doorway for a wagon to pass, for that matter); how respectfully they edged out sideways, scraping their backs against the wall and always presenting a front view of their persons to his Majesty, and never putting their hats on until they were well out of the royal presence.

He was dressed entirely in black—dress-coat and silk hat—and looked rather democratic in the midst of the showy uniforms about him. On his breast he wore a large gold star, which was half hidden by the lappel of his coat. He remained at the door a half hour, and occasionally gave an order to the men who were erecting the *kahilis* before the tomb. He had the good taste to make one of them substitute black crape for the ordinary hempen rope he was about to tie one of them to the frame-work with. Finally he entered his carriage and drove away, and the populace shortly began to drop into his wake. While he was in view there was but one man who attracted more attention than himself, and that was Harris (the Yankee Prime Minister). This feeble personage had crape enough around his hat to express the grief of an entire nation, and as usual he neglected no opportunity of making himself conspicuous and exciting the admiration of the simple Kanakas. Oh! noble ambition of this modern Richelieu!

It is interesting to contrast the funeral ceremonies of the Princess Victoria with those of her noted ancestor Kamehameha the Conqueror, who died fifty years ago—in 1819, the year before the first missionaries came.

"On the 8th of May, 1819, at the age of sixty-six, he died, as he had lived, in the faith of his country. It was his misfortune not to have come in contact with men who could have rightly influenced his religious aspirations. Judged by his advantages and compared with the most eminent of his countrymen he may be justly styled not only great, but good. To this day his memory warms the heart and elevates the national feelings of Hawaiians. They are proud of their old warrior King; they love his name; his deeds form their historical age; and an enthusiasm everywhere prevails, shared even by foreigners who knew his worth, that constitutes the firmest pillar of the throne of his dynasty.

"In lieu of human victims (the custom of that age), a sacrifice of three hundred dogs attended his obsequies—no mean holocaust when their national value and the estimation in which they were held are considered. The bones of Kamehameha, after being kept for a while, were so carefully concealed that all knowledge of their final resting place is now lost. There was a proverb current among the common people that the bones of a cruel King could not be hid; they made fish-hooks and arrows of them, upon which, in using them, they vented their abhorrence of his memory in bitter execrations."

The account of the circumstances of his death, as written by the native historians, is full of minute detail, but there is scarcely a line of it which does not mention or illustrate some by-gone custom of the country. In this respect it is the most comprehensive document I have yet met with. I will quote it entire:

"When Kamehameha was dangerously sick, and the priests were unable to cure him, they said: 'Be of good courage and build a house for the god (his own private god or idol), that thou mayest recover.' The chiefs corroborated this advice of the priests, and a place of worship was prepared for Kukailimoku, and consecrated in the evening. They proposed also to the King, with a view to prolong his life, that human victims should be sacrificed to his deity; upon which the greater part of the people absconded through fear of death, and concealed themselves in hiding places till the *tabu** in which destruction impended, was past. It is doubtful whether Kamehameha approved of the plan of the chiefs and priests to sacrifice men, as he was known to say, 'The men are sacred for the King;' meaning that they were for the service of his successor. This information was derived from Liholiho, his son.

"After this, his sickness increased to such a degree that he had not strength to turn himself in his bed. When another season, consecrated for worship at the new temple (*heiau*) arrived, he said to his son, Liholiho, 'Go thou and make supplication to thy god; I am not able to go, and will offer my prayers at home.' When his devotions to his feathered god, Kukailimoku, were concluded, a certain religiously disposed individual, who had a bird god, suggested to the King that through its influence his sickness might be removed. The name of this god was Pua; its body was made of a bird, now eaten by the Hawaiians, and called in their language *alae*. Kamehameha was willing that a trial should be made, and two houses were constructed to facilitate the experiment; but while dwelling in them he became so very weak as not to receive food. After lying there three days, his wives, children and chiefs, perceiving that he was very low, returned him to his own house. In the evening he was carried to the eating house,† where he took a little food in his mouth which he did not swallow; also a cup of water. The chiefs requested him to give them his counsel; but he made no reply, and was carried back to the dwelling house; but when near midnight—ten o'clock, perhaps—he was carried again to the place to eat; but, as before, he merely tasted of what was presented to him. Then Kaikioewa addressed him thus: 'Here we all are, your younger brethren, your son Liholiho and your foreigner; impart to us your dying charge, that Liholiho and Kaahumanu may hear.' Then Kamehameha inquired, 'What do you say?' Kaikioewa repeated, 'Your counsels for us.' He then said, 'Move on in my good way and—.' He could proceed no further. The foreigner, Mr. Young, embraced and kissed him. Hoapili also embraced him, whispering something in his ear, after which he was taken back to the house. About twelve he was carried once

---

*Tabu (pronounced tah-boo,) means prohibition (we have borrowed it,) or sacred. The tabu was sometimes permanent, sometimes temporary; and the person or thing placed under tabu was for the time being sacred to the purpose for which it was set apart. In the above case the victims selected under the tabu would be sacred to the sacrifice.

†It was deemed pollution to eat in the same hut a person slept in—the fact that the patient was dying could not modify the rigid etiquette.

more to the house for eating, into which his head entered, while his body was in the dwelling house immediately adjoining. It should be remarked that this frequent carrying of a sick chief from one house to another resulted from the *tabu* system, then in force. There were at that time six houses (huts) connected with an establishment—one was for worship, one for the men to eat in, an eating house for the women, a house to sleep in, a house in which to manufacture kapa (native cloth) and one where, at certain intervals, the women might dwell in seclusion.

"The sick was once more taken to his house, when he expired; this was at two o'clock, a circumstance from which Leleiohoku derived his name. As he breathed at last, Kalaimoku came to the eating house to order those in it to go out. There were two aged persons thus directed to depart; one went, the other remained on account of love to the King, by whom he had formerly been kindly sustained. The children also were sent away. Then Kalaimoku came to the house, and the chiefs had a consultation. One of them spoke thus: 'This is my thought—we will eat him raw.'* Kaahumanu (one of the dead King's widows) replied, 'Perhaps his body is not at our disposal; that is more properly with his successor. Our part in him—his breath—has departed; his remains will be disposed of by Liholiho.'

"After this conversation the body was taken into the consecrated house for the performance of the proper rites by the priest and the new King. The name of this ceremony is *uko*; and when the sacred hog was baked the priest offered it to the dead body, and it became a god, the King at the same time repeating the customary prayers.

"Then the priest, addressing himself to the King and chiefs, said: 'I will now make known to you the rules to be observed respecting persons to be sacrificed on the burial of this body. If you obtain one man before the corpse is removed, one will be sufficient; but after it leaves this house four will be required. If delayed until we carry the corpse to the grave there must be ten; but after it is deposited in the grave there must be fifteen. To-morrow morning there will be a *tabu*, and, if the sacrifice be delayed until that time, forty men must die.'

"Then the high priest, Hewahewa, inquired of the chiefs, 'Where shall be the residence of King Liholiho?' They replied, 'Where, indeed? You, of all men, ought to know.' Then the priest observed,

---

*This sounds suspicious, in view of the fact that all Sandwich Island historians, white and black, protest that cannibalism never existed in the islands. However, since they only proposed to "eat him raw" we "won't count that". But it would certainly have been cannibalism if they had cooked him. —[M. T.]

'There are two suitable places; one is Kau, the other is Kohala.' The chiefs preferred the latter, as it was more thickly inhabited. The priest added, 'These are proper places for the King's residence; but he must not remain in Kona, for it is polluted.' This was agreed to. It was now break of day. As he was being carried to the place of burial the people perceived that their King was dead, and they wailed. When the corpse was removed from the house to the tomb, a distance of one chain, the procession was met by a certain man who was ardently attached to the deceased. He leaped upon the chiefs who were carrying the King's body; he desired to die with him on account of his love. The chiefs drove him away. He persisted in making numerous attempts, which were unavailing. Kalaimoka also had it in his heart to die with him, but was prevented by Hookio.

"The morning following Kamehameha's death, Liholiho and his train departed for Kohala, according to the suggestions of the priest, to avoid the defilement occasioned by the dead. At this time if a chief died the land was polluted, and the heirs sought a residence in another part of the country until the corpse was dissected and the bones tied in a bundle, which being done, the season of defilement terminated. If the deceased were not a chief, the house only was defiled which became pure again on the burial of the body. Such were the laws on this subject.

"On the morning on which Liholiho sailed in his canoe for Kohala, the chiefs and people mourned after their manner on occasion of a chief's death, conducting themselves like madmen and like beasts. Their conduct was such as to forbid description. The priests, also, put into action the sorcery apparatus, that the person who had prayed the King to death might die; for it was not believed that Kamehameha's departure was the effect either of sickness or old age. When the sorcerers set up by their fire-places sticks with a strip of kapa flying at the top, the chief Keeaumoku, Kaahumanu's brother, came in a state of intoxication and broke the flag-staff of the sorcerers, from which it was inferred that Kaahumanu and her friends had been instrumental in the King's death. On this account they were subjected to abuse."

You have the contrast, now, and a strange one it is. This great Queen, Kaahumanu, who was "subjected to abuse" during the frightful orgies that followed the King's death, in accordance with ancient custom, afterward became a devout Christian and a steadfast and powerful friend of the missionaries.

Dogs were, and still are, reared and fattened for food, by the natives—hence the reference to their value in one of the above paragraphs.

Forty years ago it was the custom in the Islands to suspend all law for a certain number of days after the death of a royal personage; and then a saturnalia ensued which one may picture to himself after a fashion, but not in the full horror of the reality. The people shaved their heads, knocked out a tooth or two, plucked out an eye sometimes, cut, bruised, mutilated or burned their flesh, got drunk, burned each other's huts, maimed or murdered one another according to the caprice of the moment, and both sexes gave themselves up to brutal and unbridled licentiousness. And after it all, came a torpor from which the nation slowly emerged bewildered and dazed, as if from a hideous half-remembered nightmare. They were not the salt of the earth, those "gentle children of the sun."

The natives still keep up an old custom of theirs which cannot be comforting to an invalid. When they think a sick friend is going to die, a couple of dozen neighbors surround his hut and keep up a deafening wailing night and day till he either dies or gets well. No doubt this arrangement has helped many a subject to a shroud before his appointed time.

They surround a hut and wail in the same heart-broken way when its occupant returns from a journey. This is their dismal idea of a welcome. A very little of it would go a great way with most of us.

Chapter LXIX

BOUND FOR Hawaii (a hundred and fifty miles distant,) to visit the great volcano and behold the other notable things which distinguish that island above the remainder of the group, we sailed from Honolulu on a certain Saturday afternoon, in the good schooner Boomerang.

The Boomerang was about as long as two street cars, and about as wide as one. She was so small (though she was larger than the majority of the inter-island coasters) that when I stood on her deck I felt but little smaller than the Colossus of Rhodes must have felt when he had a man-of-war under him. I could reach the water when she lay over under a strong breeze. When the Captain and my comrade (a Mr. Billings), myself and four other persons were all assembled on the little after portion of the deck which is sacred to the cabin passengers, it was full—there was not room for any more quality folks. Another section of the deck, twice as large as ours, was full of natives of both sexes, with their customary dogs, mats, blankets, pipes, calabashes of poi, fleas, and other luxuries and baggage of minor importance. As soon as we set sail the natives all lay down on the deck as thick as negroes in a slave-pen, and smoked, conversed, and spit on each other, and were truly sociable.

The little low-ceiled cabin below was rather larger than a hearse, and as dark as a vault. It had two coffins on each side—I mean two bunks. A small table, capable of accommodating three persons at dinner, stood against the forward bulkhead, and over it hung the dingiest whale oil lantern that ever peopled the obscurity of a dungeon with ghostly shapes. The floor room unoccupied was not extensive. One might swing a cat in it, perhaps, but not a long cat. The hold forward of the bulkhead had but little freight in it, and from morning till night a portly old rooster, with a voice like Baalam's ass, and the same disposition to use it, strutted up and down in that part of the vessel and crowed. He usually took dinner at six o'clock, and then, after an hour devoted to meditation, he mounted a barrel and crowed a good part of the night. He got hoarser and hoarser all the time, but he scorned to allow any personal consideration to interfere with his duty, and kept up his labors in defiance of threatened diphtheria.

Sleeping was out of the question when he was on watch. He was a source of genuine aggravation and annoyance. It was worse than useless to shout at him or apply offensive epithets to him—he only took these things for applause, and strained himself to make more noise. Occasionally, during the day, I threw potatoes at him through an aperture in the bulkhead, but he only dodged and went on crowing.

The first night, as I lay in my coffin, idly watching the dim lamp swinging to the rolling of the ship, and snuffing the nauseous odors of bilge water, I felt something gallop over me. I turned out promptly. However, I turned in again when I found it was only a rat. Presently something galloped over me once more. I knew it was not a rat this time, and I thought it might be a centipede, because the Captain had killed one on deck in the afternoon. I turned out. The first glance at the pillow showed me a repulsive sentinel perched upon each end of it—cockroaches as large as peach leaves—fellows with long, quivering antennæ and fiery, malignant eyes. They were grating their teeth like tobacco worms, and appeared to be dissatisfied about something. I had often heard that these reptiles were in the habit of eating off sleeping sailors' toe nails down to the quick, and I would not get in the bunk any more. I lay down on the floor. But a rat came and bothered me, and shortly afterward a procession of cockroaches arrived and camped in my hair. In a few moments the rooster was crowing with uncommon spirit and a party of fleas were throwing double somersaults about my person in the wildest disorder, and taking a bite every time they struck. I was beginning to feel really annoyed. I got up and put my clothes on and went on deck.

The above is not overdrawn; it is a truthful sketch of inter-island schooner life. There is no such thing as keeping a vessel in elegant condition, when she carries molasses and Kanakas.

It was compensation for my sufferings to come unexpectedly upon so beautiful a scene as met my eye—to step suddenly out of the sepulchral gloom of the cabin and stand under the strong light of the moon—in the centre, as it were, of a glittering sea of liquid silver—to see the broad sails straining in the gale, the ship keeled over on her side, the angry foam hissing past her lee bulwarks, and sparkling sheets of spraying dashing high over her bows and raining upon her decks; to brace myself and hang fast to the first object that presented itself, with hat jammed down and coat tails whipping in the breeze, and feel that exhilaration that thrills in one's hair and quivers down his back bone when he knows that every inch of canvas is drawing and the vessel cleaving through the waves at her utmost speed. There was no darkness, no dimness, no obscurity there. All was brightness, every object was vividly defined. Every prostrate Kanaka; every coil of rope; every calabash of poi; every puppy; every seam in the flooring; every bolthead; every object, however minute, showed sharp and distinct in its every outline; and the shadow of the broad mainsail lay black as a pall upon the deck, leaving Billings's white upturned face glorified and his body in a total eclipse.

Monday morning we were close to the island of Hawaii. Two of its high mountains were in view—Mauna Loa and Hualaiai. The latter is an imposing peak, but being only ten thousand feet high is seldom mentioned or heard of. Mauna Loa is said to be sixteen thousand feet high. The rays of glittering snow and ice, that clasped its summit like a claw, looked refreshing when viewed from the blistering climate we were in. One could stand on that mountain (wrapped up in blankets and furs to keep warm), and while he nibbled a snowball or an icicle to quench his thirst he could look down the long sweep of its sides and see spots where plants are growing that grow only where the bitter cold of Winter prevails; lower down he could see sections devoted to productions that thrive in the temperate zone alone; and at the bottom of the mountain he could see the home of the tufted cocoa-palms and other species of vegetation that grow only in the sultry atmosphere of eternal Summer. He could see all the climes of the world at a single glance of the eye, and that glance would only pass over a distance of four or five miles as the bird flies!

By and by we took boat and went ashore at Kailua, designing to ride horseback through the pleasant orange and coffee region of Kona, and rejoin the vessel at a point some leagues distant. This journey is well worth taking. The trail passes along on high ground—say a thousand feet above sea level—and usually about a mile distant from the ocean, which is always in sight, save that occasionally you find yourself buried in the forest in the midst of a rank tropical vegetation and a dense growth of trees, whose great bows overarch the road and shut out sun and sea and everything, and leave you in a dim, shady tunnel, haunted with invisible singing birds and fragrant with the odor of flowers. It was pleasant to ride occasionally in the warm sun, and feast the eye upon the ever-changing panorama of the forest (beyond and below us), with its many tints, its softened lights and shadows, its billowy undulations sweeping gently down from the mountain to the sea. It was pleasant also, at intervals, to leave the sultry sun and pass into the cool, green depths of this forest and indulge in sentimental reflections under the inspiration of its brooding twilight and its whispering foliage.

We rode through one orange grove that had ten thousand trees in it! They were all laden with fruit.

At one farmhouse we got some large peaches of excellent flavor. This fruit, as a general thing, does not do well in the Sandwich Islands. It takes a sort of almond shape, and is small and bitter. It needs frost, they say, and perhaps it does; if this be so, it will have a good opportunity to go on needing it, as it will not be likely to get it. The trees from which the fine fruit I have spoken of, came, had been planted and replanted *sixteen times*, and to this treatment the proprietor of the orchard attributed his success.

We passed several sugar plantations—new ones and not very extensive. The crops were, in most cases, third rattoons. [NOTE.—The first crop is called "plant cane;" subsequent crops which spring from the original roots, without replanting, are called "rattoons."] Almost everywhere on the island of Hawaii sugar-cane matures in twelve months, both rattoons and plant, and although it ought to be taken off as soon as it tassels, no doubt, it is not absolutely necessary to do it until about four months afterward. In Kona, the average yield of an acre of ground is *two tons* of sugar, they say. This is only a moderate yield for these islands, but would be astounding for Louisiana and most other sugar growing countries. The plantations in Kona being on pretty high ground—up among the light and frequent rains—no irrigation whatever is required.

Chapter LXX

WE STOPPED some time at one of the plantations, to rest ourselves and refresh the horses. We had a chatty conversation with several gentlemen present; but there was one person, a middle aged man, with an absent look in his face, who simply glanced up, gave us good-day and lapsed again into the meditations which our coming had interrupted. The planters whispered us not to mind him—crazy. They said he was in the Islands for his health; was a preacher; his home, Michigan. They said that if he woke up presently and fell to talking about a correspondence which he had some time held with Mr. Greeley about a trifle of some kind, we must humor him and listen with interest; and we must humor his fancy that this correspondence was the talk of the world.

It was easy to see that he was a gentle creature and that his madness had nothing vicious in it. He looked pale, and a little worn, as if with perplexing thought and anxiety of mind. He sat a long time, looking at the floor, and at intervals muttering to himself and nodding his head acquiescingly or shaking it in mild protest. He was lost in his thought, or in his memories. We continued our talk with the planters, branching from subject to subject. But at last the word "circumstance," casually dropped, in the course of conversation, attracted his attention and brought an eager look into his countenance. He faced about in his chair and said:

"Circumstance? What circumstance? Ah, I know—I know too well. So you have heard of it too." [With a sigh.] "Well, no matter—all the world has heard of it. All the world. The whole world. It is a large world, too, for a thing to travel so far in—now isn't it? Yes, yes—the Greeley correspondence with Erickson has created the saddest and bitterest controversy on both sides of the ocean—and still they keep it up! It makes us famous, but at what a sorrowful sacrifice! I was so sorry when I heard that it had caused that bloody and distressful war over there in Italy. It was little comfort to me, after so much bloodshed, to know that the victors sided with me, and the vanquished with Greeley.—It is little comfort to know that Horace Greeley is responsible for the battle of

Sadowa, and not me. Queen Victoria wrote me that she felt just as I did about it—she said that as much as she was opposed to Greeley and the spirit he showed in the correspondence with me, she would not have had Sadowa happen for hundreds of dollars. I can show you her letter, if you would like to see it. But gentlemen, much as you may think you know about that unhappy correspondence, you cannot know the *straight* of it till you hear it from my lips. It has always been garbled in the journals, and even in history. Yes, even in history—think of it! Let me—*please* let me, give you the matter, exactly as it occurred. I truly will not abuse your confidence."

Then he leaned forward, all interest, all earnestness, and told his story—and told it appealingly, too, and yet in the simplest and most unpretentious way; indeed, in such a way as to suggest to one, all the time, that this was a faithful, honorable witness, giving evidence in the sacred interest of justice, and under oath. He said:

"Mrs. Beazeley—Mrs. Jackson Beazeley, widow, of the village of Campbellton, Kansas,—wrote me about a matter which was near her heart—a matter which many might think trivial, but to her it was a thing of deep concern. I was living in Michigan, then—serving in the ministry. She was, and is, an estimable woman—a woman to whom poverty and hardship have proven incentives to industry, in place of discouragements. Her only treasure was her son William, a youth just verging upon manhood; religious, amiable, and sincerely attached to agriculture. He was the widow's comfort and her pride. And so, moved by her love for him, she wrote me about a matter, as I have said before, which lay near her heart—because it lay near her boy's. She desired me to confer with Mr. Greeley about turnips. Turnips were the dream of her child's young ambition. While other youths were frittering away in frivolous amusements the precious years of budding vigor which God had given them for useful preparation, this boy was patiently enriching his mind with information concerning turnips. The sentiment which he felt toward the turnip was akin to adoration. He could not think of the turnip without emotion; he could not speak of it calmly; he could not contemplate it without exaltation. He could not eat it without shedding tears. All the poetry in his sensitive nature was in sympathy with the gracious vegetable. With the earliest pipe of dawn he sought his patch, and when the curtaining night drove him from it he shut himself up with his books and garnered statistics till sleep overcame him. On rainy days he sat and talked hours together with his mother about turnips. When company came, he made it his loving duty to put aside everything else and converse with them all the day long of his great joy in the turnip. And yet, was this joy rounded and complete? Was there no secret alloy of unhappiness in it? Alas, there was. There was a canker gnawing at his heart; the noblest inspiration of his soul eluded his endeavor—viz: he could not make of the turnip a climbing vine. Months went by; the bloom forsook his cheek, the fire faded out of his eye; sighings and abstraction usurped the place of smiles and cheerful converse. But a watchful eye noted these things and in time a motherly sympathy unsealed the secret. Hence the letter to me. She pleaded for attention—she said her boy was dying by inches.

"I was a stranger to Mr. Greeley, but what of that? The matter was urgent. I wrote and begged him to solve the difficult problem if possible and save the student's life. My interest grew, until it partook of the anxiety of the mother. I waited in much suspense.—At last the answer came.

"I found that I could not read it readily, the handwriting being unfamiliar and my emotions somewhat wrought up. It seemed to refer in part to the boy's case, but chiefly to other and irrelevant matters—such as paving-stones, electricity, oysters, and something which I took to be 'absolution' or 'agrarianism,' I could not be certain which; still, these appeared to be simply casual mentions, nothing more; friendly in spirit, without doubt, but lacking the connection or coherence necessary to make them useful.—I judged that my understanding was affected by my feelings, and so laid the letter away till morning.

"In the morning I read it again, but with difficulty and uncertainty still, for I had lost some little rest and my mental vision seemed clouded. The note was more connected, now, but did not meet the emergency it was expected to meet. It was too discursive. It appeared to read as follows, though I was not certain of some of the words:

'Polygamy dissembles majesty; extracts redeem polarity; causes hitherto exist. Ovations pursue wisdom, or warts inherit and condemn. Boston, botany, cakes, folony undertakes, but who shall allay? We fear not. Yrxwly,

HEVACE EVEELOJ.'

"But there did not seem to be a word about turnips. There seemed to be no suggestion as to how they might be made to grow like vines. There was not even a reference to the Beazeleys. I slept upon the matter; I ate no supper, neither any breakfast next morning. So I resumed my work with a brain refreshed, and was very hopeful. *Now* the letter took a different aspect—all save the signature, which latter I judged to be only a harmless affectation of Hebrew. The epistle was necessarily from Mr. Greeley, for it bore the printed heading of *The Tribune*, and I had written to no one else there. The letter, I say, had taken a different aspect, but still its language was eccentric and avoided the issue. It now appeared to say:

'Bolivia extemporizes mackerel; borax esteems polygamy; sausages wither in the east. Creation perdu, is done; for woes inherent one can damn. Buttons, buttons, corks, geology underrates but we shall allay. My beer's out. Yrxwly,

HEVACE EVEELOJ.'

"I was evidently overworked. My comprehension was impaired. Therefore I gave two days to recreation, and then returned to my task greatly refreshed. The letter now took this form:

'Poultices do sometimes choke swine; tulips reduce posterity; causes leather to resist. Our notions empower wisdom, her let's afford while we can. Butter but any cakes, fill any undertaker, we'll wean him from his filly. We feel hot.

Yrxwly,   HEVACE EVEELOJ.'

"I was still not satisfied. These generalities did not meet the question. They were crisp, and vigorous, and delivered with a confidence that almost compelled conviction; but at such a time as this, with a human life at stake, they seemed inappro-

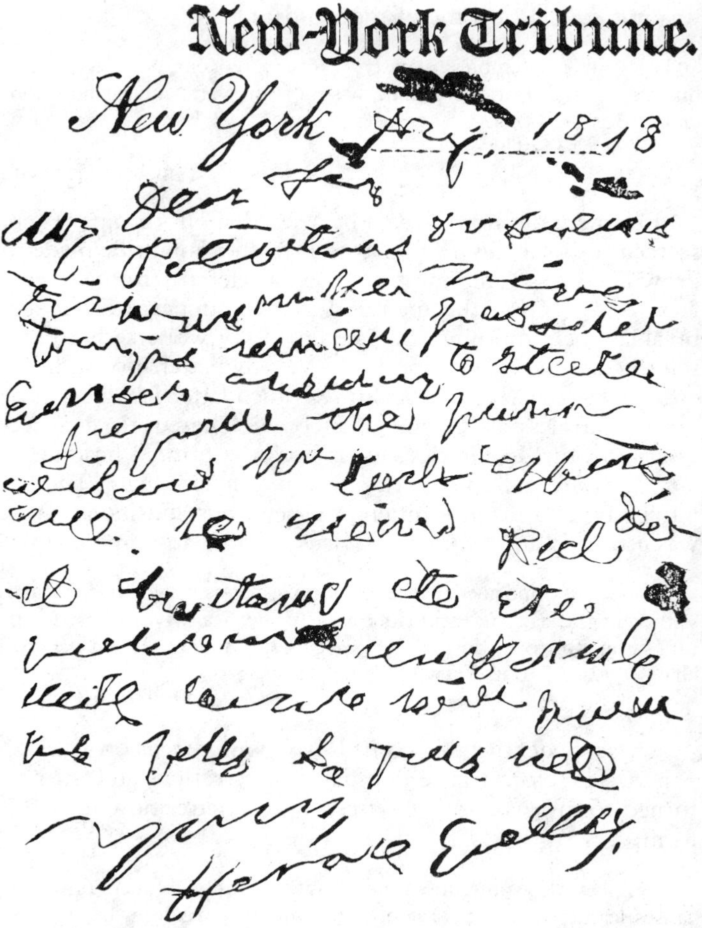

New-York Tribune.

New York

priate, worldly, and in bad taste. At any other time I would have been not only glad, but proud, to receive from a man like Mr. Greeley a letter of this kind, and would have studied it earnestly and tried to improve myself all I could; but now, with that poor boy in his far home languishing for relief, I had no heart for learning.

"Three days passed by, and I read the note again. Again its tenor had changed. It now appeared to say:

'Potations do sometimes wake wines; turnips restrain passion; causes necessary to state. Infest the poor widow; her lord's effects will be void. But dirt, bathing, etc., etc., followed unfairly, will worm him from his folly—so swear not.

Yrxwly,   HEVACE EVEELOJ.'

"This was more like it. But I was unable to proceed. I was too much worn. The word 'turnips' brought temporary joy and encouragement, but my strength was so much impaired, and the delay might be so perilous for the boy, that I relinquished the idea of pursuing the translation further, and resolved to do what I ought to have done at first. I sat down and wrote Mr. Greeley as follows:

"DEAR SIR: I fear I do not entirely comprehend your kind note. It cannot be possible, Sir, that 'turnips restrain passion'—at least the study or contemplation of turnips cannot—for it is this very employment that has scorched our poor friend's mind and sapped his bodily strength.—But if they *do* restrain it, will you bear with us a little further and explain how they should be prepared? I observe that you say 'causes necessary to state,' but you have omitted to state them.

"Under a misapprehension, you seem to attribute to me interested motives in this matter—to call it by no harsher term. But I assure you, dear sir, that if I seem to be 'infesting the widow,' it is all *seeming*, and void of reality. It is from no seeking of mine that I am in this position. She asked me, herself, to write you. I never have infested her—indeed I scarcely know her. I do not infest anybody. I try to go along, in my humble way, doing as near right as I can, never harming anybody, and never *throwing out insinuations*. As for 'her lord and his effects,' they are of no interest to me. I trust I have effects enough of my own—shall endeavor to get along with them, at any rate, and not go mousing around to get hold of somebody's that are 'void.' But do you not see?—this woman is a *widow*—she has no 'lord.' He is dead—or pretended to be, when they buried him. Therefore, no amount of 'dirt, bathing,' etc., etc., howsoever 'unfairly followed' will be likely to 'worm him from his folly'—if being dead and a ghost is 'folly.' Your closing remark is as unkind as it was uncalled for; and if report says true you might have applied it to yourself, sir, with more point and less impropriety.

Very Truly Yours, SIMON ERICKSON.

"In the course of a few days, Mr. Greeley did what would have saved a world of trouble, and much mental and bodily suffering and misunderstanding, if he had done it sooner. To-wit, he sent an intelligible rescript or translation of his original note, made in a plain hand by his clerk. Then the mystery cleared, and I saw that his heart had been right, all the time. I will recite the note in its clarified form:

[Translation.]

'Potatoes do sometimes make vines; turnips remain passive: cause unnecessary to state. Inform the poor widow her lad's efforts will be vain. But diet, bathing, etc. etc., followed uniformly, will wean him from his folly—so fear not.

Yours,   HORACE GREELEY.'

"But alas, it was too late, gentlemen—too late. The criminal delay had done its work—young Beazeley was no more. His spirit had taken its flight to a land where all anxieties shall be charmed away, all desires gratified, all ambitions realized. Poor lad, they laid him to his rest with a turnip in each hand."

So ended Erickson, and lapsed again into nodding, mumbling, and abstraction. The company broke up, and left him so. . . . But they did not say what drove him crazy. In the momentary confusion, I forgot to ask.

Chapter LXXI

AT FOUR O CLOCK in the afternoon we were winding down a mountain of dreary and desolate lava to the sea, and closing our pleasant land journey. This lava is the accumulation of ages; one torrent of fire after another has rolled down here in old times, and built up the island structure higher and higher. Underneath, it is honey-combed with caves; it would be of no use to dig wells in such a place; they would not hold water—you would not find any for them to hold, for that matter. Consequently, the planters depend upon cisterns.

The last lava flow occurred here so long ago that there are none now living who witnessed it. In one place it enclosed and burned down a grove of cocoa-nut trees, and the holes in the lava where the trunks stood are still visible; their sides retain the impression of the bark; the trees fell upon the burning river, and becoming partly submerged, left in it the perfect counterpart of every knot and branch and leaf, and even nut, for curiosity seekers of a long distant day to gaze upon and wonder at.

There were doubtless plenty of Kanaka sentinels on guard hereabouts at that time, but they did not leave casts of their figures in the lava as the Roman sentinels at Herculaneum and Pompeii did. It is a pity it is so, because such things are so interesting; but so it is. They probably went away. They went away early, perhaps. However, they had their merits; the Romans exhibited the higher pluck, but the Kanakas showed the sounder judgment.

Shortly we came in sight of that spot whose history is so familiar to every school-boy in the wide world—Kealakekua Bay—the place where Captain Cook, the great circumnavigator, was killed by the natives, nearly a hundred years ago. The setting sun was flaming upon it, a Summer shower was falling, and it was spanned by two magnificent rainbows. Two men who were in advance of us rode through one of these and for a moment their garments shone with a more than regal splendor. Why did not Captain Cook have taste enough to call his great discovery the Rainbow Islands? These charming spectacles are present to you at every turn; they are common in all the islands; they are visible every day, and frequently at night also—not the silvery bow we see once in an age in the States, by moonlight, but barred with all bright and beautiful colors, like the children of the sun and rain. I saw one of them a few nights ago. What the sailors call "raindogs"—little patches of rainbow—are often seen drifting about the heavens in these latitudes, like stained cathedral windows.

Kealakekua Bay is a little curve like the last kink of a snail-shell, winding deep into the land, seemingly not more than a mile wide from shore to shore. It is bounded on one side—where the murder was done—by a little flat plain, on which stands a cocoanut grove and some ruined houses; a steep wall of lava, a thousand feet high at the upper end and three or four hundred at the lower, comes down from the mountain and bounds the inner extremity of it. From this wall the place takes its name, *Kealakekua*, which in the native tongue signifies "The Pathway of the Gods." They say, (and still believe, in spite of their liberal education in Christianity), that the great god *Lono*, who used to live upon the hillside, always traveled that causeway when urgent business connected with heavenly affairs called him down to the seashore in a hurry.

As the red sun looked across the placid ocean through the tall, clean stems of the cocoanut trees, like a blooming whiskey bloat through the bars of a city prison, I went and stood in the edge of the water on the flat rock pressed by Captain Cook's feet when the blow was dealt which took away his life, and tried to picture in my mind the doomed man struggling in the midst of the multitude of exasperated savages—the men in the ship crowding to the vessel's side and gazing in anxious dismay toward the shore—the—but I discovered that I could not do it.

It was growing dark, the rain began to fall, we could see that the distant Boomerang was helplessly becalmed at sea, and so I adjourned to the cheerless little box of a warehouse and sat down to smoke and think, and wish the ship would make the land—for we had not eaten much for ten hours and were viciously hungry.

Plain unvarnished history takes the romance out of Captain Cook's assassination, and renders a deliberate verdict of justifiable homicide. Wherever he went among the islands, he was cordially received and welcomed by the inhabitants, and his ships lavishly supplied with all manner of food. He returned these kindnesses with insult and ill-treatment. Perceiving that the people took him for the long vanished and lamented god Lono, he encouraged them in the delusion for the sake of the limitless power it gave him; but during the famous disturbance at this spot, and while he and his comrades were surrounded by fifteen thousand maddened savages, he received a hurt and betrayed his earthly origin with a groan. It was his death-warrant. Instantly a shout went up: "He groans!—he is not a god!" So they closed in upon him and dispatched him.

His flesh was stripped from the bones and burned (except nine pounds of it which were sent on board the ships). The heart was hung up in a native hut, where it was found and eaten by three children, who mistook it for the heart of a dog. One of these children grew to be a very old man, and died in Honolulu a few years ago. Some of Cook's bones were recovered and consigned to the deep by the officers of the ships.

Small blame should attach to the natives for the killing of Cook. They treated him well. In return, he abused them. He and his men inflicted bodily injury upon many of them at different times, and killed at least three of them before they offered any proportionate retaliation.

Near the shore we found "Cook's Monument"—only a cocoanut stump, four feet high and about a foot in diameter at the butt. It had lava boulders piled around its base to hold it up and keep it in its place, and it was entirely sheathed over, from top to bottom, with rough, discolored sheets of copper, such as ships' bottoms are coppered with. Each sheet had a rude inscription scratched upon it—with a nail, apparently—and in every case the execution was wretched. Most of these merely recorded the visits of British naval commanders to the spot, but one of them bore this legend:

"Near this spot fell
CAPTAIN JAMES COOK,
The Distinguished Circumnavigator, who Discovered these
Islands A. D. 1778."

After Cook's murder, his second in command, on board
the ship, opened fire upon the swarms of natives on the
beach, and one of his cannon balls cut this cocoanut tree
short off and left this monumental stump standing. It looked
sad and lonely enough to us, out there in the rainy twilight.
But there is no other monument to Captain Cook. True, up
on the mountain side we had passed by a large inclosure like
an ample hog-pen, built of lava blocks, which marks the spot
where Cook's flesh was stripped from his bones and burned;
but this is not properly a monument, since it was erected by
the natives themselves, and less to do honor to the circumnavigator than for the sake of convenience in roasting him. A
thing like a guide-board was elevated above this pen on a tall
pole, and formerly there was an inscription upon it describing
the memorable occurrence that had there taken place; but the
sun and the wind have long ago so defaced it as to render it
illegible.

Toward midnight a fine breeze sprang up and the schooner
soon worked herself into the bay and cast anchor. The boat
came ashore for us, and in a little while the clouds and the
rain were all gone. The moon was beaming tranquilly down
on land and sea, and we two were stretched upon the deck
sleeping the refreshing sleep and dreaming the happy dreams
that are only vouchsafed to the weary and the innocent.

Chapter LXXII

I N THE BREEZY morning we went ashore and visited the ruined temple of the last god Lono. The high chief cook of this temple—the priest who presided over it and roasted the human sacrifices—was uncle to Obookia, and at one time that youth was an apprentice-priest under him. Obookia was a young native of fine mind, who, together with three other native boys, was taken to New England by the captain of a whaleship during the reign of Kamehameha I, and they were the means of attracting the attention of the religious world to their country. This resulted in the sending of missionaries there. And this Obookia was the very same sensitive savage who sat down on the church steps and wept because his people did not have the Bible. That incident has been very elaborately painted in many a charming Sunday School book—aye, and told so plaintively and so tenderly that I have cried over it in Sunday School myself, on general principles, although at a time when I did not know much and could not understand why the people of the Sandwich Islands needed to worry so much about it as long as they did not know there was a Bible at all.

Obookia was converted and educated, and was to have returned to his native land with the first missionaries, had he lived. The other native youths made the voyage, and two of them did good service, but the third, William Kanui, fell from grace afterward, for a time, and when the gold excitement broke out in California he journeyed thither and went to mining, although he was fifty years old. He succeeded pretty well, but the failure of Page, Bacon & Co. relieved him of six thousand dollars, and then, to all intents and purposes, he was a bankrupt in his old age and he resumed service in the pulpit again. He died in Honolulu in 1864.

Quite a broad tract of land near the temple, extending from the sea to the mountain top, was sacred to the god Lono in olden times—so sacred that if a common native set his sacrilegious foot upon it it was judicious for him to make his will, because his time had come. He might go around it by water, but he could not cross it. It was well sprinkled with pagan temples and stocked with awkward, homely idols carved out of logs of wood. There was a temple devoted to prayers for rain—and with fine sagacity it was placed at a point so well up on the mountain side that if you prayed there twenty-four times a day for rain you would be likely to get it every time. You would seldom get to your Amen before you would have to hoist your umbrella.

And there was a large temple near at hand which was built in a single night, in the midst of storm and thunder and rain, by the ghastly hands of dead men! Tradition says that by the wierd glare of the lightning a noiseless multitude of phantoms were seen at their strange labor far up the mountain side at dead of night—flitting hither and thither and bearing great lava-blocks clasped in their nerveless fingers—appearing and disappearing as the pallid lustre fell upon their forms and faded away again. Even to this day, it is said, the natives hold this dread structure in awe and reverence, and will not pass by it in the night.

At noon I observed a bevy of nude native young ladies bathing in the sea, and went and sat down on their clothes to keep them from being stolen. I begged them to come out, for the sea was rising and I was satisfied that they were running some risk. But they were not afraid, and presently went on with their sport. They were finished swimmers and divers, and enjoyed themselves to the last degree. They swam races, splashed and ducked and tumbled each other about, and filled the air with their laughter. It is said that the first thing an Islander learns is how to swim; learning to walk being a matter of smaller consequence, comes afterward. One hears tales of native men and women swimming ashore from vessels many miles at sea—more miles, indeed, than I dare vouch for or even mention. And they tell of a native diver who went down in thirty or forty-foot waters and brought up an anvil! I think he swallowed the anvil afterward, if my memory serves me. However I will not urge this point.

I have spoken, several times, of the god Lono—I may as well furnish two or three sentences concerning him.

The idol the natives worshiped for him was a slender, unornamented staff twelve feet long. Tradition says he was a favorite god on the Island of Hawaii—a great king who had been deified for meritorious services—just our own fashion of rewarding heroes, with the difference that we would have made him a Postmaster instead of a god, no doubt. In an angry moment he slew his wife, a goddess named Kaikilani Aiii. Remorse of conscience drove him mad, and tradition presents us the singular spectacle of a god traveling "on the shoulder;" for in his gnawing grief he wandered about from place to place boxing and wrestling with all whom he met. Of course this pastime soon lost its novelty, inasmuch as it must necessarily have been the case that when so powerful a deity sent a frail human opponent "to grass" he never came back any more. Therefore, he instituted games called maka-hiki, and ordered that they should be held in his honor, and then sailed for foreign lands on a three-cornered raft, stating that he would return some day—and that was the last of Lono. He was never seen any more; his raft got swamped, perhaps. But the people always expected his return, and thus they were easily led to accept Captain Cook as the restored god.

Some of the old natives believed Cook was Lono to the day of their death; but many did not, for they could not understand how he could die if he was a god.

Only a mile or so from Kealakekua Bay is a spot of historic interest—the place where the last battle was fought for idolatry. Of course we visited it, and came away as wise as most people do who go and gaze upon such mementoes of the past when in an unreflective mood.

While the first missionaries were on their way around the Horn, the idolatrous customs which had obtained in the island, as far back as tradition reached were suddenly broken up. Old Kamehameha I., was dead, and his son, Liholiho, the new King was a free liver, a roystering, dissolute fellow, and hated the restraints of the ancient *tabu*. His assistant in the Government, Kaahumanu, the Queen dowager, was proud and high-spirited, and hated the *tabu* because it restricted the privileges of her sex and degraded all women very nearly to the level of brutes. So the case stood. Liholiho had half a mind to put his foot down, Kaahumanu had a whole mind to badger him into doing it, and whiskey did the rest. It was probably the first time whiskey ever prominently figured as an aid to civilization. Liholiho came up to Kailua as drunk as a piper, and attended a great feast; the determined Queen spurred his drunken courage up to a reckless pitch, and then, while all the multitude stared in blank dismay, he moved deliberately forward and sat down with the women! They saw him eat from the same vessel with them, and were appalled! Terrible moments drifted slowly by, and still the King ate, still he lived, still the lightnings of the insulted gods were withheld! Then conviction came like a revelation—the superstitions of a hundred generations passed from before the people like a cloud, and a shout went up, "the *tabu* is broken! the *tabu* is broken!"

Thus did King Liholiho and his dreadful whiskey preach the first sermon and prepare the way for the new gospel that was speeding southward over the waves of the Atlantic.

The *tabu* broken and destruction failing to follow the awful sacrilege, the people, with that childlike precipitancy which has always characterized them, jumped to the conclusion that their gods were a weak and wretched swindle, just as they formerly jumped to the conclusion that Captain Cook was no god, merely because he groaned, and promptly killed him without stopping to inquire whether a god might not groan as well as a man if it suited his convenience to do it; and satisfied that the idols were powerless to protect themselves they went to work at once and pulled them down—hacked them to pieces—applied the torch—annihilated them!

The pagan priests were furious. And well they might be; they had held the fattest offices in the land, and now they were beggared; they had been great—they had stood above the chiefs—and now they were vagabonds. They raised a revolt; they scared a number of people into joining their standard, and Kekuokalani, an ambitious offshoot of royalty, was easily persuaded to become their leader.

In the first skirmish the idolaters triumphed over the royal army sent against them, and full of confidence they resolved to march upon Kailua. The King sent an envoy to try and conciliate them, and came very near being an envoy short by the operation; the savages not only refused to listen to him, but wanted to kill him. So the King sent his men forth under Major General Kalaimoku and the two hosts met at Kuamoo.

The battle was long and fierce—men and women fighting side by side, as was the custom—and when the day was done the rebels were flying in every direction in hopeless panic, and idolatry and the *tabu* were dead in the land!

The royalists marched gayly home to Kailua glorifying the new dispensation. "There is no power in the gods," said they; "they are a vanity and a lie. The army with idols was weak; the army without idols was strong and victorious!"

The nation was without a religion.

The missionary ship arrived in safety shortly afterward, timed by providential exactness to meet the emergency, and the Gospel was planted as in a virgin soil.

Chapter LXXIII

A̲T NOON, we hired a Kanaka to take us down to the ancient ruins at Honaunau in his canoe—price two dollars—reasonable enough, for a sea voyage of eight miles, counting both ways.

The native canoe is an irresponsible looking contrivance. I cannot think of anything to liken it to but a boy's sled runner hollowed out, and that does not quite convey the correct idea. It is about fifteen feet long, high and pointed at both ends, is a foot and a half or two feet deep, and so narrow that if you wedged a fat man into it you might not get him out again. It sits on top of the water like a duck, but it has an outrigger and does not upset easily, if you keep still. This outrigger is formed of two long bent sticks like plow handles, which project from one side, and to their outer ends is bound a curved beam composed of an extremely light wood, which skims along the surface of the water and thus saves you from an upset on that side, while the outrigger's weight is not so easily lifted as to make an upset on the other side a thing to be greatly feared. Still, until one gets used to sitting perched upon this knife-blade, he is apt to reason within himself that it would be more comfortable if there were just an outrigger or so on the other side also.

I had the bow seat, and Billings sat amidships and faced the Kanaka, who occupied the stern of the craft and did the paddling. With the first stroke the trim shell of a thing shot out from the shore like an arrow. There was not much to see. While we were on the shallow water of the reef, it was pastime to look down into the limpid depths at the large bunches of branching coral—the unique shrubbery of the sea. We lost that, though, when we got out into the dead blue water of the deep. But we had the picture of the surf, then, dashing angrily against the crag-bound shore and sending a foaming spray high into the air. There was interest in this beetling border, too, for it was honey-combed with quaint caves and arches and tunnels, and had a rude semblance of the dilapidated architecture of ruined keeps and castles rising out of the restless sea. When this novelty ceased to be a novelty, we turned our eyes shoreward and gazed at the long mountain with its rich green forests stretching up into the curtaining clouds, and at the specks of houses in the rearward distance and the diminished schooner riding sleepily at anchor. And when these grew tiresome we dashed boldly into the midst of a school of huge, beastly porpoises engaged at their eternal game of arching over a wave and disappearing, and then doing it over again and keeping it up—always circling over, in that way, like so many well-submerged wheels. But the porpoises wheeled themselves away, and then we were thrown upon our own resources. It did not take many minutes to discover that the sun was blazing like a bonfire, and that the weather was of a melting temperature. It had a drowsing effect, too.

In one place we came upon a large company of naked natives, of both sexes and all ages, amusing themselves with the national pastime of surf-bathing. Each heathen would paddle three or four hundred yards out to sea, (taking a short board with him), then face the shore and wait for a particularly prodigious billow to come along; at the right moment he would fling his board upon its foamy crest and himself upon the board, and here he would come whizzing by like a bombshell! It did not seem that a lightning express train could shoot along at a more hair-lifting speed. I tried surf-bathing once, subsequently, but made a failure of it. I got the board placed right, and at the right moment, too; but missed the connection myself.—The board struck the shore in three quarters of a second, without any cargo, and I struck the bottom about the same time, with a couple of barrels of water in me. None but natives ever master the art of surf-bathing thoroughly.

At the end of an hour, we had made the four miles, and landed on a level point of land, upon which was a wide extent of old ruins, with many a tall cocoanut tree growing among them. Here was the ancient City of Refuge—a vast inclosure, whose stone walls were twenty feet thick at the base, and fifteen feet high; an oblong square, a thousand and forty feet one way and a fraction under seven hundred the other. Within this inclosure, in early times, had been three rude temples; each two hundred and ten feet long by one hundred wide, and thirteen high.

In those days, if a man killed another anywhere on the island the relatives were privileged to take the murderer's life; and then a chase for life and liberty began—the outlawed criminal flying through pathless forests and over mountain and plain, with his hopes fixed upon the protecting walls of the City of Refuge, and the avenger of blood following hotly after him! Sometimes the race was kept up to the very gates of the temple, and the panting pair sped through long files of excited natives, who watched the contest with flashing eye and dilated nostril, encouraging the hunted refugee with sharp, inspiriting ejaculations, and sending up a ringing shout of exultation when the saving gates closed upon him and the cheated pursuer sank exhausted at the threshold. But sometimes the flying criminal fell under the hand of the avenger at the very door, when one more brave stride, one more brief second of time would have brought his feet upon the sacred ground and barred him against all harm. Where did these isolated pagans get this idea of a City of Refuge—this ancient Oriental custom?

This old sanctuary was sacred to all—even to rebels in arms and invading armies. Once within its walls, and confession made to the priest and absolution obtained, the wretch with a price upon his head could go forth without fear and without danger—he was *tabu*, and to harm him was death. The routed rebels in the lost battle for idolatry fled to this place to claim sanctuary, and many were thus saved.

Close to the corner of the great inclosure is a round structure of stone, some six or eight feet high, with a level top about ten or twelve in diameter. This was the place of execution. A high palisade of cocoanut piles shut out the cruel scenes from the vulgar multitude. Here criminals were killed, the flesh stripped from the bones and burned, and the bones secreted in holes in the body of the structure. If the man had been guilty of a high crime, the entire corpse was burned.

The walls of the temple are a study. The same food for speculation that is offered the visitor to the Pyramids of Egypt he will find here—the mystery of how they were constructed by a people unacquainted with science and mechanics. The natives have no invention of their own for hoisting heavy weights, they had no beasts of burden, and they have never even shown any knowledge of the properties of the lever. Yet some of the lava blocks quarried out, brought over rough, broken ground, and built into this wall, six or seven feet from the ground, are of prodigious size and would weigh tons. How did they transport and how raise them?

Both the inner and outer surfaces of the walls present a smooth front and are very creditable specimens of masonry. The blocks are of all manner of shapes and sizes, but yet are fitted together with the neatest exactness. The gradual narrowing of the wall from the base upward is accurately preserved.

No cement was used, but the edifice is firm and compact and is capable of resisting storm and decay for centuries. Who built this temple, and how was it built, and when, are mysteries that may never be unraveled.

Outside of these ancient walls lies a sort of coffin-shaped stone eleven feet four inches long and three feet square at the small end (it would weigh a few thousand pounds), which the high chief who held sway over this district many centuries ago brought thither on his shoulder one day to use as a lounge! This circumstance is established by the most reliable traditions. He used to lie down on it, in his indolent way, and keep an eye on his subjects at work for him and see that there was no "soldiering" done. And no doubt there was not any done to speak of, because he was a man of that sort of build that incites to attention to business on the part of an employee. He was fourteen or fifteen feet high. When he stretched himself at full length on his lounge, his legs hung down over the end, and when he snored he woke the dead. These facts are all attested by irrefragable tradition.

On the other side of the temple is a monstrous seven-ton rock, eleven feet long, seven feet wide and three feet thick. It is raised a foot or a foot and a half above the ground, and rests upon half a dozen little stony pedestals. The same old fourteen-footer brought it down from the mountain, merely for fun (he had his own notions about fun), and propped it up as we find it now and as others may find it a century hence, for it would take a score of horses to budge it from its position. They say that fifty or sixty years ago the proud Queen Kaahumanu used to fly to this rock for safety, whenever she had been making trouble with her fierce husband, and hide under it until his wrath was appeased. But these Kanakas will lie, and this statement is one of their ablest efforts—for Kaahumanu was six feet high—she was bulky—she was built like an ox—and she could no more have squeezed herself under that rock than she could have passed between the cylinders of a sugar mill. What could she gain by it, even if she succeeded? To be chased and abused by a savage husband could not be otherwise than humiliating to her high spirit, yet it could never make her feel so flat as an hour's repose under that rock would.

We walked a mile over a raised macadamized road of uniform width; a road paved with flat stones and exhibiting in its every detail a considerable degree of engineering skill. Some say that that wise old pagan, Kamehameha I. planned and built it, but others say it was built so long before his time that the knowledge of who constructed it has passed out of the traditions. In either case, however, as the handiwork of an untaught and degraded race it is a thing of pleasing interest. The stones are worn and smooth, and pushed apart in places, so that the road has the exact appearance of those ancient paved highways leading out of Rome which one sees in pictures.

The object of our tramp was to visit a great natural curiosity at the base of the foothills—a congealed cascade of lava. Some old forgotten volcanic eruption sent its broad river of fire down the mountain side here, and it poured down in a great torrent from an overhanging bluff some fifty feet high to the ground below. The flaming torrent cooled in the winds from the sea, and remains there to-day, all seamed, and frothed and rippled—a petrified Niagara. It is very picturesque, and withal so natural that one might almost imagine it still flowed. A smaller stream trickled over the cliff and built up an isolated pyramid about thirty feet high, which has the semblance of a mass of large gnarled and knotted vines and roots and stems intricately twisted and woven together.

We passed in behind the cascade and the pyramid, and found the bluff pierced by several cavernous tunnels, whose crooked courses we followed a long distance.

Two of these winding tunnels stand as proof of Nature's

mining abilities. Their floors are level, they are seven feet wide, and their roofs are gently arched. Their height is not uniform, however. We passed through one a hundred feet long, which leads through a spur of the hill and opens out well up in the sheer wall of a precipice whose foot rests in the waves of the sea. It is a commodious tunnel, except that there are occasional places in it where one must stoop to pass under. The roof is lava, of course, and is thickly studded with little lava-pointed icicles an inch long, which hardened as they dripped. They project as closely together as the iron teeth of a corn-sheller, and if one will stand up straight and walk any distance there, he can get his hair combed free of charge.

Chapter LXXIV

WE GOT BACK to the schooner in good time, and then sailed down to Kau, where we disembarked and took final leave of the vessel. Next day we bought horses and bent our way over the summer-clad mountain-terraces, toward the great volcano of Kilauea (Ke-low-way-ah). We made nearly a two days' journey of it, but that was on account of laziness. Toward sunset on the second day, we reached an elevation of some four thousand feet above sea level, and as we picked our careful way through billowy wastes of lava long generations ago stricken dead and cold in the climax of its tossing fury, we began to come upon signs of the near presence of the volcano—signs in the nature of ragged fissures that discharged jets of sulphurous vapor into the air, hot from the molten ocean down in the bowels of the mountain.

Shortly the crater came into view. I have seen Vesuvius since, but it was a mere toy, a child's volcano, a soup-kettle, compared to this. Mount Vesuvius is a shapely cone thirty-six hundred feet high; its crater an inverted cone only three hundred feet deep, and not more than a thousand feet in diameter, if as much as that; its fires meagre, modest, and docile.—But here was a vast, perpendicular, walled cellar, nine hundred feet deep in some places, thirteen hundred in others, level-floored, and *ten miles in circumference!* Here was a yawning pit upon whose floor the armies of Russia could camp, and have room to spare.

Perched upon the edge of the crater, at the opposite end from where we stood, was a small look-out house—say three miles away. It assisted us, by comparison, to comprehend and appreciate the great depth of the basin—it looked like a tiny martin-box clinging at the eaves of a cathedral. After some little time spent in resting and looking and ciphering, we hurried on to the hotel.

By the path it is half a mile from the Volcano House to the lookout-house. After a hearty supper we waited until it was thoroughly dark and then started to the crater. The first glance in that direction revealed a scene of wild beauty. There was a heavy fog over the crater and it was splendidly illuminated by the glare from the fires below. The illumination was two miles wide and a mile high, perhaps; and if you ever, on a dark night and at a distance beheld the light from thirty or forty blocks of distant buildings all on fire at once, reflected strongly against overhanging clouds, you can form a fair idea of what this looked like.

A colossal column of cloud towered to a great height in the air immediately above the crater, and the outer swell of every one of its vast folds was dyed with a rich crimson luster, which was subdued to a pale rose tint in the depressions between. It glowed like a muffled torch and stretched upward to a dizzy height toward the zenith. I thought it just possible that its like had not been seen since the children of Israel wandered on their long march through the desert so many centuries ago over a path illuminated by the mysterious "pillar of fire." And I was sure that I now had a vivid conception of what the majestic "pillar of fire" was like, which almost amounted to a revelation.

Arrived at the little thatched lookout house, we rested our elbows on the railing in front and looked abroad over the wide crater and down over the sheer precipice at the seething fires beneath us. The view was a startling improvement on my daylight experience. I turned to see the effect on the balance of the company and found the reddest-faced set of men I almost ever saw. In the strong light every countenance glowed like red-hot iron, every shoulder was suffused with crimson and shaded rearward into dingy, shapeless obscurity! The place below looked like the infernal regions and these men like half-cooled devils just come up on a furlough.

I turned my eyes upon the volcano again. The "cellar" was tolerably well lighted up. For a mile and a half in front of us and half a mile on either side, the floor of the abyss was magnificently illuminated; beyond these limits the mists hung down their gauzy curtains and cast a deceptive gloom over all that made the twinkling fires in the remote corners of the crater seem countless leagues removed—made them seem like the camp-fires of a great army far away. Here was room for the imagination to work! You could imagine those lights the width of a continent away—and that hidden under the intervening darkness were hills, and winding rivers, and weary wastes of plain and desert—and even then the tremendous vista stretched on, and on, and on!—to the fires and far beyond! You could not compass it—it was the idea of eternity made tangible—and the longest end of it made visible to the naked eye!

The greater part of the vast floor of the desert under us was as black as ink, and apparently smooth and level; but over a mile square of it was ringed and streaked and striped with a thousand branching streams of liquid and gorgeously brilliant fire! It looked like a colossal railroad map of the State of Massachusetts done in chain lightning on a midnight sky. Imagine it—imagine a coal-black sky shivered into a tangled net-work of angry fire!

Here and there were gleaming holes a hundred feet in diameter, broken in the dark crust, and in them the melted lava—the color a dazzling white just tinged with yellow—was boiling and surging furiously; and from these holes branched numberless bright torrents in many directions, like the spokes of a wheel, and kept a tolerably straight course for a while and then swept round in huge rainbow curves, or made a long succession of sharp worm-fence angles, which looked precisely like the fiercest jagged lightning. These streams met other streams, and they mingled with and crossed and recrossed each other in every conceivable direction, like skate tracks on a popular skating ground. Sometimes streams twenty or thirty feet wide flowed from the holes to some distance without dividing—and through the opera-glasses we could see that they ran down small, steep hills and were genuine cataracts of fire, white at their source, but soon cooling and turning to the richest red, grained with alternate lines of black and gold. Every now and then masses of the dark crust broke away and floated slowly down these streams like rafts down a river. Occasionally the molten lava flowing under the superincumbent crust broke through—split a dazzling streak, from five hundred to a thousand feet long, like a sudden flash of lightning, and then acre after acre of the cold lava parted into fragments, turned up edgewise like cakes of ice when a great river breaks up, plunged downward and were swallowed in the crimson cauldron. Then the wide expanse of the "thaw" maintained a ruddy glow for a while, but shortly cooled and became black and level again. During a "thaw," every dismembered cake was marked by a glittering white border which was superbly shaded inward by aurora borealis rays, which were a flaming yellow where they joined the white border, and from thence toward their points tapered into glowing crimson, then into a rich, pale carmine, and finally into a faint blush that held its own a moment and then dimmed and turned black. Some of the streams preferred to mingle together in a tangle of fantastic circles, and then they looked something like the confusion of ropes one sees on a ship's deck when she has just taken in sail and dropped anchor—provided one can imagine those ropes on fire.

Through the glasses, the little fountains scattered about looked very beautiful. They boiled, and coughed, and spluttered, and discharged sprays of stringy red fire—of about the consistency of mush, for instance—from ten to fifteen feet into the air, along with a shower of brilliant white sparks—a quaint and unnatural mingling of gouts of blood and snowflakes!

We had circles and serpents and streaks of lightning all twined and wreathed and tied together, without a break throughout an area more than a mile square (that amount of ground was covered, though it was not strictly "square"), and it was with a feeling of placid exultation that we reflected that many years had elapsed since any visitor had seen such a splendid display—since any visitor had seen anything more than the now snubbed and insignificant "North" and "South" lakes in action. We had been reading old files of Hawaiian newspapers and the "Record Book" at the Volcano House, and were posted.

I could see the North Lake lying out on the black floor away off in the outer edge of our panorama, and knitted to it by a web-work of lava streams. In its individual capacity it looked very little more respectable than a schoolhouse on fire. True, it was about nine hundred feet long and two or three hundred wide, but then, under the present circumstances, it necessarily appeared rather insignificant, and besides it was so distant from us.

I forgot to say that the noise made by the bubbling lava is not great, heard as we heard it from our lofty perch. It makes three distinct sounds—a rushing, a hissing, and a coughing or puffing sound; and if you stand on the brink and close your eyes it is no trick at all to imagine that you are sweeping down a river on a large low-pressure steamer, and that you hear the hissing of the steam about her boilers, the puffing from her escape-pipes and the churning rush of the water abaft her wheels. The smell of sulphur is strong, but not unpleasant to a sinner.

We left the lookout house at ten o'clock in a half cooked condition, because of the heat from Pele's furnaces, and wrapping up in blankets, for the night was cold, we returned to our Hotel.

Chapter LXXV

THE NEXT NIGHT was appointed for a visit to the bottom of the crater, for we desired to traverse its floor and see the "North Lake" (of fire) which lay two miles away, toward the further wall. After dark half a dozen of us set out, with lanterns and native guides, and climbed down a crazy, thousand-foot pathway in a crevice fractured in the crater wall, and reached the bottom in safety.

The irruption of the previous evening had spent its force and the floor looked black and cold; but when we ran out upon it we found it hot yet, to the feet, and it was likewise riven with crevices which revealed the underlying fires gleaming vindictively. A neighboring cauldron was threatening to overflow, and this added to the dubiousness of the situation. So the native guides refused to continue the venture, and then every body deserted except a stranger named Marlette. He said he had been in the crater a dozen times in daylight and believed he could find his way through it at night. He thought that a run of three hundred yards would carry us over the hottest part of the floor and leave us our shoe-soles. His pluck gave me back-bone. We took one lantern and instructed the guides to hang the other to the roof of the lookout house to serve as a beacon for us in case we got lost, and then the party started back up the precipice and Marlette and I made our run. We skipped over the hot floor and over the red crevices with brisk dispatch and reached the cold lava safe but with pretty warm feet. Then we took things leisurely and comfortably, jumping tolerably wide and probably bottomless chasms, and threading our way through picturesque lava upheavals with considerable confidence. When we got fairly away from the cauldrons of boiling fire, we seemed to be in a gloomy desert, and a suffocatingly dark one, surrounded by dim walls that seemed to tower to the sky. The only cheerful objects were the glinting stars high overhead.

By and by Marlette shouted "Stop!" I never stopped quicker in my life. I asked what the matter was. He said we were out of the path. He said we must not try to go on till we found it again, for we were surrounded with beds of rotten lava through which we could easily break and plunge down a thousand feet. I thought eight hundred would answer for me, and was about to say so when Marlette partly proved his statement by accidentally crushing through and disappearing to his arm-pits. He got out and we hunted for the path with the lantern. He said there was only one path and that it was but vaguely defined. We could not find it. The lava surface was all alike in the lantern light. But he was an ingenious man. He said it was not the lantern that had informed him that we were out of the path, but his *feet*. He had noticed a crisp grinding of fine lava-needles under his feet, and some instinct reminded him that in the path these were all worn away. So he put the lantern behind him, and began to search with his boots instead of his eyes. It was good sagacity. The first time his foot touched a surface that did not grind under it he announced that the trail was found again; and after that we kept up a sharp listening for the rasping sound and it always warned us in time.

It was a long tramp, but an exciting one. We reached the North Lake between ten and eleven o'clock, and sat down on a huge overhanging lava-shelf, tired but satisfied. The spectacle presented was worth coming double the distance to see. Under us, and stretching away before us, was a heaving sea of molten fire of seemingly limitless extent. The glare from it was so blinding that it was some time before we could bear to look upon it steadily. It was like gazing at the sun at noonday, except that the glare was not quite so white. At unequal distances all around the shores of the lake were nearly white-hot chimneys or hollow drums of lava, four or five feet high, and up through them were bursting gorgeous sprays of lava-gouts and gem spangles, some white, some red and some golden—a ceaseless bombardment, and one that fascinated the eye with its unapproachable splendor. The more distant jets, sparkling up through an intervening gossamer veil of vapor, seemed miles away; and the further the curving ranks of fiery fountains receded, the more fairy-like and beautiful they appeared.

Now and then the surging bosom of the lake under our noses would calm down ominously and seem to be gathering strength for an enterprise; and then all of a sudden a red dome of lava of the bulk of an ordinary dwelling would heave itself aloft like an escaping balloon, then burst asunder, and out of its heart would flit a pale-green film of vapor, and float upward and vanish in the darkness—a released soul soaring homeward from captivity with the damned, no doubt. The crashing plunge of the ruined dome into the lake again would send a world of seething billows lashing against the shores and shaking the foundations of our perch. By and by, a loosened mass of the hanging shelf we sat on tumbled into the lake, jarring the surroundings like an earthquake and delivering a suggestion that may have been intended for a hint, and may not. We did not wait to see.

We got lost again on our way back, and were more than an hour hunting for the path. We were where we could see the beacon lantern at the look-out house at the time, but thought it was a star and paid no attention to it. We reached the hotel at two o'clock in the morning pretty well fagged out.

Kilauea never overflows its vast crater, but bursts a passage for its lava through the mountain side when relief is necessary, and then the destruction is fearful. About 1840 it rent its overburdened stomach and sent a broad river of fire careering down to the sea, which swept away forests, huts, plantations and every thing else that lay in its path. The stream was *five miles broad*, in places, and *two hundred feet deep*, and the distance it traveled was forty miles. It tore up and bore away acre-patches of land on its bosom like rafts—rocks, trees and all intact. At night the red glare was visible a hundred miles at sea; and at a distance of forty miles fine print could be read at midnight. The atmosphere was poisoned with sulphurous vapors and choked with falling ashes, pumice stones and cinders; countless columns of smoke rose up and blended together in a tumbled canopy that hid the heavens and glowed with a ruddy flush reflected from the fires below; here and there jets of lava sprung hundreds of feet into the air and burst into rocket-sprays that returned to earth in a crimson rain; and all the while the laboring mountain shook with Nature's great palsy, and voiced its distress in moanings and the muffled booming of subterranean thunders.

Fishes were killed for twenty miles along the shore, where the lava entered the sea. The earthquakes caused some loss of human life, and a prodigious tidal wave swept inland, carrying every thing before it and drowning a number of natives. The devastation consummated along the route traversed by the river of lava was complete and incalculable. Only a Pompeii and a Herculaneum were needed at the foot of Kilauea to make the story of the irruption immortal.

Chapter LXXVI

WE RODE horseback all around the island of Hawaii (the crooked road making the distance two hundred miles), and enjoyed the journey very much. We were more than a week making the trip, because our Kanaka horses would not go by a house or a hut without stopping—whip and spur could not alter their minds about it, and so we finally found that it economized time to let them have their way. Upon inquiry the mystery was explained: the natives are such thorough-going gossips that they never pass a house without stopping to swap news, and consequently their horses learn to regard that sort of thing as an essential part of the whole duty of man, and his salvation not to be compassed without it. However, at a former crisis of my life I had once taken an aristocratic young lady out driving, behind a horse that had just retired from a long and honorable career as the moving impulse of a milk wagon, and so this present experience awoke a reminiscent sadness in me in place of the exasperation more natural to the occasion. I remembered how helpless I was that day, and how humiliated; how ashamed I was of having intimated to the girl that I had always owned the horse and was accustomed to grandeur; how hard I tried to appear easy, and even vivacious, under suffering that was consuming my vitals; how placidly and maliciously the girl smiled, and kept on smiling, while my hot blushes baked themselves into a permanent blood-pudding in my face; how the horse ambled from one side of the street to the other and waited complacently before every third house two minutes and a quarter while I belabored his back and reviled him in my heart; how I tried to keep him from turning corners, and failed; how I moved heaven and earth to get him out of town, and did not succeed; how he traversed the entire settlement and delivered imaginary milk at a hundred and sixty-two different domiciles, and how he finally brought up at a dairy depot and refused to budge further, thus rounding and completing the revealment of what the plebeian service of his life had been; how, in eloquent silence, I walked the girl home, and how, when I took leave of her, her parting remark scorched my soul and appeared to blister me all over: she said that my horse was a fine, capable animal, and I must have taken great comfort in him in my time—but that if I would take along some milk-tickets next time, and appear to deliver them at the various halting places, it might expedite his movements a little. There was a coolness between us after that.

In one place in the island of Hawaii, we saw a laced and ruffled cataract of limpid water leaping from a sheer precipice fifteen hundred feet high; but that sort of scenery finds its stanchest ally in the arithmetic rather than in spectacular effect. If one desires to be so stirred by a poem of Nature wrought in the happily commingled graces of picturesque rocks, glimpsed distances, foliage, color, shifting lights and shadows, and falling water, that the tears almost come into his eyes so potent is the charm exerted, he need not go away from America to enjoy such an experience. The Rainbow Fall, in Watkins Glen (N. Y.), on the Erie railway, is an example. It would recede into pitiable insignificance if the callous tourist drew an arithmetic on it; but left to compete for the honors simply on scenic grace and beauty—the grand, the august and the sublime being barred the contest—it could challenge the old world and the new to produce its peer.

In one locality, on our journey, we saw some horses that had been born and reared on top of the mountains, above the range of running water, and consequently they had never drank that fluid in their lives, but had been always accustomed to quenching their thirst by eating dew-laden or shower-wetted leaves. And now it was destructively funny to see them sniff suspiciously at a pail of water, and then put in their noses and try to take a *bite* out of the fluid, as if it were a solid. Finding it liquid, they would snatch away their heads and fall to trembling, snorting and showing other evidences of fright. When they became convinced at last that the water was friendly and harmless, they thrust in their noses up to their eyes, brought out a mouthful of the water, and proceeded to *chew* it complacently. We saw a man coax, kick and spur one of them five or ten minutes before he could make it cross a running stream. It spread its nostrils, distended its eyes and trembled all over, just as horses customarily do in the presence of a serpent—and for aught I know it thought the crawling stream *was* a serpent.

In due course of time our journey came to an end at Ka-waehae (usually pronounced To-a-*hi*—and before we find fault with this elaborate orthographical method of arriving at such an unostentatious result, let us lop off the *ugh* from our word "though"). I made this horseback trip on a mule. I paid ten dollars for him at Kau (Kah-oo), added four to get him shod, rode him two hundred miles, and then sold him for fifteen dollars. I mark the circumstance with a white stone (in the absence of chalk—for I never saw a white stone that a body could mark anything with, though out of respect for the ancients I have tried it often enough); for up to that day and date it was the first strictly commercial transaction I had ever entered into, and come out winner. We returned to Honolulu, and from thence sailed to the island of Maui, and spent several weeks there very pleasantly. I still remember, with a sense of indolent luxury, a picnicing excursion up a romantic gorge there, called the Iao Valley. The trail lay along the edge of a brawling stream in the bottom of the gorge—a shady route, for it was well roofed with the verdant domes of forest trees. Through openings in the foliage we glimpsed picturesque scenery that revealed ceaseless changes and new charms with every step of our progress. Perpendicular walls from one to three thousand feet high guarded the way, and were sumptuously plumed with varied foliage, in places, and in places swathed in waving ferns. Passing shreds of cloud trailed their shadows across these shining fronts, mottling them with blots; billowy masses of white vapor hid the turreted summits, and far above the vapor swelled a background of gleaming green crags and cones that came and went, through the veiling mists, like islands drifting in a fog; sometimes the cloudy curtain descended till half the cañon wall was hidden, then shredded gradually away till only airy glimpses of the ferny front appeared through it—then swept aloft and left it glorified in the sun again. Now and then, as our position changed, rocky bastions swung out from the wall, a mimic ruin of castellated ramparts and crumbling towers clothed with mosses and hung with garlands of swaying vines, and as we moved on they swung back again and hid themselves once more in the foliage. Presently a verdure-clad needle of stone, a thousand feet high, stepped out from behind a corner, and mounted guard over the mysteries of the valley. It seemed to me that if Captain Cook needed a monument, here was one ready made—therefore, why not put up his sign here, and sell out the venerable cocoanut stump?

But the chief pride of Maui is her dead volcano of Halea-kala—which means, translated, "the house of the sun." We climbed a thousand feet up the side of this isolated colossus one afternoon; then camped, and next day climbed the remaining nine thousand feet, and anchored on the summit, where we built a fire and froze and roasted by turns, all night. With the first pallor of dawn we got up and saw things that were new to us. Mounted on a commanding pinnacle, we watched Nature work her silent wonders. The sea was spread abroad on every hand, its tumbled surface seeming only wrinkled and dimpled in the distance. A broad valley below appeared like an ample checker-board, its velvety green sugar plantations alternating with dun squares of barrenness and groves of trees diminished to mossy tufts. Beyond the valley were mountains picturesquely grouped together; but bear in mind, we fancied that we were looking *up* at these things—not down. We seemed to sit in the bottom of a symmetrical bowl ten thousand feet deep, with the valley and the skirting sea lifted away into the sky above us! It was curious; and not only curious, but aggravating; for it was having our trouble all for nothing, to climb ten thousand feet toward heaven and then have to look *up* at our scenery. However, we had to be content with it and make the best of it; for, all we could do we could not coax our landscape down out of the clouds. Formerly, when I had read an article in which Poe treated of this singular fraud perpetrated upon the eye by isolated great altitudes, I had looked upon the matter as an invention of his own fancy.

I have spoken of the outside view—but we had an inside one, too. That was the yawning dead crater, into which we now and then tumbled rocks, half as large as a barrel, from our perch, and saw them go careering down the almost perpendicular sides, bounding three hundred feet at a jump; kicking up dust-clouds wherever they struck; diminishing to our view as they sped farther into distance; growing invisible, finally, and only betraying their course by faint little puffs of dust; and coming to a halt at last in the bottom of the abyss, two thousand five hundred feet down from where they started! It was magnificent sport. We wore ourselves out at it.

The crater of Vesuvius, as I have before remarked, is a modest pit about a thousand feet deep and three thousand in circumference; that of Kilauea is somewhat deeper, and *ten miles* in circumference. But what are either of them compared to the vacant stomach of Haleakala? I will not offer any figures of my own, but give official ones—those of Commander Wilkes, U. S. N., who surveyed it and testifies that it is *twenty-seven miles in circumference!* If it had a level bottom it would make a fine site for a city like London. It must have afforded a spectacle worth contemplating in the old days when its furnaces gave full rein to their anger.

Presently vagrant white clouds came drifting along, high over the sea and the valley; then they came in couples and groups; then in imposing squadrons; gradually joining their forces, they banked themselves solidly together, a thousand feet under us, and *totally shut out land and ocean*—not a vestige of *anything* was left in view but just a little of the rim of the crater, circling away from the pinnacle whereon we sat (for a ghostly procession of wanderers from the filmy hosts without had drifted through a chasm in the crater wall and filed round and round, and gathered and sunk and blended together till the abyss was stored to the brim with a fleecy fog). Thus banked, motion ceased, and silence reigned. Clear to the horizon, league on league, the snowy floor stretched without a break—not level, but in rounded folds, with shallow creases between, and with here and there stately piles of vapory architecture lifting themselves aloft out of the common plain—some near at hand, some in the middle distances, and others relieving the monotony of the remote solitudes. There was little conversation, for the impressive scene overawed speech. I felt like the Last Man, neglected of the judgment, and left pinnacled in mid-heaven, a forgotten relic of a vanished world.

While the hush yet brooded, the messengers of the coming resurrection appeared in the East. A growing warmth suffused the horizon, and soon the sun emerged and looked out over the cloud-waste, flinging bars of ruddy light across it, staining its folds and billow-caps with blushes, purpling the shaded troughs between, and glorifying the massy vapor-palaces and cathedrals with a wasteful splendor of all blendings and combinations of rich coloring.

It was the sublimest spectacle I ever witnessed, and I think the memory of it will remain with me always.

Chapter LXXVII

I STUMBLED upon one curious character in the Island of Maui. He became a sore annoyance to me in the course of time. My first glimpse of him was in a sort of public room in the town of Lahaina. He occupied a chair at the opposite side of the apartment, and sat eyeing our party with interest for some minutes, and listening as critically to what we were saying as if he fancied we were talking to him and expecting him to reply. I thought it very sociable in a stranger. Presently, in the course of conversation, I made a statement bearing upon the subject under discussion—and I made it with due modesty, for there was nothing extraordinary about it, and it was only put forth in illustration of a point at issue. I had barely finished when this person spoke out with rapid utterance and feverish anxiety:

"Oh, that was certainly remarkable, after a fashion, but you ought to have seen *my* chimney—you ought to have seen *my* chimney, sir! Smoke! I wish I may hang if—Mr. Jones, *you* remember that chimney—you *must* remember that chimney! No, no—I recollect, now, you warn't living on this side of the island then. But I am telling you nothing but the truth, and I wish I may never draw another breath if that chimney didn't smoke so that the smoke actually got *caked* in it and I had to dig it out with a pickaxe! You may smile, gentlemen, but the High Sheriff's got a hunk of it which I dug out before his eyes, and so it's perfectly easy for you to go and examine for yourselves."

The interruption broke up the conversation, which had already begun to lag, and we presently hired some natives and an out-rigger canoe or two, and went out to overlook a grand surf-bathing contest.

Two weeks after this, while talking in a company, I looked up and detected this same man boring through and through me with his intense eye, and noted again his twitching muscles and his feverish anxiety to speak. The moment I paused, he said:

"*Beg* your pardon, sir, beg your pardon, but it can only be considered remarkable when brought into strong outline by isolation. Sir, contrasted with a circumstance which occurred in my own experience, it instantly becomes commonplace. No, not that—for I will not speak so discourteously of any experience in the career of a stranger and a gentleman—but I am *obliged* to say that you could not, and you *would* not ever again refer to this tree as a *large* one, if you could behold, as I have, the great Yakmatack tree, in the island of Ounaska, sea of Kamtchatka—a tree, sir, not one inch less than four hundred and fifteen feet in solid diameter!—and I wish I may die in a minute if it isn't so! Oh, you needn't look so questioning, gentlemen; here's old Cap Saltmarsh can say whether I know what I'm talking about or not. I showed him the tree."

Captain Saltmarsh.—"Come, now, cat your anchor, lad— you're heaving too taut. You *promised* to show me that stunner, and I walked more than eleven mile with you through the cussedest jungle *I* ever see, a hunting for it; but the tree you showed me finally warn't as big around as a beer cask, and *you* know that your own self, Markiss."

"Hear the man talk! Of *course* the tree was reduced that way, but didn't I *explain* it? Answer me, didn't I? Didn't I say I wished you could have seen it when *I* first saw it? When you got up on your ear and called me names, and said I had brought you eleven miles to look at a sapling, didn't I *explain* to you that all the whale-ships in the North Seas had been wooding off of it for more than twenty-seven years? And did you s'pose the tree could last for-*ever*, con-*found* it? I don't see why you want to keep back things that way, and try to injure a person that's never done *you* any harm."

Somehow this man's presence made me uncomfortable, and I was glad when a native arrived at that moment to say that Muckawow, the most companionable and luxurious among the rude war-chiefs of the Islands, desired us to come over and help him enjoy a missionary whom he had found trespassing on his grounds.

I think it was about ten days afterward that, as I finished a statement I was making for the instruction of a group of friends and acquaintances, and which made no pretence of being extraordinary, a familiar voice chimed instantly in on the heels of my last word, and said:

"But, my dear sir, there was *nothing* remarkable about that horse, or the circumstance either—nothing in the world! I mean no sort of offence when I say it, sir, but you really do not know anything whatever about speed. Bless your heart, if you could only have seen my mare Margaretta; *there* was a beast!—*there* was lightning for you! Trot! Trot is no name for it—she flew! How she *could* whirl a buggy along! I started her out once, sir—Colonel Bilgewater, *you* recollect that animal perfectly well—I started her out about thirty or thirty-five yards ahead of the awfullest storm I ever saw in my life, and it chased us upwards of eighteen miles! It did, by the everlasting hills! And I'm telling you nothing but the unvarnished truth when I say that not one single drop of rain fell on me—not a single *drop*, sir! And I swear to it! But my dog was a-swimming behind the wagon all the way!"

For a week or two I stayed mostly within doors, for I seemed to meet this person everywhere, and he had become utterly hateful to me. But one evening I dropped in on Captain Perkins and his friends, and we had a sociable time. About ten o'clock I chanced to be talking about a merchant friend of mine, and without really intending it, the remark slipped out that he was a little mean and parsimonious about paying his workmen. Instantly, through the steam of a hot whiskey punch on the opposite side of the room, a remembered voice shot—and for a moment I trembled on the imminent verge of profanity:

"Oh, my dear sir, really you expose yourself when you parade *that* as a surprising circumstance. Bless your heart and hide, you are ignorant of the very A B C of meanness! ignorant as the unborn babe! ignorant as unborn *twins*! You don't know *any thing* about it! It is pitiable to see you, sir, a well-spoken and prepossessing stranger, making such an enormous pow-wow here about a subject concerning which your ignorance is perfectly humiliating! Look me in the eye, if you please; look me in the eye. John James Godfrey was the son of poor but honest parents in the State of Mississippi—boyhood friend of mine—bosom comrade in later years. Heaven rest his noble spirit, he is gone from us now. John James Godfrey was hired by the Hayblossom Mining Company in California to do some blasting for them—the 'Incorporated

Company of Mean Men,' the boys used to call it. Well, one day he drilled a hole about four feet deep and put in an awful blast of powder, and was standing over it ramming it down with an iron crowbar about nine foot long, when the cussed thing struck a spark and fired the powder, and scat! away John Godfrey whizzed like a sky-rocket, him and his crowbar! Well, sir, he kept on going up in the air higher and higher, till he didn't look any bigger than a boy—and he kept going on up higher and higher, till he didn't look any bigger than a doll—and he kept on going up higher and higher, till he didn't look any bigger than a little small bee—and then he went out of sight! Presently he came in sight again, looking like a little small bee—and he came along down further and further, till he looked as big as a doll again—and down further and further, till he was as big as a boy again—and further and further, till he was a full-sized man once more; and then him and his crowbar came a wh-izzing down and lit right exactly in the same old tracks and went to r-ramming down, and r-ramming down, and r-ramming down again, just the same as if nothing had happened! Now do you know, that poor cuss warn't gone only sixteen minutes, and yet that Incorporated Company of Mean Men DOCKED HIM FOR THE LOST TIME!"

I said I had the headache, and so excused myself and went home. And on my diary I entered "another night spoiled" by this offensive loafer. And a fervent curse was set down with it to keep the item company. And the very next day I packed up, out of all patience, and left the Island.

Almost from the very beginning, I regarded that man as a liar.

.   .   .   .

The line of points represents an interval of years. At the end of which time the opinion hazarded in that last sentence came to be gratifyingly and remarkably endorsed, and by wholly disinterested persons. The man Markiss was found one morning hanging to a beam of his own bedroom (the doors and windows securely fastened on the inside), dead; and on his breast was pinned a paper in his own handwriting begging his friends to suspect no innocent person of having any thing to do with his death, for that it was the work of his own hands entirely. Yet the jury brought in the astounding verdict that deceased came to his death "by the hands of some person or persons unknown!" They explained that the perfectly undeviating consistency of Markiss's character for thirty years towered aloft as colossal and indestructible testimony, that whatever statement he chose to make was entitled to instant and unquestioning acceptance as a *lie*. And they furthermore stated their belief that he was not dead, and instanced the strong circumstantial evidence of his own word that he *was* dead—and beseeched the coroner to delay the funeral as long as possible, which was done. And so in the tropical climate of Lahaina the coffin stood open for seven days, and then even the loyal jury gave him up. But they sat on him again, and changed their verdict to "suicide induced by mental aberration"—because, said they, with penetration, "he said he was dead, and he *was* dead; and would he have told the truth if he had been in his right mind? *No*, sir."

Chapter LXXVIII

AFTER HALF a year's luxurious vagrancy in the islands, I took shipping in a sailing vessel, and regretfully returned to San Francisco—a voyage in every way delightful, but without an incident: unless lying two long weeks in a dead calm, eighteen hundred miles from the nearest land, may rank as an incident. Schools of whales grew so tame that day after day they played about the ship among the porpoises and the sharks without the least apparent fear of us, and we pelted them with empty bottles for lack of better sport. Twenty-four hours afterward these bottles would be still lying on the glassy water under our noses, showing that the ship had not moved out of her place in all that time. The calm was absolutely breathless, and the surface of the sea absolutely without a wrinkle. For a whole day and part of a night we lay so close to another ship that had drifted to our vicinity, that we carried on conversations with her passengers, introduced each other by name, and became pretty intimately acquainted with people we had never heard of before, and have never heard of since. This was the only vessel we saw during the whole lonely voyage. We had fifteen passengers, and to show how hard pressed they were at last for occupation and amusement, I will mention that the gentlemen gave a good part of their time every day, during the calm, to trying to sit on an empty champagne bottle (lying on its side), and thread a needle without touching their heels to the deck, or falling over; and the ladies sat in the shade of the mainsail, and watched the enterprise with absorbing interest. We were at sea five Sundays; and yet, but for the almanac, we never would have known but that all the other days were Sundays too.

I was home again, in San Francisco, without means and without employment. I tortured my brain for a saving scheme of some kind, and at last a public lecture occurred to me! I sat down and wrote one, in a fever of hopeful anticipation. I showed it to several friends, but they all shook their heads. They said nobody would come to hear me, and I would make a humiliating failure of it. They said that as I had never spoken in public, I would break down in the delivery, anyhow. I was disconsolate now. But at last an editor slapped me on the back and told me to "go ahead." He said, "Take the largest house in town, and charge a dollar a ticket." The audacity of the proposition was charming; it seemed fraught with practical worldly wisdom, however. The proprietor of the several theatres endorsed the advice, and said I might have his handsome new opera-house at half price—fifty dollars. In sheer desperation I took it—on credit, for sufficient reasons. In three days I did a hundred and fifty dollars' worth of printing and advertising, and was the most distressed and frightened creature on the Pacific coast. I could not sleep—who could, under such circumstances? For other people there was facetiousness in the last line of my posters, but to me it was plaintive with a pang when I wrote it:

"Doors open at 7½. The trouble will begin at 8."

That line has done good service since. Showmen have borrowed it frequently. I have even seen it appended to a newspaper advertisement reminding school pupils in vacation what time next term would begin. As those three days of suspense dragged by, I grew more and more unhappy. I had sold two hundred tickets among my personal friends, but I feared they might not come. My lecture, which had seemed "humorous" to me, at first, grew steadily more and more dreary, till not a vestige of fun seemed left, and I grieved that I could not bring a coffin on the stage and turn the thing into a funeral. I was so panic-stricken, at last, that I went to three old friends, giants in stature, cordial by nature, and stormy-voiced, and said:

"This thing is going to be a failure; the jokes in it are so dim that nobody will ever see them; I would like to have you sit in the parquette, and help me through."

They said they would. Then I went to the wife of a popular citizen, and said that if she was willing to do me a very great kindness, I would be glad if she and her husband would sit prominently in the left-hand stage-box, where the whole house could see them. I explained that I should need help, and would turn toward her and smile, as a signal, when I had been delivered of an obscure joke—"and then," I added, "don't wait to investigate, but *respond!*"

She promised. Down the street I met a man I never had seen before. He had been drinking, and was beaming with smiles and good nature. He said:

"My name's Sawyer. You don't know me, but that don't matter. I haven't got a cent, but if you knew how bad I wanted to laugh, you'd give me a ticket. Come, now, what do you say?"

"Is your laugh hung on a hair-trigger?—that is, is it critical, or can you get it off *easy*?"

My drawling infirmity of speech so affected him that he laughed a specimen or two that struck me as being about the article I wanted, and I gave him a ticket, and appointed him to sit in the second circle, in the centre, and be responsible for that division of the house. I gave him minute instructions about how to detect indistinct jokes, and then went away, and left him chuckling placidly over the novelty of the idea.

I ate nothing on the last of the three eventful days—I only suffered. I had advertised that on this third day the box-office would be opened for the sale of reserved seats. I crept down to the theatre at four in the afternoon to see if any sales had been made. The ticket seller was gone, the box-office was locked up. I had to swallow suddenly, or my heart would have got out. "No sales," I said to myself; "I might have known it." I thought of suicide, pretended illness, flight. I thought of these things in earnest, for I was very miserable and scared. But of course I had to drive them away, and prepare to meet my fate. I could not wait for half-past seven—I wanted to face the horror, and end it—the feeling of many a man doomed to hang, no doubt. I went down back streets at six o'clock, and entered the theatre by the back door. I stumbled my way in the dark among the ranks of canvas scenery, and stood on the stage. The house was gloomy and silent, and its emptiness depressing. I went into the dark among the scenes again, and for an hour and a half gave myself up to the horrors, wholly unconscious of everything else. Then I heard a murmur; it rose higher and higher, and ended in a crash, mingled with cheers. It made my hair raise, it was so close to me, and so loud. There was a pause, and then another; presently came a third, and before I well knew what I was about, I was in the middle of the stage, staring at a sea of faces, bewildered by the fierce glare of the lights, and quaking in every limb with a terror that seemed like to take my life away. The house was full, aisles and all!

The tumult in my heart and brain and legs continued a full minute before I could gain any command over myself. Then I recognized the charity and the friendliness in the faces before me, and little by little my fright melted away, and I began to talk. Within three or four minutes I was comfortable, and even content. My three chief allies, with three auxiliaries, were on hand, in the parquette, all sitting together, all armed with bludgeons, and all ready to make an onslaught upon the feeblest joke that might show its head. And whenever a joke did fall, their bludgeons came down and their faces seemed to split from ear to ear; Sawyer, whose hearty countenance was seen looming redly in the centre of the second circle, took it up, and the house was carried handsomely. Inferior jokes never fared so royally before. Presently I delivered a bit of serious matter with impressive unction (it was my pet), and the audience listened with an absorbed hush that gratified me more than any applause; and as I dropped the last word of the clause, I happened to turn and catch Mrs. ——'s intent and waiting eye; my conversation with her flashed upon me, and in spite of all I could do I smiled. She took it for the signal, and promptly delivered a mellow laugh that touched off the whole audience; and the explosion that followed was the triumph of the evening. I thought that that honest man Sawyer would choke himself; and as for the bludgeons, they performed like pile-drivers. But my poor little morsel of pathos was ruined. It was taken in good faith as an intentional joke, and the prize one of the entertainment, and I wisely let it go at that.

All the papers were kind in the morning; my appetite returned; I had abundance of money. All's well that ends well.

Chapter LXXIX

I LAUNCHED out as a lecturer, now, with great boldness. I had the field all to myself, for public lectures were almost an unknown commodity in the Pacific market. They are not so rare, now, I suppose. I took an old personal friend along to play agent for me, and for two or three weeks we roamed through Nevada and California and had a very cheerful time of it. Two days before I lectured in Virginia City, two stage-coaches were robbed within two miles of the town. The daring act was committed just at dawn, by six masked men, who sprang up alongside the coaches, presented revolvers at the heads of the drivers and passengers, and commanded a general dismount. Everybody climbed down, and the robbers took their watches and every cent they had. Then they took gunpowder and blew up the express specie boxes and got their contents. The leader of the robbers was a small, quick-spoken man, and the fame of his vigorous manner and his intrepidity was in everybody's mouth when we arrived.

The night after instructing Virginia, I walked over the desolate "divide" and down to Gold Hill, and lectured there. The lecture done, I stopped to talk with a friend, and did not start back till eleven. The "divide" was high, unoccupied ground, between the towns, the scene of twenty midnight murders and a hundred robberies. As we climbed up and stepped out on this eminence, the Gold Hill lights dropped out of sight at our backs, and the night closed down gloomy and dismal. A sharp wind swept the place, too, and chilled our perspiring bodies through.

"I tell you I don't like this place at night," said Mike the agent.

"Well, don't speak so loud," I said. "You needn't remind anybody that we are here."

Just then a dim figure approached me from the direction of Virginia—a man, evidently. He came straight at me, and I stepped aside to let him pass; he stepped in the way and confronted me again. Then I saw that he had a mask on and was holding something in my face—I heard a click-click and recognized a revolver in dim outline. I pushed the barrel aside with my hand and said:

"Don't!"

He ejaculated sharply:

"Your watch! Your money!"

I said:

"You can have them with pleasure—but take the pistol away from my face, please. It makes me shiver."

"No remarks! Hand out your money!"

"Certainly—I—"

"Put up your hands! Don't you go for a weapon! Put 'em up! Higher!"

I held them above my head.

A pause. Then:

"Are you going to hand out your money or not?"

I dropped my hands to my pockets and said:

"Certainly! I—"

"Put up your *hands*! Do you want your head blown off? Higher!"

I put them above my head again.

Another pause.

"*Are* you going to hand out your money or *not*? Ah-ah—again? Put up your hands! By George, you want the head shot off you awful bad!"

"Well, friend, I'm trying my best to please you. You tell me to give up my money, and when I reach for it you tell me to put up my hands. If you would only—. Oh, now—don't! All six of you at me! That other man will get away while.—Now please take some of those revolvers out of my face—*do*, if you *please*! Every time one of them clicks, my liver comes up into my throat! If you have a mother—any of you—or if any of you have ever *had* a mother—or a—grandmother—or a—"

"Cheese it! *Will* you give up your money, or have we got to—. There-there—none of that! Put up your *hands*!"

"Gentlemen—I know you are gentlemen by your—"

"Silence! If you want to be facetious, young man, there are times and places more fitting. *This* is a serious business."

"You prick the marrow of my opinion. The funerals I have

attended in my time were comedies compared to it. Now *I* think—"

"Curse your palaver! Your money!—your money!—your money! Hold!—put up your hands!"

"Gentlemen, listen to reason. You *see* how I am situated—now *don't* put those pistols so close—I smell the powder. You see how I am situated. If I had four hands—so that I could hold up two and—"

"Throttle him! Gag him! Kill him!"

"Gentlemen, *don't*! Nobody's watching the other fellow. Why don't some of you—. Ouch! Take it away, please! Gentlemen, you see that I've got to hold up my hands; and so I can't take out my money—but if you'll be so kind as to take it out for me, I will do as much for you some—"

"Search him Beauregard—and stop his jaw with a bullet, quick, if he wags it again. Help Beauregard, Stonewall."

Then three of them, with the small, spry leader, adjourned to Mike and fell to searching him. I was so excited that my lawless fancy tortured me to ask my two men all manner of facetious questions about their rebel brother-generals of the South, but, considering the order they had received, it was but common prudence to keep still. When everything had been taken from me,—watch, money, and a multitude of trifles of small value,—I supposed I was free, and forthwith put my cold hands into my empty pockets and began an inoffensive jig to warm my feet and stir up some latent courage—but instantly all pistols were at my head, and the order came again:

"Be still! Put up your hands! And *keep* them up!"

They stood Mike up alongside of me, with strict orders to keep his hands above his head, too, and then the chief highwayman said:

"Beauregard, hide behind that boulder; Phil Sheridan, you hide behind that other one; Stonewall Jackson, put yourself behind that sage-bush there. Keep your pistols bearing on these fellows, and if they take down their hands within ten minutes, or move a single peg, let them have it!"

Then three disappeared in the gloom toward the several ambushes, and the other three disappeared down the road toward Virginia.

It was depressingly still, and miserably cold. Now this

whole thing was a practical joke, and the robbers were personal friends of ours in disguise, and twenty more lay hidden within ten feet of us during the whole operation, listening. Mike knew all this, and was in the joke, but I suspected nothing of it. To me it was most uncomfortably genuine.

When we had stood there in the middle of the road five minutes, like a couple of idiots, with our hands aloft, freezing to death by inches, Mike's interest in the joke began to wane. He said:

"The time's up, now, aint it?"

"No, you keep still. Do you want to take any chances with those bloody savages?"

Presently Mike said:

"*Now* the time's up, anyway. I'm freezing."

"Well freeze. Better freeze than carry your brains home in a basket. Maybe the time *is* up, but how do *we* know?—got no watch to tell by. I mean to give them good measure. I calculate to stand here fifteen minutes or die. Don't you move."

So, without knowing it, I was making one joker very sick of his contract. When we took our arms down at last, they were aching with cold and fatigue, and when we went sneaking off, the dread I was in that the time might not yet be up and that we would feel bullets in a moment, was not sufficient to draw all my attention from the misery that racked my stiffened body.

The joke of these highwayman friends of ours was mainly a joke upon themselves; for they had waited for me on the cold hill-top two full hours before I came, and there was very little fun in that; they were so chilled that it took them a couple of weeks to get warm again. Moreover, I never had a thought that they would kill me to get money which it was so perfectly easy to get without any such folly, and so they did not really frighten me bad enough to make their enjoyment worth the trouble they had taken. I was only afraid that their weapons would go off accidentally. Their very numbers inspired me with confidence that no blood would be intentionally spilled. They were not smart; they ought to have sent only *one* highwayman, with a double-barrelled shot gun, if they desired to see the author of this volume climb a tree.

However, I suppose that in the long run I got the largest share of the joke at last; and in a shape not foreseen by the highwaymen; for the chilly exposure on the "divide" while I was in a perspiration gave me a cold which developed itself into a troublesome disease and kept my hands idle some three months, besides costing me quite a sum in doctor's bills. Since then I play no practical jokes on people and generally lose my temper when one is played upon me.

When I returned to San Francisco I projected a pleasure journey to Japan and thence westward around the world; but a desire to see home again changed my mind, and I took a berth in the steamship, bade good-bye to the friendliest land and livest, heartiest community on our continent, and came by the way of the Isthmus to New York—a trip that was not much of a pic-nic excursion, for the cholera broke out among us on the passage and we buried two or three bodies at sea every day. I found home a dreary place after my long absence; for half the children I had known were now wearing whiskers or waterfalls, and few of the grown people I had been acquainted with remained at their hearthstones prosperous and happy—some of them had wandered to other scenes, some were in jail, and the rest had been hanged. These changes touched me deeply, and I went away and joined the famous Quaker City European Excursion and carried my tears to foreign lands.

Thus, after seven years of vicissitudes, ended a "pleasure trip" to the silver mines of Nevada which had originally been intended to occupy only three months. However, I usually miss my calculations further than that.

MORAL

If the reader thinks he is done, now, and that this book has no moral to it, he is in error. The moral of it is this: If you are of any account, stay at home and make your way by faithful diligence; but if you are "no account," go away from home, and then you will *have* to work, whether you want to or not. Thus you become a blessing to your friends by ceasing to be a nuisance to them—if the people you go among suffer by the operation.

APPENDIX

A.

MORMONISM is only about forty years old, but its career has been full of stir and adventure from the beginning, and is likely to remain so to the end. Its adherents have been hunted and hounded from one end of the country to the other, and the result is that for years they have hated all "Gentiles" indiscriminately and with all their might. Joseph Smith, the finder of the Book of Mormon and founder of the religion, was driven from State to State with his mysterious copperplates and the miraculous stones he read their inscriptions with. Finally he instituted his "church" in Ohio and Brigham Young joined it. The neighbors began to persecute, and apostasy commenced. Brigham held to the faith and worked hard. He arrested desertion. He did more—he added converts in the midst of the trouble. He rose in favor and importance with the brethren. He was made one of the Twelve Apostles of the Church. He shortly fought his way to a higher post and a more powerful—President of the Twelve. The neighbors rose up and drove the Mormons out of Ohio, and they settled in Missouri. Brigham went with them. The Missourians drove them out and they retreated to Nauvoo, Illinois. They prospered there, and built a temple which made some pretensions to architectural grace and achieved some celebrity in a section of country where a brick court-house with a tin dome and a cupola on it was contemplated with reverential awe. But the Mormons were badgered and harried again by their neighbors. All the proclamations Joseph Smith could issue denouncing polygamy and repudiating it as utterly anti-Mormon were of no avail; the people of the neighborhood, on both sides of the Mississippi, claimed that polygamy was practised by the Mormons, and not only polygamy but a little of everything that was bad. Brigham returned from a mission to England, where he had established a Mormon newspaper, and he brought back with him several hundred converts to his preaching. His influence among the brethren augmented with every move he made. Finally Nauvoo was invaded by the Missouri and Illinois Gentiles, and Joseph Smith killed. A Mormon named Rigdon assumed the Presidency of the Mormon church and government, in Smith's place, and even tried his hand at a prophecy or two. But a greater than he was at hand. Brigham seized the advantage of the hour and without other authority than superior brain and nerve and will, hurled Rigdon from his high place and occupied it himself. He did more. He launched an elaborate curse at Rigdon and his disciples; and he pronounced Rigdon's "prophecies" emanations from the devil, and ended by "handing the false prophet over to the buffetings of Satan for a thousand years"—probably the longest term ever inflicted in Illinois. The people recognized their master. They straightway elected Brigham Young President, by a prodigious majority, and have never faltered in their devotion to him from that day to this. Brigham had forecast—a quality which no other prominent Mormon has probably ever possessed. He recognized that it was better to move to the wilderness than *be* moved. By his command the people gathered together their meagre effects, turned their backs upon their homes, and their faces toward the wilderness, and on a bitter night in February filed in sorrowful procession across the frozen Mississippi, lighted on their way by the glare from their burning temple, whose sacred furniture their own hands had fired! They camped, several days afterward, on the western verge of Iowa, and poverty, want, hunger, cold, sickness, grief and persecution did their work, and many succumbed and died—martyrs, fair and true, whatever else they might have been. Two years the remnant remained there, while Brigham and a small party crossed the country and founded Great Salt Lake City, purposely choosing a land which was *outside the ownership and jurisdiction of the hated American nation*. Note that. This was in 1847. Brigham moved his people there and got them settled just in time to see disaster fall again. For the war closed and Mexico ceded Brigham's refuge to the enemy—the United States! In 1849 the Mormons organized a "free and independent" government and erected the "State of Deseret," with Brigham Young as its head. But the very next year Congress deliberately snubbed it and created the "Territory of Utah" out of the same accumulation of mountains, sage-brush, alkali and general desolation,—but made Brigham Governor of it. Then for years the enormous migration across the plains to California poured through the land of the Mormons and yet the church remained staunch and true to its lord and master. Neither hunger, thirst, poverty, grief, hatred, contempt, nor persecution could drive the Mormons from their faith or their allegiance; and even the thirst for gold, which gleaned the flower of the youth and strength of many nations was not able to entice them! That was the final test. An experiment that could survive that was an experiment with some substance to it somewhere.

Great Salt Lake City throve finely, and so did Utah. One of the last things which Brigham Young had done before leaving Iowa, was to appear in the pulpit dressed to personate the worshipped and lamented prophet Smith, and confer the prophetic succession, with all its dignities, emoluments and authorities, upon "President Brigham Young!" The people accepted the pious fraud with the maddest enthusiasm, and Brigham's power was sealed and secured for all time. Within five years afterward he openly added polygamy to the tenets of the church by authority of a "revelation" which he pretended had been received nine years before by Joseph Smith, albeit Joseph is amply on record as denouncing polygamy to the day of his death.

Now was Brigham become a second Andrew Johnson in the small beginning and steady progress of his official grandeur. He had served successively as a disciple in the ranks; home missionary; foreign missionary; editor and publisher; Apostle; President of the Board of Apostles; President of all Mormondom, civil and ecclesiastical; successor to the great Joseph by the will of heaven; "prophet," "seer," "revelator." There was but one dignity higher which he *could* aspire to, and he reached out modestly and took that—he proclaimed himself a God!

He claims that he is to have a heaven of his own hereafter, and that he will be its God, and his wives and children its goddesses, princes and princesses. Into it all faithful Mormons will be admitted, with their families, and will take rank and consequence according to the number of their wives and children. If a disciple dies before he has had time to accumulate enough wives and children to enable him to be respectable in the next world any friend can marry a few wives and raise a few children for him *after he is dead*, and they are duly credited to his account and his heavenly status advanced accordingly.

Let it be borne in mind that the majority of the Mormons have always been ignorant, simple, of an inferior order of intellect, unacquainted with the world and its ways; and let it be borne in mind that the wives of these Mormons are necessarily after the same pattern and their children likely to be fit representatives of such a conjunction; and then let it be remembered that *for forty years* these creatures have been driven, driven, driven, relentlessly! and mobbed, beaten, and shot down; cursed, despised, expatriated; banished to a remote desert, whither they journeyed gaunt with famine and disease, disturbing the ancient solitudes with their lamentations and marking the long way with graves of their dead—and all because they were simply trying to live and worship God in the way which *they* believed with all their hearts and souls to be the true one. Let all these things be borne in mind, and then it will not be hard to account for the deathless hatred which the Mormons bear our people and our government.

That hatred has "fed fat its ancient grudge" ever since Mormon Utah developed into a self-supporting realm and the church waxed rich and strong. Brigham as Territorial Governor made it plain that Mormondom was for the Mormons. The United States tried to rectify all that by appointing territorial officers from New England and other anti-Mormon localities, but Brigham prepared to make their entrance into his dominions difficult. Three thousand United States troops had to go across the plains and put these gentlemen in office. And after they were in office they were as helpless as so many stone images. They made laws which nobody minded and which could not be executed. The federal judges opened court in a land filled with crime and violence and sat as holiday spectacles for insolent crowds to gape at—for there was nothing to try, nothing to do, nothing on the dockets! And if a Gentile brought a suit, the Mormon jury would do just as it pleased about bringing in a verdict, and when the judgment of the court was rendered no Mormon cared for it and no officer could execute it. Our Presidents shipped one cargo of officials after another to Utah, but the result was always the same—they sat in a blight for awhile, they fairly feasted on scowls and insults day by day, they saw every attempt to do their official duties find its reward in darker and darker looks, and in secret threats and warnings of a more and more dismal nature—and at last they either succumbed and became despised tools and toys of the Mormons, or got scared and discomforted beyond all endurance and left the Territory. If a brave officer kept on courageously till his pluck was proven, some pliant Buchanan or Pierce would remove him and appoint a stick in his place. In 1857 General Harney came very near being appointed Governor of Utah. And so it came very near being Harney governor and Cradlebaugh judge!—two men who never had any idea of fear further than the sort of murky comprehension of it which they were enabled to gather from the dictionary. Simply (if for nothing else) for the variety they would have made in a rather monotonous history of Federal servility and helplessness, it is a pity they were not fated to hold office together in Utah.

Up to the date of our visit to Utah, such had been the Territorial record. The Territorial government established there had been a hopeless failure, and Brigham Young was the only real power in the land. He was an absolute monarch—a monarch who defied our President—a monarch who laughed at our armies when they camped about his capital—a monarch who received without emotion the news that the august Congress of the United States had enacted a solemn law against polygamy, and then went forth calmly and married twenty-five or thirty more wives.

B.

THE MOUNTAIN MEADOWS MASSACRE.

THE persecutions which the Mormons suffered so long—and which they consider they still suffer in not being allowed to govern themselves—they have endeavored and are still endeavoring to repay. The now almost forgotten "Mountain Meadows massacre" was their work. It was very famous in its day. The whole United States rang with its horrors. A few items will refresh the reader's memory. A great emigrant train from Missouri and Arkansas passed through Salt Lake City and a few disaffected Mormons joined it for the sake of the strong protection it afforded for their escape. In that matter lay sufficient cause for hot retaliation by the Mormon chiefs. Besides, these one hundred and forty-five or one hundred and fifty unsuspecting emigrants being in part from Arkansas, where a noted Mormon missionary had lately been killed, and in part from Missouri, a State remembered with execrations as a bitter persecutor of the saints when they were few and poor and friendless, here were substantial additional grounds for lack of love for these wayfarers. And finally, this train was rich, very rich in cattle, horses, mules and other property— and how could the Mormons consistently keep up their coveted resemblance to the Israelitish tribes and not seize the "spoil" of an enemy when the Lord had so manifestly "delivered it into their hand?"

Wherefore, according to Mrs. C. V. Waite's entertaining book, "The Mormon Prophet," it transpired that—

"A 'revelation' from Brigham Young, as Great Grand Archee or God, was dispatched to President J. C. Haight, Bishop Higbee and J. D. Lee (adopted son of Brigham), commanding them to raise all the forces they could muster and trust, follow those cursed Gentiles (so read the revelation), attack them disguised as Indians, and with the arrows of the Almighty make a clean sweep of them, and leave none to tell the tale; and if they needed any assistance they were commanded to hire the Indians as their allies, promising them a share of the booty. They were to be neither slothful nor negligent in their duty, and to be punctual in sending the teams back to him before winter set in, for this was the mandate of Almighty God."

The command of the "revelation" was faithfully obeyed. A large party of Mormons, painted and tricked out as Indians, overtook the train of emigrant wagons some three hundred miles south of Salt Lake City, and made an attack. But the emigrants threw up earthworks, made fortresses of their wagons and defended themselves gallantly and successfully for five days! Your Missouri or Arkansas gentleman is not much afraid of the sort of scurvy apologies for "Indians" which the southern part of Utah affords. He would stand up and fight five hundred of them.

At the end of the five days the Mormons tried military strategy. They retired to the upper end of the "Meadows," resumed civilized apparel, washed off their paint, and then, heavily armed, drove down in wagons to the beleaguered emigrants, bearing a flag of truce! When the emigrants saw white men coming they threw down their guns and welcomed them with cheer after cheer! And, all unconscious of the poetry of it, no doubt, they lifted a little child aloft, dressed in white, in answer to the flag of truce!

The leaders of the timely white "deliverers" were President Haight and Bishop John D. Lee, of the Mormon Church. Mr. Cradlebaugh, who served a term as a Federal Judge in Utah and afterward was sent to Congress from Nevada, tells in a speech delivered in Congress how these leaders next proceeded:

"They professed to be on good terms with the Indians, and represented them as being very mad. They also proposed to intercede and settle the matter with the Indians. After several hours parley they, having (apparently) visited the Indians, gave the *ultimatum* of the savages; which was, that the emigrants should march out of their camp, leaving everything behind them, even their guns. It was promised by the Mormon bishops that they would bring a force and guard the emigrants back to the settlements. The terms were agreed to, the emigrants being desirous of saving the lives of their families. The Mormons retired, and subsequently appeared with thirty or forty armed men. The emigrants were marched out, the women and children in front and the men behind, the Mormon guard being in the rear. When they had marched in this way about a mile, at a given signal the slaughter commenced. The men were almost all shot down at the first fire from the guard. Two only escaped, who fled to the desert, and were followed one hundred and fifty miles before they were overtaken and slaughtered. The women and children ran on, two or three hundred yards further, when they were overtaken and with the aid of the Indians they were slaughtered. Seventeen individuals only, of all the emigrant party, were spared, and they were little children, the eldest of them being only seven years old. Thus, on the 10th day of September, 1857, was consummated one of the most cruel, cowardly and bloody murders known in our history."

The number of persons butchered by the Mormons on this occasion was *one hundred and twenty*.

With unheard-of temerity Judge Cradlebaugh opened his court and proceeded to make Mormondom answer for the massacre. And what a spectacle it must have been to see this grim veteran, solitary and alone in his pride and his pluck, glowering down on his Mormon jury and Mormon auditory, deriding them by turns, and by turns "breathing threatenings and slaughter!"

An editorial in the *Territorial Enterprise* of that day says of him and of the occasion:

"He spoke and acted with the fearlessness and resolution of a Jackson; but the jury failed to indict, or even report on the charges, while threats of violence were heard in every quarter, and an attack on the U. S. troops intimated, if he persisted in his course.

"Finding that nothing could be done with the juries, they were discharged, with a scathing rebuke from the judge. And then, sitting as a committing magistrate, *he commenced his task alone*. He examined witnesses, made arrests in every quarter, and created a consternation in the camps of the saints greater than any they had ever witnessed before, since Mormondom was born. At last accounts terrified elders and bishops were decamping to save their necks; and developments of the most startling character were being made, implicating the highest Church dignitaries in the many murders and robberies committed upon the Gentiles during the past eight years."

Had Harney been Governor, Cradlebaugh would have been supported in his work, and the absolute proofs adduced by him of Mormon guilt in this massacre and in a number of previous murders, would have conferred gratuitous coffins upon certain citizens, together with occasion to use them. But Cumming was the Federal Governor, and he, under a curious pretense of impartiality, sought to screen the Mormons from the demands of justice. On one occasion he even went so far as to publish his protest against the use of the U. S. troops in aid of Cradlebaugh's proceedings.

Mrs. C. V. Waite closes her interesting detail of the great massacre with the following remark and accompanying summary of the testimony—and the summary is concise, accurate and reliable:

"For the benefit of those who may still be disposed to doubt the guilt of Young and his Mormons in this transaction, the testimony is here collated and circumstances given which go not merely to implicate but to fasten conviction upon them by 'confirmations strong as proofs of Holy Writ:'

"1. The evidence of Mormons themselves, engaged in the affair, as shown by the statements of Judge Cradlebaugh and Deputy U. S. Marshal Rodgers.

"2. The failure of Brigham Young to embody any account of it in his Report as Superintendent of Indian Affairs. Also his failure to make any allusion to it whatever from the pulpit, until several years after the occurrence.

"3. The flight to the mountains of men high in authority in the Mormon Church and State, when this affair was brought to the ordeal of a judicial investigation.

"4. The failure of the *Deseret News*, the Church organ, and the only paper then published in the Territory, to notice the massacre until several months afterward, and then only to deny that Mormons were engaged in it.

"5. The testimony of the children saved from the massacre.

"6. The children and the property of the emigrants found in possession of the Mormons, and that possession traced back to the very day after the massacre.

"7. The statements of Indians in the neighborhood of the scene of the massacre: these statements are shown, not only by Cradlebaugh and Rodgers, but by a number of military officers, and by J. Forney, who was, in 1859, Superintendent of Indian Affairs for the Territory. To all these were such statements freely and frequently made by the Indians.

"8. The testimony of R. P. Campbell, Capt. 2d Dragoons, who was sent in the Spring of 1859 to Santa Clara, to protect travelers on the road to California and to inquire into Indian depredations."

C.

CONCERNING A FRIGHTFUL ASSASSINATION THAT WAS NEVER CONSUMMATED.

[If ever there was a harmless man, it is Conrad Wiegand, of Gold Hill, Nevada. If ever there was a gentle spirit that thought itself unfired gunpowder and latent ruin, it is Conrad Wiegand. If ever there was an oyster that fancied itself a whale; or a jack-o'lantern, confined to a swamp, that fancied itself a planet with a billion-mile orbit; or a summer zephyr that deemed itself a hurricane, it is Conrad Wiegand. Therefore, what wonder is it that when he says a thing, he thinks the world listens; that when he does a thing the world stands still to look; and that when he suffers, there is a convulsion of nature? When I met Conrad, he was "Superintendent of the Gold Hill Assay Office"—and he was not only its Superintendent, but its entire force. And he was a street preacher, too, with a mongrel religion of his own invention, whereby he expected to regenerate the universe. This was years ago. Here latterly he has entered journalism; and his journalism is what it might be expected to be: colossal to ear, but pigmy to the eye. It is extravagant grandiloquence confined to a newspaper about the size of a double letter sheet. He doubtless edits, sets the type, and prints his paper, all alone; but he delights to speak of the concern as if it occupies a block and employs a thousand men.

[Something less than two years ago, Conrad assailed several people mercilessly in his little "People's Tribune," and got himself into trouble. Straightway he airs the affair in the "Territorial Enterprise," in a communication over his own signature, and I propose to reproduce it here, in all its native simplicity and more than human candor. Long as it is, it is well worth reading, for it is the richest specimen of journalistic literature the history of America can furnish, perhaps:]

From the Territorial Enterprise, Jan. 20, 1870.

A SEEMING PLOT FOR ASSASSINATION MISCARRIED

———

TO THE EDITOR OF THE ENTERPRISE: Months ago, when Mr. Sutro incidentally exposed mining management on the Comstock, and among others roused me to protest against its continuance, in great kindness you warned me that any attempt by publications, by public meetings and by legislative action, aimed at the correction of chronic mining evils in Storey County, must entail upon me (a) business ruin, (b) the burden of all its costs, (c) personal violence, and if my purpose were persisted in, then (*d*) assassination, and after all nothing would be effected.

YOUR PROPHECY FULFILLING

In large part at least your prophecies have been fulfilled, for (*a*) assaying, which was well attended to in the Gold Hill Assay Office (of which I am superintendent), in consequence of my publications, has been taken elsewhere, so the President of one of the companies assures me. With no reason *assigned*, other work has been taken away. With but one or two important exceptions, our assay business now consists simply of the *gleanings* of the vicinity. (*b*) Though my own personal donations to the People's Tribune Association have already exceeded $1,500, outside of our own numbers we have received (in money) less than $300 as contributions and subscriptions for the journal. (*c*) On Thursday last, on the main street in Gold Hill, near noon, with neither warning nor cause assigned, by a powerful blow I was felled to the ground, and while down I was kicked by a man who it would seem had been led to *believe* that I had spoken derogatorily of him. By whom he was so induced to believe I am as yet unable to say. On Saturday last I was again assailed and beaten by a man who first informed me why he did so, and who persisted in making his assault even after the erroneous impression under which he *also* was at first laboring had been clearly and repeatedly pointed out. This same man, after failing through intimidation to elicit from me the names of our editorial contributors, against giving which he knew me to be pledged, beat himself weary upon me with a raw hide, I not resisting, and then pantingly threatened me with permanent disfiguring mayhem, if ever again I should introduce his name into print, and who but a few minutes before his attack upon me assured me that the only reason I was "permitted" to reach home alive on Wednesday evening last (at which time the PEOPLE'S TRIBUNE was issued) was, that he deems me only half-witted, and be it remembered the very next morning I *was* knocked down and kicked by a man who seemed to be *prepared* for flight.

[*He sees doom impending:*]

WHEN WILL THE CIRCLE JOIN?

How long before the whole of your prophecy will be ful-filled I cannot say, but under the shadow of so much fulfill-ment in so short a time, and with such threats from a man who is one of the most prominent exponents of the San Fran-cisco mining-ring staring me and this whole community de-fiantly in the face and *pointing* to a completion of your augury, do you blame me for feeling that this communication is the last I shall ever write for the Press, especially when a sense alike of personal self-respect, of duty to this money-oppressed and fear-ridden community, and of American fealty to the spirit of true Liberty all command me, and each more loudly than love of life itself, to declare the name of that prominent man to be JOHN B. WINTERS, President of the Yellow Jacket Company, a political aspirant and a military Gen-eral? The name of his partially duped accomplice and abettor in this last marvelous assault, is no other than PHILIP LYNCH, Editor and Proprietor of the Gold Hill *News*.

Despite the insult and wrong heaped upon me by John B. Winters, on Saturday afternoon, only a glimpse of which I shall be able to afford your readers, so much do I deplore clinching (by publicity) a serious mistake of any one, man or woman, committed under natural and not self-wrought pas-sion, in view of his great apparent excitement at the time and in view of the almost perfect privacy of the assault, I am far from sure that I should not have given him space for repen-tance before exposing him, were it not that he himself has so far exposed the matter as to make it the common talk of the town that he has horsewhipped me. That fact having been made public, all the facts in connection need to be also, or silence on my part would seem *more* than singular, and with many would be proof either that I was conscious of some unworthy aim in publishing the article, or else that my "non-combatant" principles are but a convenient cloak alike of physical and moral cowardice. I therefore shall try to present a graphic but truthful picture of this whole affair, but shall forbear all comments, presuming that the editors of our own journal, if others do not, will speak freely and fittingly upon this subject in our next number, whether I shall then be dead or living, for my death will not stop, though it may suspend, the publication of the PEOPLE'S TRIBUNE.

[*The "non-combatant" sticks to principle, but takes along a friend or two of a conveniently different stripe:*]

THE TRAP SET

On Saturday morning John B. Winters sent verbal word to the Gold Hill Assay Office that he desired to see me at the Yellow Jacket office. Though such a request struck me as decidedly cool in view of his own recent discourtesies to me there alike as a publisher and as a stockholder in the Yellow Jacket mine, and though it seemed to me more like a summons than the courteous request by one gentleman to another for a favor, hoping that some conference with Sharon looking to the betterment of mining matters in Nevada might arise from it, I felt strongly inclined to overlook what *possibly* was simply an oversight in courtesy. But as then it had only been two days since I had been bruised and beaten under a hasty and false apprehension of facts, my caution was somewhat aroused. Moreover I remembered sensitively his contemptuousness of manner to me at my last interview in his office. I therefore felt it needful, if I went at all, to go accompanied by a friend whom he would not dare to treat with incivility, and whose presence with me might secure exemption from insult. Accordingly I asked a neighbor to accompany me.

THE TRAP ALMOST DETECTED

Although I was not then aware of this fact, it would seem that previous to my request this same neighbor had heard Dr. Zabriskie state publicly in a saloon, that Mr. Winters had told him he had decided either to kill or to horsewhip me, but had not finally decided on which. My neighbor, therefore, felt unwilling to go down with me until he had *first* called on Mr. Winters alone. He therefore paid him a visit. From that interview he assured me that he gathered the impression that he did not believe I would have any difficulty with Mr. Winters, and that he (Winters) would call on me at four o'clock in my own office.

As Sheriff Cummings was in Gold Hill that afternoon, and as I desired to converse with him about the previous assault, I invited him to my office, and he came. Although a half hour had passed beyond four o'clock, Mr. Winters had not called, and we both of us began preparing to go home. Just then, Philip Lynch, Publisher of the Gold Hill *News*, came in and said, blandly and cheerily, as if bringing good news:

"Hello, John B. Winters wants to see you."

I replied, "Indeed! Why he sent me word that he would call on me *here* this afternoon at four o'clock!"

"O, well, it don't do to be too ceremonious just now, he's in my office, and that will do as well—come on in, Winters wants to consult with you alone. He's got something to say to you."

Though slightly uneasy at this change of programme, yet believing that in an *editor's* house I ought to be safe, and anyhow that I would be within hail of the street, I hurriedly, and but partially whispered my dim apprehensions to Mr. Cummings, and asked him if he would not keep near enough to hear my voice in case I should call. He consented to do so while waiting for some other parties, and to come in if he heard my voice or thought I had need of protection.

On reaching the editorial part of the *News* office, which viewed from the street is dark, I did not see Mr. Winters, and again my misgivings arose. Had I paused long enough to consider the case, I should have invited Sheriff Cummings in, but as Lynch went down stairs, he said: "*This* way, Wiegand—it's best to be private," or some such remark.

[I do not desire to strain the reader's fancy, hurtfully, and yet it would be a favor to me if he would try to fancy this lamb in battle, or the duelling ground or at the head of a vigilance committee—M. T.:]

I followed, and *without* Mr. Cummings, and without arms, which I never do or will carry, unless as a soldier in war, or unless I should yet come to feel I must fight a duel, or to join and aid in the ranks of a *necessary* Vigilance Committee. But by following I made a fatal mistake. Following was entering a trap, and whatever animal suffers itself to be *caught* should expect the common fate of a caged rat, as I fear events to come will prove.

Traps commonly are not set for *benevolence*.

[*His body-guard is shut out:*]

THE TRAP INSIDE

I followed Lynch down stairs. At their foot a door to the left opened into a small room. From *that* room another door opened into yet *another* room, and once entered I found myself inveigled into what many will ever henceforth regard as a private subterranean Gold Hill den, admirably adapted in proper hands to the purposes of murder, raw or disguised, for from it, with both or even one door closed, when too late, I saw that I *could* not be heard by Sheriff Cummings, and from it, BY VIOLENCE AND BY FORCE, I was prevented from making a peaceable exit, when I thought I saw the studious object of this "consultation" was no other than to compass my killing, *in the presence of Philip Lynch as a witness*, as soon as by insult a proverbially excitable man should be exasperated to the point of assailing Mr. Winters, so that Mr. Lynch, by his conscience and by his well known tenderness of heart toward the rich and potent would be *compelled* to testify that he saw Gen. John B. Winters kill Conrad Wiegand in "self-defence." But I am going too fast.

OUR HOST

Mr. Lynch was present during the most of the time (say a little short of an hour), but three times he left the room. His testimony, therefore, would be available only as to the bulk of what transpired. On entering this carpeted den I was invited to a seat near one corner of the room. Mr. Lynch took a seat near the window. J. B. Winters sat (at first) near the door, and began his remarks essentially as follows:

"I have come here to exact of you a retraction, in black and white, of those damnably false charges which you have preferred against me in that —— —— infamous lying sheet of yours, and you must declare yourself their author, that you published them knowing them to be false, and that your motives were malicious."

"Hold, Mr. Winters. Your language is insulting and your demand an enormity. I trust I was not invited here either to be insulted or coerced. I supposed myself here by invitation of Mr. Lynch, at your request."

"Nor did I come here to insult you. I have already told you that I am here for a very different purpose."

"Yet your language *has* been offensive, and even now shows strong excitement. If insult is repeated I shall either leave the room or call in Sheriff Cummings, whom I just left standing and waiting for me outside the door."

"No, you won't, sir. You may just as well understand it at once as not. *Here* you are my man, and I'll tell you why! Months ago you put your property out of your hands, boasting that you did so to escape losing it on prosecution for libel."

"It is true that I did convert all my immovable property into personal property, such as I could trust safely to others, and chiefly to escape ruin through possible libel suits."

"Very good, sir. Having placed yourself beyond the pale of the law, *may God help your soul if you* DON'T make precisely such a retraction as I have demanded. I've got you now, and by —— before you can get out of this room you've *got* to both write and sign precisely the retraction I have demanded, and before you go, anyhow—you —— —— low-lived —— lying —— ——, I'll teach you what *personal* responsibility is *outside* of the law; and, by ——, Sheriff Cummings and all the friends you've got in the world besides, can't save you, you —— ——, etc.! *No*, sir. I'm *alone* now, and I'm *prepared* to be shot down just here and now rather than be villified by you as I have been, and suffer you to escape me after publishing those charges, not only here where I am known and universally respected, but where I am *not* personally known and may be injured."

I confess this speech, with its terrible and but too plainly *implied* threat of killing me if I did not sign the paper he demanded, terrified me, especially as I saw he was working himself up to the highest possible pitch of passion, and instinct told me that any reply other than one of seeming concession to his demands would only be fuel to a raging fire, so I replied:

"Well, if I've *got* to sign ——," and then I paused some time. Resuming, I said, "But, Mr. Winters, you are greatly excited. Besides, I see you are laboring under a total misapprehension. It is your duty not to inflame but to calm yourself. I am prepared to show you, if you will only point out the article that you allude to, that *you* regard as 'charges' what no calm and logical mind has any *right* to regard as such. *Show* me the charges, and I will try, at all events; and if it becomes plain that no charges *have* been preferred, then plainly there can be nothing to retract, and no one could rightly *urge* you to demand a retraction. You should beware of making so serious a mistake, for however *honest* a man may be, every one is liable to misapprehend. Besides you *assume* that *I* am the author of some certain article which you have not pointed out. It is *hasty* to do so."

He then pointed to some numbered paragraphs in a TRIBUNE article, headed "What's the Matter with Yellow Jacket?" saying "*That's* what I refer to."

To gain time for general reflection and resolution, I took up the paper and looked it over for awhile, he remaining silent, and as I hoped, cooling. I then resumed, saying, "As I supposed. I do not *admit* having written that article, nor have you any right to *assume* so important a point, and then base important action upon your assumption. You might deeply regret it afterwards. In my published Address to the People, I notified the world that no information as to the authorship of any article would be given without the consent of the writer. I therefore cannot honorably tell you *who* wrote that article, nor can you exact it."

"If you are *not* the author, then I *do* demand to know who is?"

"I must decline to say."

"Then, by ——, I brand *you* as its author, and shall treat you accordingly."

"Passing that point, the most important misapprehension which I notice is, that you regard them as 'charges' at all, when their context, both at their beginning and end, show they are not. These words introduce them: '*Such an investigation* [just before indicated], *we think MIGHT result in showing some of the following points.*' Then follow eleven specifications, and the succeeding paragraph shows that the suggested investigation 'might EXONERATE those who are generally believed guilty.' You see, therefore, the context *proves* they are not preferred as charges, and this you seem to have overlooked."

While making those comments, Mr. Winters frequently interrupted me in such a way as to convince me that he was *resolved* not to consider candidly the thoughts contained in my words. He insisted upon it that they *were* charges, and "By ——," he would make me take them back *as* charges, and he referred the question to Philip Lynch, to whom I then appealed as a literary man, as a logician, and as an editor, calling his attention especially to the introductory paragraph just before quoted.

He replied, "If they are *not* charges, they certainly are *insinuations*," whereupon Mr. Winters renewed his demands for retraction precisely such as he had before named, except that he would allow me to state who *did* write the article if I did not myself, and this time shaking his fist in my face with more cursings and epithets.

When he threatened me with his clenched fist, instinctively I tried to rise from my chair, but Winters then forcibly thrust me down, as he did every other time (at least seven or eight), when under similar imminent danger of bruising by his fist (or for aught I could know worse than that after the first stunning blow), which he could easily and safely to himself have dealt me so long as he kept me down and stood over me.

This fact it was, which more than anything else, convinced me that by plan and plot I was purposely made powerless in Mr. Winters' hands, and that he did not mean to allow me that advantage of being afoot, which he possessed. Moreover, I then became convinced, that Philip Lynch (and for what *reason* I wondered) would do absolutely nothing to protect me in his own house. I realized then the situation thoroughly. I had found it equally vain to protest or argue, and I would make no unmanly appeal for pity, still less apologize. Yet my life had been by the plainest possible implication threatened. I was a weak man. I was unarmed. I was helplessly down, and Winters was afoot and probably armed. Lynch was the only "witness." The statements demanded, if given and not explained, would utterly sink me in my own self-respect, in my family's eyes, and in the eyes of the community. On the other hand, should I give the author's name how could I ever expect that confidence of the People which I should no longer deserve, and how much dearer to me and to my family was *my* life than the life of the real author to *his* friends. Yet life seemed dear and each minute that remained seemed precious if not solemn. I sincerely trust that neither you nor any of your readers, and especially none with families, may ever be placed in such seeming *direct* proximity to death while obliged to decide the one question I was compelled to, viz.: What should I do—I, a man of family, and *not* as Mr. Winters is, "alone."

[*The reader is requested not to skip the following.—M. T.:*]

STRATEGY AND MESMERISM

To gain time for further reflection, and hoping that by a *seeming* acquiescence I might regain my personal liberty, at least till I could give an alarm, or take advantage of some momentary inadvertence of Winters, and then without a *cowardly* flight escape, I resolved to write a certain kind of retraction, but previously had inwardly decided

First.—That I would studiously avoid every action which might be *construed* into the drawing of a weapon, even by a self-infuriated man, no matter what amount of insult might be heaped upon me, for it seemed to me that this great excess of compound profanity, foulness and epithet must be more than a mere indulgence, and therefore must have some object. "Surely in vain the net is spread in the sight of any bird." Therefore, as before without thought, I thereafter by intent kept my hands away from my pockets, and generally in sight and spread upon my knees.

Second.—I resolved to make no motion with my arms or hands which could possibly be construed into aggression.

Third.—I resolved completely to govern my outward manner and suppress indignation. To do this, I must govern my spirit. To do that, by force of imagination I was obliged like actors on the boards to resolve myself into an unnatural mental state and see all things through the eyes of an assumed *character*.

Fourth.—I resolved to try on Winters, silently, and unconsciously to himself a mesmeric power which I possess over certain kinds of people, and which at times I have found to work even in the dark over the lower animals.

Does any one smile at these last counts? God save you from ever being *obliged* to beat in a game of chess, whose stake is your life, you having but four poor pawns and pieces and your adversary with his full force unshorn. But if you are, provided you have any strength with breadth of will, do not despair. Though mesmeric power may not *save* you, it may help you; *try* it at all events. In this instance I was conscious of power coming into me, and by a law of nature, I know Winters was correspondingly weakened. If I could have gained more time I am sure he would not even have struck me.

It takes time both to form such resolutions and to recite them. That time, however, I gained while thinking of my retraction, which I first wrote in pencil, altering it from time to time till I got it to suit me, my aim being to make it look like a concession to demands, while in fact it should tersely speak the truth into Mr. Winters' mind. When it was finished, I copied it in ink, and if correctly copied from my first draft it should read as follows. In copying I do not think I made any material change.

                               COPY

To Philip Lynch, Editor of the Gold Hill News: I learn that Gen. John B. Winters believes the following (pasted on) clipping from the People's Tribune of January to contain distinct charges of mine against him personally, and that as such he desires me to retract them unqualifiedly.

In compliance with his request, permit me to say that, although Mr. Winters and I see this matter differently, in view of his strong feelings in the premises, I hereby declare that I do not know those "charges" (if such they are) to be true, and I hope that a critical examination would altogether disprove them.   CONRAD WIEGAND

Gold Hill, January 15, 1870.

I then read what I had written and handed it to Mr. Lynch, whereupon Mr. Winters said:

"That's not satisfactory, and it won't do;" and then addressing himself to Mr. Lynch, he further said: "How does it strike *you*?"

"Well, I confess I don't see that it *retracts* anything."

"Nor do I," said Winters; "in fact, I regard it as adding insult to injury. Mr. Wiegand you've got to do better than that. *You* are not the man who can pull wool over *my* eyes."

"That, sir, is the only retraction I can write."

"No it isn't, sir, and if you so much as *say* so again you do it at your peril, for I'll thrash you to within an inch of your life, and, by ——, sir, I don't pledge myself to spare you even that inch either. I want you to understand I have asked you for a very different paper, and that paper you've got to sign."

"Mr. Winters, I assure you that I *do* not wish to irritate you, but, at the same time, it is utterly *impossible* for me to write any other paper than that which I have written. If you are resolved to *compel* me to *sign* something, Philip Lynch's hand must write at your dictation, and if, when written, I *can* sign it I will do so, but such a document as you say you *must* have from me, I never can sign. I mean what I say."

"Well, sir, what's to be done must be done quickly, for I've been here long enough already. I'll put the thing in another shape (and then pointing to the paper); don't you know those charges to be false?"

"I do not."

"Do you know them to be true?"

"Of my own personal knowledge I do not."

"Why then did you print them?"

"Because rightly considered in their connection they are *not* charges, but pertinent and useful *suggestions* in answer to the queries of a correspondent who stated facts which are inexplicable."

"Don't you know that *I* know they are false?"

"If you *do*, the proper course is simply to deny them and court an investigation."

"And do YOU claim the right to make ME come out and deny anything you may choose to write and print?"

To that question I think I made no reply, and he then further said: "Come, now, we've talked about the matter long enough. I want your final answer—did you write that article or not?"

"I cannot in honor tell you *who* wrote it."

"Did you not see it before it was printed?"

"Most certainly, sir."

"And did you deem it a fit thing to publish?"

"Most assuredly, sir, or I would never have consented to its appearance. Of its *authorship* I can say nothing whatever, but for its *publication* I assume full, sole and personal responsibility."

"And do you then retract it or not?"

"Mr. Winters, if my refusal to sign such a paper as you have demanded *must* entail upon me all that your language in this room fairly implies, then I ask a few minutes for prayer."

"Prayer! —— —— you, this is not your *hour* for prayer—your time to pray was when you were writing those —— lying charges. Will you sign or not?"

"You already have my answer."

"What! do you still refuse?"

"I do, sir."

"Take *that*, then," and to my amazement and inexpressible relief he drew only a rawhide instead of what I expected—a bludgeon or pistol. With it, as he spoke, he struck at my left ear downwards, as if to tear it off, and afterwards on the side of the head. As he moved away to get a better chance for a more effective shot, for the first time I gained a chance under peril to rise, and I did so pitying him from the very bottom of my soul, to think that one so naturally capable of true dignity, power and nobility could, by the temptations of this State, and by unfortunate associations and aspirations, be so deeply debased as to find in such brutality anything which he could call satisfaction—but the great hope for us all is in progress and growth, and John B. Winters, I trust, will yet be able to comprehend my feelings.

He continued to beat me with all his great force, until absolutely weary, exhausted and panting for breath. I still adhered to my purpose of non-aggressive defence, and made no other use of my arms than to defend my head and face from further disfigurement. The mere pain arising from the blows he inflicted upon my person was of course transient, and my clothing to some extent deadened its severity, as it now hides all remaining traces.

When I supposed he was through, taking the butt end of his weapon and shaking it in my face, he warned me, if I correctly understood him, of more yet to come, and furthermore said, if ever I again dared introduce his name to print, in either my own or any other public journal, he would cut off my left ear (and I do not *think* he was jesting) and send me home to my family a visibly mutilated man, to be a standing warning to all low-lived puppies who seek to blackmail gentlemen and to injure their good names. And when he *did* so operate, he informed me that his implement would not be a whip but a knife.

When he had said this, unaccompanied by Mr. Lynch, as I remember it, he left the room, for I sat down by Mr. Lynch, exclaiming: "The man is mad—he is *utterly* mad—this step is his ruin—it is a mistake—it would be ungenerous in me, despite of all the ill usage I have here received, to expose him, at least until he has had an opportunity to reflect upon the matter. I shall be in no haste."

"Winters *is* very mad just now," replied Mr. Lynch, "but when he is himself he is one of the finest men I ever met. In fact, he told me the reason he did not meet you upstairs was to spare you the humiliation of a beating in the sight of others."

I submit that that unguarded remark of Philip Lynch convicts him of having been privy in advance to Mr. Winters' intentions whatever they may have been, or at least to his meaning to make an assault upon me, but I leave to others to determine how much censure an *editor* deserves for inveigling a weak, non-combatant man, also a publisher, to a pen of his own to be horsewhipped, if no worse, for the simple printing of what is verbally in the mouth of nine out of ten men, and women too, upon the street.

While writing this account two theories have occurred to me as *possibly* true respecting this most remarkable assault:

First—The aim *may* have been simply to extort from me such admissions as in the hands of money and influence would have sent me to the Penitentiary for libel. This, however, seems unlikely, because any statements elicited by fear or force could not be evidence in law or could be so explained as to have no force. The statements wanted so badly must have been desired for some other purpose.

Second—The other theory has so dark and wilfully murderous a look that I shrink from writing it, yet as in all probability my death at the earliest practicable moment has already been decreed, I feel I should do all I can before my hour arrives, at least to show others how to break up that aristocratic rule and combination which has robbed all Nevada of true freedom, if not of manhood itself. Although I do not prefer this hypothesis as a *"charge,"* I feel that as an American citizen I still have a right both to think and to speak my thoughts even in the land of Sharon and Winters, and as much so respecting the theory of a brutal assault (especially when I have been its subject) as respecting any other apparent enormity. I give the matter simply as a suggestion which may explain to the proper authorities and to the people whom they should represent, a well ascertained but notwithstanding a darkly mysterious fact. The scheme of the assault *may* have been

First—To terrify me by making me conscious of my own helplessness after making actual though not legal threats against my life.

Second—To imply that I could save my life only by writing or signing certain specific statements which if not subsequently explained would eternally have branded me as infamous and would have consigned my family to shame and want, and to the dreadful compassion and patronage of the rich.

Third—To blow my brains out *the moment I had signed*, thereby preventing me from making any subsequent explanation such as *could* remove the infamy.

Fourth—Philip Lynch to be compelled to testify that I was killed by John B. Winters in self-defence, for the conviction of Winters would bring *him* in as an accomplice. If that *was* the programme in John B. Winters' mind nothing saved my life but my persistent *refusal* to sign, when that refusal seemed clearly to me to be the choice of death.

The remarkable assertion made to me by Mr. Winters, that pity only spared my life on Wednesday evening last, almost compels me to believe that at first he *could* not have intended me to leave that room alive; and why I was allowed to, unless through mesmeric *or some other invisible influence*, I cannot divine. The more I reflect upon this matter, the more probable as true does this horrible interpretation become.

The narration of these things I might have spared both to Mr. Winters and to the public had he himself observed silence, but as he has both verbally spoken and suffered a thoroughly garbled statement of facts to appear in the Gold Hill *News* I feel it due to myself no less than to this community, and to the entire independent press of America and Great Britain, to give a true account of what even the Gold Hill *News* has pronounced a disgraceful affair, and which it deeply regrets because of some alleged telegraphic mistake in the account of it. [Who received the erroneous telegrams?]

Though he may not deem it prudent to take my life just now, the publication of this article I feel sure must compel Gen. Winters (with his peculiar views about *his* right to exemption from criticism by *me*) to resolve on my violent death, though it may take years to compass it. Notwithstanding *I* bear *him* no ill will; and if W. C. Ralston and William Sharon, and other members of the San Francisco mining and milling Ring feel that he above all other men in this State and California is the most fitting man to supervise and control Yellow Jacket matters, until I am able to vote more than half their stock I presume he will be retained to grace his present post.

Meantime, I cordially invite all who know of any sort of important villainy which only *can* be cured by exposure (and who would expose it if they felt sure they would not be betrayed under bullying threats), to communicate with the PEO-PLE'S TRIBUNE; for until I *am* murdered, so long as I can raise the means to publish, I propose to continue my *efforts* at least to revive the liberties of the State, to curb oppression, and to benefit man's world and God's earth.

CONRAD WIEGAND

[It does seem a pity that the Sheriff was shut out, since the good sense of a general of militia and of a prominent editor failed to teach them that the merited castigation of this weak, half-witted child was a thing that ought to have been done in the street, where the poor thing could have a chance to run. When a journalist maligns a citizen, or attacks his good name on hearsay evidence, he deserves to be thrashed for it, even if he *is* a "non-combatant" weakling; but a generous adversary would at least allow such a lamb the use of his legs at such a time.—M. T.]

Chronology

1835   Samuel Langhorne Clemens born November 30 in Florida, Missouri, third of the four children of John Marshall Clemens (1798–1847) and Jane Lampton Clemens (1803–90) who survived into adulthood. The other children were: Orion (1825–97); Pamela (1827–1904); and Henry (1838–58). The Clemenses, of slaveholding but struggling Virginia farming stock, arrived about June 1 in Florida after unsuccessful efforts to establish themselves in Kentucky and Tennessee. Martha Ann Quarles, sister of Jane Clemens, and her husband, John Quarles, were already in Florida.

1839   John Clemens—austere, industrious, luckless—moves his family thirty miles from inland Florida to Hannibal, a port village about 116 miles by road (or about 130 miles by water) north of St. Louis.

1847   Unsuccessful as storekeeper, farmer, lawyer, and landowner, John Clemens dies on March 24. A few months later, Sam begins part-time work but probably receives intermittent schooling for two additional years. During the autumn is employed in the printshop of Joseph P. Ament.

1848   Works in the office of Ament's *Missouri Courier* and lives meagerly in Ament's house as an apprentice.

1851   On January 16 publishes first known sketch, the humorous anecdote "A Gallant Fireman," in the Hannibal *Western Union*. The newspaper is owned and edited by his brother Orion. Receives little or no pay as printer and editorial assistant.

1852   Writes squibs for Orion's new paper, the *Journal*, and publishes a brief example of Southwestern humor, "The Dandy Frightening the Squatter," in the Boston *Carpet Bag*, May 1. On September 9 signs a sketch "W. Epaminondas Adrastus Perkins," probably the first of his many pseudonyms.

1853–57   Leaves Hannibal at the end of May, 1853, to work as a
           printer in St. Louis, New York, Philadelphia, Keokuk,
           and Cincinnati. Publishes humorous travel letters in the
           Muscatine, Iowa, *Journal*.

1857–61   About April, 1857, becomes a cub pilot on the Mississippi
           under tutelage of Horace Bixby. Henry Clemens, a much-
           loved brother, dies (1858) as a result of an explosion on
           the steamboat *Pennsylvania*. Publishes May 17, 1859, in the
           New Orleans *Crescent* a widely read lampoon of Captain
           Isaiah Sellers, a senior pilot, from whom Clemens later
           claimed (though unconvincingly) he borrowed the pseu-
           donym "Mark Twain." License as a pilot granted him on
           September 9, 1859. Continues on the river until approxi-
           mately April 25, 1861, when river traffic is disrupted.

1861   Member of the Marion Rangers, a small Confederate mi-
           litia group, for perhaps two weeks. Through the influence
           of Edward Bates of St. Louis, Attorney General under
           Lincoln, Orion is appointed Secretary to the Nevada Ter-
           ritory. Sam accompanies Orion with some prospect of
           assisting him. They arrive in Carson City by stage on Au-
           gust 14. Sam is clerk of the Territorial Legislature October
           1 through November 29. Enters timber claims, speculates
           in mining stock, and prospects for silver.

1862   Contributes letters and sketches to the Keokuk, Iowa,
           Gate City; the Carson City, Nevada, *Silver Age*; the Vir-
           ginia City, Nevada, *Territorial Enterprise*; and the Sacra-
           mento, California, *Union*. Probably late in September
           joins the staff of the *Enterprise* as local reporter and re-
           ports on the proceedings of the legislature when it is in
           session. Quickly masters such popular forms of newspaper
           comedy as the satirical sketch, the tall tale, the hoax, and
           the burlesque; gains a reputation with Western readers.

1863   On February 3, in a letter from Carson City to the *Enter-
           prise* reporting legislative proceedings, signs himself for
           the first time as "Mark Twain." Vacations in San Fran-
           cisco during May and June. Becomes a correspondent for
           the San Francisco *Morning Call*. Contributes to the
           Golden Era, a literary weekly.

1864   Leaves Virginia City on May 29, 1864, for San Francisco. Works about four months as a local reporter for the *Morning Call* but dislikes the restraints of straight reporting. Contributes to the *Californian*, a literary weekly edited by Bret Harte. Joins storytelling prospectors in the Tuolumne hills and hears, perhaps from Ben Coon of Angel's Camp, a tale about a jumping frog.

1865   Returns to San Francisco on February 25 and remains for a year writing for newspapers and literary periodicals. Publishes "Jim Smiley and His Jumping Frog"—often called his earliest masterpiece—in the New York *Saturday Press* for November 18, 1865.

1866   Leaves San Francisco for Sacramento at the end of February, then takes five-month journey to the Sandwich Islands (Hawaii) to report in letters to the Sacramento *Union* on prospects for industry and trade. October 2 enters the lucrative business of public lecturing and reading by delivering first of many lectures on the Islands. Already he is taking on the attributes of a charismatic public figure and metaphoric Western hero. Publicized as the best of the Western humorists, he sails, with conquest in mind, for New York on December 15 as roving correspondent for the San Francisco *Alta California*.

1867   Is commissioned by the *Alta* to sail June 10 on the first cruise ship, the *Quaker City*, for Europe and the Holy Land in order to send back entertaining travel letters. Dislikes most of his affluent, religiously minded fellow passengers, but accepts from Mrs. Abel W. Fairbanks ("Mother Fairbanks") correction of his manners and purification of his prose. Young Charles Jervis Langdon (born 1849), another passenger, is said to have shown him a miniature of his sister, Olivia Lewis Langdon (born 1845). Returns to United States on November 19. Meets Olivia (Livy) in New York on December 27. Her parents, the Jervis Langdons of Elmira, New York, are newly rich from mining and marketing coal. Serves briefly in Washington as private secretary to Senator William M. Stewart of Nevada. In collaboration with Charles Henry Webb publishes *The Celebrated Jumping Frog of Calaveras County and Other Sketches*.

1868   Lectures widely. Assists in support of his mother, sister, and his always aspiring, always indigent brother, Orion. Begins courtship of the semi-invalid Livy Langdon. Re-works and expands his *Quaker City* letters. At his insis-tence, Livy begins her career as chief among his many ed-itors and censors. Livy's influence, like that of the East in general, is toward the serious and genteel, away from the vulgar and comic.

1869   With a loan from Livy's father, buys a one-third interest in the Buffalo *Express*. The thoroughly reworked *Quaker City* travel letters, published as *The Innocents Abroad*, are a great financial success and set patterns for a number of his later books.

1870   Marries Livy on February 2. The next day goes with mem-bers of the bridal party by private train to Buffalo, where he and Livy are installed in the handsome house Jervis Lang-don has bought and furnished for them. Langdon dies on August 16. Son, Langdon, born to Livy November 7.

1871   Hating the tedium of newspaper work, sells house and interest in the *Express*, both at losses. Begins residence of twenty-one years in Hartford, Connecticut, interspersed with periods abroad and working summers at Quarry Farm, near Elmira, home of Susan Crane (Mrs. Theodore Crane), Livy's sister-by-adoption.

1872   Susan Olivia Clemens (Susy), born March 19. First-born, sickly Langdon dies in June. Clemens publishes *Roughing It*.

1873   Takes family for the first of several stays in Europe, some of long duration. Economy in living is often the chief ob-ject, as speculations and lavish expenditures consume his and Livy's income and a substantial portion of Livy's in-heritance. Publishes *The Gilded Age* with co-author Charles Dudley Warner, friend and Hartford neighbor.

1874   Clara Langdon Clemens born June 8 in Elmira. In Sep-tember the family moves into their not-quite-complete, ar-chitecturally bizarre, extremely costly, luxuriously fur-nished mansion in the "Nook Farm" area of Hartford. Clemens increasingly in demand as a speaker at breakfasts, lunches, dinners, political rallies, reunions, fund raisings, and celebrations of all kinds.

1875   Publishes "Old Times on the Mississippi" (later part of *Life on the Mississippi*) in the *Atlantic Monthly*, then edited by his friend, admirer, and sometimes literary adviser and censor, William Dean Howells.

1876   In summer receives proofs of *The Adventures of Tom Sawyer* and begins writing *Adventures of Huckleberry Finn*. Is becoming deeply engaged in exploiting boyhood and the vernacular in a partly remembered, partly imagined Mississippi River valley, the post-frontier. Publishes *The Adventures of Tom Sawyer*.

1877   On December 17 delivers the "Whittier Birthday Speech," a burlesque treating the New Englanders Longfellow, Emerson, and Holmes in a way that shocks a number of listeners and is at times to be deeply regretted by Clemens.

1878–79   Travels in Europe, turns again to the writing of *Huckleberry Finn*.

1880   In this or the following year begins "investing" in the Paige typesetter, the most monetarily and psychically costly of his many speculations. Expends approximately $190,000 and untold hours before abandoning hope for this machine in January, 1895. Between late 1880 and early 1883 works once more on *Huckleberry Finn*. Publishes *A Tramp Abroad* and permits the private publication of the best known and most reprinted of his scatological writings, *1601. Conversation, as It Was by the Social Fireside, in the Time of the Tudors*. Jane Lampton Clemens (called Jean) born July 26.

1882   Makes trip on the Mississippi with James R. Osgood (at this time his publisher) and a stenographer to refresh his recollections, form new impressions, and collect information useful in completing *Life on the Mississippi*. Leaves New York on April 18, returns to Hartford on May 24. Publishes *The Prince and the Pauper,* a favorite with Livy and the children.

1883   Once again returns to writing *Huckleberry Finn*. Publishes *Life on the Mississippi*.

1884–85   Makes successful reading tour with George W. Cable,
           Louisiana writer and civil rights advocate (November
           5–February 28). On December 10, 1884, publishes *Adventures of Huckleberry Finn* in England; on February 18, 1885,
           through his own publishing house, Charles L. Webster
           & Company, in the United States.

1889   Publishes *A Connecticut Yankee in King Arthur's Court*.
           Annoyed by its mixed reception in England.

1890   Jane Clemens (his mother) and Olivia L. Langdon (Livy's
           mother) both die.

1891   Sails for Europe in June and lives there for most of the
           next decade.

1894   Charles L. Webster & Company declares itself bankrupt
           in April. Clemens loses roughly $110,000 of his own
           money and $60,000 of Livy's. With the encouragement
           of Livy and the shrewd assistance of Henry H. Rogers, a
           vice-president of the Standard Oil Company, begins the
           difficult task of setting his tangled affairs in order, making
           his copyrights secure, and paying off his creditors. His inclination toward pessimism and determinism is heightened. Publishes *Pudd'nhead Wilson, A Tale* in the *Century
           Magazine*. (In book form the novel is entitled *The Tragedy
           of Pudd'nhead Wilson*.)

1895   In August begins a lecture trip around the world to raise
           money to repay creditors. Has become a public figure
           world-wide. Tour ends in Europe in July, 1896.

1896   Publishes *Personal Recollections of Joan of Arc*. Daughter
           Susy dies in Hartford of meningitis, August 18, while Clemens is in London, Livy and Clara are en route home.
           Clemens characteristically blames himself, then inveighs
           against fate and a God whom he increasingly depicts as
           malevolent. Jean Clemens diagnosed as epileptic; thereafter often in rest homes and clinics.

1897   Publishes *Following the Equator*.

1898   In March Henry Rogers notifies Clemens in Vienna that his undisputed creditors have been repaid. Within days Clemens attempts to engage in new, grandiose speculative ventures. During these last years he places increased emphasis on the monetary value of his writings, which he has always treated as marketable products. At the same time he is strongly moved to write "seriously," to set down what he deems unprintable truths about God, religious institutions, man, politicians, tycoons, business associates, friends, and relatives.

1900   Returns to New York from England in October. Makes anti-missionary and anti-imperialist statements in connection with actions of the United States in China and the Philippines.

1901   Receives honorary degree from Yale.

1902   Receives honorary degree from the University of Missouri. Isabel Lyon, who comes into the household to be secretary to Livy, becomes Clemens' secretary and general family factotum until forced out, April, 1909, following bitter quarrels, especially with Clara. Their fortunes partly restored, the Clemenses' combined incomes for the year amount to more than $100,000.

1903   Takes a villa in Florence for the benefit of Livy's health.

1904   Olivia Clemens dies in Florence on June 5, and her body is taken to Elmira for burial. Clara enters a sanitarium in July; later undergoes a number of restorative treatments. Clemens' pleasure in the companionship of little girls becomes marked and continues until his death.

1906   Publishes *What Is Man?* privately and anonymously. In January accepts as his biographer Albert Bigelow Paine. A close association begins that lasts until Clemens' death and results in the publication of a massive biography and miscellaneous additional volumes.

1907   Receives honorary degree from Oxford University; enjoys displaying himself then and later in his crimson gown.

1908   John Howells (architect son of William Dean Howells)
        and Isabel Lyon supervise the building of a mansion called
        Stormfield near Redding, Connecticut. Clemens moves
        there from New York.

1909   Clara marries Ossip Gabrilowitsch, pianist and conductor,
        at Stormfield on October 6. Jean dies in bathtub, appar-
        ently during a seizure, on the morning of Christmas Eve.

1910   Clemens dies at Stormfield on April 21. Joseph Twichell of
        Hartford, one of Clemens' oldest friends, and Henry Van
        Dyck conduct services at the Presbyterian Brick Church in
        New York. Buried in Elmira on April 24 in the Langdon
        family plot, where little Langdon, Susy, Livy, and Jean
        had been interred before him. Left behind an enormous
        quantity of unpublished papers: autobiographical dicta-
        tions, notebooks, letters, finished and unfinished sketches,
        essays, stories, polemics, and incomplete drafts of "The
        Mysterious Stranger," generally considered even in its un-
        finished state to be the most powerful of his later writings.
        For literary executors and editors, sifting and publishing
        these literary remains becomes almost at once a major,
        long-continuing enterprise.

Note on the Texts

This volume reprints Samuel Clemens' two earliest and most popular travel books in the texts of their first American editions, distributed by the American Publishing Company of Hartford, Connecticut. Until the time of Clemens' death, *The Innocents Abroad* sold far more copies than any of his other works. *Roughing It*, although in Clemens' estimation better written, probably ranked fourth in sales, coming behind *Huckleberry Finn* and *Tom Sawyer*.

The textual history of *The Innocents Abroad* may be approached by considering certain of Clemens' activities and projected activities beginning late in 1866. When he sailed from California for New York in mid-December, he was thinking of possibly publishing a book that made use of some of the newspaper letters he had written about the Sandwich Islands and of taking a trip around the world in order to continue a series of travel letters that had been commissioned by the San Francisco *Alta California*. Though the book on the Sandwich Islands was never published, Clemens helped Charles Henry Webb collect the newspaper sketches that became his first published volume, *The Celebrated Jumping Frog of Calaveras County and Other Sketches*, 1867. In late February 1867, Clemens saw a circular advertising an "Excursion to the Holy Land, Egypt, the Crimea, Greece, and Intermediate Points of Interest" that settled for him the way to proceed with letters for the *Alta*. He promptly reserved a place on board the cruise ship and requested financing from the *Alta*. As a result of the excursion he wrote approximately sixty letters, most of them for the *Alta*, seven for the New York *Tribune*, a few for the New York *Herald*, and one for the Naples *Observer* (reprinted by the *Alta*). Several letters were lost or were left unprinted by the *Alta*. One long, general letter, written on the night of his return to New York, appeared in the *Herald* on November 2. Clemens' notebook entries constituted starting points for passages in many of the letters, and the letters themselves eventually formed the basis for *The Innocents Abroad*. Two fellow passengers on the *Quaker City*,

Mary Mason Fairbanks and Emily Severance, had helped remove "slang" and impieties from some of these letters before
Clemens mailed them to newspapers.

The letters that Clemens contributed to the *Tribune* led, he
said, to "several propositions" from publishers, including the
one that he liked "much the best." This was from Elisha P.
Bliss, Jr., of the American Publishing Company, a firm that
sold money-making books by subscription, a method many
considered rather disreputable. Clemens informed a friend
that he answered Bliss's inquiry of November 21, 1867, asking
"what they want, when they want it, & how much *bucksheesh*." Late in January 1868, he agreed to prepare a manuscript based on his travel letters. Bliss, on his side, agreed to
pay Clemens five percent of sales or about twenty cents a
copy. (The price of the books varied according to the binding.)

Gathering the materials he needed proved to be more time-
consuming than Clemens had expected. Not only were some
of his own pieces hard to find, but he also wanted to see the
letters other passengers had published. A trip to California
was necessary, moreover, before he could obtain permission
from the *Alta* to use the letters that he had written for that
paper. The first fifteen chapters were written almost entirely
without the aid of letters, but as composition proceeded,
Clemens came more and more to rely on his newspaper
pieces, at times using clippings as printer's copy, with revi-
sions marked either on the copy itself or in the margins. The
Alta articles were revised to eliminate the narrator's slang, to
cut out sexual or scatological passages, and to soften passages
that attacked patriarchs of the Bible. Descriptive passages and
narrative connections were added. When the writing was
done, Clemens found he had prepared too much, by perhaps
a thousand manuscript pages. These he cut with the help of
Bret Harte, who read the manuscript and offered suggestions.
Clemens "followed orders strictly." It was not until early October that he turned over a manuscript (now lost or destroyed) to Bliss.

Additional delays ensued, some attributable to the publishers but many to Clemens himself, for he inspected each of the
234 illustrations and continued to revise in both manuscript

and proof. On February 14, 1869, he began a "final" revision of his manuscript; on March 12 he began to receive proof, which he and his fiancée, Olivia Langdon, did not finish reading and editing until June 5; and in mid-July he received three bound copies of the book. Binding went slowly, and delays in delivery continued into 1870. Bliss gradually assembled a small army of sales agents—perhaps as many as eighteen hundred—to "invest," as Clemens said, "every hamlet and besiege every village."

Clemens suggested several possible names for the book before it appeared as *The Innocents Abroad, or The New Pilgrims' Progress* (with an analytical continuation of the subtitle). On the spine of the book, the subtitle displayed "Pilgrim's" (in the singular), which was the way Clemens had given it to Bliss. The subtitle as misprinted on the title page, if it was misprinted, remained the same, however, in subsequent printings and editions.

Only one other edition might be considered appropriate for reprinting, the one that Clemens prepared in 1872 for George Routledge & Sons, of London. (It is not known whether Clemens had any hand in the preparation of the text for the 1899 edition of the collected works, in which chapter titles are added and attempts are made to regularize punctuation.) Clemens had a double reason for wanting to see the Routledge edition published: he wanted to establish a business relationship with Routledge, and he wanted to cut into the sales of the pirated edition published in London by John Camden Hotten in 1870 (although he had been initially pleased at Hotten's attention). As a step towards accomplishing his ends, he revised the first American edition, though not very methodically, making by one count 434 substantive changes. He cancelled many long passages, added some slightly shorter ones, eliminated slighting references to foreign languages ("barbarous Italian" was changed to "fathomless Italian"), eliminated references to monetary values of architecture, toned down hyperbolic language ("uncounted treasures" became "treasures" and "all possible or conceivable" became "all conceivable"), made the narrator less materialistic and chauvinistic, less given to vulgar jokes, and less enthusiastic. Because Routledge, which paid Clemens $250 for the work, wanted to issue the book in two volumes, he wrote two new short prefaces. These revisions and the copyrighting of the book by Routledge would, Clemens hoped, protect it from further pirating in England. Some of his revisions may be judged improvements, but others are weakening adjustments intended to make the book conform to what he took to be the sophisticated and conservative taste of the English.

When Bernard von Tauchnitz asked permission in 1879 to add *The Innocents* to his Library of British and American Writers, Clemens furnished him with the Routledge text, but this may have been because he considered it suitable for a European audience or simply because he was then in Europe and found the Routledge text conveniently at hand. His special preface explains that he had considered revising the book before putting it on exhibition in so permanent a place as the Tauchnitz series but then had wiser thoughts: "How is a man to revise a boy's book and not make a botch of it?" Clemens never thought well enough of the Routledge text to substitute it for the American Publishing Company text in the many later printings in the United States.

The excellent sales of *The Innocents* encouraged Clemens to think about preparing a comparable volume. Early in 1870 he may have had in mind a book much like what turned out to be *Roughing It*. In May of 1870, Bliss was urging him on; and on July 15 Clemens wrote to his brother Orion that he had just contracted to have "another 600-page book" ready by January 1, 1871: "only began it today." Illnesses, deaths, the preparation of lectures, lecturing, and other writing interfered with the composition of the book, which went on intermittently throughout most of 1871. From March 17, 1871, Clemens and his family were at restful Quarry Farm, outside of Elmira, New York, but even in that favorable atmosphere, his progress was fitful. Early in July artists were at work on illustrations. On August 8 Clemens took what he thought was an almost completed manuscript from Elmira to Hartford, but the manuscript was less finished than he considered it. For the subscription book he and Bliss wanted, it was still too short by 300 pages. In October, when he was on a lecture tour, he continued to supplement, cut, and revise. Internal evidence suggests that Clemens corrected the proof he received with some care only up to a point and that he may not have read proof at all for the last two-fifths of the book.

No manuscript for *Roughing It* is known to exist, and all editions or excerpts published during Clemens' lifetime derive directly or indirectly from the first American edition or from late, incomplete proofs of that edition. The first complete copies of *Roughing It* were issued from the bindery on January 30, 1872. Before that time, a Canadian piracy (Toronto: The Belford Library [1872]) appeared, presumably set from proofs (lacking several chapters) smuggled out of the printing-shop in Hartford in December. In February, Routledge published an authorized English edition which used as its text proofsheets from the first American edition. This edition was not proofread or revised by Clemens. The American edition was reprinted—with a number of variants creeping in—ten or more times before 1900, and the original Routledge edition was reprinted more than once. The Routledge text was reset in 1882 (this new edition was reprinted again in 1897).

The illustrations in this volume are courtesy of the New-York Historical Society.

The standards for American English continue to fluctuate and in some ways were conspicuously different in earlier periods from what they are now. In a nineteenth-century manuscript, a word might be spelled in more than one way, and such variations might be carried into print. Commas were sometimes used expressively to suggest the movements of voice, and capitals were sometimes meant to give significances to a word beyond those that it might have in its uncapitalized form. Since modernization would remove such effects, this volume has preserved the spelling, punctuation, and capitalization, as well as the wording, of the texts reprinted here.

This volume is concerned only with presenting the texts of the editions reprinted; it does not attempt to reproduce features of typographic design—such as the display capitalization of chapter openings. Footnotes within the text are those supplied by Clemens. Open contractions are retained if they appeared in the original edition. Typographical errors have been corrected, and the following is a list of those errors by page and line number: 11.39, *Preparation*; 28.24, said; 32.25, (upper);

58.2, absolutety; 59.19, practice.; 60.8, solilopuized; 103.8, medding; 167.27, count,; 168.27, NE-VER?; 195.38, hight; 235.8, *Alleluia."*; 237.36, "This,"; 265.28, 'By; 276.19, xvii."; 299.10, disgreeably; 299.15, long.' "; 315.2, pretty; 344.17–18, Labanon; 358.16, Brake; 385.2, I; 394.29, it; 446.1, compose; 479.4, hospipitality; 522.10, npon; 565.16, mules; 565.34–35, stage,coach; 568.29–30, with insight; 580.1, statement; 650.29, feel; 684.22, Clagget; 695.35, an either; 706.2–3, [   ] was; 706.3, [   ] own; 746.34, reported,; 769.33, attempt do; 778.7, power?'; 812.18, feel; 830.7, paroxyms; 848.1, Hurs; 850.23–24, out-of-the way; 861.32, *"placer";*; 861.32, *"indications'*; 867.17, a back; 870.9, coacoanut; 874.8, Coacoanut; 876.28, collossal; 883.25, good; 885.8, guady; 885.30, tatooed; 895.24, Infantry.; 897.27, Knonohikis; 897.28, Majesty; 900.36, god'; 903.27, description; 903.31, stick; 903.32, Kaahumaun's; 915.34, 'void"; 916.15, Beazely; 919.39, 1778.; 923.38, Kaahumahu; 923.39–40, rest. It was probably the rest. It was; 924.32, Bekuokalani; 927.38, has; 930.31, rippled a; 947.3, Mani; 949.40–950.1, "Incorporated . . . Men,"; 950.23, TIME!'; 957.17, Certainly!; 957.22, *Are.*

Notes

In the notes below, numbers refer to page and line of this volume (the line count includes chapter headings). No note is made for material found in a standard desk reference book. Notes at the foot of the page in the texts are Mark Twain's. Particularly useful as sources of information about *The Innocents Abroad* are Robert Hart Hirst, *The Making of "The Innocents Abroad": 1867–1872*, unpublished dissertation, University of California, Berkeley, copyright © 1975; Dewey Ganzel, *Mark Twain Abroad: The Cruise of the "Quaker City"* (Chicago: University of Chicago Press, 1968); and *Mark Twain's Notebooks & Journals*, Vol. I (1855–1873), ed. by Frederick Anderson, Michael Frank, and Kenneth M. Sanderson (Berkeley: University of California Press, 1975). For more extensive informational and textual notes than are offered here for *Roughing It*, the reader may consult Franklin R. Rogers and Paul Baender, eds., *Roughing It* (Berkeley: University of California Press, 1961). Also useful are A. Grove Day, ed., *Mark Twain's Letters from Hawaii* (New York: Appleton Century, 1966); and Franklin R. Rogers, ed., *The Pattern for Mark Twain's Roughing It: Letters from Nevada by Samuel and Orion Clemens, 1861–1862* (Berkeley: University of California Press, 1961). The reader should be aware that when Clemens borrows from or quotes others, he often condenses, expands, invents, or otherwise departs from his source. Only a few illustrative changes are mentioned here. His quotations from the Bible frequently come from guidebooks, not directly from the Bible.

THE INNOCENTS ABROAD

17.16   sail for months] The *Quaker City* left its berth at the foot of Wall Street at 2 P.M. on June 8, 1867, and returned to New York on the morning of November 19, 1867.

18.14–16   good reason . . . acquaintances.] Henry Ward Beecher, the famous pastor of the Plymouth Church, Brooklyn, was advertised by word of mouth as going. When he withdrew, some forty members of his church withdrew likewise. Passengers came from as far away as Missouri, Louisiana, and California; but only about two-thirds as many as the minimum quota set were assembled, and the group was less Eastern, less select, and less sophisticated than Clemens, among others, had anticipated. Clemens' adverse opinion of his fellow passengers was expressed in private letters after the voyage was over. To John R. Young, of the New York *Tribune*, for example, he wrote that he yearned to ridicule "the Quaker City's strange menagerie of ignorance, imbecility, bigotry, & dotage."

18.30–31   to visit . . . Exhibition]   The first modern industrial exhibition proper was held in Paris in 1791. Beginning in 1855, the city mounted "unusual exhibitions" at eleven- or twelve-year intervals. The "Paris Universal Exhibition" of 1867, located on the Champ de Mars and displayed in an elliptical building measuring 1,608 by 1,266 feet, was considered to have incomparable éclat. Its nearly eleven million visitors included the emperors of Russia and Austria; the kings of Prussia, Belgium, Portugal, and Sweden; the sultan; and the Prince of Wales.

21.8   CHAS. C. DUNCAN]   During the voyage Clemens developed an intense dislike for Duncan. Afterwards, the two men vilified each other publically. Ten years later Clemens gave a defamatory interview to the New York *Herald*, five years after that to *The New York Times*; and in each instance Duncan brought a suit, though to little purpose, against him and the newspaper concerned.

22.1   Plymouth . . . Hymns]   *Plymouth Collection of Hymns for the Use of Christian Congregations*, comp. by Henry Ward Beecher (New York: A. S. Barnes and Co., 1855).

22.24   A popular actress]   Shortly before the cruise was to begin, Margaret Julia Mitchell (1837–1918), known as Maggie Mitchell, accepted, then rejected an offer of free transportation for herself and her mother. Miss Mitchell, who made her first important success as Oliver Twist, played up and down the Ohio and Mississippi rivers in such light dramas as *The Daughter of the Regiment*. She created her most triumphant part, the title role in *Fauchon the Cricket* (adapted from George Sand's *La Petite Fadette*), and acted in *Ingomar, the Barbarian* and *The Lady of Lyons*. Her fantastic shadow dances inspired verses by Emerson.

22.26–27   The "Drummer . . . Potomac"]   This reference appears to be to Robert Henry Hendershot (1850–c. 1925), whose heroism led Frederick Emerson Brooks to compose the verses, "The Drummer Boy of the Rappahannock."

23.16–17   "COMMISSIONER . . . AFRICA"]   Dr. William Gibson, of Jamestown, Pennsylvania, who had volunteered to collect specimens and data for the Department of Agriculture and was in return given its endorsement.

24.11   young Mr. Blucher]   Partly based on Frederick H. Greer, of Boston.

24.35–36   young . . . room mate]   Daniel Slote ("Dan"), a partner in Slote-Woodman Company, a New York banking firm. Later Slote became a business partner from whom Clemens separated in bitter disagreement. As things worked out, Clemens occupied a cabin by himself.

29.22   Capt. Bursley]   Ira Bursley. Because of the ineffectiveness of Captain Duncan, Bursley took over operational control of the *Quaker City* before the voyage was half completed.

29.32　　Capt. L****]　Daniel D. Leary, of Brooklyn.

30.8　　Capt. Jones]　William Jones, second officer.

30.10　　a man . . . brother]　The phrase was widely used. The inscription "Am I not a man and a brother?" appeared on a medallion by Wedgewood (1787) representing a Negro in chains with one knee on the ground and both hands lifted up to heaven.

33.17　　One . . . Jack]　Almost surely John A. Van Nostrand ("Jack"), of Greenville, New Jersey.

33.37　　Moult has told]　Julius Moulton, of St. Louis.

34.39　　the photographer]　William E. James, of Brooklyn, was official photographer for the cruise.

35.7　　Greenwood Cemetery]　This cemetery—located about one-half mile southwest of Prospect Park in Brooklyn—contained the graves of a number of well-known Americans.

36.33　　'Coronation']　The "Coronation March" (1863) by composer Giacomo Meyerbeer (1791–1864).

48.4　　Russ pavement]　Pavements made of blocks of granite set on a bed of crushed stone and cement.

50.17　　blackness of darkness]　Jude 13: " . . . wandering stars, to whom is reserved the blackness of darkness for ever." The phrase "blackness of darkness" may also be found in the apocryphal writings in Nicodemus 13:3.

51.14　　"clouds . . . land."]　Clemens may be conflating several Biblical passages. In Exodus 14:20, the pillar of cloud came between the Egyptians and the camp of Israel: "and it was a cloud and darkness to them." Exodus 10:21 says: "Stretch out thine hand toward heaven, that there may be darkness over the land of Egypt, even darkness which may be felt." Verbal similarities may be found in Mark 15:33: "And there was darkness over the whole land"; and in Matthew 27:45: "there was darkness over all the land."

53:15　　one . . . Spain]　The queen referred to was Maria Amelia, wife of Charles III; the siege, that of 1779–83.

56.5　　the Oracle]　Dr. Edward Andrews, of Albany, New York.

57.2　　a poet]　Bloodgood Haviland Cutter, a poetical farmer of Little Neck, Long Island, who weighed less than one hundred pounds.

57.19　　the "Interrogation Point,"]　Probably Charles Jervis Langdon, of Elmira, New York, the younger brother of Olivia L. Langdon.

58.23　　the ship's surgeon]　Dr. Abraham Reeves Jackson, whose humor sometimes goes without alteration into Clemens' text.

64.24　　the ruins . . . city]　Volubilis, near Meknès, 125 miles south of

Tangier, principal inland city of the Roman province. Impressive remains are still visible. During the period of Clemens' visit to Tangier the ruins were called Kasar Faráôn (Citadel of the Pharaoh).

65.26   Emperor of Morocco]   Muhammad XVII (1859–73).

67.6–7   may . . . increase!]   From Leigh Hunt, "Abou Ben Adhem" (or, "Abou Ben Adhem and the Angel").

71.11   our . . . Consul-General]   Usually and apparently correctly given as Jesse H. McMath, of Cadiz, Ohio, consul at Tangier from 1862 to 1869.

71.32–33   "Oh . . . face?"]   From William Cowper, "Verses Supposed to be Written by Alexander Selkirk (1782)."

71.39–40   Tangier . . . world]   Such inexact observations were freely made in guide and travel books. Harper's *Hand-Book for Travelers in Europe and the East* (New York: Harper and Brothers, 1866), p. 439, says, "*Damascus,* the oldest city in the world, was founded by Uz, grandson of Noah." Two entries in Clemens' notebooks mention the antiquity of Tangier. One observes that Tangier is one of the oldest towns in the world "except Damascus," founded about the time Hercules founded Cadiz, say four thousand years ago. The other says of Damascus: "The oldest city in the world. No time for 4,000 years that there has not been a city here. Never has changed its name. Tangier next, Cadiz or Athens next." For these notebook entries Clemens may have relied on the Reverend David A. Randall, *The Handwriting of God in Egypt, Sinai, and the Holy Land* (Philadelphia: John E. Potter and Co., 1862). In fact, a few Bronze Age remains have been found at Tangier, and there was a Phoenician settlement on the site about 1450 B.C., one of the oldest in North Africa.

82.40   the Castle d'If]   Built by Francis I in 1524 and used for several centuries as a state prison. The chateau stands on a small island opposite the harbor of Marseilles.

84.16–19   "Iron Mask" . . . St. Marguerite.]   In 1698 a new governor of the Chateau d'If, Bénigne d'Auvergne de Saint-Mars, brought with him from the Isle Ste. Marguerite, one of the Isles Lerins, nears Cannes, a masked prisoner whom he had also held at Pignerol (Italian: Pignerolo) in Piedmont. The prisoner, who died in 1703, was buried under the name Marchioly, but the identity of the prisoner is conjectural.

100.18   Sultan of Turkey]   The extravagant and incompetent Abdul Aziz (1830–76) became sultan in 1861, was deposed on May 29, 1876, and was said to have committed suicide four days later.

100.24   American . . . house]   The address of John Bigelow, the American minister plenipotentiary, was 80 Avenue de la Grande Armée.

104.22–23   christening . . . prince]   Eugène Louis Jean Joseph Bonaparte

(1856–79), son and heir apparent of Napoleon III; killed when he took part in the English expedition against the Zulus in South Africa.

106.30   *Jardin Mabille*]   "Bals" as public summer entertainments became popular with Parisians beginning with the first *bal de l'Opéra* in 1715. *Le bal Mabille*, founded in 1840, offered a dance pavilion, retired seats, and games, including games of chance. Women could attend unescorted and were admitted free.

109.5–7   trembling . . . kirk."]   The allusion is to "Tam o' Shanter," by Robert Burns.

110.10   a celebrated troubadour]   An escort sent by Philippe le Bel to conduct Arnauld de Catelan through the Bois de Boulogne, then infested with robbers, murdered the troubadour when he boasted of bringing rich treasures to the king. Suspicion was awakened, and the murderers were condemned to the stake.

110.11–12   fellow . . . name]   The unsuccessful assassin of June 6, 1867, was an emigré Pole named Berezowski. The czar was Alexander II (1818–81), who ruled 1855–81.

111.2   Père la Chaise]   A list of "great names," including those mentioned below by Clemens, appears in *Galignani's New Paris Guide for 1865* (Paris: A. and W. Galignani and Co., n.d.).

125.39   centre]   A number of *étoiles* were made. Clemens may be speaking here of the Place de la Bastille.

126.8–9   Maximilian . . . widow]   In 1863 Napoleon III placed Ferdinand Maximilian, of Austria, on the imperial throne of Mexico that had been created by French armed intervention. At the end of the Civil War, the United States obtained from France a promise that French troops would be withdrawn. The empress Carlotta (who had been Princess Charlotte, of Belgium), after trying unsuccessfully to obtain assistance for her husband and his shaky empire from France and from the pope, became insane. Porfirio Diaz and Benito Juárez combined their forces to defeat Maximilian, who was captured in Querétaro on May 15, 1867, and was executed on June 19. As Clemens indicated in his letter from New York to the *Alta* on June 5, 1867, Maximilian and his then possible execution were much talked of.

127.33   Charley in Spain]   Charles Jervis Langdon was one of a party of six that traveled in Spain.

130.30   friar . . . gray]   Because of the color of their robes, Franciscans were known as Grey Friars.

133.38   The hotel . . . in]   The Croix de Malte, which had been a private palace but had nothing to do with the Knights Templars or the Knights of Malta.

134.25   a cave]   McDowell's cave, near Hannibal, Missouri, which becomes McDougal's cave in *The Adventures of Tom Sawyer*.

134.36   Our . . . cemetery]   The *Cimitero de Staglieno*, laid out in 1867,
exhibits modern sepulchral monuments in a range of tastes.

141.11   Bartoloméo]   Clemens seems to have meant "Borroméo" here.

150.3–5   ruin . . . Supper,"]   The church of *Santa Maria della Grazie*
(dating in part from the fifteenth century) is said by *Harper's Hand-Book*,
p. 307, to present a grand appearance "although extremely dilapidated." The
Hand-Book also remarks that the *Cenacolo* (from the Latin *cenaculum*, a dining
room, and so, in painting, Leonardo's "The Last Supper") on the wall of the
associated Dominican convent "has suffered dreadfully from damp, age, and
violence, but still remains the most celebrated painting in the world." The
painting is again called "the most celebrated of any painting in the world" by
Samuel Irenaeus Prime, *Travels in Europe and the East* (New York: Harper
and Brothers, 1856), II, 35.

152.32   Matthews, the actor]   Charles Matthews the Elder (1776–1835) or
Charles Matthews the Younger (1803–78). The Elder, who toured America in
1822 and in 1834, is the more likely, as he was known for mimicry based on
observation. The Younger was prominent as a manager (of Covent Garden
and the Lyceum); he played light comedy roles and toured America in 1838.

160.19   the Lady of Lyons]   "The Lady of Lyons, or Love and Pride," a
highly popular romantic comedy by Edward G. E. Bulwer-Lytton, was first
produced in 1838. The passage that Clemens quotes is given (without all of
the line demarcations) in *Harper's Hand-Book,* p. 311.

163.2   Lago di Lecco]   The town of Lecco is near the south end of the
eastern branch of Lake Como; thus the eastern branch is frequently distinguished as the Lake of Lecco.

166.2   Godfrey]   During the first crusade, Godefroy de Bouillon (c. 1060–
1100) led a body of perhaps fifteen thousand men from the area of the Meuse
and the lower Rhine through Hungary and the Balkans to Constantinople.
In 1099 he was elected ruler of Jerusalem but refused the title of king.

168.36   tare an ouns!"]   Considered an Anglo-Irish oath, a corruption of
"By the tears and wounds of Christ!"

169.16–20   Bergamo . . . harlequin]   Arlecchino, one of the comic masks
in the *commedia dell'arte*, is possibly traceable to the devils of medieval drama,
more specifically to the medieval French Harlequin, a jester in mystery plays.
Actors of the *commedia dell'arte* gave Harlequin the part of the second *zanni,*
or clown, and established the legend that he was originally from the lower
city of Bergamo. Tristano Martinelli (c. 1557–1630) was the first recorded Arlecchino.

173.37–174.14   "There . . . o'er."]   This passage appears in Murray's

Handbook for Travellers in Northern Italy (London: John Murray, 1866), p. 363. The verses, from "Venice," by Samuel Rogers, were collected in *Italy, a Poem* (London: T. Cadell and E. Moxon, 1830).

186.21   the dim . . . light]   "Casting a dim religious light," from Milton, "Il Penseroso," line 1600.

186.37   Goliah]   A not uncommon spelling for Goliath.

200.38–201.2   the first . . . kite]   In 1866 Italian hostilities against Austria began. That summer Admiral Carlo Persano led a superior Italian fleet to defeat at Lissa. Gilderoy (a corruption of "gillie roy," a red-headed gilly), was the nickname of Patrick Macgregor, an outlaw who was hanged at Edinburgh in 1636 on a gallows higher than those used for other members of his band who died with him. In Scottish, kite (or kyte) means stomach or belly; here, by extension, body. A ballad tells how Gilderoy's captors were so afraid of him that they bound him "mickle strong" and then,

> They hong him high abone the rest,
> He was so trim a boy.

221.31   ages . . . along]   From Alexander Pope, *An Essay on Criticism*, lines 356–57:

> A needless Alexandrine ends the song
> That, like a wounded snake, drags its slow length along.

225.5–6   "butchered . . . holyday."]   From *Childe Harold's Pilgrimage*, Canto IV, Stanza 141.

225.12–13   it . . . Oliver]   See *Roughing It*, Chapters XXVI–XXVIII. Augustus W. Oliver ("Oliphant") is one of the young lawyers who makes a trip from Carson City to the Humboldt with Clemens.

225.30–31   the mosque . . . Omar]   Better known as the "Dome of the Rock." Said to have been built by Omar Ibn al-Khattab, second of the Mohammedan caliphs (c. 581–644), after Palestine and Jerusalem fell to his armies.

226.2   Forty Mile Desert]   Between Carson City, Nevada, and the Humboldt. See Chapter XX of *Roughing It*.

231.13   corpo di Baccho]   "Body of Bacchus!"; a mild oath.

233.7   We . . . catacombs.]   The catacombs of Saint Sebastian—below the church of Saint Sebastian, first mentioned under Gregory the Great—hold the remains of many martyrs. Approximately one-quarter mile away are the catacombs of Saint Calixtus, pope from c. 217–222.

237.19   discourses of Yorick]   The king's dead jester, *Hamlet*, V, i, 198–99.

240.8–9   Academy . . . New York]   The American Academy of Fine Arts was founded in 1802. In 1825 schismatic students rebelled against its restrictive policies and founded the National Academy of Design, where

Clemens saw an exhibition which he commented on at length in a letter of May 28, 1867, to the *Alta*.

242.10   *scala santa*]   The Holy Stairs consist of twenty-eight marble steps said by Church tradition to have belonged to the house of Pilate and to be the ones that Jesus descended when he left the judgment seat. In rebuilding the Lateran palace (which had been partly destroyed by fire in the time of Clement V [pope 1305–14]), Sixtus V (pope 1585–90) preserved the stairs and constructed a portico over them.

245.31   Frezzolini . . . sing]   Erminia Frezzolini (1818–84), one of the greatest Italian singers, had a magnificent voice and a talent for tragedy. Her voice began to fail in 1862.

250.10   castle of St. Elmo]   One of the fortifications of Naples, situated to the northwest.

250.23–24   the Hermitage]   A convent, where a few monks offered refreshments to visitors.

252.13   *Riviere . . . mean;*)]   Corrected later to Riviera di Chiaja. A fashionable street along the bay, begun in the sixteenth century, completed at the end of the seventeenth, and named for a quarter of the city.

254.32   Lake . . . visible]   Once a crater lake about four miles in circumference, its waters supposed to be curative for gout and rheumatism. Whether Clemens saw the lake is more than open to question, as it was drained in 1866. It contained no sunken city.

265.24   9th of November]   The culminating explosion of Vesuvius took place on August 24, A.D. 79.

266.23–24   'Rock . . . Mother.']   A poem of six stanzas entitled "Rock Me to Sleep" by "Florence Percy," pen name of Mrs. Elizabeth Akers Allen (1832–1911), appeared in the *Saturday Evening Post*, June 9, 1860, dated from Rome, May 1860. The verses were set to music by Ernest Leslie, published in Boston by Russell and Pate, and became one of the hit songs of a year that was also marked by the appearance of "Dixie" and "Old Black Joe." The poem begins: "Backward, turn backward, O Time in your flight, / Make me a child again, just for to-night!" Each stanza ends: "Rock me to sleep, mother,—rock me to sleep!" Alexander M. W. Ball and other writers claimed authorship of the poem; a second musical setting was given it by J. M. Mueller.

271.38   Denny]   Colonel William R. Denny, of Winchester, Virginia, formerly of the army of the Confederacy.

276.38   Birch]   Dr. George Bright Birch, of Hannibal, Missouri.

279.1   Two other passengers]   The two other passengers were Moses S. Beach, editor-publisher of the New York *Sun*, and the Reverend Henry Bullard, of Wayland, Massachusetts, the ship's chaplain. After bathing with others on the shore, they hid behind rocks, hired a carriage in Piraeus, and drove the five miles to Athens. They sought out a Greek classmate of Bullard's, spent the night on shore, and returned before noon the next day, ostensibly as new passengers.

281.9–15   It . . . George]   The crown was declined by Prince Leopold of Saxe-Coburg-Gotha, accepted in 1832 by Prince Otho, a younger son of King Louis I of Bavaria. Otho was followed in 1863 by Prince William George of Schleswig-Holstein-Sonderburg-Glücksburg, who became George I of Greece.

282.12   water batteries]   Meaning "floating batteries": armed and armored vessels. Constantinople was defended also by earthworks and stone fortresses.

294.35–37   The selling . . . war.]   The first newspaper was published during the Crimean War (1854–56); the first restrictive press law was promulgated in 1861; the press was placed under the control of the Foreign Office in 1866.

297.25   Five Points]   A part of New York City bordered by Broadway, Chatham, and the end of the Bowery. The district was synonymous with wretchedness, vice, and crime. Several missions were established there.

302.33   the Emperor . . . visit]   Here and below, Clemens' account of the visit to Yalta varies from what is reported elsewhere. At Odessa, Daniel D. Leary, who hoped to sell the *Quaker City* to the czar, telegraphed (apparently against the advice of Consul Timothy C. Smith) to the governor-general at Yalta. The *Quaker City* then proceeded to Yalta without having received assurances that the czar would grant an audience. That assurance came only after further negotiations at Yalta.

303.7–9   For eighteen . . . upon.]   Sevastopol, Russia's only naval base on the Black Sea, was besieged during the Crimean War by forces of the allies, beginning in September 1854, and ending in September 1855.

304.31   Darnick]   Usually *dornick*: a coarse damask of silk and wool.

308.5–8   what . . . stane."]   Matthew 7:9: "Or what man is there, of you, whom if his son ask bread, will he give him a stone?"

309.17–18   Odessa Consul]   Timothy C. Smith.

309.23   the Governor-General's]   Probably at the home of Paul Kotzebue (1801–84), son of August F. F. von Kotzebue, the German dramatist. Paul Kotzebue took part in the defense of Sevastopol and became governor of Poland, 1874–80.

318.5   Prince Dolgorouki]   Nicholas Dolgorouki, aide-de-camp to the emperor.

320.15–17   the sailors . . . royalty.]   Clemens' address to the czar—which was published in the San Francisco *Alta*, the New York *Sun*, the New York

Tribune, the London *Times*, and other periodicals—was in fact burlesqued by members of the crew, according to a letter that Mrs. Mary Mason Fairbanks published in the Cleveland *Herald*, October 8, 1867.

330.3–4   Miller's resurrection day]   William Miller (1782–1849), leader of Second Adventists in America, first set 1843 for the epiphany and when the epiphany did not take place declared that he had erred by following the Hebrew rather than Roman chronology and that the second coming would occur on October 22, 1844.

336.6   THE LEGEND . . . SLEEPERS.]   Clemens burlesques the legend of seven noble Christian youths of Ephesus who fled to a cave in Mount Celion during the time of systematic persecutions under the Emperor Decius (201–51). The youths awoke after a sleep of 230 years, died soon afterwards, and their bodies were taken to Marseilles in a large stone coffin, which was to be seen in Victor's Church. The tale is told by Gregory of Tours and others; the Koran offers an adaptation, placing the scene at Damascus. Guide and travel books mention the legend.

343.17   Jacob's Dream]   Genesis 28:10–22.

346.7   "COME . . . DEPART."]   For line 1, see *Macbeth*, IV, i, 110–111: "Show his eyes, and grieve his heart; / Come like shadows, so depart!" The lines which follow are, slightly changed, the final stanza of "The Day Is Done," by Henry Wadsworth Longfellow.

349.16–19   " * * * no man . . . there!"]   From "The Burial of Moses," by Mrs. Cecil Frances Alexander (1818–95), wife of the archbishop of Armagh. The poem begins: "By Nebo's lonely mountain, / On this side Jordan's wave, / In a vale in the land of Moab, / There lies a lonely grave; / But no man built that sepulchre, / And no man saw it e'er; / For the angels of God upturned the sod / And laid the dead man there." In August 1867, Clemens entered the entire poem in a notebook, and in September he entered the title as a reminder.

364:13–14   We . . . Ananias.]   For the story of Saul which follows see Acts 9:1–30.

364.34   Paul lay]   The shift from Saul to Paul may be explained by family history. Paul inherited Roman citizenship from his father, who had been awarded it for public service; and as a citizen he had the cognomen Paulus. His family claimed descent, however, from the tribe of Benjamin, of which King Saul was the most famous member; thus Saul was his Jewish name.

371.4   Nimrod . . . Hunter]   See Genesis 10:8–9.

371.32–33   castle of Banias]   Also called the Castle of Subeibeh.

373.4   Dr. B.]   Dr. George B. Birch.

374.4–8   "Thou . . . heaven."]   See Matthew 16:18–19.

382.17–18   "Like . . . land."]   Isaiah 32:2: "As the shadow of a great rock in a weary land."

382.40   Wm. C. Grimes']   "William C. Grimes" is William C. Prime, whose *Tent Life in the Holy Land* (New York: Harper and Brothers, 1857) contains the flamboyant passages that Clemens satirizes.

383.32–35   "And when . . . multitude,"]   Inverted from Joshua 11:4–5.

384.4–5   Deborah . . . Jabin]   Judges 4:4–16.

384.22   "For . . . died."]   Judges 4:21.

384.26–34   "Blessed . . . dead."]   Judges 5:24–27.

385.2–5   "I . . . waste."]   Leviticus 26:32–33.

389.33   the exquisite . . . Joseph.]   Genesis 37:39–50.

390.39   Esau]   Genesis 25:21–34; and chapters 26–33.

395.25   Church]   William F. Church, of Cincinnati, Ohio.

396.6–7   Jairus's . . . dead.]   Matthew 9:18–26; Mark 5:21–43; Luke 8:41–56.

396.35–36   his brothers . . . Simon]   Matthew 13:55; Mark 6:3.

397.16   he had sisters]   Matthew 13:56; Mark 6:3.

403.22–23   Wm. C. Grimes . . . follows:]   Freely adapted from Prime, *Tent Life*, pp. 374–75.

404.35–405.12   "C. W. E.," . . . misery."]   Charles Wyllys Elliott, *Remarkable Characters and Memorable Places of the Holy Land* (Hartford, Conn.: J. B. Burr and Co., 1868), pp. 455–56.

406.33–34   I found . . . Robinson.]   Clemens must be misremembering. Robinson reports that he did not visit Caesarea. See Edward Robinson, *Biblical Researches in Palestine and in the Adjacent Regions* (Boston: Crocker and Brewster, 1856), II, 241–42.

406.36   Mr. Thompson's . . . Book."]   William McClure Thomson, *The Land and the Book* (New York: Harper and Brothers, 1859), 2 vols.

412.26–36   "The Ephraimites . . . day."]   This quotation is a fairly accurate version of part of the Masonic ritual for the Fellow Craft degree.

413.9   Guide-Book,]   See Murray's *Syria* (1858), II, 417.

414.29–31   Nain . . . view.]   See Robinson, *Biblical Researches*, II, 360–61; also see Luke 7:11–15 and I Samuel 28.

419.26   "without . . . price."]   Isaiah 55:1: " . . . yea, come, buy wine and milk without money and without price."

423.9–24   "After . . . forever.' "] Prime, *Tent Life*, p. 350. The six quotations which follow may be found pp. 474, 338–39, 325, 406, 56, 488–89. Some of the transcriptions are very free.

425.40   *Scow . . . Egypt*]   William C. Prime, *Boat Life in Egypt and Nubia* (New York: Harper and Brothers, 1857), p. 146.

426.1–3   "As . . . them."]   Prime, *Tent Life*, p. 490.

426.8–16   "Then . . . Land."]   Prime, *Tent Life*, p. 60. The " weeping" within parentheses is Clemens' addition.

426.20   *"Nomadic . . . Palestine"*]   Prime, *Tent Life*.

427.15–17   I . . . Testament.]   Clemens refers not to a notebook of the period (where his only pertinent entry is the enigmatic "Apocraphal [sic] Bible") but to his letter of June 2, 1867, to the *Alta California*. Below he reproduces with slight changes both the extracts that he printed in the *Alta* and the passages that connect them. The extracts themselves are drawn—with additions (for comic emphasis), omissions, and condensations—from an edition, probably the third or fourth, of *The Apocryphal New Testament* printed for William Hone, booksellers in London. Clemens errs in stating that he used an edition of 1621. The earliest English edition appeared in 1693. The popular Hone edition first appeared in 1820. The third and fourth editions appeared in 1821. Although Clemens later owned an undated edition of apocryphal texts printed in London by S. Bagster and Sons and an edition published in Boston in 1882 by Colby and Rich, according to his letter to the *Alta*, he drew his quotations from "an edition of 1621" (a misreading for 1821) which he found in a New York library. In a fourth edition of Hone (bearing the date 1821) the passages quoted by Clemens may be found as follows: First extract: First Gospel of the Infancy of Jesus Christ, summaries prefixed to Chapters 6, p. 25; 7, p. 27; 16, p. 36; 19, p. 38; and 20, p. 39. Second extract: I Corinthians 11:1–5, pp. 102–03. Third extract: Hermas III, Similitude 9:199, p. 237.

430.29   worse . . . *campoodie*]   Or *campoody*; Southwestern American (Paiute from the Spanish *campo*), meaning an Indian village.

431.15   "Necessity . . . law."]   Proverbial expressions to this effect may be found in many places, including Publius Syrus, Maxim 553 ("Necessity knows no law except to conquer"); Rabelais; John Skelton; and Shakespeare.

432.1–12   "Now . . . people."]   Luke 7:12–16.

435.6   Ahab . . . Samaria]   Clemens summarizes I Kings 21 and II Kings 9–10.

437.35–438.8   Samaria . . . son."]   See II Kings 6:24–29.

440.34–37   "And . . . silver."]   Joshua 24:32; Genesis 50:25, 26.

446.39   the great Rotunda]   See Matthew 28:1–2.

450.22–24   But . . . *earth.*]   Several books used by Clemens comment on the stone. See especially Murray's *Syria* (1858), I, 164–65, which repeats the tale of the skeptic who tested whether the sun gave him a shadow at noon and the tradition that from this spot came the clay from which Adam was modeled. Compare the sacred stone, flanked by two eagles (?), in the temple of Apollo at Delphi, supposed to mark the middle point of the earth. It was commonly thought that Zeus started two eagles from the opposite ends of the earth and that they met at the point marked by the stone. The ancients also conceived that the stone marked the grave of the Python or of Dionysus and was magical as well as commemorative. This navel-stone or omphalos at Delphi was only one of several such conical or pyramidical sacred stones in the Greek world and elsewhere. Their connections are with primitive earth deities and the spirits of the dead. In their aspects as gravestones, they are ultimately of phallic origin.

454.17   Saewulf]   Murray's *Syria* (1858), I, 158, identifies Saewulf as an English monk who followed the crusaders and visited Jerusalem about 1103; but whether he was in fact a religious has not been established. In describing the Chapel of the Mocking, Murray's says, p. 166, that the Jews blindfolded Christ, smote Him on the face, and gibed in barbarous derision, "Prophesy who it is that smote thee." Murray's reference is to Thomas Wright, ed., *Early Travels in Palestine* (London: H. G. Bohn, 1848), which contains Saewulf's *Relatio de Peregrinatione ad Hierosolymam et Terram Sanctam.*

457.28   a war . . .]   Apparently a jesting reference to a quarrel. Harper's *Hand-Book*, p. 428, refers to Greeks and Latins quarreling for the privilege of repairing the dome, with neither party being successful.

473.33–36   "On Jordan's . . . lie."]   Loosely quoted from Hymn 1272 in *Plymouth Collection of Hymns* (1866), p. 775.

482.9   all the Lamartines]   Alphonse de Lamartine (1790–1869) was notably sentimental in both prose and verse. From 1820–23 he was attached to the French embassy in Naples; during 1824–29 he was in Florence; and for sixteen months beginning in May 1832, he traveled in the Near East. His first book in prose was *Voyage en Orient* (1835), translated as *A Pilgrimage to the Holy Land*. In 1835 the popular book was printed in London for R. Bentley and in Philadelphia for Carey, Lea and Blanchard. In 1848 it was reprinted in New York for D. Appleton and Company.

484.4–5   "Sun . . . Ajalon."]   Joshua 10:12.

484.18   [For description . . . Gazetteer.]]   *Universal Gazetteer of the World* (North Middleboro, Mass.: Z. and B. F. Pratt, 1852).

485.1–7   A writer . . . different."]   Elliott, *Remarkable Characters,* p. 353.

489.29   the Jaffa Colonists]   Clemens' very incomplete account of the colonists is rewritten and condensed from his more detailed, skeptical, hostile letter written in Alexandria on October 2 for the New York *Tribune* of November 2. Additional material is available elsewhere, perhaps most conveniently in *The New York Times*: February 17, 1867; March 20; August 19; August 22; September 2; October 1; October 22; and November 14. George J. Adams, born, he claimed, in England, became a Millerite, a Methodist "exhorter," a Baptist, a Campbellite, a Mormon elder in Jonesport, Maine, and an actor, playing at Purdy's theater in Boston, mainly in Shakespearian roles. He published a newspaper called the *Sword of Truth*. As founder and high priest of a charismatic, messianic sect, the "New Church of the Messiah," he enlisted some one hundred and sixty followers to establish a colony in the Holy Land, near Jaffa. Most of Adams' attendants were plain people from Washington County, Maine, who sold their farms, entrusted their money to their prophetic leader, and embarked on what proved to be an impractical venture that lasted in all approximately one year.

491.12–13   It . . . note-book]   The sketch is not in a notebook but does appear in a letter of April 19, 1867, to the *Alta California*. There Clemens identifies the hotel as bad as Shepherd's as the Heming House in Keokuk, Iowa.

503.22–23   One . . . reptiles]   A notebook entry indicates that Dr. William Gibson may have been this "Iconoclast."

507.14   What . . . at sea]   Only a few phrases in the sample entries which follow actually appear in the notebooks.

507.35   Harry caught him]   Henry (or Harry) E. Duncan, a boy of eleven, one of the sons of Captain and Mrs. Duncan.

508.12–13   Dr. C.]   Dr. Albert Crane, of New Orleans, Louisiana.

513.2–3   an article . . . *Herald*]   The article appeared in the *Herald* on November 20, 1867.

517.32   Gideon's Band]   That is, proverbially, a small, selected group. The story of Gideon is told in Judges 6–8.

ROUGHING IT

541.30–31   he offered . . . secretary]   Only after the opening of the First Territorial Legislature did Orion Clemens employ Samuel Clemens for a time as his clerk (at eight dollars a day).

541.32–33   the heavens . . . scroll!]   Rev. 6:14 and 21:1.

542.11   steamboat . . . River.]   After waiting in St. Louis because of the tardy arrival from Washington of Orion's handbook and instructions (and probably delayed also by Confederate General Sterling G. Price's efforts to sever the river route to St. Joseph), on July 18, 1861, Samuel and Orion Clemens began their western journey on the steamboat *Sioux City*. From St. Joseph they proceeded by stagecoach, fares for two coming to $400. Orion's journal, used by Clemens when he wrote *Roughing It* for reminders of events, dates, names, and distances, has disappeared; but an extant letter of September 8, 1861, from Orion to his wife duplicates the entries for July 26 through August 14, that is, from leaving St. Joseph until arriving in Carson City after an overland journey that Orion estimated at 1,700 miles.

557.36   Nicholson pavement]   Samuel Nicholson (1791–1868), of Boston, author and inventor, devised a wooden-block paving that was adopted by many towns, as it was well-suited for light traffic.

567.27   Mr. Ben Holliday]   Ben Holladay (1819–87), the quintessential Western businessman-speculator, made and lost fortunes in mining and transportation. In 1849 he was part owner of a wagon-freight line from Missouri to Salt Lake City, a business which he expanded rapidly. In 1863 he began to buy steamships, ending with a fleet of twenty-three plying from Alaska to Mexico. The freighting business suffered during the Indian uprisings in 1864–65, and in 1866 Holladay sold his interests to Wells, Fargo & Company. Using proceeds from his holdings in the Ophir mine in Nevada, he purchased land in Westchester County, New York, where he built a million-dollar house. In 1868 he began to invest in railroads, but in 1876, following the Panic of 1873, he lost his Oregon railroad system and his Westchester house. His two daughters contracted disastrous marriages to titled Europeans.

575.17   blackness of darkness]   See note 50.17.

577.30–31   Indian mail . . . massacre]   The most reliable reports indicate that Colonel Almon (or Almond) W. Babbitt, secretary of the Utah Territory, and two companions, acting against advice, separated from a wagon train waiting at Fort Kearny for a cavalry escort and left the fort on September 2, 1856, taking documents and currency with them. The scalped and mutilated bodies of three men were found later. In 1850 Babbitt had been elected a delegate to Congress from the State of Deseret but was refused admission.

579.3–4   the Black Hills]   The Laramie Mountains; not the range now called the Black Hills in South Dakota and Wyoming.

582.14   Slade himself]   "Captain" J. A. Slade. Clemens writes of Slade in a letter of January 22, 1870, for the Buffalo *Express*. For the extended, partly fictitious account below he draws heavily upon a letter of March 11, 1871, from Orion and on Thomas J. Dimsdale, *The Vigilantes of Montana* (1866).

603.6   Mormon "Destroying Angel"]   Eph Hanks, in charge of the Big Canyon Creek station, was reputed to be quiet and pleasant. On the other hand, the young Kimball mentioned immediately below, when asked by Orion if he were related to Heber C. Kimball, replied abruptly, "I'm his hell-roaring son."

604.16   the Acting Governor]   Francis H. Wootton, of Maryland, was appointed secretary of the Nevada Territory and became acting governor for a brief period following the departure on May 17, 1861, of Governor Alfred Cumming, but resigned shortly after the South seceded from the Union.

605.19–22   The armorial . . . FALL."]   The "armorial achievement," or seal, of the state of Missouri exhibits "a white or grizzly bear of Missouri" on each side of what for comic purposes could be construed as the head of a cask of whiskey.

606.22   Heber C. Kimball]   Heber Chase Kimball (1801–68), born in Sheldon, Vermont, was converted in 1832 by itinerant Mormon elders, joined Joseph Smith in Ohio, did important missionary work in England, and was chosen to be one of the twelve apostles. In Utah he became a member of the governing council and lieutenant governor.

606.24   the "Lion House,"]   Residence of Brigham Young, who led the Mormons from Illinois to Utah, 1846–48.

606.30   Mr. Street]   James Street, construction superintendent for the Pacific Telegraph Company, not met in fact until the Clemenses reached Camp Floyd.

606.32   state visit . . . king]   In a letter of August 19, 1861, to the St. Louis *Missouri Democrat*, Orion reported on this visit made at the request of the United States State Department in an effort to establish the intentions of the Mormons following the secession of the Southern states. Orion noted that " we" visited Brigham Young, First President of the Church; Heber C. Kimball, Second President; and David Hammer Wells, Third President. His conversation about the political sympathies of the Mormons was with Kimball, not Young. He quotes Kimball as saying, "I'd like to see the South give the North a grubbing, and I'd like to see the North give the South a grubbing, but I want the South to grub a little the hardest. . . ." Kimball also remarked, "I ain't given to prophesying" but in his opinion the United States would go all to pieces and the Mormons would "take charge of the country." Wells was a High Priest, Second Counselor to Brigham Young, and Lieutenant-General of the Nauvoo Legion.

611.7   "Morisites"]   Joseph Morris declared himself, not Brigham Young, to be Prophet and founded a schismatic sect on April 6, 1861. A tenet of the sect was a belief in millenarianism and the imminent coming of the Saviour (in 1862). When three dissatisfied members tried to leave the Morrisite settlement at South Weber and were imprisoned, a force of Mormon militia was sent to serve a writ for the arrest of the schismatic leaders. During fighting on June 13–15, 1862, perhaps six to eight members of the settlement (including Joseph Morris) and two members of the posse were killed.

614.10–11   St. Parley Pratt]   Parley P. Pratt (1807–57), born in Burlington, New York, was converted to Mormonism about 1830 and rose rapidly in the church. He was ordained one of the twelve apostles in 1835. When charged with murder in 1838 for his part in the hostilities between Mormons and Missourians, he escaped, worked for the church in the United States and England, joined the migration of 1847, and helped to frame the constitution of the State of Deseret. He was killed by three men near Van Buren, Arkansas, one of his attackers being Hector McLean, husband of a woman who had left him to join Pratt.

614.24   Nephi]   There are alternative explanations of the identity of Nephi. He is said to have been the son of Lehi, a Hebrew prophet who led his followers to the New World about 600 B.C.; but it is also said that the name *Nephi* was corrected to *Moroni* and that Nephi is the founder of the tribe of Nephites, whereas Moroni was the son of Mormon.

614.39   Orson Hyde]   In 1855 Hyde, president of the Quorum of Twelve Apostles, was appointed probate judge for the newly constituted Carson County, Utah Territory, by Governor Brigham Young. Later during 1855 the act establishing Carson County was repealed and Hyde was recalled, leaving Carson County without a court until 1858. These circumstances contributed to the formation of the Nevada Territory.

617.2   the Mormon Bible]   The Book of Mormon has appeared in a number of editions since its first publication in 1830. In his not entirely accurate account, Clemens seems to have used the third European edition, published for Orson Pratt (brother of Parley P. Pratt; excommunicated in 1842, rebaptized in 1843) by F. D. Richards in Liverpool in 1852. Some editions of the Mormon Bible are divided into chapters but not into verses. The Bible comprises fifteen main divisions, known, with one exception, as books. The exception—"The Words of Mormon," which falls between the Book of Omni and the Book of Mosiah—is the seventh of the fifteen divisions.

625.10   "Mountain Meadows Massacre"]   See Appendix B, pp. 965–69.

632.8   Goshoot Indians]   Usually spelled Gosiute.

632.13   Kytches of Africa]   A tribe of the upper valley of the White Nile. John George Wood, cited below by Clemens, asserted that it is hardly possible to conceive of "a more miserable and degraded set of people than the Kytch tribe." He does, however, consider the tribe to be remarkable for keeping cattle for show, not for food, and for the observance of strict marriage laws in the practice of polygamy.

633.15   attacked . . . stage-coach]   On March 22, 1863, Indians killed the keeper of a stage station eight miles from the Nevada border and a little later ambushed the stage. The driver was Henry ("Happy Harry") Harper. Gordon Newell Mott, associate justice of the Nevada Supreme Court, took the stage on to Deep Creek Station, just across the border in Utah. The stage carried three passengers in addition to the judge: an old man and two children. The old man was severely wounded but recovered.

634.7   Emerson Bennett's works]   Bennett (1822–1905) was the prolific writer of far-western adventure stories. When Clemens was in New York between December 10–17, 1870, he probably saw a dramatized version of Bennett's *The Prairie Flower* at the Bowery Theatre.

635.2–3   the highest . . . peaks]   The Schell Creek and Egan mountain ranges.

635.8   Gov. Nye]   James W. Nye (1814–76), first president of the New York City metropolitan police board, was appointed by Lincoln in 1861 to be first governor of the Nevada Territory. He left the governorship in 1864 to serve as senator from Nevada, 1864–73.

636.2   Ragtown]   So called because emigrants hurrying for water littered the desert thereabouts with abandoned possessions.

639.18   sozodont]   A popular dentifrice.

639.25–26   Bayard Taylor . . . written]   The anecdote is not mentioned by any of the actual authors named here.

640.4–10   And what . . . Aha!]   Clemens first mentions the anecdote in a letter of December 12, 1863, to the Virginia City *Territorial Enterprise*. Apparently he considered it to be authentic until an editor—probably Joseph T. Goodman of the *Enterprise*—informed him that the incident never occurred. Clemens then made inquiry of Horace Greeley, who seems to have answered, denying the story. It may be noted that in Clemens' version of the King James Bible, Daniel has only twelve chapters, whereas in other versions it has fifteen. Beginning with the fourth printing of the first edition of *Roughing It*, the reference was changed from "thirteenth" to "sixteenth" in order to preserve the joke.

644.2   Bridget O'Flannigan]   In fact, Mrs. M. Murphy.

646.32   Bob H——]   Probably Robert M. Howland, said to be a nephew of Governor Nye. Regularly in Aurora but paid frequent visits to Carson City.

649.16   Johnny K——]   John D. Kinney, from Cincinnati, who had come west with Chief Justice Turner; at this time gave his occupation as "real estate."

649.24–25   a wood ranch]   In August 1861, Clemens established a claim on the borders of Lake Bigler (Tahoe) in his own name and in those of five others.

658.26   *tapidaros*]   *Tapaderas,* Mexican Spanish for leather stirrup covers.

662.3   two . . . fifty]   In his letter of August 28, 1861, to the Keokuk *Gate City,* Orion reports that the charge for stabling and haying a horse for one night was $1.50.

662.14–15   Carson and Eagle valleys]   The Carson River flows through the Carson Valley. Carson City is in Eagle Valley.

664.25   the Organic Act]   This act establishing the Nevada Territory was signed into law on March 2, 1861, by President James Buchanan. The First Territorial Legislature convened on October 1, 1861.

670.7–8   "Esmeralda" . . . "Humboldt"]   The Esmeralda mining district (around Aurora, Nevada) was in the Sierra Nevada foothills, approximately one hundred miles southeast of Carson City. The Humboldt district was approximately one hundred and seventy-five miles to the northeast of Carson City.

670.20   *Daily Territorial Enterprise*]   Probably in late November or early December 1861. No complete file of the *Territorial Enterprise* is known to be extant; articles from issues not available in complete form may sometimes be found reprinted in other newspapers or preserved in scrapbooks.

673.3   four persons]   William H. Clagett, newly appointed notary public for Unionville; Augustus W. Oliver, probate judge for the newly formed Humboldt County; and Cornbury S. Tillou, blacksmith. Clagett had studied law in Keokuk, and Clemens had known him there.

687.27–28   Mr. Ballou . . . Ollendorff]   His companions were Attorney General Benjamin B. Bunker and, in all probability, Captain Edwin A. Rowe, 2nd California Cavalry, commandant of Fort Churchill, and Lieutenant Colonel James N. Olney, commanding officer of the 2nd California Infantry.

705.13   General Buncombe]   The same Benjamin B. Bunker as above, originally from New Hampshire, appointed attorney general of the Nevada Territory by Lincoln in 1861, removed from office in 1863 for inattention to his duties and for spending much time out of the Territory.

709.21   Hoosac Tunnel]   For years the longest tunnel (4.73 miles) in America. On the line of the Fitchburg (Massachusetts) railroad; begun in 1855, completed in 1876.

715.17   The first . . . Canyon]   Actually the first mill in Nevada was established by Hugh Logan and John P. Holmes at Gold Hill in October 1859.

739.6   the Tennessee land]   John Marshall Clemens purchased 70,000 or more acres that members of his family long expected to make them rich. Their hopes were completely disappointed.

744.30   Esmeralda *Union*]   The Aurora, Nevada, *Esmeralda Union*; first published in March 1864; ended publication in November 1867.

746.28   Mr. Goodman]   Joseph T. Goodman and Denis McCarthy purchased partnerships in the *Enterprise* in 1861. Goodman became a valued friend and associate of Clemens.

747.11   Dan]   "Dan De Quille," pen name of William Wright, who, like Goodman, became a close friend. Clemens encouraged and advised Wright during the composition (much of it in Hartford) of *The Big Bonanza* (1876), which was issued by Clemens' subscription publisher.

749.14–15   Boggs . . . *Union*]   Clemens and Clement T. Rice, reporter for the *Virginia Daily Union*, were friendly rivals. They sometimes collaborated to report on legislative sessions.

752.5   "hurdy-gurdy houses,"]   Dance halls, ordinarily with bars, girls, and music; usually disreputable.

756.25   Mr. Stewart]   William M. Stewart, senator 1864–75 and 1887–1905. Clemens served as his secretary in Washington beginning about November 22, 1867, and ending in February or March 1868.

758.29–30   McKean Buchanan]   Buchanan (1823–72) was educated for the Navy and served three years as a midshipman before making his first appearance as an actor in New Orleans. He made his New York debut as Hamlet in 1849. His "sombre and antiquated" style was not pleasing to New Yorkers, and in his later years he acted mainly in the West, where he was popular.

761.8   A Sanitary Committee]   Clemens turned over an appeal for funds that he had received from his sister, Pamela, to the president of the Storey County Sanitary Commission. After Reuel Gridley devoted himself to forwarding the project, contributions increased markedly.

773.19   a very Warwick]   Richard Neville, Earl of Warwick (1428–71), known as "the Kingmaker."

774.9–10   short-haired brotherhood]   Firemen wore their hair short to keep it from catching on fire.

774.14   the minister]   Drawn from the Reverend Franklin S. Rising, whom Clemens knew in Nevada, "stumbled on" in Hawaii, returned to San Francisco with, and encountered again in New York in 1867. Rising died in December 1868, when two steamers collided on the Ohio River.

786.2   Mr. —— of Cariboo]   In 1858 Cariboo, on the Fraser River in British Columbia, was the site of a gold rush.

787.4   last evening]   Apparently in March 1862.

787.39   Charles Hurtzal]   Charles Hutzel.

788.20–21   Five . . . assassinated]   Williams was killed on December 10, 1862.

792.12   Capt. Ned Blakely]   Clemens modeled Blakely and a number of other characters on Captain Edgar (Ned) Wakeman (1818–75), who commanded the *America* when Clemens sailed on that steamer from San Francisco to Nicaragua in 1866.

798.11   The *Weekly Occidental*]   First published March 6, 1864; seems to have continued for only four issues.

798.13   Mr. F.]   Thomas Fitch, an attorney who held various offices in California and Nevada, a member of the United States Congress (1869–71), and, with his wife, the author of a novel, *Better Days: or, a Millionaire of Tomorrow* (1891).

799.5 Mr. D.] Rollin M. Daggett, a newspaper and magazine editor, a United States congressman (1879–81), and a minister to Hawaii (1882–83).

799.18–19 a dissolute stranger] Charles Henry Webb, who arrived in California in April 1864 as a correspondent for *The New York Times*. He founded a regionally important literary weekly, the San Francisco *Californian*.

804.16–17 "The Raging Canal"] A popular ballad (with "canal" pronounced "canawl"), versions of which may be found in several collections.

810.16–42 Mr. Valentine . . . M. T.]] Revised from an editorial in the *Territorial Enterprise* for August 27, 1863.

814.17 the Sutro Tunnel] Adolph Sutro (1830–98) began the tunnel in October 1869 and completed it in 1878.

816.38 Dorcas S'iety] Dorcas Society, named like others for the Dorcas who "was full of good works and almsdeeds" (Acts 9:36–41).

820.22 news comes] *New York Times*, June 3, 1871. In 1864 Clemens himself reported a similar incident for the San Francisco *Call*, but his story was, he said, suppressed by his employer.

821.32 "foreign" mining tax] A tax, which varied from $3 a month to $20 a month, directed first at the Spanish-Americans, later at the Chinese.

822.9–10 Mr. Burlingame] Clemens met Anson Burlingame (1820–70), first American minister to China, in Hawaii in June 1864.

822.25 several great companies] Most Chinese immigrants to California came from the Pearl River delta region (Kwantung Province). Beginning about 1851 there were formed in San Francisco "companies" like those of Chinese who emigrated to Southeast Asia. The first companies, based on a clan system and regional loyalties, served various social and benevolent functions but were also used by their chiefs to exploit laborers, especially those who came to America on an indentured basis. Violence among feuding factions diminished in the early 1860s, and a coordinating council known as the Chung Wah Kung Saw, or the Chinese Six Companies, was formed. The number of companies and their names changed from time to time; their governance was often challenged by secret societies whose members had no loyalty to family or district.

822.40 passed or not] Adopted April 1, 1877; ostensibly permits were needed to ascertain the cause of death and to prevent the spread of smallpox.

825.2–3 vaccinated . . . wharf] A city and county ordinance adopted in 1870. The ordinance mentions no fee.

823.10 item . . . printed] Probably about September 15, 1864.

823.19   Josh-lights]   Joss lights.

828.40   Marshall]   G. M. Marshall, a reporter for the Virginia City *Daily Union*.

830.23   Toodles]   The principal character in a sketch performed by the R. G. Marsh Juvenile Comedians, seen by Clemens on January 12, 1864, in Carson City.

837.29   John Phenix]   "John Phoenix," pseudonym of George Derby (1823–61), soldier by profession, writer by avocation, notable for his development of the boisterous Western style of humor. Died deranged from a sunstroke while on duty in Florida.

844.31   my first earthquake]   It began at 12:45 P.M. on November 8, 1865.

847.15   an Oakland Minister]   The Reverend Mr. Harmon, of the Pacific Female Seminary.

848.1   NEVADA MINES . . . NEW YORK]   Probably in the *Enterprise* for November 8, 1864.

849.2   *Golden Era*]   Established December 19, 1852, in San Francisco by Rollin M. Daggett; ended publication in 1893.

849.3–4   C. H. Webb . . . *Californian*]   Established May 28, 1864; ceased publication in 1868.

849.8   Captain Ogden]   Richard L. Ogden, for a time a captain in the Quartermaster Corps; he engaged in several business enterprises.

854.2   an old . . . mine]   James M. Gillis, brother of Steven E. Gillis, an even closer friend.

858.5   Dick Baker]   Dick Stoker, mining partner of James ("Jim") Gillis. The story of the cat is revised from a letter for the Buffalo *Express*, which in turn was derived from an earlier sketch.

861.16   paust]   Probably from the German *Posten*, a parcel, lot, or batch of ore.

862.15   We sailed . . . winter.]   March 7, 1866.

862.20   sea-worn . . . captains]   The sea captains were: James Smith, W. H. Phillips, and A. W. Fish, each of whom sailed with his vessel from Honolulu in April for the Arctic fishing grounds.

865.23   "The Old Guard"]   First published in June 1862; ended publication in December 1870.

870.31   the "Willows,"]   A privately operated park that offered a menagerie, singing, and dancing.

876.35   a dozen cottages]   The village of Waikiki.

878.8–10   When Kamehameha . . . Oahu]   The king of the island of Hawaii died in 1782, leaving his kingdom to his son Kiwalao, some say jointly with his nephew, Kamehameha. Disagreements between the two powerful men provoked conflict and ended in the death of Kiwalao. Kahekili, King of Maui—who had conquered the islands of Molokai, Lanai, and Oahu—and his son Kalanikupule began hostilities against Kamehameha in 1794. Kamehameha defeated the major force of his enemies on Oahu in 1795, driving many of them over a six-hundred-foot precipice, the Nuuanu *Pali*. Kamehameha died on May 8, 1819. The name Kamehameha (meaning "The Lonely One"), like nearly all Hawaiian words, has been variously spelled.

880.20   Pari]   The word *Pari* seems to be either Clemens' error or a printer's error for *Pali*, or precipice.

880.22   Mr. Jarves' . . . history]   Clemens owned a copy of one edition: James Jackson Jarves, *History of the Hawaiian or Sandwich Islands*, 2nd ed. (Boston: James Munroe and Co., 1844).

882.33   Mr. L.]   Lewis Leland, manager of the Occidental Hotel, San Francisco.

885.26   *ohia*]   This word, which has a variety of meanings both explicit and figurative, refers here to the *ohi'a-lehua* tree (*metrosideros macropus*). Its flowers are much used for the making of leis.

890.7–9   David Kalakaua . . . Vice President]   Kalakaua was named King of Hawaii after the death of King Lunalilo in 1874. Prince William was William C. Lunalilo, who became King William, or King Lunalilo, following the death of Kamehameha V in 1873 and who ruled until his death in 1874. Mataias Kekuanoa (or Mataio Kekuanaoa), the father of kings Kamehameha IV and V, died in 1868. The Vice President was Godfrey Rhodes, an Englishman who was a long-time resident of the islands.

892.22   the Great Shark God]   Moa-alii, the celebrated and rapacious shark god for whom numerous temples were built on headlands.

895.5   his Excellency . . . Minister]   Although he did not hold this title, Charles Coffin Harris, an attorney originally from Portsmouth, New Hampshire, was Attorney General in 1862 and was appointed Minister of Finance in 1867.

895.12–13   Minister of Finance]   Charles Coffin Harris was Minister of Finance. Clemens may mean Charles de Varigny, who had given up his position as Minister of Finance in 1865 to become Minister of Foreign Affairs; he was also charged with the combined ministries of War and Navy.

895.32   Lord Bishop . . . Honolulu]   Thomas Nettleship Staley, Anglican Bishop of Hawaii beginning in 1861.

896.1–2   Minister of . . . Information]   No such ministry existed from 1855 to 1865, when a Bureau of Public Instruction was created. The President of the Board of Education was Mataio Kekuanoa; the Inspector General of Schools, Abraham Fornander.

897.4   Princess Victoria]   Victoria Kamehamalu, commonly called Ka-mamalu, born November 1, 1838, died May 29, 1866. In 1857 she assumed the office of *kuhina-nui* ("important guardian of the temple"), which became he-reditary. The office was abolished in 1864. At the time of Victoria's death she was next in line of succession to her brother, Kamehameha V.

898.24   Ahahui Kaahumanu]   In his letter of June 22, 1866, to the Sacra-mento *Union*, Clemens reports that this was a benevolent association of women of the islands, founded and presided over by Princess Victoria Ka-mehamalu. Its chief objects had to do with the nursing of "its members when sick, and their decent burial after death." When members marched in proces-sion at a funeral, a scarf indicated by its color the official rank of the wearer.

899.6–7   Burlingame and . . . Van Valkenburgh]   Anson Burlingame, en route to China, and General Robert B. Van Valkenburgh, en route to his post as United States Minister to Japan.

900.7   On . . . 1819,]   The slightly revised quoted matter is from James J. Jarves, *History of the Hawaiian Islands,* 3rd ed. (Honolulu: Charles Edwin Hitchcock, 1847), pp. 105–06, as is that beginning 900.34, which is taken by Jarves from an account in the Hawaiian *Spectator*, II, 227.

900.38   Kukailimoku]   A large wooden image of the most honored war god. The image had been entrusted to Kamehameha long before by his uncle, Kalaniopuu.

901.28   Kaikioewa]   A chieftain who was guardian for Liholiho.

901.31   Kaahumanu]   In 1793 Kaahumanu was about sixteen, very hand-some, and the favorite queen of Kamehameha, but she was estranged from him in 1794 because of her alleged infidelity. She and the king were recon-ciled through the good offices of Captain George Vancouver, the famous British explorer, whom the queen persuaded to induce Kamehameha to promise to forego beating her. She was the first to assume the office of *ku-hina-nui*, a position that Kamehameha apparently devised for her to hold following his death. The term is usually translated as "premier" or "prime minister," but the authority of the *kuhina-nui* was greater than that which has ordinarily accompanied these offices. Kaahumanu served during the reigns of Liholiho (a son of Kamehameha by another wife) and of his brother Kanikeaouli (Kamehameha III) until her death in 1832. She is said to have been inordinately fond of alcohol, yet she is also declared to have been the ablest member of the royal line after Kamehameha I.

901.34   Mr. Young]   In 1789 two chiefs of Maui stole the small boat of the American trading snow *Eleanora* and killed its watchman. In retaliation Captain Simon Metcalf fired on the natives of a neighboring village and burned their huts. When trading was resumed, in order to punish the natives further, he fired on the amassed canoes crowded with islanders come to trade, killing perhaps a hundred and wounding many more. Metcalf then sailed for Hawaii. Unknown to Metcalf, the *Eleanora*'s tender, a small schooner named the *Fair American* with six on board, was taken off Hawaii by natives under a chief who had been whipped by Metcalf. Metcalf's son and four others were killed, and Isaac Davis, the only survivor, was taken captive. At approximately the same time John Young, boatswain of the *Eleanora*, was taken while on shore. Kamehameha held both men, treated them well, made them chiefs, and they served him loyally in both war and peace. Young was governor of the island of Hawaii from 1802 to 1812.

901.34–35   Hoapili]   A chieftain whose name, meaning "intimate friend," had been given him by Kamehameha, concealed the bones of the dead king, married two of his widows, and became governor of Maui.

902.12   Kalaimoku]   The name is usually spelled Kalanimoku. Sometimes called Billy Pitt, he was an able prime minister and treasurer.

905.6   Boomerang]   In fact, the *Emeline*, commanded by Captain Crane.

918.20   the great god *Lono*]   God of the harvest, one of the four major gods brought from Tahiti. In addition to being the god of agriculture, he is regarded as the god of medicine, and his name occurs in chants relating to cloud signs and other weather phenomena.

918.26–28   Captain Cook's . . . life]   Clemens takes his account and interpretation of the death of Cook on February 14, 1779, mainly from Jarves, *History of the Hawaiian Islands*.

921.5   Obookia]   Opukahaia (d. 1818), or Henry Obookiah, as he was called in New England, was taken to New Haven in 1809, became the ward of the Reverend Edwin W. Dwight, of Yale College, was converted to Christianity, and took part in a campaign for the establishment of a mission in Hawaii.

921.24   The other . . . youths]   William Kanui, Thomas Hopu, and John Honolii, who were educated in New England by the American Board of Commissioners for Foreign Missions.

921.29   the failure . . . Co.]   A banking firm with its main office in St. Louis.

923.12–13   makahiki]   The harvest season.

924.32   Kekuokalani]   This conservative rival for the throne was killed about December 20, 1819, in the battle over Liholiho's breaking of *tabu*, or *kapu*.

936.10   the heat . . . furnaces]   The "most fearful of all their deities," Pele, made her home in the crater of Kilauea. She and her chief followers were said to bathe in the red surge of the fiery billows.

944.31–32 an article . . . fraud] In "The Balloon Hoax," the narrator says, "The sea does not seem convex (as one might suppose) but absolutely and most unequivocally concave."

944.11–12 Commander Wilkes, U. S. N.] Charles Wilkes (1798–1877), when only a lieutenant, led an exploring expedition (1838–42), charted 1600 miles of the coast of the Antarctic continent, mapped some 280 islands in the Pacific and adjacent waters, and surveyed 800 miles of streams and coasts in the Oregon country.

947.2 one curious character] F. A. Oudinot, resident of Lahaina, Maui, claimed descent from a marshal of France under Napoleon and is the prototype for Markiss in this chapter.

961.3 BRIEF SKETCH . . . HISTORY] Condensed and paraphrased from Mrs. Catharine V. Waite, *The Mormon Prophet and His Harem; or an Authentic History of Brigham Young, His Numerous Wives and Children* (1866).

962.2 Mormon . . . Rigdon] Sidney Rigdon. After the murder of Smith on June 27, 1844, Rigdon assumed the presidency but was deposed on August 8 by Brigham Young and excommunicated on September 8. A short time later he was welcomed back into the church.

964.21 "fed . . . grudge"] "I will feed fat the ancient grudge I bear him." *Merchant of Venice*, I, ii, 48.

964.28 Three thousand . . . troops] In 1857–58 Colonel Albert S. Johnston (later a Confederate general) commanded these troops.

965.10 In 1857 . . . Harney] General William S. Harney was not "near" to being governor. He was appointed to lead the troops that were in fact commanded by Colonel Albert S. Johnston; but his orders were revoked.

965.12 Cradlebaugh] In 1858 President Buchanan appointed John Cradlebaugh associate justice of the Second Judicial District, Territory of Utah.

965.37 A great . . . train] Known as the Faucher party.

966.6 a noted . . . missionary] Parley P. Pratt. See note 614.10–11.

966.19–20 President . . . Lee] Isaac C. Haight, president of the Cedar City Stake ("stake" meaning a territorial unit of church jurisdiction), John M. Higbee, and John D. Lee, bishops from Cedar City and Fort Harmony, respectively. Lee, who was executed on March 23, 1877, for his part in the massacre, wrote a posthumously published book, *Mormonism Unveiled, or the Life and Confessions of John D. Lee* (1877).

967.10–11 President Haight] Haight was in Cedar City, not at the scene of the massacre.

967.13–14 a speech . . . Congress] On February 7, 1863, in the House of Representatives.

967.38   10th day]   Historians now say it happened on September 11.

968.32   Cumming . . . Governor]   Alfred Cumming (1802–73), of Georgia, was appointed territorial governor of Utah in the spring of 1857 by President Buchanan, replacing Brigham Young. Following the inauguration of Lincoln he left for his home near Augusta, Georgia.

969.5   'confirmations . . . Writ:']   *Othello*, III, iii, 323–24.

969.8   Deputy . . . Rodgers]   William H. Rogers assisted Judge Cradlebaugh in the investigation of the massacre.

969.37   Conrad Wiegand]   Wiegand won local notoriety for his socialistic politics, anti-vice crusades, and general impracticality.

970.22   "People's Tribune"]   Published beginning January 13, 1870, for five issues (through June).

970.31–32   when . . . management]   Adolph Sutro spoke in Virginia City on September 20, 1869, attacking the Bank of California and officials of large mines. Wiegand and others continued the attack.

971.15   On Thursday last]   On January 13, 1870, one Griffith Williams beat Wiegand severely, was arrested, and was fined $7.50.

973.13   conference with Sharon]   William E. Sharon, general agent in Virginia City and Gold Hill for the Bank of California.

977.29   Address to the People]   Title of the prospectus for the *Tribune* which Wiegand circulated on November 3, 1869.

LIBRARY OF CONGRESS CATALOGING IN PUBLICATION DATA

Clemens, Samuel Langhorne (Mark Twain), 1835–1910
    The innocents abroad; Roughing it.

    (The Library of America; 21)
    Edited by Guy Cardwell.
    Contents: The innocents abroad—Roughing it.
    I. Cardwell, Guy, 1905–   .   II. Title: Innocents abroad.
III. Title: Roughing it. IV. Twain, Mark. V. Series: The
Library of America.
PS1302   1984   813'.4   84–11296
ISBN 0–940450–25–9

This book is set in 10 point Linotron Galliard, a face designed for photocomposition by Matthew Carter and based on the sixteenth-century face Granjon. The paper is Olin Nyalite and conforms to guidelines adopted by the Committee on Book Longevity of the Council on Library Resources. The binding material is Brillianta, a 100% rayon cloth made by Van Heek-Scholco Textielfabrieken, Holland. Composition by Haddon Craftsmen, Inc. and The Clarinda Company. Printing and binding by R. R. Donnelley & Sons Company. Designed by Bruce Campbell.

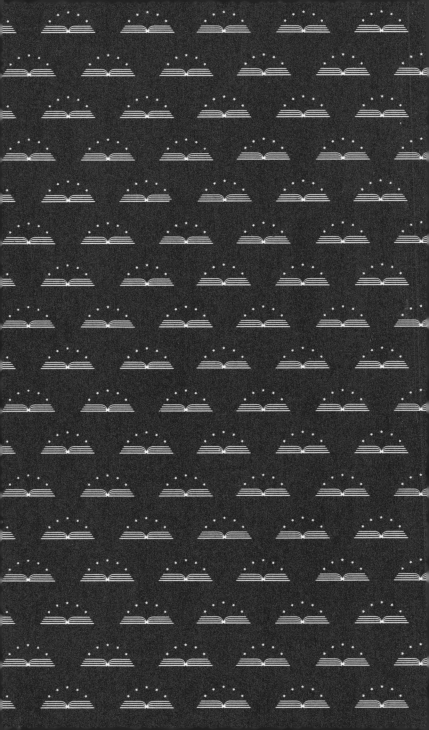